THE
OXFORD GUIDE
TO THE
ENGLISH
LANGUAGE

THE
OXFORD GUIDE
TO THE
ENGLISH
LANGUAGE

E. S. C. WEINER
J. M. HAWKINS

with a foreword by
ROBERT BURCHFIELD

Oxford   New York
OXFORD UNIVERSITY PRESS

Oxford University Press, Walton Street, Oxford OX2 6DP

Oxford New York Toronto
Delhi Bombay Calcutta Madras Karachi
Kuala Lumpur Singapore Hong Kong Tokyo
Nairobi Dar es Salaam Cape Town
Melbourne Auckland

and associated companies in
Beirut Berlin Ibadan Mexico City Nicosia

Oxford is a trade mark of Oxford University Press

Preliminary material and compilation © Oxford University Press 1984
The Oxford Guide to English Usage © Oxford University Press 1983
Dictionary Text © Oxford University Press 1981

First published 1984
Reprinted (with corrections) 1984
First issued as an Oxford University Press paperback 1985

British Library Cataloguing in Publication Data
Weiner, Eva S.
The Oxford guide to the English language.—
Repr. (with corrections)—(Oxford paperback reference)
1. English language—Usage
I. Title   II. Hawkins, Joyce
428   PE1460
ISBN 0–19–281499–0

Printed in Great Britain
at the University Press, Oxford
by David Stanford
Printer to the University

CONTENTS

THE
ENGLISH LANGUAGE

THE English language is the property of some 300 million people round the world, and, as a second language, it is spoken, with varying degrees of proficiency, by as many more.

It started out as a collection of Germanic dialects, brought by marauding tribes to islands that were already inhabited by Celtic speakers—the ancestors of the Scots, the Welsh, the Irish, and the Cornish—and that had undergone and benefited from the earlier occupation by the Romans.

These Germanic dialects had affinities with the speech of related tribes in what is now Germany, the Netherlands, and Scandinavia. At the time of the migrations all the dialects were probably mutually intelligible. They shared a common system of vowels and consonants, scarcely distinguished in quality and differing only in their distribution. They also shared fundamental features like grammatical gender (the nouns were 'masculine', 'feminine', and 'neuter' with different forms of the definite article prefixed to them, and adjectives 'agreed' in case and number with the nouns to which they were affixed); 'strong' and 'weak' verbs (the first changing tense internally, e.g. sing/sang, and the second by the addition of ancestral forms of -ed, e.g. look/looked); and a moderately complicated set of endings or inflexions to indicate case-relationships (dative = 'to, from' someone or something, genitive = 'belonging to, owned by' someone or something, and so on), and used them either in combination with prepositions, or more often, in place of them.

In the period of some 1,500 years since the arrival of the semi-legendary tribes of Hengist, Horsa, and other tribal leaders, English as a spoken language has burgeoned into thousands of differentiated varieties in the British Isles and, from the sixteenth century onwards, in many countries abroad, especially in North America, Australasia, and South Africa.

Now no single variety of English is comprehensible to the descendants of the Germanic tribes who migrated to other parts of the continent of Europe and outlying islands, that is from the Elbe and the Vistula in the East to Norway, Denmark, and Iceland in the West.

It has not always been so, but at present two main varieties of English are politically and linguistically dominant—the Received

Standard of southern Britain, and a generalized form of American English spoken along the eastern seaboard of the United States of America, and in particular the variety spoken by educated Americans in the great cities of Boston, Washington, and New York.

Foreigners who learn English must first decide which variety to learn. It is interesting to observe the choices made. Visiting scholars from China and the USSR seem mostly to speak British English; Japanese and German scholars are divided, and some can adapt with reasonable success to both. Foreign scholars from the Pacific—Malaysians, Indonesians, those from Papua New Guinea, and so on—assimilate their speech to that of the Australians if they learn their English, or improve it, in Canberra or Sydney.

All speakers of English, native or foreign, are faced with the problem that the language changes all the time. The ancient division of verbs into strong, weak, and irregular has not changed in itself, but the strong class has withered away (witness our uncertainty about the past tense of verbs like *to bet, to crow, to thrive*), the weak class has prospered, and the irregular verbs have undergone splinterings, mergings, and other developments that make them still seem extremely unstable and unpredictable (how successfully do we all manage to control the tenses and modes of *may, can, dare, shall, will*, and so on?).

Scholars of the last two hundred years or so have edited and analysed the written language of all past generations. We now have immense dictionaries, like the twelve-volume *Oxford English Dictionary* (1884–1928) and its supplementary volumes (A–Scz in three volumes, 1972–82, the final volume to be published in 1985) and *Webster's Third New International Dictionary* (1961 and later impressions), as well as compendious dictionaries of special periods (Old English, Middle English, etc.) and of regional areas (USA, Scotland, Canada, etc.). We also have complex analyses of English grammar, both of the past and of the present day; and scholarly descriptions of the pronunciation systems of all periods since the beginning of recorded English in the early eighth century.

There was a time, before 1600, when there were no general dictionaries of English and no English grammars. We now live in a world strewn with reference books—*The Dictionary of National Biography, Who's Who*, telephone directories, encyclopaedias, dictionaries of music, quotations, proverbs, and so on, and manuals of this and that. Vast computerized data bases have been established in the United States which are available at present for special purposes but will soon be available to anyone who has a home computer.

Paradoxically there has never been a time when people needed guidance about the English language more than they do at present. The prescriptivism of eighteenth-century grammarians like Robert Lowth and Lindley Murray has been challenged by the descriptivism of twentieth-century linguistic scholars like Ferdinand de Saussure and Noam Chomsky. In this splintering battle, the Oxford dictionaries, from the largest to the smallest, stand like sentinels or marshals, setting the words and meanings in order, defining them and showing how they are pronounced, indicating where the limits of acceptable usage lie, and providing the fullest amount of information about the history of words and constructions. They necessarily place emphasis on the written word because before 1900 or so the written word is all we have, but they give due prominence to the informal felicities and grossness of specialized and generalized slang and colloquial expressions.

The two sections that follow, *The Oxford Guide to English Usage* and the *Dictionary*, fall firmly into the scholarly tradition that is associated with the word 'Oxford'. It is impossible to think of two works of the same size that deal as authoritatively as these do with lexical and grammatical matters.

William Cobbett, the author of *Rural Rides*, wrote *A Grammar of the English Language* in 1819. He set it out as a series of letters to his son, whom he addresses as 'My Dear James'. He reminded James that 'a sound mind in a sound body is the greatest blessing that God can give to man'. But 'mere soundness of mind, without any mental requirements, is possessed by millions; it is an ordinary possession'. The prize beyond measure is knowledge:

In the immense field of this kind of knowledge, innumerable are the paths, and Grammar is the gate of entrance to them all.

To grammar, I would add lexicography, and in so far as they are separable from both, the broad principles of pronunciation.

Despite the remarkable and irreversible changes that have come upon the English language since the Anglo-Saxon period, it has not yet reached a point of perfection and stability that we sometimes associate with Latin of the Golden Age, the language of Virgil, Horace, and others. Equally it is not entering a period of decline. From earliest times, linguistic radicals have looked at fashionable change and liked it or have not objected to it. Linguistic conservatives have fought to preserve old ways of speaking and writing. The battle continues unabated. The issue is one of sovereignty. Who decides whether it is right to confuse *infer* and *imply*, *disinterested* and *uninterested,* or *refute* and *deny*? Is *hopefully,* in its new use as a sentence adverb, acceptable, and to whom? Should we all say *kílometre* and condemn *kilómetre*? Is *privatization* to be admitted to the language without dissent?

Battles like these have been fought for centuries. Grievous alterations to the structure of the language, and to individual words, have occurred. These old ambuscades and assaults on the language have been forgotten, but the new ones, here and now, are once more seen by many people as subversive and destructive.

Yet is it not true that our language, far from bleeding to death, still lies ready to hand as a flexible and noble instrument of majesty and strength? The works of modern writers like Virginia Woolf, Iris Murdoch, and T. S. Eliot are as linguistically potent as those of great writers of the past. The oratory of Winston Churchill was not inferior to that of Edmund Burke or Thomas Babington Macaulay. And everyday English, as it is spoken and written by ordinary people, looks like remaining an effective communicative force, though existing in many varieties each of which is subject to perpetual change, for many centuries to come.

ROBERT BURCHFIELD
Chief Editor
Oxford
August 1983
The Oxford English Dictionaries

THE
OXFORD GUIDE
TO
ENGLISH USAGE

INTRODUCTION

It is one thing to use language; it is quite another to
understand how it works.

(Anthony Burgess, *Joysprick*)

ENGLISH usage is a subject as wide as the English language itself. By
far the greater part of usage, however, raises no controversies and
poses no problems for native speakers of English, just because it *is*
their natural idiom. But there are certain limited areas—particularly
sounds, spellings, words, and constructions—about which there
arises uncertainty, difficulty, or disagreement. The proper aim of a
usage guide is to resolve these problems, rather than describe the
whole of current usage.

The *Oxford Guide to English Usage* has this aim. Within the limits
just indicated, it offers guidance in as clear, concise, and systematic a
manner as possible. In effecting its aims it makes use of five special
features, explained below.

1. *Layout.* In the *Guide* the subject of usage is divided into four fields:
word formation, *pronunciation*, *vocabulary*, and *grammar*. Each field
is covered by a separate section of the book, and each of the four
sections has its own alphabetical arrangement of entries. Each entry
is headed by its title in **bold type.** All the words that share a particular
kind of spelling, sound, or construction can therefore be treated
together. This makes for both economy and comprehensiveness of
treatment. Note that Section II is in two parts: A deals with the
pronunciation of particular letters, or groups of letters, while B is an
alphabetical list of words whose pronunciation gives trouble.

2. *Explanation.* The explanations given in each entry are intended
to be simple and straightforward. Where the subject is inevitably
slightly complicated, they begin by setting out familiar facts as a basis
from which to untangle the complexities. The explanations take into
account the approaches developed by modern linguistic analysis, but
employ the traditional terms of grammar as much as possible. (A
glossary of all grammatical terms used will be found on pp. xviiff.)
Technical symbols and abbreviations, and the phonetic alphabet, are
not used at all.

3. *Exemplification.* Throughout Sections III and IV, and where
appropriate elsewhere, example sentences are given to illustrate the

point being discussed. The majority of these are real, rather than invented, examples. Many of them have been drawn from the works of some of the best twentieth-century writers (many equally good writers happen not to have been quoted). Even informal or sub-standard usage has been illustrated in this way; such examples frequently come from speeches put into the mouths of characters in novels, and hence no censure of the style of the author is implied. The aim is to illustrate the varieties of usage and to display the best, thereby making it more memorable than a mere collection of lapses and solecisms would be able to do.

4. *Recommendation*. Recommendations are clearly set out. The blob ● is used in the most clear-cut cases where a warning, restriction, or prohibition is stated. The square □ is occasionally employed where no restriction needs to be enforced. The emphasis of the recommenda-tions is on the degree of acceptability in standard English of a particular use, rather than on a dogmatic distinction of right and wrong. Much that is sometimes condemned as 'bad English' is better regarded as appropriate in informal contexts but inappropriate in formal ones. The appropriateness of usage to context is indicated by the fairly rough categories 'formal' and 'informal', 'standard', 'regional', and 'non-standard', 'jocular', and so on. Some of the ways in which American usage differs from British are pointed out.

5. *Reference*. Ease of access to the entry sought by the user is a priority of the *Guide*. The division into four sections, explained above, means that (roughly speaking) only a quarter of the total range of pages need be looked through in order to find a particular entry. But this should rarely be necessary, since there are two indexes: a *subject index* in which every subject covered by the *Guide* can be found (and this includes all endings, prefixes, and spellings), and a *word index* in which every word cited can be found. Within each section there are many cross-references to other entries; these are indicated by **bold type** and followed by the page number if necessary.

In addition to the four main sections described at 1 above, the *Guide* has three *appendices*: I is an outline of the principles of punctuation; II lists some of the clichés and overworked diction most widely dis-liked at present; and III gives a brief description of the character-istics of the five major overseas varieties of English.

Concise as it is, the *Guide* may be found by individual users to cover some ground that is already familiar and some that they consider it unnecessary to know about. It is impossible for an entry (especially in the field of grammar) not to include more facts than are strictly part of the question which the entry is designed to answer. Language is a closely woven, seamless fabric, not a set of building blocks or pigeon-holes, capable of independent treatment; hence there are bound to be some redundancies and some overlap between different entries. Moreover, every user has a different degree of knowledge and interest. It is the compiler's hope, however, that all will be instructed and enriched by any incidental gains in understanding of the language that the use of this *Guide* may afford.

GRAMMATICAL TERMS
USED IN THIS BOOK

WHERE an example is partly in italics and partly in roman type, it is the words in roman that exemplify the term being defined.

absolute used independently of its customary grammatical relationship or construction, e.g. Weather permitting, *I will come*.

acronym a word formed from the initial letters of other words, e.g. *NATO*.

active applied to a verb whose subject is also the source of the action of the verb, e.g. *We* saw *him*; opposite of **passive**.

adjective a word that names an attribute, used to describe a noun or pronoun, e.g. small *child, it is* small.

adverb a word that modifies an adjective, verb, or another adverb, expressing a relation of place, time, circumstance, manner, cause, degree, etc., e.g. *gently, accordingly, now, here, why*.

agent noun a noun denoting the doer of an action, e.g. *builder*.

agent suffix a suffix added to a verb to form an agent noun, e.g. *-er*.

agree to have the same grammatical number, gender, case, or person as another word.

analogy the formation of a word, derivative, or construction in imitation of an existing word or pattern.

animate denoting a living being.

antecedent a noun or phrase to which a relative pronoun refers back.

antepenultimate last but two.

antonym a word of contrary meaning to another.

apposition the placing of a word, especially a noun, syntactically parallel to another, e.g. *William the Conqueror*.

article *a/an* (**indefinite** article) or *the* (**definite** article).

attributive designating a noun, adjective, or phrase expressing an attribute, characteristically preceding the word it qualifies, e.g. *old* in *the old dog*; opposite of **predicative**.

auxiliary verb a verb used in forming tenses, moods, and voices of other verbs.

case the form (**subjective, objective,** or **possessive**) of a noun or pronoun, expressing relation to some other word.

clause a distinct part of a sentence including a **subject** (sometimes by implication) and **predicate**.

collective noun a singular noun denoting many individuals; see p. 142.

collocation an expression consisting of two (or more) words frequently juxtaposed, especially adjective + noun.

comparative the form of an adjective or adverb expressing a higher degree of a quality, e.g. *braver, worse.*

comparison the differentiation of the **comparative** and **superlative** degrees from the positive (basic) form of an adjective or adverb.

complement a word or words necessary to complete a grammatical construction: the complement of a clause, e.g. *John is* (a) thoughtful (man), *Solitude makes John* thoughtful; of an adjective, e.g. *John is glad* of your help; of a preposition, e.g. *I thought of* John.

compound preposition a preposition made up of more than one word, e.g. *with regard to.*

concord agreement between words in gender, number, or person, e.g. *the girl* who is *here, you who* are *alive,* Those *men* work.

conditional designating (1) a clause which expresses a condition, or (2) a mood of the verb used in the consequential clause of a conditional sentence, e.g. (1) *If he had come,* (2) *I should have seen him.*

consonant (1) a speech sound in which breath is at least partly obstructed, combining with a **vowel** to form a syllable; (2) a letter usually used to represent (1); e.g. *ewe* is written with vowel + consonant + vowel, but is pronounced as consonant (y) + vowel (oo).

co-ordination the linking of two or more parts of a compound sentence that are equal in importance, e.g. *Adam delved and Eve span.*

correlative co-ordination co-ordination by means of pairs of corresponding words regularly used together, e.g. *either . . or.*

countable designating a noun that refers in the singular to one and in the plural to more than one, and can be qualified by *a, one, every,* etc. and *many, two, three,* etc.; opposite of **mass (noun)**.

diminutive denoting a word describing a small, liked, or despised specimen of the thing denoted by the corresponding root word, e.g. *ringlet, Johnny, princeling.*

diphthong: see **digraph,** p. 102.

direct object the **object** that expresses the primary object of the action of the verb, e.g. *He sent* a present *to his son.*

disyllabic having two syllables.

double passive: see p. 148.

elide to omit by **elision**.

elision the omission of a vowel or syllable in pronouncing, e.g. *let's.*

ellipsis the omission from a sentence of words needed to complete a construction or sense.

elliptical involving **ellipsis**.

feminine the gender proper to female beings.

finite designating (part of) a verb limited by person and number, e.g. *I* am, *He* comes.

formal designating the type of English used publicly for some serious purpose, either in writing or in public speeches.

future the tense of a verb referring to an event yet to happen: **simple future,** e.g. *I shall go*; **future in the past**, referring to an event that was yet to happen at a time prior to the time of speaking, e.g. *He said he* would go.

gerund the part of the verb which can be used like a noun, ending in -*ing*, e.g. *What is the use of my* scolding *him?*

govern (said of a verb or preposition) to have (a noun or pronoun, or a case) dependent on it.

group possessive: see p. 151.

hard designating a letter, chiefly *c* or *g*, that indicates a guttural sound, as in *cot* or *got*.

if-**clause** a clause introduced by *if*.

imperative the mood of a verb expressing command, e.g. Come *here!*

inanimate opposite of **animate**.

indirect object the person or thing affected by the action of the verb but not primarily acted upon, e.g. *I gave* him *the book*.

infinitive the basic form of a verb that does not indicate a particular tense or number or person; the *to*-**infinitive,** used with preceding *to*, e.g. *I want* to know; the **bare infinitive,** without preceding *to*, e.g. *Help me* pack.

inflexion a part of a word, usually a suffix, that expresses grammatical relationship, such as number, person, tense, etc.

informal designating the type of English used in private conversation, personal letters, and popular public communication.

intransitive designating a verb that does not take a direct object, e.g. *I must* think.

intrusive *r*: see p. 59.

linking *r*: see p. 58.

loan-word a word adopted by one language from another.

main clause the principal clause of a sentence.

masculine the gender proper to male beings.

mass noun a noun that refers to something regarded as grammatically indivisible, treated only as singular, and never qualified by *those*, *many*, *two*, *three*, etc.; opposite of **countable** noun.

modal relating to the **mood** of a verb; used to express mood.

mood form of a verb serving to indicate whether it is to express fact, command, permission, wish, etc.

monosyllabic having one syllable.

nominal designating a phrase or clause that is used like a noun, e.g. What you need *is a drink*.

nonce-word a word coined for one occasion.

non-finite designating (a part of) a verb not limited by person and number, e.g. the infinitive, gerund, or participle.

non-restrictive: see p. 170.

noun a word used to denote a person, place, or thing.

noun phrase a phrase functioning within the sentence as a noun, e.g. The one over there *is mine*.

object a noun or its equivalent governed by an active transitive verb, e.g. *I will take that one*.

objective the case of a pronoun typically used when the pronoun is the object of a verb or governed by a preposition, e.g. *me*, *him*.

paradigm the complete pattern of inflexion of a noun, verb, etc.

participle the part of a verb used like an adjective but retaining some verbal qualities (tense and government of an object) and also used to form compound verb forms: the **present participle** ends in *-ing*, the **past participle** of regular verbs in *-ed*, e.g. *While* doing *her work she had* kept *the baby* amused.

passive designating a form of the verb by which the verbal action is attributed to the person or thing to whom it is actually directed (i.e. the logical object is the grammatical subject), e.g. *He* was seen *by us*; opposite of **active**.

past a tense expressing past action or state, e.g. *I* arrived *yesterday*.

past perfect a tense expressing action already completed prior to the time of speaking, e.g. *I* had arrived *by then*.

pejorative disparaging, depreciatory.

penultimate last but one.

perfect a tense denoting completed action or action viewed in relation to the present, e.g. *I* have finished *now*; **perfect infinitive**, e.g. *He seems* to have finished *now*.

periphrasis a roundabout way of expressing something.

person one of the three classes of personal pronouns or verb-forms, denoting the person speaking **(first person)**, the person spoken to **(second person)**, and the person or thing spoken about **(third person)**.

phrasal verb an expression consisting of a verb and an adverb (and preposition), e.g. *break down, look forward to*.

phrase a group of words without a predicate, functioning like an adjective, adverb, or noun.

plural denoting more than one.

polysyllabic having more than one syllable.

possessive the case of a noun or a pronoun indicating possession, e.g. *John's*; **possessive pronoun**, e.g. *my*, *his*.

predicate the part of a clause consisting of what is said of the subject, including verb + complement or object.

predicative designating (especially) an adjective that forms part or the whole of the predicate, e.g. *The dog is* old.

prefix a verbal element placed at the beginning of a word to qualify its meaning, e.g. *ex-*, *non-*.

preposition a word governing a noun or pronoun, expressing the relation of the latter to other words, e.g. *seated* at *the table*.

prepositional phrase a phrase consisting of a preposition and its complement, e.g. *I am surprised* at your reaction.

present a tense expressing action now going on or habitually performed in past and future, e.g. *He* commutes *daily*.

pronoun a word used instead of a noun to designate (without naming) a person or thing already known or indefinite, e.g. *I*, *you*, *he*, etc., *anyone*, *something*, etc.

proper name a name used to designate an individual person, animal, town, ship, etc.

qualify (of an adjective or adverb) to attribute some quality to (a noun or adjective/verb).

reflexive implying the subject's action on himself or itself; **reflexive pronoun**, e.g. *myself*, *yourself*, etc.

relative: see p. 169.

restrictive: see p. 170.

semivowel a sound intermediate between vowel and consonant, e.g. the sound of *y* and *w*.

sentence adverb an adverb that qualifies or comments on the whole sentence, not one of the elements in it, e.g. Unfortunately, *he missed his train*.

simple future: see **future**.

singular denoting a single person or thing.

soft designating a letter, chiefly *c* or *g*, that indicates a sibilant sound, as in *city* or *germ*.

split infinitive: see p. 174.

stem the essential part of a word to which inflexions and other suffixes are added, e.g. *un*limit*ed*.

stress the especially heavy vocal emphasis falling on one (the **stressed**) syllable of a word more than on the others.

subject the element in a clause (usually a noun or its equivalent) about which something is predicated (the latter is the **predicate**).

subjective the case of a pronoun typically used when the pronoun is the subject of a clause.

subjunctive the mood of a verb denoting what is imagined, wished, or possible, e.g. *I insist that it* be *finished*.

subordinate clause a clause dependent on the main clause and functioning like a noun, adjective, or adverb within the sentence, e.g. *He said* that you had gone.

substitute verb the verb *do* used in place of another verb, e.g. '*He likes chocolate*.' 'Does *he?*'

suffix a verbal element added at the end of a word to form a derivative, e.g. *-ation*, *-ing*, *-itis*, *-ize*.

superlative the form of an adjective or adverb expressing the highest or a very high degree of a quality, e.g. *brave*, *worst*.

synonym a word identical in sense and use with another.

transitive designating a verb that takes a direct object, e.g. *I* said *nothing*.

unreal condition (especially in a conditional sentence) a condition which will not be or has not been fulfilled.

unstressed designating a word, syllable, or vowel not having **stress**.

variant a form of a word etc. that differs in spelling or pronunciation from another (often the main or usual) form.

verb a part of speech that predicates.

vowel (1) an open speech sound made without audible friction and capable of forming a syllable with or without a consonant; (2) a letter usually used to represent (1), e.g. *a*, *e*, *i*, *o*, *u*.

***wh*-question word** a convenient term for the interrogative and relative words, most beginning with *wh*: *what*, *when*, *where*, *whether*, *which*, *who*, *whom*, *whose*, *how*.

ABBREVIATIONS

Amer.	American
COD	*The Concise Oxford Dictionary* (edn. 7, Oxford, 1982)
Hart's Rules	*Hart's Rules for Compositors and Readers* (edn. 39, Oxford, 1983)
MEU	H. W. Fowler, *A Dictionary of Modern English Usage* (edn. 2, revised by Sir Ernest Gowers, Oxford, 1965)
NEB	*The New English Bible* (Oxford and Cambridge, 1970)
ODWE	*The Oxford Dictionary for Writers and Editors* (Oxford, 1981)
OED	*The Oxford English Dictionary* (Oxford, 1933) and its supplementary volumes, A–G (1972); H–N (1976); O–Scz (1982).
TLS	*The Times Literary Supplement*

I

WORD FORMATION

THIS section is concerned with the ways in which the forms of English words and word elements change or vary. It deals primarily with their written form, but in many cases the choice between two or more possible written forms is also a choice between the corresponding spoken forms. What follows is therefore more than merely a guide to spelling, although it is that too. A great part is taken up with guidance on the way in which words change when they are inflected (e.g. the possessive case and plural of nouns, the past tense and past participle of verbs) or when derivational prefixes and suffixes are added (e.g. the adjectival *-able* and *-ible* suffixes, the adverbial *-ly* suffix). Because this is intended as a very basic outline, little space has been given to the description of the meanings and uses of the inflected and compounded forms of words. Instead, the emphasis is on the identification of the correct, or most widely acceptable, written form. Particular attention is given to the dropping, doubling, and alteration of letters when derivatives are formed. Space has also been given to problems of spelling that are not caused by derivation, especially the different ways of spelling the same sound in different words (e.g. *y* or *i* in *cider*, *cipher*, *gypsy*, *pygmy*, etc.). A comprehensive coverage of all words requiring hyphens or capitals would require more space than is available here. The entries for these two subjects attempt only to offer guidelines in certain difficult but identifiable cases. For a fuller treatment the reader is referred to the *Oxford Dictionary for Writers and Editors* and *Hart's Rules for Compositors and Readers*. Wherever possible, notes are added to indicate where the conventions of American spelling differ from those recommended here.

In cases where there is widespread variation in the spelling of a particular word or form, the spelling recommended here is that preferred (as its 'house style') by the Oxford University Press.

abbreviations

It is usual to indicate an abbreviation by placing a point (full stop) after it, e.g.

H. G. Wells, five miles S. (= south), *B.Litt., Kt., Sun.* (= Sunday), *Jan.* (= January), *p. 7* (= page 7), *ft., in., lb., cm.*

However, no point is necessary:

1. With a sequence of capitals alone, e.g. *BBC, MA, QC, NNE,* BC, AD, *PLC* (and not, of course, with acronyms, e.g. *Aslef, Naafi*).

2. With the numerical abbreviations *1st, 2nd,* etc.

3. *C, F* (of temperature), chemical symbols, and measures of length, weight, time, etc. in scientific and technical use.

4. *Dr, Revd, Mr, Mrs, Ms, Mme, Mlle, St, Hants, Northants, p* (= penny or pence).

5. In words that are colloquial abbreviations, e.g. *co-op, demo, recap, trad, vac.*

-ability and -ibility

Nouns ending in these suffixes undergo the same changes in the stem as adjectives in *-able* and *-ible* (see next entry).

-able and -ible

Words ending in *-able* generally owe their form to the Latin termination *-abilis* or the Old French *-able* (or both), and words in *-ible* to the Latin *-ibilis.* The suffix *-able* is also added to words of 'distinctly French or English origin' (*OED,* s.v. *-ble*), and as a living element to English roots.

A. Words ending in *-able.* The following alterations are made to the stem:

1. Silent final *-e* is dropped (see p. 9).

Exceptions: words whose stem ends in *-ce, -ee, -ge, -le,* and the following:

blameable	*rateable*
dyeable	*ropeable*
giveable (but *forgivable*)	*saleable*
hireable	*shareable*
holeable	*sizeable*
likeable	*tameable*
liveable	*tuneable*
nameable	*unshakeable*

● Amer. spelling tends to omit *-e-* in the words above.

2. Final -*y* becomes -*i*- (see p. 34).
Exception: *flyable*.

3. A final consonant may be doubled (see pp. 8 f.).
Exceptions:

inferable	*referable*
preferable	*transferable*
(but *conferrable*)	

4. Most verbs of more than two syllables ending in -*ate* drop this ending when forming adjectives in -*able*, e.g. *alienable*, *calculable*, *demonstrable*, etc. Verbs of two syllables ending in -*ate* form adjectives in -*able* regularly, e.g. *creatable*, *debatable*, *dictatable*, etc.

For a list of -*able* words, see *Hart's Rules*, pp. 83–4.

B. Words ending in -*ible*. These are fewer, since -*ible* is not a living suffix. Below is a list of the commonest. Almost all form their negative in *in*-, *il*-, etc., so that the negative form can be inferred from the positive in the list below; the exceptions are indicated by (*un*).

accessible	*edible*	*perfectible*
adducible	*eligible*	*permissible*
admissible	*exhaustible*	*persuasible*
audible	*expressible*	*plausible*
avertible	*extensible*	*possible*
collapsible	*fallible*	*reducible*
combustible	(*un*)*feasible*	*repressible*
compatible	*flexible*	*reproducible*
comprehensible	*forcible*	*resistible*
contemptible	*fusible*	*responsible*
corrigible	*gullible*	*reversible*
corruptible	*indelible*	*risible*
credible	(*un*)*intelligible*	*sensible*
defensible	*irascible*	(*un*)*susceptible*
destructible	*legible*	*tangible*
digestible	*negligible*	*vendible*
dirigible	*ostensible*	*vincible*
discernible	*perceptible*	*visible*
divisible		

ae and *oe*

In words derived from Latin and Greek, these are now always written as separate letters, not as the ligatures æ, œ, e.g. *aeon*, *Caesar*, *gynaecology*; *diarrhoea*, *homoeopathy*, *Oedipus*. The simple *e* is preferable in several words once commonly spelt with *ae*, *oe*, especially *medieval* (formerly with *ae*) and *ecology*, *ecumenical* (formerly with initial *oe*).

● In Amer. spelling, *e* replaces *ae*, *oe* in many words, e.g. *gynecology*, *diarrhea*.

American spelling

Differences between Amer. and British spelling are mentioned at the following places: **-able** and **-ible** (p. 2); **ae** and **oe** (p. 4); **-ce** or **-se** (p. 7); **doubling of final consonant** (pp. 8 f.); **dropping of silent -e** (pp. 9 ff.); **hyphens** (p. 17); **l** and **ll** (pp. 20 f.); **-oul-** (p. 22); **-our** or **-or** (p. 22); **past of verbs, formation of** (pp. 23 f.); **-re** or **-er** (pp. 30 f.); **-xion** or **-ction** (p. 32); **-yse** or **-yze** (p. 34).

See also **difficult and confusable spellings** (pp. 35 ff.) passim.

ante- and anti-

ante- (from Latin) = 'before'; *anti-* (from Greek) = 'against, opposite to'. Note especially *antechamber* and *antitype*.

-ant or -ent

-ant is the noun ending, *-ent* the adjective ending in the following:

dependant	*dependent*
descendant	*descendent*
pendant	*pendent*
propellant	*propellent*

independent is both adjective and noun; *dependence*, *independence* are the abstract nouns.

The following are correct spellings:

ascendant, -nce, -ncy	*relevant, -nce*
attendant, -nce	*repellent*
expellent	*superintendent, -ncy*
impellent	*tendency*
intendant, -ncy	*transcendent, -nce*

a or an

A. Before *h*.

1. Where *h* is aspirated, use *a*, e.g. *a harvest, hero, hope*.

2. Where *h* is silent, use *an*, e.g. *an heir, honour, honorarium.*
3. In words in which the first syllable is unstressed, use *a*, e.g. *a historic occasion, a hotel.*

● The older usage was not to pronounce *h* and to write *an*, but this is now almost obsolete.

B. Before capital letter abbreviations.

Be guided by the pronunciation.

1. Where the abbreviation is pronounced as one or more letter-names, e.g.

a B road	*a UN resolution*
a PS	*a VIP*

but

an A road	*an MP*
an H-bomb	*an SOS*

2. Where the abbreviation is pronounced as a word (an acronym), e.g.

a RADA student	*a SABENA airline typist*

but

an ACAS official	*an OPEC minister*

But where the abbreviation would in speech be expanded to the full word, use *a* or *an* as appropriate to the latter, e.g. *a MS* 'a manuscript'.

-ative or *-ive*

Correct are:

(*a*)	*authoritative*	*qualitative*
	interpretative	*quantitative*
(*b*)	*assertive*	*preventive*
	exploitive	

by- prefix

'Tending to form one word with the following noun, but a hyphen is still frequently found' (*ODWE*).

One word: *bygone, byline, byname, bypass, bypath, bystander, byway, byword*; the others (e.g. *by-election, by-road*) are hyphened.

● *Bye* (noun) in sport, *bye-bye* (= good-bye) are the chief words with final *-e.*

c and *ck*

Words ending in -*c* interpose *k* before suffixes which otherwise would indicate a soft *c*, chiefly -*ed*, -*er*, -*ing*, -*y*, e.g.:

bivouacker, -ing	*panicky*
colicky	*picnicked, -er, -ing*
frolicked, -ing	*plasticky*
mimicked, -ing	*trafficked, -ing*

Exceptions: *arced, -ing, zinced, zincify, zincing*.

Before -*ism*, -*ist*, -*ity*, and -*ize c* (chiefly occurring in the suffix -*ic*) remains and is pronounced soft, e.g. *Anglicism, physicist, domesticity, italicize*.

capital or small initials

There are four classes of word that especially give trouble.

A. Compass points. Use capitals:

1. When abbreviated, e.g. *NNE* for *north-north-east*.
2. When denoting a region, e.g. *unemployment in the North*.
3. When part of a geographical name with recognized status, e.g. *Northern Ireland, East Africa, Western Australia*.
4. In Bridge.

Otherwise use small initials, e.g. *facing (the) south, the wind was south, southbound, a southeaster*.

B. Parties, denominations, and organizations.

'The general rule is: capitalization makes a word more specific and limited in its reference: contrast a Christian scientist (man of science) and a Christian Scientist (member of the Church of Christ Scientist).' (*Hart's Rules*, pp. 10–11.)

So, for example, *Conservative, Socialist, Democratic* (names of parties); *Roman Catholic, Orthodox, Congregational*; but *conservative, socialist, democratic* (as normal adjectives), *catholic sympathies, orthodox views, congregational singing*.

C. Words derived from proper names.

When connection with the proper name is indirect (the meaning associated with or suggested by the proper name), use a small initial letter, e.g.

(nouns) *boycott, jersey, mackintosh, quisling*;

(adjectives) *herculean* (*labours*), *platonic* (*love*), *quixotic* (*temperament*)*;

(verbs) *blarney, bowdlerize, pasteurize*.

When the connection of a derived adjective or verb with a proper name is immediate and alive, use a capital, e.g.

Christian, Platonic (*philosophy*), *Rembrandtesque, Roman*;
Anglicize, Christianize, Russify.

● Adjectives of nationality usually retain the capital even when used in transferred senses, e.g. *Dutch courage, go Dutch, Russian salad, Turkish delight*. The chief exceptions are *arabic* (*numeral*), *roman* (*numeral, type*).

D. Proprietary names.

The name of a product or process, if registered as a trade mark, is a proprietary name, and should be given a capital initial, e.g. *Araldite, Coca-Cola, Marmite, Olivetti, Pyrex, Quaker Oats, Vaseline, Xerox*.

-cede or -ceed

Exceed, proceed, succeed; the other verbs similarly formed have *-cede*, e.g. *concede, intercede, recede*. Note also *supersede*.

-ce or -se

Advice, device, licence, and *practice* are nouns; the related verbs are spelt with *-se*: *advise, devise, license, practise*. Similarly *prophecy* (noun), *prophesy* (verb).

● Amer. spelling favours *licence, practice* for both noun and verb; but the nouns *defence, offence, pretence* are spelt with *c* in Britain, *s* in America.

co- prefix

Most words with this prefix have no hyphen (even if a vowel, other than *o*, follows the prefix). Those that have a hyphen are:

1. Words with *o* following, e.g. *co-operate* (and derivatives; but *uncooperative*), *co-opt, co-ordinate* (often *coordinate* in Mathematics; also *uncoordinated*).

2. Words in which the hyphen preserves correct syllabication, so

aiding recognition, e.g. *co-latitude*, *co-religionist*, *co-respondent* (distinguished from *correspondent*).

3. Words, especially recent or nonce coinages, in which *co-* is a living prefix meaning 'fellow-', e.g. *co-author*, *co-pilot*, *co-wife*.

doubling of final consonant

1. When certain suffixes beginning with a vowel are added to nouns, adjectives, adverbs, and verbs, the final consonant of the stem word is doubled before the suffix:

(*a*) if the preceding vowel is written with a single letter (or single letter preceded by *qu*) and

(*b*) if that vowel bears the main stress (hence all monosyllables are included).

So *bed*, *bedding* but *head*, *heading*; *occúr*, *occúrred* but *óffer*, *óffered*; *befít*, *befítted* but *bénefit*, *bénefited*.

Suffixes which cause this doubling include:

(*a*) The verb inflexions *-ed*, *-ing*, e.g

begged, *begging*	*revved*, *revving*
equipped, *equipping*	*trek*, *trekking*

(*b*) The adjective and adverb suffixes *-er*, *-est*, e.g. *sadder*, *saddest*.

(*c*) Various derivational suffixes, especially *-able*, *-age*, *-en*, *-er*, *-ery*, *-ish*, *-y*, e.g.

clubbable	*waggery*
tonnage	*priggish*
sadden	*shrubby*
trapper	

Exception: *bus* makes *bused*, *busing*.

2. Words of more than one syllable, not stressed on the last syllable, do not double the final consonant, unless it is *l*, when a suffix beginning with a vowel is added, e.g.

biased	*gossipy*	*wainscoted*
blossoming	*lettered*	*wickedest*
combated	*pilotage*	*womanish*
focusing		

Exception: *worship* makes *worshipped*, *-ing*.

Note that some other words in which the final syllable has a full vowel (not obscure *e* or *i*), some of which are compounds, also double the final consonant, e.g.

handicap	*kidnap*	*periwig*
hobnob	*leapfrog*	*sandbag*
horsewhip	*nonplus*	*zigzag*
humbug		

● Amer. sometimes *kidnaped, kidnaping, worshiped, worshiping.*

3. Consonants that are never doubled are *h, w, x, y.*

4. When endings beginning with a vowel are added, *l* is *always* doubled after a single vowel wherever the stress falls, e.g.

controllable	*jeweller*
flannelled	*panelling*

Note also *woollen, woolly.*

Exceptions: *parallel* makes *paralleled, -ing; devil* makes *devilish;* some (rare) superlatives such as *brutalest, loyalest, civil(l)est.*

● In Amer. spelling *l* obeys the same rules as the other consonants (except *h, w, x, y*), e.g. *traveler, marvelous,* but *compelling, pally.*

Note also Amer. *woolen* (but *woolly*).

5. A silent final consonant is not doubled. Endings are added as if the consonant were pronounced, e.g.

crocheted, -ing	*rendezvouses* (third
précised	person singular)
	rendezvousing

dropping of silent -e

A. When a suffix beginning with a vowel (including -*y*) is added to a word ending in silent -*e* (including *e* following another vowel), the -*e* is dropped.

So:

1. Before suffixes beginning with *e*- (i.e. -*ed*, -*er*, -*ery*, -*est*), e.g.

braver, bravery, bravest	*hoed*
dyed, dyer	*issued*
eeriest	*manœuvred*
freer, freest	*queued*

2. Before -*able*, e.g.

adorable	*bribable*	*manœuvrable*
analysable	*imaginable*	*usable*

Exceptions:

(a) Words ending in -ce and -ge retain the e to indicate the softness of the consonant, e.g. *bridgeable*, *peaceable*.

(b) In a number of -able adjectives, e is retained in order to make the root word more easily recognizable. See list on p. 2.

(c) ee is retained, e.g. *agreeable*, *feeable*, *foreseeable*.

(d) The few adjectives formed on verbs ending in consonant + -le; e.g. *handleable*.

3. Before -age, e.g. *cleavage*, *dotage*, *linage* (number of lines).

Exceptions: *acreage*, *mileage*.

4. Before -ing, e.g. *centring*, *fatiguing*, *housing*, *manœuvring*. With change of *i* to *y*: *dying*, *lying*, etc. (see p. 19).

Exceptions:

(a) ee, oe, and ye remain, e.g.

agreeing	*eyeing*	*shoeing*
canoeing	*fleeing*	*tiptoeing*
dyeing	*hoeing*	

(b) *blueing*, *cueing* (*gluing*, *issuing*, *queuing*, etc. are regular).

(c) *ageing* (*raging*, *staging*, etc. are regular).

(d) *routeing*, *singeing*, *swingeing*, *tingeing* are distinguished from *routing* 'putting to flight', *singing*, *swinging*, and *tinging* 'tinkling'.

5. Before -ish, e.g.

bluish	*nicish*	*roguish*
latish	*purplish*	*whitish*

Exception: *moreish*.

6. Before -y, e.g.

bony	*chancy*	*mousy*
caky	*cliquy*	*stagy*

Exceptions: see **-y or -ey adjectives,** p. 33.

B. When a suffix beginning with a consonant (e.g. -ful, -ling, -ly, -ment, -ness, -some) is added to a word ending in silent -e, the -e is retained, e.g.

abridgement	*definitely*	*judgement* (*judgment*
acknowledgement	*fledgeling*	often in legal works)
amazement	*houseful*	*useful*
awesome		*whiteness*

Exceptions: *argument*, *awful*, *duly*, *eerily*, *eeriness*, *truly*, *wholly*.

● In Amer. spelling *e* is dropped after *dg* and before a suffix beginning with a consonant, e.g. *fledgling*, *judgment*.

C. Final silent *-e* is omitted in Amer. spelling in several words in which it is found in British spelling, and so often is final silent *-ue* in the endings *-gogue*, *-logue*, e.g.

ax	*adz*	*program*
analog	*epilog*	*pedagog*

-efy or *-ify*

The chief words with *-efy* (*-efied*, *-efication*, etc.) are:

liquefy	*rarefy*	*torrefy*
obstupefy	*rubefy*	*tumefy*
putrefy	*stupefy*	

All the others have *-ify* etc. See also **-ified or -yfied,** p. 17.

-ei- or *-ie-*

The rule '*i* before *e* except after *c*' holds good for nearly all words in which the vowel-sound is *ee*, as *Aries*, *hygienic*, *yield*.

Exceptions where *ie* follows *c* are: *prima facie*, *specie*, *species*, *superficies*.

Note also *friend*, *adieu*, *review*, *view*.

The following words which are, or can be, pronounced with the *ee*-sound have *ei*:

caffeine	*either*	*protein*
casein	*forfeit*	*receipt*
ceiling	*heinous*	*receive*
codeine	*inveigle*	*seise*
conceit	*Madeira*	*seize*
conceive	*neither*	*seizure*
counterfeit	*perceive*	*surfeit*
deceit	*peripeteia*	*weir*
deceive	*plebeian*	*weird*

en- or *in-*

The following pairs of words can give trouble:

encrust (verb)	*incrustation*
engrain (verb) to dye in the raw state	*ingrain* (adjective) dyed in the yarn
	ingrained deeply rooted

enquire ask	*inquire* undertake a formal investigation
enquiry question	*inquiry* official investigation
ensure make sure	*insure* take out insurance (against risk: note *assurance* of life)

-er and -est

These suffixes of comparison may require the following changes in spelling:

1. Doubling of final consonant (see p. 8).
2. Dropping of silent -e (see p. 9).
3. *Y* to *i* (see p. 34).

-erous or -rous

The ending *-erous* is normal in adjectives related to nouns ending in *-er*, e.g. *murderous, slanderous, thunderous*. The exceptions are:

ambidextrous	*disastrous*	*monstrous*
cumbrous	*leprous*	*slumbrous*
dextrous	*meandrous*	*wondrous*

final vowels before suffixes

A. For treatment of final *-e* and *-y* before suffixes, see **dropping of silent -e**, pp. 9 ff., and **y to i**, pp. 34 f.

B. For treatment of final *-o* before *-s* (suffix), see **plural formation**, p. 25 and **-s suffix**, p. 31.

C. In nearly all other cases, the final vowels *-a, -i, -o,* and *-u* are unaffected by the addition of suffixes and do not themselves affect the suffixes. So:

bikinied (girls)	*mascaraed*	*(they) rumbaed*
echoed	*mustachioed*	*taxied*
hennaed	*radioed*	
echoer	*skier*	*vetoer*
areas	*emus*	*(he) skis*
cameras	*gnus*	*taxis*
corgis	*(he) rumbas*	
echoing	*scubaing*	*taxiing*
radioing	*skiing*	*vetoing*

Exceptions: *idea'd* (having ideas); past *ski'd* from *ski* (contrast *skied* from *sky*).

D. Final *-é* in words taken from French is retained before all suffixes; the *e* of *-ed* is dropped after it, e.g.

appliquéd	*canapés*	*communiqués*
appliquéing	*chasséing*	*émigrés*
attachés	*clichéd*	*soufflés*
cafés		

for- and *fore-*

The prefix *for-* 'means away, out, completely, or implies prohibition or abstention' (*MEU*). *Fore-* is the same as the ordinary word so spelt, = 'beforehand, in front'.

Note especially:

forbear refrain	*forebear* ancestor
forgather	*foreclose*
forgo abstain from	*forego* (esp. in *foregoing* (*list*),
	foregone (*conclusion*)
forfeit	

f to *v*

Certain nouns that end in *f* or *f* followed by silent *e* change this *f* to *v* in some derivatives. Most are familiar, but with a few derivatives there is variation between *f* and *v* or uncertainty about which consonant is correct; only these are dealt with below.

beef: plural *beeves* oxen, *beefs* kinds of beef.

calf (young bovine animal): *calfish* calflike; *calves-foot jelly*.

calf (of leg): (*enormously*) *calved* having (enormous) calves.

corf (basket): plural *corves*.

dwarf: plural *dwarfs*. ● *Dwarves* only in J. R. R. Tolkien's writings.

elf: *elfish* and *elvish* are both acceptable; *elfin* but *elven*.

handkerchief: plural *handkerchiefs*.

hoof: plural usually *hoofs*, but *hooves* is commonly found, e.g. *The useless tool for horses' hooves* (Graham Greene); *Listening for Sebastian's retreating hooves* (Evelyn Waugh); adjective *hoofed* or *hooved*.

knife: verb *knife*.

leaf: *leaved* having leaves (*broad-leaved*, etc.) but *leafed* as past of *leaf* (*through a book*, etc.).

life: *lifelong* lasting a lifetime; *livelong* (*day*, etc., poetic: the *i* is short); the plural of *still life* is *still lifes*.

oaf: plural *oafs*.

roof: plural *roofs*. ● *Rooves* is commonly heard and sometimes written, e.g. *Several acres of bright red rooves* (George Orwell). Its written use should be avoided.

scarf (garment): plural *scarves*; *scarfed* wearing a scarf.

scarf (joint): plural and verb keep *f*.

sheaf: plural *sheaves*; verb *sheaf* or *sheave*; *sheaved* made into a sheaf.

shelf: plural *shelves*; *shelvy* having sandbanks.

staff: plural *staffs* but archaic and musical *staves*.

turf: plural *turfs* or *turves*; verb *turf*; *turfy*.

wharf: plural *wharfs* or *wharves*.

wolf: *wolfish* of a wolf.

-ful suffix

The adjectival suffix *-ful* may require the following changes in spelling:

1. Change of *y* to *i* (see p. 35).

2. Simplification of *-ll* (see *l* and *ll*, p. 20).

hyphens

A. Hyphens are used to connect words that are more closely linked to each other than to the surrounding syntax. Unfortunately their use is not consistent. Some pairs or groups of words are written as a single word (e.g. *motorway*, *railwayman*), others, despite their equally close bond, as separate words (e.g. *motor cycle*, *pay phone*); very similar pairs may be found with a hyphen (e.g. *motor-cyclist*, *pay-bed*). There are no hard and fast rules that will predict in every case whether a group of words should be written as one, with a hyphen, or separately. Useful lists can be found in *Hart's Rules*, pp. 76–81; numerous individual items are entered in *ODWE*.

1. Groups consisting of attributive noun + noun are probably the most unpredictable. It is the nature of English syntax to produce limitless numbers of groups of this kind. Such a group generally remains written as separate words until it is recognized as a lexical item with a special meaning, when it may receive a hyphen. Eventually it may be written as one word, but this usually happens when the two nouns are monosyllabic and there is no

clash between the final letter of the first and the first letter of the second.

This generalization is, however, a very weak guide to what happens in practice. Compare, for example, *coal tar*, *coal-face*, *coalfield*; *oil well*, *oil-painting*, *oilfield*; *blood cell*, *blood-pressure*, *bloodstream*.

2. Nouns derived from phrasal verbs, consisting of verb + adverb, are slightly more predictable. They are never written as two words, frequently hyphened, and sometimes written as one, e.g. *fall-out*, *play-off*, *set-back*, *turn-out*; *feedback*, *layout*, *runoff*, *turnover*. Phrases consisting of agent-noun in *-er* + adverb are usually hyphened, e.g. *picker-up*, *runner-up*; those consisting of gerund in *-ing* + adverb are usually left as two words, e.g. *Your coming back so soon surprised me*, unless they have become a unit with a special meaning, e.g. *Gave him a going-over*.

3. Various collocations which are not hyphened when they play their normal part in the sentence are given hyphens when they are transferred to attributive position before a noun, e.g.

   (*a*) adjective + noun: *a common-sense argument* (but *This is common sense*), *an open-air restaurant* (but *eating in the open air*).

   (*b*) preposition + noun: *an out-of-date aircraft* (but *This is out of date*), *an in-depth interview* (but *interviewing him in depth*).

   (*c*) participle + adverb: *The longed-for departure* and *Tugged-at leaves and whirling branches* (Iris Murdoch) (but *the departure greatly longed for*; *leaves tugged at by the wind*).

   (*d*) other syntactic groups used attributively, e.g. *A tremendous wrapping-up-and-throwing-away gesture* (J. B. Priestley); *An all-but-unbearable mixture* (Lynne Reid Banks).

4. Collocations of adverb + adjective (or participle) are usually written as two words when attributive as well as when predicative, e.g. *a less interesting topic*, *an amazingly good performance*, but may very occasionally take a hyphen to avoid misunderstanding, e.g. *Sir Edgar, who had heard one or two more-sophisticated rumours* (Angus Wilson) (this does not mean 'one or two additional sophisticated rumours').

   See also **well,** p. 135.

5. When two words that form a close collocation but are not normally joined by a hyphen enter into combination with another

word that requires a hyphen, it may be necessary to join them with a hyphen as well in order to avoid an awkward or even absurd result, e.g. *natural gas* needs no hyphen in *natural gas pipeline*, but *natural-gas-producer* may be preferred to the ambiguous *natural gas-producer*; *crushed ice* + *-making* looks odd in *crushed ice-making machine*, and so *crushed-ice-making machine* may be preferred. Occasionally a real distinction in meaning may be indicated, e.g. *The non-German-speakers at the conference used interpreters* versus *The non-German speakers at the conference were all Austrians.* Many people, however, prefer to avoid the use of long series of hyphened words.

6. A group of words that has been turned into a syntactic unit, often behaving as a different part of speech from the words of which it is composed, normally has hyphens, e.g. *court-martial* (verb), *happy-go-lucky* (adjective), *good-for-nothing*, *stick-in-the-mud*, *ne'er-do-well* (nouns).

7. A hyphen is used to indicate a common second element in all but the last word of a list, e.g. *two-*, *three-*, or *fourfold*.

B. Hyphens are also used within the word to connect a prefix or suffix to the stem. With most prefixes and suffixes it is normal to write the whole compound as a single word; the use of the hyphen is exceptional, and the writing of prefix or suffix and stem as two words virtually unknown.

The hyphen is used in the following cases:

1. After a number of prefixes that are considered to be living formative elements, i.e. prefixes that can be freely used to form new compounds:

   ex- (= formerly), e.g. *ex-President*; *neo-* (denoting a revived movement), e.g. *neo-Nazism*; *non-*, e.g. *non-stick*; *pro-* (= in favour of), e.g. *pro-marketeer*; *self-*, e.g. *self-destructive*.

   Exceptions: *Neoplatonism* (*-ic*, etc.); *selfsame*, *unselfconscious*.

2. After a number of prefixes to aid recognition of the second element, e.g. *anti-g*, or to distinguish the compound from another word identically spelt, e.g. *un-ionized* (as against *unionized*); see also **co- prefix, re- prefix**.

3. Between a prefix ending with a vowel and a stem beginning with the same vowel, e.g. *de-escalate*, *pre-empt*; see also **co- prefix, re-prefix**.

4. Between a prefix and a stem beginning with a capital letter, e.g. *anti-Darwinian, hyper-Calvinism, Pre-Raphaelite*.

5. With some living suffixes forming specially coined compounds, e.g. *Mickey Mouse-like*; or still regarded to some extent as full words, such as *-wise* (= as regards ——), e.g. *Weather-wise we have had a good summer*.

6. With suffixes in irregularly formed compounds, e.g. *unget-at-able*.

7. With the suffix *-like* after a stem ending in *-l*, e.g. *eel-like*, when attached to a word of two or more syllables, e.g. *cabbage-like*, and with the suffix *-less* after a stem ending in double *-l*, e.g. *bell-less, will-lessness*.

Note. In Amer. spelling there is a greater tendency than in British spelling to write compounds as one word, rather than hyphened, e.g. *nonplaying, nonprofit, roundhouse, runback, sandlot*.

-ified or *-yfied*

-ified is usual, whatever the stem of the preceding element, e.g.

citified	*dandified*	*townified*
countrified	*Frenchified*	*whiskified*

But *ladyfied*.

in- or *un-*

There is no comprehensive set of rules governing the choice between these two negative prefixes. The following guidelines are offered. Note that *in-* takes the form of *il-, im-*, or *ir-* before initial *l, m*, or *r*.

1. *in-* is from Latin and properly belongs to words derived from Latin, whereas *un-*, as a native prefix, has a natural ability to combine with any English word. Hence

(*a*) *un-* may be expected to spread to words originally having *in-*. This has happened when the *in-* word has developed a sense more specific than merely the negative of the stem word:

unapt	*inept*
unartistic	*inartistic*
unhuman	*inhuman*
unmaterial	*immaterial*
unmoral	*immoral*
unreligious	*irreligious*
unsanitary	*insanitary*
unsolvable	*insoluble*

(*b*) It is always possible, for the sake of a particular effect, for a writer to coin a nonce-word with *un-*:

> *A small bullied-looking woman with unabundant brown hair* (Kingsley Amis)
>
> *Joyce's arithmetic is solid and unnonsensical* (Anthony Burgess)

2. Adjectives ending in *-ed* and *-ing* rarely accept *in-* (while participles can of course be formed from verbs like *inactivate*, *indispose*, etc.).

Exception: *inexperienced*.

3. *in-* seems to be preferred before the prefixes *ad-*, *co-* (*col-*, *com-*, *con-*, *cor-*), *de-*, *di(s)-*, *ex-*, *per-*.

Important exceptions are:

unadventurous	*uncooperative*	*undevout*
uncommunicative	*undemonstrative*	*unexceptionable*
unconditional	*undeniable*	*unexceptional*
unconscionable	*undesirable*	*unpersuasive*
unconscious	*undetectable*	

4. *un-* is preferred before the prefixes *em-*, *en-*, *im-*, *in-*, *inte(r)-*.

5. Adjectives ending in *-able* usually take *in-* if the stem preceding the suffix *-able* is not, by itself, an English word:

> *educable*, stem *educ-*, negative *in-*
> *palpable*, stem *palp-*, negative *im-*

Exceptions: *unamenable*, *unamiable*, *unconscionable*.

They usually take *un-* if the stem has only one syllable and is an English word:

> *unbridgeable*   *unreadable*
> *unlovable*   *unsaleable*

Exceptions: *incurable*, *immovable*, *impassable* (that cannot be traversed: *impassible* = unfeeling).

But no generalization covers those with a polysyllabic English stem:

> *illimitable*   *undeniable*
> *invariable*   *unmistakable*

Note: Rule 2 overrides rule 3 (e.g. *uncomplaining*, *undisputed*, *unperturbed*); rule 3 overrides rule 5 (*unconscionable*); rule 4 overrides rule 5 (*unimpressible*).

i to *y*

When the suffix *-ing* is added to words (chiefly verbs) that end in *-ie*, *e* is dropped (see **dropping of silent -e**, p. 10), and *i* becomes *y*, e.g.

> *dying*   *lying*   *tying*   *vying*

Exceptions: *hie, sortie, stymie* make *hieing, sortieing, stymieing*.

-ize and *-ise*

-ize should be preferred to *-ise* as a verbal ending in words in which both are in use.

1. The choice arises only where the ending is pronounced *eyes*, not where it is *ice, iss* or *eez*. So: *precise, promise, expertise, remise*.

2. The choice applies only to the verbal suffix (of Greek origin), added to nouns and adjectives with the sense 'make into, treat with, or act in the way of (that which is indicated by the stem word)'.

Hence are eliminated

(*a*) nouns in *-ise*:

compromise	*exercise*	*revise*
demise	*franchise*	*surmise*
disguise	*merchandise*	*surprise*
enterprise		

(*b*) verbs corresponding to a noun which has *-is-* as a part of the stem (e.g. in the syllables *-vis-*, *-cis-*, *-mis-*), or identical with a noun in *-ise*. Some of the more common verbs in *-ise* are:

advertise	*despise*	*incise*
advise	*devise*	*merchandise*
apprise	*disguise*	*premise*
arise	*emprise*	*prise (open)*
chastise	*enfranchise*	*revise*
circumcise	*enterprise*	*supervise*
comprise	*excise*	*surmise*
compromise	*exercise*	*surprise*
demise	*improvise*	*televise*

3. In most cases, *-ize* verbs are formed on familiar English stems, e.g. *authorize, familiarize, symbolize*; or with a slight alteration to the stem, e.g. *agonize, dogmatize, sterilize*. A few words have no such immediate stem: *aggrandize* (cf. *aggrandizement*), *appetize*

(cf. *appetite*), *baptize* (cf. *baptism*), *catechize* (cf. *catechism*), *recognize* (cf. *recognition*); and *capsize*.

l and *ll*

Whether to write a single or double *l* can be a problem in the following cases:

1. Where a suffix is added to single final *l*: see **doubling of final consonants**, p. 9.

2. *l* is single when it is the last letter of the following verbs:

annul	*enrol*	*fulfil*
appal	*enthral*	*instil*
distil	*extol*	

These double the *l* before suffixes beginning with a vowel (see p. 9), but not before *-ment*:

annulment	*enthralment*	*distillation*
enrolment	*fulfilment*	*enthralling*

● In Amer. spelling *l* is usually double in all these words except *annul*(*ment*), *extol*.

3. Final *-ll* is usually simplified to *l* before suffixes or word elements that begin with a consonant, e.g.

almighty, almost, etc.	*fulfil*	*skilful*
chilblain	*gratefully*	*thraldom*
dully	*instalment*	*wilful*

Exception: Before *-ness*, *-ll* remains in *dullness, fullness*.

● In Amer. spelling *ll* is usual in *skillful, thralldom, willful*.

-ly

The suffix *-ly* is added to words (mainly nouns and adjectives) to form adjectives and adverbs, e.g. *earth, earthly*; *part, partly*; *sad, sadly*. With certain words one of the following spelling changes may be required:

1. If the word ends in double *ll*, add only *-y*, e.g. *fully, shrilly*.

2. If the word ends in consonant + *le*, change *e* to *y*, e.g. *ably, singly, terribly*.

Exception: *supplely* (distinguished from the noun and verb *supply*).

3. If the word ends in consonant + *y*, change *y* to *i* and add *-ly*, e.g. *drily*, *happily*.

Exceptions: *shyly*, *slyly*, *spryly*, *wryly*.

4. If the word ends in unstressed *-ey*, change *ey* to *i* and add *-ly*, e.g. *matily*.

5. If the word has more than one syllable and ends in *-ic*, add *-ally*, even if there is no corresponding adjective in *-ical*, e.g. *basically*, *scientifically*.

Exceptions: *politicly* (from the adjective *politic*, distinguished from *politically*, from the adjective *political*), *publicly* (● not *publically*).

6. Final *-e* is exceptionally dropped before *-ly* in *duly*, *eerily*, *truly*, *wholly* (*palely*, *puerilely*, *vilely*, etc., are regular).

7. Final *-y* is exceptionally changed to *i* before *-ly* in *daily*, *gaily* (*greyly*, *coyly* are regular).

-ness

As a suffix added to adjectives, it may require the change of *y* to *i*: see p. 35.

-or and -er

These two suffixes, denoting 'one who or that which performs (the action of the verb)' are from Latin (through French) and Old English respectively, but their origin is not a sure guide to their distribution.

1. *-er* is the living suffix, forming most newly-coined agent nouns; but *-or* is frequently used with words of Latin origin to coin technical terms.

2. *-er* is usual after doubled consonants (except *-ss-*), after soft *c* and *g*, after *-i-*, after *ch* and *sh*, and after *-er*, *-graph*, *-ion*, and *-iz-*, e.g.

   chopper, *producer*, *avenger*, *qualifier*, *launcher*, *furnisher*, *discoverer*, *photographer*, *executioner*, *organizer*.

Principal exceptions: *counsellor*, *carburettor*, *conqueror*.

3. *-or* follows *-at-* to form a suffix *-ator*, often but not always in words related to verbs in *-ate*, e.g. *duplicator*, *incubator*.

Exception: *debater*.

Note: nouns in *-olater*, as *idolater*, do not contain the agent suffix.

4. No rule can predict whether a given word having -s-, -ss-, or -t- (apart from -at-) before the suffix requires -or or -er. So *supervisor*, *compressor*, *prospector*, but *adviser*, *presser*, *perfecter*. -tor usually follows -c, unstressed *i*, and *u*, e.g. *actor*, *compositor*, *executor*; -ter usually follows *f*, *gh*, *l*, *r*, and *s*, e.g. *drifter*, *fighter*, *defaulter*, *exporter*, *protester*; but there are numerous exceptions.

5. A functional distinction is made between -or and -er in the following:

accepter one who accepts	*acceptor* (in scientific use)
adapter one who adapts	*adaptor* electrical device
caster one who casts, casting machine	*castor* beaver; plant giving oil; sugar (sprinkler); wheel
censer vessel for incense	*censor* official
conveyer one who conveys	*conveyor* device
resister one who resists	*resistor* electrical device
sailer ship of specified power	*sailor* seaman

6. A number of words have -er in normal use but -or in Law:

abetter	*mortgager* (*mortgagor*)
accepter	*settler*
granter	

-oul-

In the words *mould*, *moulder*, *moult*, and *smoulder*, Amer. spelling favours *o* alone instead of *ou*.

-our or -or

1. In agent nouns, only -or occurs as the ending (cf. **-or and -er**), e.g. *actor*, *counsellor*.

Exception: *saviour*.

2. In abstract nouns, -our is usual, e.g. *colour*, *favour*, *humour*. Only the following end in -or:

error	*pallor*	*terror*
horror	*squalor*	*torpor*
languor	*stupor*	*tremor*
liquor		

● In Amer. English -or is usual in nearly all words in which British English has -our (*glamour* and *saviour* are the main exceptions).

3. Nouns in *-our* change this to *-or* before the suffixes *-ation*, *-iferous*, *-ific*, *-ize*, and *-ous*, e.g.

> *coloration, humorous, odoriferous, soporific, vaporize, vigorous.*

But *-our* keeps the *u* before *-able*, *-er*, *-ful*, *-ism*, *-ist*, *-ite*, and *-less*, e.g.

> *armourer, behaviourism, colourful, favourite, honourable, labourite, odourless, rigourist.*

past of verbs, formation of

A. Regular verbs add *-ed* for the past tense and past participle, and may make the following spelling changes:

1. Doubling of final consonant (see pp. 8 f.).
2. Dropping of silent *-e* (see p. 9).
3. Change of *y* to *i* (see p. 34).

Note *laid*, *paid*, and *said* from *lay*, *pay*, and *say*.

B. A number of verbs vary in their past tense and past participle between a regular form and a form with *-t* (and in some cases a different vowel-sound in the stem):

burn	*kneel*	*leap*	*smell*	*spill*
dream	*lean*	*learn*	*spell*	*spoil*

The *-t* form is usual in Received Pronunciation* and should be written by those who pronounce it. The regular form is usual in Amer. English.

Bereave is regular when the reference is to the loss of relatives by death; *bereft* is used when to loss of immaterial possessions.

Cleave is a rare word with two opposite meanings: (i) = stick; *A man . . shall cleave unto his wife* (Genesis 2: 24) (regular). (ii) = split; past tense *clave* is archaic; *clove*, *cleft*, and regular *cleaved* are all permissible, but *cleaved* is usual in scientific and technical contexts; past participle, in fixed expressions, *cloven-footed*, *cloven hoof*, *cleft palate*, *cleft stick*; *cleaved* is technical, but probably also best used outside the fixed expressions.

● *Earn* is regular. There is no form *earnt*.

C. A number of verbs vary in the past participle only between the regular form and one ending in *-(e)n*:

> *hew, mow, saw, sew, shear, show, sow, strew, swell.*

* See p. 45.

In most of these the latter form is to be preferred; in British English it is obligatory when the participle is used attributively as an adjective. So *new-mown hay*, *a sawn-off* (Amer. *sawed-off*) *shotgun*, *shorn* (not *sheared*) *of one's strength*, *a swollen gland*; *swollen* or *swelled head* (= conceit) is a colloquial exception.

D. The past tense has *-a-*, the past participle *-u-*, in

begin	*shrink*	*stink*
drink	*sing*	*swim*
ring	*sink*	

● It is an error to use *begun*, *drunk*, etc. for the past tense, as if they followed *clung*, *flung*, *spun*, etc.

E. The past tense and past participle of the following verbs can cause difficulty:

abide (*by*) makes *abided*
alight makes *alighted*
bet: *betted* is increasingly common beside *bet*
bid (make a bid): *bid*
bid (command; say (goodnight, etc.)): *bid* is usual (*bade*, *bidden* are archaic)
broadcast unchanged in past tense and past participle
chide: *chided* is now usual (older *chid*)
forecast unchanged in past tense and past participle
hang: *hanged* is frequent for the capital punishment; otherwise only *hung*
knit: *knitted* is usual, but *knit* is common in metaphorical use (*he knit his brows*)
light makes past *lit*, past participle *lit* in predicative use (*a fire was lit*) but *lighted* attributively (*a lighted match*)
quit makes *quitted* ● Amer. *quit*
reeve (nautical) makes *rove*
rid unchanged in past tense and past participle
speed makes *sped*, but *speeded* in the senses 'cause to go at (a certain) speed' and 'travel at illegal or dangerous speed'
spit makes *spat* ● Amer. *spit*
stave (to dent) *staved* or *stove*; (to ward off) *staved*
sweat makes *sweated* ● Amer. *sweat*
thrive: *thrived* is increasingly common beside *throve*, *thriven*

plural formation

Most nouns simply add *-s*, e.g. *cats*, *dogs*, *horses*, *cameras*.

A. The regular plural suffix -s is preceded by -e-:

1. After sibilant consonants, where ease of pronunciation requires a separating vowel, i.e. after

    ch: e.g. *benches, coaches, matches* (but not *conchs, lochs, stomachs* where the *ch* has a different sound)
    s: e.g. *buses, gases, pluses, yeses* (note that single *s* is not doubled)
    sh: e.g. *ashes, bushes*
    ss: e.g. *grasses, successes*
    x: e.g. *boxes, sphinxes*
    z: e.g. *buzzes, waltzes* (note *quizzes* with doubling of *z*)

Proper names follow the same rule, e.g. *the Joneses, the Rogerses, the two Charleses.*

● *-es* should not be replaced by an apostrophe, as *the Jones'.*

2. After -*y* (not preceded by a vowel), which changes to *i*, e.g. *ladies, soliloquies, spies.*

Exceptions: proper names, e.g. *the Willoughbys, the three Marys*; also *trilbys, lay-bys, standbys, zlotys* (Polish currency).

3. After -*o* in certain words:

bravoes (= ruffians; *bravos* = shouts of 'bravo!')	*haloes*	*potatoes*
buffaloes	*heroes*	*salvoes* (= discharges; *salvos* = reservations, excuses)
calicoes	*innuendoes*	
cargoes	*mangoes*	
dingoes	*mementoes*	*stuccoes*
dominoes	*mosquitoes*	*tomatoes*
echoes	*mottoes*	*tornadoes*
embargoes	*Negroes*	*torpedoes*
goes	*noes*	*vetoes*
grottoes	*peccadilloes*	*volcanoes*
	porticoes	

Words not in this list add only -*s*.

It is helpful to remember that -*e*- is never inserted:

(*a*) when the *o* is preceded by another vowel, e.g. *cuckoos, embryos, ratios.*

(*b*) when the word is an abbreviation, e.g. *hippos, kilos.*

(*c*) with proper names, e.g. *Lotharios, Figaros, the Munros.*

4. With words which change final *f* to *v* (see pp. 13 f.), e.g. *calves, scarves.*

B. Plural of compound nouns.

1. Compounds made up of a noun followed by an adjective, a prepositional phrase, or an adverb attach -s to the noun, e.g.

   (a) *courts martial*   *heirs presumptive*
        cousins-german   *poets laureate*

   But *brigadier-generals, lieutenant-colonels, sergeant-majors.*

   (b) *men-of-war*   *tugs of war*
        sons-in-law

   (c) *hangers-on*   *whippers-in*
        runners-up

Note: In informal usage -s is not infrequently transferred to the second element of compounds of type (a).

2. Compounds which contain no noun, or in which the noun element is now disguised, add -s at the end. So also do nouns formed from phrasal verbs and compounds ending in -ful, e.g.

   (a) *ne'er-do-wells*   *will-o'-the-wisps*
        forget-me-nots

   (b) *pullovers*   *set-ups*
        run-throughs

   (c) *handfuls*   *spoonfuls*

3. Compounds containing *man* or *woman* make both elements plural, as usually do those made up of two words linked by *and*, e.g.

   (a) *gentlemen ushers*   *women doctors*
        menservants

   (b) *pros and cons*   *ups and downs*

C. The plural of the following nouns with a singular in -s is unchanged:

biceps	*means*	*species*
congeries	*mews*	*superficies*
forceps	*series*	*thrips*
innings		

The following are mass nouns, not plurals:

            bona fides (= 'good faith'), *kudos*

● The singulars *bona-fide* (as a noun; there is an adjective *bona-fide*), *congery, kudo,* sometimes seen, are erroneous.

D. Plural of nouns of foreign origin. The terminations that may form their plurals according to a foreign pattern are given in alphabetical order below; to each is added a list of the words that normally follow this pattern. It is recommended that the regular plural (in -s) should be used for all the other words with these terminations, even though some are found with either type of plural.

1. -a (Latin and Greek) becomes -ae:

alga	lamina	nebula
alumna	larva	papilla

Note: formula has -ae in mathematical and scientific use.

2. -eau, -eu (French) add -x:

beau	château	plateau
bureau	milieu	tableau

3. -ex, -ix (Latin) become -ices:

appendix	cortex	matrix
calix	helix	radix

Note: index, vortex have -ices in mathematical and scientific use (otherwise regular).

4. -is (Greek and Latin) becomes -es (pronounced eez):

amanuensis	crisis	oasis
analysis	ellipsis	parenthesis
antithesis	hypothesis	synopsis
axis	metamorphosis	thesis
basis		

5. -o (Italian) becomes -i:

concerto grosso (concerti grossi)

graffito	ripieno
maestro	virtuoso

Note: solo and soprano sometimes have -i in technical contexts (otherwise regular).

6. -on (Greek) becomes -a:

criterion	parhelion	phenomenon

Note: The plural of automaton is in -a when used collectively (otherwise regular).

7. *-s* (French) is unchanged in the plural (note: it is silent in the singular, but pronounced *-z* in the plural):

chamois	*corps*	*fracas*
chassis	*faux pas*	*patois*

Also (not a noun in French): *rendezvous*.

8. *-um* (Latin) becomes *-a*:

addendum	*datum*	*maximum*
bacterium	*desideratum*	*minimum*
candelabrum	*dictum*	*quantum*
compendium	*effluvium*	*scholium*
corrigendum	*emporium*	*spectrum*
cranium	*epithalamium*	*speculum*
crematorium	*erratum*	*stratum*
curriculum		

Note: *medium* in scientific use, and in the sense 'a means of communication' (as *mass medium*) has plural in *-a*; the collective plural of *memorandum* 'things to be noted' is in *-a*; *rostrum* has *-a* in technical use; otherwise these words are regular. In the technical sense 'starting-point' *datum* has a regular plural.

9. *-us* (Latin) becomes *-i*:

alumnus	*fungus*	*nucleus*
bacillus	*gladiolus*	*radius*
bronchus	*locus*	*stimulus*
cactus	*narcissus*	*terminus*
calculus		

Note: *focus* has plural in *-i* in scientific use, but otherwise is regular; *genius* has plural *genii* when used to mean 'guardian spirit', but in its usual sense is regular; *corpus*, *genus*, *opus* become *corpora*, *genera*, *opera*.

● The following words of foreign origin are plural nouns; they should normally not be construed as singulars (see also as separate entries in Section III):

bacteria	*graffiti*	*phenomena*
candelabra	*insignia*	*regalia*
criteria	*media*	*strata*
data		

E. There is no need to use an apostrophe before *-s*:

1. After figures: *the 1890s*.
2. After abbreviations: *MPs*, *SOSs*.

But it is needed in: *dot the i's and cross the t's, fair do's, do's and don'ts*.

possessive case

To form the possessive:

1. Normally, add -'s in the singular and -s' (i.e. apostrophe following the plural suffix -s) in the plural, e.g.

> Bill's book   the Johnsons' dog
> his master's voice   a girls' school

Nouns that do not form plural in -s add -'s to the plural form, e.g.

> children's books   women's liberation

2. Nouns ending in s add 's for the singular possessive, e.g.

> boss's   Hicks's
> Burns's   St James's Square
> Charles's   Tess's
> Father Christmas's   Thomas's

To form the plural possessive, they add an apostrophe to the s of the plural in the normal way, e.g.

> bosses'   the octopuses' tentacles
> the Joneses' dog   the Thomases' dog

French names ending in silent s or x add -'s, which is pronounced as z, e.g.

> Dumas's (= Dumah's)   Crémieux's

Names ending in -es pronounced iz are treated like plurals and take only an apostrophe (following the pronunciation, which is iz, not iziz), e.g.

> Bridges'   Moses'
> Hodges'   Riches'

Polysyllables not accented on the last or second last syllable can take the apostrophe alone, but the form with -'s is equally acceptable, e.g.

> Barnabas'   or   Barnabas's
> Nicholas'   or   Nicholas's

It is the custom in classical works to use the apostrophe only, irrespective of pronunciation, for ancient classical names ending in -s, e.g.

> Ceres'   Herodotus'   Venus'
> Demosthenes'   Mars'   Xerxes'

Jesus' 'is an accepted liturgical archaism' (Hart's Rules, p. 31). But in non-liturgical use, Jesus's is acceptable (used, e.g., in the NEB, John 2: 3).

With the possessive preceding the word *sake*, be guided by the pronunciation, e.g.

for goodness' sake	but	*for God's sake*
for conscience' sake (!)		*for Charles's sake*

After -*x* and -*z*, use -'*s*, e.g. *Ajax's, Berlioz's music, Leibniz's law, Lenz's law*.

3. Expressions such as:

a fortnight's holiday	*two weeks' holiday*
a pound's worth	*two pounds' worth*
your money's worth	

contain possessives and should have apostrophes correctly placed.

4. In *I'm going to the butcher's, grocer's*, etc. there is a possessive with ellipsis of the word 'shop'. The same construction is used in *I'm going to Brown's, Green's*, etc., so that properly an apostrophe is called for. Where a business calls itself *Brown, Green*, or the like (e.g. *Marks and Spencer, J. Sainsbury*) the apostrophe would be expected before -*s*. But many businesses use the title *Browns, Greens*, etc., without an apostrophe (e.g. *Debenhams, Barclays Bank*). No apostrophe is necessary in *a Debenhams store* or in (*go to* or *take to*) *the cleaners*.

5. The apostrophe must not be used:

(*a*) with the plural non-possessive -*s*: notices such as *TEA'S* are often seen, but are wrong.

(*b*) with the possessive of pronouns: *hers, its, ours, theirs, yours*; the possessive of *who* is *whose*.

● *it's* = *it is*; *who's* = *who is*.

● There are no words *her's, our's, their's, your's*.

-re or -er

The principal words in which the ending -*re* (with the unstressed *er* sound—there are others with the sound *ruh*, e.g. *macabre*, or *ray*, e.g. *padre*) is found are:

accoutre	*centre*	*louvre*
* *acre*	* *euchre*	* *lucre*
amphitheatre	*fibre*	*lustre*
* *cadre*	*goitre*	*manœuvre*
calibre	*litre*	* *massacre*

* meagre	ochre	sepulchre
* mediocre	* ogre	sombre
metre (note meter	philtre	spectre
the measuring	reconnoitre	theatre
device)	sabre	titre
mitre	sceptre	* wiseacre
nitre		

● All but those marked * are spelt with -er in Amer. English.

re- prefix

This prefix is followed by a hyphen:

1. Before another e, e.g. re-echo, re-entry.

2. So as to distinguish the compound so formed from the more familiar identically spelt word written solid, e.g.

> re-cover (put new cover on):   recover
> re-form (form again):   reform
> re-sign (sign again):   resign

silent final consonants

Words borrowed from French having silent final consonants give difficulty when inflexions are added to them:

A. In the plural: see p. 28.

B. In the possessive: see p. 29.

C. With verbal inflexions: see p. 9.

-s suffix

A. As the inflexion of the plural of nouns: see **plural formation**.

B. As the inflexion of the third person singular present indicative of verbs, it requires the same changes in the stem as the plural ending, namely the insertion of -e-:

1. After sibilants (ch, s, sh, x, z), e.g. catches, tosses, pushes, fixes, buzzes; note that single s and z are subject to doubling of final consonant (see pp. 8 f.), though the forms in which they occur are rare, e.g. gasses, nonplusses, quizzes, whizzes.

2. After y, which is subject to the change of y to i (see p. 35), e.g. cries, flies, carries, copies.

3. After o: echo, go, torpedo, veto, like the corresponding nouns, insert -e- before -s; crescendo, radio, solo, zero should follow their nouns in having -s, but in practice there is variation.

-xion or -ction

Complexion, crucifixion, effluxion, fluxion, genuflexion, inflexion all have -*x*-; *connection, reflection* (which formerly sometimes had -*ct*-) have -*ct*-; *deflexion* is increasingly being replaced by *deflection*.

● In Amer. spelling -*ction* is more usual in *connection, deflection, genuflection, inflection, reflection*.

-y, -ey, or -ie nouns

The diminutive or pet form of nouns can be spelt -*y*, -*ey*, or -*ie*. The majority of nouns which end in the sound of -*y* are so spelt (whether diminutives or of other origin), e.g.

aunty	*granny*	*nappy*
baby	*missy*	*potty*

The following are the main diminutives spelt with -*ey* (-*ey* nouns of other kinds are excluded from the list):

goosey	*lovey-dovey*	*Sawney*
housey-housey	*matey*	*slavey*
Limey	*nursey*	

The following list contains the diminutives in -*ie*, together with a number of similar nouns that are not in fact diminutives but do end in -*ie*. Note that most Scottish diminutives are spelt with -*ie*, e.g. *corbie, kiltie*.

beanie	*genie* (spirit; plural *genii*)	*movie*
birdie		*nightie*
bookie	*Geordie*	*oldie*
brownie	*gillie*	*pinkie* (little finger)
budgie	*girlie*	
caddie (golf; *tea caddy*)	*goalie*	*pixie*
chappie	*hippie*	*quickie*
charlie	*junkie*	*rookie*
clippie	*Kewpie* (doll)	*sheltie*
cookie	*laddie*	*softie*
coolie	*lassie*	*Tin Lizzie*
dearie	*mealie* (maize; *mealy* adjective)	*walkie-talkie*
doggie (noun; *doggy* adjective)	*mountie*	*zombie*

Note: *bogie* (wheeled undercarriage), *bogey* (golf), *bogy* (ghost).

-y or -ey adjectives

When -y is added to a word to form an adjective, the following changes in spelling occur:

1. Doubling of final consonant (see pp. 8 f.).

2. Dropping of silent -e (see p. 10).

Exceptions:

(a) After u:

> bluey gluey tissuey

(b) In words that are not well established in the written language, where the retention of -e helps to clarify the sense:

> cagey dikey pricey
> cottagey matey villagey
> dicey pacey

Note also *holey* (distinguished from *holy*); *phoney* (of unknown origin).

3. Insertion of -e- when -y is also the final letter of the stem:

> clayey skyey sprayey wheyey

Also in *gooey*.

4. Adjectives ending in unstressed -ey (2 (a) and (b) and 3 above) change this -ey to -i- before the comparative and superlative suffixes -er and -est and the adverbial suffix -ly, e.g.

> cagey: cagily matey: matily pricey: pricier
> dicey: dicier pacey: pacier phoney: phonily
> gooey: gooier

Before -ness there is variation, e.g.

> cagey: cageyness matey: mateyness, phoney: phoniness
> clayey: clayeyness matiness wheyey: wheyiness

y or i

There is often uncertainty about whether y or i should be written in the following words:

> Write i in: Write y in:
> cider gypsy
> cipher lyke-wake
> dike lynch law

Write *i* in:	Write *y* in:
Libya	*pygmy*
lich-gate	*style* (manner)
linchpin	*stylus*
sibyl (classical)	*stymie*
sillabub	*Sybil* (frequently as
silvan	Christian name)
siphon	*syrup*
siren	*tyke*
stile (in fence)	*tympanum* (ear-drum)
timpani (drums)	*tyre* (of wheel)
tiro	*wych-elm*
	wych-hazel

-*yse* or -*yze*

This verbal ending (e.g. in *analyse*, *catalyse*, *paralyse*) is not a suffix but part of the Greek stem -*lyse*. It should not be written with *z* (though *z* is normally used in such words in America).

y to *i*

Words that end in -*y* change this to -*i*- before certain suffixes. The conditions are:

A. When the -*y* is not preceded by a vowel (except -*u*- in -*guy*, -*quy*).

-*y* does not change to -*i*- when preceded by a vowel (other than *u* in -*guy*, -*quy*). So *enjoyable*, *conveyed*, *parleyed*, *gayer*, *gayest*, *donkeys*, *buys*, *employer*, *joyful*, *coyly*, *enjoyment*, *greyness*.

Exceptions: *daily*, *gaily*, and adjectives ending in unstressed -*ey* (see p. 33).

B. When the suffix is:

   1. -*able*, e.g. *deniable*, *justifiable*, *variable*.

Exception: *flyable*.

   2. -*ed* (the past tense and past participle), e.g. *carried*, *denied*, *tried*.

   3. -*er* (agent-noun suffix), e.g. *carrier*, *crier*, *supplier*.

Exceptions: *flyer*, *fryer*, *shyer* (one who, a horse which, shies), *skyer* (in cricket). Note that *drier*, *prier*, *trier* (one who tries) are regular.

   4. -*er*, -*est* (comparative and superlative); e.g. *drier*, *driest*; *happier*, *happiest*.

5. *-es* (noun plural and third person singular present indicative), e.g. *ladies, soliloquies, spies; carries, denies, tries.*

Exceptions: see p. 25.

6. *-ful* (adjectives), e.g. *beautiful, fanciful.* (*Bellyful* is a noun, not an adjective.)

7. *-less* (adjectives), e.g. *merciless, remediless.*

Exceptions: some rare compounds, e.g. *countryless, hobbyless, partyless.*

8. *-ly* (adverbs), e.g. *drily, happily, plaguily.*

Exceptions: *shyly, slyly, spryly, wryly.*

9. *-ment* (nouns), e.g. *embodiment, merriment.*

10. *-ness* (nouns), e.g. *happiness, cliquiness.*

Exceptions: *dryness, flyness, shyness, slyness, spryness, wryness; busyness* (distinguished from *business*).

Difficult and confusable spellings (not covered in previous entries)

The list below contains words (i) which occasion difficulty in spelling; (ii) of which various spellings exist; or (iii) which need to be distinguished from other words spelt similarly. In each case the recommended form is given, and in some cases, for the sake of clarity, is followed by the rejected variant. Where the rejected variant is widely separated in alphabetical position from the recommended form, the former has been given an entry preceded by the mark ● and followed by 'use' and the recommended form. The wording added to some entries constitutes a guide to the sense, not an exhaustive definition or description.

accommodation

adaptation ● not *adaption*

adviser

● *aerie*: use *eyrie*

affront

agriculturist

ait ● not *eyot*

align, alignment ● not *aline, alinement*

alleluia

almanac (*almanack* only in some titles)

aluminium ● Amer. *aluminum*

ambiance (term in art)

ambience surroundings

amok ● not *amuck*

ampere

annex (verb)

annexe (noun)

any one (of a number)

anyone anybody

any time

any way any manner

anyway at all events

apophthegm ● Amer. *apothegm*
apostasy
archaeology
artefact
aubrietia
aught anything
autarchy despotism
autarky self-sufficiency
auxiliary
ay yes (plural *the ayes have it*)
aye always
babu ● not *baboo*
bachelor
bail out obtain release, relieve
    financially
bale out parachute from air-
    craft
balk (verb)
balmy like balm
barmy (informal) mad
baulk timber
bayoneted, -ing
behove ● Amer. *behoove*
bivouac (noun and verb)
bivouacked, bivouacking
blond (of man or his hair)
blonde (of woman or her hair)
born: *be born* (of child)
borne: *have borne* have carried
    or given birth to; *be borne* be
    carried; *be borne by* be
    carried by or given birth to
    by (a mother)
brand-new
brier ● not *briar*
bur clinging seed
burr rough edge, drill, rock,
    accent, etc.
cabbala, cabbalistic
caftan
calendar almanac
calender press

caliph
calligraphy
calliper leg support; (plural)
    compasses ● not *caliper*
callous (adjective)
callus (noun)
camellia shrub
canvas (noun) cloth
canvas (verb) cover with canvas
    (past *canvased*)
canvass (verb) (past *canvassed*)
carcass
caviare
chameleon
chancellor
chaperon
Charollais
cheque (bank)
chequer (noun) pattern (verb)
    variegate; ● Amer. *checker*
chilli pepper
choosy
chord combination of notes,
    line joining points on curve
chukka boot
chukker (polo)
clarinettist ● Amer. *clarinetist*
coco palm
cocoa chocolate
coconut
colander strainer
commit(ment)
comparative
complement make complete,
    that which makes complete
compliment praise
computer
conjuror
connection
conqueror
conscientious
consensus

cord string, flex, spinal *cord*, rib of cloth

cornelian ● not *carnelian*

corslet armour, underwear

cosy ● Amer. *cozy*

council assembly

councillor member of council

counsel advice, barrister

counsellor adviser

court martial (noun)

court-martial (verb)

crape black fabric

crêpe crape fabric other than black; rubber; pancake

crevasse large fissure in ice

crevice small fissure

crosier

crumby covered in crumbs

crummy (informal) dirty, inferior

curb restrain, restraint

curtsy

● *czar*: use *tsar*

dare say ● not *daresay*

debonair

depositary (person)

depository (place)

descendant

desiccated

● *despatch*: use *dispatch*

deterrable

devest (only Law: gen. use *divest*)

didicoi (tinker)

dilatation (medical)

dilator

dinghy boat

dingy grimy

disc ● Amer. *disk*

discreet judicious

discrete separate

disk (sometimes in computing) ● Amer. in all senses of *disc*

dispatch

dissect

dissociate ● not *disassociate*

disyllable

divest

doily

douse quench

dowse use divining rod

draft (noun) military party, money order, rough sketch (verb) sketch ● Amer. in all senses of *draught*

draftsman one who drafts documents

draught act of drawing, take of fish, act of drinking, vessel's depth, current of air ● Amer. *draft*

draughtsman one who makes drawings, plans, etc.; piece in game of draughts

duffel

ecology

ecstasy

ecumenical

educationist ● not *educationalist*

effrontery

● *eikon*: use *icon*

eirenicon ● not *irenicon*

embarrassment

embed

employee (masculine and feminine; no accent)

enclose

enclosure (but *Inclosure Acts*)

encroach

encyclopaedia

envelop (verb)

envelope (noun)

erector

every one (of a number)

everyone everybody

exalt raise, praise
exult rejoice
● *eyot*: use *ait*
eyrie ● not *aerie*
faecal
faeces
fee'd (*a fee'd lawyer*)
feldspar
feldspathic
felloe (of wheel) ● not *felly*
ferrule cap on stick
ferule cane
fetid ● not *foetid*
flotation
flu ● not *'flu*
foetal, *foetus* ● Amer. *fetal*,
  fetus
fogy
forbade (past tense of *forbid*)
forestall
for ever for always
forever continually
forty
fount (type) ● Amer. *font*
fungous (adjective)
fungus (noun)
furore ● Amer. *furor*
fusilier
fusillade
gaol (official use) ● Amer. *jail*
  (both forms found in Brit.
  literary use)
gaoler (as for *gaol*)
gauge measure
gazump ● not *gazoomph*, etc.
gibe jeer
gild make gold
● *gild* association: use *guild*
glycerine
gormandize eat greedily
gormless
gourmand glutton

gram
gramophone
grandad
granddaughter
grayling (fish, butterfly)
grey ● Amer. *gray*
griffin fabulous creature ● not
  gryphon
griffon vulture, dog
grill for cooking
grille grating
grisly terrible
grizzly grey-haired; bear
groin (anatomy; architecture)
grommet ● not *grummet*
groyne breakwater
guerrilla
guild association
gybe (nautical) ● Amer. *jibe*
haema-, *haemo-* (prefix
  meaning 'blood')
haemorrhage
haemorrhoids
hallelujah
hallo
harass
hark
harum-scarum
haulm stem
hearken
hiccup
Hindu
homoeopathy
homogeneous having parts all
  the same
homogenize make
  homogeneous
homogenous having common
  descent
honorific
● *hooping cough*: use *whooping*
  cough

horsy
horticulturist
hurrah, hurray ● not *hoorah, hooray*
hussy ● not *huzzy*
hypocrisy
hypocrite
icon
idiosyncrasy
idyll
ignoramus plural *ignoramuses*
● *imbed*: use *embed*
impinging
impostor
● *inclose, inclosure*: use *en-*
incommunicado
in so far
insomuch
inure
investor
irenic
● *irenicon*: use *eirenicon*
its of it
it's it is
jail (see *gaol*)
jailor (see *gaol*)
jalopy
jam pack tightly; conserve
jamb door-post
● *jibe*: use *gibe, gybe* ● Amer. also = accord with
joust combat ● not *just*
● *kabbala*: use *cabbala*
● *kaftan*: use *caftan*
kebab
kerb pavement ● Amer. *curb*
ketchup
● *khalif*: use *caliph*
kilogram
kilometre
koala
Koran

kowtow
labyrinth
lachrymal of tears
lachrymose tearful
lackey
lacquer
lacrimal (in science)
lacrimate, -ation, -atory (in science)
largess
ledger account book
leger line (in music)
licensee
lickerish greedy
lightening making light
lightning (accompanying thunder)
limeade
linage number of lines
lineage ancestry
lineament feature
liniment embrocation
liqueur flavoured alcoholic liquor
liquor
liquorice
litchi Chinese fruit
literate
literature
littérateur
littoral
loadstone
loath(some) (adjectives)
loathe (verb)
lodestar
longevity
longitude ● not *longtitude*
lour frown
Mac (prefix) spelling depends on the custom of the one bearing the name, and this must be followed; in

alphabetical arrangement,
treat as Mac however spelt,
Mac, Mc, Mᶜ or *M'*

mac (informal) mackintosh

mackintosh

maharaja

maharanee

● *Mahomet*: use *Muhammad*

mamma

mandolin

manikin dwarf, anatomical
model

manila hemp, paper

manilla African bracelet

mannequin (live) model

manœuvrable ● Amer.
maneuverable

mantel(piece)

mantle cloak

marijuana

marquis

marshal (noun and verb)

marten weasel

martial of war (*martial law*)

martin bird

marvellous ● Amer. *marvelous*

matins

matt lustreless

medieval ● not *mediaeval*

menagerie

mendacity lying

mendicity the state of being a
beggar

millenary of a thousand;
thousandth anniversary

millennium thousand years

millepede

milli- (prefix meaning one-
thousandth)

milometer ● not *mileometer*

miniature

minuscule ● not *miniscule*

mischievous ● not *mischievious*

miscible (in science)

missel-thrush

missis (slang) ● not *missus*

misspell

mistletoe

mixable

mizen (nautical)

moneyed

moneys

mongoose (plural *mongooses*)

moustache ● Amer. *mustache*

mouth (verb) ● not *mouthe*

mucous (adjective)

mucus (noun)

Muhammad

murky

Muslim ● not *Moslem*

naïve, naïvety

naught nothing

négligé

negligible

net not subject to deduction

nonet

nonsuch unrivalled person or
thing

no one nobody

nought the figure zero

numskull

nurseling ● Amer. *nursling*

O (interjection) used to form a
vocative (*O Caesar*) and
when not separated by
punctuation from what
follows (*O for the wings of
a dove*)

octet

● *of*: not to be written instead of
have in such constructions as
'*Did you go?*' '*I would* have,
if it hadn't rained.'

omelette

on to ● not *onto*
orangeade
Orangeism
orang-utan
outcast person cast out
outcaste (India) person with no
    caste
ouzel
oyez!
paediatric
palaeo- (prefix = ancient)
palate roof of mouth
palette artist's board
pallet mattress, part of
    machine, organ valve,
    platform for loads
pallor
panda animal
pander pimp; to gratify
panellist ● Amer. *panelist*
paraffin
parakeet
parallel, paralleled, paralleling
partisan
pasha
pastel (crayon)
pastille
pavior
pawpaw (fruit) ● not *papaw*
pedal (noun) foot lever (verb)
    operate pedal
peddle follow occupation of
    pedlar; trifle
pederast
pedigreed
pedlar vendor of small wares
    ● Amer. *peddler*
peen (verb) strike with pein
peewit
pein of hammer
Pekingese dog, inhabitant of
    Peking ● not *Pekinese*

peninsula (noun)
peninsular (adjective)
pennant (nautical) piece of
    rigging, flag
pennon (military) long narrow
    flag
phone (informal) telephone
    ● not *'phone*
phoney
pi pious
pidgin simplified language
pie jumbled type
piebald
pigeon bird; *not one's pigeon*
    not one's affair
piggy back ● not *pick-a-back*
pi-jaw
pilaff ● not *pilau, pilaw*
pimento ● not *pimiento*
plane (informal) aeroplane
    ● not *'plane*
plenitude ● not *plentitude*
plimsoll (shoe) not *plimsole*
plough ● Amer. *plow*
pommel knob, saddle-bow
poppadam
postilion
powwow
predacious ● not *predaceous*
predominant(ly) ● not *pre-
    dominate(ly)*
premise (verb) to say as
    introduction
premises (plural noun) fore-
    going matters, building
premiss (in logic) proposition
primeval
principal chief
principle fundamental truth,
    moral basis
prise force open
Privy Council

Privy Counsellor
program (in computing)
  ● Amer. in all senses
programme (general)
proletariat
promoter
pukka
pummel pound with fists
pupillage
putt (in golf)
pyjamas ● Amer. *pajamas*
quadraphony, quadraphonic
  ● not *quadri-* or *quadro-*
quartet
quatercentenary ● not *quarter-*
questionnaire
quintet
rabbet groove in woodwork
  (also *rebate*)
racket (for ball games) ● not
  racquet
rackets game
racoon ● not *raccoon*
radical (chemistry)
radicle (botany)
raja ● not *rajah*
rarity
rattan plant, cane (also
  rotan)
raze ● not *rase*
razzmatazz
recce (slang) reconnaissance
recompense
Renaissance ● not *Renascence*
renege ● not *renegue*
repairable (of material) able to
  be repaired
reparable (of loss) able to be
  made good
reverend (deserving reverence;
  title of clergy)
reverent (showing reverence)

review survey, reconsideration,
  report
revue musical entertainment
rhyme ● not *rime*
riband (sport, heraldry)
ribbon
rigor (medical) shivering-fit
rigour severity
Riley (slang: *the life of Riley*)
rill stream
rille (on moon)
rime frost
rogues' gallery
role (no accent)
roly-poly
Romania
rule the roost ● not *roast*
rumba ● not *rhumba*
saccharin (noun)
saccharine (adjective)
salutary beneficial
salutatory welcoming
sanatorium ● Amer. *sanitarium*
Sanhedrin
satire literary work
satiric(al) of satire
satyr woodland deity
satyric of Greek drama with
  satyrs
savannah
scallop ● not *scollop*
scallywag ● Amer. *scalawag*
sceptic ● Amer. *skeptic*
scrimmage tussle ● also term
  in Amer. football
scrummage (Rugby)
sear to scorch, wither(ed)
secrecy
seigneur feudal lord
seigneurial of a seigneur
seigniory lordship
selvage

septet

sere catch of gun-lock; term in ecology

sergeant (military, police)

serjeant (law)

sestet (in a sonnet)

● *sett* (noun): use *set*

sextet (in music, etc.)

Shakespearian

shanty hut, song

sheath (noun)

sheathe (verb)

sheikh

shemozzle rumpus

sherif Muslim leader

sheriff county officer

show ● not *shew*

sibylline

Sinhalese

slew turn ● not *slue*

smart alec

smooth (adjective and verb) ● not *smoothe*

sobriquet

somersault

some time (*come and see me some time*)

sometime former, formerly

spirituel (masculine and feminine) having refinement of mind

spurt

squirearchy

stanch (verb) stop a flow

State (capital S for the political unit)

stationary (adjective) at rest

stationery (noun) paper, etc.

staunch loyal

stoep (South Africa) veranda

storey division of building ● Amer. *story*

storeyed having storeys

storied celebrated in story

stoup for holy water, etc.

straight without curve

strait narrow

sty for pigs; swelling on eyelid ● not *stye*

subsidiary

sulphur ● Amer. *sulfur*

sumac

summons (noun) a command to appear (plural *summonses*)

summons (verb) issue a summons (inflected *summonsed*)

swap ● not *swop*

sycamine, *sycomore* (Biblical trees)

sycamore (member of maple genus)

syllabication ● not *syllabification*

synthesist, *synthesize* ● not *synthet-*

teasel (plant)

teetotalism

teetotaller

tehee (laugh)

tell (archaeology)

template ● not *templet*

tetchy

thank you ● not *thankyou*

tic contraction of muscles

tick-tack semaphore

titbit ● Amer. *tidbit*

titillate excite

titivate smarten up

today

tomorrow

tonight

tonsillar, *tonsillitis*

t'other

toupee
Trades Union Congress
trade union
traipse trudge ● not *trapes*
tranquil
tranquillity, tranquillize
transferable
tranship(ment)
transonic
transsexual
trolley
troop assembly of soldiers
trooper member of troop
troupe company of performers
trouper member of troupe
tsar
Turco- (combining form of
  Turkish)
tympanum ear-drum
'un (informal for *one*)
underlie, underlying
unequivocal, -ally ● not
  unequivocable, -ably
valance curtain, drapery
valence (in chemistry)
Vandyke beard, brown
veld
vendor
veranda

vermilion
vice tool ● Amer. *vise*
villain evil-doer
villein serf
visor ● not *vizor*
wagon
waiver forgoing of legal right
warrior
wastable
waver be unsteady
way: under way ● not *under
  weigh*
whiskey (Irish)
whisky (Scotch)
Whit Monday, Sunday
Whitsunday (Scottish; not a
  Sunday)
whiz
whooping cough
who's who is
whose of whom
wistaria ● not *wisteria*
withhold
woeful ● not *woful*
wrath anger
wreath (noun)
wreathe (verb)
wroth angry
yoghurt

II

PRONUNCIATION

> For one thing, you speak quite differently from Roy. Now
> mind you, I'm not saying that one kind of voice is better
> than another kind, although . . the B.B.C. seems to have
> very definite views on the subject.
>
> (Marghanita Laski, *The Village*)

THIS section aims at resolving the uncertainty felt by many speakers
both about some of the general variations in the pronunciation of
English, and about a large number of individual words whose
pronunciation is variable. Accordingly, the section is in two parts:
A, general points of pronunciation, and B, a list of preferred
pronunciations.

The aim of recommending one type of pronunciation rather than
another, or of giving a word a recommended spoken form, naturally
implies the existence of a standard. There are of course many varieties
of English, even within the limits of the British Isles, but it is not
the business of this section to describe them. The treatment here is
based upon Received Pronunciation (RP), namely 'the pronunciation of that variety of British English widely considered to be least
regional, being originally that used by educated speakers in southern
England'.* This is not to suggest that other varieties are inferior;
rather, RP is here taken as a neutral national standard, just as it
is in its use in broadcasting or in the teaching of English as a foreign
language.

A. *General points of pronunciation*

This first part of Section II is concerned with general variations and
uncertainties in pronunciation. Even when RP alone is taken as the
model, it is impossible to lay down a set of rules that will establish the
correct pronunciation of every word and hold it constant, since
pronunciation is continually changing. Some changes affect a particular sound in its every occurrence throughout the vocabulary,

---

* *A Supplement to the OED*, Volume 3.

while others occur only in the environment of a few other sounds. Some changes occur gradually and imperceptibly; some are limited to a section of the community. At any time there is bound to be considerable variation in pronunciation. One of the purposes of the entries that follow is to draw attention to such variation and to indicate the degree of acceptability of each variant in standard English. Uncertainty about pronunciation also arises from the irregularity of English spelling. It is all too often impossible to guess how a particular letter or group of letters in an unfamiliar word should be pronounced. Broadly speaking, there are particular letters and letter sequences which repeatedly cause such uncertainty (e.g. *g* (hard and soft); final *-ed*; final *-ade*). To settle these uncertainties is the other main purpose of the entries that follow.

The entries are arranged in alphabetical order of heading; the headings are not, of course, complete words, but are either individual letters of the alphabet or sequences of letters making up parts (usually the beginnings or endings) of words. Some entries cover sounds that are spelt in various ways: the heading given is the typical spelling. There are also three entries of a different sort: they deal with (*a*) the main distinguishing features of American pronunciation, (*b*) the reduction of common words in rapid speech, and (*c*) patterns of stress.

a

1. There is variation in the pronunciation of *a* between the sound heard in *calm, father* and that heard in *cat, fan,* in

(*a*) the suffix *-graph* (in *photograph, telegraph,* etc.) and

(*b*) the prefix *trans-* (as in *transfer, translate,* etc.).

(*a*) In *-graph, a* as in *calm* seems to be the more generally acceptable form in RP. Note that when the suffix *-ic* is added (e.g. in *photographic*), only *a* as in *cat* can be used.

(*b*) In *trans-,* either kind of *a* is acceptable.

2. The word endings *-ada, -ade,* and *-ado* occasion difficulty, since in some words the pronunciation of the *a* is as in *calm,* in others as in *made.*

(*a*) In *-ada* words, *a* is as in *calm,* e.g. *armada, cicada.*

(*b*) In most *-ade* words, *a* is as in *made,* e.g. *accolade, barricade, cavalcade.*
Exceptions: *a* as in *calm* in

aubade	*façade*	*roulade*
ballade	*pomade*	*saccade*
charade	*promenade*	

and in unassimilated loan-words from French, e.g. *dégringolade*, *œillade*.

(*c*) In most *-ado* words, *a* is as in *calm*, e.g.

aficionado	*avocado*	*desperado*
amontillado	*bravado*	*Mikado*

Exceptions: *a* as in *made* in *bastinado*, *gambado*, *tornado*.

3. *a* in the word-ending *-alia* is like *a* in *alien*, e.g. in *marginalia*, *pastoralia*, *penetralia*.

4. *a* before *ls* and *lt* in many words is pronounced either like *aw* in *bawl* or *o* in *doll*, e.g. in

alter	*halt*	*salt*
false	*palsy*	*waltz*

The same variation occurs with *au* in *fault*, *vault*.
Note: in several words *a* before *ls* and *lt* can only be pronounced like *a* in *sally*, e.g.

Alsation	*altruism*	*salsify*
alter ego	*caltrop*	*saltation*

5. The word endings *-ata*, *-atum*, and *-atus* occasion difficulty. In most words the *a* is pronounced as in *mate*, e.g. in

apparatus	*flatus*
datum (plural *data*)	*hiatus*
desideratum (plural	*meatus*
desiderata)	*ultimatum*

Exceptions: *cantata*, *erratum*, *sonata*, *toccata* with *a* as in *calm*; *stratum*, *stratus* with *a* as in *mate* or as in *calm*.

-age

The standard pronunciation of the following words of French origin ending in *-age* is with stress on the first syllable, *a* as in *calm*, and *g* as in *régime*.

barrage	*fuselage*	*mirage*
camouflage	*garage*	*montage*
dressage	*massage*	*sabotage*

Note that *collage* is stressed on the second syllable.

● The pronunciation of -*age* as in *cabbage* in any of these words is non-standard. The placing of the stress on the final syllable in some of these words is a feature of Amer. pronunciation.

□ The substitution of the sound of *g* as in *large* for that in *régime* by some speakers in several of these words is acceptable.

American pronunciation

Where the Amer. pronunciation of individual forms and words significantly differs from the British, this is indicated as part of the individual entries in this Section. There remain certain constant features of 'General American'* pronunciation that, being generally distributed, are not worth noting for every word or form in which they occur. The principal features are these:

1. *r* is sounded wherever it is written, i.e. after vowels finally and before consonants, as well as before vowels, e.g. in *burn, car, form*.

2. The sound of *l* is 'dark' (as in British *bell, fill*) everywhere; the British sound of *l* as in *land, light* is not used.

3. (*t*)*t* between vowels sounds like *d* (and this *d* often sounds like a kind of *r*), e.g. in *latter, ladder, tomato*.

4. The vowel of *boat, dote, know, no*, etc. is a pure long vowel, not a diphthong as in British English.

5. Where British English has four vowels, (i) *a* as in *bat*, (ii) *ah* as in *dance, father*, (iii) *o* as in *hot, long*, and (iv) *aw* as in *law*, Amer. English has only three, differently distributed, viz.: (i) *a* as in *bat, dance*, (ii) *ah* as in *father, hot*, and (iii) *aw* as in *long, law*.

6. The sound of *you* (spelt *u, ew*, etc.) after *s, t, d, n*, is replaced by the sound of *oo*, e.g. in *resume, Tuesday, due, new*, etc.

7. The sound of *u* as in *up* (also spelt *o* in *come*, etc.) sounds like the obscure sound of *a* as in *aloft, china*.

8. *er* is pronounced as in *herd* in words where it is like *ar* in *hard* in British English, e.g. in *clerk, derby*.

9. The vowels in the first syllables of (*a*) *ferry, herald, merry*, etc., (*b*) *fairy, hairy, Mary*, etc., and (*c*) *carry, Harry, marry*, etc. (i.e. when

---

 * 'A form of U.S. speech without marked dialectal or regional characteristics' (*A Supplement to the OED*, Volume 1).

r follows) are not distinguished from one another by most General American speakers.

10. In words of four syllables and over, in which the main stress falls on the first or second syllable, there is a strong secondary stress on the last syllable but one, the vowel of which is fully enunciated, not reduced as in British English, e.g. *cóntemplàtive, témporàry, térritòry*.

-arily

In a few adverbs that end in the sequence *-arily* there is a tendency to place the stress on the *a* rather than the first syllable of the word. The reason lies in the stress pattern of four- and five-syllable words.

Adjectives of four syllables ending in *-ary* which are stressed on the first syllable are generally pronounced with elision of one of the middle syllables, e.g. *military, necessary, temporary* pronounced milit'ry, necess'ry, temp'rary. This trisyllabic pattern is much easier to pronounce.

The addition of the adverbial suffix *-ly* converts the word back into an unwieldly tetrasyllable that cannot be further elided: *milit(a)rily, necess(a)rily, temp(o)rarily*. Hence the use of these adverbs is some-times avoided by saying *in a military fashion, in a solitary way*, etc.

A number of these adverbs are, however, in common use, e.g.

arbitrarily	*necessarily*	*temporarily*
momentarily	*ordinarily*	*voluntarily*

Because of the awkwardness of placing the stress on the first syllable, colloquial speech has adopted a pronunciation with stress on the third syllable, with the *a* sounding like *e* in *verily*. This is probably a borrowing from Amer. English, in which this pronunciation problem does not arise. In adjectives like *necessary* the ending *-ary* quite regularly receives a secondary stress (see **American pronunciation** above), which can then be converted into a main stress when *-ly* is added.

This pronunciation is much easier and more natural in rapid, colloquial speech, in which it would be pedantic to censure it.

● In formal and careful speech, the standard pronunciation of *arbitrarily, momentarily, necessarily, ordinarily, temporarily*, and *voluntarily* is with stress on the first syllable.

The case of the word *primarily* is somewhat different. It contains only four syllables, which, with stress on the first, can be reduced by elision of the second syllable to the easily pronounced spoken form prim'rily.

● There is therefore no need to pronounce the word with stress on the second syllable, pri-*merr*-ily, or even worse, pri-*marr*-ily. These are widely unacceptable.

-ed

1. In the following adjectives the ending *-ed* is pronounced as a separate syllable:

accursed	*naked*	*wicked*
cragged	*rugged*	*wretched*
deuced	*sacred*	

Note: *deuced* can also be pronounced as one syllable.

2. The following words represent two different spoken forms each with meanings that differ according to whether *-ed* is pronounced as a separate syllable or not. In most cases the former pronunciation indicates an adjective (as with the list under 1 above), the latter the past tense and past participle of a verb, but some are more complicated.

(*a*) *-ed* as separate syllable	(*b*) *-ed* pronounced '*d*
aged	
= very old (*he is very aged, an aged man*)	= having the age of (one, etc.) (*he is aged three, a boy aged three*); past of *to age* (*he has aged greatly*)
beloved	
used before noun (*beloved brethren*); = beloved person (*my beloved is mine*)	used as predicate (*he was beloved by all*)
blessed	
= fortunate, holy, sacred (*blessed are the meek, the blessed saints*); = blessed person (*Isles of the blessed*)	part of *to bless*; sometimes also in senses listed in left-hand column
crabbed	
= cross-grained, hard to follow, etc.	past of *to crab*

crooked
    = not straight, dishonest   = having a transverse handle (*crooked stick*); past of *to crook*

cursed
    before noun = damnable   past of *to curse*

dogged
    = tenacious   past of *to dog*

jagged
    = indented   past of *to jag*

learned
    = erudite   past of *to learn* (usually *learnt*)

ragged
    = rough, torn, etc.   past of *to rag*

-edly, -edness

When the further suffixes *-ly* (forming adverbs) and *-ness* (forming nouns) are added to adjectives ending in the suffix *-ed*, an uncertainty arises about whether to pronounce this *-ed-* as a separate syllable or not. The adjectives to which these suffixes are added can be divided into three kinds.

1. Those in which *-ed* is already a separate syllable (*a*) because it is preceded by *d* or *t* or (*b*) because the adjective is one of those discussed in the entry for *-ed* above; e.g. *belated, decided, excited, levelheaded, wicked*. When both *-ly* and *-ess* are added, *-ed-* remains a separate syllable, e.g. (i) *belatedly, decidedly, excitedly, wickedly*; (ii) *belatedness, levelheadedness, wickedness*.

2. Those in which the syllable preceding *-ed* is unstressed, i.e. if *-(e)d* is removed the word ends in an unstressed syllable; e.g. *bad-tempered, embarrassed, hurried, self-centred*. When both *-ly* and *-ness* are added, *-ed-* remains non-syllabic (i.e. it sounds like 'd), e.g.

(i)
abandonedly	*frenziedly*	*old-fashionedly*
bad-temperedly	*good-humouredly*	*self-centredly*
biasedly	*hurriedly*	*shamefacedly*
dignifiedly	*ill-naturedly*	*worriedly*
embarrassedly		

(ii) *bad-temperedness*   *self-centredness* (= -center'dness)
    hurriedness   *shamefacedness*

3. Those in which the syllable preceding *-ed* is stressed, i.e. if *-(e)d* is removed the word ends in a stressed syllable, or is a monosyllable, e.g. *assured, fixed.*

● (i) When *-ly* is added *-ed* becomes an extra syllable, e.g.

advisedly	*declaredly*	*professedly*
allegedly	*deservedly*	*resignedly*
amusedly	*designedly*	*surprisedly*
assuredly	*displeasedly*	*undisguisedly*
avowedly	*fixedly*	*unfeignedly*
constrainedly	*markedly*	*unreservedly*

Exceptions:

There are a few definite exceptions to this rule, e.g. *subduedly, tiredly* (*ed* is not a separate syllable). There are also several words in which variation is found, e.g. *confessedly, depravedly, depressedly* (three or four syllables according to *OED*); *inspiredly* (four syllables in *OED*, but now probably three).

● Note that some adverbs formed on adjectives in *-ed* sound awkward and ugly whether *-ed-* is pronounced as a separate syllable or not. Because of this, some authorities (e.g. *MEU*) discourage the formation of words like *boredly, charmedly, discouragedly, experiencedly.*

(ii) When *-ness* is added, there is greater variation. The older usage seems to have been to make *-ed-* an extra syllable. In *OED* the following are so marked:

absorbedness	*estrangedness*	*forcedness*
assuredness	*exposedness*	*markedness*
confirmedness	*fixedness*	*surprisedness*

The following have *ed* or *'d* as alternative pronunciation:

ashamedness	*pleasedness*
detachedness	*preparedness*

But *'d* is the only pronunciation in *blurredness, subduedness.* However, many other words are not specially marked, and it seems likely that it has become increasingly rare for *-ed-* to be separately sounded.

□ It is acceptable *not* to make *-ed-* a separate syllable in words of this type.

-ein(e)

The ending -ein(e) (originally disyllabic) is now usually pronounced like -ene in *polythene* in

    caffeine   *casein*   *codeine*   *protein*

-eity

The traditional pronunciation of *e* in this termination is as in *me*, e.g. in

contemporaneity	*heterogeneity*	*spontaneity*
corporeity	*homogeneity*	*velleity*
deity	*simultaneity*	

Among younger speakers there is a marked tendency to substitute the sound of *e* in *café*, *suede*. The reasons for this are probably:

1. The difficulty of making the sounds of *e* (as in *me*) and *i* distinct when they come together. Cf. the words *rabies*, *species*, *protein*, etc. in which *e* and *i* were originally separate syllables but have now fused. Because of this difficulty, many users of the traditional pronunciation of *e* actually make the first two syllables of *deity* sound like *deer*, and so with the other words.

2. The influence of the reformed pronunciation of Latin in which *e* has the sound of *e* in *café*.

The same variation is found in the sequence -ei- in the words *deism*, *deist*, *reify*, *reification* (but not *theism*, *theist*).

● The pronunciation of *e* as in *me* is the only generally acceptable one in all these words.

-eur

This termination, occurring in words originally taken from French, in which it is the agent suffix, normally carries the stress and sounds like *er* in *deter*, *refer*, e.g. in:

agent provocateur	*entrepreneur*	*restaurateur*
coiffeur	*litterateur*	*sabreur*
colporteur	*masseur*	*seigneur*
connoisseur	*poseur*	*tirailleur*
(con-a-*ser*)	*raconteur*	*voyeur*

Stress is on the first syllable usually in

> *amateur* (and *amateurish*: *am*-a-ter-ish)
> *chauffeur*   *saboteur*

Stress can be either on the first or the third syllable in *secateurs*.

Feminine nouns can be formed from some of these by the substitution of *-se* for *-r*: the resulting termination is pronounced like *urze* in *furze*, e.g. *coiffeuse, masseuse, saboteuse*.

liqueur is pronounced li-*cure* (Amer. li-*cur*).

g

A. In certain less familiar words and words taken from foreign languages, especially Greek, there is often uncertainty as to whether *g* preceding *e, i,* and (especially) *y* is pronounced hard as in *get* or soft as in *gem*.

1. The prefix *gyn(o)-* meaning 'woman' now always has a hard *g*.

2. The element *-gyn-* with the same meaning, occurring inside the word, usually has a soft *g*, as in *androgynous, misogynist*.

3. The elements *gyr-* (from a root meaning 'ring') and *-gitis* (in names of diseases) always have a soft *g*, as in

> *gyrate*   *gyro* (-*scope,*
> *gyration*   *compass*, etc.)
> *gyre* (poetic, =   *laryngitis*
>   gyrate, gyration)   *meningitis*

4. The following, among many other more familiar words, have a hard *g*:

> *gibbous*   *gill* (fish's organ)
> *gig* (all senses)   *gingham*

5. The following have a soft *g*:

> *gibber*   *giro*   *gypsum*
> *gibe*   (payment system)   *gyrfalcon*
> *gill* (measure) *gybe*   *gyve*
> *gillyflower*   *gypsophila*   *panegyric*

6. There is variation in:
> *demagogic, -y, gibberish, hegemony, pedagogic, -y*.

● *g* should be hard in *analogous*.

B. See *-age,* p. 47.

-gm

g is silent in the sequence *gm* at the end of the word:

   apophthegm   *paradigm*
   diaphragm   *phlegm*

But *g* is pronounced when this sequence comes between vowels:

   apophthegmatic *paradigmatic*
   enigma   *phlegmatic*

h

1. Initial *h* is silent in *heir*, *honest*, *honour*, *hour*, and their derivatives; also in *honorarium*. It is sounded in *habitué*.

2. Initial *h* used commonly to be silent if the first syllable was unstressed, as in *habitual*, *hereditary*, *historic*, *hotel*. This pronunciation is now old-fashioned. (See also **a or an**, p. 5.)

-ies

The ending *-ies* is usually pronounced as one syllable (like *ies* in *diesel*) in:

   caries   *rabies*   *series*
   congeries *scabies* *species*
   facies

● The reduction of this ending to a sound like the ending of the plural words *armies*, *babies*, etc., is best avoided.

-ile

The ending *-ile* is normally pronounced like *isle*, e.g. in

   docile   *fertile*   *sterile*
   domicile *missile* *virile*

● The usual Amer. pronunciation in most words of this kind is with the sound of *il* in *daffodil* or *pencil*.

The pronunciation is like *eel* in:

   automobile *-mobile* (suffix)
   imbecile

-ile forms two syllables in *campanile* (rhyming with *Ely*), *cantabile* (pronounced can-*tah*-bi-ly), and *sal volatile* (rhyming with *philately*).

ng

There is a distinction in Standard English between *ng* representing a single sound (which is represented by *n* alone before *c*, *k*, *q*, and *x*, as in *zinc*, *ink*, *tranquil*, and *lynx*) and *ng* representing a compound consisting of this sound followed by the sound of hard *g*.

1. The single sound is the only one to occur at the end of a word, e.g. in

bring *furlong* *song* *writing*

2. The single sound also occurs in the middle of words, but usually in words that are a compound of a word ending in *-ng* (as in 1 above) + a suffix, e.g.

bringer	*kingly*	*stringy*
bringing	*longish*	*wrongful*
hanged	*singable*	

3. The compound sound, *ng* + *g*, is otherwise normal in the middle of words, e.g.

anger *hungry* *language* *singly*

And exceptionally, according to rule 2, in *diphthongize*, *longer*, *-est*, *prolongation*, *stronger*, *-est*, *younger*, *-est*.

● 4. It is non-standard:

(*a*) To use *-in* for *-ing* (suffix), i.e. to pronounce *bringing*, *writing* as bringin, writin.

(*b*) To use *n* for *ng* in *length*, *strength*. (The pronunciation lenkth, strenkth is acceptable.)

(*c*) To use *nk* for *ng* in *anything*, *everything*, *nothing*, *something*.

(*d*) To use the compound sound *ng* + *g* in all cases of *ng*, i.e. in words covered by rules 1 and 2 as well as 3. This pronunciation is, however, normal in certain regional forms of English.

o

1. In many words the sound normally represented in English by *u* as in *butter*, *sun* is written instead with *o*, e.g. *above*, *come*, *front*. There are a few words in which there is variation in pronunciation between the above sound (as in *come*, etc.) and the more usual sound of *o* (as in *body*, *lot*, etc.). The earlier pronunciation of most of these was with the *u*-sound; the *o*-sound was introduced under the influence of the spelling.

(*a*) More usually with the *u*-sound:

accomplice	frontier	pommel
accomplish	mongrel	

(*b*) More usually with the *o*-sound:

combat	hovel	pomegranate
conduit	hover	sojourn
dromedary		

(*c*) Still variable (either is acceptable):

comrade   constable

2. Before *ff*, *ft*, *ss*, *st*, and *th*, in certain words, there was formerly a variety of RP in which *o* was pronounced like *aw* in *law* or *oa* in *broad*, so that *off*, *often*, *cross*, *lost*, and *cloth* sounded like *orf*, *orphan*, etc.

● This pronunciation is now non-standard.

3. Before double *ll*, *o* has the long sound (as in *pole*) in some words, and the short sound (as in *Polly*) in others.

(*a*) With the long sound:

boll	roll	toll
droll	scroll	troll
knoll	stroll	wholly
poll	swollen	

(*b*) With the short sound:

doll, *loll*, and most words in which another syllable follows, e.g. *collar*, *holly*, etc.

4. Before *lt*, *o* is pronounced long, as in *pole*, e.g. *bolt*, *colt*, *molten*, *revolt*.

● The substitution of short *o*, as in *doll*, in these words is non-standard.

5. Before *lv*, *o* is pronounced short, as in *doll*, e.g.

absolve	evolve	revolve
devolve	involve	revolver
dissolve	resolve	solve

● The substitution of long *o*, as in *pole*, in these words is non-standard.

ough

Difficult though this spelling is for foreign learners, most words in which it occurs are familiar to the ordinary English speaker. Pronunciation difficulties may arise, however, with the following words:

brougham	(a kind of carriage) *broo*-am or broom
chough	(bird) chuff
clough	(ravine) cluff
hough	(animal's joint), same as, and sounds like, *hock*
slough	(bog) rhymes with *plough*
slough	(snake's skin) sluff
sough	(sound) suff (can also rhyme with *plough*)

phth

This sequence should sound like *fth* (in *fifth*, *twelfth*), e.g. in *diphtheria*, *diphthong*, *monophthong*, *naphtha*, *ophthalmic*.

● It is non-standard to pronounce these as if written *dip-theria*, etc.

Initially, as in the words *phthisical*, *phthisis*, the *ph* can be silent; it is also usually silent in *apophthegm*.

pn-, ps-, pt-

These sequences occur at the beginning of many words taken from Greek. In all of them it is normal not to pronounce the initial *p-*. The exception is *psi* representing the name of a Greek letter, used, e.g., as a symbol.

r

1. When *r* is the last letter of a word (always following a vowel, or another *r*) or precedes 'silent' final *e* (where it may follow a consonant, e.g. in *acre* which really = aker), it is normally silent in RP, e.g. in

aware	*four*	*pure*
err	*here*	*runner*
far	*kilometre*	

But when another word, beginning with a vowel sound, follows in the same sentence, it is normal to pronounce the final *r*, e.g. in

aware of it	*four hours*	*pure air*
to err is human	*here it is*	*runner-up*
far away	*a kilometre of track*	

This is called the 'linking *r*'.

● It is standard to use linking *r* and unnatural to try to avoid it.

2. A closely connected feature of the spoken language is what is called 'intrusive *r*'.

(*a*) The commonest occurrence of this is when a word ending with the obscure sound of *a*, as *china, comma, Jonah, loofah*, etc. is immediately followed by a word beginning with a vowel sound. An intrusive *r* is added to the end of the first word as if it were spelt with *-er* so as to ease the passage from one word to the next. Typical examples are:

> *the area-*r *of the island*   *an umbrella-*r
> *the pasta-*r *is cooked*   *organization*
> *sonata-*r *in E flat*   *a villa-*r *in Italy*

Here the sound spelt *-a* at the end of *area, pasta*, etc., which sounds the same as *-er, -re* at the end of *runner, kilometre*, is treated as if it were spelt with an *r* following.

(*b*) In the same way, some speakers unconsciously equate (i) the spelling *a* or *ah* in *grandma, Shah* with the identical-sounding *ar* in *far*, (ii) the spelling *aw* in *law, draw* with the similar *our* in *four* or *ore* in *bore, tore*, and (iii) the spelling *eu* in *milieu, cordon bleu* with the similar *er(r)* in *err, prefer*. Thus, just as linking *r* is used with *far, four, bore, tore, err*, and *prefer*, such speakers introduce an intrusive *r* in, e.g.

> *is grandma-*r *at home?*   *a milieu-*r *in*
> *The Shah-*r *of Iran*   *which . .*
> *draw-*r *a picture*   *a cordon bleu-*r
> *law-*r *and order*   *in the kitchen*

(*c*) Intrusive *r* is often introduced before inflexional endings, e.g.

> *The boys are keen on scubering* (i.e.
>   *scubaing*) (Berkely Mather)
> *oohing and ah-*r*-ing*
> *draw-*r*-ing room*

and even within the word *withdraw-*r*-al*.

(*d*) Intrusive *r* has been noted since the end of the eighteenth century. In the mid-nineteenth century it was regarded as unpardonable in an educated person, but acknowledged to occur widely even among the cultivated. Its use after obscure *a* (as described under (*a*) above), where it greatly aids the flow of the sentence and is relatively unobtrusive, is acceptable in rapid, informal speech. The avoidance of intrusive *r* here by the insertion of a hiatus or a catch in the breath would sound affected and pedantic.

● The use of intrusive *r* after the sounds of *ah*, *aw*, and *eu* (described under (*b*)) is very widely unacceptable and should be avoided if possible. Its use before inflexional endings ((*c*) above) is illiterate or jocular.

● In formal speech, the use of intrusive *r* in any context conveys an impression of unsuitable carelessness and should not be used at all.

3. There is a tendency in certain words to drop *r* if it is closely followed (or in a few cases, preceded) by another *r* at the beginning of an unstressed syllable, e.g. in

> *deteriorate* mispronounced deteriate
> *February* mispronounced Febuary
> *honorary* mispronounced honary (prefer hon'rary)
> *itinerary* mispronounced itinery
> *library* mispronounced lib'ry
> *secretary* mispronounced seketry or seketerry
> *temporary* mispronounced tempary (prefer temp'rary)

● This pronunciation should be avoided, especially in formal speech.

reduced forms

In rapid speech, many of the shorter words whose function is essentially grammatical rather than lexical, being lightly stressed, tend to be reduced either by the obscuring of their vowels or the loss of a consonant or both. They may even be attached to one another or to more prominent words. Similarly, some words such as pronouns and auxiliary verbs are in rapid speech omitted altogether, while longer words of frequent occurrence are shortened by the elision of unstressed syllables. Typical examples are:

> *gunna, wanna* = going to, want to
> *kinda, sorta* = kind of, sort of
> *gimme, lemme* = give me, let me
> *'snot* = it's not
> *innit, wannit* = isn't it, wasn't it
> *doncha, dunno* = don't you, I don't know
> *what's he say, where d'you find it, we done it, what you want it for?*
> *'spect* or *I'xpect* = I expect
> *(I) spose* = I suppose
> *cos, course, on'y, praps, probly* = because, of course, only, perhaps, probably

● Most of these reduced forms (with the possible exception of *innit*, *wannit*) are natural in informal RP, but severely mar the quality and clarity of careful and prepared discourse, where they should be avoided.

s, *sh*, *z*, and *zh*

In certain kinds of word, where the spelling is *ci*, *si*, or *ti*, or where it is *s* before long *u*, there is variation between two or more of the four sounds which may be phonetically represented as:

s as in *sun*	*zh* representing the
sh as in *ship*	sound of *s* in *leisure*
z as in *zone*	or *g* in *régime*

1. There is variation between *s* and *sh* in words such as:

appreciate	*association*	*negotiation*
appreciation	*negotiate*	*sociology*
associate		

This variation does not occur in all words with a similar structure: only *s* is used in *glaciation*, *pronunciation* (= -see-*ay*-shon), and only *sh* in *partiality* (par-shee-*al*-ity). Note that there can be a variant having the sound of *s* only with words in which the following *i* constitutes a separate syllable; hence only *sh* occurs in *initial*, *racial*, *sociable*, *spatial*, *special*, etc. It is possible that speakers avoid using *sh* in words that end in *-tion*, which also contains the *sh*-sound, so as to prevent the occurrence of this sound in adjacent syllables, e.g. in *appreciation* = appreshi-ashon.

2. There is variation between *s* and *sh* in *sensual*, *sexual*, *issue*, *tissue*, and between *z* and *zh* in *casual*, *casuist*, *visual*.

3. There is variation between *sh* and *zh* in *aversion*, *equation*, *immersion*, *transition*, *version*.

□ Either variant is acceptable in each of these kinds of word, although in all of them *sh* is the traditional pronunciation.

4. In the names of some countries and regions ending in *-sia*, and in the adjectives derived from them, there is variation between *sh* and *zh*, and in some cases *z* and *s* as well. So:

Asian	= *A*-shan or *A*-zhan
Asiatic	= A-shi-*at*-ic or A-zhi-*at*-ic or A-zi-*at*-ic or A-si-*at*-ic
Friesian	= *Free*-zi-an or *Free*-zhan
Indonesian	= Indo-*nee*-shan or -zhan or -zi-an or -si-an
Persian	= *Per*-shan or *Per*-zhan

Polynesian (varies like *Indonesian*)
Rhodesian = Ro-*dee*-shan or -zhan or -zi-an or -si-an

● In all except *Friesian* the pronunciation with *sh* is traditional in RP and therefore the most widely acceptable. The pronunciation with *zh* is also generally acceptable.

stress

1. The position of the stress accent is the key to the pronunciation of many English polysyllabic words. If it is known on which syllable the stress falls, it is very often possible to deduce the pronunciation of the vowels. This is largely because the vowels of unstressed syllables in English are subject to reduction in length, obscuration of quality, and, quite often, complete elision. Compare the sound of the vowel in the stressed syllable in the words on the left with that of the vowel in the same syllable, unstressed, in the related words on the right:

a:	humánity	húman
	monárchic	mónarch
	practicálity	práctically (-ic'ly)
	secretárial	sécretary (-t'ry)
e:	presént (verb)	présent (noun)
	protést	protestátion
	mystérious	mýstery (= myst'ry)
i:	satírical	sátirist
	combíne	combinátion
	anxíety	ánxious (= anksh'ous)
o:	ecónomy	económic
	oppóse	ópposite
	histáric	hístory (= hist'ry)
u:	luxúrious	lúxury
	indústrial	índustry

Because the position of the stress has such an important effect on the phonetic shape of the word, it is not surprising that many of the most hotly disputed questions of pronunciation centre on the placing of the stress. For example, in *controversy*, stress on the first syllable causes the four vowels to sound like those of *collar turning*, while stress on the second causes them to sound like those of *an opposite*: two quite different sequences of vowels.

2. It is impossible to formulate rules accounting for the position of the stress in every English word, whether by reference to the spelling or on the basis of grammatical function. If it were, most of

the controversies about pronunciation could be cleared up overnight. Instead, three very general observations can be made.

(*a*) Within very broad limits, the stress can fall on any syllable. These limits are roughly defined by the statement that more than three unstressed syllables cannot easily be uttered in sequence. Hence, for example, five-syllable words with stress on the first or last syllable are rare. Very often in polysyllabic words at least one syllable besides the main stressed syllable bears a medium or secondary stress, e.g. *cáterpìllar*, *còntrovèrtibílity*.

(*b*) Although there is such fluidity in the occurrence of stress, some patterns of stress are clearly associated with some patterns of spelling or with grammatical function (or, especially, with variation of grammatical function in a single word). For example, almost all words ending in the suffixes *-ic* and *-ical* are stressed on the syllable immediately preceding the suffix. There is only a handful of exceptions: *Arabic*, *arithmetic* (noun), *arsenic*, *catholic*, *choleric*, *heretic*, *lunatic*, *politic*(*s*), *rhetoric*.

(*c*) If the recent and current changes and variations in stress in a large number of words are categorized, a small number of general tendencies can be discerned. Most of these can be ascribed to the influence exerted by the existing fixed stress patterns over other words (many of which may conform to other existing patterns of stress). It will be the purpose of the remaining part of this entry to describe some of these tendencies and to relate them to the existing canons of acceptibility.

3. *Two-syllable words*

While there is no general rule that says which syllable the stress will fall on, there is a fixed pattern to which quite a large number of words conform, by which nouns and adjectives are stressed on the first syllable, and verbs on the second.

A large number of words beginning with a (Latin) prefix have stress on the first syllable if they are nouns or adjectives, but on the second if they are verbs, e.g.

accent	import	transfer
compound	present	transport
conflict	suspect	

The same distinction is made in some words ending in *-ment*, e.g.

ferment	segment
fragment	torment

And words ending in -*ate* with stress on the first syllable are usually nouns, while those with stress on the second are mainly verbs, e.g.

nouns:	verbs:
climate	*create*
curate	*dictate*
dictate	*frustrate*
mandate	*vacate*

This pattern has recently exercised an influence over several other words not originally conforming to it. The words

ally	*defect*	*rampage*
combine	*intern*	

were all originally stressed on the second syllable; as verbs, they still are, but as nouns, they are all usually stressed on the first. Exactly the same tendency has affected

dispute   *recess*   *research*   *romance*

but in these words, the pronunciation of the noun with stress on the first syllable is rejected in good usage. The following nouns and adjectives (not corresponding to identically spelt verbs) show the same transference of stress: *adept*, *adult*, *chagrin*, *supine*.

In the verbs *combat*, *contact*, *harass*, and *traverse*, originally stressed on the first syllable, a tendency towards stress on the second syllable is discernible, but the new stress has been accepted only in the word *traverse*.

4. *Three-syllable words*

Of the three possible stress patterns in three-syllable words, that with stress on the first syllable is the strongest and best-established, exercising an influence over words conforming to the other two patterns.

(*a*) Words with stress on the final syllable are relatively rare. A number of them have been attracted to the dominant pattern; in some this pattern (stress on the first syllable) is acceptable in RP, e.g. *artisan*, *commandant*, *confidant*, *partisan*, *promenade*; in others it is not, e.g. *cigarette*, *magazine*.

(*b*) Many words originally having stress on the second syllable now normally or commonly have stress on the first, e.g.

abdomen	*decorous*	*recondite*
acumen	*obdurate*	*remonstrate*
albumen	*precedence*	*secretive*
aspirant	*precedent*	*sonorous*
communal	(noun)	*subsidence*
composite	*quandary*	*vagary*

Other words are also affected by this tendency, but the pronunciation with stress on the first syllable has not been accepted as standard, e.g. in

Byzantine	*contribute*
clandestine	*distribute*

Note: This tendency to move the stress back from the second to the first syllable of three-syllable words has been observed for at least a century. A case that typically illustrates it is the word *sonorous*. In 1884 W. W. Skeat, in his *Etymological Dictionary of the English Language* (edn. 2), wrote: 'Properly *sonórous*; it will probably, sooner or later, become *sónorous*.' The first dictionary to recognize the change was *Webster's New International* of 1909, which adds the newer pronunciation with the comment 'now often, esp. in British usage'. Fifty years after Skeat, G. B. Shaw wrote to *The Times* (2 Jan. 1934): 'An announcer who pronounced decadent and sonorous as dekkadent and sonnerus would provoke Providence to strike him dumb'—testifying both to the prevalence of the new pronunciation and to the opposition it aroused. In 1956 Compton Mackenzie, in an Oxford Union Debate, protested against the pronunciation of *quandary*, *sonorous*, and *decorous* with stress on the first syllable (B. Foster, *The Changing English Language*, 1968, p. 243). Foster (ibid.), however, records his surprise in about 1935 at hearing a schoolmaster use the older pronunciation of *sonorous*. The newer pronunciation was first mentioned in the *Concise Oxford Dictionary* in 1964; the two pronunciations are both heard, but the newer one probably now prevails.

(*c*) There is a tendency in a few words to move the stress from the first to the second syllable. It is generally resisted in standard usage, e.g. in

combatant	*exquisite*	*urinal*
deficit	*stigmata*	

all of which have stress on the first syllable. But it has prevailed in *aggrandize*, *chastisement*, *conversant*, *doctrinal*, *environs*, *pariah*.

5. *Four-syllable words*

In a very large group of four-syllable words there is a clash between two opposing tendencies. One is the impulse to place the stress on the first syllable; the other is the influence of antepenultimate stress which is so prevalent in three-syllable words. Broadly speaking, it has been traditional in RP to favour stress on the first syllable, so that the shift to the second syllable has been strongly resisted in:

applicable	*demonstrable*	*intricacy*
aristocrat	*formidable*	*kilometre*
capitalist	*hospitable*	*lamentable*
controversy	*illustrative*	*remediless*
contumacy		

In many words the two tendencies can be reconciled by the elision of one of the two middle unstressed syllables:

adversary	*necessary*	*promissory*
comparable	*participle*	*referable*
migratory	*preferable*	*voluntary*
momentary	*primarily*	

However, many words traditionally stressed on the first syllable have been, or are being, adapted to the antepenultimate stress pattern, e.g.

centenary	*hegemony*	*nomenclature*
despicable	*metallurgy*	*pejorative*
disputable	*miscellany*	*peremptory*
explicable		

Because antepenultimate stress has been accepted in most of these words, it is difficult to reject it in the words in the first list simply on the ground of tradition. Analogy is the obvious argument in some cases, i.e. the analogy of *capital*, *demonstrate*, *illustrate*, *intricate*, *kilocycle* (or *centimetre*), and *remedy* for the words related to them in the list, but this cannot be used with the remaining words.

6. *Five-syllable words*

Five-syllable words originally stressed on the first syllable have been affected by the difficulty of uttering more than three unstressed syllables in sequence (see 2(*a*) above). The stress has been shifted to the second syllable in *laboratory*, *obligatory*, whereas in *veterinary* the fourth syllable is elided, and usually the second as well. For *arbitrarily*, *momentarily*, etc., see **-arily,** pp. 49 ff.

t

1. In rapid speech, *t* is often dropped from the sequence *cts*, so that *acts*, *ducts*, *pacts* sound like *axe*, *ducks*, *packs*.

● This should be avoided in careful speech.

2. The sounding of *t* in *often* is a spelling pronunciation: the traditional form in RP rhymes with *soften*.

th

1. Monosyllabic nouns ending in *-th* after a vowel sound (or vowel + *r*) form the plural by adding *-s* in the usual way, but the resulting sequence *ths* is pronounced in two different ways. In some words it is voiceless as in *myths*, in others voiced as in *mouths*.

(*a*) The following are like *myth*:

berth	girth	sleuth
birth	growth	sloth
breath	hearth	(animal)
death	heath	smith
faith	moth	wraith
fourth		

(*b*) The following are like *mouth*:

bath	sheath	wreath
oath	swath	youth
path	truth	

cloth, *lath* vary, but are now commonly like *myth*.

2. Note that final *th* is like *th* in *bathe*, *father* in:

bequeath	booth
betroth	mouth (verb)

u

The sound of long *u*, as in *cube*, *cubic*, *cue*, *use* is also spelt *eu*, *ew*, and *ui*, as in *feud*, *few*, *pursuit*. It is properly a compound of two sounds, the semivowel *y* followed by the long vowel elsewhere written *oo*. Hence the word *you* (= y + oo) sounds like the name of the letter *U*, *ewe*, and *yew*.

When this compound sound follows certain consonants the *y* is lost, leaving only the *oo*-sound.

1. Where it follows *ch*, *j*, *r*, and the sound of *sh*, the *y* element was lost in the mid-eighteenth century.

So *brewed*, *chews*, *chute*, *Jules*, *rude*, sound like *brood*, *choose*, *shoot*, *joules*, *rood*.

The *y* element was also lost at about the same time or a little later where it follows an *l* preceded by another consonant; so *blew*, *clue*, *glue*, etc. sound as if they were spelt *bloo*, *cloo*, *gloo*, etc.

2. Where this compound sound follows an *l* not preceded by another

consonant, loss of the *y*-element is now very common in a syllable that bears the main or secondary stress. *COD*, for instance, gives only the *oo* pronunciation in many words, e.g. *Lewis, Lucifer, lucrative, lucre*, etc., and either pronunciation for many others, e.g. *lubricate, Lucan, lucid, ludicrous*, etc.

It is equally common in internal stressed syllables; in *COD* the words *allude, alluvial, collusion, voluminous*, etc. are given both pronunciations. So also in a syllable which bears a secondary stress: *absolute, interlude*.

□ In all syllables of these kinds, the *oo*-sound is probably the predominant type, but either is acceptable.

● In *unstressed* syllables, however, it is not usual for the *y*-element to be lost. The *yoo*-sound is the only one possible in, e.g.

curlew	*purlieu*	*value*
deluge	*soluble*	*volume*
prelude	*valuable*	

Contrast *solute* (= *sol*-yoot) with *salute* (= sa-*loot*).

3. After *s*, there is again variation between the compound sound and the *oo*-sound. The latter has now a very strong foothold. Very few people, if any, pronounce *Susan* and *Sue* with a *yoo*, and most people pronounce *super* (the word and the prefix) with *oo*. On the other hand, most people probably use *yoo* in *pseudo-* and in internal syllables, as in *assume, presume, pursue*. Common words such as *sewage, sewer, suet, suicide, sue*, and *suit* show wide variation: some people pronounce the first four (in which another vowel follows *ew* or *u*) with *oo*, but the last two with *yoo*.

In an unstressed syllable, the *y*-sound is kept, as with *l* in 2 above:

capsule	*consular*	*insulate*
chasuble	*hirsute*	*peninsula*

□ Apart from in *Susan, Sue*, and *super*, and the words in which the vowel occurs in an unstressed syllable, either pronunciation is acceptable, although *yoo* is the traditional one.

4. After *d, n, t*, and *th*, the loss of the *y*-sound is non-standard, e.g. in *due, new, tune, enthusiasm*.

Note: In Amer. English loss of the *y*-sound is normal after these consonants and *l* and *s*.

● The tendency to make *t* and *d* preceding this sound in stressed syllables sound like *ch* and *j*, e.g. *Tuesday, duel* as if *Choosday, jewel*, should be avoided in careful speech. In unstressed syllables (e.g. in *picture*, *procedure*) it is normal.

ul

After *b*, *f*, and *p*, the sequence *ul* sounds like *ool* in *wool* in some words, e.g. in *bull*, *full*, *pull*, and like *ull* in *hull* in others, e.g. in *bulk*, *fulminate*, *pulp*. In a few words there is uncertainty about the sound of *u*, or actual variation.

(*a*) Normally with *u* as in *hull*:

Bulgarian	*fulminate*	*pulmonary*
ebullient	*pullulate*	*pulverize*
effulgent		

(*b*) Normally with *u* as in *bull*:

bulwark	*fulmar*	*fulsome*	*fulvous*

(*c*) With variation: *fulcrum*

urr

In Standard English the stressed vowel of *furry* and *occurring* is like that of *stirring*, not that of *hurry* and *occurrence*.

● The identity of the two sounds is normal in Amer. English.

wh

In some regions *wh* is distinguished from *w* by being preceded or accompanied by an *h*-sound.

□ This pronunciation is not standard in RP, but is acceptable to most RP-speakers.

B. *Preferred pronunciations*

The entries in this list are of three kinds. Some of the words in it have only one current pronunciation, which cannot, however, be deduced with certainty from the written form. These are mainly words that are encountered in writing and are not part of the average person's spoken vocabulary. Another class of words included here have a single, universally accepted pronunciation, which, in rapid or careless speech, undergoes a significant slurring or reduction. These reduced forms are noted, with a warning to use the fully enunciated form in careful speech so as to avoid giving an impression of sloppiness or casualness. Much the largest group are words for which two or more different pronunciations exist. Both (or all) are given, with notes giving a rough guide to the currency and acceptability of each.

The approach adopted here is fairly flexible, allowing for the inevitable subjectivity of judgements about pronunciation and the fact that there is variation and inconsistency even in the speech of an individual person.

Where the American pronunciation is significantly different from the British (disregarding the differences that are constant, such as the American pronunciation of *r* where it is silent in British speech), a note of it has been added, usually in brackets at the end of the entry. In a few cases the American pronunciation stands alone after the recommended one, implying that the use of the American form is incorrect in British speech. It will be found that in many cases the American pronunciation coincides with an older British one that is now being ousted. It is hoped that this will dispel the impression that all innovations are Americanisms, and give a clearer idea of the relationship between the two varieties of English pronunciation.

The symbol ● is used to warn against forms especially to be avoided; □ introduces most of the cases of peaceful coexistence of two variant pronunciations.

abdomen: stress on 1st syllable in general use; on 2nd in the speech of many members of the medical profession.

accomplice, accomplish: the older (and Amer.) pronunciation has 2nd syllable as in *comma*; but pronunciation as *come* is now predominant.

acoustic: 2nd syllable as *coo*, not *cow*.

acumen: stress on 1st syllable.

adept, adult (adjective and noun): stress on 1st syllable.

adversary: stress on 1st syllable.

aficionado: a-fiss-eon-*ah*-do.

aggrandize: stress on 2nd syllable.

ague: 2 syllables.

albumen: stress on 1st syllable.

ally (noun): stress on 1st syllable; (verb) on 2nd syllable; **allied** preceding a noun is stressed on 1st syllable.

analogous: *g* as in *log*; not a-*na*-lo-jus.

Antarctic: ● do not drop the first *c*.

anti- (prefix): rhymes with *shanty*, not, as often Amer., *ant eye*.

antiquary: stress on 1st syllable.

apache (Indian): rhymes with *patchy*; (street ruffian) rhymes with *cash*.

apartheid: 3rd syllable like *hate*. ● Not *apart-ite* or *apart-hide*.

apophthegm: *a*-po-them.

apparatus: 3rd syllable like *rate*; not appar-*ah*-tus.

applicable: stress on 1st syllable.

apposite: 3rd syllable like that of *opposite*.

arbitrarily: stress properly on 1st syllable, in informal speech on 3rd.

Arctic: ● do not drop the first *c*.

Argentine: 3rd syllable as in *turpentine*.

aristocrat: stress on 1st syllable. ● Not (except Amer.) a-*rist*-ocrat.

artisan: stress originally on 3rd syllable; pronunciation with stress on 1st syllable is Amer., and now common in Britain.

aspirant: stress on 1st syllable.

asthma: *ass*-ma is the familiar pronunciation; to sound the *th* is didactic (Amer. *az*-ma).

ate: rhymes with *bet* (Amer. with *bate*).

audacious: *au* as in *audience*, not as in *gaucho*.

auld lang syne: 3rd word like *sign*, not *zine*.

azure: the older pronunciation was with -*zure* like -*sure* in *pleasure*; now usually *az*-yoor.

banal: 2nd syllable like that of *canal* or *morale* (Amer. rhymes with *anal*).

basalt: 1st *a* as in *gas*, 2nd as in *salt*; stress on either.

bathos: *a* as in *paper*.

blackguard: *blagg*-ard.

bolero (dance): stress on 2nd syllable; (jacket) stress on 1st.

booth: rhymes with *smooth* (Amer. with *tooth*).

bouquet: first syllable as *book*, not as *beau*.

Bourbon (dynasty): 1st syllable as that of *bourgeois*; (US whisky) 1st syllable as *bur*.

breeches: rhymes with *pitches*.

brochure: stress on 1st syllable.

brusque: should be Anglicized: broosk or brusk.

bureau: stress on 1st syllable.

burgh (in Scotland): sounds like *borough*.

Byzantine: stress on 2nd syllable.

cadaver: 2nd syllable as in *waver*.

cadaverous: 2nd syllable like 1st of *average*.

cadre: rhymes with *harder*.

caliph: rhymes with *bailiff*.

camellia: rhymes with *Amelia*.

canine: ▢ 1st syllable may be as *can* or *cane* (the latter probably prevails).

canton (subdivision): 2nd syllable as 1st of *tonic*; (military, also in **cantonment**) 2nd syllable as that of *cartoon*.

capitalist: stress on 1st syllable.

carillon: rhymes with *trillion* (Amer. *carry*-lon).

caryatid: stress on 2nd *a*.

catacomb: 3rd syllable, in the older pronunciation, as *comb*; now frequently rhyming with *tomb*.

centenary: sen-*tee*-nary (Amer. *sen*-te-nary).

cento: *c* as in *cent*, not *cello*.

centrifugal, centripetal: stress originally on 2nd syllable; but pronunciation with stress on 3rd syllable seems to be usual among younger speakers.

certification: stress on 1st and 4th syllables, not 2nd and 4th.

cervical: ▢ stress either on 1st syllable (with last two syllables as in *vertical*) or on 2nd (rhyming with *cycle*): both pronunciations have been common for at least a century and a half (Amer. only the first pronunciation).

chaff: rhymes with *staff*.

chagrin: stress on 1st syllable; 2nd as *grin* (Amer. stress on 2nd syllable).

chamois (antelope): *sham*-wah; (leather) shammy.

chastisement: traditionally with stress on 1st syllable; now often on 2nd.

chimera: *ch* = k, not sh.

chiropodist: strictly *ch* = k, but pronunciation as sh is common.

choleric: 1st two syllables like *collar*.

cigarette: stress on 3rd syllable (Amer. on 1st).

clandestine: stress on 2nd syllable.

clangour: rhymes with *anger*.

clientele: kleeon-*tell*.

clique: rhymes with *leak*, not *lick*.

coccyx: *cc* = ks.

colander: 1st syllable as *cull*.

combat (verb), **combatant, -ive:** stress on 1st syllable (Amer. on 2nd).

combine (noun): stress on 1st syllable.

commandant: stress originally on 3rd syllable; now often on 1st.

communal: stress on 1st syllable.

commune (noun): stress on 1st syllable.

comparable: stress on 1st syllable, not on 2nd.

compensatory: the older (and Amer.) pronunciation has stress on 2nd syllable, but stress on 3rd is now common.

compilation: 2nd syllable as *pill*.

composite: stress on 1st syllable; 3rd as that of *opposite* (Amer. stress on 2nd syllable).

conch: originally = *conk*; now often with *ch* as in *lunch*.

conduit: last three letters like those of *circuit* (Amer. *con*-doo-it).

confidant(e): the older pronunciation has stress on last syllable, which rhymes with *ant*; stress on 1st syllable is now common.

congener: stress on 1st syllable; *o* as in *con*; *g* as in *gin*.

congeries: □ con-*jeer*-eez or con-*jeer*-y-eez.

congratulatory: stress on 2nd syllable; pronunciation with stress on 4th syllable is also common.

conjugal: stress on 1st syllable.

consuetude: stress on 1st syllable; *sue* like *swi* in *swift*.

consummate (adjective): stress on 2nd syllable; (verb) on 1st syllable, 3rd syllable as *mate*.

contact (noun and verb): stress on 1st syllable.

contemplative: stress on 2nd syllable.

contrarily (on the contrary): stress on 1st syllable; (perversely) stress on 2nd syllable.

contribute: stress on 2nd syllable. ● The former pronunciation with stress on 1st syllable has survived in dialect and is frequently heard, but is not standard.

controversy: stress on 1st syllable. ● The pronunciation with stress on 2nd syllable seems to be increasingly common, but is strongly disapproved by many users of RP.

contumacy: stress on 1st syllable (Amer. on 2nd).

contumely: 3 syllables with stress on the 1st.

conversant: now usually stressed on 2nd syllable; formerly on 1st.

courier: *ou* as in *could*.

courteous: 1st syllable like *curt*.

courtesan: 1st syllable like *court*.

courtesy: 1st syllable like *curt*.

covert: 1st syllable like that of *cover*. ● Does not rhyme with *overt*.

culinary: *cul-* now usually as in *culprit*; formerly as in *peculiar*.

dais: originally one syllable; now only with two.

data: 1st syllable as *date*. ● Does not rhyme with *sonata*.

decade: stress on 1st syllable.

defect (noun): stress on 1st syllable is now usual.

deficit: stress on 1st syllable.

deify, deity: *e* as in *me*. ● Pronunciation with *e* as in *suede*, *fête* is common among younger speakers, but is disapproved of by many users of RP.

delirious: 2nd syllable as 1st of *lyrical*, not *Leary*.

demesne: 2nd syllable sounds like *main*.

demonstrable: stress on 1st syllable.

deprivation: 1st two syllables like those of *depreciation*.

derisive, derisory: 2nd syllable like *rice*.

despicable: in formal speech, stress on 1st syllable; informally, especially for greater emphasis, on 2nd.

desuetude: as for **consuetude**.

desultory: stress on 1st syllable.

deteriorate: ● do not drop 4th syllable, i.e. not deteri-ate.

detour: *dee*-tour not *day*-tour (Amer. de-*tour*).

deus ex machina: *day*-us ex *mak*-ina, not ma-*shee*-na.

dilemma: 1st syllable like *dill*.

dinghy: ding-gy, not rhyming with *stringy*.

diphtheria, diphthong: *ph* = f not p.

disciplinary: the older (and Amer.) pronunciation has stress on 1st syllable, but it is now usually on the 3rd (with *i* as in *pin*).

disputable: stress on 2nd syllable.

dispute (noun): stress on 2nd syllable, not on 1st.

dissect: 1st syllable as *Diss*. ● Does not rhyme with *bisect*.

distribute: stress on 2nd syllable.

doctrinal: the older pronunciation has stress on 1st syllable, but it is now usually on the 2nd (with *i* as in *mine*).

dolorous, dolour: 1st syllable like *doll* (Amer. like *dole*).

dour: rhymes with *poor* not *power*.

dubiety: last 3 syllables like those of *anxiety*.

ducat: 1st syllable like *duck*.

dynast, dynastic, dynasty: 1st syllable like *din* (Amer. like *dine*).

ebullient: *u* as in *dull*, not as in *bull*.

economic: □ *e* as in *extra* or as in *equal*: both are current.

Edwardian: 2nd syllable as *ward*.

e'er (poetry, = *ever*): sounds like *air*.

efficacy: stress on 1st syllable, not 2nd.

ego: 1st syllable as that of *eager*.

egocentric, egoism, etc.: 1st syllable like *egg* (Amer. usually as **ego**).

either: *ei* as in *height* or *seize*: both are widely current (Amer. only the second pronunciation).

elixir: rhymes with *mixer*.

enclave: *en-* as in *end*, *a* as in *slave*.

entirety: now usually entire-ety; formerly entire-ty.

envelope: *en-* as in *end*, not *on*.

environs: rhymes with *sirens*.

epos: *e* as in *epic*.

epoxy: stress on 2nd syllable.

equerry: stress properly on 2nd syllable, but commonly on 1st.

espionage: now usually with *-age* as in *camouflage*.

et cetera: etsetera. ● Not eksetera.

explicable: stress originally on 1st syllable, but now usually on 2nd.

exquisite: stress on 1st syllable.

extraordinary: 1st *a* is silent.

fakir: sounds like *fake*-ear.

falcon: *a* as in *talk*, not as in *alcove*.

fascia: rhymes with *Alsatia*.

fascism, fascist: 1st syllable like that of *fashion*.

February: ● do not drop the 1st *r*: feb-roor-y, not *feb*-yoor-y or *feb*-wa-ry or *feb*-yoo-erry (Amer. *feb*-roo-erry).

fetid, fetish: *e* as in *fetter*.

fifth: in careful speech, do not drop the 2nd *f*.

finance: □ stress on 1st syllable (only with *i* as in *fine*) or on 2nd (with *i* as in *fin* or *fine*).

forbade: 2nd syllable like *bad*.

formidable: in careful speech, stress on 1st syllable; informally, on 2nd.

forte (one's strong point): originally (and Amer.) like *fort*, but now usually like the musical term *forte*.

foyer: *foy*-ay or *fwah*-yay (Amer. *foy*-er).

fracas (singular): *frack*-ah, (plural) *frack*-ahz (Amer. *frake*-us).

fulminate: *u* as in *dull*.

fulsome: *u* formerly as in *dull*, now always as in *full*.

furore: 3 syllables (Amer. **furor** with 2).

Gaelic: 1st syllable as *gale*.

gala: 1st *a* as in *calm*. ● The former pronunciation with *a* as in *gale* is still used in the North and US.

gallant (brave, etc.): stress on 1st syllable; (polite and attentive to ladies) stress on 1st or 2nd syllable.

garage: stress on 1st syllable, *age* as in *camouflage* (or rhyming with *large*). ● Pronunciation so as to rhyme with *carriage* is non-standard (Amer. ga-*rahge*).

garrulity: stress on 2nd syllable, which sounds like *rule*.

garrulous: stress on 1st syllable.

gaseous: 1st syllable like *gas*.

genuine: *ine* as in *engine*.

genus: *e* as in *genius*; **genera** (plural) has *e* as in *general*.

gibber, gibberish: now usually with *g* as in *gin*; *g* as in *give* was formerly frequent in the first word and normal in the second.

glacial: 1st *a* as in *glade*.

golf: *o* as in *got*. ● The pronunciation goff is old-fashioned.

gone: *o* as in *on*. ● The pronunciation gawn is non-standard.

government: ● In careful speech, do not drop the 1st *n* (or the whole 2nd syllable).

gratis: *a* properly as in *grate*; but grahtis and grattis are commonly heard.

greasy: □ *s* may be as in *cease* or *easy*.

grievous: ● does not rhyme with *previous*.

gunwale: gunn'l.

half-past: ● In careful speech, avoid saying hah past or hoff posst.

harass(ment): stress on 1st syllable (Amer. often on 2nd).

have: in rapid speech, the weakly stressed infinitive *have* is reduced to *'ve* and sounds like the weakly stressed form of the preposition *of*. When stress is restored to it, it should become *have*, not *of*, as in '*You couldn't 've done it*', '*I could* have' (not '*I could* of').

hectare: 2nd syllable like *tar*, not tare.

hegemony: stress on 2nd syllable, *g* as in *get* or (as also Amer.) as in *gem*.

Hegira: stress on 1st syllable, which is like *hedge*.

heinous: *ei* as in *rein*.

homo- (prefix = same): *o* as in *from*.

homoeopath: 1st two syllables rhyme with *Romeo*.

homogeneous: last three syllables sound like *genius*.

honorarium: *h* silent, *a* as in *rare*.

hospitable: stress properly on 1st syllable.

hotel: *h* to be pronounced.

housewifery: stress on 1st syllable, *i* as in *whiff*.

hovel, hover: *o* as in *hot*. ● The former pronunciation with *o* as in *love* is now only Amer.

idyll: *i* as in *idiot*; it may be like *i* in *idea* in **idyllic** (with stress on 2nd syllable) and usually is in **idyllist** (with stress on 1st syllable).

illustrative: stress on 1st syllable (Amer. on 2nd).

imbroglio: *g* is silent; rhymes with *folio*.

impious: stress on 1st syllable; on 2nd in **impiety**.

importune: stress on 3rd syllable or (with some speakers) on 2nd.

inchoate: stress on 1st syllable.

indict: *c* is silent; rhymes with *incite*.

indisputable: stress on 3rd syllable.

inexplicable: stress originally on 2nd syllable, but now usually on 3rd.

infamous: stress on 1st syllable.

inherent: 1st *e* as in *here*.

intaglio: *g* is silent, *a* as in *pal* or *pass*.

integral: stress on 1st syllable.

intern (verb): stress on 2nd syllable; (noun, Amer.) on 1st.

internecine: stress on 3rd syllable, last two syllables like *knee sign*.

interstice: stress on 2nd syllable.

intestinal: stress on 2nd syllable; 3rd syllable like *tin*.

intricacy: stress on 1st syllable.

invalid (sick person): stress on 1st syllable, 2nd *i* as in *lid* or *machine;* (verb) stress on 1st or 3rd syllable, 2nd *i* as in *machine*; (not valid) stress on 2nd syllable.

inveigle: originally rhyming with *beagle*, but now commonly with *Hegel*.

inventory: like *infantry* with *v* instead of *f*.

irrefragable: stress on 2nd syllable.

irrelevant: ● not *irrevalent*, a blunder sometimes heard.

irreparable: stress on 2nd syllable.

irrevocable: stress on 2nd syllable.

issue: *ss* as in *mission*; but pronunciation to rhyme with *miss you* is very common.

isthmus: do not drop the *th*.

January: *jan*-yoor-y (Amer. *jan*-yoo-erry).

jejune: stress on 2nd syllable.

jewellery: jewel-ry. ● Not jool-ery.

joule (unit): rhymes with *fool*.

jubilee: stress on 1st syllable ● Not 3rd.

jugular: 1st syllable like *jug*: formerly as in *conjugal*.

junta: pronounce as written. ● Hoonta, an attempt to reproduce the Spanish pronunciation, is chiefly Amer.

kilometre: stress on 1st syllable, as with *kilocycle, kilolitre*. ● Not on

2nd syllable; the pattern is that of *millimetre*, *centimetre* (units), not that of *speedometer*, *milometer*, etc. (devices).

knoll: *o* as in *no*.

laboratory: stress on 2nd syllable. ● The former pronunciation, with stress on 1st syllable, is now chiefly used by Amer. speakers (with *o* as in *Tory*).

lamentable: stress on 1st syllable.

languor: as for **clangour**.

lasso: stress on 2nd syllable, *o* as in *do*.

lather: rhymes with *gather*, not *rather*.

launch: rhymes with *haunch*, not *branch*.

leeward (in general use): *lee*-ward; (nautical) like *lured*.

leisure: rhymes with *pleasure* (Amer. with *seizure*).

length: *ng* as in *long*. ● Not lenth.

levee (reception, assembly): like *levy*; (Amer., embankment) may be stressed on 2nd syllable.

library: in careful speech avoid dropping the 2nd syllable (li-bry).

lichen: sounds like *liken*.

lieutenant: 1st syllable like *left*; in Navy, like *let* (Amer. like *loot*).

liquorice: licker-iss.

longevity: *ng* as in *lunge*.

longitude: *ng* as in *lunge*. ● Not (*latitude and*) longtitude, an error sometimes heard.

long-lived: originally rhyming with *arrived*, but now usually like past tense *lived*.

lour: rhymes with *hour*.

lugubrious: loo-*goo*-brious.

machete: *ch* as in *attach*; rhymes with *Betty* (or with some speakers, *Katie*).

machination: *ch* as in *mechanical*, not as in *machine*.

machismo, macho: *ch* as in *attach*, not as in *mechanical*.

magazine: stress on 3rd syllable (Amer. and Northern pronunciation has stress on 1st).

maieutic: 1st syllable like *may*.

mandatory: stress on 1st syllable.

margarine: *g* as in *Margery*.

marital: stress on 1st syllable.

massage: stress on 1st syllable (Amer. on 2nd).

matrix: *a* as in *mate*; **matrices** (plural) the same, with stress on 1st syllable.

medicine: two syllables (med-sin). ● The pronunciation with three syllables is normal in Scotland and the US, but disapproved of by many users of RP.

mediocre: 1st syllable like *mead*.

metallurgy, -ist: stress on 2nd syllable. ● The older pronunciation with stress on 1st syllable, becoming rare in Britain, is chiefly Amer.

metamorphosis: stress on 3rd syllable.

metope: two syllables.

midwifery: stress on 1st syllable, *i* as in *whiff*.

mien: sounds like *mean*.

migraine: 1st syllable like *me* (Amer. like *my*).

migratory: stress on 1st syllable.

millenary: stress on 2nd syllable, which is like *Len* or *lean*.

miscellany: stress on 2nd syllable (Amer. on 1st).

mischievous: stress on 1st syllable. ● Not rhyming with *previous*.

misericord: stress on 2nd syllable.

mocha (coffee): originally (and Amer.) rhyming with *coca*, now often like *mocker*.

momentary, -ily: stress on 1st syllable.

municipal: stress on 2nd syllable.

nadir: *nay*-dear.

naïve: nah-*Eve* or nigh-*Eve*.

naïvety: has 3 syllables.

nascent: *a* as in *fascinate*.

necessarily: in formal speech, has stress on 1st syllable, with reduction or elision of *a*; informally, especially in emphatic use, stressed on 3rd syllable (e.g. *not necess*ar*ily!*).

neither: as for **either**.

nephew: *ph* sounds like *v* (Amer. like *f*).

nicety: has three syllables.

niche: nitch has been the pronunciation for two or three centuries; neesh, now common, is remodelled on the French form.

nomenclature: stress on 2nd syllable. The pronunciation with stress on 1st and 3rd syllables is now chiefly Amer.

nonchalant: stress on 1st syllable, *ch* as in *machine*.

nuclear: *newk*-lee-er. ● Not as if spelt *nucular*.

nucleic: stress on 2nd syllable, which has *e* as in *equal*.

obdurate: stress on 1st syllable.

obeisance: 2nd syllable like *base*.

obligatory: stress on 2nd syllable.

obscenity: *e* as in *scent*.

occurrence: 2nd syllable like the 1st in *current*.

o'er (poetry, = over): sounds like *ore*.

of: see **have**.

often: the *t* is silent, as in *soften*.

ominous: 1st syllable as that of *omelette*.

ophthalmic: *ph* = f not p.

opus: *o* as in *open*.

ormolu: *orm*-o-loo with weak 2nd *o* as in *Caroline*.

p (abbreviation for *penny, pence*): in formal context, say *penny* (after 1) or *pence*. ● 'Pee' is informal only.

pace (with all due respect to): like *pacey*.

paella: pah-*ell*-a.

panegyric: stress on 3rd syllable, *g* as in *gin*, *y* as in *lyric*.

paprika: stress on 1st syllable (Amer. on 2nd).

pariah: the older pronunciation has the stress on 1st syllable, rhyming with *carrier*; the pronunciation with stress on 2nd syllable, rhyming with *Isaiah*, is now common (and normal Amer.).

participle: stress on 1st syllable; 1st *i* may be dropped.

particularly: in careful speech, avoid dropping the 4th syllable (particuly).

partisan: as **artisan**.

pasty (pie): *a* now usually as in *lass*; the older sound, as in *past*, is sometimes used in *Cornish pasty*.

patent: 1st syllable like *pate*. ● Some who use this pronunciation for the general sense, have 1st syllable like *pat* in *Patent Office, letters patent*.

pathos: as for **bathos**.

patriarch: 1st *a* as in *paper*.

patriot(ic): *a* as in *pat* or *paper*.

patron, patroness: *a* as in *paper*.

patronage, patronize: *a* as in *pat*.

pejorative: stress on 2nd syllable.

peremptory: stress on 2nd syllable (Amer. on 1st).

perhaps: in careful speech, two syllables with *h*, not *r*, sounded; informally praps.

pharmacopoeia: stress on *oe*; *-poeia* rhymes with *idea*.

philharmonic: 2nd *h* is silent.

phthisis: *ph* is silent.

pianist: stress on 1st *i*, *ia* as in *Ian*.

piano (instrument): *a* as in *man*; (musical direction) *a* as in *calm*.

piazza: *zz* = ts.

pistachio: *a* as in *calm* or *man*, *ch* as in *machine*.

plaid, plait: rhyme with *lad, flat*.

plastic: rhymes with *fantastic.* ● The pronunciation with *a* as in *calm* sounds affected to many people.

pogrom: originally with stress on the 2nd syllable (as in Russian); now usually on the 1st.

pomegranate: the older pronunciation was with 1st *e* silent, *o* as in *come* or *from*, and stress either on *o* or the 1st *a*; the pronunciation *pom*-gran-it is still used by some speakers, but *pommy*-gran-it is now usual.

porpoise: *oise* like *ose* in *purpose.*

posthumous: *h* is silent.

pot-pourri: stress on 2nd syllable (Amer. on 3rd), *pot-* like *Poe.*

precedence: originally with stress on 2nd syllable, now usually on 1st, which sounds like *press.*

precedent (adjective): stress on 2nd syllable; (noun) as for **precedence**.

precedented: as for **precedence**.

preferable: stress on 1st syllable.

premise (verb): stress on 2nd syllable, rhyming with *surmise.*

prestige: stress on 2nd syllable, *i* and *g* as in *régime.*

prestigious: rhymes with *religious.*

prima facie: *pry*-ma *fay*-shee.

primarily: stress on 1st syllable, with *a* reduced or elided. ● The pronunciation with stress on the 2nd syllable, used by some (but not all) Americans, is disapproved of by many users of RP.

Primates: (order of mammals) originally with 3 syllables, but now often with 2.

primer (elementary school-book): *i* as in *prime.* ● The older pronunciation with *i* as in *prim* survives in Australia and New Zealand.

privacy: □ *i* as in *privet* or *private*; the former is probably commoner; the latter is the older and Amer. pronunciation.

probably: in careful speech, 3 syllables; informally often probbly.

proboscis: pro-*boss*-iss.

process (noun): *o* as in *probe.* ● An older pronunciation with *o* as in *profit* is now only Amer.

process (verb, to treat): like the noun; (to walk in procession) stress on 2nd syllable.

promissory: stress on 1st syllable.

pronunciation: 2nd syllable like *nun.* ● Not pro-*noun*-ciation.

prosody: 1st syllable like that of *prospect.*

protean: stress on 1st syllable.

protégé: 1st syllable like that of *protestant* (Amer. like that of *protest*).

proven: *o* as in *prove.*

proviso: 2nd syllable as that of *revise*.

puissance (show-jumping): pronounced with approximation to French, *pui* = pwi, *a* nasalized; (in poetry) may be *pwiss*-ance or *pew*-iss-ance, depending on scansion.

pursuivant: *Percy*-vant.

pyramidal: stress on 2nd syllable.

quaff: rhymes with *scoff*.

quagmire: *a* originally as in *wag*, now usually as in *quad*.

qualm: rhymes with *calm*; the older pronunciation, rhyming with *shawm*, is now rare.

quandary: stress on 1st syllable; the older pronunciation, with stress on 2nd syllable, is rarely, if ever, heard.

quasi: the vowels are like those in *wayside*.

quatercentenary: *kwatt*-er-, not *quarter*-.

questionnaire: 1st two syllables like *question*.

rabid: 1st syllable like that of *rabbit*.

rabies: 2nd syllable like *bees*, not like the 2nd syllable of *babies*.

rampage (verb): stress on 2nd syllable; (noun) on 1st syllable.

rapport: stress on 2nd syllable, which sounds like *pore* (Amer. like *port*).

ratiocinate: 1st two syllables like *ratty*, stress on 3rd.

rationale: *ale* as in *morale*.

really: rhymes with *ideally*, *clearly*, not with *freely*.

recess (noun and verb): stress on 2nd syllable.

recognize: ● do not drop the *g*.

recondite: stress on 1st or 2nd syllable. The former is the commoner, the latter, the older, pronunciation.

recuperate: 2nd syllable like the 1st of *Cupid*.

referable: stress on 1st syllable.

remediable, -al: stress on 2nd syllable, *e* as in *medium*.

remonstrate: stress on 1st syllable; the older pronunciation, with stress on 2nd syllable, is rare.

Renaissance: stress on 2nd syllable, *ai* as in *plaice*.

renege: the traditional pronunciation rhymes with *league*. □ A pronunciation to rhyme with *plague*, for long dialectal, is now common. ● *g* is hard as in *get*, not as in *allege*.

reportage: *age* as in *camouflage*, but with stress.

research (noun): stress on 2nd syllable (Amer. on 1st).

respite: stress on 1st syllable, 2nd like *spite* (Amer. like *spit*).

restaurant: pronunciation with final *t* silent and second *a* nasalized is preferred by many, but that with *ant* = ont is widespread.

revanchism: *anch* as in *ranch*.

ribald: 1st syllable like *rib*.

risible: rhymes with *visible*.

risqué: □ *rees*-kay or *riss*-kay.

romance: stress on 2nd syllable. ● Pronunciation with stress on 1st syllable, usually in sense 'love affair, love story', is non-standard (except when used jocularly).

Romany: 1st syllable as that of *Romulus*.

rotatory: stress on 1st syllable.

rowan: *ow* often as in *low*, although in Scotland, whence the word comes, it is as in *cow*.

rowlock: rhymes with *Pollock*.

sacrilegious: now always rhymes with *religious*.

sahib: *sah*-ib.

salsify: *sal*-si-fee.

salve (noun, ointment; verb, soothe): properly rhymes with *halve*, but now usually with *valve* (Amer. with *have*).

salve (save ship): rhymes with *valve*.

satiety: as for **dubiety**.

Saudi: rhymes with *rowdy*, not *bawdy*.

scabies: as for **rabies**.

scabrous: 1st syllable like that of *scabious* (Amer. like *scab*).

scallop: rhymes with *wallop*.

scarify (make an incision): rhymes with *clarify*. ● Not to be confused with slang *scarify* (terrify) pronounced *scare*-ify.

scenario: *sc* as in *scene*, *ario* as in *impresario* (Amer. with *a* as in *Mary*).

schedule: *sch* as in *Schubert* (Amer. as in *school*).

schism: properly, *ch* is silent (siz'm); but skiz'm is often heard.

schist (rock): *sch* as in *Schubert*.

schizo-: skitso.

scilicet: 1st syllable like that of *silent*.

scone: rhymes with *on*.

second (to support): stress on 1st syllable; (to transfer) on 2nd.

secretary: *sek*-re-try. ● Not *sek*-e-try or *sek*-e-terry or (Amer.) *sek*-re-terry.

secretive: stress on 1st syllable.

seise, seisin: *ei* as in *seize*.

seismic: 1st syllable like *size*.

seraglio: *g* silent, *a* as in *ask*.

sheikh: sounds like *shake* (Amer. like *chic*).

simultaneous: *i* as in *simple* (Amer. as in *Simon*).

sinecure: properly, *i* as in *sign*, but *i* as in *sin* is common.

Sinhalese: sin-hal-*ese*.

Sioux: soo.

sisal: 1st syllable like the 2nd of *precise*.

sixth: in careful speech, avoid the pronunciation sikth.

slalom: *a* as in *spa*.

slaver (dribble): *a* as in *have*.

sleight: sounds like *slight*.

sloth: rhymes with *both*.

slough (bog): rhymes with *bough*; (to cast a skin) with *tough*.

sobriquet: 1st syllable like that of *sober*.

sojourn: 1st *o* as in *sob* (Amer. as in *sober*).

solder: *o* as in *sob* (Amer. pronunciation is sodder or sawder).

solecism: *o* as in *sob*.

solenoid: stress on 1st syllable, *o* as in *sober* or as in *sob*.

sonorous: stress on 1st syllable, 1st *o* as in *sob*.

soporific: 1st *o* now usually as in *sob* (formerly also as in *sober*).

sough (rushing sound): rhymes with *tough*.

sovereignty: *sov*'renty. ● Not sov-*rain*-ity.

Soviet: *o* as in *sober*. The pronunciation with *o* as in *sob* is also very common.

species: *ci* as in *precious*. ● Not *spee*-seez.

spinet: □ may be stressed on either syllable.

spontaneity: as for **deify, deity.**

stalwart: 1st syllable like *stall*.

status: 1st syllable like *stay*. ● Not *statt*-us.

stigmata: stress on 1st syllable. ● Not with *ata* as in *sonata*.

strafe: rhymes with *staff*.

stratosphere: *a* as in *Stratford*.

stratum, strata: *a* of first syllable like 1st *a* of *sonata*.

strength: *ng* as in *strong*. ● Not *strenth*.

suave, suavity: *a* as 1st *a* in *lava*.

subsidence: stress originally on 2nd syllable with *i* as in *side*; pronunciation with stress on 1st syllable and *i* as in *sit* is increasingly common.

substantial: 1st *a* as in *ant*, not *aunt*.

substantive (in grammar): stress on 1st syllable; (having separate existence, permanent) on 2nd syllable.

suffragan: *g* as in *get*.

supererogatory: stress on 4th syllable.

superficies: super-*fish*-(i-)eez.

supine (adjective): stress on 1st syllable (Amer. on 2nd).

suppose: ● in careful speech, avoid the elision of the *u*; informal *I s'pose so, s'posing it happens?*

surety: now usually three syllables (*sure*-et-y); originally two (*sure*-ty).

surveillance: ● do not drop the *l*; = sur-*vey*-lance, not sur-*vey*-ance.

suzerain: *u* as in *Susan*.

swath: *a* as in *water*; in plural, *th* as in *paths*.

syndrome: two syllables (formerly three).

taxidermist: □ stress on 1st or 3rd syllable.

temporarily: stress on 1st syllable (with weakening or dropping of *o*): *temp*-ra-rily. ● Not tempo-*rar*-ily.

Tibetan: 2nd syllable like *bet*, not *beat*.

tirade: tie-*raid*.

tissue: as for **issue**.

tonne: sounds like *ton*. ● To avoid misunderstanding, *metric* can be prefixed; but in most spoken contexts the slight difference between the imperial and metric weights will not matter.

tortoise: as for **porpoise**.

tourniquet: 3rd syllable like the 2nd of *croquet* (Amer. like *kit*).

towards: the form with two syllables is now the most common; some speakers use the pronunciation tords in all contexts, others only in some.

trachea: stress on *e* (Amer. on 1st *a*, pronounced as in *trade*).

trait: 2nd *t* is silent (in Amer. pronunciation, it is sounded).

trajectory: stress properly on 1st syllable; now often (and Amer.) on 2nd.

transferable: stress on 1st syllable is implied by the single *r* (see p. 8); but the form *transferrable* was formerly common, and accounts for the common pronunciation with stress on 2nd syllable.

transition: □ tran-*sizh*-on or tran-*zish*-on.

transparent: □ last two syllables either like those of *apparent* or like *parent*.

trauma, traumatic: *au* as in *cause* (Amer. as in *gaucho*).

traverse (noun): stress on 1st syllable; (verb) on 2nd syllable. (The original pronunciation of the verb exactly like the noun is still usual in Amer. English.)

trefoil: stress on 1st syllable, *e* as in *even* or as in *ever*.

triumvir: 1st two syllables like those of *triumphant*.

troth: rhymes with *both* (Amer. with *cloth*).

trow: rhymes with *know*.

truculent: 1st *u* as in *truck;* formerly as in *true*.

turquoise: □ *tur*-kwoyz or *tur*-kwahz.

ululate: *yool*-yoo-late. The alternative pronunciation *ull*-yoo-late seems now to be chiefly Amer.

umbilical: stress on 2nd syllable.

unprecedented: 2nd syllable like *press*.

untoward: the older pronunciation rhymed with *lowered*, but the pronunciation with stress on the 3rd syllable is now usual.

Uranus: stress on 1st syllable.

urinal: stress on 1st syllable.

usual: in careful speech, avoid complete loss of *u* (*yoo*-zh'l).

uvula: *yoo*-vyoo-la.

uxorious: 1st *u* as *Uxbridge*.

vagary: the original pronunciation was with stress on 2nd syllable, but this has been almost entirely superseded by that with stress on 1st syllable.

vagina, vaginal: stress on 2nd syllable, *i* as in *china*.

valance: rhymes with *balance*.

valence, -cy (chemistry): *a* as in *ale*.

valet: those who employ them sound the *t*.

Valkyrie: stress on 1st syllable.

vase: *a* as in *dance* (Amer. rhymes with *face* or *phase*).

veld: sounds like *felt*.

venison: the old pronunciation *ven*-z'n is now rare; *ven*-i-z'n or *ven*-i-s'n are usual.

veterinary: stress on 1st syllable, with reduction or elision of 2nd *e* and *a* (*vet*-rin-ry). ● Not *vet*-nary or (Amer.) *vet*-rin-ery.

vice (in the place of): rhymes with *spicy*.

vicegerent: three syllables, 2nd *e* as in *errant*.

victualler, victuals: sound like *vitt*-ell-er, vittles.

viola (instrument): stress on 2nd syllable, *i* as in *Fiona*; (flower) stress on 1st syllable, *i* as in *vie*.

vitamin: *i* as in *hit* (Amer. as in *vital*).

viz. (= videlicet): when reading aloud, it is customary to substitute *namely*; 'viz' is chiefly jocular.

voluntarily: stress on 1st syllable.

waistcoat: the older pronunciation was *wess*-kot (with 2nd syllable like that of *mascot*); but the pronunciation as spelt has replaced it, except among older speakers.

walnut, walrus: ● do not drop the *l*.

werewolf: 1st syllable like *weir*.

whoop (cry of excitement, *whoop it up*): = woop; (cough, *whooping cough*) = hoop; both rhyme with *loop*.

wrath: rhymes with *cloth* (Amer. with *hath*).

wroth: as for **troth**.

yoghurt: *yogg*-urt (Amer. *yoh*-gurt).

zoology: in careful speech, best pronounced with 1st *o* as in *zone*; there are a number of other compounds of *zoo-* in technical use, in which this is the normal pronunciation.

III

VOCABULARY

> The perfect use of language is that in which every word
> carries the meaning that it is intended to, no less and
> no more.
>
> (C. Connolly, *Enemies of Promise*)

THIS section is concerned with problems of meaning, construction, derivation, and diction, associated with individual words. The main aim is to recommend the meaning or construction most appropriate for serious writing or formal speaking, but some attention is paid to informal and American usage.

aboriginal (noun) should be used in formal contexts as the singular of *aborigines*; *Aboriginal, Aboriginals* (with capitals) are preferable for singular and plural when referring to the aboriginal inhabitants of Australia.

● *Aborigine* is informal only.

account, to reckon, consider, is not followed by *as*, e.g. *Mere morality . . was once accounted a shameful and cynical thing* (G. B. Shaw).

affect, to have an influence on, e.g. *Hugh was immensely affected by the way Randall had put it* (Iris Murdoch).

● Do not confuse with *effect* to accomplish, e.g. *He picked at the German's lapel, hoping to effect a closer relationship by touch* (Patrick White).

● There is a noun *effet* 'result, property', e.g. *to good effect, personal effects, sound effects*; but there is no noun *affect* except in the specialized language of Psychology.

affinity *between* or *with*, not *to* or *for*, since mutual relationship or attraction is meant, e.g. *Ann felt an affinity with them, as if she too were an old dusty object* (Iris Murdoch); *Points of affinity between Stephen and Bloom* (Anthony Burgess).

afflict: see **inflict**.

aftermath can be used of any after-effects, e.g. *The aftermath of the wedding seemed to mean different things to different people (The*

Times). It is pedantic to object to the sense 'unpleasant consequences' on the ground of derivation.

agenda (from a Latin plural) is usually a singular noun (with plural *agendas*), e.g. *It's a short agenda, by the way* (Edward Hyams). But it is occasionally found in its original use as a plural meaning 'things to be done' or 'items of business to be considered' (singular *agend*).

aggravate (1) To make worse, e.g. *The war . . simply aggravates the permanent human situation* (C. S. Lewis). (2) To annoy, exasperate.

● Sense (2) is regarded by some people as incorrect, but is common informally. The participial adjective *aggravating* is often used in sense (2) by good writers, e.g. *He had pronounced and aggravating views on what the United States was doing for the world* (Graham Greene).

ain't (= are not, is not, have not, has not) is not used in Standard English except in representations of dialect speech, or humorously. *Aren't* (= are not) is also a recognized colloquialism for *am not* in the interrogative construction *aren't I*.

alibi, a plea that when an alleged act took place one was elsewhere.

● The sense 'an excuse' is informal and to many people unacceptable, e.g. *Low spirits make you seem complaining . . I have an alibi because I'm going to have a baby* (L. P. Hartley).

all of (= the whole of, the entirety of, every one of) is usual before pronouns, e.g. *And so say all of us*, or emphatically, often paralleling *none of* etc., before nouns, e.g. *Marshall Stone has all of the problems but none of the attributes of a star* (Frederic Raphael). Otherwise *all* + noun is normal, e.g. *All the King's men*.

● The general use of *all of* before nouns is Amer. only.

all right. This phrase is popularly thought of as a unit, e.g. *an all-right bloke*, but its unitary nature has not yet been recognized in spelling by the standard language, probably because the expression remains largely an informal one.

● *Alright*, though widely seen in the popular press, remains non-standard, even where the standard spelling is somewhat cumbersome, as in: *I just wanted to make sure it was all all right* (Iris Murdoch).

allude means 'refer indirectly'; an *allusion* is 'an indirect reference', e.g. *He would allude to her, and hear her discussed, but never mention her by name* (E. M. Forster).

● The words are not, except very informally, mere synonyms for *refer, reference*.

alternative (adjective and noun). The use of *alternative* with reference to more than two options, though sometimes criticized, is acceptable, e.g. *We have been driven to Proletarian Democracy by the failure of all the alternative systems* (G. B. Shaw).

● Do not confuse with *alternate* happening or following in turns, e.g. *Just as every sense is afflicted with a fitting torment so is every spiritual faculty; . . the sensitive faculty with alternate longing and rage* (James Joyce).

altogether. ● Beware of using this when *all* (adjective) *together* (adverb) is meant, e.g. *The dogs were now running, all together.* The reverse error, of using *all together* for the adverb *altogether*, should also be avoided; *altogether* is correct in *There's too much going on altogether at the moment* (Evelyn Waugh).

amend, to alter to something that sounds better, make improvements in; to make better, e.g. *If you consider my expression inadequate I am willing to amend it* (G. B. Shaw); *I have amended my life, have I not?* (James Joyce); noun *amendment*.

● Do not confuse with *emend* to remove errors from (something written), e.g. *An instance of how the dictionary may be emended or censored* (Frederic Raphael); noun *emendation*. An *emendation* will almost always be an *amendment*, but the converse is not true.

analogous means 'similar in certain respects'. It is not a mere synonym for *similar*.

anticipate (1) To be aware of (something) in advance and take suitable action, to deal with (a thing) or perform (an action) before someone else has had time to act so as to gain an advantage, to take action appropriate to (an event) before the due time, e.g. *His power to . . anticipate every change of volume and tempo* (C. Day Lewis); *I shall anticipate any such opposition by tendering my resignation now* (Angus Wilson); *She had anticipated execution by suicide* (Robert Graves); *Some unknown writer in the second century . . suddenly anticipated the whole technique of modern . . narrative* (C. S. Lewis).

(2) To take action before (another person) has had the opportunity to do so, e.g. *I'm sorry—do go on. I did not mean to anticipate you* (John le Carré).

(3) To expect (used only with an event as a direct object), e.g. *Serious writers . . anticipated that the detective story might supersede traditional fiction; Left-wing socialists really anticipated a Fascist dictatorship* (A. J. P. Taylor).

● Sense (3) is well established in informal use, but is regarded as incorrect by many people. Use *expect* in formal contexts. In any case, *anticipate* cannot be followed, as *expect* can, by infinitive constructions (*I expect to see him* or *him to come*) or a personal object (*I expect him today*) and cannot mean 'expect as one's due' (*I expect good behaviour from pupils*).

antithetical to means 'characterized by direct opposition to'; it is not a mere synonym for *opposed to*.

approve (1) (Followed by direct object) authorize, e.g. *I will give letters of introduction to persons approved by you* (NEB).

(2) (Followed by *of*) consider good, e.g. *All the books approved of by young persons of cultivated taste* (C. P. Snow).

● *Approve* should not be used in sense (2) with a direct object, as (wrongly) in *Laziness, rudeness, and untidiness are not approved in this establishment* (correctly, *approved of*).

apt, followed by the *to*-infinitive, carries no implication that the state or action expressed by the infinitive is undesirable from the point of view of its grammatical subject (though it often is from that of the writer), e.g. *In weather like this he is apt to bowl at the batsman's head* (Robert Graves). It indicates that the subject of the sentence is habitually predisposed to doing what is expressed by the verb, e.g. *Time was apt to become confusing* (Muriel Spark). Compare **liable,** which, however, is not complementary to *apt to*, but overlaps with it; *apt to*, followed by a verb with undesirable overtones, = 'habitually or customarily liable to'.

aren't: see **ain't**.

Argentine, Argentinian can be both noun (= a native of Argentina) and adjective (= belonging to Argentina).

● Only the former is used in *Argentine Republic*, and it also has the advantage of brevity when used in other contexts. It rhymes with *turpentine*.

artiste, a professional singer, dancer, or similar public performer: used of persons of either sex.

as (1) = *that, which,* or *who* (relative) is now non-standard except after *same, such,* e.g. *Such comments as seem to be needed* (George Orwell); but not *I know somebody who knows this kid as went blind* (Alan Sillitoe, representing regional speech).

(2) = *that* (conjunction), introducing a noun clause, is now non-standard, e.g. in *I don't know as you'll like it.*

Asian is to be preferred when used of persons to *Asiatic*, which is now widely considered derogatory; the formation of *Asian* is in any case more closely parallel to that of *European, African,* etc. *Asiatic* is acceptable in other contexts, e.g. *Asiatic coastal regions; The Royal Asiatic Society; Asiatic cholera*.

as from is used in formal dating to mean 'from' or 'after' and followed by an actual date, e.g. *As from 10 p.m. on 15 October. As of*, originally Amer., has the same meaning and use.

● *As of now, yesterday*, and the like, are informal and humorous only.

aside from: Amer., = apart from, except for.

as if, as though (1) Followed by the past tense when the verb refers to an unreal possibility (i.e. when the statement introduced by *as if, as though* is untrue, or unlikely), e.g. *Every critic writes as if he were infallible* (Cyril Connolly); *It's not as though he lived like a Milord* (Evelyn Waugh). (2) Followed by the present tense when the statement is true, or might be true; this is especially common when the verbs *look* or *sound* precede, e.g. *I suppose you get on pretty well with your parents. You look as though you do* (Kingsley Amis); *He speaks as though even the rules which we freely invent are somehow suggested to us in virtue of their being right* (Mary Warnock).

attention. *Someone called it to my attention* (Alison Lurie) represents an illogical reversal of the idiom, not uncommon in speech; *someone called* (or *drew*) *my attention to it* or *someone brought it to my attention* would be better in formal contexts.

author (verb) is a rarely required synonym for *write*; *co-author*, however, is acceptable as a verb.

avenge: one avenges an injured person or oneself *on* (occasionally *against*) an offender, or a wrong *on* an offender; the noun is *vengeance* (*on*), and the idea is usually of justifiable retribution, as distinct from **revenge,** though the distinction is not absolute.

aware is normally a predicative adjective followed by an *of*-phrase or a *that*-clause, but can also be preceded by an adverb in the sense 'aware of, appreciative of (the subject indicated by the adverb)', a chiefly Amer. use, e.g. *The most intellectually ambitious and the most technically aware* (W. S. Graham).

● To use *aware* without any qualifying word at all is modish but meaningless, e.g. *Aware, provincial, intelligent, tall Englishman* (*New Statesman*).

bacteria is the plural of *bacterium*, not a singular noun.

baluster, a short pillar with a curving outline, especially in a balustrade; *banister*, an upright supporting a stair handrail (usually in the plural).

beg the question, to assume the truth of the thing which is to be proved, e.g. *I scoffed at that pompous question-begging word 'Evolution'* (H. G. Wells).

● It does not mean (1) to avoid giving a straight answer; or (2) to invite the obvious question (that . .).

behalf: *on behalf of X* (= in X's interest, as X's representative) should not be confused with *on the part of X* (= proceeding from or done by X); *behalf* cannot replace *part* in *His death was largely due to panic on his part.*

benign (in Medicine) has *malignant* as its antonym.

beside (preposition) is used of spatial relationships, or in figurative adaptations of these, e.g. *Beside oneself with joy*; *Quite beside the question*; *We all seemed children beside him* (Evelyn Waugh); *besides* = in addition to, other than, e.g. *Besides this I started my second year by joining the Ruskin School of Art* (Evelyn Waugh).

between. There are no grounds for objection to the use of *between* 'to express the relation of a thing to many surrounding things severally and collectively' (*OED*); *among* should not be substituted in, e.g., *Cordial relations between Britain, Greece, and Turkey.*

See also **choose between**.

bi- (prefix). *Biannual* = appearing (etc.) twice a year, half-yearly; *biennial* = recurring (etc.) every two years, two-yearly. *Bimonthly*, *bi-weekly*, and *bi-yearly* are ambiguous in sense, meaning either 'twice a month (etc.)' or 'every two months (etc.)'; they are best avoided.

● Use *twice a month* or *semi-monthly*, *twice a week* or *semi-weekly*, and *twice a year* in the first sense, and *every two months*, *fortnightly* or *every two weeks*, and *every two years* in the second sense.

billion, etc. (1) Traditional British usage has a *billion* = a million million ($1,000,000,000,000 = 10^{12}$), a *trillion* = a million^3 (10^{18}), and a *quadrillion* = a million^4 (10^{24}); the logic is that the initial *bi-*, *tri-*, *quadri-*, etc. relate to the powers of a million.

(2) The US usage makes each 'step' from *million* to *quadrillion*, and beyond, a power of 1,000; i.e. *million* = 1000^2, *billion* = 1000^3, *trillion* = 1000^4, *quadrillion* = 1000^5.

(3) For the quantity 'thousand million' ($1000^3 = 10^9$), the older British term *milliard* is now rare. Many people who have frequent need to refer to the quantity, namely astronomers and economists, use the American *billion* for this. Most British national newspapers have officially adopted it too.

● In general contexts it is probably safer to use *thousand million* (X,000 m.). But where the sense is vague, e.g. *A billion miles away*, *Billions of stars*, the exact value is immaterial. Note that American *trillion* (10^{12}) = traditional British *billion*.

but = 'except', followed by a pronoun: see pp. 141 f.

candelabra is properly the plural of *candelabrum* and is best kept so in written English.

● *Candelabra* (singular), *candelabras* (plural) are frequent informally.

censure, to criticize harshly and unfavourably, e.g. *Laura censured his immoral marriage* (E. M. Forster).

● Do not confuse with *censor* to suppress (the whole or parts of books, plays, etc.).

centre about, (a)round, meaning (figuratively) 'to gather, revolve, or turn around' is criticized by many authorities, though used by good writers, e.g. *A rather restless, cultureless life, centring round tinned food*, Picture Post, *the radio and the internal combustion engine* (George Orwell). It can be avoided by using *to be centred in* or *on*, e.g. *My universe was still centred in my mother's fragrant person* (Richard Church).

century. Strictly, since the first century ran from the year 1 to the year 100, the first year of a given century should be that ending in the digits 01, and the last year of the preceding century should be the year before, ending in two noughts.

● In popular usage, understandably, the reference of these terms has been moved back one year, so that one will expect the twenty-first century to run from 2000 to 2099. Beware of ambiguity in their written use.

character. The use of this word after an adjective as a substitute for an abstract-noun termination (*-ness*, *-ty*, or the like), or for the word *kind*, devalues it and should be avoided, e.g. *the uniqueness and antiquity of the fabric*, not *the unique and ancient character of the fabric*.

charisma (1) Properly, a theological word (plural *charismata*) designating any of the gifts of the Holy Spirit (see I Corinthians 12). (2) In general use (usually as a mass noun, with no plural), a term (drawn from the works of the German sociologist Max Weber) for the capacity to inspire followers with devotion and enthusiasm.

charismatic (1) Designating a Christian movement that lays stress on the *charismata*. (2) Generally, 'having the capacity to inspire with devotion and enthusiasm', e.g. *A forcefully charismatic hero compensating in physical presence for what he politically lacks* (Terry Eagleton).

choose between: this construction, and *choice between*, are normally followed by *and* in written English; informally *or* is sometimes used, e.g. *The poorest girl alive may not be able to choose between being Queen of England or Principal of Newnham; but she can choose between ragpicking and flowerselling* (G. B. Shaw).

chronic is used of a disease that is long-lasting, though its manifestations may be intermittent (the opposite is *acute* 'coming sharply to a crisis'); it is used in much the same way of other conditions, e.g. *The chronic unemployment of the nineteen-twenties* (A. J. P. Taylor); *The commodities of which there is a chronic shortage* (George Orwell).

● The sense 'objectionable, bad, severe' is very informal.

comparable is followed by *with* in sense (1) of **compare** and by *to* in sense (2). The latter is much the more usual use, e.g. *The little wooden crib-figures . . were by no means comparable to the mass-produced figures* (Muriel Spark).

compare. In formal use, the following distinctions of sense are made:

(1) 'Make a comparison of x with y', followed by *with*, e.g. *You've got to compare method with method, and ideal with ideal* (John le Carré).

(2) 'Say to be similar to, liken to', followed by *to*, e.g. *To call a bishop a mitred fool and compare him to a mouse* (G. B. Shaw).

(3) Intransitively, = 'to be compared', followed by *with*, e.g. *None can compare with thee* (NEB).

● *Compare with* is loosely used in sense (2); the senses overlap, e.g. *How can you compare the Brigadier with my father?* (John Osborne). Conversely, in the separate clause (*as*) *compared with* or *to x*, only sense (1) is possible, but *to* occurs as well as *with*, e.g. *Tarzan . . bewails his human ugliness as compared to the beauty of the apes* (Tom Stoppard); *Earth is tractable stuff compared with coal* (George Orwell).

comparison is usually followed by *with*, especially in *by* or *in comparison with*. It is followed by *to* when the sense is 'the action of likening (to)', e.g. *The comparison of philosophy to a yelping she-dog* (Jowett).

complaisant, disposed to please others or comply with others' wishes; noun *complaisance*, e.g. *The indulgent complaisance which Horace did not bother to disguise* (Frederic Raphael).

● Do not confuse with *complacent* self-satisfied (noun *complacency*).

compose can be used to mean 'constitute, make up' with the constituents as subject and the whole as object, e.g. *The* *tribes which composed the German nation.* It is more commonly used in the passive with the whole as subject and the constituents as object, e.g. *His face was . . composed of little layers of flesh like pallid fungus* (Iris Murdoch).

comprise. The proper constructions with *comprise* are the converse of those used with **compose.** (1) In the active, meaning 'consist of', with the whole as subject and the constituents as objects, e.g. *The faculty comprises the following six departments.*

● In sense (1), *comprise* differs from *consist* in not being followed by *of.* Unlike *include*, *comprise* indicates a comprehensive statement of constituents.

(2) In the passive, meaning 'to be embraced or comprehended *in*', with the constituents as subject and the whole as object, e.g. *Fifty American dollars comprised in a single note* (Graham Greene).

● *Comprise* is often used as a synonym of **compose,** e.g. *The twenty-odd children who now comprise the school* (Miss Read). This is regarded as incorrect by many people. It is especially objectionable in the passive, since *comprise* is not followed by *of*; write *The faculty is composed* (not *comprised*) *of six departments.*

condole, to express sympathy, is always followed by *with*, e.g. *Many . . had come . . to condole with them on their brother's death* (NEB).

● Do not confuse with *console* 'to comfort', followed by direct object, e.g. *Console one another . . with these words* (NEB).

conduce, to lead or contribute (to a result), is always followed by *to*; similarly *conducive* (adjective); e.g. *The enterprise was popular, since it conduced to cut-price jobs* (J. I. M. Stewart).

conform may be followed by *to* or *with*, e.g. *The United Nations . . conformed to Anglo-American plans* (A. J. P. Taylor); *Having himself no particular opinions or tastes he relied upon whatever conformed with those of his companion* (John le Carré).

congeries, a collection of things massed together, is a singular noun, e.g. *A congeries of halls and inns on the site* (J. I. M. Stewart); it is unchanged in the plural.

● The form *congery*, formed in the misapprehension that *congeries* is plural only, is erroneous.

connote, denote. *Connote* means 'to imply in addition to the primary meaning, to imply as a consequence or condition', e.g. *Literature has needed to learn how to exploit all the connotations that lie latent in a word* (Anthony Burgess).

Denote means 'to be the sign of, indicate, signify', e.g. *A proper name . . will convey no information beyond the bare fact that it denotes a person* (Stephen Ullman).

● The two terms are kept rigidly distinct in Logic, but in popular usage *connote* is frequently used to mean 'convey to the mind', or 'mean in actual use' and hence verges on the sense of *denote*. *Denote* cannot be used in the senses of *connote*, e.g. in *His silence does not connote hesitation* (Iris Murdoch).

consequent, following as a result, adverb *consequently*, e.g. *Two engaged in a common pursuit do not consequently share personal identity* (Muriel Spark). These are nearly always to be used rather than *consequential* 'following as an indirect result' and *consequentially*, which are rarer and more specialized.

consist: *consist of* = be composed of, made up of; *consist in* = have as its essential quality, e.g. *All enjoyment consists in undetected sinning* (G. B. Shaw).

continual, always happening, very frequent and without cessation; *continuous*, connected, unbroken, uninterrupted; similarly the adverbs; e.g. *He was continually sending Tiberius not very helpful military advice* (Robert Graves); *There was a continuous rattle from the one-armed bandits* (Graham Greene).

continuance, continuation. The former relates mainly to the intransitive senses of *continue* (to be still in existence), the latter to its transitive senses (to keep up, to resume), e.g. *The great question of our continuance after death* (J. S. Huxley); *As if contemplating a continuation of her assault* (William Trevor).

cousin (1) The children of brothers or sisters are *first cousins* to each other. (2) The children of first cousins are *second cousins* to each other. (3) The child of one's first cousin, and the first cousin of one's parent, is one's *first cousin once removed*. (4) The grandchild of one's first cousin, or the first cousin of one's grandparent, is one's *first cousin twice removed*; and so on. (5) *Cousin-german* = first cousin.

credible, able to be believed.

● Do not confuse with *credulous*, too ready to believe things, as e.g. in *Even if one is credible* (correctly *credulous*) *enough to believe in their ability* (*Daily Telegraph*).

crescendo, used figuratively, means 'a progressive increase in force or effect'. Do not use it when *climax* is meant, e.g. in *The storm reached a crescendo* (correctly *a climax*) *at midnight*.

criteria is the plural of *criterion*, not a singular noun.

crucial, decisive, critical, e.g. *His medical studies were not merely an*

episode in the development of his persona but crucial to it
(Frederic Raphael).

● The weakened sense 'important' is informal only.

data (1) In scientific, philosophical, and general use, usually considered as a number of items and treated as plural, e.g. *Let us
give the name of 'sense-data' to the things which are immediately known in sensation: such things as colours, sounds,* (etc.)
(Bertrand Russell); *The optical data are incomplete* (*Nature*); the
singular is *datum*, e.g. *Personality is not a datum from which we
start* (C. S. Lewis).

(2) In computing and allied disciplines it is treated as a mass
noun (i.e. a collective item), and used with words like *this, that,*
and *much,* and with singular verbs; it is sometimes so treated in
general use, e.g. *Useful data has been obtained* (Winston
Churchill).

● Some people object to use (2).

● *Data* is not a singular countable noun and therefore cannot be
preceded by *a, every, each, either, neither,* and cannot be given
a plural form *datas.*

decidedly, decisively. *Decidedly,* definitely, undoubtedly, e.g. *The
bungalow had a decidedly English appearance* (Muriel Spark).
Decisively (1) conclusively, so as to decide the question, e.g.
*The definition of 'capital' itself depends decisively on the level of
technology employed* (E. F. Schumacher); (2) resolutely, un-
hesitatingly, e.g. *The young lady, whose taste has to be considered,
decisively objected to him* (G. B. Shaw).

decimate, (originally) to kill or destroy one in every ten of; (now
usually) to destroy or remove a large proportion of, e.g. *All my
parents' friends, my friends' brothers were getting killed. Our
circle was decimated* (Rosamond Lehmann).

● *Decimate* does not mean 'defeat utterly'.

decline (verb: to refuse an invitation) has no derived noun; we have
to make do with *refusal* if *declining* cannot be used.

definitive, decisive, unconditional, final; (of an edition) authoritative;
e.g. *The Gold Cup flat handicap, the official and definitive result of
which he had read in the Evening Telegraph* (James Joyce).

● Do not use instead of *definite* (= having exact limits, distinct,
precise); it cannot replace the latter in *We finally received a
definite no.*

delusion, illusion. A general distinction can be drawn, though it is not
absolute. *Delusion* would naturally occur in psychiatric contexts, and is used similarly outside them, to denote a false idea,

impression, or belief held tenaciously, arising mainly from the internal workings of the mind; e.g. *delusions of grandeur*, and *He's been sent here for delusions. His most serious delusion is that he's a murderer* (Robert Graves).

Illusion denotes a false impression derived either from the external world, e.g. *optical illusion*, and *A partition making two tiny boxes, giving at least the illusion of privacy* (Doris Lessing), or from faulty thinking, e.g. *I still imagine I could live in Rome, but it may be an illusion* (Iris Murdoch).

It is in this second sense that *illusion* is almost equivalent to *delusion*; cf. *I hope to strike some small blows for what I believe to be right, but I have no delusions that knock-outs are likely* (Frederic Raphael). It should be remembered that *delusion* carries the sense of *being deluded* (by oneself or another), whereas no verb is implied in *illusion*; on the other hand, one can be said to be *disillusioned*, whereas *delusion* forms no such derivative.

demean (1) *Demean oneself* = conduct oneself (usually with adverbial expression), e.g. *Even on the scaffold he demeaned himself with dignity*. (2) *Demean* (*someone* or *something*) = lower in status, especially with *oneself*, e.g. *Their nobles would not demean themselves to serve their governor* (NEB).

denote: see **connote**.

depend, to be contingent on (a condition or cause), is followed by *on* or *upon*.

● The use of *it depends* followed, without *on* or *upon*, by an interrogative clause, is informal only, e.g. *It depends what you have . . in mind in forming a library of gramophone records whether you think it worth acquiring* (*The Times*).

depreciate, deprecate. *Depreciate* (1) to make or become lower in value; (2) to belittle, disparage, e.g. *To defend our record we seem forced to depreciate the Africans* (Listener); *To become a little more forthcoming and less self-depreciating* (Richard Adams).

Deprecate (1) (with a plan, proceeding, purpose, etc. as the object) to express a wish against or disapproval of, e.g. *I deprecate this extreme course, because it is good neither for my pocket nor for their own souls* (G. B. Shaw); *Polly . . patted her father's head in deprecation of such forcible metaphor* (Anthony Powell). (2) (with a person as the object) to express disapproval of, to reprove; to disparage, e.g. *Anyone who has reprinted his reviews is in no position to deprecate our reprinter* (Christopher Ricks).

● Sense (2) of *deprecate* tends to take on the sense of *depreciate* (2), especially in conjunction with *self*. This use is frequently found in good writers, e.g. *A humorous self-deprecation about one's own advancing senility* (Aldous Huxley); *The old, self-deprecating expression* (Susan Hill). It is, however, widely regarded as incorrect.

derisive = scoffing; *derisory* = (1) scoffing, (2) so small or un-important as to be ridiculous (now the more usual sense), e.g. *A part . . once looked upon as discreditable and derisory* (Anthony Powell).

dialect (form of speech) forms *dialectal* as its adjective; *dialectic* (form of reasoning) can be adjective as well as noun, or can have *dialectical* as its adjective.

dice is the normal singular as well as the plural (*one dice, two dice*); the old singular, *die*, is found only in *the die is cast, straight* (or *true*) *as a die*, and in mathematical discussions, e.g. *Rolling a die will generate a stream of random numbers.*

dichotomy in non-technical use means 'differentiation into contrasting categories' and is frequently followed by *between*, e.g. *An absolute dichotomy between science and reason on the one hand and faith and poetry on the other.*

● It does not mean *dilemma* or *ambivalence*.

die (noun): see **dice**.

different can be followed by *from*, *to*, or *than*.

(1) *Different from* is the most usual expression in both written and spoken English; it is the most favoured by good writers, and is acceptable in all contexts, e.g. *It is also an 'important' book, in a sense different from the sense in which that word is generally used* (George Orwell).

(2) *Different to* is common informally. It sometimes sounds more natural than *different from*, and should then be used; e.g. when yoked with *similar* and followed by a phrase introduced by *to*: *His looks are neither especially similar nor markedly different to those of his twin brother.*

(3) *Different than* is an established idiom in American English, but is not uncommon in British use, e.g. *Both came from a different world than the housing estate outside London* (Doris Lessing). Both *different to* and *different than* are especially valuable as a means of avoiding the repetition and the relative construction required after *different from* in sentences like *I was a very different man in 1935 from what I was in 1916* (Joyce Cary). This could be recast as *I was a very different man in 1935 than I was in 1916* or *than in 1916*. Compare *The American theatre, which is suffering from a different malaise than ours*, which is

greatly preferable to *suffering from a different malaise from that which ours is suffering from.*

This construction is especially common when *different* is part of an adverbial clause (e.g. *in a different way*) or when the adverb *differently* is used, and has been employed by good writers since the seventeenth century, e.g. *Things were constructed very differently now than in former times* (Trollope); *Sebastian was a drunkard in quite a different sense to myself* (Evelyn Waugh); *Puts one in a different position to your own father* (John Osborne).

differential, a technical term in Mathematics, an abbreviation for *differential gear*, or a term for a maintained difference in wage between groups of workers.

● It is not a synonym for *difference.*

digraph = a group of two letters standing for a single sound, e.g. *ea* in *head*, *gh* in *cough*; *ligature* = a typographical symbol consisting of two letters joined together, e.g. fi, fl. The term *diphthong* is best restricted to the sense for which there is no synonym, namely 'a union of two vowels pronounced in one syllable', which is something primarily spoken and heard, not written; *i* in *find*, *ei* in *rein*, and *eau* in *bureau* all *represent* diphthongs. One cause of confusion is that Latin had two *diphthongs* (*ae* and *oe*) often printed as the *ligatures* æ and œ; in English words derived from Latin these are now *digraphs ae* and *oe* (sometimes modified into *e*: see pp. 3–4) representing single vowel sounds.

dilemma (1) A choice between two (or sometimes more than two) undesirable or awkward alternatives, e.g. *The unpleasant dilemma of being obliged either to kill the father or give up the daughter.* (2) More loosely, a perplexing situation in which a choice has to be made, e.g. *The dilemma of the 1960s about whether nice girls should sleep with men* (Alan Watkins).

● It is not merely a synonym for *problem.*

diphthong: see **digraph.**

direct is used as an adverb in two of the main senses of the adjective: (1) straight, e.g. *Another door led direct to the house* (Evelyn Waugh); (2) without intermediaries, e.g. *I appeal now, over your head, . . direct to the august oracle* (G. B. Shaw).

directly is used in most of the main senses of the adjective, e.g. *Why don't you deal directly with the wholesalers?* (G. B. Shaw); *The wind is blowing directly on shore*; *directly opposite, opposed.*

● It is not usually used to mean 'straight', since it has an extra sense, used in similar contexts, 'immediately, without delay', e.g. *Just a night in London—I'll be back directly* (Iris Murdoch).

discomfit, to thwart, disconcert; similarly *discomfiture*; e.g. *He discomfited his opponents by obliging them to disagree with a great logician* (Frederic Raphael).

● Do not confuse with *discomfort* (now rare as a verb, = make uneasy).

disinterest, lack of interest, indifference, e.g. *Buried the world under a heavy snowfall of disinterest* (Christopher Fry).

● The use of *disinterest* in this sense may be objected to on the same grounds as sense (2) of **disinterested**; but the word is rarely used in any other sense, and the possible alternative *uninterest* is very rare indeed.

disinterested (1) Impartial, unbiased, e.g. *Thanks to his scientific mind he understood—a proof of disinterested intelligence which had pleased her* (Virginia Woolf). The noun is *disinterestedness*. (2) Uninterested, indifferent, e.g. *It is not that we are disinterested in these subjects, but that we are better qualified to talk about our own interests* (*The Times*). The noun is **disinterest**.

● Sense (2) is common in informal use, but is widely regarded as incorrect and is avoided by careful writers, who prefer *uninterested*.

disposal is the noun from *dispose of* (get off one's hands, deal with); *disposition* is the noun from *dispose* (arrange, incline).

distinctive, serving to distinguish, characteristic, e.g. *It had smelled like this soap today, a light, entirely distinctive smell* (Susan Hill).

● Do not confuse with *distinct*, separate, individual, definite, e.g. *Trying to put into words an impression that was not distinct in my own mind* (W. Somerset Maugham).

drunk, drunken. In older and literary usage, the predicative and attributive forms respectively; now usually allocated to distinct senses, namely 'intoxicated' and 'given to drink', e.g. *They were lazy, irresponsible, and drunken; but on this occasion they were not drunk. Drunken* also means 'caused by or exhibiting drunkenness', e.g. *a drunken brawl.*

due to (1) That ought to be given to, e.g. *Pay Caesar what is due to Caesar* (NEB). (2) To be ascribed to, e.g. *Half the diseases of modern civilization are due to starvation of the affections in the young* (G. B. Shaw). *Due* is here an adjective with a complementary prepositional phrase, like *liable* (*to*), *subject* (*to*). As an adjective it needs to be attached to a noun as complement (see example above), or as part of a verbless adjective clause, e.g. *A few days' temporary absence of mind due to sunstroke was . . nothing to worry about* (Muriel Spark).

(3) = *owing to*. A sentence conforming to type (2) above like *He suffered a few days' absence of mind due to sunstroke* can be equated with *He suffered a few days' absence of mind, owing to sunstroke*. In this way *due to* has borrowed from *owing to* the status of independent compound preposition, a use not uncommon even with good writers, e.g. *It . . didn't begin until twenty past due to a hitch* (William Trevor); *Due to an unlikely run of nineteens and zeros, I gained the equivalent of three hundred pounds* (Graham Greene).

● The use of *due to* as a compound preposition is widely regarded as unacceptable. It can often be avoided by the addition of the verb *to be* and *that*, e.g. It is *due to your provident care* that . . *improvements are being made* (NEB).

effect: see **affect**.

e.g., i.e.: *E.g.* (short for Latin *exempli gratia*) = for example, for instance; it introduces one or more typical examples of what precedes it: *Many countries of Asia, e.g. India, Indonesia, and Malaysia, were once ruled by European powers. I.e.* (short for Latin *id est*) = that is; it introduces an amplification or explanation of what precedes it: *It was natural that the largest nation (i.e. India) should take the lead; The United States presence, i.e. the maintenance of American military personnel, in south-east Asia.*

egoism, -ist(ic), egotism, -ist(ic). *Egoism* is the term used in Philosophy and Psychology, and denotes self-interest (often contrasted with *altruism*), e.g. *Egoistic instincts concerned with self-preservation or the good of the Ego* (Gilbert Murray). *Egotism* is the practice of talking or thinking excessively about oneself, self-centredness, e.g. *He is petty, selfish, vain, egotistical; he is spoilt; he is a tyrant* (Virginia Woolf).

● In practice the senses tend to merge, e.g. *Human loves don't last, . . they are far too egoistic* (Iris Murdoch); *A complete egotist in all his dealings with women* (Joyce Cary).

egregious, remarkable in a bad sense; gross, outrageous; used mainly with words like *ass, impostor, liar, blunder, folly, waste*, e.g. *Wark tenderly forgives her most egregious clerical errors* (Martin Amis).

either (adjective and pronoun). (1) One or other of the two, e.g. *Simple explanations are for simple minds. I've no use for either* (Joe Orton). (2) Each of the two, e.g. *Every few kilometres on either side of the road, there were Haitian and Dominican guardposts* (Graham Greene).

● *Either* is frequently used in sense (2), in preference to *each*, with reference to a thing that comes naturally in a pair, e.g. *end*, *hand*, *side*. This use is sometimes ignorantly condemned but is both the older sense of *either* and commonly found in good writers of all periods.

elder (adjective) the earlier-born (of two related or indicated persons), e.g. *The first and elder wife . . returned . . to Jericho* (Muriel Spark); *He is my elder by ten years. Eldest* first-born or oldest surviving (member of family, son, daughter, etc.).

elusive (rather than *elusory*) is the usual adjective related to *elude*; *illusory* (rather than *illusive*) is the usual adjective related to *illusion*.

enjoin: one can enjoin an action, etc., *on* someone, or enjoin someone *to* do something; the former is more usual; e.g. *To . . enjoin celibacy on its laity as well as on its clergy* and *That enables and enjoins the citizen to earn his own living* (G. B. Shaw).

enormity (1) Great wickedness (of something), e.g. *Hugh was made entirely speechless . . by the enormity of the proposal* (Iris Murdoch); a serious crime or offence, e.g. *They had met to pass sentence on Wingfield for his enormities* (David Garnett). (2) Enormousness, e.g. *The war in its entire magnitude did not exist for the average civilian . . The enormity of it was quite beyond most of us* (G. B. Shaw).
● Sense (2) is commonly found, but is regarded by many people as incorrect.

enthuse, to show or fill with enthusiasm, is chiefly informal.

● **equally as** (+ adjective) should not be used for *equally*, e.g. in *How to apply it in a calm, unruffled manner was equally as important* (G. F. Newman), or for *as*, e.g. *The Government are equally as guilty as the Opposition.*

event: *in the event of* is followed by a noun or gerund, e.g. *In the event of the earl's death, the title will lapse.*
● *In the event that*, treated as a compound conjunction, is ungainly and avoided by good writers; it is even worse with *that* omitted, e.g. *In the event the car overturns.*

ever. When placed after a *wh*-question word in order to intensify it, *ever* should be written separately, e.g. *Where ever have you been?*, *when ever is he coming?*, *who ever would have thought it?*, *why ever did you do it?*, *how ever shall I escape?* When used with a relative pronoun or adverb to give it indefinite or general force, *ever* is written as one word with it, e.g. *Wherever you go I'll follow; whenever he washes up he breaks something; there's a reward for whoever* (not *whomever*) *finds it; whatever else you do, don't get lost; however it's done, it's difficult.*

evidence, evince. *Evidence* (verb), to serve as evidence for the existence or truth of, e.g. *There was an innate refinement . . about Gerty which was unmistakably evidenced in her delicate hands* (James Joyce).

Evince, to show that one has a (hidden or unseen) quality, e.g. *Highly evolved sentiments and needs* (*sometimes said to be distinctively human, though birds and animals . . evince them*) (G. B. Shaw).

● *Evince* should not be confused with *evoke* to call up (a response, a feeling, etc.), e.g. *A timely and generous act which evoked a fresh outburst of emotion* (James Joyce).

exceedingly, extremely; *excessively*, beyond measure, immoderately, e.g. *The excessively rational terms employed by people with a secret panic* (Muriel Spark).

excepting (preposition) is only used after *not* and *always*.

exceptionable, to which exception may be taken; *unexceptionable* with which no fault may be found, e.g. *The opposite claim would seem to him unexceptionable even if he disagreed with it* (George Orwell).

● Do not confuse with (*un*)*exceptional*, that is not an exception, unusual.

excess. *In excess of* 'to a greater amount or degree than' forms an adverbial phrase.

● Prefer *more than* where the phrase qualified is the subject or object, e.g. in *The Data Centre, which processes in excess of 1200 jobs per week*.

expect (1) in the sense 'suppose, think' is informal; (2) see **anticipate**.

explicit, express. *Explicit*, distinctly expressing all that is meant, leaving nothing implied, e.g. *I had been too tactful, . . too vague . . But I now saw that I ought to have been more explicit* (Iris Murdoch); *express*, definite, unmistakable in import, e.g. *Idolatry fulsome enough to irritate Jonson into an express disavowal of it* (G. B. Shaw).

exposure (to) may be used figuratively to mean 'being made subject (to an influence, etc.)' but should not be used for *experience (of)*, e.g. in *Candidates who have had exposure to North American markets*.

express (adjective): see **explicit**.

facility in the sense 'ease in doing something', e.g. *I knew that I had a facility with words* (George Orwell), should not be confused with a similar sense of *faculty*, viz. 'a particular kind of ability', e.g. *Hess . . had that odd faculty, peculiar to lunatics, of falling into strained positions* (Rebecca West).

factious: see **fractious**.

factitious, made for a special purpose; not natural; artificial; e.g. *Heroic tragedy is decadent because it is factitious; it substitutes violent emotionalism for emotion* (and) *the purple patch for poetry* (L. C. Knights); *fictitious*, feigned, simulated; imaginary, e.g. *Afraid of being suspected, he gave a fictitious account of his movements.*

farther, farthest: though originally interchangeable with *further, furthest*, these words are now only used where the sense of 'distance' is involved, e.g. *One whose actual dwelling lay presumably amid the farther mysteries of the cosmos* (J. I. M. Stewart).

● Even in this sense many people prefer *further, furthest*.

feasible, capable of being done, achieved, or dealt with, e.g. *Young people believing that niceness and innocence are politically as well as morally feasible* (J. I. M. Stewart).

● It is sometimes used to mean 'possible' or 'probable', but whichever of these two words is appropriate should be used instead.

fewer: see **less**.

fictitious: see **factitious**.

flammable, easily set on fire; preferable as a warning of danger to *inflammable*, which may be mistaken for a negative (= not easily set on fire). The real negatives are *non-flammable* and *non-inflammable*.

flaunt, to display proudly or ostentatiously, e.g. *The wicked flaunt themselves on every side* (NEB); *As though to defy reason, as though to flaunt a divine indestructibility, the question will not go away: is God?* (Tom Stoppard).

● Do not confuse with *flout* 'to disobey openly and scornfully', e.g. *His deliberate flouting of one still supposedly iron rule* (Frederic Raphael): *flout* should have been used by the public figure reported as having said *Those wanting to flaunt the policy would recognize that public opinion was not behind them.*

following, as a sequel to, consequent on, is used in two ways. (1) Properly, as an adjective, dependent on a preceding noun, e.g. *During demonstrations following the hanging of two British soldiers.* (2) By extension, as an independent quasi-preposition, e.g. *The prologue was written by the company following an incident witnessed by them.*

● Many people regard use (2) as erroneous (cf. **due to** (3)). It can also give rise to ambiguity, e.g. *Police arrested a man following* *the hunt*. In any case, *following* should not be used as a mere synonym for *after* (e.g. *Following supper they went to bed*).

for: The subject of a clause of which the verb is the *to*-infinitive is normally preceded by *for*, e.g. *For him to stay elsewhere is unthinkable* (contrast *that he should stay elsewhere* . .). But if the clause is a direct object in a main sentence, *for* is omitted: hence *I could not bear for him to stay elsewhere* (*Daily Mail*) is non-standard.

forensic (1) of or used in courts of law, e.g. *forensic medicine, forensic science*; (2) of or involving forensic science, e.g. *An object which has been sent for forensic examination*.

● Sense (2) is often deplored as an illogical extension, but is widespread.

former (latter). When referring to the first (last) of three or more, *the first* (*the last*) should be used, not *the former* (*the latter*).

fortuitous means 'happening by chance, accidental', e.g. *His presence is not fortuitous. He has a role to play* (André Brink).

● It does not mean either 'fortunate' or 'timely', as (incorrectly) in *He could not believe it. It was too fortuitous to be chance*.

fractious, unruly; peevish; e.g. *Block tackle and a strangling pully will bring your lion to heel, no matter how fractious* (James Joyce).

● Do not confuse with *factious* 'given to, or proceeding from, faction', e.g. *In spite of such a divisive past and a fractious* (correctly, *factious*) *present* (*New York Times*).

fruition, fulfilment, especially in the phrase *be brought to, come to, grow to, reach*, etc. *fruition*, once stigmatized as a misuse, is now standard.

fulsome is a pejorative term, applied to nouns such as *flattery, servility, affection*, etc., and means 'cloying, excessive, disgusting by excess', e.g. *They listened to fulsome speeches, doggedly translated by a wilting Olga Fiodorovna* (Beryl Bainbridge).

● *Fulsome* is not now regarded as a synonym of *copious*, though this was its original meaning.

further, furthest: see **farther, farthest.**

geriatric means 'pertaining to the health and welfare of the elderly'; it is incorrect to use it as a synonym of *senile* or *elderly*, or as a noun meaning 'elderly or senile person'.

gourmand, glutton; *gourmet*, connoisseur of good food.

graffiti is the plural of *graffito*; it is not a singular mass noun.

half. The use of *half* in expressions of time to mean *half-past* is indigenous to Britain and has been remarked on since the 1930s, e.g. *We'd easily get the half-five bus* (William Trevor); it is to be distinguished from the use of *half* + the succeeding hour (i.e. *half-nine* = half-past eight) in parts of Scotland and Ireland. It remains non-standard.

hardly. (1) *Hardly* is not used with negative constructions.

● Expressions like *Without hardly a word of comment* (substitute *with hardly* or *almost without a word . .*) and *I couldn't hardly tell what he meant* (substitute *I could hardly tell . .*) are non-standard.

(2) *Hardly* and *scarcely* are followed by *when* or *before*, not *than*, e.g. *Hardly had Grimes left the house when a tall young man . . presented himself at the front door* (Evelyn Waugh).

heir apparent, one whose right of inheritance cannot be superseded by the birth of another heir; as opposed to an *heir presumptive*, whose right can be so superseded.

● *Heir apparent* does not mean 'seeming heir'.

help. *More than*, or *as little as*, *one can help* are illogical but established idioms, e.g. *They will not respect more than they can help treaties extracted from them under duress* (Winston Churchill).

hoi polloi can be preceded by *the*, even though *hoi* represents the Greek definite article, e.g. *The screens with which working archaeologists baffle the* hoi polloi (Frederic Raphael).

● **homogenous** is a frequent error for *homogeneous*, and is probably due partly to the form of the related verb *homogenize*. A word *homogenous* exists, but has a technical meaning that is quite different and very restricted in its use. *Homogeneous* means 'of the same kind, uniform', e.g. *The style throughout was homogeneous but the authors' names were multiform* (Evelyn Waugh).

hopefully, thankfully. These adverbs are used in two ways: (1) As adverbs of manner = 'in a hopeful/thankful way', 'with hope/gratitude', e.g. *The prevailing mentality of that deluded time was still hopefully parliamentary* (G. B. Shaw); *When it thankfully dawned on her that the travel agency . . would be open* (Muriel Spark). (2) As sentence adverbs, outside the clause structure and conveying the speaker's comment on the statement, e.g. *Hopefully they will be available in the autumn* (*Guardian*); *The editor, thankfully, has left them as they were written* (TLS).

● Use (2) is widely regarded as unacceptable. The main reason is that other commenting sentence adverbs, such as *regrettably*, *fortunately*, etc., can be converted to the form *it is regrettable*, *fortunate*, etc., *that —*, but these are to be resolved as *it is to be hoped* or *one hopes that —* and *one is thankful that —*. (The same objection could be, but is not, made to *happily* and *unhappily* which mean *one is (un)happy* not *it is (un)happy that* —, e.g. in *Unhappily children do hurt flies* (Jean Rhys).) A further objection is that absurdity or ambiguity can arise from the interplay of senses (1) and (2), e.g. *There is also a screen, hopefully forming a backdrop to the whole stage* (Tom Stoppard); *Any decision to trust Egypt . . and move forward hopefully toward peace . . in the Middle East* (*Guardian Weekly*). This use of *hopefully* probably arose as a translation of German *hoffentlich*, used in the same way, and first became popular in America in the late 1960s; the same American provenance, but not the German, holds good for *thankfully*. It is recommended that sense (2) should be restricted to informal contexts.

i.e.: see **e.g., i.e.**

if in certain constructions (usually linking two adjectives or adverbs that qualify the same noun or verb) can be ambiguous, e.g. *A great play, if not the greatest, by this author*.

● It is best to paraphrase such sentences as, e.g., either *A great play, though not the greatest by this author* or *A great play, perhaps* (or *very nearly*) *the greatest by this author*.

ignorant is better followed by *of* than by *about*, e.g. *Is this famous teacher of Israel ignorant of such things?* (NEB).

ilk. *Of that ilk* is a Scots term, meaning 'of the same place, territorial designation, or name', e.g. *Wemyss of that ilk* = Wemyss of Wemyss.

● By a misunderstanding *ilk* has come to mean 'sort, lot' (usually pejorative), e.g. *Joan Baez and other vocalists of that ilk* (David Lodge). This should be avoided in formal English.

ill used predicatively = 'unwell'; *sick* used predicatively = 'about to or likely to vomit, in the act of vomiting', e.g. *I felt sick*; *I was violently sick*; used attributively = 'unwell', e.g. *a sick man*, except in collocations like *sick bay*, *sick leave*.

● It is non-standard to use *ill* predicatively for 'in the act of vomiting' or *sick* predicatively for 'unwell' (though the latter is standard Amer.), except in the phrase *off sick* 'away on sick leave'.

illusion: see **delusion**.

illusory: see **elusive**.

impact, used figuratively, is best confined to contexts in which someone or something is imagined as striking another, e.g. *The most dynamic colour combination if used too often loses its impact* (i.e., on the eye). It is weakened if used as a mere synonym for *effect*, *impression*, or *influence*.

impedance. The total resistance of an electric circuit to the flow of alternating current.

● Do not confuse with *impediment*, a hindrance, a defect (in speech, etc.), e.g. *Convinced of the existence of a serious impediment to his marriage* (Evelyn Waugh).

imply, infer. *Imply* (1) to involve the truth or existence of; (2) to express indirectly, insinuate, hint at. *Infer* (1) to reach (an opinion), deduce, from facts and reasoning, e.g. *She left it to my intelligence to infer her meaning. I inferred it all right* (W. Somerset Maugham); *He is a philosopher's God, logically inferred from self-evident premises* (Tom Stoppard).

(2) = *imply*, sense (2), e.g. *I have inferred once, and I repeat, that Limehouse is the most overrated excitement in London* (H. V. Morton).

● Sense (2) of *infer* is generally unacceptable, since it is the reverse of the primary sense of the verb.

imprimatur, official licence to print.

● Do not confuse with *imprint*, the name of the publisher/printer, place of publication/printing, etc., on the title-page or at the end of a book.

inapt, inept. *Inapt* = 'not apt', 'unsuitable'; *inept* = (1) without aptitude, unskilful, e.g. *Fox-trots and quicksteps, at which he had been so inept* (David Lodge); (2) inappropriate, e.g. *Not much less than famous for looking ineptly dressed* (Anthony Powell); (3) absurd, silly, e.g. *Here I was, awkward and tongue-tied, and all the time in danger of saying something inept or even rude* (Siegfried Sassoon).

inchoate means 'just begun, underdeveloped', e.g. *Trying to give his work a finished look—and all the time it's pathetically obvious . . that the stuff's fatally inchoate* (John Wain).

● It does not mean *chaotic* or *incoherent*.

include: see **comprise** (1).

industrial action is an imprecise, often inappropriate, and sometimes socially divisive expression. If possible, use *strike, work-to-rule, overtime ban*, etc., as appropriate.

infer: see **imply**.

inflammable: see **flammable**.

inflict, afflict. One *inflicts* something *on* someone or *afflicts* someone *with* something; something is *inflicted on* one, or one is *afflicted with* something.

● Do not use *inflict with* where *afflict with* is meant, e.g. in *The miners are still out, and industry is inflicted* (correctly, *afflicted*) *with a kind of creeping paralysis.*

ingenious, clever at inventing, etc.; noun *ingenuity*; *ingenuous* open, frank, innocent; noun *ingenuousness*.

insignia is a plural noun, e.g. *Fourteen different airline insignia* (David Lodge); its singular, rarely encountered, is *insigne*.

insinuendo, a blend of *insinuation* and *innuendo*, is at best only jocular.

intense, existing, having some quality, in a high degree, e.g. *The intense evening sunshine* (Iris Murdoch); *intensive* employing much effort, concentrated, e.g. *Intensive care*; *The intensive geological surveys of the Sahara* (Margaret Drabble).

interface (noun) (1) A surface forming a common boundary between two regions, e.g. *The concepts of surface tension apply to the interfaces between solid and solid, solid and liquid,* (etc.). (2) A piece of equipment in which interaction occurs between two systems, processes, etc., e.g. *Modular interfaces can easily be designed to adapt the general-purpose computer to the equipment.* (3) A point or area of interaction between two systems, organizations, or disciplines, e.g. *The interface between physics and music is of direct relevance to . . the psychological effects of hearing* (*Nature*).

● Sense (3) is widely regarded as unacceptable, since it is often debased into a high-sounding synonym for *boundary, meeting-point, interaction, liaison, link,* etc., e.g. *The need for the interface of lecturer and student will diminish.*

interface (verb), to connect (equipment) with (equipment) by means of an interface; (of equipment) to be connected by an interface; e.g. *A multiplexed analog-to-digital converter interfaced to a PDP 11-40 computer* (*Lancet*).

● *Interface* should not be used as a synonym for *interact* (*with*), as, e.g., in *The ideal candidate will have the ability to interface effectively with the heads of staff of various departments.*

internment, confinement (from verb *intern*).

● Do not confuse with *interment*, burial (from verb *inter*).

into: it is common informally, but incorrect in formal prose, to use *in* where *into* is required, especially after verbs of motion, e.g. *Practically knocked me over in his eagerness to get in the house* (David Lodge).

invite (noun = 'invitation'), although over three centuries old, remains informal (and somewhat non-standard) only.

ironic, ironical, ironically. The noun *irony* can mean (1) a way of speaking in which the intended meaning (for those with insight) is the opposite to, or very different from, that expressed by the words used (and apprehended by the victim of the irony); or (2) a condition of affairs or events that is the opposite of what might be expected, especially when the outcome of an action appears as if it is in mockery of the agent's intention.

The adjectives *ironic*, *ironical*, and the adverb *ironically* are commonly used in sense (1) of *irony*, e.g. *Ironical silent apology for the absence of naked women and tanks of gin from the amenities* (Kingsley Amis). They are also frequently found in sense (2), e.g. *The outcome was ironic. The expenditure of British treasure served to rearm the United States rather than to strengthen Great Britain* (A. J. P. Taylor); *The fact that after all she had been faithful to me was ironic* (Graham Greene).

● Some people object to this use, especially when *ironically* is used to introduce a trivial oddity, e.g. *It was ironic that he thought himself locked out when the key was in his pocket all the time.*

kind of, sort of (1) *A kind of*, *a sort of* should not be followed by *a* before the noun, e.g. *a kind of shock*, not *a kind of a shock*. (2) *Kind of*, *sort of*, etc., followed by a plural noun, are often treated as plural and qualified by plural words like *these*, *those*, or followed by a plural verb, e.g. *They would be on those sort of terms* (Anthony Powell). This is widely regarded as incorrect except in informal use: substitute *that* (etc.) *kind* (or *sort*) *of* or *of that kind* (or *sort*), e.g. *this kind of car is unpopular* or *cars of this kind are unpopular*. (3) *Kind of*, *sort of* used adverbially, e.g. *I kind of expected it*, are informal only.

kudos is a mass noun like *glory* or *fame*, e.g. *He's made a lot of kudos out of the strike* (Evelyn Waugh).

● It is not a plural noun and there is no singular *kudo*.

latter: see **former**.

laudable, praiseworthy, e.g. *The Opposition's abstention from criticism of the Government in this crisis was laudable*; *laudatory*, expressing praise, e.g. *One politician's remarks about another are not always laudatory*.

lay (verb), past *laid*, = 'put down, arrange', etc. is only transitive, e.g. *Lay her on the bed*; *They laid her on the bed*; (reflexive, somewhat archaic): *I will both lay me down in peace, and sleep* (Authorized Version).

● To use *lay* intransitively, to mean 'lie', e.g. *She wants to lay down*; *She was laying on the bed*, is non-standard, even though fairly common in spoken English. Cf. *lie*.

leading question, in Law, is a question so worded that it prompts a person to give the desired answer, e.g. *The solicitor . . at once asked me some leading questions . . I had to try to be both forthcoming and discreet* (C. P. Snow).

● It does not mean a 'principal' (or 'loaded' or 'searching') 'question'.

learn with a person as the object, = 'teach', is non-standard, or occasionally jocular as in *I'll learn you*.

less (adjective) is the comparative of (*a*) *little*, and, like the latter, is used with mass nouns, e.g. *I owe him little duty and less love* (Shakespeare); *fewer* is the comparative of (*a*) *few*, and both are used with plural countable nouns, e.g. *Few people have their houses broken into; and fewer still have them burnt* (G. B. Shaw).

● *Less* is quite often used informally as the comparative of *few*, probably on the analogy of *more*, which is the comparative both of *much* (with mass nouns) and *many* (with plural countable nouns), e.g. *I wish that they would send less delicacies and frills and some more plain and substantial things* (Susan Hill). This is regarded as incorrect in formal English.

● *Less* should not be used as the comparative of *small* (or some similar adjective such as *low*), e.g. *a lower price* not *a less price*.

lesser, not so great as the other or the rest, e.g. *He opened* The Times *with the rich crackle that drowns all lesser sounds* (John Galsworthy).

● *Lesser* should not be used when the meaning is 'not so big' or 'not so large': its opposition to *greater* is essential. It cannot replace *smaller* in *A smaller prize will probably be offered*.

lest is very formal (in ordinary English, *so that . . not* or *in case* is used); it is followed by *should* or (in exalted style) the subjunctive, e.g. *Lest the eye wander aimlessly, a Doric temple stood by the water's edge* (Evelyn Waugh); *Lest some too sudden gesture or burst of emotion should turn the petals brown* (Patrick White).

let, to allow (followed by the bare infinitive) is rarely used in the passive: the effect is usually unidiomatic, e.g. *Halfdan's two sons . . are let owe their lives to a trick* (Gwyn Jones). *Allowed to* is usual.

liable (1) can be followed by *to* + a noun or noun phrase in the sense 'subject to, likely to suffer from', or by an infinitive; (2) carries the implication that the action or experience expressed by the infinitive is undesirable, e.g. *Receiving in the bedroom is liable to get a woman talked about* (Tom Stoppard); (3) can indicate either the mere possibility, or the habituality, of what is expressed by the verb, e.g. *The cruellest question which a novelist is liable . . to be asked* (Frederic Raphael); *The kind of point that one is always liable to miss* (George Orwell).

● The sense 'likely to' is Amer., e.g. *Boston is liable to be the ultimate place for holding the convention.*

Contrast **apt**.

lie (verb) past *lay*, *lain*, = 'recline', 'be situated', is only intransitive, e.g. *Lie down on the bed*; *The ship lay at anchor until yesterday*; *Her left arm, on which she had lain all night, was numb*.

● To use *lie* transitively, to mean 'lay', e.g. *Lie her on the bed*, is non-standard. The past *lay* and participle *lain* are quite often wrongly used for *laid* out of over-correctness, e.g. *He had lain this peer's honour in the dust*. Cf. **lay**.

ligature: see digraph.

like, indicating resemblance between two things: (1) It is normally used as an adjective followed by a noun, noun phrase, or pronoun (in the objective case), e.g. *A man with human frailties like our own* (NEB); *He loathes people like you and me* (not . . *and I*). It can be used to mean 'such as' (introducing a particular example of a class about which something is said), e.g. *With a strongly patterned dress like that you shouldn't really wear any jewellery* (Iris Murdoch).

● In formal contexts some people prefer *such as* to be used if more than one example is mentioned, e.g. *British composers such as Elgar, Vaughan Williams, and Britten*.

(2) It is often used as a conjunction with a dependent clause, e.g. *Everything went wrong* . . *like it does in dreams* (Iris Murdoch); *Not with a starched apron like the others had* (Jean Rhys), or with an adverbial phrase, e.g. *With glossy hair, black, and a nose like on someone historical* (Patrick White); *It was as if I saw myself. Like in a looking-glass* (Jean Rhys).

● Although this is not uncommon in formal writing, it is often 'condemned as vulgar or slovenly' (*OED*), and is best avoided, except informally. Use *as*, e.g. *Are you going to kill me as you killed the Egyptian?* (NEB), or recast the sentence, e.g. *A costume like those that the others wore*.

(3) It is often informally used to mean 'as if', e.g. *The light at either end of the tunnel was like you were looking through a sheet of yellow cellophane* (Patrick White); *You wake like someone hit you on the head* (T. S. Eliot).

● This use is very informal.

likely (adverb), in the sense 'probably', must be preceded by *more*, *most*, or *very*, e.g. *Its inhabitants* . . *very likely do make that claim for it* (George Orwell).

● The use without the qualifying adverb is Amer., e.g. *They'll likely turn ugly* (Eugene O'Neill).

linguist means 'one whose subject is linguistics' as well as 'one skilled in the use of languages'; there is no other suitable term (*linguistician* is disfavoured).

literally. In very informal speech, *literally* is used as an intensifying adverb without meaning apart from its emotive force.

● This use should be avoided in writing or formal speech, since it almost invariably involves absurdity, e.g. *The dwarfs mentioned here are literally within a stone's throw of the Milky Way* (*New Scientist*). The appropriate use is seen in *She emerged, fully armed, from the head of Zeus who was suffering from a literally splitting headache* (Frederic Raphael).

loan (verb) has some justification where a businesslike loan is in question, e.g. *The gas industry is using a major part of its profits to benefit the PSBR by loaning money to Government* (*Observer*). Otherwise it is a needless variant for *lend*.

locate can mean 'discover the place where someone or somebody is', e.g. *She had located and could usefully excavate her Saharan highland emporium* (Margaret Drabble); it should not be used to mean merely 'find'.

lot. *A lot of*, though somewhat informal, is acceptable in serious writing; *lots of* is not.

luncheon is an especially formal variant of *lunch*; the latter should normally be used, except in fixed expressions like *luncheon voucher*.

luxuriant, growing profusely, prolific, profuse, exuberant, e.g. *His hair . . does not seem to have been luxuriant even in its best days* (G. B. Shaw).

● Do not confuse with *luxurious* (the adjective relating to *luxury*), e.g. *The food, which had always been good, was now luxurious* (C. P. Snow).

majority can mean 'the greater number of a countable set', and is then followed by the plural, e.g. *The majority of the plays produced were failures* (G. B. Shaw).

● *Great* (or *huge*, *vast*, etc.) can precede *majority* in this sense, e.g. *The first thing you gather from the vast majority of the speakers* (C. S. Lewis); but not *greater*, *greatest* (since 'more' is already contained in the word).

● *Majority* is not used to mean 'the greater part of an uncountable mass', e.g. *I was doing most* (or *the greater part*) *of the cooking* (not *the majority of the cooking*).

masterful, domineering, e.g. *People might say she was tyrannical, domineering, masterful* (Virginia Woolf).

● Do not confuse with *masterly*, very skilful, e.g. *A masterly compound of friendly argumentation and menace* (Iris Murdoch).

maximize, to make as great as possible.

● It should not be used for 'to make as good, easy, (etc). as possible' or 'to make the most of' as in *To maximize customer service*; *To maximize this situation*.

means (1) Money resources: a plural noun, e.g. *You might find out from Larry . . what his means are* (G. B. Shaw).

(2) That by which a result is brought about. It may be used either as a singular noun or as a plural one, without any change in form, e.g. (singular) *The press was, at this time, the only means . . of influencing opinion at home* (A. J. P. Taylor); (plural) *All the time-honoured means of meeting the opposite sex* (Frederic Raphael).

● Beware of mixing singular and plural, as in *The right to resist by every* (singular) *means that are* (plural) *consonant with the law of God*.

media, agency, means (of communication etc.), is a plural noun, e.g. *The communication media inflate language because they dare not be honest* (Anthony Burgess). Its singular is *medium* (rare except in *mass medium*).

● *Media* cannot be treated as a singular noun or form a plural *medias*. *Medium* (in Spiritualism) forms its plural in *-s*.

militate: see **mitigate**.

milliard: see **billion**.

minimize, to reduce to, or estimate at, the smallest possible amount or degree, e.g. *Each side was inclined to minimize its own losses in battle*.

● It does not mean *lessen* and therefore cannot be qualified by adverbs like *greatly*.

minority. *Large*, *vast*, etc. *minority* can mean either 'a considerable number who are yet less than half', or 'a number who are very much the minority': it is best to avoid the ambiguity.

mitigate, appease, alleviate, moderate (usually transitive), e.g. *Its heat mitigated by the strong sea-wind* (Anthony Burgess).

● Do not confuse with *militate* (intransitive) *against*, to serve as a strong influence against, e.g. *The very fact that Leamas was a professional could militate against his interests* (John le Carré): it is only the idea of countering that they have in common.

momentum, impetus.

> ● Do not confuse with *moment* 'importance', e.g. *He has marked his entrance with an error of some moment* (not *momentum*).

more than one is followed by a singular verb and is referred back to by singular pronouns, e.g. *More than one popular dancing man inquired anxiously at his bank* (Evelyn Waugh).

motivate, to cause (a person) to act in a particular way.

> ● It does not mean 'supply a motive, justify', e.g. (wrongly) in *The publisher motivates the slim size of these volumes by claiming it makes them more likely to be read.*

mutual (1) Felt, done, etc., by each to(wards) the other, e.g. *The mutual affection of father and son was rather touching* (W. Somerset Maugham).

(2) Standing in a (specified) relation to each other, e.g. *Kings and subjects, mutual foes* (Shelley). This sense is now rare.

(3) Common to two (or more) parties, e.g. *a mutual friend* or *acquaintance.*

> ● Sense (3) is acceptable in a small number of collocations, such as the two indicated, in which *common* might be ambiguous; cf. *They had already formed a small island of mutual Englishness* (Muriel Spark): *common Englishness* might imply vulgarity. Otherwise *common* is preferable, e.g. in *By common* (rather than *mutual*) *consent the Chinese meal had been abandoned.*

nature. ● Avoid using adjective + *nature* as a periphrasis for an abstract noun, e.g. write *The dangerousness of the spot*, not *The dangerous nature of the spot.*

need (*this needs changing*, etc.): see **want**.

neighbourhood. *In the neighbourhood of* is an unnecessarily cumbersome periphrasis for *round about.*

neither (adverb). ● It is non-standard to use it instead of *either* to strengthen a preceding negative, e.g. *There were no books either* (not *neither*).

non-flammable: see **flammable**.

normalcy is chiefly Amer.

> ● Prefer *normality.*

not only: see **only** (4).

no way (1) (Initially, followed by inversion of verb and subject) = 'not at all, by no means', e.g. *No way will you stop prices or unemployment going up again* (James Callaghan). ● Informal only. (2) (Emphatic) = 'certainly not', e.g. '*Did you go up in the elevator?*' '*No way.*' ● Chiefly Amer.; informal only.

number. *A number* (*of*) is constructed with the plural, *the number* (*of*) the singular, e.g. *Many of you are feeble and sick, and a number have died* (NEB); *The number of men who make a definite contribution to anything whatsoever is small* (Virginia Woolf).

obligate (verb) is in Britain only used in Law.

● There is no gain in using it (as often in Amer. usage) for *oblige*.

oblivious, in the sense 'unaware of, unconscious of', may be followed by *of* or *to*, e.g. *'When the summer comes,' said Lord Marchmain, oblivious of the deep corn and swelling fruit . . outside his windows* (Evelyn Waugh); *Rose seemed oblivious to individuals* (Angus Wilson).

● This sense, which developed from the older sense 'forgetful', is sometimes censured, but is now fully established in the language.

of used for *have*: see **of**, p. 40, and **have,** p. 76.

off of used for the preposition *off*, e.g. *Picked him off of the floor*, is non-standard.

one (pronoun) (1) = 'any person, the speaker or writer as representing people in general' has *one*, *one's*, and *oneself* as objective, possessive, and reflexive forms.

● These forms should be used to point back to a previous use of *one*, e.g. *One always did, in foreign parts, become friendly with one's fellow-countrymen more quickly than one did at home* (Muriel Spark). *One* should not be mixed with *he* (*him*, *his*, etc.) (acceptable Amer. usage) or *we*, *you*, etc.

(2) = single thing or person, following *any* and *every*; the resulting phrase is written as two words and is distinct from *anyone*, *everyone* (= anybody, everybody), e.g. *Any one* (*of these*) *will do*; *Perhaps every one of my conclusions would be negatived by other observers* (George Orwell).

ongoing has a valid use as an adjective meaning 'that goes on', i.e. 'that is happening and will continue' (just as *oncoming* means 'that comes on'), e.g. *The refugee problem in our time is an ongoing problem* (Robert Kee).

● The vague or tautologous use of *ongoing* should be avoided, as in the cliché *ongoing situation*, or in *We have an ongoing military relationship which we are continuing* (*Guardian*).

only (1) In spoken English, it is usual to place *only* between subject and verb, e.g. *He only saw Bill yesterday*: intonation is used to show whether *only* limits *he*, *saw*, *Bill*, or *yesterday*.

(2) It is an established idiom that, in a sentence containing *only* + verb + another item, in the absence of special intonation, *only* is understood as limiting, not the subject or verb, but the other item. *I only want some water* is the natural way of saying

I want only some water. If there is more than one item following the verb, *only* often limits the item nearest the end of the sentence, e.g. *A type of mind that can only accept ideas if they are put in the language he would use himself* (Doris Lessing) (= only if . .); but not always, e.g. *The captain was a thin unapproachable man . . who only appeared once at table* (Graham Greene) (= only once). This idiom is tacitly recognized by all good writers, e.g. *They only met on the most formal occasions* (C. P. Snow); *The contractors were only waiting for the final signature to start their work of destruction* (Evelyn Waugh); *The Nonconformist sects only influenced minorities* (George Orwell).

(3) Despite the idiom described under (2), there are often sentences in which confusion can arise, e.g. *Patrick only talked as much as he did, which was not as much as all that, to keep the ball in the air* (Kingsley Amis), where at first sight *only* might appear to limit *he* (referring to some other person) but really limits *to keep . . air*. If confusion or ambiguity is likely to arise, *only* should be placed before the item which it limits, e.g. *They sought to convert others only by the fervour of their sentiments and the earnestness of their example* (Frederic Raphael); *The coal-miner is second in importance only to the man who ploughs the soil* (George Orwell).

(4) *Not only* should always be placed next to the item which it qualifies, and not in the position before the verb. This is a fairly common slip, e.g. *Katherine's marriage not only kept her away, but at least two of Mr. March's cousins* (C. P. Snow); *kept not only her* would be better. If placing it before the verb is inevitable, the verb should be repeated after *but* (*also*), e.g. *It not only brings the coal out but brings the roof down as well* (George Orwell).

orient, orientate. In meaning the two words are virtually synonymous. In general, as opposed to technical, use, *orientate* seems to be predominant, but either is acceptable.

other than can be used where *other* is an adjective or pronoun, e.g. *He was no other than the rightful lord*; *The acts of any person other than myself*.

● *Other* cannot be treated as an adverb: *otherwise than* should be used instead, e.g. in *It is impossible to refer to them other than very cursorily*.

out used as a preposition instead of *out of*, e.g. *You should of* [sic] *pushed him out the nest long ago* (character in work by Muriel Spark), is non-standard.

outside of (1) = apart from (a sense *outside* cannot have) is informal only, e.g. *The need of some big belief outside of art* (Roger Fry, in a letter).

(2) = beyond the limits of, e.g. *The most important such facility outside of Japan* (*Gramophone*).

● In sense (2) *outside* alone is preferable: the *of* is redundant.

outstanding. ● Do not use in the sense 'remaining undetermined, unpaid, etc.' in contexts where ambiguity with the sense 'eminent, striking' can arise, e.g. *The other outstanding result* (in sport).

overly, excessively, too, is still regarded as an unassimilated Americanism, e.g. *Those overly rationalistic readers* (TLS).

● Use *excessively*, *too*, or *over-* instead; for *not overly*, *not very* or *none too* make satisfactory replacements.

overseas (adjective and adverb) is now more usual than *oversea*.

overview is an Americanism that has not found acceptance in Britain: *survey*, *review*, or *outline* are adequate substitutes.

owing to, unlike **due to,** has for long been established as a compound preposition, e.g. *My rooms became uninhabitable, owing to a burst gas-pipe* (C. P. Snow).

● *Owing to the fact that* should be avoided: use a conjunction like *because*.

pace means 'despite (someone)'s opinion', e.g. *Our civilization, pace Chesterton, is founded on coal* (George Orwell).

● It does not mean 'according to (someone)' or 'notwithstanding (something)'.

parameter. (1) (In technical use, especially in Mathematics and Computing) (roughly) a quantity constant in the case considered, but varying between different cases.

(2) (In extended use) a defining characteristic, especially one that can be measured, e.g. *The three major parameters of colour— brightness, hue, and saturation.*

(3) (Loosely) a limit or boundary, e.g. *The considerable element of indeterminacy which exists within the parameters of the parole system* (*The Times*); an aspect or feature, e.g. *The main parameters of the problem.*

● Use (3) is a popular dilution of the word's meaning, probably influenced (at least in the first quotation) by *perimeter*; it should be avoided.

parricide refers to the killing of one's father, one's close relative, or a person regarded as sacred, or to treason; *patricide* only to the killing of one's father.

part (on the part of): see **behalf.**

partially, partly. Apart from the (rare) use of *partially* to mean 'in a partial or biased way', these two words are largely interchangeable. Note, however, that *partly . . partly* is more usual than *partially . . partially*, e.g. *Partly in verse and partly in prose.*

peer, as in *to have no peer*, means 'equal', not 'superior'.

pence is sometimes informally used as a singular, e.g. *How Fine Fare, on lard, is one pence up on Sainsbury's* (Malcolm Bradbury).

● This use is very informal. Normally *penny* should be used in the singular.

perquisite (informal abbreviation *perk*) a casual profit, incidental benefit attaching to an employment, thing to which a person has sole right, e.g. *Free travel by train was a perquisite of railway managerial staff.*

● Do not confuse with *prerequisite* 'something required as a previous condition (*for*, *of*, or *to* something)', e.g. *Her mere comforting presence beside me which was already a prerequisite to peaceful sleep* (Lynne Reid Banks).

persistency is limited in sense to 'the action of persisting in one's course', e.g. *They made repeated requests for compensation, but an official apology was the only reward for their persistency*; *persistence* is sometimes used in that sense, but more often for 'continued existence', e.g. *One of the more surprising things about the life-ways of primitive societies is their persistence* (Sean O'Faolain).

perspicuous, easily understood, clearly expressed; expressing things clearly; similarly *perspicuity*; e.g. *There is nothing more desirable in composition than perspicuity* (Southey).

● Do not confuse with *perspicacious*, having or showing insight, and *perspicacity*, e.g. *Her perspicacity at having guessed his passion* (Vita Sackville-West).

petit bourgeois, **petty bourgeois.** The meaning (and with many people, the pronunciation) of these is the same. If the former is used, the correct French inflections should be added: *petits bourgeois* (plural), *petite(s) bourgeoise(s)* (feminine (plural)); also *petite bourgeoisie.* With *petty bourgeois* it should be remembered that the sense of the original French *petit* is not English *petty*, although that may be one of its main connotations.

phenomena is the plural of *phenomenon*.

● It cannot be used as a singular and cannot form a plural *phenomenas*.

picaresque (of a style of fiction) dealing with the adventures of rogues.

● It does not mean 'transitory' or 'roaming'.

pivotal, being that on which anything pivots or turns, e.g. *The pardon of Richard Nixon was pivotal to those who made up their minds at the last minute.*

● Do not use it merely to mean *vital*.

plaid, shawl-like garment; *tartan*, woollen cloth with distinctive pattern; the pattern itself.

● **plus** (conjunction), = 'and in addition', is an Amer. colloquialism of little acceptability, e.g. —— *have big names at big savings. Plus you get one year manufacturer's guarantee* (Advertisement).

polity, a form of civil government, e.g. *A republican polity*; a state.

● It does not mean *policy* or *politics*.

portentous can mean: (1) Like a portent, ominous, e.g. *Fiery-eyed with a sense of portentous utterance* (Muriel Spark). (2) Prodigious, e.g. *Every movement of his portentous frame* (James Joyce). (3) Solemn, ponderous, and somewhat pompous, e.g. *Our last conversation must have sounded to you rather portentous* (Iris Murdoch); *A portentous commentary on Holy Scripture* (Lord Hailsham).

● Sense (3) is sometimes criticized, but is an established, slightly jocular use.

● The form *portentious* (due to the influence of *pretentious*) is erroneous.

post, pre. Their use as full words (not prefixes) to mean 'after' and 'before' is unnecessary and disagreeable, e.g. in *Post the Geneva meeting of Opec* (*Daily Telegraph*); *Pre my being in office* (Henry Kissinger).

practicable, practical. When applied to things, *practicable* means 'able to be done', e.g. (with the negative *impracticable*), *Schemes which look very fine on paper, but which, as we well know, are impracticable* (C. S. Lewis); *practical* 'concerned with practice, suitable for use, suited to the conditions', e.g. *Having considered the problem, he came up with several practical suggestions; It is essential that the plan should cover all the practical details.*

pre: see **post, pre.**

precipitous, like a precipice, e.g. *Our rooms were . . reached by a precipitous marble staircase* (Evelyn Waugh).

● Do not confuse with *precipitate*, hasty, rash, e.g. *They were all a little out of breath from precipitate arrival* (Patrick White).

predicate (verb): (1) (Followed by *of*) to assert as a property of, e.g. *That easy Bohemianism—conventionally predicated of the 'artistic' temperament* (J. I. M. Stewart). (2) (Followed by *on*) to found or base (something) on, e.g. *A new conception* *of reality . . predicated on dissatisfaction. with formalist litera-ture* (TLS)

● Sense (2) tends to sound pretentious. Use *found*, or *base*, *on*.

pre-empt (1) To obtain beforehand, secure for oneself in advance, e.g. *Sound allows the mind an inventive role systematically pre-empted by the cinema* (Frederic Raphael). (2) To preclude, forestall, e.g. *The Nazi régime by its own grotesque vileness pre-empted fictional effort* (Listener).

● Sense (2) is better expressed by a verb such as *preclude* or *forestall*.

● *Pre-empt* is not a synonym for *prevent*.

prefer. The rejected alternative is introduced by *to*, e.g. *Men preferred darkness to light* (NEB). But when the rejected alternative is an infinitive, it is preceded by *rather than* (not *than* alone), e.g. *I'd prefer to be stung to death rather than to wake up . . with half of me shot away* (John Osborne).

preferable to means 'more desirable than' and is therefore intensified by *far*, *greatly*, or *much*, not *more*, e.g. *After a hundred and eighty* (skips) *an unclear head seemed much preferable to more skips* (Kingsley Amis).

preference. The alternatives are introduced by *for* and *over*, e.g. *The preference for a single word over a phrase or clause* (Anthony Burgess); but *in preference* is followed by *to*, e.g. *Both were sensitive to artistic impressions musical in preference to plastic or pictorial* (James Joyce).

prejudice (1) = bias, is followed by *against* or *in favour of*; (2) = detriment, is followed by *to*; (3) = injury, is followed by *of* (in the phrase *to the prejudice of*).

prepared: *to be prepared to*, to be willing to, has been criticized as officialese by some authorities, but is now established usage, e.g. *One should kill oneself, which, of course, I was not prepared to do* (Cyril Connolly).

prerequisite: see **perquisite**.

prescribe, to lay down as a rule to be followed; *proscribe*, to forbid by law.

presently (1) After a short time, e.g. *Presently we left the table and sat in the garden-room* (Evelyn Waugh). (2) At present, currently, e.g. *The praise presently being heaped upon him* (*The Economist*).

● Sense (2) (for long current in American English) is regarded as incorrect by some people but is widely used and often sounds more natural than *at present*.

prestigious (1) Characterized by juggling or magic, delusive, deceptive, e.g. *The prestigious balancing act which he was constantly obliged to perform* (TLS): now rare. (2) Having or showing prestige, e.g. *A career in pure science is still more socially prestigious . . than one in engineering* (*The Times*): a fully acceptable sense.

prevaricate, to speak or act evasively or misleadingly, e.g. *I never have told a lie . . On many occasions I have resorted to prevarication; but on great occasions I have always told the truth* (G. B. Shaw); *procrastinate*, to postpone action, e.g. *Hamlet . . pronounces himself a procrastinator, an undecided man, even a coward* (C. S. Lewis).

prevent is followed by the objective case and *from* + the gerund, or by the possessive case + the gerund, e.g. *prevent me from going* or *prevent my going*.

● *Prevent me going* is informal only.

● **pre-war** as an adverb, in, e.g., *Some time pre-war there was a large contract out for tender* (*Daily Telegraph*): prefer *before the war*.

pristine (1) Ancient, original, e.g. *Stone which faithfully reproduced its pristine alternations of milk and cream* (J. I. M. Stewart). (2) Having its original, unspoilt condition, e.g. *Pristine snow reflects about 90 per cent of incident sunlight* (Fred Hoyle).

● *Pristine* does not mean 'spotless', 'pure', or 'fresh'.

procrastinate: see prevaricate.

prone (followed by *to*) is used like, and means much the same as, **liable**, except that it usually qualifies a personal subject, e.g. *My literary temperament rendering me especially prone to 'all that kind of poisonous nonsense'* (Cyril Connolly).

proportion means 'a comparative part, share, or ratio'; it is not a mere synonym for *part*.

proscribe: see prescribe.

protagonist, the leading character in a story or incident.

● In Greek drama there was only one protagonist, but this is no reason to debar the use of the word in the plural, e.g. *We . . sometimes mistook a mere supernumerary in a fine dress for one of the protagonists* (C. S. Lewis).

● Do not confuse with *proponent*: the word contains the Greek prefix *prot-* 'first', not the prefix *pro-* 'in favour of', and does not mean 'champion, advocate'.

protest (verb, transitive) to affirm solemnly, e.g. *He barely attempted to protest his innocence* (George Orwell).

● The sense 'protest against', e.g. in *The residents have protested the sale*, is Amer. only.

proven. It is not standard to use this as the ordinary past participle of *prove* in British English (it is standard Scots and Amer.); it is, however, common attributively in certain expressions, such as *of proven ability*.

provenance, origin, place of origin, is used in Britain; the form *provenience* is its usual Amer. equivalent.

prudent, showing carefulness and foresight, e.g. *It seemed prudent to inform him of my plans rather than let him hear about them indirectly*; *prudential*, involving or marked by prudence, e.g. *The humble little outfit of prudential maxims which really underlay much of the talk about Shakespeare's characters* (C. S. Lewis).

pry, to prise (open, etc.): chiefly Amer., but occasionally in British literary use, e.g. *For her to pry his fingers open* (David Garnett). The normal sense is 'peer' or 'inquire'.

quadrillion: see **billion**.

question: (1) *No question that* (sometimes *but*), no doubt that, e.g. *There can be no question that the burning of Joan of Arc must have been a most instructive and interesting experiment* (G. B. Shaw); *There is no question but Leslie was an unusually handsome boy* (Anthony Powell).

(2) *No question of*, no possibility of, e.g. *There can be no question of tabulating successes and failures and trying to decide whether the successes are too numerous to be accounted for by chance* (C. S. Lewis). See also **beg the question, leading question.**

quote (noun = quotation) is informal only (except in Printing and Commerce).

● **re** (in the matter of, referring to) is better avoided and should not be used for 'about, concerning'.

reason. *The reason* (*why*) . . *is* . . should be followed by *that*, not *because*, e.g. *The reason why such a suggestion sounds hopeless . . is that few people are able to imagine the radio being used for the dissemination of anything except tripe* (George Orwell).

recoup (1) (transitive) to recompense (oneself or a person) *for* (a loss or expenditure), e.g. *Dixon felt he could recoup himself a little for the expensiveness of the drinks* (Kingsley Amis); also *to recoup one's losses*; (2) (intransitive) to make good one's loss, e.g. *I had . . acquired so many debts that if I didn't return to England to recoup, we might have to run for it* (Chaim Bermant). ● This word is not synonymous with *recuperate* except partly in sense (2) above ('to make good one's loss').

recuperate (1) (intransitive) to recover from exhaustion, ill-health, financial loss, etc., e.g. *I've got a good mind . . to put all my* *winnings on red and give him a chance to recuperate* (Graham Greene); (2) (transitive) to recover (health, a loss, material). In sense (2) *recover* is preferable.

redolent, smelling *of* something, e.g. *Corley's breath redolent of rotten cornjuice* (James Joyce); also used figuratively to mean 'strongly suggestive or reminiscent of', e.g. *The missive most redolent of money and sex* (Martin Amis).

referendum. ● For the plural, *referendums* is preferable to *referenda*.

refute, to prove (a statement, opinion, accusation, etc.), to be false, e.g. *The case against most of them must have been so easily refuted that they could hardly rank as suspects* (Rebecca West); to prove (a person) to be in error, e.g. *One of those German scholars whose function is to be refuted in a footnote* (Frederic Raphael).
● *Refute* does not mean 'deny' or 'repudiate' (an allegation etc.).

regalia is a plural noun, meaning 'emblems of royalty or of an order'. It has no singular in ordinary English.

region: *in the region of*, an unwieldy periphrasis for *round about*, is better avoided.

register office is the official term for the institution informally often called the *registry office*.

regretfully, in a regretful manner; *regrettably*, it is to be regretted (that).
● *Regretfully* should not be used where *regrettably* is intended: *The investigators, who must regretfully remain anonymous* (TLS), reads as a guess at the investigators' feelings instead of an expression of the writer's opinion, which was what was intended. The influence of **hopefully** (2) may be discernible here.

renege (intransitive), to fail to fulfil an agreement or undertaking, is usually constructed with *on*, e.g. *It . . reneged on Britain's commitment to the East African Asians* (*The Times*).

resource is often confused with *recourse* and *resort*. *Resource* means (1) a reserve upon which one can draw (often used in the plural); (2) an action or procedure to which one can turn in difficulty, an expedient; (3) mental capabilities for amusing oneself, etc. (often used in the plural, e.g. *Left to his own resources*); (4) ability to deal with a crisis, e.g. *A man of infinite resource. Recourse* means the action of turning to a possible source of help; frequently in the phrases *have recourse to*, *without recourse to. Resort* means (1) the action of turning to a possible source of help(= *recourse*; but *resorting* is more usual than *resort* after *without*); frequently in the phrase *in the last resort*, as a last expedient, in the end; (2) a thing to which one can turn in difficulty.

responsible for (1) Liable to be called to account for, e.g. *I'm not responsible for what uncle Percy does* (E. M. Forster).

(2) Obliged to take care of or carry out, e.g. *Both they and the singers, who were responsible for their respective duties* (NEB).

(3) Being the cause of, e.g. *A war-criminal responsible for so many unidentified deaths* (Graham Greene).

● Beware of using senses (1) or (2) in expressions in which sense (3) can be understood, with absurd results, e.g. *Now, as Secretary for Trade, he is directly responsible for pollution* (*The Times*).

restive (1) Unmanageable, rejecting control, obstinate, e.g. *The I.L.P. . . had been increasingly restive during the second Labour government, and now, refusing to accept Labour-party discipline in the house of commons, voluntarily disaffiliated from the Labour party* (A. J. P. Taylor).

(2) Restless, fidgety, e.g. *The audiences were not bad, though apt to be restive and noisy at the back* (J. B. Priestley).

● Sense (2) is objected to by some authorities but is quite commonly used by good writers.

revenge: one revenges oneself or a wrong (*on* an offender); one is revenged (*for* a wrong): the noun is *revenge*, and the idea is usually of satisfaction of the offended party's resentment. Cf. **avenge**.

reverend, deserving reverence; *reverent*, showing reverence.

(*The*) *Revd*, plural *Revds*, is the abbreviation of *Reverend* as a clergy title (not *Rev.*).

reversal is the noun corresponding to the verb *reverse*; *reversion* is the noun corresponding to the verb *revert*.

same. ● It is non-standard to use the phrase *same as* as a kind of conjunction meaning 'in the same way as, just as', e.g. *But I shouldn't be able to serve them personally, same as I do now* (L. P. Hartley).

● The phrase *same like*, used for *just like* or *in the same way as*, is illiterate, e.g. *I have rich friends, same like you* (Iris Murdoch).

sanction (verb) to give approval to, to authorize, e.g. *This council sanctioned the proclamation of a state of war with Germany from 11 p.m.* (A. J. P. Taylor).

● It does not mean 'impose sanctions on'.

sc. (short for Latin *scilicet* = *scire licet* one is permitted to know) introduces (1) a word to be supplied, e.g. *He asserted that he had met him* (*sc. the defendant*) *on that evening*, or (2) a word to be substituted for one already used, in order to render an

expression intelligible, e.g. *'I wouldn't of (sc. have) done'* was
her answer.

scabrous (1) (In Botany and Zoology) having a rough surface. (2)
Encrusted with dirt, grimy, e.g. *The streaky green distempered
walls and the scabrous wooden W.C. seat* (John Braine). (3)
Risqué, salacious, indecent, e.g. *Silly and scabrous titters about
Greek pederasty* (C. S. Lewis).

● *Scabrous* does not mean 'scathing, abusive, scurrilous'.

scarify, to loosen the surface of (soil, etc.); to make slight cuts in
(skin, tissue) surgically.

● The verb *scarify* (pronounced scare-ify) 'scare, terrify', e.g.
To be on the brink of a great happiness is a scarifying feeling
(Noel Coward), is informal only.

scenario (1) An outline of the plot of a play. (2) A film script giving
details of scenes, stage-directions, etc. (3) An outline of an
imagined (usually future) sequence of events, e.g. *Several of
the computer 'scenarios' include a catastrophic and sudden
collapse of population* (*Observer*).

● Sense (3) is valid when a detailed narrative of events that might
happen under certain conditions is denoted. The word should
not be used as a loose synonym for *scene, situation, circumstance,*
etc.

scilicet: see sc.

Scottish is now the usual adjective; *Scotch* is restricted to a fairly
large number of fixed expressions, e.g. *Scotch broth, egg, whisky*;
Scots is used mainly for the Scottish dialect of English, in the
names of regiments, and in *Scotsman, Scotswoman* (*Scotchman,
-woman* are old-fashioned). To designate the inhabitants of
Scotland, the plural noun *Scots* is normal.

seasonable, suitable for the time of year, occurring at the right time
or season, opportune; *unseasonable* occurring at the wrong
time or season, e.g. *You are apt to be pressed to drink a glass of
vinegary port at an unseasonable hour* (Somerset Maugham).

● Do not confuse with *seasonal*, occurring at or associated with
a particular season, e.g. *There is a certain seasonal tendency to
think better of the Government . . in spring* (*The Economist*)

senior, superior are followed by *to*. They contain the idea of 'more'
(advanced in years, exalted in position, etc.) and so cannot be
constructed with *more . . than*, e.g. *There are several officers
senior*, or *superior in rank*, *to him*, not . . *more senior*, or *more
superior in rank, than him*.

sensibility, ability to feel, sensitiveness, delicacy of feeling, e.g. *The* *man's moving fingers . . showed no sign of acute sensibility* (Graham Greene).

● *Sensibility* is not the noun corresponding to *sensible* meaning 'having good sense'; i.e. it does not mean 'possession of good sense'.

sensual, gratifying to the body; indulging oneself with physical pleasures, showing that one does this, e.g. *His sensual eye took in her slim feminine figure* (Angus Wilson); *sensuous*, affecting or appealing to the senses (without the pejorative implications of *sensual*), e.g. *I got up and ran about the . . meadow in my bare feet. I remember the sensuous pleasure of it* (C. Day Lewis).

serendipity, the making of pleasant discoveries by accident, or the knack or fact of doing this; the adjective (usually applied to a discovery, event, fact, etc.) is *serendipitous*.

● *Serendipitous* does not mean merely 'fortunate'.

sic (Latin for *thus*) is placed in brackets after a word that appears odd or erroneous to show that the word is quoted exactly as it stands in the original, e.g. *Daisy Ashford's novel* The Young Visiters (*sic*).

sick: see **ill**.

● **sit, stand.** The use of the past participle *sat, stood* with the verb *to be*, meaning *to be sitting, standing*, is non-standard, e.g. *No really, I'd be sat there falling asleep if I did come* (Kingsley Amis).

situation. A useful noun for expressing the sense 'position of affairs, combination of circumstances' which may validly be preceded by a defining adjective, e.g. *the financial, industrial, military, political, situation*.

● The substitution of an attributive noun for an adjective before *situation* should be carefully considered. It should not be used when the resulting phrase will be tautologous (e.g. *a crisis situation, people in work situations*: *crises* and *work* are themselves *situations*). The placing of an attributive phrase before *situation* is nearly always ugly and should be avoided, e.g. *The deep space situation, a balance-of-terror situation, a standing credit situation*.

● The combination of **ongoing** with *situation* is a cliché to be avoided.

sled is Amer. for *sledge*; *sleigh* is a sledge for passengers that is drawn by horses (or reindeer).

so used adverbially as a means of linking two clauses and meaning 'therefore' may be preceded by *and* but need not be; e.g. *Leopold Bloom is a modern Ulysses, so he has to encounter Sirens and* *a Cyclops* (Anthony Burgess); *I had received no word from Martha all day, so I was drawn back to the casino* (Graham Greene).

so-called (1) has long been used in the sense 'called by this term, but not entitled to it'; (2) is now often used quite neutrally, without implication of incorrectness, especially in Science.

sort of: see **kind of**.

specialty, except for its use in Law, is an equivalent of *speciality* restricted to North America.

spectate, to be a spectator, is at best informal.

● *Watch* is usually an adequate substitute, e.g. in *A spectating, as opposed to a reading, audience* (*Listener*).

strata is the plural of *stratum*.

● It is incorrect to treat it as a singular noun, e.g. in *The movement has . . sunk to a wider and more anonymous strata.*

style. (1) Adjective + -*style* used to qualify a noun, e.g. *European-style clothing, contemporary-style dancing,* is acceptable.

(2) Adjective or noun + -*style,* forming an adverb, is somewhat informal, e.g. *A revolution, British-style* (A. J. P. Taylor).

substantial, actually existing; of real value; of solid material; having much property; in essentials; e.g. *substantial damages, progress; a substantial house, yeoman; substantial agreement.*

● It is not merely a synonym of *large*.

substantive (adjective) is used mainly in technical senses; e.g. *substantive rank,* in the services, is permanent, not acting or temporary.

substitute (verb) to put (someone or something) in place of another: constructed with *for*; e.g. *Democracy substitutes election by the incompetent many for appointment by the corrupt few* (G. B. Shaw).

● The sense 'replace (someone or something) *by* or *with* another' is incorrect, or at best highly informal, e.g. in *Having substituted her hat with a steel safety helmet, she went on a tour of the site* (better, *Having replaced her hat with . .* or *Having substituted a steel safety helmet for . .*).

such as: see **like**.

superior: see **senior**.

suppositious, hypothetical, conjectural; *supposititious,* fraudulently substituted (especially of a child displacing a real heir), e.g. *Russia . . is the supposititious child of necessity in the household of theory* (H. G. Wells).

synchronize (transitive), to make to occur at the same time, e.g.

Everyday cordialities would be synchronized with gazes of rapt ardour (Martin Amis).

● It is not a synonym for *combine* or *co-ordinate*.

than: see **different, other than, prefer, senior.**

thankfully: see **hopefully.**

the (article). When a name like *The Times* or *The Hague* is used attributively, *The* is dropped, e.g. *A* Times *correspondent, Last year's* Hague *conference*. If *the* precedes the name in such a construction, it belongs to the succeeding noun, not to the name, and is therefore not given a capital initial (or italics), e.g. *A report from the* Times *correspondent*.

the (adverb) prefixed to a comparative means 'thereby' or 'by so much', e.g. *What student is the better for mastering these futile distinctions?* This combination can enter into the further construction seen in *The more the merrier* (i.e. 'by how much more, by that much merrier'). It cannot enter into a construction with *than*: the tendency to insert it before *more* and *less* (putting *any the more, none the less* for *any more, no less*) should be resisted, e.g. in *The intellectual release had been no less* (not *none the less*) *marked than the physical*.

then may be used as an adjective preceding a noun as a neat alternative to *at that time* or similar phrase, e.g. *Hearing that they were on personal terms with the then Prime Minister* (Frederic Raphael).

● It should not be placed before the noun if it would sound equally well in its usual position, e.g. *Harold Macmillan was the then Prime Minister* could equally well be . . *was then the Prime Minister*. The same applies to an adverbial use of *then* before attributive adjectives, e.g. *The then existing constitution*: write *The constitution then existing.*

there- adverbs, e.g. *therein, thereon, thereof*, etc., belong mainly to very formal diction and should be avoided in ordinary writing (apart from certain idiomatic adverbs, e.g. *thereabouts, thereby, thereupon*); e.g. *We did not question this reasoning, and there lay our mistake* (Evelyn Waugh): a lesser writer might have written *therein*. But such adverbs can be employed for special effectiveness, e.g. *This idea brought him rocketing back to earth. But he stood thereupon like a giant* (Iris Murdoch).

through, up to and including, e.g. *Friday through Tuesday*, though useful, is Amer. only.

too followed by an adjective used attributively should be confined to poetry or special effects in prose, e.g. *Metropolis, that too-great* *city* (W. H. Auden); *A small too-pretty house* (Graham Greene).

● In normal prose it is a clumsy construction, e.g. *The crash came during a too-tight loop.*

tooth-comb and *fine tooth-comb*, arising from a misapprehension of *fine-tooth comb*, are now established expressions whose illogicality it is pedantic to object to.

tortuous, torturous. Do not confuse: *tortuous* means (1) twisting, e.g. *Through tortuous lanes where the overhanging boughs whipped the windscreen* (Evelyn Waugh); (2) devious, e.g. *Control had his reasons; they were usually so bloody tortuous it took you a week to work them out* (John le Carré). *Torturous* means 'involving torture, excruciating', e.g. *Torturously original inlay-work* (TLS).

transcendent, surpassing (e.g. *Of transcendent importance*), (of God) above and distinct from the universe, e.g. *Such transcendent power does not come from us, but is God's alone* (NEB); *transcendental*, visionary, idealistic, beyond experience, etc., e.g. *Most of those who have been near death have also described some kind of mystical or transcendental experience* (British Medical Journal). (Other more technical senses of each word are ignored here.)

transpire (figuratively): (1) To leak out, come to be known, e.g. *What had transpired concerning that father was not so reassuring* (John Galsworthy). (2) To come about, take place, e.g. *What transpired between them is unknown* (David Cecil).

● Sense (2), probably arising from the misunderstanding of sentences like 'What had transpired during his absence he did not know', is chiefly informal. It is regarded by many people as unacceptable, especially if the idea of something emerging from ignorance is absent: it should therefore not be used in sentences like *A storm transpired.*

trillion: see **billion.**

triumphal, of or celebrating a triumph, e.g. *A triumphal arch*; *triumphant*, conquering, exultant.

try (verb) in writing normally followed by the *to*- infinitive: *try and* + bare infinitive is informal.

turbid (1) thick, dense; (2) confused, disordered, e.g. *In an access of despair had sought death in the turbid Seine* (W. Somerset Maugham).
Turgid (1) swollen; (2) (of language) inflated, grandiloquent, e.g. *Some of them are turgid, swollen with that kind of intellectual bombast which never rises to gusto* (G. H. Vallins).

underlay (verb) (past *underlaid*) to lay something under (a thing), e.g. *Underlaid the tiles with felt*: a somewhat rare verb; *underlie* (past tense *underlay*, past participle *underlain*) to lie under; to be the basis of; to exist beneath the surface of, e.g. *The arrogance that underlay their cool good manners* (Doris Lessing).

unequivocal, not ambiguous, unmistakable; similarly *unequivocally* adverb, e.g. *Made her intentions unequivocally clear*.

● The forms *unequivocable, -ably*, sometimes seen, are erroneous.

unexceptionable, -al: see **exceptionable**.

unique: (1) Being the only one of its kind, e.g. *The fighting quality that gives war its unique power over the imagination* (G. B. Shaw): in this sense *unique* cannot be qualified by adverbs like *absolutely, most, quite, so, thoroughly*, etc. (2) Unusual, remarkable, singular, e.g. *A passionate human insight so unique in her experience that she felt it to be unique in human experience* (Muriel Spark).

● Sense (2) is regarded by many people as incorrect. Substitute one of the synonyms given above, or whatever other adjective is appropriate.

unlike (adverb) may govern a noun, noun phrase, or pronoun, just as *like* may, e.g. *A sarcasm unlike ordinary sarcasm* (V. S. Pritchett).

● It may not govern a clause with or without ellipsis of the verb, e.g. *He was unlike he had ever been*; *Unlike in countries of lesser economic importance*.

● **various** cannot be used as a pronoun followed by *of* (as, for example, *several* can), as (wrongly) in *The two ministers concerned . . have been paying private visits to various of the Commonwealth representatives*.

venal, able to be bribed, influenced by bribery; *venial*, pardonable.

vengeance: see **avenge**.

verbal (1) of or in words; (2) of a verb; (3) spoken rather than written.

● Some people reject sense (3) as illogical and prefer *oral*. However, *verbal* is the usual term in a number of idioms, such as *verbal communication, contract, evidence*.

verge (verb) in *verge on, upon*, to border on, e.g. *He told two or three stories verging on the improper* (John Galsworthy), is in origin a different word from *verge* in *verge to, towards* to incline towards, approach, e.g. *The London docks, where industrial disputes always verged towards violence* (A. J. P. Taylor). Both are acceptable.

vermin is usually treated as plural, e.g. *A lot of parasites, vermin who feed on God's love and charity* (Joyce Cary).

via (1) By way of (a place), e.g. *To London via Reading*. (2) By means of, through the agency of, e.g. *Other things can . . be taught . . via the air, via television, via teaching machines, and so on* (E. F. Schumacher); *I sent it via my secretary*.

● Sense (2) is sometimes criticized, but is certainly acceptable in informal use.

waive to refrain from using or insisting on, to forgo or dispense with, e.g. *The satisfaction . . of waiving the rights which my preaching gives me* (NEB).

● Do not confuse this with *wave*, chiefly in conjunction with *aside*, *away*, as (wrongly) in *But the Earl simply waived the subject away with his hand* (Trollope).

want, need (verbs) in the sense 'require' can be followed (1) by a gerund as object, e.g. *Your hair needs* or *wants cutting* or (2) by an object and a past participle as complement to the object (with the verb 'to be' omitted), e.g. *We want* or *need this changed*.

● The idiom *We want* or *need this changing* (perhaps a mixture of the two constructions, but having the sense of (2)) is informal only.

well is joined by a hyphen to a following participle when the combination is used attributively, e.g. *A well-worn argument*. Predicatively a hyphen is not necessary unless the combination is to be distinguished in meaning from the two words written separately, e.g. *He is well-spoken* but *The words were well spoken*.

what ever, when ever, where ever: see **ever**.

whence meaning 'from where', does not need to be preceded by *from*.

who ever: see **ever**.

whoever, any one who, no matter who: use *whoever* for the objective case as well as the subjective, rather than *whomever*, which is rather stilted.

-wise (suffix) added to nouns (1) forming adverbs of manner, is very well established, but is now, except in fixed expressions like *clockwise*, rather literary or poetic, e.g. *The Saint wears tight yellow trousers . . and is silkily shaven Romanwise* (TLS); (2) forming viewpoint adverbs (meaning 'as regards —'), e.g. *I can eat only Cox's Orange Pippins, and am in mourning applewise from April to October* (Iris Murdoch).

● (2) is widely regarded as unacceptable in formal usage.

● Adverbs of type (2) are formed on nouns only, not on adjectives: hence sentences like *The rate-payers would have to shoulder an extra burden financial-wise* are incorrect (substitute . . *burden finance-wise* or *financial burden*).

- **without** = 'unless' is illiterate, e.g. *Without you have a bit of class already, your town gets no new theatre* (*Listener*).
  See also **hardly**.

womankind is better than *womenkind* (cf. *mankind*).

worth while is usually written as two words predicatively, but as one attributively, e.g. *He thought it worth while*, or *a worthwhile undertaking, to publish the method.*

write (to compose a letter) with indirect personal object, e.g. *I will write you about it*, is not acceptable British English (but is good Amer. English).

IV

GRAMMAR

Language is an instrument for communication. The
language which can with the greatest ease make the finest
and most numerous distinctions of meaning is the best.
(C. S. Lewis, *Studies in Words*)

THIS section deals with specific problems of grammar; it makes no
attempt at a systematic exposition of English syntax.

It is notoriously difficult to find convenient labels for many of the
topics on which guidance is needed. Wherever possible, the headings
chosen for the entries are, or include, the words which actually cause
grammatical problems (e.g. *as, may* or *might*). Some headings include
the grammatical endings involved (e.g. *-ing*). But inevitably many
entries have had to be given abstract labels (e.g. *double passive,
subjunctive*). To compensate for this, a number of cross-references are
included, by which the user can find a way to the required entry. The
aim throughout is to tackle a particular problem immediately and to
give a recommendation as soon as the problem has been identified.
Explanations entailing wider grammatical principles are postponed
or even omitted.

adverbial relative clauses

A relative clause, expressing time, manner, or place, can follow a
noun governed by a preposition (*on the day* in the example below):

On the day that you eat from it, *you will certainly die* (NEB)

It is possible for the relative clause to begin with the same preposition
and *which*, e.g.

On the day on which this occurred, *I was away*

But it is a perfectly acceptable idiom to use a relative clause introduced by *that* without repetition of the preposition, especially after
the nouns *day, morning, night, time, year*, etc., *manner, sense, way* (see
p. 183), *place*, e.g.

Envy in the consuming sense that certain persons display *the trait* (Anthony Powell)

It is, if anything, even more usual for *that* to be omitted:

He cannot have been more than thirty at the time we met him (Evelyn Waugh)
If he would take it in the sense she meant it (L. P. Hartley)
On the day you pass over the Jordan (NEB)

adverbs without *-ly*

Most adverbs consist of an adjective + the ending *-ly*, e.g. *badly*, *differently*. For the changes in spelling that the addition of *-ly* may require, see pp. 20f.

Normally the use of the ordinary adjective as an adverb, without *-ly*, is non-standard, e.g.

I was sent for special
The Americans speak different *from us*
They just put down their tools sudden *and cut and run*

There are, however, a number of words which are both adjective and adverb and cannot add the adverbial ending *-ly*:

early	*fast*	*much*
enough	*little*	*straight*
far	*low*	

Some other adjectives can be used as adverbs both with and without *-ly*. The two forms have different meanings:

deep	*high*	*near*
hard	*late*	

The forms without *-ly* are the adverbs more closely similar in meaning to the adjectives, as the following examples illustrate:

deep: *Still waters run deep*
He read deep into the night

hard: *They hit me hard in the chest*
He lost his hard-earned money
We will be hard put to it to be ready by Christmas

high: *It soared high above us*
Don't fix your hopes too high

late: *I will stay up late to finish it*
A drawing dated as late as 1960

near: *He won't come near me*
    As near as makes no difference
    Near-famine conditions

The forms with *-ly* have meanings more remote from those of the adjectives:

deeply is chiefly figurative, e.g. *Deeply in love*
hardly = 'scarcely', e.g. *He hardly earned his money*
highly is chiefly figurative, e.g. *Don't value possessions too highly*
lately = 'recently', e.g. *I have been very tired lately*
nearly = 'almost', e.g. *The conditions were nearly those of a famine*

● The forms with and without *-ly* are not interchangeable and should not be confused.

See also *-lily* **adverbs**.

article, omission of

To omit, or not to omit, *a* (*an*) and *the*?

Omission of the definite or indefinite article before a noun or noun phrase in apposition to a name is a journalistic device, e.g.

Clarissa, American business woman, comes to England (*Radio Times*)
Nansen, hero and humanitarian, moves among them (*The Times*)

It is more natural to write *an American business woman, the hero and humanitarian*.

Similarly, when the name is in apposition to the noun or noun phrase, and the article is omitted, the effect is of journalistic style, e.g.

NUM President Arthur Scargill
Best-selling novelist Barbara Cartland
Unemployed labourer William Smith

Preferably write: *The NUM President, The best-selling novelist, An unemployed labourer* (with a comma before and after the name which follows).

After *as* it is possible to omit *a* or *the*, e.g.

As manipulator of words, the author reminded me of X.Y.
The Soviet system could no longer be regarded as sole model for Communism everywhere

It is preferable not to omit these words, however, except where the noun or noun phrase following is treated as a kind of generic mass noun, e.g.

> *The vivid relation between himself, as man, and the sunflower, as sunflower* (D. H. Lawrence)

as, case following

In the following sentences, formal usage requires the *subjective* case (*I, he, she, we, they*) because the pronoun would be the subject if a verb were supplied:

> *You are just as intelligent as* he (in full, *as he is*)
> *Widmerpool . . might not have heard the motif so often as* I (Anthony Powell) (in full, *as I had*)

Informal usage permits *You are just as intelligent as* him.

Formal English uses the *objective* case (*me, him, her, us, them*) only when the pronoun would be the object if a verb were supplied:

> *I thought you preferred John to Mary, but I see that you like her just as much* as him (which means . . *just as much as you like him*)

In real usage, sentences like this are rare and not very natural. It is more usual for the verb to be included in the sentence or for the thought to be expressed in a different construction.

as if, as though

For the tense following these see p. 93.

auxiliary verbs

There are sixteen auxiliary verbs in English, three primary auxiliaries (used in the compounding of ordinary verbs) and thirteen modal auxiliaries (used to express mood, and, to some extent, tense).

Primary:	*be, do, have*	
Modal:	*can*	*ought* (*to*)
	could	*shall*
	dare	*should*
	may	*used* (*to*)
	might	*will*
	must	*would*
	need	

Auxiliaries differ from regular verbs in the following ways:

(1) They can precede the negative *not*, instead of taking the *do not* construction, e.g. *I cannot* but *I do not know*;
(2) They can precede the subject in questions, instead of taking the *do* construction, e.g. *Can you hear* but *Do you know*.

The modal auxiliaries additionally differ from regular verbs in the following ways:

(3) They are invariable: they do not add *-s* for the third person present, and do not form a separate past tense in *-ed*; e.g. *He must go; he must have seen it.*
(4) They are usually followed by the bare infinitive; e.g. *He will go, he can go* (not 'to go' as with other verbs, e.g. *He intends to go, he is able to go*).

Use of auxiliaries

In reported speech and some other *that*-clauses *can, may, shall*, and *will* become *could, might, should*, and *would* for the past tense:

> *He said that he* could *do it straight away*
> *I told you that I* might *arrive unexpectedly*
> *I knew that when I grew up I* should *be a writer* (George Orwell)
> *Did you think that the money you brought* would *be enough?*

In clauses of this kind, the auxiliaries *must, need*, and *ought*, which normally refer to the present tense, can also be used for the past tense:

> *I had meant to return direct to Paris, but this business . . meant that I* must *go to London* (Evelyn Waugh)
> *To go to church had made her feel she* need *not reproach herself for impropriety* (V. S. Pritchett)
> *She was quite aware that she* ought *not to quarter Freddy there* (G. B. Shaw)

Note that this use is restricted to *that*-clauses. It would not be permissible to use *must, need*, or *ought* for the past tense in a main sentence; for example, one could not say: *Yesterday I must go.*

Further discussion of the use of auxiliary verbs will be found under **can** and **may, dare, have, need, ought, shall** and **will, should** and **would, used to, were** or **was**.

but, case following

The personal pronoun following *but* (= 'except') should be in the case it would have if a verb were supplied.

I walked through the mud of the main street. Who but I? (Kipling)
Our uneducated brethren who have, under God, no defence but us
   (C. S. Lewis)

In the Kipling example *I* is used because it would be the subject of *I walked*. In the Lewis example *us* is used because it would be the object of *who have* (i.e. 'who have *us* as their only defence').

can and *may*

The auxiliary verbs *can* and *may* are both used to express permission, but *may* is more formal and polite:

I'm going to come and see you some time—may I? (Evelyn Waugh)

collective nouns

Collective nouns are singular words that denote many individuals, e.g.

army	crowd	navy
audience	family	orchestra
board (of directors, examiners, etc.)	fleet	parliament
choir	flock	party (i.e. body of persons)
clan	gang	squad
class	government	swarm
club	group	team
committee	herd	tribe
company	jury	union (i.e. trade union)
congregation	majority	
	militia	

the aristocracy	the laity
the bourgeoisie	the nobility
the Cabinet	the proletariat
the clergy	the public
the élite	the upper class
the gentry	the working class
the intelligentsia	

It is normal for collective nouns, being singular, to be followed by singular verbs and pronouns (*is*, *has*, *consists*, and *it* in the examples below):

The Government is *determined to beat inflation, as* it has *promised*
Their family is *huge:* it consists *of five boys and three girls*
The bourgeoisie is *despised for not being proletarian* (C. S. Lewis)

The singular verb and pronouns are preferable unless the collective is clearly and unmistakably used to refer to separate individuals rather than to a united body, e.g.

> *The Cabinet has made* its *decision*, but
> *The Cabinet are resuming* their *places around the table at Number 10 Downing Street*
> *The Brigade of Guards* is *on parade*, but
> *The Brigade of Guards* are *above average height*

The singular should always be used if the collective noun is qualified by a singular word like *this, that, every*, etc.:

> *This family* is *divided*
> *Every team* has its *chance to win*

If a relative clause follows, it must be *which* + singular verb or *who* + plural verb, e.g.

> *It was not the intelligentsia, but just intellectual society*, which was *gathered there* (John Galsworthy)
> *The working party* who *had been preparing the decorations* (Evelyn Waugh)

● Do not mix singular and plural, as (wrongly) in

> *The congregation* were *now dispersing. It tended to form knots and groups*

comparison of adjectives and adverbs

Whether to use *-er, -est* or *more, most*.

The two ways of forming the comparative and superlative of adjectives and adverbs are:

(*a*) The addition of the comparative and superlative suffixes *-er* and *-est* (for spelling changes that may be required see p. 12). Monosyllabic adjectives and adverbs almost always require these suffixes, e.g. *big* (*bigger, biggest*), *soon* (*sooner, soonest*), and so normally do many adjectives of two syllables, e.g. *narrow* (*narrower, narrowest*), *silly* (*sillier, silliest*).

(*b*) The placing of the comparative and superlative adverbs *more* and *most* before the adjective or adverb. These are used with adjectives of three syllables or more (e.g. *difficult, memorable*), participles (e.g. *bored, boring*), many adjectives of two syllables (e.g. *afraid, awful, childish, harmless, static*), and adverbs ending in *-ly* (e.g. *highly, slowly*).

Adjectives with two syllables vary between the use of the suffixes and of the adverbs.

There are many which never take the suffixes, e.g.

antique	*breathless*	*futile*
bizarre	*constant*	*steadfast*

There is also a large class which is acceptable with either, e.g.

clever	*handsome*	*polite*
common	*honest*	*solemn*
cruel	*pleasant*	*tranquil*
extreme		

The choice is largely a matter of style. Some examples will show how much variation there is in literary English.

With the suffixes:

> *An attitude of* completest *indifference* (George Orwell)
> *The* extremest *forms of anti-Semitism* (Lewis Namier)
> *You are so much* honester *than I am* (Iris Murdoch)
> *Now the* stupidest *of us knows* (C. S. Lewis)

With the adverbs:

> *I was a bit* more clever *than the other lads* (Angus Wilson)
> *The* most solemn *of Jane Austen's beaux* (Iris Murdoch)
> *Those periods which we think* most tranquil (C. S. Lewis)

With a mixture in one sentence:

> *Only the* dirtiest *and* most tipsy *of cooks* (Evelyn Waugh)

Even monosyllabic adjectives can sometimes take *more* and *most*:

(i) When two adjectives are compared with each other, e.g.

> *More dead than alive*
> *More good than bad*
> *More well-known than popular*

This is standard (we would not say 'better than bad' or 'better-known than popular').

(ii) Occasionally, for stylistic reasons, e.g.

> *I am the more bad because I realize where my badness lies* (L. P. Hartley)
> *This was never more true than at present*

(iii) Thoughtlessly, e.g.

> *Facts that should be more well known*
> *The most well-dressed man in town*
> *Wimbledon will be yet more hot tomorrow*

● These are not acceptable: substitute *better known*, *best dressed*, and *hotter*.

comparisons

Comparisons between two persons or things require the comparative (*-er* or *more*) in constructions like the following:

> *I cannot tell which of the two is the* elder (not *eldest*)
> *Of the two teams, they are the* slower-moving (not *slowest-moving*)

The superlative is of course used when more than two are compared.

compound subject

A subject consisting of two singular nouns or noun phrases joined by *and* normally takes a plural verb:

> *My son and daughter are twins*
> *Where to go and what to see were my main concern*

If one half of the subject is the pronoun *I* or the pronoun *you*, and the other is a noun or third person singular pronoun (*he*, *she*, or *it*), or if the subject is *you and I*, the verb must be plural.

> *He and I are good friends*
> *Do my sister and I look alike?*
> *You and your mother have similar talents*
> *You and I are hardly acquainted*

But if the phrase containing *and* represents a single item, it is followed by a singular verb:

> *The bread and butter was scattered on the floor* (W. Somerset Maugham)

And similarly if the two parts of the subject refer to a single individual:

> *His friend and legal adviser, John Smith, was present*
> *My son and heir is safe!*

See also **neither . . nor** and **subjects joined by (either . .) or**.

co-ordination

The linking of two main clauses by a comma alone, without any connecting conjunction, is sometimes said to be incorrect. It is on occasion used by good writers, however, as the examples show. It should be regarded as acceptable if used sparingly.

> *The peasants possess no harrows, they merely plough the soil several times over* (George Orwell)
>
> *Charles carried a mackintosh over his arm, he was stooping a little* (C. P. Snow)
>
> *I began to wonder when the Presidential Candidate would appear, he must have had a heavy handicap* (Graham Greene)

correlative conjunctions

The correct placing of the pairs

> *both . . and*   *neither . . nor*
>
> *either . . or*   *not only . . but* (*also*)

A sentence containing any of these pairs must be so constructed that the part of the sentence introduced by the first member of the pair (*both*, *either*, *neither*, or *not only*) is parallel in structure to the part introduced by the second member (*and*, *or*, *neither*, or *but* (*also*)).

The rule is that if one covers up the two correlative words and all the words between them, the remaining sentence should still be grammatical.

The following sentence from a typical newspaper advertisement illustrates this rule:

> *Candidates will have a background in* either *commercial electronics* or *university research*

Because *in* precedes *either*, it need not be repeated after *or*. If it had followed *either*, it would have had to be inserted after *or* as well. But the sentence as given is the most economical structure possible.

In the following example the preposition *of* comes after *either* and must therefore be repeated after *or*:

> *He did not wish to pay the price* either *of peace* or *of war* (George Orwell)

This conforms with the rule stated above, while perhaps sounding better than *of either peace or war* (which would be as good grammatically).

It is, however, not uncommon for the conjunctions to be placed so that the two halves are not quite parallel, even in the writings of careful authors, e.g.

> *I end* neither *with a death* nor *a marriage* (W. Somerset Maugham)
> *People who* either *hadn't been asked to pay* or *who were simply not troubling themselves* (V. S. Pritchett)

In the first example, *with* belongs to both halves and needs to be repeated after *nor*. In the second, *who* precedes *either* and strictly need not be repeated after *or*.

These sentences exhibit fairly trivial slips that rarely cause difficulty (except in the case of *not only*: see p. 120).

● A more serious error is the placing of the first correlative conjunction too late, so that words belonging only to the first half are carried over to the second, resulting in a grammatical muddle, e.g.

> *The other Exocet was either destroyed or blew up* (BBC News)

This should be carefully avoided.

dare

The verb *to dare* can be used either like a regular verb or like an auxiliary verb. Either use is entirely acceptable (though in a particular context, one may sound better than the other).

As an ordinary verb it forms such parts as:

I dare	*I do not dare*	*do I dare?*
he dares	*he does not dare*	*does he dare?*
he dared	*he did not dare*	*did he dare?*
I would dare	*I have dared*	

As an auxiliary verb it forms:

I dare not	*he dared not*
he dare not	*dared he?*
dare he?	

The first use, as an ordinary verb, is always acceptably followed by the *to*-infinitive, e.g.

> *I knew what I would find if I dared to look* (Jean Rhys)
> *James did not dare to carry out the sentence* (Frederic Raphael)

But many of the forms can also be followed by the bare infinitive. This sometimes sounds more natural:

> *None of which they'd dare go near* (John Osborne)
> *Don't you dare put that light on* (Shelagh Delaney)

The second use, as an auxiliary verb, normally requires the bare infinitive, e.g.

> *How dare he keep secrets from me?* (G. B. Shaw)
> *He dared not risk being carried past his destination* (C. S. Forester)

double passive

The construction whereby a passive infinitive directly follows a passive verb is correctly used in the following:

> *The prisoners were ordered to be shot*
> *This music is intended to be played on a piano*

The rule is that if the subject and the first passive verb can be changed into the active, leaving the passive infinitive intact, the sentence is correctly formed. The examples above (if a subject, say *he*, is supplied) can be changed back to:

> *He* ordered the prisoners *to be shot*
> *He* intends this music *to be played on a piano*

In other words, the passive infinitive is not part of the passive construction. An active infinitive could equally well be part of the sentence, e.g.

> *The prisoners were ordered* to march

The examples below violate the rule because both the passive verb and the passive infinitive have to be made active in order to form a grammatical sentence:

> *The order was attempted to be carried out*
> (active: *He attempted to carry out the order*)

> *A new definition was sought to be inserted in the Bill*
> (active: *He sought to insert a new definition in the Bill*)

This 'double passive' construction is unacceptable.

The passive of the verbs *to fear* and *to say* can be followed by either an active or a passive infinitive, e.g.

> (i) *The passengers are feared* to have drowned
> *The escaped prisoner is said* to be very dangerous

or

(ii) *The passengers are feared to have been killed*
The escaped prisoner is said to have been sighted

The construction at (ii) is not the double passive and is entirely acceptable. Both constructions are sometimes found with other verbs of saying (e.g. *to allege, to assert, to imply*):

Morris demonstrated that Mr Elton was obviously implied to be impotent (David Lodge)

either .. or: see **subjects joined by (*either ..*) or.**

either (pronoun)

Either is a singular pronoun and should be followed by a singular verb:

Enormous evils, either of which depends on somebody else's voice (Louis MacNeice)

In the following example the plural verb accords with the notional meaning 'both parents were not'.

It was improbable that either of our parents were giving thought to the matter (J. I. M. Stewart)

This is quite common in informal usage, but should not be carried over into formal prose.

gender of indefinite expressions

It is often uncertain what personal pronoun should be used to refer back to the indefinite pronouns and adjectives in the following list:

any	*no* (+ noun)
anybody	*nobody*
anyone	*none*
each	*no one*
every (+ noun)	*some* (+ noun)
everybody	*somebody*
everyone	*someone*

and also to refer back to (*a*) *person*, used indefinitely, or a male and female noun linked by (*either ..*) *or* or *neither .. nor*, e.g.

Has anybody eaten his/their *lunch yet?*
A person who is upset may vent his/their *feelings on* his/their *family*
Neither John nor Mary has a home of their/his or her *own*

If it is known that the individuals referred to are all of the same sex, there is no difficulty; use *he* or *she* as appropriate:

> *Everyone in the women's movement has had* her *own experience of sexual discrimination*

If, however, the sex of those referred to is unknown or deliberately left indefinite, or if the reference is to a mixed group, the difficulty arises that English has no singular pronoun to denote common gender.

The grammarians' recommendation, during the past two centuries, has been that *he* (*him*, *himself*, *his*) should be used. Many good writers follow this:

> *Everyone talked at the top of* his *voice* (W. Somerset Maugham)
> *Everyone took* his *place in a half-circle about the fire* (Malcolm Bradbury)
> (The context of each shows that the company was mixed.)

> *The long street in which nobody knows* his *neighbour* (G. B. Shaw)
> *Each person should give as* he *has decided for* himself (NEB)

Popular usage, however, has for at least five centuries favoured the plural pronoun *they* (*them*, *themselves*, *their*).

This is entirely acceptable in informal speech:

> *Nobody would ever marry if* they *thought it over* (G. B. Shaw)
> *It's the sort of thing any of us would dislike, wouldn't* they? (C. P. Snow)

It is by no means uncommon in more formal contexts:

> *Nobody stopped to stare, everyone had* themselves *to think about* (Susan Hill)
> *His own family were occupied, each with* their *particular guests* (Evelyn Waugh)
> *Delavacquerie allowed everyone to examine the proofs as long as* they *wished* (Anthony Powell)

(The context of the second and third example shows that the company was mixed.)

Many people regard it as inequitable that the masculine pronoun *he* should be used to include both sexes, and therefore prefer to use *they*.

One can avoid the difficulty from time to time by writing *he or she*, as many writers do on awkward occasions:

> *Nobody has room in* his or her *life for more than one such relationship at a time* (G. B. Shaw)

But this grows unwieldy with repetition:

> *If I ever wished to disconcert anyone, all I had to do was to ask* him (or her) *how many friends* he/she *had* (Frederic Raphael)

There are some contexts in which neither *he* nor *they* will seem objectionable. In others, where *he* and *they* both seem inappropriate for the reasons given, it may be necessary simply to recast the sentence.

group possessive

The group possessive is the construction by which the ending -'s of the possessive case can be added to the last word of a noun phrase, which is regarded as a single unit, e.g.

> *The king of Spain's daughter*
> *John and Mary's baby*
> *Somebody else's umbrella*
> *A quarter of an hour's drive*

Expressions like these are natural and acceptable.

Informal language, however, permits the extension of the construction to long and complicated phrases:

> *The people in the house opposite's geraniums*
> *The woman I told you about on the phone yesterday's name is Thompson*
> *The man who called last week's umbrella is still in the hall*

In these, the connection between the words forming the group possessive is much looser and more complicated than in the earlier examples. The effect is often somewhat ludicrous.

● Expressions of this sort should not be used in serious prose. Substitute:

> *The geraniums of the people in the house opposite*
> *The name of the woman I told you about on the phone yesterday is Thompson*
> *The umbrella of the man who called last week is still in the hall*

have

1. The verb *to have*, in some of its uses, can form its interrogative and negative either with or without the verb *to do*, e.g. *Do you have/have you?*, *You don't have/you haven't.*

In sentences like those below, *have* is a verb of event, meaning 'experience'. The interrogative (in the first example) and the negative (in the second example) are always formed in the regular way, using the verb *do*:

> Do you *ever* have *nightmares?*
> *We* did not have *an easy time getting here*

In the next pair of sentences, *have* is a verb of state, meaning 'possess'. When used in this sense, the interrogative (in the first example) and negative (in the second example) can be formed in the manner of an auxiliary verb, without the verb *do*:

> *What* have you *in common with the child of five whose photograph your mother keeps?* (George Orwell)
> *The truth was that he* hadn't *the answer* (Joyce Cary)

In more informal language, the verb *got* is added, e.g. *What have you got*, *He hadn't got the answer*. This is not usually suitable for formal usage.

It was formerly usual to distinguish the sense 'experience' from the sense 'possess' by using the *do*-formation for the first and the auxiliary formation for the second (but only in the present tense). Hence *I don't have indigestion* (as a rule) was kept distinct from *I haven't (got) indigestion* (at the moment). The use of the *do*-construction when the meaning was 'possess' was an Americanism, but it is now generally acceptable.

● However, the use of *do* as a substitute verb for *have*, common informally, is not acceptable in formal prose:

> *I had stronger feelings than she* did (substitute *than she had*)
> *Some have money, some* don't (substitute *some haven't*)

2. *Have* is often wrongly inserted after *I'd* in sentences like:

> *If I'd* have *known she'd be here I don't suppose I'd have come* (Character in play by John Osborne)

This is common, and hardly noticed, in speech, but should not occur in formal writing. The correct construction is:

If I'd known *she'd be here* . .

Without the contraction, the clause would read: *If I had known*, with the past perfect, which is the correct form in this kind of *if*-clause. The only expression that the mistaken *If I'd have known* could stand for is *If I would have known*, which is impossible in this context.

he who, she who

He who and *she who* are correctly used when *he* and *she* are the subject of the main clause, and *who* is the subject of the relative clause:

He who *hesitates is lost*
She who *was a star in the old play may find herself a super in the new* (C. S. Lewis)

In these examples *he* and *she* are the subjects of *is lost* and *may find* respectively; *who* is the subject of *hesitates* and *was*.

He who and *she who* should not be treated as invariable. They should change to *him who* and *her who* if the personal pronouns are not the subject of the main clause:

The distinction between the man who gives with conviction and him (not *he*) *who is simply buying a title*

Similarly *who* must become *whom* if it is not the subject of the relative clause:

I sought him whom *my soul loveth* (Authorized Version)

See also **who and whom (interrogative and relative pronouns)**.

ics, nouns in

Nouns ending in *-ics* denoting subjects or disciplines are sometimes treated as singular and sometimes as plural. Examples are:

apologetics	*genetics*	*optics*
classics (as	*linguistics*	*phonetics*
a study)	*mathematics*	*physics*
dynamics	*mechanics*	*politics*
economics	*metaphysics*	*statistics*
electronics	*obstetrics*	*tactics*
ethics		

When used strictly as the name of a discipline they are treated as singular:

> *Psychometrics* is *unable to investigate the nature of intelligence* (*Guardian*)
> *The quest for a hermeneutics* (TLS)

So also when the complement is singular:

> *Mathematics* is *his strong point*

When used more loosely, to denote a manifestation of qualities, often accompanied by a possessive, they are treated as plural:

> *His politics* were *a mixture of fear, greed and envy* (Joyce Cary)
> *I don't understand the mathematics of it, which* are *complicated*
> *The acoustics in this hall* are *dreadful*
> *Their tactics* were *cowardly*

So also when they denote a set of activities or pattern of behaviour, as commonly with words like

acrobatics	dramatics	heroics
athletics	gymnastics	hysterics
callisthenics		

E.g. *The mental gymnastics required to believe this* are *beyond me*

These words usually retain a plural verb even with a singular complement:

> *The acrobatics* are *just the social side* (Tom Stoppard)

infinitive, present or perfect

The perfect infinitive is correctly used when it refers to a state or action earlier in time than that referred to by the verb on which it depends, e.g.

> *If it were real life and not a play, that is the part it would be best* to have acted (C. S. Lewis)
> *Someone seems* to have been making *a beast of himself here* (Evelyn Waugh)

In the above examples, the infinitives *to have acted* and *to have been making* relate to actions earlier in time than the verbs *would be best* and *seems*.

Only if the first verb relates to the past and the infinitive relates to a state or action prior to that should a perfect infinitive follow a past or perfect verb, forming a sort of 'double past', e.g.

> *When discussing sales with him yesterday*, I should have liked to have seen *the figures beforehand*

In this example *I should have liked* denotes the speaker's feelings during the discussion and *to have seen* denotes an action imagined as occurring before the discussion.

If the state or action denoted by the infinitive is thought of as occurring at the same time as the verb on which it depends, then the present infinitive should be used:

> *She* would have liked to see *what was on the television* (Kingsley Amis)

The 'double past' is often accidentally used in this kind of sentence informally, e.g.

> *I should have liked to have gone to the party*

A literary example is:

> *Mr. McGregor threw down the sack on the stone floor in a way that would have been extremely painful to the Flopsy Bunnies, if they had happened to have been inside it* (Beatrix Potter)

This should be avoided.

-ing (gerund and participle)

1. The *-ing* form of a verb can in some contexts be used in either of two constructions:

(i) as a gerund (verbal noun) with a noun or pronoun in the possessive standing before it, e.g.

> *In the event of* Randall's not going (Iris Murdoch)
> *She did not like* his being *High Church* (L. P. Hartley)

(ii) as a participle with a noun in its ordinary form or a pronoun in the objective case standing before it, e.g.

> *What further need would there have been to speak of another priest arising?* (NEB)
> *Dixon did not like* him doing *that* (Kingsley Amis)

The option of using either arises only when the word before the *-ing* form is a proper or personal noun (e.g. *John, father, teacher*) or a personal pronoun.

It is sometimes said that the construction with the possessive (as in (i) above) is obligatory. This rule, in its strict form, should be disregarded. Instead one should, in formal usage, try to employ the possessive construction wherever it is possible and natural:

> *To whom, without* its being *ordered, the waiter immediately brought a plate of eggs and bacon* (Evelyn Waugh)
> *The danger of* Joyce's turning *them into epigrams* (Anthony Burgess)

But it is certainly not wrong to use the non-possessive construction if it sounds more natural, as in the New English Bible quotation above. Moreover, there is sometimes a nuance of meaning. *She did not like his being High Church* suggests that she did not like the fact that he was High Church, and need not imply personal antipathy, whereas *Dixon did not like him doing that* suggests an element of repugnance to the person as well as to his action.

When using most non-personal nouns (e.g. *luggage, meaning, permission*), groups of nouns (e.g. *father and mother, surface area*), non-personal pronouns (e.g. *anything, something*), and groups of pronouns (e.g. *some of them*), there is no choice of construction: the possessive would not sound idiomatic at all. Examples are:

> *Travellers in Italy could depend on their* luggage *not* being *stolen* (G. B. Shaw)
> *Altogether removing possibility of its* meaning being *driven home* (Anthony Powell)
> *His lines were cited . . without his* permission having *been asked* (*The Times*)
> *Due to her* father and mother being *married* (Compton Mackenzie)
> *Owing to its* surface area being *so large relative to its weight* (George Orwell)
> *The air of* something *unusual* having *happened* (Arthur Conan Doyle)
> *He had no objection to* some of them listening (Arnold Bennett)

When the word preceding the *-ing* form is a regular plural noun ending in *-s*, there is no spoken distinction between the possessive and the non-possessive form. It is unnecessary to write an apostrophe:

> *If she knew about her* daughters *attending the party* (Anthony Powell)

2. There is also variation between the gerundial and the participial uses of the *-ing* form after nouns like *difficulty, point, trouble,* and *use.*

Formal English requires the gerundial use, the gerund being introduced by *in* (or *of* after *use*):

> *There was . . no difficulty* in finding *parking space* (David Lodge)
> *There doesn't seem much point* in trying *to explain everything* (John Osborne)

Informal usage permits the placing of the *-ing* form immediately after the noun, forming a participial construction, e.g.

> *He had some trouble* convincing *Theo Craven* (Lynne Reid Banks)
> *The chairman had difficulty* concealing *his irritation*

● This is not acceptable in formal usage.

I or *me, we* or *us,* etc.

There is often confusion about which case of a personal pronoun to use when the pronoun stands alone or follows the verb *to be*.

1. When the personal pronoun stands alone, as when it forms the answer to a question, formal usage requires it to have the case it would have if the verb were supplied:

> *Who killed Cock Robin?*—I (in full, *I killed him*)
> *Which of you did he approach?*—Me (in full, *he approached me*)

Informal usage permits the objective case in both kinds of sentence, but this is not acceptable in formal style. It so happens that the subjective case often sounds stilted. It is then best to avoid the problem by providing the substitute verb *do*, or, if the preceding sentence contains an auxiliary, by repeating the auxiliary, e.g.

> *Who likes cooking?*—I do
> *Who can cook?*—I can

2. When a personal pronoun follows *it is, it was, it may be, it could have been*, etc., it should always have the subjective case:

> *Nobody could suspect that* it was *she* (Agatha Christie)
> *We are given no clue as to what it must have felt like to be* he (C. S. Lewis)

Informal usage favours the objective case:

> *I thought it might have been* him *at the door*
> *Don't tell me it's* them *again!*

● This is not acceptable in formal usage.

When *who* or *whom* follows, the subjective case is obligatory in formal usage and quite usual informally:

> *It was* I *who painted the back door purple*
> *It's* they *whom I shall be staying with in London*

The informal use of the objective case often sounds substandard:

> *It was* her *who would get the blood off* (Character in work by Patrick White)

(For agreement between the personal pronoun antecedent and the verb in *It is I who* etc., see *I who, you who,* **etc.**)

In constructions which have the form *I am* + noun or noun phrase + *who*, the verb following *who* agrees with the noun (the antecedent of *who*) and is therefore always in the third person (singular or plural):

> *I am the sort of person who* likes *peace and quiet*
> *You are the fourth of my colleagues who's told me that* (Character in work by Angus Wilson) (*'s = has*, agreeing with *the fourth*)

The following is not standard, but must be explained by the uniqueness of the person denoted by the subject:

> *How then canst thou be a god that* hidest *thyself?* (NEB)

I should or *I would*

There is often uncertainty whether to use *should* or *would* in the first person singular and plural before verbs such as *like* or *think* and before the adverbs *rather* and *sooner*.

1. *Should* is correct before verbs of liking, e.g. *be glad, be inclined, care, like,* and *prefer*:

> *Would you like a beer?*—I should prefer *a cup of coffee, if you don't mind*
> *The very occasions on which* we should *most like to write a slashing review* (C. S. Lewis)

2. *Should* is correct in tentative statements of opinion, with verbs such as *guess, imagine, say,* and *think*:

> I should imagine *that you are right*
> I should say *so*
> I shouldn't have *thought it was difficult*

3. *Would* is correct before the adverbs *rather* and *sooner*, e.g.

> I would *truly* rather *be in the middle of this than sitting in that church in a tight collar* (Susan Hill)

Would is always correct with persons other than the first person singular and plural.

See also **should and would**.

I who, you who, etc.

The verb following a personal pronoun (*I, you, he*, etc.) + *who* should agree with the pronoun and should not be in the third person singular unless the third person singular pronoun precedes *who*:

> *I, who* have *no savings to speak of, had to pay for the work*

This remains so even if the personal pronoun is in the objective case:

> *They made me, who* have *no savings at all, pay for the work* (not *who has*)

When *it is* (*it was*, etc.) precedes *I who*, etc., the same rule applies: the verb agrees with the personal pronoun:

> *It's I who* have *done it*
> *It could have been we who* were *mistaken*

Informal usage sometimes permits the third person to be used (especially when the verb *to be* follows *who*):

> *You* who's *supposed to be so practical!*
> *Is it me* who's *supposed to be keeping an eye on you?* (Character in work by David Lodge)

● This is not acceptable in formal usage.

like

The objective case of personal pronouns is always used after the adjectives *like* and *unlike*:

> *Unlike my mother and* me, *my sister is fair-haired* (not *Unlike my mother and* I)

-lily adverbs

When the adverbial suffix *-ly* is added to an adjective which already ends in *-ly*, the resulting adverb tends to have an unpleasant jingling sound, e.g. *friendlily*.

Adverbs of this kind are divided into three groups, here arranged in order of decreasing acceptability:

(i) Those formed from adjectives in which the final -*ly* is an integral part of the word, not a suffix, e.g. *holily, jollily, sillily.* These are the least objectionable and are quite often used.

(ii) Those of three syllables formed from adjectives in which the final -*ly* is itself a suffix, e.g. *friendlily, ghastlily, statelily, uglily.* These are occasionally found.

(iii) Those of four (or more) syllables formed from adjectives in which the final -*ly* is itself a suffix, e.g. *heavenlily, scholarlily.* Such words have been recorded but are deservedly rare.

The adverbs of groups (ii) and (iii) should be avoided if possible, by using the adjective with a noun like *manner* or *way*, e.g. *In a scholarly manner.*

A few adjectives in -*ly* can be used adverbially to qualify other adjectives, e.g. *beastly cold, ghastly pale.* Occasionally, to avoid the use of an adverb in -*lily*, the plain adjective has been used to qualify a verb, e.g.

> *Then I strolled* leisurely *along those dear, dingy streets* (W. Somerset Maugham)

This does not usually sound natural. It is recommended that *in a leisurely* (etc.) *way* should be used instead.

may or *might*

There is sometimes confusion about whether to use *may* or *might* with the perfect infinitive referring to a past event, e.g. *He may have done* or *He might have done.*

1. If uncertainty about the action or state denoted by the perfect infinitive remains, i.e. at the time of speaking or writing the truth of the event is still unknown, then either *may* or *might* is acceptable:

> *As they all wore so many different clothes of identically the same kind . . , there* may *have been several more or several less* (Evelyn Waugh)
> *For all we knew we were both bastards, although of course there* might *have been a ceremony* (Graham Greene)

2. If there is no longer uncertainty about the event, or the matter

was never put to the test, and therefore the event did not in fact occur, use *might*:

> *If that had come ten days ago my whole life* might *have been different* (Evelyn Waugh)
> *You should not have let him come home alone; he* might *have got lost*

● It is a common error to use *may* instead of *might* in these circumstances:

> *If he (President Galtieri) had not invaded, then eventually the islands* may *have fallen into their lap*
> *I am grateful for his intervention without which they* may *have remained in the refugee camp indefinitely*
> *Schoenberg* may *never have gone atonal but for the break-up of his marriage*

(These are all from recent newspaper articles. *Might* should be substituted for *may* in each.)

measurement, nouns of

There is some uncertainty about when to use the singular form, and when the plural, of nouns of measurement.

1. All nouns of measurement remain in the singular form when compounded with a numeral and used attributively before another noun:

> *A six*-foot *wall*   *A five*-pound *note*
> *A three*-mile *walk*   *A 1,000*-megaton *bomb*

This rule includes metric measurements:

> *A ten*-hectare *field*   *A three*-litre *bottle*

2. *Foot* remains in the singular form in expressions such as:

> *I am six foot*   *She is five foot two*

But *feet* is used where an adjective, or the word *inches*, follows, e.g.

> *I am six feet tall*   *She is five feet three inches*
> *It is ten feet long*

Stone and *hundredweight* remain in the singular form in plural expressions, e.g.

> *I weigh eleven stone*   *Three hundredweight of coal*

Metric measurements always take the plural form when not used attributively:

> *This measures three metres by two metres*
> *Two kilos of sugar*

Informally, some other nouns of measurement are used in the singular form in plural expressions, e.g.

> *That will be two pound fifty, please*

● This is non-standard.

See also **quantity, nouns of**.

need

The verb *to need*, when followed by an infinitive, can be used either like an ordinary verb or like an auxiliary.

1. *Need* is used like an ordinary verb, and followed by the *to*-infinitive, in the present tense when the sentence is neither negative nor interrogative, in the past tense always, and in all compound tenses (e.g. the future and perfect):

> *One needs friends, one* needs to *be a friend* (Susan Hill)
> *One* did not need to *be a clairvoyant to see that war . . was coming* (George Orwell)

2. *Need* can be used like an auxiliary verb in the present tense in negative and interrogative sentences. This means that:

(*a*) The third person singular need not add *-s*:

> *I do not think one* need *look farther than this* (George Orwell)

(*b*) For the negative, *need not* can replace *does not need*:

> *One* need not *be an advocate of censorship to recommend the cautious use of poison* (Frederic Raphael)

(*c*) For the interrogative, *need I* (*you*, etc.) can replace *do I need*:

> Need I *add that she is my bitterest enemy?* (G. B. Shaw)

(*d*) The bare infinitive can follow instead of the *to*-infinitive:

> *Company that keeps them smaller than they need* be (*Bookseller*) (This is negative in sense, for it implies *They need not be as small as this*)

This auxiliary verb use is optional, not obligatory. The regular constructions are equally correct:

I do not think one needs to look . .
One does not need to be . .
Do I need to add . .
Smaller than they need to be . .

One should choose whichever sounds more natural. It is important, however, to avoid mixing the two kinds of construction, as in the two following examples:

One needs not be *told that* (etc.)
What proved vexing, it needs be *said, was* (etc.)

neither . . nor

Two singular subjects linked by *neither . . nor* can be constructed with either a singular or a plural verb. Strictly and logically a singular verb is required (since both subjects are not thought of as governing the verb at the same time). When the two subjects are straightforward third person pronouns or nouns, it is best to follow this rule:

Neither he nor his wife has *arrived*
There is *neither a book nor a picture in the house*

Informal usage permits the plural and it has been common in the writings of good authors for a long time:

Neither painting nor fighting feed *men* (Ruskin)

When one of the two subjects is plural and the other singular, the verb should be made plural and the plural subject placed nearer to it:

Neither the teacher nor the pupils understand *the problem*

When one of the subjects is *I* or *you* and the other is a third person pronoun or a noun, or when one is *I* and the other *you*, the verb can be made to agree with the subject that is nearer to it. However, this does not always sound natural, e.g.

Neither my son nor I am *good at figures*

One can recast the sentence, but this can spoil the effect intended by using *neither . . nor*. It is often better to use the plural, as good writers do:

Neither Isabel nor I are *timid people* (H. G. Wells)

Neither Emily nor I were *quite prepared for the title* (Anthony Powell)

This is not illogical if *neither . . nor* is regarded as the negative of *both . . and.*

neither (pronoun)

Neither is a singular pronoun and strictly requires a singular verb:

Neither of us likes *to be told what to do*

Informal usage permits not only a plural verb, but also a plural complement:

Neither of us like *tennis*
Neither of us are good players

Although this is widely regarded as incorrect, it has been an established construction for three or four centuries:

Thersites' body is as good as Ajax', When neither are *alive* (Shakespeare)
Neither were great inventors (Dryden)

It is recommended that one should follow the rule requiring the singular unless it leads to awkwardness, as when neither *he* nor *she* is appropriate:

John and Mary will have to walk. Neither of them have *brought* their *cars*

none (pronoun)

The pronoun *none* can be followed either by singular verb and singular pronouns, or by plural ones. Either is acceptable, although the plural tends to be more common.

Singular: *None of them* was *allowed to forget for a moment* (Anthony Powell)
Plural: *None of the fountains ever* play (Evelyn Waugh)
None of the authors expected their *books to become best-sellers* (Cyril Connolly)

ought

Oughtn't or *didn't ought?*

The standard form of the negative of *ought* is *ought not* or *oughtn't*:

A look from Claudia showed me I ought not *to have begun it* (V. S. Pritchett)

Being an auxiliary verb, *ought* can precede *not* and does not require the verb *do*. It is non-standard to form the negative with *do* (*didn't ought*):

I hope that none here will say I did anything I didn't ought. *For I only done my duty* (Character in work by Michael Innes)

When the negative is used to reinforce a question in a short extra clause or 'question tag', the negative should be formed according to the rule above:

You ought to be pleased, oughtn't you? (not *didn't you?*)

In the same way *do* should not be used as a substitute verb for *ought*, e.g.

Ought he to go?— Yes, he ought (not *he did*)
You ought not to be pleased, ought you? (not *did you?*)

participles

A participle used in place of a verb in a subordinate clause must have an explicit subject to qualify. If no subject precedes the participle within the clause, the participle is understood to qualify the subject of the main sentence. In the following sentences the participles *running* and *propped* qualify the subjects *she* and *we*:

Running *to catch a bus, she just missed it* (Anthony Powell)
We both lay there, propped *on our elbows* (Lynne Reid Banks)

It is a frequent error to begin a sentence with a participial clause, with no subject expressed, and to continue it with a main clause in which the subject is not the word which the participle qualifies:

Driving *along the road, the church* appeared on our left
(*We*, not *the church*, is the subject of *driving*)

Having been relieved *of his portfolio in 1976, the scheme was left to his successor at the Ministry to complete*
(*He*, or a proper name, is the subject of *having been relieved*)

In sentences like these one must either recast the main clause so that its subject is the same as that of the subordinate clause, or recast the subordinate clause using a finite verb:

Driving along the road, we saw the church appear *on our left*
As we were driving along the road, the church appeared on our left

Sometimes a subject can be supplied in the participial clause, the clause remaining otherwise unchanged. This is usually only possible when the participle is *being* or *having*:

> Jones *having been relieved of his portfolio in 1976, the scheme was left to his successor at the Ministry to complete*

If the subject supplied in accordance with this rule is a personal pronoun it should be in the subjective case:

> He being *such a liar, no one will believe him when he tells the truth*
> He rose bearing her, she *still weeping, and the others formed a procession behind* (Iris Murdoch)

When the participial clause includes a subject it should not be separated by a comma from the participle:

> Bernadette being her niece, *she feels responsible for the girl's moral welfare* (David Lodge) (Not: *Bernadette, being her niece, she* . .)

This is in contrast with the punctuation of the other kind of participial clause, in which the participle qualifies the subject of the main sentence. If this type of participial clause follows the subject, it is either marked off by a pair of commas or not marked off at all:

> *The man*, hoping to escape, *jumped on to a bus*
> *A man* carrying a parcel *jumped on to the bus*

The rule that a participle must have an explicit subject does not apply to participial clauses whose subject is indefinite (= 'one' or 'people'). In these the clause is used adverbially, standing apart from and commenting on the content of the sentence:

> Judging *from his appearance, he has had a night out*
> Taking *everything into consideration, you were lucky to escape*
> Roughly speaking, *this is how it went*

The participial clauses here are equivalent to 'If one judges . .', 'If one takes . .', 'If one speaks . .' Expressions of this kind are entirely acceptable.

preposition at end

It is a natural feature of the English language that many sentences and clauses end with a preposition, and has been since the earliest times. The alleged rule that forbids the placing of the preposition at the end of a clause or sentence should be disregarded.

The preposition *cannot* be moved to an earlier place in many sentences, e.g.

> *What did you do that* for?
> *What a mess this room is* in!
> *The bed had not been slept* in
> *She was good to look* at *and easy to talk* to (W. Somerset Maugham)

There are other kinds of construction which, generally speaking, allow a choice between placing the preposition at the end or placing it earlier—principally relative clauses, in which the preposition can stand before the relative pronoun if it is not placed finally. The choice is very often a matter of style. The preposition has been placed before the relative pronoun in:

> *The present is the only time* in which *any duty can be done* (C. S. Lewis)
> *The . . veteran* for whom *nothing has been real since the Big Push* (David Lodge)

But it stands at or near the end in:

> *Harold's Philistine outlook, which she had acquiesced* in *for ten years* (L. P. Hartley)
> *The sort of attentive memory . . that I should have become accustomed* to (C. P. Snow)

But notice that some prepositions cannot come at the end:

> *An annual sum*, in return for *which she agreed to give me house room* (William Trevor)
> During *which week will the festival be held?*

It would be unnatural to write *Which she agreed to give me house room* in return for, and *Which week will the festival be held* during?

Conversely, some relative clauses will not allow the preposition to stand before the relative pronoun:

> *The opposition* (*that*) *I ran up* against *was fierce*
> *A sort of world apart which one can quite easily go through life without ever hearing* about (George Orwell)

These cannot be changed to:

> *The opposition* against *which I ran up . .*
> *A sort of world apart without ever hearing* about *which . .*

One should be guided by what sounds natural. There is no need to alter the position of the preposition merely in deference to the alleged rule.

quantity, nouns of

The numerals *hundred, thousand, million, billion, trillion*, and the words *dozen* and *score* are sometimes used in the singular and sometimes in the plural.

1. They always have the singular form if they are qualified by a preceding word, whether it is singular (e.g. *a, one*) or plural (e.g. *many, several, two, three*, etc.), and whether or not they are used attributively before a noun or with nothing following:

> *A hundred days*
> *Three hundred will be enough*
> *I will take two dozen*
> *Two dozen eggs*

● The use of the plural form after a plural qualifier and when nothing follows is incorrect:

> *The population is now three millions* (correctly *three million*)

Although they have the singular form, they always take plural verbs, even after the indefinite article:

> *There* were *about a dozen of them approaching* (Anthony Powell)
> *There* were *a score of them at a table apart* (J. I. M. Stewart)

2. They take the plural form when they denote indefinite quantities. Usually they are followed by *of* or stand alone:

> *Are there any errors?— Yes, hundreds*
> *He has dozens of friends*
> *Many thousands of people are homeless*

reflexive pronouns

The reflexive pronouns are normally used to refer back to the subject of the clause or sentence in which they occur, e.g.

> I *congratulated* myself *on outwitting everyone else*
> *Can't* you *do anything for* yourself?

Sometimes it is permissible to use a reflexive pronoun to refer to someone who is not the subject. Very often the person referred to may be the subject of a preceding or following clause, e.g.

It was their success, both with myself *and others, that confirmed* me
  in what has since been my career (Evelyn Waugh)

You *have the feeling that all their adventures have happened to*
  yourself (George Orwell)

He was furious with the woman, with a rancorous anger that sur-
  prised himself (Joyce Cary)

In each of the above, there is a nearby *me*, *you*, or *he* to which the
reflexive refers, but to have written *me*, *you*, and *him* respectively in
these sentences would not have been grammatically incorrect.

A reflexive pronoun is often used after such words as

as	*but for*	*like*
as for	*except*	*than*
but	*except for*	

E.g. *For those who*, like himself, *felt it indelicate to raise an umbrella*
  in the presence of death (Iris Murdoch)

It can be a very useful way to avoid the difficult choice between *I*, *he*,
she, etc. (which often sounds stilted) and *me*, *him*, *her*, etc. (which are
grammatically incorrect) after the words *as*, *but*, and *than*, e.g.

None of them was more surprised than myself *that I'd spoken*
  (Lynne Reid Banks)

Here *than I* would be strictly correct, while *than me* would be
informal.

Naturally a reflexive pronoun cannot be used in the ways outlined
above if confusion would result. One would not write:

John was as surprised as himself *that he had been appointed*

but would substitute the person's name, or *he himself was*, for *himself*,
or recast the sentence.

relative clauses

A relative clause is a clause introduced by a relative pronoun and
used to qualify a preceding noun or pronoun (called its antecedent),
e.g. *The visitor* (antecedent) *whom* (relative pronoun) *you were*
expecting (remainder of relative clause) *has arrived*; *He* who hesitates
is lost.

Exceptionally, there are nominal relative clauses in which the antecedent and relative pronoun are combined in one *wh*-pronoun, e.g.
What you need *is a drink*: see **what** (relative pronoun).

Relative clauses can be either restrictive or non-restrictive. A restrictive relative clause serves to restrict the reference of the antecedent, e.g. *A suitcase* which has lost its handle *is useless*. Here the antecedent *suitcase* is defined or restricted by the clause.

A non-restrictive relative clause is used not to narrow the reference of the antecedent, but to add further information, e.g. *He carried the suitcase*, which had lost its handle, *on one shoulder*. Here the suitcase is already identified, and the relative clause adds explanatory information.

Notice that no commas are used to mark off a restrictive relative clause from the rest of the sentence, but when, as above, a non-restrictive relative clause comes in the middle of the sentence, it is marked off by a comma at each end.

There are two kinds of relative pronouns:

(i) The *wh*-type: *who*, *whom*, *whose*, *which*, and, in nominal relative clauses only, *what*.

(ii) The pronoun *that* (which can be omitted in some circumstances: see ***that* (relative pronoun), omission of**).

When one relative clause is followed by another, the second relative pronoun

    (*a*) may or may not be preceded by a conjunction; and

    (*b*) may or may not be omitted.

(*a*) A conjunction is not required if the second relative clause qualifies an antecedent which is a word inside the first relative clause:

    I found a firm which *had a large quantity of components* for which *they had no use*

Here *for which . . use* qualifies *components* which is part of the relative clause qualifying *firm*. *And* or *but* should not be inserted before *for which*.

But if the two clauses are parallel, both qualifying the same antecedent, a conjunction is required:

    Help me with these shelves which *I have to take home* but *which will not fit in my car*

(*b*) The second relative pronoun can be omitted if (i) it qualifies the same antecedent as the first, and (ii) it plays the same part in its clause as the first (i.e. subject or object):

> *George*, who *takes infinite pains and* (who) *never cuts corners, is our most dependable worker*

Here the second *who* qualifies the same antecedent (*George*) as the first *who*, and, like it, is the subject of its clause. It can therefore be omitted.

But if the second relative pronoun plays a different part in its clause, it cannot be omitted:

> *George*, whom *everybody likes but* who *rarely goes to a party, is shy*

Here the first relative pronoun, *whom*, is the object, the second, *who*, is the subject, in their clauses. The second relative pronoun must be kept. This rule applies even if the two pronouns have the same form; it is the function that counts:

> *Like a child spelling out the letters of a word* which *he cannot read and* which *if he could would have no meaning* (Jean Rhys)

The second *which* cannot be omitted.

See also **preposition at end,** *that* **(relative pronoun), omission of,** *what* **(relative pronoun),** *which* **or** *that* **(relative pronouns),** *who* **and** *whom* **(interrogative and relative pronouns),** *who* **or** *which* **(relative pronouns),** *whose* **or** *of which* **in relative clauses,** *who/whom* **or** *that* **(relative pronouns).**

shall and *will*

'*The horror of that moment*', *the King went on, '*I shall never*, never forget!' '*You will, though,*' *the Queen said, '*if you don't make a memorandum of it.*' (Lewis Carroll)

There is considerable confusion about when to use *shall* and *will*. Put simply, the traditional rule in standard British English is:

1. In the first person, singular and plural.

(*a*) *I shall*, *we shall* express the simple future, e.g.

> *I am not a manual worker and please God I never* shall *be one* (George Orwell)
> *In the following pages we* shall *see good words . . losing their edge* (C. S. Lewis)

(*b*) *I will*, *we will* express intention or determination on the part of the speaker (especially a promise made by him or her), e.g.

> *I* will *take you to see her tomorrow morning* (P. G. Wodehouse)

> *I* will *no longer accept responsibility for the fruitless loss of life*
> (Susan Hill)
> '*I don't think we* will *ask Mr. Fraser's opinion*', *she said coldly*
> (V. S. Pritchett)

2. For the second and third persons, singular and plural, the rule is exactly the converse.

(*a*) *You*, *he*, *she*, *it*, or *they* will express the simple future, e.g.

> Will *it disturb you if I keep the lamp on for a bit?* (Susan Hill)
> *Seraphina* will *last much longer than a car. She'll probably last longer than you* will (Graham Greene)

(*b*) *You*, *he*, *she*, *it*, or *they* shall express intention or determination on the part of the speaker or someone other than the actual subject of the verb, especially a promise made by the speaker to or about the subject, e.g.

> *Today you* shall *be with me in Paradise* (NEB)
> *One day you* shall *know my full story* (Evelyn Waugh)
> Shall *the common man be pushed back into the mud, or* shall *he not?* (George Orwell)

The two uses of *will*, and one of those of *shall*, are well illustrated by:

> '*I* will *follow you to the ends of the earth*,' *replied Susan, passionately.* '*It* will *not be necessary*,' *said George.* '*I am only going down to the coal-cellar. I* shall *spend the next half-hour or so there.*' (P. G. Wodehouse)

In informal usage *I will* and *we will* are quite often used for the simple future, e.g.

> *I* will *be a different person when I live in England* (Character in work by Jean Rhys)

More often the distinction is covered up by the contracted form '*ll*, e.g.

> *I don't quite know when* I'll *get the time to write again* (Susan Hill)

● The use of *will* for *shall* in the first person is not regarded as fully acceptable in formal usage.

should and *would*

When used for (*a*) the future in the past or (*b*) the conditional,

> *should* goes with *I* and *we*
> *would* goes with *you*, *he*, *she*, *it*, and *they*

(*a*) The future in the past.

First person:

> *I had supposed these to be the last* . . I should *ever set eyes on* (Anthony Powell)
> *Julia and I, who had left* . . , *thinking* we should *not return* (Evelyn Waugh)

The person's imagined statement or thought at the time was:

> *These are the last* I shall *ever set eyes on*
> We shall *not return*

with *shall*, not *will* (see **shall and will**).

Second and third persons:

> *I told you that* you would *find Russian difficult to learn*
> *He was there. Later*, he would *not be there* (Susan Hill)

The person's statement or thought at the time was

> You will *find Russian difficult to learn*
> He will *not be there*

(*b*) The conditional.

First person:

> I should *view with the strongest disapproval any proposal to abolish manhood suffrage* (C. S. Lewis)
> *If we had not hurried* we should *never have got a seat*

Second and third persons:

> *If you cared about your work*, you would *make more effort*
> *Isobel* would *almost certainly have gone in any case* (Anthony Powell)

In informal usage, *I would* and *we would* are very common in both kinds of sentence:

> *I wondered whether* I would *have to wear a black suit*
> I would *have been content, I would never have repeated it* (Both examples from Graham Greene)

The use of *would* with the first person is understandable, because *should* (in all persons) has a number of uses which can clash with the conditional and the future in the past; sometimes the context does not make it clear, for example, whether *I should do* means 'it would be the case that I did' or 'I ought to do', e.g.

> *I wondered whether, when I was cross-examined,* I should *admit that I knew the defendant*

● This use of *I would* and *we would* is not, however, regarded as fully acceptable in formal language.

See also *I should* or *I would*.

singular or plural

1. When subject and complement are different in number (i.e. one is singular, the other plural), the verb normally agrees with the subject, e.g.

(Plural subject)

> *Ships* are *his chief interest*
> *Their wages* were *a mere pittance*
> *Liqueur chocolates* are *our speciality*

The Biblical *The wages of sin* is *death* reflects an obsolete idiom by which *wages* took a singular verb.

(Singular subject)

> *The ruling passion of his life* was *social relationships*
> *What we need* is *customers*
> *Our speciality* is *liqueur chocolates*

2. A plural word or phrase used as a name, title, or quotation counts as singular, e.g.

> Sons and Lovers has *always been one of Lawrence's most popular novels*
> Coloured persons is *the term applied to those of mixed white and native blood*

3. A singular phrase that happens to end with a plural word should nevertheless be followed by a singular verb, e.g.

> *Everyone except the French* wants (not *want*) *Britain to join*
> *One in six* has (not *have*) *this problem*

See also *-ics,* **nouns in, quantity, nouns of, -s plural or singular,** *what* **(relative pronoun).**

split infinitive

The split infinitive is the name given to the separation of *to* from the infinitive by means of an adverb (or sometimes an adverbial phrase), e.g. *He used* to continually refer *to the subject*. In this the adverb *continually* splits the infinitive *to refer* into two parts.

It is often said that an infinitive should never be split. This is an artificial rule that can produce unnecessarily contorted sentences. Rather, it is recommended that a split infinitive should be avoided by placing the adverb before or after the infinitive, unless this leads to clumsiness or ambiguity. If it does, one should either allow the split infinitive to stand, or recast the sentence.

1. Good writers usually avoid splitting the infinitive by placing the adverb before the infinitive:

> *I am not able, and I do not want*, completely to abandon *the world-view that I acquired in childhood* (George Orwell)
> *One meets people who have learned* actually to prefer *the tinned fruit to the fresh* (C. S. Lewis)
> *He did not want* positively to suggest *that she was dominant* (Iris Murdoch)

On the other hand, it is quite natural in speech, and permissible in writing, to say:

> *What could it be like* to actually live *in France?*
> To really let *the fact that these mothers were mothers sink in*
>   (Both examples from Kingsley Amis)
> *Only one thing stops me from jumping up and screaming . . , it is* to deliberately think *myself back into that hot light* (Doris Lessing)

2. Avoidance of ambiguity.

When an adverb closely qualifies the infinitive verb it may often be better to split the infinitive than to move the adverb to another position. The following example is ambiguous in writing, though in speech stress on certain words would make the meaning clear:

> *It fails completely to carry conviction*

Either it means 'It totally fails . .', in which case *completely* should precede *fails*, or it means 'It fails to carry complete conviction', in which case that should be written, or the infinitive should be split.

3. Avoidance of clumsiness.

> *It took more than an excited elderly man . . socially to discompose him . .* (Anthony Powell)

In this example *socially* belongs closely with *discompose*: it is not 'to discompose in a social way' but 'to cause social discomposure' or 'to

destroy social composure'. There are quite a number of adverb +
verb collocations of this kind. When they occur in the infinitive, it
may be better either to split the infinitive or to recast the sentence
than to separate the adverb from the verb.

4. Unavoidable split infinitive.

There are certain adverbial constructions which must immediately
precede the verb and therefore split the infinitive, e.g. *more than*:

> *Enough new ships are delivered* to more than make up *for the old
> ones being retired*

And a writer may have sound stylistic reasons for allowing a parenthetic expression to split an infinitive:

> *It would be an act of gratuitous folly* to, as he had put it to Mildred,
> make *trouble for himself at this stage* (Iris Murdoch)

-s plural or singular

Some nouns, though they have the plural ending -s, are nevertheless
treated as singulars, taking singular verbs and pronouns referring
back to them.

1. *News*

2. Diseases:

measles	*mumps*	*rickets*	*shingles*

Measles and *rickets* can also be treated as ordinary plural nouns.

3. Games:

billiards	*dominoes*	*ninepins*
bowls	*draughts*	*skittles*
darts	*fives*	

4. Countries:

the Bahamas	*the Philippines*
the Netherlands	*the United States*

These are treated as singular when considered as a unit, which they
commonly are in a political context, or when the complement is
singular, e.g.

> *The Philippines* is *a predominantly agricultural country*
> *The United States* has *withdrawn its ambassador*

The Bahamas and *the Philippines* are also the geographical names of the groups of islands which the two nations comprise, and in this use can be treated as plurals, e.g.

The Bahamas were *settled by British subjects*

Flanders and *Wales* are always singular. So are the city names *Athens*, *Brussels*, *Naples*, etc.

See also *-ics,* **nouns in**.

subjects joined by (*either . .*) *or*

When two singular subjects (either may be a noun, a pronoun, or a noun phrase) are joined by *or* or *either . . or*, the strict rule is that they require a singular verb and singular pronouns, since *or* (or *either . . or*) indicates that only one of them is the logical subject:

Either Peter or John has *had* his *breakfast already*
A traffic warden or a policeman is *always on the watch in this street*

However, 'at all times there has been a tendency to use the plural with two or more singular subjects when their mutual exclusion is not emphasized' (*OED*), e.g.

On which rage or wantonness vented themselves (George Eliot)

When one of the subjects joined by *or* is plural, it is best to put the verb in the plural, and place the plural subject nearer to the verb:

Either the child or the parents are *to blame*

When one subject is *I, we,* or *you*, and the other is a noun or a third person pronoun, or when the subjects are *you* and *I*, the verb is usually made to agree with the nearer of the two subjects:

Either he or I am *going to win*
Either he or you have *got to give in*
Either you or your teacher has *made a mistake*

This form of expression very often sounds awkward, especially when the sentence is a question:

Am *I or he going to win?*
Is *he or we wrong?*

It is usually best to recast the sentence by adding another verb:

Am I going to win, or is he?
Is he wrong, or are we?
Either he has got to give in, or you have

subjunctive

The subjunctive mood is indicated by the basic form of the verb, a form that is identical with the bare infinitive and imperative. In most verbs, e.g. *do*, *give*, and *make*, this will be the same as all the persons of the present tense except the third, which ends in *-s*. In the verb *to be*, however, the subjunctive is *be*, whereas the present tense is *am*, *are*, or *is*. For the past subjunctive of *to be* (*were*) see **were or was**.

The subjunctive is normal, and quite familiar, in a number of fixed expressions which cause no problems:

Be *that as it may*	*Heaven* help *us*
Come *what may*	*Long* live *the Queen*
God bless *you*	*So* be *it*
God save *the Queen*	Suffice *it to say that*
Heaven forbid	

There are two other uses of the subjunctive that may cause difficulty, but they are entirely optional. This means that the ordinary user of English need not be troubled by the use of the subjunctive, apart from the past subjunctive *were*.

1. In *that*-clauses after words expressing command, hope, intention, wish, etc. Typical introducing words are

be adamant that	*propose that*
demand that	*proposal that*
insist that	*resolve that*
be insistent that	*suggest that*
insistence that	*suggestion that*

Typical examples are:

> *He had been insisting that they* keep *the night of the twenty-second free* (C. P. Snow)
>
> *Joseph was insistent that his wishes* be *carried out* (W. Somerset Maugham)
>
> *Chance . . dictated that I* be *reading Sterne when . . Bellow's new novel arrived* (Frederic Raphael)
>
> *Your suggestion that I* fly *out* (David Lodge)

Until recently this use of the subjunctive was restricted to very formal language, where it is still usual, e.g.

> *The Lord Chancellor put the motion that the House* go *into Committee*

It is, however, a usual American idiom, and is now quite acceptable in British English, but there is no necessity to use the subjunctive in such contexts. *Should* or *may* with the infinitive, or (especially in informal use) the ordinary indicative, depending on the context, will do equally well:

> *Your demand that he* should *pay the money back surprised him*
> *I insist that the boy* goes *to school this minute*

● Beware of constructions in which the sense hangs on a fine distinction between subjunctive and indicative, e.g.

> *The most important thing for Argentina is that Britain* recognize *her sovereignty over the Falklands*

The implication is that Britain does not recognize it. A small slip that changed *recognize* to *recognizes* would disastrously reverse this implication. The use of *should recognize* would render the sense quite unmistakable.

2. In certain concessive and conditional clauses, i.e. clauses introduced by *though* and *if*, the subjunctive can be used to express reserve on the part of the speaker about an action or state which is contemplated or in prospect, e.g.

> *Though he* be *the devil himself he shall do as I say*
> *Though your sins* be *as scarlet, they shall be as white as snow* (Authorized Version)
> *It is a fine thing if a man* endure *the pain of undeserved suffering* (NEB)
> *The University is a place where a poor man, if he* be *virtuous, may live a life of dignity and simplicity* (A. C. Benson)
> *If this* be *true, then we are all to blame*

As the examples show, this is restricted to very formal and exalted language. It should not be used in ordinary prose, where sometimes the indicative and sometimes an auxiliary such as *may* are entirely acceptable, e.g.

> *Though he* may be *an expert, he should listen to advice*
> *If this* is *the case, then I am in error*

than, case following

A personal pronoun following *than* should have the case that it would have if a verb were supplied. In the following sentences, the subjective case is required because the personal pronoun would be the subject:

> *Other people have failed to grasp this, people much cleverer than* I (in full, *than I am*)
>
> *We pay more rent than* they (in full, *than they do*)

In the sentence below, the objective case is used, because the pronoun would be the object if there were a verb:

> *Jones treated his wife badly. I think that he liked his dog better than* her (in full, *than he liked her*)

Informal English permits the objective case to be used, no matter what case the pronoun would have if a verb were supplied:

> *You do it very well. Much better than* me

This is unacceptable in formal usage. The preferred alternative, with the subjective, often sounds stilted. When this is so, it can be avoided by supplying the verb:

> *We pay more rent than* they do

The interrogative and relative pronoun *whom* is always used after *than*, rather than the subjective form *who*:

> *Professor Smith*, than whom *there is scarcely anyone better qualified to judge*, *believes it to be pre-Roman*

that (conjunction), omission of

1. The conjunction *that* introducing a noun clause and used after verbs of saying, thinking, knowing, etc., can often be omitted in informal usage:

> *I told him* (that) *he was wrong*
>
> *He knew* (that) *I was right*
>
> *Are you sure* (that) *this is the place?*

Generally speaking, the omission of *that* confers a familiar tone on the sentence, and is not usually appropriate in formal prose.

That should never be omitted if other parts of the sentence (apart from the indirect object) intervene:

> *I told him, as I have told everyone*, that *he was wrong*
>
> *Are you sure in your own mind* that *this is the place?*

The omission of *that* makes it difficult, in written prose, to follow the sense.

2. When the conjunction *that* is part of the correlative pairs of conjunctions *so . . that* and *such . . that*, or of the compound conjunctions *so that*, *now that*, it can be omitted in informal usage.

● It should not be omitted in formal style:

> *He walked so fast* (or *at such a speed*) that *I could not keep up*
> *I'll move my car so* that *you can park in the drive*
> *Are you lonely now* that *your children have left home?*

that (relative pronoun), omission of

The relative pronoun *that* can often be omitted. Its omission is much more usual informally than formally.

In formal contexts the omission of *that* is best limited to relative clauses which are fairly short and which stand next to their antecedents:

> *The best thing* (that) *you can do is make up for lost time*
> *None of the cars* (that) *I saw had been damaged*
> *Nothing* (that) *I could say made any difference*

That cannot be omitted when it is the subject of the relative clause, e.g.

> *Nothing* that *occurred to me made any difference*
> *None of the cars* that *were under cover had been damaged*

See also **adverbial relative clauses** and **way, relative clause following**.

there is or *there are*

In a sentence introduced by *there* + part of the verb *to be*, the latter agrees in number with the noun, noun phrase, or pronoun which follows:

> *There was a great deal to be said for this scheme*
> *There are many advantages in doing it this way*

In very informal language *there is* or *there was* is often heard before a plural:

> *There's two coloured-glass windows in the chapel* (Character in work by Evelyn Waugh)

● This is non-standard.

to

The preposition *to* can stand at the end of a clause or sentence as a substitute for an omitted *to*-infinitive, e.g.

> *He had tried not to think about Emma . . , but of course it was impossible not* to (Iris Murdoch)
> *I gave him her message, as I should have been obliged* to *if she had died* (C. P. Snow)

This is standard usage.

unattached phrases

An adjectival or adverbial phrase, introducing a sentence, must qualify the subject of the sentence, e.g.

> While not entirely in agreement with the plan, *he had no serious objections to it*
> After two days on a life-raft, *the survivors were rescued by helicopter*

The introductory phrases *While . . plan* and *After . . life-raft* qualify the subjects *he* and *the survivors* respectively.

It is a common error to begin a sentence with a phrase of this kind, anticipating a suitable subject, and then to continue the sentence with a quite different subject, e.g.

> After six hours without food in a plane on the perimeter at Heathrow, *the flight was cancelled*

The phrase *After . . Heathrow* anticipates a subject like *the passengers*: a flight cannot spend six hours without food in a plane on an airport perimeter. Such a sentence should either have a new beginning, e.g.

> *After* the passengers had spent *six hours . .*

or a new main clause, e.g.

> *After six hours . . Heathrow*, the passengers learnt that *the flight had been cancelled*

used to

The negative and interrogative of *used to* can be formed in two ways:

(i) Negative: *used not to*
   Interrogative: *used X to?*

This formation follows the pattern of the other auxiliary verbs.

Examples:

> *Used you to beat your mother?* (G. B. Shaw)
> *You used not to have a moustache, used you?* (Evelyn Waugh)

(ii) Negative: *did not use to, didn't use to*

> Interrogative: *did X use to?*

This formation is the same as that used with regular verbs.

Examples:

> *She didn't use to find sex revolting* (John Braine)
> *Did you use to be a flirt?* (Eleanor Farjeon)

□ Either form is acceptable. On the whole *used you to*, *used he to*, etc. tend to sound rather stilted.

● The correct spellings of the negative forms are:

> *usedn't to* and *didn't use to*

not:

> *usen't to* and *didn't used to*

way, relative clause following

(*The*) *way* can be followed by a relative clause with or without *that*. There is no need for the relative clause to contain the preposition *in*:

> *It may have been* the way he smiled (Jean Rhys)
> *Whatever* way they happened *would be an ugly way* (Iris Murdoch)
> *She couldn't give a dinner party* the way the young lad's mother could (William Trevor)

were or was

There is often confusion about whether to use the past subjunctive *were* or the past indicative *was*.

Formal usage requires *were*

1. In conditional sentences where the condition is 'unreal', e.g.

> *It would probably be more marked if the subject* were *more dangerous* (George Orwell)
> (The condition is unreal because 'the subject' is not very 'dangerous' in fact)

If anyone were *to try to save me, I would refuse* (Jean Rhys)
(The condition is regarded as unlikely)

2. Following *as if* and *as though*, e.g.

He wore it with an air of melancholy, as though it were *court mourning* (Evelyn Waugh)
(For a permissible exception see p. 93)

3. In *that*-clauses after *to wish*, e.g.

I wish I were *going instead of you*

4. In the fixed expressions *As it were, If I were you*

Notice that in all these constructions the clause with *were* refers to something unreal, something that in fact is not or will not be the case.

Were may also be used in dependent questions, where there is doubt of the answer, e.g.

Hilliard wondered whether Barton were *not right after all* (Susan Hill)
Her mother suddenly demanded to know if she were *pregnant* (Joyce Cary)

□ This is not obligatory even in very formal prose. *Was* is acceptable instead.

we (with phrase following)

Expressions consisting of *we* or *us* followed by a qualifying word or phrase, e.g. *we English, us English*, are often misused with the wrong case of the first person plural pronoun. In fact the rules are exactly the same as for *we* or *us* standing alone.

If the expression is the subject, *we* should be used:

(Correct)   *Not always laughing as heartily as* we English *are supposed to do* (J. B. Priestley)
(Incorrect) *We all make mistakes, even* us anarchists (Character in work by Alison Lurie) (Substitute *we anarchists*)

If the expression is the object or the complement of a preposition, *us* should be used:

(Correct)   *To* us English, *Europe is not a very vivid conception*
(Incorrect) *The Manchester Guardian has said some nice things about* we in the North-East

what (relative pronoun)

What can be used as a relative pronoun only when introducing nominal relative clauses, e.g.

> *So much of* what you tell me *is strange, different from* what I was led to expect (Jean Rhys)

In this kind of relative clause, the antecedent and relative pronoun are combined in the one word *what*, which can be regarded as equivalent to *that which* or *the thing(s) which*.

● *What* cannot act as a relative pronoun qualifying an antecedent in standard English. This use is found only in non-standard speech, e.g.

> *The young gentleman* what's *arranged everything* (Character in work by Evelyn Waugh)

A *what*-clause used as the subject of a sentence almost always takes a singular verb, even if there is a plural complement, e.g.

> *What one first became aware of* was *the pictures* (J. I. M. Stewart)
> *What interests him* is *less events . . than the reverberations they set up* (Frederic Raphael)

Very occasionally the form of the sentence may render the plural more natural, e.g.

> *What once were great houses* are *now petty offices*
> *I have few books, and what there are* do *not help me*

which or *that* (relative pronouns)

There is a degree of uncertainty about whether to use *which* or *that* as the relative pronoun qualifying a non-personal antecedent (for personal antecedents see *who/whom* or *that*).

The general rule is that *which* is used in relative clauses to which the reader's attention is to be drawn, while *that* is used in clauses which mention what is already known or does not need special emphasis.

Which is almost always used in non-restrictive clauses, i.e. those that add further information about an antecedent already defined by other words or the context. Examples:

> *The men are getting rum issue*, which they deserve (Susan Hill)
> *Narrow iron beds with blue rugs on them*, which *Miss Fanshawe has to see are all kept tidy* (William Trevor)

● The use of *that* in non-restrictive clauses should be avoided. It is not uncommon in informal speech, and is sometimes employed by good writers to suggest a tone of familiarity, e.g.

> *Getting out of Alec's battered old car* that *looked as if it had been in collision with many rocks, Harold had a feeling of relief* (L. P. Hartley)

It should not, however, be used in ordinary prose.

Both *which* and *that* can be used in restrictive relative clauses, i.e. clauses that limit or define the antecedent.

There is no infallible rule to determine which should be used. Some guidelines follow:

1. *Which* preferred.

(*a*) Clauses which add significant information often sound better with *which*, e.g.

> *Was I counting on Israel to work some miracle* which *would give me the strength?* (Lynne Reid Banks)
> *Not nearly enough for the social position* which *they had to keep up* (D. H. Lawrence)

(*b*) Clauses which are separated from their antecedent, especially when separated by another noun, sound better with *which*, e.g.

> *Larry told her the story of the young airman* which *I narrated at the beginning of this book* (W. Somerset Maugham)

(*c*) When a preposition governs the relative pronoun, *which* preceded by the preposition is often a better choice than *that* with the preposition at the end of the sentence (see also **preposition at end**), e.g.

> *I'm telling you about a dream* in which *ordinary things are marvellous* (William Trevor)
> (*A dream that ordinary things are marvellous in* would not sound natural)
>
> *The inheritance* to which *we are born is one that nothing can destroy* (NEB)
> (*The inheritance that we are born to* would sound very informal and unsuited to the context)

2. *That* preferred.

In clauses that do not fall into the above categories *that* can usually be used. There is no reason to reject *that* if

(*a*) the antecedent is impersonal,
(*b*) the clause is restrictive,
(*c*) no preposition precedes the relative pronoun, and
(*d*) the sentence does not sound strained or excessively colloquial.

Examples:

> *I read the letters, none of them very revealing,* that *littered his writing table* (Evelyn Waugh)
> *He fell back on the old English courtesy* that *he had consciously perfected to combat the increasing irritability* that *came with old age and arthritis* (Angus Wilson)

In these examples, *which* would be acceptable, but is not necessary.

When the antecedent is an indefinite pronoun (e.g. *anything, everything, nothing, something*) or contains a superlative adjective qualifying the impersonal antecedent (e.g. *the biggest car, the most expensive hat*) English idiom tends to prefer *that* to *which*:

> *Is there nothing small* that *the children could buy you for Christmas?*
> *This is the most expensive hat* that *you could have bought*

Note that *that* can sometimes be used when one is not sure whether to use *who* or *which*:

> *This was the creature, neither child nor woman,* that *drove me through the dusk that summer evening* (Evelyn Waugh)

who and *whom* (interrogative and relative pronouns)

1. Formal usage restricts the use of the interrogative and relative pronoun *who* to the subject of the clause only, e.g.

> *I* who'*d never read anything before but the newspaper* (W. Somerset Maugham)

When the pronoun is the object or the complement of a preposition, *whom* must be used:

> *Why are we being served by a man* whom *neither of us likes?* (William Trevor)
> *The real question is food (or freedom) for* whom (C. S. Lewis)
> *A midget nobleman to* whom *all doors were open* (Evelyn Waugh)

● The use of *who* as object or prepositional complement is acceptable informally, but should not be carried over into serious prose, e.g.

Who *are you looking for?*
The person who *I'm looking for is rather elusive*

See also *than,* **case following**.

2. *Whom* for *who.*

Whom is sometimes mistakenly used for *who* because the writer believes it to be the object, or the complement of a preposition.

(*a*) For the interrogative pronoun the rule is: the case of the pronoun *who/whom* is determined by its role in the interrogative clause, not by any word in the main clause:

> *He never had any doubt about* who *was the real credit to the family* (J. I. M. Stewart)

Who here is the subject of *was*. One should not be confused by *about*, which governs the whole clause, not *who* alone.

The error is seen in:

> Whom *among our poets . . could be called one of the interior decorators of the 1950s?*
> (Read *Who . .* because it is the subject of the passive verb *be called*)

Whom is correct in:

> *He knew* whom *it was from* (L. P. Hartley)
> (Here *whom* is governed by *from*)

> Whom *he was supposed to be fooling, he couldn't imagine* (David Lodge)
> (Here *whom* is the object of *fooling*)

(*b*) For the relative pronoun, when followed by a parenthetic clause such as *they say*, *he thinks*, *I believe*, etc., the rule is: the case of the pronoun *who/whom* is determined by the part it plays in the relative clause if the parenthetic statement is omitted:

> *Sheikh Yamani* who *they say is the richest man in the Middle East*
> (Not *whom they say* since *who* is the subject of *is*, not the object of *say*)

But *whom* is correct in:

> *Sheikh Yamani* whom *they believe to be the richest man in the Middle East*

Here *they believe* is not parenthetic, since it could not be removed leaving the sentence intact. *Whom* is its object: the simple clause would be *They believe* him to be *the richest man*.

See also *I who, you who,* etc.

who or *which* (relative pronouns)

If a *wh*-pronoun is used to introduce a relative clause it must be *who* (*whom*) if the antecedent is personal, e.g.

> *Suzanne was a woman* who *had no notion of reticence* (W. Somerset Maugham)

But it must be *which* if the antecedent is non-personal. e.g.

> *There was a suppressed tension about her* which *made me nervous* (Lynne Reid Banks)

If the relative clause is non-restrictive, i.e. it adds significant new information about an antecedent already defined, the *wh*-type of pronoun *must* be used (as above).

If the relative clause is restrictive, i.e. it defines or limits the reference of the antecedent, one can use either the appropriate *wh*-pronoun (as indicated above), or the non-variable pronoun *that*. For guidance about this choice see *which* or *that* (relative pronouns) and *who/whom* or *that* (relative pronouns).

whose or *of which* in relative clauses

The relative pronoun *whose* can be used as the possessive of *which*, i.e. with reference to a non-personal antecedent, just as much as it can as the possessive of *who*. The rule sometimes enunciated that *of which* must always be used after a non-personal antecedent should be ignored, as it is by good writers, e.g.

> *The little book* whose *yellowish pages she knew* (Virginia Woolf)
> *A robe* whose *weight and stiff folds expressed her repose* (Evelyn Waugh)
> *A narrow side street,* whose *windows had flower boxes and painted shutters* (Doris Lessing)

In some sentences, *of which* would be almost impossible, e.g.

> *The lawns about* whose *closeness of cut his father worried the gardener daily* (Susan Hill)

There is, of course, no rule prohibiting *of which* if it sounds natural, e.g.

> *A little town the name* of which *I have forgotten* (W. Somerset Maugham)

Whose can only be used as the non-personal possessive in *relative* clauses. Interrogative *whose* refers only to persons, as in *Whose book is this?*

who/whom or that (relative pronouns)

In formal usage, *who/whom* is always acceptable as the relative pronoun following an antecedent that denotes a person. (For the choice between *who* and *whom* see **who and whom (interrogative and relative pronouns).**

In non-restrictive relative clauses, i.e. those which add significant new information about an antecedent already defined, *who/whom* is obligatory, e.g.

> *It was not like Coulter,* who *was a cheerful man* (Susan Hill)

In restrictive relative clauses, i.e those which define or limit the reference of the antecedent, *who/whom* is usually quite acceptable:

> *The masters* who *taught me Divinity told me that biblical texts were highly untrustworthy* (Evelyn Waugh)

It is generally felt that the relative pronoun *that* is more impersonal than *who/whom*, and is therefore slightly depreciatory if applied to a person. Hence it tends to be avoided in formal usage.

However, if

(i) the relative pronoun is the object, and
(ii) the personality of the antecedent is suppressed

that may well be appropriate, e.g.

> *Then the woman* that *they actually caught and pinned down would not have been Margot* (Evelyn Waugh)
> *They looked now just like the GIs* that *one saw in Viet Nam* (David Lodge)

Informally *that* is acceptable with any personal antecedent, e.g.

> *You got it from the man* that *stole the horse* (G. B. Shaw)
> *Honey, it's me* that *should apologize* (David Lodge)

● This should be avoided in formal style.

you and *I* or *you* and *me*

When a personal pronoun is linked by *and* or *or* to a noun or another pronoun there is often confusion about which case to put the pronoun in. In fact the rule is exactly as it would be for the pronoun standing alone.

1. If the two words linked by *and* or *or* constitute the subject, the pronoun should be in the subjective case, e.g.

> *Only* she *and her mother cared for the old house*
> *That's what we would do, that is, John* and I
> *Who could go?—Either you or* he

The use of the objective case is quite common in informal speech, but it is non-standard, e.g. (examples from the speech of characters in novels)

> *Perhaps only* her *and Mrs Natwick had stuck to the christened name* (Patrick White)
> *That's how we look at it*, me *and Martha* (Kingsley Amis)
> *Either Mary had to leave or* me (David Lodge)

2. If the two words linked by *and* or *or* constitute the object of the verb, or the complement of a preposition, the objective case must be used:

> *The afternoon would suit* her *and John better*
> *It was time for Sebastian and* me *to go down to the drawing-room* (Evelyn Waugh)

The use of the subjective case is very common informally. It probably arises from an exaggerated fear of the error indicated under 1 above.

● It remains, however, non-standard, e.g.

> *It was this that set Charles and* I *talking of old times*
> *Why is it that people like you and* I *are so unpopular?* (Character in work by William Trevor)
> *Between you and* I

This last expression is very commonly heard. *Between you and me* should always be substituted.

PRINCIPLES OF PUNCTUATION

apostrophe

1. Used to indicate the possessive case: see pp. 29 f.

2. Used to mark an omission, e.g. *e'er, we'll, he's, '69.*

● Sometimes written, but unnecessary, in a number of curtailed words, e.g. *bus, cello, flu, phone, plane* (not *'bus*, etc.). See also p. 28.

brackets

See: 1. **parentheses.**
     2. **square brackets.**

colon

1. Links two grammatically complete clauses, but marks a step forward, from introduction to main theme, from cause to effect, or from premiss to conclusion, e.g. *To commit sin is to break God's law: sin, in fact, is lawlessness.*

2. Introduces a list of items (a dash should not be added), e.g. *The following were present: J. Smith, J. Brown, P. Thompson, M. Jones.*
   It is used after such expressions as *for example, namely, the following, to resume, to sum up.*

comma

The least emphatic separating mark of punctuation, used:

1. Between adjectives which each qualify a noun in the same way, e.g. *A cautious, eloquent man.*
But when adjectives qualify the noun in different ways, or when one adjective qualifies another, no comma is used, e.g. *A distinguished foreign author, a bright red tie.*

2. To separate items (including the last) in a list of more than two items, e.g. *Potatoes, peas, and carrots; Potatoes, peas, or carrots; Potatoes, peas, etc.; Red, white, and blue.*

● But *A black and white TV set.*

3. To separate co-ordinated main clauses, e.g. *Cars will turn here,*

and coaches will go straight on. But not when they are closely linked, e.g. *Do as I tell you and you'll never regret it.*

4. To mark the beginning and end of a parenthetical word or phrase, e.g. *I am sure, however, that it will not happen*; *Fred, who is bald, complained of the cold.*

● Not with restrictive relative clauses, e.g. *Men who are bald should wear hats.*

5. After a participial or verbless clause, a salutation, or a vocative, e.g. *Having had breakfast, I went for a walk*; *The sermon over, the congregation filed out* or *The sermon being over,* (etc.); *My son, give me thy heart.*

● Not *The sermon, being over,* (etc.)

● No comma with expressions like *My friend Lord X* or *My son John.*

6. To separate a phrase or subordinate clause from the main clause so as to avoid misunderstanding, e.g. *In the valley below, the villages looked very small*; *He did not go to church, because he was playing golf*; *In 1982, 1918 seemed a long time ago.*

● A comma should not be used to separate a phrasal subject from its predicate, or a verb from an object that is a clause: *A car with such a high-powered engine, should not let you down* and *They believed, that nothing could go wrong* are both incorrect.

7. Following words introducing direct speech, e.g. *They answered, 'Here we are.'*

8. Following *Dear Sir, Dear John,* etc., in letters, and after *Yours sincerely,* etc.

● No comma is needed between month and year in dates, e.g. *In December 1982* or between number and road in addresses, e.g. *12 Acacia Avenue.*

dash

1. The *en rule* is distinct (in print) from the **hyphen** (see pp. 14 ff.) and is used to join pairs or groups of words wherever movement or tension, rather than co-operation or unity, is felt: it is often equivalent to *to* or *versus*, e.g. *The 1914–18 war*; *current–voltage characteristic*; *The London–Horsham–Brighton route*; *The Fischer–Spassky match*; *The Marxist–Trotskyite split.*

● Note *The Marxist-Leninist position*; *The Franco-Prussian war* with hyphens.

It is also used for joint authors, e.g. *The Lloyd–Jones hypothesis* (two men), distinct from *The Lloyd-Jones hypothesis* (one man with double-barrelled name).

2. The *em rule* (the familiar dash) is used to mark an interruption in the structure of a sentence. A pair of them can be used to enclose a parenthetic remark or to make the ending and resumption of a statement interrupted by an interlocutor; e.g. *He was not—you may disagree with me, Henry—much of an artist*; '*I didn't—*' '*Speak up, boy!*' '*—hear anything; I was just standing near by.*' It can be used informally to replace the **colon** (use 1).

exclamation mark

Used after an exclamatory word, phrase, or sentence. It usually counts as the concluding full stop, but need not, e.g. *Hail source of Being! universal Soul!* It may also be used within square brackets, after a quotation, to express the editor's amusement, dissent, or surprise.

full stop

1. Used at the end of all sentences which are not questions or exclamations. The next word should normally begin with a capital letter.

2. Used after **abbreviations**: see pp. 1 f. If a point making an abbreviation comes at the end of a sentence, it also serves as the closing full stop, e.g. *She also kept dogs, cats, birds, etc.* but *She also kept pets (dogs, cats, birds, etc.).*

3. When a sentence concludes with a quotation which itself ends with a full stop, question mark, or exclamation mark, no further full stop is needed, e.g. *He cried 'Be off!' But the child would not move.* But if the quotation is a short statement, and the introducing sentence has much greater weight, the full stop is put outside the quotation marks, e.g. *Over the entrance to the temple at Delphi were written the words 'Know thyself'.*

hyphen: see pp. 14 ff.

parentheses

Enclose:

1. Interpolations and remarks made by the writer of the text himself, e.g. *Mr. X (as I shall call him) now spoke.*

2. An authority, definition, explanation, reference, or translation.

3. In the report of a speech, interruptions by the audience.

4. Reference letters or figures (which do not then need a full stop), e.g. (1), (*a*).

period: see **full stop**.

question mark

1. Follows every question which expects a separate answer. The next word should begin with a capital letter.

● Not used after indirect questions, e.g. *He asked me why I was there.*

2. May be placed before a word, etc., whose accuracy is doubted, e.g. *T. Tallis ?1505–85.*

quotation marks

1. Single quotation marks are used for a first quotation; double for a quotation within this; single again for a further quotation inside that.

2. The closing quotation mark should come before all punctuation marks unless these form part of the quotation itself, e.g. *Did Nelson really say* 'Kiss me, Hardy'? but *Then she asked* 'What is your name?' (see also **full stop,** 3).

The comma at the end of a quotation, when words such as *he said* follow, is regarded as equivalent to the final full stop of the speaker's utterance, and is kept inside the quotation, e.g. '*That is nonsense,*' *he said.* The commas on either side of *he said,* etc., when these words interrupt the quotation, should be outside the quotation marks, e.g. '*That*', *he said,* '*is nonsense.*' But the first comma goes inside the quotation marks if it would be part of the utterance even if there were no interruption, e.g. '*That, my dear fellow,*' *he said,* '*is nonsense.*'

3. Quotation marks (and roman type) are used when citing titles of articles in magazines, chapters of books, poems not published separately, and songs.

● Not for titles of books of the Bible; nor for any passage that represents only the substance of an extract, or has any grammatical alterations, and is not a verbatim quotation.

Titles of books and magazines are usually printed in italic.

semicolon

Separates those parts of a sentence between which there is a more distinct break than would call for a comma, but which are too closely connected to be made into separate sentences. Typically these will be clauses of similar importance and grammatical construction, e.g. *To err is human; to forgive, divine.*

square brackets

Enclose comments, corrections, explanations, interpolations, notes, or translations, which were not in the original text, but have been added by subsequent authors, editors, or others, e.g. *My right honourable friend [John Smith] is mistaken.*

CLICHÉS AND MODISH AND INFLATED DICTION

A CLICHÉ is a phrase that has become worn out and emptied of meaning by over-frequent and careless use. Never to use clichés at all would be impossible: they are too common, and too well embedded in the fabric of the language. On many occasions they can be useful in communicating simple ideas economically, and are often a means of conveying general sociability. When writing serious prose, however, in which clear and precise communication is intended, one should guard against allowing clichés to do the work which the words of one's own choosing could do better. 'Modish and inflated diction' is a rough and ready way of referring to a body of words and phrases that is familiar, but hard to delineate and delimit. In origin some of these expressions are often scientific or technical and are, in their original context, assigned a real and useful meaning; others are the creation of popular writers and broadcasters. What they all have in common is their grip on the popular mind, so that they have come to be used in all kinds of general contexts where they are unnecessary, ousting ordinary words that are better but sound less impressive. As their popularity and frequency increases, so their real denotative value drains away, a process that closely resembles monetary inflation. As with clichés, it would be difficult, and not necessarily desirable, to ban these expressions from our usage completely, but, again, one should carefully guard against using them either because they sound more learned and up to date than the more commonplace words in one's vocabulary, or as a short cut in communicating ideas that would be better set out in simple, clear, basic vocabulary.

The list that follows does not claim to be an exhaustive collection of clichés or of modish diction, but presents some contemporary expressions which are most frequently censured and are avoided by good writers.

actual (tautologous or meaningless, e.g. *Is this an actual Roman coin?*)
actually (as a filler, e.g. *Actually it's time I was going*)
articulate (verb = express)
at the end of the day
at this moment (or *point*) *in time*
-awareness (e.g. *brand-awareness*)

ball game (*a different*, etc., ——)
basically (as a filler)
by and large (sometimes used with no meaning)
-centred (e.g. *discovery-centred*)
conspicuous by one's absence
constructive (used tautologously, e.g. *A constructive suggestion*)
definitely
-deprivation (e.g. *status-deprivation*)
dialogue
dimension (= feature, factor)
-directed (e.g. *task-directed*)
dispense (= give)
environment
escalate (= increase, intensify)
eventuate (= result)
framework (in the framework of)
fresh (= new, renewed, etc.)
grind to a halt (= end, stop)
identify (= find, discover)
if you like (explanatory tag)
integrate, integrated
in terms of
in the order of (= about)
in this day and age
-ize (suffix, forming vogue words, e.g. *normalize, permanentize, prioritize, respectabilize*)
leave severely alone
life-style
look closely at
loved ones (= relatives)
low profile (*keep, or maintain, a* ——)
massive (= huge)
matrix
meaningful (can often be omitted without any change in meaning)
methodology (= method)
-minded (e.g. *company-minded*)
name of the game, the
-oriented (e.g. *marketing-oriented*)
overkill
participate in
persona (= character)
proliferation (= a number)

proposition
quantum jump
real (especially in *very real*)
-related (e.g. *church-related*)
simplistic (= oversimplified)
sort of (as a filler)
spell (= mean, involve)
target (figuratively used)
terminate (= end)
totality of, the
track-record (= record)
until such time as
utilize (= use)
viability
vibrant
you know (as a filler)
you name it

See also the entries in Section III for:

antithetical
author
aware
character
crucial
decimate
dichotomy
differential
dilemma
event (in the event that)
excess (in excess of)
exposure
feasible
following

hopefully
impact
industrial action
interface
ironic
limited
literally
locate
maximize
nature
neighbourhood (in the neighbourhood of)
no way
obligate

ongoing
overly
overview
parameter
pivotal
predicate
pre-empt
pristine
proportion
region (in the region of)
scenario
situation
substantial

APPENDIX III

ENGLISH OVERSEAS

OUTSIDE the United Kingdom and the Republic of Ireland, English is an important language in many countries, and the major language of four—the United States, Canada, Australia, and New Zealand—and of a large minority in another, South Africa. Despite the great distances separating these five English-speaking communities from each other and from the British Isles, and the great social and cultural differences between them, the forms of English which they use remain mutually intelligible to a remarkable degree. Partly this is because all English-speaking communities have held to a standard spelling system. There are a number of points of difference in spelling between the English of the United States and that of Britain (the other communities follow the British mode, except that many US spellings are usual, or acceptable, in Canada); but these are all relatively minor. The major differences are in pronunciation, vocabulary, and, to a lesser degree, grammar.

1. *The United States*

The main differences between General American pronunciation and British Received Pronunciation are set out on pp. 48–9. The General American accent is a supra-regional way of speaking acceptable throughout the country, but there are very marked differences of accent between different regions of the United States. Two varieties familiar in Great Britain are 'Brooklynese' (the New York City accent), in which *earl* and *oil* sound alike (the sound is somewhere between the two), and the southern 'drawl' (the accent of the states from Virginia southward) in which *I* and *time* sound like *ah* and *tahm*.

The difference in vocabulary between American and British English is too well known to need extensive illustration. Most British people are familiar with many American equivalents for British terms, e.g. *bathrobe* (dressing gown), *checkers* (draughts), *cookie* (biscuit), *elevator* (lift), *flyer* (handbill), *gas* (petrol), *vest* (waistcoat). It is not so often realized that many words and phrases now normal in Britain originated in North America, e.g. *to fall for*, *to fly off the handle*, *off-beat*, *punch line*, *quiz* (as a noun), *round trip*, *round-up*, *to snoop*. Nor is it fully realized how many words and phrases used every day in the United States are unknown, or nearly so, in Britain, and show no sign of being adopted here. Many, but not all, are colloquial, e.g. *realtor* (estate agent), *rotunda* (concourse), *running gear* (vehicle's wheels and axles), *sassy* (cheeky), *scam* (fraud), *scofflaw* (habitual law-breaker), *to second-guess* (be wise after the event), *tacky* (seedy, tatty). Many words have slightly different meanings in the United States, e.g. *jelly* (jam), *mean* (nasty, *not* stingy), *nervy* (impudent, *not* nervous). Some familiar words have a slightly different form, e.g. *behoove, crawfish, dollhouse, math, normalcy, rowboat, sanitarium* (British *sanatorium*), *tidbit*. There are some notable differences between American and British grammar and construction, e.g. *aside from* (apart from), *back of* (behind), *different than, in school, most* (almost), *protest* (protest against), *some* (to some extent), *through* (up to and including); *he ordered them arrested, I just ate* (I have just eaten), *to teach school, on the street, a quarter of ten*.

While, therefore, the formal and literary varieties of British and American English are mutually intelligible, the most colloquial spoken varieties of each are in some ways very different, and each can, in some contexts, be almost incomprehensible to a speaker of the other.

2. *Canada*

Canadian English is subject to the conflicting influences of British and American English. On the whole British English has a literary influence, while American has a spoken one. The Canadian accent is in most respects identical with General American. But where British English has four vowels in (i) *bat*, (ii) *dance, father*, (iii) *hot, long*, (iv) *law*, and General American three, Canadian has only two: *bat* and *dance* with a front *a*, and *father, hot, long*, and *law* with a back *ah*-sound. Peculiar to the Canadian accent is a distinction between two varieties of the *I*-sound and two of the *ow*-sound: *light* does not have the same vowel as *lied*, nor *lout* as *loud*. Canadians pronounce some words in the American way, e.g. *dance, half, clerk, tomato*, but others in the British way, e.g. *lever, ration, process, lieutenant*, and the name of the letter *Z*. Some American spellings have caught on, e.g. *honor, jail, plow, program, tire*, but many, such as *-er* in words like *center*, single *l* in *traveled, jeweler*, and the short *ax, catalog, check*, have not. In vocabulary there is much US influence: Canadians use *billboard, gas, truck, wrench* rather than *hoarding, petrol, lorry, spanner*; but on the other hand, they agree with the British in using *blinds, braces, porridge, tap*, rather than *shades, suspenders, oatmeal, faucet*. The Canadian vocabulary, like the American, reflects the contact between English and various American Indian peoples, e.g. *pekan* (a kind of weasel), *sagamite* (broth or porridge), *saskatoon* (a kind of bush, or its berry). It also reflects close contact with the large French-speaking community of Canada and with Eskimo peoples, e.g. *aboiteau* (dike), *inconnu* (a kind of fish), *to mush* (travel by dog-sled); *chimo* (an Eskimo greeting), *kuletuk* (a garment resembling a parka). And as there have been different degrees of settlement by the various non-English-speaking European nationalities in Canada than in the United States, so the range of European loan-words in Canadian English is markedly different, many American colloquialisms being unknown. On the other hand, there are several regional dialects that differ markedly from the standard language, notably that of Newfoundland.

3. *Australia and New Zealand*

There are no important differences in written form between the English of Great Britain and that of Australia, New Zealand, or indeed South Africa. The literary language of the four communities is virtually identical. Grammatically, too, the English of all four is uniform, except that each has developed its own colloquial idioms. Thus it is in the everyday spoken language that the main differences lie. The Australian accent is marked by a number of divergences from the British. (i) The vowels of *fleece*, *face*, *price*, *goose*, *goat*, and *mouth* all begin with rather open, slack sounds not unlike those used in Cockney speech. (ii) The vowels of *dress*, *strut*, *start*, *dance*, *nurse* have a much closer, tighter, more fronted sound than in RP. (iii) In unstressed syllables, typically -*es* or -*ed* (*boxes*, *studded*), where RP would have a sound like *i* in *pin*, Australian English has a sound like *e* in *open* or *a* in *comma*. (iv) In unstressed syllables, typically -*y*, or -*ie* + consonant (*study*, *studied*), where RP has the sound of *i* in *pin*, Australian English has a close -*ee* sound, as in *tree*. The result of (iii) and (iv) is that in Australia *boxes* and *boxers* sound the same, but *studded* and *studied*, which are the same in RP, sound different. (v) -*t*- between vowels, and *l*, are often sounded rather as they are in American English. A number of individual words are differently pronounced, e.g. *aquatic* and *auction* with an *o* sound as in *hot* in the stressed syllable; *Melbourne* with a totally obscured second syllable, but *Queensland* with a fully pronounced one (the reverse of the RP). Australian vocabulary reflects, of course, the very different nature of the landscape, climate, natural history, and way of life. Familiar English words like *brook*, *dale*, *field*, and *forest* are unusual, whereas *bush*, *creek*, *paddock*, and *scrub* are normal. There are of course a large number of terms (often compounded from English elements) for the plants and animals peculiar to the country, e.g. *blue gum*, *stringybark* (plants), *flathead*, *popeye mullet* (fish). The borrowings from Aboriginal languages hardly need extensive illustration; many are familiar in Britain, e.g. *billabong*, *boomerang*, *budgerigar*, *didgeridoo*, *wallaby*. Many of them have taken on transferred meanings and have lost their Aboriginal associations, e.g. *gibber* (boulder, stone), *mulga* (an inhospitable region), *warrigal* (wild, untamed person or animal). But above all it is in the colloquial language that Australian English differs from British. Not only are there terms relating to Australian life and society, e.g. *jackaroo*, *rouseabout*, *walkabout*, but ordinary terms, e.g. *to chiack* (tease), *crook* (bad, irritable, ill), *dinkum*, *furphy* (rumour), *to smoodge* (fawn, caress); formations and compounds like those ending in *-o* (e.g. *arvo* (afternoon), *Commo* (communist), *smoko* (teabreak)); *to overland*, *ratbag* (eccentric, troublemaker), *ropeable* (angry); and expressions like *come the raw prawn*, *she'll be right*, *have a shingle short*. While it is true that many Australianisms are known in Britain, and form the basis of various kinds of humorous entertainment, and while British English has borrowed some Australian vocabulary (e.g. the verb *to barrack* or the noun *walkabout*), there is yet a wide gap between the popular spoken forms of the two kinds of English.

The gap is less wide in the case of New Zealand English, where British influence has on the whole remained stronger. To a British ear, the New Zealand accent is hardly distinguishable from the Australian. Its main peculiarities are: (i) *i* as in *kit* is a very slack sound almost like *a* in *cadet*; (ii) *a* as in *trap* and *e* as in *dress* are almost like British *e* in *pep* and *i* in *this*; (iii) the vowels of *square* and *near* are very tense and close, and may even be sounded alike; (iv) the vowels of *smooth* and *nurse* are sounded forward in the mouth, and rather close. The chief differences between New Zealand and Australian English are lexical. The words of aboriginal origin are mostly unknown in New Zealand, while the New Zealand words drawn from Maori are unknown in Australia. Many of the latter, naturally, refer to natural history and landscape specific to the country, e.g. *bid-a-bid* (kind of plant), *cockabully*, *tarakihi* (kinds of fish), *pohutukawa* (kind of tree). There is a large everyday vocabulary, much of it, but by no means all, colloquial or slang, used neither in Britain nor in Australia, e.g. *booay* (remote rural district), *greenstone* (stone used for ornaments), *return to the mat* (resume Maori way of life), *shake* (earthquake), *tar-sealed* (surfaced with tar macadam), *Taranaki gate* (gate made of wire strands attached to upright battens). While a fair amount of colloquial vocabulary is shared by Australia and New Zealand (e.g. *sheila*, *Pommy*, *paddock* (field), *shout* (to treat to drinks)), there are important nuances. In both *to bach* is to live as a bachelor, but in New Zealand only is there a noun *bach*, a small beach or holiday house. Similar organizations are the *RSA* (Returned Servicemen's Association) in New Zealand, but the *RSL* (Returned Servicemen's League) in Australia; the initials of the one would be meaningless to a member of the other. *Mopoke* or *morepork* is the name for a kind of owl in New Zealand, but for either a nightjar, or a different kind of owl, in Australia.

4. *South Africa*

English is one of the two official languages of the Republic of South Africa, the other being Afrikaans (derived from Dutch, but now an entirely independent language). Afrikaans has had a fairly strong influence on the English of the Republic: the South African accent is distinctly 'clipped'; *r* is often rolled, and the consonants *p*, *t*, and *k* have a sharper articulation, usually lacking the aspiration (a faint *h* sound) found in other varieties of English. *I* is sometimes very lax (like *a* in *along*), e.g. in *bit*, *lip*, at other times very tense (like *ee*), e.g. in *kiss*, *big*; the vowels of *dress*, *trap*, *square*, *nurse* are very tense and close, while that of *part* is very far back, almost like *port*. As in the other forms of English of the Southern Hemisphere, the different landscape, flora and fauna, and way of life are reflected in the South African vocabulary, e.g. *dorp* (village), *go-away bird*, *kopje*, *nartjie* (tangerine), *rand*, *rhenosterbos* (a kind of plant), *roman*, *snoek* (both fish), *springbok*, *stoep* (veranda), *veld*. There are many loan-words from Afrikaans and African languages, e.g. (besides most of those above) *braai* (barbecue), *donga* (eroded watercourse), *erf* (building plot), *gogga* (insect), *impala* (kind of antelope), *indaba* (meeting for discussion), *lekker* (nice), *rondavel* (hut). There are also many general colloquial words and phrases, e.g. *the farm* (the country), *homeboy* (African from one's own area), *location* (Black township), *robot* (traffic light), *tackies* (plimsolls). Some of these reflect the influence of Afrikaans idiom, e.g. *to come there* (arrive), *just now* (in a little while), *land* (a field), *to wait on* (wait for). Only a few words have entered the main stream of English, but they are important ones, including *apartheid*, *commandeer*, *commando*, *laager*, *trek*, and the slang *scoff* (to eat; food).

The spoken language of each of the main English-speaking communities, as well as of the smaller communities scattered around the world, manifests enormous differences in pronunciation, vocabulary, and idiom. The relative uniformity of the written, and especially the literary, language, stands in tension with this. The outcome is a world language of unparalleled richness and variety.

SUBJECT INDEX

WORD INDEX

Words and phrases are entered in strict alphabetical order, ignoring spaces between two or more words forming a compound or phrase (hence *as for* follows *ascendant* and *court martial* follows *courtesy*).

An asterisk is placed in front of forms or spellings that are not recommended; reference to the page(s) indicated will show the reason for this ruling in each case.

ampere 35
amphitheatre 30
*amuck 35
amusedly 52
an 4, 5, 139
*analog 11
analogous 54, 71, 91
analysable 9
analyse 34
analysis 27
and 26, 145, 170, 191
androgynous 54
anger 56
Anglicism 6
Anglicize 7
annex 35
annexe 35
annul 20
annulment 20
Antarctic 71
antechamber 4
anticipate 91
anti-Darwinian 17
anti-g 16
antiquary 71
antique 144
antithesis 27
antithetical 92
antitype 4
anxiety 62
anxious 62
any 149
anybody 149
any one 35, 119
anyone 35, 149
anything 56, 156, 187
any time 35
any way 35
anyway 35
apache 71
apartheid 71, 205
apologetics 153
apophthegm 35, 55, 58, 71
apophthegmatic 55
*apothegm 36
apostasy 36
appal 20
apparatus 47, 71
appendix 27
appetite 20
appetize 19
applicable 66, 71
appliquéd 13
appliquéing 13
apposite 71
appreciate 61

appreciation 61
apprise 19
approve 92
apt 92
aquatic 203
arabic 7
Arabic 63
Araldite 7
arbitrarily 49, 66, 71
arced 6
archaeology 36
arcing 6
Arctic 71
are 178
area 59
areas 12
aren't 92
Argentine 71, 92
Argentinian 92
argument 10
Aries 11
arise 19
aristocracy 142
aristocrat 66, 71
arithmetic 63
armada 46
armourer 23
army 142
arsenic 63
artefact 36
articulate 198
artisan 64, 71
artiste 92
arvo 204
as 92, 105, 115, 140, 169
ascendance 4
ascendancy 4
ascendant 4
as for 169
as from 93
ashamedness 52
ashes 25
Asian 61, 92
Asiatic 61, 92
aside from 93, 202
as if 93, 184
as it were 184
Aslef 2
as of 93
aspirant 64, 71
assert 149
assertive 5
associate 61
association 61
assume 68
assurance 12

assured 52
assuredly 52
assuredness 52
asthma 71
as though 93, 184
ate 71
Athens 177
athletics 154
attachés 13
attendance 4
attendant 4
attention 93
at the end of the day 198
at this moment in time 198
at this point in time 198
aubade 47
aubrietia 36
auction 203
audacious 71
audible 3
audience 142
aught 36
auld lang syne 71
aunty 32
autarchy 36
autarky 36
author 93
authoritative 5
authorize 19
automaton 27
automobile 55
auxiliary 36
avenge 93
avenger 21
aversion 61
avertible 3
avocado 47
avowedly 52
aware 58, 93
-awareness 198
awesome 10
awful 10, 143
*ax 11, 202
axis 27
ay 36
aye 36
ayes 36
azure 71

B

*baboo 36
babu 36
baby 32

breeches 71
brewed 67
*briar 36
bribable 9
bridgeable 10
brier 36
brigadier-generals 26
bring 56
bringer 56
bringing 56
broadcast 24
broad-leaved 13
brochure 72
bronchus 28
brood 67
brook 203
brougham 58
brownie 32
brusque 72
Brussels 177
brutalest 9
budgerigar 204
budgie 32
buffaloes 25
Bulgarian 69
bulwark 69
bur 36
bureau 27, 72
burgh 72
burn 23, 48
burr 36
bus 8, 200
bused 8
buses 25
bush 203
bushes 25
business 35
busing 8
busyness 35
but 141, 169, 170
but for 169
buys 34
buzzes 25, 31
by and large 199
bye 5
bye-bye 5
by-election 5
bygone 5
byline 5
byname 5
bypass 5
bypath 5
by-road 5
bystander 5
byway 5
byword 5
Byzantine 65, 72

C

C 2
cabbage-like 17
cabbala 36, 39
cabbalistic 36
Cabinet 142
cactus 28
cadaver 72
cadaverous 72
caddie 32
caddy 32
cadre 30, 72
Caesar 3
cafés 13
caffeine 11, 53
caftan 36, 39
cagey 33
cageyness 33
cagily 33
caky 10
calculable 3
calculus 28
calendar 36
calender 36
calf 13
calfish 13
calibre 30
calicoes 25
*caliper 36
caliph 36, 39, 72
calix 27
calligraphy 36
calliper 36
callisthenics 154
callous 36
callus 36
caltrop 47
calved 13
calves 25
calves-foot jelly 13
camellia 36, 72
cameras 12, 24
camouflage 47
campanile 55
canapés 13
candelabra 28, 95
candelabras 95
candelabrum 28, 95
canine 72
canoeing 10
cantabile 55
cantata 47
canton 72
cantonment 72

canvas 36
canvased 36
canvass 36
canvassed 36
capital 66
capitalist 66, 72
capsize 20
capsule 68
car 48
carburettor 21
carcass 36
care 158
cargoes 25
caries 55
carillon 72
*carnelian 37
carried 34
carrier 34
carries 31, 35
carry 48
caryatid 72
casein 11, 53
caster 22
castor 22
casual 61
casuist 61
catacomb 72
*catalog 202
catalyse 34
catches 31
catechism 20
catechize 20
caterpillar 63
catholic 63
cats 24
cavalcade 46
caviare 36
ceiling 11
cello 193
censer 22
censor 22, 95
censure 95
centenary 66, 72
*center 202
centimetre 66
cento 72
centre 30
centre about 95
centre around 95
-centred 199
centre round 95
centrifugal 72
centring 10
centripetal 72
century 95
certification 72
cervical 72

chaff 72
chagrin 64, 72
chameleon 36
chamois 28, 72
chancellor 36
chancy 10
chaperon 36
chappie 32
character 95
charade 47
charisma 95
charismata 95
charismatic 95
Charleses 25
charlie 32
charmedly 52
Charollais 36
chasséing 13
chassis 28
chastise 19
chastisement 65, 72
chasuble 68
château 27
chauffeur 54
check 202
checker 36
checkers 201
cheque 36
chequer 36
chews 67
chiack 204
chid 24
chide 24
chided 24
chilblain 20
childish 143
chilli 36
chimera 72
chimo 203
china 59
chiropodist 72
choice between 96
choir 142
choleric 63, 72
choose 67
choose between 96
choosy 36
chopper 21
chord 36
chough 58
Christian 7
Christianize 7
chronic 96
chukka boot 36
chukker 36
chute 67
cicada 46

cider 33
cigarette 64, 72
cipher 33
circumcise 19
citified 17
civil(l)est 9
clan 142
clandestine 64, 72
clangour 72
*clarinetist 36
clarinettist 36
class 142
classics 153
clave 23
clayey 33
clayeyness 33
cleavage 10
cleave 23
cleaved 23
cleft 23
clergy 142
clerk 48, 202
clever 144
clichéd 13
clientele 72
climate 64
clippie 32
clique 73
cliquiness 35
cliquy 10
cloth 57, 67
clough 58
clove 23
cloven 23
club 142
clubbable 8
clue 67
clung 24
coaches 25
coal-face 15
coalfield 15
coal tar 15
co-author 8, 93
Coca-Cola 7
coccyx 73
cockabully 204
coco 36
cocoa 36
coconut 36
codeine 11, 53
coiffeur 53
coiffeuse 54
colander 36, 73
co-latitude 8
colicky 6
collage 47
collapsible 3

collar 57
collusion 68
coloration 23
colour 22
colourful 23
colporteur 53
colt 57
combat 57, 64, 73
combatant 65, 73
combated 8
combative 73
combination 62
combine 62, 64, 73
combustible 3
come 48
come the raw prawn 204
come there, to 205
comma 59
commandant 64, 73
commandeer 205
commando 205
commit 36
commitment 36
committee 142
Commo 204
common 118, 144
common-sense 15
communal 64, 73
commune 73
communiqués 13
company 142
comparable 66, 73, 96
comparative 36
compared to 96
compared with 96
compare to 96
compare with 96
comparison 96
compatible 3
compelling 9
compendium 28
compensatory 73
compilation 73
complacency 96
complacent 96
complaisance 96
complaisant 96
complement 36
complexion 32
compliment 36
compose 96
composite 64, 73
compositor 22
compound 63
comprehensible 3
compressor 22
comprise 19, 97

elude 105
elusive 105
elusory 105
elven 13
elvish 13
embargoes 25
embarrassed 51
embarrassedly 51
embarrassment 37
embed 37, 39
embodiment 35
embryos 25
emend 91
emendation 91
émigrés 13
employee 37
employer 34
emporium 28
emprise 19
emus 12
enclave 75
enclose 37, 39
enclosure 37, 39
encroach 37
encrust 11
encyclopaedia 37
enfranchise 19
engrain 11
enigma 55
enjoin 105
enjoyable 34
enjoyment 34
enormity 105
enough 138
enquire 12
enquiry 12
enrol 20
enrolment 20
ensure 12
enterprise 19
enthral 20
enthralling 20
enthralment 20
enthuse 105
enthusiasm 68
entirety 75
entrepreneur 53
envelop 37
envelope 37, 75
environment 199
environs 65, 75
*epilog 11
epithalamium 28
epos 75
epoxy 75
equally 105
equally as 105

equation 61
equerry 75
equipped 8
equipping 8
erector 37
erf 205
err 58
erratum 28, 47
error 22
escalate 199
espionage 75
estrangedness 52
et cetera 75
ethics 153
euchre 30
event of, in the 105
event that, in the 105
eventuate 199
ever 105
every 143, 149
everybody 149
every one 37, 119
everyone 37, 149
everything 56, 187
evidence 106
evince 106
evoke 106
evolve 57
exalt 38
exceed 7
exceedingly 106
except 169
except for 169
excepting 106
exceptionable 106
exceptional 106
excess 106
excessively 106
excise 19
excited 51
excitedly 51
executioner 21
executor 22
exercise 19
exhaustible 3
expect 106
expellent 4
experiencedly 52
expertise 19
explicable 66, 75
explicit 106
exploitive 7
exporter 22
exposedness 52
exposure 106
ex-President 16
express 106

expressible 3
exquisite 65, 75
extensible 3
extol 20
extraordinary 75
extreme 144
exult 38
eyeing 10
*eyot 35, 38
eyrie 35, 38

F

F 2
façade 47
facies 55
facility 106
factious 108
factitious 107
faculty 106
faecal 38
faeces 38
fair do's 28
fairy 48
faith 67
fakir 75
falcon 75
fall for, to 201
fallible 3
fall-out 15
false 47
familiarize 19
family 142
fanciful 35
far 58, 138
farm 205
farther 107
farthest 107
fascia 75
fascism 75
fascist 75
fast 138
father 48, 67, 155
father and mother 156
fatiguing 10
faucet 202
fault 47
faux pas 28
favour 22
favourite 23
fear 148
feasible 3, 107
February 60, 75
feeable 10
fee'd 38

H

I

DICTIONARY

PRONUNCIATION

A guide to this is given, by means of the International Phonetic Alphabet, for a word or part of a word that is difficult to pronounce, or is spelt the same as another word but pronounced differently. The stressed syllable in words of two or more syllables is shown by the mark ˈ placed immediately before it.

The pronunciation indicated represents the standard speech of southern England.

Key to phonetic symbols

CONSONANTS ·

The following consonants have their usual English sound values:
b, d, f, h, k, l, m, n, p, r, t, v, w, z.

g as in go	ʃ as in ship	x (Scottish) as in loch
ŋ as in sing	ʒ as in vision	(in general use often
θ as in thin	j as in yet	pronounced as k)
ð as in then		tʃ as in chin
s as in hiss		dʒ as in jam

VOWELS

æ as in fat	ʌ as in dug	aɪə(r) as in fire
ɑ as in cart	ʊ as in book	aʊə(r) as in sour
e as in met	u as in boot	eɪ as in fate
ɪ as in bit	ɜ(r) as in fur	eə(r) as in fair
i as in meet	ə as in ago	ɔɪ as in boil
o as in got	aɪ as in bite	ʊə(r) as in poor
ɔ as in port	aʊ as in brow	əʊ as in goat

The symbol ˜ over a vowel indicates nasalization as in French *vin blanc* (væ̃ blɑ̃).

ABBREVIATIONS

a. adjective
abbr. abbreviation
adjs. adjectives
adv. adverb
advs. adverbs
Amer. American
attrib. attributively
Austr. Australian
colloq. colloquial
conj. conjunction
Dec. December
esp. especially
fem. feminine
imper. imperative
Ind. Indian
int. interjection
ints. interjections
iron. ironically
Ir. Irish
Jan. January

joc. jocularly
n. noun
N. Engl. northern
England
n. fem. noun feminine
Nov. November
ns. nouns
orig. originally
[P.] proprietary term
pl., *pl.* plural
poss. possessive
p.p. past participle
pr. pronounced
pref. prefix
prep. preposition
preps. prepositions
pres. present
pres. p. present
participle
pron. pronoun

p.t. past tense
rel.pron. relative
pronoun
S. Afr. South African
Sc. Scottish
Sept. September
sing. singular
sl. slang
U.S. United States
usu. usually
v. aux. auxiliary verb
v.i. intransitive verb
v. imper. imperative
verb
v. refl. reflexive verb
v.t. transitive verb
v.t./i. transitive and
intransitive verb
vulg. vulgar

Abbreviations that are in general use (such as ft., R.C.) appear in the dictionary itself.

Proprietary Terms

This dictionary includes some words which are, or are asserted to be, proprietary terms or trade marks. Their inclusion does not mean that they have acquired for legal purposes a non-proprietary or general significance, nor is any other judgement implied concerning their legal status. In cases where the editor has some evidence that a word is used as a proprietary name or trade mark this is indicated by the letter [P.], but no judgement concerning the legal status of such words is made or implied thereby.

A

a *a.* one, any; each.

aback *adv.* **taken ~,** disconcerted.

abacus *n.* (pl. *-cuses*) frame with balls sliding on rods, used for counting.

abandon *v.t.* leave without intending to return; give up. —*n.* careless freedom of manner. **abandonment** *n.*

abandoned *a.* (of manner etc.) showing abandon, depraved.

abase *v.t.* humiliate, degrade. **abasement** *n.*

abashed *a.* embarrassed, ashamed.

abate *v.t./i.* make or become less intense. **abatement** *n.*

abattoir /-twa(r)/ *n.* slaughterhouse.

abbey *n.* building occupied by a community of monks or nuns; church formerly belonging to this.

abbot *n.* head of a community of monks. **abbess** *n.fem.*

abbreviate *v.t.* shorten.

abbreviation *n.* shortened form of word(s).

ABC *n.* alphabet; alphabetical guide; rudiments (of a subject).

abdicate *v.i.* renounce a throne or right etc. **abdication** *n.*

abdomen /ˈæ-/ *n.* part of the body containing the digestive organs. **abdominal** /-ˈdɒm-/ *a.*

abduct *v.t.* kidnap. **abduction** *n.*, **abductor** *n.*

aberration /-ˈreɪ-/ *n.* deviation from what is normal; mental or moral lapse; distortion.

abet *v.t.* (p.t. *abetted*) encourage or assist in wrongdoing. **abettor** *n.*

abeyance *n.* **in ~,** not being used or dealt with for a time.

abhor *v.t.* (p.t. *abhorred*) detest. **abhorrence** /-ˈhɒ-/ *n.*

abhorrent /-ˈhɒ-/ *a.* detestable.

abide *v.t./i.* (*old use*; p.t. *abode*) remain, dwell; (p.t. *abided*) tolerate. **~ by,** keep (a promise); accept (consequences etc.).

abiding *a.* lasting, permanent.

ability *n.* quality that makes an action or process possible, power to do something; cleverness.

abject /ˈæ-/ *a.* wretched; lacking all pride. **abjectly** *adv.*

ablaze *a.* blazing.

able *a.* (*-er, -est*) having ability. **ably** *adv.*

ablutions *n.pl.* process of washing oneself; place for this.

abnormal *a.* not normal, not usual. **abnormally** *adv.*, **abnormality** *n.*

aboard *adv. & prep.* on board.

abode *see* **abide**. —*n.* (*old use*) dwelling-place.

abolish *v.t.* put an end to. **abolition** *n.*

abominable *a.* detestable; very bad or unpleasant. **abominably** *adv.*

abominate *v.t.* detest. **abomination** *n.*

aboriginal *a.* existing in a country from its earliest times. —*n.* aboriginal inhabitant.

aborigines /-niz/ *n.pl.* aboriginal inhabitants. **aborigine** /-ni/ *n.* (*colloq.*) one of these.

abort *v.t./i.* cause or suffer abortion; end prematurely and unsuccessfully.

abortion *n.* premature expulsion of a foetus from the womb; operation to cause this; misshapen creature.

abortionist *n.* person who favours permitting abortions; one who performs abortions.

abortive *a.* producing abortion; unsuccessful.

abound *v.i.* be plentiful. **~ in,** be rich in.

about *adv. & prep.* all round; near; here and there; in circulation; approximately; in connection with; so as to face in the opposite direction; in rotation. **~-face, ~-turn** *ns.* reversal of direction or policy. **be ~ to,** be on the point of (doing).

above *adv. & prep.* at or to a higher point (than); over; beyond the level or understanding etc. of. **~-board** *a.* without deception.

abrasion *n.* rubbing or scraping away; injury caused by this.

abrasive *a.* causing abrasion; harsh. —*n.* substance used for grinding or polishing surfaces.

abreast *adv.* side by side. **~ of,** level with, not behind.

abridge *v.t.* shorten by using fewer words. **abridgement** *n.*

abroad *adv.* away from one's country; far and wide.

abrupt *a.* sudden; curt; steep. **abruptly** *adv.*, **abruptness** *n.*

abscess *n.* collection of pus formed in the body.

abscond *v.i.* go away secretly.

absence *n.* being absent; lack.

absent[1] /ˈæ-/ *a.* not present; lacking, non-existent; absent-minded. **~-minded** *a.* with one's mind on other things; forgetful. **absently** *adv.*

absent[2] /-ˈsent/ *v.refl.* **~ oneself,** stay away.

absentee *n.* person who is absent from work etc. **absenteeism** *n.*

absinthe *n.* a green liqueur.

absolute *a.* complete; unrestricted; independent. **absolutely** *adv.*

absolution *n.* priest's formal declaration of forgiveness of sins.

absolve *v.t.* clear of blame or guilt; free from an obligation.

absorb *v.t.* take in, combine into itself or oneself; reduce the intensity of; occupy the attention or interest of. **absorber** *n.*, **absorption** *n.*

absorbent *a.* able to absorb moisture etc. **absorbency** *n.*

abstain *v.i.* refrain, esp. from drinking alcohol; decline to use one's vote. **abstainer** *n.*, **abstention** *n.*

abstemious /-ˈsti-/ *a.* not self-indulgent. **abstemiously** *adv.*

abstinence *n*. abstaining esp. from food or alcohol. **abstinent** *a*.

abstract[1] /ˈæ-/ *a*. having no material existence; theoretical; (of art) not representing things pictorially. —*n*. abstract quality or idea; summary; piece of abstract art.

abstract[2] /-ˈstrækt/ *v.t*. take out, remove. **abstracted** *a*. with one's mind on other things. **abstraction** *n*.

abstruse /-ˈstrus/ *a*. profound.

absurd *a*. not in accordance with common sense, ridiculous. **absurdly** *adv*., **absurdity** *n*.

abundant *a*. plentiful; having plenty of something. **abundantly** *adv*., **abundance** *n*.

abuse *v.t*. make bad use of; ill-treat; attack with abusive language. —*n*. abusing; abusive language.

abusive *a*. using harsh words or insults. **abusively** *adv*.

abut *v.t./i*. (p.t. *abutted*) border upon; have a common boundary.

abysmal *a*. extreme; (*colloq*.) very bad. **abysmally** *adv*.

abyss /-ˈbɪs/ *n*. bottomless chasm.

acacia *n*. a kind of flowering tree or shrub.

academic *a*. of a college or university; scholarly; of theoretical interest only. —*n*. academic person. **academically** *adv*.

academician *n*. member of an Academy.

academy *n*. school, esp. for specialized training; A∼, a society of scholars or artists.

accede /-ˈsid/ *v.i*. ∼ **to,** agree to; enter upon (office).

accelerate *v.t./i*. increase the speed (of). **acceleration** *n*.

accelerator *n*. device (esp. a pedal of a vehicle) for increasing speed.

accent[1] /ˈæ-/ *n*. emphasis; mark showing emphasis or quality of a vowel; national or local etc. way of pronouncing words.

accent[2] /-ˈsent/ *v.t*. pronounce with an accent; emphasize.

accentuate *v.t*. emphasize. **accentuation** *n*.

accept *v.t./i*. take willingly, say yes to an offer or invitation; agree to; take as true. **acceptance** *n*.

acceptable *a*. worth accepting; tolerable. **acceptably** *adv*.

access *n*. way in; right or means of approaching or entering; attack of emotion.

accessible *a*. able to be reached. **accessibly** *adv*., **accessibility** *n*.

accession *n*. reaching a rank or position; thing added.

accessory *a*. additional. —*n*. accessory fitment or decoration etc.; person who helps in a crime.

accident *n*. unexpected event, esp. one causing damage; chance. **accidental** *a*., **accidentally** *adv*.

acclaim *v.t*. welcome or applaud enthusiastically. —*n*. shout of welcome, applause. **acclamation** *n*.

acclimatize *v.t./i*. make or become used to a new climate. **acclimatization** *n*.

accolade *n*. bestowal of a knighthood or other honour; praise.

accommodate *v.t*. supply; provide lodging or room for; adapt, make harmonize. **accommodating** *a*. willing to do as asked.

accommodation *n*. process of accommodating; living-premises. ∼ **address,** one to which letters may be sent for a person not living there.

accompany *v.t*. go with; be present with; provide in addition; play an instrumental part supporting (a solo voice or choir). **accompaniment** *n*., **accompanist** *n*.

accomplice *n*. partner in crime.

accomplish *v.t*. succeed in doing or achieving.

accomplished *a*. skilled; having many accomplishments.

accomplishment *n*. accomplishing; useful ability.

accord *v.t./i*. be consistent; grant. —*n*. consent, agreement. **of one's own** ∼**,** without being asked or compelled.

accordance *n*. conformity.

according *adv*. ∼ **as,** in proportion as. ∼ **to,** as stated by; in proportion to. **accordingly** *adv*.

accordion *n*. portable musical instrument with bellows and a keyboard.

accost *v.t*. approach and speak to.

account *n*. statement of money paid or owed; credit arrangement with a bank or firm; importance; ground, reason; description, report. —*v.t*. regard as. ∼ **for,** give a reckoning of; explain the cause of; kill, overcome.

accountable *a*. obliged to account for one's actions. **accountability** *n*.

accountant *n*. person who keeps or inspects business accounts. **accountancy** *n*.

accoutrements /-ˈkutrə-/ *n.pl*. equipment, trappings.

accredited *a*. holding credentials.

accrue *v.i*. accumulate. **accrual** *n*.

accumulate *v.t./i*. acquire more and more of; increase in amount. **accumulation** *n*.

accumulator *n*. rechargeable electric battery.

accurate *a*. free from error. **accurately** *adv*., **accuracy** *n*.

accusative *n*. grammatical case indicating the object of an action.

accuse *v.t*. state that one lays the blame for a crime or fault etc. upon. **accusation** *n*., **accuser** *n*.

accustom *v.t*. make used to.

accustomed *a*. usual; customary.

ace *n*. playing-card with one spot; expert; unreturnable stroke in tennis.

acetate *n*. synthetic textile fibre.

acetone /ˈæsɪ-/ *n*. colourless liquid used as a solvent.

ache *n*. dull continuous pain. —*v.i*. suffer an ache.

achieve *v.t*. accomplish; reach or gain by effort. **achievement** *n*.

acid *a*. sour. —*n*. any of a class of substances that contain hydrogen and neutralize alkalis. **acidly** *adv*., **acidity** *n*.

acknowledge *v.t*. admit the truth of; show

recognition of; announce the receipt of. **acknowledgement** *n*.

acme /-mɪ/ *n*. peak (of perfection).

acne /-nɪ/ *n*. eruption of pimples.

aconite *n*. plant with a poisonous root.

acorn *n*. oval nut of the oak-tree.

acoustic /-ˈku-/ *a*. of sound; of acoustics. **acoustics** *n.pl*. qualities of a room etc. that affect the way sound carries in it. **acoustical** *a*.

acquaint *v.t*. make known to. **be acquainted with,** know slightly.

acquaintance *n*. slight knowledge; person one knows slightly.

acquiesce /-ˈes/ *v.i*. assent. **acquiescent** *a*., **acquiescence** *n*.

acquire *v.t*. get possession of. **acquirement** *n*.

acquisition *n*. acquiring; thing acquired.

acquisitive *a*. eager to acquire things. **acquisitiveness** *n*.

acquit *v.t*. (p.t. *acquitted*) declare to be not guilty. ~ **oneself,** perform one's part. **acquittal** *n*.

acre *n*. measure of land, 4,840 sq. yds. **acreage** /ˈeɪkərɪdʒ/ *n*. number of acres.

acrid *a*. bitter.

acrimony /ˈæ-/ *n*. bitterness of manner. **acrimonious** /-ˈməʊ-/ *a*.

acrobat *n*. performer of acrobatics. **acrobatic** *a*. involving spectacular gymnastic feats. **acrobatics** *n.pl*. acrobatic feats.

acronym *n*. word formed from the initial letters of others.

across *prep. & adv*. from side to side (of); to or on the other side (of); crosswise.

acrostic *n*. poem etc. in which the first and/or last letters of lines form word(s).

acrylic *a. & n*. (synthetic fibre) made from an organic substance.

act *n*. thing done; law made by parliament; section of a play; item in a circus or variety show. —*v.t./i*. perform actions, behave; play the part of, be an actor.

action *n*. process of doing something or functioning; thing done; lawsuit; battle.

actionable *a*. giving cause for a lawsuit.

activate *v.t*. make active. **activation** *n*., **activator** *n*.

active *a*. doing things; energetic; in operation. **actively** *adv*.

activity *n*. being active; action, occupation.

actor *n*. performer in stage play(s) or film(s). **actress** *n.fem*.

actual *a*. existing in fact, current. **actually** *adv*.

actuality /-ˈæl-/ *n*. reality.

actuary *n*. insurance expert who calculates risks and premiums. **actuarial** /-ˈeər-/ *a*.

actuate *v.t*. activate; be a motive for. **actuation** *n*.

acumen /əˈkjuːmen/ *n*. shrewdness.

acupuncture *n*. pricking the body with needles to relieve pain etc. **acupuncturist** *n*.

acute *a*. sharp; intense, (of illness) severe for a time; quick at understanding. ~ **accent,** the accent ´. ~ **angle,** angle of less than 90°. **acutely** *adv*., **acuteness** *n*.

ad *n*. (*colloq*.) advertisement.

A.D. *abbr*. (Latin *anno domini*) of the Christian era.

adage /ˈædɪdʒ/ *n*. proverb, saying.

adamant *a*. not yielding to requests.

Adam's apple prominent cartilage at the front of the neck.

adapt *v.t./i*. make or become suitable for new use or conditions. **adaptation** *n*., **adaptor** *n*.

adaptable *a*. able to be adapted or to adapt oneself. **adaptability** *n*.

add *v.t./i*. join as an increase or supplement; say further; put together to get a total.

addenda *n*. list of things to be added to a book etc.

adder *n*. small poisonous snake.

addict *n*. one who is addicted, esp. to drug(s).

addicted *a*. doing or using something as a habit or compulsively; devoted (to a hobby or interest). **addiction** *n*.

addictive *a*. causing addiction.

addition *n*. adding; thing added. **in** ~, as an added thing.

additional *a*. added, extra. **additionally** *adv*.

additive *n*. substance added.

addle *v.t*. make (an egg) rotten.

address *n*. particulars of where a person lives or where mail should be delivered; a speech. —*v.t*. write the address on; speak to; apply (oneself) to a task.

addressee *n*. person to whom a letter etc. is addressed.

adenoids *n.pl*. enlarged tissue at the back of the throat. **adenoidal** *a*.

adept /ˈæ-/ *a. & n*. very skilful (person).

adequate *a*. enough; satisfactory but not excellent. **adequately** *adv*., **adequacy** *n*.

adhere *v.i*. stick; continue to give one's support. **adherence** *n*., **adherent** *a. & n*.

adhesion *n*. adhering; abnormal union of inflamed tissue.

adhesive *a*. sticking, sticky. —*n*. adhesive substance.

ad hoc for a specific purpose.

adieu /əˈdjuː/ *int. & n*. goodbye.

ad infinitum /-ˈnaɪ-/ for ever.

adjacent *a*. lying near; adjoining.

adjective *n*. descriptive word. **adjectival** *a*., **adjectivally** *adv*.

adjoin *v.t*. be next to.

adjourn /-ˈdʒɜːn/ *v.t./i*. move (a meeting etc.) to another place or time. **adjournment** *n*.

adjudge *v.t*. decide or award judicially.

adjudicate *v.t./i*. act as judge (of); adjudge.

adjunct *n*. thing that is subordinate or incidental to another.

adjust *v.t./i*. alter slightly so as to be correct or in the proper position; adapt (oneself) to new conditions; assess (loss or damages). **adjuster** *n*., **adjustment** *n*.

adjustable *a*. able to be adjusted.

adjutant /ˈædʒʊ-/ *n*. army officer assisting in administrative work.

ad lib as one pleases. **ad-lib** *v.i*. (p.t. *-libbed*) (*colloq*.) improvise remarks or actions.

administer *v.t./i*. manage (business affairs); formally give or hand out.

administrate *v.t./i.* act as administrator (of).
administration *n.* administering; management of public or business affairs. **administrative** *a.*
administrator *n.* person responsible for administration.
admirable *a.* worthy of admiration. **admirably** *adv.*
admiral *n.* naval officer of the highest rank. **red** ∼, **white** ∼, kinds of butterfly.
Admiralty *n.* former name for the government department superintending the Royal Navy.
admire *v.t.* regard with pleasure; think highly of; compliment a person on. **admiration** *n.*, **admirer** *n.*
admissible *a.* able to be admitted or allowed. **admissibility** *n.*
admission *n.* admitting; statement admitting something.
admit *v.t.* (p.t. *admitted*) allow to enter; accept as valid; state reluctantly. ∼ **of**, leave room for (doubt, improvement, etc.).
admittance *n.* admitting, esp. to a private place.
admonish *v.t.* exhort; reprove. **admonition** *n.*, **admonitory** /-ˈmon-/ *a.*
ad nauseam /ˈnɔːzɪæm/ to a sickening extent.
ado *n.* fuss, trouble.
adolescent *a. & n.* (person) between childhood and maturity. **adolescence** *n.*
adopt *v.t.* take as one's own; accept responsibility for maintenance of (a road etc.); accept, approve (a report etc.). **adoption** *n.*
adoptive *a.* related by adoption.
adorable *a.* very lovable.
adore *v.t.* love deeply; worship as divine; (*colloq.*) like very much. **adoration** *n.*
adorn *v.t.* decorate with ornaments; be an ornament to. **adornment** *n.*
adrenal /-ˈdri-/ *a.* close to the kidneys.
adrenalin /-ˈdren-/ *n.* stimulant hormone produced by the adrenal glands.
adrift *adj. & adv.* drifting; loose.
adroit *a.* skilful, ingenious.
adulation *n.* excessive flattery.
adult /ˈæ-/ *a. & n.* fully grown (person etc.). **adulthood** *n.*
adulterate *v.t.* make impure by adding substance(s). **adulteration** *n.*
adulterer *n.* person who commits adultery. **adulteress** *n.fem.*
adultery *n.* infidelity to one's wife or husband by voluntarily having sexual intercourse with someone else. **adulterous** *a.*
advance *v.t./i.* move or put forward; make progress; lend (money). —*n.* forward movement; progress; increase in price or amount; loan; attempt to establish a friendly relationship. —*a.* going or done in advance. **in** ∼, ahead. **advancement** *n.*
advanced *a.* far on in time or progress etc.; not elementary.
advantage *n.* favourable circumstance; benefit; next point won after deuce in tennis. **take** ∼ **of**, make use of; exploit.
advantageous *a.* profitable, beneficial. **advantageously** *adv.*
Advent *n.* coming of Christ; season before

Christmas. **advent** *n.* arrival of an important development etc.
adventure *n.* exciting or dangerous experience. **adventurous** *a.*
adventurer *n.* person who seeks adventures; one living by his wits.
adverb *n.* word qualifying a verb, adjective, or other adverb. **adverbial** *a.*, **adverbially** *adv.*
adversary /ˈæ-/ *n.* opponent, enemy.
adverse /ˈæ-/ *a.* unfavourable, bringing harm. **adversely** *adv.*, **adversity** *n.*
advertise *v.t./i.* make publicly known, esp. to encourage sales; seek by public notice. **advertiser** *n.*
advertisement *n.* advertising; public notice advertising something.
advice *n.* opinion given about what should be done; piece of information.
advisable *a.* worth recommending as a course of action. **advisability** *n.*
advise *v.t./i.* give advice to; recommend; inform. **adviser** *n.*
advisory *a.* giving advice.
advocate[1] /-kət/ *n.* person who pleads on behalf of another.
advocate[2] /-keɪt/ *v.t.* recommend.
aegis /ˈiːdʒɪs/ *n.* protection, sponsorship.
aeon /ˈiːən/ *n.* immense time.
aerate *v.t.* expose to the action of air; add carbon dioxide to. **aeration** *n.*, **aerator** *n.*
aerial *a.* of or like air; existing or moving in the air; by or from aircraft. —*n.* wire or rod for transmitting or receiving radio waves.
aerobatics *n.pl.* spectacular feats by aircraft in flight.
aerodrome *n.* airfield.
aerodynamic *a.* of the interaction between air-flow and the movement of solid bodies through air.
aeronautics *n.* study of the flight of aircraft. **aeronautical** *a.*
aeroplane *n.* mechanically driven aircraft with wings.
aerosol *n.* container holding a substance sealed into it for release as a fine spray; its contents.
aerospace *n.* earth's atmosphere and space beyond this.
aesthete /ˈiːsθiːt/ *n.* person claiming to understand and appreciate beauty, esp. in the arts.
aesthetic /iːsˈθe-/ *a.* of or showing appreciation of beauty; artistic, tasteful. **aesthetically** *adv.*
afar *adv.* far off, far away.
affable *a.* polite and friendly. **affably** *adv.*, **affability** *n.*
affair *n.* thing to be done, matter; business; temporary sexual relationship.
affect *v.t.* pretend to have or feel or be; use for show; have an effect on.
affectation *n.* pretence, esp. in behaviour.
affected *a.* full of affectation.
affection *n.* love, liking; disease.
affectionate *a.* loving. **affectionately** *adv.*
affidavit /-ˈdeɪ-/ *n.* written statement sworn on oath to be true.
affiliate *v.t.* connect as a subordinate member or branch. **affiliation** *n.*

affinity *n.* close resemblance or connection; strong liking, attraction; tendency to combine.

affirm *v.t./i.* state as a fact; declare formally and solemnly instead of on oath. **affirmation** *n.*

affirmative *a. & n.* saying 'yes'.

affix *v.t.* attach; add (a signature etc.).

afflict *v.t.* distress physically or mentally.

affliction *n.* distress; thing causing this.

affluence *n.* wealth.

affluent *a.* wealthy.

afford *v.t.* have enough money or time etc. for; provide.

affray *n.* public fight or riot.

affront *v.t. & n.* insult.

afield *adv.* at or to a distance.

aflame *adv. & a.* burning.

afloat *adv. & a.* floating; on the sea.

afoot *adv. & a.* going on.

aforesaid *a.* mentioned previously.

aforethought *a.* premeditated.

afraid *a.* frightened; regretful.

afresh *adv.* anew, with a fresh start.

African *a.* of Africa. —*n.* African (esp. dark-skinned) person.

Afrikaans /-ˈkɑns/ *n.* language of South Africa, developed from Dutch.

Afro- *pref.* African.

aft *adv.* at or towards the rear of a ship or aircraft.

after *prep., adv., & a.* behind; later (than); in pursuit of; concerning; according to. —*conj.* at a time later than. **~-effect** *n.* effect persisting after its cause has gone.

afterbirth *n.* placenta discharged from the womb after childbirth.

aftermath *n.* after-effects.

afternoon *n.* time between morning and about 6 p.m. or sunset.

aftershave *n.* lotion for use after shaving.

afterthought *n.* thing thought of or added later.

afterwards *adv.* at a later time.

again *adv.* another time, once more; besides.

against *prep.* in opposition or contrast to; in preparation or return for; into collision or contact with.

agate /ˈægət/ *n.* hard stone with patches or bands of colour.

age *n.* length of life or existence; later part of life; historical period; (*colloq., usu. pl.*) very long time. —*v.t./i.* (pres. p. *ageing*) grow old, show signs of age; cause to do this.

aged /eɪdʒd/ *a.* of the age of; /ˈeɪdʒɪd/ old.

ageless *a.* not growing or seeming old.

agency *n.* business or office of an agent; means of action by which something is done.

agenda *n.* list of things to be dealt with, esp. at a meeting.

agent *n.* person who does something; thing producing an effect; one who acts on behalf of another.

agglomeration *n.* mass.

aggravate *v.t.* make worse; (*colloq.*) annoy. **aggravation** *n.*

aggregate[1] /-ət/ *a.* combined, total. —*n.* total; collected mass; broken stone etc. used in making concrete.

aggregate[2] /-eɪt/ *v.t./i.* collect into an aggregate, unite; (*colloq.*) amount to. **aggregation** *n.*

aggression *n.* unprovoked attacking; hostile act(s) or behaviour.

aggressive *a.* showing aggression; forceful. **aggressively** *adv.*, **aggressiveness** *n.*

aggressor *n.* one who begins hostilities.

aggrieved *a.* having a grievance.

aghast *a.* filled with consternation.

agile *a.* nimble, quick-moving. **agilely** *adv.*, **agility** *n.*

agitate *v.t.* shake briskly; cause anxiety to; stir up interest or concern. **agitation** *n.*, **agitator** *n.*

agnostic *a.* person holding that nothing can be known about the existence of God. **agnosticism** *n.*

ago *adv.* in the past.

agog *a.* eager, expectant.

agonize *v.t./i.* cause agony to; suffer agony, worry intensely.

agony *n.* extreme suffering.

agoraphobia *n.* abnormal fear of crossing open spaces.

agree *v.t./i.* consent; approve as correct or acceptable; hold or reach a similar opinion; get on well together; be consistent. **~ with,** suit the health or digestion of.

agreeable *a.* pleasing; willing to agree. **agreeably** *adv.*

agreement *n.* agreeing; arrangement agreed between people.

agriculture *n.* large-scale cultivation of land. **agricultural** *a.*

aground *adv. & a.* (of a ship) on the bottom of shallow water.

ah, aha *ints.* exclamations of surprise, triumph, etc.

ahead *adv.* further forward in position or time.

ahoy *int.* seaman's shout to call attention.

aid *v.t. & n.* help.

aide *n.* aide-de-camp; (*U.S.*) assistant.

aide-de-camp /-ˈkã/ *n.* (pl. *aides-de-camp*, pr. eɪdz-) officer assisting a senior officer.

ail *v.t./i.* make or become ill.

ailment *n.* slight illness.

aim *v.t./i.* point, send, or direct towards a target; attempt; have ambition. —*n.* aiming; intention.

aimless *a.* without a purpose. **aimlessly** *adv.*, **aimlessness** *n.*

air *n.* mixture of oxygen, nitrogen, etc., surrounding the earth; atmosphere overhead; aircraft operating there; light wind; impression given; impressive manner; melody. —*v.t./i.* expose to air; dry off; express publicly. **~-conditioned** *a.* supplied with **~-conditioning,** system controlling the humidity and temperature of air. **~ force,** branch of the armed forces using aircraft in attack and defence. **~ hostess,** stewardess in an aircraft. **~ mail,** mail carried by aircraft. **~ raid,** attack by aircraft dropping bombs.

in the ~, prevalent; not yet decided. **on the ~,** broadcast(ing) by radio or TV.

airborne *a.* carried by air or aircraft; (of aircraft) in flight.

aircraft *n.* machine or structure capable of flight in air; (as *pl.*) such craft collectively.

Airedale *n.* large rough-coated terrier.

airfield *n.* area with runways etc. for aircraft.

airgun *n.* gun with a missile propelled by compressed air.

airlift *n.* large-scale transport of supplies etc. by aircraft, esp. in an emergency. —*v.t.* transport thus.

airline *n.* public air transport service; company providing this.

airlock *n.* stoppage of the flow in a pump or pipe, caused by an air-bubble; airtight compartment giving access to a pressurized chamber.

airman *n.* (pl. *-men*) member of an air force, esp. below the rank of officer.

airport *n.* airfield with facilities for passengers and goods.

airtight *a.* not allowing air to enter or escape.

airworthy *a.* (of aircraft) fit to fly. **airworthiness** *n.*

airy *a.* (*-ier, -iest*) well-ventilated; light as air; careless and lighthearted. **airily** *adv.*, **airiness** *n.*

aisle /aɪl/ *n.* side part of a church; gangway between rows of seats.

ajar *adv.* & *a.* slightly open.

akimbo *adv.* with hands on hips and elbows pointed outwards.

akin *a.* related, similar.

alabaster *n.* translucent usu. white form of gypsum.

à la carte (of a meal) ordered as separate items from a menu.

alacrity *n.* eager readiness.

alarm *n.* warning sound or signal; device giving this; alarm-clock; fear caused by expectation of danger. —*v.t.* cause alarm to. **~-clock** *n.* clock with a device that rings at a set time.

alarmist *n.* person who raises unnecessary or excessive alarm.

alas *int.* exclamation of sorrow.

albatross *n.* sea-bird with long wings.

albino /-ˈbiː-/ *n.* (pl. *-os*) person or animal with no natural colouring matter in the hair or skin.

album *n.* blank book for holding photographs, postage-stamps, etc.; set of recordings, holder for these.

albumen *n.* white of egg.

alchemy *n.* medieval form of chemistry, seeking to turn other metals into gold. **alchemist** *n.*

alcohol *n.* colourless inflammable liquid, intoxicant present in wine, beer, etc.; liquor containing this; compound of this type.

alcoholic *a.* of alcohol. —*n.* person addicted to continual heavy drinking of alcohol. **alcoholism** *n.*

alcove *n.* recess in a wall or room.

alder *n.* a kind of tree.

ale *n.* beer.

alert *a.* watchful, observant. —*n.* warning to be ready for action or danger. —*v.t.* rouse to be alert. **on the ~,** watchful. **alertness** *n.*

alfresco *adv.* & *a.* in the open air.

alga *n.* (pl. *-gae,* pr. -dʒiː) water plant with no true stems or leaves.

algebra *n.* branch of mathematics using letters etc. to represent quantities. **algebraic** *a.*, **algebraically** *adv.*

alias *n.* (pl. *-ases*) false name. —*adv.* also falsely called.

alibi *n.* (pl. *-is*) evidence that an accused person was elsewhere when a crime was committed; (*loosely*) excuse. —*v.t.* (p.t. *alibied,* pres.p. *alibiing*) provide an alibi for.

alien *n.* one who is not a subject of the country where he lives. —*a.* foreign; unfamiliar.

alienate *v.t.* cause to become unfriendly. **alienation** *n.*

alight[1] *v.i.* get down from (a vehicle etc.); descend and settle.

alight[2] *a.* on fire.

align *v.t.* place or bring into line; join as an ally. **alignment** *n.*

alike *adj.* like one another. —*adv.* in the same way.

alimentary *a.* **~ canal,** tubular passage by which food passes through the body.

alimony *n.* allowance paid by a man to his divorced or separated wife.

alive *a.* living; alert; lively.

alkali /-laɪ/ *n.* (pl. *-is*) any of a class of substances that neutralize acids. **alkaline** *a.*

all *a.* whole amount or number or extent of. —*n.* all those concerned, everything. —*adv.* entirely, quite. **~but,** almost. **~-clear** *n.* signal that danger is over. **~ in,** exhausted; including everything. **~ out,** using maximum effort. **~ over,** in or on all parts of; excessively attentive to (a person); being very characteristic. **~ right,** satisfactorily; in good condition; I consent. **~ round,** in all respects; for each person. **~-round** *a.* general, not specialized. **~-rounder** *n.* person with all-round abilities. **~ there,** mentally alert; sane. **~ the same,** in spite of that. **~ up,** (*colloq.*) ended.

Allah *n.* Muslim name of God.

allay *v.t.* lessen (fears).

allegation *n.* thing alleged.

allege *v.t.* declare without proof.

allegedly /-ɪdlɪ/ *adv.* according to allegation.

allegiance *n.* support given to a government, sovereign, or cause.

allegory /ˈælɪ-/ *n.* story symbolizing an underlying meaning. **allegorical** *a.*, **allegorically** *adv.*

allegro /əˈleɪɡrəʊ/ *adv.* & *n.* (pl. *-os*) (passage to be played) briskly.

alleluia *int.* & *n.* praise to God.

allergic *a.* having or caused by an allergy; having a strong dislike.

allergy *n.* condition causing an unfavourable reaction to certain foods, pollens, etc.

alleviate *v.t.* lessen (pain or distress etc.). **alleviation** *n.*

alley *n.* (pl. *-eys*) narrow street, passage; long enclosure for ten-pin bowling etc.

alliance *n.* union or association formed for mutual benefit.

allied *a.* of allies; of the same general kind.

alligator *n.* reptile of the crocodile family.

alliteration *n.* occurrence of the same sound at the start of adjacent words. **alliterative** /-ˈlɪtərə-/ *a.*

allocate *v.t.* allot. **allocation** *n.*

allot *v.t.* (p.t. *allotted*) distribute officially, give as a share.

allotment *n.* allotting; share allotted; small area of public land let for cultivation.

allow *v.t./i.* permit; give a limited quantity or sum; add or deduct in estimating; admit, agree.

allowable *a.* able to be allowed.

allowance *n.* allowing; amount or sum allowed. **make allowances for,** be lenient because of.

alloy *n.* mixture of metals. —*v.t.* mix (with another metal); spoil or weaken (pleasure etc.).

allude *v.i.* refer briefly or indirectly.

allure *v.t.* entice, attract. —*n.* attractiveness. **allurement** *n.*

allusion *n.* statement alluding to something. **allusive** *a.*

alluvium *n.* deposit left by a flood. **alluvial** *a.*

ally[1] /ˈæ-/ *n.* country or person in alliance with another.

ally[2] /-ˈlaɪ/ *v.t.* join as an ally.

almanac /ˈɔl-/ *n.* calendar with astronomical or other data.

almighty *a.* all-powerful; (*colloq.*) very great; *the A~,* God.

almond *n.* kernel of a fruit related to the peach; tree bearing this.

almost *adv.* very little short of, as the nearest thing to.

alms /ɑmz/ *n.* (*old use*) money etc. given to the poor.

almshouse /ˈɑm-/ *n.* house founded by charity for poor (usu. elderly) people.

aloe *n.* plant with bitter juice.

aloft *adv.* high up; upwards.

alone *a.* not with others; without company or help. —*adv.* only.

along *adv.* through part or the whole of a thing's length; onward; in company, in addition. —*prep.* close to the side of.

alongside *adv.* close to the side of a ship or wharf etc. —*prep.* beside.

aloof *adv.* apart. —*a.* showing no interest, unfriendly. **aloofness** *n.*

aloud *adv.* in a voice that can be heard, not in a whisper.

alpha *n.* first letter of the Greek alphabet, = a.

alphabet *n.* letters used in writing a language; signs indicating these. **alphabetical** *a.*, **alphabetically** *adv.*

alphabetize *v.t.* put into alphabetical order. **alphabetization** *n.*

Alpine *a.* of the Alps.

alpine *a.* of high mountains. —*n.* plant growing on mountains or rock gardens.

already *adv.* before this time; as early as this.

Alsatian *n.* dog of a large strong smooth-haired breed.

also *adv.* in addition, besides. **~-ran** *n.* horse or dog not in the first three to finish a race.

altar *n.* structure on which offerings are made to a god; table used in the Communion service.

alter *v.t./i.* make or become different. **alteration** *n.*

altercation *n.* noisy dispute.

alternate[1] /-nət/ *a.* first one then the other successively. **alternately** *adv.*

alternate[2] /-neɪt/ *v.t./i.* place or occur etc. alternately. **alternation** *n.*

alternative *a.* & *n.* (thing that is) one of two or more possibilities. **alternatively** *adv.*

although *conj.* though.

altimeter /ˈæ-/ *n.* instrument (esp. in an aircraft) showing altitude.

altitude *n.* height above sea level or above the horizon.

alto *n.* (pl. *-os*) highest adult male voice; contralto; musical instrument with the second highest pitch in its group.

altogether *adv.* entirely; on the whole.

altruism /ˈæl-/ *n.* unselfishness.

altruist /ˈæl-/ *n.* unselfish person. **altruistic** *a.*, **altruistically** *adv.*

aluminium *n.* lightweight silvery metal.

always *adv.* at all times; whatever the circumstances.

alyssum /ˈælɪ-/ *n.* plant with small usu. yellow or white flowers.

am *see* **be.**

a.m. *abbr.* (Latin *ante meridiem*) before noon.

amalgam *n.* alloy of mercury; soft pliable mixture.

amalgamate *v.t./i.* mix, combine. **amalgamation** *n.*

amaryllis *n.* lily-like plant.

amass *v.t.* heap up, collect.

amateur *n.* person who does something as a pastime not as a profession.

amateurish *a.* lacking professional skill.

amaze *v.t.* overwhelm with wonder. **amazement** *n.*

amazon *n.* tall strong woman.

ambassador *n.* highest-ranking diplomat representing his country in another.

amber *n.* hardened brownish-yellow resin; its colour; yellow traffic-light used as a cautionary signal.

ambidextrous *a.* able to use either hand equally well.

ambience *n.* surroundings.

ambiguous *a.* having two or more possible meanings; uncertain. **ambiguously** *adv.*, **ambiguity** *n.*

ambit *n.* bounds, scope.

ambition *n.* strong desire to achieve something; object of this.

ambitious *a.* full of ambition. **ambitiously** *adv.*

ambivalent /-ˈbɪv-/ *a.* with mixed feelings towards something. **ambivalence** *n.*

amble *v.i.* walk slowly.

ambrosia *n.* something delicious.

ambulance *n.* vehicle equipped to carry sick or injured persons.

ambush *n.* troops etc. lying concealed to make a surprise attack; this attack. —*v.t.* attack thus.

amen /a- *or* eɪ-/ *int.* so be it.

amenable /-ˈmi-/ *a.* responsive.

amend *v.t.* make minor alteration(s) in. **make amends**, compensate for something. **amendment** *n.*

amenity /-ˈmi- *or* -ˈme-/ *n.* pleasant feature of a place etc.

American *a.* of America; of the U.S.A. —*n.* American person; form of English used in the U.S.A.

Americanism *n.* American word or phrase.

Americanize *v.t.* make American in character. **Americanization** *n.*

amethyst *n.* precious stone, purple or violet quartz; its colour.

amiable *a.* likeable; friendly. **amiably** *adv.*, **amiability** *n.*

amicable /ˈæ-/ *a.* friendly. **amicably** *adv.*

amid, amidst *preps.* in the middle of, during.

amiss *a.* & *adv.* wrong(ly), badly.

ammonia *n.* strong-smelling gas; solution of this in water.

ammonite *n.* fossil of a spiral shell.

ammunition *n.* bullets, shells, etc.; facts used in argument.

amnesia *n.* loss of memory.

amnesty *n.* general pardon.

amoeba *n.* (pl. *-bae* or *-bas*) simple microscopic organism changing shape constantly.

amok *adv.* **run ∼**, be out of control and do much damage.

among, amongst *preps.* surrounded by; in the number of; between.

amoral /eɪˈmo-/ *a.* not based on moral standards.

amorous *a.* showing or readily feeling sexual love.

amorphous *a.* shapeless.

amount *n.* total of anything; quantity. —*v.i.* **∼ to**, add up to; be equivalent to.

amp *n.* (*colloq.*) ampere; amplifier.

ampere /-peə(r)/ *n.* unit of electric current.

ampersand *n.* the sign & (= and).

amphetamine /-mɪn/ *n.* stimulant drug.

amphibian *n.* amphibious animal or vehicle.

amphibious *a.* able to live or operate both on land and in water; using both sea and land forces.

amphitheatre *n.* oval or circular unroofed building with tiers of seats round a central arena.

ample *a.* (*-er*, *-est*) plentiful, quite enough; large. **amply** *adv.*

amplify *v.t.* increase the strength of, make louder; add details to (a statement). **amplification** *n.*, **amplifier** *n.*

amplitude *n.* breadth; abundance.

ampoule /-puːl/ *n.* small sealed container holding liquid for injection.

amputate *v.t.* cut off by surgical operation. **amputation** *n.*

amuse *v.t.* cause to laugh or smile; make time pass pleasantly for. **amusement** *n.*

an *a.* form of *a* used before vowel sounds other than long 'u'.

anachronism *n.* thing that is out of harmony with the period in which it is placed.

anaemia /-ˈni-/ *n.* lack of haemoglobin in blood.

anaemic /-ˈni-/ *a.* suffering from anaemia; lacking strong colour or characteristics.

anaesthesia *n.* loss of sensation, esp. induced by anaesthetics.

anaesthetic *n.* substance causing loss of sensation.

anaesthetist /-ˈni-/ *n.* person trained to administer anaesthetics.

anagram *n.* word formed from the rearranged letters of another.

anal *a.* of the anus.

analgesic /-ˈdʒi-/ *a.* & *n.* (drug) relieving pain.

analogous *a.* similar in certain respects. **analogously** *adv.*

analogue /-log/ *n.* analogous thing.

analogy *n.* partial likeness between things that are compared.

analyse *v.t.* make an analysis of; psychoanalyse. **analyst** *n.*

analysis *n.* separation of a substance into parts for study and interpretation; detailed examination.

analytic, analytical *adjs.* of or using analysis. **analytically** *adv.*

anarchist *n.* person who believes that laws are undesirable and should be abolished.

anarchy *n.* total lack of organized control, resulting in disorder or lawlessness.

anathema /-ˈnæθə-/ *n.* formal curse; detested thing.

anatomy *n.* bodily structure; study of this. **anatomical** *a.*, **anatomically** *adv.*

ancestor *n.* person from whom one's father or mother is descended. **ancestral** *a.*

ancestry *n.* line of ancestors.

anchor *n.* heavy metal structure for mooring a ship to the sea-bottom. —*v.t./i.* moor with an anchor; fix firmly.

anchorage *n.* place where ships may anchor.

anchovy *n.* small rich-flavoured fish.

ancient *a.* belonging to times long past; very old.

ancillary *a.* helping in a subsidiary way.

and *conj.* connecting words, phrases, or sentences.

anecdote *n.* short amusing or interesting usu. true story.

anemone *n.* plant with white, red, or purple flowers.

anew *adv.* again; in a new way.

angel *n.* attendant or messenger of God; very kind person. **angelic** *a.*

angelica *n.* candied stalks of a fragrant plant; this plant.

anger *n.* extreme displeasure. —*v.t.* make angry.

angle[1] *n.* space between two lines or surfaces that meet; point of view. —*v.t.* place obliquely; present from a particular point of view.

angle[2] *v.i.* fish with hook and bait; try to obtain by hinting. **angler** *n.*

Anglican *a.* & *n.* (member) of the Church of England or a Church in communion with it.

Anglo- *pref.* English, British.

Anglo-Saxon *n.* English person or language of the period before the Norman Conquest; person of English descent. —*a.* of Anglo-Saxon(s).

angora *n.* long-haired variety of cat, goat, or rabbit; yarn or fabric made from the hair of such goats or rabbits.

angry *a.* (*-ier, -iest*) feeling or showing anger; inflamed. **angrily** *adv.*

ångström /ˈæŋstrəm/ *n.* unit of measurement for wavelengths.

anguish *a.* severe physical or mental pain. **anguished** *a.*

angular *a.* having angles or sharp corners; measured by angle.

aniline /-lɪn/ *n.* oily liquid used in making dyes and plastics.

animal *n.* living thing that can move voluntarily, esp. other than man; quadruped. —*a.* of animals or their nature.

animate[1] /-ət/ *a.* living.

animate[2] /-eɪt/ *v.t.* give life or movement to; make lively; motivate. **animated cartoon,** film made by photographing a series of drawings. **animation** *n.*

animosity *n.* hostility.

animus *n.* animosity.

aniseed *n.* fragrant seed of a plant (*anise*), used for flavouring.

ankle *n.* joint connecting the foot with the leg; part of the leg below the calf.

annals *n.pl.* narrative of events year by year; historical records.

annex *v.t.* take possession of; add as a subordinate part. **annexation** *n.*

annexe *n.* supplementary building.

annihilate *v.t.* destroy completely. **annihilation** *n.*

anniversary *n.* yearly return of the date of an event.

annotate *v.t.* add explanatory notes to. **annotation** *n.*

announce *v.t.* make known publicly; make known the presence or arrival of. **announcement** *n.*

announcer *n.* person who announces items in a broadcast.

annoy *v.t.* cause slight anger to; be troublesome to. **annoyance** *n.*

annoyed *a.* slightly angry.

annual *a.* yearly. —*n.* plant that lives for one year or one season; book etc. published in yearly issues. **annually** *adv.*

annuity *n.* yearly allowance, esp. provided by a form of investment.

annul *v.t.* (p.t. *annulled*) make null and void. **annulment** *n.*

Annunciation *n.* announcement by the angel Gabriel to the Virgin Mary that she was to be the mother of Christ.

anode *n.* electrode by which current enters a device.

anodize *v.t.* coat (metal) with a protective layer by electrolysis.

anodyne *n.* something that relieves pain or distress.

anoint *v.t.* apply ointment or oil etc. to, esp. in religious consecration.

anomaly *n.* something irregular or inconsistent. **anomalous** *a.*

anon *adv.* (*old use*) soon, presently.

anon. *abbr.* anonymous.

anonymous *a.* of unknown or undisclosed name or authorship. **anonymously** *adv.*, **anonymity** /-ˈnɪm-/ *n.*

anorak *n.* waterproof jacket with hood attached.

anorexia *n.* loss of appetite for food; reluctance to eat.

another *a.* one more; different; any other. —*pron.* another one.

answer *n.* thing said, written, needed, or done to deal with a question, problem, etc.; figure etc. produced by calculation. —*v.t./i.* make or be an answer to; act in response to; take responsibility; correspond (to a description etc.).

answerable *a.* able to be answered; having to account for something.

ant *n.* small insect living in a highly organized group. **~-eater** *n.* mammal that eats ants.

antagonism *n.* active opposition, hostility. **antagonistic** *a.*

antagonist *n.* opponent.

antagonize *v.t.* rouse antagonism in.

Antarctic *a.* & *n.* (of) regions round the South Pole.

ante *n.* stake put up by a poker player before drawing new cards.

ante- *pref.* before.

antecedent *n.* preceding thing or circumstance. —*a.* previous.

antedate *v.t.* put an earlier date on; precede in time.

antediluvian *a.* of the time before Noah's Flood; antiquated.

antelope *n.* (pl. *antelope*) animal resembling a deer.

antenatal *a.* before birth; of or during pregnancy.

antenna *n.* (pl. *-ae*) insect's feeler; (*U.S.*, pl. *-as*) aerial.

anterior *a.* coming before in position or time.

ante-room *n.* room leading to a more important one.

anthem *n.* piece of music to be sung in a religious service.

anther *n.* part of a stamen containing pollen.

anthill *n.* mound over an ants' nest.

anthology *n.* collection of passages from literature, esp. poems.

anthracite *n.* form of coal burning with little flame or smoke.

anthrax *n.* disease of sheep and cattle, transmissible to people.

anthropoid *a.* & *n.* man-like (ape).

anthropology *n*. study of the origin and customs of mankind. **anthropological** *a*., **anthropologist** *n*.

anthropomorphic *a*. attributing human form or personality to a god, animal, etc.

anti- *pref*. opposed to; counteracting. ∼**-aircraft** *a*. used against enemy aircraft.

antibiotic *n*. substance that destroys bacteria or prevents their growth.

antibody *n*. protein formed in the blood in reaction to a substance which it then destroys.

antic *n*. absurd movement or behaviour.

anticipate *v.t.* look forward to; deal with or use etc. in advance; forestall; (*loosely*) expect. **anticipation** *n*., **anticipatory** *a*.

anticlimax *n*. dull ending where a climax was expected.

anticlockwise *a*. & *adv*. in the direction opposite to clockwise.

anticyclone *n*. outward flow of air from an area of high atmospheric pressure, producing fine weather.

antidote *n*. substance that counteracts the effects of poison etc.

antifreeze *n*. substance added to water to prevent freezing.

antihistamine /-mɪn/ *n*. substance counteracting the effect of histamine.

antimony /ˈæ-/ *n*. brittle silvery metallic element.

antipathy /-ˈtɪp-/ *n*. strong settled dislike; object of this.

antiperspirant *n*. substance that prevents or reduces sweating.

antipodes /-ˈtɪpədiz/ *n.pl.* places on opposite sides of the earth, esp. Australia and New Zealand (opposite Europe). **antipodean** /-ˈdiən/ *a*.

antiquarian *a*. of the study of antiques. —*n*. person who studies antiques.

antiquated *a*. very old; very old-fashioned.

antique *a*. belonging to the distant past. —*n*. antique interesting or valuable object.

antiquity *n*. ancient times; great age; object dating from ancient times.

antirrhinum /-ˈraɪ-/ *n*. snapdragon.

anti-Semitic *a*. hostile to Jews.

antiseptic *a*. & *n*. (substance) preventing things from becoming septic.

antisocial *a*. opposed to existing social practices; interfering with social amenities; not sociable.

antistatic *a*. counteracting the effects of static electricity.

antithesis /-ˈtɪθə-/ *n*. (pl. *-eses*) contrast.

antitoxin *n*. substance that neutralizes a toxin. **antitoxic** *a*.

antivivisectionist *n*. person opposed to making experiments on live animals.

antler *n*. branched horn of a deer etc.

antonym *n*. word opposite to another in meaning.

anus *n*. opening at the excretory end of the alimentary canal.

anvil *n*. iron block on which a smith hammers metal into shape.

anxiety *n*. state of being anxious; cause of this.

anxious *a*. troubled and uneasy in mind; eager. **anxiously** *adv*.

any *a*. one or some from three or more or from a quantity; every; in a significant amount. —*pron*. any one, some. —*adv*. at all.

anybody *n*. & *pron*. any person; person of importance.

anyhow *adv*. anyway; not in an orderly manner.

anyone *n*. & *pron*. anybody.

anything *n*. & *pron*. any thing. ∼ **but,** far from being.

anyway *adv*. in any way; in any case.

anywhere *adv*. & *pron*. (in or to) any place.

Anzac *n*. member of the Australian and New Zealand Army Corps (1914–18); Australian or New Zealander.

aorta /eɪˈɔːtə/ *n*. great artery carrying blood from the heart.

apace *adv*. swiftly.

apart *adv*. separately, so as to become separated; to or at a distance; into pieces.

apartheid /-heɪt/ *n*. policy of racial segregation in South Africa.

apartment *n*. set of rooms; (*U.S.*) flat.

apathy *n*. lack of interest or concern. **apathetic** *a*., **apathetically** *adv*.

ape *n*. tailless monkey. —*v.t.* imitate, mimic.

aperient /-ˈpɪər-/ *a*. & *n*. laxative.

aperitif /əˈperɪtif/ *n*. alcoholic drink taken as an appetizer.

aperture *n*. opening, esp. one that admits light.

apex *n*. tip, highest point; pointed end.

aphid /ˈeɪfɪd/ *n*. small insect destructive to plants.

aphis /ˈeɪfɪs/ *n*. (pl. *-ides*, pr. *-ɪdiz*) aphid.

aphorism /ˈæf-/ *n*. pithy saying.

aphrodisiac *a*. & *n*. (substance) arousing sexual desire.

apiary /ˈeɪ-/ *n*. place where bees are kept.

apiece *adv*. to or for or by each.

aplomb /əˈplom/ *n*. dignity and confidence.

apocalyptic /-ˈlɪp-/ *a*. prophesying great and dramatic events like those in the **Apocalypse** (last book of the New Testament).

Apocrypha /əˈpokrɪfə/ *n*. books of the Old Testament not accepted as part of the Hebrew scriptures.

apocryphal *a*. untrue, invented.

apologetic *a*. making an apology. **apologetically** *adv*.

apologize *v.i.* make an apology.

apology *n*. statement of regret for having done wrong or hurt; explanation of one's beliefs; poor specimen.

apoplectic /-ˈplek-/ *a*. of or liable to suffer apoplexy; liable to fits of red-faced rage.

apoplexy /ˈæ-/ *n*. sudden loss of ability to feel and move, caused by rupture or blockage of the brain artery.

Apostle *n*. any of the twelve men sent forth by Christ to preach the gospel. **apostolic** /-ˈstol-/ *a*.

apostrophe /əˈpostrəfi/ *n*. the sign ' used esp. to show the possessive case or omission of a letter; passage (in a speech) pointedly addressing someone. **apostrophize** *v.t.* address in this way.

apothecary /-'poθ-/ *n.* (*old use*) pharmaceutical chemist.

appal *v.t.* (p.t. *appalled*) fill with horror or dismay. **appalling** *a.*

apparatus /-'reɪ-/ *n.* equipment for scientific or other work.

apparel *n.* clothing.

apparent /-'pæ-/ *a.* clearly seen or understood; seeming but not real. **apparently** *adv.*

apparition *n.* appearance, thing appearing, esp. of a startling or remarkable kind; ghost.

appeal *v.i.* make an earnest or formal request; apply to a higher court for reversal of a lower court's decision; seem attractive. —*n.* act of appealing; attractiveness.

appear *v.i.* be or become visible; present oneself; be published; seem. **appearance** *n.*

appease *v.t.* soothe or conciliate, esp. by giving what was asked. **appeasement** *n.*

appellation *n.* name, title.

append *v.t.* attach, add at the end.

appendage *n.* thing appended.

appendicitis *n.* inflammation of the intestinal appendix.

appendix *n.* (pl. *-ices*) section at the end of a book, giving extra information; (pl. *-ixes*) small blind tube of tissue attached to the intestine.

appertain *v.i.* belong; be relevant.

appetite *n.* desire, esp. for food.

appetizer *n.* thing eaten or drunk to stimulate the appetite.

appetizing *a.* stimulating the appetite. **appetizingly** *adv.*

applaud *v.t./i.* express approval (of), esp. by clapping; praise. **applause** *n.*

apple *n.* round fruit with firm flesh. **~-pie order,** perfect order.

appliance *n.* device, instrument.

applicable /'æ-/ *a.* able to be applied, appropriate.

applicant *n.* person who applies, esp. for a job.

application *n.* applying; thing applied; ability to apply oneself.

applicator *n.* device for applying something.

applied *a.* put to practical use.

appliqué /æ'pliːkeɪ/ *n.* piece of fabric attached ornamentally. **appliquéd** *a.*

apply *v.t./i.* put into contact with another thing; bring into use or action; be relevant; make a formal request. **~ oneself,** give one's attention and energy.

appoint *v.t.* fix or decide by authority; choose (a person or persons) for a job, committee, etc. **well-appointed** *a.* well equipped.

appointment *n.* arrangement to meet or visit at a specified time; appointing a person to a job, the job itself; (*pl.*) equipment.

apportion *v.t.* divide into shares, allot.

apposite /-zɪt/ *a.* appropriate.

apposition *n.* relationship of words that are syntactically parallel.

appraise *v.t.* estimate the value or quality of. **appraisal** *n.*

appreciable *a.* perceptible; considerable. **appreciably** *adv.*

appreciate *v.t./i.* value greatly, be grateful for; enjoy intelligently; understand; increase in value. **appreciation** *n.*, **appreciative** *a.*

apprehend *v.t.* seize, arrest; grasp the meaning of; expect with fear or anxiety. **apprehension** *n.*

apprehensive *a.* feeling apprehension, anxious. **apprehensively** *adv.*

apprentice *n.* person learning a craft and bound to an employer by a legal agreement. —*v.t.* bind as an apprentice. **apprenticeship** *n.*

apprise *v.t.* inform.

approach *v.t./i.* come nearer (to); set about doing; go to with a request or offer. —*n.* approaching; way or means of this.

approachable *a.* able to be approached; easy to talk to.

approbation *n.* approval.

appropriate[1] /-ət/ *a.* suitable, proper. **appropriately** *adv.*

appropriate[2] /-eɪt/ *v.t.* take and use; set aside for a special purpose. **appropriation** *n.*

approval *n.* approving. **on ~,** (of goods) supplied without obligation to buy if not satisfactory.

approve *v.t./i.* say or feel that (a thing) is good or suitable; agree to.

approximate[1] /-ət/ *a.* almost but not quite exact. **approximately** *adv.*

approximate[2] /-eɪt/ *v.t./i.* be almost the same; make approximate. **approximation** *n.*

appurtenance *n.* minor thing that goes with a more important one.

après-ski /æpreɪ-'skiː/ *a. & n.* (of or for) evening period after skiing.

apricot *n.* stone-fruit related to the peach; its orange-pink colour.

April *n.* fourth month of the year. **~ fool,** person hoaxed on April Fool's Day (1 April).

apron *n.* garment worn over the front of the body to protect clothes; hard-surfaced area on an airfield, where aircraft are manœuvred, loaded, etc.

apropos /æprə'pəʊ/ *adv. & a.* appropriate(ly). **~ of,** concerning.

apse *n.* recess usu. with an arched or domed roof, esp. in a church.

apt *a.* suitable; having a certain tendency; quick at learning. **aptly** *adv.*, **aptness** *n.*

aptitude *n.* natural ability.

aqualung *n.* diver's portable breathing-apparatus.

aquamarine /-'riːn/ *n.* bluish-green beryl; its colour.

aquarium *n.* (pl. *-ums*) tank for keeping living fish etc.; building containing such tanks.

aquatic *a.* living in or near water; taking place in or on water.

aquatint *n.* a kind of etching.

aqueduct *n.* artificial channel on a raised structure, carrying water across country.

aquilegia /-'liː-/ *n.* columbine.

aquiline /-laɪn/ *a.* like an eagle, (of a nose) hooked.

Arab *n.* member of a Semitic people of the Middle East. —*a.* of Arabs.

arabesque /-ˈbesk/ *n.* decoration with intertwined lines etc.; dancer's posture with the body bent forward and leg and arm extended in line.

Arabian *a.* of Arabia.

Arabic /ˈæ-/ *a.* & *n.* (of) the language of the Arabs. **arabic numerals,** the symbols 1, 2, 3, etc.

arable /ˈæ-/ *a.* & *n.* (land) suitable for growing crops.

arachnid /-ˈræk-/ *n.* member of the class to which spiders belong.

arbiter *n.* person with power to decide what shall be done or accepted; arbitrator.

arbitrary *a.* based on random choice. **arbitrarily** *adv.*

arbitrate *v.i.* act as arbitrator. **arbitration** *n.*

arbitrator *n.* impartial person chosen to settle a dispute.

arboreal /-ˈbɔr-/ *a.* of or living in trees.

arboretum /-ˈri-/ *n.* (pl. *-ta* or *-tums*) place where trees are grown for study and display.

arbour *n.* shady shelter under trees or a framework with climbing plants.

arc *n.* part of a curve; luminous electric current crossing a gap between terminals. ∼ **lamp, light, welding,** that using an electric arc.

arcade *n.* covered area between shops; series of arches. **amusement** ∼, area with pin-tables, gambling machines, etc.

arcane /-ˈkem/ *a.* mysterious.

arch[1] *n.* curved structure, esp. as a support. —*v.t./i.* form (into) an arch.

arch[2] *a.* consciously or affectedly playful. **archly** *adv.*, **archness** *n.*

archaeology *n.* study of civilizations through their material remains. **archaeological** *a.*, **archaeologist** *n.*

archaic *a.* belonging to former or ancient times.

archangel *n.* angel of the highest rank.

archbishop *n.* chief bishop.

archdeacon *n.* priest ranking next below bishop.

arch-enemy *n.* chief enemy.

archer *n.* person who shoots with bow and arrows. **archery** *n.* sport of shooting thus.

archetype /-kɪ-/ *n.* prototype; typical specimen.

archipelago /-kɪˈpel-/ *n.* (pl. *-os*) group of islands; sea round this.

architect *n.* designer of buildings.

architecture *n.* designing of buildings; style of building(s). **architectural** *a.*

archives /-kaɪvz/ *pl.n.* historical documents.

archivist /-kɪv-/ *n.* person trained to deal with archives.

archway *n.* arched entrance or passage.

Arctic *a.* & *n.* (of) regions round the North Pole. **arctic** *a.* very cold.

ardent *a.* full of ardour, enthusiastic. **ardently** *adv.*

ardour *n.* great warmth of feeling, enthusiasm.

arduous *a.* needing much effort. **arduously** *adv.*

are *see* **be.**

area *n.* extent or measure of a surface; region; sunken courtyard.

arena *n.* level area in the centre of an amphitheatre or sports stadium; scene of conflict.

aren't = are not.

argue *v.t./i.* express disagreement; exchange angry words; give as reason(s); indicate.

argument *n.* discussion involving disagreement, quarrel; reason put forward; chain of reasoning.

argumentative *a.* fond of arguing.

aria /ˈɑr-/ *n.* solo in opera.

arid /ˈæ-/ *a.* dry, parched. **aridly** *adv.*, **aridness** *n.*, **aridity** /-ˈrɪd-/ *n.*

arise *v.i.* (p.t. *arose*, p.p. *arisen*) come into existence or to people's notice; (*old use*) rise.

aristocracy *n.* hereditary upper classes; form of government in which these rule. **aristocratic** *a.*

aristocrat /ˈæ-/ *n.* member of the aristocracy.

arithmetic *n.* calculating by means of numbers. **arithmetical** *a.*

ark *n.* Noah's boat in which he and his family and animals were saved from the Flood; wooden chest in which the writings of Jewish Law were kept.

arm[1] *n.* upper limb of the human body; similar projection.

arm[2] *v.t.* equip with weapon(s); make (a bomb etc.) ready to explode.

armada /-ˈmɑ-/ *n.* fleet of warships.

armadillo *n.* (pl. *-os*) burrowing animal of South America with a body encased in bony plates.

Armageddon *n.* decisive conflict.

armament *n.* military weapons; process of equipping for war.

armchair *n.* chair with raised sides.

armful *n.* as much as an arm can hold.

armistice *n.* agreement to stop fighting temporarily.

armlet *n.* band worn round an arm or sleeve.

armour *n.* protective metal covering, esp. that formerly worn in fighting.

armoured *a.* protected by armour; equipped with armoured vehicles.

armoury *n.* place where weapons are kept.

armpit *n.* hollow under the arm at the shoulder.

arms *n.pl.* weapons; coat of arms (see *coat*).

army *n.* organized force for fighting on land; vast group; body of people organized for a purpose.

aroma *n.* smell, esp. a pleasant one. **aromatic** *a.*

arose *see* **arise.**

around *adv.* & *prep.* all round, on every side (of); near at hand; (*U.S.*) approximately.

arouse *v.t.* rouse.

arpeggio /-ˈpedʒ-/ *n.* (pl. *-os*) notes of a musical chord played in succession.

arrange *v.t.* put into order; form plans, settle the details of; adapt. **arrangement** *n.*

arrant /ˈæ-/ *a.* downright.

array *v.t.* arrange in order; dress, adorn. —*n.* imposing series, display.

arrears *n.pl.* money owed and overdue for repayment; work overdue for being finished.

arrest *v.t.* stop (a movement or moving thing); catch and hold (attention); seize by authority of law. —*n.* stoppage; seizure, legal arresting of an offender.

arrestable *a.* (of an offence) such that the offender may be arrested.

arrival *n.* arriving; person or thing that has arrived.

arrive *v.i.* reach a destination or other point on a journey; (of time) come; (*colloq.*, of a baby) be born; be recognized as having achieved success.

arrogant *a.* proud and overbearing. **arrogantly** *adv.*, **arrogance** *n.*

arrow *n.* straight pointed shaft to be shot from a bow; line with an outward-pointing V at the end, indicating direction etc.

arrowroot *n.* edible starch made from the root of an American plant.

arsenal *n.* place where weapons and ammunition are stored or made.

arsenic *n.* semi-metallic element; strongly poisonous compound of this. **arsenical** /-ˈsen-/ *a.*

arson *n.* intentional and unlawful setting on fire of a house etc.

arsonist *n.* person guilty of arson.

art[1] *n.* production of something beautiful; skill or ability; paintings or sculptures etc.; (*pl.*) subjects other than sciences, requiring sensitive understanding rather than use of measurement.

art[2] (*old use*, with *thou*) = are.

artefact *n.* man-made object, simple prehistoric tool or weapon.

arterial /-ˈtiər-/ *a.* of an artery. ~ **road**, trunk road as a channel of transport.

artery *n.* large blood-vessel conveying blood away from the heart.

artesian well /-ˈtizjən/ a well that is bored vertically into oblique strata so that water rises with little or no pumping.

artful *a.* crafty. **artfully** *adv.*, **artfulness** *n.*

arthritis *n.* condition in which there is inflammation, pain, and stiffness in the joints. **arthritic** /-ˈrɪt-/ *a.*

artichoke *n.* plant with a flower of leaf-like scales used as a vegetable. **Jerusalem ~,** sunflower with an edible root.

article *n.* particular or separate thing; prose composition in a newspaper etc.; clause in an agreement. —*v.t.* bind by articles of apprenticeship. **definite ~,** the word 'the'. **indefinite ~,** 'a' or 'an'.

articulate[1] /-ət/ *a.* spoken distinctly; able to express ideas clearly.

articulate[2] /-eɪt/ *v.t./i.* say or speak distinctly; form a joint, connect by joints. **articulated lorry,** one with sections connected by a flexible joint. **articulation** *n.*

artifice *n.* trickery; device.

artificial *a.* not originating naturally; made in imitation of something. **artificially** *adv.*, **artificiality** *n.*

artillery *n.* large guns used in fighting on land; branch of an army using these.

artisan /-ˈzæn *or* ˈa-/ *n.* skilled workman.

artist *n.* person who produces works of art, esp. paintings; one who does something with exceptional skill; professional entertainer.

artiste /-ˈtist/ *n.* professional entertainer.

artistic *a.* of art or artists; showing or done with good taste. **artistically** *adv.*

artistry *n.* artistic skill.

artless *a.* free from artfulness, simple and natural. **artlessly** *adv.*

arty *a.* (*colloq.*) with an exaggerated or affected display of artistic style or interests.

arum /ˈeər-/ *n.* a kind of plant with a large spathe.

Aryan *a.* of the original Indo European language; of its speakers or their descendants. —*n.* Aryan person.

as *adv.* & *conj.* in the same degree, similarly; in the form or function of; while, when; because. —*rel.pron.* that, who, which. ~ **for,** ~ **to,** with regard to. ~ **well,** in addition; desirable, desirably.

asbestos *n.* soft fibrous mineral substance; fireproof material made from this.

ascend *v.t./i.* go or come up. ~ **the throne,** become king or queen.

ascendancy *n.* being dominant.

ascendant *a.* rising. **in the ~,** rising in power or influence.

ascension *n.* ascent; *A~,* that of Christ to heaven.

ascent *n.* ascending; way up, upward slope or path.

ascertain *v.t.* find out by enquiring.

ascertainable *a.* able to be ascertained.

ascetic /-ˈset-/ *a.* not allowing oneself pleasures and luxuries. —*n.* person who is ascetic esp. for religious reasons. **asceticism** *n.*

ascribe *v.t.* attribute, **ascription** *n.*

aseptic /eɪ-/ *a.* free from harmful bacteria. **aseptically** *adv.*

ash[1] *n.* tree with silver-grey bark.

ash[2] *n.* powder that remains after something has burnt. **~-bin** *n.* dustbin. **Ash Wednesday,** first day of Lent.

ashamed *a.* feeling shame.

ashen *a.* pale as ashes.

ashore *adv.* to or on shore.

ashtray *n.* receptacle for tobacco ash.

ashy *a.* ashen; covered with ash.

Asian *a.* of Asia or its people. —*n.* Asian person.

Asiatic *a.* of Asia.

aside *adv.* to or on one side, away from the main part or group. —*n.* words spoken so that only certain people will hear. ~ **from,** (*U.S.*) apart from.

asinine /ˈæsɪnaɪn/ *a.* silly.

ask *v.t./i.* call for an answer to or about; address a question to; seek to obtain; invite.

askance *adv.* **look ~ at,** look at with distrust or displeasure.

askew *adv.* & *a.* crooked(ly).

asleep *adv.* & *a.* in or into a state of sleep; numbed.

asp *n.* small poisonous snake.

asparagus *n*. plant whose shoots are used as a vegetable; these shoots.

aspect *n*. look or appearance; feature of a complex matter; direction a thing faces, side facing this way.

aspen *n*. a kind of poplar.

asperity /-ˈspe-/ *n*. harshness.

aspersions *n.pl*. attack on a reputation.

asphalt /ˈæsfælt/ *n*. black substance like coal-tar; mixture of this with gravel etc. for paving. —*v.t*. surface with asphalt.

asphyxia *n*. suffocation.

asphyxiate *v.t*. suffocate. **asphyxiation** *n*.

aspic *n*. savoury jelly for coating cooked meat, eggs, etc.

aspidistra *n*. plant with broad tapering leaves.

aspirant /ˈæ-/ *n*. person who aspires to something.

aspirate¹ /-ət/ *n*. sound of h.

aspirate² /-eɪt/ *v.t*. pronounce with an h.

aspiration *n*. aspirating; aspiring; earnest desire or ambition.

aspire *v.i*. feel an earnest ambition.

aspirin *n*. drug that relieves pain and reduces fever; tablet of this.

ass *n*. donkey; (*colloq*.) stupid person.

assail *v.t*. attack violently.

assailant *n*. attacker.

assassin *n*. person who assassinates another.

assassinate *v.t*. kill (an important person) by violent means. **assassination** *n*., **assassinator** *n*.

assault *n*. & *v.t*. attack.

assay /-ˈseɪ/ *n*. test of metal for quality. —*v.t*. make an assay of.

assemblage *n*. assembly; things assembled.

assemble *v.t./i*. bring or come together; put or fit together.

assembly *n*. assembling; assembled group.

assent *v.i*. consent; express agreement. —*n*. consent, permission.

assert *v.t*. state, declare to be true; use (power etc.) effectively. **assertion** *n*.

assess *v.t*. decide the amount or value of; estimate the worth or likelihood etc. of. **assessment** *n*., **assessor** *n*.

asset *n*. property with money value, esp. as available to meet debts; useful quality, person or thing having this.

assiduous *a*. diligent and persevering. **assiduously** *adv*., **assiduity** *n*.

assign *v.t*. allot; designate to perform a task etc.; ascribe.

assignation *n*. assigning; arrangement to meet.

assimilate *v.t./i*. absorb or be absorbed into the body or a group etc., or into the mind as knowledge. **assimilation** *n*.

assist *v.t./i*. help. **assistance** *n*.

assistant *n*. helper; person who serves customers in a shop. —*a*. assisting, esp. as a subordinate.

associate¹ /-eɪt/ *v.t./i*. join as a companion or supporter etc.; have frequent dealings; connect in one's mind.

associate² /-ət/ *n*. companion, partner; subordinate member. —*a*. associated; having subordinate membership.

association *n*. associating; group organized for a common purpose; mental connection between ideas. **Association football,** that played with a spherical ball not handled in play except by the goalkeeper.

assorted *a*. of different sorts put together.

assortment *n*. collection composed of several sorts.

assume *v.t*. take as true, without proof; take or put upon oneself.

assumption *n*. assuming; thing assumed to be true; *A*∼, reception of the Virgin Mary in bodily form into heaven.

assurance *n*. positive assertion; self-confidence; life insurance.

assure *v.t*. tell confidently, promise; make certain.

assured *a*. sure, confident; insured.

assuredly /-ɪdlɪ/ *adv*. certainly.

aster *n*. garden plant with daisy-like flowers.

asterisk *n*. star-shaped symbol *.

astern *adv*. at or towards the stern; backwards.

asteroid *n*. any of the small planets revolving round the sun.

asthma /-sm-/ *n*. chronic condition causing difficulty in breathing. **asthmatic** /-sˈmæ-/ *a*. & *n*.

astigmatism /-ˈstɪg-/ *n*. defect in an eye or lens, preventing proper focusing. **astigmatic** /-ˈmæ-/ *a*.

astonish *v.t*. surprise very greatly. **astonishment** *n*.

astound *v.t*. shock with surprise.

astrakhan /-ˈkæn/ *n*. dark curly fleece of lambs from Astrakhan in Russia; fabric imitating this.

astray *adv*. & *a*. away from the proper path. **go** ∼, be mislaid.

astride *adv*. with legs wide apart; with one leg on each side of something. —*prep*. astride of; extending across.

astringent *a*. causing tissue to contract; harsh, severe. —*n*. astringent substance. **astringency** *n*.

astrology *n*. study of the supposed influence of stars on human affairs. **astrologer** *n*., **astrological** *a*.

astronaut *n*. person who operates a spacecraft in which he travels.

astronautics *n*. study of space travel and its technology.

astronomer *n*. person skilled in astronomy.

astronomical *a*. of astronomy; enormous in amount. **astronomically** *adv*.

astronomy *n*. study of stars and planets and their movements.

astute *a*. shrewd, quick at seeing how to gain an advantage. **astutely** *adv*., **astuteness** *n*.

asunder *adv*. apart, into pieces.

asylum *n*. refuge; (*old use*) mental institution.

asymmetrical *a*. not symmetrical. **asymmetrically** *adv*.

at *prep*. having as position, time of day, condition, or price. ∼ **all,** in any way; of any kind. ∼ **once,** immediately; simultaneously.

ate *see* **eat.**

atheist /ˈeɪθɪ-/ n. person who does not believe in the existence of God or god(s). **atheism** n.

athlete n. person who is good at athletics.

athletic a. of athletes; muscular and physically active.

athletics n.pl. or sing. sports, esp. running, jumping, etc.

Atlantic a. & n. (of) the ∼ **Ocean** (east of the American continent).

atlas n. book of maps.

atmosphere n. mixture of gases surrounding the earth or a heavenly body; air in any place; mental feeling conveyed by an environment etc.; unit of pressure. **atmospheric** a.

atmospherics n.pl. electrical disturbances in the air, causing interference in telecommunications.

atoll /ˈæ-/ n. ring-shaped coral reef enclosing a lagoon.

atom n. smallest particle of a chemical substance; very small quantity or thing. ∼ **bomb**, atomic bomb.

atomic a. of atom(s). ∼ **bomb**, bomb deriving its power from atomic energy. ∼ **energy**, that obtained from nuclear fission.

atomize v.t. reduce to atoms or fine particles. **atomizer** n.

atonal /eɪˈtəʊnəl/ a. (of music) not written in any key.

atone v.i. make amends for an error or deficiency. **atonement** n.

atrocious a. extremely wicked; very bad. **atrociously** adv.

atrocity n. wickedness; wicked or cruel act etc.

atrophy /ˈæ-/ n. wasting away through lack of nourishment or of use. —v.t./i. cause atrophy in; suffer atrophy.

attach v.t./i. fix to something else; join; attribute, be attributable. **attached** a. bound by affection or loyalty. **attachment** n.

attaché /-ʃeɪ/ n. person attached to an ambassador's staff. ∼ **case**, small rectangular case for carrying documents etc.

attack n. violent attempt to hurt, overcome, or defeat; strong criticism; sudden onset of illness. —v.t./i. make an attack (on); act harmfully on. **attacker** n.

attain v.t. achieve. **attainment** n.

attempt v.t. make an effort to accomplish or overcome. —n. this effort.

attend v.t./i. give attention to; be present at; accompany as an attendant. **attendance** n.

attendant a. accompanying. —n. person present as a companion or to provide service.

attention n. applying one's mind; awareness; consideration, care; erect attitude in military drill.

attentive a. giving attention. **attentively** adv., **attentiveness** n.

attenuate v.t. make slender or thin or weaker. **attenuation** n.

attest v.t./i. provide proof of; declare true or genuine. **attestation** n.

attic n. room in the top storey of a house.

attire n. clothes. —v.t. clothe.

attitude n. position of the body; way of thinking or behaving.

attorney /-ˈtɜ-/ n. (pl. -eys) person appointed to act for another in legal or business matters; (U.S.) lawyer.

attract v.t. draw towards itself by unseen force; arouse the interest or pleasure of. **attraction** n.

attractive a. attracting; pleasing in appearance. **attractively** adv.

attribute[1] /-ˈtrɪb-/ v.t. ∼ **to**, regard as belonging to or caused by. **attribution** n.

attribute[2] /ˈæ-/ n. characteristic quality; object regularly associated with a person or thing.

attributive a. qualifying a noun and placed before it.

attrition n. wearing away.

aubergine /ˈəʊbəʒiːn/ n. deep-purple vegetable; its colour.

aubrietia /-ˈbriːʃə/ n. perennial rock-plant flowering in spring.

auburn a. (of hair) reddish-brown.

auction n. public sale where articles are sold to the highest bidder. —v.t. sell by auction.

auctioneer n. person who conducts an auction.

audacious a. bold, daring. **audaciously** adv., **audacity** n.

audible a. loud enough to be heard. **audibly** adv., **audibility** n.

audience n. group of listeners or spectators; formal interview.

audio n. sound reproduced mechanically; its reproduction. ∼ **typist**, one who types from a recording. ∼**-visual** a. using both sight and sound.

audit n. official examination of accounts. —v.t. make an audit of.

audition n. test of a prospective performer's ability. —v.t./i. test in an audition.

auditor n. one who audits accounts.

auditorium n. part of a building where the audience sits.

auger n. boring-tool.

augment /-ˈment/ v.t. increase. **augmentation** n.

augur v.i. bode.

august /-ˈɡʌst/ a. majestic, imposing.

August n. eighth month of the year.

auk n. northern sea-bird.

aunt n. sister or sister-in-law of one's father or mother. **Aunt Sally,** target in a throwing-game; target of general abuse.

auntie n. (colloq.) aunt.

au pair /əʊ-/ young woman from overseas helping with housework in return for board and lodging.

aura n. atmosphere surrounding a person or thing.

aural a. of the ear. **aurally** adv.

au revoir /əʊ rəˈvwɑ(r)/ goodbye for the moment.

auspicious a. showing signs that promise success. **auspiciously** adv.

austere a. severely simple and plain. **austerely** adv., **austerity** /-ˈste-/ n.

Australasian a. of Australia, New Zealand, and neighbouring islands.

Australian *a. & n.* (native or inhabitant) of Australia.

authentic *a.* genuine, known to be true. **authentically** *adv.*, **authenticity** *n.*

authenticate *v.t.* prove the truth or authenticity of. **authentication** *n.*

author *n.* writer of a book etc.; originator. **authoress** *n.fem.*, **authorship** *n.*

authoritarian *a.* favouring complete obedience to authority.

authoritative *a.* having or using authority. **authoritatively** *adv.*

authority *n.* power to enforce obedience; person(s) with this; person with specialized knowledge.

authorize *v.t.* give authority to or permission for. **authorization** *n.*

autistic *a.* suffering from a mental disorder that prevents proper response to one's environment. **autism** *n.* this disorder.

autobiography *n.* story of a person's life written by himself. **autobiographical** *a.*

autocracy /-ˈtok-/ *n.* despotism.

autocrat *n.* person with unrestricted power; dictatorial person. **autocratic** *a.*, **autocratically** *adv.*

autocross *n.* motor-racing across country.

autograph *n.* person's signature; manuscript in the author's handwriting. —*v.t.* write one's name in or on.

automate *v.t.* control by automation.

automatic *a.* mechanical, self-regulating; done without thinking. —*n.* automatic machine or firearm etc. **automatically** *adv.*

automation *n.* use of automatic equipment in industry etc.

automaton /-ˈtom-/ *n.* robot.

automobile *n.* (*U.S.*) car.

automotive *a.* concerning motor vehicles.

autonomous /-ˈton-/ *a.* self-governing.

autonomy /-ˈton-/ *n.* self-government.

autopsy *n.* post-mortem.

autumn *n.* season between summer and winter. **autumnal** *a.*

auxiliary *a.* giving help or support. —*n.* helper; (*pl.*) foreign troops employed by a country at war. ∼ **verb**, one used in forming tenses etc. of other verbs.

avail *v.t./i.* be of use or help (to). —*n.* effectiveness, advantage. ∼ **oneself of**, make use of.

available *a.* ready to be used; obtainable. **availability** *n.*

avalanche *n.* mass of snow pouring down a mountain; great onrush.

avarice *n.* greed for gain. **avaricious** *a.*

avenge *v.t.* take vengeance for. **avenger** *n.*

avenue *n.* wide street or road; way of approach.

average *n.* value arrived at by adding several quantities together and dividing by the number of these; standard regarded as usual. —*a.* found by making an average; of ordinary standard. —*v.t./i.* calculate the average of; amount to or produce as an average.

averse *a.* unwilling, disinclined.

aversion *n.* strong dislike.

avert *v.t.* turn away; ward off.

aviary *n.* large cage or building for keeping birds.

aviation *n.* flying an aircraft.

aviator *n.* (*old use*) pilot or member of an aircraft crew.

avid *a.* eager, greedy. **avidly** *adv.*, **avidity** *n.*

avocado /-ˈkɑ-/ *n.* (pl. *-os*) pear-shaped tropical fruit.

avoid *v.t.* keep oneself away from; refrain from. **avoidance** *n.*

avoidable *a.* able to be avoided.

avoirdupois /ˌævədəˈpɔɪz/ *n.* system of weights based on the pound of 16 ounces.

avuncular *a.* of or like a kindly uncle.

await *v.t.* wait for.

awake *v.t./i.* (p.t. *awoke*, p.p. *awoken*) wake. —*a.* not asleep; alert.

awaken *v.t./i.* awake.

award *v.t.* give by official decision as a prize or penalty etc. —*n.* awarding; thing awarded.

aware *a.* having knowledge or realization. **awareness** *n.*

awash *a.* washed over by water.

away *adv.* to or at a distance; into non-existence; persistently. —*a.* played on an opponent's ground. —*n.* away match or win.

awe *n.* respect combined with fear or wonder. —*v.t.* fill with awe.

awesome *a.* causing awe.

awestricken, awestruck *adjs.* suddenly filled with awe.

aweigh *adv.* (of anchor) raised just clear of the sea bottom.

awful *a.* extremely bad or unpleasant; (*colloq.*) very great. **awfully** *adv.*

awhile *adv.* for a short time.

awkward *a.* difficult to use or handle; clumsy, having little skill; inconvenient; embarrassed. **awkwardly** *adv.*, **awkwardness** *n.*

awl *n.* small pricking-tool.

awning *n.* roof-like canvas shelter.

awoke, awoken *see* **awake**.

awry /əˈraɪ/ *adv. & a.* twisted to one side; amiss.

axe *n.* chopping-tool. —*v.t.* (pres.p. *axing*) remove by abolishing or dismissing.

axil *n.* angle where a leaf joins a stem.

axiom *n.* accepted general truth or principle. **axiomatic** /-ˈmæ-/ *a.*

axis *n.* (pl. *axes*) line through the centre of an object, round which it rotates if spinning. **axial** *a.*

axle *n.* rod on which wheels turn.

ay /aɪ/ *adv. & n.* (pl. *ayes*) aye.

ayatollah /aɪəˈtolə/ *n.* senior Muslim religious leader.

aye /aɪ/ *adv.* yes. —*n.* vote in favour of a proposal.

azalea *n.* shrub-like flowering plant.

Aztec *n.* member of a former Indian people of Mexico.

B

B.A. *abbr.* Bachelor of Arts.

baa *n.* & *v.i.* bleat.

babble *v.i.* chatter indistinctly or foolishly; (of a stream) murmur. —*n.* babbling talk or sound.

babe *n.* baby.

baboon *n.* a kind of large monkey.

baby *n.* very young child or animal; thing small of its kind; (*U.S. sl.*) person, esp. a man's girl-friend. **∼-sit** *v.i.* act as **∼-sitter,** person employed to look after a child while its parents are out.

babyish *a.* like a baby.

baccarat /-rɑ/ *n.* gambling card-game.

bachelor *n.* unmarried man. **Bachelor of Arts** etc., person with the lowest university degree.

bacillus /-ˈsɪl-/ *n.* (pl. *-li*) rod-like bacterium.

back *n.* hinder surface or part furthest from the front; defensive player positioned near the goal in football etc. —*a.* situated behind; of or for past time. —*adv.* at or towards the rear; in check; in or into a previous time, position, or state; in return. —*v.t./i.* move backwards; help, support; lay a bet on; cover the back of. **∼-bencher** M.P. not entitled to sit on front benches. **∼ down,** withdraw a claim or argument. **∼ of beyond,** very remote place. **∼ out,** withdraw from an agreement. **backer** *n.*

backache *n.* pain in one's back.

backbiting *n.* spiteful talk.

backbone *n.* column of small bones down the centre of the back.

backchat *n.* answering back.

backdate *v.t.* regard as valid from an earlier date.

backfire *v.i.* make an abnormal explosion, e.g. in an exhaust pipe; produce an undesired effect.

backgammon *n.* game played on a board with draughts and dice.

background *n.* back part of a scene or picture; conditions surrounding and influencing something.

backhand *n.* backhanded stroke.

backhanded *a.* performed with the back of the hand turned forwards; (of a compliment) with underlying sarcasm.

backhander *n.* backhanded stroke; (*sl.*) bribe, reward for services.

backlash *n.* violent hostile reaction.

backlog *n.* arrears of work.

backside *n.* (*colloq.*) buttocks.

backslide *v.i.* slip back from good behaviour into bad.

backstage *a.* & *adv.* behind a theatre stage.

backstroke *n.* stroke used in swimming on one's back.

backward *a.* directed backwards; having made less than normal progress; diffident. —*adv.* backwards.

backwards *adv.* towards the back; with the back foremost; in a reverse direction or order. **∼ and forwards,** each way alternately.

backwater *n.* stagnant water joining a stream; place unaffected by new ideas or progress.

bacon *n.* salted or smoked meat from a pig.

bacterium *n.* (pl. *-ia*) microscopic organism. **bacterial** *a.*

bad *a.* (*worse, worst*) having undesirable qualities; wicked, evil; unpleasant; harmful; serious; of poor quality; diseased, decayed. —*adv.* (*U.S.*) badly. **∼ language,** swear-words. **badly** *adv.*, **badness** *n.*

bade *see* **bid**[2].

badge *n.* thing worn to show membership, rank, etc.

badger *n.* burrowing animal of the weasel family. —*v.t.* pester.

badinage /-ɑʒ/ *n.* banter.

badminton *n.* game like lawn tennis, played with a shuttlecock.

baffle *v.t.* be too difficult for; frustrate. —*n.* screen. **bafflement** *n.*

bag *n.* flexible container; amount of game shot by a sportsman; (*pl., sl.*) large amount, (*old use*) trousers. —*v.t./i.* (p.t. *bagged*) put into bag(s); hang loosely; (*colloq.*) take for oneself.

bagatelle *n.* game played with small balls on a board with holes.

baggage *n.* luggage.

baggy *a.* hanging in loose folds.

bagpipes *n.pl.* wind instrument with air stored in a bag and pressed out through pipes.

bail[1] *n.* money pledged as security that an accused person will return for trial. —*v.t.* obtain or allow the release of (a person) on bail; relieve by financial help.

bail[2] *n.* one of two cross-pieces resting on the stumps in cricket.

bail[3] *v.t.* scoop water out of.

bailiff *n.* officer assisting a sheriff, e.g. with legal seizure of goods; landlord's agent or steward.

bairn *n.* (*Sc.*) child.

bait *n.* food etc. placed to attract prey. —*v.t.* place bait on or in; torment by jeers.

baize *n.* thick woollen green cloth for covering tables etc.

bake *v.t./i.* cook or harden by dry heat.

baker *n.* person who bakes and sells bread.

bakery *n.* place where bread is baked for sale.

baking-powder *n.* mixture of powders used to make cake etc. rise.

balance *n.* weighing-apparatus with hanging pans; regulating-apparatus of a clock; even distribution of weight or amount; difference between credits and debits; remainder. —*v.t./i.* consider by comparing; be or put or keep in a state of balance; equalize.

balcony *n.* projecting platform with a rail or parapet; upper floor of seats in a cinema etc.

bald *a.* (*-er, -est*) with scalp wholly or partly hairless; (of tyres) with tread worn away; without details. **baldly** *adv.*, **baldness** *n.*

balderdash *n.* nonsense.

balding *a.* becoming bald.

bale[1] *n.* large bound bundle of straw etc.; large package of goods. —*v.t.* make into a bale or bales.

bale[2] *v.t.* ~ **out,** descend by parachute from an aircraft.

baleful *a.* menacing, destructive. **balefully** *adv.*

balk *v.t./i.* shirk; frustrate.

ball[1] *n.* solid or hollow sphere, esp. used in a game; rounded part or mass; single delivery of a ball by a bowler. —*v.t./i.* form into a ball. ~**-bearing** *n.* bearing using small steel balls; one such ball. ~**-cock** *n.* device with a floating ball controlling the water-level in a cistern. ~**-point** *n.* pen with a tiny ball as its writing-point.

ball[2] *n.* social assembly for dancing.

ballad *n.* simple song or poem telling a story.

ballast *n.* heavy material placed in a ship's hold to steady it.

ballerina *n.* female ballet-dancer.

ballet /-leɪ/ *n.* performance of dancing and mime to music.

ballistic *a.* ~ **missile,** one that is powered and guided at first but falls to its target by gravity.

ballistics *n.pl.* study of projectiles.

balloon *n.* bag inflated with air or lighter gas. —*v.i.* swell like this.

balloonist *n.* person who travels by balloon.

ballot *n.* vote recorded on a slip of paper; voting by this. —*v.t./i.* (p.t. *balloted*) vote by ballot; cause to do this.

ballroom *n.* large room where dances are held.

ballyhoo *n.* vulgar or misleading publicity.

balm *n.* soothing influence; fragrant herb; (*old use*) ointment.

balmy *a.* (*-ier, -iest*) fragrant; (of air) soft and warm; (*sl.*) crazy.

baloney *n.* (*sl.*) nonsense.

balsa *n.* tropical American tree; its lightweight wood.

balsam *n.* soothing oil; a kind of flowering plant.

baluster *n.* short stone pillar in a balustrade.

balustrade *n.* row of short pillars supporting a rail or coping.

bamboo *n.* giant tropical grass with hollow stems.

bamboozle *v.t.* (*sl.*) mystify, trick.

ban *v.t.* (p.t. *banned*) forbid officially. —*n.* order banning something.

banal /-ˈnɑl/ *a.* commonplace, uninteresting. **banality** /-ˈnæ-/ *n.*

banana *n.* finger-shaped fruit; tropical tree bearing this.

band *n.* strip, hoop, loop; range of values or wavelengths etc.; organized group of people; set of musicians esp. playing wind or percussion instruments. —*v.t./i.* put a band on; form an organized group.

bandage *n.* strip of material for binding a wound. —*v.t.* bind with this.

bandit *n.* member of a band of robbers.

bandstand *n.* covered outdoor platform for a band playing music.

bandwagon *n.* **climb on the** ~**,** seek to join a thing heading for success.

bandy[1] *v.t.* pass to and fro.

bandy[2] *a.* (*-ier, -iest*) curving apart at the knees. **bandiness** *n.*

bane *n.* cause of trouble or anxiety. **baneful** *a.*, **banefully** *adv.*

bang *n.* noise of or like an explosion; sharp blow. —*v.t./i.* make this noise; strike; shut noisily. —*adv.* abruptly; exactly.

banger *n.* firework that explodes noisily; (*sl.*) noisy old car; (*sl.*) sausage.

bangle *n.* bracelet of rigid material.

banian *n.* Indian fig-tree with branches that root.

banish *v.t.* condemn to exile; dismiss from one's presence or thoughts. **banishment** *n.*

banisters *n.pl.* uprights and handrail of a staircase.

banjo *n.* (pl. *-os*) guitar-like musical instrument.

bank[1] *n.* slope, esp. at the side of a river; raised mass of earth etc.; row of lights, switches, etc. —*v.t./i.* form or build up into a bank; tilt sideways in rounding a curve.

bank[2] *n.* establishment for safe keeping of money which it pays out on a customer's order; money held by the keeper of a gaming-table; place storing a reserve supply. —*v.t./i.* place money in a bank; base one's hopes. ~ **holiday,** public holiday when banks are officially closed.

banking *n.* business of running a financial bank. **banker** *n.*

banknote *n.* printed strip of paper issued by a bank as currency.

bankrupt *a.* unable to pay one's debts. —*n.* bankrupt person. —*v.t.* make bankrupt. **bankruptcy** *n.*

banner *n.* a kind of flag carried in processions; any flag.

banns *n.pl.* announcement in church about a forthcoming marriage.

banquet *n.* elaborate ceremonial public meal. **banqueting** *n.* taking part in a banquet.

banshee *n.* (*Ir. & Sc.*) spirit whose wail is said to foretell a death.

bantam *n.* small kind of fowl.

bantamweight *n.* boxing-weight (54 kg).

banter *n.* good-humoured joking. —*v.i.* joke thus.

Bantu /-ˈtu/ *a. & n.* (pl. *-u* or *-us*) (member) of a group of African Negroid peoples or their languages.

bap *n.* large soft bread roll.

baptism *n.* religious rite of sprinkling with water as a sign of purification and admission to the Church. **baptismal** *a.*

Baptist *n.* member of a Protestant sect believing that baptism should be by immersion.

baptize *v.t.* perform baptism on; name, nickname.

bar *n.* long piece of solid material; strip; barrier; sandbank; vertical line dividing music into units, this unit; barristers, their profession; counter where alcohol or refreshments are served, room containing this. —*v.t.* (p.t. *barred*) fasten or keep in or out with bar(s); obstruct; prohibit. —*prep.* except.

barb *n.* backward-pointing part of an arrow etc.; wounding remark.

barbarian *n.* uncivilized person.

barbaric *a.* suitable for barbarians, rough and wild.

barbarity *n.* savage cruelty.

barbarous *a.* uncivilized, cruel. **barbarously** *adv.*, **barbarism** *n.*

barbecue *n.* frame for grilling food above an open fire; this food; open-air party where such food is served. —*v.t.* cook on a barbecue.

barbed *a.* having barb(s). ∼ **wire,** wire with many short sharp points.

barber *n.* men's hairdresser.

barbiturate *n.* sedative drug.

bard *n.* Celtic minstrel; poet.

bare *a.* (-*er*, -*est*) not clothed or covered; not adorned; scanty. —*v.t.* uncover, reveal. **barely** *adv.*, **bareness** *n.*

bareback *adv.* on horseback without a saddle.

barefaced *a.* shameless, undisguised.

bareheaded *a.* not wearing a hat.

bargain *n.* agreement with obligations on both or all sides; thing obtained cheaply. —*v.i.* discuss the terms of an agreement; expect.

barge *n.* large flat-bottomed boat used on rivers and canals. —*v.i.* move clumsily. ∼ **in,** intrude.

baritone *n.* male voice between tenor and bass.

barium *n.* white metallic element.

bark[1] *n.* outer layer of a tree. —*v.t.* scrape skin off accidentally.

bark[2] *n.* sharp harsh sound made by a dog. —*v.t./i.* make this sound; utter in a sharp commanding voice.

barley *n.* a kind of cereal plant; its grain. ∼ **sugar,** sweet made of boiled sugar. ∼**water** *n.* drink made from pearl barley.

barmaid *n.* female attendant at a bar serving alcohol.

barman *n.* (pl. -*men*) male attendant at a bar serving alcohol.

barmy *a.* (*sl.*) crazy.

barn *n.* simple roofed farm building for storing grain and hay etc.

barnacle *n.* shellfish that attaches itself to objects under water.

barometer *n.* instrument measuring atmospheric pressure, used in forecasting weather. **barometric** *a.*

baron *n.* member of the lowest rank of nobility; magnate. **baroness** *n.fem.*, **baronial** /-ˈrəʊ-/ *a.*

baroque /bəˈrɒk/ *a.* of the ornate architectural style of the 17th–18th centuries. —*n.* this style.

barrack *v.t./i.* shout protests; jeer at.

barracks *n.pl.* building(s) for soldiers to live in.

barrage *n.* heavy bombardment; artificial barrier.

barrel *n.* large round container with flat ends; tube-like part esp. of a gun. ∼**organ** *n.* mechanical instrument producing music by a pin-studded cylinder and keys.

barren *a.* not fertile, unable to bear fruit or young. **barrenness** *n.*

barricade *n.* barrier. —*v.t.* block or defend with a barricade.

barrier *n.* thing that prevents or controls advance or access.

barrister *n.* lawyer entitled to represent clients in the higher courts.

barrow[1] *n.* wheelbarrow; cart pushed or pulled by hand.

barrow[2] *n.* prehistoric burial mound.

barter *n.* & *v.t./i.* trade by exchange of goods for other goods.

basalt /ˈbæsɔlt/ *n.* dark rock of volcanic origin.

base *n.* lowest part; part on which a thing rests or is supported; starting-point; basis; headquarters; main ingredient of a mixture; substance capable of combining with an acid to form a salt; one of four stations to be reached by a runner in baseball. —*v.t.* use as a base or foundation or evidence for a forecast etc. —*a.* dishonourable; of inferior value. **baseless** *a.*

baseball *n.* American ball-game resembling rounders.

basement *n.* storey below ground level.

bash *v.t.* strike violently; attack. —*n.* violent blow or knock; (*sl.*) attempt.

bashful *a.* shy and self-conscious. **bashfully** *adv.*, **bashfulness** *n.*

basic *a.* forming a basis; fundamental. **basically** *adv.*

basil *n.* sweet-smelling herb.

basilica *n.* oblong hall or church with an apse at one end.

basilisk *n.* small American lizard; mythical reptile said to cause death by its glance or breath.

basin *n.* round open dish for holding liquids or soft substances; wash-basin; sunken place, area drained by a river; almost land-locked harbour. **basinful** *n.*

basis *n.* (pl. *bases*) foundation or support; main principle.

bask *v.i.* sit or lie comfortably exposed to pleasant warmth.

basket *n.* container for holding or carrying things, made of inter-woven cane or wire etc.

basketball *n.* game like netball.

basketwork *n.* structure of baskets; art of making this.

Basque *n.* & *a.* (member) of a people living in the western Pyrenees; (of) their language.

bas-relief /ˈbæs-/ *n.* sculpture or carving in low relief.

bass[1] /bæs/ *n.* (pl. *bass*) fish of the perch family.

bass[2] /beɪs/ *a.* deep-sounding, of the lowest pitch in music. —*n.* (pl. *basses*) lowest male voice; bass pitch; double-bass.

basset *n.* short-legged hound used for hunting hares etc.

bassoon /-ˈsun/ *n.* woodwind instrument with a deep tone.

bastard *n.* illegitimate child; (*sl.*) unpleasant person or thing.

baste[1] *v.t.* sew together temporarily with loose stitches.

baste² *v.t.* moisten with fat during cooking; thrash.

bastion *n.* projecting part of a fortified place; stronghold.

bat¹ *n.* wooden implement for striking a ball in games; batsman. —*v.t./i.* (p.t. *batted*) perform or strike with the bat in cricket etc.

bat² *n.* flying animal with a mouse-like body.

bat³ *v.t.* (p.t. *batted*) flutter.

batch *n.* set of people or things dealt with as a group.

bated *a.* **with ∼ breath,** with breath held anxiously.

bath *n.* washing (esp. of the whole body) by immersion; container used for this; (*pl.*) public swimming-pool. —*v.t./i.* wash in a bath.

bathe *v.t./i.* apply liquid to, immerse in liquid; make wet or bright all over; swim for pleasure. —*n.* swim. **bather** *n.*

bathos /ˈbeɪθɒs/ *n.* anticlimax, descent from an important thing to a trivial one.

bathroom *n.* room containing a bath.

batik *n.* method of printing designs on textiles by waxing parts not to be dyed; fabric printed thus.

batman *n.* (pl. *-men*) soldier acting as an officer's personal servant.

baton *n.* short stick, esp. used by a conductor; truncheon.

batsman *n.* (pl. *-men*) player batting in cricket.

battalion *n.* army unit of several companies.

batten¹ *n.* bar of wood or metal, esp. holding something in place. —*v.t.* fasten with batten(s).

batten² *v.i.* feed greedily, thrive at the expense of others.

batter¹ *v.t.* hit hard and often. —*n.* beaten mixture of flour, eggs, and milk, used in cooking.

batter² *n.* player batting in baseball.

battering-ram *n.* iron-headed beam formerly used in war for breaking through walls or gates.

battery *n.* group of big guns; artillery unit; set of similar or connected units of equipment, poultry cages, etc.; electric cell(s) supplying current; unlawful blow or touch.

battle *n.* fight between large organized forces; contest. —*v.i.* engage in battle, struggle.

battleaxe *n.* heavy axe used as a weapon in ancient times; (*colloq.*) formidable woman.

battlefield *n.* scene of battle.

battlements *n.pl.* parapet with gaps at intervals, orig. for firing from.

battleship *n.* warship of the most heavily armed kind.

batty *a.* (*sl.*) crazy.

bauble *n.* showy valueless ornament.

baulk *n.* ridge between furrows; timber beam.

bawdy *a.* (*-ier, -iest*) humorous in a coarse way. **bawdiness** *n.*

bawl *v.t./i.* shout; weep noisily. **∼ out,** (*U.S. colloq.*) scold.

bay¹ *n.* a kind of laurel.

bay² *n.* part of a sea or lake within a wide curve of the shore.

bay³ *n.* recess, compartment. **∼ window,** one projecting from an outside wall.

bay⁴ *n.* deep cry of a large dog or of hounds. —*v.i.* make this sound. **at ∼,** forced to face attackers.

bay⁵ *a.* & *n.* reddish-brown (horse).

bayonet *n.* dagger-like blade that can be fixed to the muzzle of a rifle. —*v.t.* stab with this.

bazaar *n.* series of shops or stalls in an Oriental country; large shop selling a variety of cheap goods; sale of goods to raise funds.

B.C. *abbr.* Before Christ; British Columbia.

be *v.i.* (pres. tense *am, are, is*; p.t. *was, were*; p.p. *been*) exist, occur; have a certain position or quality or condition; become. —*v.aux.* (used to form tenses of other verbs). **have been to,** have visited.

beach *n.* shore between high and low water marks. —*v.t.* bring on shore from water. **∼ head** *n.* fortified position set up on a beach by an invading army.

beachcomber *n.* person who salvages stray articles along a beach.

beacon *n.* signal-fire on a hill; large light used as a signal or warning.

bead *n.* small shaped piece of hard material pierced for threading with others on a string; drop or bubble of liquid; (*pl.*) necklace, rosary.

beading *n.* moulding or carving like beads; strip of trimming for wood.

beady *a.* (of eyes) small and bright.

beagle *n.* small hound used for hunting hares.

beak *n.* bird's horny projecting jaws; any similar projection. **beaked** *a.*

beaker *n.* glass vessel with a lip, used in laboratories; tall drinking-cup.

beam *n.* long piece of timber or metal carrying the weight of part of a house etc.; ship's breadth; ray of light or other radiation; radio signal; bright look, smile. —*v.i.* send out light etc.; look or smile radiantly. **on one's ∼-ends,** near the end of one's resources.

bean *n.* plant with kidney-shaped seeds in long pods; seed of this or of coffee etc.

beano *n.* (pl. *-os*) jolly party.

bear¹ *n.* large heavy animal with thick fur; child's toy like this.

bear² *v.t./i.* (p.t. *bore*, p.p. *borne*) carry, support; have in one's heart or mind; endure; be fit for; produce, give birth to; take (a specified direction); exert pressure. **∼ on,** be relevant to. **∼ out,** confirm. **bearer** *n.*

bearable *a.* endurable.

beard *n.* hair on and round a man's chin; similar growth on an animal or plant. —*v.t.* confront boldly.

beargarden *n.* scene of uproar.

bearing *n.* deportment, behaviour; relevance; compass direction; device reducing friction where a part turns; heraldic emblem.

beast *n.* large four-footed animal; unpleasant person or thing. **∼ of burden,** animal that carries packs on its back.

beastly *a.* (*-ier, -iest*) (*colloq.*) very unpleasant.

beat *v.t./i.* (p.t. *beat*, p.p. *beaten*) hit repeatedly, strike strongly; mix vigorously; (of the heart) pump rhythmically; do better than, defeat. —*n.* regular repeated stroke; its sound; recurring emphasis marking rhythm; appointed course of a policeman or sentinel. ∼ **a retreat,** go away defeated. ∼ **up,** assault violently. **beater** *n.*

beatific *a.* showing great happiness.

beatify *v.t.* (*R.C. Church*) declare blessed, as first step in canonization. **beatification** *n.*

beatitude *n.* blessedness.

beautician *n.* person whose job is to give beautifying treatment.

beautiful *a.* having beauty; very satisfactory. **beautifully** *adv.*

beautify *v.t.* make beautiful.

beauty *n.* combination of qualities giving pleasure to the sight or other senses or to the mind; beautiful person or thing.

beaver *n.* small amphibious rodent; its brown fur. —*v.i.* work hard.

becalmed *a.* unable to move because there is no wind.

became *see* **become.**

because *conj.* for the reason that. —*adv.* ∼ **of,** by reason of.

beck *n.* **at the** ∼ **and call of,** always ready and waiting to obey.

beckon *v.t.* summon by a gesture.

become *v.t./i.* (p.t. *became,* p.p. *become*) come or grow to be, begin to be; give a pleasing appearance or effect upon; befit.

bed *n.* thing to sleep or rest on; framework with a mattress and coverings; flat base, foundation; bottom of a sea or river etc.; layer; garden plot. —*v.t./i.* (p.t. *bedded*) provide with a bed; put or go into a bed.

bedbug *n.* bug infesting beds.

bedclothes *n.pl.* sheets, blankets, etc.

bedevil *v.t.* (p.t. *bedevilled*) afflict with difficulties.

bedfellow *n.* person sharing one's bed; associate.

bedlam *n.* scene of uproar.

Bedouin /ˈbedʊɪn/ *n.* (pl. *Bedouin*) member of an Arab people living in tents in the desert.

bedpan *n.* pan for use as a lavatory by a person confined to bed.

bedpost *n.* upright support of a bed.

bedraggled *a.* limp and untidy.

bedridden *a.* permanently confined to bed through illness or weakness.

bedrock *n.* solid rock beneath loose soil; basic facts.

bedroom *n.* room for sleeping in.

bedside *n.* position by a bed.

bed-sitting-room *n.* room used for both living and sleeping in. **bedsit, bedsitter** *ns.* (*colloq.*).

bedsore *n.* sore developed by lying in bed for a long time.

bedspread *n.* covering spread over a bed during the day.

bedstead *n.* framework of a bed.

bedtime *n.* hour for going to bed.

bee *n.* insect that produces wax and honey. **make a** ∼**line for,** go straight or rapidly towards.

beech *n.* tree with smooth bark and glossy leaves.

beef *n.* meat from ox, bull, or cow; muscular strength; (*sl.*) grumble. —*v.i.* (*sl.*) grumble.

beefburger *n.* hamburger.

beefeater *n.* warder in the Tower of London, wearing Tudor dress.

beefsteak *n.* slice of beef.

beefy *a.* (*-ier, -iest*) having a solid muscular body. **beefiness** *n.*

beehive *n.* hive.

been *see* **be.**

beer *n.* alcoholic drink made from malt and hops. **beery** *a.*

beeswax *n.* yellow substance secreted by bees, used as polish.

beet *n.* plant with a fleshy root used as a vegetable or for making sugar; (*U.S.*) beetroot.

beetle *n.* insect with hard wing-covers.

beetling *a.* overhanging, projecting.

beetroot *n.* (pl. *beetroot*) root of beet as a vegetable.

befall *v.t./i.* (p.t. *befell,* p.p. *befallen*) happen; happen to.

befit *v.t.* (p.t. *befitted*) be suitable for.

before *adv., prep.,* & *conj.* at an earlier time (than); ahead, in front of; in preference to.

beforehand *adv.* in advance.

befriend *v.t.* show kindness towards.

beg *v.t./i.* (p.t. *begged*) ask for as a gift or charity; obtain a living thus; request earnestly or humbly; ask for formally; (of a dog) sit up expectantly with forepaws off the ground. ∼ **the question,** use circular reasoning. **go begging,** be available but unwanted.

began *see* **begin.**

beget *v.t.* (p.t. *begot,* p.p. *begotten,* pres.p. *begetting*) be the father of; give rise to.

beggar *n.* person who lives by begging; very poor person; (*sl.*) person. —*v.t.* reduce to poverty. **beggary** *n.*

beggarly *a.* mean and insufficient.

begin *v.t./i.* (p.t. *began,* p.p. *begun,* pres.p. *beginning*) perform the first or earliest part of (an activity etc.); be the first to do a thing; come into existence; have its first element or starting-point.

beginner *n.* person just beginning to learn a skill.

beginning *n.* first part; starting-point, source or origin.

begone *int.* go away.

begonia *n.* garden plant with bright leaves and flowers.

begot, begotten *see* **beget.**

begrudge *v.t.* grudge.

beguile *v.t.* deceive; entertain pleasantly. **beguilement** *n.*

begun *see* **begin.**

behalf *n.* **on** ∼ **of,** in aid of; as the representative of.

behave *v.i.* act or react in a specified way; show good manners.

behaviour *n.* way of behaving.

behead *v.t.* cut the head from, execute (a person) thus.

beheld *see* **behold.**

behind *adv.* & *prep.* in or to the rear (of); behindhand; remaining after others' departure. —*n.* buttocks.

behindhand *adv.* & *a.* in arrears; late; out of date.

behold *v.t.* (p.t. *beheld*) (*old use*) see, observe. **beholder** *n.*

beholden *a.* owing thanks.

beige *a.* & *n.* light fawn (colour).

being *n.* existence; thing that exists and has life, person.

belated *a.* coming very late or too late.

belch *v.t./i.* send out wind noisily from the stomach through the mouth; send out from an opening or funnel, gush. —*n.* act or sound of belching.

belfry *n.* bell tower; space for bells in a tower.

belief *n.* believing; thing believed.

believe *v.t./i.* accept as true or as speaking or conveying truth; think, suppose. ∼ **in,** have faith in the existence of; feel sure of the worth of. **believer** *n.*

belittle *v.t.* disparage.

bell *n.* cup-shaped metal instrument that makes a ringing sound when struck; its sound, esp. as a signal; bell-shaped thing.

belle *n.* beautiful woman.

belligerent *a.* & *n.* (person or country) waging war; aggressive. **belligerently** *adv.*, **belligerence** *n.*, **belligerency** *n.*

bellow *n.* loud deep sound made by a bull; deep shout. —*v.t./i.* make this sound.

bellows *n.pl.* apparatus for driving air into something; part that expands or flattens in a series of folds.

belly *n.* abdomen; stomach; bulging or rounded part. —*v.t./i.* swell out.

bellyful *n.* as much as one wants or rather more.

belong *v.i.* be rightly assigned as property, part, duty, etc.; be a member; have a rightful place.

belongings *n.pl.* personal possessions.

beloved /-'lʌvɪd/ *a.* & *n.* dearly loved (person).

below *adv.* & *prep.* at or to a lower position or amount (than).

belt *n.* strip of cloth or leather etc., esp. worn round the waist; long narrow region. —*v.t./i.* put a belt round; (*sl.*) hit; (*sl.*) rush.

bemused *a.* bewildered; lost in thought.

bench *n.* long seat of wood or stone; long working-table; judges or magistrates hearing a case.

bend *v.t./i.* (p.t. & p.p. *bent*) make or become curved or angular; turn downwards, stoop; turn in a new direction. —*n.* curve, turn.

beneath *adv.* & *prep.* below, underneath; not worthy of.

Benedictine /-tɪn/ *n.* monk of an order founded by St. Benedict.

benedictine /-tin/ *n.* liqueur originally made by Benedictines.

benediction *n.* spoken blessing.

benefactor *n.* one who gives financial or other help. **benefaction** *n.*

beneficial *a.* having a helpful or useful effect. **beneficially** *adv.*

beneficiary *n.* one who receives a benefit or legacy.

benefit *n.* something helpful or favourable or profitable; allowance payable in accordance with an insurance plan. —*v.t./i.* (p.t. *benefited*, pres. p. *benefiting*) do good to; receive benefit.

benevolent *a.* kindly and helpful. **benevolently** *adv.*, **benevolence** *n.*

benign *a.* kindly; mild and gentle; not malignant. **benignly** *adv.*

bent *see* **bend.** —*n.* natural skill or liking. —*a.* (*sl.*) dishonest. ∼ **on,** seeking or determined to do.

benzene *n.* liquid obtained from petroleum and coal-tar, used as a solvent, fuel, etc.

benzine /-zin/ *n.* liquid mixture of hydrocarbons used in dry-cleaning.

bequeath *v.t.* leave as a legacy.

bequest *n.* legacy.

bereave *v.t.* deprive, esp. of a relative, by death. **bereavement** *n.*

bereft *a.* deprived.

beret /'bereɪ/ *n.* round flat cap with no peak.

berry *n.* small round juicy fruit with no stone.

berserk *a.* **go** ∼, go into an uncontrollable destructive rage.

berth *n.* bunk or sleeping-place in a ship or train; place for a ship to anchor or tie up at a wharf. —*v.t.* moor at a berth. **give a wide** ∼ **to,** keep a safe distance from.

beryl *n.* transparent usu. green precious stone.

beseech *v.t.* (p.t. *besought*) implore.

beset *v.t.* (p.t. *beset*, pres.p. *besetting*) hem in, surround; habitually affect or trouble.

beside *prep.* at the side of, close to; compared with. **be** ∼ **oneself,** be at the end of one's self control. ∼ **the point,** irrelevant.

besides *prep.* in addition to, other than. —*adv.* also.

besiege *v.t.* lay siege to; crowd round.

besotted *a.* infatuated.

besought *see* **beseech.**

bespoke *a.* making or (of clothes) made to a customer's order.

best *a.* of the most excellent kind. —*adv.* in the best way; most usefully. —*n.* best thing, victory. ∼ **man,** bridegroom's chief attendant. ∼ **part of,** most of.

bestial /'bes-/ *a.* of or like a beast, savage. **bestiality** *n.*

bestow *v.t.* present. **bestowal** *n.*

bet *n.* agreement pledging a thing that will be forfeited if one's forecast is wrong; money etc. pledged. —*v.t./i.* (p.t. *bet* or *betted*) make a bet; (*colloq.*) predict.

beta *n.* second letter of the Greek alphabet, = b.

betake *v.refl.* (p.t. *betook*, p.p. *betaken*) ∼ **oneself,** go.

bête noire /beɪt 'nwɑ(r)/ person or thing one most dislikes.

betide *v.t.* happen to.

betray *v.t.* give up or reveal disloyally to an enemy; be disloyal to; reveal unintentionally. **betrayal** *n.*

betroth *v.t.* cause to be engaged to marry. **betrothal** *n.*

better[1] *a.* of a more excellent kind; recovered from illness. —*adv.* in a better manner; more usefully. —*n.* better thing; (*pl.*) persons of higher status than oneself. —*v.t.* improve; do better than. ~ **half,** (*joc.*) one's wife. ~ **part,** more than half. **get the** ~ **of,** overcome. **betterment** *n.*

better[2] *n.* person who bets.

betting-shop *n.* bookmaker's office.

between *prep.* in the space or time or quality etc. bounded by (two limits); separating; to and from; connecting; shared by; taking one and rejecting the other of. —*adv.* between points or limits etc.

bevel *n.* sloping edge. —*v.t.* (p.t. *bevelled*) give a sloping edge to.

beverage *n.* any drink.

bevy *n.* company, large group.

beware *v.i.* be on one's guard.

bewilder *v.t.* puzzle, confuse. **bewilderment** *n.*

bewitch *v.t.* put under a magic spell; delight very much.

beyond *adv.* & *prep.* at or to the further side (of); outside the range of; besides. ~ **doubt,** certain.

biannual *a.* happening twice a year. **biannually** *adv.*

bias *n.* influence favouring one of a group; diagonal across threads of woven fabric; tendency of a bowl to swerve because of its lopsided form. —*v.t.* (p.t. *biased*) give bias to, influence.

bib *n.* covering put under a young child's chin to protect its clothes while feeding; front part of an apron, above the waist.

Bible *n.* Christian or Jewish scriptures; copy of these.

biblical *a.* of or in the Bible.

bibliography *n.* list of books about a subject or by a specified author; study of the history of books. **bibliographer** *n.*, **bibliographical** *a.*

bicarbonate *n.* a kind of carbonate.

bicentenary /-'ti-/ *n.* 200th anniversary.

bicentennial /-'ten-/ *a.* happening every 200 years. —*n.* bicentenary.

biceps /'baɪs-/ *n.* large muscle at the front of the upper arm.

bicker *v.i.* quarrel constantly about unimportant things.

bicycle *n.* two-wheeled vehicle driven by pedals. —*v.i.* ride a bicycle.

bid[1] *n.* offer of a price, esp. at an auction; statement of the number of tricks a player proposes to win in a card game; attempt. —*v.t./i.* (p.t. *bid*, pres.p. *bidding*) make a bid (of), offer. **bidder** *n.*

bid[2] *v.t.* (p.t. *bid* (old use *bade*, pr. bæd), p.p. *bidden*, pres.p. *bidding*) command; say as a greeting etc.

biddable *a.* willing to obey.

bidding *n.* command.

bide *v.t.* await (one's time).

bidet /'biːdeɪ/ *n.* low washbasin that one can sit astride to wash the genital and anal regions.

biennial *a.* lasting for two years; happening every second year. —*n.* plant that flowers and dies in its second year. **biennially** *adv.*

bier *n.* movable stand for a coffin.

biff *v.t.* & *n.* (*sl.*) hit.

bifocals *n.pl.* spectacles with lenses that have two segments, assisting both distant and close focusing.

big *a.* (*bigger*, *biggest*) large in size, amount, or intensity; elder; important; boastful; (*sl.*) generous. —*adv.* (*U.S. sl.*) on a large scale.

bigamist *n.* person guilty of bigamy.

bigamy *n.* crime of going through a form of marriage while a previous marriage is still valid. **bigamous** *a.*

bight *n.* loop of rope; recess of a coast, bay.

bigot *n.* person who holds an opinion obstinately and is intolerant towards those who disagree. **bigoted** *a.*, **bigotry** *n.*

bigwig *n.* (*colloq.*) important person.

bike *n.* (*colloq.*) bicycle, motor cycle.

bikini *n.* (pl. *-is*) woman's scanty two-piece beach garment.

bilateral *a.* having two sides; existing between two groups. **bilaterally** *adv.*

bilberry *n.* small round dark blue fruit; shrub producing this.

bile *n.* bitter yellowish liquid produced by the liver.

bilge *n.* ship's bottom; water collecting there; (*sl.*) worthless talk.

bilingual *a.* written in or able to speak two languages.

bilious *a.* sick, esp. from trouble with bile or liver. **biliousness** *n.*

bilk *v.t.* defraud of payment.

bill[1] *n.* written statement of charges to be paid; poster; programme; certificate; draft of a proposed law; (*U.S.*) banknote. —*v.t.* announce, advertise; send a bill to. ~ **of exchange,** written order to pay a sum of money on a specified date.

bill[2] *n.* bird's beak.

billet *n.* lodging for troops. —*v.t.* place in a billet.

billiards *n.* game played with cues and three balls on a table.

billion *n.* one million million; (orig. *U.S.*) thousand million.

billow *n.* great wave. —*v.i.* rise or move like waves.

billy *n.* can used by campers etc. as a kettle or cooking-pot.

billy-goat *n.* male goat.

bin *n.* large rigid container or receptacle.

binary *a.* dual, of two. ~ **scale,** system of numbers using only two digits (0 and 1).

bind *v.t./i.* (p.t. *bound*) tie, fasten together; cover the edge of so as to strengthen or decorate; fasten into a cover; place under an obligation or legal agreement; (*sl.*) grumble. —*n.* (*sl.*) bore, nuisance. **binder** *n.*

bindery *n.* workshop where books are bound.

binding *n.* book-cover; braid etc. used to bind an edge.

bindweed *n.* wild convolvulus.

binge *n.* (*sl.*) spree, eating and drinking and making merry.

bingo *n.* gambling game using cards marked with numbered squares.

binocular *a.* using two eyes.

binoculars *n.pl.* instrument with lenses for both eyes, making distant objects seem larger.

biochemistry *n.* chemistry of living organisms. **biochemical** *a.*, **biochemist** *n.*

biographer *n.* writer of a biography.

biography *n.* story of a person's life. **biographical** *a.*

biology *n.* study of the life and structure of living things. **biological** *a.*, **biologically** *adv.*, **biologist** *n.*

bionic *a.* (of a person or faculties) operated electronically.

biopsy *n.* examination of tissue cut from a living body.

biorhythm *n.* any of the recurring cycles of activity said to occur in a person's life.

bipartite *a.* consisting of two parts; involving two groups.

biped /ˈbaɪped/ *n.* two-footed animal.

biplane *n.* old type of aeroplane.

birch *n.* tree with smooth bark; bundle of birch twigs for flogging delinquents. —*v.t.* flog with this.

bird *n.* feathered animal; (*colloq.*) person; (*sl.*) young woman.

birdseed *n.* special seeds used as food for caged birds.

Biro *n.* [P.] ball-point pen.

birth *n.* emergence of young from the mother's body; parentage. **∼-control** *n.* prevention of unwanted pregnancy. **give ∼ to,** produce as young from the body.

birthday *n.* anniversary of the day of one's birth.

birthmark *n.* unusual coloured mark on the skin at birth.

birthright *n.* thing that is one's right through being born into a certain family or country.

biscuit *n.* small flat thin piece of pastry baked crisp.

bisect *v.t.* divide into two equal parts. **bisection** *n.*, **bisector** *n.*

bishop *n.* clergyman of high rank; mitre-shaped chess piece.

bishopric *n.* diocese of a bishop.

bismuth *n.* metallic element; compound of this used in medicines.

bison *n.* (pl. *bison*) wild ox; buffalo.

bit[1] *n.* small piece or quantity; short time or distance; mouthpiece of a bridle; part of a tool that cuts or bores or grips when twisted.

bit[2] *see* bite.

bitch *n.* female dog; (*colloq.*) spiteful woman, difficult thing. —*v.i.* (*colloq.*) speak spitefully or sourly. **bitchy** *a.*, **bitchiness** *n.*

bite *v.t./i.* (p.t. *bit*, p.p. *bitten*) cut with the teeth; penetrate; grip or act effectively. —*n.* act of biting; wound made by this; small meal.

biting *a.* causing a smarting pain; sharply critical.

bitter *a.* tasting sharp, not sweet or mild; with

mental pain or resentment; piercingly cold. **bitterly** *adv.*, **bitterness** *n.*

bittern *n.* a kind of marsh bird.

bitty *a.* made up of unrelated bits.

bitumen *n.* black substance made from petroleum. **bituminous** *a.*

bivalve *n.* shellfish with a hinged double shell.

bivouac /ˈbɪvʊæk/ *n.* temporary camp without tents or other cover. —*v.i.* (p.t. *bivouacked*) camp thus.

bizarre *a.* strikingly odd in appearance or effect.

blab *v.i.* (p.t. *blabbed*) talk indiscreetly.

black *a.* (-er, -est) of the very darkest colour, like coal or soot; having a black skin; dismal, gloomy; hostile; evil; not to be handled by trade unionists. —*n.* black colour or thing; *B*∼, Negro. —*v.t.* make black; declare (goods etc.) 'black'. **∼ coffee,** coffee without milk. **∼ eye,** bruised eye. **∼ hole,** region in outer space from which matter and radiation cannot escape. **∼ list,** list of persons who are disapproved of. **∼ market,** illegal buying and selling. **∼ out,** cover windows etc. so that no light can penetrate; suffer a blackout. **∼ sheep,** scoundrel. **∼ spot,** place of danger or difficulty. **in the ∼,** with a credit balance, not in debt.

blackball *v.t.* reject as a member.

blackberry *n.* bramble; its edible dark berry.

blackbird *n.* European songbird, male of which is black.

blackboard *n.* board for writing on with chalk in front of a class.

blacken *v.t./i.* make or become black; say evil things about.

blackfly *n.* insect infesting plants.

blackguard /ˈblægɑd/ *n.* scoundrel.

blackhead *n.* small dark lump blocking a pore in the skin.

blackleg *n.* person who works while fellow workers are on strike.

blacklist *v.t.* enter in a black list.

blackmail *v.t.* demand payment or action from (person) by threats. —*n.* this demand, money demanded, thus. **blackmailer** *n.*

blackout *n.* being blacked out; temporary loss of consciousness or memory; suspension of radio reception.

blacksmith *n.* smith who works in iron.

blackthorn *n.* thorny shrub bearing white flowers and sloes.

bladder *n.* sac in which urine collects in the body; inflatable bag.

blade *n.* flattened cutting-part of a knife or sword etc.; flat part of an oar, propeller, etc.; flat narrow leaf esp. of grass; broad bone.

blame *v.t.* hold responsible and criticize for a fault. —*n.* responsibility or criticism for a fault.

blameless *a.* not subject to blame.

blanch *v.t./i.* make or become white or pale; immerse in boiling water.

blancmange /bləˈmɒnʒ/ *n.* flavoured jelly-like pudding made with milk.

bland *a.* (-er, -est) mild; gentle and casual, not

irritating or stimulating. **blandly** adv., **blandness** n.

blandishments n.pl. flattering or coaxing words.

blank a. not written or printed on; without interest or expression, without result. —n. blank space or paper; blank cartridge. ~ **cartridge,** one containing no bullet. ~ **verse,** verse without rhyme, usu. in lines of ten syllables. **blankly** adv., **blankness** n.

blanket n. warm covering made of woollen or similar material; thick covering mass. —v.t. (p.t. **blanketed**) cover with a blanket.

blare v.t./i. sound loudly and harshly. —n. this sound.

blarney n. smooth talk that flatters and deceives.

blasé /'blɑːzeɪ/ a. bored or unimpressed by things.

blaspheme v.t./i. utter blasphemies (about). **blasphemer** n.

blasphemy n. irreverent talk about sacred things. **blasphemous** a., **blasphemously** adv.

blast n. strong gust; wave of air from an explosion; sound of a wind instrument or whistle or car horn etc. —v.t. blow up with explosives; cause to wither, destroy. ~ **furnace** n. furnace for smelting ore, with compressed hot air driven in. ~ **off,** be launched by firing of rockets. ~-**off** n.

blatant /'bleɪt-/ a. very obvious; shameless. **blatantly** adv.

blaze¹ n. bright flame or fire; bright light or display; outburst; (pl., sl.) hell. —v.i. burn or shine brightly; have an intense outburst of feeling.

blaze² n. white mark on an animal's face; mark chipped in the bark of a tree to mark a route. —v.t. mark (a tree or route) with blazes. ~ **a trail,** make such marks; pioneer.

blaze³ v.t. proclaim (news).

blazer n. loose-fitting jacket, esp. in the colours or bearing the badge of a school, team, etc.

blazon n. heraldic shield, coat of arms. —v.t. inscribe ornamentally; proclaim.

bleach v.t./i. whiten by sunlight or chemicals. —n. bleaching substance or process.

bleak a. (-er, -est) cold and cheerless. **bleakly** adv., **bleakness** n.

bleary a. (of eyes) watery and seeing indistinctly.

bleat n. cry of a sheep, goat, or calf. —v.t./i. utter this cry; speak or say plaintively.

bleed v.t./i. (p.t. **bled**) leak blood or other fluid; draw blood or fluid from; extort money from.

bleep n. short high-pitched sound. —v.i. make this sound. **bleeper** n.

blemish n. flaw or defect that spoils the perfection of a thing. —v.t. spoil with a blemish.

blench v.i. flinch.

blend v.t./i. mix into a uniform or harmonious compound or combination. —n. mixture.

bless v.t. call God's favour upon; make sacred or holy; praise (God). **be blessed with,** be fortunate in having.

blessed /-sɪd/ a. holy, sacred; in paradise; (colloq.) damned. **blessedness** n.

blessing n. God's favour; prayer for this; something one is glad of.

blest a. (old use) blessed.

blew see **blow**¹.

blight n. disease, fungus, or insect that withers plants; malignant influence. —v.t. affect with blight; spoil.

blighter n. (sl.) person or thing, esp. an annoying one.

blind a. without sight; without foresight or understanding or adequate information; failing to flower; (in cookery) without filling. —adv. blindly. —v.t./i. make blind; take away power of judgement from; (sl.) go along recklessly. —n. screen, esp. on a roller, for a window; pretext. ~ **alley,** alley closed at one end; job with no prospects of advancement. **blindly** adv., **blindness** n.

blindfold a. & adv. with eyes covered with a cloth to block one's sight. —n. cloth used for this. —v.t. cover the eyes of (a person) thus.

blink v.t./i. open and shut one's eyes rapidly; shine unsteadily; shirk facing (facts). —n. act of blinking; quick gleam.

blinker n. leather piece fixed to a bridle to prevent a horse from seeing sideways. —v.t. obstruct the sight or understanding of.

blip v.t. (p.t. **blipped**) strike briskly. —n. small image on a radar screen.

bliss n. perfect happiness. **blissful** a., **blissfully** adv.

blister n. bubble-like swelling on skin; raised swelling on a surface. —v.t./i. cause blister(s) on; be affected with blister(s).

blithe a. casual and carefree. **blithely** adv.

blithering a. (colloq.) contemptible.

blitz n. violent attack, esp. from aircraft. —v.t. attack in a blitz.

blizzard n. severe snowstorm.

bloated a. swollen with fat, gas, or liquid.

bloater n. salted smoked herring.

blob n. drop of liquid; round mass.

bloc n. group of parties or countries who combine for a purpose.

block n. solid piece of hard substance; log of wood; (sl.) head; pulley(s) mounted in a case; compact mass of buildings; large building divided into flats or offices; large quantity treated as a unit; pad of paper for drawing or writing on; obstruction. —v.t. obstruct, prevent the movement or use of. ~ **in,** sketch in roughly. ~ **letters,** plain capital letters.

blockade n. blocking of access to a place, to prevent entry of goods etc. —v.t. set up a blockade of.

blockage n. blocking; thing that blocks.

blockhead n. stupid person.

bloke n. (sl.) man.

blond a. & n. fair-haired (man).

blonde a. & n. fair-haired (woman).

blood n. red liquid circulating in the bodies of animals; bloodshed; temper, courage; race, descent, parentage; kindred. —v.t. give a first taste of blood to (a hound); initiate (a person). ~-**bath** n. massacre. ~-**curdling** a. horrifying. ~ **sports,** sports involving killing. ∿-**vessel** n. tubular structure conveying blood within the body.

bloodhound n. large keen-scented dog, formerly used in tracking.

bloodless a. without blood; drained of blood; without bloodshed.

bloodshed n. killing or wounding.

bloodshot a. (of eyes) red from dilated veins.

bloodstock n. thoroughbred horses.

bloodstream n. blood circulating in the body.

bloodsucker n. creature that sucks blood; person who extorts money.

bloodthirsty a. eager for bloodshed.

bloody a. (-ier, -iest) blood-stained; with much bloodshed. —v.t. stain with blood. ∿-**minded** a. (colloq.) deliberately uncooperative.

bloom n. flower; beauty, perfection; fine powder on grapes etc. —v.i. bear flowers; be in full beauty.

bloomer n. (sl.) blunder.

bloomers n.pl. (colloq.) knickers.

blossom n. flower(s), esp. of a fruit tree. —v.i. open into flowers; develop and flourish.

blot n. spot of ink etc.; something ugly or disgraceful. —v.t. (p.t. blotted) make blot(s) on; dry with blotting-paper, soak up; obscure.

blotch n. large irregular mark. **blotched** a., **blotchy** a.

blotter n. pad of blotting-paper; device holding this.

blotting-paper n. absorbent paper for drying ink writing.

blotto n. (sl.) very drunk.

blouse n. shirt-like garment worn by women and children; waist-length coat forming part of military uniform.

blow¹ v.t./i. (p.t. blew, p.p. blown) move or flow as a current of air does; send out a current of air or breath; propel, shape, or sound by this; be moved or carried by air; puff and pant; (of a fuse) melt; cause (a fuse) to melt; break with explosives; (sl.) reveal; (sl.) spend recklessly. —n. blowing. ∿-**dry** v.t. dry and style (hair) with a hand-held drier. ∿ **in**, (colloq.) arrive casually or unexpectedly. ∿-**out** n. burst tyre; melted fuse; (sl.) large meal. ∿ **over**, die down. ∿ **up**, inflate; exaggerate; enlarge (a photograph); explode, shatter by an explosion; lose one's temper; reprimand severely; become a crisis.

blow² n. hard stroke with a hand or tool or weapon; shock, disaster.

blower n. (colloq.) telephone.

blowfly n. fly that lays its eggs on meat.

blowlamp n. portable burner for directing a very hot flame.

blown see blow¹. —a. breathless.

blowpipe n. tube through which air etc. is blown, e.g. to heat a flame or send out a missile.

blowy a. windy.

blowzy /-ɔʊ-/ a. red-faced and coarse-looking.

blubber¹ n. whale fat.

blubber² v.i. weep noisily.

bludgeon n. heavy stick used as a weapon. —v.t. strike with a bludgeon; compel forcefully.

blue a. (-er, -est) of a colour like the cloudless sky; unhappy; indecent. —n. blue colour or thing; (pl.) melancholy jazz melodies, state of depression. —v.t. (pres.p. blueing) make blue; (sl.) spend recklessly. ∿-**blooded** a. of aristocratic descent. ∿ **cheese**, cheese with veins of blue mould. ∿-**pencil** v.t. censor. **out of the** ∿, unexpectedly.

bluebell n. plant with blue bell-shaped flowers.

blueberry n. edible blue berry; shrub bearing this.

bluebottle n. large bluish fly.

blueprint n. blue photographic print of building plans; detailed scheme.

bluff¹ a. with a broad steep front; abrupt, frank, and hearty. —n. bluff cliff etc. **bluffness** n.

bluff² v.t./i. deceive by a pretence esp. of strength. —n. bluffing.

bluish a. rather blue.

blunder v.i. move clumsily and uncertainly; make a blunder. —n. mistake.

blunderbuss n. old type of gun firing many balls at one shot.

blunt a. without a sharp edge or point; speaking or expressed plainly. —v.t./i. make or become blunt. **bluntly** adv., **bluntness** n.

blur n. smear; indistinct appearance. —v.t./i. (p.t. blurred) smear; make or become indistinct.

blurb n. written description praising something.

blurt v.t. utter abruptly.

blush v.i. become red-faced from shame or embarrassment. —n. blushing.

bluster v.i. blow in gusts; talk aggressively, with empty threats. —n. blustering talk. **blustery** a.

boa /ˈbəʊə/ n. large South American snake that crushes its prey.

boar n. male pig.

board n. long piece of sawn wood; flat piece of wood or stiff material; notice-board; thick stiff card used for book covers; daily meals supplied in return for payment or services; committee. —v.t./i. cover or block with boards; enter (a ship, aircraft, or vehicle); provide with or receive meals and accommodation for payment. **go by the** ∿, be ignored or rejected. **on** ∿, on or in a ship, aircraft, or vehicle.

boarder n. person who boards with someone; resident pupil.

boarding-house n., **boarding-school** n. one taking boarders.

boast v.t./i. speak with great pride, trying to impress people; be the proud possessor of. —n. boastful statement; thing one is proud of. **boaster** n.

boastful a. boasting frequently. **boastfully** adv., **boastfulness** n.

boat n. vessel for travelling on water; boat-shaped serving-dish for sauce etc. **in the same** ∿, suffering the same troubles.

boater n. flat-topped straw hat.

boating n. going out in a rowing-boat for pleasure.

boatman *n.* (pl. *-men*) man who rows or sails or rents out boats.

boatswain /'bəʊsən/ *n.* ship's officer in charge of rigging, boats, etc.

bob[1] *v.t./i.* (p.t. *bobbed*) move quickly up and down; cut (hair) short to hang loosely. —*n.* bobbing movement; bobbed hair.

bob[2] *n.* (pl. *bob*) (*sl.*) shilling, 5p.

bobbin *n.* small spool holding thread or wire in a machine.

bobby *n.* (*colloq.*) policeman.

bobsled, bobsleigh *ns.* sledge with two sets of runners in tandem.

bode *v.t./i.* be a sign of, promise.

bodice *n.* part of a dress from shoulder to waist.

bodily *a.* of the human body or physical nature. —*adv.* in person, physically; as a whole.

bodkin *n.* thick blunt needle with a large eye for threading tape etc.

body *n.* structure of bones and flesh etc. of man or an animal; corpse; main part; group regarded as a unit; separate piece of matter; strong texture or quality. ∼**-blow** *n.* severe blow.

bodyguard *n.* escort or personal guard of an important person.

Boer /'bəʊə(r)/ *n.* (*old use*) South African of Dutch descent.

boffin *n.* (*sl.*) person engaged in technical research.

bog *n.* permanently wet spongy ground. —*v.t.* (p.t. *bogged*) make or become stuck and unable to progress. **boggy** *a.*

bogey *n.* (pl. *-eys*) bogy; (in golf) one stroke above par at a hole.

boggle *v.i.* hesitate in fright; raise objections.

bogus *a.* false.

bogy *n.* evil spirit; something causing fear.

boil[1] *n.* inflamed swelling producing pus.

boil[2] *v.t./i.* bubble up with heat; heat so that liquid does this.

boiler *n.* container in which water is heated. ∼ **suit,** one-piece suit for rough work.

boisterous *a.* windy; noisy and cheerful. **boisterously** *adv.*

bold *a.* (*-er, -est*) confident and courageous; (of colours) strong and vivid. **boldly** *adv.*, **boldness** *n.*

bole *n.* trunk of a tree.

bolero /-'leər-/ *n.* (pl. *-os*) Spanish dance; /'bɒlə-/ woman's short jacket with no fastening.

bollard *n.* short thick post.

Bolshie *a. & n.* (*sl.*) Communist; rebellious (person).

bolster *n.* long pad placed under a pillow. —*v.t.* support.

bolt *n.* sliding bar for fastening a door; sliding part of a rifle-breech; strong metal pin; shaft of lightning; roll of cloth; act of bolting. —*v.t./i.* fasten with bolt(s); run away; gulp (food) hastily. ∼**-hole** *n.* place into which one can escape. ∼ **upright,** quite upright.

bomb *n.* case of explosive or incendiary material to be set off by impact or a timing device; (*sl.*) large sum of money. —*v.t./i.* attack with bombs.

bombard *v.t.* attack with artillery; send a stream of particles against; attack with questions etc. **bombardment** *n.*

bombardier *n.* artillery N.C.O.

bombastic *a.* using pompous words.

bomber *n.* aircraft that carries and drops bombs; person who throws or places bombs.

bombshell *n.* great shock.

bona-fide /bəʊnə 'faɪdɪ/ *adj.* genuine.

bona fides /bəʊnə 'faɪdiz/ honest intention, sincerity.

bonanza *n.* sudden great wealth or luck.

bond *n.* thing that unites or restrains; binding agreement; document issued by a government or public company acknowledging that money has been lent to it and will be repaid; high-quality writing-paper. —*v.t.* unite with a bond. **in** ∼, stored in a Customs warehouse until duties are paid.

bondage *n.* slavery, captivity.

bonded *a.* stored or (of a warehouse) storing goods in bond.

bone *n.* one of the hard parts making up the skeleton of a body; substance of this. —*v.t.* remove bones from. ∼ **china,** made of clay and bone ash. ∼**-dry** *a.* quite dry. ∼ **idle,** very lazy. ∼**-meal** *n.* powdered bones used as a fertilizer.

bonehead *n.* (*sl.*) stupid person.

bonfire *n.* fire built in the open air to destroy rubbish or in celebration.

bonhomie /'bɒnəmɪ/ *n.* geniality.

bonnet *n.* hat with strings that tie under the chin; Scotch cap; hinged cover over the engine etc. of a motor vehicle.

bonny *a.* (*-ier, -iest*) healthy-looking; (*Sc.*) good-looking.

bonus *n.* extra payment or benefit.

bony *a.* (*-ier, -iest*) like bones; having bones with little flesh; full of bones.

boo *int.* exclamation of disapproval. —*v.t./i.* shout 'boo' (at).

boob *n. & v.i.* (*sl.*) blunder.

booby *n.* foolish person. ∼ **prize,** one given as a joke to the competitor with the lowest score. ∼ **trap,** hidden trap rigged up as a practical joke; hidden bomb. ∼**-trap** *v.t.* place a booby trap in or on.

book *n.* set of sheets of paper bound in a cover; literary work filling this; main division of a literary work or of the Bible; record of bets made. —*v.t./i.* enter in a book or list; reserve; buy a ticket in advance.

bookable *a.* able to be booked.

bookcase *n.* piece of furniture with shelves for books.

bookie *n.* (*colloq.*) bookmaker.

bookkeeping *n.* systematic recording of business transactions.

booklet *n.* small thin book.

bookmaker *n.* person whose business is the taking of bets.

bookmark *n.* strip of paper etc. to mark a place in a book.

bookworm *n.* grub that eats holes in books; person fond of reading.

boom[1] *v.i.* make a deep resonant sound; have a period of prosperity. —*n.* booming sound; prosperity.

boom[2] *n.* long pole; floating barrier.

boomerang *n.* Australian missile of curved wood that can be thrown so as to return to the thrower. —*v.i.* (of a scheme etc.) cause harm to the originator.

boon[1] *n.* benefit.

boon[2] *a.* ~ **companion,** pleasant companion.

boor *n.* ill-mannered person. **boorish** *a.,* **boorishness** *n.*

boost *v.t.* push upwards; increase the strength or reputation of. —*n.* upward thrust; increase. **booster** *n.*

boot *n.* covering of leather etc. for the foot and ankle or leg; covered luggage-compartment in a car; (*sl.*) dismissal. —*v.t.* kick.

bootee *n.* baby's knitted boot.

booth *n.* small shelter.

booty *n.* loot.

booze *v.i.* (*colloq.*) drink alcohol. —*n.* (*colloq.*) alcoholic drink; drinking spree. **boozer** *n.*

boracic /-ˈræs-/ *a.* boric.

borax *n.* compound of boron used in detergents etc.

border *n.* edge, boundary; part near this; edging; flower-bed round part of a garden. —*v.t./i.* put or be a border to. ~ **on,** be next to; come close to being.

borderline *n.* line of demarcation.

bore[1] *see* **bear**[2].

bore[2] *v.t./i.* make (a hole) with a revolving tool or by digging; pierce thus; thrust one's way. —*n.* hole bored; hollow inside of a cylinder.

bore[3] *v.t.* weary by dullness. —*n.* boring person or thing. **boredom** *n.*

bore[4] *n.* tidal wave in an estuary.

boric *a.* ~ **acid,** substance derived from boron, used as an antiseptic.

born *a.* brought forth by birth; having a specified natural quality.

borne *see* **bear**[2].

boron *n.* chemical element very resistant to high temperatures.

borough /ˈbʌrə/ *n.* town or district with certain rights of self-government; administrative area of London.

borrow *v.t./i.* get temporary use of (a thing or money); use (an idea etc.) without being the inventor. **borrowed time,** extension of one's life. **borrower** *n.*

Borstal *n.* institution where young offenders may be sent for reformative training.

bosh *int.* & *n.* (*sl.*) nonsense.

bo's'n /ˈbəʊsən/ *n.* boatswain.

bosom *n.* breast. ~ **friend,** very dear friend.

boss[1] *n.* (*colloq.*) master, manager, overseer. —*v.t.* (*colloq.*) be the boss of; give orders to.

boss[2] *n.* projecting knob.

bossy *a.* (*-ier, -iest*) fond of giving orders to people. **bossiness** *n.*

botany *n.* study of plants. **botanical** *a.,* **botanist** *n.*

botch *v.t.* spoil by poor work.

both *a., pron.,* & *adv.* the two, not only the one.

bother *v.t./i.* cause trouble, worry, or annoyance to; pester; take trouble, feel concern. —*int.* exclamation of annoyance. —*n.* worry, minor trouble.

bottle *n.* narrow-necked glass or plastic container for liquid. —*v.t.* store in bottles; preserve in jars.

bottleneck *n.* narrow place where traffic cannot flow freely; obstruction to an even flow of work etc.

bottom *n.* lowest part or place; buttocks; ground under a stretch of water. —*a.* lowest in position, rank, or degree.

bottomless *a.* extremely deep.

botulism *n.* poisoning by bacteria in food.

bouclé /ˈbuːkleɪ/ *n.* yarn or fabric with thread looped at intervals.

boudoir /ˈbuːdwɑː(r)/ *n.* woman's small private room.

bougainvillaea /buːɡənˈvɪlɪə/ *n.* tropical shrub with red or purple bracts.

bough *n.* large branch coming from the trunk of a tree.

bought *see* **buy.**

boulder *n.* large rounded stone.

boulevard /ˈbuːləvɑːd/ *n.* wide street.

bounce *v.t./i.* spring back or up when sent against something hard; cause to do this; (*sl.,* of a cheque) be sent back by a bank as worthless; move in a lively manner. —*n.* bouncing movement or power; lively manner. **bouncer** *n.*

bouncing *a.* big and healthy.

bound[1] *v.t.* limit, be a boundary of.

bound[2] *v.i.* spring, run with a jumping movement. —*n.* bounding movement.

bound[3] *see* **bind.** —*a.* obstructed by a specified thing (*snow-*~). ~ **to,** certain to. **I'll be** ~, I feel certain.

boundary *n.* line that marks a limit; hit to the boundary in cricket.

bounden *a.* ~ **duty,** duty dictated by conscience.

boundless *a.* without limits.

bounds *n.pl.* limits. **out of** ~, beyond the area one is allowed to enter.

bountiful *a.* giving generously; abundant.

bounty *n.* generosity; generous gift; gratuity, reward.

bouquet /bʊˈkeɪ/ *n.* bunch of flowers for carrying; perfume of wine.

bourbon /ˈbɜːbən/ *n.* whisky made mainly from maize.

bourgeois /ˈbʊəʒwɑː/ *a.* (*derog.*) middle-class, conventional. **bourgeoisie** /-ziː/ *n.*

bout *n.* period of exercise or work or illness; boxing contest.

boutique /buːˈtiːk/ *n.* small shop selling fashionable clothes etc.

bovine *a.* of oxen; dull and stupid.

bow[1] /bəʊ/ *n.* strip of wood curved by a tight string joining its ends, for shooting arrows;

rod with horse-hair stretched between its ends, for playing a violin etc.; knot with loop(s), ribbon etc. tied in this way. ~-legged a. bandy. ~-tie n. man's necktie tied in a bow. ~-window n. curved bay window.

bow² /bau/ n. bending of the head or body in greeting, respect, agreement, etc. —v.t./i. bend thus; bend downwards under weight; submit.

bow³ /bau/ n. front end of a boat or ship; oarsman nearest the bow.

bowdlerize /ˈbau-/ v.t. expurgate.

bowel n. intestine; (pl.) intestines, innermost parts.

bower n. leafy shelter.

bowl¹ n. basin; hollow rounded part of a spoon, tobacco-pipe, etc.

bowl² n. heavy ball weighted to roll in a curve, (pl.) game played with such balls; ball used in skittles etc. —v.t./i. send rolling along the ground; go fast and smoothly; send a ball to a batsman, dismiss by knocking bails off with this. ~ over, knock down; overwhelm with surprise or emotion.

bowler¹ n. person who bowls in cricket; one who plays at bowls.

bowler² n. ~ hat, hard felt hat with a rounded top.

bowling n. playing bowls or skittles or a similar game.

box¹ n. container or receptacle with a flat base; numbered receptacle at a newspaper office for holding replies to an advertisement; compartment in a theatre, stable, etc.; small shelter. —v.t. put into a box. ~ in, shut into a small space. ~-office n. office for booking seats at a theatre etc. ~-pleat n. two parallel pleats folded to form a raised band. ~-room n. room for storing empty boxes etc.

box² v.t./i. slap (a person's ears); fight with fists as a sport, usu. in padded gloves. —n. slap.

box³ n. small evergreen shrub; its wood.

boxer n. person who engages in the sport of boxing; dog of a breed resembling a bulldog.

Boxing Day first weekday after Christmas Day.

boy n. male child; young man; male native servant. ~-friend n. woman's usual male companion. boyhood n., boyish a.

boycott v.t. refuse to deal with or trade with. —n. boycotting.

bra n. woman's undergarment worn to support the breasts.

brace n. device that holds things together or in position; pair; (pl.) straps to keep trousers up, passing over the shoulders. —v.t. give support or firmness to.

bracelet n. ornamental band worn on the arm.

bracing a. invigorating.

bracken n. large fern that grows on waste land; mass of such ferns.

bracket n. support projecting from an upright surface; any of the marks used in pairs for enclosing words or figures, ( ), [ ], { }; group bracketed together as similar. —v.t. enclose by brackets; put together as similar.

brackish a. slightly salt.

bract n. leaf-like part of a plant.

bradawl n. small boring-tool.

brag v.i. (p.t. bragged) boast.

braggart n. person who brags.

brahmin n. member of the Hindu priestly caste.

braid n. woven ornamental trimming; plait of hair. —v.t. trim with braid; plait.

Braille n. system of representing letters etc. by raised dots which blind people read by touch.

brain n. mass of soft grey matter in the skull, centre of the nervous system in animals; (also pl.) mind, intelligence. —v.t. kill by a heavy blow on the head. ~-child n. person's invention or plan.

brainstorm n. violent mental disturbance; (U.S.) bright idea.

brainwash v.t. force (a person) to change his views by subjecting him to great mental pressure.

brainwave n. bright idea.

brainy a. (-ier, -iest) clever.

braise v.t. cook slowly with little liquid in a closed container.

brake n. device for reducing speed or stopping motion. —v.t./i. slow by use of this.

bramble n. shrub with long prickly shoots, blackberry.

bran n. ground inner husks of grain, sifted from flour.

branch n. arm-like part of a tree; similar part of a road, river, etc.; subdivision of a family or subject; local shop or office belonging to a large organization. —v.i. send out or divide into branches. ~ off, leave a main route. ~ out, begin a new line of activity.

brand n. trade mark; goods of a particular make; mark of identification made with hot metal; piece of burning or charred wood. —v.t. mark with a brand; give a bad name to. ~-new a. new, unused.

brandish v.t. wave.

brandy n. strong alcoholic spirit distilled from wine or fermented fruit-juice. ~ snap, crisp curled gingerbread wafer.

brash a. vulgarly self-assertive.

brass n. yellow alloy of copper and zinc; thing(s) made of this; (sl.) money. —a. made of brass. ~ tacks, basic facts, practical details. top ~, (sl.) important officers.

brassière /-siǝ(r)/ n. bra.

brassy a. (-ier, -iest) like brass; bold and vulgar. brassiness n.

brat n. (derog.) child.

bravado /-ˈvɑ-/ n. show of boldness.

brave a. (-er, -est) able to face and endure danger or pain; spectacular. —n. American Indian warrior. —v.t. face and endure bravely. bravely adv., bravery n.

bravo int. well done!

brawl n. noisy quarrel or fight. —v.i. take part in a brawl.

brawn n. muscular strength; pressed meat from a pig's or calf's head.

brawny a. (-ier, -iest) muscular.

bray *n.* donkey's cry; similar sound. —*v.i.* make this cry or sound.

brazen *a.* like or made of brass; shameless, impudent. —*v.t.* ~ **it out,** behave (after doing wrong) as if one has no need to be ashamed.

brazier *n.* basket-like stand for holding burning coals.

breach *n.* breaking or neglect of a rule or contract; estrangement; broken place, gap. —*v.t.* break through, make a breach in.

bread *n.* food made of flour and liquid, usu. leavened by yeast, and baked; (*sl.*) money. ~**-fruit** *n.* tropical fruit with bread-like pulp. ~**-winner** *n.* member of a family who earns money to support the other(s).

breadcrumbs *n.pl.* bread crumbled for use in cooking.

breadline *n.* **on the** ~, living in extreme poverty.

breadth *n.* width, broadness.

break *v.t./i.* (p.t. *broke,* p.p. *broken*) fall into pieces, come apart, cause to do this; damage; become unusable; fail to keep (a promise or law); make or become discontinuous; make a way suddenly or violently; appear suddenly; reveal (news); surpass (a record); subdue; weaken, destroy; (of a boy's voice) become suddenly deeper at puberty; (of a ball) change direction after touching the ground. —*n.* breaking; sudden dash; gap; interval; points scored continuously in billiards; (*colloq.*) opportunity, piece of luck. ~ **down,** fail, collapse; give way to emotion; analyse. ~ **even,** make gains and losses that balance exactly. ~ **up,** bring or come to an end; become weaker; begin holidays at the end of school term. ~ **with,** give up; end one's friendship with.

breakable *a.* able to be broken.

breakage *n.* breaking.

breakdown *n.* mechanical failure; weakening; collapse of health or mental stability; analysis.

breaker *n.* heavy ocean wave that breaks on a coast.

breakfast *n.* first meal of the day. —*v.i.* eat breakfast.

breakneck *a.* dangerously fast.

breakthrough *n.* major advance in knowledge or negotiation.

breakwater *n.* wall built out into the sea to break the force of waves.

bream *n.* fish of the carp family.

breast *n.* upper front part of the body; either of the two milk-producing organs on a woman's chest. —*v.t.* face and advance. ~**stroke** *n.* swimming-stroke performed face downwards.

breastbone *n.* bone down the centre of the upper front of the body.

breath *n.* air drawn into and sent out of the lungs in breathing; breathing in; gentle blowing. **out of** ~, panting after exercise. **under one's** ~, in a whisper.

breathalyser *n.* device measuring the alcohol in a person's breath.

breathe *v.t./i.* draw (air etc.) into the lungs or body or tissues and send it out again; utter.

breather *n.* pause for rest; short period in fresh air.

breathless *a.* out of breath.

breathtaking *a.* amazing.

bred *see* **breed.**

breech *n.* back part of a gun barrel. ~ **birth,** birth in which a baby's buttocks emerge first.

breeches *n.pl.* trousers reaching to just below the knees.

breed *v.t./i.* (p.t. *bred*) produce offspring; train, bring up; give rise to. —*n.* variety of animals etc. within a species. **breeder** *n.*

breeder-reactor *n.* nuclear reactor that produces fissile material.

breeding *n.* good manners resulting from training or background.

breeze *n.* light wind. **breezy** *a.*

breeze-blocks *n.pl.* lightweight building-blocks.

brethren *n.pl.* (*old use*) brothers.

Breton *a. & n.* (native) of Brittany.

breviary /ˈbriːvjərɪ/ *n.* book of prayers to be said by R.C. priests.

brevity *n.* briefness.

brew *v.t./i.* make (beer) by boiling and fermentation; make (tea) by infusion; bring about, develop. —*n.* liquid or amount brewed.

brewer *n.* person whose trade is brewing beer.

brewery *n.* building where beer is brewed commercially.

briar *n.* = **brier.**

bribe *n.* thing offered to influence a person to act in favour of the giver. —*v.t.* persuade by this. **bribery** *n.*

bric-à-brac *n.* odd items of ornaments, furniture, etc.

brick *n.* block of baked or dried clay used to build walls; rectangular block; (*sl.*) kind-hearted person. —*v.t.* block with a brick structure. ~**-red** *a.* reddish.

bricklayer *n.* workman who builds with bricks.

bridal *a.* of a bride or wedding.

bride *n.* woman on her wedding-day or when newly married.

bridegroom *n.* man on his wedding-day or when newly married.

bridesmaid *n.* girl or unmarried woman attending a bride.

bridge[1] *n.* structure providing a way across something; captain's platform on a ship; bony upper part of the nose. —*v.t.* make or be a bridge over, span as if with a bridge.

bridge[2] *n.* card-game developed from whist.

bridgehead *n.* fortified area established in enemy territory, esp. on the far side of a river.

bridle *n.* harness on a horse's head. —*v.t./i.* put a bridle on; restrain; draw up one's head in pride or scorn. ~**-path** *n.* path suitable for riders but not for vehicles.

brief[1] *a.* (-*er*, -*est*) lasting only for a short time; concise; short. **briefs** *n.pl.* very short pants or knickers. **briefly** *adv.,* **briefness** *n.*

brief[2] *n.* set of instructions and information,

esp. to a barrister about a case. —*v.t.* employ (a barrister); inform or instruct in advance.

briefcase *n.* case for carrying documents.

brier *n.* thorny bush, wild rose; bush with a woody root, pipe made of this.

brig *n.* two-masted sailing-vessel.

brigade *n.* army unit forming part of a division; organized group.

brigadier *n.* officer commanding a brigade or of similar status.

brigand *n.* member of a band of robbers.

bright *a.* (-*er*, -*est*) giving out or reflecting much light, shining; cheerful; quick-witted, clever. **brightly** *adv.*, **brightness** *n.*

brighten *v.t./i.* make or become brighter.

brill *n.* flat-fish like turbot.

brilliant *a.* very bright, sparkling; very clever. —*n.* cut diamond with many facets. **brilliantly** *adv.*, **brilliance** *n.*

brilliantine /-tin/ *n.* substance used to make hair glossy.

brim *n.* edge of a cup or hollow or channel; projecting edge of a hat. —*v.i.* (p.t. *brimmed*) be full to the brim.

brimstone *n.* (*old use*) sulphur.

brindled *a.* brown with streaks of another colour.

brine *n.* salt water.

bring *v.t.* (p.t. *brought*) cause to come; put forward (charges etc.) in a lawcourt. **~ about,** cause to happen. **~ off,** do successfully. **~ out,** show clearly; publish. **~ up,** look after and train (growing children); vomit; cause to stop suddenly. **~ up the rear,** come last in a line. **bringer** *n.*

brink *n.* edge of a steep place or of a stretch of water; point just before a change.

brisk *a.* (-*er*, -*est*) lively, moving quickly. **briskly** *adv.*, **briskness** *n.*

brisket *n.* joint of beef from the breast.

brisling *n.* small herring or sprat.

bristle *n.* short stiff hair; one of the stiff pieces of hair or wire etc. in a brush. —*v.i.* raise bristles in anger or fear; show indignation; be thickly set with bristles. **~ with,** be full of. **bristly** *a.*

Britannic *a.* of Britain.

British *a.* of Britain or its people.

Briton *n.* British person.

brittle *a.* hard but easily broken. **brittleness** *n.*

broach *v.t.* open and start using; begin discussion of.

broad *a.* (-*er*, -*est*) large across, wide; measuring from side to side; full and complete; in general terms; (of humour) rather coarse. —*n.* broad part. **~ bean,** edible bean with flat seeds. **~-minded** *a.* having tolerant views. **broadly** *adv.*, **broadness** *n.*

broadcast *v.t./i.* (p.t. *broadcast*) send out by radio or TV; speak on radio or TV; make generally known; sow (seed) by scattering. —*n.* broadcast programme. **broadcaster** *n.*

broaden *v.t./i.* make or become broader.

broadside *n.* firing of all guns on one side of a ship. **~ on,** sideways on.

brocade *n.* fabric woven with raised patterns.

broccoli /-lɪ/ *n.* (pl. -*li*) hardy kind of cauliflower.

brochure /ˈbrəʊʃ-/ *n.* booklet or leaflet giving information.

broderie anglaise /brəʊdərɪ ɑnˈɡleɪz/ fabric with openwork embroidery.

brogue *n.* strong shoe with ornamental perforated bands; dialectal esp. Irish accent.

broke *see* **break.** —*a.* (*sl.*) having spent all one's money; bankrupt.

broken *see* **break.** —*a.* **~ English,** English spoken imperfectly by a foreigner. **~-hearted** *a.* crushed by grief.

broker *n.* agent who buys and sells on behalf of others; stockbroker; official licensed to sell the goods of persons unable to pay their debts.

brolly *n.* (*colloq.*) umbrella.

bromide *n.* chemical compound used to calm nerves.

bronchial *a.* of the branched tubes into which the windpipe divides.

bronchitis *n.* inflammation of the bronchial tubes.

bronco *n.* (pl. -*os*) wild or half-tamed horse of western North America.

bronze *n.* brown alloy of copper and tin; thing made of this; its colour. —*a.* made of bronze, bronze-coloured. —*v.t./i.* make or become sun-tanned.

brooch *n.* ornamental hinged pin fastened with a clasp.

brood *n.* young produced at one hatching or birth; (*joc.*) family of children. —*v.i.* sit on eggs and hatch them; think long and deeply or resentfully.

broody *a.* (of a hen) wanting to brood; thoughtful and depressed.

brook[1] *n.* small stream.

brook[2] *v.t.* tolerate, allow.

broom *n.* shrub with white or yellow flowers; long-handled brush for sweeping floors.

broomstick *n.* broom-handle.

broth *n.* thin meat or fish soup.

brothel *n.* house where women work as prostitutes.

brother *n.* son of the same parents as another person; man who is a fellow member of a group or Church etc.; monk who is not a priest. **~-in-law** *n.* (pl. **~s-in-law**) brother of one's husband or wife; husband of one's sister. **brotherly** *a.*

brotherhood *n.* relationship of brothers; comradeship; association of men.

brought *see* **bring.**

brow *n.* eyebrow; forehead; projecting or overhanging part.

browbeat *v.t.* (p.t. -*beat*, p.p. -*beaten*) intimidate.

brown *a.* (-*er*, -*est*) of a colour between orange and black; dark-skinned. —*n.* brown colour or thing. —*v.t./i.* make or become brown. **browned off,** (*sl.*) bored, fed up. **brownish** *a.*

Brownie *n.* junior Guide.

browse *v.i.* feed on leaves or grass etc.; read casually.

bruise n. injury that discolours skin without breaking it. —v.t./i. cause bruise(s) on; become bruised.

brunette n. woman with brown hair.

brunt n. chief stress or strain.

brush n. implement with bristles; fox's tail; skirmish; brushing; undergrowth. —v.t./i. use a brush on; touch lightly in passing. ~ **off**, reject curtly; snub. ~ **up**, smarten; study and revive one's knowledge of.

brushwood n. undergrowth; cut or broken twigs.

brusque /brʊsk/ a. curt and offhand. **brusquely** adv., **brusqueness** n.

Brussels sprouts edible buds of a kind of cabbage.

brutal a. very cruel, without mercy. **brutally** adv., **brutality** n.

brutalize v.t. make brutal.

brute n. animal other than man; brutal person; (colloq.) unpleasant person or thing. **brutish** a.

bryony n. climbing hedge-plant.

B.Sc. abbrev. Bachelor of Science.

Bt. abbrev. Baronet.

bubble n. thin ball of liquid enclosing air or gas; transparent domed cover. —v.t./i. send up or rise in bubbles; show great liveliness. **bubbly** a.

buccaneer n. pirate; adventurer.

buck[1] n. male of deer, hare, or rabbit. —v.i. (of a horse) jump with the back arched. ~ **up**, (sl.) make haste; make or become more cheerful.

buck[2] n. article placed before the dealer in a game of poker. **pass the ~**, shift the responsibility (and possible blame). ~**-passing** n.

buck[3] n. (U.S. & Austr. sl.) dollar.

bucked a. (sl.) cheered and encouraged.

bucket n. round open container with a handle, for carrying or holding liquid. —v.i. move fast and bumpily; pour heavily. **bucketful** n.

buckle n. device through which a belt or strap is threaded to secure it. —v.t./i. fasten with a buckle; crumple under pressure. ~ **down to**, set about doing.

bucolic a. rustic.

bud n. leaf or flower not fully open. —v.i. (p.t. budded) put forth buds.

Buddhism n. Asian religion based on the teachings of Buddha. **Buddhist** a. & n.

budding a. beginning to develop.

buddleia /-lɪə/ n. tree or shrub with purple or yellow flowers.

buddy n. (colloq.) friend.

budge v.t./i. move slightly.

budgerigar n. a kind of Australian parakeet.

budget n. plan of income and expenditure, esp. of a country. —v.t./i. (p.t. budgeted) allow or arrange for in a budget.

buff n. fawn colour; bare skin; (U.S. colloq.) enthusiast. —v.t. polish with soft material.

buffalo n. (pl. -oes) a kind of ox.

buffer n. thing that lessens the effect of impact; (sl.) man. —v.t. act as a buffer to. ~ **zone**, region between hostile areas, preventing direct interaction.

buffet[1] /ˈbʊfeɪ/ n. counter where food and

drink are served; meal where guests serve themselves.

buffet[2] /ˈbʌfɪt/ n. blow, esp. with a hand. —v.t. (p.t. buffeted) deal blows to.

buffoon n. person who plays the fool. **buffoonery** n.

bug n. small unpleasant insect; (sl.) microbe; (sl.) secret microphone; (sl.) defect. —v.t. (p.t. bugged) (sl.) install a secret microphone in; (U.S. sl.) annoy.

bugbear n. thing feared or disliked.

buggy n. (old use) light carriage; small sturdy vehicle.

bugle n. brass instrument like a small trumpet. **bugler** n.

build v.t./i. (p.t. built) construct by putting parts or material together. —n. bodily shape. ~ **on**, rely on. ~ **up**, establish gradually; fill in with buildings; increase in height or thickness; boost with praise. ~**-up** n. this process. **builder** n.

building n. house or similar structure. ~ **society,** organization that accepts deposits of money and lends to people buying houses.

built see **build**.

bulb n. rounded base of the stem of certain plants, from which roots grow downwards; thing (esp. an electric lamp) shaped like this. **bulbous** a.

bulge n. rounded swelling; outward curve. —v.t./i. form a bulge, swell.

bulk n. size, esp. when great; greater part; bulky thing. —v.t. increase the size or thickness of. ~ **large**, seem important. **in ~**, in large amounts; in a mass, not packaged.

bulkhead n. partition in a ship etc.

bulky a. (-ier, -iest) taking up much space. **bulkiness** n.

bull[1] n. male of ox, whale, elephant, etc.; bull's-eye of a target. ~**'s-eye** n. centre of a target; hard round peppermint sweet. ~**-terrier** n. terrier resembling a bulldog.

bull[2] n. pope's official edict.

bull[3] n. (sl.) absurd statement, unnecessary routine tasks.

bulldog n. powerful dog with a short thick neck.

bulldoze v.t. clear with a bulldozer.

bulldozer n. powerful tractor with a device for clearing ground.

bullet n. small missile used in a rifle or revolver. ~**-proof** a. able to keep out bullets.

bulletin n. short official statement of news.

bullfight n. sport of baiting and killing bulls as an entertainment.

bullfinch n. song-bird with a strong beak and pinkish breast.

bullion n. gold or silver in bulk or bars, before manufacture.

bullock n. castrated bull.

bullring n. arena for bullfights.

bully[1] n. one who uses his strength or power to hurt or intimidate others. —v.t. behave as a bully towards.

bully[2] v.i. ~ **off,** put the ball into play in hockey by two opponents striking sticks together.

bulrush *n.* a kind of tall rush.

bulwark *n.* wall of earth built as a defence; ship's side above the deck.

bum[1] *n.* (*sl.*) buttocks.

bum[2] *n.* (*U.S. sl.*) beggar, loafer.

bumble *v.i.* move or act in a blundering way. **~-bee** *n.* large bee.

bump *v.t./i.* knock with a dullsounding blow; travel with a jolting movement. —*n.* bumping sound or knock; swelling, esp. left by a blow. **bumpy** *a.*

bumper *n.* something unusually large; horizontal bar at the front or back of a motor vehicle to lessen the effect of collision.

bumpkin *n.* country person with awkward manners.

bumptious *a.* conceited. **bumptiously** *adv.*, **bumptiousness** *n.*

bun *n.* small round sweet cake; hair twisted into a bun shape at the back of the head.

bunch *n.* cluster; number of small things fastened together; (*sl.*) group. —*v.t./i.* make into bunch(es); form a group.

bundle *n.* collection of things loosely fastened or wrapped together; (*sl.*) much money. —*v.t.* make into a bundle; push hurriedly.

bung *n.* stopper for closing the hole in a barrel or jar. —*v.t.* close with a bung; block; (*sl.*) throw.

bungalow *n.* one-storeyed house.

bungle *v.t.* spoil by lack of skill, mismanage. —*n.* bungled attempt. **bungler** *n.*

bunion *n.* swelling at the base of the big toe, with thickened skin.

bunk[1] *n.* shelf-like bed.

bunk[2] *v.* (*sl.*) run away.—*n.* **do a ~**, (*sl.*) run away.

bunk[3] *n.* (*sl.*) bunkum.

bunker *n.* container for fuel; sandy hollow forming a hazard on a golf-course; reinforced underground shelter.

bunkum *n.* nonsense.

bunny *n.* (*children's use*) rabbit.

bunt *v.t.* & *n.* push with the head.

bunting[1] *n.* bird related to finches.

bunting[2] *n.* decorative flags.

buoy *n.* anchored floating object serving as a navigation mark; lifebuoy. —*v.t.* mark with buoy(s). **~ up**, keep afloat; sustain, hearten.

buoyant *a.* able to float; cheerful. **buoyancy** *n.*

bur *n.* plant's seed-case or flower that clings to clothing etc.

burble *v.i.* make a gentle murmuring sound; speak lengthily.

burden *n.* thing carried; heavy load or obligation; trouble; theme. —*v.t.* put a burden on. **burdensome** *a.*

bureau /ˈbjʊərəʊ/ *n.* (pl. -eaux, pr. -əʊz) writing-desk with drawers; office, department.

bureaucracy /-ˈrɒk-/ *n.* government by State officials not by elected representatives; excessive official routine. **bureaucratic** *a.*

bureaucrat *n.* official in a government office.

burgeon *v.i.* begin to grow rapidly.

burglar *n.* person who breaks into a building, esp. in order to steal. **burglary** *n.*

burgle *v.t.* rob as a burglar.

burgundy *n.* red or white wine from Burgundy; similar wine.

burial *n.* burying.

burlesque *n.* mocking imitation. —*v.t.* imitate mockingly.

burly *a.* (-ier, -iest) with a strong heavy body. **burliness** *n.*

Burmese *a.* & *n.* (native, language) of Burma.

burn[1] *v.t./i.* (p.t. *burned* or *burnt*) damage, destroy, or mark by fire, heat, or acid; be damaged or destroyed thus; use as fuel; produce heat or light. —*n.* mark or sore made by burning; firing of a spacecraft's rockets.

burn[2] *n.* (*Sc.*) brook.

burner *n.* part that shapes the flame in a lamp or cooker.

burning *a.* intense; hotly discussed.

burnish *v.t.* polish by rubbing.

burnt *see* **burn**[1].

burp *n.* & *v.i.* (*colloq.*) belch.

burr *n.* whirring sound; rough pronunciation of 'r'; country accent using this; small drill; bur. —*v.i.* make a whirring sound.

burrow *n.* hole dug by a fox or rabbit etc. as a dwelling. —*v.t./i.* dig a burrow, tunnel; form by tunnelling; search deeply, delve.

bursar *n.* person who manages the finances and other business of a college etc.

bursary *n.* grant given to a student.

burst *v.t./i.* (p.t. *burst*) force or be forced open; fly violently apart; begin or appear or come suddenly. —*n.* bursting; outbreak; brief violent effort, spurt.

bury *v.t.* place (a dead body) in the earth or a tomb or the sea; put or hide underground; cover up.

bus *n.* (pl. *buses*) long-bodied passenger vehicle. —*v.t./i.* (p.t. *bused*) travel by bus; transport (children) to a distant school by bus.

busby *n.* tall fur cap worn as part of military ceremonial uniform.

bush[1] *n.* shrub; thick growth; wild uncultivated land. **~ telegraph**, way news is spread unofficially.

bush[2] *n.* perforated plug; metal-lined hole.

bushel *n.* measure for grain and fruit (8 gallons).

bushy *a.* (-ier, -iest) covered with bushes; growing thickly. **bushiness** *n.*

business *n.* task, duty; occupation, trade; thing to be dealt with; process, affair, structure; buying and selling, trade; commercial establishment. **~-like** *a.* practical, systematic. **~ man**, one engaged in trade or commerce. **have no ~ to**, have no right to (do something).

busker *n.* entertainer performing in the street.

busman *n.* (pl. *-men*) driver of a bus. **~'s holiday**, leisure time spent in something similar to one's work.

bust[1] *n.* sculptured head, shoulders, and chest; bosom, measurement round a woman's body there.

bust[2] *v.t./i.* (p.t. *busted* or *bust*) (*sl.*) burst, break. —*n.* (*sl.*) failure; spree. ~**-up** *n.* (*sl.*) quarrel. **go** ~, (*sl.*) become bankrupt. **buster** *n.*

bustard *n.* large swift-running bird.

bustle[1] *v.t./i.* make a show of activity; cause to hurry. —*n.* excited activity.

bustle[2] *n.* padding used to puff out the top of a skirt at the back.

busy *a.* (-*ier*, -*iest*) working, occupied; having much to do; full of activity. **busily** *adv.*

busybody *n.* meddlesome person.

but *adv.* only. —*prep. & conj.* however; except.

butane *n.* inflammable liquid used as fuel.

butcher *n.* person who cuts up and sells animal flesh for food; one who butchers people. —*v.t.* kill needlessly or brutally. **butchery** *n.*

butler *n.* chief manservant, in charge of the wine-cellar.

butt[1] *n.* large cask or barrel.

butt[2] *n.* thicker end of a tool or weapon; short remnant, stub.

butt[3] *n.* mound behind a target, (*pl.*) shooting-range; target for ridicule or teasing. —*v.t./i.* push with the head; meet or place edge to edge. ~ **in**, interrupt; meddle.

butter *n.* fatty food substance made from cream. —*v.t.* spread with butter. ~**-bean** *n.* dried haricot bean. ~**-fingers** *n.* person likely to drop things. ~ **muslin**, thin loosely woven fabric. ~ **up**, (*colloq.*) flatter.

buttercup *n.* wild plant with yellow cup-shaped flowers.

butterfly *n.* insect with four large often brightly coloured wings. ~ **stroke**, swimming-stroke with both arms lifted at the same time.

buttermilk *n.* liquid left after butter is churned from milk.

butterscotch *n.* hard toffee-like sweet.

buttock *n.* either of the two fleshy rounded parts at the lower end of the back of the body.

button *n.* knob or disc sewn to a garment as a fastener or ornament; small rounded object; knob pressed to operate a device. —*v.t.* fasten with button(s).

buttonhole *n.* slit through which a button is passed to fasten clothing; flower worn in the buttonhole of a lapel. —*v.t.* accost and talk to.

buttress *n.* support built against a wall; thing that supports or reinforces. —*v.t.* reinforce, prop up.

buxom *n.* plump and healthy.

buy *v.t.* (p.t. *bought*) obtain in exchange for money or by sacrifice; bribe; (*sl.*) accept, believe; (*sl.*) receive as punishment. —*n.* purchase. **buyer** *n.*

buzz *n.* vibrating humming sound. —*v.t./i.* make or be filled with a buzz; go about busily; threaten (an aircraft) by flying close to it.

buzzard *n.* a kind of hawk.

buzzer *n.* device that produces a buzzing sound as a signal.

by *prep. & adv.* near, beside, in reserve; along, via, past; during; through the agency or means of; having as another dimension; not later than; according to; after, succeeding; to the extent of; in respect of; (of an animal) having as its sire. ~ **and by,** before long. ~ **and large,** on the whole. ~**-election** *n.* election of an M.P. to replace one who has died or resigned. ~**-law** *n.* regulation made by a local authority or corporation. ~ **one-self,** alone, without help. ~**-play** *n.* minor action in a drama etc. ~**-product** *n.* thing produced while making something else. ~**-road, byway** *ns.* minor road.

bye *n.* run scored by a ball that passes the batsman; state of having no opponent for one round of a tournament.

bye-bye *int.* (*colloq.*) goodbye.

bygone *a.* belonging to the past.

bygones *n.pl.* bygone things.

bypass *n.* road taking traffic round a congested area; secondary channel for use when the main route is blocked. —*v.t.* provide with a bypass; use a bypass round; avoid.

byre *n.* cow-shed.

bystander *n.* person standing near when something happens.

byword *n.* notable example; familiar saying.

Byzantine /baɪ-/ *a.* of Byzantium or the eastern Roman Empire; complicated, underhand.

C

C *abbr.* Centigrade.

cab *n.* taxi; compartment for the driver of a train, lorry, etc.

cabaret /-reɪ/ *n.* entertainment provided in a night-club etc.

cabbage *n.* vegetable with a round head of green or purple leaves.

caber *n.* trimmed tree-trunk used in the sport of *tossing the caber*.

cabin *n.* small hut; compartment in a ship or aircraft.

cabinet *n.* cupboard or case with drawers or shelves; *C*~, central group of a government, formed from the most important ministers. ~**-maker** *n.* skilled joiner.

cable *n.* thick rope of fibre or wire; set of insulated wires for carrying electricity or telegraph messages; telegram sent abroad. —*v.t./i.* telegraph by cable. ~**-car** *n.* car of a ~ **railway,** drawn on an endless cable by a stationary engine.

cache /kæʃ/ *n.* hiding-place for treasure or stores; things in this. —*v.t.* put into a cache.

cackle *n.* clucking of hens etc.; chattering talk; loud silly laugh. —*v.i.* utter a cackle.

cacophony /-'kof-/ *n.* harsh discordant sound. **cacophonous** *a.*

cactus *n.* (pl. -*ti* or -*tuses*) fleshy plant, often with prickles, from a hot dry climate.

cad *n.* man who behaves dishonourably. **caddish** *a.*

cadaverous /-'dæ-/ *a.* gaunt and pale.

caddie *n.* golfer's attendant carrying clubs. —*v.i.* act as caddie.

caddy *n.* small box for tea.

cadence /'keɪ-/ *n.* rhythm in sound; rise and fall of the voice in speech; end of a musical phrase.

cadet *n.* young person being trained for service in the armed forces or police.

cadge *v.t./i.* ask for as a gift, beg things. **cadger** *n.*

cadmium *n.* soft metallic element.

cadre /'kɑdə(r)/ *n.* small group forming a nucleus that can be expanded.

Caesarean /-'zeər-/ *a.* ∼ **section,** operation to deliver a child by cutting the walls of the mother's abdomen and womb.

café *n.* shop selling refreshments, informal restaurant.

cafeteria *n.* self-service restaurant.

caffeine /-fin/ *n.* stimulant found in tea and coffee.

caftan *n.* long loose robe or dress.

cage *n.* enclosure of wire or with bars, esp. for birds or animals; enclosed platform carrying people in a lift or mine-shaft. —*v.t.* place or keep in a cage.

cagey *a.* (*colloq.*) secretive; shrewd; wary. **cagily** *adv.*, **caginess** *n.*

cairn *n.* mound of stones as a memorial or landmark etc. ∼ **terrier,** small shaggy short-legged terrier.

cairngorm *n.* yellow or wine-coloured gemstone.

cajole /-'dʒəʊl/ *v.t.* coax. **cajolery** *n.*

cake *n.* baked sweet bread-like food; small flattened mass. —*v.t./i.* form into a compact mass; encrust.

calamine /-maɪn/ *n.* lotion containing zinc carbonate.

calamity *n.* disaster. **calamitous** *a.*

calcium *n.* whitish metallic element.

calculable *a.* able to be calculated.

calculate *v.t./i.* reckon mathematically; estimate; plan deliberately; (*U.S.*) suppose. **calculation** *n.*

calculator *n.* electronic device used in mathematical calculations.

calculus *n.* (pl. -*li*) method of calculating in mathematics; stone formed in the body.

calendar *n.* chart showing dates of days of the year; method of fixing these; device displaying the date; register or list (e.g. of events).

calf¹ *n.* (pl. *calves*) young of cattle, also of elephant, whale, and seal; leather from calf-skin. ∼**love** *n.* immature romantic affection.

calf² *n.* (pl. *calves*) fleshy hind part of the human leg below the knee.

calibrate *v.t.* mark or correct the units of measurement on (a gauge). **calibration** *n.*

calibre *n.* diameter of a gun or tube or bullet etc.; level of ability.

calico *n.* (pl. -*oes*) a kind of cotton cloth.

call *v.t./i.* shout to attract attention; utter a characteristic cry; read (a list) aloud for checking; summon; command, invite; rouse from sleep; communicate (with) by telephone or radio; name, describe or address as; make a brief visit. —*n.* shout; bird's cry; signal on a bugle etc.; vocation; invitation, demand; need; telephone communication; short visit. ∼**box** *n.* telephone kiosk. ∼ **for,** demand; need. ∼ **off,** cancel. ∼ **up,** summon to join the armed forces. **caller** *n.*

calligraphy *n.* beautiful handwriting.

calliper *n.* splint for a weak leg; (*pl.*) compasses for measuring cavities.

callous *a.* feeling no pity or sympathy. **callously** *adv.*, **callousness** *n.*

callow /-əʊ/ *a.* (-*er*, -*est*) immature and inexperienced. **callowness** *n.*

callus *n.* patch of hardened skin.

calm *a.* (-*er*, -*est*) still, not windy; not excited or agitated. —*n.* calm condition. —*v.t./i.* make calm. **calmly** *adv.*, **calmness** *n.*

calorie *n.* unit of heat; unit of the energy-producing value of food.

calumny *n.* slander.

calve *v.i.* give birth to a calf.

Calvinism *n.* teachings of the Protestant reformer John Calvin or his followers. **Calvinist** *n.*

calypso *n.* (pl. -*os*) topical West Indian song.

calyx /'keɪ-/ *n.* ring of sepals covering a flower-bud.

cam *n.* device changing rotary to to-and-fro motion. **camshaft** *n.*

camber *n.* slight convex curve given to a surface esp. of a road.

cambric *n.* thin linen or cotton cloth.

came *see* **come.**

camel *n.* quadruped with one hump or two; fawn colour.

camellia /-'mil-/ *n.* evergreen flowering shrub.

Camembert /-beə/ *n.* a kind of soft rich cheese.

cameo *n.* (pl. -*os*) stone with coloured layers carved in a raised design; short well-executed description or part in a play etc.

camera *n.* apparatus for taking photographs or TV pictures. **cameraman** *n.* (pl. -*men*).

camisole *n.* woman's cotton bodice-like garment or undergarment.

camouflage *n.* disguise, concealment, esp. by colouring or covering. —*v.t.* disguise or conceal thus.

camp¹ *n.* temporary accommodation for travellers etc., esp. in tents; place where troops are lodged or trained; fortified site. —*v.i.* encamp, be in a camp. ∼**bed** *n.* portable folding bed. **camper** *n.*

camp² *a.* affected, exaggerated, bizarre; homosexual. —*n.* camp behaviour. —*v.t./i.* act or behave in a camp way.

campaign *n.* series of military operations;

organized course of action. —*v.i.* conduct or take part in a campaign.

camphor *n.* strong-smelling white substance used in medicine and moth-balls. **camphorated** *a.*

campion *n.* wild plant with pink or white flowers.

campus *n.* (pl. *-puses*) grounds of a university or college.

can¹ *n.* metal vessel for liquids; tinplate container in which food etc. is hermetically sealed. —*v.t.* (p.t. *canned*) put or preserve in a can. **canned music,** music recorded for reproduction.

can² *v.aux.* is or are able or allowed to.

Canadian *a.* & *n.* (native, inhabitant) of Canada.

canal *n.* artificial watercourse; duct.

canapé /ˈkænəpeɪ/ *n.* small piece of bread etc. with savoury topping.

canary *n.* small yellow song-bird.

cancan *n.* lively high-kicking dance performed by women.

cancel *v.t./i.* (p.t. *cancelled*) cross out; mark (a stamp etc.) to prevent re-use; declare that (something arranged) will not take place; order to be discontinued. ～ **out,** neutralize. **cancellation** *n.*

cancer *n.* malignant tumour; spreading evil. **cancerous** *a.*

candelabrum *n.* (pl. *-bra*) large branched candlestick or stand for a lamp.

candid *a.* frank. **candidly** *adv.*, **candidness** *n.*

candidate *n.* person applying for a job etc., or taking an examination. **candidacy, candidature** *ns.*

candied *a.* encrusted or preserved in sugar.

candle *n.* stick of wax enclosing a wick which is burnt to give light.

candlestick *n.* holder for a candle.

candlewick *n.* fabric with a tufted pattern.

candour *n.* frankness.

candy *n.* (*U.S.*) sweets, a sweet. ～**-floss** *n.* fluffy mass of spun sugar. ～**-striped** *a.* patterned with alternate stripes of white and colour.

candytuft *n.* garden plant with flowers in flat clusters.

cane *n.* stem of a tall reed or grass or slender palm; light walking-stick; rod with which children are struck as a punishment. —*v.t.* strike with a cane.

canine /ˈkeɪnaɪn *or* ˈkæ-/ *a.* of dog(s). —*n.* canine tooth. ～ **tooth,** pointed tooth between incisors and molars.

canister *n.* small metal container.

canker *n.* disease of animals or plants; influence that corrupts.

cannabis *n.* hemp plant; drug made from this.

canned *see* **can**¹.

cannibal *n.* person who eats human flesh; animal that eats others of its own kind. **cannibalism** *n.*

cannibalize *v.t.* use parts from (a machine) to repair another.

cannon *n.* large mounted gun (pl. *cannon*);

hitting of two balls in one shot in billiards. —*v.i.* bump heavily (into an obstacle).

cannot negative form of **can**².

canny *a.* shrewd. **cannily** *adv.*

canoe *n.* light boat propelled by paddles. —*v.i.* go in a canoe. **canoeist** *n.*

canon *n.* member of cathedral clergy; general rule or principle; set of writings etc. accepted as genuine. **canonical** *a.*

canonize *v.* declare officially to be a saint. **canonization** *n.*

canopy *n.* covering hung or held up over a throne, bed, person, etc.; spreading fabric of a parachute.

cant¹ *v.t./i.* tilt, slope.

cant² *n.* insincere talk.

can't = cannot.

cantankerous *a.* perverse, peevish.

cantata /-ˈtɑ-/ *n.* choral composition.

canteen *n.* restaurant for employees in a factory etc.; case of cutlery.

canter *n.* gentle gallop. —*v.t./i.* go or cause to go at a canter.

canticle *n.* song or chant with words from the Bible.

cantilever *n.* projecting beam or girder supporting a structure.

canton *n.* division of Switzerland.

canvas *n.* strong coarse cloth; a painting on this. —*v.t.* cover with canvas.

canvass *v.t./i.* ask for political support, orders, etc.; propose (a plan).

canyon *n.* deep gorge.

cap *n.* soft brimless hat, often with a peak; head-dress worn as part of uniform etc.; cap-like cover or top; explosive device for a toy pistol. —*v.t.* (p.t. *capped*) put or confer a cap on; cover or form the top or end of; surpass.

capable *a.* having a certain ability or capacity; competent. **capably** *adv.*, **capability** *n.*

capacious *a.* roomy.

capacitor *n.* device storing a charge of electricity.

capacity *n.* ability to contain or accommodate; amount that can be contained or produced; mental power; function or character.

cape¹ *n.* cloak; short similar part.

cape² *n.* coastal promontory.

caper¹ *v.* move friskily. —*n.* frisky movement; (*sl.*) activity.

caper² *n.* bramble-like shrub; one of its buds, pickled for use in sauces.

capillary *n.* very fine hair-like tube or blood-vessel.

capital *a.* chief, very important; (*colloq.*) excellent; involving the death penalty; (of a letter of the alphabet) of the kind used to begin a name or sentence etc. —*n.* chief town of a country; capital letter; top part of a pillar; accumulated wealth; money with which a business is started.

capitalism /ˈkæp-/ *n.* system in which trade and industry are controlled by private owners.

capitalist /ˈkæp-/ *n.* rich person, one who has much capital invested.

capitalize *v.t.* convert into or provide with

capital; write as or with a capital letter. **~ on,** make advantageous use of.

capitulate *v.i.* surrender, yield. **capitulation** *n.*

capon /ˈkeɪ-/ *n.* domestic cock castrated and fattened.

caprice /-ˈpriːs/ *n.* whim; piece of music in a lively fanciful style.

capricious *a.* guided by caprice, impulsive; unpredictable.

capsicum *n.* tropical plant with pungent seeds.

capsize *v.t./i.* overturn.

capstan *n.* revolving post or spindle on which a cable etc. winds.

capsule *n.* plant's seed-case; gelatine case enclosing medicine for swallowing; detachable compartment of a spacecraft.

captain *n.* leader of a group or sports team; person commanding a ship or civil aircraft; naval officer next below rear-admiral; army officer next below major. — *v.t.* be captain of. **captaincy** *n.*

caption *n.* short title or heading; description or explanation on an illustration etc.

captious *a.* fond of finding fault, esp. about trivial matters. **captiously** *adv.*, **captiousness** *n.*

captivate *v.t.* capture the fancy of, charm. **captivation** *n.*

captive *a.* taken prisoner, unable to escape. — *n.* captive person or animal. **captivity** *n.*

captor *n.* one who takes a captive.

capture *v.t.* take prisoner; take or obtain by force or skill or attraction. — *n.* capturing; person or thing captured.

car *n.* motor car; (*U.S.*) railway carriage; passenger compartment of a cable railway.

carafe /-ˈræf/ *n.* glass bottle for serving wine or water.

caramel *n.* brown syrup made from heated sugar; toffee tasting like this.

caramelize *v.t./i.* make into or become caramel.

carapace /ˈkæ-/ *n.* upper shell of a tortoise or crustacean.

carat *n.* unit of purity of gold or of weight of precious stones.

caravan *n.* dwelling on wheels, able to be towed by a horse or car; company travelling together across desert. **caravanning** *n.*

caraway *n.* plant with spicy seeds that are used for flavouring cakes.

carbine /-baɪn/ *n.* automatic rifle.

carbohydrate *n.* energy-producing compound (e.g. starch) in food.

carbolic *n.* a kind of disinfectant.

carbon *n.* non-metallic element occurring as diamond, graphite, and charcoal, and in all living matter; sheet of carbon paper; carbon copy. **~ copy,** copy made with carbon paper; exact copy. **~ paper,** paper coated with carbon etc. for making a copy as something is typed or written.

carbonate *n.* compound releasing carbon dioxide when mixed with acid.

carborundum *n.* compound of carbon and silicon used for grinding and polishing things.

carboy *n.* large round bottle with a protective framework, for transporting liquids.

carbuncle *n.* severe abscess; garnet cut in a round knob shape.

carburettor *n.* apparatus mixing air and petrol vapour in a motor engine.

carcass *n.* dead body of an animal; bony part of the body of a bird before or after cooking; framework.

carcinogen *n.* cancer-producing substance. **carcinogenic** *a.*

card[1] *n.* piece of cardboard or thick paper; this printed with a greeting or invitation etc.; postcard; playing-card; list of races etc.; (*colloq.*) odd or amusing person; (*pl.*) card-game(s); (*pl.*, *colloq.*) employee's official documents, held by his employer. **~-index** *n.* index on cards. **~-sharper** *n.* professional swindler at card-games.

card[2] *v.t.* clean or comb (wool) with a wire brush or toothed instrument.

cardboard *n.* stiff substance made by pasting together sheets of paper.

cardiac *a.* of the heart.

cardigan *n.* knitted jacket.

cardinal *a.* chief, most important. — *n.* member of the Sacred College of the R.C. Church, which elects the pope; deep scarlet. **~ numbers,** whole numbers 1, 2, 3, etc.

care *n.* serious attention and thought; caution to avoid damage or loss; protection, supervision; worry, anxiety. — *v.i.* feel concern, interest, affection, or liking. **take ~ of,** take charge of; see to the safety or well-being of; deal with.

careen *v.t./i.* tilt or keel over; (*U.S.*) swerve.

career *n.* way of making one's living, profession; course through life; swift course. — *v.i.* go swiftly or wildly.

careerist *n.* person intent on advancement in his career.

carefree *a.* light-hearted through being free from anxieties.

careful *a.* acting or done with care. **carefully** *adv.*, **carefulness** *n.*

careless *a.* not careful. **carelessly** *adv.*, **carelessness** *n.*

caress *n.* loving touch, kiss. — *v.t.* give a caress to.

caret /ˈkærət/ *n.* omission-mark.

caretaker *n.* person employed to look after a building.

careworn *a.* showing signs of prolonged worry.

cargo *n.* (pl. *-oes*) goods carried by ship or aircraft.

Caribbean *a.* of the West Indies or their inhabitants.

caribou /-buː/ *n.* (pl. *caribou*) North American reindeer.

caricature *n.* exaggerated portrayal of a person etc., esp. for comic effect. — *v.t.* make a caricature of.

caries /ˈkeəriːz/ *n.* (pl. *caries*) decay of tooth or bone.

Carmelite *n.* member of an order of white-cloaked friars or nuns.

carmine /-maɪn/ *a. & n.* vivid crimson.

carnage *n.* great slaughter.

carnal a. of the body or flesh, not spiritual. **carnally** adv.

carnation n. cultivated clove-scented pink.

carnet /-neɪ/ n. permit allowing a vehicle to cross a frontier or enter a camping site.

carnival n. public festivities, usu. with a procession.

carnivore n. carnivorous animal.

carnivorous a. eating flesh as food.

carol n. Christmas hymn. —v.i. (p.t. *carolled*) sing carols; sing joyfully.

carouse /-'raʊz/ v.i. drink and be merry. **carousal** n.

carousel /kæru'sel/ n. (*U.S.*) merry-go-round; rotating conveyor.

carp[1] n. (pl. *carp*) freshwater fish.

carp[2] v.i. keep finding fault.

carpenter n. person who makes or repairs wooden objects and structures. **carpentry** n.

carpet n. textile fabric for covering a floor. —v.t. (p.t. *carpeted*) cover with a carpet. ∼ **slippers,** slippers with cloth uppers. ∼-**sweeper** n. household device with revolving brushes for sweeping carpets. **on the** ∼, (*colloq.*) being reprimanded.

carport n. roofed open-sided shelter for a car.

carriage n. wheeled vehicle or support; moving part carrying or holding something in a machine; conveying of goods etc., cost of this. ∼ **clock,** small portable clock with a handle on top.

carriageway n. that part of the road on which vehicles travel.

carrier n. person or thing carrying something; paper or plastic bag with handles, for holding shopping. ∼ **pigeon,** homing pigeon transporting messages.

carrion n. dead decaying flesh.

carrot n. tapering orange-red root vegetable; incentive.

carry v.t./i. transport, convey; support; be the bearer of; involve, entail; take (a process etc.) to a specified point; get the support of; win acceptance for (a motion etc.); capture (a fortress etc.); stock (goods for sale); be heard at a distance. ∼ **away,** arouse great emotion in. ∼-**cot** n. baby's portable cot. ∼ **off,** remove by force; win; manage well. ∼ **on,** continue; (*colloq.*) behave excitedly, flirt. ∼ **out,** put into practice.

cart n. wheeled structure for carrying loads. —v.t. carry, transport. ∼-**horse** n. horse of heavy build. ∼-**track** n. track suitable for carts.

carte blanche /kɑt blɑ̃ʃ/ full power to do as one thinks best.

cartilage n. firm elastic tissue in skeletons of vertebrates, gristle.

cartography /-'tɒg-/ n. map-drawing. **cartographer** n., **cartographic** a.

carton n. cardboard or plastic container.

cartoon n. humorous drawing in a newspaper etc.; sequence of these; animated cartoon; preliminary sketch for a painting etc. —v.t. draw a cartoon of. **cartoonist** n.

cartridge n. case containing explosive for firearms; sealed cassette; head of pick-up on record-player. ∼ **paper,** thick strong paper.

cartwheel n. handspring with limbs spread like spokes of a wheel.

carve v.t./i. make or inscribe or decorate by cutting; cut (meat) into slices for eating.

Casanova n. man noted for his love affairs.

cascade n. waterfall; thing falling or hanging like this. —v.i. fall thus.

cascara n. a purgative tree-bark.

case[1] n. instance of a thing's occurring; situation; crime being investigated; lawsuit; set of facts or arguments supporting something; form of a noun, adjective, or pronoun showing its relationship to another word. **in** ∼, lest.

case[2] n. container or protective covering; this with its contents; suitcase. —v.t. enclose in a case; (*sl.*) examine (a house etc.) in preparation for a crime.

casement n. window opening on hinges.

cash n. money in the form of coins or banknotes. —v.t. give or obtain cash for (a cheque etc.). ∼ **in (on),** get profit or advantage (from).

cashew n. a kind of edible nut.

cashier[1] n. person employed to receive and pay out money in a bank or receive payments in a shop.

cashier[2] v.t. dismiss from military service in disgrace.

cashmere n. very fine soft wool; fabric made from this.

casino n. (pl. *-os*) public building or room for gambling.

cask n. barrel for liquids.

casket n. small usu. ornamental box for valuables; (*U.S.*) coffin.

cassava /-'sɑ-/ n. tropical plant; flour made from its roots.

casserole n. covered dish in which meat etc. is cooked and served; food cooked in this. —v.t. cook in a casserole.

cassette n. small case containing a reel of film or magnetic tape.

cassock n. long robe worn by clergy and choristers.

cast v.t./i. (p.t. *cast*) throw; shed; direct (a glance etc.); register (one's vote); shape (molten metal) in a mould; calculate; select actors for a play or film, assign a role to. —n. throw of dice, fishing-line, etc.; moulded mass of solidified material; heap of earth excreted by a worm; set of actors in a play etc.; type, quality; slight squint. ∼-**iron** a. made of cast iron; very strong. ∼-**off** a. & n. discarded (thing).

castanets n.pl. pair of shell-shaped pieces of wood etc. clicked in the hand to accompany dancing.

castaway n. shipwrecked person.

caste n. exclusive social class, esp. in the Hindu system.

castigate v.t. punish or rebuke or criticize severely. **castigation** n.

casting a. ∼ **vote,** deciding vote when those on each side are equal.

castle *n.* large fortified residence; rook in chess. —*v.i.* make a special move with a chess king and rook.

castor *n.* small swivelling wheel on a leg of furniture; small container with a perforated top for sprinkling sugar etc. ∼ **sugar,** finely granulated white sugar.

castor oil purgative and lubricant oil from seeds of a tropical plant.

castrate *v.t.* remove the testicles of. **castration** *n.*

casual *a.* happening by chance; not serious or formal or methodical; not permanent. **casually** *adv.*, **casualness** *n.*

casualty *n.* person killed or injured; thing lost or destroyed.

cat *n.* small furry domesticated animal; wild animal related to this; (*colloq.*) spiteful or malicious woman; whip with knotted lashes formerly used for flogging people. ∼'s-**cradle** *n.* child's game with string. ∼'s-**eyes** *pl.n.* reflector studs on a road. ∼'s-**paw** *n.* person used as a tool by another.

cataclysm *n.* violent upheaval or disaster. **cataclysmic** *a.*

catacomb *n.* underground gallery with recesses for tombs.

catafalque *n.* platform for the coffin of a distinguished person before or during a funeral.

catalepsy *n.* seizure or trance with rigidity of the body. **cataleptic** *a.*

catalogue *n.* systematic list of items. —*v.t.* list in a catalogue.

catalyst *n.* substance that aids a chemical reaction while remaining unchanged.

catamaran *n.* boat with twin hulls.

catapult *n.* device with elastic for shooting small stones. —*v.t./i.* hurl from or as if from a catapult; rush violently.

cataract *n.* large waterfall; opaque area clouding the lens of the eye.

catarrh *n.* inflammation of mucous membrane, esp. of the nose, with a watery discharge.

catastrophe /-əfɪ/ *n.* sudden great disaster. **catastrophic** *a.*

catcall *n.* whistle of disapproval.

catch *v.t./i.* (p.t. *caught*) capture, seize; come unexpectedly upon, detect; surprise, trick; overtake; be in time for; grasp and hold; make or become fixed, check suddenly; become infected with; hit. —*n.* act of catching; thing caught or worth catching; concealed difficulty; fastener. ∼ **fire,** begin to burn. ∼ **it,** (*sl.*) be scolded or punished. ∼ **on,** (*colloq.*) become popular; understand what is meant. ∼-**phrase** *n.* phrase in frequent current use, slogan. ∼ **up,** come abreast with; do arrears of work.

catching *a.* infectious.

catchment *n.* ∼ **area,** area from which rainfall drains into a river etc.; area from which a hospital draws patients or a school draws pupils.

catchword *n.* catch-phrase.

catchy *a.* (of a tune) pleasant and easy to remember.

catechism *n.* series of questions; *C*∼, summary of the principles of a religion in the form of questions and answers.

catechize /ˈkætɪkaɪz/ *v.t.* put a series of questions to.

categorical *a.* unconditional, absolute. **categorically** *adv.*

category *n.* class of things.

cater *v.i.* supply food; provide what is needed or wanted. **caterer** *n.*

caterpillar *n.* larva of butterfly or moth. ∼ **track,** ∼ **tread,** steel band with treads, passing round a vehicle's wheels.

caterwaul *v.i.* make a cat's howling cry.

catgut *n.* gut as thread.

cathedral *n.* principal church of a diocese.

catheter /ˈkæθ-/ *n.* tube inserted into the bladder to extract urine.

cathode *n.* electrode by which current leaves a device. ∼ **ray,** beam of electrons from the cathode of a vacuum tube.

catholic *a.* universal, including many or most things; *C*∼, of all Churches or all Christians. **Catholic** *a.* & *n.* Roman Catholic.

catholicism *n.* being catholic; adherence to the Catholic Church.

catkin *n.* hanging flower of willow, hazel, etc.

catmint *n.* strong-smelling plant attractive to cats.

catnap *n.* short nap.

cattle *n.pl.* large ruminant animals with horns and cloven hoofs.

catty *a.* slightly spiteful. **cattily** *adv.*, **cattiness** *n.*

catwalk *n.* narrow strip for walking on to gain access to machinery etc.

caucus *n.* (usu. *derog.*) local committee of a political party; (*U.S.*) meeting of party leaders.

caudal *a.* of or at the tail.

caught *see* **catch.**

caul *n.* membrane sometimes found on a child's head at birth.

cauldron *n.* large deep pot for boiling things in.

cauliflower *n.* cabbage with a white flowerhead.

caulk *v.t.* stop up (a ship's seams) with waterproof material or by driving edges of plating together.

causal *a.* of or forming a cause.

cause *n.* what produces an effect; reason or motive for action etc.; lawsuit, party's case in this; movement or principle supported. —*v.t.* be the cause of, make happen.

causeway *n.* raised road across low or wet ground.

caustic *a.* burning by chemical action, corrosive; sarcastic. —*n.* caustic substance. **caustically** *adv.*

cauterize *v.t.* burn the surface of (tissue) to destroy infection or stop bleeding. **cauterization** *n.*

caution *n.* avoidance of rashness, attention to safety; warning; (*colloq.*) amusing person. —*v.t.* warn; reprimand with a warning not to repeat an offence.

cautionary *a.* conveying a warning.

cautious *a.* having or showing caution. **cautiously** *adv.*

cavalcade *n.* procession, esp. on horseback or in cars.

Cavalier *n.* supporter of Charles I in the English Civil War.

cavalier *a.* arrogant, offhand.

cavalry *n.* troops who fight on horseback.

cave *n.* natural hollow in a hill. —*v.t./i.* ∼ **in,** collapse; yield.

caveat /ˈkævɪæt/ *n.* warning.

caveman *n.* (pl. *-men*) person of prehistoric times living in caves.

cavern *n.* large cave; hollow part.

cavernous *a.* like a cavern.

caviare *n.* pickled roe of sturgeon or other large fish.

cavil *v.i.* (p.t. *cavilled*) raise petty objections. —*n.* petty objection.

caving *n.* sport of exploring caves.

cavity *n.* hollow within a solid body.

cavort *v.i.* caper excitedly.

caw *n.* harsh cry of a rook etc. —*v.i.* utter a caw.

cayenne *n.* hot red pepper.

cc *abbr.* cubic centimetre(s).

cease *v.t./i.* come to an end, discontinue, stop. ∼**-fire** *n.* signal to stop firing guns. **without** ∼, not ceasing.

ceaseless *a.* not ceasing.

cedar *n.* evergreen tree; its hard fragrant wood. **cedarwood** *n.*

cede *v.t.* surrender (territory etc.).

cedilla *n.* mark written under c (ç) to show that it is pronounced as s.

ceiling *n.* interior surface of the top of a room; upper limit or level.

celandine /-daɪn/ *n.* small wild plant with yellow flowers.

celebrate *v.t./i.* mark or honour with festivities; engage in festivities; officiate at (a religious ceremony). **celebration** *n.*

celebrated *a.* famous.

celebrity *n.* famous person; fame.

celeriac /sɪˈle-/ *n.* celery with a turnip-like root.

celerity /sɪˈle-/ *n.* swiftness.

celery *n.* plant with edible crisp juicy stems.

celestial *a.* of the sky; of heaven.

celibate *a.* remaining unmarried, esp. for religious reasons. **celibacy** *n.*

cell *n.* small room for a monk or prisoner; compartment in a honeycomb; device for producing electric current chemically; microscopic unit of living matter; small group as a nucleus of political activities.

cellar *n.* underground room; stock of wine, place where this is stored.

cello /ˈtʃe-/ *n.* (pl. *-os*) bass instrument like a violin. **cellist** *n.* its player.

Cellophane *n.* [P.] thin transparent wrapping material.

cellular *a.* of or consisting of cells; woven with open mesh.

celluloid *n.* plastic made from cellulose nitrate and camphor.

cellulose *n.* organic substance in plant tissues, used in making plastics; paint made from this.

Celt /k-/ *n.* member of an ancient European people or their descendants. **Celtic** *a.*

cement *n.* substance of lime and clay setting like stone; similar material used as an adhesive. —*v.t.* put cement on; join with cement; unite firmly.

cemetery *n.* burial ground other than a churchyard.

cenotaph *n.* tomb-like monument to persons buried elsewhere.

censer *n.* container for burning incense, swung on chains.

censor *n.* person authorized to examine letters, books, films, etc., and remove or ban anything regarded as harmful. —*v.t.* remove or ban thus. **censorial** *a.*, **censorship** *n.*

censorious *a.* severely critical.

censure *n.* severe criticism and rebuke. —*v.t.* criticize and rebuke severely.

census *n.* official counting of population or traffic etc.

cent *n.* hundredth part of a dollar or other currency; coin worth this.

centenarian /-ˈneər-/ *n.* person 100 years old or more.

centenary /-ˈtin-/ *n.* 100th anniversary.

centennial /-ˈten-/ *a.* of a centenary. —*n.* (*U.S.*) centenary.

centigrade *a.* using a temperature scale of 100°, with 0° as the freezing-point and 100° as the boiling-point of water.

centilitre *n.* 100th of a litre.

centimetre *n.* 100th of a metre.

centipede *n.* small segmented crawling creature with many legs.

central *a.* of, at, or forming a centre; most important. ∼ **heating,** heating of a building from one source. **centrally** *adv.*, **centrality** *n.*

centralize *v.t.* bring under control of central authority. **centralization** *n.*

centre *n.* middle point or part; point or place where things are concentrated or from which they are dispersed; holders of moderate political views; centre-forward. —*a.* at or of the centre. —*v.t./i.* (p.t. *centred*) place in or at a centre; concentrate at one point.

centrifugal /-ˈtrɪf- *or* -ˈfju-/ *a.* moving away from the centre.

centrifuge *n.* machine using centrifugal force for separating substances. —*v.t.* separate by this.

centripetal /-ˈtrɪp- *or* -ˈpe-/ *a.* moving towards the centre.

century *n.* period of 100 years; 100 runs at cricket.

ceramic *a.* of pottery or a similar substance. **ceramics** *n.* art of making pottery.

cereal *n.* grass-plant with edible grain; this grain, breakfast food made from it.

cerebral *a.* of the brain; intellectual.

ceremonial *a.* of or used in ceremonies, formal. —*n.* ceremony; rules for this. **ceremonially** *adv.*

ceremonious *a.* full of ceremony. **ceremoniously** *adv.*

ceremony *n.* set of formal acts.

certain *a.* feeling sure; believed firmly; able to be relied on to happen or be effective; specific but not named; some. **make ~,** make sure.

certainly *adv.* without doubt; yes.

certainty *n.* being certain; thing that is certain.

certifiable *a.* able to be certified.

certificate *n.* official document attesting certain facts. **certificated** *a.*

certify *v.t.* declare formally, show on a certificate or other document.

certitude *n.* feeling of certainty.

cervix *n.* neck; neck-like structure, esp. of womb. **cervical** /ˈsɜːvɪkəl *or* -ˈvaɪ-/ *a.*

cessation *n.* ceasing.

cession *n.* ceding.

cesspit, cesspool *ns.* covered pit to receive liquid waste or sewage.

chafe *v.t./i.* warm by rubbing; make or become sore by rubbing; become irritated or impatient.

chaff *n.* corn-husks separated from seed; chopped hay and straw; banter. —*v.t./i.* banter, tease.

chaffinch *n.* European finch.

chafing-dish *n.* heated pan for cooking or keeping food warm at the table.

chagrin /ˈʃæɡrɪn/ *n.* annoyance and embarrassment or disappointment. **chagrined** *a.*

chain *n.* series of connected metal links; connected series or sequence. —*v.t.* fasten with chain(s). **~ reaction,** change causing further changes. **~ store,** one of a set of similar shops owned by one firm.

chair *n.* movable seat, with a back, for one person; position of chairman; position of a professor. —*v.t.* seat in the chair of honour; carry in triumph on the shoulders of a group; act as chairman of.

chairman *n.* (pl. *-men*) person who presides over a meeting or committee. **chairwoman** *n.fem.*

chaise longue /ʃeɪz ˈlɒ̃ŋ/ chair with a very long seat to support a sitter's legs.

chalet /ˈʃæleɪ/ *n.* Swiss hut or cottage; small villa; small hut in a holiday camp etc.

chalice *n.* large goblet.

chalk *n.* white soft limestone; piece of this or similar coloured substance used for drawing. —*v.t.* rub, mark, or draw with chalk. **~-striped** *a.* patterned with thin white stripes. **chalky** *a.*

challenge *n.* call to try one's skill or strength; demand to respond or identify oneself; formal objection; demanding task. —*v.t.* make a challenge to; question the truth or rightness of. **challenger** *n.*

chamber *n.* (*old use*) room, bedroom; (*pl.*) set of rooms; hall used for meetings of an assembly, the assembly itself; chamber-pot; cavity or compartment. **~ music,** music for performance in a room rather than a hall. **~-pot** *n.* bedroom receptacle for urine.

chamberlain *n.* official managing a sovereign's or noble's household.

chambermaid *n.* woman cleaner of hotel bedrooms.

chameleon /kəˈmiːljən/ *n.* small lizard that changes colour according to its surroundings.

chamfer *v.t.* (p.t. *chamfered*) bevel the edge of.

chamois /ˈʃæmwɑː/ *n.* small mountain antelope; /ˈʃæmɪ/ a kind of soft leather, a piece of this.

champ *v.t./i.* munch noisily, make a chewing action; show impatience.

champagne *n.* sparkling white wine; its pale straw colour.

champion *n.* person or thing that defeats all others in a competition; person who fights or speaks in support of another or of a cause. —*a.* & *adv.* (*colloq.* or *dial.*) splendid, splendidly. —*v.t.* support as champion. **championship** *n.*

chance *n.* way things happen through no known cause or agency; luck; likelihood; opportunity. —*a.* happening by chance. —*v.t./i.* happen; risk.

chancel *n.* part of a church near the altar.

chancellor *n.* State or law official of various kinds; non-resident head of a university.

Chancery *n.* division of the High Court of Justice.

chancy *a.* risky, uncertain.

chandelier /ʃændəˈlɪə(r)/ *n.* hanging support for several lights.

chandler *n.* dealer in ropes, canvas, etc., for ships.

change *v.t./i.* make or become different; interchange, exchange, substitute; put fresh clothes or coverings etc. on; go from one of two (sides, trains, etc.) to another; get or give small money or different currency for. —*n.* changing; money in small units or returned as balance of that offered in payment; menopause. **changeable** *a.*

changeling *n.* child or thing believed to have been substituted secretly for another.

channel *n.* sunken bed of a stream; stretch of water connecting two seas; course in which anything moves; passage for liquid; medium of communication; band of broadcasting frequencies. —*v.t.* (p.t. *channelled*) form channel(s) in; direct through a channel.

chant *n.* melody for psalms; monotonous singing; rhythmic shout. —*v.t./i.* sing, esp. to a chant; shout rhythmically.

chantry *n.* chapel founded for priests to sing masses for the founder's soul.

chaos *n.* great disorder. **chaotic** *a.,* **chaotically** *adv.*

chap[1] *n.* (*colloq.*) man.

chap[2] *n.* crack in skin. —*v.t./i.* (p.t. *chapped*) cause chaps in; suffer chaps.

chap[3] *n.* lower jaw or half of cheek, esp. of a pig, as food.

chapel *n.* place used for Christian worship, other than a cathedral or parish church; religious service in this; place with a separate altar within a church; section of a trade union in a printing works.

chaperon /ˈʃæp-/ n. older woman in charge of a young unmarried woman on social occasions. —v.t. act as chaperon to. **chaperonage** n.

chaplain n. clergyman of an institution, private chapel, ship, regiment, etc. **chaplaincy** n.

chaplet n. short rosary.

chapter n. division of a book; canons of a cathedral; members of a monastic order. ∼-**house** n. building used for meetings of a cathedral chapter.

char[1] n. charwoman.

char[2] v.t./i. (p.t. *charred*) make or become black by burning.

charabanc /ˈʃæ-/ n. early form of bus used for outings.

character n. qualities making a person or thing what he or it is; moral strength; noticeable or eccentric person; person in a novel or play etc.; reputation; testimonial; biological characteristic; letter or sign used in writing, printing, etc.

characteristic a. & n. (feature) forming part of the character of a person or thing. **characteristically** adv.

characterize v.t. describe the character of; be a characteristic of. **characterization** n.

charade /ʃəˈrɑd/ n. scene acted as a clue to a word in the game of *charades*; absurd pretence.

charcoal n. black substance made by burning wood slowly in an oven.

charge n. price asked for goods or services; appropriate quantity of material put into a receptacle etc. at one time, esp. of an explosive; electricity contained in a substance; task, duty; custody; person or thing entrusted; formal instructions about one's responsibility; accusation; rushing attack. —v.t./i. ask as a price or from (a person); record as a debt; load or fill with a charge of explosive etc.; give an electric charge to, store energy in (a battery etc.); give as a task or duty, entrust; accuse formally; rush forward in attack. **in** ∼, in command. **take** ∼, take control.

chargeable a. able to be charged.

chargé d'affaires /ʃɑʒeɪ dæˈfeə(r)/ (pl. -gés, pr. -ʒeɪ-) ambassador's deputy; envoy to a minor country.

chariot n. two-wheeled horse-drawn vehicle used in ancient times in battle and in racing.

charioteer n. driver of a chariot.

charisma /kəˈrɪzmə/ n. power to inspire devotion and enthusiasm.

charismatic /kærɪzˈmæ-/ a. having charisma. **charismatically** adv.

charitable a. full of charity; of or belonging to charities. **charitably** adv.

charity n. loving kindness; unwillingness to think badly of others; institution or fund for helping the needy, help so given.

charlady n. charwoman.

charlatan /ˈʃɑlətən/ n. person falsely claiming to be an expert, esp. in medicine.

charlotte n. pudding of cooked fruit with a covering of breadcrumbs.

charm n. attractiveness, power of arousing love or admiration; act, object, or words believed to have magic power; small ornament worn on a bracelet etc. —v.t. give pleasure to; influence by personal charm; influence as if by magic. **charmer** n.

charming a. delightful.

chart n. map for navigators; table, diagram, or outline map showing special information; list of recordings that are currently most popular. —v.t. make a chart of.

charter n. official document granting rights or defining the form of an institution; chartering of aircraft etc. —v.t. grant a charter to; let or hire (an aircraft, ship, or vehicle). ∼ **flight**, flight by chartered aircraft. **chartered accountant** etc., one qualified according to the rules of an association holding a royal charter.

chartreuse /ʃɑˈtrɜz/ n. fragrant green or yellow liqueur.

charwoman n. (pl. -*women*) woman employed to clean a house etc.

chary /ˈtʃeərɪ/ a. cautious.

chase[1] v.t./i. go quickly after in order to capture or overtake or drive away; hurry; (*colloq.*) try to obtain. —n. chasing, pursuit; hunting; steeplechase.

chase[2] v.t. engrave, emboss.

chaser n. horse for steeplechasing.

chasm n. deep cleft.

chassis /ˈʃæsɪ/ n. (pl. *chassis*, pr. -sɪz) baseframe, esp. of a vehicle.

chaste a. virgin, celibate; not sexually immoral; simple in style, not ornate. **chastely** adv.

chasten v.t. discipline by punishment; subdue the pride of.

chastise v.t. punish, esp. by beating. **chastisement** n.

chastity n. being chaste.

chasuble n. loose garment worn over other vestments by a priest celebrating the Eucharist.

chat n. informal conversation. —v.i. (p.t. *chatted*) have a chat.

château /ˈʃætəʊ/ n. (pl. -*eaux*, pr. -əʊz) French castle or large country house.

chatelaine /ˈʃætəleɪn/ n. mistress of a large house.

chattel n. movable possession.

chatter v.i. talk quickly and continuously about unimportant matters; (of teeth) rattle together. —n. chattering talk. **chatterer** n.

chatterbox n. talkative person.

chatty a. fond of chatting; resembling chat. **chattily** adv., **chattiness** n.

chauffeur n. person employed to drive a car.

chauvinism /ˈʃəʊ-/ n. exaggerated patriotism. **male** ∼, some men's prejudiced belief in their superiority over women. **chauvinist** n., **chauvinistic** a.

cheap a. (-*er*, -*est*) low in cost or value; poor in quality. —adv. cheaply. **cheaply** adv., **cheapness** n.

cheapen v.t./i. make or become cheap.

cheapjack a. of poor quality, shoddy.

cheat v.t./i. act dishonestly or unfairly to win

profit or advantage; trick, deprive by deceit. —*n.* person who cheats; deception.

check[1] *v.t./i.* stop, slow the motion (of); test or examine for correctness etc.; (*U.S.*) correspond when compared. —*n.* process of checking; pause; restraint; exposure of a chess king to capture; receipt; bill in a restaurant; (*U.S.*) cheque. **~ in,** register on arrival. **~ out,** register on departure or dispatch; (*U.S.*) test for correctness etc. **checker** *n.*

check[2] *n.* pattern of squares or crossing lines. **checked** *a.*

checkmate *n.* = mate[2]; complete defeat, deadlock. —*v.t.* put into checkmate; defeat, foil.

Cheddar *n.* firm cheese of a kind orig. made at Cheddar in England.

cheek *n.* side of the face below the eye; impudent speech, quiet arrogance. —*v.t.* speak cheekily to. **~ by jowl,** close together.

cheeky *a.* (-*ier*, -*iest*) showing bold or cheerful lack of respect; coquettish. **cheekily** *adv.*, **cheekiness** *n.*

cheep *n.* weak shrill cry like that of a young bird. —*v.i.* make this cry.

cheer *n.* shout of applause; cheerfulness. —*v.t./i.* utter a cheer, applaud with a cheer; gladden. **~ up,** make or become more cheerful.

cheerful *a.* happy, contented; pleasantly bright. **cheerfully** *adv.*, **cheerfulness** *n.*

cheerio *int.* (*colloq.*) goodbye.

cheerless *a.* gloomy, dreary.

cheese *n.* food made from pressed milk curds; shaped mass of this. **~-paring** *a.* stingy, (*n.*) stinginess. **cheesy** *a.*

cheesecake *n.* open tart filled with sweetened curds; (*sl.*) display of a woman's shapely body in an advertisement etc.

cheesecloth *n.* thin loosely-woven cotton fabric.

cheetah *n.* a kind of leopard.

chef *n.* professional cook.

chef d'œuvre /ʃeɪ ˈdɜvr/ *n.* (pl. *chefs d' œuvre*, pr. ʃeɪ ˈd-) masterpiece.

chemical *a.* of or made by chemistry. —*n.* substance obtained by or used in a chemical process. **chemically** *adv.*

chemist *n.* person skilled in chemistry; dealer in medicinal drugs.

chemistry *n.* study of substances and their reactions; structure and properties of a substance.

chenille /ʃəˈniːl/ *n.* fabric with velvety pile, used for furnishings.

cheque *n.* written order to a bank to pay out money from an account; printed form for this. **~ card,** card guaranteeing payment of a bank customer's cheques.

chequer *n.* pattern of squares, esp. of alternating colours.

chequered *a.* marked with a chequer pattern; having frequent changes of fortune.

cherish *v.t.* take loving care of; be fond of; cling to (hopes etc.).

cheroot /ʃəˈruːt/ *n.* cigar with both ends open.

cherry *n.* small soft round fruit with a stone;

tree bearing this or grown for its ornamental flowers; deep red. —*a.* deep red.

cherub *n.* angelic being (pl. *cherubim*); (in art) representation of a chubby infant with wings; angelic child. **cherubic** /-ˈruː-/ *a.*

chess *n.* game for two players using 32 **~-men** on a chequered board (**~-board**) with 64 squares.

chest *n.* large strong box for storing or shipping things in; upper front surface of the body, part containing the heart and lungs. **~ of drawers,** piece of furniture with drawers for storing clothes etc.

chesterfield *n.* sofa with a padded back, seat, and ends.

chestnut *n.* tree with a hard brown nut; this nut; reddish-brown, horse of this colour; old joke or anecdote. —*a.* reddish-brown.

chevron /ˈʃev-/ *n.* V-shaped symbol.

chew *v.t./i.* work or grind between the teeth; make this movement.

chewing-gum *n.* flavoured gum used for prolonged chewing.

chewy *a.* suitable for chewing.

Chianti /kɪ-/ *n.* dry usu. red Italian wine.

chic /ʃiːk/ *a.* (-*er*, -*est*) stylish and elegant. —*n.* stylishness, elegance.

chicane /ʃɪˈkeɪn/ *n.* chicanery; artificial barrier or obstacle on a motor-racing course. —*v.t./i.* use chicanery, cheat.

chicanery /ʃɪˈkeɪnərɪ/ *n.* trickery.

chick *n.* young bird before or after hatching.

chicken *n.* young domestic fowl; its flesh as food; (*sl.*) game testing courage. —*a.* (*sl.*) cowardly. —*v.i. out,* (*sl.*) withdraw through cowardice. **~-pox** *n.* disease with a rash of small red blisters.

chickweed *n.* weed with small white flowers.

chicory *n.* blue-flowered plant used for salad; its root, roasted and ground for use with coffee.

chide *v.t./i.* (p.t. *chided* or *chid*, p.p. *chidden*) (*old use*) scold, rebuke.

chief *n.* leader, ruler; person with the highest rank etc. —*a.* highest in rank etc.; most important.

chiefly *adv.* mainly.

chieftain *n.* chief of a clan or tribe.

chiffon /ˈʃɪ-/ *n.* thin almost transparent fabric.

chignon /ˈʃiːnjɔ̃/ *n.* coil of hair worn at the back of the head.

chihuahua /tʃɪˈwɑwə/ *n.* very small smooth-haired dog.

chilblain *n.* painful swelling caused by exposure to cold.

child *n.* (pl. *children*) young human being; son or daughter. **childhood** *n.*

childbirth *n.* process of giving birth to a child.

childish *a.* like a child, unsuitable for a grown person.

childlike *a.* simple and innocent.

childless *a.* having no children.

chill *n.* unpleasant coldness; illness with feverish shivering. —*a.* chilly. —*v.t./i.* make or become chilly; preserve at a low temperature without freezing.

chilli *n.* (pl. *-ies*) dried pod of red pepper.

chilly *a.* (*-ier*, *-iest*) rather cold, unpleasantly cold; cold and unfriendly in manner. **chilliness** *n.*

chime *n.* tuned set of bells; series of notes from these. —*v.t./i.* ring as a chime; show (the hour) by chiming.

chimney *n.* (pl. *-eys*) structure for carrying off smoke or gases. **~-pot** *n.* pipe at the top of a chimney. **~-sweep** *n.* person whose trade is to remove soot from inside chimneys.

chimp *n.* (*colloq.*) chimpanzee.

chimpanzee *n.* African ape.

chin *n.* front of the lower jaw. **~-wag** *n.* (*colloq.*) chat.

china *n.* fine earthenware, porcelain; things made of this.

chinchilla *n.* small squirrel-like South American animal; its grey fur.

chine *n.* animal's backbone; ravine in southern England.

Chinese *a. & n.* (native, language) of China.

chink[1] *n.* narrow opening, slit.

chink[2] *n.* sound like glasses or coins striking together. —*v.t./i.* make or cause to make this sound.

chintz *n.* cotton usu. glazed cloth used for furnishings.

chip *n.* small piece cut or broken off something hard; microchip; fried oblong strip of potato; basket made of thin strips of wood; counter used in a gambling game. —*v.t./i.* (p.t. *chipped*) break or cut the edge or surface of; shape thus; make (potato) into chips; (*colloq.*) tease. **~ in**, (*colloq.*) interrupt; contribute money. **~ on one's shoulder,** feeling of resentment.

chipmunk *n.* striped squirrel-like animal of North America.

chipolata /-ˈlɑ-/ *n.* small spicy sausage.

chiropody /kɪ- *or* ʃɪ-/ *n.* treatment of minor ailments of the feet. **chiropodist** *n.*

chirp *n.* short sharp sound made by a small bird or grasshopper. —*v.i.* make this sound.

chirpy *a.* lively and cheerful.

chisel *n.* tool with a sharp bevelled end for shaping wood or stone etc. —*v.t.* (p.t. *chiselled*) cut with this.

chit[1] *n.* young child; small young woman.

chit[2] *n.* short written note.

chit-chat *n.* chat, gossip.

chitterlings *n.pl.* pig's small intestines, cooked as food.

chivalry *n.* courtesy and considerate behaviour, inclination to help weaker persons. **chivalrous** *a.*

chive *n.* small herb with onion-flavoured leaves.

chivvy *v.t.* (*colloq.*) urge to hurry.

chloride *n.* compound of chlorine and another element.

chlorinate *v.t.* treat or sterilize with chlorine. **chlorination** *n.*

chlorine *n.* chemical element, heavy yellowish-green gas.

chloroform /ˈklo-/ *n.* liquid giving off vapour that causes unconsciousness when inhaled. —*v.t.* make unconscious with this.

chlorophyll /ˈklo-/ *n.* green colouring-matter in plants.

choc *n.* (*colloq.*) chocolate. **~-ice** *n.* bar of ice cream coated with chocolate.

chock *n.* block or wedge for preventing something from moving. —*v.t.* wedge with chock(s). **~-a-block** *a. & adv.* crammed, crowded together. **~-full** *a.* crammed full.

chocolate *n.* edible substance made from cacao seeds; drink made with this, sweet made of or coated with this; dark brown colour.

choice *n.* choosing, right of choosing; variety from which to choose; person or thing chosen. —*a.* of especially good quality.

choir *n.* organized band of singers, esp. in church; part of a church where these sit, chancel.

choirboy *n.* boy singer in a church choir.

choke *v.t./i.* stop (a person) breathing, esp. by squeezing or blocking the windpipe; be unable to breathe; clog, smother. —*n.* valve controlling the flow of air into a petrol engine. **~ off,** (*colloq.*) silence, discourage, esp. by a snub.

choker *n.* high stiff collar; close-fitting necklace.

cholera *n.* serious often fatal disease caused by bacteria.

choleric /ˈkol-/ *a.* easily angered.

cholesterol /kəˈles-/ *n.* fatty animal substance thought to cause hardening of arteries.

choose *v.t./i.* (p.t. *chose*, p.p. *chosen*) select out of a greater number of things; decide, prefer.

choosey *a.* (*colloq.*) careful in choosing, hard to please.

chop[1] *v.t./i.* (p.t. *chopped*) cut by a blow with an axe or knife; hit with a short downward movement. —*n.* chopping stroke; thick slice of meat, usu. including a rib.

chop[2] *n.* = chap[3].

chopper *n.* chopping tool; (*sl.*) helicopter.

choppy *a.* full of short broken waves; jerky. **choppiness** *n.*

chopstick *n.* one of a pair of sticks used in China to lift food to the mouth.

chop-suey *n.* Chinese dish of meat or fish fried with vegetables.

choral *a.* of or for or sung etc. by a chorus. **chorally** *adv.*

chorale /kɒˈrɑl/ *n.* choral composition using the words of a hymn.

chord[1] *n.* string of a harp etc.; straight line joining two points on a curve.

chord[2] *n.* combination of notes sounded together.

chore /tʃɔ(r)/ *n.* routine task.

choreography /kori-/ *n.* composition of stage dances. **choreographer** *n.*

chorister /ˈko-/ *n.* member of a choir.

chortle *n.* loud chuckle. —*v.i.* utter a chortle.

chorus *n.* group of singers; thing spoken or sung by many together; refrain of a song; group of singing dancers in a musical comedy. —*v.t./i.* speak or sing as a group. **in ~,** speaking or singing together.

chose, chosen see **choose.**

choux pastry /ʃu-/ light pastry for making small cakes.

chow n. long-haired dog of a Chinese breed.

christen v.t. admit to the Christian Church by baptism; name.

Christendom n. all Christians or Christian countries.

christening n. ceremony of baptism.

Christian a. of or believing in Christianity; kindly, humane. —n. believer in Christianity. ∼ **name,** name given at a christening. ∼ **Science,** religious system by which health and healing are sought by Christian faith, without medical treatment.

Christianity n. religion based on the teachings of Christ.

Christmas n. festival (25 Dec.) commemorating Christ's birth. **∼-box** n. Christmas present. ∼ **Day,** 25 Dec. ∼ **Eve,** 24 Dec. ∼ **tree,** evergreen or artificial tree decorated at Christmas. **Christmassy** a.

chromatic a. of colour, in colours. ∼ **scale,** music scale proceeding by semitones. **chromatically** adv.

chrome n. chromium; yellow pigment from a compound of this.

chromium n. metallic element that does not rust.

chromosome /ˈkrəʊ-/ n. thread-like structure carrying genes in animal and plant cells.

chronic a. constantly present or recurring; having a chronic disease or habit. **chronically** adv.

chronicle n. record of events in order of their occurrence. —v.t. record in a chronicle. **chronicler** n.

chronological a. arranged in the order in which things occurred. **chronologically** adv.

chronology n. arrangement of events in order of occurrence.

chronometer n. time-measuring instrument, esp. one unaffected by temperature changes.

chrysalis n. form of an insect in the stage between grub and adult insect; case enclosing it.

chrysanthemum n. garden plant flowering in autumn.

chub n. (pl. chub) river fish with a thick body.

chubby a. (-ier, -iest) round and plump. **chubbiness** n.

chuck[1] v.t. (colloq.) throw carelessly or casually; touch playfully under the chin. ∼ **out,** expel.

chuck[2] n. part of a lathe holding the drill; part of a drill holding the bit; cut of beef from neck to ribs.

chuckle n. quiet laugh. —v.i. utter a chuckle.

chuffed a. (sl.) pleased; displeased.

chug v.i. (p.t. chugged) make or move with a dull short repeated sound. —n. this sound.

chum n. (colloq.) close friend. —v.i. (p.t. chummed) ∼ **up,** form a close friendship. **chummy** a.

chump n. (sl.) head; foolish person. ∼ **chop,** chop from the thick end of a loin of mutton.

chunk n. thick piece; substantial amount.

chunky a. short and thick; in chunks, containing chunks. **chunkiness** n.

church n. building for public Christian worship; religious service in this. —v.t. perform the church service of thanksgiving for (a woman after childbirth). **Church** n. Christians collectively; particular group of these; clergy, clerical profession.

churchwarden n. representative of a parish, assisting with church business.

churchyard n. enclosed land round a church, often used for burials.

churlish a. ill-mannered, surly. **churlishly** adv., **churlishness** n.

churn n. machine in which milk is beaten to make butter; very large milk-can. —v.t./i. beat (milk) or make (butter) in a churn; stir or swirl violently. ∼ **out,** produce.

chute n. sloping channel down which things can be slid or dropped.

chutney n. (pl. -eys) seasoned mixture of fruit, vinegar, spices, etc., eaten with meat or cheese.

cicada /sɪˈkɑːdə/ n. chirping insect resembling a grasshopper.

C.I.D. abbr. Criminal Investigation Department.

cider n. fermented drink made from apples.

cigar n. roll of tobacco-leaf for smoking.

cigarette n. roll of shredded tobacco in thin paper for smoking.

cinch /sɪntʃ/ n. (U.S. sl.) certainty, easy task.

cinder n. piece of partly burnt coal or wood.

cine /ˈsɪnɪ/ a. cinematographic.

cinema n. theatre where films are shown; films as an art form or industry.

cinematography n. process of making and projecting moving pictures. **cinematographic** a.

cinerary a. ∼ **urn,** urn for holding ashes after cremation.

cinnamon n. spice made from the bark of a south-east Asian tree.

cipher n. symbol 0 representing nought or zero; any Arabic numeral; person or thing of no importance; system of letters or numbers used to represent others for secrecy.

circa /ˈsɜːkə/ prep. about.

circle n. perfectly round plane figure, line, or shape; curved tier of seats at a theatre etc.; group with similar interests. —v.t./i. move in a circle; form a circle round.

circlet n. small circle; circular band worn as an ornament.

circuit /ˈsɜːkɪt/ n. line, route, or distance round a place; judge's journey through a district to hold courts, this district; path of an electric current, apparatus through which a current passes.

circuitous /səˈkjuːɪtəs/ a. roundabout, indirect.

circuitry /ˈsɜːkɪtrɪ/ n. circuits.

circular a. shaped like or moving round a circle. —n. letter or leaflet etc. sent to a circle of people. **circularity** n.

circularize v.t. send circular(s) to.

circulate v.t./i. go or send round.

circulation n. circulating; movement of blood

round the body; number of copies sold, esp. of a newspaper. **circulatory** *a.*

circumcise *v.t.* cut off the foreskin of. **circumcision** *n.*

circumference *n.* boundary of a circle, distance round this.

circumflex *a.* ~ **accent,** the accent ˆ.

circumlocution *n.* roundabout, verbose, or evasive expression. **circumlocutory** /-ˡlok-/ *a.*

circumnavigate *v.t.* sail completely round. **circumnavigation** *n.*

circumscribe *v.t.* draw a line round; restrict. **circumscription** *n.*

circumspect *a.* cautious and watchful, wary. **circumspection** *n.*

circumstance *n.* occurrence or fact connected with an event or person.

circumstantial *a.* detailed; consisting of facts that strongly suggest something but do not prove it. **circumstantially** *adv.*

circumvent *v.t.* evade (a difficulty etc.). **circumvention** *n.*

circus *n.* travelling show with performing animals, acrobats, etc.; group performing in a series of sports matches etc.

cirrhosis /sɪˡrəʊsɪs/ *n.* disease of the liver.

cistern *n.* tank for storing water.

citadel *n.* fortress overlooking a city.

cite *v.t.* quote or mention as an example etc. **citation** *n.*

citizen *n.* inhabitant of a city; person with full rights in a country or Commonwealth. **citizenship** *n.*

citric *a.* ~ **acid,** acid in the juice of lemons, limes, etc.

citrus *n.* tree of a group including lemon, orange, etc.

city *n.* important town; town with special rights given by charter; *the C*~, oldest part of London, now a centre of finance.

civet /ˡsɪvɪt/ *n.* cat-like animal of central Africa; musky substance obtained from its glands.

civic *a.* of a city or citizenship.

civics *n.pl.* study of municipal government and of citizens' rights and duties.

civil *a.* of citizens; not of the armed forces or the Church; polite and obliging. ~ **engineering,** designing and construction of roads, bridges, etc. ~ **list,** annual allowance for the sovereign's household expenses. ~ **servant,** employee of the **Civil Service,** government departments other than the armed forces. ~ **war,** war between citizens of the same country. **civilly** *adv.*

civilian *n.* person not in the armed forces.

civility *n.* politeness.

civilization *n.* making or becoming civilized; stage in the evolution of society; civilized conditions.

civilize *v.t.* cause to improve from a primitive to a developed stage of society; improve the behaviour of.

civvies *n.pl.* (*sl.*) civilian clothes.

cl *abbr.* centilitre(s).

clack *n.* short sharp sound; noise of chatter. —*v.i.* make this sound.

clad *see* **clothe.**

cladding *n.* boards or metal plates applied as a protective covering.

claim *v.t.* demand as one's right; assert. —*n.* demand; assertion.

claimant *n.* person making a claim.

clairvoyance *n.* power of seeing in the mind events etc. that are in the future or out of sight. **clairvoyant** *n.* person thought to have this.

clam *n.* shellfish with a hinged shell. —*v.i.* (p.t. *clammed*) ~ **up,** (*U.S. sl.*) refuse to talk.

clamber *v.i.* climb with difficulty.

clammy *a.* (-*ier*, -*iest*) unpleasantly moist and sticky. **clamminess** *n.*

clamour *n.* loud confused noise; loud protest etc. **clamorous** *a.*

clamp¹ *n.* device for holding things tightly. —*v.t.* grip with a clamp, fix firmly. ~ **down on,** become firmer about, put a stop to.

clamp² *n.* pile of bricks for burning; pile of potatoes stored under straw and earth.

clan *n.* group of families with a common ancestor; large family forming a close group.

clandestine /-ˡdestɪn/ *a.* kept secret, done secretly. **clandestinely** *adv.*

clang *n.* loud ringing sound. —*v.i.* make this sound.

clanger *n.* (*sl.*) blunder.

clangour *n.* clanging noise.

clank *n.* sound like metal striking metal. —*v.t./i.* make or cause to make this sound.

clannish *a.* united in close group.

clap *v.t./i.* (p.t. *clapped*) strike palms loudly together, esp. in applause; strike or put quickly or vigorously. —*n.* act or sound of clapping; sharp noise of thunder. **clapped out,** (*sl.*) worn out.

clapper *n.* tongue or striker of a bell.

claptrap *n.* insincere talk.

claret *n.* a dry red wine.

clarify *v.t./i.* make or become clear. **clarification** *n.*

clarinet *n.* wood-wind instrument with finger-holes and keys. **clarinettist** *n.* its player.

clarion *a.* loud, rousing.

clarity *n.* clearness.

clash *n.* loud harsh sound as of cymbals; conflict; discordant effect of colours. —*v.t./i.* make or cause to make a clash; conflict.

clasp *n.* device for fastening things, with interlocking parts; grasp, hand-shake. —*v.t./i.* fasten, join with a clasp; grasp, embrace closely. ~**-knife** *n.* folding knife with a catch for fixing it open.

class *n.* set of people or things with characteristics in common; standard of quality; rank of society; set of students taught together. —*v.t.* place in a class.

classic *a.* of recognized high quality; typical; simple in style. —*n.* classic author or work etc.

classical *a.* classic; of the ancient Greeks and Romans; traditional and standard in style. **classically** *adv.*

classics *n.* study of ancient Greek and Roman literature, history, etc.

classifiable *a.* able to be classified.

classify *v.t.* arrange systematically, class. **classification** *n.*

classless *a.* without distinctions of social class.

classroom *n.* room where a class of students is taught.

classy *a.* (*sl.*) of high quality.

clatter *n.* rattling sound. —*v.t./i.* make or cause to make this sound.

clause *n.* single part in a treaty, law, or contract; distinct part of a sentence, with its own verb.

claustrophobia *n.* abnormal fear of being in an enclosed space.

claustrophobic *a.* causing or suffering from claustrophobia.

clavicle *n.* collar-bone.

claw *n.* pointed nail on an animal's or bird's foot; claw-like device for grappling or holding things. —*v.t.* scratch or pull with a claw or hand.

clay *n.* stiff sticky earth, used for making bricks and pottery. **clayey** *a.*

clean *a.* (-*er*, -*est*) free from dirt or impurities; not soiled or used; without projections; free from indecency; complete. —*adv.* completely. —*v.t.* make clean; dry-clean; gut (fish etc.). **cleaner** *n.*

cleanly[1] /ˈkli-/ *adv.* in a clean way.

cleanly[2] /ˈkle-/ *a.* attentive to cleanness. **cleanliness** *n.*

cleanse /klenz/ *v.t.* clean. **cleanser** *n.*

clear *a.* (-*er*, -*est*) transparent; free from doubt, difficulties, obstacles, etc.; easily seen or heard or understood; complete, net. —*adv.* clearly; completely; apart. —*v.t./i.* make or become clear; prove innocent; get past or over; make as net profit. ~ **off**, **out**, get rid of; (*sl.*) go away. **clearly** *adv.*, **clearness** *n.*

clearance *n.* clearing; permission; space allowed for one object to pass or move within another.

clearing *n.* space cleared of trees in a forest.

clearway *n.* road where vehicles must not stop on the carriageway.

cleavage *n.* split, separation; hollow between full breasts.

cleave[1] *v.t./i.* (p.t. *cleaved*, *clove*, or *cleft*; p.p. *cloven* or *cleft*) split.

cleave[2] *v.* (*old use*) stick, cling.

clef *n.* symbol on a stave in music, showing the pitch of notes.

cleft *see* **cleave**[1]. —*n.* split, cleavage. **in a ~ stick**, unable to evade difficulties.

clematis /ˈklemə- *or* klɪˈmeɪ-/ *n.* climbing plant with showy flowers.

clemency *n.* mildness, esp. of weather; mercy. **clement** *a.*

clench *v.t.* close (teeth or fingers) tightly; grasp firmly; clinch (a nail etc.). —*n.* clenching, clenched state.

clerestory /ˈklɪəstɔrɪ/ *n.* upper row of windows in a large church.

clergy *n.* persons ordained for religious duties. **clergyman** *n.* (pl. -*men*).

cleric /ˈklerɪk/ *n.* clergyman.

clerical *a.* of clerks; of clergy.

clerihew *n.* witty verse in four lines of unequal length.

clerk /klɑk/ *n.* person employed to do written work in an office.

clever *a.* (-*er*, -*est*) quick at learning and understanding things; showing skill. **cleverly** *adv.*, **cleverness** *n.*

cliché /ˈkliːʃeɪ/ *n.* hackneyed phrase or idea.

click *n.* short sharp sound. —*v.t./i.* make or cause to make a click; (*sl.*) be a success, be understood.

client *n.* person using the services of a professional person; customer.

clientele /kliːɒnˈtel/ *n.* clients.

cliff *n.* steep rock-face, esp. on a coast. ~**hanger** *n.* story or contest full of suspense.

climacteric /klaɪˈmæktərɪk/ *n.* period of life when physical powers begin to decline.

climate *n.* regular weather conditions of an area.

climax *n.* point of greatest interest or intensity; sexual orgasm. —*v.i.* reach a climax. **climactic** *a.*

climb *v.t./i.* go up or over. —*n.* ascent made by climbing. **climber** *n.*

clinch *v.t./i.* fasten securely; secure (a nail etc.) by driving the point sideways when through; settle conclusively; (of boxers) be too close together for strong blows. —*n.* clinching.

cling *v.i.* (p.t. *clung*) hold on tightly; stick.

clinic *n.* place or session at which medical treatment is given to visiting persons; private or specialized hospital.

clinical *a.* of or used in treatment of patients. **clinically** *adv.*

clink *n.* thin sharp sound. —*v.t./i.* make or cause to make this sound.

clinker *n.* fused ash of coal etc., piece of this.

clip[1] *n.* device for holding things tightly or together. —*v.t.* (p.t. *clipped*) fix or fasten with clip(s).

clip[2] *v.t.* cut, esp. with shears or scissors; (*colloq.*) hit sharply. —*n.* clipping; piece clipped from something; (*colloq.*) sharp blow.

clipper *n.* fast ship.

clippers *n.pl.* instrument for clipping things.

clique /-ik/ *n.* small exclusive group.

clitoris /ˈklɪ-/ *n.* small erectile part of female genitals.

cloak *n.* loose sleeveless outer garment. —*v.t.* cover, conceal.

cloakroom *n.* room where outer garments and packages etc. can be left, often containing a lavatory.

clobber *n.* (*sl.*) equipment. —*v.t.* (*sl.*) hit repeatedly; defeat heavily.

cloche /kloʃ *or* -əʊʃ/ *n.* transparent portable cover for protecting plants.

clock[1] *n.* instrument indicating time; clock-like measuring device. —*v.t.* time; (*colloq.*) achieve as speed.

clock[2] *n.* ornamental pattern on the side of a stocking or sock.

clockwise *adv.* & *a.* moving in the direction of the hands of a clock.

clockwork *n.* mechanism with wheels and springs.

clod *n.* lump of earth.

clog *n.* wooden-soled shoe. —*v.t./i.* (p.t. *clogged*) cause an obstruction in; become blocked.

cloister *n.* covered walk along the side of a church etc.; life in a monastery or convent.

clone *n.* group of plants or organisms produced asexually from one ancestor. —*v.t./i.* grow thus.

close[1] /kləʊs/ *a.* (-*er*, -*est*) near; near together; dear to each other; dense; concentrated; secretive; stingy; stuffy. —*adv.* closely; in a near position. —*n.* street closed at one end; grounds round a cathedral or abbey. **~ season,** period when killing of game is forbidden by law. **~-up** *n.* photograph etc. showing a subject as at close range. **closely** *adv.*, **closeness** *n.*

close[2] /kləʊz/ *v.t./i.* shut; bring or come to an end; bring or come nearer together. —*n.* conclusion, end. **closed shop,** system whereby employees must be members of a specified trade union.

closet *n.* (*U.S.*) cupboard; store room.

closeted *a.* in private conference or study.

closure *n.* closing, closed condition.

clot *n.* thickened mass of liquid; (*sl.*) stupid person. —*v.i.* (p.t. *clotted*) form clot(s).

cloth *n.* woven or felted material; piece of this; table-cloth.

clothe *v.t.* (p.t. *clothed* or *clad*) put clothes on, provide with clothes.

clothes *n.pl.* things worn to cover the body; bedclothes.

clothing *n.* clothes for the body.

cloud *n.* visible mass of watery vapour floating in the sky; mass of smoke or dust etc.; state of gloom. —*v.t./i.* make or become covered with clouds or gloom.

cloudburst *n.* violent storm of rain.

cloudy *a.* (-*ier*, -*iest*) covered with clouds; (of liquid) not transparent.

clout *n.* blow; (*colloq.*) power of effective action. —*v.t.* hit.

clove[1] *n.* dried bud of a tropical tree, used as spice.

clove[2] *n.* one division of a compound bulb such as garlic.

clove[3] *see* **cleave**[1]. —*a.* **~ hitch,** knot used to fasten a rope round a pole etc.

cloven *see* **cleave**[1]. —*a.* **~ hoof,** divided hoof like that of sheep etc.

clover *n.* plant with three-lobed leaves. **in ~,** in ease and luxury.

clown *n.* person who does comical tricks. —*v.i.* perform or behave as a clown.

cloy *v.t.* sicken by glutting with sweetness or pleasure.

club *n.* heavy stick used as a weapon; stick with a wooden or metal head, used in golf; playing-card of the suit marked with black clover-leaves; group who meet for social or sports etc. purposes, their premises; organization offering benefit to subscribers. —*v.t./i.* (p.t.

clubbed) strike with a club. **~ together,** join in subscribing.

cluck *n.* throaty cry of hen. —*v.i.* utter a cluck.

clue *n.* fact or idea giving a guide to the solution of a problem.

clump *n.* cluster, mass. —*v.t./i.* tread heavily; form into a clump; (*colloq.*) hit.

clumsy *a.* (-*ier*, -*iest*) large and ungraceful or difficult to handle; not skilful. **clumsily** *adv.*, **clumsiness** *n.*

clung *see* **cling**.

cluster *n.* small close group. —*v.t./i.* make into or form a cluster.

clutch[1] *v.t./i.* grasp tightly; try to grasp. —*n.* tight grasp; clutching movement; device for connecting and disconnecting moving parts.

clutch[2] *n.* set of eggs for hatching; chickens hatched from these.

clutter *n.* things lying about untidily. —*v.t.* fill with clutter.

cm *abbr.* centimetre(s).

Co. *abbr.* Company; County.

c/o *abbr.* care of.

co- *pref.* joint, jointly.

coach *n.* large horse-drawn carriage; railway carriage; private or long-distance bus; private tutor; instructor in sports. —*v.t.* train, teach.

coagulate *v.t./i.* change from liquid to semi-solid, clot. **coagulation** *n.*

coal *n.* hard black mineral used esp. for burning as fuel; piece of this.

coalesce *v.i.* combine. **coalescence** *n.*

coalfield *n.* area where coal occurs.

coalition *n.* union, esp. temporary union of political parties.

coarse *a.* (-*er*, -*est*) composed of large particles; rough or loose in texture; rough or crude in manner, vulgar. **~ fish,** freshwater fish other than salmon and trout. **coarsely** *adv.*, **coarseness** *n.*

coarsen *v.t./i.* make or become coarse.

coast *n.* sea-shore and land near it. —*v.i.* sail along a coast; ride a bicycle or drive a motor vehicle without using power. **coastal** *a.*

coaster *n.* ship trading along a coast; tray for bottle(s); mat for a glass.

coastguard *n.* public organization that keeps watch on the coast to report passing ships, prevent smuggling, etc.; member of this.

coastline *n.* line of a coast.

coat *n.* outdoor garment with sleeves; fur or hair covering an animal's body; covering layer. —*v.t.* cover with a layer. **~ of arms,** design on a shield as the emblem of a family or institution.

coatee *n.* woman's short coat.

coating *n.* covering layer.

coax *v.t.* persuade gently; manipulate carefully or slowly.

coaxial /-'æks-/ *a.* **~ cable,** electric cable in which a central conductor is surrounded by an insulated tubular conductor.

cob *n.* sturdy short-legged horse for riding; a kind of hazel-nut; stalk of an ear of maize; small round loaf.

cobalt *n.* metallic element; deep-blue pigment made from it.

cobber *n.* (*Austr. colloq.*) friend, mate.

cobble[1] *n.* rounded stone formerly used for paving roads.

cobble[2] *v.t.* mend roughly.

cobbler *n.* (*old use*) shoe-mender.

cobra /ˈkəʊ- *or* ˈkɒ-/ *n.* poisonous snake of India and Africa.

cobweb *n.* network spun by a spider.

cocaine *n.* drug used as a local anaesthetic or as a stimulant.

cochineal *n.* red colouring-matter used in food.

cock *n.* male bird; tap or valve controlling a flow; lever in a gun. —*v.t.* tilt or turn upwards; set the cock of (a gun) for firing, set (a camera shutter) ready for release. **~-a-hoop** *a.* pleased and triumphant. **~-and-bull story,** foolish story that no one should believe. **~-eyed** *a.* (*sl.*) askew.

cockade *n.* rosette etc. worn on a hat as badge.

cockatoo *n.* (pl. -*oos*) crested parrot.

cockchafer *n.* flying beetle.

cockerel *n.* young male fowl.

cocked *a.* **~ hat,** triangular hat worn as part of a uniform.

cockle *n.* edible shellfish. —*v.t./i.* make or become puckered.

Cockney *n.* (pl. -*eys*) native or dialect of the East End of London.

cockpit *n.* compartment for the pilot and crew in an aircraft.

cockroach *n.* beetle-like insect that infests kitchens etc.

cocksure *a.* very self-confident.

cocktail *n.* mixed alcoholic drink; appetizer containing shellfish. **fruit ~,** mixed chopped fruit.

cocky *a.* (-*ier*, -*iest*) conceited and arrogant. **cockily** *adv.,* **cockiness** *n.*

cocoa *n.* powder of crushed cacao seeds; drink made from this.

coconut *n.* nut of a tropical palm; its edible lining. **~ matting,** that made from fibre of its husk.

cocoon *n.* silky sheath round a chrysalis; protective wrapping. —*v.t.* wrap completely.

cod *n.* (pl. *cod*) large edible sea-fish. **~-liver oil,** rich oil from its liver.

coddle *v.t.* cherish and protect; cook (an egg) slowly in hot water.

code *n.* set of laws, rules, or signals; pre-arranged word or phrase used to represent a message, esp. for secrecy; cipher. —*v.t.* put into code.

codeine *n.* substance made from opium, used to relieve pain.

codfish *n.* cod.

codger *n.* (*colloq.*) fellow, person.

codicil /ˈkəʊ-/ *n.* appendix to a will.

codify /ˈkəʊ-/ *v.t.* arrange (laws etc.) into a code. **codification** *n.*

codling *n.* a kind of cooking apple; moth whose larva feeds on apples.

co-education *n.* education of boys and girls in the same classes. **co-educational** *a.*

coefficient *n.* multiplier; mathematical factor.

coelacanth /ˈsil-/ *n.* a kind of fish extinct except for one species.

coerce *v.t.* compel by threats or force. **coercion** *n.,* **coercive** *a.*

coexist *v.i.* exist together, esp. harmoniously. **coexistence** *n.,* **coexistent** *a.*

coextensive *a.* extending over same space or time.

coffee *n.* bean-like seeds of a tropical shrub, roasted and ground for making a drink; this drink; light-brown colour. **~ bar,** place serving coffee and light refreshments from a counter. **~-table** *n.* small low table.

coffer *n.* large strong box for holding money and valuables; (*pl.*) financial resources.

coffin *n.* box in which a corpse is placed for burial or cremation.

cog *n.* one of a series of projections on the edge of a wheel, engaging with those of another. **cog-wheel** *n.*

cogent /ˈkəʊ-/ *a.* convincing. **cogently** *adv.,* **cogency** *n.*

cogitate *v.i.* think deeply. **cogitation** *n.*

cognac /ˈkɒnjæk/ *n.* French brandy.

cognate *a.* akin, related. —*n.* relative; cognate word.

cognizant *a.* aware, having knowledge. **cognizance** *n.*

cohabit *v.i.* live together as man and wife. **cohabitation** *n.*

cohere *v.i.* stick together.

coherent *a.* cohering; connected logically, not rambling. **coherently** *adv.,* **coherence** *n.*

cohesion *n.* tendency to cohere.

coiffure /kwɑ-/ *n.* hair-style.

coil *v.t./i.* wind into rings or a spiral. —*n.* something coiled; one ring or turn in this.

coin *n.* metal money; piece of this. —*v.t.* make (coins) by stamping metal; get (money) in large quantities as profit; invent (a word or phrase).

coinage *n.* coining; coins, system of these; coined word or phrase.

coincide *v.i.* occupy the same portion of time or space; be in agreement or identical.

coincidence *n.* coinciding; remarkable occurrence of similar or corresponding events at the same time by chance. **coincident, coincidental** *adjs.,* **coincidentally** *adv.*

coition *n.* sexual intercourse.

coitus *n.* coition.

coke[1] *n.* solid substance left after gas and tar have been extracted from coal, used as fuel.

coke[2] *n.* (*sl.*) cocaine.

colander *n.* bowl-shaped perforated vessel for draining food.

cold *a.* (-*er*, -*est*) at or having a low temperature; not affectionate, not enthusiastic; (of scent in hunting) grown faint; (*colloq.*) at one's mercy; (*sl.*) unconscious. —*n.* low temperature; cold condition; illness causing catarrh and sneezing. **~-blooded** *a.* having a blood temperature varying with that of the surroundings; unfeeling, ruthless. **~ cream,** ointment for softening the skin. **~ feet,** fear.

∼-**shoulder** v.t. treat with deliberate un-friendliness. ∼ **war,** intense hostility between nations without fighting. **coldly** adv., **coldness** n.

coleslaw n. salad of shredded raw cabbage coated in dressing.

colic n. severe abdominal pain. **colicky** a.

colitis /kə'laɪ-/ n. inflammation of the colon.

collaborate v.i. work in partnership. **collaboration** n., **collaborator** n.

collage /kɒ'lɑʒ/ n. artistic composition in which objects are glued to a backing to form a picture.

collapse v.t./i. fall down or in suddenly; lose strength suddenly; fold; cause to collapse. —n. collapsing; breakdown.

collapsible a. made so as to fold up.

collar n. upright or turned-over band round the neck of a garment; strap put round an animal's neck; band holding part of a machine; cut of bacon from near the head. —v.t. (colloq.) seize, take for oneself. ∼-**bone** n. bone joining breast-bone and shoulder-blade.

collate v.t. compare in detail; collect and arrange systematically. **collation** n., **collator** n.

collateral a. parallel; additional but subordinate. —n. collateral security. ∼ **security,** additional security pledged. **collaterally** adv.

colleague n. fellow worker esp. in a business or profession.

collect[1] /-'lekt/ v.t./i. bring or come together; seek and obtain from a number of sources; obtain specimens of, esp. as a hobby; fetch.

collect[2] /'kɒ-/ n. short prayer for use on an appointed day.

collected a. calm and controlled.

collection n. collecting; objects or money collected.

collective a. of a group taken or working as a unit. —n. collective farm; collective noun. ∼ **farm,** group of smallholdings run jointly by their workers. ∼ **noun,** noun (singular in form) denoting a group (e.g. army, herd). **collectively** adv.

collector n. one who collects things.

colleen n. (Ir.) girl.

college n. educational establishment for higher or professional education; organized body of professional people. **collegiate** a.

collide v.i. come into collision.

collie n. dog with a pointed muzzle and shaggy hair.

colliery n. coal-mine.

collision n. violent striking of one body against another; clash of interests; disagreement.

colloid n. gluey substance.

collop n. escalope.

colloquial a. suitable for informal speech or writing. **colloquially** adv., **colloquialism** n.

collusion n. agreement made for a deceitful or fraudulent purpose.

cologne /-'ləʊn/ n. eau-de-Cologne or similar scented liquid.

colon[1] n. lower part of the large intestine. **colonic** /-'lɒn-/ a.

colon[2] n. punctuation-mark : .

colonel /'kɜːnəl/ n. army officer next below brigadier.

colonial a. of a colony or colonies. —n. inhabitant of a colony.

colonialism n. policy of acquiring or maintaining colonies.

colonize v.t. establish a colony in. **colonization** n., **colonist** n.

colonnade n. row of columns.

colony n. settlement or settlers in new territory, remaining subject to the parent State; people of one nationality or occupation etc. living in a particular area; birds etc. congregated similarly.

coloration n. colouring.

colossal a. immense. **colossally** adv.

colossus n. (pl. -ssi) immense statue.

colostomy /-'lɒs-/ n. opening made surgically in the surface of the abdomen, through which the bowel can empty.

colour n. sensation produced by rays of light of different wavelengths; one or more varieties of this; ruddiness of complexion; pigmentation of skin, esp. if dark; pigment, paint; (usu. pl.) flag of a ship or regiment; (pl.) award to a regular member of a sports team. —v.t./i. put colour on; paint, stain, dye; change colour, blush; give a special character or bias to. ∼-**blind** a. unable to distinguish between certain colours. **lend** ∼ **to,** give an appearance of truth to.

colourant n. colouring-matter.

coloured a. & n. (person) wholly or partly of non-white descent.

colourful a. full of colour; with vivid details. **colourfully** adv.

colourless a. without colour; lacking vividness.

colt n. young male horse.

columbine n. garden flower with pointed projections on its petals.

column n. round pillar; thing shaped like this; vertical division of a page, printed matter in this; long narrow formation of troops, vehicles, etc.

columnist n. journalist who regularly writes a column of comments.

coma n. deep unconsciousness.

comatose a. in a coma; drowsy.

comb n. toothed strip of stiff material for tidying hair, separating strands, etc.; fowl's fleshy crest; honeycomb. —v.t. tidy or separate with a comb; search thoroughly.

combat n. battle, contest. —v.t. (p.t. combated) counter.

combatant a. & n. (person etc.) engaged in fighting.

combination n. combining; set of people or things combined; (pl.) undergarment covering body and legs. ∼ **lock,** lock controlled by a series of positions of dial(s).

combine[1] /-'baɪn/ v.t./i. join into a group or set or mixture.

combine[2] /'kɒm-/ n. combination of people or firms acting together in business. ∼ **harvester,** combined reaping and threshing machine.

combustible *a.* capable of catching fire.

combustion *n.* burning; process in which substances combine with oxygen and produce heat.

come *v.i.* (p.t. *came*, p.p. *come*) move towards a speaker or place or point; begin to develop; arrive, reach a point or condition; occupy a specified position; occur; originate from; (*sl.*) behave as; (*imper.*) exclamation of mild protest or of encouragement. ~ **about,** happen. ~ **across,** meet or find unexpectedly. ~-**back,** *n.* return to a former successful position; retort. ~ **by,** obtain. ~-**down** *n.* fall in status. ~ **into,** inherit. ~ **off,** fare; be successful. ~ **out,** become visible or revealed or known etc. ~ **out with,** utter. ~ **round,** recover from fainting; be converted to the speaker's opinion. ~ **to,** amount to; regain consciousness. ~ **to pass,** happen. ~ **up,** arise for discussion etc. ~-**uppance** *n.* (*U.S.*) deserved punishment or rebuke. ~ **up with,** contribute (a suggestion etc.). **comer** *n.*

comedian *n.* humorous entertainer or actor. **comedienne** /-'en/ *n.fem.*

comedy *n.* light amusing drama; amusing incident.

comely *a.* (-*ier*, -*iest*) (*old use*) good-looking.

comestibles /-'mest-/ *n.pl.* things to eat.

comet *n.* heavenly body with a tail of light.

comfort *n.* state of ease and contentment; relief of suffering or grief; person or thing giving this. —*v.t.* give comfort to. **comforter** *n.*

comfortable *a.* providing or having ease and contentment; not close or restricted. **comfortably** *adv.*

comfy *a.* (*colloq.*) comfortable.

comic *a.* causing amusement; of comedy. —*n.* comedian; children's periodical with a series of strip cartoons. **comical** *a.*, **comically** *adv.*

coming *n.* arrival. —*a.* approaching, next. ~ **man,** one likely to be important in the near future.

comma *n.* punctuation-mark , .

command *n.* statement, given with authority, that an action must be performed; tenure of authority; mastery; forces or district under a commander. —*v.t.* give a command to; have authority over; deserve and get; dominate from a strategic position, look down over.

commandant /'ko-/ *n.* officer in command of a fortress etc.

commandeer *v.t.* seize for use.

commander *n.* person in command; naval officer next below captain; police officer next below commissioner.

commandment *n.* divine command.

commando *n.* (pl. -*os*) member of a military unit specially trained for making raids and assaults.

commemorate *v.t.* keep in the memory by a celebration or memorial. **commemoration** *n.*, **commemorative** *a.*

commence *v.t./i.* begin. **commencement** *n.*

commend *v.t.* praise; recommend; entrust. **commendation** *n.*

commendable *a.* worthy of praise. **commendably** *adv.*

commensurate /kə'menʃərət/ *a.* of the same size; proportionate.

comment *n.* opinion given; explanatory note. —*v.i.* make comment(s) on.

commentary *n.* series of comments.

commentate *v.i.* act as commentator.

commentator *n.* person who writes or speaks a commentary.

commerce *n.* all forms of trade and the services (e.g. banking, insurance) that assist trading.

commercial *a.* of or engaged in commerce; (of broadcasting) financed by firms whose advertisements are included. **commercially** *adv.*

commercialize *v.t.* make commercial, alter so as to make profitable. **commercialization** *n.*

commiserate *v.t./i.* express pity for; sympathize. **commiseration** *n.*

commissariat /-'sear-/ *n.* stock of food; department supplying this.

commission *n.* committing; giving of authority to perform a task; task given; body of people given such authority; warrant conferring authority, esp. on officers in the armed forces; payment to an agent selling goods or services. —*v.t.* give commission to; place an order for. ~-**agent** *n.* bookmaker. **in** ~, ready for service. **out of** ~, not in commission; not in working order.

commissionaire *n.* uniformed attendant at the door of a theatre, business premises, etc.

commissioner *n.* member of a commission; head of Scotland Yard; government official in charge of a district abroad.

commit *v.t.* (p.t. *committed*) do, perform; entrust, consign; pledge or bind to a course of action etc. ~ **to memory,** memorize. **committal** *n.*

commitment *n.* committing; obligation or pledge, state of being involved in this.

committee *n.* group of people appointed to attend to special business or manage the affairs of a club etc.

commode *n.* chest of drawers; chamber-pot mounted in a chair or box, with a cover.

commodious *a.* roomy.

commodity *n.* article of trade, product.

commodore *n.* naval officer next below rear-admiral; commander of a division of a fleet.

common *a.* (-*er*, -*est*) of or affecting all; occurring often; ordinary; of inferior quality; ill-bred. —*n.* area of unfenced grassland for all to use. ~ **law,** unwritten law based on custom and former court decisions. **Common Market,** European Economic Community, association of countries with internal free trade. ~-**room** *n.* room shared by students or teachers for social purposes. ~ **sense,** normal good sense in practical matters. ~ **time,** 4 crotchets in the bar in music. **commonness** *n.*

commoner *n.* one of the commonpeople, not a noble.

commonly *adv.* usually, frequently.

commonplace *a.* ordinary; lacking originality. —*n.* commonplace thing.

commonwealth *n.* independent State; republic; federation of States.

commotion *n.* fuss and disturbance.

communal /ˈkom-/ *a.* shared among a group. **communally** *adv.*

commune¹ /-ˈmjun/ *v.i.* communicate mentally or spiritually.

commune² /ˈkom-/ *n.* group (not all of one family) sharing accommodation and goods; district of local government in France etc.

communicable *a.* able to be communicated.

communicant *n.* person who receives Holy Communion; one who communicates information.

communicate *v.t./i.* make known; transfer, transmit; pass news and information to and fro, have social dealings with; have or be a means of access.

communication *n.* communicating; letter or message; means of access. ⁓ **cord,** chain for pulling by a passenger to stop a train in an emergency.

communicative *a.* talkative, willing to give information.

communion *n.* fellowship; social dealings; branch of the Christian Church; *C*⁓, sacrament in which bread and wine are consumed.

communiqué /-keɪ/ *n.* official communication giving a report.

communism *n.* social system based on common ownership of property, means of production, etc.; *C*⁓, political doctrine or movement seeking a form of this, such a system in the U.S.S.R. etc. **Communist** *n.*, **communistic** *a.*

community *n.* body of people living in one district etc. or having common interests or origins; state of being shared or alike.

commutable *a.* exchangeable.

commute *v.t./i.* exchange or change for something else; travel regularly by train or car etc. to and from one's work. **commuter** *n.*

compact¹ /ˈkom-/ *n.* pact, contract.

compact² /-ˈpækt/ *a.* closely or neatly packed together; concise. —*v.t.* make compact.

compact³ /ˈkom-/ *n.* small flat case for face-powder.

companion *n.* one who accompanies another; member of certain orders of knighthood; thing that matches or accompanies another. ⁓**-way** *n.* staircase from a ship's deck to cabins etc. **companionship** *n.*

companionable *a.* sociable.

company *n.* companionship; people assembled; guests; associate(s); people working together or united for business purposes, firm; subdivision of an infantry battalion.

comparable /ˈkom-/ *a.* suitable to be compared, similar.

comparative *a.* involving comparison; of the grammatical form expressing 'more'. —*n.* comparative form of a word. **comparatively** *adv.*

compare *v.t./i.* estimate similarity of; liken, declare to be similar; be worthy of comparison; form the comparative and superlative of. ⁓ **notes,** exchange ideas.

comparison *n.* comparing.

compartment *n.* partitioned space.

compass *n.* device showing the direction of the magnetic or true north; range, scope; (*pl.*) hinged instrument for drawing circles. —*v.t.* encompass.

compassion *n.* feeling of pity. **compassionate** *a.*, **compassionately** *adv.*

compatible *a.* able to exist or be used together; consistent; able to be together harmoniously. **compatibly** *adv.*, **compatibility** *n.*

compatriot /-ˈpæ-/ *n.* fellow-countryman.

compel *v.t.* (p.t. *compelled*) force; arouse (a feeling) irresistibly.

compendious *a.* giving much information concisely.

compendium *n.* summary; package of table-games or writing-paper.

compensate *v.t./i.* make payment to (a person) in return for loss or damage; counterbalance. **compensation** *n.*, **compensatory** *a.*

compère /-peə(r)/ *n.* person who introduces performers in a variety show etc. —*v.t.* act as compère to.

compete *v.i.* take part in a competition or other contest.

competent *a.* having ability or authority to do what is required; adequate. **competently** *adv.*, **competence** *n.*

competition *n.* friendly contest; competing; those who compete.

competitive *a.* involving competition. **competitively** *adv.*

competitor *n.* one who competes.

compile *v.t.* collect and arrange into a list or book etc.; make (a book) thus. **compilation** *n.*, **compiler** *n.*

complacent /-ˈpleɪ-/ *a.* self-satisfied. **complacently** *adv.*, **complacency** *n.*

complain *v.i.* say one is dissatisfied; say one is suffering from pain etc.

complaint *n.* statement that one is dissatisfied; illness.

complaisant /-ˈpleɪz-/ *a.* willing to please others. **complaisance** *n.*

complement *n.* that which completes or fills something; degrees required to make up a given angle to 90°. —*v.t.* form a complement to. **complementary** *a.*

complete *a.* having all its parts; finished; thorough, in every way. —*v.t.* make complete; fill in (a form etc.). **completely** *adv.*, **completeness** *n.*, **completion** *n.*

complex *a.* made up of parts; complicated. —*n.* complex whole; set of feelings that influence behaviour; set of buildings. **complexity** *n.*

complexion *n.* colour and texture of the skin of the face; general character of things.

compliant /-ˈplaɪ-/ *a.* complying, obedient. **compliance** *n.*

complicate *v.t.* make complicated. **complicated** *a.* complex; difficult because of this. **complication** *n.*

complicity *n.* involvement in wrong-doing.

compliment *n.* polite expression of praise; (*pl.*)

formal greetings in a message. —*v.t.* pay compliment to.

complimentary *a.* expressing a compliment; given free of charge.

comply *v.i.* ∼ **with,** act in accordance with (a command etc.).

component *n.* one of the parts of which a thing is composed. —*a.* being a component.

compose *v.t.* form, make up; create in music or literature; arrange in good order; calm. **composer** *n.*

composite /-zɪt/ *a.* made up of parts.

composition *n.* composing; thing composed; compound artificial substance.

compositor *n.* type-setter.

compos mentis sane.

compost *n.* decayed matter used as a fertilizer; mixture of soil or peat for growing seedlings etc.

composure *n.* calmness.

compound[1] /ˈkom-/ *a.* made up of two or more parts or ingredients. —*n.* compound thing or substance.

compound[2] /-ˈpaʊ-/ *v.t./i.* combine; add to; settle by agreement; condone (a felony etc.).

compound[3] /ˈkom-/ *n.* (in India, China, etc.) fenced enclosure.

comprehend *v.t.* understand; include.

comprehensible *a.* intelligible.

comprehension *n.* understanding.

comprehensive *a.* including much or all. —*n.* comprehensive school. ∼ **school,** one providing secondary education for children of all abilities. **comprehensively** *adv.*

compress[1] /-ˈpres/ *v.t.* squeeze, force into less space. **compression** *n.,* **compressor** *n.*

compress[2] /ˈkom-/ *n.* pad to stop bleeding or to cool inflammation.

comprise *v.t.* include; consist of; form, make up.

compromise /ˈkom-/ *n.* settlement reached by making concessions on each side. —*v.t./i.* make a settlement etc.; expose to suspicion or commit to a policy etc. unwisely.

compulsion *n.* compelling, being compelled; irresistible urge. **compulsive** *a.,* **compulsively** *adv.*

compulsory *a.* that must be done, required by rules etc.

compunction *n.* regret, scruple.

compute *v.t./i.* calculate; use a computer. **computation** *n.*

computer *n.* electronic machine for making calculations, controlling machinery, etc.

computerize *v.t.* equip with or perform or operate by computer. **computerization** *n.*

comrade *n.* companion, associate; fellow socialist. **comradeship** *n.*

con[1] *v.t.* (p.t. *conned*) (*colloq.*) persuade or swindle after winning confidence. —*n.* (*sl.*) confidence trick.

con[2] *v.t.* (p.t. *conned*) direct the steering of (a ship).

con[3] *see* pro and con.

concatenation *n.* combination.

concave *a.* curved like the inner surface of a ball. **concavity** *n.*

conceal *v.t.* hide, keep secret. **concealment** *n.*

concede *v.t.* admit to be true; grant (a privilege etc.); admit defeat in (a contest).

conceit *n.* too much pride in oneself; affectation of style. **conceited** *a.*

conceivable *a.* able to be imagined or believed true. **conceivably** *adv.*

conceive *v.t./i.* become pregnant; form (an idea etc.) in the mind, think.

concentrate *v.t./i.* employ all one's thought or effort; bring or come together; make less dilute. —*n.* concentrated substance.

concentration *n.* concentrating; concentrated thing. ∼ **camp,** camp for detention of internees or political prisoners, esp. in Nazi Germany.

concentric *a.* having the same centre.

concept *n.* idea, general notion.

conception *n.* conceiving; idea.

conceptual *a.* of concepts.

concern *v.t.* be about; be relevant or important to; involve. —*n.* thing that concerns one; anxiety; business or firm; (*colloq.*) thing.

concerned *a.* anxious.

concerning *prep.* with reference to.

concert *n.* musical entertainment. **in** ∼, in combination.

concerted *a.* done in concert.

concertina *n.* portable musical instrument with bellows and keys. —*v.t./i.* fold like bellows.

concerto /-ˈtʃeə-/ *n.* (pl. -*os*) musical composition for solo instrument(s) and orchestra.

concession *n.* conceding; thing conceded.

conciliate *v.t.* soothe the hostility of; reconcile. **conciliation** *n.,* **conciliatory** /-ˈsɪlɪə/ *a.*

concise *a.* brief and comprehensive. **concisely** *adv.,* **conciseness** *n.*

conclave *n.* assembly for discussion.

conclude *v.t./i.* end; settle finally; reach an opinion by reasoning.

conclusion *n.* concluding; ending; opinion reached.

conclusive *a.* ending doubt, convincing. **conclusively** *adv.*

concoct *v.t.* prepare from ingredients; invent. **concoction** *n.*

concomitant /-ˈkom-/ *a.* accompanying.

concord *n.* agreement, harmony.

concordance *n.* agreement; index of words.

concordant *a.* being in concord.

concourse *n.* crowd, gathering; open area at a railway terminus etc.

concrete *n.* mixture of gravel and cement etc. used for building. —*a.* existing in material form; definite. —*v.t./i.* cover with or embed in concrete; solidify.

concretion *n.* solidified mass.

concubine *n.* woman who cohabits with a man without marriage.

concur *v.i.* (p.t. *concurred*) agree in opinion; coincide. **concurrence** *n.,* **concurrent** *a.*

concussion *n.* injury to the brain caused by a hard blow.

condemn *v.t.* express strong disapproval of; convict; sentence; doom; declare unfit for use. **condemnation** *n.*

condense *v.t./i.* make denser or briefer; change from gas or vapour to liquid. **condensation** *n.*

condenser *n.* capacitor.

condescend *v.i.* consent to do something less dignified or fitting than is usual. **condescension** *n.*

condiment *n.* seasoning for food.

condition *n.* thing that must exist if something else is to exist or occur; state of being; (*pl.*) circumstances. —*v.t.* bring to the desired or good condition; have a strong effect on; accustom. **on ∼ that,** with the stipulation that. **conditioner** *n.*

conditional *a.* subject to specified conditions. **conditionally** *adv.*

condole *v.i.* express sympathy. **condolence** *n.*

condone *v.t.* forgive or overlook (a fault etc.). **condonation** *n.*

conduce *v.t.* help to cause or produce. **conducive** *a.*

conduct[1] /-'dʌkt/ *v.t.* lead, guide; be the conductor of; manage; transmit (heat, electricity, etc.).

conduct[2] /'kon-/ *n.* behaviour; way of conducting business etc.

conduction *n.* conducting of heat etc. **conductive** *a.*, **conductivity** *n.*

conductor *n.* person who controls an orchestra's or choir's performance by gestures; one who collects fares in a bus etc. (fem. *conductress*); thing that conducts heat etc.

conduit /'kondɪt/ *n.* pipe or channel for liquid; tube protecting wires.

cone *n.* tapering object with a circular base; cone-shaped thing; dry scaly fruit of pine or fir.

coney *n.* (*shop term*) rabbit-fur.

confab *n.* (*colloq.*) chat.

confection *n.* thing made of various items put together.

confectioner *n.* maker or seller of confectionery.

confectionery *n.* sweets, cakes, and pastries.

confederacy *n.* league of States.

confederate *a.* joined by treaty or agreement. —*n.* member of a confederacy; accomplice.

confederation *n.* union of States or people or organizations.

confer *v.t./i.* (p.t. *conferred*) grant; hold a discussion. **conferment** *n.*

conference *n.* meeting for discussion.

confess *v.t./i.* acknowledge, admit; declare one's sins, esp. to a priest; hear the confession of.

confession *n.* acknowledgement of a fact, sin, guilt, etc.; statement of one's principles.

confessional *n.* enclosed stall in a church, for hearing of confessions.

confessor *n.* priest who hears confessions and gives counsel.

confetti *n.* bits of coloured paper thrown at a bride and bridegroom.

confidant /'kon-/ *n.* person one confides in. **confidante** *n.fem.*

confide *v.t./i.* tell or talk confidentially; entrust.

confidence *n.* firm trust; feeling of certainty,

boldness; thing told confidentially. **∼ trick,** swindle worked by gaining a person's trust. **in ∼,** confidentially.

confident *a.* feeling confidence. **confidently** *adv.*

confidential *a.* to be kept secret; entrusted with secrets. **confidentially** *adv.*, **confidentiality** *n.*

configuration *n.* shape, outline.

confine /-'faɪn/ *v.t.* keep within limits; keep shut up.

confinement *n.* confining, being confined; time of childbirth.

confines /'kon-/ *n.pl.* boundaries.

confirm *v.t.* make firmer or definite; corroborate; administer the rite of confirmation to. **confirmatory** /-'fɜ-/ *a.*

confirmation *n.* confirming; thing that confirms; rite in which a person confirms the vows made for him at baptism.

confiscate *v.t.* take or seize by authority. **confiscation** *n.*

conflagration *n.* great fire.

conflict[1] /'kon-/ *n.* fight, struggle; disagreement.

conflict[2] /'flɪkt/ *v.i.* have a conflict.

confluence *n.* place where two rivers unite.

conform *v.t./i.* make similar; act or be in accordance, keep to rules or custom. **conformity** *n.*

conformation *n.* conforming; structure.

conformist *n.* person who conforms to rules or custom.

confound *v.t.* astonish and perplex; confuse.

confront *v.t.* be or come or bring face to face with; face boldly. **confrontation** *n.*

confuse *v.t.* throw into disorder; make unclear; bewilder; destroy the composure of. **confusion** *n.*

confute *v.t.* prove wrong. **confutation** *n.*

conga *n.* dance in which people form a long winding line.

congeal *v.t./i.* coagulate, solidify. **congelation** *n.*

congenial *a.* pleasant, agreeable to oneself. **congeniality** *n.*

congenital /-'dʒen-/ *a.* being so from birth. **congenitally** *adv.*

conger *n.* large sea eel.

congested *a.* too full; abnormally full of blood. **congestion** *n.*

conglomeration *n.* mass of different things put together.

congratulate *v.t.* tell (a person) that one admires his success. **congratulation** *n.*, **congratulatory** *a.*

congregate *v.i.* flock together.

congregation *n.* people assembled esp. at a church service.

congress *n.* formal meeting of delegates for discussion; *C∼,* law-making assembly, esp. of the U.S.A. **congressional** *a.*

conic *a.* of a cone.

conical *a.* cone-shaped.

conifer /'kəʊ-/ *n.* tree bearing cones. **coniferous** *a.*

conjecture *n.* & *v.t./i.* guess. **conjectural** *a.*, **conjecturally** *adv.*

conjugal /'kon-/ *a.* of marriage.

conjugate v.t. inflect (a verb). **conjugation** n.

conjunction n. word that connects others; combination.

conjure v.t./i. do sleight-of-hand tricks; produce. **conjuror** n.

conk n. (sl.) nose, head. —v.t. (sl.) hit. ∼ **out**, (sl.) break down; become unconscious, die.

conker n. fruit of the horse-chestnut.

connect v.t./i. join, be joined; associate mentally; (of a train etc.) arrive so that passengers are in time for another conveyance. **connection** n., **connective** a.

conning-tower n. raised structure on a submarine.

connive v.i. ∼ **at,** tacitly consent to. **connivance** n.

connoisseur /konə'sɜ(r)/ n. person with expert understanding esp. of artistic subjects.

connote v.t. imply in addition to its basic meaning. **connotation** n.

connubial a. of marriage.

conquer v.t. overcome in war or by effort. **conqueror** n.

conquest n. conquering; thing won by conquering.

consanguinity n. kinship.

conscience n. person's sense of right and wrong; feeling of remorse.

conscientious a. showing careful attention. **conscientiously** adv.

conscious a. with mental faculties awake; aware; intentional. **consciously** adv., **consciousness** n.

conscript[1] /-'skrɪpt/ v.t. summon for compulsory military service. **conscription** n.

conscript[2] /'kon-/ n. conscripted person.

consecrate v.t. make sacred; dedicate to the service of God. **consecration** n.

consecutive a. following continuously. **consecutively** adv.

consensus n. general agreement.

consent v.i. say one is willing to do or allow what is asked. —n. willingness; permission.

consequence n. result; importance.

consequent a. resulting.

consequently adv. as a result.

consequential a. consequent; self-important. **consequentially** adv.

conservancy n. commission controlling a river etc.; conservation.

conservation n. conserving.

conservationist n. one who seeks to preserve the natural environment.

conservative a. opposed to great change; avoiding extremes. **conservatively** adv., **conservatism** n.

Conservative a. & n. (member) of the U.K. political party favouring freedom from State control.

conservatory n. greenhouse, esp. forming an extension of a house.

conserve[1] /-'sɜv/ v.t. keep from harm, decay, or loss.

conserve[2] /'kon-/ n. jam made from fresh fruit and sugar.

consider v.t. think about, esp. in order to decide; allow for; be of the opinion.

considerable a. fairly great in amount etc. **considerably** adv.

considerate a. careful not to hurt or inconvenience others. **considerately** adv.

consideration n. considering; careful thought; being considerate; fact that must be kept in mind; payment given as a reward.

considering prep. taking into account.

consign v.t. deposit, entrust; send (goods etc.). **consignor** n.

consignment n. consigning; batch of goods etc.

consist v.i. ∼ **in,** have as its essential feature. ∼ **of,** be composed of.

consistency n. being consistent; degree of thickness or solidity.

consistent a. unchanging; not contradictory. **consistently** adv.

consolation n. consoling; thing that consoles. ∼ **prize,** one given to a runner-up.

console[1] /-'səʊl/ v.t. comfort in time of sorrow.

console[2] /'kon-/ n. bracket supporting a shelf; frame or panel holding the controls of equipment; cabinet for a TV set etc.

consolidate v.t./i. make or become secure and strong; combine. **consolidation** n.

consommé /-meɪ/ n. clear meat soup.

consonant n. letter other than a vowel; sound it represents. —a. consistent, harmonious.

consort[1] /-'kon-/ n. husband or wife, esp. of a monarch.

consort[2] /-'sɔt/ v.i. keep company.

consortium n. (pl. -tia) combination of firms etc. acting together.

conspicuous a. easily seen, attracting attention. **conspicuously** adv., **conspicuousness** n.

conspiracy n. conspiring; plan made by conspiring.

conspirator n. one who conspires. **conspiratorial** a., **conspiratorially** adv.

conspire v.i. plan secretly and usu. unlawfully against others; (of events) seem to combine.

constable n. policeman or police-woman of the lowest rank.

constabulary n. police force.

constancy n. quality of being unchanging; faithfulness.

constant a. continuous; occurring repeatedly; unchanging; faithful. —n. unvarying quantity. **constantly** adv.

constellation n. group of fixed stars.

consternation n. great surprise and anxiety or dismay.

constipate v.t. affect with constipation. **constipation** n. difficulty in emptying the bowels.

constituency n. body of voters who elect a representative; area represented thus.

constituent a. forming part of a whole. —n. constituent part; member of a constituency.

constitute v.t. make up, form; establish, be; appoint.

constitution n. constituting; composition; principles by which a State is organized; bodily condition.

constitutional a. of or in accordance with a

constitution. —*n.* walk as exercise. **constitutionally** *adv.*

constrain *v.t.* compel, oblige.

constraint *n.* constraining; restriction; strained manner.

constrict *v.t.* tighten by making narrower, squeeze. **constriction** *n.*, **constrictor** *n.*

construct *v.t.* make by placing parts together.

construction *n.* constructing; thing constructed; words put together to form a phrase etc.; interpretation. **constructional** *a.*

constructive *a.* constructing; making useful suggestions. **constructively** *adv.*

construe *v.t.* interpret; combine grammatically.

consul *n.* official appointed by a State to live in a foreign city to protect its subjects there and assist commerce. **consular** *a.*

consulate *n.* consul's position or premises.

consult *v.t./i.* seek information or advice from. **consultation** *n.*

consultant *n.* specialist consulted for professional advice.

consultative *a.* of or for consultation.

consume *v.t.* use up; eat or drink up; destroy (by fire); dominate by a feeling.

consumer *n.* person who buys or uses goods or services.

consumerism *n.* protection of consumers' interests.

consummate[1] /-'sʌm-/ *a.* perfect.

consummate[2] /'kon-/ *v.t.* accomplish, complete (esp. marriage by sexual intercourse). **consummation** *n.*

consumption *n.* consuming; (*old use*) tuberculosis.

consumptive *a.* suffering from tuberculosis.

contact *n.* touching, meeting, communicating; electrical connection; one who has been near an infected person; one who may be contacted for information or help. —*v.t.* get in touch with.

contagion *n.* spreading of disease by contact; disease etc. spread thus. **contagious** *a.*

contain *v.t.* have within itself; include; control, restrain.

container *n.* receptacle, esp. of standard design to transport goods.

containerize *v.t.* use containers for transporting (goods). **containerization** *n.*

containment *n.* prevention of hostile expansion.

contaminate *v.t.* pollute. **contamination** *n.*

contemplate *v.t./i.* gaze at; consider as a possibility, intend; meditate. **contemplation** *n.*

contemplative /-'tem-/ *a.* meditative.

contemporary *a.* of the same period or age; modern in style. —*n.* person of the same age.

contempt *n.* despising, being despised; disrespect.

contemptible *a.* deserving contempt.

contemptuous *a.* showing contempt. **contemptuously** *adv.*

contend *v.t./i.* strive, compete; assert. **contender** *n.*

content[1] /-'ten-/ *a.* satisfied with what one has.

—*n.* being content. —*v.t.* make content. **contented** *a.*, **contentment** *n.*

content[2] /'kon-/ *n.* what is contained in something.

contention *n.* contending; assertion made in argument.

contentious *a.* quarrelsome; likely to cause contention.

contest[1] /'kon-/ *n.* struggle for victory; competition.

contest[2] /-'test/ *v.t./i.* compete for or in; dispute. **contestant** *n.*

context *n.* what precedes or follows a word or statement and fixes its meaning; circumstances.

contiguous *a.* adjacent, next. **contiguously** *adv.*, **contiguity** *n.*

continent *n.* one of the main land masses of the earth; *the* C∼, Europe as distinct from the British Isles. —*a.* able to control one's excretions. **continence** *n.*

continental *a.* of a continent.

contingency *n.* something unforeseen; thing that may occur.

contingent *a.* happening by chance; possible but not certain; conditional. —*n.* body of troops or ships etc. contributed to a larger group.

continual *a.* never ending. **continually** *adv.*

continuance *n.* continuing.

continue *v.t./i.* not cease; remain in a place or condition; resume. **continuation** *n.*

continuous *a.* without interval. **continuously** *adv.*, **continuity** *n.*

continuum *n.* (pl. *-tinua*) continuous thing.

contort *v.t.* force or twist out of normal shape. **contortion** *n.*

contortionist *n.* performer who can twist his body dramatically.

contour *n.* outline; line on a map joining points of the same altitude.

contra- *pref.* against.

contraband *n.* smuggled goods.

contraception *n.* prevention of conception.

contraceptive *a.* & *n.* (drug or device) preventing conception.

contract[1] /'kon-/ *n.* formal agreement. **contractual** *a.*

contract[2] /-'trækt/ *v.t./i.* make a contract; arrange (work) to be done by contract; catch (an illness), acquire (a habit, debt, etc.); make or become smaller or shorter. **contraction** *n.*, **contractor** *n.*

contradict *v.t.* say that (a statement) is untrue or (a person) is wrong; be contrary to. **contradiction** *n.*, **contradictory** *a.*

contradistinction *n.* distinguishing by contrast.

contralto *n.* (pl. *-os*) lowest female voice.

contraption *n.* (*colloq.*) strange device or machine.

contrary[1] /'kon-/ *a.* opposite in nature or tendency or direction. —*n.* the opposite. —*adv.* in opposition. **on the** ∼, as the opposite of what was just stated.

contrary[2] /-'treə-/ *a.* perverse. **contrariness** *n.*

contrast[1] /ˈkon-/ *n.* difference shown by comparison; thing showing this.

contrast[2] /-ˈtrɑ-/ *v.t./i.* show contrast, compare so as to do this.

contravene *v.t.* break (a rule etc.). **contravention** *n.*

contretemps /ˈkɔntrətã/ *n.* unfortunate happening.

contribute *v.t./i.* give to a common fund or effort etc.; help to bring about. **contribution** *n.*, **contributor** *n.*, **contributory** *a.*

contrite /ˈkon-/ *a.* deeply penitent. **contritely** *adv.*, **contrition** *n.*

contrivance /-ˈtraɪ-/ *n.* contriving; contrived thing, device.

contrive *v.t./i.* plan or make or do something resourcefully.

control *n.* power to give orders or restrain something; means of restraining or regulating; check. —*v.t.* (p.t. *controlled*) have control of; regulate; restrain. **controllable** *a.*, **controller** *n.*

controversial *a.* causing controversy.

controversy /ˈkon- *or* -ˈtrov-/ *n.* prolonged dispute.

controvert *v.t.* deny the truth of. **controvertible** *a.*

contusion *n.* bruise.

conundrum *n.* riddle, puzzle.

conurbation *n.* large urban area formed where towns have spread and merged.

convalesce *v.i.* regain health after illness. **convalescence** *n.*, **convalescent** *a.* & *n.*

convection *n.* transmission of heat within a liquid or gas by movement of heated particles.

convector *n.* heating appliance that circulates warmed air.

convene *v.t./i.* assemble. **convener** *n.*

convenience *n.* being convenient; convenient thing; lavatory.

convenient *a.* easy to use or deal with; with easy access. **conveniently** *adv.*

convent *n.* residence of a community of nuns.

convention *n.* assembly; formal agreement; accepted custom. **conventional** *a.*, **conventionally** *adv.*

converge *v.i.* come to or towards the same point. **convergence** *n.*, **convergent** *a.*

conversant *a.* ~ **with**, having knowledge of.

conversation *n.* informal talk between people. **conversational** *a.*, **conversationally** *adv.*

conversationalist *n.* person who is good at conversation.

converse[1] /-ˈvəs/ *v.i.* hold a conversation.

converse[2] /ˈkon-/ *a.* opposite, contrary. —*n.* converse idea or statement. **conversely** *adv.*

convert[1] /-ˈvət/ *v.t./i.* change from one form or use etc. to another; cause to change an attitude or belief. **conversion** *n.*

convert[2] /ˈkon-/ *n.* person converted, esp. to a religious faith.

convertible *a.* able to be converted. —*n.* car with a folding or detachable roof. **convertibility** *a.*

convex *a.* curved like the outer surface of a ball. **convexity** *n.*

convey *v.t.* carry, transport, transmit; communicate as an idea.

conveyance *n.* conveying; means of transport, vehicle.

conveyancing *n.* business of transferring legal ownership of land.

conveyor *n.* person or thing that conveys; continuous moving belt conveying objects in a factory etc.

convict[1] /-ˈvɪkt/ *v.t.* prove or declare guilty.

convict[2] /ˈkon-/ *n.* convicted person in prison.

conviction *n.* convicting; firm opinion. **carry** ~, be convincing.

convince *v.t.* make (a person) feel certain that something is true.

convivial *a.* sociable and lively. **convivially** *adv.*, **conviviality** *n.*

convocation *n.* convoking; assembly convoked.

convoke *v.t.* summon to assemble.

convoluted *a.* coiled, twisted.

convolution *n.* coil, twist.

convolvulus *n.* twining plant with trumpet-shaped flowers.

convoy *n.* ships or vehicles travelling under escort or together. —*v.t.* escort in a convoy.

convulse *v.t.* cause violent movement or a fit of laughter in.

convulsion *n.* violent involuntary movement of the body; upheaval.

convulsive *a.* like or causing convulsion. **convulsively** *adv.*

coo *v.i.* make a soft murmuring sound like a dove. —*n.* this sound. —*int.* (*sl.*) exclamation of surprise.

cooee *int.* cry to attract attention.

cook *v.t./i.* prepare (food) by heating; undergo this process; (*colloq.*) falsify (accounts etc.). —*n.* person who cooks, esp. as a job. ~ **up**, (*colloq.*) concoct.

cooker *n.* stove for cooking food; apple suitable for cooking.

cookery *n.* art and practice of cooking.

cookie *n.* (*U.S.*) sweet biscuit.

cool *a.* (*-er*, *-est*) fairly cold; providing coolness; calm, unexcited; not enthusiastic; (of a large sum of money) no less than. —*n.* coolness; (*sl.*) calmness. —*v.t./i.* make or become cool. **coolly** *adv.*, **coolness** *n.*

coolant *n.* fluid for cooling machinery etc.

coolie *n.* unskilled native labourer in eastern countries.

coop *n.* cage for poultry. —*v.t.* confine, shut in.

Co-op *n.* (*colloq.*) Co-operative Society; shop etc. run by this.

co-operate *v.i.* work or act together. **co-operation** *n.*

co-operative *a.* co-operating; willing to help; based on economic co-operation. —*n.* farm or firm etc. run on this basis.

co-opt *v.t.* appoint to a committee etc. by invitation of existing members. **co-option** *n.*

co-ordinate[1] /-ət/ *a.* equal in importance. —*n.* (also *coordinate*) one of the magnitudes used to give the position of a point.

co-ordinate[2] /-eɪt/ v.t. bring into a proper relation; cause to function together efficiently. **co-ordination** n., **co-ordinator** n.

coot n. a kind of water-bird.

cop v.t. (p.t. copped) (sl.) catch. —n. (sl.) capture; policeman.

cope[1] v.i. (colloq.) manage successfully. ∼ **with**, deal successfully with.

cope[2] n. long loose cloak worn by clergy in certain ceremonies.

copeck /ˈkɔʊ-/ n. Russian coin, one hundredth of a rouble.

copier n. copying machine.

coping n. top (usu. sloping) row of masonry in a wall. ∼**-stone** n.

copious a. plentiful. **copiously** adv.

copper[1] n. reddish-brown metallic element; coin containing this; its colour. —a. made of copper.

copper[2] n. (sl.) policeman.

copperplate n. neat handwriting.

coppice, copse ns. group of small trees and undergrowth.

Coptic a. of the Egyptian branch of the Christian Church.

copula n. part of the verb be connecting subject and predicate.

copulate v.i. come together sexually as in mating. **copulation** n., **copulatory** a.

copy n. thing made to look like another; specimen of a book etc.; material for printing. —v.t. make a copy of; imitate. **copyist** n.

copyright n. sole right to print, publish, perform, etc., a work. —a. protected by copyright.

coquette /-ˈket/ n. woman who flirts. **coquettish** a., **coquetry** n.

coral n. hard red, pink, or white substance built by tiny sea creatures; reddish-pink colour.

corbel n. stone or wooden support projecting from a wall. **corbelled** a.

cord n. long thin flexible material made from twisted strands; piece of this; similar structure in the body; corduroy.

corded a. with raised ridges.

cordial a. warm and friendly. —n. fruit-flavoured essence diluted to make a drink. **cordially** adv., **cordiality** n.

cordite n. smokeless explosive used as a propellant.

cordon n. line of police, soldiers, etc., enclosing something; cord or braid worn as a badge; fruit tree pruned to grow as a single stem. —v.t. enclose by a cordon.

cordon bleu /kɔːdɔ̃ ˈblɜː/ of the highest degree of excellence in cookery.

corduroy n. cloth with velvety ridges; (pl.) trousers made of this.

core n. central or most important part; horny central part of an apple etc., containing seeds. —v.t. remove the core from. **corer** n.

co-respondent n. person with whom the respondent in a divorce suit is said to have committed adultery.

corgi n. (pl. -is) dog of a small Welsh breed with short legs.

coriander n. plant with seeds used for flavouring.

Corinthian a. of the most ornate style in Greek architecture.

cork n. light tough bark of a South European oak; piece of this used as a float; bottle-stopper. —v.t. stop up with a cork.

corker n. (sl.) excellent person or thing.

corkscrew n. tool for extracting corks from bottles; spiral thing.

corm n. bulb-like underground stem from which buds grow.

cormorant n. large black sea-bird.

corn[1] n. wheat, oats, or maize; its grain; (sl.) something corny.

corn[2] n. small area of horny hardened skin, esp. on the foot.

corncrake n. bird with a harsh cry.

cornea n. transparent outer covering of the eyeball. **corneal** a.

corned a. preserved in salt.

cornelian /-ˈniː-/ n. reddish or white semi-precious stone.

corner n. angle or area where two lines, sides, or streets meet; remote place; free kick or hit from the corner of the field in football or hockey; monopoly. —v.t./i. drive into a position from which there is no escape; move round a corner; obtain a monopoly of. ∼**-stone** n. basis; vital foundation.

cornet n. brass instrument like a small trumpet; cone-shaped wafer holding ice-cream.

cornflakes n.pl. breakfast cereal of toasted maize flakes.

cornflour n. flour made from maize.

cornflower n. plant (esp. blue-flowered) that grows among corn.

cornice n. ornamental moulding round the top of an indoor wall.

Cornish a. of Cornwall. —n. Celtic language of Cornwall.

cornucopia n. horn-shaped container overflowing with fruit and flowers, symbol of abundance.

corny a. (colloq.) hackneyed.

corollary n. proposition that follows logically from another.

corona n. ring of light round something.

coronary n. one of the arteries supplying blood to the heart; thrombosis in this.

coronation n. ceremony of crowning a monarch or consort.

coroner n. officer holding inquests.

coronet n. small crown.

corporal[1] n. non-commissioned officer next below sergeant.

corporal[2] a. of the body. ∼ **punishment,** whipping or beating.

corporate a. shared by members of a group; united in a group.

corporation n. group constituted to act as an individual or elected to govern a town; (colloq.) protruding abdomen.

corps /kɔ(r)/ *n.* (pl. *corps*, pr. kɔz) military unit; organized body of people.

corpse *n.* dead body.

corpulent *a.* having a bulky body, fat. **corpulence** *n.*

corpuscle *n.* blood-cell.

corral /-'rɑl/ *n.* (*U.S.*) enclosure for cattle etc. —*v.t.* (p.t. *corralled*) put or keep in a corral.

correct *a.* true, accurate; in accordance with an approved way of behaving or working. —*v.t.* make correct; mark errors in; reprove; punish. **correctly** *adv.*, **correctness** *n.*, **corrector** *n.*

correction *n.* correcting; alteration correcting something.

corrective *a.* & *n.* (thing) correcting what is bad or harmful.

correlate *v.t./i.* compare or connect or be connected systematically. **correlation** *n.*

correspond *v.i.* be similar or equivalent or in harmony; write letters to each other.

correspondence *n.* similarity; writing letters; letters written.

correspondent *n.* person who writes letters; person employed by a newspaper etc. to gather news and send reports.

corridor *n.* passage in a building or train; strip of territory or air space giving access to a point or area.

corrigenda *n.pl.* corrections.

corroborate *v.t.* get or give supporting evidence. **corroboration** *n.*, **corroborative** *a.*, **corroboratory** *a.*

corrode *v.t.* destroy (metal etc.) gradually by chemical action. **corrosion** *n.*, **corrosive** *a.*

corrugated *a.* shaped into alternate ridges and grooves.

corrupt *a.* dishonest, accepting bribes; immoral, wicked; decaying. —*v.t.* make corrupt; spoil, taint. **corruption** *n.*, **corruptible** *a.*

corsair *n.* (*old use*) pirate.

corset *n.* close-fitting undergarment worn to shape or support the body.

cortège /-'teɪʒ/ *n.* funeral procession.

cortex *n.* (pl. *-ices*) outer part of the kidney or brain.

cortisone *n.* hormone produced by adrenal glands or synthetically.

corvette *n.* small fast gunboat.

cos[1] *n.* long-leaved lettuce.

cos[2] *abbr.* cosine.

cosh *n.* weighted weapon for hitting people. —*v.t.* hit with a cosh.

cosine *n.* sine of the complement of a given angle.

cosmetic *n.* substance for beautifying the complexion etc. —*a.* improving the appearance.

cosmic *a.* of the universe. ⁓ **rays,** radiation from outer space.

cosmonaut *n.* Russian astronaut.

cosmopolitan *a.* of or from all parts of the world; free from national prejudices. —*n.* cosmopolitan person.

cosmos *n.* universe.

Cossack *n.* member of a people of South Russia, famous as horsemen.

cosset *v.t.* (p.t. *cosseted*) pamper.

cost *v.t.* (p.t. *cost*) have as its price; involve the sacrifice or loss of; (p.t. *costed*) fix or estimate the cost of. —*n.* what a thing costs; (*pl.*) expenses of a lawsuit.

costermonger *n.* person selling fruit etc. from a barrow in the street.

costly *a.* (*-ier, -iest*) costing much, expensive. **costliness** *n.*

costume *n.* style of clothes, esp. that of a historical period; garment(s) for a specified activity.

cosy *a.* (*-ier, -iest*) warm and comfortable. —*n.* cover to keep a teapot hot. **cosily** *adv.*, **cosiness** *n.*

cot *n.* child's bed with high sides.

coterie /'kəʊtərɪ/ *n.* select group of people.

cotoneaster /kətəʊnɪ'æ-/ *n.* shrub or tree with red berries.

cottage *n.* small simple house in the country. ⁓ **cheese,** that made from curds without pressing. ⁓ **hospital,** one without resident doctors. ⁓ **loaf,** loaf with a small round mass on top of a larger one. ⁓ **pie,** dish of minced meat topped with mashed potato.

cottager *n.* country person living in a cottage.

cotton *n.* soft white substance round the seeds of a tropical plant; this plant; thread or fabric made from cotton. —*v.i.* ⁓ **on,** (*sl.*) understand. ⁓ **wool,** raw cotton prepared as wadding. **cottony** *a.*

cotyledon *n.* first leaf growing from a seed.

couch *n.* long piece of furniture for lying or sitting on, usu. with a head-rest at one end. —*v.t.* express in a specified way.

couchette /ku'ʃet/ *n.* railway sleeping-berth convertible to seats.

couch-grass *n.* weed with long creeping roots.

cougar /'kuːgə(r)/ *n.* (*U.S.*) puma.

cough *v.t./i.* expel air etc. from lungs with a sudden sharp sound. —*n.* act or sound of coughing; illness causing coughing.

could *p.t.* of **can**[2]; feel inclined to.

couldn't, could not.

council *n.* assembly to advise on or discuss or organize something. ⁓ **house,** one owned and let by a municipal council.

councillor *n.* member of a council.

counsel *n.* advice, suggestions; (pl. *counsel*) barrister. —*v.t.* (p.t. *counselled*) advise.

counsellor *n.* adviser.

count[1] *v.t./i.* find the total of; say numbers in order; include or be included in a reckoning; be important; regard as. —*n.* counting, number reached by this; point being considered. ⁓**-down** *n.* counting seconds etc. backwards to zero. ⁓ **on,** rely on; expect confidently.

count[2] *n.* foreign nobleman.

countenance *n.* expression of the face; appearance of approval. —*v.t.* give approval to.

counter[1] *n.* apparatus for counting things; small disc etc. used for keeping account in table-games; flat-topped fitment over which goods are sold or business transacted with customers.

counter[2] *adv.* in the opposite direction. —*a.*

opposed. —*v.t./i.* hinder or defeat by an opposing action.

counter- *pref.* rival; retaliatory; reversed; opposite.

counteract *v.t.* reduce or prevent the effects of. **counteraction** *n.*

counter-attack *n.* & *v.t./i.* attack in reply to an opponent's attack.

counterbalance *n.* weight or influence balancing another. —*v.t.* act as a counterbalance to.

counterblast *n.* powerful retort.

counterfeit *a.*, *n.*, & *v.t.* fake.

counterfoil *n.* section of a cheque or receipt kept as a record.

countermand *v.t.* cancel.

countermeasure *n.* action taken to counteract danger etc.

counterpane *n.* bedspread.

counterpart *n.* person or thing corresponding to another.

counterpoint *n.* method of combining melodies.

counterpoise *n.* & *v.t.* counterbalance.

counter-productive *a.* having the opposite of the desired effect.

countersign *n.* password. —*v.t.* add a confirming signature to.

countersink *v.t.* (p.t. *-sunk*) sink (a screw-head) into a shaped cavity so that the surface is level.

counterweight *n.* & *v.t.* counterbalance.

countess *n.* count's or earl's wife or widow; woman with the rank of count or earl.

countless *a.* too many to be counted.

countrified *a.* like the countryside or country life.

country *n.* nation's or State's land; people of this; State of which one is a member; region; land consisting of fields etc. with few buildings. **~ dance** folk-dance. **go to the ~,** hold a general election.

countryman *n.* (pl. *-men*) man living in the country; man of one's own country. **countrywoman** *n.fem.*

countryside *n.* country district.

county *n.* major administrative division of a country; its residents; families of high social level long-established in a county.

coup /ku/ *n.* sudden action taken to obtain power etc.

coup d'état /ku deɪˈta/ sudden overthrow of a government by force or illegal means.

coupé /ˈkupeɪ/ *n.* two-door car with a sloping back.

couple *n.* two people or things; married or engaged pair; partners in a dance. —*v.t./i.* fasten or link together; join by coupling; copulate. **coupler** *n.*

couplet *n.* two successive rhyming lines of verse.

coupling *n.* device connecting railway carriages or machine parts.

coupon *n.* form or ticket entitling the holder to something; entry-form for a football pool etc.

courage *n.* ability to control fear when facing danger or pain. **courageous** *a.*, **courageously** *adv.*

courgette /kʊəˈʒet/ *n.* a kind of small vegetable marrow.

courier *n.* messenger carrying documents; person employed to guide and assist tourists.

course *n.* onward progress; direction taken or intended; series of lessons or treatments etc.; area on which golf is played or a race takes place; layer of stone etc. in a building; one part of a meal. —*v.t./i.* hunt with hounds that follow game by sight not scent; move or flow freely. **of ~,** without doubt.

court *n.* courtyard; area marked out for certain games; sovereign's establishment with attendants; lawcourt. —*v.t.* try to win the favour or support or love of; invite (danger etc.). **~ martial,** (pl. *courts martial*) court trying offences against military law; trial by this. **~-martial** *v.t.* (p.t. *-martialled*) try by court martial. **pay ~ to,** court.

courteous *a.* polite. **courteously** *adv.*

courtesan /kɔtɪˈzæn/ *n.* (*old use*) prostitute with upper-class clients.

courtesy *n.* courteous behaviour or act. **by ~ of,** by permission of.

courtier *n.* (*old use*) one of a sovereign's companions at court.

courtship *n.* courting, esp. of an intended wife or mate.

courtyard *n.* space enclosed by walls or buildings.

cousin *n.* (also **first ~**) child of one's uncle or aunt. **second ~,** child of one's parent's cousin. **cousinly** *adv.*

couture /kuˈtjʊə(r)/ *n.* design and making of fashionable clothes.

couturier /kuˈtjʊərɪeɪ/ *n.* designer of fashionable clothes.

cove *n.* small bay.

coven *n.* assembly esp. of witches.

covenant *n.* formal agreement, contract. —*v.i.* make a covenant.

Coventry *n.* **send to ~,** refuse to speak to or associate with.

cover *v.t.* place or be or spread over; conceal or protect thus; travel over (a distance); have within range of gun(s); protect by insurance or a guarantee; be enough to pay for; deal with (subject etc.); report for a newspaper etc. —*n.* thing that covers; wrapper, envelope, binding of a book; screen, shelter, protection; place laid at a meal. **~ up,** conceal (a thing or fact). **~-up** *n.*

coverage *n.* process of covering; area or risk etc. covered.

covert *n.* thick undergrowth where animals hide; feather covering the base of a bird. —*a.* concealed, done secretly. **covertly** *adv.*

covet *v.t.* desire eagerly (esp. a thing belonging to another person). **covetous** *a.*, **covetously** *adv.*

covey (pl. *-eys*) group of partridges.

cow[1] *n.* fully grown female of cattle or other large animals.

cow[2] *v.t.* intimidate.

coward *n.* person who lacks courage. **cowardly** *a.*, **cowardliness** *n.*

cowardice *n.* lack of courage.

cowboy *n.* man in charge of grazing cattle on a ranch; (*colloq.*) person with reckless or unscrupulous methods in business.

cower *v.i.* crouch or shrink in fear.

cowl *n.* monk's hood or hooded robe; hood-shaped covering.

cowling *n.* removable metal cover on an engine.

cowrie *n.* a kind of sea-shell.

cowshed *n.* shed for cattle not at pasture.

cowslip *n.* wild plant with small fragrant yellow flowers.

cox *n.* coxswain. —*v.t.* act as cox of (a racing-boat).

coxswain /ˈkoksweɪn, *nautical pr.* ˈkoksn/ steersman.

coy *a.* (-*er*, -*est*) pretending to be shy or embarrassed. **coyly** *adv.*, **coyness** *n.*

coypu *n.* beaver-like water animal.

crab *n.* ten-legged shellfish. —*v.t./i.* (p.t. *crabbed*) find fault with; grumble. **~-apple** *n.* a kind of small sour apple.

crabbed /-bɪd/ *a.* bad-tempered; (of handwriting) hard to read.

crack *n.* sudden sharp noise; sharp blow; line where a thing is broken but not separated; (*sl.*) joke. —*a.* (*colloq.*) first-rate. —*v.t./i.* make or cause to make the sound of a crack; knock sharply; break into or through; find a solution to (a problem); tell (a joke); break without parting completely; (of the voice) become harsh; give way under strain; break down (heavy oils) to produce lighter ones. **~-brained** *a.* (*colloq.*) crazy. **~ down on,** (*colloq.*) take severe measures against. **~ up,** (*colloq.*) praise; have a physical or mental breakdown. **get cracking,** (*colloq.*) start working.

cracked *a.* (*sl.*) crazy.

cracker *n.* small explosive firework; toy paper tube made to give an explosive crack when pulled apart; thin dry biscuit.

crackers *a.* (*sl.*) crazy.

cracking *a.* (*sl.*) very good.

crackle *v.t./i.* make or cause to make a series of light crackling sounds. —*n.* these sounds.

crackling *n.* crisp skin on roast pork.

crackpot *n.* (*sl.*) person with crazy or impractical ideas.

cradle *n.* baby's bed usu. on rockers; place where something originates; supporting structure. —*v.t.* hold or support gently.

craft *n.* skill, technique; occupation requiring this; cunning, deceit; (pl. *craft*) ship, boat, raft, aircraft, or spacecraft.

craftsman *n.* (pl. -*men*) workman skilled in a craft. **craftsmanship** *n.*

crafty *a.* (-*ier*, -*iest*) cunning, using underhand methods. **craftily** *adv.*, **craftiness** *n.*

crag *n.* steep or rugged rock.

craggy *a.* rugged.

cram *v.t.* (p.t. *crammed*) force into too small a space; overfill thus; study intensively for an examination.

cramp *n.* painful involuntary tightening of a muscle etc.; metal bar with bent ends for

holding masonry etc. together. —*v.t.* keep within too narrow limits.

crampon *n.* spiked plate worn on boots for climbing on ice.

cranberry *n.* small red acid berry; shrub bearing this.

crane *n.* large wading bird; apparatus for lifting and moving heavy objects. —*v.t./i.* stretch (one's neck) to see something. **~-fly** *n.* long-legged flying insect.

cranium *n.* (pl. -*ia*) skull. **cranial** *a.*

crank¹ *n.* L-shaped part for converting to-and-fro into circular motion. —*v.t.* turn with a crank. **crankshaft** *n.* shaft turned thus.

crank² *n.* person with very strange ideas. **cranky** *a.*

cranny *n.* crevice.

craps *n.pl.* (*U.S.*) gambling game played with a pair of dice.

crash *n.* loud noise as of breakage; violent collision or fall; financial collapse. —*v.t./i.* make a crash; move or go with a crash; be or cause to be involved in a crash; (*colloq.*) gatecrash. —*a.* involving intense effort to achieve something rapidly. **~-helmet** *n.* padded helmet worn to protect the head in a crash. **~-land** *v.t./i.* land (an aircraft) in emergency, esp. with damage to it. **~-landing** *n.*

crass *a.* very stupid.

crate *n.* packing-case made of wooden slats; (*sl.*) old aircraft or car. —*v.t.* pack in crate(s).

crater *n.* bowl-shaped cavity.

cravat *n.* short scarf; neck-tie.

crave *v.t./i.* feel an intense longing (for); ask earnestly for.

craven *a.* cowardly.

craving *n.* intense longing.

crawl *v.i.* move on hands and knees or with the body on the ground; move very slowly; (*colloq.*) seek favour by servile behaviour; be covered or feel as if covered with crawling things. —*n.* crawling movement or pace; overarm swimming-stroke. **crawler** *n.*

crayfish *n.* freshwater shellfish like a small lobster.

crayon *n.* stick of coloured wax etc. —*v.t.* draw or colour with crayon(s).

craze *n.* temporary enthusiasm; its object.

crazed *a.* driven insane.

crazy *a.* (-*ier*, -*iest*) insane; very foolish; (*colloq.*) madly eager. **~ paving,** paving made of irregular pieces. **crazily** *adv.*, **craziness** *n.*

creak *n.* harsh squeak. —*v.i.* make this sound. **creaky** *a.*

cream *n.* fatty part of milk; its colour, yellowish-white; cream-like substance; best part. —*a.* cream-coloured. —*v.t.* remove the cream from; beat to a creamy consistency; apply cosmetic cream to. **~ cheese,** soft rich cheese. **creamy** *a.*

crease *n.* line made by crushing or pressing; line marking the limit of the bowler's or batsman's position in cricket. —*v.t./i.* make a crease in; develop creases.

create *v.t./i.* bring into existence; produce by

what one does; give a new rank to; (*sl.*) make a fuss. **creation** *n.*, **creative** *a.*, **creator** *n.*

creature *n.* animal, person.

crèche /kreɪʃ/ *n.* day nursery for babies.

credence /ˈkriː-/ *n.* belief.

credentials *n.pl.* documents showing that a person is who or what he claims to be.

credible *a.* believable. **credibly** *adv.*, **credibility** *n.*

credit *n.* belief that a thing is true; honour for an achievement etc., good reputation; source of this; system of allowing payment to be deferred; sum at a person's disposal in a bank; entry in an account for a sum paid; acknowledgement of services to a book or film etc. —*v.t.* (p.t. *credited*) believe; attribute; enter as credit. ～ **card**, card authorizing a person to buy on credit.

creditable *a.* deserving praise. **creditably** *adv.*

creditor *n.* person to whom money is owed.

credulous *a.* too ready to believe things. **credulity** *n.*

creed *n.* set of beliefs or principles.

creek *n.* narrow inlet of water, esp. on a coast; (*U.S.*) tributary. **up the** ～, (*sl.*) in difficulties.

creel *n.* fisherman's wicker basket for carrying fish.

creep *v.i.* (p.t. *crept*) move with the body close to the ground; move timidly, slowly, or stealthily; develop gradually; (of a plant) grow along the ground or a wall etc.; feel creepy. —*n.* creeping; (*sl.*) person one dislikes.

creeper *n.* creeping plant.

creepy *a.* (*-ier, -iest*) feeling or causing a nervous shivering sensation.

cremate *v.t.* burn (a corpse) to ashes. **cremation** *n.*

crematorium /krem-/ *n.* (pl. *-ia*) place where corpses are cremated.

crème de menthe /krem də mɑnt/ peppermint-flavoured liqueur.

Creole /ˈkriːəʊl/ *n.* descendant of European settlers in the West Indies or in Central or South America; their dialect.

creosote *n.* brown oily liquid distilled from coal tar, used as a preservative for wood; colourless antiseptic liquid distilled from wood tar. —*v.t.* treat with this.

crêpe *n.* fabric with a wrinkled surface; rubber with a wrinkled texture, used for shoe-soles. ～ **paper**, thin crêpe-like paper. **crêpey** *a.*

crept *see* **creep**.

crescendo *adv.* & *n.* (pl. *-os*) increasing in loudness.

crescent *n.* narrow curved shape tapering to a point at each end; curved street of houses.

cress *n.* plant with hot-tasting leaves used in salads.

crest *n.* tuft or outgrowth on a bird's or animal's head; plume on a helmet; top of a slope or hill, white top of a large wave; design above a shield on a coat of arms or used separately. **crested** *a.*

crestfallen *a.* disappointed at failure.

cretin /ˈkre-/ *n.* person who is deformed and mentally defective through lack of thyroid hormone. **cretinous** *a.*

cretonne /kreˈton/ *n.* heavy cotton cloth used in furnishings.

crevasse *n.* deep open crack esp. in a glacier.

crevice *n.* narrow gap in a surface.

crew[1] *see* **crow**.

crew[2] *n.* people working a ship or aircraft; group working together; gang. —*v.i.* act as crew (of). ～ **cut**, man's closely-cropped haircut.

crib *n.* rack for fodder; model of the manger-scene at Bethlehem; cot; cribbage; (*colloq.*) piece of cribbing; translation for students' use. —*v.t./i.* (p.t. *cribbed*) copy unfairly.

cribbage *n.* a card-game.

crick *n.* painful stiffness in the neck or back. —*v.t.* cause this to.

cricket[1] *n.* outdoor game for two teams of 11 players with ball, bats, and wickets. **not** ～, (*colloq.*) not fair play. **cricketer** *n.*

cricket[2] *n.* brown insect resembling a grasshopper.

crime *n.* serious offence, act that breaks a law; illegal acts.

criminal *n.* person guilty of a crime. —*a.* of or involving crime.

criminology *n.* study of crime. **criminologist** *n.*

crimp *v.t.* press into ridges.

crimson *a.* & *n.* deep red.

cringe *v.i.* cower; behave obsequiously.

crinkle *n.* & *v.t./i.* wrinkle.

crinoline *n.* light framework formerly worn to make a long skirt stand out.

cripple *n.* lame person. —*v.t.* make a cripple; weaken seriously.

crisis *n.* (pl. *crises*) decisive moment; time of acute difficulty.

crisp *a.* (*-er, -est*) brittle; slightly stiff; cold and bracing; brisk and decisive. —*n.* thin slice of potato fried crisp. —*v.t./i.* make or become crisp. **crisply** *adv.*, **crispness** *n.*

criss-cross *n.* pattern of crossing lines. —*a.* & *adv.* in this pattern. —*v.t./i.* mark or form or move thus, intersect.

criterion *n.* (pl. *-ia*) standard of judgement.

critic *n.* person who points out faults; one skilled in criticism.

critical *a.* looking for faults; expressing criticism; of or at a crisis. **critically** *adv.*

criticism *n.* pointing out faults; judging of merit, esp. of literary or artistic work.

criticize *v.t.* express criticism of.

critique /-ˈtiːk/ *n.* critical essay.

croak *n.* deep hoarse cry or sound like that of a frog. —*v.t./i.* utter or speak with a croak; (*sl.*) die, kill.

crochet /ˈkrəʊʃeɪ/ *n.* a kind of knitting done with one hooked needle. —*v.t./i.* make by or do such work.

crock[1] *n.* earthenware pot; broken piece of this.

crock[2] *n.* (*colloq.*) person who is disabled or often ill; worn-out vehicle etc. —*v.i.* (*colloq.*) disable. ～ **up**, become a crock.

crockery *n.* household china.

crocodile *n.* large amphibious tropical reptile;

its skin; line of children walking in pairs. **~ tears,** pretence of sorrow.

crocus *n.* (pl. *-uses*) spring-flowering plant growing from a corm.

croft *n.* small enclosed field or rented farm in Scotland.

crofter *n.* tenant of a croft.

crony *n.* close friend or companion.

crook *n.* hooked stick; bent thing; (*colloq.*) criminal. —*v.t.* bend.

crooked /-ɪd/ *a.* not straight; dishonest. **crookedly** *adv.*

croon *v.t./i.* sing softly.

crop *n.* batch of plants grown for their produce; harvest from this; group or amount produced at one time; bird's gullet where food is broken up for digestion; whip-handle; very short haircut. —*v.t./i.* (p.t. *cropped*) cut or bite off; produce or gather as harvest. **~ up,** occur unexpectedly.

cropper *n.* (*sl.*) heavy fall.

croquet /ˈkrəʊkeɪ/ *n.* game played on a lawn with balls and mallets.

croquette /-ˈket/ *n.* fried ball or roll of potato, meat, or fish.

crore *n.* (*Ind.*) 100 lakhs.

crosier *n.* bishop's hooked staff.

cross *n.* mark made by drawing one line intersecting another; thing shaped like this; *the C~*, that on which Christ was crucified; affliction to be borne with Christian patience; hybrid animal or plant; mixture of or compromise between two things. —*v.t./i.* place cross-wise; draw line(s) across, mark (a cheque) thus so that it must be paid into a bank; make the sign of the Cross on or over; go or extend across; oppose the wishes of; cause to interbreed; cross-fertilize. —*a.* passing from side to side; showing bad temper. **at ~ purposes,** misunderstanding or conflicting. **~ off** *or* **out,** draw a line through (an item) to make it invalid. **crossly** *adv.*, **crossness** *n.*

crossbar *n.* horizontal bar.

cross-bred *a.* produced by inter-breeding. **cross-breed** *n.* cross-bred animal. **cross-breeding** *n.*

cross-check *v.t./i.* check again by a different method.

crosse *n.* netted crook used in lacrosse.

cross-examine *v.t.* cross-question, esp. in a lawcourt. **cross-examination** *n.*

cross-eyed *a.* squinting.

cross-fertilize *v.t.* fertilize (a plant) from one of a different kind. **cross-fertilization** *n.*

crossfire *n.* gunfire crossing other line(s) of fire.

cross-grained *a.* bad-tempered.

crossing *n.* journey across water; place where things cross; place for pedestrians to cross a road.

cross-patch *n.* bad-tempered person.

cross-question *v.t.* question closely so as to test earlier answers.

cross-reference *n.* reference to another place in the same book etc.

crossroads *n.* place where roads intersect.

cross-section *n.* diagram showing internal structure; representative sample.

crosswise *adv.* in the form of a cross.

crossword *n.* puzzle in which intersecting words have to be inserted into a diagram.

crotch *n.* place where things fork, esp. where legs join the trunk.

crotchet *n.* note in music, half a minim.

crotchety *a.* peevish.

crouch *v.i.* stoop low with legs tightly bent.

croup *n.* laryngitis in children, with a hard cough.

croupier /ˈkruːpɪə(r)/ *n.* person who rakes in stakes and pays out winnings at a gaming-table.

croûton /ˈkruːtɔ̃/ *n.* small piece of fried or toasted bread.

crow *n.* large black bird; crowing cry or sound. —*v.i.* utter a cock's cry (p.t. *crew*); (of a baby) make sounds of pleasure; exult. **as the ~ flies,** in a straight line. **~'s-feet,** wrinkles beside the eyes. **~'s nest,** protected platform on the mast of a ship.

crowbar *n.* bar of iron with a bent end, used as a lever.

crowd *n.* large group. —*v.t./i.* come together in a crowd; fill or occupy fully.

crown *n.* monarch's ceremonial headdress, usu. a circlet of gold etc.; *the C~*, supreme governing power in a monarchy; crown-shaped object or ornament; top part of a head, hat, or arched thing. —*v.t.* place a crown on; form or cover or ornament the top part of; be a climax to; (*sl.*) hit on the head. **Crown Court,** court where criminal cases are tried in England and Wales. **Crown prince** *or* **princess,** heir to a throne.

crucial *a.* very important, decisive. **crucially** *adv.*

crucible *n.* pot in which metals are melted.

crucifix *n.* model of the Cross or of Christ on this.

crucifixion *n.* crucifying; *the C~*, that of Christ.

crucify *v.t.* put to death by nailing or binding to a transverse bar; cause extreme mental pain to.

crude *a.* (*-er, -est*) in a natural or raw state; not well finished; lacking good manners, vulgar. **crudely** *adv.*, **crudity** *n.*

cruel *a.* (*crueller, cruellest*) feeling pleasure in another's suffering; hard-hearted; causing suffering. **cruelly** *adv.*, **cruelty** *n.*

cruet *n.* set of containers for oil, vinegar, or salt etc. at the table; stand holding these.

cruise *v.i.* sail for pleasure or on patrol; travel at a moderate speed. —*n.* cruising voyage.

cruiser *n.* fast warship; motor boat with a cabin.

crumb *n.* small fragment, esp. of bread or similar food.

crumble *v.t./i.* break into small fragments. —*n.* pudding of fruit with crumbly topping.

crumbly *a.* easily crumbled.

crummy *a.* (*-ier, -iest*) (*sl.*) dirty; inferior.

crumpet *n.* flat soft yeast cake eaten toasted.

crumple *v.t./i.* crush or become crushed into creases; collapse.

crunch *v.t.* crush noisily with the teeth; make this sound. —*n.* sound of crunching; decisive event.

crusade *n.* medieval Christian military expedition to recover the Holy Land from Muslims; campaign against an evil. —*v.i.* take part in a crusade. **crusader** *n.*

crush *v.t./i.* press so as to break or injure or wrinkle; pound into fragments; become crushed; defeat or subdue completely. —*n.* crowded mass of people; drink made from crushed fruit; (*sl.*) infatuation.

crust *n.* hard outer layer, esp. of bread.

crustacean *n.* animal with a hard shell (e.g. lobster).

crusty *a.* (-*ier*, -*iest*) with a crisp crust; having a harsh manner.

crutch *n.* support for a lame person; crotch.

crux *n.* (pl. *cruxes*) vital part of a problem; difficult point.

cry *n.* loud wordless sound uttered; appeal; rallying call; spell of weeping. —*v.t./i.* shed tears; call loudly; appeal for help etc. **~-baby** *n.* person who weeps easily. **~ off**, withdraw from a promise.

crypt *n.* room below the floor of a church.

cryptic *a.* concealing its meaning in a puzzling way. **cryptically** *adv.*

cryptogam *n.* non-flowering plant such as a fern, moss, or fungus.

cryptogram *n.* thing written in cipher.

crystal *a.* glass-like mineral; piece of this; high-quality glass; symmetrical piece of a solidified substance.

crystalline /-aɪn/ *a.* like or made of crystal; clear.

crystallize *v.t./i.* form into crystals; make or become definite in form. **crystallized fruit**, fruit preserved in sugar. **crystallization** *n.*

cub *n.* young of certain animals. **Cub (Scout)**, member of the junior branch of the Scout Association.

cubby-hole *n.* small compartment.

cube *n.* solid object with six equal square sides; product of a number multiplied by itself twice. —*v.t.* cut into small cubes; find the cube of. **~ root**, number which produces a given number when cubed.

cubic *a.* of three dimensions. **~ centimetre**, volume of a cube with sides 1 cm long, used as a unit.

cubical *a.* cube-shaped.

cubicle *n.* small division of a large room, screened for privacy.

cubism *n.* style of painting in which objects are shown as geometrical shapes. **cubist** *n.*

cuckold *n.* man whose wife has committed adultery. —*v.t.* make a cuckold of.

cuckoo *n.* bird with a call that is like its name.

cucumber *n.* long green-skinned fruit eaten as salad; plant producing this.

cud *n.* food that cattle bring back from the stomach into the mouth and chew again.

cuddle *v.t./i.* hug lovingly; nestle. —*n.* gentle hug. **cuddlesome, cuddly** *adjs.* pleasant to cuddle.

cudgel *n.* short thick stick used as a weapon. —*v.t.* (p.t. *cudgelled*) **~ one's brains**, think hard about a problem.

cue[1] *n.* & *v.t.* (pres.p. *cueing*) signal to do something.

cue[2] *n.* long rod for striking balls in billiards etc.

cuff *n.* band of cloth round the edge of a sleeve; cuffing blow. —*v.t.* strike with the open hand. **~-link** *n.* device of two linked discs etc. to hold cuff edges together. **off the ~**, without preparation.

cui bono? /kwi ˈbəʊnəʊ/ who gains?

cuisine /kwɪˈziːn/ *n.* style of cooking.

cul-de-sac *n.* street closed at one end.

culinary /ˈkʌlɪ-/ *a.* of or used in cooking.

cull *v.t.* pick (flowers); select; select and kill (surplus animals). —*n.* culling; thing(s) culled.

culminate *v.i.* reach its highest point or degree. **culmination** *n.*

culottes /kjuˈlɒt/ *n.pl.* women's trousers styled to resemble a skirt.

culpable *a.* deserving blame.

culprit *n.* person who has committed a slight offence.

cult *n.* system of religious worship; worship of a person or thing.

cultivate *v.t.* prepare and use (land) for crops; produce (crops) by tending them; develop by practice; further one's acquaintance with (a person). **cultivation** *n.*, **cultivator** *n.*

culture *n.* developed understanding of literature, art, music, etc.; type of civilization; artificial rearing of bees, bacteria, etc.; bacteria grown for study. —*v.t.* grow in artificial conditions. **cultural** *a.*, **culturally** *adv.*

cultured *a.* exhibiting culture.

culvert *n.* drain under a road etc.

cumbersome *a.* clumsy to carry or use.

cummerbund *n.* sash for the waist.

cumulative /ˈkjuː-/ *a.* increasing by additions. **cumulatively** *adv.*

cuneiform /ˈkjuːnɪfɔːm/ *n.* ancient writing done in wedge-shaped strokes cut into stone etc.

cunning *a.* skilled at deception, crafty; ingenious; (*U.S.*) attractive. —*n.* craftiness, ingenuity.

cup *n.* drinking-vessel usu. with a handle at the side; amount it holds; ornamental goblet as a prize; rounded cavity; wine or fruit-juice with added flavourings. —*v.t.* (p.t. *cupped*) form into a cup-like shape; hold as if in a cup.

cupful *n.* (pl. *cupfuls*).

cupboard *n.* recess or piece of furniture with a door, in which things may be stored.

cupidity *n.* greed for gain.

cupola /ˈkjuː-/ *n.* small dome.

cur *n.* worthless dog.

curable *a.* able to be cured.

curaçao /ˈkjʊərəsəʊ/ *n.* orange-flavoured liqueur.

curacy *n.* position of curate.

curate *n.* clergyman who assists a parish priest.

curative *a*. curing illness.

curator *n*. person in charge of a museum or other collection.

curb *n*. means of restraint. —*v.t*. restrain.

curd *n*. thick soft substance, esp. (*pl*.) that formed when milk turns sour.

curdle *v.t./i*. form or cause to form curds.

cure *v.t*. restore to health; get rid of (a disease or trouble etc.); preserve by salting, drying, etc. —*n*. curing; substance or treatment that cures disease etc.

curettage /ˈkjʊərɪtɪdʒ/ *n*. scraping surgically.

curfew *n*. signal or time after which people must stay indoors.

curio *n*. (pl. *-os*) unusual and therefore interesting object.

curiosity *n*. desire to find out and know things; curio.

curious *a*. eager to learn or know something; strange, unusual. **curiously** *adv*.

curl *v.t./i*. curve, esp. in a spiral shape or course. —*n*. curled thing or shape; coiled lock of hair.

curler *n*. device for curling hair.

curlew *n*. wading bird with a long curved bill.

curling *n*. game like bowls played on ice.

curly *a*. (*-ier*, *-iest*) curling, full of curls.

curmudgeon /kəˈmʌdʒən/ *n*. bad-tempered person.

currant *n*. dried grape used in cookery; small round edible berry, shrub producing this.

currency *n*. money in use; state of being widely known.

current *a*. belonging to the present time; in general use. —*n*. body of water or air moving in one direction; flow of electricity. **currently** *adv*.

curriculum *n*. (pl. *-la*) course of study.

curry[1] *n*. seasoning made with hot-tasting spices; dish flavoured with this. —*v.t*. flavour with curry.

curry[2] *v.t*. groom with a ∼-comb, a pad with rubber or plastic projections; win (favour) by flattery.

curse *n*. call for evil to come on a person or thing; a great evil; violent exclamation of anger. —*v.t./i*. utter a curse (against); afflict.

cursory *a*. hasty and not thorough. **cursorily** *adv*.

curt *a*. noticeably or rudely brief. **curtly** *adv*., **curtness** *n*.

curtail *v.t*. cut short, reduce. **curtailment** *n*.

curtain *n*. piece of cloth etc. hung as a screen, esp. at a window; fall of a stage-curtain at the end of an act or scene. —*v.t*. provide or shut off with curtain(s).

curtsy *n*. movement of respect made by bending the knees. —*v.i*. make a curtsy.

curvature *n*. curving; curved form.

curve *n*. line or surface with no part straight or flat. —*v.t./i*. form (into) a curve.

curvet /-ˈvet/ *n*. horse's frisky leap. —*v.i*. (p.t. *curvetted*) make this.

cushion *n*. stuffed bag used as a pad, esp. for leaning against; padded part. —*v.t*. protect with a pad; lessen the impact of, protect thus.

cushy *a*. (*-ier*, *-iest*) (*colloq*.) pleasant and easy.

cusp *n*. pointed part where curves meet.

cuss *n*. (*colloq*.) curse; perverse person. **cussed** /-ɪd/ *a*. perverse.

custard *n*. dish or sauce made with milk and eggs or flavoured cornflour.

custodian *n*. guardian, keeper.

custody *n*. safe-keeping; imprisonment.

custom *n*. usual way of behaving or acting; regular dealing by customer(s); (*pl*.) duty on imported goods, officials dealing with these.

customary *a*. usual. **customarily** *adv*.

customer *n*. person buying goods or services from a shop etc.

cut *v.t./i*. (p.t. *cut*, pres.p. *cutting*) divide, wound, or shape etc. by pressure of an edge; reduce; intersect; divide (a pack of cards); switch off (an engine etc.); ignore, absent oneself from; (*sl*.) go quickly. —*n*. cutting, wound etc. made by this; piece cut off; stroke of a whip etc.; style of cutting; hurtful remark; reduction; (*sl*.) share.

cute *a*. (*-er*, *-est*) (*colloq*.) sharp-witted; ingenious; (*U.S.*) quaint. **cutely** *adv*., **cuteness** *n*.

cuticle *n*. skin at the base of a nail.

cutlass *n*. short curved sword.

cutlery *n*. table knives, forks, and spoons.

cutlet *n*. neck-chop; mince cooked in this shape; thin piece of veal.

cutter *n*. person or thing that cuts; a kind of small boat.

cutting *a*. (of remarks) hurtful. —*n*. piece cut from something; passage cut through high ground for a road etc.; piece of a plant for re-planting.

cuttlefish *n*. sea creature that ejects black fluid when attacked.

cyanide *n*. a strong poison.

cybernetics /saɪ-/ *n*. science of systems of control and communication in animals and machines.

cyclamen /ˈsɪk-/ *n*. plant with petals that turn back.

cycle *n*. recurring series of events; bicycle, motor cycle. —*v.i*. ride a bicycle. **cyclist** *n*.

cyclic, cyclical /ˈsaɪ-/ *adjs*. happening in cycles. **cyclically** *adv*.

cyclone *n*. violent wind rotating round a central area.

cyclostyle *n*. device printing copies from a stencil. —*v.t*. print thus.

cyclotron /ˈsaɪ-/ *n*. apparatus for accelerating charged particles in a spiral path.

cygnet /ˈsɪg-/ *n*. young swan.

cylinder *n*. object with straight sides and circular ends. **cylindrical** *a*.

cymbal *n*. brass plate struck with another or with a stick as a percussion instrument.

cynic *n*. person who believes motives are bad or selfish. **cynical** *a*., **cynically** *adv*., **cynicism** *n*.

cynosure /ˈsaɪnəzjʊ(r)/ *n*. centre of attention.

cypress *n*. evergreen tree with dark feathery leaves.

cyst /sɪst/ *n*. abnormal sac of fluid on or in the body. **cystic** *a*.

cystitis /sɪs-/ *n*. inflammation of the bladder.

czar *n*. = tsar.

D

dab[1] *n.* quick light blow or pressure; small lump of a soft substance. —*v.t./i.* (p.t. *dabbed*) strike or press lightly or feebly.

dab[2] *n.* a kind of flat-fish.

dab[3] *n. & a.* adept.

dabble *v.t./i.* move (feet etc.) lightly in water or mud; splash; work at something in an amateur way.

dachshund /ˈdæks-/ *n.* small dog with a long body and short legs.

dad *n.* (*colloq.*) father.

daddy *n.* (*children's use*) father.

daddy-long-legs *n.* crane-fly.

dado /ˈdeɪdəʊ/ *n.* (pl. *-oes*) lower part of a wall decorated differently from the upper part.

daffodil *n.* yellow flower with a trumpet-shaped central part.

daft *a.* (*-er, -est*) silly, crazy.

dagger *n.* short pointed two-edged weapon used for stabbing.

dago *n.* (pl. *-oes*) (*sl., derog.*) foreigner, esp. from southern Europe.

dahlia *n.* garden plant with bright flowers.

daily *a.* happening or appearing on every day or every weekday. —*adv.* once a day. —*n.* daily newspaper; (*colloq.*) charwoman.

dainty *a.* (*-ier, -iest*) small and pretty; fastidious. —*n.* choice food, delicacy. **daintily** *adv.*, **daintiness** *n.*

dairy *n.* place where milk and its products are processed or sold. ～ **farm,** one producing chiefly milk.

dais /ˈdeɪɪs/ *n.* low platform, esp. at the end of a hall.

daisy *n.* flower with many petal-like rays.

dale *n.* valley.

dally *v.i.* idle, dawdle; flirt. **dalliance** *n.*

Dalmatian *a.* of Dalmatia in Yugoslavia. —*n.* large white dog with dark spots.

dam[1] *n.* barrier built across a river to hold back water. —*v.t.* (p.t. *dammed*) hold back with a dam; obstruct (a flow).

dam[2] *n.* mother of an animal.

damage *n.* something done that reduces the value or usefulness of the thing affected, or spoils its appearance; (*pl.*) money as compensation for injury. —*v.t.* cause damage to.

damask *n.* fabric woven with a pattern visible on either side. ～ **rose,** old fragrant variety of rose.

dame *n.* (*old use* or *U.S. sl.*) woman; *D*～, title of a woman with an order of knighthood.

damn *v.t.* condemn to hell; condemn as a failure; swear at. —*int. & n.* uttered curse. —*a. & adv.* damned.

damnable *a.* hateful, annoying. **damnably** *adv.*

damnation *n.* eternal punishment in hell.

damp *n.* moisture in air or in or on a thing. —*a.* (*-er, -est*) slightly wet. —*v.t.* make damp; discourage; stop the vibration of. ～ **course,** layer of damp-proof material in a wall, to keep damp from rising. **dampness** *n.*

damper *n.* metal plate controlling the flow of air into a flue; depressing influence; pad that damps the vibration of a piano string.

damsel *n.* (*old use*) young woman.

damson *n.* small dark-purple plum.

dance *v.t./i.* move with rhythmical steps and gestures, usu. to music; move in a quick or lively way. —*n.* piece of dancing, music for this; social gathering for dancing. ～ **attendance on,** follow about and help dutifully. **dancer** *n.*

dandelion *n.* wild plant with bright yellow flowers.

dandified *a.* like a dandy.

dandle *v.t.* dance or nurse (a child) in one's arms.

dandruff *n.* scurf from the scalp.

dandy *n.* man who pays excessive attention to the smartness of his appearance. —*a.* (*colloq.*) very good.

Dane *n.* native of Denmark.

danger *n.* liability or exposure to harm or death; thing causing this.

dangerous *a.* causing danger, not safe. **dangerously** *adv.*

dangle *v.t./i.* hang or swing loosely; hold out (hopes) temptingly.

Danish *a. & n.* (language) of Denmark.

dank *a.* (*-er, -est*) damp and cold.

daphne *n.* flowering shrub.

dapper *a.* neat and smart.

dapple *v.t.* mark with patches of colour or shade. ～**grey** *a.* grey with darker markings.

Darby and Joan devoted old married couple.

dare *v.t.* be bold enough (to do something); challenge to do something risky. —*n.* this challenge. **I** ～ **say,** I am prepared to believe.

daredevil *n.* recklessly daring person.

daring *a.* bold. —*n.* boldness.

dark *a.* (*-er, -est*) with little or no light; of deep shade or colour, closer to black than to white; having dark hair or dark skin; gloomy; secret; mysterious. —*n.* absence of light; time of darkness, nightfall; dark colour. **Dark Ages,** early Middle Ages in Europe. ～ **horse,** competitor etc. of whose abilities little is known. ～**room** *n.* room with daylight excluded, for processing photographs. **darkly** *adv.*, **darkness** *n.*

darken *v.t./i.* make or become dark.

darling *n. & a.* dearly loved or lovable (person or thing); favourite.

darn *v.t.* mend by weaving thread across a hole. —*n.* place darned.

dart *n.* small pointed missile, esp. for throwing at the target in the game of *darts*; darting movement; tapering tuck. —*v.t./i.* run suddenly; send out (a glance etc.) rapidly.

dartboard *n.* target in the game of darts.

dash *v.t./i.* run rapidly, rush; knock or throw forcefully against something; destroy (hopes); write hastily. —*n.* rapid run, rush;

small amount of liquid or flavouring added; dashboard; vigour; punctuation mark — showing a break in the sense; longer signal in the Morse code.

dashboard *n.* board below the windscreen of a motor vehicle, carrying various instruments and controls.

dashing *a.* spirited, showy.

dastardly *a.* contemptible.

data /ˈdeɪ-/ *n.pl.* facts on which a decision is to be based; facts prepared for being processed by computer. **database,** quantity of data available for use.

datable *a.* able to be dated.

date[1] *n.* day, month, or year of a thing's occurrence; period to which a thing belongs; (*colloq.*) appointment to meet socially. —*v.t./i.* mark with a date; assign a date to; originate from a particular date; become out of date; (*U.S. colloq.*) make a social appointment with. **~-line** *n.* north-to-south line in the Pacific, east and west of which the date differs. **to ~,** until now.

date[2] *n.* small brown edible fruit. **~-palm** *n.* palm tree bearing this.

dative *n.* grammatical case indicating the indirect object of a verb.

daub *v.t.* smear roughly. —*n.* clumsily painted picture; smear; clay coating for walls.

daughter *n.* female in relation to her parents. **~-in-law** *n.* son's wife.

daunt *v.t.* make afraid or discouraged.

dauntless *a.* brave, not daunted.

davit /ˈdæ-/ *n.* small crane on a ship.

dawdle *v.i.* walk slowly and idly, take one's time. **dawdler** *n.*

dawn *n.* first light of day; beginning. —*v.i.* begin to grow light; begin to appear.

day *n.* time while the sun is above the horizon; period of 24 hours; hours given to work during a day; specified day; time, period.

day-dream *n.* pleasant idle thoughts. —*v.i.* have day-dreams.

daylight *n.* light of day.

daytime *n.* time of daylight.

daze *v.t.* cause to feel stunned or bewildered. —*n.* dazed state.

dazzle *v.t.* make unable to see because of too much light; impress by a splendid display.

deacon *n.* clergyman ranking below priest; layman attending to church business in Nonconformist churches. **deaconess** *n.fem.*

dead *a.* no longer alive; numb; no longer used; without brightness or resonance or warmth; not functioning; dull; exact; (of the ball in games) out of play. —*adv.* completely, exactly. —*n.* dead person; inactive or silent time. **~-alive** *a.* very dreary. **~ beat,** tired out. **~ end,** blind alley. **~ heat,** race in which two or more competitors finish exactly even. **~ letter,** letter that cannot be delivered; law or rule no longer observed. **~ march,** funeral march. **~ nettle,** nettle-like plant that does not sting. **~-pan** *a.* expressionless. **~ reckoning,** calculating a ship's position by log and compass etc. **~ weight,** heavy inert weight.

deaden *v.t./i.* deprive of or lose vitality, loudness, feeling, etc.

deadline *n.* time limit.

deadlock *n.* state when no progress can be made. —*v.i.* reach this.

deadly *a.* (*-ier, -iest*) causing death or serious damage; death-like; very dreary. —*adv.* as if dead; extremely. **~ nightshade,** plant with poisonous black berries. **deadliness** *n.*

deaf *a.* (*-er, -est*) wholly or partly unable to hear; refusing to listen. **~-aid** *n.* hearing-aid. **deafness** *n.*

deafen *v.t.* make unable to hear by a very loud noise.

deal[1] *n.* fir or pine timber.

deal[2] *v.t./i.* (p.t. *dealt*) distribute; hand out (cards) to players in a card game; give, inflict; do business; trade. —*n.* dealing; player's turn to deal; business transaction; treatment; (*colloq.*) large amount. **~ with,** take action about; treat (a subject) in a book or speech etc.

dealer *n.* person who deals; trader.

dean *n.* clergyman who is head of a cathedral chapter; university official. **rural ~,** clergyman in charge of a group of parishes.

deanery *n.* dean's position or residence; rural dean's parishes.

dear *a.* (*-er, -est*) much loved, cherished; costing more than it is worth. —*n.* dear person. —*adv.* dearly. —*int.* exclamation of surprise or distress. **dearly** *adv.*, **dearness** *n.*

dearth /dɜːθ/ *n.* scarcity.

death *n.* process of dying, end of life; state of being dead; ending of something, destruction. **~ duty,** tax levied on property after the owner's death. **~'s head,** picture of a skull as a symbol of death. **~-trap** *n.* very dangerous place. **~-watch beetle,** beetle whose larvae bore into wood and make a ticking sound.

deathly *a.* (*-ier, -iest*) like death.

débâcle /deɪˈbɑkl/ *n.* general collapse.

debar *v.t.* (p.t. *debarred*) exclude.

debase *v.t.* lower in quality or value. **debasement** *n.*

debatable *a.* questionable.

debate *n.* formal discussion. —*v.t.* hold a debate about, consider.

debauch /-ˈbɒtʃ/ *v.t.* make dissolute, lead into over-indulgence in harmful or immoral pleasures. **debauchery** *n.*

debenture *n.* bond acknowledging a debt on which fixed interest is being paid.

debilitate *v.t.* weaken.

debility *n.* weakness of health.

debit *n.* entry in an account for a sum owing. —*v.t.* (p.t. *debited*) enter as a debit, charge.

debonair /-ˈneə(r)/ *a.* having a carefree self-confident manner.

debrief *v.t.* question to obtain facts about a completed mission.

debris /ˈdebriː/ *n.* scattered broken pieces or rubbish.

debt *n.* something owed. **in ~,** owing something.

debtor *n.* person who owes money.

debug v.t. (p.t. *debugged*) remove bugs from.

debunk v.t. (*colloq.*) show up as exaggerated or false.

début /ˈdeɪbjuː/ n. first public appearance.

debutante /ˈdebjutɑnt/ n. (*old use*) young woman making her first appearance in society.

decade /ˈdek-/ n. ten-year period.

decadent a. deteriorating in standard. **decadence** n.

Decalogue n. the Ten Commandments.

decamp v.i. go away suddenly or secretly.

decant /-ˈkæ-/ v.t. pour (liquid) into another container, leaving sediment behind; (*colloq.*) transfer.

decanter n. stoppered bottle into which wine etc. may be decanted before serving.

decapitate v.t. behead. **decapitation** n.

decathlon /dɪˈkæ-/ n. athletic contest involving ten events.

decay v.t./i. rot; lose quality or strength. —n. decaying, rot.

decease n. death.

deceased a. dead.

deceit n. deceiving, deception.

deceitful a. deceiving people. **deceitfully** adv.

deceive v.t. cause to believe something that is not true; be sexually unfaithful to. **deceiver** n.

decelerate v.t./i. reduce the speed (of). **deceleration** n.

December n. twelfth month of the year.

decent a. conforming to accepted standards of what is proper; respectable; (*colloq.*) quite good; (*colloq.*) kind, obliging. **decently** adv., **decency** n.

decentralize v.t. transfer from central to local control. **decentralization** n.

deception n. deceiving.

deceptive a. deceiving; misleading. **deceptively** adv.

decibel /ˈdes-/ n. unit for measuring the relative loudness of sound.

decide v.t./i. think about and make a choice or judgement; settle by giving victory to one side; cause to reach a decision.

decided a. having firm opinions; clear, definite. **decidedly** adv.

deciduous /-ˈsɪd-/ a. (of a tree) shedding its leaves annually.

decimal a. reckoned in tens or tenths. —n. decimal fraction. ∼ **currency,** that with each unit 10 or 100 times the value of the one next below it. ∼ **fraction,** fraction with 10 as denominator, expressed in figures after a dot. ∼ **point,** this dot.

decimate v.t. destroy one tenth of; (*loosely*) destroy a large proportion of. **decimation** n.

decipher v.t. make out the meaning of (a coded message, bad hand-writing, etc.). **decipherment** n.

decision n. deciding, judgement reached by this; ability to form firm opinions and act on them.

decisive a. conclusive; showing decision and firmness. **decisively** adv.

deck¹ n. horizontal floor in a ship; similar floor or platform, esp. one of two or more. ∼-**chair** n. folding canvas chair for outdoors.

deck² v.t. decorate, dress up.

declaim v.t./i. speak or say impressively or dramatically.

declare v.t./i. make known, announce openly or formally; state firmly; end one's side's innings at cricket before ten wickets have fallen. **declaration** n.

decline v.t./i. refuse; slope downwards; decrease, lose strength or vigour. —n. gradual decrease or loss of strength.

decoction n. boiling to extract essence; the essence itself.

decode v.t. put (a coded message) into plain language.

decoder n. person or machine that decodes; device analysing and distributing stereophonic signals.

decoke v.t. (*colloq.*) remove the carbon deposit from (an engine). —n. (*colloq.*) this process.

decompose v.t./i. separate (a substance) into its parts; rot. **decomposition** n.

decompression n. release from compression; gradual reduction of air pressure.

decongestant n. medicinal substance that relieves congestion.

decontaminate v.t. rid of (esp. radioactive) contamination. **decontamination** n.

décor /ˈdeɪ-/ n. style of decoration used in a room etc.

decorate v.t. make (a thing) look attractive by adding objects or details; paint or paper the walls of; confer a medal or award on. **decoration** n.

decorative a. ornamental, pleasant to look at. **decoratively** adv.

decorator n. tradesman who paints and papers rooms etc.

decorous a. polite and well-behaved, decent. **decorously** adv.

decorum /-ˈkɔr-/ n. correctness and dignity of behaviour.

decoy¹ /ˈdiː-/ n. thing used to lure a person or animal into a trap etc.

decoy² /-ˈkɔɪ/ v.t. lure by a decoy.

decrease v.t./i. make or become smaller or fewer. —n. decreasing; amount of this.

decree n. order given by a government or other authority. —v.t. (p.t. *decreed*) order by decree.

decrepit a. make weak by old age or use; dilapidated. **decrepitude** n.

decry v.t. disparage.

dedicate v.t. devote to a sacred person or use, or to a special purpose. **dedication** n.

deduce v.t. arrive at (knowledge) by reasoning. **deducible** a.

deduct v.t. subtract. **deductible** a.

deduction n. deducting; thing deducted; deducing; conclusion deduced.

deductive a. based on reasoning.

deed n. thing done, act; written or printed legal agreement. ∼ **poll,** deed made by one party only, as a formal declaration.

deem v.t. believe, consider to be.

deep *a.* (*-er*, *-est*) going or situated far down or in; intense; low-pitched; absorbed; profound. **~-freeze** *n.* freezer. **deeply** *adv.*, **deepness** *n.*

deepen *v.t./i.* make or become deeper.

deer *n.* (pl. *deer*) ruminant swift-footed animal, male of which usu. has antlers.

deerstalker *n.* cloth cap with a peak in front and at the back.

deface *v.t.* spoil or damage the surface of. **defacement** *n.*

defamatory /-'fæm-/ *a.* defaming.

defame *v.t.* attack the good reputation of. **defamation** *n.*

default *v.i.* fail to fulfil one's obligations or to appear. —*n.* this failure. **defaulter** *n.*

defeat *v.t.* win victory over; cause to fail, frustrate; baffle. —*n.* defeating others; being defeated.

defeatist *n.* person who pessimistically expects or accepts defeat.

defecate /'difi-/ *v.i.* discharge faeces from the body.

defect[1] /'di- *or* di'fekt/ *n.* deficiency, imperfection.

defect[2] /-'fekt/ *v.i.* desert one's country, abandon one's allegiance to a cause. **defection** *n.*, **defector** *n.*

defective *a.* having defect(s); incomplete.

defence *n.* defending; protection; justification put forward against an accusation; defendant's case.

defenceless *a.* having no defences.

defend *v.t.* protect, esp. by warding off an attack; uphold by argument; represent (the defendant) in a lawsuit. **defender** *n.*

defendant *n.* person accused or sued in a lawsuit.

defensible *a.* able to be defended. **defensibility** *n.*

defensive *a.* used or done for defence. **on the ~,** in an attitude of defence. **defensively** *adv.*

defer[1] *v.t.* (p.t. *deferred*) postpone. **deferment** *n.*, **deferral** *n.*

defer[2] *v.i.* (p.t. *deferred*) yield to a person's wishes or authority.

deference *n.* polite respect. **deferential** *a.*, **deferentially** *adv.*

defiance *n.* defying; open disobedience. **defiant** *a.*, **defiantly** *adv.*

deficiency *n.* lack, shortage; thing or amount lacking.

deficient *a.* not having enough; insufficient, lacking.

deficit *n.* amount by which a total falls short of what is required; excess of liabilities over assets.

defile *v.t.* make dirty, pollute. **defilement** *n.*

define *v.t.* give a definition of; state precisely; outline clearly, mark the boundary of. **definable** *a.*

definite *a.* having exact limits; clear and unmistakable, not vague; certain. **definitely** *adv.*

definition *n.* statement of a thing's precise meaning; making or being distinct, clearness of outline.

definitive *a.* finally fixing or settling something; most authoritative.

deflate *v.t./i.* let out air from; counteract inflation in; become deflated. **deflation** *n.*, **deflationary** *a.*

deflect *v.t./i.* turn aside. **deflexion** *n.*, **deflector** *n.*

defoliant *n.* chemical substance that destroys foliage.

deform *v.t.* spoil the shape of. **deformation** *n.*

deformity *n.* abnormality of shape, esp. of a part of the body.

defraud *v.t.* deprive by fraud.

defray *v.t.* provide money to pay (costs). **defrayal** *n.*

defrost *v.t./i.* remove frost from; thaw.

deft *a.* (*-er*, *-est*) skilful, handling things neatly. **deftly** *adv.*, **deftness** *n.*

defunct *a.* dead; no longer existing or functioning.

defuse *v.t.* remove the fuse from (an explosive); reduce the dangerous tension in (a situation).

defy *v.t.* resist; refuse to obey; challenge to do something.

degenerate[1] /-eit/ *v.i.* become worse. **degeneration** *n.*

degenerate[2] /-at/ *a.* having degenerated.

degrade *v.t.* reduce to a lower rank; bring disgrace or humiliation on. **degradation** *n.*

degree *n.* stage in a series or of intensity; academic rank given for proficiency or as an honour; unit of measurement for angles or temperature.

dehumanize *v.t.* remove human qualities from; make impersonal. **dehumanization** *n.*

dehydrate *v.t./i.* remove moisture from; lose moisture. **dehydration** *n.*

de-ice *v.t.* remove or prevent formation of ice on. **de-icer** *n.*

deify /'di:i-/ *v.t.* treat as a god. **deification** *n.*

deign *v.i.* condescend.

deity /'di:iti/ *n.* god, goddess.

déjà vu /deiʒɑ 'vju:/ feeling of having experienced the present situation before.

dejected *a.* in low spirits.

dejection *n.* lowness of spirits.

delay *v.t./i.* make or be late; postpone. —*n.* delaying.

delectable *a.* delightful.

delectation *n.* enjoyment.

delegacy /'del-/ *n.* body of delegates.

delegate[1] /-gət/ *n.* representative.

delegate[2] /-geit/ *v.t.* entrust (a task or power) to an agent.

delegation *n.* delegating; body of delegates.

delete *v.t.* strike out (a word etc.). **deletion** *n.*

delft *n.* a kind of earthenware.

deliberate[1] /-ət/ *a.* intentional; slow and careful. **deliberately** *adv.*

deliberate[2] /-eit/ *v.t./i.* think over or discuss carefully.

deliberation *n.* deliberating; being deliberate.

deliberative *a.* for the purpose of deliberating or discussing.

delicacy *n.* being delicate; choice food.

delicate *a.* fine, slender; not intense; easily

harmed, liable to illness; requiring carefulness or tact; not coarse. **delicately** *adv.*

delicatessen *n.* shop selling prepared delicacies.

delicious *a.* delightful, esp. to taste or smell. **deliciously** *adv.*

delight *n.* great pleasure; thing giving this. —*v.t./i.* please greatly; feel delight. **delightful** *a.*, **delightfully** *adv.*

delineate *v.t.* outline. **delineation** *n.*

delinquent *a. & n.* (person) guilty of an offence or neglect of duty. **delinquency** *n.*

delirium *n.* disordered state of mind, esp. during fever; wild excitement. **delirious** *a.*, **deliriously** *adv.*

deliver *v.t.* take to an addressee or purchaser; transfer, hand over; utter; aim (a blow or attack); bowl; rescue, set free; assist (a female giving birth). **deliverer** *n.*, **delivery** *n.*

deliverance *n.* rescue, freeing.

dell *n.* small wooded hollow.

delphinium *n.* tall garden plant with usu. blue flowers.

delta *n.* Greek letter D, written *Δ*; triangular patch of alluvial land at the mouth of a river.

delude *v.t.* deceive.

deluge *n. & v.t.* flood.

delusion *n.* false belief or impression; this as a symptom of madness.

delusive *a.* deceptive, raising false hopes.

de luxe /də ˈlʌks/ of superior quality; luxurious.

delve *v.i.* search deeply.

demagogue *n.* person who wins support by appealing to popular feelings and prejudices.

demand *n.* request made imperiously or by authority; customers' desire for goods or services; claim. —*v.t.* make a demand for; need.

demarcation *n.* marking of a boundary or limits, esp. of work for different trades.

demean *v.t.* lower the dignity of.

demeanour *n.* way a person behaves.

demented *a.* driven mad, crazy.

demerara /-ˈreərə/ *n.* brown raw cane sugar.

demerit *n.* fault, defect.

demilitarized *a.* with military forces and installations removed.

demise /-ˈmaɪz/ *n.* death.

demisemiquaver *n.* note equal to half a semiquaver.

demist *v.t.* clear mist from (a windscreen etc.). **demister** *n.*

demo *n.* (pl. *-os*) (*colloq.*) demonstration.

demob *v.t.* (p.t. *demobbed*) (*colloq.*) demobilize. —*n.* (*colloq.*) demobilization.

demobilize *v.t.* release from military service. **demobilization** *n.*

democracy *n.* government by all the people, usu. through elected representatives; country governed thus.

democrat *n.* person favouring democracy; *D~*, member of the Democratic Party in the U.S.A.

democratic *a.* of or according to democracy; *D~*, of one of the two main political parties in the U.S.A. **democratically** *adv.*

demolish *v.t.* pull or knock down; destroy. **demolition** *n.*

demon *n.* devil, evil spirit; cruel or forceful person. **demonic** /-ˈmon-/ *a.*, **demoniacal** /-ˈnaɪ-/ *a.*

demonstrable /ˈdem-/ *a.* able to be demonstrated. **demonstrably** *adv.*

demonstrate *v.t./i.* show evidence of, prove; show the working of; take part in a procession etc. to express a group's opinion publicly. **demonstration** *n.*, **demonstrator** *n.*

demonstrative /-ˈmonstrə-/ *a.* showing, proving; showing one's feelings. **demonstratively** *adv.*

demoralize *v.t.* weaken the morale of, dishearten. **demoralization** *n.*

demote *v.t.* reduce to a lower rank or category. **demotion** *n.*

demur *v.i.* (p.t. *demurred*) raise objections. —*n.* objection raised.

demure *a.* quiet and serious or pretending to be so. **demurely** *adv.*, **demureness** *n.*

den *n.* wild animal's lair; person's small private room.

denatured *a.* (of alcohol) made unfit for drinking.

deniable *a.* able to be denied.

denial *n.* denying; statement that a thing is not true.

denier /ˈdenjə(r)/ *n.* unit of weight by which the fineness of yarn is measured.

denigrate *v.t.* blacken the reputation of. **denigration** *n.*

denim *n.* strong twilled fabric; (*pl.*) trousers made of this.

denizen *n.* person or plant living in a specified place.

denomination *n.* name, title; specified Church or sect; class of units of measurement or money.

denominational *a.* of a particular religious denomination.

denominator *n.* number written below the line in a vulgar fraction.

denote *v.t.* be the sign, symbol, or name of; indicate. **denotation** *n.*

dénouement /deɪˈnuːmɑ̃/ *n.* clearing up of a plot's complications, at the end of a play or story.

denounce *v.t.* speak against; inform against; announce one's withdrawal from (a treaty etc.).

dense *a.* (*-er, -est*) thick; closely massed; stupid. **densely** *adv.*, **denseness** *n.*

density *n.* denseness; relation of weight to volume.

dent *n.* depression left by a blow or pressure. —*v.t./i.* make a dent in; become dented.

dental *a.* of or for teeth; of dentistry.

dentifrice *n.* substance for cleaning teeth.

dentist *n.* person qualified to treat decay and malformations of teeth.

dentistry *n.* dentist's work.

denture *n.* set of artificial teeth.

denude *v.t.* strip of covering or property. **denudation** *n.*

denunciation *n.* denouncing.

deny *v.t.* say that (a thing) is untrue or does

not exist; disown; prevent from having. **~ oneself,** restrict one's food, drink, or pleasure.

deodorant /di'əʊ-/ *n.* substance that removes or conceals unwanted odours. —*a.* deodorizing.

deodorize /dɪ'əʊ-/ *v.t.* destroy the odour of. **deodorization** *n.*

depart *v.t./i.* go away, leave.

department *n.* section of an organization. **~ store,** large shop with departments each selling a separate type of goods.

departmental *a.* of a department.

departure *n.* departing; setting out on a new course of action.

depend *v.i.* **~ on,** be controlled or determined by; be unable to do without; trust confidently.

dependable *a.* reliable.

dependant *n.* one who depends on another for support.

dependence *n.* depending.

dependency *n.* dependent State.

dependent *a.* depending; controlled by another.

depict *v.t.* represent in a picture or in words. **depiction** *n.*

depilatory /-'pɪlə-/ *a.* & *n.* (substance) removing hair.

deplete *v.t.* reduce by using quantities of. **depletion** *n.*

deplorable *a.* regrettable; very bad. **deplorably** *adv.*

deplore *v.t.* find or call deplorable.

deploy *v.t./i.* spread out, organize for effective use. **deployment** *n.*

depopulate *v.t.* reduce the population of. **depopulation** *n.*

deport *v.t.* remove (an unwanted person) from a country. **deportation** *n.*

deportment *n.* behaviour, bearing.

depose *v.t./i.* remove from power; testify, state on oath.

deposit *v.t.* (p.t. *deposited*) put down; leave as a layer of matter; entrust for keeping; pay as a deposit. —*n.* thing or substance deposited; sum paid into a bank or as a guarantee or first instalment. **depositor** *n.*

deposition *n.* deposing from power; sworn statement; depositing.

depository *n.* storehouse.

depot /'depəʊ/ *n.* storehouse; headquarters; (*U.S.*) bus or railway station.

deprave *v.t.* make morally bad, corrupt. **depravation** *n.*

depravity /-'præ-/ *n.* moral corruption, wickedness.

deprecate *v.t.* express disapproval of; disclaim politely. **deprecation** *n.*, **deprecatory** *a.*

depreciate *v.t./i.* make or become lower in value; disparage. **depreciation** *n.*

depreciatory /-'priʃə-/ *a.* disparaging.

depredation /depri-/ *n.* plundering, destruction.

depress *v.t.* press down; reduce (trade etc.); make sad.

depression *n.* pressing down; state of sadness; long period of inactivity in trading; area of low atmospheric pressure; sunken place. **depressive** *a.*

deprive *v.t.* take a thing away from; prevent

from using or enjoying something **deprival** *n.*, **deprivation** *n.*

depth *n.* deepness, measure of this; deepest or most central part. **~-charge** *n.* bomb that will explode under water. **out of one's ~,** in water too deep to stand in; attempting something beyond one's ability.

deputation *n.* body of people sent to represent others.

depute /-'pjuːt/ *v.t.* delegate; appoint to act as one's representative.

deputize *v.i.* act as deputy.

deputy *n.* person appointed to act as a substitute or representative.

derail *v.t.* cause (a train) to leave the rails. **derailment** *n.*

derange *v.t.* disrupt; make insane. **derangement** *n.*

Derby *n.* annual horse-race at Epsom; important race or contest.

derelict *a.* abandoned; left to fall into ruin.

dereliction *n.* abandonment; neglect of duty.

deride *v.t.* scoff at.

derision *n.* scorn, ridicule.

derisive *a.* scornful, showing derision. **derisively** *adv.*

derisory *a.* showing derision; deserving derision.

derivative *a.* & *n.* derived (thing).

derive *v.t./i.* obtain from a source; have its origin. **derivation** *n.*

dermatitis *n.* inflammation of the skin.

dermatology *n.* study of the skin and its diseases. **dermatologist** *n.*

derogatory *a.* disparaging.

derrick *n.* crane with an arm pivoted to the floor or base; framework holding drilling machinery over an oil-well etc.

derris *n.* an insecticide.

derv *n.* fuel for diesel engines.

dervish *n.* member of a Muslim religious order vowed to poverty.

descant *n.* treble accompaniment to a main melody.

descend *v.t./i.* go or come down; stoop to unworthy behaviour. **be descended from,** have origin from (an ancestor, family, etc.).

descendant *n.* person etc. descended from another.

descent *n.* descending; downward route or slope; sudden attack; lineage, family origin.

describe *v.t.* give a description of; mark the outline of, move in (a specified pattern).

description *n.* statement of what a person or thing is like; sort.

descriptive *a.* describing.

desecrate /'desɪ-/ *v.t.* treat (a sacred thing) irreverently. **desecration** *n.*, **desecrator** *n.*

desert[1] /'dez-/ *n.* & *a.* barren uninhabited often sand-covered (area). .

desert[2] /-'zɜːt/ *v.t./i.* abandon; leave one's service in the armed forces without permission. **deserter** *n.*, **desertion** *n.*

deserts /-'zɜːts/ *n.pl.* what one deserves.

deserve *v.t.* be worthy of or entitled to, because of actions or qualities. **deservedly** /-vɪdlɪ/ *adv.*

desiccate *v.t.* dry out moisture from. **desiccation** *n.*

design *n.* drawing that shows how a thing is to be made; general form or arrangement; lines or shapes forming a decoration; mental plan. —*v.t.* prepare a design for; plan, intend. **designedly** /-ɪdlɪ/ *adv.*, **designer** *n.*

designate[1] /-ət/ *a.* appointed but not yet installed.

designate[2] /-eɪt/ *v.t.* describe or name as; specify; appoint to a position. **designation** *n.*

designing *a.* scheming.

desirable *a.* arousing desire, worth desiring. **desirability** *n.*

desire *n.* feeling that one would get pleasure or satisfaction from something; thing desired. —*v.t.* feel a desire for; ask for.

desirous *a.* desiring.

desist *v.i.* cease.

desk *n.* piece of furniture for reading or writing at.

desolate *a.* solitary, lonely; deserted, uninhabited. **desolated** *a.* feeling very distressed. **desolation** *n.*

despair *n.* complete lack of hope; cause of this. —*v.i.* feel despair.

desperado /-ˈrɑ-/ *n.* (pl. *-oes*) reckless criminal.

desperate *a.* hopelessly bad; reckless through despair. **desperately** *adv.*, **desperation** *n.*

despicable /ˈdes- or -ˈspɪk-/ *a.* contemptible. **despicably** *adv.*

despise *v.t.* regard as inferior or worthless.

despite *prep.* in spite of.

despondent *a.* dejected. **despondently** *adv.*, **despondency** *n.*

despot *n.* tyrant, ruler with unrestricted power. **despotic** *a.*, **despotically** *adv.*

despotism *n.* tyranny.

dessert /-ˈzɜt/ *n.* sweet course of a meal; fruit etc. at the end of dinner. **∼-spoon** *n.* medium-sized spoon for eating puddings etc.

destination *n.* place to which a person or thing is going.

destine *v.t.* settle the future of, set apart for a purpose.

destiny *n.* fate considered as a power; what is destined by fate to happen to a person or thing.

destitute *a.* penniless, without the necessaries of life; devoid. **destitution** *n.*

destroy *v.t.* pull or break down; make useless, spoil completely; kill (an animal) deliberately. **destruction** *n.*, **destructive** *a.*

destroyer *n.* one who destroys; fast warship.

desultory /ˈdes-/ *a.* going from one subject to another, not systematic. **desultorily** *adv.*

detach *v.t.* release or remove from something else or from a group.

detachable *a.* able to be detached.

detached *a.* not joined to another; free from bias or emotion.

detachment *n.* detaching; being detached; group detached from a larger one for special duty.

detail *n.* small fact or item; such items collectively; small military detachment. —*v.t.* relate in detail; assign to special duty.

detain *v.t.* keep in confinement; cause delay to.

detainee *n.* person detained in custody.

detect *v.t.* discover the presence or activity of. **detection** *n.*

detective *n.* person whose job is to investigate crimes.

detector *n.* device for detecting something.

détente /ˈdeɪtɑnt/ *n.* easing of strained relations between States.

detention *n.* detaining; imprisonment.

deter *v.t.* (p.t. *deterred*) discourage from action. **determent** *n.*

detergent *a. & n.* cleansing (substance, esp. other than soap).

deteriorate *v.i.* become worse. **deterioration** *n.*

determinant *n.* decisive factor.

determination *n.* firmness of purpose; process of deciding.

determine *v.t.* decide; calculate precisely; resolve firmly.

determined *a.* full of determination.

deterrent /-ˈte-/ *n.* thing that deters; nuclear weapon deterring attack.

detest *v.t.* dislike intensely. **detestable** *a.*, **detestation** *n.*

detonate *v.t./i.* explode. **detonation** *n.*, **detonator** *n.*

detour /ˈdiːtʊə(r)/ *n.* deviation from a direct or intended course.

detract *v.t./i.* **∼ from**, reduce, lessen. **detraction** *n.*

detractor *n.* person who criticizes a thing unfavourably.

detriment *n.* harm.

detrimental *a.* harmful. **detrimentally** *adv.*

de trop /də ˈtrəʊ/ not wanted.

deuce[1] *n.* score of 40-all in tennis.

deuce[2] *n.* (in exclamations of annoyance) the Devil.

deuterium *n.* heavy form of hydrogen.

Deutschmark /ˈdɔɪtʃ-/ *n.* unit of money in West Germany.

devalue *v.t.* reduce the value of. **devaluation** *n.*

devastate *v.t.* cause great destruction to. **devastation** *n.*

devastating *a.* overwhelming.

develop *v.t./i.* (p.t. *developed*) make or become larger or more mature or organized; bring or come into existence; make usable or profitable, build on (land); treat (a film etc.) so as to make a picture visible. **developer** *n.*, **development** *n.*

deviant *a. & n.* (person or thing) deviating from normal behaviour.

deviate *v.i.* turn aside from a course of action, truth, etc. **deviation** *n.*

device *n.* thing made or used for a purpose; scheme; design used as a decoration or emblem.

devil *n.* evil spirit; *the D∼*, supreme spirit of evil; cruel or annoying person; person of mischievous energy or cleverness; (*colloq.*) difficult person or problem. —*v.t./i.* (p.t. *devilled*) cook (food) with hot seasoning; do research for an author or barrister. **devilish** *a.*

devilment *n.* mischief.

devilry *n.* wickedness; devilment.

devious *a.* roundabout; not straightforward, underhand. **deviously** *adv.*, **deviousness** *n.*

devise *v.t.* plan; invent.

devoid *a.* ∼ **of,** lacking, free from.

devolution *n.* devolving; delegation of power from central to local or regional administration.

devolve *v.t./i.* pass or be passed to a deputy or successor.

devote *v.t.* give or use for a particular purpose.

devoted *a.* showing devotion.

devotee *n.* enthusiast.

devotion *n.* great love or loyalty; zeal; worship; (*pl.*) prayers.

devotional *a.* used in worship.

devour *v.t.* eat hungrily or greedily; consume; take in greedily with the eyes or ears.

devout *a.* earnestly religious; earnest, sincere. **devoutly** *adv.*

dew *n.* drops of moisture on a surface, esp. condensed during the night from water vapour in air.

dew-claw *n.* small claw on the inner side of a dog's leg.

dewdrop *n.* drop of dew.

dewlap *n.* fold of loose skin at the throat of cattle etc.

dewy *a.* wet with dew. ∼**-eyed** *a.* innocently trusting or sentimental.

dexterity *n.* skill.

dextrous *a.* skilful. **dextrously** *adv.*

diabetes *n.* disease in which sugar and starch are not properly absorbed by the body. **diabetic** /-ˈbet-/ *a. & n.*

diabolic *a.* of the Devil.

diabolical *a.* very cruel, wicked, or cunning. **diabolically** *adv.*

diadem *n.* crown.

diaeresis /daɪˈɪərɪsɪs/ *n.* mark ¨ over a vowel sounded separately.

diagnose *v.t.* make a diagnosis of.

diagnosis *n.* (pl. *-oses*) identification of a disease or condition after observing its signs. **diagnostic** *a.*

diagonal *a. & n.* (line) crossing from corner to corner. **diagonally** *adv.*

diagram *n.* drawing that shows the parts of thing or how it works, or represents the operation of a process etc. **diagrammatic** *a.*

dial *n.* face of a clock or watch; similar plate or disc with a movable pointer; movable disc manipulated to connect one telephone with another; (*sl.*) face. —*v.t./i.* (p.t. *dialled*) select or regulate or operate by using a dial.

dialect *n.* words and pronunciation peculiar to a district. **dialectal** *a.*

dialectic *n.* investigation of truths in philosophy etc. by systematic reasoning.

dialogue *n.* talk between people.

dialysis /daɪˈælɪ-/ *n.* purification of blood by causing it to flow through a suitable membrane.

diamanté /diəˈmɒnteɪ/ *a.* decorated with sparkling fragments of crystal etc.

diameter *n.* straight line from side to side through the centre of circle or sphere; its length.

diametrical *a.* of or along a diameter; (of opposition) direct. **diametrically** *adv.*

diamond *n.* very hard brilliant precious stone; four-sided figure with equal sides and with angles that are not right angles; thing shaped thus, playing-card of suit marked with such shapes. ∼ **wedding** etc., 60th (or 75th) anniversary.

diaper *n.* baby's napkin.

diaphanous *a.* almost transparent.

diaphragm *n.* a kind of partition, esp. that between chest and abdomen; vibrating disc in a microphone etc.; device for varying the aperture of a lens.

diarrhoea *n.* condition with frequent fluid faeces.

diary *n.* daily record of events; book for noting these.

diathermy *n.* medical heat treatment by electric currents.

diatonic *a.* using notes of the major and minor (not chromatic) scales.

diatribe *n.* violent verbal attack.

dibber *n.* tool to make holes in ground for young plants.

dice *n.* (pl. *dice*) small cube marked on each side with 1–6 spots, used in games of chance; game played with these. —*v.i.* gamble using dice; take great risks; cut into small cubes.

dicey *a.* (*sl.*) risky; unreliable.

dichotomy /daɪˈkɒt-/ *n.* division into two parts or kinds.

dickens *n.* (*colloq.*, in exclamations) the deuce, the Devil.

dicker *v.i.* (*colloq.*) haggle.

dicotyledon *n.* plant with two cotyledons.

dictate *v.t./i.* say (words) aloud to be written by a person or recorded by a machine; state or order authoritatively; give orders officiously. **dictation** *n.*

dictates /ˈdɪk-/ *n.pl.* commands.

dictator *n.* ruler with unrestricted authority; domineering person. **dictatorship** *n.*

dictatorial *a.* of or like a dictator. **dictatorially** *adv.*

diction *n.* manner of uttering or pronouncing words.

dictionary *n.* book that lists and explains the words of a language or the topics of a subject.

dictum *n.* (pl. *-ta*) formal saying.

did *see* do.

didactic *a.* meant or meaning to instruct. **didactically** *adv.*

diddle *v.t.* (*sl.*) cheat, swindle.

didn't = did not.

die[1] *v.i.* (pres.p. *dying*) cease to be alive; cease to exist or function; fade away. **be dying to** or **for,** feel an intense longing to or for.

die[2] *n.* (*old use*) dice.

die[3] *n.* device that stamps a design or that cuts or moulds material into shape. ∼**-cast** *a.* made by casting metal in a mould.

die-hard *n.* very conservative or stubborn person.

diesel *n.* diesel engine; vehicle driven by this. **~-electric** *a.* using an electric generator driven by a diesel engine. **~ engine,** oil-burning engine in which ignition is produced by the heat of compressed air.

diet[1] *n.* habitual food; restricted selection of food. —*v.t./i.* keep to a restricted diet. **dietary** *a.,* **dieter** *n.*

diet[2] *n.* congress, parliamentary assembly in certain countries.

dietetic /-ˈtet-/ *a.* of diet and nutrition. **dietetics** *n.pl.* study of diet and nutrition.

dietician *n.* expert in dietetics.

differ *v.i.* be unlike; disagree.

difference *n.* being different or unlike; amount of this; remainder after subtraction; disagreement.

different *a.* unlike, not the same; separate. **differently** *adv.*

differential *a.* of, showing, or depending on a difference. —*n.* agreed difference in wage-rates; arrangement of gears allowing a vehicle's rear wheels to revolve at different speeds when cornering.

differentiate *v.t./i.* be a difference between; distinguish between; develop differences. **differentiation** *n.*

difficult *a.* needing much effort or skill to do or deal with; troublesome. **difficulty** *n.*

diffident *a.* lacking self-confidence. **diffidently** *adv.,* **diffidence** *n.*

diffraction *n.* breaking up of a beam of light into a series of coloured or dark-and-light bands.

diffuse[1] /-ˈfjus/ *a.* diffused, not concentrated; wordy. **diffusely** *adv.,* **diffuseness** *n.*

diffuse[2] /-ˈfjuz/ *v.t./i.* spread widely or thinly; mix slowly. **diffuser** *n.,* **diffusion** *n.*

dig *v.t./i.* (p.t. **dug,** pres.p. **digging**) break up and move soil; make (a way or hole) thus; remove by digging; excavate; seek or discover by investigation; thrust, poke. —*n.* piece of digging; excavation; thrust, poke; cutting remark; (*pl., colloq.*) lodgings.

digest[1] /-ˈdʒe-/ *v.t* dissolve (food) in the stomach etc. for absorption by the body; absorb into the mind.

digest[2] /ˈdaɪ-/ *n.* methodical summary; publication giving excerpts of news, writings, etc.

digestible *a.* able to be digested.

digestion *n.* process or power of digesting food.

digestive *a.* of or aiding digestion. **~ biscuit,** wholemeal biscuit.

digger *n.* one who digs; mechanical excavator.

digit *n.* any numeral from 0 to 9; finger or toe.

digital *a.* of or using digits. **~ clock,** one that shows the time as a row of figures.

digitalin /-ˈteɪ-/ *n.* poisonous substance prepared from foxglove leaves.

digitalis /-ˈteɪ-/ *n.* heart stimulant prepared from foxglove leaves.

dignified *a.* showing dignity.

dignify *v.t.* give dignity to.

dignitary *n.* person holding high rank or position.

dignity *n.* calm and serious manner or style; worthiness; high rank or position.

digress *v.i.* depart from the main subject temporarily. **digression** *n.*

dike *n.* long wall or embankment to prevent flooding; drainage ditch.

dilapidated *a.* in disrepair.

dilapidation *n.* dilapidated state.

dilate *v.t./i.* make or become wider. **~ upon,** speak or write lengthily about. **dilation, dilatation** *ns.,* **dilator** *n.*

dilatory /ˈdɪlə-/ *a.* delaying, not prompt. **dilatoriness** *n.*

dilemma /dɪl-/ *n.* situation in which a choice must be made between unwelcome alternatives.

dilettante /dɪlɪˈtæntɪ/ *n.* person who dabbles in a subject for pleasure.

diligent *a.* working or done with care and effort. **diligently** *adv.,* **diligence** *n.*

dill *n.* herb with spicy seeds.

dilly-dally *v.i.* (*colloq.*) dawdle; waste time by indecision.

dilute *v.t.* reduce the strength of (fluid) by adding water etc; reduce the forcefulness of. **dilution** *n.*

dim *a.* (**dimmer, dimmest**) lit faintly; indistinct; (*colloq.*) stupid. —*v.t./i.* (p.t. **dimmed**) make or become dim. **dimly** *adv.,* **dimness** *n.*

dime *n.* 10-cent coin of the U.S.A.

dimension *n.* measurable extent; scope. **dimensional** *a.*

diminish *v.t./i.* make or become less.

diminuendo *adv. & n.* (pl. *-os*) decreasing in loudness.

diminution *n.* decrease.

diminutive *a.* tiny. —*n.* word for a small specimen of a thing; affectionate form of a name.

dimple *n.* small dent, esp. in the skin. —*v.t./i.* show dimple(s); produce dimples in.

din *n.* loud annoying noise. —*v.t./i.* (p.t. **dinned**) make a din; force (information) into a person by constant repetition.

dinar /ˈdi-/ *n.* unit of money in Yugoslavia and various countries esp. in the Middle East.

dine *v.t./i.* eat dinner; entertain to dinner.

diner *n.* one who dines; dining-room.

ding-dong *n.* sound of clapper bell(s). —*adj. & adv.* with vigorous action; with success alternating between contestants.

dinghy *n.* small open boat or inflatable rubber boat.

dingo *n.* (pl. *-oes*) Australian wild dog.

dingy *a.* (*-ier, -iest*) dirty-looking. **dingily** *adv.,* **dinginess** *n.*

dining-room *n.* room in which meals are eaten.

dinkum *a.* (*Austr. colloq.*) true, real.

dinky *a.* (*-ier, -iest*) (*colloq.*) attractively small and neat.

dinner *n.* chief meal of the day; formal evening meal. **~-jacket** *n.* man's usu. black jacket for evening wear.

dinosaur *n.* extinct lizard-like creature.

dint *n.* dent. **by ~ of,** by means of.

diocese *n.* district under the care of a bishop. **diocesan** /-ˈɒs-/ *a.*

dioxide *n.* oxide with two atoms of oxygen to one of a metal or other element.

dip *v.t./i.* (p.t. *dipped*) put into liquid; go under water and emerge quickly; lower, go downwards. —*n.* dipping; short bathe; liquid or mixture into which something is dipped; downward slope. ~ **into**, read briefly from (a book).

diphtheria /dɪf-/ *n.* infectious disease with inflammation of the throat.

diphthong *n.* compound vowel-sound (as *ou* in *loud*).

diploma *n.* certificate awarded by a college etc. to a person completing a course of study.

diplomacy *n.* handling of international relations; tact.

diplomat *n.* member of the diplomatic service; tactful person.

diplomatic *a.* of or engaged in diplomacy; tactful. **diplomatically** *adv.*

dipper *n.* diving bird; ladle.

dipsomania *n.* uncontrollable craving for alcohol. **dipsomaniac** *n.* person suffering from this.

dire *a.* (-*er*, -*est*) dreadful; ominous; extreme and urgent.

direct *a.* straight, not crooked or roundabout; with nothing or no one between; straightforward, frank. —*adv.* by a direct route. —*v.t.* tell or show how to do something or reach a place; address (a letter etc.); cause to have a specified direction or target; control, manage; command. **directness** *n.*

direction *n.* directing; line along which a thing moves or faces; instruction.

directional *a.* of direction; operating in one direction only.

directive *n.* general instruction issued by authority.

directly *adv.* in a direct line; in a direct manner; very soon. —*conj.* (*colloq.*) as soon as.

director *n.* supervisor; member of a board directing a business company's affairs; one who supervises acting and filming. **directorship** *n.*

directory *n.* list of telephone subscribers, inhabitants, members, etc.

dirge *n.* song of mourning.

dirk *n.* a kind of dagger.

dirndl *n.* full skirt gathered into a tight waistband.

dirt *n.* unclean matter; soil; anything worthless; foul words, scandal. ~**-track** *n.* racing track made of earth or cinders etc.

dirty *a.* (-*ier*, -*iest*) soiled, not clean; producing impurities or much fallout; dishonourable; stormy; lewd, obscene. —*v.t./i.* make or become dirty.

disability *n.* thing that disables or disqualifies a person.

disable *v.t.* deprive of some ability, make unfit. **disabled** *a.* having a physical disability. **disablement** *n.*

disabuse *v.t.* disillusion.

disadvantage *n.* unfavourable condition or circumstance. **disadvantaged** *a.*, **disadvantageous** *a.*

disaffected *a.* discontented, having lost one's feelings of loyalty. **disaffection** *n.*

disagree *v.i.* have a different opinion; fail to agree; quarrel. **disagreement** *n.*

disagreeable *a.* unpleasant; bad-tempered. **disagreeably** *adv.*

disallow *v.t.* refuse to sanction.

disappear *v.i.* pass from sight or existence. **disappearance** *n.*

disappoint *v.t.* fail to do what was desired or expected by. **disappointment** *n.*

disapprobation *n.* disapproval.

disapprove *v.i.* have or express an unfavourable opinion. **disapproval** *n.*

disarm *v.t./i.* deprive of weapon(s); disband or reduce armed forces; defuse (a bomb); make less hostile.

disarmament *n.* reduction of a country's forces or weapons.

disarrange *v.t.* put into disorder. **disarrangement** *n.*

disarray *n.* & *v.t.* disorder.

disaster *n.* sudden great misfortune; great failure. **disastrous** *a.*, **disastrously** *adv.*

disband *v.t./i.* separate, disperse. **disbandment** *n.*

disbar *v.t.* (p.t. *disbarred*) deprive of the status of barrister.

disbelieve *v.t./i.* refuse or be unable to believe. **disbelief** *n.*

disbud *v.t.* (p.t. *disbudded*) remove unwanted buds from.

disburden *v.t.* relieve of a burden.

disburse *v.t.* pay out (money). **disbursement** *n.*

disc *n.* thin circular plate or layer; thing shaped thus; record bearing recorded sound. ~ **jockey**, (*colloq.*) compère of a broadcast programme of recorded light music.

discard[1] /-ˈkɑd/ *v.t.* throw away, put aside as useless or unwanted.

discard[2] /ˈdɪs-/ *n.* discarded thing.

discern *v.t.* perceive with the mind or senses. **discernment** *n.*

discernible *a.* able to be discerned.

discerning *a.* perceptive, showing sensitive understanding.

discharge *v.t./i.* send or flow out; unload; release the electric charge (of); allow to leave; dismiss; pay (a debt), perform (a duty etc.). —*n.* discharging; substance discharged.

disciple *n.* one of the original followers of Christ; person accepting the teachings of another.

disciplinarian *n.* person who enforces strict discipline.

disciplinary /ˈdɪs-*or*-ˈplɪn-/ *a.* of or for discipline.

discipline *n.* orderly or controlled behaviour; training or control producing this; branch of learning. —*v.t.* train to be orderly; punish.

disclaim *v.t.* disown.

disclaimer *n.* statement disclaiming something.

disclose *v.t.* reveal. **disclosure** *n.*

disco *n.* (pl. -*os*) (*colloq.*) discothèque.

discolour *v.t./i.* spoil the colour of; become discoloured or changed in colour. **discoloration** *n.*

discomfit v.t. (p.t. *discomfited*) disconcert. **discomfiture** n.

discomfort n. being uncomfortable; thing causing this.

disconcert v.t. upset the self-confidence of, fluster.

disconnect v.t. break the connection of; put out of action by disconnecting parts. **disconnection** n.

disconsolate a. unhappy, disappointed. **disconsolately** adv.

discontent n. dissatisfaction.

discontented a. feeling discontent.

discontinue v.t./i. put an end to; cease. **discontinuance** n.

discontinuous a. not continuous. **discontinuity** n.

discord n. disagreement, quarrelling; harsh sound. **discordant** a.

discothèque /ˈdɪskətek/ n. club or party where amplified recorded music is played for dancing; equipment for playing such music.

discount[1] /ˈdɪs-/ n. amount of money taken off the full price.

discount[2] /-ˈkaʊnt/ v.t. disregard partly or wholly; purchase (a bill of exchange) for less than its value will be when matured.

discourage v.t. dishearten; dissuade (from).

discourse[1] /ˈdɪs-/ n. speech, lecture; treatise.

discourse[2] /-ˈkɔs/ v.i. utter or write a discourse.

discourteous a. lacking courtesy. **discourteously** adv., **discourtesy** n.

discover v.t. obtain sight or knowledge of. **discovery** n.

discredit v.t. (p.t. *discredited*) damage the reputation of; refuse to believe; cause to be disbelieved. —n. damage to a reputation; thing causing this; doubt.

discreditable a. bringing discredit.

discreet a. cautious and prudent; not giving away secrets; unobtrusive, not showy. **discreetly** adv.

discrepancy n. failure to tally. **discrepant** a.

discrete a. separate.

discretion n. being discreet; freedom to decide something.

discretionary a. done or used at a person's discretion.

discriminate v.t./i. make a distinction. **~ against,** treat unfairly. **discriminating** a. having good judgement. **discrimination** n.

discursive a. rambling, not keeping to the main subject.

discus n. heavy disc thrown in contests of strength.

discuss v.t. examine by argument, talk or write about. **discussion** n.

disdain v.t. & n. scorn.

disdainful a. showing disdain. **disdainfully** adv.

disease n. unhealthy condition; specific illness. **diseased** a.

disembark v.t./i. put or go ashore. **disembarkation** n.

disembodied a. (of a spirit) freed from the body.

disembowel v.t. (p.t. *disembowelled*) take out the bowels of. **disembowelment** n.

disenchant v.t. free from enchantment, disillusion. **disenchantment** n.

disengage v.t. free from engagement; detach. **disengagement** n.

disentangle v.t. free from tangles or confusion; separate.

disfavour n. dislike, disapproval.

disfigure v.t. spoil the appearance of. **disfigurement** n.

disfranchise v.t. deprive of the right to vote for a parliamentary representative. **disfranchisement** n.

disgorge v.t./i. eject, pour forth; (*colloq.*) hand over.

disgrace n. loss of favour or respect; thing causing this. —v.t. bring disgrace upon. **disgraceful** a., **disgracefully** adv.

disgruntled a. discontented, resentful.

disguise v.t. conceal the identity of; conceal. —n. disguising, disguised condition; thing that disguises.

disgust n. strong dislike. —v.t. cause disgust in.

dish n. shallow flat-bottomed object for holding food; food prepared for the table; shallow concave object. —v.t. (*colloq.*) ruin (hopes etc.). **~ out,** (*colloq.*) distribute. **~ up,** put food into dishes for serving.

disharmony n. lack of harmony.

dishcloth n. cloth for washing dishes.

dishearten v.t. cause to lose hope or confidence.

dished a. concave.

dishevelled a. ruffled and untidy. **dishevellment** n.

dishonest a. not honest. **dishonestly** adv., **dishonesty** n.

dishonour v.t. & n. disgrace.

dishonourable a. not honourable, shameful. **dishonourably** adv.

dishwasher n. machine for washing dishes etc. automatically.

disillusion v.t. free from pleasant but mistaken beliefs. **disillusionment** n.

disincentive n. thing that discourages an action or effort.

disinclination n. unwillingness.

disincline v.t. cause to feel reluctant or unwilling.

disinfect v.t. cleanse by destroying harmful bacteria. **disinfection** n.

disinfectant n. substance used for disinfecting things.

disingenuous a. insincere.

disinherit v.t. reject from being one's heir.

disintegrate v.t./i. break into small parts or pieces. **disintegration** n.

disinter v.t. (p.t. *disinterred*) dig up, unearth.

disinterested a. unbiased.

disjoin v.t. separate.

disjointed a. (of talk) lacking orderly connection.

disk n. = disc.

dislike n. feeling of not liking something. —v.t. feel dislike for.

dislocate v.t. displace from its position; disrupt. **dislocation** n.

dislodge *v.t.* move or force from an established position.

disloyal *a.* not loyal. **disloyally** *adv.*, **disloyalty** *n.*

dismal *a.* gloomy; (*colloq.*) feeble. **dismally** *adv.*

dismantle *v.t.* take away equipment from; take to pieces.

dismay *n.* feeling of surprise and discouragement. —*v.t.* cause dismay to.

dismember *v.t.* remove the limbs of; partition (a country etc.). **dismemberment** *n.*

dismiss *v.t.* send away from one's presence or employment; reject; put (a batsman or side) out in cricket. **dismissal** *n.*

dismount *v.i.* get off or down from a thing on which one is riding.

disobedient *a.* not obedient. **disobediently** *adv.*, **disobedience** *n.*

disobey *v.t./i.* disregard orders, fail to obey.

disorder *n.* lack of order or of discipline; ailment. —*v.t.* throw into disorder; upset. **disorderly** *a.*

disorganize *v.t.* upset the orderly system or arrangement of.

disorientate *v.t.* cause (a person) to lose his bearings. **disorientation** *n.*

disown *v.t.* refuse to acknowledge as one's own; reject all connection with.

disparage *v.t.* speak slightingly of. **disparagement** *n.*

disparate /ˈdɪs-/ *a.* different in kind.

disparity /-ˈpæ-/ *n.* inequality, difference.

dispassionate *a.* free from emotion; impartial. **dispassionately** *adv.*

dispatch *v.t.* send off to a destination or for a purpose; kill; complete (a task etc.) quickly. —*n.* dispatching; promptness; official message; news report. **~-box** *n.* container for carrying official documents. **~-rider** *n.* messenger who travels by motor cycle.

dispel *v.t.* (p.t. *dispelled*) drive away.

dispensable *a.* not essential.

dispensary *n.* place where medicines are dispensed.

dispensation *n.* dispensing; distributing; management, esp. of the world by Providence; exemption.

dispense *v.t./i.* distribute, deal out; prepare and give out (medicine etc.). **~ with**, do without; make unnecessary. **dispenser** *n.*

disperse *v.t./i.* go or send in different directions, scatter. **dispersal** *n.*, **dispersion** *n.*

dispirited *a.* dejected.

displace *v.t.* shift from its place; take the place of; oust. **displacement** *n.*

display *v.t.* show, arrange conspicuously. —*n.* displaying; thing(s) displayed.

displease *v.t.* arouse displeasure of.

displeasure *n.* disapproval.

disport *v.refl.* **~ oneself,** frolic.

disposable *a.* able to be disposed of; at one's disposal; designed to be thrown away after use.

disposal *n.* disposing. **at one's ~,** available for one's use.

dispose *v.t./i.* place, arrange; make willing or ready to do something. **~ of,** get rid of; finish off. **be well disposed,** be friendly or favourable.

disposition *n.* arrangement; person's character; tendency.

dispossess *v.t.* deprive of the possession of. **dispossession** *n.*

disproportion *n.* disproportionate condition.

disproportionate *a.* relatively too large or too small. **disproportionately** *adv.*

disprove *v.t.* show to be wrong.

disputable /-ˈpju-/ *a.* questionable.

disputant /-ˈpju-/ *n.* person engaged in a dispute.

disputation *n.* argument, debate.

dispute /-ˈpjut/ *v.t./i.* argue, debate; quarrel; question the truth or validity of. —*n.* argument, debate; quarrel. **in ~,** being disputed.

disqualify *v.t.* make ineligible or unsuitable. **disqualification** *n.*

disquiet *n.* uneasiness, anxiety. —*v.t.* cause disquiet to.

disquisition *n.* long discourse.

disregard *v.t.* pay no attention to. —*n.* lack of attention.

disrepair *n.* bad condition caused by lack of repair.

disreputable *a.* not respectable. **disreputably** *adv.*

disrepute *n.* discredit.

disrobe *v.t./i.* undress.

disrupt *v.t.* cause to break up; interrupt the flow or continuity of. **disruption** *n.*, **disruptive** *a.*

dissatisfaction *n.* lack of satisfaction or of contentment.

dissatisfied *a.* not satisfied.

dissect /dɪs-/ *v.t.* cut apart so as to examine the internal structure. **dissection** *n.*, **dissector** *n.*

dissemble *v.t./i.* conceal (feelings).

disseminate *v.t.* spread widely. **dissemination** *n.*

dissension *n.* disagreement that gives rise to strife.

dissent *v.i.* have or express a different opinion. —*n.* difference in opinion. **dissenter** *n.*

dissertation *n.* detailed discourse.

disservice *n.* harmful action done by a person intending to help.

dissident *a.* disagreeing. —*n.* person who disagrees; one who opposes the authorities. **dissidence** *n.*

dissimilar *a.* unlike. **dissimilarity** *n.*

dissimulation *n.* dissembling.

dissipate *v.t./i.* dispel; fritter away. **dissipated** *a.* living a dissolute life. **dissipation** *n.*

dissociate *v.t.* separate, esp. in one's thoughts; declare to be unconnected. **dissociation** *n.*

dissolute *a.* lacking moral restraint or self-discipline.

dissolution *n.* dissolving of an assembly or partnership.

dissolve *v.t./i.* make or become liquid or dispersed in liquid; disappear gradually; disperse (an assembly); end (a partnership, esp. marriage); give way to emotion.

dissonant *a.* discordant.

dissuade *v.t.* persuade against a course of action. **dissuasion** *n.*

distance *n.* length of space between two points; distant part; remoteness. —*v.t.* outdistance.

distant *a.* at a specified or considerable distance away; aloof. **distantly** *adv.*

distaste *n.* dislike.

distasteful *a.* arousing distaste. **distastefully** *adv.*

distemper *n.* disease of dogs and certain other animals; a kind of paint for use on plaster etc. —*v.t.* paint with distemper.

distend *v.t./i.* swell from pressure within. **distension** *n.*

distil *v.t./i.* (p.t. *distilled*) treat or make by distillation; undergo distillation.

distillation *n.* process of vaporizing, condensing, and re-collecting a liquid so as to purify it or to extract elements; something distilled.

distiller *n.* one who makes alcoholic liquor by distillation.

distillery *n.* place where alcohol is distilled.

distinct *a.* clearly perceptible; different in kind. **distinctly** *adv.*

distinction *n.* distinguishing; difference; thing that differentiates; mark of honour; excellence.

distinctive *a.* distinguishing, characteristic.

distinguish *v.t./i.* be or see or point out a difference between; discern; make notable.

distort *v.t.* pull or twist out of shape; misrepresent. **distortion** *n.*

distract *v.t.* draw away the attention of.

distracted *a.* distraught.

distraction *n.* thing that distracts the attention; entertainment; distraught state, frenzy.

distraught *a.* nearly crazy with grief or worry.

distress *n.* suffering, unhappiness. —*v.t.* cause distress to. **in ~**, in danger and needing help.

distribute *v.t.* divide and share out; scatter, place at different points. **distribution** *n.*

distributive *a.* of or concerned with distribution.

distributor *n.* one who distributes things; device for passing electric current to sparking-plugs.

district *n.* part (of a country, county, or city) with a particular feature or regarded as a unit.

distrust *n.* lack of trust, suspicion. —*v.t.* feel distrust in.

disturb *v.t.* break the quiet or rest or calm of; cause to move from a settled position. **disturbance** *n.*

disturbed *a.* mentally or emotionally unstable or abnormal.

disunity *n.* lack of unity.

disuse *n.* state of not being used.

disused *a.* no longer used.

ditch *n.* long narrow trench for drainage or as a boundary. —*v.t./i.* make or repair ditches; (*sl.*) abandon; (*sl.*) make a forced landing of (an aircraft) on the sea.

dither *v.i.* tremble; hesitate indecisively. —*n.* state of dithering.

ditto *n.* (in lists) the same again.

ditty *n.* short simple song.

divan *n.* low couch without a raised back or ends; bed resembling this.

dive *v.t./i.* plunge head first into water; plunge or move quickly downwards; go under water; rush headlong. —*n.* diving; sharp downward movement or fall; (*sl.*) disreputable place.

diver *n.* one who dives; person who works underwater in a special suit with an air supply.

diverge *v.i.* go in different directions from a point or each other; depart from a path etc. **divergence** *n.*, **divergent** *a.*

diverse /-ˈvɜːs/ *a.* of differing kinds.

diversify *v.t.* introduce variety into; vary. **diversification** *n.*

diversion *n.* diverting; thing that diverts attention; entertainment; route round a closed road.

diversity *n.* variety.

divert *v.t.* turn from a course or route; entertain, amuse.

divest *v.t.* **~ of**, strip of.

divide *v.t./i.* separate into parts or groups or from something else; cause to disagree; find how many times one number contains another; be able to be divided. —*n.* dividing line; watershed.

dividend *n.* number to be divided; share of profits payable esp. as interest; benefit from an action.

divider *n.* thing that divides; (*pl.*) measuring-compasses.

divination *n.* divining.

divine *a.* (-*er*, -*est*) of, from, or like God or a god; (*colloq.*) excellent, very beautiful. —*v.t.* discover by intuition or allegedly magical means. **divinely** *adv.*, **diviner** *n.*

divinity *n.* being divine; god.

divisible *a.* able to be divided. **divisibility** *n.*

division *n.* dividing; separation of M.P.s into two sections for counting votes in parliament; dividing line, partition; one of the parts into which a thing is divided. **divisional** *a.*

divisive /-ˈvaɪ-/ *a.* tending to cause disagreement.

divisor *n.* number by which another is to be divided.

divorce *n.* legal termination of a marriage; separation. —*v.t.* end the marriage of (a person) by divorce; separate.

divorcee *n.* divorced person.

divot *n.* piece of turf dislodged by a club-head in golf.

divulge *v.t.* reveal (information). **divulgation** *n.*

D.I.Y. *abbr.* do-it-yourself.

dizzy *a.* (-*ier*, -*iest*) giddy, feeling confused; causing giddiness. **dizzily** *adv.*, **dizziness** *n.*

D.J. *abbr.* disc jockey.

do *v.t./i.* (3 sing. pres. tense *does*, p.t. *did*, p.p. *done*) perform, complete; deal with; cover (a distance) in travelling; undergo; provide food etc. for; act, proceed; fare; be suitable or acceptable; (*sl.*) swindle, rob, attack. —*v.aux.* (used to form present or past tense, for emphasis, or to avoid repeating a verb just used.) —*n.* (pl. *dos* or *do's*) entertainment, party; dealing. **∼ away with,** abolish, get rid of. **∼ down,** (*colloq.*) swindle. **∼ for,** (*colloq.*) ruin, destroy. **∼-gooder** *n.* well-meaning but unrealistic promoter of social work or reform. **∼ in,** (*sl.*) ruin, kill; tire out. **∼-it-yourself** *a.* for use by an amateur handyman. **∼ out,** clean, redecorate. **∼ up,** fasten, wrap; repair, redecorate; tire out. **∼ with,** tolerate; need, want. **∼ without,** manage without.

docile /ˈdəʊ-/ *a.* willing to obey. **docilely** *adv.*, **docility** *n.*

dock[1] *n.* enclosed body of water where ships are admitted for loading, unloading, or repair. —*v.t./i.* bring or come into dock; join (spacecraft) together in space, be joined thus.

dock[2] *n.* enclosure for the prisoner in a criminal court.

dock[3] *v.t.* cut short; reduce, take away part of.

dock[4] *n.* tall weed with broad leaves.

docker *n.* labourer who loads and unloads ships in a dockyard.

docket *n.* document or label listing goods delivered; voucher. —*v.t.* (p.t. *docketed*) enter on a docket; label with a docket.

dockyard *n.* area and buildings round a shipping dock.

dockyard see **dock**[1].

doctor *n.* person qualified to give medical treatment; person holding a doctorate. —*v.t.* treat medically; castrate; patch up; tamper with, falsify.

doctorate *n.* highest degree at a university.

doctrinaire *a.* applying theories or principles rigidly.

doctrine *n.* principle(s) of a religious, political, or other group. **doctrinal** /-ˈtraɪ-/ *a.*

document *n.* piece of paper giving information or evidence. —*v.t.*-provide or prove with documents. **documentation** *n.*

documentary *a.* consisting of documents; giving a factual filmed report. —*n.* documentary film.

dodder *v.i.* totter because of age or frailty. **doddery** *a.*

dodge *v.t./i.* move quickly to one side so as to avoid (a thing); evade. —*n.* dodging movement; (*colloq.*) clever trick, ingenious action. **dodger** *n.*

dodgem *n.* one of the small cars in an enclosure at a fun-fair, driven so as to bump or dodge others.

dodgy *a.* (*-ier, -iest*) (*colloq.*) cunning, artful; awkward.

dodo *n.* (pl. *-os*) large extinct bird.

doe *n.* female of deer, hare, or rabbit.

doesn't = does not.

doff *v.t.* (*old use*) take off (one's hat).

dog *n.* four-legged carnivorous wild or domesticated animal; male of this or of fox or wolf; (*colloq.*) person; mechanical device for gripping things; (*pl.*) greyhound racing. —*v.t.* (p.t. *dogged*) follow persistently. **∼-collar** *n.* (*colloq.*) clerical collar. **∼-eared** *a.* with page-corners crumpled through use. **∼-star** *n.* the star Sirius.

doge /dəʊdʒ/ *n.* former ruler of Venice.

dogged /ˈdɒgɪd/ *a.* determined. **doggedly** *adv.*

doggerel *n.* bad verse.

doggo *adv.* lie **∼,** (*sl.*) remain motionless or making no sign.

doghouse *n.* (*U.S.*) kennel. **in the ∼,** (*sl.*) in disgrace.

dogma *n.* doctrine(s) put forward by authority.

dogmatic *a.* of or like dogmas; stating things in an authoritative way. **dogmatically** *adv.*, **dogmatism** *n.*

dogmatize *v.i.* make dogmatic statement(s).

dogrose *n.* wild hedge-rose.

dogsbody *n.* (*colloq.*) drudge.

dogwood *n.* shrub with dark-red branches.

doh *n.* name for the keynote of a scale in music, or the note C.

doily *n.* small ornamental mat.

doldrums *n.pl.* ocean regions near the equator, with little or no wind. **in the ∼,** in low spirits.

dole *v.t.* distribute. —*n.* (*colloq.*) unemployment benefit.

doleful *a.* mournful. **dolefully** *adv.*

doll *n.* small model of a human figure, esp. as a child's toy. —*v.t.* **∼ up,** (*colloq.*) dress smartly.

dollar *n.* unit of money in the U.S.A. and various other countries.

dollop *n.* (*colloq.*) mass of a soft substance.

dolly *n.* (*children's use*) doll; movable platform for a cine camera.

dolman *a.* **∼ sleeve,** loose sleeve cut in one piece with the body of a garment.

dolphin *n.* sea animal like a large porpoise, with a beak-like snout.

domain *n.* area under a person's control; field of thought or activity.

dome *n.* rounded roof with a circular base; thing shaped like this. **domed** *a.*

domestic *a.* of home or household; of one's own country; domesticated. —*n.* servant in a household. **∼ science,** study of household management. **domestically** *adv.*

domesticated *a.* (of animals) trained to live with and be kept by man; (of people) enjoying household work and home life.

domesticity *n.* domestic life.

domicile *n.* place of residence.

domiciled *a.* dwelling.

dominant *a.* dominating. **dominance** *n.*

dominate *v.t./i.* have a commanding influence over; be the most influential or conspicuous person or thing; tower over. **domination** *n.*

domineer *v.i.* behave forcefully, making others obey.

Dominican *n.* friar of the order founded by St. Dominic.

dominion *n.* authority to rule, control; ruler's territory.

domino *n.* (pl. *-oes*) small oblong piece marked with pips, used in the game of *dominoes.*

don[1] *v.t.* (p.t. *donned*) put on.

don[2] *n.* head or fellow or tutor of a college. **donnish** *a.*

Don *n.* Spanish title put before a man's Christian name.

donate *v.t.* give as a donation.

donation *n.* gift (esp. of money) to a fund or institution.

done *see* do.

donkey *n.* animal of the horse family, with long ears. ～ **engine,** small auxiliary engine. ～ **jacket,** thick weatherproof jacket. ～-**work** *n.* drudgery.

donor *n.* one who gives or donates something.

don't = do not.

doodle *v.i.* scribble idly. —*n.* drawing or marks made thus.

doom *n.* grim fate; death or ruin. —*v.t.* destine to a grim fate.

doomsday *n.* day of the Last Judgement.

door *n.* hinged, sliding, or revolving barrier closing an opening; doorway.

doormat *n.* mat placed at a doorway, for wiping dirt from shoes.

doorstep *n.* step or ground just outside a door.

doorway *n.* opening filled by a door.

dope *n.* (*colloq.*) medicine, drug; (*sl.*) information; (*sl.*) stupid person. —*v.t./i.* (*colloq.*) drug.

dopey *n.* (*sl.*) half asleep, stupid.

Doric *a.* of the simplest style in Greek architecture.

dormant *a.* sleeping; temporarily inactive.

dormer *n.* upright window under a small gable on a sloping roof.

dormitory *n.* room with several beds, esp. in a school. ～ **town,** one from which most residents travel to work elsewhere.

dormouse *n.* (pl. -*mice*) mouse-like animal that hibernates.

dorsal *a.* of or on the back.

dosage *n.* giving of medicine; size of a dose.

dose *n.* amount of medicine to be taken at one time; amount of radiation received. —*v.t.* give dose(s) of medicine to.

doss *v.i.* (*sl.*) sleep in a doss-house or on a makeshift bed etc. ～-**house,** *n.* cheap hostel. **dosser** *n.*

dossier /ˈdɒsɪə(r)/ *n.* set of documents about a person or event.

dot *n.* small round mark; shorter signal in the Morse code. —*v.t.* (p.t. *dotted*) mark with dot(s); scatter here and there. **on the ～,** exactly on time.

dotage *n.* senility with mental weakness.

dote *v.i.* ～ **on,** feel great fondness for.

dottle *n.* unburnt tobacco left in a pipe.

dotty *a.* (-*ier*, -*iest*) (*colloq.*) feeble-minded; eccentric; silly.

double *a.* consisting of two things or parts; twice as much or as many; designed for two persons or things; having two or more circles of petals. —*adv.* twice as much; in twos. —*n.* double quantity or thing; person or thing very like another; (*pl.*) game with two players on each side. —*v.t./i.* make or become twice as much or as many; fold in two; turn back sharply from a course; act two parts in the same play etc. **at the ～,** running, hurrying. ～-**bass** *n.* lowest pitched instrument of the violin family. ～-**breasted** *a.* (of a coat) with fronts overlapping. ～ **chin,** chin with a roll of fat below. ～ **cream,** thick cream. ～-**cross** *v.t.* cheat, deceive. ～-**dealing** *n.* deceit, esp. in business. ～-**decker** *n.* bus with two decks. ～ **Dutch,** unintelligible talk. ～ **figures,** numbers from 10 to 99. ～-**jointed** *a.* have unusually flexible joints. ～ **take,** delayed reaction just after one's first reaction. ～-**talk** *n.* talk that means something very different from its apparent meaning. **doubly** *adv.*

double entendre /dubl ɑnˈtɑndr/ phrase with two meanings, one of which is usu. indecent.

doubt *n.* feeling of uncertainty or disbelief; being undecided —*v.t./i.* feel doubt about, hesitate to believe. **doubter** *n.*

doubtful *a.* feeling or causing doubt; unreliable. **doubtfully** *adv.*

doubtless *a.* certainly.

douche /duʃ/ *n.* jet of water applied to the body; device for applying this. —*v.t./i.* use a douche (on).

dough *n.* thick mixture of flour etc. and liquid, for baking; (*sl.*) money. **doughy** *a.*

doughnut *n.* small cake of fried sweetened dough.

dour /dʊə(r)/ *a.* stern, gloomy-looking. **dourly** *adv.*, **dourness** *n.*

douse /daʊs/ *v.t.* extinguish (a light); throw water on, put into water.

dove *n.* bird with a thick body and short legs; person favouring a policy of peace and negotiation rather than violence.

dovecote *n.* shelter for domesticated pigeons.

dovetail *n.* wedge-shaped joint interlocking two pieces of wood. —*v.t./i.* join by this; combine neatly.

dowager *n.* woman holding a title or property from her dead husband.

dowdy *a.* (-*ier*, -*iest*) unattractively dull, not stylish; dressed in dowdy clothes. **dowdily** *adv.*, **dowdiness** *n.*

dowel *n.* headless wooden or metal pin holding pieces of wood or stone together. **dowelling** *n.* rod for cutting into dowels.

dower *n.* widow's share of her husband's estate. ～ **house,** small house near a larger one, forming part of a dower.

down[1] *n.* area of open undulating land, esp. (*pl.*) chalk uplands.

down[2] *n.* very fine soft furry feathers or short hairs.

down[3] *adv.* to, in, or at a lower place or state etc.; to a smaller size; from an earlier to a later time; recorded in writing etc.; to the source or place where a thing is; as (partial) payment at the time of purchase. —*prep.* downwards along or through or into; at a lower part of. —*a.* directed downwards; travelling away from a central place. —*v.t.* (*colloq.*) knock or bring or put down; swallow. ～-**and-out** *n.* destitute person. ～-**hearted** *a.* in low spirits. ～ **on,** hostile to. ～-**to-earth** *a.* sensible and practical. ～ **under,** in Australia or other countries of the antipodes.

downcast *a.* dejected; (of eyes) looking downwards.

downfall *n.* fall from prosperity or power; thing causing this.

downgrade *v.t.* reduce to a lower grade.

downhill *a.* & *adv.* going or sloping downwards.

downpour *n.* great fall of rain.

downright *a.* frank, straightforward; thorough. —*adv.* thoroughly.

downstairs *adv.* & *a.* to or on a lower floor.

downstream *a.* & *adv.* in the direction in which a stream flows.

downtrodden *a.* oppressed.

downward *a.* moving or leading down. —*adv.* downwards.

downwards *adv.* towards a lower place etc.

downy *a.* (-*ier*, -*iest*) like or covered with soft down.

dowry *n.* property or money brought by a bride to her husband.

dowse /daʊz/ *v.i.* search for underground water or minerals by using a forked stick. **dowser** *n.*

doyen /ˈdɔɪən/ *n.* senior member of a staff or profession. **doyenne** *n.fem.*

doze *v.i.* sleep lightly. —*n.* short light sleep.

dozen *n.* set of twelve; (*pl.*, *colloq.*) very many.

Dr. *abbr.* Doctor; debtor.

drab *a.* dull, uninteresting.

drachm /dræm/ *n.* one eighth of an ounce or of a fluid ounce.

drachma *n.* (pl. -*as* or -*ae*) unit of money in Greece.

draft[1] *n.* rough preliminary written version; written order to a bank to pay money; group detached for special duty, selection of these; (*U.S.*) conscription. —*v.t.* prepare a draft of; select; (*U.S.*) conscript.

draft[2] *n.* (*U.S.*) draught.

drag *v.t./i.* (p.t. *dragged*) pull along; trail on the ground; bring or proceed with effort; search (the bottom of water) with grapnels, nets, etc.; draw at a cigarette or pipe. —*n.* heavy harrow; net for dragging water; thing that slows progress; (*sl.*) draw at a cigarette etc.; (*sl.*) women's clothes worn by men.

dragon *n.* mythical reptile able to breathe out fire; fierce person.

dragonfly *n.* long-bodied insect with gauzy wings.

dragoon *v.t.* force into action.

drain *v.t./i.* draw off (liquid) by channels or pipes etc.; flow away; deprive gradually of (strength or resources); drink all of. —*n.* channel or pipe carrying away water or sewage; thing that drains one's strength etc.

drainage *n.* draining; system of drains; what is drained off.

drake *n.* male duck.

dram *n.* drachm; small drink of spirits.

drama *n.* play(s) for acting on the stage or broadcasting; dramatic quality or series of events.

dramatic *a.* of drama; exciting, impressive. **dramatics** *n.pl.* performance of plays. **dramatically** *adv.*

dramatist *n.* writer of plays.

dramatize *v.t.* make into a drama. **dramatization** *n.*

drank *see* **drink.**

drape *v.t.* cover or arrange loosely.

draper *n.* retailer of cloth or clothing.

drapery *n.* draper's trade or fabrics; fabric draped in folds.

drastic *a.* having a strong or violent effect. **drastically** *adv.*

draught *n.* current of air; pulling; fish caught in a net; depth of water needed to float a ship; drawing of liquor from a cask etc.; one continuous act of swallowing, amount swallowed; (*pl.*) game played with 24 round pieces on a chess-board. **~ beer**, beer drawn from a cask.

draughtsman *n.* (pl. -*men*) one who draws plans or sketches.

draughty *a.* (-*ier*, -*iest*) letting in sharp currents of air.

draw *v.t./i.* (p.t. *drew*, p.p. *drawn*) pull; attract; take in (breath etc.); take from or out; draw lots, obtain by a lottery; seek to get information from (a person); finish a contest with scores equal; require (a specified depth) in which to float; produce (a picture or diagram) by making marks; formulate; write out (a cheque) for encashment; search (a covert) for game; make one's way, come; infuse. —*n.* act of drawing; thing that draws custom or attention; drawing of lots; drawn game. **~ at**, suck in smoke from (a pipe etc.). **~ in**, (of days) become shorter. **~ out**, prolong; (of days) become longer. **~-sheet** *n.* sheet that can be taken from under a patient without remaking the bed. **~-string** *n.* string that can be pulled to tighten an opening. **~ the line at,** refuse to do or tolerate. **~ up**, halt; compose (a contract etc.); make (oneself) stiffly erect.

drawback *n.* disadvantage.

drawbridge *n.* bridge over a moat, hinged for raising.

drawer *n.* person who draws something; one who writes a cheque; horizontal sliding compartment; (*sl.*) knickers, underpants.

drawing *n.* picture etc. drawn but not coloured. **~-pin** *n.* pin with a broad flat head, for fastening paper etc. to a surface. **~-room** *n.* formal sitting-room.

drawl *v.t./i.* speak lazily or with drawn-out vowel sounds. —*n.* drawling manner of speaking.

drawn *see* **draw.** —*a.* looking strained from tiredness or worry.

dray *n.* strong low cart for heavy loads. **drayman** *n.*

dread *n.* great fear. —*v.t.* fear greatly. —*a.* (*old use*) dreaded.

dreadful *a.* very bad. **dreadfully** *adv.*

dream *n.* series of pictures or events in a sleeping person's mind; day-dream; beautiful person or thing. —*v.t./i.* (p.t. *dreamed* or *dreamt*) have dream(s); have an ambition; think of as a possibility. **~ up**, imagine; invent. **dreamer** *n.*, **dreamless** *a.*

dreamy *a.* day-dreaming.

dreary *a.* (-*ier*, -*iest*) dull, boring; gloomy. **drearily** *adv.*, **dreariness** *n.*

dredge[1] *n.* apparatus for scooping things from the bottom of a river or sea. —*v.t./i.* bring up or clean with a dredge. **dredger**[1] *n.* boat that dredges.

dredge[2] *v.t.* sprinkle with flour or sugar. **dredger**[2] *n.* container with a perforated lid for sprinkling flour etc.

dregs *n.pl.* bits of worthless matter that sink to the bottom of liquid; worst and useless part.

drench *v.t.* wet all through.

dress *n.* outer clothing; woman's or girl's garment with a bodice and skirt. —*v.t./i.* put clothes on; clothe oneself; arrange, decorate, trim; put a dressing on. **~ circle,** first gallery in a theatre. **~ rehearsal,** final one, in costume. **~ shirt,** shirt for wearing with evening dress.

dressage /-ɑʒ/ *n.* management of a horse to show its obedience and deportment.

dresser[1] *n.* one who dresses a person or thing.

dresser[2] *n.* kitchen sideboard with shelves for dishes etc.

dressing *n.* sauce or stuffing for food; fertilizer etc. spread over land; bandage or ointment etc. for a wound; substance for stiffening fabric in manufacture. **~-case** *n.* case for brushes, cosmetics, etc., while travelling. **~ down,** scolding. **~-gown** *n.* loose gown worn when one is not fully dressed. **~-table** *n.* table with a mirror, for use while dressing.

dressmaker *n.* woman who makes women's clothes. **dressmaking** *n.*

dressy *a.* (-*ier*, -*iest*) wearing stylish clothes; elegant, elaborate.

drew *see* **draw.**

drey *n.* squirrel's nest.

dribble *v.t./i.* have saliva flowing from the mouth; flow or let flow in drops; (in football etc.) move the ball forward with slight touches.

driblet *n.* small amount.

dried *a.* (of food) preserved by removal of moisture.

drier *n.* device for drying things.

drift *v.t./i.* be carried by a current of water or air; go casually or aimlessly; pile or be piled into drifts. —*n.* drifting movement; mass of snow piled up by the wind; deviation from a set course; general meaning of a speech etc.

drifter *n.* aimless person.

driftwood *n.* wood floating on the sea or washed ashore.

drill[1] *n.* tool or machine for boring holes or sinking wells; training; (*colloq.*) routine procedure. —*v.t./i.* use a drill, make (a hole) with a drill; train, be trained.

drill[2] *n.* furrow; machine for making this or sowing seeds in furrows. —*v.t.* plant in drills.

drill[3] *n.* strong twilled fabric.

drily *adv.* in a dry way.

drink *v.t./i.* (p.t. *drank*, p.p. *drunk*) swallow (liquid); take alcoholic drink, esp. in excess; pledge good wishes (to) by drinking. —*n.* liquid for drinking; alcoholic liquors. **~ in,** watch or listen to eagerly. **drinker** *n.*

drip *v.t./i.* (p.t. *dripped*) fall or let fall in drops.

—*n.* liquid falling in drops; sound of this; (*sl.*) weak or dull person. **~-dry** *v.i. & a.* (able to) dry easily without ironing.

dripping *n.* fat melted from roast meat.

drive *v.t./i.* (p.t. *drove*, p.p. *driven*) send or urge onwards; propel; force to penetrate; operate (a vehicle) and direct its course; travel or convey in a private vehicle; keep (machinery) going; cause, compel; make (a bargain). —*n.* journey in a private vehicle; stroke hitting a ball strongly; transmission of power to machinery; energy, urge; organized effort; road; track for a car, leading to a private house. **~ at,** intend to convey as a meaning. **~-in** *a.* (of a cinema etc.) able to be used without getting out of one's car.

drivel *n.* silly talk, nonsense.

drizzle *n. & v.i.* rain in very fine drops.

drogue *n.* funnel-shaped piece of fabric used as a wind-sock, brake, target, etc.

droll *a.* (-*er*, -*est*) amusing in an odd way. **drolly** *adv.,* **drollery** *n.*

dromedary *n.* camel with one hump, bred for riding.

drone *n.* male honey-bee; idler; deep humming sound. —*v.i.* make this sound; speak monotonously.

drool *v.i.* slaver, dribble; show gushing appreciation.

droop *v.t./i.* bend or hang down limply. —*n.* drooping attitude.

drop *n.* small rounded mass of liquid; thing shaped like this; very small quantity; fall; steep descent, distance of this; painted curtain or scenery let down on to a stage; (*pl.*) medicine measured by drops. —*v.t./i.* (p.t. *dropped*) fall; shed, let fall; sink from exhaustion; make or become lower; utter or send casually; omit; reject, give up. **~ in,** pay a casual visit. **~-kick** *n.* kicking of a football as it falls when dropped from one's hands; **~ off,** fall asleep. **~ out,** cease to participate. **~-out** *n.* one who drops out from a course of study or from conventional society.

droppings *n.pl.* animal dung.

dropsy *n.* disease in which fluid collects in the body. **dropsical** *a.*

dross *n.* scum on metal; impurities, rubbish.

drought *n.* continuous dry weather.

drove *see* **drive.** —*n.* moving herd or flock or crowd.

drown *v.t./i.* kill or be killed by suffocating in water or other liquid; flood, drench; deaden (grief etc.) with drink; overpower (sound) with greater loudness.

drowse *v.i.* be half asleep. **drowsy** *a.,* **drowsily** *adv.,* **drowsiness** *n.*

drubbing *n.* thrashing, defeat.

drudge *n.* person who does laborious or menial work. —*v.i.* do such work. **drudgery** *n.*

drug *n.* substance used in medicine or as a stimulant or narcotic. —*v.t./i.* (p.t. *drugged*) add or give a drug to; take drugs as an addict.

drugstore *n.* (*U.S.*) chemist's shop also selling various goods.

Druid n. priest of an ancient Celtic religion. **Druidism** n.

drum n. percussion instrument, a round frame with skin stretched across; cylindrical object; eardrum. —v.t./i. (p.t. **drummed**) tap or thump continually; din. ~ **up,** obtain by vigorous effort.

drummer n. person who plays drum(s).

drumstick n. stick for beating a drum; lower part of a cooked fowl's leg.

drunk see **drink.** —a. excited or stupefied by alcoholic drink. —n. drunken person.

drunkard n. person who is often drunk.

drunken a. intoxicated, frequently in this condition. **drunkenly** adv., **drunkenness** n.

drupe n. fruit with juicy flesh round a kernel (e.g. peach).

dry a. (**drier, driest**) without water or moisture or rainfall; thirsty; uninteresting; not allowing the sale of alcohol; expressed with pretended seriousness; (of wine) not sweet. —v.t./i. make or become dry; preserve (food) by removing its moisture. ~**-clean** v.t. clean by solvent that evaporates quickly. ~ **rot,** decay of wood that is not ventilated. ~ **run,** (colloq.) dummy run. ~ **up,** dry washed dishes; (colloq.) cease talking. **dryness** n.

dual a. composed of two parts, double. ~ **carriageway,** road with a dividing strip between traffic travelling in opposite directions. **duality** n.

dub v.t. (p.t. **dubbed**) make into a knight by touching on the shoulders with a sword; nickname; replace or add to the sound-track of (a film).

dubbin n. thick grease for softening and waterproofing leather.

dubious a. doubtful. **dubiously** adv.

ducal a. of a duke.

duchess n. duke's wife or widow; woman with the rank of duke.

duchy n. territory of a duke.

duck[1] n. swimming-bird of various kinds; female of this; (colloq.) dear; batsman's score of 0; ducking movement. —v.t./i. push (a person) or dip one's head under water; bob down, esp. to avoid being seen or hit; dodge (a task etc.). ~**-boards** n.pl. boards forming a narrow path, esp. over mud.

duck[2] n. strong linen or cotton cloth; (pl.) trousers made of this.

duckling n. young duck.

duct n. channel or tube conveying liquid or air etc. —v.t. convey through a duct.

ductile a. (of metal) able to be drawn into fine strands.

dud n. & a. (sl.) (thing) that is useless or counterfeit or fails to work.

dude n. (U.S.) dandy. ~ **ranch,** ranch used as a holiday centre.

dudgeon n. indignation.

due a. owed; payable immediately; merited; scheduled to do something or to arrive. —adv. exactly. —n. a person's right, what is owed to him; (pl.) fees. ~ **to,** because of.

duel n. fight or contest between two persons or sides. **duelling** n., **duellist** n.

duet n. musical composition for two performers.

duff a. (sl.) dud.

duffer n. inefficient or stupid person.

duffel n. heavy woollen cloth with thick nap.

dug[1] see **dig.** —a. ~**-out** n. underground shelter; canoe made from a hollowed treetrunk.

dug[2] n. udder, teat.

duke n. nobleman of the highest rank. **dukedom** n.

dulcet a. sounding sweet.

dulcimer n. musical instrument with strings struck by two hammers.

dull a. (**-er, -est**) lacking intelligence or liveliness; stupid; not sharp; not resonant. —v.t./i. make or become dull. **dully** adv., **dullness** n.

dullard n. stupid person.

duly adv. in a correct or suitable way.

dumb a. (**-er, -est**) unable to speak; silent; (colloq.) stupid. ~**-bell** n. short bar with weighted ends, lifted to exercise muscles. **dumbly** adv., **dumbness** n.

dumbfound v.t. astonish, strike dumb with surprise.

dummy n. sham article; model of the human figure, used to display clothes; rubber teat for a baby to suck; card-player whose cards are exposed and played by his partner. —a. sham. ~ **run,** trial run.

dump v.t./i. deposit as rubbish; put down carelessly; (colloq.) abandon; market abroad at a lower price than at home. —n. rubbishheap; temporary store; (colloq.) dull place; (pl.) low spirits.

dumpling n. ball of dough cooked in stew or with fruit inside.

dumpy a. (**-ier, -iest**) short and fat. **dumpiness** n.

dun[1] a. & n. greyish-brown.

dun[2] v.t. (p.t. **dunned**) ask persistently for payment of a debt.

dunce n. person slow at learning.

dune n. mound of drifted sand.

dung n. animal excrement.

dungarees n.pl. overalls of coarse cotton cloth.

dungeon n. strong underground cell for prisoners.

dunk v.t. dip into liquid.

duo n. (pl. **-os**) pair of performers.

duodenum n. part of the intestine next to the stomach. **duodenal** a.

dupe v.t. deceive, trick. —n. duped person.

duplicate[1] /-kət/ n. one of two or more things that are exactly alike; exact copy. —a. exactly like another or others.

duplicate[2] /-keit/ v.t. make or be a duplicate; do twice. **duplication** n.

duplicator n. machine for copying documents.

duplicity n. deceitfulness.

durable a. likely to last. **durables** n.pl. durable goods. **durably** adv., **durability** n.

duration n. time during which a thing continues.

duress n. use of force or threats.

during *prep.* throughout; at a point in the continuance of.

dusk *n.* darker stage of twilight.

dusky *a.* (-*ier*, -*iest*) shadowy, dim; dark-coloured. **duskiness** *n.*

dust *n.* fine particles of earth or other matter. —*v.t./i.* sprinkle with dust or powder; clear of dust by wiping, clean a room etc. thus. **∼-cover** *n.* paper jacket on a book.

dustbin *n.* bin for household rubbish.

duster *n.* cloth for dusting things.

dustman *n.* (pl. -*men*) man employed by a local authority to empty dustbins and cart away rubbish.

dustpan *n.* pan into which dust is brushed from a floor.

dusty *a.* (-*ier*, -*iest*) like dust; covered with dust. **∼ answer**, sharp rejection. **dustiness** *n.*

Dutch *a. & n.* (language) of the Netherlands. **∼ courage**, that obtained by drinking alcohol. **∼ treat**, outing in which each person pays his own expenses. **go ∼**, share expenses thus. **Dutchman** *n.*, **Dutchwoman** *n.*

dutch *n.* (*costermongers' sl.*) wife.

dutiable *a.* on which customs or other duties must be paid.

dutiful *a.* doing one's duty, showing due obedience. **dutifully** *adv.*

duty *n.* moral or legal obligation; task etc. that must be done; tax on certain goods or imports. **on ∼**, actually engaged in one's regular work.

duvet /ˈduveɪ/ *n.* thick soft quilt used instead of bedclothes.

dwarf *n.* (pl. -*fs*) person or thing much below the usual size; (in fairy-tales) small being with magic powers. —*a.* very small. —*v.t.* stunt; make seem small.

dwell *v.i.* (p.t. *dwelt*) live as an inhabitant. **∼ on**, write or speak or think lengthily about. **dweller** *n.*

dwelling *n.* house etc. to live in.

dwindle *v.i.* become less or smaller.

dye *v.t./i.* (pres.p. *dyeing*) colour, esp. by dipping in liquid. —*n.* substance used for dyeing things; colour given by dyeing. **dyer** *n.*

dying *see* **die**[1].

dynamic *a.* of force producing motion; energetic, forceful. **dynamically** *adv.*

dynamics *n.* branch of physics dealing with matter in motion.

dynamite *n.* powerful explosive made of nitroglycerine. —*v.t.* fit or blow up with a charge of dynamite.

dynamo *n.* (pl. -*os*) small generator producing electric current.

dynasty /ˈdɪn-/ *n.* line of hereditary rulers. **dynastic** /-ˈnæ-/ *a.*

dysentery *n.* disease causing severe diarrhoea.

dyslexia *n.* abnormal difficulty in reading and spelling. **dyslexic** *a. & n.*

dyspepsia *n.* indigestion. **dyspeptic** *a.*

dystrophy *n.* progressive weakness of muscles.

E

E. *abbr.* east; eastern.

each *a. & pron.* every one of two or more. **∼ way**, (of a bet) backing a horse to win or be placed.

eager *a.* full of desire, enthusiastic. **eagerly** *adv.*, **eagerness** *n.*

eagle *n.* large bird of prey.

ear[1] *n.* organ of hearing; external part of this; ability to distinguish sounds accurately; listening, attention; ear-shaped thing. **∼-drum** *n.* membrane inside the ear, vibrating when sound-waves strike it. **∼-ring** *n.* ornament worn on the ear-lobe.

ear[2] *n.* seed-bearing part of corn.

earache *n.* pain in the ear-drum.

earl *n.* British nobleman ranking between marquis and viscount. **earldom** *n.*

early *a.* (-*ier*, -*iest*) *a. & adv.* before the usual or expected time; not far on in development or in a series.

earmark *n.* distinguishing mark. —*v.t.* put such mark on; set aside for a particular purpose.

earn *v.t.* get or deserve as a reward for one's work or merit; (of money) gain as interest.

earnest *a.* showing serious feeling or intention. **in ∼**, seriously. **earnestly** *adv.*, **earnestness** *n.*

earnings *n.pl.* money earned.

earphone *n.* headphone.

earshot *n.* range of hearing.

earth *n.* the planet we live on; its surface, dry land; soil; hole of a fox or badger; connection to ground as completion of an electrical circuit. —*v.t.* heap earth over (roots etc.); connect an electrical circuit to earth. **run to ∼**, find after a long search. **earthworm** *n.*

earthen *a.* made of earth or of baked clay.

earthenware *n.* pottery made of coarse baked clay.

earthly *a.* of this earth, of man's life on it.

earthquake *n.* violent movement of part of the earth's crust.

earthwork *n.* bank built of earth.

earthy *a.* like earth or soil; (of humour etc.) gross, coarse.

earwig *n.* small insect with pincers at the end of its body.

ease *n.* freedom from pain or trouble or anxiety; absence of painful effort. —*v.t./i.* relieve from pain etc.; make or become less tight or forceful or burdensome; move gently or gradually.

easel *n.* frame to support a painting or blackboard etc.

east *n.* point on the horizon where the sun rises; direction in which this lies; eastern part. —*a.*

in the east; (of wind) from the east. —*adv.* towards the east.

Easter *n.* festival commemorating Christ's resurrection. ∼ **egg,** chocolate egg given as a gift at Easter.

easterly *a.* towards or blowing from the east.

eastern *a.* of or in the east.

easternmost *a.* furthest east.

eastward *a.* towards the east. **eastwards** *adv.*

easy *a.* (*-ier, -iest*) done or got without great effort; free from pain or trouble or anxiety. —*adv.* in an easy way. ∼ **chair,** large comfortable chair. ∼**going** *a.* tolerant, not strict. **go** ∼ **with,** (*colloq.*) do not use too much of. **easily** *adv.*, **easiness** *n.*

eat *v.t./i.* (p.t. **ate,** p.p. **eaten**) chew and swallow (food); have a meal; destroy gradually. **eater** *n.*

eatable *a.* fit to be eaten.

eatables *n.pl.* food.

eau-de-Cologne / əʊ də kəˈləʊn / *n.* delicate perfume originally made at Cologne.

eaves *n.pl.* overhanging edge of a roof.

eavesdrop *v.i.* (p.t. *-dropped*) listen secretly to a private conversation. **eavesdropper** *n.*

ebb *n.* outward movement of the tide, away from the land; decline. —*v.i.* flow away; decline.

ebony *n.* hard black wood of a tropical tree. —*a.* black as ebony.

ebullient *a.* full of high spirits. **ebulliently** *adv.*, **ebullience** *n.*

eccentric *a.* unconventional; not concentric; not placed centrally; (of an orbit) not circular. —*n.* eccentric person. **eccentrically** *adv.*, **eccentricity** *n.*

ecclesiastical *a.* of the Church or clergy.

echelon /ˈeʃə-/ *n.* staggered formation of troops etc.; level of rank or authority.

echo *n.* (pl. *-oes*) repetition of sound by reflection of sound-waves; close imitation. —*v.t./i.* (p.t. **echoed,** pres.p. **echoing**) repeat by an echo; imitate.

éclair /eɪ-/ *n.* finger-shaped cake of choux pastry with cream filling.

eclectic *a.* choosing or accepting from various sources.

eclipse *n.* blocking of light from one heavenly body by another; loss of brilliance or power etc. —*v.t.* cause an eclipse of; outshine.

ecliptic *n.* sun's apparent path among the stars.

ecology *n.* study of living things in relation to their environment; this relationship. **ecological** *a.*, **ecologist** *n.*

economic /i- or e-/ *a.* of economics; enough to give a good return for money or effort outlaid. **economics** *n.* science of the production and consumption or use of goods or services; (as *pl.*) financial aspects.

economical /i- or e-/ *a.* thrifty, avoiding waste. **economically** *adv.*

economist *n.* expert in economics.

economize *v.i.* use or spend less.

economy *n.* being economical; community's system of using its resources to produce wealth; state of a country's prosperity.

ecru /ˈeɪkru/ *n.* light fawn colour.

ecstasy *n.* intense delight. **ecstatic** *a.*, **ecstatically** *adv.*

ectoplasm *n.* substance supposed to be exuded from a spiritualist medium in a trance.

ecumenical /ikjuˈmen-/ *a.* of the whole Christian Church; seeking world-wide Christian unity.

eczema *n.* skin disease causing scaly itching patches.

eddy *n.* swirling patch of water or air etc. —*v.i.* swirl in eddies.

edelweiss /ˈeɪdlvaɪs/ *n.* alpine plant with white flowers.

edge *n.* sharpened side of a blade; sharpness; line where two surfaces meet at an angle; rim, narrow surface of a thin or flat object; outer limit of an area. —*v.t./i.* border; move gradually. **on** ∼, tense and irritable. **have the** ∼ **on,** (*colloq.*) have an advantage over.

edgeways *adv.* with the edge forwards or outwards.

edging *n.* something placed round an edge to define or decorate it.

edgy *a.* tense and irritable.

edible *a.* suitable for eating.

edict *n.* order proclaimed by authority.

edifice *n.* large building.

edify *v.t.* be an uplifting influence on the mind of. **edification** *n.*

edit *v.t.* (p.t. *edited*) be the editor of; prepare for publication; prepare (a film or recording) by arranging sections in sequence.

edition *n.* form in which something is published; copies printed from one set of type.

editor *n.* person responsible for the contents of a newspaper etc. or a section of this; one who edits.

editorial *a.* of an editor. —*n.* newspaper article giving the editor's comments.

educate *v.t.* train the mind and abilities of; provide such training for. **education** *n.*, **educational** *a.*

educationist *n.* expert in educational methods.

Edwardian /-ˈwɔː-/ *a.* of the reign of Edward VII (1901–10).

E.E.C. *abbr.* European Economic Community.

eel *n.* snake-like fish.

eerie *a.* (*-ier, -iest*) causing a feeling of mystery and fear. **eerily** *adv.*, **eeriness** *n.*

efface *v.t.* rub out, obliterate; make inconspicuous. **effacement** *n.*

effect *n.* change produced by an action or cause; impression; state of being operative; (*pl.*) property. —*v.t.* cause to occur.

effective *a.* producing an effect; striking; operative. **effectively** *adv.*

effectual *a.* answering its purpose. **effectually** *adv.*

effectuate *v.t.* cause to happen.

effeminate *a.* not manly, womanish. **effeminacy** *n.*

effervesce *v.i.* give off bubbles of gas. **effervescence** *n.*, **effervescent** *a.*

effete /-ˈfiːt/ *a.* having lost its vitality.

efficacious *a.* producing the desired result. **efficaciously** *adv.*, **efficacy** *n.*

efficient *a.* producing results with little waste of effort. **efficiently** *adv.*, **efficiency** *n.*

effigy *n.* model of person.

effluent *n.* outflow, sewage.

effort *n.* use of energy; thing produced.

effortless *a.* done without effort.

effrontery *n.* shameless insolence.

effusive *a.* expressing emotion in an unrestrained way. **effusively** *adv.*

e.g. *abbr.* (Latin *exempli gratia*) for example.

egalitarian *a.* & *n.* (person) holding the principle of equal rights for all persons.

egg[1] *n.* reproductive cell produced by a female; bird's (esp. domestic hen's) hard-shelled egg. **~-plant** *n.* aubergine. **egg-shell** *n.*

egg[2] *v.t.* **~ on,** (*colloq.*) urge on.

ego /'i- *or* 'eg-/ *n.* self; self-esteem.

egocentric /eg-/ *a.* self-centred.

egoism /'eg-/ *n.* self-interest, selfishness.

egotism /'eg-/ *n.* practice of talking too much about oneself, conceit, selfishness.

egotist /'eg-/ *n.* conceited person. **egotistic** *a.*, **egotistical** *a.*

egret /'igrɪt/ *n.* a kind of heron.

Egyptian *a.* & *n.* (native) of Egypt.

eh /eɪ/ *int.* (*colloq.*) exclamation of enquiry.

eiderdown *n.* quilt stuffed with soft material.

eight *a.* & *n.* one more than seven (8, VIII); crew of eight. **eighth** *a.* & *n.*

eighteen *a.* & *n.* one more than seventeen (18, XVIII). **eighteenth** *a.* & *n.*

eighty *a.* & *n.* ten times eight (80, LXXX). **eightieth** *a.* & *n.*

eisteddfod /aɪs'teðvod/ *n.* Welsh gathering of poets and musicians for competitions.

either /'aɪ- *or* 'i-/ *a.* & *pron.* one or other of two; each of two. *—adv.* & *conj.* as the first alternative; likewise.

ejaculate *v.t./i.* utter suddenly; eject fluid (esp. semen) from the body. **ejaculation** *n.*

eject *v.t.* send out forcefully; expel. **ejection** *n.*, **ejectment** *n.*, **ejector** *n.*

eke *v.t.* **~ out,** supplement; make (a living) laboriously.

elaborate[1] /-ət/ *a.* with many parts or details. **elaborately** *adv.*

elaborate[2] /-eɪt/ *v.t./i.* work out or describe in detail. **elaboration** *n.*

elapse *v.i.* (of time) pass away.

elastic *a.* going back to its original length or shape after being stretched or squeezed; adaptable. *—n.* cord or material made elastic by interweaving strands of rubber etc. **elasticity** *n.*

elated *a.* feeling very pleased or proud. **elation** *n.*

elbow *n.* joint between the forearm and upper arm; part of a sleeve covering this; sharp bend. *—v.t.* thrust with one's elbow.

elder[1] *a.* older. *—n.* older person; official in certain Churches.

elder[2] *n.* tree with dark berries. **elderberry** *n.* its berry.

elderly *a.* old.

eldest *a.* oldest; first-born.

elect *v.t.* choose by vote; choose as a course. *—a.* chosen.

election *n.* electing; process of electing representative(s), esp. as M.P.s.

electioneering *n.* busying oneself in an election campaign.

elector *n.* person entitled to vote in an election. **electoral** *a.*

electorate *n.* whole body of electors.

electric *a.* of, producing, or worked by electricity; startling. **electrics** *n.pl.* electrical fittings.

electrical *a.* of electricity; startling. **electrically** *adv.*

electrician *n.* person whose job is to deal with electrical equipment.

electricity *n.* form of energy occurring in certain particles and in bodies containing these; supply of electric current.

electrify *v.t.* charge with electricity; convert to the use of electric power; startle. **electrification** *n.*

electrocute *v.t.* kill by electricity. **electrocution** *n.*

electrode *n.* solid conductor through which electricity enters or leaves a vacuum tube etc.

electrolysis /-'trolɪ-/ *n.* decomposition or breaking up (e.g. of hair-roots) by electric current.

electrolyte *n.* solution that conducts electric current, esp. in an electric cell or battery.

electromagnet *n.* magnet consisting of a metal core magnetized by a current-carrying coil round it.

electromagnetic *a.* having both electrical and magnetic properties.

electromotive *a.* producing electric current.

electron *n.* particle with a negative electric charge. **~ microscope,** very powerful one using beams of electrons instead of light.

electronic *a.* produced or worked by a flow of electrons; of electronics. **electronically** *adv.*

electronics *n.* use of electronic devices; (as *pl.*) electronic circuits.

electroplate *v.t.* coat with a thin layer of silver etc. by electrolysis. *—n.* objects plated thus.

elegant *a.* tasteful and dignified. **elegantly** *adv.*, **elegance** *n.*

elegy *n.* sorrowful or serious poem.

element *n.* component part; one of about 100 substances that cannot be split up by chemical means into simpler substances; suitable or satisfying environment; trace; wire that gives out heat in an electrical appliance; (*pl.*) atmospheric forces, basic principles, bread and wine in the Eucharist. **elemental** *a.*

elementary *a.* dealing with the simplest facts of a subject. **~ particle,** one not consisting of simpler ones.

elephant *n.* very large animal with a trunk and ivory tusks.

elephantiasis *n.* disease in which the legs become grossly enlarged.

elephantine /-'fæn-/ *a.* of or like elephants; very large, clumsy.

elevate *v.t.* raise to a higher position or level.

elevation *n.* elevating; altitude; hill; drawing showing one side of a structure.

elevator *n.* thing that hoists something; (*U.S.*) lift.

eleven *a. & n.* one more than ten (11, XI); team of eleven players. **eleventh** *a. & n.*

elevenses *n.pl.* refreshments about 11 a.m.

elf *n.* (pl. *elves*) imaginary small being with magic powers. **elfin** *a.*

elicit *v.t.* draw out (information or a response).

eligible *a.* qualified to be chosen or allowed something; regarded as desirable. **eligibility** *n.*

eliminate *v.t.* get rid of; exclude. **elimination** *n.*, **eliminator** *n.*

elision *n.* omission of part of a word in pronouncing it.

élite /eɪˈliːt/ *n.* group regarded as superior and favoured; size of letters in typewriting.

elixir *n.* fragrant liquid used as medicine or flavouring.

Elizabethan *a.* of Elizabeth I's reign (1558–1603). —*n.* person of this time.

elk *n.* large deer.

ellipse *n.* regular oval.

ellipsis *n.* (pl. *-pses*) omission of words.

elliptical *a.* shaped like an ellipse; containing an ellipsis, having omissions. **elliptically** *adv.*

elm *n.* tree with rough serrated leaves; its wood.

elocution *n.* style or art of speaking.

elongate *v.t.* lengthen. **elongation** *n.*

elope *v.i.* run away secretly with a lover. **elopement** *n.*

eloquence *n.* fluent speaking. **eloquent** *a.*, **eloquently** *adv.*

else *adv.* besides; otherwise.

elsewhere *adv.* somewhere else.

elucidate *v.t.* throw light on (a problem), explain. **elucidation** *n.*

elude *v.t.* escape skilfully from; avoid; escape the memory or understanding of. **elusion** *n.*

elusive *a.* eluding, escaping.

elver *n.* young eel.

emaciated *a.* thin from illness or starvation. **emaciation** *n.*

emanate *v.i.* issue, originate from a source. **emanation** *n.*

emancipate *v.t.* liberate, free from restraint. **emancipation** *n.*

emasculate *v.t.* deprive of force, weaken. **emasculation** *n.*

embalm *v.t.* preserve (a corpse) by using spices or chemicals.

embankment *n.* bank or stone structure to keep a river from spreading or to carry a railway etc.

embargo *n.* (pl. *-oes*) order forbidding commerce or other activity.

embark *v.t./i.* put or go on board ship; begin an undertaking. **embarkation** *n.* embarking on a ship.

embarrass *v.t.* cause to feel awkward or ashamed. **embarrassment** *n.*

embassy *n.* ambassador and his staff; their headquarters.

embattled *a.* prepared for battle; fortified.

embed *v.t.* (p.t. *embedded*) fix firmly in a surrounding mass.

embellish *v.t.* ornament; improve (a story) with invented details. **embellishment** *n.*

embers *n.pl.* small pieces of live coal or wood in a dying fire.

embezzle *v.t.* take (money etc.) fraudulently for one's own use. **embezzlement** *n.*, **embezzler** *n.*

embitter *v.t.* rouse bitter feelings in.

emblazon *v.t.* ornament with heraldic or other devices.

emblem *n.* symbol, design used as a badge etc.

emblematic *a.* serving as an emblem, symbolic.

embody *v.t.* express (principles or ideas) in visible form; incorporate. **embodiment** *n.*

embolden *v.t.* make bold, encourage.

embolism *n.* obstruction of a blood-vessel by a clot or air-bubble.

emboss *v.t.* decorate by a raised design; mould in relief.

embrace *v.t./i.* hold closely and lovingly, hold each other thus; accept, adopt; include. —*n.* act of embracing, hug.

embrocation *n.* liquid for rubbing on the body to relieve aches.

embroider *v.t.* ornament with needlework; embellish (a story). **embroidery** *n.*

embroil *v.t.* involve in an argument or quarrel etc.

embryo *n.* (pl. *-os*) animal developing in a womb or egg; thing in a rudimentary stage. **embryonic** *a.*

emend *v.t.* alter to remove errors. **emendation** *n.*

emerald *n.* bright green precious stone; its colour.

emerge *v.i.* come up or out into view; become known. **emergence** *n.*, **emergent** *a.*

emergency *n.* serious situation needing prompt attention.

emery *n.* coarse abrasive for smoothing wood etc. **∼-board** *n.* strip of cardboard coated with emery, used for filing the nails.

emetic *n.* medicine used to cause vomiting.

emigrate *v.i.* leave one country and go to settle in another. **emigration** *n.*, **emigrant** *n.*

eminence *n.* state of being eminent; piece of rising ground; *His E∼* cardinal's title.

eminent *a.* famous, distinguished; outstanding. **eminently** *adv.*

emir /eˈmɪə(r)/ *n.* Muslim ruler. **emirate** *n.* his territory.

emissary *n.* person sent to conduct negotiations.

emit *v.t.* (p.t. *emitted*) send out (light, heat, fumes, etc.); utter. **emission** *n.*, **emitter** *n.*

emollient *a.* softening, soothing. —*n.* emollient substance.

emolument *n.* fee or salary.

emotion *n.* intense mental feeling.

emotional *a.* of emotion(s); showing great emotion. **emotionally** *adv.*

emotive *a.* rousing emotion.

empathy *n.* ability to identify oneself mentally with, and so understand, a person or thing.

emperor *n.* male ruler of an empire.

emphasis *n.* (pl. *-ases*) special importance; vigour of expression etc.; stress on a sound or word.

emphasize *v.t.* lay emphasis on.

emphatic *a.* using or showing emphasis. **emphatically** *adv.*

empire *n.* group of countries ruled by a supreme authority; controlling power; large organization controlled by one person or group.

empirical *a.* based on observation or experiment, not on theory. **empirically** *adv.*

emplacement *n.* place or platform for a gun or battery of guns.

employ *v.t.* give work to; use the services of; make use of. **employment** *n.*, **employer** *n.*

employee *n.* person employed by another in return for wages.

emporium *n.* (pl. *-a*) centre of commerce; shop.

empower *v.t.* authorize, enable.

empress *n.* woman ruler of an empire; wife or widow of an emperor.

empty *a.* containing nothing; without occupant(s); lacking good sense; (*colloq.*) hungry. —*v.t./i.* make or become empty; transfer contents of. **empties** *n.pl.* emptied boxes or bottles etc. **emptiness** *n.*

emu *n.* large Australian bird resembling an ostrich.

emulate *v.t.* try to do as well as, imitate. **emulation** *n.*, **emulator** *n.*

emulsify *v.t./i.* convert or be converted into emulsion. **emulsifier** *n.*

emulsion *n.* creamy liquid; light-sensitive coating on photographic film.

enable *v.t.* give the means or authority to do something.

enact *v.t.* decree, make into a law; perform (a play etc.). **enactment** *n.*

enamel *n.* glass-like substance for coating metal or pottery; paint that dries hard and glossy; hard outer covering of teeth. —*v.t.* (p.t. *enamelled*) coat with enamel.

enamoured *a.* fond.

en bloc /ã ˈblok/ in a block.

encamp *v.t./i.* settle in a camp.

encampment *n.* camp.

encase *v.t.* enclose in a case.

enchant *v.t.* bewitch. **enchantment** *n.*, **enchantress** *n.fem.*

encircle *v.t.* surround. **encirclement** *n.*

enclave *n.* small territory wholly within the boundaries of another.

enclose *v.t.* put a fence etc. round, shut in on all sides, seclude; shut up in a receptacle; put into an envelope or parcel along with other contents.

enclosure *n.* enclosing; enclosed area; thing enclosed.

encomium /-ˈkəʊ-/ *n.* formal praise.

encompass *v.t.* surround, encircle.

encore /ˈoŋk-/ *int.* & *v.* call for repetition of a performance. —*n.* this call; thing performed in response to it.

encounter *v.t.* meet, esp. by chance; find oneself faced with. —*n.* unexpected meeting; battle.

encourage *v.t.* give hope or confidence or stimulus to; urge. **encouragement** *n.*

encroach *v.i.* intrude on someone's territory or rights etc.; advance beyond proper limits. **encroachment** *n.*

encrust *v.t.* cover with a crust of hard material; ornament with a layer of jewels etc. **encrustation** *n.*

encumber *v.t.* be a burden to, hamper.

encumbrance *n.* thing that encumbers.

encyclical /-ˈsɪk-/ *n.* pope's letter for circulation to churches.

encyclopaedia *n.* book of information on all branches of knowledge or of one subject. **encyclopaedic** *a.*

end *n.* limit; furthest point or part; final part; destruction, death; purpose. —*v.t./i.* bring or come to an end. **make ∼s meet,** keep expenditure within income. **no ∼ of,** (*colloq.*) much, many.

endanger *v.t.* cause danger to.

endear *v.t.* cause to be loved.

endearment *n.* word(s) expressing love.

endeavour *v.t.* & *n.* attempt.

endemic *a.* commonly found in a specified area or people.

ending *n.* final part.

endive /-dɪv/ *n.* curly-leaved plant used as salad; (*U.S.*) chicory.

endless *a.* without end, continual.

endocrine /-kraɪn/ *a.* **∼ gland,** gland pouring secretions straight into the blood, not through a duct.

endorse *v.t.* sign or write comment on (a document); sign the back of (a cheque); enter particulars of an offence on (a driving-licence etc.); confirm, declare approval of. **endorsement** *n.*

endow *v.t.* provide with a permanent income; provide with an ability or quality. **endowment** *n.*

endurable *a.* able to be endured.

endurance *n.* power of enduring.

endure *v.t./i.* experience and survive (pain or hardship); tolerate; last.

enema /ˈen-/ *n.* liquid injected into the rectum through the anus by a syringe.

enemy *n.* one who is hostile to and seeks to harm another.

energetic *a.* full of energy; done with energy. **energetically** *adv.*

energize *v.t.* give energy to; cause electricity to flow into.

energy *n.* capacity for vigorous activity; ability of matter or radiation to do work; oil etc. as fuel.

enervate *v.t.* cause to lose vitality.

enfant terrible /ãfã teˈribl/ person whose behaviour is embarrassing or irresponsible.

enfeeble *v.t.* make feeble.

enfold *v.t.* wrap up; clasp.

enforce *v.t.* compel obedience to. **enforceable** *a.*, **enforcement** *n.*

enfranchise *v.t.* give (a person) the right to vote. **enfranchisement** *n.*

engage *v.t./i.* take as an employee; reserve;

promise; take part; occupy the attention of; begin a battle against; interlock.

engaged *a.* having promised to marry a specified person; occupied; in use.

engagement *n.* engaging something; promise to marry a specified person; appointment; battle.

engaging *a.* attractive.

engender *v.t.* give rise to.

engine *n.* mechanical contrivance using fuel and supplying power; part of a railway train containing this; fire-engine.

engineer *n.* person skilled in engineering; one in charge of machines and engines. —*v.t.* contrive; bring about.

engineering *n.* application of science for the use of power in machines, road-building etc.

English *a.* & *n.* (language) of England. **Englishman** *n.*, **Englishwoman** *n.*

engrave *v.t.* cut (a design) into a hard surface; ornament thus. **engraver** *n.*

engraving *n.* print made from an engraved metal plate.

engross /-ˈgrəʊs/ *v.t.* occupy fully by absorbing the attention.

engulf *v.t.* swamp.

enhance *v.t.* increase the quality or power etc. of. **enhancement** *n.*

enigma *n.* enigmatic person or thing.

enigmatic *a.* mysterious and puzzling. **enigmatically** *adv.*

enjoy *v.t.* get pleasure from; have as an advantage or benefit. ∼ **oneself,** experience pleasure from what one is doing. **enjoyment** *n.*

enjoyable *a.* giving enjoyment.

enlarge *v.t./i.* make or become larger; reproduce on a larger scale. ∼ **upon,** say more about. **enlargement** *n.*, **enlarger** *n.*

enlighten *v.t.* inform; free from ignorance etc. **enlightenment** *n.*

enlist *v.t.* enrol for military service; get the support of. **enlistment** *n.*

enliven *v.t.* make more lively. **enlivenment** *n.*

en masse /ā ˈmæs/ all together.

enmity *n.* hostility of enemies.

ennoble *v.t.* make noble.

enormity *n.* great wickedness or crime.

enormous *a.* very large.

enough *a.*, *adv.*, & *n.* as much or as many as necessary.

enquire *v.t./i.* ask. **enquiry** *n.*

enrage *v.t.* make furious. **enragement** *n.*

enrapture *v.t.* delight intensely.

enrich *v.t.* make richer. **enrichment** *n.*

enrol *v.t./i.* (p.t. *enrolled*) admit as or become a member. **enrolment** *n.*

en route /ā ˈruːt/ on the way.

ensconce *v.t.* establish securely or comfortably.

ensemble /ā ˈsãmbl/ *n.* thing viewed as a whole; set of performers; outfit.

enshrine *v.t.* set in a shrine. **enshrinement** *n.*

ensign *n.* military or naval flag.

enslave *v.t.* make slave(s) of. **enslavement** *n.*

ensnare *v.t.* snare, trap as if in a snare.

ensue *v.i.* happen afterwards or as a result.

ensure *v.t.* make safe or certain.

entail *v.t.* make necessary; leave (land) to a line of heirs so that none can give away or sell it. —*n.* entailing; entailed land. **entailment** *n.*

entangle *v.t.* tangle; entwine and trap. **entanglement** *n.*

entente /ã ˈtãt/ *n.* friendly understanding between countries.

enter *v.t./i.* go or come in or into; put on a list or into a record etc.; register as a competitor.

enteritis *n.* inflammation of the intestines.

enterprise *n.* bold undertaking; initiative; business activity.

enterprising *a.* full of initiative.

entertain *v.t.* amuse, occupy pleasantly; receive with hospitality; have in one's home; consider favourably. **entertainer** *n.*, **entertainment** *n.*

enthral *v.t.* (p.t. *enthralled*) hold spellbound.

enthrone *v.t.* place on a throne. **enthronement** *n.*

enthuse *v.t./i.* fill with or show enthusiasm.

enthusiasm *n.* eager liking or interest, **enthusiastic** *a.*, **enthusiastically** *adv.*

enthusiast *n.* person who is full of enthusiasm for something.

entice *v.t.* attract by offering something pleasant. **enticement** *n.*

entire *a.* complete. **entirely** *adv.*

entirety *n.* **in its** ∼, as a whole.

entitle *v.t.* give a title to (a book etc.); give (a person) a right. **entitlement** *n.*

entity *n.* something that exists as a separate thing.

entomb *v.t.* place in a tomb.

entomology *n.* study of insects. **entomological** *a.*, **entomologist** *n.*

entourage /ontʊˈrɑʒ/ *n.* people accompanying an important person.

entrails *n.pl.* intestines.

entrance[1] /ˈen-/ *n.* entering; door or passage by which one enters; right of admission, fee for this.

entrance[2] /-ˈtrɑns/ *v.t.* fill with intense delight.

entrant *n.* one who enters.

entreat *v.t.* request earnestly or emotionally. **entreaty** *n.*

entrée /ˈontreɪ/ *n.* right or privilege of admission; dish served between the fish and meat courses.

entrench *v.t.* establish firmly. **entrenchment** *n.*

entrepreneur /ontrəprəˈnɜː(r)/ *n.* person who organizes a commercial undertaking, esp. involving risk.

entrust *v.t.* give as a responsibility, place in a person's care.

entry *n.* entering; entrance; alley; item entered in a list etc. or for a competition; entrant.

entwine *v.t.* twine round.

enumerate *v.t.* count, mention (items) one by one. **enumeration** *n.*

enunciate *v.t.* pronounce (words); state clearly. **enunciation** *n.*

envelop /-ˈvel-/ *v.t.* (p.t. *enveloped*) wrap, cover on all sides. **envelopment** *n.*

envelope /ˈen-/ *n.* folded gummed cover for a letter.

enviable *a.* desirable enough to arouse envy. **enviably** *adv.*

envious *a.* full of envy. **enviously** *adv.*

environment *n.* surroundings. **environmental** *a.*

environs /-'vaɪər-/ *n.pl.* surrounding districts, esp. of a town.

envisage *v.t.* imagine; foresee.

envoy *n.* messenger; diplomatic minister ranking below ambassador.

envy *n.* discontent aroused by another's possession of a thing one would like to have; object of this. —*v.t.* feel envy of.

enzyme *n.* protein formed in living cells (or produced synthetically) and assisting chemical processes.

epaulette *n.* ornamental shoulder-piece.

ephemeral /ɪ'fi-/ *a.* lasting only a very short time.

epic *n.* long poem, story, or film about heroic deeds or history. —*a.* of or like an epic.

epicentre *n.* point where an earthquake reaches the earth's surface.

epicure *n.* person who enjoys delicate food and drink. **epicurean** *a.*

epidemic *n.* outbreak of a disease etc. spreading through a community.

epidermis *n.* outer layer of the skin.

epidural /-'djʊər-/ *a. & n.* (anaesthetic) injected round the nerves of the spine, anaesthetizing the lower part of the body.

epigram *n.* short witty saying. **epigrammatic** *a.*

epilepsy *n.* disorder of the nervous system, causing fits. **epileptic** *a. & n.*

epilogue *n.* short concluding section.

Epiphany *n.* festival (6 Jan.) commemorating the showing of Christ to the Magi.

episcopal /ɪ'pɪsk-/ *a.* of or governed by bishop(s).

episode *n.* event forming one part of a sequence; one part of a serial.

epistle *n.* letter.

epitaph *n.* words inscribed on a tomb or describing a dead person.

epithet *n.* descriptive word(s).

epitome /ɪ'pɪtəmɪ/ *n.* thing that shows on a small scale the qualities of something much larger.

epoch /'iːpok/ *n.* particular period. **∼-making** *a.* very important.

equable /'ek-/ *a.* (of climate) even, free from extremes; even-tempered.

equal *a.* same in size, amount, value, etc.; having the same rights or status. —*n.* person or thing equal to another. —*v.t.* (p.t. *equalled*) be the same in size etc. as; do something equal to. **be ∼ to,** have the strength or ability for (a task). **equally** *adv.,* **equality** *n.*

equalize *v.t./i.* make or become equal; equal an opponent's score.

equalizer *n.* equalizing goal etc.

equanimity /ek-/ *n.* calmness of mind or temper.

equate *v.t.* consider to be equal or equivalent.

equation /-ʒən/ *n.* mathematical statement that two expressions are equal; equating, making equal.

equator *n.* imaginary line round the earth at an

equal distance from the North and South Poles. **equatorial** *a.*

equerry /'ekwərɪ/ *n.* official of the British royal household, attending members of the royal family.

equestrian *a.* of horse-riding; on horseback.

equidistant /i-/ *a.* at an equal distance.

equilateral /i-/ *a.* having all sides equal.

equilibrium /i-/ *n.* state of balance.

equine /'ekwaɪn/ *a.* of or like a horse.

equinox /'ekwɪ-/ *n.* time of year when night and day are of equal length. **equinoctial** *a.*

equip *v.t.* (p.t. *equipped*) supply with what is needed.

equipment *n.* equipping; tools or outfit etc. needed for a job or expedition.

equitable /'ek-/ *a.* fair and just.

equity *n.* fairness, impartiality; (*pl.*) stocks and shares not bearing fixed interest.

equivalent *a.* equal in amount, value, or meaning etc. —*n.* equivalent thing. **equivalence** *n.*

equivocal *a.* ambiguous; questionable. **equivocally** *adv.*

equivocate *v.i.* use words ambiguously, esp. to conceal truth. **equivocation** *n.*

era *n.* period of history.

eradicate *v.t.* get rid of completely. **eradication** *n.*

erase *v.t.* rub or wipe out. **eraser** *n.,* **erasure** *n.*

erect *a.* upright; rigid from sexual excitement. —*v.t.* set up, build. **erector** *n.*

erectile *a.* able to become rigid from sexual excitement.

erection *n.* erecting; becoming erect; thing erected, building.

ergonomics *n.* study of work and its environment in order to achieve maximum efficiency.

ermine /-mɪn/ *n.* stoat; its white winter fur.

erode *v.t.* wear away gradually. **erosion** *n.*

erotic *a.* of or arousing sexual desire. **erotically** *adv.,* **eroticism** *n.*

err /ɜː(r)/ *v.i.* (p.t. *erred*) make a mistake; be incorrect; sin.

errand *n.* short journey to take or fetch something; its purpose.

errant /'e-/ *a.* misbehaving; travelling in search of adventure.

erratic *a.* irregular, uneven. **erratically** *adv.*

erratum /e'rɑː-/ *n.* (pl. *-ta*) error in printing or writing.

erroneous *a.* incorrect. **erroneously** *adv.*

error *n.* mistake; being wrong; amount of inaccuracy.

erudite *a.* learned. **erudition** *n.*

erupt *v.i.* break out or through; shoot forth lava. **eruption** *n.*

escalate *v.t./i.* increase in intensity or extent. **escalation** *n.*

escalator *n.* staircase with a line of steps moving up or down.

escalope /'eskələʊp/ *n.* slice of boneless meat, esp. veal.

escapade *n.* piece of reckless or mischievous conduct.

escape *v.t./i.* get free; get out of its container; avoid; be forgotten or unnoticed by; be uttered unintentionally. —*n.* act or means of escaping; temporary distraction from reality or worry.

escapee *n.* one who escapes.

escapement *n.* mechanism regulating the movement of a watch or clock.

escapism *n.* escape from the realities of life. **escapist** *n.* & *a.*

escarpment *n.* steep slope at the edge of a plateau etc.

escort[1] /ˈes-/ *n.* person(s) or ship(s) accompanying another as a protection or honour; man accompanying a woman socially.

escort[2] /-ˈkɔt/ *v.t.* act as escort to.

escudo /-ˈkju-/ *n.* (pl. *-os*) unit of money in Portugal.

escutcheon /ɪˈskʌtʃən/ *n.* shield bearing a coat of arms.

Eskimo *n.* (pl. *-os* or *-o*) member or language of a people living in Arctic regions.

esoteric /esəʊˈte-/ *a.* intended only for people with special knowledge or interest.

espadrille /ˈes-/ *n.* canvas shoe with a sole of plaited fibre.

espalier /ɪˈspæljə(r)/ *n.* trellis; shrub or tree trained on this.

esparto *n.* a kind of grass used in making paper.

especial *a.* special, outstanding. **especially** *adv.*

Esperanto *n.* artificial language designed for international use.

espionage /ˈespɪɒnaʒ/ *n.* spying.

esplanade /-ˈneɪd/ *n.* level area, promenade.

espresso *n.* (pl. *-os*) coffee made by forcing steam through powdered coffee-beans.

esprit de corps /espri də kɔ(r)/ loyalty uniting a group.

espy *v.t.* catch sight of.

Esq. *abbr.* Esquire, courtesy title placed after a man's surname.

essay[1] /ˈe-/ *n.* short literary composition in prose.

essay[2] /-ˈseɪ/ *v.t.* attempt.

essayist *n.* writer of essays.

essence *n.* thing's nature; indispensable quality or element; concentrated extract; liquid perfume.

essential *a.* unable to be dispensed with; of a thing's essence. —*n.* essential thing. **essentially** *adv.*

establish *v.t.* set up; settle; cause people to accept (a custom, belief, etc.); prove.

establishment *n.* establishing; staff of employees; firm or institution; *the E*~, people established in authority and resisting change.

estate *n.* landed property; residential or industrial district planned as a unit; all a person owns, esp. that left at his death; (*old use*) state. ~ **car,** car that can carry passengers and goods in one compartment.

esteem *v.t.* think highly of. —*n.* favourable opinion, respect.

ester *n.* a kind of chemical compound.

estimable *a.* worthy of esteem.

estimate[1] /-ət/ *n.* judgement of a thing's approximate value or amount or cost etc.

estimate[2] /-eɪt/ *v.t.* form an estimate of. **estimation** *n.*

estranged *a.* no longer friendly or loving. **estrangement** *n.*

estuary *n.* mouth of a large river, affected by tides.

etc. *abbr.* = et cetera /-ˈset-/, and other things of the same kind.

etch *v.t.* engrave with acids. **etching** *n.*

eternal *a.* existing always; unchanging. **eternally** *adv.*

eternity *n.* infinite time; endless period of life after death. ~ **ring,** finger-ring with gems set all round it, symbolizing eternity.

ether /ˈiθ-/ *n.* upper air; liquid used as an anaesthetic and solvent.

ethereal /-ˈθɪər-/ *a.* light and delicate; heavenly.

ethic *n.* moral principle. **ethics** *n.* moral philosophy.

ethical *a.* of ethics; morally correct, honourable; (of medicines) not advertised to the public. **ethically** *adv.*

ethnic *a.* of a racial group; resembling the peasant clothes of primitive peoples. **ethnically** *adv.*

ethnology *n.* study of human races and their characteristics. **ethnological** *a.*, **ethnologist** *n.*

ethos /ˈiθɒs/ *n.* characteristic spirit and beliefs.

etiquette *n.* rules of correct behaviour.

etymology *n.* account of a word's origin and development. **etymological** *a.*, **etymologically** *adv.*

eucalyptus *n.* (pl. *-tuses*) evergreen tree with leaves that yield a strong-smelling oil.

Eucharist *n.* Christian sacrament in which bread and wine are consumed; this bread and wine. **Eucharistic** *a.*

eulogize *v.t.* write or utter a eulogy of. **eulogistic** *a.*

eulogy *n.* piece of spoken or written praise.

eunuch *n.* castrated man.

euphemism *n.* mild word(s) substituted for improper or blunt one(s). **euphemistic** *a.*, **euphemistically** *adv.*

euphonium *n.* tenor tuba.

euphony *n.* pleasantness of sounds, esp. in words.

euphoria *n.* feeling of happiness. **euphoric** *a.*

Eurasian *a.* of Europe and Asia; of mixed European and Asian parentage. —*n.* Eurasian person.

eureka /jʊəˈriːkə/ *int.* I have found it.

European *a.* of Europe or its people. —*n.* European person.

euthanasia *n.* bringing about a gentle and easy death, esp. to end suffering.

evacuate *v.t.* send away from a place considered dangerous; empty of contents or occupants. **evacuation** *n.*

evacuee *n.* evacuated person.

evade *v.t.* avoid by cleverness or trickery.

evaluate *v.t.* find out or state the value of; assess. **evaluation** *n.*

evangelical *a.* of or preaching the gospel.

evangelist *n.* author of a Gospel; person who preaches the gospel.

evaporate *v.t./i.* turn into vapour; cease to exist. **evaporated milk,** milk thickened by partial evaporation and tinned. **evaporation** *n.*

evasion *n.* evading; evasive answer or excuse.

evasive *a.* evading; not frank. **evasively** *adv.*, **evasiveness** *n.*

eve *n.* evening or day just before a festival; time just before an event.

even *a.* level, smooth; uniform; calm; equal; (of an amount) not involving fractions; (of a number) divisible by two without remainder. —*v.t./i.* make or become even. —*adv.* (used for emphasis or in comparing things). **evenly** *adv.*, **evenness** *n.*

evening *n.* latter part of the day, before nightfall.

evensong *n.* service of evening prayer in the Church of England.

event *n.* something that happens, esp. something important; item in a sports programme.

eventful *a.* full of incidents.

eventide *n.* (*old use*) evening.

eventual *a.* coming at last, ultimate. **eventually** *adv.*

eventuality *n.* possible event.

ever *adv.* always; at any time; in any possible way. ∼ **so,** (*colloq.*) very; very much.

evergreen *a.* having green leaves throughout the year. —*n.* evergreen tree or shrub.

everlasting *a.* lasting for ever or for a very long time.

evermore *adv.* for ever, always.

every *a.* each one without exception; each in a series; all possible. ∼ **other,** with one between each two selected.

everybody *pron.* every person.

everyday *a.* worn or used on ordinary days; usual, commonplace.

everyone *pron.* everybody.

everything *pron.* all things; all that is important.

everywhere *adv.* in every place.

evict *v.t.* expel (a tenant) by legal process. **eviction** *n.*

evidence *n.* anything that establishes a fact or gives reason for believing something; statements made in a lawcourt to support a case. —*v.t.* be evidence of. **be in** ∼, be conspicuous.

evident *a.* obvious to the eye or mind. **evidently** *adv.*

evil *a.* morally bad; harmful; very unpleasant. —*n.* evil thing, sin, harm. **evilly** *adv.*

evoke *v.t.* bring to one's mind, produce. **evocation** *n.*, **evocative** *a.*

evolution *n.* process of developing into a different form; origination of living things by development from earlier forms. **evolutionary** *a.*

evolve *v.t./i.* develop or work out gradually. **evolvement** *n.*

ewe *n.* female sheep.

ex *prep.* excluding; (of goods) as sold from.

ex- *pref.* former.

exacerbate /-ˈsæs-/ *v.t.* make worse; irritate. **exacerbation** *n.*

exact[1] *a.* accurate; giving all details. **exactness** *n.*

exact[2] *v.t.* insist on and obtain. **exaction** *n.*

exacting *a.* making great demands, requiring great effort.

exactitude *n.* exactness.

exactly *adv.* in an exact manner; quite so, as you say.

exaggerate *v.t.* make seem larger or better or worse etc. than it really is. **exaggeration** *n.*

exalt *v.t.* raise in rank or power etc.; praise highly; make joyful. **exaltation** *n.*

exam *n.* (*colloq.*) examination.

examination *n.* examining; testing of knowledge etc. by this.

examine *v.t.* look at closely, esp. in order to learn about or from; put questions or exercises to (a person) to test his knowledge or ability; question formally. **examiner** *n.*

examinee *n.* person being tested in an examination.

example *n.* fact illustrating a general rule; thing showing what others of the same kind are like; person or thing worthy of imitation. **make an** ∼ **of,** punish as a warning to others.

exasperate *v.t.* annoy greatly. **exasperation** *n.*

excavate *v.t.* make (a hole) by digging, dig out; reveal by digging. **excavation** *n.*, **excavator** *n.*

exceed *v.t.* be greater than; go beyond the limit of.

exceedingly *adv.* very.

excel *v.t./i.* (p.t. *excelled*) be or do better than; be very good at something.

excellent *a.* extremely good. **excellently** *adv.*, **excellence** *n.*

except *prep.* not including. —*v.t.* exclude from a statement etc.

excepting *prep.* except.

exception *n.* excepting; thing that does not follow the general rule. **take** ∼ **to,** object to.

exceptionable *a.* open to objection.

exceptional *a.* very unusual; outstandingly good. **exceptionally** *adv.*

excerpt[1] /ˈek-/ *n.* extract from a book or film or piece of music etc.

excerpt[2] /-ˈsɜpt/ *v.t.* select excerpts from.

excess *n.* exceeding of due limits; amount by which one quantity etc. exceeds another; agreed amount deductible by an insurer from the total claimed by the insured person; (*pl.*) immoderation in eating or drinking.

excessive *a.* too much. **excessively** *adv.*

exchange *v.t./i.* give or receive in place of another thing or from another person. —*n.* exchanging; price at which one currency is exchanged for another; place where merchants or stockbrokers assemble to do business; central telephone office where connections are made between lines involved in calls. **exchangeable** *a.*

exchequer *n.* government department in charge of national revenue; country's or person's supply of money.

excise[1] /ˈeksaɪz/ *n.* duty or tax on certain goods and licences.

excise[2] /-ˈsaɪz/ *v.t.* cut out or away. **excision** *n.*

excitable *a.* easily excited. **excitability** *n.*

excite *v.t.* rouse the emotions of, make eager; cause (a feeling or reaction); stimulate to activity. **excitement** *n.*

exclaim *v.t./i.* cry out or utter suddenly from pain, pleasure, etc.

exclamation *n.* exclaiming; word(s) exclaimed. ∼ **mark,** punctuation mark ! placed after an exclamation.

exclude *v.t.* keep out from a place or group or privilege etc.; omit, ignore as irrelevant; make impossible. **exclusion** *n.*

exclusive *a.* excluding others; selective; catering only for the wealthy; not obtainable elsewhere. ∼ **of,** not including. **exclusively** *adv.,* **exclusiveness** *n.*

excommunicate *v.t.* cut off from participation in a Church or its sacraments. **excommunication** *n.*

excrement /ˈekskrɪ-/ *n.* faeces.

excrescence /ɪksˈkres-/ *n.* outgrowth on an animal body or plant; ugly addition, e.g. to a building.

excreta /-ˈkri-/ *n.pl.* matter (esp. faeces) excreted from the body.

excrete *v.t.* expel (waste matter) from the body or tissues. **excretion** *n.,* **excretory** *a.*

excruciating *a.* intensely painful.

exculpate /ˈeks-/ *v.t.* free from blame. **exculpation** *n.*

excursion *n.* short journey or outing, returning afterwards to the starting-point.

excusable *a.* able to be excused. **excusably** *adv.*

excuse[1] /-ˈkjuz/ *v.t.* pardon, overlook (a slight offence); be a justification of (a fault or error); release from an obligation.

excuse[2] /-ˈkjus/ *n.* reason put forward for excusing a fault etc.

ex-directory *a.* deliberately not listed in a telephone directory.

execrable /ˈeksɪ-/ *a.* abominable. **execrably** *adv.*

execute *v.t.* carry out (an order); perform; produce (a work of art); put (a condemned person) to death. **execution** *n.,* **executant** *n.*

executioner *n.* one who executes condemned person(s).

executive /ɪgˈzek-/ *n.* person or group with managerial powers, or with authority to put government decisions into effect. —*a.* having such power or authority.

executor /ɪgˈzek-/ *n.* person appointed by a testator to carry out the terms of his will. **executrix** *n.fem.*

exemplary *a.* fit to be imitated; serving as a warning to others.

exemplify *v.t.* serve as an example of.

exempt *a.* free from a customary obligation or payment etc. —*v.t.* make exempt. **exemption** *n.*

exercise *n.* use of one's powers or rights; activity, esp. designed to train the body or mind, or requiring physical exertion. —*v.t.* use (powers etc.); take or cause to take exercise, train by exercises; perplex, worry. ∼ **book,** book for writing in, with limp covers.

exert *v.t.* bring into use. ∼ **oneself,** make an effort.

exertion *n.* exerting; great effort.

exeunt /ˈeksɪənt/ (*stage direction*) they leave the stage.

ex gratia /eks ˈgreɪʃə/ done or given as a concession, without legal obligation.

exhale *v.t./i.* breathe out. **exhalation** *n.*

exhaust *v.t.* use up completely; tire out. —*n.* expulsion of waste gases from an engine etc.; these gases; device through which they are expelled.

exhaustion *n.* exhausting; being tired out.

exhaustive *a.* thorough, trying all possibilities. **exhaustively** *adv.*

exhibit *v.t.* display, present for the public to see. —*n.* thing exhibited. **exhibitor** *n.*

exhibition *n.* exhibiting; public display.

exhibitionism *n.* tendency to behave in a way designed to attract attention. **exhibitionist** *n.*

exhilarate *v.t.* make joyful or lively. **exhilaration** *n.*

exhort *v.t.* urge or advise earnestly. **exhortation** *n.*

exhume /ɪgˈzjum/ *v.t.* dig up (a buried corpse etc.). **exhumation** *n.*

exigency /ˈeks-/ *n.* urgent need; emergency.

exigent /ˈeks-/ *a.* urgent; requiring much, exacting.

exiguous /egˈzɪg-/ *a.* very small.

exile *n.* being sent away from one's country as a punishment; long absence from one's country or home; exiled person. —*v.t.* send into exile.

exist *v.i.* have place as part of what is real; occur in specified conditions; continue living. **existence** *n.,* **existent** *a.*

existentialism *n.* philosophical theory emphasizing that man is free to choose his actions.

exit (*stage direction*) he or she leaves the stage. —*n.* departure from a stage or place; way out.

exodus *n.* departure of many people.

ex officio /eks əˈfɪʃɪəʊ/ because of his official position.

exonerate *v.t.* declare or show to be blameless. **exoneration** *n.*

exorbitant *a.* (of a price or demand) much too great.

exorcize *v.t.* drive out (an evil spirit) by prayer; free (a person or place) of an evil spirit. **exorcism** *n.,* **exorcist** *n.*

exotic *a.* introduced from abroad; colourful, unusual. **exotically** *adv.*

expand *v.t./i.* make or become larger; spread out; give a fuller account of, write out in full; become genial. **expansion** *n.*

expanse *n.* wide area or extent.

expansive *a.* able to expand; genial, communicative. **expansiveness** *n.*

expatiate /-ˈpeɪʃɪeɪt/ *v.i.* speak or write at length about a subject.

expatriate /-ˈpætrɪət/ *a.* living abroad. —*n.* expatriate person.

expect *v.t.* think or believe that (a person or thing) will come or (a thing) will happen; wish for and be confident of receiving; think, suppose. **expecting a baby,** pregnant.

expectant *a.* filled with expectation. ~ **mother,** pregnant woman. **expectantly** *adv.*, **expectancy** *n.*

expectation *n.* expecting; thing expected; probability.

expectorant *n.* medicine for causing a person to expectorate.

expectorate *v.i.* cough and spit phlegm; spit. **expectoration** *n.*

expedient *a.* suitable, advisable; advantageous rather than right or just. **expediency** *n.*

expedite /ˈeks-/ *v.t.* help or hurry the progress of.

expedition *n.* journey or voyage for a purpose; people or ships etc. making this; promptness, speed.

expeditionary *a.* of or used in an expedition.

expeditious *a.* speedy and efficient. **expeditiously** *adv.*

expel *v.t.* (p.t. *expelled*) send or drive out; compel to leave.

expend *v.t.* spend; use up.

expendable *a.* able to be expended; not worth saving.

expenditure *n.* expending of money etc.; amount expended.

expense *n.* cost; cause of spending money; (*pl.*) reimbursement.

expensive *a.* involving great expenditure; costing or charging more than average. **expensively** *adv.*, **expensiveness** *n.*

experience *n.* observation of fact(s) or event(s), practice in doing something; knowledge or skill gained by this. —*v.t.* feel or have an experience of.

experienced *a.* having knowledge or skill gained by much experience.

experiment *n.* & *v.i.* test to discover how a thing works or what happens, or to demonstrate a known fact. **experimentation** *n.*

experimental *a.* of or used in experiments; still being tested. **experimentally** *adv.*

expert *n.* person with great knowledge or skill in a particular thing. —*a.* having great knowledge or skill. **expertly** *adv.*

expertise /-ˈtiz/ *n.* expert knowledge or skill.

expiate *v.t.* make amends for (wrongdoing). **expiation** *n.*

expire *v.t./i.* breathe out (air); die; come to the end of a period of validity. **expiration** *n.*

expiry *n.* termination of validity.

explain *v.t.* make clear, show the meaning of; account for. **explanation** *n.*, **explanatory** *a.*

expletive /-ˈplitɪv/ *n.* violent exclamation, oath.

explicable /ˈeks- or -ˈplɪ/ *a.* able to be explained.

explicit /-ˈsplɪs-/ *a.* stated plainly. **explicitly** *adv.*, **explicitness** *n.*

explode *v.t./i.* expand and break with a loud noise; cause to do this; burst out, show sudden violent emotion; increase suddenly; destroy (a theory) by showing it to be false. **explosion** *n.*

exploit[1] /ˈeks-/ *n.* bold or notable deed.

exploit[2] /-ˈsplɔɪt/ *v.t.* make good use of; use selfishly. **exploitation** *n.*

explore *v.t.* travel into (a country etc.) in order to learn about it; examine. **exploration** *n.*, **exploratory** /-ˈplɔ-/ *a.*, **explorer** *n.*

explosive *a.* & *n.* (substance) able or liable to explode.

exponent /-ˈpəʊ-/ *n.* person who expounds something; one who favours a specified theory etc.

export *v.t.* send (goods etc.) to another country for sale. —*n.* exporting; thing exported. **exportation** *n.*, **exporter** *n.*

expose *v.t.* leave uncovered or unprotected; subject to a risk etc.; allow light to reach (photographic film); reveal. **exposure** *n.*

exposition *n.* expounding; explanation; large exhibition.

expostulate *v.i.* protest, remonstrate. **expostulation** *n.*

expound *v.t.* set forth or explain in detail.

express[1] *a.* definitely stated; travelling rapidly, designed for high speed. —*adv.* at high speed. —*n.* train or bus travelling rapidly to its destination with few or no stops.

express[2] *v.t.* make (feelings or qualities) known; put into words; represent by symbols; press or squeeze out.

expression *n.* expressing; word or phrase; look or manner that expresses feeling; mathematical symbols expressing a quantity.

expressionism *n.* style of painting, drama, or music seeking to express feelings rather than represent objects realistically. **expressionist** *n.*

expressive *a.* expressing something; full of expression. **expressively** *adv.*

expressly *adv.* explicitly; for a particular purpose.

expulsion *n.* expelling; being expelled.

expunge *v.t.* wipe out.

expurgate /ˈeks-/ *v.t.* remove (objectionable matter) from (a book etc.). **expurgation** *n.*

exquisite /ˈeks-/ *a.* having exceptional beauty; acute, keenly felt. **exquisitely** *adv.*

ex-service *a.* formerly a member of the armed services.

exserviceman *n.* (pl. *-men*) former member of armed services.

extant /-ˈstæ-/ *a.* still existing.

extempore /-ˈstempərɪ/ *a.* & *adv.* impromptu, without preparation.

extend *v.t./i.* make longer; stretch; reach, be continuous; enlarge; offer, grant.

extendible, extensible *adjs.* able to be extended.

extension *n.* extending; extent, range; additional part or period; subsidiary telephone, its number; extramural instruction.

extensive *a.* extending far, large in area or scope. **extensively** *adv.*

extent *n.* space over which a thing extends; scope; large area.

extenuate *v.t.* make (an offence) seem less great by providing a partial excuse. **extenuation** *n.*

exterior *a.* on or coming from the outside. —*n.* exterior surface or appearance.

exterminate *v.t.* destroy all members or examples of. **extermination** *n.*

external *a.* of or on the outside; from an independent source. **externally** *adv.*

extinct *a.* no longer burning or active or existing in living form.

extinction *n.* extinguishing; making or becoming extinct.

extinguish *v.t.* put out (a light or flame); end the existence of.

extinguisher *n.* device for discharging liquid chemicals or foam to extinguish a fire.

extol *v.t.* (p.t. *extolled*) praise enthusiastically.

extort *v.t.* obtain by force or threats. **extortion** *n.*

extortionate *a.* excessively high in price, exorbitant.

extra *a.* additional, more than is usual or expected. —*adv.* more than usually; in addition. —*n.* extra thing; person employed as one of a crowd in a cinema film.

extract[1] /-'stræ-/ *v.t.* take out or obtain by force or effort; obtain (juice etc.) by suction or pressure or chemical treatment. **extractor** *n.*

extract[2] /'eks-/ *n.* substance extracted from another; passage from a book, play, film, or music.

extraction *n.* extracting; lineage.

extraditable *a.* liable to or warranting extradition.

extradite *v.t.* hand over or obtain (an accused person) for trial or punishment in the country where a crime was committed. **extradition** *n.*

extramarital *a.* of sexual relationships outside marriage.

extramural *a.* for students who are non-resident or not members of a university.

extraneous /-'treɪ-/ *a.* of external origin; not belonging to the subject being discussed.

extraordinary *a.* very unusual or remarkable; beyond what is usual. **extraordinarily** *adv.*

extrapolate /-'træ-/ *v.t./i.* estimate on the basis of available data. **extrapolation** *n.*

extra-sensory *a.* achieved by some means other than the known senses.

extravagant *a.* spending or using much more than is necessary; going beyond what is reasonable. **extravagantly** *adv.*, **extravagance** *n.*

extravaganza /-'gæn-/ *n.* fanciful composition; lavish spectacular film or theatrical production.

extreme *a.* very great or intense; at the end(s), outermost; going to great lengths in actions or views. —*n.* end; extreme degree or act or condition. **extremely** *adv.*

extremist *n.* person holding extreme views, esp. in politics.

extremity /-'strem-/ *n.* extreme point; end; extreme degree of need or danger etc.; (*pl.*) hands and feet.

extricable /'eks-/ *a.* able to be extricated.

extricate *v.t.* take out or release from an entanglement or difficulty etc. **extrication** *n.*

extrovert *n.* lively sociable person.

extrude *v.t.* thrust or squeeze out. **extrusion** *n.*

exuberant *a.* full of high spirits; growing profusely. **exuberantly** *adv.*, **exuberance** *n.*

exude *v.t./i.* ooze; give off like sweat or a smell. **exudation** *n.*

exult *v.i.* rejoice greatly. **exultant** *a.* exulting. **exultation** *n.*

eye *n.* organ of sight; iris of this; region round it; power of seeing; thing like an eye, spot, hole. —*v.t.* (p.t. *eyed*, pres.p. *eyeing*) look at, watch. **~-opener** *n.* thing that brings enlightenment or great surprise. **~-shade** *n.* device to protect the eyes from strong light. **~-shadow** *n.* cosmetic applied to the skin round the eyes. **~-tooth** *n.* canine tooth in the upper jaw, below the eye.

eyeball *n.* whole of the eye within the eyelids.

eyebrow *n.* fringe of hair on the ridge above the eye-socket.

eyeful *n.* something thrown or blown into one's eye; (*colloq.*) thorough look, remarkable or attractive sight.

eyelash *n.* one of the hairs fringing the eyelids.

eyeless *a.* without eyes.

eyelet *n.* small hole; ring strengthening this.

eyelid *n.* either of the two folds of skin that can be moved together to cover the eye.

eyepiece *n.* lens(es) to which the eye is applied in a telescope or microscope etc.

eyesight *n.* ability to see; range of vision.

eyesore *n.* ugly object.

eyewash *n.* (*sl.*) talk or behaviour intended to give a misleadingly good impression.

eyewitness *n.* person who actually saw something happen.

eyrie /'aɪrɪ/ *n.* eagle's nest; house etc. perched high up.

F

F *abbr.* Fahrenheit.

fable *n.* story not based on fact, often conveying a moral.

fabric *n.* cloth or knitted material; plastic used similarly; walls etc. of a building.

fabricate *v.t.* construct, manufacture; invent (a story etc.). **fabrication** *n.*

fabulous *a.* incredibly great; (*colloq.*) marvellous. **fabulously** *adv.*

façade /fə'sɑd/ *n.* principal (esp. front) face of a building; outward appearance.

face *n.* front of the head; expression shown by its features; grimace; outward aspect; front or right side; dial-plate of a clock; coal-face. —*v.t./i.* have or turn the face towards; meet firmly; meet as an opponent; put a facing on. **∼-flannel** *n.* cloth for washing one's face. **∼-lift** *n.* operation for tightening the skin of the face; alteration that improves the appearance. **∼-pack** *n.* paste for improving the skin of the face.

faceless *a.* without identity; purposely not identifiable.

facer *n.* sudden great difficulty.

facet /'fæsɪt/ *n.* one of many sides of a cut stone or jewel; one aspect.

facetious *a.* intended or intending to be amusing. **facetiously** *adv.*, **facetiousness** *n.*

facia /'feɪʃə/ *n.* dashboard.

facial *a.* of the face. —*n.* beauty treatment for the face.

facile /'fæsaɪl/ *a.* done or doing something easily; superficial.

facilitate *v.t.* make easy or easier. **facilitation** *n.*

facility *n.* ease, absence of difficulty; means for doing something.

facing *n.* covering made of different material.

facsimile *n.* a reproduction of a document etc.

fact *n.* thing known to have happened or to be true or to exist. **in ∼,** in reality, indeed.

faction *n.* small united group within a larger one.

factor *n.* circumstance that contributes towards a result; one of the numbers etc. by which a given number can be divided exactly; (*Sc.*) land-agent.

factory *n.* building(s) in which goods are manufactured.

factotum /-'təʊt-/ *n.* servant or assistant doing all kinds of work.

factual *a.* based on or containing facts. **factually** *adv.*

faculty *n.* any of the powers of the body or mind; department teaching a specified subject in a university or college; authorization given by Church authorities.

fad *n.* person's particular like or dislike; craze.

faddy *a.* having petty likes and dislikes, esp. about food.

fade *v.t./i.* lose or cause to lose colour, freshness, or vigour; disappear gradually; cause

(a cinema picture or sound) to decrease or increase gradually.

faeces /'fiːsiz/ *n.pl.* waste matter discharged from the bowels.

fag *v.t./i.* (p.t. *fagged*) toil; make tired. —*n.* tiring work, drudgery; exhaustion; pupil who does services for a senior in certain schools; (*sl.*) cigarette.

fagged *a.* tired.

faggot *n.* tied bundle of sticks or twigs; ball of chopped seasoned liver, baked or fried.

Fahrenheit *a.* of a temperature scale with the freezing-point of water at 32° and boiling-point at 212°.

faience /faɪ'ɑns/ *n.* painted glazed earthenware.

fail *v.t./i.* be unsuccessful; become weak, cease functioning; neglect or be unable; disappoint; become bankrupt; declare to be unsuccessful. —*n.* failure.

failing *n.* weakness or fault. —*prep.* in default of.

failure *n.* failing, lack of success; person or thing that fails.

faint *a.* (*-er, -est*) indistinct; not intense; weak, feeble; about to faint. —*v.i.* collapse unconscious. —*n.* act or state of fainting. **∼-hearted** *a.* timid. **faintly** *adv.*, **faintness** *n.*

fair[1] *n.* gathering for a sale of goods, often with entertainments; exhibition of commercial goods; funfair. **∼-ground** *n.* open space where a fair is held.

fair[2] *a.* (*-er, -est*) light in colour, having light-coloured hair; (*old use*) beautiful; (of weather) fine, (of wind) favourable; just, unbiased; of moderate quality or amount. —*adv.* fairly. **∼ play,** equal opportunities etc. for all.

Fair Isle /aɪl/ knitted or knitwear in a pattern of coloured wools.

fairly *adv.* in a fair manner; moderately; actually.

fairway *n.* navigable channel; smooth part of a golf-course between tee and green.

fairy *n.* imaginary small being with magical powers. **∼ godmother,** benefactress. **∼ lights,** strings of small coloured lights used as decorations. **∼ story, ∼-tale** *n.* tale about fairies or magic; falsehood.

fairyland *n.* world of fairies; very beautiful place.

fait accompli /feɪt ə'kɒmpliː/ thing already done and not reversible.

faith *n.* reliance, trust; belief in religious doctrine; loyalty, sincerity. **∼-healing** *n.* healing by prayer. **∼-healer** *n.*

faithful *a.* loyal, trustworthy; true, accurate. **faithfully** *adv.*, **faithfulness** *n.*

fake *n.* thing that looks genuine but is not, a forgery; person pretending to be something he is not. —*a.* faked. —*v.t.* make an imitation of; pretend. **faker** *n.*

fakir /'feɪkɪə(r)/ *n.* Muslim or Hindu religious beggar regarded as a holy man.

falcon /ˈfɔlkən/ n. a kind of small hawk.
falconry n. breeding and training of hawks.

fall v.i. (p.t. *fell*, p.p. *fallen*) come or go down freely; lose one's position or office; decrease; die in battle; pass into a specified state; occur; (of the face) show dismay; be captured or conquered. —n. falling; amount of this; (*U.S.*) autumn; (*pl.*) waterfall; *the F~* (*of man*), Adam's sin and its results. **~ back on**, retreat or have recourse to. **~ for**, (*colloq.*) fall in love with; be deceived by. **~ in**, take one's place in a military formation, order to do this; (of a lease) end. **~ in with**, meet by chance; agree to. **~ off**, decrease, degenerate. **~ out**, quarrel; happen; leave one's place in a military formation, order to do this. **~out** n. airborne radioactive debris. **~ short**, be inadequate. **~ through**, (of a plan) fail to be achieved. **~ to**, begin working, fighting, or eating.

fallacious /-ˈleɪʃəs/ a. containing a fallacy.
fallacy n. false belief or reasoning.
fallible a. liable to make mistakes. **fallibility** n.
fallow[1] a. (of land) left unplanted for a time.
fallow[2] a. **~ deer**, deer of pale brownish yellow colour.
false a. incorrect; deceitful, unfaithful; not genuine, sham. **falsely** adv., **falseness** n.
falsehood n. lie(s).
falsetto n. (pl. -os) voice above one's natural range.
falsify v.t. alter fraudulently; misrepresent. **falsification** n.
falsity n. falseness; falsehood.
falter v.i. go or function unsteadily; become weaker; speak hesitantly.
fame n. condition of being known to many people; good reputation.
famed a. famous.
familiar a. well known; well acquainted; too informal. **familiarly** adv., **familiarity** n.
familiarize v.t. make familiar. **familiarization** n.
family n. parents and their children; a person's children; set of relatives; group of related plants or animals, or of things that are alike.
famine n. extreme scarcity (esp. of food) in a region.
famished, famishing adjs. suffering from extreme hunger.
famous a. known to very many people.
famously adv. (*colloq.*) extremely well.
fan[1] n. device waved in the hand or operated mechanically to create a current of air. —v.t. (p.t. *fanned*) drive a current of air upon; spread from a central point. **~ belt**, belt driving a fan that cools a car engine.
fan[2] n. enthusiastic admirer or supporter. **~ mail**, letters from fans.
fanatic n. person filled with excessive enthusiasm. **fanatical** a., **fanatically** adv.
fanaticism n. excessive enthusiasm.
fancier n. person who likes animals or plants, or who breeds or grows these as a hobby.
fanciful a. imaginative; imaginary. **fancifully** adv.
fancy n. imagination; thing imagined, un-

founded idea; desire; liking. —a. ornamental, elaborate; arbitrary. —v.t. imagine; suppose; (*colloq.*) like, find attractive. **~ dress**, costume representing an animal, historical character, etc., worn for a party.
fanfare n. short showy or ceremonious sounding of trumpets.
fang n. long sharp tooth; snake's tooth that injects venom.
fanlight n. small window above a door or larger window.
fantasia /-ˈteɪz-/ n. imaginative musical or other composition.
fantasize v.i. day-dream.
fantastic a. absurdly fanciful; (*colloq.*) excellent. **fantastically** adv.
fantasy n. imagination; thing imagined; fanciful design, fantasia.
far adv. at or to or by a great distance. —a. distant, remote. **Far East**, countries of east and south-east Asia. **~-fetched** a. not obvious, very unlikely.
farce n. light comedy; absurd and useless proceedings, pretence. **farcical** a., **farcically** adv.
fare n. price charged for a passenger to travel; passenger paying this; food provided. —v.i. have good or bad treatment etc., progress.
farewell int. & n. goodbye.
farm n. unit of land used for raising crops or livestock; farmhouse. —v.t./i. grow crops, raise livestock; use (land) for this. **~ out**, delegate (work).
farmer n. owner or manager of a farm.
farmhouse n. farmer's house on a farm.
farmstead /-sted/ n. farm and its buildings.
farmyard n. enclosed area round farm buildings.
farrago /-ˈrɑːgəʊ/ n. hotchpotch.
farrier n. smith who shoes horses.
farrow v.i. give birth to young pigs. —n. farrowing; litter of pigs.
farther adv. & a. at or to a greater distance, more remote.
farthest adv. & a. at or to the greatest distance, most remote.
farthing n. former coin worth one quarter of a penny.
fascicle /ˈfæsɪkəl/ n. one section of a book that is issued in sections.
fascinate v.t. attract and hold the interest of; charm greatly; make (a victim) powerless by a fixed look. **fascination** n., **fascinator** n.
fascism n. system of extreme right-wing dictatorship. **fascist** n.
fashion n. manner or way of doing something; style popular at a given time.
fashionable a. in or using a currently popular style; used by stylish people. **fashionably** adv.
fast[1] a. (-er, -est) moving or done quickly; allowing quick movement; showing a time ahead of the correct one; pleasure-seeking and immoral; firmly fixed. —adv. quickly; firmly, tightly.
fast[2] v.i. go without food or without certain kinds of food. —n. fasting; day or season appointed for this.

fasten *v.t./i.* fix firmly, tie or join together; become fastened.

fastener, fastening *ns.* device used for fastening something.

fastidious *a.* choosing only what is good; easily disgusted. **fastidiously** *adv.*, **fastidiousness** *n.*

fastness *n.* being fast or firmly fixed; stronghold, fortress.

fat *n.* white or yellow substance found in animal bodies and certain seeds. —*a.* (*fatter, fattest*) containing much fat; excessively plump; fattened; thick; profitable. ∼-**head** *n.* (*sl.*) stupid person. **a** ∼ **lot**, (*sl.*) very little. **fatness** *n.*

fatal *a.* causing or ending in death or disaster; fateful. **fatally** *adv.*

fatalist *n.* person who submits to what happens, regarding it as inevitable. **fatalism** *n.*, **fatalistic** *a.*

fatality /fəˈtæl-/ *n.* death caused by accident or in war etc.

fate *n.* power thought to control all events; person's destiny.

fated *a.* destined by fate; doomed.

fateful *a.* bringing great usu. unpleasant events.

father *n.* male parent or ancestor; founder, originator; title of certain priests; *the F*∼, God, first person of the Trinity. —*v.t.* beget; originate; fix the paternity of (a child) on person. ∼-**in-law** *n.* (pl. ∼*s-in-law*) father of one's wife or husband. **fatherhood** *n.*, **fatherly** *adj.*

fatherland *n.* one's native country.

fatherless *a.* without a living or known father.

fathom *n.* measure (6 ft.) of the depth of water. —*v.t.* measure the depth of; find the cause of, understand.

fatigue *n.* tiredness; weakness in metal etc., caused by stress; soldier's non-military task. —*v.t.* cause fatigue to.

fatstock *n.* livestock fattened for slaughter as food.

fatten *v.t./i.* make or become fat.

fatty *a.* like fat, containing fat. —*n.* (*colloq.*) fat person.

fatuity *n.* being fatuous; fatuous remark etc.

fatuous *a.* foolish, silly. **fatuously** *adv.*, **fatuousness** *n.*

faucet *n.* tap.

fault *n.* defect, imperfection; offence; responsibility for something wrong; break in layers of rock; incorrect serve in tennis. —*v.t.* find fault(s) in; make imperfect. **at** ∼, responsible for a mistake etc.

faultless *a.* without fault. **faultlessly** *adv.*

faulty *a.* (-*ier*, -*iest*) having fault(s). **faultily** *adv.*, **faultiness** *n.*

faun *n.* Latin rural deity with a goat's legs and horns.

fauna *n.pl.* animals of an area or period.

faux pas /fəʊ ˈpɑ/ (pl. *faux pas*, pr. -ˈpɑz) embarrassing blunder.

favour *n.* liking, approval; kindly or helpful act beyond what is due; favouritism; badge or ornament worn to show that one supports a certain party. —*v.t.* regard or treat with favour; oblige; resemble (one parent etc.).

favourable *a.* giving or showing approval; pleasing, satisfactory; advantageous. **favourably** *adv.*

favourite *a.* liked above others. —*n.* favoured person or thing; competitor generally expected to win.

favouritism *n.* unfair favouring of one at the expense of others.

fawn[1] *n.* fallow deer in its first year; light yellowish brown. —*a.* fawn-coloured.

fawn[2] *v.i.* (of a dog) show affection; try to win favour by obsequiousness.

fealty /ˈfiːəltɪ/ *n.* loyalty.

fear *n.* unpleasant sensation caused by nearness of danger or pain; awe felt for God. —*v.t./i.* feel fear of; be afraid.

fearful *a.* terrible; feeling fear; (*colloq.*) extreme. **fearfully** *adv.*

fearless *a.* feeling no fear. **fearlessly** *adv.*, **fearlessness** *n.*

fearsome *a.* frightening, alarming.

feasible *a.* able to be done; plausible. **feasibly** *adv.*, **feasibility** *n.*

feast *n.* large elaborate meal; joyful festival; treat. —*v.t./i.* eat heartily; give a feast to.

feat *n.* remarkable achievement.

feather *n.* one of the structures with a central shaft and fringe of fine strands, growing from a bird's skin; long silky hair on a dog's or horse's legs. —*v.t.* cover or fit with feathers; turn (an oar-blade etc.) to pass through the air edgeways. ∼-**bed** *v.t.* make things financially easy for. ∼-**brained** *a.* silly. ∼ **one's nest**, enrich oneself. **feathery** *a.*

featherweight *n.* boxing-weight (58 kg); very lightweight thing or person.

feature *n.* one of the named parts of the face; noticeable quality; prominent article in a newspaper etc.; full-length cinema film; documentary broadcast. —*v.t.* give prominence to; be a feature of or in.

February *n.* second month of the year.

feckless *a.* incompetent and irresponsible. **fecklessness** *n.*

fecund /ˈfek-/ *a.* fertile. **fecundity** /fɪˈkʌnd-/ *n.*

fed *see* **feed**. —*a.* **fed up**, (*sl.*) discontented, displeased.

federal *a.* of a system in which States unite under a central authority but are independent in internal affairs.

federate *v.t./i.* unite on a federal basis or for a common purpose.

federation *n.* federating; federated society or group of States.

fee *n.* sum payable for a person's advice or services, or for a privilege or instruction etc.

feeble *a.* (-*er*, -*est*) weak; ineffective. ∼-**minded** *a.* mentally deficient. **feebly** *adv.*, **feebleness** *n.*

feed *v.t./i.* (p.t. *fed*) give food to; give as food; (of animals) take food; nourish; supply; send passes to (a player) in football etc. —*n.* meal; food for animals; pipe or channel carrying material to a machine; this material.

feedback *n.* return of part of a system's output

to its source; return of information about a product etc. to its supplier.

feeder *n.* one that feeds; bottle with a teat for feeding babies; baby's bib; feeding-apparatus in a machine; branch road or railway line etc. linking outlying areas to a central system.

feel *v.t./i.* (p.t. *felt*) explore or perceive by touch; be conscious of (being); give a sensation; have a vague conviction or impression; have as an opinion. —*n.* sense of touch; act of feeling; sensation produced by a thing touched. ~ **like**, be in the mood for.

feeler *n.* long slender part in certain animals, used for testing things by touch; tentative suggestion. ~ **gauge**, set of blades used for measuring narrow gaps.

feeling *n.* power to feel things; mental or physical awareness; idea or belief not based on reasoning; opinion; readiness to feel, sympathy.

feet *see* **foot.**

feign /feɪn/ *v.t.* pretend.

feint /feɪ-/ *n.* sham attack made to divert attention. —*v.i.* make a feint. —*a.* (of ruled lines) faint.

felicitate *v.t.* congratulate. **felicitation** *n.*

felicitous *a.* well-chosen, apt. **felicitously** *adv.*

felicity *n.* happiness; pleasing manner or style.

feline /ˈfiːlaɪn/ *a.* of cats, cat-like. —*n.* animal of the cat family.

fell[1] *n.* stretch of moor or hilly land, especially in north England.

fell[2] *a.* ruthless. **at one ~ swoop,** in a single deadly action.

fell[3] *v.t.* strike down; cut down (a tree), stitch down (a seam).

fell[4] *see* **fall.**

fellow *n.* associate, comrade; thing like another; member of a learned society or governing body of a college; (*colloq.*) man, boy. ~ **traveller,** non-Communist who sympathizes with Communist aims.

fellowship *n.* friendly association with others; society, membership of this; position of a college fellow.

felon *n.* person who has committed a felony.

felony *n.* (*old use*) serious crime.

felt[1] *n.* cloth made by matting and pressing fibres. —*v.t./i.* make or become matted; cover with felt.

felt[2] *see* **feel.**

female *a.* of the sex that can bear offspring or produce eggs; (of plants) fruit-bearing. —*n.* female animal or plant.

feminine *a.* of, like, or suitable for women; of the grammatical form suitable for names of females. —*n.* feminine word. **femininity** *n.*

feminist *n.* supporter of women's claims to be given rights equal to those of men.

femur /ˈfiːmə(r)/ *n.* thigh-bone.

fen *n.* low-lying marshy or flooded tract of land.

fence *n.* barrier round the boundary of a field or garden etc.; person who knowingly buys and re-sells stolen goods. —*v.t./i.* surround with a fence; act as a fence for (stolen goods); engage in the sport of fencing. **fencer** *n.*

fencing *n.* fences, their material; sport of fighting with foils.

fend *v.t./i.* ~ **for,** provide a livelihood for, look after. ~ **off,** ward off.

fender *n.* low frame bordering a fireplace; pad hung over a moored vessel's side to prevent bumping.

fennel *n.* fragrant herb.

ferment[1] /-ˈment/ *v.t./i.* undergo fermentation; cause fermentation in; seethe with excitement.

ferment[2] /ˈfɜː-/ *n.* fermentation; thing causing this; excitement.

fermentation *n.* chemical change caused by an organic substance, producing effervescence and heat.

fern *n.* flowerless plant with feathery green leaves.

ferocious *a.* fierce, savage. **ferociously** *adv.*, **ferocity** *n.*

ferret *n.* small animal of the weasel family. —*v.t./i.* (p.t. *ferreted*) search, rummage. ~ **out,** discover by searching.

ferroconcrete *n.* reinforced concrete.

ferrule /ˈferul/ *n.* metal ring or cap on the end of a stick or tube.

ferry *v.t.* convey (esp. in a boat) across water; transport. —*n.* boat etc. used for ferrying; place where it operates; service it provides.

fertile *a.* able to produce vegetation or fruit or young; capable of developing into a new plant or animal; inventive. **fertility** *n.*

fertilize *v.t.* make fertile; introduce pollen or sperm into. **fertilization** *n.*

fertilizer *n.* material added to soil to make it more fertile.

fervent *a.* showing fervour. **fervently** *adv.*

fervid *a.* fervent. **fervidly** *adv.*

fervour *n.* intensity of feeling.

fester *v.t./i.* make or become septic; cause continuing resentment.

festival *n.* day or period of celebration; series of performances of music or drama etc.

festive *a.* of or suitable for a festival, gaily decorated.

festivity *n.* festive proceedings.

festoon *n.* hanging chain of flowers or ribbons etc. —*v.t.* decorate with hanging ornaments.

fetch *v.t.* go for and bring back; cause to come out; be sold for (a price); (*colloq.*) deal (a blow). ~ **up,** end up.

fetching *a.* attractive.

fête /feɪt/ *n.* festival; outdoor entertainment or sale, esp. in aid of charity. —*v.t.* entertain in celebration of an achievement.

fetid /ˈfet-/ *a.* stinking.

fetish /ˈfet-/ *n.* object worshipped by primitive peoples; thing given foolishly excessive respect.

fetlock *n.* part of a horse's leg above and behind the hoof.

fetter *n.* & *v.t.* shackle.

fettle *n.* condition, trim.

feud *n.* lasting hostility.

feudal *a*. of or like the feudal system. ～ **system,** medieval system of holding land by giving one's services to the owner. **feudalism** *n*.

fever *n*. abnormally high body-temperature; disease causing this; nervous excitement. **feverish** *a*.

few *a. & n*. not many. **a** ～, some. **a good** ～, quite **a** ～, (*colloq*.) a fairly large number. **fewness** *n*.

fez *n*. (pl. *fezzes*) Muslim man's high flat-topped red cap.

fiancé *n*., **fiancée** /fɪˈɑːnseɪ/ *n.fem*. person one is engaged to marry.

fiasco *n*. (pl. *-os*) ludicrous failure.

fiat /ˈfaɪæt/ *n*. order, decree.

fib *n*. unimportant lie. **fibbing** *n*. telling fibs. **fibber** *n*.

fibre *n*. thread-like strand; substance formed of fibres; strength of character. **fibrous** *a*.

fibreboard *n*. board made of compressed fibres.

fibreglass *n*. textile fabric made of glass fibres; plastic containing glass fibres.

fibroid /ˈfaɪ-/ *a*. consisting of fibrous tissue. —*n*. benign fibroid tumour.

fibrositis *n*. rheumatic pain in tissue other than bones and joints.

fickle *a*. often changing, not loyal. **fickleness** *n*.

fiction *n*. invented story; class of literature consisting of books containing such stories. **fictional** *a*.

fictitious *a*. imaginary, not true.

fiddle *n*. (*colloq*.) violin; (*sl*.) piece of cheating, swindle. —*v.t./i*. (*colloq*.) play the violin; fidget with something; (*sl*.) cheat, falsify. **fiddler** *n*.

fiddlesticks *n*. nonsense.

fidelity *n*. faithfulness, loyalty, accuracy.

fidget *v.t./i*. (p.t. *fidgeted*) make small restless movements; make or be uneasy. —*n*. one who fidgets. **fidgety** *a*.

field *n*. piece of open ground, esp. for pasture or cultivation; sports ground; area rich in a natural product; area or sphere of action, operation, or interest etc.; all competitors in an outdoor contest or sport; fielders. —*v.t./i*. be a fielder, stop and return (a ball); put (a team) into the field. ～-**day** *n*. day of much activity. ～ **events,** athletic contests other than races. ～-**glasses** *n.pl*. binoculars. **F**～ **Marshal,** army officer of the highest rank.

fielder *n*. person who fields a ball; member of the side not batting.

fieldsman *n*. (pl. *-men*) fielder.

fieldwork *n*. practical work done by surveyors, social workers, etc. **fieldworker** *n*.

fiend /fɪnd/ *n*. evil spirit; wicked, mischievous, or annoying person; devotee. **fiendish** *a*.

fierce *a*. (*-er, -est*) violent in temper, manner, or action; eager, intense. **fiercely** *adv*., **fierceness** *n*.

fiery *a*. (*-ier, -iest*) consisting of fire, flaming; bright red; intensely hot; intense, spirited.

fiesta /fɪˈe-/ *n*. festival in Spanish-speaking countries.

fife *n*. small shrill flute.

fifteen *a. & n*. one more than fourteen (15, XV); team of fifteen players. **fifteenth** *a. & n*.

fifth *a. & n*. next after fourth. ～ **column,** organized body working for the enemy in a country at war. **fifthly** *adv*.

fifty *a. & n*. five times ten (50, L). ～-**fifty** *a. & adv*. half-and-half, equally. **fiftieth** *a. & n*.

fig *n*. tree with broad leaves and soft pear-shaped fruit; this fruit.

fight *v.t./i*. (p.t. *fought*) struggle against, esp. in physical combat or war; contend; strive to obtain or accomplish something or to overcome. —*n*. fighting; battle, contest, struggle; boxing-match; ～ **shy of,** avoid.

fighter *n*. one who fights; aircraft designed for attacking others.

figment *n*. thing that does not exist except in the imagination.

figurative *a*. metaphorical. **figuratively** *adv*.

figure *n*. written symbol of a number; diagram; decorative pattern; representation of a person or animal; bodily shape; geometrical shape; (*pl*.) arithmetic. —*v.t./i*. represent in a diagram or picture; imagine; form part of a plan etc.; be mentioned; work out by arithmetic or logic. ～-**head** *n*. carved image at the prow of a ship; leader with only nominal power. ～ **of speech,** word(s) used for vivid effect and not literally.

figured *a*. with a woven pattern.

figurine /ˈfɪɡjʊərɪn/ *n*. statuette.

filament *n*. strand; fine wire giving off light in an electric lamp.

filbert *n*. nut of cultivated hazel.

filch *v.t*. pilfer, steal.

file[1] *n*. tool with a rough surface for smoothing things. —*v.t*. shape or smooth with a file.

file[2] *n*. cover or box etc. for keeping papers for reference; its contents; line of people or things one behind another. —*v.t./i*. place in a file; place on record; march in a file.

filial *a*. of or due from a son or daughter.

filibuster *v.i*. delay or prevent the passing of a law by making a long speech. —*n*. this process.

filigree *n*. lace-like work in metal.

filings *n.pl*. particles filed off.

fill *v.t./i*. make or become full; block; spread over or through; occupy; appoint a person to (a vacant post). —*n*. enough to fill a thing; enough to satisfy a person's appetite or desire. ～ **in,** complete; (*colloq*.) inform; act as substitute. ～ **out,** enlarge; become enlarged or plumper. ～ **up,** fill completely.

filler *n*. thing or material used to fill a gap or increase bulk.

fillet *n*. piece of boneless meat or fish. —*v.t*. (p.t. *filleted*) remove bones from.

filling *n*. substance used to fill a cavity etc. ～ **station,** place selling petrol to motorists.

fillip *n*. quick blow with a finger; boost.

filly *n*. young female horse.

film *n*. thin layer; sheet or rolled strip of light-sensitive material for taking photographs; drama or events shown by a cinematographic process. —*v.t./i*. cover or become covered with a thin layer; make a film of. ~ **star,** star actor or actress in films. **~-strip** *n.* series of transparencies in a strip for projection.

filmy *a.* thin and almost transparent.

filter *n.* device or substance for holding back impurities in liquid or gas passing through it; screen for absorbing or modifying light or electrical or sound waves; arrangement for filtering traffic. —*v.t./i.* pass through a filter, remove impurities thus; make a way in or out gradually; (of traffic) be allowed to pass while other traffic is held up. **~-bed** *n.* tank or reservoir for filtering liquid. **~-tip** *n.* cigarette with a filter at the mouth end.

filth *n.* disgusting dirt; obscenity. **filthy** *a.*, **filthily** *adv.*, **filthiness** *n.*

filtrate *n.* filtered liquid. —*v.t./i.* filter. **filtration** *n.*

fin *n.* thin projection from a fish's body, used for propelling and steering itself; similar projection to improve the stability of aircraft etc.

finagle /fɪˈneɪ-/ *v.t./i.* (*U.S. colloq.*) behave or obtain dishonestly.

final *a.* at the end, coming last; conclusive. —*n.* last contest in a series; last edition of a day's newspaper; (*pl.*) final examinations. **finally** *adv.*

finale /fɪˈnɑːlɪ/ *n.* final section of a drama or musical composition.

finalist *n.* competitor in a final.

finality /faɪˈnæ-/ *n.* quality or fact of being final.

finalize *v.t.* bring to an end; put in final form. **finalization** *n.*

finance /faɪ-/ *n.* management of money; money resources. —*v.t.* provide money for. **financial** *a.*, **financially** *adv.*

financier /faɪ-/ *n.* person engaged in financing businesses.

finch *n.* a kind of small bird.

find *v.t./i.* (p.t. *found*) discover; obtain; supply; (of a jury etc.) decide and declare. —*n.* discovery; thing found. ~ **out,** get information about; detect, discover. **finder** *n.*

fine¹ *n.* sum of money to be paid as a penalty. —*v.t.* punish by a fine.

fine² *a.* (*-er, -est*) of high quality or merit; bright, free from rain; slender, in small particles; delicate, subtle; excellent. —*adv.* finely. —*v.t./i.* make or become finer. ~ **arts,** painting, sculpture, and architecture. **finely** *adv.*, **fineness** *n.*

finery *n.* showy clothes etc.

finesse /fɪˈnes/ *n.* delicate manipulation; tact.

finger *n.* one of the five parts extending from each hand; one of these other than the thumb; finger-like object or part; measure (about ¾ inch) of alcohol in a glass. —*v.t.* touch or feel with the fingers. **~-stall** *n.* sheath to cover an injured finger.

fingerprint *n.* impression of ridges on the pad of a finger.

fingertip *n.* tip of a finger.

finicking *a. & n.* giving or needing extreme care about details. **finical** *a.*, **finicky** *a.*

finish *v.t./i.* bring or come to an end, complete; reach the end of a task or race etc.; consume

all of; put final touches to. —*n.* last stage; point where a race etc. ends; completed state.

finite /ˈfaɪnaɪt/ *a.* limited.

fiord /fjɔd/ *n.* narrow inlet of the sea between cliffs esp. in Norway.

fir *n.* evergreen cone-bearing tree.

fire *n.* combustion; flame; burning fuel; heating device with a flame or glow; destructive burning; angry or excited feeling. —*v.t./i.* set fire to; catch fire; bake (pottery etc.); excite; send a bullet or shell from (a gun), detonate; discharge (a missile); dismiss from a job. ~ **away,** (*colloq.*) begin. ~ **brigade,** organized body of people trained and employed to extinguish fires. **~-engine** *n.* vehicle fitted with equipment for putting out large fires. **~-escape** *n.* special staircase or apparatus for escape from a burning building. **~-irons** *n.pl.* poker, tongs, and shovel for tending a domestic fire.

firearm *n.* gun, pistol, etc.

firebrand *n.* person who stirs up trouble.

firedamp *n.* explosive mixture of methane and air in mines.

firefly *n.* phosphorescent beetle.

firelight *n.* light from a fire.

fireman *n.* (pl. *-men*) member of a fire brigade; man employed to tend a furnace.

fireplace *n.* grate, hearth.

fireside *n.* space round a fireplace; this as the centre of a home.

firewood *n.* wood for use as fuel.

firework *n.* device containing chemicals. that burn or explode spectacularly.

firing-squad *n.* group detailed to fire rifles as a salute during a military funeral, or to shoot a condemned man.

firm¹ *n.* business company.

firm² *a.* (*-er, -est*) not yielding when pressed or pushed; steady, not shaking; securely established; resolute. —*adv.* firmly. —*v.t./i.* make or become firm.

firmament *n.* sky with its clouds and stars.

first *a.* coming before all others in time or order or importance. —*n.* first thing or occurrence; first day of a month. —*adv.* before all others or another; in preference; first-class. **at ~,** at the beginning. ~ **aid,** treatment given for an injury before a doctor arrives. **~-class** *a. & adv.* of the best quality; in the best category or accommodation. ~ **cousin** (see *cousin*). **at ~ hand,** directly from the original source. ~ **name,** personal or Christian name. **~-rate** *a.* excellent.

firstly *adv.* first.

firth *n.* estuary or narrow inlet of the sea in Scotland.

fiscal *a.* of public revenue.

fish *a.* (pl. usu. *fish*) cold-blooded animal living wholly in water; its flesh as food. —*v.t./i.* try to catch fish (from); make a search by reaching into something, (*colloq.*) bring out; try to obtain something by hints or indirect questioning.

fishery *n.* area of sea where fishing is done; business of fishing.

fishmonger *n.* shopkeeper who sells fish.

fishy *a.* (*-ier*, *-iest*) like fish; (*colloq.*) causing disbelief or suspicion.

fissile *a.* tending to split; capable of undergoing nuclear fission.

fission *n.* splitting (esp. of an atomic nucleus, with release of energy).

fissionable *a.* fissile.

fissure *n.* cleft.

fist *n.* hand when tightly closed.

fisticuffs *n.* fighting with fists.

fit[1] *n.* sudden attack of illness or its symptoms, or of convulsions or loss of consciousness; short period of a feeling or activity.

fit[2] *a.* (*fitter*, *fittest*) suitable, good enough; right and proper; in good physical condition or health. —*v.t./i.* (p.t. *fitted*) be or adjust to be the right shape and size for; put into place; make or be suitable or competent. —*n.* way a thing fits. ~ **out**, ~ **up**, supply, equip. **fitly** *adv.*, **fitness** *n.*

fitful *a.* occurring in short periods not steadily. **fitfully** *adv.*

fitment *n.* piece of fixed furniture.

fitter *n.* person who supervises the fitting of clothes; mechanic.

fitting *a.* right and proper.

fittings *n.pl.* fixtures and fitments.

five *a. & n.* one more than four (5, V).

fiver *n.* (*colloq.*) £5; five-pound note.

fix *v.t./i.* make firm or stable or permanent; direct steadily; establish, specify; repair; (*sl.*) deal with, arrange or influence fraudulently; (*sl.*) inject oneself with a narcotic. —*n.* awkward situation; position determined by taking bearings; (*sl.*) addict's dose of a narcotic. ~ **up**, organize; provide for. **fixer** *n.*

fixated *a.* having an obsession.

fixation *n.* fixing; obsession.

fixative *n.* substance for keeping things in position, or preventing fading or evaporation.

fixedly /-ɪdlɪ/ *adv.* intently.

fixity *n.* fixed state, stability, permanence.

fixture *n.* thing fixed in position; firmly established person or thing; match; race; date fixed for this.

fizz *v.i.* hiss or splutter, esp. when gas escapes in bubbles from a liquid. —*n.* this sound; fizzing drink. **fizzy** *a.*

fizzle *v.i.* fizz feebly. ~ **out**, end feebly or unsuccessfully.

flab *n.* (*colloq.*) flabbiness, fat.

flabbergast *v.t.* astound.

flabby *a.* (*-ier*, *-iest*) fat and limp, not firm. **flabbiness** *n.*

flaccid /'flæksɪd/ *a.* hanging loose or wrinkled, not firm. **flaccidly** *adv.*, **flaccidity** *n.*

flag[1] *n.* piece of cloth attached by one edge to a staff or rope, used as a signal or symbol; similarly shaped device. —*v.t.* (p.t. *flagged*) mark or signal with or as if with a flag.

flag[2] *v.i.* (p.t. *flagged*) droop; lose vigour.

flag[3] *n.* flagstone. **flagged** *a.* paved with flagstones.

flagellation /-ædʒ-/ *n.* whipping.

flagon *n.* large bottle in which wine or cider is sold; vessel with a handle, lip, and lid for serving wine.

flagrant /'fleɪ-/ *a.* (of an offence or offender) very bad and obvious. **flagrantly** *adv.*, **flagrance** *n.*

flagship *n.* ship carrying an admiral and flying his flag.

flagstone *n.* large paving-stone.

flail *n.* strong stick hinged on a long handle, formerly used for threshing grain. —*v.t./i.* beat with or as if with a flail; swing about wildly.

flair *n.* natural ability.

flak *n.* anti-aircraft shells.

flake *n.* small thin piece, esp. of snow. —*v.i.* come off in flakes. ~ **out**, (*colloq.*) faint, fall asleep from exhaustion. **flaky** *a.*, **flakiness** *n.*

flamboyant *a.* showy in appearance or manner. **flamboyantly** *adv.*, **flamboyance** *n.*

flame *n.* bright tongue-shaped portion of gas burning visibly; bright red. —*v.i.* burn with flames; become bright red. **old** ~, (*colloq.*) former sweetheart.

flamingo *n.* (pl. *-os*) wading bird with long legs and pink feathers.

flammable *a.* able to be set on fire.

flan *n.* open pastry or sponge case with filling.

flange *n.* projecting rim.

flank *n.* side, esp. of the body between ribs and hip. —*v.t.* place or be at the side of.

flannel *n.* a kind of woollen fabric; face-flannel; (*pl.*) trousers of flannel or similar fabric.

flannelette *n.* cotton fabric made to look and feel like flannel.

flap *v.t./i.* (p.t. *flapped*) sway or move up and down with a sharp sound; strike lightly with something flat; (*sl.*) show agitation. —*n.* act or sound of flapping; hanging or hinged piece; (*sl.*) agitation.

flare *v.i.* blaze suddenly; burst into sudden activity or anger; widen outwards. —*n.* sudden blaze; device producing a flaring light as a signal or illumination; flared shape.

flash *v.t./i.* give out a sudden bright light; come suddenly into sight or mind; move rapidly; cause to shine briefly; signal with light(s); send (news etc.) by radio or telegraph. —*n.* sudden burst of flame or light; sudden show of wit or feeling; very brief time; brief news item; device producing a bright brief light in photography; coloured patch of cloth as an emblem. ~ **flood**, sudden destructive flood.

flashback *n.* change of scene in a story or film to an earlier period.

flashing *n.* strip of metal covering a joint in a roof etc.

flashlight *n.* electric torch.

flashy *a.* showy, gaudy. **flashily** *adv.*, **flashiness** *n.*

flask *n.* narrow-necked bottle; vacuum flask.

flat *a.* (*flatter*, *flattest*) horizontal, level; spread out, lying at full length; absolute; dull, monotonous; dejected; having lost its effervescence or its power to generate electric current; below the correct pitch in music. —*adv.* in a flat manner; (*colloq.*) completely, exactly. —*n*. flat thing or part, level ground; set of rooms on one floor, used as a residence; music note a semitone lower than the corresponding one of natural pitch, sign indicating this. ～**fish** *n*. fish with a flattened body, swimming on its side. ～ **rate**, rate that is the same in all cases, not proportional.

flatlet *n*. small flat.

flatten *v.t./i.* make or become flat.

flatter *v.t.* compliment, esp. in order to win favour; cause to feel honoured; exaggerate the good looks of. **flatterer** *n*., **flattery** *n*.

flatulent *a*. causing or suffering from formation of gas in the digestive tract. **flatulence** *n*.

flatworm *n*. type of worm with a flattened body.

flaunt *v.t./i.* display proudly or ostentatiously.

flautist *n*. flute-player.

flavour *n*. distinctive taste; special characteristic. —*v.t.* give flavour to.

flavouring *n*. substance used to give flavour to food.

flaw *n*. imperfection, blemish. —*v.t.* spoil with a flaw.

flawless *a*. without a flaw.

flax *n*. blue-flowered plant; textile fibre from its stem.

flaxen *a*. made of flax; pale yellow like dressed flax.

flay *v.t.* strip off the skin or hide of; criticize severely.

flea *n*. small jumping insect that feeds on blood. ～ **market**, (*joc.*) street market.

fleck *n*. very small patch of colour; speck.

flecked *a*. marked with flecks.

fled *see* **flee**.

fledged *a*. (of a young bird) with fully grown wing-feathers, able to fly; (of a person) fully trained.

fledgeling *n*. bird just fledged.

flee *v.t./i.* (p.t. *fled*) run or hurry away (from).

fleece *n*. sheep's woolly hair; soft fabric used for linings. —*v.t.* defraud, rob by trickery. **fleecy** *a*.

fleet[1] *n*. navy; ships sailing together; vehicles or aircraft under one command or ownership.

fleet[2] *a*. (-er, -est) moving swiftly, nimble. **fleetness** *n*.

fleeting *a*. passing quickly, brief.

Flemish *a*. & *n*. (language) of Flanders in north-west Belgium.

flesh *n*. soft substance of animal bodies; body as opposed to mind or soul; pulpy part of fruits and vegetables. ～ **and blood,** human nature; one's relatives.

fleshy *a*. of or like flesh; having much flesh, plump, pulpy.

fleur-de-lis /flɜdə'liː/ *n*. (pl. *fleurs-de-lis*, pr. flɜd-) heraldic design of three petal-like parts.

flew *see* **fly**[2].

flex[1] *v.t.* bend; move (a muscle) so that it bends a joint.

flex[2] *n*. flexible insulated wire for carrying electric current.

flexible *a*. able to bend easily; adaptable, able to be changed. **flexibly** *adv*., **flexibility** *n*.

flexitime *n*. system of flexible working hours.

flick *n*. quick light blow or stroke; (*colloq.*) film. —*v.t./i.* move or strike or remove with a flick. ～**knife** *n*. knife with a blade that springs out.

flicker *v.i.* burn or shine unsteadily; occur briefly; quiver. —*n*. flickering light or movement; brief occurrence.

flier *n*. = flyer.

flight[1] *n*. flying; movement or path of a thing through the air; journey in or of an aircraft; flock of birds or insects; set of aircraft; series of stairs; feathers etc. on a dart or arrow. ～**deck** *n*. cockpit of a large aircraft.

flight[2] *n*. fleeing. **put to** ～, cause to flee. **take** ～, **take to** ～, flee.

flightless *a*. non-flying.

flighty *a*. (-ier, -iest) frivolous.

flimsy *a*. (-ier, -iest) light and thin; fragile; unconvincing. **flimsily** *adv*., **flimsiness** *n*.

flinch *v.i.* draw back in fear, wince; shrink from one's duty etc.

fling *v.t./i.* (p.t. *flung*) throw violently or hurriedly; rush, go angrily. —*n*. act or movement of flinging; spell of indulgence in pleasure.

flint *n*. very hard stone producing sparks when struck with steel; piece of hard alloy used to produce a spark. **flinty** *a*.

flip *v.t./i.* (p.t. *flipped*) flick; toss with a sharp movement. —*n*. action of flipping; (*colloq.*) short flight, quick tour. ～ **side**, reverse side of a gramophone record.

flippant *a*. not showing proper seriousness. **flippantly** *adv*., **flippancy** *n*.

flipper *n*. sea animal's limb used in swimming; large flat rubber attachment to the foot for underwater swimming.

flirt *v.t./i.* pretend lightheartedly to court a person; toy; move (a thing) rapidly to and fro. —*n*. person who flirts. **flirtation** *n*.

flirtatious *a*. flirting; fond of flirting. **flirtatiously** *adv*.

flit *v.i.* (p.t. *flitted*) fly or move lightly and quickly; decamp stealthily. —*n*. act of flitting.

flitch *n*. a side of bacon.

float *v.t./i.* rest or drift on the surface of liquid; be held up freely in gas or air; have or allow (currency) to have a variable rate of exchange; start (a company or scheme). —*n*. thing designed to float on liquid; low cart; money for minor expenditure or giving change. **floating voter,** one not attached to any political party.

flock[1] *n*. number of animals or birds together; large number of people, congregation. —*v.i.* gather or go in a flock.

flock[2] *n*. tuft of wool or cotton; wool or cotton waste.

floe *n*. sheet of floating ice.

flog *v.t.* (p.t. *flogged*) beat severely; (*sl.*) sell. **flogging** *n*.

flood *n*. great quantity of water coming over a place usually dry; great outpouring. —*v.t./i.* cover or fill with a flood; overflow; come in great quantities. ～**tide** *n*. advancing tide.

floodgate *n*. gate controlling a flow of water.

floodlight *n.* lamp producing a broad bright beam to light up a stage or building. —*v.t.* (p.t. *floodlit*) illuminate with this.

floor *n.* lower surface of a room, part on which one stands; part of a legislative assembly hall where members sit; storey. —*v.t.* provide with a floor; knock down; baffle.

flop *v.i.* (p.t. *flopped*) hang or fall heavily and loosely; (*sl.*) be a failure. —*n.* flopping movement or sound; (*sl.*) failure. **floppy** *a.*

flora *n.pl.* plants of an area or period.

floral *a.* of flowers.

florid /ˈflo-/ *a.* ornate; ruddy.

florin *n.* guilder; former British coin worth two shillings (10p).

florist /ˈflo-/ *n.* person who sells or grows flowers as a business.

floss *n.* mass of silky fibres; silk thread with little twist. **flossy** *a.*

flotation *n.* floating, esp. of a commercial venture.

flotilla *n.* small fleet; fleet of small ships.

flotsam *n.* floating wreckage. **~ and jetsam,** odds and ends.

flounce[1] *v.i.* go in an impatient annoyed manner. —*n.* flouncing movement.

flounce[2] *n.* deep frill attached by its upper edge. **flounced** *a.*

flounder[1] *n.* small flat-fish.

flounder[2] *v.i.* move or struggle clumsily, as in mud; become confused when trying to do something.

flour *n.* fine powder made from grain, used in cooking. —*v.t.* cover with flour. **floury** *a.*

flourish *v.t./i.* grow vigorously; prosper, be successful; be alive and active; wave dramatically. —*n.* dramatic gesture; ornamental curve; fanfare.

flout *v.t.* disobey openly.

flow *v.i.* glide along as a stream; proceed evenly; hang loosely; curve smoothly; gush forth. —*n.* flowing movement or mass; amount flowing; outpouring; inward movement of the tide, towards the land.

flower *n.* part of a plant where fruit or seed develops; this and its stem; best part. —*v.t./i.* produce or allow to produce flowers. **in ~,** with flowers opened.

flowered *a.* ornamented with a design of flowers.

flowerless *a.* non-flowering.

flowerpot *n.* pot in which a plant may be grown.

flowery *a.* full of flowers; full of ornamental phrases.

flown *see* **fly**[2].

flu *n.* (*colloq.*) influenza.

fluctuate *v.i.* vary irregularly. **fluctuation** *n.*

flue *n.* smoke-duct in a chimney; channel for conveying heat.

fluent *a.* speaking or spoken smoothly and readily. **fluently** *adv.*, **fluency** *n.*

fluff *n.* fluffy substance. —*v.t./i.* shake into soft mass; (*sl.*) bungle.

fluffy *a.* (-ier, -iest) having or covered with a soft mass of fur or fibres. **fluffiness** *n.*

fluid *a.* consisting of particles that move freely among themselves; not stable. —*n.* fluid substance. **fluidity** *n.*

fluke[1] *n.* success due to luck.

fluke[2] *n.* barbed arm of an anchor etc.; lobe of a whale's tail.

fluke[3] *n.* a kind of flat-fish; flat-worm.

flummox *v.i.* (*sl.*) baffle.

flung *see* **fling.**

flunk *v.t./i.* (*U.S. colloq.*) fail.

flunkey *n.* (pl. *-eys*) (*colloq.*) servant wearing livery.

fluorescent *a.* taking in radiations and sending them out as light. **fluorescence** *n.*

fluoridation *n.* addition of fluoride to drinking-water.

fluoride *n.* substance that prevents or reduces tooth-decay.

flurry *n.* short rush of wind, rain, or snow; commotion; nervous agitation. —*v.t.* fluster.

flush[1] *v.t./i.* become red in the face; fill with pride; cleanse or dispose of with a flow of water; rush out in a flood. —*n.* flushing of the face, blush; rush of emotion; rush of water; fresh growth of vegetation. —*a.* level, in the same plane; (*colloq.*) well supplied with money.

flush[2] *n.* (in poker) hand of cards all of one suit.

flush[3] *v.t.* drive out.

fluster *v.t.* make nervous or confused. —*n.* flustered state.

flute *n.* wind-instrument, pipe with a mouth-hole at the side; ornamental groove. —*v.t./i.* speak or utter in flute-like tones; make ornamental grooves in.

flutter *v.t./i.* move wings hurriedly; wave or flap quickly; (of the heart) beat irregularly. —*n.* fluttering movement or beat; nervous excitement; stir.

flux *n.* flow; continuous succession of changes.

fly[1] *n.* two-winged insect. **~-blown** *a.* tainted by flies' eggs.

fly[2] *v.t./i.* (p.t. *flew*, p.p. *flown*) move through the air, esp. on wings or in an aircraft; control the flight of; wave, mount (a flag) to wave; go quickly; pass suddenly; flee. —*n.* flying; flap covering an opening or containing a fastening, (*pl.*, *colloq.*) fastening down the front of trousers; speed-regulating device in machinery.

fly[3] *a.* (*sl.*) astute, knowing.

flycatcher *n.* bird that catches insects in the air.

flyer *n.* one that flies; airman.

flying *a.* able to fly. **~ buttress,** one based on separate structure, usu. forming an arch. **~ colours,** great credit. **~ fox,** fruit-eating bat. **~ saucer,** unidentified object reported as seen in the sky. **~ squad,** detachment of police etc. organized for rapid movement. **~ start,** vigorous start giving an initial advantage.

flyleaf *n.* blank leaf at the beginning or end of a book.

flyover *n.* bridge carrying one road or railway over another.

flyweight *n.* boxing-weight (51 kg).

flywheel *n.* heavy wheel revolving on a shaft to regulate machinery.

foal *n.* young of the horse or a related animal. —*v.i.* give birth to a foal.

foam *n.* collection of small bubbles; spongy rubber or plastic. —*v.i.* form foam. **foamy** *a.*

fob[1] *n.* ornament worn hanging from a key or watch-chain etc.

fob[2] *v.t.* (p.t. *fobbed*) ∼ **off,** palm off; get (a person) to accept something inferior.

focal *a.* of or at a focus.

fo'c's'le /ˈfoksəl/ *n.* forecastle.

focus *n.* (pl. *-cuses* or *-ci*, pr. *-saɪ*) point where rays meet; distance at which an object is most clearly seen; adjustment on a lens to produce a clear image; centre of activity or interest. —*v.t./i.* (p.t. *focused*) adjust the focus of; bring into focus; concentrate.

fodder *n.* dried food, hay, etc. for horses or other animals.

foe *n.* enemy.

foetal /ˈfi-/ *a.* of a foetus.

foetus /ˈfi-/ *n.* (pl. *-tuses*) developed embryo in a womb or egg.

fog *n.* thick mist that is difficult to see through. —*v.t./i.* (p.t. *fogged*) cover or become covered with fog or condensed vapour; perplex. **∼-horn** *n.* sounding-instrument for warning ships in fog. **foggy** *a.,* **fogginess** *n.*

fogy *n.* (pl. *-gies*) person with old-fashioned ideas.

foible *n.* harmless peculiarity in a person's character.

foil[1] *n.* paper-thin sheet of metal; person or thing emphasizing another's qualities by contrast.

foil[2] *v.t.* thwart, frustrate.

foil[3] *n.* long thin sword with a button on the point.

foist *v.t.* cause a person to accept (an inferior or unwelcome thing).

fold[1] *v.t./i.* bend or turn (a flexible thing) so that one part lies on another; close by pressing parts together; become folded; clasp; envelop; cease to function. —*n.* folded part; hollow between thicknesses; line made by folding.

fold[2] *n.* enclosure for sheep.

folder *n.* folding cover for loose papers; leaflet.

foliage *n.* leaves.

folio *n.* (pl. *-os*) largest-sized book; page-number.

folk *n.* people; one's relatives. **∼-dance,** **∼ song,** etc., dance, song, etc., in the traditional style of a country.

folklore *n.* traditional beliefs and tales of a community.

folkweave *n.* loosely woven fabric used chiefly for furnishings.

follicle *n.* very small cavity containing a hair-root.

follow *v.t./i.* go or come after; go along (a road etc.); use as a guide or leader, conform to; take an interest in the progress of; grasp the meaning of; result from; be true in consequence of something else. **∼ suit,** play a card of the suit led; follow a person's example.

follower *n.*

following *n.* body of believers or supporters. —*a.* now to be mentioned. —*prep.* as a sequel to.

folly *n.* foolishness, foolish act; ornamental building serving no practical purpose.

foment *v.t.* stir up (trouble).

fomentation *n.* hot lotion used to bathe a painful or inflamed part.

fond *a.* (*-er, -est*) affectionate; doting; (of hope) cherished but unlikely to be fulfilled. **∼ of,** having a liking for; much inclined to. **fondly** *adv.,* **fondness** *n.*

fondant *n.* soft sugary sweet.

fondle *v.t.* touch or stroke lovingly.

fondue *n.* dish of flavoured melted cheese.

font *n.* basin in a church, holding water for baptism.

food *n.* substance (esp. solid) that can be taken into the body of an animal or plant to maintain its life.

fool *n.* foolish person; jester in a medieval household; creamy fruit-flavoured pudding. —*v.t.* joke, tease; play about idly; trick.

foolery *n.* foolish acts.

foolhardy *a.* taking foolish risks.

foolproof *a.* simple and easy to use, unable to go wrong.

foolish *a.* lacking good sense or judgement; ridiculous. **foolishly** *adv.,* **foolishness** *n.*

foolscap *n.* size of paper ($17 \times 13\frac{1}{2}$ in.).

foot *n.* (pl. *feet*) end part of the leg below the ankle; similar part in animals; lower part or end; measure of length, = 12 inches (30·48 cm); unit of rhythm in a line of verse. —*v.t.* walk; be the one to pay (a bill). **∼-bridge** *n.* bridge for pedestrians. **∼-slogging** *n.* (*colloq.*) walking. **on ∼,** walking. **to one's feet,** to a standing position. **under one's feet,** in danger of being trodden on, in the way.

footage *n.* length measured in feet.

football *n.* large round or elliptical inflated ball; game played with this. **∼ pool,** form of gambling on the results of football matches. **footballer** *n.,* **footballing** *n.*

footfall *n.* sound of footsteps.

foothills *n.pl.* low hills near the bottom of a mountain or range.

foothold *n.* place just wide enough to put a foot on when climbing; small but secure position gained.

footing *n.* foothold; balance; status, conditions.

footlights *n.pl.* row of lights along the front of a stage floor.

footling /ˈfu-/ *a.* (*sl.*) trivial, petty.

footloose *a.* independent, without responsibilities.

footman *n.* (pl. *-men*) manservant, usu. in livery.

footmark *n.* footprint.

footnote *n.* note printed at the bottom of a page.

footpath *n.* path for pedestrians, pavement.

footplate *n.* platform for the driver and fireman in a locomotive.

footprint *n.* impression left by a foot or shoe.

footsore *a.* with feet sore from walking.

footstep *n.* step; sound of this.

footstool *n.* stool for resting the feet on while sitting.

footwear *n.* shoes and stockings.

footwork *n.* manner of moving or using the feet in sports etc.

fop *n.* dandy.

for *prep.* in place of; as the price or penalty of; in defence or favour of; with a view to; in the direction of; intended to be received or used by; because of; so as to happen at (a time); during. —*conj.* because.

forage /ˈfo-/ *v.i.* go searching; rummage. —*n.* foraging; food for horses and cattle.

foray /ˈfo-/ *n.* sudden attack, raid.

forbade *see* **forbid.**

forbear *v.t./i.* (p.t. *forbore*, p.p. *forborne*) refrain (from).

forbearance *n.* patience, tolerance.

forbearing *a.* patient, tolerant.

forbid *v.t.* (p.t. *forbade* /-ˈbæd/, p.p. *forbidden*) order not to; refuse to allow.

forbidding *a.* having an uninviting appearance, stern.

force *n.* strength; intense effort; influence tending to cause movement; body of troops or police; organized or available group; compulsion; effectiveness. —*v.t.* use force upon, esp. in order to get or do something; break open by force; strain to the utmost, overstrain; impose; produce by effort; cause (plants etc.) to reach maturity early. **forced landing,** emergency landing. **forced march,** lengthy march requiring special effort.

force-feed *v.t.* (p.t. *-fed*) feed (a prisoner etc.) against his will.

forceful *a.* powerful and vigorous. **forcefully** *adv.*, **forcefulness** *n.*

forcemeat *n.* finely-chopped seasoned meat used as stuffing.

forceps *n.* (pl. *forceps*) small tongs.

forcible *a.* done by force. **forcibly** *adv.*

ford *n.* shallow place where a stream may be crossed by wading or driving through. —*v.t.* cross thus. **fordable** *a.* able to be forded.

fore *a.* & *adv.* in or at or towards the front. —*n.* fore part. **to the ~,** in front, conspicuous.

forearm[1] *n.* arm from the elbow downwards.

forearm[2] *v.t.* arm or prepare in advance against possible danger.

forebears *n.pl.* ancestors.

foreboding *n.* feeling that trouble is coming.

forecast *v.t.* (p.t. *forecast*) tell in advance (what is likely to happen). —*n.* statement that does this.

forecastle /ˈfəʊksəl/ *n.* forward part of certain ships.

foreclose *v.t.* take possession of property and prevent (a mortgage) from being redeemed when a loan is not duly repaid. **foreclosure** *n.*

forecourt *n.* enclosed space in front of a building; outer courtyard.

forefathers *n.pl.* ancestors.

forefinger *n.* finger next to the thumb.

forefoot *n.* (pl. *-feet*) animal's front foot.

forefront *n.* the very front.

foregoing *a.* preceding.

foregone *a.* **~ conclusion,** result that can be foreseen easily.

foreground *n.* part of a scene etc. that is nearest to the observer.

forehand *a.* & *n.* (stroke) played with the palm of the hand turned forwards.

forehead /ˈforɪd *or* ˈfohed/ *n.* part of the face above the eyes.

foreign *a.* of, from, or dealing with a country that is not one's own; not belonging naturally.

foreigner *n.* person born in or coming from another country.

foreknowledge *n.* knowledge of a thing before it occurs.

foreland *n.* cape, promontory.

foreleg *n.* animal's front leg.

foreman *n.* (pl. *-men*) workman superintending others; president and spokesman of a jury.

foremost *a.* most advanced in position or rank; most important. —*adv.* in the foremost position etc.

forensic /fəˈren-/ *a.* of or used in lawcourts. **~ medicine,** medical knowledge used in police investigations etc.

foreordain *v.t.* destine beforehand.

forerunner *n.* person or thing that comes in advance of another which it foreshadows.

foresee *v.t.* (p.t. *-saw*, p.p. *-seen*) be aware of or realize beforehand.

foreseeable *a.* able to be foreseen.

foreshadow *v.t.* be an advance sign of (a future event etc.).

foreshore *n.* shore that the tide flows over; empty land near a shore.

foreshorten *v.t.* show or portray (an object) with apparent shortening giving an effect of distance.

foresight *n.* ability to foresee and prepare for future needs.

foreskin *n.* loose skin at the end of the penis.

forest *n.* trees and undergrowth covering a large area. **forested** *a.*

forestall *v.t.* prevent or foil by taking action first.

forester *n.* officer in charge of a forest or of growing timber.

forestry *n.* science of planting and caring for forests.

foretaste *n.* experience in advance of what is to come.

foretell *v.t.* (p.t. *foretold*) forecast.

forethought *n.* careful thought and planning for the future.

forewarn *v.t.* warn beforehand.

forewoman *n.* (pl. *-women*) woman equivalent of a foreman.

forfeit /-fɪt/ *n.* thing that has to be paid or given up as a penalty. —*v.t.* give or lose as a forfeit. —*a.* forfeited. **forfeiture** *n.*

forgather *v.i.* assemble.

forgave *see* **forgive.**

forge[1] *v.i.* advance by effort.

forge[2] *n.* blacksmith's workshop; furnace where metal is heated. —*v.t.* shape (metal) by heating and hammering; make a fraudulent imitation or copy of. **forger** *n.*

forgery *n.* forging; thing forged.

forget *v.t./i.* (p.t. *forgot*, p.p. *forgotten*) lose remembrance (of); stop thinking about. **~-me-not** *n.* plant with small blue flowers. **~ oneself,** behave without suitable dignity.

forgetful *a.* tending to forget.

forgive *v.t.* (p.t. *forgave*, p.p. *forgiven*) cease to feel angry or bitter towards or about. **forgiveness** *n.*

forgo *v.t.* (p.t. *forwent*, p.p. *forgone*) give up, go without.

fork *n.* pronged instrument or tool; thing or part divided like this, one of its divisions. —*v.t./i.* lift or dig with a fork; separate into two branches; follow one of these branches. **~-lift truck,** truck with a forked device for lifting and carrying loads. **~ out,** (*sl.*) pay.

forlorn *a.* left alone and unhappy. **~ hope,** the only faint hope left. **forlornly** *adv.*

form *n.* shape, appearance; way in which a thing exists; class in a school; usual method, formality, ritual; document with blank spaces to be filled in with information; condition, style; bench; hare's lair. —*v.t./i.* shape, produce; bring into existence, constitute; take shape; develop; arrange in a formation.

formal *a.* conforming to accepted rules or customs; of form; regular in design. **formally** *adv.*

formality *n.* being formal; formal act, esp. one required by rules.

formalize *v.t.* make formal or official. **formalization** *n.*

format *n.* shape and size of a book etc.

formation *n.* forming; thing formed; particular arrangement.

formative *a.* forming.

former *a.* of an earlier period; mentioned first of two.

formerly *adv.* in former times.

formidable /ˈfɔː-/ *a.* inspiring fear or awe; difficult to do.

formless *a.* without regular form.

formula *n.* (pl. *-ae* or *-as*) fixed series of words for use on social or ceremonial occasions; list of ingredients; symbols showing chemical constituents or a mathematical statement; classification of a racing car.

formulate *v.t.* express systematically. **formulation** *n.*

fornicate *v.t.* have sexual intercourse while unmarried. **fornication** *n.*, **fornicator** *n.*

forsake *v.t.* (p.t. *forsook*, p.p. *forsaken*) renounce; withdraw one's help or companionship etc. from.

forswear *v.t.* (p.t. *forswore*, p.p. *forsworn*) renounce.

forsythia *n.* shrub bearing yellow flowers in spring.

fort *n.* fortified place or building.

forte /-tɪ/ *n.* person's strong point.

forth *adv.* out; onwards. **back and ~,** to and fro.

forthcoming *a.* about to occur or appear; available; (*colloq.*) communicative, responsive.

forthright *a.* frank, outspoken.

forthwith *adv.* immediately.

fortification *n.* fortifying; defensive wall or building etc.

fortify *v.t.* strengthen, esp. against attack; increase the vigour of.

fortissimo *adv.* very loudly.

fortitude *n.* courage in bearing pain or trouble.

fortnight *n.* period of two weeks.

fortnightly *a. & adv.* (happening or appearing) once a fortnight.

fortress *n.* fortified building or town.

fortuitous /-ˈtjuː-/ *a.* happening by chance. **fortuitously** *adv.*

fortunate *a.* lucky. **fortunately** *adv.*

fortune *n.* chance as a power in mankind's affairs; events it brings; destiny; prosperity, success; much wealth. **~-teller** *n.* person who claims to fortell future events in people's lives.

forty *a. & n.* four times ten (40, XL). **~ winks,** a nap. **fortieth** *a. & n.*

forum *n.* place or meeting where a public discussion is held.

forward *a.* directed towards the front; having made more than normal progress; presumptuous. —*n.* attacking player (= striker) in football or hockey. —*adv.* forwards; towards the future; in advance, ahead. —*v.t.* send on (a letter etc.) to a new address or (goods) to a customer; help to advance (interests). **forwardness** *n.*

forwards *adv.* towards the front; so as to make progress; with the front foremost.

fosse *n.* ditch as a fortification.

fossil *n.* hardened remains or traces of a prehistoric animal or plant.

fossilize *v.t.* turn or be turned into a fossil. **fossilization** *n.*

foster *v.t.* promote the growth of; rear (a child that is not one's own). **~-child** *n.* child reared thus. **~-mother** *n.* woman who fosters a child.

fought *see* **fight.**

foul *a.* (*-er, -est*) causing disgust; clogged; entangled; unfair; against the rules of a game. —*n.* stroke or blow etc. that breaks rules. —*v.t./i.* make or become foul; entangle with; obstruct; commit a foul against. **~-mouthed** *a.* using foul language. **foully** *adv.*, **foulness** *n.*

found[1] *see* **find.**

found[2] *v.t.* establish; provide money for starting (an institution etc.); base. **founder** *n.*, **foundress** *n.fem.*

found[3] *v.t.* melt or mould (metal), fuse (materials for glass); make (an object) in this way. **founder** *n.*

foundation *n.* founding; institution or fund founded; base, first layer; underlying principle.

founder[1, 2] *see* **found**[1, 2].

founder[3] *v.i.* stumble or fall; (of a ship) fill with water and sink; fail completely.

foundling *n.* deserted child of unknown parents.

foundry *n.* workshop where metal or glass founding is done.

fount *n.* fountain, source; one size and style of printing-type.

fountain *n.* spring or jet of water; structure provided for this. ∼**-pen** *n.* pen that can be filled with a supply of ink.

four *a.* & *n.* one more than three (4, IV); four-oared boat or its crew. ∼**-poster** *n.* bed with four posts that support a canopy.

fourfold *a.* & *adv.* four times as much or as many.

foursome *n.* party of four people.

fourteen *a.* & *n.* one more than thirteen (14, XIV). **fourteenth** *a.* & *n.*

fourth *a.* next after the third. —*n.* fourth thing, class, etc.; quarter, one of four equal parts. **fourthly** *adv.*

fowl *n.* kind of bird kept to supply eggs and flesh for food.

fowling *n.* catching or shooting wildfowl. **fowler** *n.*

fox *n.* wild animal of the dog family with a bushy tail; its fur; crafty person. —*v.t.* deceive or puzzle by acting craftily. ∼**-terrier** *n.* short-haired terrier. **foxy** *a.*

foxglove *n.* tall plant with flowers like glove-fingers.

foxtrot *n.* dance with slow and quick steps; music for this.

foyer /ˈfɔɪeɪ/ *n.* entrance hall of a theatre, cinema, or hotel.

fracas /-kɑ/ *n.* (pl. *-cas*, pr. -kɑz) noisy quarrel or disturbance.

fraction *n.* number that is not a whole number; small part or amount. **fractional** *a.*, **fractionally** *adv.*

fractious *a.* irritable, peevish. **fractiously** *adv.*, **fractiousness** *n.*

fracture *n.* break, esp. of bone. —*v.t./i.* break.

fragile *a.* easily broken or damaged; not strong. **fragility** *n.*

fragment[1] /ˈfræ-/ *n.* piece broken off something; isolated part.

fragment[2] /-ˈment/ *v.t./i.* break into fragments. **fragmentation** *n.*

fragmentary /ˈfræ-/ *a.* consisting of fragments.

fragrance *n.* being fragrant; perfume.

fragrant *a.* having a pleasant smell.

frail *a.* (*-er*, *-est*) not strong; physically weak. **frailty** *n.*

frame *n.* rigid structure supporting other parts; open case or border enclosing a picture or pane of glass etc.; single exposure on cine film; box-like structure for protecting plants. —*v.t.* put or form a frame round; construct; express in words; (*sl.*) arrange false evidence against. ∼ **of mind,** temporary state of mind.

framework *n.* supporting frame.

franc *n.* unit of money in France, Belgium, and Switzerland.

franchise *n.* right to vote in public elections; authorization to sell a company's goods or services in a certain area.

Franciscan *n.* friar of the order founded by St. Francis.

Franco- *pref.* French.

frank[1] *a.* (*-er*, *-est*) showing one's thoughts and feelings unmistakably. **frankly** *adv.*, **frankness** *n.*

frank[2] *v.t.* mark (a letter etc.) to show that postage has been paid.

frankfurter *n.* highly seasoned smoked sausage.

frankincense *n.* sweet-smelling gum burnt as incense.

frantic *a.* wildly excited by anxiety etc. **frantically** *adv.*

fraternal *a.* of a brother or brothers. **fraternally** *adv.*

fraternity *n.* brotherhood.

fraternize *v.i.* associate with others in a friendly way. **fraternization** *n.*

fraud *n.* criminal deception; dishonest trick; person or thing that is not what he or it seems or pretends to be. **fraudulence** *n.*, **fraudulent** *a.*, **fraudulently** *adv.*

fraught *a.* ∼ **with,** filled with, involving.

fray[1] *n.* fight, conflict.

fray[2] *v.t./i.* make or become worn so that there are loose threads; strain or upset (nerves or temper).

frazzle *n.* exhausted state.

freak *n.* person or thing that is abnormal in form; something very unusual; person who dresses absurdly. **freakish** *a.*

freckle *n.* light brown spot on the skin. —*v.t./i.* spot or become spotted with freckles.

free *a.* (*freer*, *freest*) not a slave, not in the power of another; having freedom; not fixed, able to move; without, not subject to; costing nothing to the recipient; not occupied, not in use; lavish. —*v.t./i.* (*p.t. freed*) make free; rid of; clear, disentangle. ∼ **hand,** right of taking what action one chooses. ∼**-hand** *a.* (of drawing) done without ruler or compasses etc. ∼ **house,** inn or public house not controlled by one brewery. ∼ **lance,** person who sells his services to various employers. ∼**-range** *a.* (of hens) allowed to range freely in search of food; (of eggs) from such hens. ∼**-wheel** *v.i.* ride a bicycle without pedalling.

freedom *n.* being free; independence; frankness; unrestricted use.

freehold *n.* holding of land or a house etc. in absolute ownership. **freeholder** *n.*

Freemason *n.* member of a fraternity with elaborate ritual and secret signs. **Freemasonry** *n.* their system and institutions.

freemasonry *n.* sympathy and mutual help between people of similar interests.

freesia *n.* a kind of fragrant flower.

freeze *v.t./i.* (p.t. *froze*, p.p. *frozen*) change from liquid to solid by extreme cold; be so cold that water turns to ice; chill or be chilled by extreme cold or fear; preserve by refrigeration; make (assets) unable to be realized; hold (prices or wages) at a fixed level. —*n.* period of freezing weather; freezing of prices etc. ∼ **on to,** (*sl.*) take or keep tight hold of.

freezer *n.* refrigerated container for preserving and storing food.

freight *n.* cargo; transport of goods in containers or by water or air (in U.S.A. also by land). —*v.t.* load with freight.

freighter *n.* ship or aircraft carrying mainly freight.

French *a. & n.* (language) of France. **~ chalk,** powdered talc. **~ horn,** brass wind instrument with a coiled tube. **~ leave,** absence without permission. **~-polish** *v.t.* polish (wood) with shellac polish. **~ window,** one reaching to the ground, used also as a door. **Frenchman** *n.*, **Frenchwoman** *n.*

frenzied *a.* in a state of frenzy. **frenziedly** *adv.*

frenzy *n.* violent excitement or agitation.

frequency *n.* frequent occurrence; rate of repetition; number of cycles of a carrier wave per second, band or group of such values.

frequent[1] /'fri-/ *a.* happening or appearing often. **frequently** *adv.*

frequent[2] /-'kwe-/ *v.t.* go frequently to, be often in (a place).

fresco *n.* (pl. -*oes*), picture painted on a wall or ceiling before the plaster is dry.

fresh *a.* (-*er*, -*est*) new, not stale or faded; not preserved by tinning or freezing etc.; not salty; refreshing; vigorous; (*U.S.*) presumptuous. **freshly** *adv.*, **freshness** *n.*

freshen *v.t./i.* make or become fresh.

freshwater *adj.* of rivers or lakes, not of the sea.

fret[1] *v.t./i.* (p.t. *fretted*) worry; vex; wear away by rubbing or gnawing.

fret[2] *n.* one of the ridges on the finger-board of a guitar etc.

fretful *a.* constantly worrying or crying. **fretfully** *adv.*

fretsaw *n.* very narrow saw used for fretwork.

fretwork *n.* woodwork cut in decorative patterns.

Freudian /'froi-/ *a.* of Freud or his theories of psychoanalysis.

friable /'frai-/ *a.* easily crumbled.

friar *n.* member of certain religious orders of men.

friary *n.* monastery of friars.

fricassee *n.* dish of pieces of meat served in a thick sauce.

friction *n.* rubbing; resistance of one surface to another that moves over it; conflict of people who disagree. **frictional** *a.*

Friday *n.* day after Thursday.

fridge *n.* (*colloq.*) refrigerator.

fried *see* **fry**[1].

friend *n.* person (other than a relative or lover) with whom one is on terms of mutual affection; helper, sympathizer. **friendship** *n.*

friendly *a.* (-*ier*, -*iest*) like a friend; favourable. **Friendly Society,** one providing benefits for its members e.g. during illness or old age. **friendliness** *n.*

Friesian /'friːʒən/ *n.* one of a breed of black-and-white dairy cattle.

frieze *n.* band of sculpture or decoration round the top of a wall.

frigate *n.* small fast naval ship.

fright *n.* sudden great fear; ridiculous-looking person or thing.

frighten *v.t./i.* cause fright to; feel fright; drive or compel by fright.

frightened *a.* afraid.

frightful *a.* causing horror; ugly; (*sl.*) extremely great or bad. **frightfully** *adv.*

frigid *a.* intensely cold; very cold in manner; unresponsive sexually. **frigidly** *adv.*, **frigidity** *n.*

frill *n.* gathered or pleated strip of trimming attached at one edge; unnecessary extra. **frilled** *a.*, **frilly** *a.*

fringe *n.* ornamental edging of hanging threads or cords; front hair cut short to hang over the forehead; edge of an area or group etc. —*v.t.* edge. **~ benefits,** those provided by an employer in addition to wages or salary.

frisk *v.t./i.* leap or skip playfully; pass hands over (a person) to search for concealed weapons etc.

frisky *a.* (-*ier*, -*iest*) lively, playful. **friskily** *adv.*, **friskiness** *n.*

fritillary /-'tɪl-/ *n.* plant with speckled flowers; spotted butterfly.

fritter[1] *n.* fried batter-coated slice of fruit or meat etc.

fritter[2] *v.t.* waste little by little on trivial things.

frivol *v.i.* (p.t. *frivolled*) spend time frivolously.

frivolous *a.* lacking a serious purpose, pleasure-loving. **frivolously** *adv.*, **frivolity** *n.*

frizz *v.t./i.* curl into a wiry mass. **frizzy** *a.*, **frizziness** *n.*

frizzle *v.t./i.* fry crisp.

fro *see* **to and fro.**

frock *n.* woman's or girl's dress.

frog *n.* small jumping animal living both in water and on land; horny substance in the sole of a horse's foot; looped cord and button as a fastener. **~ in one's throat,** hoarseness. **~-march** *v.t.* hustle (a person) forcibly, holding his arms.

frogman *n.* (pl. -*men*) swimmer with a rubber suit and oxygen supply for use under water.

frolic *v.i.* (p.t. *frolicked*) play about in a lively way. —*n.* such play.

from *prep.* having as the starting-point, source, or cause; as separated, distinguished, or unlike. **~ time to time,** at intervals of time.

frond *n.* leaf-like part of a fern or palm-tree etc.

front *n.* side or part normally nearer or towards the spectator or line of motion; area where fighting takes place in a war; outward appearance; cover for secret activities; promenade of a seaside resort. —*a.* of the front; situated in front. —*v.t./i.* face, have the front towards; serve as a cover for secret activities. **in ~,** at the front.

frontage *n.* front of a building; land bordering this.

frontal *a.* of or on the front.

frontier *n.* boundary between countries.

frontispiece *n.* illustration opposite the title-page of a book.

frost *n.* freezing weather-condition; white frozen dew or vapour. —*v.t./i.* injure with frost; cover with frost or frosting; make (glass) opaque by roughening its surface. **~-bite** n. injury to body-tissue from freezing. **~-bitten** a., **frosty** a.

frosting n. sugar icing.

froth n. & v.t./i. foam. **frothy** a.

frown v.i. wrinkle one's brow in thought or disapproval. —n. frowning movement or look. **~ on,** disapprove of.

frowsty a. fusty, stuffy.

froze, frozen see **freeze.**

frugal a. careful and economical; scanty, costing little. **frugally** adv., **frugality** n.

fruit n. seed-containing part of a plant; this used as food; product of labour; currants etc. used in food. —v.t./i. produce or allow to produce fruit. **~ machine,** coin operated gambling machine. **~ salad,** fruits cut up and mixed.

fruiterer n. shopkeeper selling fruit.

fruitful a. producing much fruit or good results. **fruitfully** adv., **fruitfulness** n.

fruition /fruˈɪʃən/ n. fulfilment of hopes; results of work.

fruitless a. producing little or no result. **fruitlessly** adv., **fruitlessness** n.

fruity a. (-ier, -iest) like fruit in smell or taste; (colloq.) of full rich quality.

frump n. dowdy woman. **frumpish** a.

frustrate v.t. prevent from achieving something or from being achieved. **frustration** n.

fry[1] v.t./i. (p.t. fried) cook or be cooked in very hot fat.

fry[2] n. (pl. fry) young fishes. **small ~,** people of little importance.

frying-pan n. shallow pan used in frying.

ft. abbr. foot or feet (as a measure).

fuchsia /ˈfjuːʃə/ n. ornamental shrub with drooping flowers.

fuddle v.t. stupefy, esp. with drink.

fuddy-duddy a. & n. (sl.) (person who is) out of date and unable to accept new ideas.

fudge n. soft sweet made of milk, sugar, and butter.

fuel n. material burnt as a source of warmth, light, or energy, or used as a source of nuclear energy; thing that increases anger etc. —v.t. (p.t. fuelled) supply with fuel.

fug n. stuffy atmosphere in a room etc. **fuggy** a., **fugginess** n.

fugitive n. person who is fleeing or escaping. —a. fleeing, escaping; transient.

fugue /fjuːg/ n. musical composition with theme(s) repeated in a complex pattern.

fulcrum n. point of support on which a lever pivots.

fulfil v.t. (p.t. fulfilled) accomplish, carry out (a task); satisfy, do what is required by (a contract etc.); make (a prophecy) come true. **~ oneself,** develop and use one's abilities fully. **fulfilment** n.

full a. (-er, -est) holding or having as much as the limits will allow; copious; complete; plump; made with material hanging in folds; (of tone) deep and mellow. —adv. completely; exactly. **~-blown** a. fully developed. **~-**

blooded a. vigorous, hearty. **~ moon,** moon with the whole disc illuminated. **~-scale** a. of actual size, not reduced. **~ stop,** dot used as a punctuation-mark at the end of a sentence or abbreviation; complete stop. **fullness** n., **fully** adv.

fulmar n. Arctic sea-bird.

fulminate v.i. protest loudly and bitterly. **fulmination** n.

fulsome a. praising excessively and sickeningly.

fumble v.i. touch or handle a thing awkwardly; grope about.

fume n. strong-smelling smoke or gas or vapour. —v.i. emit fumes; seethe with anger.

fumigate v.t. disinfect by means of fumes. **fumivation** n.

fun n. light-hearted amusement. **~-fair** n. fair consisting of amusements and side-shows. **make ~ of,** cause people to laugh at.

function n. special activity or purpose of a person or thing; important ceremony. —v.i. perform a function; be in action.

functional a. of function(s); practical and not decorative or luxurious. **functionally** adv.

functionary n. official.

fund n. sum of money for a special purpose; stock, supply. —v.t. provide with money.

fundamental a. of the basis or foundation of a subject etc.; essential. —n. fundamental fact or principle. **fundamentally** adv.

funeral n. ceremony of burial or cremation; procession to this.

funerary a. of or used for a burial or funeral.

funereal /-nɪər-/ a. suitable for a funeral, dismal, dark.

fungicide /-dʒɪ-/ n. substance that kills fungus. **fungicidal** a.

fungoid a. like a fungus.

fungus n. (pl. -gi, pr. -gaɪ) plant without green colouring-matter (e.g. mushroom, mould).

funicular (fjuˈnɪk-/ n. cable railway with ascending and descending cars counterbalancing each other.

funk n. (sl.) fear; coward. —v.t./i. (sl.) show fear; fear and shirk.

funky a. (sl.) (of jazz etc.) uncomplicated, emotional; having a strong smell.

funnel n. tube with a wide top for pouring liquid etc. into small openings; metal chimney on a steam engine or ship. —v.t./i. (p.t. funnelled) move through a funnel or narrowing space.

funny a. (-ier, -iest) causing amusement; puzzling, odd. **~-bone** n. part of the elbow where a very sensitive nerve passes. **~ business,** trickery. **funnily** adv.

fur n. short fine hair covering the bodies of certain animals; skin with this, or fabric imitating it, used for clothing; coating, incrustation. —v.t./i. (p.t. furred) cover or become covered with fur.

furbelows n.pl. showy trimmings.

furbish v.t. polish, clean, renovate.

furious a. full of anger; violent, intense. **furiously** adv.

furl v.t. roll up and fasten.

furnace *n.* closed fireplace for central heating; enclosed space for heating metals etc.

furnish *v.t.* equip with furniture; provide, supply. **furnishings** *n.pl.* furniture and fitments etc.

furniture *n.* movable articles (e.g. chairs, beds) for use in a room.

furore /fjʊˈrɔːrɪ/ *n.* uproar of enthusiastic admiration or fury.

furrier /ˈfʌ-/ *n.* person who deals in furs or fur clothes.

furrow *n.* long cut in the ground; groove. —*v.t.* make furrows in.

furry *a.* like fur; covered with fur.

further *adv.* & *a.* more distant; to a greater extent; additional. —*v.t.* help the progress of. **furtherance** *n.* **furthermore** *adv.* moreover.

furthermost *a.* most distant.

furthest *a.* most distant. —*adv.* at or to the greatest distance.

furtive *a.* sly, stealthy. **furtively** *adv.*, **furtiveness** *n.*

fury *n.* wild anger, rage; violence; violently angry person.

furze *n.* gorse.

fuse[1] *v.t./i.* blend (metals etc.), become blended; unite; fit with a fuse; stop functioning through melting of a fuse. —*n.* strip of wire placed in an electric circuit to melt and interrupt the current when the circuit is overloaded.

fuse[2] *n.* length of easily burnt material for igniting a bomb or explosive. —*v.t.* fit a fuse to.

fuselage /-lɑːʒ/ *n.* body of an aeroplane.

fusillade /-ˈleɪd/ *n.* continuous firing of guns; outburst of questions etc.

fusion *n.* fusing; union of atomic nuclei, with release of energy.

fuss *n.* unnecessary excitement or activity; vigorous protest. —*v.t./i.* complain vigorously; agitate. **make a ∼ of**, treat with a great display of attention or affection.

fussy *a.* (**-ier, -iest**) often fussing; fastidious; with much unnecessary detail or decoration. **fussily** *adv.*, **fussiness** *n.*

fusty *a.* (**-ier, -iest**) smelling stale and stuffy; old-fashioned in ideas etc. **fustiness** *n.*

futile *a.* producing no result. **futility** *n.*

future *a.* belonging to the time after the present. —*n.* future time or events or condition. **in ∼**, from now on.

futuristic *a.* looking suitable for the distant future, not traditional.

futurity /-ˈtjʊər-/ *n.* future time.

fuzz *n.* fluff, fluffy or frizzy thing; (*sl.*) police.

fuzzy *a.* (**-ier, -iest**) like or covered with fuzz; frizzy; blurred, indistinct. **fuzziness** *n.*

G

g *abbr.* gram(s).

gab *n.* (*colloq.*) chatter.

gabardine *n.* twilled fabric.

gabble *v.t./i.* talk or utter quickly and indistinctly. —*n.* gabbled talk.

gable *n.* triangular part of an outside wall, between sloping roofs. **gabled** *a.*

gad *v.i.* (p.t. *gadded*) ∼ **about**, travel constantly for pleasure.

gadabout *n.* person who gads about.

gadfly *n.* fly that bites cattle.

gadget *n.* small mechanical device or tool. **gadgetry** *n.* gadgets.

Gaelic /ˈgæ-/ *n.* Celtic language of Scots; /ˈgeɪ-/ Irish language.

gaff *n.* stick with a hook for landing large fish. —*v.t.* seize with a gaff.

gaffe *n.* blunder.

gaffer *n.* (*colloq.*) elderly man; boss, foreman.

gag *n.* thing put in or over a person's mouth to silence him; surgical device to hold the mouth open; joke. —*v.t./i.* (p.t. *gagged*) put a gag on; deprive of freedom of speech; tell jokes; retch.

gaga *a.* (*sl.*) senile.

gaggle *n.* flock (of geese).

gaiety *n.* cheerfulness, bright appearance; merrymaking.

gaily *adv.* with gaiety.

gain *v.t./i.* obtain; acquire gradually; profit; get nearer in racing or pursuit; reach; (of a clock) become fast. —*n.* increase in wealth or possessions etc.

gainful *a.* profitable. **gainfully** *adv.*

gainsay *v.t.* (p.t. *gainsaid*) (*formal*) deny, contradict.

gait *n.* manner of walking or running.

gaiter *n.* cloth or leather covering for the lower part of the leg.

gala /ˈgɑː-/ *n.* festive occasion; fête.

galaxy *n.* system of stars; brilliant company of people; *the G∼*, the Milky Way. **galactic** *a.*

gale *n.* very strong wind.

gall[1] *n.* bile; bitterness of feeling; (*sl.*) impudence. **∼-bladder** *n.* organ storing bile.

gall[2] *n.* sore made by rubbing. —*v.t.* rub and make sore; vex, humiliate.

gall[3] *n.* abnormal growth on a plant, esp. on an oak-tree.

gallant /ˈgæ-/ *a.* brave, chivalrous. **gallantly** *adv.*, **gallantry** *n.*

galleon *n.* large Spanish sailing-ship in the 15th–17th centuries.

gallery *n.* balcony in a hall or theatre etc.; long room or passage, esp. used for special purpose; room or building for showing works of art.

galley *n.* (pl. *-eys*) ancient ship, esp. propelled by oars; kitchen in a ship or aircraft; oblong tray holding type for printing.

Gallic *a.* of ancient Gaul; French.

gallivant *v.i.* (*colloq.*) gad about.

gallon *n.* measure for liquids, = 4 quarts (4.546 litres).

gallop *n.* horse's fastest pace; ride at this. —*v.t./i.* (p.t. *galloped*) go or ride at a gallop; progress rapidly.

gallows *n.* framework with a noose for hanging criminals.

gallstone *n.* small hard mass formed in the gall-bladder.

galore *adv.* in plenty.

galosh *n.* rubber overshoe.

galvanic /-ˈvæn-/ *a.* producing electric current by chemical action; stimulating people into activity.

galvanize *v.t.* stimulate into activity; coat with zinc. **galvanization** *n.*

gambit *n.* opening move or remark.

gamble *v.t./i.* play games of chance for money; risk in hope of gain. —*n.* gambling; risky undertaking. **~ on,** act in the hope of. **gambler** *n.*

gambol *v.i.* (p.t. *gambolled*) jump about in play. —*n.* gambolling movement.

game[1] *n.* play or sport, esp. with rules; section of this as a scoring unit; scheme; wild animals hunted for sport or food. —*v.i.* gamble for money stakes. —*a.* brave; willing. **gamely** *adv.*, **gameness** *n.*

game[2] *a.* lame.

gamekeeper *n.* person employed to protect and breed game.

gamesmanship *n.* art of winning games by upsetting the confidence of one's opponent.

gamete *n.* sexual cell.

gamma *n.* third letter of the Greek alphabet, = g.

gammon *n.* cured or smoked ham.

gamut *n.* whole range of notes used in music; whole series or scope.

gander *n.* male goose.

gang *n.* group of people working or going about together. —*v.i.* **~ up,** combine in a gang.

gangling *a.* tall and awkward.

ganglion *n.* (pl. -*ia*) group of nerve-cells from which nerve-fibres radiate; cyst on the sheath of a tendon.

gangplank *n.* plank placed for walking into or out of a boat.

gangrene *n.* decay of body tissue. **gangrenous** *a.*

gangster *n.* member of a gang of violent criminals.

gangway *n.* gap left for people to pass, esp. between rows of seats; passageway, esp. on a ship; movable bridge from a ship to land.

gannet *n.* large sea-bird.

gantry *n.* overhead bridge-like framework supporting railway signals or a travelling crane etc.

gaol *n.* prison. —*v.t.* put into gaol.

gaolbird *n.* person who has been in gaol, esp. frequently.

gaoler *n.* person in charge of a gaol or its prisoners.

gap *n.* opening, space, interval; deficiency; wide difference.

gape *v.i.* open the mouth wide; stare in surprise; be wide open.

garage /ˈgæraʒ/ *n.* building for storing motor vehicle(s); commercial establishment where motor vehicles are repaired and serviced, or selling petrol and oil. —*v.t.* put or keep in a garage.

garb *n.* clothing. —*v.t.* clothe.

garbage *n.* domestic waste; rubbish.

garble *v.t.* distort or confuse (a message or story etc.).

garden *n.* piece of cultivated ground, esp. attached to a house; (*pl.*) ornamental public grounds. —*v.i.* tend a garden. **gardener** *n.*

gardenia *n.* fragrant white or yellow flower; tree or shrub bearing this.

gargantuan /-ˈgæn-/ *a.* gigantic.

gargle *v.i.* wash the inside of the throat with liquid held there by the breath. —*n.* liquid used for this.

gargoyle *n.* grotesque carved face or figure on a building.

garish /ˈgeər-/ *a.* gaudy.

garland *n.* wreath of flowers etc. as a decoration. —*v.t.* deck with garland(s).

garlic *n.* onion-like plant. **garlicky** *a.*

garment *n.* article of clothing.

garner *v.t.* store up, collect.

garnet *n.* red semi-precious stone.

garnish *v.t.* decorate (esp. food). —*n.* thing used for garnishing.

garret *n.* attic, esp. a poor one.

garrison *n.* troops stationed in a town or fort to defend it; building they occupy. —*v.t.* place a garrison in.

garrotte /-ˈrot/ *n.* cord, wire, or a metal collar used to strangle a victim. —*v.t.* strangle or (in Spain) execute with this.

garrulous *a.* talkative. **garrulously** *adv.*, **garrulousness** *n.*, **garrulity** *n.*

garter *n.* band worn round the leg to keep a stocking up.

gas *n.* (pl. *gases*) substance with particles that can move freely; such a substance used as a fuel or anaesthetic; (*sl.*) empty talk; (*U.S. colloq.*) gasoline, petrol. —*v.t./i.* (p.t. *gassed*) kill or overcome by poisonous gas; (*colloq.*) talk lengthily. **~ chamber,** room that can be filled with poisonous gas to kill prisoners. **~ mask,** device worn over face as a protection against poisonous gas. **~ ring,** hollow perforated ring through which gas flows for cooking on.

gaseous /ˈgæ-/ *a.* of or like a gas.

gash *n.* long deep cut. —*v.t.* make a gash in.

gasholder *n.* gasometer.

gasket *n.* sheet or ring of rubber, asbestos, etc., sealing a joint between metal surfaces.

gasoline /-lin/ *n.* (*U.S.*) petrol.

gasometer /-ˈsomɪ-/ *n.* large round storage tank from which gas is piped to a district.

gasp *v.t./i.* draw breath in sharply in exhaustion or surprise; speak breathlessly. —*n.* breath drawn in thus.

gastric *a.* of the stomach.

gastronomy *n.* science of good eating and drinking. **gastronomic** *a.*

gasworks *n.* place where fuel gas is made.

gate *n.* hinged movable barrier in a wall or fence etc.; gateway; slots controlling the movement of gear lever; number of spectators entering by payment to see a football match etc., amount of money taken. —*v.t.* confine to a college or school after certain hours, as a punishment. **~-legged** *a.* (of a table) with legs in a frame that can be moved to support leaves.

gateaux /ˈgætəʊ/ *n.* (pl. *-eaux* pr. *-əʊz*) large rich cream cake.

gatecrash *v.t./i.* go to (a private party) un-invited. **gatecrasher** *n.*

gated *a.* fitted with gates.

gateway *n.* opening or structure framing a gate; entrance.

gather *v.t./i.* bring or come together; collect; obtain gradually; understand, conclude; draw together in folds; swell and form pus. **gathers** *n.pl.* gathered folds of fabric.

gathering *n.* people assembled; inflamed swelling containing pus.

gauche /gəʊʃ/ *a.* lacking ease and grace of manner. **gaucherie** /-rɪ/ *n.*

gaudy *a.* (*-ier*, *-iest*) showy or bright in a tasteless way. **gaudily** *adv.*, **gaudiness** *n.*

gauge /geɪdʒ/ *n.* standard measure esp. of contents or thickness; device for measuring things; distance between pairs of rails or wheels. —*v.t.* measure; estimate.

gaunt *a.* lean and haggard; grim, desolate. **gauntness** *n.*

gauntlet[1] *n.* glove with a long wide cuff; this cuff.

gauntlet[2] *n.* **run the ~**, be exposed to continuous criticism or risk.

gauze *n.* thin transparent fabric; fine wire mesh. **gauzy** *a.*

gave *see* **give.**

gavotte *n.* old French dance.

gawky *a.* (*-ier*, *-iest*) awkward and ungainly. **gawkiness** *n.*

gawp *v.i.* (*colloq.*) stare stupidly.

gay *a.* (*-er*, *-est*) happy and full of fun; brightly coloured; (*colloq.*) homosexual. **gayness** *n.*

gaze *v.i.* look long and steadily. —*n.* long steady look.

gazebo /-ˈziː-/ *n.* (pl. *-os*) turret or summerhouse with a wide view.

gazelle *n.* small antelope.

gazette *n.* title of certain newspapers or of official journals containing public notices.

gazetteer /-ˈtɪə(r)/ *n.* index of places, rivers, mountains, etc.

gazump *v.t.* disappoint (an intended purchaser) by raising the price after accepting his offer.

G.B. *abbr.* Great Britain.

G.C.E. *abbr.* General Certificate of Education.

G.D.R. *abbr.* German Democratic Republic.

gear *n.* equipment; apparatus; set of toothed wheels working together in machinery. —*v.t.* provide with gear(s); adapt (to a purpose). **in**

~, with gear mechanism engaged. **out of ~**, with it disengaged.

gearbox, **gearcase** *ns.* case enclosing gear mechanism.

gecko *n.* (pl. *-os*) tropical lizard.

geese *see* **goose.**

gee-up *int.* command to a horse to move on or go faster.

geezer *n.* (*sl.*) person, old man.

Geiger counter device for detecting and measuring radioactivity.

geisha /ˈgeɪ-/ *n.* Japanese woman trained to entertain men.

gel /dʒel/ *n.* jelly-like substance.

gelatine *n.* clear substance made by boiling bones. **gelatinous** /-ˈlæ-/ *a.*

geld *v.t.* castrate, spay.

gelding *n.* gelded horse.

gelignite /ˈdʒel-/ *n.* explosive containing nitroglycerine.

gem *n.* precious stone; thing of great beauty or excellence.

gen *n.* (*sl.*) information.

gender *n.* grammatical classification corresponding roughly to the two sexes and sex-lessness.

gene *n.* one of the factors controlling heredity.

genealogy /-nɪˈæl-/ *n.* list of ancestors; study of family pedigrees. **genealogical** *a.*, **genealogist** *n.*

genera *see* **genus.**

general *a.* of or involving all or most parts, things, or people; involving main features only, not detailed or specific; (in titles) chief. —*n.* army officer next below field marshal. **~ election**, election of parliamentary representatives from the whole country. **~ practitioner**, doctor treating cases of all kinds in a section of the community. **~ staff**, army officers assisting a commander at headquarters. **in ~**, as a general rule, usually; for the most part. **generally** *adv.*

generality *n.* being general; general statement without details.

generalize *v.t./i.* draw a general conclusion; speak in general terms; bring into general use. **generalization** *n.*

generate *v.t.* bring into existence, produce.

generation *n.* generating; single stage in descent or pedigree; all persons born at about the same time; period of about 30 years.

generator *n.* machine converting mechanical energy into electricity.

generic /dʒɪˈne-/ *a.* of a whole genus or group. **generically** *adv.*

generous *a.* giving or given freely; not small-minded; plentiful. **generously** *adv.*, **generosity** *n.*

genesis *n.* origin.

genetic *a.* of genes or genetics. **genetically** *adv.*

genetics *n.* science of heredity.

genial *a.* kindly and cheerful; pleasantly warm. **genially** *adv.*, **geniality** *n.*

genie /ˈdʒiːnɪ/ *n.* (pl. *genii*) spirit or goblin in Arabian tales.

genital /ˈdʒenɪ-/ *a.* of animal reproduction; of genitals. **genitals** *n.pl.* external sex organs.

genitive *n.* grammatical case showing source or possession.

genius *n.* (pl. *-uses*) exceptionally great natural ability; person having this; (pl. *-ii*) guardian spirit.

genocide /ˈdʒen-/ *n.* deliberate extermination of a race of people.

genre /ʒɑnr/ *n.* kind, esp. of art or literature.

gent *n.* (*sl.*) gentleman.

genteel *a.* affectedly polite and refined. **genteelly** *adv.*

gentian *n.* alpine plant with usu. deep-blue flowers. ~ **violet,** dye used as an antiseptic.

Gentile *n.* non-Jewish person.

gentility *n.* good manners and elegance.

gentle *a.* (*-er, -est*) mild, moderate, not rough or severe; of good family. —*v.t.* coax. —*n.* maggot used as bait. **gently** *adv.*, **gentleness** *n.*

gentlefolk *n.pl.* people of good family.

gentleman *n.* (pl. *-men*) man, esp. of good social position; well-mannered man. **gentlemanly** *a.*

gentlewoman *n.* (pl. *-women*) woman of good family.

gentry *n.pl.* people ranking next below nobility; (*derog.*) people.

genuflect *v.i.* bend the knee and lower the body, esp. in worship. **genuflexion** *n.*

genuine *a.* really what it is said to be. **genuinely** *adv.*, **genuineness** *n.*

genus /ˈdʒiː-/ *n.* (pl. *genera,* pr. dʒen-) group of animals or plants, usu. containing several species; kind.

geography *n.* study of earth's surface and its physical features, climate, etc.; features and arrangement of a place. **geographical** *a.*, **geographically** *adv.*, **geographer** *n.*

geology *n.* study of earth's crust; features of earth's crust. **geological** *a.*, **geologically** *adv.*, **geologist** *n.*

geometry *n.* branch of mathematics dealing with properties and relations of lines, angles, surfaces, and solids. **geometric** *a.*, **geometrical** *a.*, **geometrically** *adv.*

georgette *n.* thin silky fabric.

Georgian *a.* of the time of the Georges, kings of England, esp. 1714–1830.

geranium *n.* garden plant with red, pink, or white flowers.

gerbil /ˈdʒɜː-/ *n.* rodent with long hind legs for leaping.

geriatrics /dʒerɪˈæ-/ *n.* branch of medicine dealing with the diseases and care of old people. **geriatric** *a.*

germ *n.* micro-organism, esp. one capable of causing disease; portion (of an organism) capable of developing into a new organism; basis from which a thing may develop.

German *a.* & *n.* (native, language) of Germany.

germane /-ˈmeɪn/ *a.* relevant.

Germanic /-ˈmæ-/ *a.* having German characteristics.

germicide *n.* substance that kills germs. **germicidal** *a.*

germinate *v.t./i.* begin or cause to develop and grow. **germination** *n.*

gerontology /dʒe-/ *n.* study of ageing and of old people's problems.

gerrymander /-ˈmæn-/ *v.i.* arrange boundaries of constituencies so as to gain unfair electoral advantage.

gerund /ˈdʒe-/ *n.* English verbal noun ending in *-ing.*

Gestapo *n.* German secret police of the Nazi regime.

gestation *n.* carrying in the womb between conception and birth; period of this.

gesticulate /dʒes-/ *v.i.* make expressive movements with the hands and arms. **gesticulation** *n.*

gesture *n.* expressive movement or action. —*v.i.* make a gesture.

get *v.t./i.* (p.t. *got,* pres.p. *getting*) come into possession of; earn; win; fetch; capture, catch; establish communication with by radio or telephone; (*colloq.*) understand; prepare (a meal); bring or come into a certain state; succeed in coming or going or bringing; persuade. ~ **at,** reach; (*colloq.*) imply; (*sl.*) imply criticism of; (*sl.*) tamper with, bribe. ~ **away,** escape. ~ **by,** (*colloq.*) pass; manage to survive. ~ **off,** be acquitted; obtain an acquittal for. ~ **on,** manage; make progress; be on harmonious terms; advance in age. ~ **out of,** evade. ~**-out** *n.* means of evading something. ~ **over,** recover from. ~ **round,** influence in one's favour; evade (a law or rule). ~ **up,** stand after sitting, kneeling, or lying down; get out of bed; prepare, organize; dress. ~**-up** *n.* outfit.

getaway *n.* escape after a crime.

geyser /ˈɡaɪz-/ *n.* natural spring that spouts hot water or steam; /giz-/ a kind of water-heater.

ghastly *a.* (*-ier, -iest*) causing horror; (*colloq.*) very bad; pale and ill-looking. **ghastliness** *n.*

ghat /ɡæt/ *n.* (in India) steps down to a river; landing-place.

gherkin /ˈɡɜː-/ *n.* small cucumber used for pickling.

ghetto *n.* (pl. *-os*) slum area occupied by a particular group.

ghost *n.* person's spirit appearing after his death. —*v.t./i.* write as a ghost-writer. ~**writer** *n.* person who writes a book etc. for another to pass off as his own. **ghostly** *a.*, **ghostliness** *n.*

ghoul /ɡuːl/ *n.* (in Muslim stories) spirit that robs and devours corpses; person who enjoys gruesome things. **ghoulish** *a.*, **ghoulishly** *adv.*

giant *n.* (in fairy-tales) a being of superhuman size; abnormally large person, animal, or thing; person of outstanding ability. —*a.* very large. **giantess** *n.fem.*

gibber *v.i.* make meaningless sounds, esp. when shocked or terrified.

gibberish *n.* unintelligible talk, nonsense.

gibbet *n.* gallows; post with an arm from which an executed criminal was hung.

gibbon *n.* long-armed ape.

gibe /dʒaɪb/ *n.* & *v.t./i.* jeer.

giblets *n.pl.* edible organs from a bird.

giddy *a.* (*-ier*, *-iest*) having or causing the feeling that everything is spinning round. **giddily** *adv.*, **giddiness** *n.*

gift *n.* thing given or received without payment; natural ability; easy task. **~-wrap** *v.t.* (p.t. *-wrapped*) wrap attractively as a gift.

gifted *a.* having great natural ability.

gig[1] /g-/ *n.* light two-wheeled horse-drawn carriage.

gig[2] /g-/ *n.* (*colloq.*) engagement to play jazz etc.

gigantic *a.* very large.

giggle *v.i.* laugh in a silly or nervous way. —*n.* this laugh.

gigolo /ˈdʒɪ-/ *n.* (pl. *-os*) man paid by a woman to be her escort or lover.

gild[1] *v.t.* (p.t. & p.p. *gilded*) cover with a thin layer of gold or gold paint.

gild[2] *n.* old spelling of **guild.**

gill[1] /g-/ *n.* (usu. *pl.*) respiratory opening on the body of a fish etc.; one of the vertical plates on the underside of a mushroom cap.

gill[2] /dʒɪ-/ *n.* one quarter of a pint.

gillie /ˈgɪ-/ *n.* man or boy attending a person hunting or fishing in Scotland.

gilt[1] *a.* gilded, gold-coloured. —*n.* substance used in gilding; gilt-edged investment. **~-edged** *a.* (of an investment etc.) very safe.

gilt[2] *n.* young sow.

gimbals /ˈgɪ-/ *n.pl.* contrivance of rings to keep instruments horizontal in a moving ship etc.

gimcrack /ˈdʒɪ-/ *a.* cheap and flimsy.

gimlet *n.* small tool with a screw-like tip for boring holes.

gimmick /ˈgɪ-/ *n.* trick or device to attract attention or publicity. **gimmicky** *a.*

gin[1] *n.* trap, snare; machine for separating raw cotton from its seeds. —*v.t.* (p.t. *ginned*) treat (cotton) in a gin.

gin[2] *n.* alcoholic spirit flavoured with juniper berries.

ginger *n.* hot-tasting root of a tropical plant; liveliness; reddish yellow. —*a.* ginger-coloured. —*v.t.* make more lively. **~ ale, ~ beer,** ginger-flavoured fizzy drinks.

gingerbread *n.* ginger-flavoured cake or biscuit.

gingerly *a.* & *adv.* cautious(ly).

gingham *n.* cotton fabric, often with a checked or striped pattern.

gipsy *n.* = gypsy.

giraffe *n.* long-necked African animal.

gird *v.t.* encircle, attach with a belt or band.

girder *n.* metal beam supporting part of a building or bridge.

girdle[1] *n.* belt or cord worn round the waist; elastic corset; ring of bones in the body. —*v.t.* surround.

girdle[2] *n.* round iron plate for cooking things over heat.

girl *n.* female child; young woman; female assistant or employee; man's girl-friend. **~-friend** *n.* female friend, esp. man's usual companion. **girlhood** *n.*, **girlish** *a.*

girlie *n.* (*colloq.*) girl. **~ magazines,** those containing erotic pictures of young women.

giro /ˈdʒaɪ-/ *n.* (pl. *-os*) banking system by which payment can be made by transferring credit from one account to another.

girt *a.* (*poet.*) girded.

girth *n.* distance round something; band passing under a horse's belly, holding a saddle in place.

gist /dʒɪ-/ *n.* essential points or general sense of a speech etc.

give *v.t./i.* (p.t. *gave*, p.p. *given*) cause to receive or have; supply; provide; utter; pledge; make over in exchange or payment; present (a play etc.) in public; yield as a product or result; permit a view or access; declare (judgement) authoritatively; be flexible. —*n.* springiness, elasticity. **~ away,** give as a gift; hand over (a bride) to a bridegroom; reveal (a secret etc.) unintentionally. **~ in,** acknowledge that one is defeated. **~ off,** emit. **~ out,** announce; become exhausted or used up. **~ over,** devote; (*colloq.*) cease. **~ tongue,** speak; (of hounds) bark. **~ up,** cease; part with, hand over; abandon hope or an attempt. **~ way,** yield; allow other traffic to go first; collapse. **giver** *n.*

given *see* **give.** —*a.* specified; having a tendency. **~ name,** Christian name, first name (given in addition to the family name).

gizzard *n.* bird's second stomach, in which food is ground.

glacé /ˈglæseɪ/ *a.* iced with sugar; preserved in sugar.

glacial /ˈgleɪʃəl/ *a.* icy; of or from glaciers or other ice.

glacier /ˈglæ-/ *n.* mass or river of ice moving very slowly.

glad *a.* pleased, joyful. **gladly** *adv.*, **gladness** *n.*

gladden *v.t.* make glad.

glade *n.* open space in a forest.

gladiator *n.* man trained to fight at public shows in ancient Rome. **gladiatorial** *a.*

gladiolus *n.* (pl. *-li*) garden plant with spikes of flowers.

glamorize *v.t.* make glamorous.

glamour *n.* alluring beauty; attractive exciting qualities. **glamorous** *a.*

glance *v.i.* look briefly; strike and glide off. —*n.* brief look.

gland *n.* organ that extracts from the blood substances to be used or expelled by the body. **glandular** *a.*

glare *v.i.* shine with a harsh dazzling light; stare angrily or fiercely. —*n.* glaring light or stare.

glass *n.* hard brittle usu. transparent substance; things made of this; mirror; glass drinking-vessel; barometer; (*pl.*) spectacles, binoculars. **glassy** *a.*

glasshouse *n.* greenhouse; (*sl.*) military prison.

glaucoma *n.* condition caused by increased pressure of fluid within the eyeball.

glaze *v.t./i.* fit or cover with glass; coat with a glossy surface; become glassy. —*n.* shiny surface or coating.

glazier *n.* person whose trade is to fit glass in windows etc.

gleam *n.* beam or ray of soft light; brief show of a quality. —*v.i.* send out gleams.

glean *v.t./i.* pick up grain left by harvesters; gather scraps of. **gleaner** *n.*

glee *n.* lively or triumphant joy; part-song. **~ club,** type of choral society. **gleeful** *a.,* **gleefully** *adv.*

glen *n.* narrow valley.

glengarry *n.* Scotch cap with a pointed front.

glib *a.* ready with words but insincere or superficial.

glide *v.i.* move smoothly; fly in a glider or aircraft without engine power. *—n.* gliding movement.

glider *n.* aeroplane with no engine.

glimmer *n.* faint gleam. *—v.i.* gleam faintly.

glimpse *n.* brief view. *—v.t.* catch a glimpse of.

glint *n.* very brief flash of light. *—v.i.* send out a glint.

glissade /-'seɪd/ *v.i.* slide skilfully. *—n.* glissading movement.

glisten *v.i.* shine like something wet.

glitter *v.i. & n.* sparkle.

gloat *v.i.* be full of greedy or malicious delight.

global *a.* world-wide. **globally** *adv.*

globe *n.* ball-shaped object, esp. with a map of the earth on it; the world; hollow round glass object. **~-trotting** *n.* travelling widely as a tourist.

globular *a.* shaped like a globe.

globule *n.* small rounded drop.

glockenspiel *n.* musical instrument of tuned steel bars or tubes struck by hammers.

gloom *n.* semi-darkness; feeling of sadness and depression. **gloomy** *a.* (*-ier, -iest*), **gloomily** *adv.*

glorify *v.t.* praise highly; worship; make (a thing) seem grander than it is. **glorification** *n.*

glorious *a.* possessing or bringing glory; splendid. **gloriously** *adv.*

glory *n.* fame and honour won by great deeds; adoration and praise in worship; beauty, magnificence; thing deserving praise and honour. *—v.i.* rejoice, pride oneself. **~-hole** *n.* (*sl.*) untidy room or cupboard etc.

gloss *n.* shine on a smooth surface; explanatory comment. *—v.t.* make glossy. **~ over,** cover up (a mistake or fault).

glossary *n.* list of technical or special words, with definitions.

glossy *a.* (*-ier, -iest*) shiny. **glossily** *adv.,* **glossiness** *n.*

glove *n.* covering for the hand, usu. with separate divisions for fingers and thumb.

gloved *a.* wearing a glove.

glover *n.* maker of gloves.

glow *v.i.* send out light and heat without flame; have a warm or flushed look, colour, or feeling. *—n.* glowing state, look, or feeling. **~-worm** *n.* beetle that can give out a greenish light at its tail.

glower /'glaʊ-/ *v.i.* scowl.

glowing *a.* (of a description etc.) very enthusiastic or favourable.

gloxinia *n.* tropical plant with bell-shaped flowers.

glucose *n.* form of sugar found in fruit-juice.

glue *n.* sticky substance used for joining things together. *—v.t.* (pres.p. *gluing*) fasten with glue; attach closely. **gluey** *a.*

glum *a.* (*glummer, glummest*) sad and gloomy.

glut *v.t.* (p.t. *glutted*) supply with more than is needed; satisfy fully with food. *—n.* excessive supply.

gluten /'glu-/ *n.* sticky protein substance left when starch is washed out of flour.

glutinous *a.* glue-like, sticky.

glutton *n.* one who eats far too much; one who is eager for something; animal of the weasel family. **gluttonous** *a.,* **gluttony** *n.*

glycerine /-ɪn/ *n.* thick sweet liquid used in medicines etc.

G.M.T. *abbr.* Greenwich Mean Time.

gnarled *a.* knobbly; twisted and misshapen.

gnash *v.t./i.* (of teeth) strike together; grind (one's teeth).

gnat *n.* small biting fly.

gnaw *v.t./i.* bite persistently (at something hard).

gnome *n.* dwarf in fairy-tales, living underground and guarding treasure; *G~,* (*colloq.*) one of the important influential financiers.

gnu /nu/ *n.* ox-like antelope.

go *v.i.* (p.t. *went,* p.p. *gone*) move; leave; extend; be in a specified state; be functioning; make a specified movement or sound; (of time) pass; be allowable or acceptable; belong in a specified place; be, on average; become; proceed; be sold; be spent or used up; be abolished or lost; fail, die; be able to be put; be given or allotted; be guided or directed; contribute, serve. *—n.* (pl. *goes*) energy; turn, try; success; attack of illness. **be going to,** be about or likely to (do something). **~-ahead** *n.* signal to proceed; (*a.*) energetic. **~ back on,** fail to keep (a promise). **~-between** *n.* one who acts as messenger or negotiator. **~ cart** *n.* simple four-wheeled structure for a child to play on. **~ for,** (*sl.*) attack. **~-getter** *n.* (*colloq.*) pushful enterprising person. **~-go** *a.* (*colloq.*) very active or energetic. **~-kart** *n.* miniature racing-car. **~-karting** *n.* racing in this. **~ out,** be extinguished. **~ round,** be enough for everyone. **~-slow** *n.* deliberately slow pace of work as a form of industrial protest. **~ under,** succumb; fail. **~ up,** rise in price; explode; burn rapidly. **~ with,** match, harmonize with. **on the ~,** in constant motion, active.

goad *n.* pointed stick for prodding cattle to move; stimulus to activity. *—v.t.* stimulate by annoying.

goal *n.* structure or area into which players try to send the ball in certain games; point scored thus; objective. **~-post** *n.* either of the posts marking the limit of a goal.

goalie *n.* (*colloq.*) goalkeeper.

goalkeeper *n.* player whose task is to keep the ball out of the goal.

goat *n.* small horned animal.

goatee *n.* short pointed beard.

gobble *v.t./i.* eat quickly and greedily; make a throaty sound like a turkey-cock.

gobbledegook *n.* (*sl.*) pompous language used by officials.

goblet *n.* drinking-glass with a stem and foot; container for the liquid in a liquidizer.

goblin *n.* mischievous ugly elf.

God *n.* creator and ruler of the universe in Christian, Jewish, and Muslim teaching. **god** *n.* superhuman being worshipped as having power over nature and human affairs; person or thing that is greatly admired or adored. **God-fearing** *a.* sincerely religious. **God-forsaken** *a.* wretched, dismal.

godchild *n.* (pl. *-children*) child in relation to its godparent(s).

god-daughter *n.* female godchild.

goddess *n.* female god.

godfather *n.* male godparent; (*U.S.*) mastermind of an illegal organization.

godhead *n.* divine nature; *the G~*, God.

godlike *a.* like God or a god. **godliness** *n.*

godly *a.* sincerely religious. **godliness** *n.*

godmother *n.* female godparent.

godparent *n.* person who undertakes, when a child is baptized, to see that it is brought up as a Christian.

godsend *n.* piece of unexpected good fortune.

godson *n.* male godchild.

goggle *v.i.* stare with wide-open eyes.

goggles *n.pl.* spectacles for protecting the eyes from wind, water, etc.

going *pres.p.* of **go**.

goitre *n.* enlarged thyroid gland.

gold *n.* yellow metal of high value; coins or articles made of this; its colour. —*a.* made of or coloured like gold. **~-digger** *n.* woman who uses her attractions to obtain money from men. **~-mine** *n.* place where gold is mined; source of great wealth.

golden *a.* gold; precious, excellent. **~ handshake,** generous cash payment to a person dismissed or forced to retire. **~ jubilee, ~ wedding,** 50th anniversary.

goldfinch *n.* song-bird with a band of yellow across each wing.

goldfish *n.* (pl. *goldfish*) small reddish Chinese carp kept in a bowl or pond.

goldsmith *n.* person whose trade is making articles in gold.

golf *n.* game in which a ball is struck with clubs towards and into a series of holes. **~-course, ~-links** *ns.* area of land on which golf is played. **golfer** *n.*

golliwog *n.* a kind of black male doll with fuzzy hair.

golosh *n.* = galosh.

gondola *n.* boat with high pointed ends, used on canals in Venice; structure slung beneath a balloon, for carrying passengers etc.

gondolier *n.* man who propels a gondola by means of a pole.

gone *see* **go**.

gong *n.* metal plate that resounds when struck, esp. as a signal for meals.

goo *n.* (*sl.*) sticky wet substance.

good *a.* (*better, best*) having the right or desirable qualities; proper, expedient; morally correct, kindly; well-behaved; enjoyable, beneficial; efficient; thorough; considerable, full. —*n.* morally right thing; profit, benefit; (*pl.*) movable property, articles of trade, things to be carried by road or rail. **as ~ as,** practically, almost. **~-for-nothing** *a.* & *n.* worthless (person). **Good Friday,** Friday before Easter, commemorating the Crucifixion. **~ name,** good reputation. **~ will,** intention that good shall result.

goodwill *n.* friendly feeling; established popularity of a business, treated as a saleable asset.

goodbye *int.* & *n.* expression used when parting.

goodish *a.* fairly good; rather large or great.

goodness *n.* quality of being good; good element; (in exclamations) God.

goody *n.* (*colloq.*) something good or attractive, esp. to eat. **~-goody** *a.* & *n.* smugly virtuous (person).

gooey *a.* (*sl.*) wet and sticky.

goofy *a.* (*sl.*) stupid.

googly *n.* ball bowled to break in an unexpected direction.

goose *n.* (pl. *geese*) web-footed bird larger than a duck. **~-flesh, ~-pimples** *ns.* bristling skin caused by cold or fear. **~ step,** way of marching without bending the knees.

gooseberry *n.* thorny shrub; its edible berry.

Gordian *a.* **cut the ~ knot,** solve a problem forcefully.

gore[1] *n.* clotted blood from a wound.

gore[2] *v.t.* pierce with a horn.

gore[3] *n.* triangular or tapering section of a skirt or sail. **gored** *a.*

gorge *n.* narrow steep-sided valley. —*v.t./i.* eat greedily; fill full, choke up. **one's ~ rises,** one is sickened or disgusted.

gorgeous *a.* richly coloured, magnificent; (*colloq.*) very pleasant, beautiful. **gorgeously** *adv.*

gorgon *n.* terrifying woman.

Gorgonzola *n.* rich strong blue-veined cheese.

gorilla *n.* large powerful ape.

gormandize *v.i.* eat greedily.

gormless *a.* (*sl.*) stupid.

gorse *n.* wild evergreen thorny shrub with yellow flowers.

gory *a.* (*-ier, -iest*) covered with blood; involving bloodshed.

gosh *int.* (*sl.*) exclamation of surprise.

gosling *n.* young goose.

gospel *n.* teachings of Christ; thing one may safely believe; set of principles believed in. **Gospel** *n.* book(s) of the New Testament recording Christ's life and teachings.

gossamer *n.* fine filmy piece of cobweb; flimsy delicate material.

gossip *n.* casual talk, esp. about other people's affairs; person fond of gossiping. —*v.i.* (p.t. *gossiped*) engage in gossip. **gossipy** *a.*

got *see* **get**. — **have ~,** possess. **have ~ to do it,** must do it.

Goth *n.* one of the Germanic invaders of the Roman Empire in the 3rd–5th centuries.

Gothic *a.* of an architectural style of the 12th–16th centuries, with pointed arches.

gouge *n.* chisel with a concave blade. —*v.t.* cut out with a gouge; scoop or force out.

goulash *n.* stew of meat and vegetables, seasoned with paprika.

gourd *n.* fleshy fruit of a climbing plant; container made from its dried rind.

gourmand /ˈgʊə-/ *n.* glutton.

gourmet /ˈgʊə-/ *n.* connoisseur of good food and drink.

gout *n.* disease causing inflammation of the joints. **gouty** *a.*

govern *v.t./i.* rule with authority; conduct the affairs of a country or organization; keep under control; influence, direct. **governor** *n.*

governance *n.* governing, control.

governess *n.* woman employed to teach children in a private household.

government *n.* governing; group or organization governing a country; State as an agent. **governmental** *a.*

gown *n.* loose flowing garment; woman's long dress; official robe.

G.P. *abbr.* general practitioner.

grab *v.t./i.* (p.t. *grabbed*) grasp suddenly; take greedily; operate harshly. —*n.* sudden clutch or attempt to seize; mechanical device for gripping things.

grace *n.* attractiveness and elegance, esp. of manner or design or ease of movement; favour; mercy; short prayer of thanks said at a meal; title of a duke, duchess, or archbishop. —*v.t.* confer honour or dignity on, be an ornament to.

graceful *a.* having or showing grace. **gracefully** *adv.*, **gracefulness** *n.*

graceless *a.* inelegant; ungracious.

gracious *a.* kind and pleasant towards inferiors; merciful; elegant. **graciously** *adv.*, **graciousness** *n.*

gradation *n.* process of gradual change; stage in this.

grade *n.* level of rank, quality, or value; class of people or things of the same grade; mark given to a student for his standard of work; slope. —*v.t.* arrange in grades; assign a grade to; adjust the slope of (a road).

gradient *n.* slope, amount of this.

gradual *a.* taking place by degrees, not sudden. **gradually** *adv.*

graduate[1] /-ət/ *n.* person who holds a university degree.

graduate[2] /-eɪt/ *v.t./i.* take a university degree; divide into graded sections; mark into regular divisions. **graduation** *n.*

graffito *n.* (pl. *-ti*) words or a drawing scribbled or scratched on a wall.

graft[1] *n.* shoot fixed into a cut in a tree to form a new growth; living tissue transplanted surgically; (*sl.*) hard work. —*v.t./i.* put a graft in or on; join inseparably; (*sl.*) work hard.

graft[2] *n.* obtaining an advantage by bribery or unfair means; this bribe or bribery; the advantage gained.

Grail *n.* Holy ~, cup or platter used by Christ at the Last Supper.

grain *n.* small hard seed(s) of a food plant such as wheat or rice; these plants; small hard particle; unit of weight (about 65 mg); texture produced by particles in stone etc.; pattern of lines made by fibres or layers. **grainy** *a.*

gram *n.* one thousandth of a kilogram.

grammar *n.* use of words in their correct forms and relationships. ~ **school,** secondary school for pupils with academic ability.

grammatical *a.* according to the rules of grammar. **grammatically** *adv.*

gramophone *n.* record-player.

grampus *n.* dolphin-like sea animal.

gran *n.* (*colloq.*) grandmother.

granary *n.* storehouse for grain.

grand *a.* (*-er*, *-est*) great; splendid; imposing; (*colloq.*) very good. —*n.* grand piano; (*sl.*) one thousand pounds or dollars. ~ **piano,** large full-toned piano with horizontal strings. **Grand Prix** /grã pri/, important international motor race. **grandly** *adv.*, **grandness** *n.*

grandad *n.* (*colloq.*) grandfather.

grandchild *n.* (pl. *-children*) child of one's son or daughter.

granddaughter *n.* female grandchild.

grandee *n.* person of high rank.

grandeur *n.* splendour, grandness.

grandfather *n.* male grandparent. ~ **clock,** one in a tall wooden case.

grandiloquent /-ˈdɪl-/ *a.* using pompous language. **grandiloquence** *n.*

grandiose *a.* imposing; planned on a large scale; pompous.

grandma *n.* (*colloq.*) grandmother.

grandmother *n.* female grandparent. ~ **clock,** one like a grandfather clock but in a smaller case.

grandpa *n.* (*colloq.*) grandfather.

grandparent *n.* parent of one's father or mother.

grandson *n.* male grandchild.

grandstand *n.* principal roofed building for spectators at races and sports.

grange *n.* country house with farm-buildings that belong to it.

granite *n.* hard grey stone.

granny *n.* (*colloq.*) grandmother. ~ **knot,** reef-knot with threads crossed the wrong way.

grant *v.t.* give or allow as a privilege; admit to be true. —*n.* thing granted; student's allowance from public funds. **take for granted,** assume to be true or sure to happen or continue.

granular *a.* like grains.

granulated *a.* formed into grains. **granulation** *n.*

granule *n.* small grain.

grape *n.* green or purple berry used for making wine. ~**vine** *n.* vine bearing this; way news spreads unofficially.

grapefruit *n.* large round yellow citrus fruit.

graph *n.* diagram of line(s) showing the relationship between quantities. —*v.t.* draw a graph of.

graphic *a.* of drawing, painting, or engraving; giving a vivid description. **graphically** *adv.*

graphical *a.* using diagrams or graphs. **graphically** *adv.*

graphite *n.* a form of carbon.

graphology *n.* study of handwriting. **graphologist** *n.*

grapnel *n.* small anchor with several hooks; hooked device for dragging a river-bed.

grapple *v.t./i.* seize, hold firmly; struggle. **grappling-iron** *n.* grapnel.

grasp *v.t./i.* seize and hold; understand. —*n.* firm hold or grip; understanding. ∼ **at,** snatch at.

grasping *a.* greedy for money or possessions.

grass *n.* wild low-growing plant with green blades eaten by animals; species of this (e.g. a cereal plant); ground covered with grass; (*sl.*) person who grasses, betrayal. —*v.t.* cover with grass; (*sl.*) betray a conspiracy etc. ∼ **roots,** fundamental level or source; rank-and-file members. ∼ **widow,** wife whose husband is absent for some time. **grassy** *a.*

grasshopper *n.* jumping insect that makes a chirping noise.

grassland *n.* wide grass-covered area with few trees.

grate[1] *n.* metal framework keeping fuel in a fireplace; hearth.

grate[2] *v.t./i.* shred finely by rubbing against a jagged surface; make a harsh noise by rubbing; sound harshly; have an irritating effect.

grateful *a.* feeling that one values a kindness or benefit received. **gratefully** *adv.*

grater *n.* device for grating food.

gratify *v.t.* give pleasure to; satisfy (wishes). **gratification** *n.*

grating *n.* screen of spaced bars placed across an opening.

gratis /-eɪ- *or* -ɑ-/ *a.* & *adv.* free of charge.

gratitude *n.* being grateful.

gratuitous *a.* given or done free of charge; uncalled for.

gratuity *n.* money given as a present for services rendered.

grave[1] *n.* hole dug to bury a corpse.

grave[2] *a.* (-*er*, -*est*) serious, causing great anxiety; solemn. ∼ **accent** /grɑv/, the accent ˋ. **gravely** *adv.*

gravel *n.* coarse sand with small stones, used for paths.

graven *a.* carved.

gravestone *n.* stone placed over a grave.

graveyard *n.* burial ground.

gravitate *v.i.* move or be attracted towards something.

gravitation *n.* gravitating; force of gravity.

gravity *n.* seriousness; solemnity; force that attracts bodies towards the centre of the earth.

gravy *n.* juice from cooked meat; sauce made from this.

grayling *n.* grey freshwater fish.

graze[1] *v.t./i.* feed on growing grass; pasture animals in (a field).

graze[2] *v.t./i.* touch or scrape lightly in passing; scrape skin from. —*n.* grazed place on the skin.

grease *n.* animal fat melted soft; any thick oily substance. —*v.t.* put grease on. ∼**-paint** *n.* make-up used by actors. **greasy** *a.*

great *a.* (-*er*, -*est*) much above average in size or amount or intensity; of remarkable ability or character, important; (*colloq.*) very good; (of family relationship) one generation removed in ancestry or descent. **greatly** *adv.*, **greatness** *n.*

greatcoat *n.* heavy overcoat.

grebe *n.* a diving bird.

Grecian *a.* Greek.

greed *n.* excessive desire, esp. for food or wealth. **greedy** *a.* (-*ier*, -*iest*), **greedily** *adv.*, **greediness** *n.*

Greek *a.* & *n.* (native, language) of Greece.

green *a.* (-*er*, -*est*) of the colour between blue and yellow, coloured like grass; unripe, not seasoned, (of bacon) not smoked; immature, inexperienced, easily deceived. —*n.* green colour or thing; piece of grassy public land; grassy area; (*pl.*, *colloq.*) green vegetables. ∼ **belt,** area of open land round a town. ∼ **fingers,** skill in making plants grow. ∼ **light,** signal or (*colloq.*) permission to proceed. **Green Paper,** government report of proposals being considered. ∼ **pound,** agreed value of the £ used for reckoning payments to E.E.C. agricultural producers. ∼**-room** *n.* room in a theatre for the use of actors when off stage. **greenness** *n.*

greenery *n.* green foliage or plants.

greenfinch *n.* finch with green and yellow feathers.

greenfly *n.* (pl. -*fly*) small green insect that sucks juices from plants.

greengage *n.* round plum with a greenish skin.

greengrocer *n.* shopkeeper selling vegetables and fruit. **greengrocery** *n.* his shop or goods.

greenhorn *n.* inexperienced person.

greenhouse *n.* building with glass sides and roof, for rearing plants.

greenish *a.* rather green.

greenstick *n.* ∼ **fracture,** bone-fracture in which the bone is partly broken and partly bent.

greet *v.t.* address politely on meeting or arrival; react to; present itself to (sight or hearing).

gregarious *a.* living in flocks or communities; fond of company.

gremlin *n.* mischievous spirit said to cause mishaps to machinery.

grenade *n.* small bomb thrown by hand or fired from a rifle.

grew *see* **grow.**

grey *a.* (-*er*, -*est*) of the colour between black and white, coloured like ashes. —*n.* grey colour or thing. —*v.t./i.* make or become grey. **greyness** *n.*

greyhound *n.* slender smooth-haired dog noted for its swiftness.

greyish *a.* rather grey.

greylag *n.* grey wild goose.

grid *n.* grating; system of numbered squares for map references; network of lines, power-cables, etc.; gridiron. **gridded** *a.*

griddle *n.* = **girdle**².

gridiron *n.* framework of metal bars for cooking on; field for American football, marked with parallel lines.

grief *n.* deep sorrow. **come to** ∼, meet with disaster; fail; fall.

grievance *n.* ground of complaint.

grieve *v.t./i.* cause grief to; feel grief.

grievous *a.* causing grief; serious.

griffin *n.* mythological creature with an eagle's head and wings on a lion's body.

griffon *n.* small terrier-like dog; a kind of vulture.

grill *n.* metal grid, grating; device on a cooker for radiating heat downwards; grilled food; grill-room. —*v.t./i.* cook under a grill or on a gridiron; question closely and severely. ∼-**room** *n.* restaurant or room where grills and other foods are served.

grille *n.* grating, esp. in a door or window.

grilse *n.* young salmon returning from sea to spawn for the first time.

grim *a.* (*grimmer, grimmest*) stern, severe; without cheerfulness, unattractive. **grimly** *adv.*, **grimness** *n.*

grimace *n.* contortion of the face in pain or disgust, or done to cause amusement. —*v.i.* make a grimace.

grime *n.* ingrained dirt. —*v.t.* blacken with grime. **grimy** *a.* (*-ier, -iest*), **griminess** *n.*

grin *v.i.* (p.t. *grinned*) smile broadly, showing the teeth. —*n.* broad smile.

grind *v.t./i.* (p.t. *ground*) crush into grains or powder; produce thus; crush or oppress by cruelty; sharpen or smooth by friction; rub harshly together; make a grating sound; produce with effort; study hard. —*n.* grinding process; hard monotonous work. **grinder** *n.*

grindstone *n.* thick revolving disc for sharpening or grinding things.

grip *v.t./i.* (p.t. *gripped*) take firm hold of; hold the attention of. —*n.* firm grasp or hold; way of or thing for grasping or holding; understanding, mental hold or control; (*U.S.*) suitcase, travelling-bag.

gripe *v.t./i.* cause colic; (*sl.*) grumble. —*n.* (*sl.*) grumble.

grisly *a.* (*-ier, -iest*) causing fear, horror, or disgust.

grist *n.* grain to be ground or already ground.

gristle *n.* tough flexible tissue of animal bodies, esp. in meat. **gristly** *a.*

grit *n.* particles of stone or sand; courage and endurance. —*v.t./i.* (p.t. *gritted*) make a grating sound; clench; spread grit on. **gritty** *a.*, **grittiness** *n.*

grizzle *v.i. & n.* whimper, whine.

grizzled *a.* grey; grey-haired.

grizzly *a.* grizzled. ∼ **bear**, large grey bear of North America.

groan *v.i.* make a long deep sound in pain, grief, or disapproval; make a deep creaking sound. —*n.* sound made by groaning.

groats *n.pl.* crushed oats.

grocer *n.* shopkeeper selling foods and household stores.

grocery *n.* grocer's shop or goods.

grog *n.* drink of spirits mixed with water.

groggy *a.* weak and unsteady, esp. after illness. **groggily** *adv.*

groin *n.* groove where each thigh joins the trunk; curved edge where two vaults meet in a roof; arch supporting a vault.

groom *n.* person employed to look after horses; official of the royal household; bridegroom. —*v.t.* clean and brush (an animal); make neat and trim; prepare (a person) for a career or position.

groove *n.* long narrow channel. —*v.t.* make groove(s) in.

grope *v.i.* feel about as one does in the dark.

grosgrain /ˈgrəʊ-/ *n.* silky corded fabric used for ribbons etc.

gross *a.* (*-er, -est*) thick, large-bodied; vulgar; outrageous; total, without deductions.—*n.* (pl. *gross*) twelve dozen. —*v.t.* produce or earn as total profit. ∼ **up**, work out the gross amount by re-adding to the net amount the tax etc. deducted. **grossly** *adv.*

grotesque *a.* very odd or ugly.

grotto *n.* (pl. *-oes*) picturesque cave.

grouch *v.i. & n.* (*colloq.*) grumble.

ground¹ *n.* solid surface of earth; area, position, or distance on this, (*pl.*) enclosed land of a large house or institution; foundation for a theory, reason for action; underlying part; (*pl.*) solid particles (e.g. of coffee) that do not dissolve. —*v.t./i.* run aground; prevent (an aircraft or airman) from flying; base; give basic training to. ∼-**nut** *n.* peanut. ∼-**rent** *n.* rent paid for land leased for building. ∼ **swell**, slow heavy waves.

ground² *see* **grind.** —*a.* ∼ **glass**, glass made opaque by grinding.

grounding *n.* basic training.

groundless *a.* without foundation.

groundsel *n.* a kind of weed.

groundsheet *n.* waterproof sheet for spreading on the ground.

groundsman *n.* (pl. *-men*) man employed to look after a sports ground.

groundwork *n.* preliminary or basic work.

group *n.* number of persons or things near, belonging, classed, or working together. —*v.t./i.* form or gather into group(s).

grouper *n.* sea-fish used as food.

grouse¹ *n.* a kind of game-bird.

grouse² *v.i. & n.* (*colloq.*) grumble. **grouser** *n.*

grout *n.* thin fluid mortar. —*v.t.* fill with grout.

grove *n.* group of trees.

grovel *v.i.* (p.t. *grovelled*) lie or crawl face downwards; humble oneself.

grow *v.t./i.* (p.t. *grew*, p.p. *grown*) increase in size or amount; develop or exist as a living plant; become; allow to grow; produce by cultivation. ∼ **up**, become adult or mature. **grower** *n.*

growl *v.i.* make a low threatening sound as a dog does. —*n.* this sound.

grown *see* **grow.** —*a.* adult; covered with a growth. **~-up** *a.* & *n.* adult.

growth *n.* process of growing; thing that grows or has grown; tumour.

groyne *n.* solid structure projecting towards the sea to prevent sand and pebbles from being washed away.

grub *n.* worm-like larva of certain insects; (*sl.*) food. —*v.t./i.* (p.t. *grubbed*) dig the surface of soil; dig up by the roots; rummage. **~-screw** *n.* headless screw.

grubby *a.* (*-ier, -iest*) infested with grubs; dirty. **grubbiness** *n.*

grudge *v.t.* resent having to give or allow. —*n.* feeling of resentment or ill will.

gruel *n.* thin oatmeal porridge, esp. for invalids.

gruelling *a.* very tiring.

gruesome *a.* filling one with horror or disgust.

gruff *a.* (*-er, -est*) (of the voice) low and hoarse; having a gruff voice; surly. **gruffly** *adv.*, **gruffness** *n.*

grumble *v.i.* complain in a bad-tempered way; rumble. —*n.* complaint, esp. a bad-tempered one; rumble. **grumbler** *n.*

grumpy *a.* (*-ier, -iest*) bad-tempered. **grumpily** *adv.*, **grumpiness** *n.*

grunt *n.* gruff snorting sound made by a pig. —*v.t./i.* make this sound; speak or utter with such a sound.

G-string *n.* narrow strip of cloth etc. covering the genitals, attached to a string round the waist.

guano *n.* dung of sea-birds, used as manure; artificial manure esp. made from fish.

guarantee *n.* formal promise to do something or that a thing is of specified quality and durability; thing offered as security; guarantor. —*v.t.* give or be a guarantee of or to.

guarantor *n.* giver of a guarantee.

guard *v.t./i.* watch over and protect or supervise; restrain; take precautions. —*n.* state of watchfulness for danger; defensive attitude in boxing, cricket, etc.; person guarding something; railway official in charge of a train; body of soldiers guarding a place or person, or (*pl.*) as a section of an army; protecting part or device.

guarded *a.* cautious, discreet.

guardian *n.* one who guards or protects; person undertaking legal responsibility for an orphan.

guardsman *n.* (pl. *-men*) soldier acting as guard.

guava /ˈgwɑ-/ *n.* orange-coloured fruit of a tropical American tree.

gudgeon[1] *n.* small freshwater fish.

gudgeon[2] *n.* a kind of pivot; socket for a rudder; metal pin.

guelder /ˈge-/ *n.* **~ rose,** shrub with round white flowers.

guerrilla *n.* person who takes part in **~ warfare,** fighting or harassment by small groups acting independently.

guess *v.t./i.* form an opinion or state without definite knowledge or without measuring; think likely; (*U.S.*) suppose. —*n.* opinion formed by guessing.

guesstimate *n.* (*colloq.*) estimate formed by guesswork.

guesswork *n.* guessing.

guest *n.* person entertained at another's house or table etc., or lodging at a hotel; visiting performer. **~-house** *n.* superior boarding-house.

guff *n.* (*sl.*) empty talk.

guffaw *n.* coarse noisy laugh. —*v.i.* give a guffaw.

guidance *n.* guiding; advising or advice on problems.

guide *n.* person who shows others the way; one employed to point out interesting sights to travellers; guidebook, book of information about a subject; directing principle; thing marking a position or steering moving parts. —*v.t.* act as guide to. **~-book** *n.* book of information about a place, for visitors.

Guide *n.* member of the Girl Guides Association.

guild *n.* association of craftsmen or merchants.

guilder *n.* unit of money of the Netherlands.

Guild-hall *n.* town hall.

guile *n.* treacherous cunning, craftiness. **guileful** *a.*, **guileless** *a.*

guillemot /ˈgɪlɪmɒt/ *n.* a kind of auk.

guillotine *n.* machine used in France for beheading criminals; machine with a long blade for cutting paper or metal; fixing of times for voting in Parliament, to prevent a lengthy debate. —*v.t.* use a guillotine on.

guilt *n.* fact of having committed an offence; feeling that one is to blame. **guiltless** *a.*

guilty *a.* (*-ier, -iest*) having done wrong; feeling or showing guilt. **guiltily** *adv.*

guinea *n.* former British coin worth 21 shillings (£1·05); this amount. **~-fowl** *n.* bird of the pheasant family. **~-pig** *n.* rat-like animal kept as a pet or for biological experiments; person or thing used as a subject for an experiment.

guise *n.* false outward manner or appearance; pretence.

guitar *n.* a kind of stringed musical instrument. **guitarist** *n.*

gulf *n.* large area of sea partly surrounded by land; deep hollow; wide difference in opinion.

gull *n.* sea-bird with long wings.

gullet *n.* passage by which food goes from mouth to stomach.

gullible *a.* easily deceived. **gullibility** *n.*

gully *n.* narrow channel cut by water or carrying rainwater from a building; fielding position in cricket.

gulp *v.t./i.* swallow (food etc.) hastily or greedily; make a gulping movement. —*n.* act of gulping; large mouthful of liquid gulped.

gum[1] *n.* firm flesh in which teeth are rooted.

gum[2] *n.* sticky substance exuded by certain trees, used for sticking things together; chewing-gum; gum-drop; gum-tree. —*v.t.* (p.t. *gummed*) smear or stick together with gum. **~-drop** *n.* hard gelatine sweet.

∼-tree *n.* tree that exudes gum; eucalyptus. **gummy** *a.*

gumboil *n.* small abscess on the gum.

gumboot *n.* rubber boot, wellington.

gumption *n.* (*colloq.*) common sense.

gumshoe *n.* (*U.S.*) galosh.

gun *n.* weapon that sends shells or bullets from a metal tube; device operating similarly. —*v.t./i.* (p.t. *gunned*) shoot with a gun. **∼-running** *n.* smuggling of firearms.

gunboat *n.* small armed vessel with heavy guns.

gunfire *n.* firing of guns.

gunman *n.* (pl. *-men*) man armed with a gun.

gunner *n.* artillery soldier, esp. a private; naval warrant officer in charge of a battery of guns; member of an aircraft crew who operates a gun.

gunnery *n.* construction and operating of large guns.

gunny *n.* coarse material for making sacks; sack made of this.

gunpowder *n.* explosive of saltpetre, sulphur, and charcoal.

gunroom *n.* room where sporting guns are kept; room for junior officers in a warship.

gunshot *n.* shot fired from a gun.

gunsmith *n.* maker and repairer of small firearms.

gunwale /ˈgʌnəl/ *n.* upper edge of a small ship's or boat's side.

gurgle *n.* low bubbling sound. —*v.i.* make this sound.

Gurkha *n.* member of a Hindu people in Nepal, forming regiments in the British army.

guru *n.* (pl. *-us*) Hindu spiritual teacher; revered teacher.

gush *v.t./i.* flow or pour suddenly or in great quantities; talk effusively. —*n.* sudden or great outflow; effusiveness. **gusher** *n.*

gusset *n.* triangular or diamond-shaped piece of cloth inserted to strengthen or enlarge a garment. **gusseted** *a.*

gust *n.* sudden rush of wind, rain, smoke, or sound. —*v.i.* blow in gusts. **gusty** *a.*, **gustily** *adv.*

gusto *n.* zest.

gut *n.* intestine; thread made from animal intestines; (*pl.*) abdominal organs, (*colloq.*) courage and determination. —*a.* fundamental; instinctive. —*v.t.* (p.t. *gutted*) remove guts from (fish); remove or destroy internal fittings or parts of.

gutta-percha *n.* rubbery substance made from the juice of Malayan trees.

gutter *n.* trough round a roof, or channel at a roadside, for carrying away rain-water; slum environment. —*v.i.* (of a candle) burn unsteadily so that melted wax runs freely down the sides.

guttering *n.* material for a gutter.

guttersnipe *n.* dirty child who plays in slum streets.

guttural *a.* throaty, harsh-sounding. **gutturally** *adv.*

guy[1] *n.* effigy of Guy Fawkes burnt on 5 Nov.; oddly dressed person; (*sl.*) man. —*v.t.* ridicule, esp. by comic imitation.

guy[2] *n.* rope or chain used to keep a thing steady or secured.

guzzle *v.t./i.* eat or drink greedily.

gym *n.* (*colloq.*) gymnasium. gymnastics. **∼-slip, ∼-tunic** *ns.* sleeveless tunic worn as part of a girl's school uniform.

gymkhana *n.* public display of sports competitions, esp. horse-riding.

gymnasium *n.* room equipped for physical training and gymnastics.

gymnast *n.* expert in gymnastics.

gymnastics *n.pl.* exercises to develop the muscles or demonstrate agility. **gymnastic** *a.*

gynaecology /gaɪ-/ *n.* study of the female reproductive system. **gynaecological** *a.*, **gynaecologist** *n.*

gypsophila *n.* garden plant with many small white flowers.

gypsum *n.* chalk-like substance.

gypsy *n.* member of a wandering race in Europe.

gyrate /dʒaɪ-/ *v.i.* move in circles or spirals, revolve. **gyration** *n.*

gyratory /ˈdʒaɪ-/ *a.* gyrating, following a circular or spiral path.

gyro /ˈdʒaɪ-/ *n.* (pl. *-os*) (*colloq.*) gyroscope.

gyrocompass /ˈdʒaɪ-/ *n.* navigation compass using a gyroscope.

gyroscope /ˈdʒaɪ-/ *n.* rotating device used to keep navigation instruments steady. **gyroscopic** *a.*

H

ha *int.* exclamation of triumph.

habeas corpus /heɪbɪəs/ order requiring a person to be brought before a judge or into court, esp. to investigate the authorities' right to keep him imprisoned.

haberdashery *n.* sewing-goods etc.

habit *n.* settled way of behaving; monk's or nun's long dress; a woman's riding-dress.

habitable *a.* suitable for living in.

habitat *n.* animal's or plant's natural environment.

habitation *n.* place to live in.

habitual *a.* done or doing something constantly, esp. as a habit; usual. **habitually** *adv.*

habituate *v.t.* accustom.

habitué /-tjueɪ/ *n.* one who visits a place frequently or lives there.

hack[1] *n.* horse for ordinary riding; person

doing routine work, esp. as a writer. —*v.i.* ride on horseback at an ordinary pace.

hack[2] *v.t./i.* cut, chop, or hit roughly. **~-saw** *n.* saw for metal.

hacking *a.* (of a cough) dry and frequent.

hackles *n.pl.* long feathers on a cock's neck. **with his ~ up,** angry.

hackney *n.* **~ carriage,** taxi.

hackneyed *a.* (of sayings) over-used and therefore lacking impact.

had *see* **have.**

haddock *n.* (pl. *haddock*) sea-fish like a cod, used as food.

haemoglobin *n.* red oxygen-carrying substance in blood.

haemophilia *n.* tendency to bleed excessively. **haemophiliac** *n.*

haemorrhage *n.* profuse bleeding. —*v.i.* bleed profusely.

haemorrhoids *n.pl.* varicose veins at or near the anus.

haft *n.* handle of a knife or dagger.

hag *n.* ugly old woman.

haggard *a.* looking ugly from exhaustion.

haggis *n.* Scottish dish made from sheep's heart, lungs, and liver.

haggle *v.i.* argue about price or terms when settling a bargain.

ha-ha *n.* sunk fence.

haiku /ˈhaɪkʊ/ *n.* (pl. *haiku*) three-line poem of 17 syllables.

hail[1] *v.t./i.* greet; call to; signal to and summon. **~ from,** originate or have come from.

hail[2] *n.* pellets of frozen rain falling in a shower; shower of blows, questions, etc. —*v.t./i.* pour down as or like hail. **hailstone** *n.*

hair *n.* fine thread-like strand growing from the skin; mass of these, esp. on the head. **~-do** *n.* (*colloq.*) arrangement of the hair. **~-raising** *a.* terrifying. **~-trigger** *n.* trigger operated by the slightest pressure.

hairbrush *n.* brush for grooming the hair.

haircut *n.* shortening hair by cutting it; style of this.

hairdresser *n.* person whose job is to cut and arrange hair.

hairless *a.* without hair.

hairpin *n.* U-shaped pin for keeping hair in place. **~ bend,** sharp U-shaped bend in a road.

hairspring *n.* very fine spring in a watch.

hairy *a.* (-*ier*, -*iest*) covered with hair; (*sl.*) hair-raising, difficult.

Haitian /ˈhaɪ-/ *a. & n.* (native) of Haiti.

hake *n.* (pl. *hake*) sea-fish of the cod family, used as food.

halcyon *a.* calm and peaceful; (of a period) happy and prosperous.

hale *a.* strong and healthy.

half *n.* (pl. *halves*) one of two equal parts; this amount. —*a.* amounting to a half. —*adv.* to the extent of a half, partly. **~ a dozen,** six. **~ and half,** half of one thing and half another. **~-back** *n.* player between forwards and full back(s). **~-baked** *a.* (*colloq.*) not competently planned; foolish. **~-breed** *n.* half-caste. **~-**

brother *n.* brother with only one parent in common with another. **~-caste** *n.* person of mixed race. **~-hearted** *a.* not very enthusiastic. **~-term** *n.* short holiday half-way through a school term. **~-timbered** *a.* built with a timber frame with brick or plaster filling. **~-time** *n.* interval between two halves of a game. **~-tone** *n.* illustration in which light and dark shades are represented by means of small and large dots. **~-way** *a. & adv.* at a point equidistant between two others. **~-wit** *n.* half-witted person. **~-witted** *a.* mentally retarded; stupid.

halfpenny *n.* (pl. -*pennies* for single coins, -*pence* for a sum of money) coin worth half a penny.

halibut *n.* (pl. *halibut*) large flat-fish used as food.

halitosis *n.* breath that smells unpleasant.

hall *n.* large room or building for meetings, concerts, etc.; large country house; space inside the front entrance of a house.

hallelujah *int. & n.* = alleluia.

hallmark *n.* official mark put on gold, silver, and platinum to indicate its standard; distinguishing characteristic. **hallmarked** *a.*

hallo *int. & n.* = hullo.

halloo *int. & v.i.* shout to urge on hounds or call attention.

hallow *v.t.* make holy; honour as holy.

Hallowe'en *n.* 31 Oct., eve of All Saints' Day.

hallucination *n.* illusion of seeing or hearing something not actually present. **hallucinatory** *a.*

hallucinogenic /-ˈdʒen-/ *a.* causing hallucinations.

halo *n.* (pl. -*oes*) circle of light shown round the head of a sacred figure; corona.

halt *n. & v.t./i.* stop.

halter *n.* strap round the head of a horse for leading or fastening it.

halting *a.* slow and hesitant.

halve *v.t.* divide or share equally between two; reduce by half.

halyard *n.* rope for raising or lowering a sail or flag.

ham *n.* upper part of a pig's leg, dried and salted or smoked; meat from this; back of thigh; (*sl.*) poor actor or performer; (*sl.*) operator of an amateur radio station. —*v.t./i.* (p.t. *hammed*) (*sl.*) over-act. **~-handed** *a.* (*sl.*) clumsy.

hamburger *n.* flat round cake of minced beef.

hamlet *n.* small village.

hammer *n.* tool with a heavy metal head for breaking things or driving nails in; thing shaped or used like this; metal ball attached to a wire for throwing as an athletic contest. —*v.t./i.* hit or beat with a hammer; strike loudly. **~ and tongs,** with great energy and noise. **~-toe** *n.* toe permanently bent downwards.

hammock *n.* hanging bed of canvas or netting.

hamper[1] *n.* basketwork packing-case.

hamper[2] *v.t.* prevent free movement or activity of, hinder.

hamster *n.* small rodent with cheek-pouches for carrying grain.

hamstring *n.* tendon at the back of a knee or hock. —*v.t.* (p.t. *hamstrung*) cripple by cutting hamstring(s); cripple the activity of.

hand *a.* end part of the arm, below the wrist; control, influence, or help in doing something; pledge of marriage; manual worker, member of a ship's crew; style of handwriting; signature; pointer on a dial etc.; (right or left) side; unit of 4 inches as a measure of a horse's height; round of a card-game, player's cards; (*colloq.*) applause. —*v.t.* give or pass by hand or otherwise. **at ~,** close by. **~out** *n.* thing distributed free of charge. **on ~,** available. **on one's hands,** resting on one as a responsibility. **out of ~,** out of control; without delay. **to ~,** within reach.

handbag *n.* bag to hold a purse and small personal articles; travelling-bag.

handbook *n.* small book giving useful facts.

handcuff *n.* metal ring linked to another, for securing a prisoner's wrists. —*v.t.* put handcuffs on.

handful *n.* quantity that fills the hand; a few; person difficult to control; difficult task.

handicap *n.* disadvantage imposed on a superior competitor to equalize chances; race etc. in which handicaps are imposed; thing that makes progress difficult or lessens the chance of success; physical or mental disability. —*v.t.* (p.t. *handicapped*) impose or be a handicap on. **handicapped** *a.* suffering from a physical or mental disability. **handicapper** *n.*

handicraft *n.* work needing skill with the hands and artistic design.

handily *adv.* in a handy way.

handiwork *n.* thing made or done by the hands or by a named person.

handkerchief *n.* (pl. *-fs*) small square of cloth for wiping the nose etc.

handle *n.* part by which a thing is to be held, carried, or controlled. —*v.t.* touch or move with the hands; deal with; manage; deal in.

handlebar *n.* steering-bar of a bicycle etc.

handshake *n.* act of shaking hands as a greeting etc.

handsome *a.* good-looking; generous; (of a price etc.) very large.

handspring *n.* somersault involving a handstand.

handstand *n.* balancing on one's hands with feet in the air.

handwriting *n.* writing by hand with pen or pencil; style of this.

handy *a.* (*-ier, -iest*) convenient; clever with one's hands.

handyman *n.* (pl. *-men*) person who does odd jobs.

hang *v.t./i.* (p.t. *hung*) support or be supported from above with the lower end free; rest on hinges; stick (wallpaper) to a wall; kill or be killed by suspension from a rope that tightens round the neck (p.t. *hanged*); droop; remain. —*n.* way a thing hangs. **get the ~ of,** (*colloq.*) get the knack of, understand. **~ about,** loiter.

~ back, hesitate. **~ fire,** be slow in developing. **~-glider** *n.* frame used in **~-gliding,** sport of being suspended in an airborne frame controlled by one's own movements. **~ on,** hold tightly; depend on; pay close attention to; remain; (*sl.*) wait. **~ out,** (*sl.*) have one's home. **~-up** *n.* (*sl.*) difficulty, inhibition.

hangar *n.* shed for an aircraft.

hangdog *a.* shamefaced.

hanger *n.* loop or hook by which a thing is hung; shaped piece of wood etc. to hang a garment on. **~-on** *n.* person who attaches himself to another for personal gain.

hangings *n.pl.* draperies hung on walls.

hangman *n.* man whose job is to hang persons condemned to death.

hangover *n.* unpleasant after-effects from drinking much alcohol; thing left from an earlier time.

hank *n.* coil or length of thread.

hanker *v.i.* crave, feel a longing.

hanky-panky *n.* (*sl.*) trickery.

haphazard *a.* done or chosen at random. **haphazardly** *adv.*

hapless *a.* unlucky.

happen *v.i.* occur; chance. **~ to,** be the fate or experience of.

happy *a.* (*-ier, -iest*) contented, pleased; fortunate; pleasing. **~-go-lucky** *a.* taking events cheerfully. **happily** *adv.*, **happiness** *n.*

hara-kiri *n.* suicide as formerly practised by Japanese military officers.

harangue *n.* lengthy earnest speech. —*v.t.* make a harangue to.

harass /ˈhæ-/ *v.t.* worry or annoy continually; make repeated attacks on. **harassment** /ˈhæ-/ *n.*

harbinger /-dʒə(r)/ *n.* person or thing whose presence announces the approach of another.

harbour *n.* place of shelter for ships. —*v.t.* give shelter or refuge to; keep (evil thoughts) in one's mind.

hard *a.* (*-er, -est*) firm, not easily cut; difficult; not easy to bear; harsh; strenuous; (of drugs) strong and addictive; (of currency) not likely to drop suddenly in value; (of drinks) strongly alcoholic; (of water) containing mineral salts that prevent soap from lathering freely. —*adv.* intensively; with difficulty; so as to be hard. **~ by,** close by. **~-headed** *a.* shrewd and practical. **~ lines,** worse luck than is deserved. **~ of hearing,** slightly deaf. **~ shoulder,** extra strip of road beside a motorway, for use in an emergency. **~ up,** (*colloq.*) short of money. **hardness** *n.*

hardboard *n.* stiff board made of compressed wood-pulp.

harden *v.t./i.* make or become hard or hardy.

hardly *adv.* only with difficulty; scarcely.

hardship *n.* harsh circumstance.

hardware *n.* tools and household implements sold by a shop; weapons; machinery.

hardwood *n.* hard heavy wood of deciduous trees.

hardy *a.* (*-ier, -iest*) capable of enduring cold or harsh conditions.

hare *n.* field animal like a large rabbit. —*v.i.* run rapidly. **~-brained** *a.* wild and foolish, rash.

harebell *n.* wild plant with blue bell-shaped flowers.

harelip *n.* deformed lip with a vertical slit like that of a hare.

harem /ˈheərəm/ *n.* women of a Muslim household; their apartments.

haricot /-kəʊ/ *n.* **~ bean,** white dried seed of a kind of bean.

hark *v.i.* listen. **~ back,** return to an earlier subject.

harlequin *a.* in varied colours.

harlot *n.* (*old use*) prostitute.

harm *n.* damage, injury. —*v.t.* cause harm to. **harmful** *a.*, **harmless** *a.*

harmonic *a.* full of harmony.

harmonica *n.* mouth-organ.

harmonious *a.* forming a pleasing or consistent whole; free from disagreement or ill-feeling; sweet-sounding. **harmoniously** *adv.*

harmonium *n.* musical instrument like a small organ.

harmonize *v.t./i.* make or be harmonious; add notes to (a melody) to form chords. **harmonization** *n.*

harmony *n.* being harmonious; combination of musical notes to form chords; melodious sound.

harness *n.* straps and fittings by which a horse is controlled; similar fastenings. —*v.t.* put harness on, attach by this; control and use.

harp *n.* musical instrument with strings in a roughly triangular frame. —*v.i.* **~ on,** talk repeatedly and tiresomely about. **harpist** *n.*

harpoon *n.* spear-like missile with a rope attached. —*v.t.* spear with a harpoon.

harpsichord *n.* piano-like instrument with strings sounded by mechanism that plucks them.

harpy *n.* mythical monster with a woman's head and body and bird's wings and claws; grasping unscrupulous person.

harrow *n.* heavy frame with metal spikes or discs for breaking up clods. —*v.t.* draw a harrow over (soil); distress greatly.

harry *v.t.* harass.

harsh *a.* (-er, -est) rough and disagreeable; severe, cruel. **harshly** *adv.*, **harshness** *n.*

hart *n.* adult male deer.

harvest *n.* gathering of crop(s); season for this; season's yield of a natural product; product of action. —*v.t./i.* gather a crop; reap. **harvester** *n.*

has *see* have.

hash *n.* dish of chopped re-cooked meat; jumble. —*v.t.* make into hash. **make a ~ of,** (*sl.*) make a mess of, bungle. **settle a person's ~,** (*sl.*) deal with and subdue him.

hashish *n.* hemp dried for chewing or smoking as a narcotic.

hasp *n.* clasp fitting over a staple, secured by a pin or padlock.

hassle *n.* & *v.i.* (*colloq.*) quarrel, struggle.

hassock *n.* thick firm cushion for kneeling on in church.

hast (*old use*, with *thou*) = have.

haste *n.* hurry. **make ~,** hurry.

hasten *v.t./i.* hurry.

hasty *a.* (-ier, -iest) hurried; acting or done too quickly. **hastily** *adv.*, **hastiness** *n.*

hat *n.* covering for the head, worn out of doors. **~ trick,** three successes in a row, esp. taking of three wickets by three successive balls.

hatband *n.* band of ribbon round a hat.

hatch[1] *n.* opening in a door, floor, ship's deck, etc.; its cover.

hatch[2] *v.t./i.* emerge or produce (young) from an egg; devise (a plot). —*n.* brood hatched.

hatch[3] *v.t.* mark with close parallel lines. **hatching** *n.* these marks.

hatchback *n.* sloping back of a car, hinged at the top so that it can be opened; car with this.

hatchery *n.* place for hatching eggs.

hatchet *n.* small axe. **bury the ~,** cease quarrelling and become friendly. **~-faced** *a.* having a narrow face with sharp features. **~-man** *n.* person employed to attack and destroy reputations.

hatchway *n.* cover on a hatch in a ship's deck.

hate *n.* hatred. —*v.t.* feel hatred towards; dislike greatly. **hater** *n.*

hateful *a.* arousing hatred.

hatless *a.* not wearing a hat.

hatred *n.* violent dislike or enmity.

hatter *n.* maker or seller of hats.

haughty *a.* (-ier, -iest) proud of oneself and looking down on others. **haughtily** *adv.*, **haughtiness** *n.*

haul *v.t.* pull or drag forcibly; transport by truck etc. —*n.* process of hauling; amount gained by effort, booty; distance to be traversed.

haulage *n.* transport of goods.

haulier *n.* person or firm whose trade is the transporting of goods by road.

haunch *n.* fleshy part of the buttock and thigh; leg and loin of meat.

haunt *v.t.* be persistently in (a place); linger in the mind of; (of a ghost) manifest its presence in (a place). —*n.* place often visited by person(s) named. **haunted** *a.*

hauteur /əʊˈtɜ(r)/ *n.* haughtiness.

have *v.t.* (3 sing. pres. *has*; p.t. *had*) possess; contain; experience, undergo; give birth to; cause to be or do or be done; engage in; allow; be under the obligation of; show (a quality); receive, accept; (*sl.*) cheat, deceive. —*v.aux.* (used with p.p. to form past tenses). **~ it out,** settle a problem by frank discussion. **~ up,** bring (a person) before a court of justice. **haves and have-nots,** people with and without wealth or privilege.

haven *n.* refuge.

haver /ˈheɪ-/ *v.i.* hesitate.

haversack *n.* strong bag carried on the back or slung from a shoulder.

havoc *n.* great destruction or disorder.

haw[1] *n.* hawthorn berry.

haw[2] *see* hum[2].

hawk[1] n. bird of prey; person who favours an aggressive policy. **~-eyed** a. having very keen sight.

hawk[2] v.i. clear one's throat of phlegm noisily.

hawk[3] v.t. carry (goods) about for sale. **hawker** n.

hawser n. heavy rope or cable for mooring or towing a ship.

hawthorn n. thorny tree or shrub with small red berries.

hay n. grass mown and dried for fodder. **~ fever,** catarrh caused by pollen or dust. **make ~ of,** throw into confusion.

haystack n. regular pile of hay firmly packed for storing.

haywire a. badly disorganized.

hazard n. risk, danger; source of this; obstacle. —v.t. risk. **hazardous** a.

haze n. thin mist.

hazel n. bush with small edible nuts; light brown. **hazel-nut** n.

hazy a. (-ier, -iest) misty; indistinct; vague. **hazily** adv., **haziness** n.

H-bomb n. hydrogen bomb.

he pron. male previously mentioned; person of unspecified sex. —n. male animal.

head n. part of the body containing the eyes, nose, mouth, and brain; intellect; individual person or animal; (colloq.) headache; thing like the head in form or position, top or leading part or position; chief person; headmaster, headmistress; body of water or steam confined for exerting pressure; heads, side of a coin showing a head, turned upwards after being tossed. —v.t./i. be at the head or top of; strike (a ball) with one's head in football; direct one's course; force to turn by getting in front. **~-dress** n. ornamental covering or band worn on the head. **~-on** a. & adv. with head or front foremost. **~ over heels,** in a somersault. **~ wind,** wind blowing from directly in front.

headache n. continuous pain in the head; problem causing worry.

header n. dive with the head first; heading of the ball in football.

headgear n. hat or head-dress.

heading n. word(s) at the top of printed or written matter as a title etc.; passage in a mine.

headlamp n. headlight.

headland n. promontory.

headless a. having no head.

headlight n. powerful light on the front of a vehicle etc.; its beam.

headline n. heading in a newspaper.

headlong a. & adv. falling or plunging with the head first; in a hasty and rash way.

headmaster, headmistress ns. principal teacher in a school, responsible for organizing it.

headphone n. receiver held over the ear(s) by a band over the head.

headquarters n.pl. place from which an organization is controlled.

headstone n. stone set up at the head of a grave.

headstrong a. self-willed and obstinate.

headway n. progress.

headword n. word forming the heading of an entry in a dictionary.

heady a. (-ier, -iest) likely to cause intoxication.

heal v.t./i. form healthy flesh again, unite after being cut or broken; cause to do this; (old use) cure. **healer** n.

health n. state of being well and free from illness; condition of the body.

healthy a. (-ier, -iest) having or showing or producing good health; beneficial; functioning well. **healthily** adv., **healthiness** n.

heap n. a number of things or particles lying one on top of another; (pl., colloq.) plenty. —v.t./i. pile or become piled in a heap; load with large quantities.

hear v.t./i. (p.t. heard) perceive (sounds) with the ear; listen, pay attention to; listen to and try (a lawsuit); receive information or a letter etc. **hear! hear!** I agree. **not ~ of,** refuse to allow. **hearer** n.

hearing n. ability to hear; opportunity of being heard, trial of a lawsuit. **~-aid** n. small sound-amplifier worn by a deaf person to improve the hearing.

hearsay n. things heard in rumour.

hearse n. vehicle for carrying the coffin at a funeral.

heart n. muscular organ that keeps blood circulating by contracting rhythmically; centre of a person's emotions, affections, or inmost thoughts; courage; enthusiasm; central part; symmetrical figure representing a heart; playing-card of the suit marked with these. **break the ~ of,** cause overwhelming grief to. **by ~,** memorized thoroughly. **~ attack,** sudden failure of the heart to function normally. **~-break** n. overwhelming grief. **~-broken** a. broken-hearted. **~-searching** n. examination of one's own feelings and motives. **~-strings** n.pl. one's deepest feelings of love or pity. **~-to-heart** a. frank and personal. **~-warming** a. emotionally moving and encouraging.

heartache n. mental pain, sorrow.

heartburn n. burning sensation in the lower part of the chest.

heartburning n. jealousy.

hearten v.t. cause to feel encouraged.

heartfelt a. felt deeply, sincere.

hearth n. floor of a fireplace; fireside.

hearthrug n. rug laid in front of a fireplace.

heartless a. not feeling pity or sympathy. **heartlessly** adv.

hearty a. (-ier, -iest) showing warmth of feeling, enthusiastic; vigorous; (of meals) large. **heartily** adv., **heartiness** n.

heat n. form of energy produced by movement of molecules; sensation produced by this, hotness; intense feeling, anger; preliminary contest. —v.t./i. make or become hot. **~-stroke** n. illness caused by over-exposure to sun. **~ wave,** period of very hot weather.

heated a. (of a person or discussion) angry. **heatedly** adv.

heater n. device supplying heat.

heath *n.* flat uncultivated land with low shrubs; small shrubby plant of the heather kind.

heathen *n.* person who is neither Christian, Jewish, Muslim, nor Buddhist.

heather *n.* evergreen plant with purple, pink, or white flowers.

heave *v.t./i.* lift or haul with great effort; utter (a sigh); (*colloq.*) throw; rise and fall like waves at sea; pant, retch. —*n.* act of heaving. ~ **in sight,** (p.t. *hove*) come into view. ~ **to,** (p.t. *hove*) come or bring (a ship) to a stand-still with head to wind.

heaven *n.* abode of God; place or state of supreme bliss; *the heavens,* the sky as seen from the earth.

heavenly *a.* of heaven, divine; of or in the heavens; (*colloq.*) very pleasing.

heavy *a.* (-*ier*, -*iest*) having great weight; of more than average weight or force or intensity; dense; stodgy; serious in tone, dull and tedious. ~-**hearted** *a.* sad. **heavily** *adv.*, **heaviness** *n.*

heavyweight *a.* having great weight or influence. —*n.* heavyweight person; heaviest boxing-weight.

Hebrew *n. & a.* (member) of a Semitic people in ancient Palestine; (of) their language or a modern form of this.

heckle *v.t.* interrupt (a public speaker) with aggressive questions and abuse. **heckler** *n.*

hectare /-tɑ(r)/ *n.* unit of area, 10,000 sq. metres. (about 2½ acres).

hectic *a.* with feverish activity. **hectically** *adv.*

hectogram *n.* 100 grams.

hector *v.t.* intimidate by bullying.

hedge *n.* fence of bushes or shrubs; barrier. —*v.t./i.* surround with a hedge; make or trim hedges; protect oneself against loss on (a bet etc.); avoid giving a direct answer or commitment.

hedgehog *n.* small animal with a back covered in stiff spines.

hedgerow *n.* bushes etc. forming a hedge.

hedonist /ˈhiː-/ *n.* person who believes pleasure is the chief good.

heed *v.t.* pay attention to. —*n.* careful attention. **heedless** *a.*, **heedlessly** *adv.*, **heedlessness** *n.*

heel[1] *n.* back part of the human foot; part of a stocking or shoe covering or supporting this; (*sl.*) dishonourable man. —*v.t.* make or repair the heel(s) of; kick (a ball) with the heel. **down at** ~, shabby. **take to one's heels,** run away.

heel[2] *v.t./i.* tilt (a ship) or become tilted to one side.

hefty *a.* (-*ier*, -*iest*) large and heavy.

hegemony /hɪˈgɛ-/ *n.* leadership, esp. by one country.

heifer /ˈhɛf-/ *n.* young cow.

height *n.* measurement from base to top or head to foot; distance above ground or sea level; high place; highest degree of something.

heighten *v.t./i.* make or become higher or more intense.

heinous /ˈheɪ-/ *a.* very wicked.

heir /eə(r)/ *n.* person who inherits property or a rank etc. ~ **apparent,** legal heir whose claim cannot be set aside by the birth of another heir. ~ **presumptive,** one whose claim may be set aside thus.

heiress /ˈeər-/ *n.* female heir, esp. to great wealth.

heirloom /ˈeər-/ *n.* possession handed down in a family for several generations.

Hejira /ˈhedʒ-/ *n.* Muhammad's flight from Mecca (A.D. 622), from which the Muslim era is reckoned.

held *see* **hold**[1].

helical /ˈhel-/ *a.* like a helix.

helicopter *n.* aircraft with blades that revolve horizontally.

heliotrope /ˈhi-/ *n.* plant with small purple flowers; light purple.

heliport *n.* helicopter station.

helium /ˈhi-/ *n.* light colourless gas that does not burn.

helix /ˈhi-/ *n.* (pl. -*ices*) spiral.

hell *n.* place of punishment for the wicked after death; place or state of supreme misery. ~-**bent** *a.* recklessly determined. ~ **for leather,** at great speed.

hellebore /ˈhelɪ-/ *n.* plant with white or greenish flowers.

Hellenistic *a.* of Greece in the 4th–1st centuries B.C.

hello *int. & n.* hullo.

helm *n.* tiller or wheel by which a ship's rudder is controlled.

helmet *n.* protective head-covering.

helmsman *n.* (pl. -*men*) person controlling a ship's helm.

help *v.t./i.* be useful (to); make easier; prevent; serve with food. —*n.* act of helping; person or thing that helps. ~ **oneself to,** take without seeking assistance or permission. **helper** *n.*

helpful *a.* giving help, useful. **helpfully** *adv.*, **helpfulness** *n.*

helping *n.* portion of food served.

helpless *a.* unable to manage without help; powerless. **helplessly** *adv.*, **helplessness** *n.*

helpmate *n.* helper.

helter-skelter *adv.* in disorderly haste. —*n.* spiral slide at a fun-fair.

hem *n.* edge (of cloth) turned under and sewn or fixed down. —*v.t.* (p.t. *hemmed*) sew thus. ~ **in** *or* **round,** surround and restrict.

hemisphere *n.* half a sphere; half the earth, esp. as divided by the equator or a line through the poles. **hemispherical** *a.*

hemlock *n.* poisonous plant.

hemp *n.* plant with coarse fibres used in making rope and cloth; narcotic drug made from it.

hempen *a.* made of hemp.

hemstitch *v.t.* decorate with an ornamental open-work stitch.

hen *n.* female bird, esp. of the domestic fowl. ~-**party** *n.* (*colloq.*) party of women only.

hence *adv.* from this time; for this reason; (*old use*) from here.

henceforth, henceforward *advs.* from this time on, in future.

henchman *n.* (pl. -*men*) trusty supporter.

henna *n.* reddish dye used esp. on the hair; tropical plant from which it is obtained.
hennaed *a.*

henpecked *a.* nagged by one's wife.

heptagon *n.* geometric figure with seven sides.

her *pron.* objective case of *she.* —*a.* belonging to her.

herald *n.* officer in former times who made State proclamations; official of the corporation (*Heralds' College*) concerned with pedigrees and coats of arms; person or thing 'heralding something. —*v.t.* proclaim the approach of.

heraldic /-'ræl-/ *a.* of heralds or heraldry.

heraldry *n.* study of coats of arms.

herb *n.* plant with a soft stem that dies down to the ground after flowering; one used in making medicines or flavourings. **herbal** *a.*

herbaceous *a.* of or like herbs.

herbalist *n.* dealer in medicinal herbs.

herbicide *n.* substance used to destroy unwanted vegetation.

herbivore /'hɜ-/ *n.* herbivorous animal.

herbivorous /-'bɪv-/ *a.* feeding on plants.

herculean /-'li-/ *a.* needing or showing great strength or effort.

herd *n.* group of animals feeding or staying together; mob. —*v.t./i.* gather, stay, or drive as a group; tend (a herd). **herdsman** *n.*

here *adv.* in, at, or to this place; at this point. —*n.* this place.

hereabouts *adv.* near here.

hereafter *adv.* from now on.

hereby *adv.* by this act or decree etc.

hereditary *a.* inherited; holding a position by inheritance.

heredity *n.* inheritance of characteristics from parents.

heresy *n.* opinion contrary to accepted beliefs; holding of this.

heretic *n.* person who holds a heresy. **heretical** /-'ret-/ *a.*

herewith *adv.* with this.

heritage *n.* thing(s) inherited.

hermaphrodite /-'mæ-/ *n.* creature with male and female sexual organs.

hermetic *a.* with airtight closure. **hermetically** *adv.*

hermit *n.* person living in solitude.

hermitage *n.* hermit's dwelling.

hernia *n.* abnormal protrusion of part of an organ through the wall of the cavity (esp. the abdomen) containing it.

hero *n.* (pl. -*oes*) man admired for his brave deeds; chief male character in a story etc.

heroic *a.* very brave. **heroically** *adv.*

heroin *n.* powerful drug prepared from morphine.

heroine *n.* female hero.

heroism *n.* heroic conduct.

heron *n.* long-legged wading-bird.

heronry *n.* place where herons breed.

herring *n.* North Atlantic fish much used for food. **~-bone** *n.* zigzag pattern or arrangement.

hers *poss.pron.* belonging to her.

herself *pron.* emphatic and reflexive form of *she* and *her.*

hertz *n.* (pl. *hertz*) unit of frequency of electromagnetic waves.

hesitant *a.* hesitating. **hesitantly** *adv.*, **hesitancy** *n.*

hesitate *v.i.* pause in doubt; be reluctant, scruple. **hesitation** *n.*

hessian *n.* strong coarse cloth of hemp or jute.

het *a.* ~ **up**, (*sl.*) excited, agitated.

heterogeneous *a.* made up of people or things of various sorts.

heterosexual *a.* sexually attracted to people of the opposite sex.

hew *v.t.* (p.p. *hewn*) chop or cut with an axe etc.; cut into shape.

hexagon *n.* geometric figure with six sides. **hexagonal** *a.*

hexameter /-'sæm-/ *n.* line of verse with six metrical feet.

hey *int.* exclamation of surprise or inquiry, or calling attention. ~ **presto!,** conjuror's formula, calling attention.

heyday *n.* time of greatest success.

hi *int.* exclamation calling attention or (*U.S.*) greeting.

hiatus *n.* (pl. -*tuses*) break or gap in a sequence or series.

hibernate *v.i.* spend the winter in sleep-like state. **hibernation** *n.*

hibiscus *n.* shrub or tree with trumpet-shaped flowers.

hiccup *n.* cough-like stopping of breath. —*v.i.* make this sound.

hickory *n.* tree related to the walnut; its wood.

hide[1] *v.t./i.* (p.t. *hid*, p.p. *hidden*) put or keep out of sight; keep secret; conceal oneself. ~-**out** *n.* (*colloq.*) hiding-place.

hide[2] *n.* animal's skin.

hidebound *a.* rigidly conventional.

hideous *a.* very ugly. **hideously** *adv.*, **hideousness** *n.*

hiding *n.* (*colloq.*) thrashing.

hierarchy /'haɪ-/ *n.* system with grades of status. **hierarchical** *a.*

hieroglyph /'haɪ-/ *n.* pictorial symbol used in ancient Egyptian and other writing. **hieroglyphic** *a.*, **hieroglyphics** *n.pl.*

hi-fi *a.* & *n.* (*colloq.*) high fidelity, (equipment) reproducing sound with little or no distortion.

higgledy-piggledy *a.* & *adv.* in complete confusion.

high *a.* (-*er*, -*est*) extending far or a specified distance upwards; far above ground or sea level; ranking above others; extreme, greater than normal; (of sound or a voice) with rapid vibrations, not deep or low; (of meat) slightly decomposed; (*sl.*) intoxicated, under the influence of a drug. —*n.* high level; area of high pressure. —*adv.* in, at, or to a high level. **High Church,** section of the Church of England giving an important place to ritual and the authority of priests. ~ **explosive,** that with a violently shattering effect. ~-**falutin** *a.* (*colloq.*) pompous. ~-**handed** *a.* using authority arrogantly. $\sim$ **priest,** chief priest. $\sim$**-rise** a. with many storeys. $\sim$ **road,** main road. $\sim$ **school,** secondary (usu. grammar) school. $\sim$ **sea(s),** sea outside territorial waters. $\sim$ **season,** busiest season. $\sim$**-speed** a. operating at great speed. $\sim$**-spirited** a. lively. $\sim$ **spot,** (sl.) important place or feature. $\sim$ **street,** principal shopping-street. $\sim$ **tea,** evening meal with tea and cooked food. $\sim$**water mark,** level reached by the tide at its highest level. **higher education,** education above the level given in schools.

highball n. (U.S.) drink of spirits and soda served in a tall glass.

highbrow a. very intellectual, cultured. —n. highbrow person.

highlands n.pl. mountainous region. **highland** a., **highlander** n.

highlight n. bright or light area in a picture; best or most outstanding feature. —v.t. emphasize.

highly adv. in a high degree, extremely; very favourably. $\sim$**-strung** a. (of a person) easily upset.

Highness n. title of a prince or princess.

highway n. public road; main route.

highwayman n. (pl. -men) man (usu. on horse-back) who robbed passing travellers in former times.

hijack v.t. seize control illegally of (a vehicle or aircraft in transit). —n. hijacking. **hijacker** n.

hike n. long walk. —v.i. go for a hike. **hiker** n.

hilarious /-ˈleər-/ a. noisily merry; extremely funny. **hilariously** adv., **hilarity** /-ˈlæ-/ n.

hill n. raised part of earth's surface, less high than a mountain; slope in a road etc.; mound. $\sim$**-billy** n. (U.S.) rustic person; folk music like that of the southern U.S.A.

hillock n. small hill, mound.

hillside n. sloping side of a hill.

hilly a. full of hills.

hilt n. handle of a sword or dagger. **to the** $\sim$, completely.

him pron. objective case of he.

Himalayan /-ˈleɪ-/ a. of the Himalaya Mountains.

himself pron. emphatic and reflexive form of he and him.

hind[1] n. female deer.

hind[2] a. situated at the back.

hinder[1] /ˈhɪn-/ v.t. delay progress of.

hinder[2] /ˈhaɪ-/ a. = hind[2].

Hindi n. a form of Hindustani; group of spoken languages of northern India.

hindmost a. furthest behind.

hindrance n. thing that hinders; hindering, being hindered.

hindsight n. wisdom about an event after it has occurred.

Hindu n. person whose religion is Hinduism. —a. of Hindus.

Hinduism n. a religion and philosophy of India.

Hindustani n. language of much of northern India and Pakistan.

hinge n. movable joint such as that on which a door or lid etc. turns. —v.t./i. attach or be attached by hinge(s). $\sim$ **on,** depend on.

hint n. slight indication, suggestion made in-directly; small piece of practical information. —v.i. make a hint.

hinterland n. district behind a coast etc. or served by a port or other centre.

hip[1] n. projection of the pelvis on each side of body. **hipped** a.

hip[2] n. fruit of wild rose.

hip[3] int. introducing a cheer.

hippie n. (sl.) young person who adopts an un-conventional style of dress and living-habits.

hippopotamus n. (pl. -muses or -mi) large African river-animal with tusks and a thick skin.

hire v.t. engage or grant temporary use of, for payment. —n. hiring. $\sim$**-purchase** n. system by which a thing becomes the hirer's after a number of payments. **hirer** n.

hireling n. (derog.) hired helper.

hirsute /ˈhɜː-/ a. hairy, shaggy.

his a. & poss.pron. belonging to him.

hiss n. sound like 's'. —v.t./i. make this sound; utter with a hiss; express disapproval in this way.

histamine /-mɪn/ n. substance present in the body and causing some allergic reactions.

historian n. expert in or writer of history.

historic a. famous in history.

historical a. of or concerned with history. **historically** adv.

history n. past events; methodical record of these; study of past events. **make** $\sim$, do something memorable.

histrionic a. of acting; theatrical in manner. **histrionics** n.pl. theatricals; theatrical be-haviour.

hit v.t./i. (p.t. hit, pres.p. hitting) strike with a blow or missile, come forcefully against; have a bad effect upon (a person etc.); come to, find, encounter. —n. blow, stroke; shot that hits its target; success. $\sim$ **it off,** get on well with a person. $\sim$ **off,** represent exactly. $\sim$ **on,** discover. $\sim$**-or-miss** a. aimed or done care-lessly.

hitch v.t./i. move (a thing) with a slight jerk; fasten or be fastened with a loop or hook etc.; hitch-hike, obtain (a lift) in this way. —n. slight jerk; noose or knot of various kinds; temporary stoppage, snag. **get hitched,** (sl.) get married. $\sim$**-hike** v.i. travel by begging lifts in vehicles. $\sim$**-hiker** n.

hither adv. to or towards this place. $\sim$ **and thither,** to and fro.

hitherto adv. until this time.

hive n. container for bees to live in; bees living in this. —v.t./i. $\sim$ **off,** separate from a larger group. $\sim$ **of industry,** place full of people working busily.

ho int. exclamation of triumph or scorn, or calling attention.

hoard v.t. save and store away. —n. things hoarded. **hoarder** n.

hoarding n. fence of boards, often bearing advertisements.

hoar-frost *n.* white frost.

hoarse *a.* (*-er*, *-est*) (of a voice) sounding rough as if from a dry throat; having such a voice. **hoarsely** *adv.*, **hoarseness** *n.*

hoary *a.* (*-ier*, *-iest*) grey with age; (of a joke etc.) old.

hoax *v.t.* deceive jokingly. —*n.* joking deception. **hoaxer** *n.*

hob *n.* metal shelf on the side of a grate where a pan can be kept hot.

hobble *v.t./i.* walk lamely; fasten the legs of (a horse) to limit its movement. —*n.* hobbling walk.

hobby *n.* thing done often and for pleasure in one's spare time.

hobby-horse *n.* figure of a horse used in a morris dance; stick with a horse's head, as a toy; rocking-horse; favourite topic.

hobgoblin *n.* mischievous or evil spirit.

hobnail *n.* heavy-headed nail for boot-soles. **hobnailed** *a.*

hob-nob *v.i.* (p.t. *-nobbed*) spend time together in a friendly way.

hock[1] *n.* middle joint of an animal's hind leg.

hock[2] *n.* German white wine.

hock[3] *v.t.* (*U.S. sl.*) pawn. **in ~,** in pawn; in debt; in prison.

hockey *n.* field-game played with curved sticks and a small hard ball; ice-hockey.

hocus-pocus *n.* trickery.

hod *n.* trough on a pole for carrying mortar or bricks; container for shovelling and holding coal.

hoe *n.* tool for loosening soil or scraping up weeds. —*v.t./i.* (pres.p. *hoeing*) dig or scrape with a hoe.

hog *n.* castrated male pig reared for meat; (*colloq.*) greedy person. —*v.t.* (p.p. *hogged*) (*colloq.*) take greedily; hoard selfishly.

hogmanay *n.* (*Sc.*) New Year's Eve.

hoick *v.t.* (*sl.*) lift or bring out, esp. with a jerk.

hoist *v.t.* raise or haul up. —*n.* apparatus for hoisting things; pull or haul.

hoity-toity *a.* haughty.

hokey-pokey *n.* (*sl.*) trickery.

hold[1] *v.t./i.* (p.t. *held*) keep in one's arms or hands etc. or in one's possession or control; keep in a position or condition; contain; bear the weight of; remain unbroken under strain; continue; occupy; cause to take place; believe. —*n.* act, manner, or means of holding; means of exerting influence. **get ~ of,** acquire; make contact with. **~ forth,** speak lengthily. **~ one's tongue,** be or keep silent. **~ out,** offer; last; continue to make a demand. **~ over,** postpone. **~ up,** hinder; stop and rob by use of threats or force. **~-up** *n.* delay; stoppage and robbery. **~ water,** (of reasoning) be sound. **~ with,** (*sl.*) approve of. **holder** *n.*

hold[2] *n.* storage cavity below a ship's deck.

holdall *n.* portable case for miscellaneous articles.

holding *n.* something held or owned; land held by an owner or tenant.

hole *n.* hollow place; burrow; aperture; wretched place; (*sl.*) awkward situation;

—*v.t.* make hole(s) in; send (a golf-ball) into the hole. **~-and-corner** *a.* underhand. **~ up,** (*U.S. sl.*) hide oneself.

holey *a.* full of holes.

holiday *n.* day(s) of recreation. —*v.i.* spend a holiday.

holiness *n.* being holy; *His H~,* title of the pope.

hollow *a.* empty within, not solid; sunken; echoing as if in something hollow; worthless. —*n.* hollow or hollow place; valley. —*adv.* completely. —*v.t.* make hollow.

holly *n.* evergreen shrub with prickly leaves and red berries.

hollyhock *n.* plant with large flowers on a tall stem.

holocaust *n.* large-scale destruction, esp. by fire.

holster *n.* leather case holding a pistol or revolver.

holy *a.* (*-ier*, *-iest*) belonging or devoted to God and reverenced; consecrated. **~ of holies,** most sacred place. **Holy Ghost, Holy Spirit,** third person of the Trinity. **Holy Week,** week before Easter Sunday. **Holy Writ,** the Bible.

homage *n.* things said or done as a mark of respect or loyalty.

home *n.* place where one lives; dwelling-house; institution where those needing care may live; place to be reached by a runner or in certain games. —*a.* of one's home or country; played on one's own ground. —*adv.* at or to one's home; to the point aimed at. —*v.i.* make its way home or to a target. **Home Counties,** those nearest London. **Home Office,** British government department dealing with law and order in England and Wales. **Home Secretary,** minister in charge of this. **home truth,** unpleasant truth about oneself.

homeland *n.* native land.

homeless *a.* lacking a dwelling.

homely *a.* (*-ier*, *-iest*) simple and informal; (*U.S.*) plain, not beautiful. **homeliness** *n.*

Homeric *a.* of or in the style of the Greek poet Homer.

homesick *a.* longing for home.

homestead *n.* house (esp. a farmhouse) with surrounding land and buildings.

homeward *a.* & *adv.* going towards home. **homewards** *adv.*

homework *n.* work set for a pupil to do away from school.

homicide *n.* killing of one person by another. **homicidal** *a.*

homily *n.* moralizing lecture.

homing *a.* (of a pigeon) trained to fly home from a distance.

homoeopathic /hɔʊmɪəˈpæ-/ *a.* treating a disease by very small doses that in a healthy person would produce its symptoms.

homogeneous /-ˈdʒin-/ *a.* of the same kind, uniform. **homogeneity** /-ˈniː-/ *n.*

homogenize /-ˈmɒdʒ-/ *v.t.* treat (milk) so that cream does not separate and rise to top.

homonym /ˈhɒm-/ *n.* word of the same spelling as another.

homophone /'hom-/ *n.* word with the same sound as another.

homosexual *a.* sexually attracted only to people of the same sex as oneself. —*n.* homosexual person.

Hon. *abbr.* Honorable; Honorary.

hone *v.t.* sharpen on a whetstone.

honest *a.* truthful, trustworthy; fairly earned. ∼**-to-goodness** *a.* (*colloq.*) real, straightforward. **honestly** *adv.*, **honesty** *n.*

honey *n.* (pl. -*eys*) sweet substance made by bees from nectar; its yellowish colour; sweetness, pleasantness; (*colloq.*) darling. ∼**-bee** *n.* common bee living in a hive.

honeycomb *n.* bees' wax structure for holding their honey and eggs; pattern of six-sided sections.

honeycombed *a.* filled with holes or tunnels.

honeydew *n.* ∼ **melon,** melon with pale skin and sweet green flesh.

honeymoon *n.* holiday spent together by a newly-married couple. —*v.i.* spend a honeymoon.

honeysuckle *n.* climbing shrub with fragrant pink and yellow flowers.

honk *n.* noise like the cry of a wild goose or the sound of an old-style motor horn. —*v.i.* make this noise.

honorarium /onə'reər-/ *n.* (pl. -*ums*) voluntary payment for services where no fee is legally required.

honorary *a.* given as an honour; unpaid.

honour *n.* great respect or public regard; mark of this, privilege; good personal character or reputation; title of respect, esp. given to certain judges. —*v.t.* feel honour for; confer honour on; acknowledge and pay (a cheque) or fulfil (a promise etc.).

honourable *a.* deserving, possessing, or showing honour; *H*∼, a courtesy title. **honourably** *adv.*

hood *n.* covering for the head and neck, esp. forming part of a garment; hood-like thing or cover, folding roof over a car. **hooded** *a.*

hoodlum *n.* hooligan, young thug.

hoodwink *v.t.* deceive.

hoof *n.* (pl. *hoofs* or *hooves*) horny part of a quadruped's foot.

hook *n.* bent or curved piece of metal etc. for catching hold or hanging things on; thing shaped like this; curved cutting-tool; hooking movement, short blow made with the elbow bent. —*v.t./i.* grasp, catch, or fasten with hook(s); scoop or propel with a curving movement. **by** ∼ **or by crook,** by some means no matter what. ∼ **it,** (*sl.*) run away. ∼**-up** *n.* interconnection. **off the** ∼, freed from a difficulty. **hooker** *n.*

hookah *n.* oriental tobacco-pipe with a long tube passing through water.

hooked *a.* hook-shaped. ∼ **on,** (*sl.*) addicted to.

hookey *n.* **play** ∼, (*U.S. sl.*) play truant.

hookworm *n.* parasitic worm, male of which has hook-like spines.

hooligan *n.* young ruffian. **hooliganism** *n.*

hoop *n.* circular band of metal or wood; metal arch used in croquet. **go or be put through the hoops,** undergo a test or ordeal.

hoop-la *n.* game in which rings are thrown to encircle a prize.

hoopoe *n.* bird with a crest and striped plumage.

hooray *int.* & *n.* = hurrah.

hoot *n.* owl's cry; sound of a hooter; cry of scorn or disapproval; (*colloq.*) laughter. —*v.t./i.* make or cause to make a hoot.

hooter *n.* siren or steam-whistle used as a signal; car horn.

Hoover *n.* [P.] a kind of vacuum cleaner. **hoover** *v.t.* clean with a vacuum cleaner.

hop[1] *v.t./i.* (p.t. *hopped*) jump on one foot or (of an animal) from both or all feet; (*colloq.*) make a quick short trip. ∼ **in** *or* **out,** (*colloq.*) get into or out of a car. ∼ **it,** (*sl.*) go away. **on the** ∼, (*colloq.*) unprepared.

hop[2] *n.* plant cultivated for its cones (*hops*) which are used to give a bitter flavour to beer.

hope *n.* feeling of expectation and desire; person or thing giving cause for this; what one hopes for. —*v.t./i.* feel hope. **hopeful** *a.*, **hopefully** *adv.*

hopeless *a.* without hope; inadequate, incompetent. **hopelessly** *adv.*, **hopelessness** *n.*

hopper *n.* one who hops; container with an opening at its base through which its contents can be discharged.

hopsack *n.* a kind of coarsely woven fabric.

hopscotch *n.* game involving hopping over marked squares.

horde *n.* large group or crowd.

horizon *n.* line at which earth and sky appear to meet; limit of knowledge or interests.

horizontal *a.* parallel to the horizon, going straight across. **horizontally** *adv.*

hormone *n.* secretion (or synthetic substance) that stimulates an organ or growth. **hormonal** *a.*

horn *n.* hard pointed growth on the heads of certain animals; substance of this; similar projection; wind instrument with a trumpet-shaped end; device for sounding a warning signal. —*v.t.* cut off the horns of; gore with horn(s). ∼ **in,** (*sl.*) intrude, interfere. ∼**-rimmed** *a.* with frames of material like horn or tortoiseshell.

horned *a.* having horns.

hornet *n.* a kind of large wasp.

hornpipe *n.* lively solo dance traditionally associated with sailors.

horny *a.* (-*ier*, -*iest*) of or like horn; hardened and calloused.

horoscope *n.* astrologer's diagram of relative positions of stars; forecast of events, based on this.

horrible *a.* causing horror; (*colloq.*) unpleasant. **horribly** *adv.*

horrid *a.* horrible.

horrific *a.* horrifying. **horrifically** *adv.*

horrify *v.t.* arouse horror in, shock.

horror *n.* loathing and fear; intense dislike or

dismay; person or thing causing horror. ~-stricken, ~-struck *adjs.* horrified.

hors-d'œuvre /ɔ'dɜvr/ *n.* food served as an appetizer.

horse *n.* quadruped with a mane and tail; frame for hanging things on; padded structure for vaulting over in a gymnasium. ~-box *n.* closed vehicle for transporting a horse. ~-chestnut *n.* brown shiny nut; tree bearing this. ~-laugh *n.* loud coarse laugh. ~-radish *n.* plant with a hot-tasting root used to make sauce. ~ sense, (*colloq.*) common sense.

horseback *n.* on ~, riding on a horse.

horsehair *n.* hair from a horse's mane or tail, used for padding furniture.

horseman *n.* (pl. *-men*) rider on horseback. horsewoman *n.fem.* (pl. *-women*).

horseplay *n.* boisterous play.

horsepower *n.* unit for measuring the power of an engine.

horseshoe *n.* U-shaped strip of metal nailed to a horse's hoof; thing shaped like this.

horsy *a.* of or like a horse; interested in horses and horse-racing.

horticulture *n.* art of garden cultivation. horticultural *a.*, horticulturist *n.*

hosanna *int.* & *n.* cry of adoration to God and the Messiah.

hose *n.* stockings and socks; hose-pipe. —*v.t.* water or spray with a hose-pipe. ~-pipe *n.* flexible tube for conveying water.

hosiery *n.* stockings, socks, etc.

hospice *n.* lodging for travellers; home for destitute or sick people.

hospitable /'hɒs-/ *a.* giving hospitality. hospitably *adv.*

hospital *n.* institution for treatment of sick or injured people.

hospitality *n.* friendly and generous entertainment of guests.

host[1] *n.* large number of people or things.

host[2] *n.* person who entertains another as his guest; organism on which another lives as a parasite. —*v.t.* act as host to.

host[3] *n.* bread consecrated at the Eucharist.

hostage *n.* person held as security that the holder's demands will be satisfied.

hostel *n.* lodging-house for students or other special group.

hostess *n.* woman host.

hostile *a.* of an enemy; unfriendly.

hostility *n.* being hostile, enmity; (*pl.*) acts of warfare.

hot *a.* (*hotter*, *hottest*) at or having a high temperature; producing a burning sensation to the taste; eager, angry; excited, excitable; (of scent in hunting) fresh and strong; (of news) fresh; (*colloq.*) very skilful; (of jazz) strongly rhythmical and emotional; (*sl.*) radioactive; (*sl.*, of goods) recently stolen and risky to handle. —*v.t./i.* (p.t. *hotted*) (*colloq.*) make or become hot or exciting. ~ air, (*sl.*) excited or boastful talk. ~ dog, hot sausage in a bread roll. ~ line, direct line of communication, esp. between heads of governments. ~-pot *n.* stew of meat, potatoes, and other

vegetables. ~-water bottle, container to be filled with hot water for warmth in bed. in ~ water, (*colloq.*) in trouble or disgrace.

hotbed *n.* place favourable to the growth of something evil.

hotchpotch *n.* jumble.

hotel *n.* building where meals and rooms are provided for travellers.

hotelier *n.* hotel-keeper.

hotfoot *adv.* in eager haste.

hothead *n.* impetuous person.

hothouse *n.* heated greenhouse.

hotplate *n.* heated surface on which food may be heated or kept hot.

Hottentot *n.* member of a negroid people of South Africa.

hound *n.* dog used in hunting. —*v.t.* pursue, harass; urge, incite.

hour *n.* one twenty-fourth part of a day and night; point of time; occasion; (*pl.*) period for daily work.

hourglass *n.* glass containing sand that takes one hour to trickle from upper to lower section through a narrow opening.

houri /'hʊərɪ/ *n.* (pl. *-is*) beautiful young woman of the Muslim paradise.

hourly *a.* done or occurring once an hour; continual. —*adv.* every hour.

house[1] /-s/ *n.* building for people (usu. one family) to live in, or for a particular purpose; household; legislative assembly; business firm; theatre audience or performance; family, dynasty; one of twelve astrological divisions of the heavens. ~-proud *a.* giving great attention to the appearance of one's home. ~ surgeon, surgeon resident at a hospital. ~-trained *a.* trained to be clean in the house. ~-warming *n.* party to celebrate occupation of a new home.

house[2] /-z/ *v.t.* provide accommodation or storage-space for; encase.

houseboat *n.* barge-like boat fitted up as a dwelling.

housebreaker *n.* burglar; person employed in demolition of houses. housebreaking *n.*

housecoat *n.* woman's long dress-like garment for informal wear.

housecraft *n.* skill in housekeeping.

household *n.* occupants of a house living as a family. Household troops, those nominally employed to guard the sovereign. ~ word, familiar saying or name.

householder *n.* person owning or renting a house or flat.

housekeeper *n.* woman employed to look after a household.

housekeeping *n.* management of household affairs; (*colloq.*) money to be used for this.

housemaid *n.* woman servant in a house, esp. one who cleans rooms.

housemaster, housemistress *ns.* teacher in charge of a school boarding-house.

housewife *n.* woman managing a household. housewifely *adv.*

housewifery /-wɪf-/ *n.* housekeeping.

housework *n.* cleaning and cooking etc. done in housekeeping.

housing *n.* accommodation; rigid case enclosing machinery.

hove *see* **heave.**

hovel *n.* miserable dwelling.

hover *v.i.* (of a bird etc.) remain in one place in the air; linger, wait close at hand. **~-fly** *n.* wasp-like insect that hovers.

hovercraft *n.* vehicle supported by air thrust downwards from its engines.

how *adv.* by what means, in what way; to what extent or amount etc.; in what condition. **~ about,** what is your feeling about (this thing). **~ do you do,** formal greeting. **~-d'ye-do** *n.* (*colloq.*) awkward state of affairs. **~ many,** what total. **~ much,** what amount or price.

however *adv.* in whatever way, to whatever extent; nevertheless.

howl *n.* long loud wailing cry or sound. —*v.t./i.* make or utter with a howl; weep loudly.

howler *n.* (*colloq.*) stupid mistake.

hoyden *n.* girl who behaves boisterously. **hoydenish** *a.*

h.p. *abbr.* hire-purchase; horse-power.

H.R.H. *abbr.* His or Her Royal Highness.

hub *n.* central part of a wheel; central point of activity. **~-cap** *n.* cover for the hub of a car wheel.

hubble-bubble *n.* hookah.

hubbub *n.* confused noise of voices.

huddle *v.t./i.* crowd into a small place. —*n.* close mass.

hue[1] *n.* colour.

hue[2] *n.* **~ and cry,** outcry.

huff *n.* fit of annoyance. —*v.i.* blow. **huffy** *a.*

hug *v.t.* (p.t. *hugged*) squeeze tightly in one's arms; keep close to.

huge *a.* extremely large.

hugger-mugger *a.* & *adv.* full of secrecy; in disorder.

hulk *n.* body of an old ship; large clumsy-looking person or thing.

hulking *a.* (*colloq.*) large and clumsy.

hull[1] *n.* framework of a ship.

hull[2] *n.* pod of a pea or bean; cluster of leaves on a strawberry. —*v.t.* remove the hull of.

hullabaloo *n.* uproar.

hullo *int.* exclamation used in greeting or to call attention.

hum *v.t./i.* (p.t. *hummed*) sing with closed lips; make a similar sound; (*colloq.*) be in state of activity; (*sl.*) smell bad. —*n.* humming sound; (*sl.*) bad smell. **~ and haw,** hesitate.

human *a.* of mankind. —*n.* human being. **humanly** *adv.*

humane /-'meɪn/ *a.* kind-hearted, merciful. **humanely** *adv.*

humanism *n.* system of thought concerned with human affairs and ethics (not theology); promotion of human welfare. **humanist** *n.,* **humanistic** *a.*

humanitarian *a.* promoting human welfare and the reduction of suffering.

humanity *n.* human nature or qualities; kindness; human race; (*pl.*) arts subjects.

humanize *v.t.* make human; make humane. **humanization** *n.*

humble *a.* (*-er, -est*) having or showing a modest estimate of one's own importance; of low rank; not large or expensive. —*v.t.* lower the rank or self-importance of. **eat ~ pie,** make a humble apology. **humbly** *adv.*

humbug *n.* misleading behaviour or talk to win support or sympathy; person behaving thus; hard *usu.* peppermint-flavoured boiled sweet.

humdrum *n.* dull, commonplace.

humerus *n.* bone of upper arm.

humid *a.* (of air) damp. **humidity** *n.*

humidifier *n.* device for keeping air moist in a room etc.

humiliate *v.t.* cause to feel disgraced. **humiliation** *n.*

humility *n.* humble condition or attitude of mind.

hummock *n.* hump in the ground.

humoresque *n.* light and lively musical composition.

humorist *n.* person noted for his humour.

humour *n.* quality of being amusing; ability to perceive and enjoy this; state of mind. —*v.t.* keep (a person) contented by doing as he wishes. **humorous** *a.,* **humorously** *adv.*

hump *n.* rounded projecting part; curved deformity of the spine; *the ~,* (*sl.*) fit of depression or annoyance. —*v.t.* form into a hump; hoist and carry. **humped** *a.*

humpback *n.* hunchback. **~ bridge,** small steeply arched bridge.

humus /'hju-/ *n.* soil-fertilizing substance formed by decay of dead leaves and plants etc.

hunch *v.t./i.* bend into a hump. —*n.* hump; hunk; intuitive feeling.

hunchback *n.* person with a hump back.

hundred *n.* ten times ten (100, C). **hundredth** *a.* & *n.*

hundredfold *a.* & *adv.* one hundred times as much or as many.

hundredweight *n.* measure of weight, 112 lb or (**metric ~**) 50 kg (110.25 lb).

hung *see* **hang.** —*a.* **~-over** *a.* (*sl.*) having a hangover.

Hungarian *a.* & *n.* (native, language) of Hungary.

hunger *n.* uneasy sensation felt when one has not eaten for some time; strong desire. —*v.i.* feel hunger. **~-strike** *a.* refusal of food as a form of protest.

hungry *a.* (*-ier, -iest*) feeling hunger. **hungrily** *adv.*

hunk *n.* large or clumsy piece.

hunt *v.t./i.* pursue (wild animals) for food or sport; pursue with hostility; use (a horse or hounds) in hunting; seek; search; (of an engine) run fast and slow alternately. —*n.* process of hunting; hunting district or group.

hunter *n.* one who hunts; horse used for hunting; watch with a hinged cover over the dial.

huntsman *n.* (pl. *-men*) hunter.

hurdle *n.* portable frame with bars, used as a

temporary fence; frame to be jumped over in a race; obstacle, difficulty. **hurdler** *n.*

hurdy-gurdy *n.* barrel-organ.

hurl *v.t.* throw violently. —*n.* violent throw.

hurly-burly *n.* rough bustle.

hurrah, hurray *int.* & *n.* exclamation of joy or approval.

hurricane *n.* violent storm-wind.

hurried *a.* done with great haste. **hurriedly** *adv.*

hurry *v.t./i.* act or move with eagerness or too quickly; cause to do this. —*n.* hurrying.

hurt *v.t./i.* (p.t. *hurt*) cause pain, harm, or injury to; cause or feel pain. —*n.* injury, harm. **hurtful** *a.*

hurtle *v.t./i.* move or hurl rapidly.

husband *n.* married man in relation to his wife. —*v.t.* use economically, try to save.

husbandry *n.* farming; management of resources.

hush *v.t./i.* make or become silent or quiet. —*n.* silence. **~-hush** *a.* (*colloq.*) kept very secret.

husk *n.* dry outer covering of certain seeds and fruits. —*v.t.* remove the husk from.

husky[1] *a.* (-*ier*, -*iest*) dry; hoarse; burly. **huskily** *adv.*, **huskiness** *n.*

husky[2] *n.* Eskimo dog.

hussy *n.* cheeky young woman.

hustings *n.* parliamentary election proceedings.

hustle *v.t./i.* push roughly; hurry. —*n.* hustling. **hustler** *n.*

hut *n.* small simple or roughly made house or shelter.

hutch *n.* box-like pen for rabbits.

hyacinth *n.* plant with fragrant bell-shaped flowers.

hybrid *n.* offspring of two different species or varieties; thing made by combining different elements. —*a.* produced in this way.

hydrangea *n.* shrub with pink, blue, or white flowers in clusters.

hydrant *n.* pipe from a water-main (esp. in a street) to which a hose can be attached.

hydrate *n.* chemical compound of water with another substance.

hydraulic *a.* of water conveyed by pipes etc.; involving water-power; hardening under water. **hydraulically** *adv.*

hydro *n.* (pl. -*os*) hotel etc. providing hydrotherapy; hydro-electric power-plant.

hydrocarbon *n.* compound of hydrogen and carbon.

hydrochloric /-ˈklɔr-/ *a.* **~ acid**, corrosive acid containing hydrogen and chlorine.

hydroelectric *a.* using water-power to produce electricity.

hydrofoil *n.* boat with a structure that raises its hull out of the water when the boat is in motion; this structure.

hydrogen *n.* odourless gas, the lightest element. **~ bomb**, powerful bomb releasing energy by fusion of hydrogen nuclei.

hydrometer /-ˈdrom-/ *n.* instrument measuring the density of liquids.

hydrophobia *n.* abnormal fear of water, esp. as a symptom of rabies; rabies.

hydrostatic *a.* of the pressure and other characteristics of liquid at rest.

hydrotherapy *n.* use of water to treat diseases and abnormalities.

hyena *n.* wolf-like animal with a howl that sounds like laughter.

hygiene *n.* cleanliness as a means of preventing disease. **hygienic** *a.*, **hygienically** *adv.*

hygrometer /-ˈgrom-/ *n.* instrument measuring humidity.

hymen *n.* membrane partly closing the opening of the vagina of a virgin girl or woman.

hymn *n.* song of praise to God or a sacred being. **~-book** *n.* book of hymns.

hymnal *n.* hymn-book.

hyper- *pref.* excessively.

hyperactive *a.* abnormally active.

hyperbola /-ˈpɜ-/ *n.* a kind of curve. **hyperbolic** /-ˈbol-/ *a.*

hyperbole /-ˈpɜbəlɪ/ *n.* rhetorical exaggeration. **hyperbolical** /-ˈbol-/ *a.*

hypermarket *n.* very large self-service store selling a wide variety of goods and services.

hyphen *n.* the sign - used to join words together or divide a word into parts. —*v.t.* hyphenate.

hyphenate *v.t.* join or divide with a hyphen. **hyphenation** *n.*

hypnosis *n.* sleep-like condition produced in a person who then obeys suggestions; production of this.

hypnotic *a.* of or producing hypnosis or a similar condition; producing sleep. —*n.* drug producing sleep. **hypnotically** *adv.*

hypnotize *v.t.* produce hypnosis in; fascinate, dominate the mind or will of. **hypnotist** *n.*

hypnotism *n.* hypnosis.

hypocaust /ˈhaɪ-/ *n.* ancient Roman system of under-floor heating by hot air.

hypochondria /-ˈkon-/ *n.* state of constantly imagining that one is ill. **hypochondriac** *n.* person suffering from this.

hypocrisy *n.* falsely pretending to be virtuous; insincerity.

hypocrite *n.* person guilty of hypocrisy. **hypocritical** *a.*

hypodermic *a.* injected beneath the skin; used for such injections. —*n.* hypodermic syringe.

hypotenuse /-ˈpot-/ *n.* longest side of a right-angled triangle.

hypothermia *n.* condition of having an abnormally low body-temperature.

hypothesis /-ˈpoθ-/ *n.* (pl. -*theses*) supposition put forward as a basis for reasoning or investigation.

hypothetical *a.* supposed but not necessarily true. **hypothetically** *adv.*

hysterectomy *n.* surgical removal of the womb.

hysteria *n.* wild uncontrollable emotion. **hysterical** *a.*, **hysterically** *adv.*

hysterics *n.pl.* hysterical outburst.

I

I *pron.* person speaking or writing and referring to himself.

ibex *n.* (pl. *ibex* or *ibexes*) mountain goat with curving horns.

ibis /ˈaɪ-/ *n.* wading bird found in warm climates.

ice *n.* frozen water, brittle transparent solid; portion of ice-cream. —*v.t./i.* become frozen; make very cold; decorate with icing. ∼**cream** *n.* sweet creamy frozen food. ∼**hockey,** game like hockey played on ice by skaters. ∼**lolly,** water-ice or ice-cream on a stick.

iceberg *n.* mass of ice floating in the sea.

Icelandic *a.* & *n.* (language) of Iceland.

icicle *n.* hanging ice formed when dripping water freezes.

icing *n.* mixture of powdered sugar etc. used to decorate food.

icon /ˈaɪkon/ *n.* (in the Eastern Church) sacred painting or mosaic.

iconoclast /aɪˈkon-/ *n.* person who attacks cherished beliefs.

icy *a.* (-*ier*, -*iest*) very cold; covered with ice; very unfriendly. **icily** *adv.*

idea *n.* plan etc. formed in the mind by thinking; opinion; mental impression; vague belief.

ideal *a.* satisfying one's idea of what is perfect. —*n.* person or thing regarded as perfect or as a standard to aim at. **ideally** *adv.*

idealist *n.* person with high ideals. **idealism** *n.*, **idealistic** *a.*

idealize *v.t.* regard or represent as perfect.

identical *a.* the same; exactly alike. **identically** *adv.*

identify *v.t./i.* recognize as being a specified person or thing; consider to be identical; associate (oneself) closely in feeling or interest. **identifiable** *a.*, **identification** *n.*

identikit *n.* set of pictures of features that can be put together to form a likeness.

identity *n.* who or what a person or thing is; sameness.

ideogram /ˈɪdɪ-/ *n.* symbol indicating something.

ideology /aɪdɪ-/ *n.* ideas that form the basis of a political or economic theory. **ideological** *a.*

idiocy *n.* state of being an idiot; extreme foolishness.

idiom *n.* phrase or usage peculiar to a language; characteristic mode of expression in art or music.

idiomatic *a.* in accordance with or full of idioms. **idiomatically** *adv.*

idiosyncrasy /-ˈsɪŋk-/ *n.* person's own characteristic way of behaving. **idiosyncratic** /-ˈkræt-/ *a.*

idiot *n.* mentally deficient person incapable of rational conduct; (*colloq.*) very stupid person.

idiotic *a.* very stupid. **idiotically** *adv.*

idle *a.* (-*er*, -*est*) doing no work; not employed or in use; lazy; having no special purpose.

—*v.t./i.* be idle, pass (time) without working; (of an engine) run slowly in neutral gear. **idly** *adv.*, **idleness** *n.*, **idler** *n.*

idol *n.* image worshipped as a god; idolized person or thing.

idolatry /-ˈdol-/ *n.* worship of idols. **idolater** *n.*

idolize *v.t.* love or admire excessively.

idyll /ˈɪdɪl/ *n.* peaceful or romantic scene or incident; description of this, usu. in verse. **idyllic** /-ˈdɪl-/ *a.*, **idyllically** *adv.*

i.e. *abbr.* (Latin *id est*) that is.

if *conj.* on condition that; supposing that; whether; used in exclamations of wish or surprise. —*n.* condition, supposition.

igloo *n.* Eskimo's snow hut.

igneous *a.* (of rock) formed by volcanic action.

ignite *v.t./i.* set fire to; catch fire.

ignition *n.* igniting; mechanism producing a spark to ignite the fuel in an engine.

ignoble *a.* not noble in character, aims, or purpose. **ignobly** *adv.*

ignominy /ˈɪg-/ *n.* disgrace, humiliation. **ignominious** /-ˈmɪn-/ *a.*, **ignominiously** *adv.*

ignoramus /-ˈreɪ-/ *n.* (pl. -*muses*) ignorant person.

ignorant *a.* lacking knowledge; behaving rudely through not knowing good manners. **ignorantly** *adv.*, **ignorance** *n.*

ignore *v.t.* take no notice of.

iguana /ɪˈgwɑ-/ *n.* tropical tree-climbing lizard.

ileostomy /ɪlɪˈos-/ *n.* opening made surgically in the surface of the abdomen, through which the small intestine can empty.

ilk *n.* (*colloq.*) kind.

ill *a.* unwell; bad; harmful; hostile, unkind. —*adv.* badly. —*n.* evil, harm, injury. ∼ **advised** *a.* unwise. ∼ **at ease,** uncomfortable, embarrassed. ∼**bred** *a.* ill-mannered. ∼**gotten** *a.* gained by evil or unlawful means. ∼**mannered** *a.* having bad manners. ∼**natured** *a.* unkind. ∼**starred** *a.* unlucky. ∼**treat** *v.t.* treat badly or cruelly. ∼ **will,** hostility, unkind feeling.

illegal *a.* against the law. **illegally** *adv.*, **illegality** *n.*

illegible *a.* not legible. **illegibly** *adv.*, **illegibility** *n.*

illegitimate *a.* born of parents not married to each other; contrary to a law or rule. **illegitimately** *adv.*, **illegitimacy** *n.*

illicit /-ˈlɪs-/ *a.* unlawful, not allowed. **illicitly** *adv.*

illiterate *a.* unable to read and write; uneducated. **illiteracy** *n.*

illness *n.* state of being ill; particular form of ill health.

illogical *a.* not logical. **illogically** *adv.*, **illogicality** *n.*

illuminate *v.t.* light up; throw light on (a subject); decorate with lights; decorate (a manuscript) with coloured designs. **illumination** *n.*

illusion *n.* false belief; thing wrongly supposed to exist.

illusionist *n.* conjuror.

illusory *a.* based on illusion, not real.

illustrate *v.t.* supply (a book etc.) with drawings or pictures; make clear by example(s) or picture(s) etc.; serve as an example of. **illustration** *n.*, **illustrator** *n.*

illustrative /'ɪl-/ *a.* serving as an illustration or example.

illustrious *a.* distinguished.

image *n.* statue; optical appearance of a thing produced in a mirror or through a lens; likeness; mental picture; general reputation.

imagery *n.* images; metaphorical language evoking mental pictures.

imaginable *a.* able to be imagined.

imaginary *a.* existing only in the imagination, not real.

imagination *n.* imagining; ability to imagine or to plan creatively. **imaginative** *a.*, **imaginatively** *adv.*

imagine *v.t.* form a mental image of; think, suppose; guess.

imam /ɪ'mɑm/ *n.* Muslim spiritual leader.

imbalance *n.* lack of balance.

imbecile /-siːl/ *n.* mentally deficient person; stupid person. —*a.* idiotic. **imbecility** *n.*

imbibe *v.t.* drink; absorb into the mind.

imbroglio /-'brəʊ-/ *n.* (pl. *-os*) confused situation, usu. with disagreement.

imbue *v.t.* fill with feelings, qualities, or emotions.

imitate *v.t.* try to act or be like; copy. **imitation** *n.*, **imitator** *n.*

imitative *a.* imitating.

immaculate *a.* free from stain, blemish, or fault. **immaculately** *adv.*, **immaculacy** *n.*

immanent *a.* inherent. **immanence** *n.*

immaterial *a.* having no physical substance; of no importance.

immature *a.* not mature. **immaturity** *n.*

immeasurable *a.* not measurable, immense. **immeasurably** *adv.*

immediate *a.* with no delay; nearest, with nothing between. **immediately** *adv. & conj.*, **immediacy** *n.*

immemorial *a.* existing from before what can be remembered.

immense *a.* extremely great. **immensely** *adv.*, **immensity** *n.*

immerse *v.t.* put completely into liquid; absorb deeply in thought or business etc.

immersion *n.* immersing. **~ heater,** electric heating element designed to be placed in the liquid to be heated.

immigrate *v.i.* come into a foreign country as a permanent resident. **immigrant** *a. & n.*, **immigration** *n.*

imminent *a.* about to occur. **imminence** *n.*

immobile *a.* immovable; not moving. **immobility** *n.*

immobilize *v.t.* make or keep immobile. **immobilization** *n.*

immoderate *a.* excessive, lacking moderation. **immoderately** *adv.*

immodest *a.* not modest.

immoral *a.* morally wrong. **immorally** *adv.*, **immorality** *n.*

immortal *a.* living for ever, not mortal; famous for all time. —*n.* immortal being. **immortality** *n.*

immortalize *v.t.* make immortal.

immovable *a.* unable to be moved; unyielding. **immovably** *adv.*

immune *a.* having immunity.

immunity *n.* ability to resist infection; special exemption.

immunize *v.t.* make immune to infection. **immunization** *n.*

immure *v.t.* imprison, shut in.

immutable *a.* unchangeable. **immutably** *adv.*, **immutability** *n.*

imp *n.* small devil; mischievous child.

impact[1] /'ɪm-/ *n.* collision, force of this; strong effect.

impact[2] /-'pæ-/ *v.t.* press or wedge firmly. **impaction** *n.*

impair *v.t.* damage, weaken. **impairment** *n.*

impala /-'pɑ-/ *n.* (pl. *-a*) small antelope.

impale *v.t.* fix or pierce with a pointed object. **impalement** *n.*

impalpable *a.* intangible.

impart *v.t.* give; make (information etc.) known.

impartial *a.* not favouring one more than another. **impartially** *adv.*, **impartiality** *n.*

impassable *a.* impossible to travel on or over.

impasse /'æmpɑs/ *n.* deadlock.

impassioned *a.* passionate.

impassive *a.* not feeling or showing emotion. **impassively** *adv.*

impatient *a.* feeling or showing lack of patience; intolerant. **impatiently** *adv.*, **impatience** *n.*

impeach *v.t.* accuse of a serious crime against the State and bring for trial; disparage. **impeachment** *n.*

impeccable *a.* faultless. **impeccably** *adv.*

impecunious *a.* having little or no money.

impedance *n.* resistance of an electric circuit to the flow of current.

impede *v.t.* hinder.

impediment *n.* hindrance, obstruction; lisp or stammer.

impedimenta *n.pl.* encumbrances, baggage.

impel *v.t.* (p.t. *impelled*) urge; drive forward.

impending *a.* imminent.

impenetrable *a.* unable to be penetrated. **impenetrability** *n.*

impenitent *a.* not penitent.

imperative *a.* expressing a command; essential. —*n.* command; essential thing.

imperceptible *a.* not perceptible; too slight to be noticed. **imperceptibly** *adv.*

imperfect *a.* not perfect. **imperfectly** *adv.*, **imperfection** *n.*

imperial *a.* of an empire or emperor or empress; majestic; (of measures) used by statute in the U.K.

imperialism *n.* policy of having or extending an empire. **imperialist** *n.*, **imperialistic** *a.*

imperil *v.t.* (p.t. *imperilled*) endanger.
imperious *a.* commanding, bossy. **imperiously** *adv.*
impermanent *a.* not permanent.
impermeable *a.* not permeable.
impersonal *a.* not showing or influenced by personal feeling; not involving a person. **impersonally** *adv.*, **impersonality** *n.*
impersonate *v.t.* pretend to be (another person). **impersonation** *n.*, **impersonator** *n.*
impertinent *a.* not showing proper respect. **impertinently** *adv.*, **impertinence** *n.*
imperturbable *a.* not excitable, calm. **imperturbably** *adv.*, **imperturbability** *n.*
impervious *a.* ~ **to,** not able to be penetrated or influenced by.
impetigo /-'taɪ-/ *n.* contagious skin disease causing spots.
impetuous *a.* acting or done on impulse or with sudden energy. **impetuously** *adv.*, **impetuosity** *n.*
impetus *n.* moving force.
impiety *n.* lack of reverence.
impinge *v.i.* make an impact; encroach.
impious /'ɪmpɪ-/ *a.* not reverent, wicked. **impiously** *adv.*
impish *a.* of or like an imp.
implacable *a.* not able to be placated, relentless. **implacably** *adv.*, **implacability** *n.*
implant[1] /-'plɑ-/ *v.t.* plant, insert; insert (tissue) in a living thing. **implantation** *n.*
implant[2] /'ɪm-/ *n.* implanted tissue.
implausible *a.* not plausible.
implement[1] *n.* tool.
implement[2] *v.t.* put into effect. **implementation** *n.*
implicate *v.t.* involve.
implication *n.* implicating; implying; thing implied.
implicit *a.* implied but not made explicit; absolute. **implicitly** *adv.*
implore *v.t.* request earnestly.
imply *v.t.* suggest without stating directly; mean; involve the existence or truth of.
impolite *a.* not polite. **impolitely** *adv.*, **impoliteness** *n.*
impolitic *a.* unwise; inexpedient.
imponderable *a.* not able to be estimated.
import[1] /-'pɔ-/ *v.t.* bring in from abroad or from an outside source; imply. **importation** *n.*, **importer** *n.*
import[2] /'ɪm-/ *n.* importing; thing imported; meaning; importance.
important *a.* having a great effect; having great authority or influence; pompous. **importance** *n.*
importunate *a.* making persistent requests. **importunity** *n.*
impose *v.t./i.* put (a tax, obligation, etc.); inflict; force acceptance of. ~ **on,** take unfair advantage of.
imposing *a.* impressive.
imposition *n.* act of imposing something; thing imposed; burden imposed unfairly.
impossible *a.* not possible; unendurable. **impossibly** *adv.*, **impossibility** *n.*

impostor *n.* person who fraudulently pretends to be someone else.
imposture *n.* fraudulent deception.
impotent *a.* powerless, unable to take action; (of a male) unable to copulate successfully or to procreate. **impotently** *adv.*, **impotence** *n.*
impound *v.t.* take (property) into legal custody; confiscate.
impoverish *v.t.* cause to become poor; exhaust the natural strength or fertility of. **impoverishment** *n.*
impracticable *a.* not practicable. **impracticability** *n.*
impractical *a.* not practical.
imprecation *n.* spoken curse.
imprecise *a.* not precise. **imprecisely** *adv.*, **imprecision** *n.*
impregnable *a.* safe against attack. **impregnability** *n.*
impregnate *v.t.* introduce sperm or pollen into and fertilize; penetrate all parts of. **impregnation** *n.*
impresario /-'sɑr-/ *n.* (pl. *-os*) manager of an operatic or concert company.
impress *v.t.* cause to form a strong (usu. favourable) opinion; fix in the mind; press a mark into.
impression *n.* effect produced on the mind; uncertain idea; imitation done for entertainment; impressed mark; making of this; reprint.
impressionable *a.* easily influenced.
impressionism *n.* style of painting etc. giving a general impression without detail. **impressionist** *n.*
impressive *a.* making a strong favourable impression. **impressively** *adv.*
imprint[1] /'ɪm-/ *n.* mark made by pressing on a surface.
imprint[2] /-'prɪnt/ *v.t.* impress or stamp a mark etc. on.
imprison *v.t.* put into prison; keep in confinement. **imprisonment** *n.*
improbable *a.* not likely to be true or to happen. **improbably** *adv.*, **improbability** *n.*
impromptu *a. & adv.* without preparation or rehearsal. —*n.* impromptu musical composition.
improper *a.* unsuitable; incorrect; not conforming to social conventions; indecent. ~ **fraction,** fraction greater than unity, with the numerator greater than the denominator. **improperly** *adv.*
impropriety /-'praɪ-/ *n.* being improper; improper act, remark, etc.
improve *v.t./i.* make or become better. **improvement** *n.*
improver *n.* person working at a trade for a low wage to improve his skill.
improvident *a.* not providing for future needs. **improvidently** *adv.*, **improvidence** *n.*
improvise *v.t.* compose impromptu; provide from whatever materials are at hand. **improvisation** *n.*
imprudent *a.* unwise, rash. **imprudently** *adv.*, **imprudence** *n.*

impudent *a.* impertinent, cheeky. **impudently** *adv.*, **impudence** *n.*

impugn /-'pjun/ *v.t.* express doubts about the truth or honesty of.

impulse *n.* push, thrust; impetus; stimulating force in a nerve; sudden inclination to act, without thought for the consequences.

impulsive *a.* acting or done on impulse. **impulsively** *adv.*, **impulsiveness** *n.*

impunity *n.* freedom from punishment or injury.

impure *a.* not pure.

impurity *n.* being impure; substance that makes another impure.

impute *v.t.* attribute (a fault etc.). **imputation** *n.*

in *prep.* having as a position or state within (limits of space, time, surroundings, etc.); having as a state or manner; into, towards. —*adv.* in a position bounded by limits, or to a point enclosed by these; inside; in fashion, season, or office; batting; (of a fire) burning; having arrived or been gathered or received. —*a.* internal; living etc. inside; fashionable. ~ **for,** about to experience; competing in. ~ **laws** *n.pl.* (*colloq.*) one's relatives by marriage. ~ **memoriam,** in memory of one who has died. ~**patient** *n.* person resident in a hospital for treatment. **ins and outs,** passages; details of activity or procedure. ~ **so far,** to such an extent. ~**tray** *n.* tray for documents awaiting attention.

in. *abbr.* inch(es).

inability *n.* being unable.

inaccessible *a.* not accessible.

inaccurate *a.* not accurate. **inaccurately** *adv.*, **inaccuracy** *n.*

inaction *n.* lack of action.

inactive *a.* not active. **inactivity** *n.*

inadequate *a.* not adequate; not sufficiently able. **inadequately** *adv.*, **inadequacy** *n.*

inadmissible *a.* not allowable.

inadvertent *a.* unintentional.

inadvisable *a.* not advisable.

inalienable *a.* not able to be given away or taken away.

inane *a.* silly, lacking sense. **inanely** *adv.*, **inanity** *n.*

inanimate *a.* lacking animal life; showing no sign of being alive.

inapplicable *a.* not applicable.

inappropriate *a.* unsuitable.

inarticulate *a.* not expressed in words; unable to speak distinctly; unable to express ideas clearly.

inartistic *a.* not artistic.

inattention *n.* lack of attention.

inattentive *a.* not paying attention.

inaudible *a.* not audible.

inaugural *a.* of an inauguration.

inaugurate *v.t.* admit to office ceremonially; begin (an undertaking), open (a building etc.) formally; be the beginning of. **inauguration** *n.*, **inaugurator** *n.*

inauspicious *a.* not auspicious.

inborn *a.* existing in a person or animal from birth, natural.

inbred *a.* produced by inbreeding; inborn.

inbreeding *n.* breeding from closely related individuals.

Inc. *abbr.* (*U.S.*) Incorporated.

Inca *n.* member of a former American Indian people in Peru.

incalculable *a.* unable to be calculated.

incandescent *a.* glowing with heat, shining. **incandescence** *n.*

incantation *n.* words or sounds uttered as a magic spell.

incapable *a.* not capable; helpless. **incapability** *n.*

incapacitate *v.t.* disable; make ineligible. **incapacitation** *n.*

incapacity *n.* inability, lack of sufficient strength or power.

incarcerate *v.t.* imprison. **incarceration** *n.*

incarnate *a.* embodied, in human form.

incarnation *n.* embodiment, esp. in human form; *the I~,* that of God as Christ.

incautious *a.* rash. **incautiously** *adv.*

incendiary *a.* designed to cause fire. —*n.* incendiary bomb; arsonist.

incense[1] /'ɪn-/ *n.* substance burnt to produce fragrant smoke, esp. in religious ceremonies; this smoke.

incense[2] /-'sens/ *v.t.* make angry.

incentive *n.* thing that encourages an action or effort.

inception *n.* beginning.

incertitude *n.* uncertainty.

incessant *a.* not ceasing.

incest *n.* sexual intercourse between very closely related people. **incestuous** *a.*

inch *n.* measure of length (= 2·54 cm). —*v.t./i.* move gradually.

inchoate /'ɪnkəʊət/ *a.* just begun, undeveloped.

incidence *n.* rate at which a thing occurs; falling.

incident *n.* event, esp. one causing trouble. —*a.* liable to happen; falling.

incidental *a.* occurring in connection with something; casual.

incidentally *adv.* in an incidental way; by the way.

incinerate *v.t.* burn to ashes. **incineration** *n.*, **incinerator** *n.*

incipient *a.* beginning to exist.

incise *v.t.* make a cut in; engrave. **incision** *n.*

incisive *a.* clear and decisive.

incisor *n.* one of the front teeth.

incite *v.t.* urge on to action; stir up. **incitement** *n.*

incivility *n.* impoliteness.

inclement *a.* (of weather) cold, wet.

inclination *n.* slope; bending; tendency; liking, preference.

incline[1] /-'klaɪn/ *v.t./i.* slope; bend; have or cause to have a certain tendency; influence.

incline[2] /'ɪn-/ *n.* slope.

include *v.t.* have or treat as part of a whole; put into a specified category. **inclusion** *n.*

inclusive *a.* & *adv.* including what is mentioned; including everything.

incognito /-'kɒgnɪ-/ *a.* & *adv.* with one's identity kept secret. —*n.* pretended identity.

incoherent *a.* rambling in speech or in reasoning. **incoherently** *adv.*

incombustible *a.* not able to be burnt.

income *n.* money received during a period as wages, interest, etc.

incoming *a.* coming in.

incommode *v.t.* inconvenience.

incommunicado /-ˈkɑ-/ *a.* not allowed to communicate with others.

incomparable /-ˈkom-/ *a.* beyond comparison, without an equal.

incompatible *a.* not compatible. **incompatibility** *n.*

incompetent *a.* not competent. **incompetently** *adv.*, **incompetence** *n.*

incomplete *a.* not complete. **incompletely** *adv.*

incomprehensible *a.* not able to be understood. **incomprehension** *n.*

inconceivable *a.* unable to be imagined; (*colloq.*) most unlikely.

inconclusive *a.* not fully convincing.

incongruous *a.* unsuitable, not harmonious. **incongruity** *n.*

inconsequential *a.* unimportant; not following logically, irrelevant. **inconsequentially** *adv.*

inconsiderable *a.* negligible.

inconsiderate *a.* not considerate.

inconsistent *a.* not consistent. **inconsistently** *adv.*, **inconsistency** *n.*

inconsolable *a.* not able to be consoled.

inconspicuous *a.* not conspicuous. **inconspicuously** *adv.*

incontestable *a.* indisputable. **incontestably** *adv.*

incontinent *a.* unable to control one's excretion of urine and faeces; lacking self-restraint. **incontinence** *n.*

incontrovertible *a.* indisputable.

inconvenience *n.* lack of convenience; thing causing this. —*v.t.* cause inconvenience to.

inconvenient *a.* not convenient, slightly troublesome. **inconveniently** *adv.*

incorporate *v.t.* include as a part; form into a corporation. **incorporation** *n.*

incorrect *a.* not correct. **incorrectly** *adv.*, **incorrectness** *n.*

incorrigible /-ˈko-/ *a.* not able to be reformed. **incorrigibly** *adv.*

incorruptible *a.* not liable to decay; not corruptible morally. **incorruptibility** *n.*

increase¹ /-ˈkris/ *v.t./i.* make or become greater.

increase² /ˈin-/ *n.* increasing; amount by which a thing increases.

increasingly *adv.* more and more.

incredible *a.* unbelievable. **incredibly** *adv.*, **incredibility** *n.*

incredulous *a.* unbelieving, showing disbelief. **incredulously** *adv.*, **incredulity** *n.*

increment *n.* increase, added amount.

incriminate *v.t.* indicate as involved in wrongdoing. **incrimination** *n.*, **incriminatory** *a.*

incrustation *n.* encrusting; crust or deposit formed on a surface.

incubate *v.t.* hatch (eggs) by warmth; cause (bacteria etc.) to develop. **incubation** *n.*

incubator *n.* apparatus for incubating eggs or bacteria; enclosed heated compartment in which a baby born prematurely can be kept.

incubus *n.* (pl. *-uses*) burdensome person or thing.

inculcate *v.t.* implant (a habit etc.) by constant urging. **inculcation** *n.*

inculpate *v.t.* incriminate.

incumbent *a.* forming an obligation or duty. —*n.* holder of an office; rector, vicar.

incur *v.t.* (p.t. *incurred*) bring upon oneself.

incurable *a.* unable to be cured. **incurably** *adv.*

incurious *a.* feeling or showing no curiosity. **incuriously** *adv.*

incursion *n.* brief invasion, raid.

indebted *a.* owing a debt.

indecent *a.* offending against standards of decency; unseemly. **indecently** *adv.*, **indecency** *n.*

indecipherable *a.* unable to be deciphered.

indecision *n.* inability to decide something, hesitation.

indecisive *a.* not decisive.

indecorous /-ˈdek-/ *a.* unseemly.

indeed *adv.* in truth, really.

indefatigable *a.* untiring.

indefensible *a.* unable to be defended; not justifiable.

indefinable *a.* unable to be defined or described clearly.

indefinite *a.* not clearly stated or fixed, vague. **~ article,** the word 'a' or 'an'.

indefinitely *adv.* in an indefinite way; for an unlimited period.

indelible *a.* (of a mark) unable to be removed or washed away; making such a mark. **indelibly** *adv.*

indelicate *a.* slightly indecent; tactless. **indelicately** *adv.*

indemnify *v.t.* provide indemnity to.

indemnity *n.* protection against penalties incurred by one's actions; compensation for injury.

indent *v.t./i.* make notches or recesses in; start inwards from a margin; place an official order (for goods etc.). **indentation** *n.*

indenture *n.* written contract, esp. of apprenticeship.

independent *a.* not dependent on or controlled by another person or thing; (of broadcasting) not financed by licence-fees. **independently** *adv.*, **independence** *n.*

indescribable *a.* unable to be described. **indescribably** *adv.*

indestructible *a.* unable to be destroyed.

indeterminable *a.* impossible to discover or decide.

indeterminate *a.* not fixed in extent or character.

index *n.* (pl. *indexes*) list (usu. alphabetical) of names, subjects, etc., with references; figure indicating the current level of prices etc. compared with a previous level. —*v.t.* make an index to; enter in an index; adjust (wages etc.) according to a price-index. **~ finger,** forefinger. **indexation** *n.*

Indian *a.* of India or Indians. —*n.* native of India; one of the original inhabitants of the American continent or their descendants. ~ **corn,** maize. ~ **file,** single file. ~ **ink,** a black pigment. ~ **summer,** dry sunny weather in autumn.

indiarubber *n.* rubber for rubbing out pencil or ink marks.

indicate *v.t.* point out; be a sign of; show the need of; state briefly. **indication** *n.*

indicative *a.* giving an indication; (of a form of a verb) used in statements. —*n.* this form of verb.

indicator *n.* thing that indicates something; pointer; device on a vehicle showing when the direction of travel is about to be altered.

indict /-ˈdaɪt/ *v.t.* make a formal accusation against. **indictment** *n.*

indifferent *a.* showing no interest or sympathy; neither good nor bad; not very good. **indifferently** *adv.*, **indifference** *n.*

indigenous /-ˈdɪdʒ-/ *a.* native.

indigent /ˈɪn-/ *a.* needy.

indigestible *a.* difficult or impossible to digest.

indigestion *n.* pain caused by difficulty in digesting food.

indignant *a.* feeling or showing indignation. **indignantly** *adv.*

indignation *n.* anger aroused by something unjust or wicked.

indignity *n.* unworthy treatment, humiliation.

indigo *n.* deep-blue dye or colour.

indirect *a.* not direct. **indirectly** *adv.*

indiscreet *a.* revealing secrets; not cautious. **indiscreetly** *adv.*, **indiscretion** *n.*

indiscriminate *a.* not discriminating, not making a careful choice. **indiscriminately** *adv.*

indispensable *a.* essential.

indisposed *a.* slightly ill; unwilling. **indisposition** *n.*

indisputable /-ˈpju-/ *a.* undeniable. **indisputably** *adv.*

indissoluble *a.* firm and lasting, not able to be destroyed.

indistinct *a.* not distinct. **indistinctly** *adv.*, **indistinctness** *n.*

indistinguishable *a.* not distinguishable.

individual *a.* single, separate; characteristic of one particular person or thing. —*n.* one person or animal or plant considered separately; (*colloq.*) person. **individually** *adv.*, **individuality** *n.*

individualist *n.* person who is very independent in thought or action.

indivisible *a.* not divisible.

indoctrinate *v.t.* fill (a person's mind) with particular ideas or doctrines. **indoctrination** *n.*

indolent *a.* lazy. **indolence** *n.*

indomitable *a.* unyielding, untiringly persistent.

indoor *a.* situated, used, or done inside a building. **indoors** *adv.* inside a building.

indubitable *a.* that cannot reasonably be doubted. **indubitably** *adv.*

induce *v.t.* persuade; produce, cause. **inducement** *n.* inducing; incentive.

induct *v.t.* install (a clergyman) ceremonially into a benefice.

induction *n.* inducting; inducing; reasoning (from observed examples) that a general law exists; production of an electric or magnetic state by proximity of an electrified or magnetic object; drawing of a fuel mixture into the cylinder(s) of an engine. **inductive** *a.*

indulge *v.t./i.* allow (a person) to have what he wishes; gratify. **indulgence** *n.*

indulgent *a.* indulging a person's wishes too freely; kind, lenient. **indulgently** *adv.*

industrial *a.* of, for, or full of industries. **industrially** *adv.*

industrialist *n.* owner or manager of an industrial business.

industrialized *a.* full of highly developed industries.

industrious *a.* hard-working. **industriously** *adv.*

industry *n.* manufacture or production of goods; business activity; being industrious.

inebriated /-ˈni-/ *a.* drunken.

inedible *a.* not edible.

ineducable *a.* incapable of being educated.

ineffable *a.* too great to be described.

ineffective *a.* not effective.

ineffectual *a.* not effectual.

inefficient *a.* not efficient. **inefficiently** *adv.*, **inefficiency** *n.*

inelegant *a.* not elegant.

ineligible *a.* not eligible.

inept *a.* unsuitable, absurd; unskilful. **ineptly** *adv.*, **ineptitude** *n.*

inequality *n.* lack of equality.

inequitable /-ˈnek-/ *a.* unfair, unjust.

ineradicable *a.* not able to be eradicated.

inert *a.* without the power of moving; without active properties; not moving or taking action.

inertia *n.* being inert; property by which matter continues in its state of rest or line of motion.

inescapable *a.* unavoidable.

inessential *a.* not essential. —*n.* inessential thing.

inestimable *a.* too great or intense to be estimated.

inevitable *a.* not able to be prevented, sure to happen or appear. **inevitably** *adv.*, **inevitability** *n.*

inexact *a.* not exact. **inexactitude** *n.*

inexcusable *a.* not able to be excused. **inexcusably** *adv.*

inexhaustible *a.* available in unlimited quantity.

inexorable /-ˈneks-/ *a.* relentless.

inexpedient *a.* not expedient.

inexpensive *a.* not expensive. **inexpensively** *adv.*

inexperience *n.* lack of experience. **inexperienced** *a.*

inexpert *a.* not expert, unskilful. **inexpertly** *adv.*

inexplicable /-ˈneks-/ *a.* unable to be explained. **inexplicably** *adv.*

inextricable /-ˈneks-/ *a.* unable to be extricated or disentangled. **inextricably** *adv.*

infallible *a.* incapable of being wrong; never failing. **infallibility** *n.*

infamous /ˈɪnfə-/ a. having a bad reputation. **infamy** n.

infancy n. early childhood, babyhood; early stage of development.

infant n. child during the earliest stage of its life.

infanticide /-ˈfæ-/ n. murder of an infant soon after its birth.

infantile a. of infants or infancy; very childish.

infantry n. troops who fight on foot.

infatuated a. filled with intense unreasoning love. **infatuation** n.

infect v.t. affect or contaminate with a disease or its germs; affect with one's feeling.

infection n. process of infecting; disease or diseased condition.

infectious a. (of disease) able to spread by air or water; infecting others.

infer v.t. (p.t. *inferred*) reach (an opinion) from facts or reasoning. **inference** n.

inferior a. low or lower in rank, importance, quality, or ability. —n. person inferior to another, esp. in rank. **inferiority** n.

infernal a. of hell; (*colloq.*) detestable, tiresome. **infernally** adv.

inferno n. (pl. -os) hell; intensely hot place; raging fire.

infertile a. not fertile. **infertility** n.

infest v.t. be numerous or troublesome in (a place). **infestation** n.

infidel /ˈɪn-/ n. person with no religious faith; opponent of Christianity.

infidelity n. unfaithfulness.

infighting n. boxing closer than at arm's length; hidden conflict within an organization.

infiltrate v.t. enter gradually and unperceived. **infiltration** n., **infiltrator** n.

infinite a. having no limit; too great or too many to be measured. **infinitely** adv.

infinitesimal a. extremely small.

infinitive n. form of a verb not indicating tense, number, or person (e.g. *to go*).

infinity n. infinite number, extent, or time.

infirm a. weak from age or illness. **infirmity** n.

infirmary n. hospital.

inflame v.t. arouse strong feeling or emotion in; cause inflammation in.

inflammable a. able to be set on fire.

inflammation n. redness and heat produced in a part of the body.

inflammatory a. arousing strong feeling or anger.

inflatable a. able to be inflated.

inflate v.t./i. fill with air or gas so as to swell; increase artificially.

inflation n. inflating; general increase in prices and fall in the purchasing power of money.

inflationary a. causing inflation.

inflect v.t. change the pitch of (a voice) in speaking; change the ending or form of (a word) grammatically. **inflexion** n.

inflexible a. not flexible; unyielding. **inflexibly** adv., **inflexibility** n.

inflict v.t. cause (a blow, penalty, etc.) to be suffered. **infliction** n.

inflow n. inward flow.

influence n. ability to produce an effect, or to affect character, beliefs, or actions; person or thing with this. —v.t. exert influence on.

influential a. having great influence.

influenza n. virus disease causing fever, muscular pain, and catarrh.

influx n. inflow.

inform v.t./i. give information to; reveal secret or criminal activities to police etc. **informer** n.

informal a. not formal, without formality or ceremony. **informally** adv., **informality** n.

informant n. giver of information.

information n. facts told or heard or discovered.

informative a. giving information.

infra-red a. of or using radiation with a wavelength longer than that of visible light-rays.

infrastructure n. subordinate parts forming the basis of an enterprise.

infrequent a. not frequent. **infrequently** adv., **infrequency** n.

infringe v.t. break (a rule or agreement); encroach. **infringement** n.

infuriate v.t. make very angry.

infuse v.t. imbue, instil; steep (tea or herbs etc.) in liquid, (of tea etc.) undergo this.

infusion n. infusing; liquid made by this; thing added to a stock.

ingenious a. clever at inventing things; cleverly contrived. **ingeniously** adv., **ingenuity** n.

ingenuous a. without artfulness, unsophisticated. **ingenuously** adv., **ingenuousness** n.

ingest v.t. take in as food.

ingle-nook n. nook beside a deeply recessed fireplace.

inglorious a. not bringing glory.

ingot n. oblong lump of cast metal.

ingrained a. deeply fixed in a surface or character.

ingratiate v.refl. bring (oneself) into a person's favour, esp. to gain advantage.

ingratitude n. lack of gratitude.

ingredient n. one element in a mixture or combination.

ingrowing a. growing abnormally into the flesh.

inhabit v.t. live in as one's home or dwelling-place. **inhabitable** a., **inhabitant** n.

inhalant /-ˈheɪ-/ n. medicinal substance to be inhaled.

inhale v.t./i. breathe in, draw (tobacco-smoke) into the lungs. **inhalation** n.

inhaler n. device producing a medicinal vapour to be inhaled.

inherent /-ˈhɪər-/ a. existing in a thing as a permanent quality. **inherently** adv.

inherit v.t. receive by legal right from its former owner; receive from a predecessor; derive from parents etc. **inheritance** n.

inhibit v.t. restrain, prevent; cause inhibitions in.

inhibition n. inhibiting; resistance to an instinct, impulse, or feeling.

inhospitable /-ˈhɒs-/ a. not hospitable.

inhuman a. brutal, lacking qualities of kindness etc. **inhumanity** n.

inhumane a. not humane.

inimical *a*. hostile.

inimitable *a*. impossible to imitate.

iniquitous *a*. very unjust.

iniquity *n*. great injustice; wickedness.

initial *n*. first letter of a word or name. —*v.t.* (p.t. *initialled*) mark or sign with initials. —*a*. of the beginning. **initially** *adv*.

initiate *v.t.* cause to begin; admit into membership; give basic instruction to. —*n*. initiated person. **initiation** *n*., **initiator** *n*.

initiative *n*. first step in a process; right or power to take this; readiness to initiate things.

inject *v.t.* force or drive (a liquid etc.) into something, esp. by a syringe. **injection** *n*.

injudicious *a*. unwise.

injunction *n*. command.

injure *v.t.* cause injury to.

injurious *a*. causing injury.

injury *n*. damage, harm; form of this; wrong or unjust act.

injustice *n*. lack of justice; unjust action or treatment.

ink *n*. coloured liquid or paste used in writing with a pen, printing, etc. —*v.t.* apply ink to. **inky** *a*.

inkling *n*. hint, slight knowledge or suspicion.

inlaid *see* **inlay**[1].

inland *a*. & *adv*. in or towards the interior of a country. **Inland Revenue,** government department assessing and collecting taxes.

in-laws *n.pl.* (*colloq.*) one's relatives by marriage.

inlay[1] /-ˈleɪ/ *v.t.* (p.t. *inlaid*) set (one thing in another) so that the surfaces are flush and form a design.

inlay[2] /ˈɪn-/ *n*. inlaid material or design.

inlet *n*. strip of water extending into land; piece inserted; way in (e.g. for water into a tank).

inmate *n*. inhabitant, esp. of an institution.

inmost *a*. furthest inward.

inn *n*. hotel, esp. in the country; public house. **Inns of Court,** four law societies with exclusive right of admitting people to practise as barristers in England.

innards *n.pl.* (*colloq.*) entrails; inner parts.

innate *a*. inborn.

inner *a*. nearer to the centre or inside; interior, internal.

innermost *a*. furthest inward.

innings *n*. (pl. *innings*) turn at batting; period of power or opportunity.

innkeeper *n*. keeper of an inn.

innocent *a*. not guilty, free of evil or wrongdoing; harmless; foolishly trustful. —*n*. innocent person. **innocently** *adv*., **innocence** *n*.

innocuous *a*. harmless.

innovate *v.i.* introduce something new. **innovation** *n*., **innovator** *n*.

innuendo *n*. (pl. *-oes*) insinuation.

innumerable *a*. too many to be counted.

inoculate *v.t.* protect (against disease) with vaccines or serums. **inoculation** *n*.

inoffensive *a*. not offensive.

inoperable *a*. unable to be cured by surgical operation.

inoperative *a*. not functioning.

inopportune *a*. happening at an unsuitable time.

inordinate *a*. excessive. **inordinately** *adv*.

inorganic *a*. of mineral origin, not organic.

input *n*. what is put in.

inquest *n*. judicial investigation to establish facts esp. about a sudden death; (*colloq.*) detailed discussion of a thing that is over.

inquire *v.i.* make an inquiry. **inquirer** *n*.

inquiry *n*. investigation.

inquisition *n*. detailed questioning; *the I~*, tribunal of the medieval R.C. Church, esp. in Spain, to discover and punish heretics.

inquisitive *a*. eagerly seeking knowledge; prying.

inquisitor *n*. person who questions another searchingly.

inroad *n*. incursion.

inrush *n*. violent influx.

insalubrious *a*. unhealthy.

insane *a*. not sane, mad; extremely foolish. **insanely** *adv*., **insanity** *n*.

insanitary *a*. not clean, not hygienic.

insatiable /-ˈseɪʃ-/ *a*. unable to be satisfied. **insatiably** *adv*.

inscribe *v.t.* write or engrave.

inscription *n*. words or names inscribed on a coin, stone, etc.

inscrutable *a*. baffling, impossible to understand or interpret.

insect *n*. small creature with six legs, no backbone, and a segmented body.

insecticide *n*. substance for killing insects.

insectivorous *a*. feeding on insects.

insecure *a*. not secure. **insecurely** *adv*., **insecurity** *n*.

inseminate *v.t.* insert semen into. **insemination** *n*.

insensible *a*. unconscious; unaware; callous; imperceptible.

insensitive *a*. not sensitive.

inseparable *a*. unable to be separated or kept apart.

insert[1] /-ˈsɜːt/ *v.t.* put into or between or among. **insertion** *n*.

insert[2] /ˈɪn-/ *n*. thing inserted.

inset[1] /-ˈset/ *v.t.* (p.t. *inset*, pres.p. *insetting*) set or place in; decorate with an inset.

inset[2] /ˈɪn-/ *n*. thing set into a larger thing.

inshore *a*. & *adv*. near or nearer to the shore.

inside *n*. inner side, surface, or part. —*a*. of or from the inside. —*adv*. on, in, or to the inside. —*prep*. on or to the inside of; within. *~ out*, with the inner side turned outwards; thoroughly.

insidious *a*. proceeding inconspicuously but with harmful effect. **insidiously** *adv*., **insidiousness** *n*.

insight *n*. perception and understanding of a thing's nature.

insignia *n.pl.* symbols of authority or office; identifying badge.

insignificant *a*. unimportant. **insignificantly** *adv*., **insignificance** *n*.

insincere *a*. not sincere. **insincerely** *adv*., **insincerity** *n*.

insinuate v.t. insert gradually or craftily; hint artfully. **insinuation** n.

insipid a. lacking flavour, interest, or liveliness. **insipidity** n.

insist v.t./i. declare or demand emphatically.

insistent a. insisting; forcing itself on one's attention. **insistently** adv., **insistence** n.

insole n. inner sole of a boot or shoe; loose piece of material laid in the bottom of a shoe.

insolent a. behaving insultingly, arrogant. **insolently** adv., **insolence** n.

insoluble a. unable to be dissolved; unable to be solved.

insolvent a. unable to pay one's debts. **insolvency** n.

insomnia n. inability to sleep sufficiently.

insomniac n. sufferer from insomnia.

inspect v.t. examine critically or officially. **inspection** n.

inspector n. person whose job is to inspect or supervise things; police officer next above sergeant.

inspiration n. inspiring; inspiring influence; sudden brilliant idea.

inspire v.t. stimulate to creative or other activity; instil (a feeling or idea) into.

instability n. lack of stability.

install v.t. place (a person) into office ceremonially; set in position and ready for use; establish.

installation n. process of installing; apparatus etc. installed.

instalment n. one of the parts in which a thing is presented or a debt paid over a period of time.

instance n. example of something. —v.t. mention as an instance. **in the first ∼,** firstly.

instant a. immediate; (of food) designed to be prepared quickly and easily. —n. exact point of time; moment. **instantly** adv.

instantaneous a. occurring or done instantly. **instantaneously** adv.

instead adv. as an alternative or substitute.

instep n. upper surface of the foot; part of a shoe etc. covering this.

instigate v.t. incite; initiate. **instigation** n., **instigator** n.

instil v.t. (p.t. **instilled**) implant (ideas etc.) gradually.

instinct n. inborn impulse; natural tendency or ability. **instinctive** a., **instinctively** adv.

institute n. society or organization for promotion of a specified activity; its premises. —v.t. establish; cause to be started.

institution n. process of instituting; institute, esp. for a charitable or social activity; established rule or custom. **institutional** a.

institutionalized a. living or used to living in an institution.

instruct v.t. give instruction to (a person) in a subject or skill; inform; give instructions to. **instructor** n., **instructress** n.fem.

instruction n. process of teaching; knowledge or teaching imparted; (pl.) statements telling a person what he is required to do.

instructive a. giving instruction, enlightening.

instrument n. tool or implement for delicate work; measuring-device used in operation of an engine or aircraft etc.; device for producing musical sounds; person used and controlled by another; formal document.

instrumental a. serving as a means; performed on musical instruments.

instrumentalist n. player of a musical instrument.

insubordinate a. disobedient, rebellious. **insubordination** n.

insubstantial a. lacking reality or solidity.

insufferable a. unbearable.

insufficient a. not sufficient. **insufficiently** adv., **insufficiency** n.

insular a. of an island; of islanders, narrow-minded. **insularity** n.

insulate v.t. cover with a substance that prevents the passage of electricity, sound, or heat; isolate from influences. **insulation** n., **insulator** n.

insulin n. hormone controlling the body's absorption of sugar.

insult[1] /-'sʌlt-/ v.t. speak or act so as to hurt the feelings and rouse the anger of.

insult[2] /'ɪn-/ n. insulting remark or action.

insuperable a. unable to be overcome.

insupportable a. unbearable.

insurance n. contract to provide compensation for loss, damage, or death; sum payable as a premium for this, or in compensation; safeguard against loss or failure.

insure v.t. protect by insurance; (U.S.) ensure. **insurer** n.

insurgent a. rebellious, rising in revolt. —n. rebel.

insurmountable a. insuperable.

insurrection n. rebellion.

insusceptible a. not susceptible.

intact a. undamaged, complete.

intake n. process of taking thing(s) in; place or amount of this.

intangible a. not tangible.

integer n. whole number, not fraction.

integral /'ɪn-/ a. forming or necessary to form a whole.

integrate v.t./i. combine (parts) into a whole; bring or come into full membership of a community. **integration** n.

integrity n. honesty.

intellect n. mind's power of reasoning and acquiring knowledge.

intellectual a. of or using the intellect; having a strong intellect. —n. intellectual person. **intellectually** adv.

intelligence n. mental ability to learn and understand things; information, esp. that of military value; people collecting this.

intelligent a. having mental ability. **intelligently** adv.

intelligentsia /-'dʒen-/ n. intellectual people regarded as a class.

intelligible a. able to be understood. **intelligibly** adv., **intelligibility** n.

intemperate a. drinking alcohol excessively. **intemperance** n.

intend *v.t.* have in mind as what one wishes to do or achieve.

intense *a.* strong in quality or degree; feeling strong emotion. **intensely** *adv.*, **intensity** *n.*

intensify *v.t.* make or become more intense. **intensification** *n.*

intensive *a.* employing much effort; concentrated. **intensively** *adv.*

intent *n.* intention. —*a.* with concentrated attention. **~ on**, concentrating on; having as an intention. **intently** *adv.*, **intentness** *n.*

intention *n.* what one intends to do.

intentional *a.* done on purpose, not accidental. **intentionally** *adv.*

inter /-ˈtɜ(r)/ *v.t.* (p.t. *interred*) bury.

inter- *prep.* between, among.

interact *v.i.* have an effect upon each other. **interaction** *n.*

interbreed *v.t./i.* breed with each other, cross-breed.

intercede *v.i.* intervene on someone's behalf.

intercept *v.t.* stop or catch between starting-point and destination. **interception** *n.*, **interceptor** *n.*

intercession *n.* interceding.

interchange¹ /-ˈtʃeɪ-/ *v.t./i.* put (each of two things) into the other's place; exchange; alternate.

interchange² /ˈɪn-/ *n.* process of interchanging; road junction designed so that streams of traffic do not intersect on the same level.

interchangeable *a.* able to be interchanged.

intercom *n.* communication system operating like a telephone.

interconnected *a.* connected.

inter-continental *a.* between continents.

intercourse *n.* dealings between people or countries; copulation.

interdict *n.* formal prohibition.

interest *n.* feeling of curiosity or concern; quality causing this; object of it; advantage; legal share; financial stake; money paid for use of money borrowed. —*v.t.* arouse the interest of; cause to take an interest in.

interested *a.* feeling interest; having a private interest, not impartial.

interesting *a.* arousing interest.

interface *n.* surface forming a common boundary between two portions of matter or space; apparatus connecting two devices.

interfere *v.i.* take part in dealing with others' affairs without right or invitation; be an obstruction.

interference *n.* interfering; disturbance of radio signals.

interferon /-ˈfɪər-/ *n.* protein preventing the development of a virus.

interim *n.* intervening period. —*a.* of or in such a period, temporary.

interior *a.* inner. —*n.* interior part.

interject *v.t.* put in (a remark) when someone is speaking.

interjection *n.* process of interjecting; remark interjected; exclamation.

interlace *v.t./i.* weave or lace together.

interlard *v.t.* insert contrasting remarks into.

interlock *v.t./i.* fit into each other. —*n.* fine machine-knitted fabric.

interlocutor /-ˈlok-/ *n.* person taking part in a conversation.

interloper *n.* intruder.

interlude *n.* interval; thing happening or performed in this.

intermarry *v.i.* marry members of the same or another group. **intermarriage** *n.*

intermediary *n.* mediator, go-between. —*a.* acting as intermediary; intermediate.

intermediate *a.* coming between two things in time, place, or order.

interment *n.* burial.

intermezzo /-ˈmets-/ *n.* (pl. *-os*) a kind of short musical composition.

interminable *a.* very long and boring. **interminably** *adv.*

intermission *n.* interval, pause.

intermittent *a.* occurring at intervals. **intermittently** *adv.*

intern *v.t.* compel (an enemy alien or prisoner) to live in a special area.

internal *a.* of or in the inside; of a country's domestic affairs. **internally** *adv.*

international *a.* between countries. —*n.* sports contest between players representing different countries; one of these players. **internationally** *adv.*

internecine /-ˈniːsaɪn/ *a.* mutually destructive.

internee *n.* interned person.

internment *n.* interning.

interplanetary *a.* between planets.

interplay *n.* interaction.

interpolate *v.t.* interject; insert (esp. misleadingly). **interpolation** *n.*

interpose *v.t./i.* insert; intervene.

interpret *v.t./i.* explain the meaning of; act as interpreter. **interpretation** *n.*

interpreter *n.* person who orally translates speech between persons speaking different languages.

interregnum *n.* period between the rule of two successive rulers.

interrelated *a.* related.

interrogate *v.t.* question closely. **interrogation** *n.*, **interrogator** *n.*

interrogative *a.* forming or having the form of a question.

interrupt *v.t.* break the continuity of; break the flow of (speech etc.) by a remark. **interruption** *n.*

intersect *v.t./i.* divide or cross by passing or lying across. **intersection** *n.*

intersperse *v.t.* insert here and there.

interstice /ˈɪntəstɪs/ *n.* small intervening space. **interstitial** *a.*

intertwine *v.t./i.* entwine, be entwined.

interval *n.* time or pause between two events or parts of an action; space between two things; difference in musical pitch. **at intervals**, with some time or space between.

intervene *v.i.* occur between events; cause hindrance by occurring; enter a dispute etc. to change its course or resolve it. **intervention** *n.*

interview *n.* formal meeting or conversation

with a person to assess his merits or obtain information. —*v.t.* hold an interview with. **interviewer** *n.*

interweave *v.t.* (p.t. *interwove*, p.p. *interwoven*) weave together.

intestate *a.* not having made a valid will before death occurs.

intestine *n.* long tubular section of the alimentary canal between stomach and anus. **intestinal** *a.*

intimate[1] /-ət/ *a.* closely acquainted or familiar; having a sexual relationship (esp. outside marriage) with a person; private and personal. —*n.* intimate friend. **intimately** *adv.*, **intimacy** *n.*

intimate[2] /-eɪt/ *v.t.* make known, esp. by hinting. **intimation** *n.*

intimidate *v.t.* influence by frightening. **intimidation** *n.*

into *prep.* to the inside of, to a point within; to a particular state or occupation; dividing (a number) mathematically.

intolerable *a.* unbearable.

intolerant *a.* not tolerant. **intolerantly** *adv.*, **intolerance** *n.*

intonation *n.* intoning; pitch of the voice in speaking; slight accent.

intone *v.t.* chant, esp. on one note.

intoxicant *n.* intoxicating drink.

intoxicated *a.* drunk. **intoxication** *n.*

intra- *pref.* within.

intractable *a.* hard to deal with or control. **intractability** *n.*

intransigent *a.* stubborn. **intransigence** *n.*

intransitive *a.* (of verb) used without a direct object. **intransitively** *adv.*

intravenous /-ˈviː-/ *a.* into a vein. **intravenously** *adv.*

intrepid *a.* fearless, brave. **intrepidly** *adv.*, **intrepidity** *n.*

intricate *a.* very complicated. **intricately** *adv.*, **intricacy** *n.*

intrigue *v.t./i.* plot in an underhand way; rouse the interest or curiosity of. —*n.* underhand plot or plotting; secret love affair.

intrinsic *a.* belonging to a person's or thing's basic nature. **intrinsically** *adv.*

introduce *v.t.* make (a person) known to others; present to an audience; bring into use; insert.

introduction *n.* introducing; introductory section or treatise.

introductory *a.* introducing; preliminary.

introspection *n.* examination of one's own thoughts and feelings. **introspective** *a.*

introvert *n.* introspective and shy person. **introverted** *a.*

intrude *v.t./i.* come or join in without being invited or wanted; thrust in. **intruder** *n.*, **intrusion** *n.*

intrusive *a.* intruding.

intuition *n.* power of knowing without reasoning or being taught. **intuitive** *a.*, **intuitively** *adv.*

inundate *v.t.* flood. **inundation** *n.*

inure *v.t.* accustom, esp. to something unpleasant.

invade *v.t.* enter (territory) with hostile intent; crowd into; penetrate harmfully. **invader** *n.*

invalid[1] /ˈɪn-/ *n.* person suffering from ill health. —*v.t.* remove from active service because of ill health or injury.

invalid[2] /-ˈvæl-/ *a.* not valid.

invalidate *v.t.* make no longer valid. **invalidation** *n.*, **invalidity** /-ˈlɪ-/ *n.*

invaluable *a.* having value too great to be measured.

invariable *a.* not variable, always the same. **invariably** *adv.*

invasion *n.* invading.

invasive *a.* tending to encroach.

invective *n.* violent attack in words; abusive language.

inveigh /-ˈveɪ/ *v.i.* attack violently or bitterly in words.

inveigle /-ˈveɪgəl/ *v.t.* entice.

invent *v.t.* create by thought, make, or design (a thing not previously known); construct (a false or fictional story). **inventor** *n.*

inventive *a.* able to invent things.

inventory /ˈɪn-/ *n.* detailed list of goods or furniture.

inverse *a.* reversed in position, relation, or order. —*n.* inverted thing, opposite. **inversely** *adv.*

invert *v.t.* turn upside down; reverse the position, order, or relationship of. **inverted commas**, quotation-marks. **inversion** *n.*

invertebrate /-ət/ *a.* & *n.* (animal) having no backbone.

invest *v.t./i.* use (money) to buy shares or property etc. to earn interest or bring profit; confer rank or power upon; endow with a quality. ∼ **in**, (*colloq.*) buy (a useful thing). **investment** *n.*, **investor** *n.*

investigate *v.t.* study (a thing) carefully to discover facts about it. **investigation** *n.*, **investigator** *n.*

investiture *n.* formal investing of a person with a rank or office etc.

inveterate *a.* habitual; firmly established.

invidious *a.* liable to cause resentment. **invidiously** *adv.*

invigilate *v.i.* supervise candidates at an examination. **invigilation** *n.*, **invigilator** *n.*

invigorate *v.t.* fill with vigour, give strength or courage to.

invincible *a.* unconquerable. **invincibly** *adv.*, **invincibility** *n.*

inviolable *a.* not to be violated. **inviolability** *n.*

invisible *a.* not able to be seen. **invisibly** *adv.*, **invisibility** *n.*

invite *v.t.* ask (a person) politely to come or to do something; ask for; attract, tempt. —*n.* (*sl.*) invitation. **invitation** *n.*

inviting *a.* pleasant and tempting.

invocation *n.* invoking; calling to God in prayer.

invoice *n.* list of goods or services supplied, with prices. —*v.t.* make an invoice of; send an invoice to.

invoke *v.t.* call for the help or protection of; summon (a spirit).

involuntary *a.* done without intention or without conscious effort. **involuntarily** *adv.*

involve *v.t.* have as a consequence; include or affect in its operation; show to be concerned in a crime etc. **involvement** *a.*

involved *a.* complicated; concerned.

invulnerable *a.* not vulnerable. **invulnerability** *n.*

inward *a.* situated on or going towards the inside; in the mind or spirit. —*adv.* inwards. **inwardly** *adv.*, **inwards** *adv.*

iodine /-dɪn/ *n.* chemical substance used in solution as an antiseptic.

iodize *v.t.* impregnate with iodine.

ion *n.* electrically charged particle.

Ionic *a.* of the order of architecture using scroll-like ornamentation.

ionize *v.t./i.* convert or be converted into ions.

ionosphere *n.* ionized region of the upper atmosphere.

iota *n.* Greek letter i; very small amount.

IOU *n.* signed paper given as a receipt for money borrowed.

ipecacuanha *n.* dried root used esp. as an emetic.

ipso facto by that very fact.

I.Q. *abbr.* intelligence quotient.

I.R.A. *abbr.* Irish Republican Army.

irascible /-'ræs-/ *a.* irritable, hot-tempered. **irascibly** *adv.*, **irascibility** *n.*

irate *a.* angry. **irately** *adv.*

ire *n.* anger.

iridescent *a.* coloured like a rainbow; shimmering. **iridescence** *n.*

iris *n.* coloured part of the eyeball, round the pupil; lily-like flower.

Irish *a. & n.* (language) of Ireland. **Irishman** *n.*, **Irishwoman** *n.*

irk *v.t.* annoy, be tiresome to.

irksome *a.* tiresome.

iron *n.* hard grey metal; tool etc. made of this; implement with a flat base heated for smoothing cloth or clothes; (*pl.*) fetters. —*a.* made of iron; strong as iron. **Iron Curtain,** barrier of secrecy and restriction round the Soviet sphere of influence. **∼-mould** *n.* brown spot on fabric, caused by iron rust.

ironic, ironical *adjs.* using irony.

ironmonger *n.* shopkeeper selling tools and household implements. **ironmongery** *n.* his shop or goods.

ironwork *n.* things made of iron.

ironworks *n.* place where iron is smelted or heavy iron goods made.

irony *n.* expression of meaning by use of words normally conveying the opposite; apparent perversity of fate or circumstances.

irradiate *v.t.* throw light or other radiation on. **irradiation** *n.*

irrational *a.* not rational. **irrationally** *adv.*, **irrationality** *n.*

irreconcilable *a.* not reconcilable.

irrecoverable *a.* unable to be recovered. **irrecoverably** *adv.*

irredeemable *a.* unable to be redeemed. **irredeemably** *adv.*

irreducible *a.* not reducible.

irrefutable /-'ref-/ *a.* unable to be refuted. **irrefutably** *adv.*

irregular *a.* not regular; contrary to rules or custom. **irregularly** *adv.*, **irregularity** *n.*

irrelevant *a.* not relevant. **irrelevantly** *adv.*, **irrelevance** *n.*

irreligious *a.* not religious; irreverent.

irreparable /-'rep-/ *a.* unable to be repaired. **irreparably** *adv.*

irreplaceable *a.* unable to be replaced.

irrepressible *a.* unable to be repressed.

irreproachable *a.* blameless, faultless.

irresistible *a.* too strong or delightful to be resisted. **irresistibly** *adv.*

irresolute *a.* unable to make up one's mind. **irresolutely** *adv.*, **irresolution** *n.*

irrespective *a.* ∼ of, not taking (a thing) into account.

irresponsible *a.* not showing a proper sense of responsibility.

irretrievable *a.* not retrievable. **irretrievably** *adv.*

irreverent *a.* not reverent; not respectful. **irreverently** *adv.*, **irreverence** *n.*

irreversible *a.* not reversible, unable to be altered or revoked.

irrevocable /-'rev-/ *a.* unable to be revoked, unalterable. **irrevocably** *adv.*

irrigate *v.t.* supply (land) with water by streams, pipes, etc. **irrigation** *n.*

irritable *a.* easily annoyed, bad-tempered. **irritably** *adv.*, **irritability** *n.*

irritant *a. & n.* (thing) causing irritation.

irritate *v.t.* annoy; cause itching in. **irritation** *n.*

is *see* be.

Islam *n.* Muslim religion; Muslim world. **Islamic** *a.*

island *n.* piece of land surrounded by water. **traffic ∼,** paved or raised area in a road, where people crossing may be safe from traffic.

islander *n.* inhabitant of an island.

isle *n.* island.

isobar *n.* line on a map, connecting places with the same atmospheric pressure.

isolate *v.t.* place apart or alone; separate from others or from a compound. **isolation** *n.*

isosceles /aɪ'sɒsɪliz/ *a.* (of a triangle) having two sides equal.

isotherm *n.* line on a map, connecting places with the same temperature.

isotope *n.* one of two or more forms of a chemical element differing in their atomic weight.

issue *n.* outgoing, outflow; issuing, quantity issued; one publication (e.g. of a magazine) in a series; result, outcome; important topic; offspring. —*v.t./i.* come or flow out; supply for use; publish; send out; result, originate. **at ∼,** being discussed or disputed or risked. **join** *or* **take ∼,** proceed to argue.

isthmus *n.* (pl. *-muses*) narrow strip of land with water on each side, connecting two masses of land.

it *pron.* thing mentioned or being discussed; impersonal subject of a verb.

Italian *a. & n.* (native, language) of Italy.

italic *a.* (of type) sloping like *this*; of a compact pointed form of writing. **italics** *n.pl.* italic type.

itch *n.* tickling sensation in the skin, causing a desire to scratch; restless desire. —*v.i.* have or feel an itch. **itchy** *a.*

item *n.* single thing in a list or collection; single piece of news.

itemize *v.t.* list, state the individual items of.

itinerant /ɪ'tɪn-/ *a.* travelling.

itinerary /aɪ-/ *n.* route, list of places to be visited on a journey.

its *poss. pron.* of it.

it's = it is, it has.

itself *pron.* emphatic and reflexive form of *it*.

ivory *n.* hard creamy-white substance forming tusks of elephant etc.; object made of this; its colour. —*a.* creamy-white. ∼ **tower,** seclusion from the harsh realities of life.

ivy *n.* climbing evergreen shrub.

J

jab *v.t.* (p.t. *jabbed*) poke roughly. —*n.* rough poke; (*colloq.*) injection.

jabber *v.i.* talk rapidly, often unintelligibly. —*n.* jabbering talk.

jack *n.* portable device for raising heavy weights off the ground; ship's small flag showing nationality; playing-card next below queen; small ball aimed at in bowls; male donkey. —*v.t.* raise with a jack.

jackal *n.* dog-like wild animal.

jackass *n.* **laughing** ∼, Australian giant kingfisher with a harsh cry.

jackdaw *n.* bird of the crow family.

jacket *n.* short coat usu. reaching to the hips; outer covering.

jack-knife *n.* large folding knife. —*v.i.* fold accidentally.

jackpot *n.* large prize of money that has accumulated until won. **hit the** ∼, have a sudden success.

Jacobean *a.* of the reign of James I of England (1603–25).

Jacobite *n.* & *a.* (of) a supporter of the exiled Stuart kings of England.

jacquard /-kɑd/ *n.* fabric with an intricate woven pattern.

jade *n.* hard green, blue, or white stone; its green colour.

jaded *a.* tired and bored.

jag *n.* (*sl.*) drinking-bout, spree.

jagged *a.* having sharp projections.

jaguar *n.* large flesh-eating animal of the cat family.

jail *n.* = gaol.

jalopy /-'lop-/ *n.* battered old car.

jam¹ *n.* thick sweet substance made by boiling fruit with sugar; (*colloq.*) something easy or pleasant. —*v.t.* (p.t. *jammed*) spread with jam; make into jam.

jam² *v.t./i.* (p.t. *jammed*) squeeze or wedge into a space; become wedged; crowd or block (an area); apply forcibly; make (a broadcast) unintelligible by causing interference. —*n.* squeeze, crush; stoppage caused by jamming; crowded mass; (*colloq.*) difficult situation. ∼**-packed** *a.* (*colloq.*) very full. ∼ **session,** improvising playing of jazz.

jamb *n.* side-post of a door or window.

jamboree *n.* large party; rally.

jammy *a.* smeared with jam.

jangle *n.* harsh metallic sound. —*v.t./i.* make or cause to make this sound; upset by discord.

janitor *n.* caretaker of a building.

January *n.* first month of the year.

Japanese *a.* & *n.* (native, language) of Japan.

japonica *n.* ornamental shrub with red flowers.

jar¹ *n.* cylindrical glass or earthenware container.

jar² *v.t./i.* (p.t. *jarred*) jolt; have a harsh or disagreeable effect (upon). —*n.* jarring movement or effect.

jargon *n.* words or expressions developed for use within a particular group of people.

jasmine *n.* shrub with white or yellow flowers.

jasper *n.* a kind of quartz.

jaundice *n.* condition in which the skin becomes abnormally yellow.

jaundiced *a.* affected by jaundice; filled with resentment.

jaunt *n.* short trip. —*v.i.* make a jaunt.

jaunty *a.* (-*ier*, -*iest*) cheerful, self-confident. **jauntily** *adv.*, **jauntiness** *n.*

javelin *n.* a light spear.

jaw *n.* bone(s) forming the framework of the mouth; (*colloq.*) lengthy talk; (*pl.*) gripping-parts. —*v.t./i.* talk lengthily (to).

jay *n.* bird of the crow family. ∼**-walker** *n.* person walking carelessly in a road. ∼**-walking** *n.*

jazz *n.* type of music with strong rhythm and much syncopation; (*sl.*) pretentiousness. —*v.t.* play or arrange as jazz; liven. **jazzy** *a.*

jealous *a.* resentful towards a rival; taking watchful care. **jealously** *adv.*, **jealousy** *n.*

jeans *n.pl.* denim trousers.

jeer *v.t./i.* laugh or shout rudely or scornfully (at). —*n.* jeering.

Jehovah *n.* name of God in the Old Testament.

jell *v.i.* set as a jelly; take definite form.

jellied *a.* set in jelly.

jelly *n.* soft solid food made of liquid set with gelatine; substance of similar consistency; jam made of strained fruit-juice.

jellyfish *n.* sea animal with a jelly-like body.

jemmy *n.* burglar's short crowbar.

jenny *n.* female donkey.

jeopardize /'dʒep-/ *v.t.* endanger.

jeopardy /'dʒep-/ *n.* danger.

jerboa *n.* rat-like desert animal with long hind legs.

jeremiad *n.* long mournful complaint.

jerk *n.* sudden sharp movement or pull. —*v.t./i.* move or pull or stop with jerk(s). **jerky** *a.*, **jerkily** *adv.*, **jerkiness** *n.*

jerkin *n.* sleeveless jacket.

jerry-built *a.* built badly and with poor materials.

jerrycan *n.* five-gallon can for petrol or water.

jersey *n.* (pl. *-eys*) knitted woollen pullover with sleeves; machine-knitted fabric.

jest *n.* & *v.i.* joke.

jester *n.* person who makes jokes; entertainer at a medieval court.

Jesuit *n.* member of the Society of Jesus (an R.C. religious order).

jet[1] *n.* hard black mineral; glossy black. **∼ black** *a.*

jet[2] *n.* stream of water, gas, or flame from a small opening; burner on a gas cooker; engine or aircraft using jet propulsion. **∼ propulsion,** propulsion by engines that send out a high-speed jet of gases at the back. **∼ propelled** *a.*

jetsam *n.* goods jettisoned by a ship in distress and washed ashore.

jettison *v.t.* throw overboard; discard.

jetty *n.* breakwater; landing-stage.

Jew *n.* person of Hebrew descent or whose religion is Judaism. **∼'s harp,** small metal frame held in the teeth for twanging. **Jewess** *n.fem.*

jewel *n.* precious stone cut or set as an ornament; person or thing that is highly valued. **jewelled** *a.*

jeweller *n.* person who makes or deals in jewels or jewellery.

jewellery *n.* jewels or similar ornaments to be worn.

Jewish *a.* of Jews.

Jewry *n.* the Jewish people.

jib *n.* triangular sail stretching forward from a mast; projecting arm of a crane. —*v.i.* (p.t. *jibbed*) refuse to proceed. **∼ at,** object to.

jiffy *n.* (*colloq.*) moment.

jig *n.* lively jumping dance; device that holds work and guides tools working on it; template. —*v.t./i.* (p.t. *jigged*) move quickly up and down.

jigger *n.* measure of spirits.

jiggery-pokery *n.* (*colloq.*) trickery.

jiggle *v.t./i.* rock or jerk lightly.

jigsaw *n.* picture cut into pieces which are then shuffled and reassembled for amusement.

jilt *v.t.* abandon (a person) after having courted him or her.

jingle *v.t./i.* make or cause to make a ringing or clinking sound. —*n.* this sound; simple rhyme.

jingoism *n.* excessive patriotism and contempt for other countries.

jink *v.i.* dodge by a sudden turn. **high jinks,** boisterous fun.

jinx *n.* (*colloq.*) influence causing bad luck.

jitter *v.i.* (*colloq.*) be nervous. **jitters** *n.pl.* (*colloq.*) nervousness. **jittery** *a.*

jive *n.* fast lively jazz; dance to this. —*v.i.* dance to this music.

job *n.* piece of work; paid position of employment; (*colloq.*) difficult task. **good** *or* **bad ∼,** fortunate or unfortunate state of affairs. **∼ lot,** miscellaneous articles sold together.

jobber *n.* stockjobber.

jobbing *a.* doing single pieces of work for payment.

jobcentre *n.* government office in a town centre, where notices about jobs available are displayed.

jobless *a.* out of work.

jockey *n.* (pl. *-eys*) person who rides in horse-races. —*v.t./i.* manœuvre to gain advantage; force by skilful or unfair means.

jocose /-ˈkəʊs/ *a.* joking.

jocular *a.* joking. **jocularly** *adv.*, **jocularity** *n.*

jocund *a.* merry, cheerful.

jodhpurs *n.pl.* riding-breeches fitting closely from knee to ankle.

jog *v.t./i.* (p.t. *jogged*) push or shake slightly; stimulate; proceed at a slow regular pace, run thus for exercise. —*n.* jogging movement or pace; nudge.

joggle *v.t./i.* shake slightly. —*n.* slight shake.

jogtrot *n.* slow regular trot.

join *v.t./i.* put or come together, unite; come into the company of; take one's place in; become a member of. —*n.* place where things join. **∼ battle,** begin fighting. **∼ up,** enlist in the forces.

joiner *n.* maker of furniture and light woodwork. **joinery** *n.* this work.

joint *a.* shared or done by two or more people together; sharing. —*n.* join; structure where parts or bones fit together; section of an animal's carcass as food; (*sl.*) place where people meet for gambling or drinking etc. —*v.t.* connect by joint(s); divide into joints. **out of ∼,** dislocated; in disorder. **jointly** *adv.*

joist *n.* one of the beams on which floor boards or ceiling laths are fixed.

joke *n.* thing said or done to cause laughter; ridiculous person or thing. —*v.i.* make jokes.

joker *n.* person who jokes; (*sl.*) fellow; extra playing-card used as the highest trump.

jollification *n.* merry-making.

jollity *n.* being jolly; merry-making.

jolly *a.* (*-ier, -iest*) cheerful, merry; very pleasant. —*adv.* (*colloq.*) very. —*v.t.* keep (a person) in good humour.

jolt *v.t./i.* shake or dislodge with a jerk; move jerkily. —*n.* jolting movement; shock.

jonquil *n.* a kind of narcissus.

joss-stick *n.* thin stick that burns with a smell of incense.

jostle *v.t./i.* push roughly.

jot *n.* very small amount. —*v.t.* (p.t. *jotted*) write down briefly.

jotter *n.* note-pad, notebook.

joule /dʒuːl/ *n.* unit of energy.

journal *n.* daily record of events; newspaper or periodical.

journalese *n.* style of language used in inferior journalism.

journalist *n.* person employed in writing for a newspaper or magazine. **journalism** *n.* this work.

journey *n.* (pl. *-eys*) continued course of going or travelling. —*v.i.* make a journey.

journeyman *n.* (pl. *-men*) workman who has completed his apprenticeship.

joust /dʒaʊst/ *v.i.* fight on horseback with lances.

jovial *a.* full of cheerful good humour. **jovially** *adv.*, **joviality** *n.*

jowl *n.* jaw, cheek; dewlap, loose skin on the throat.

joy *n.* deep emotion of pleasure; thing causing delight. **~-ride** *n.* car ride taken for pleasure, usu. without the owner's permission.

joyful *a.* full of joy. **joyfully** *adv.*, **joyfulness** *n.*

joyous *a.* joyful. **joyously** *adv.*

J.P. *abbr.* Justice of the Peace.

jubilant *a.* rejoicing. **jubilation** *n.*

jubilee *n.* special anniversary.

Judaism *n.* religion of the Jewish people, based on the teachings of the Old Testament and Talmud.

judder *v.i.* shake noisily or violently. —*n.* this movement.

judge *n.* public officer appointed to hear and try cases in lawcourts; person appointed to decide who has won a contest; person able to give an authoritative opinion. —*v.t.* try (a case) in a lawcourt; act as judge of; give an opinion about; estimate.

judgement *n.* (in law contexts **judgment**) judging; judge's decision.

judicature *n.* administration of justice; a body of judges.

judicial *a.* of the administration of justice; of a judge or judgement. **judicially** *adv.*

judiciary /-'drɪʃ-/ *n.* the whole body of judges in a country.

judicious *a.* judging wisely, showing good sense. **judiciously** *adv.*

judo *n.* Japanese system of unarmed combat.

jug *n.* vessel with a handle and a shaped lip, for holding and pouring liquids. —*v.t.* (p.t. *jugged*) stew (hare). **jugful** *n.*

juggernaut *n.* large overwhelmingly powerful object or institution; very large transport vehicle.

juggle *v.t./i.* toss and catch objects skilfully for entertainment; manipulate skilfully; re-arrange (facts etc.), esp. deceitfully. **juggler** *n.*

jugular *a.* **~ vein,** one of the two great veins in the neck.

juice *n.* fluid content of fruits, vegetables, or meat; fluid secreted by an organ of the body. **juicy** *a.*

jujube *n.* jelly-like sweet.

juke-box *n.* machine that plays a selected record when a coin is inserted.

July *n.* seventh month of the year.

jumble *v.t.* mix in a confused way. —*n.* jumbled articles; items for a jumble sale. **~ sale,** sale of miscellaneous second-hand goods to raise money for charity.

jumbo *n.* (pl. *-os*) very large thing. **~ jet,** very large jet aircraft.

jump *v.t./i.* make a sudden upward movement; rise suddenly; move up off the ground etc. by muscular movement of the legs; pass over by jumping; use (a horse) for jumping; pass over to a point beyond; leave (rails or track) accidentally; abscond from; pounce on. —*n.* jumping movement; sudden rise or change; gap in a series; obstacle to be jumped. **~ at,** accept eagerly. **~ the gun,** act before the permitted time. **~ the queue,** obtain something without waiting one's turn. **~ to conclusions,** reach them too hastily.

jumper[1] *n.* one who jumps.

jumper[2] *n.* woman's knitted garment for the upper part of the body; upper part of a sailor's uniform.

jumpy *a.* nervous.

junction *n.* join; place where roads or railway lines unite.

juncture *n.* point of time, convergence of events.

June *n.* sixth month of the year.

jungle *n.* land overgrown with tangled vegetation, esp. in the tropics; tangled mass; scene of ruthless struggle.

junior *a.* younger in age; lower in rank or authority; for younger children. —*n.* junior person.

juniper *n.* evergreen shrub with dark berries.

junk[1] *n.* useless or discarded articles, rubbish. **~-shop** *n.* shop selling miscellaneous second-hand goods.

junk[2] *n.* flat-bottomed ship with sails, used in China seas.

junket *n.* sweet custard-like food made of milk and rennet.

junketing *n.* merry-making.

junkie *n.* (*sl.*) drug addict.

junta *n.* group who combine to rule a country, esp. after a revolution.

jurisdiction *n.* authority to administer justice or exercise power.

jurisprudence *n.* skill in law.

juror *n.* member of a jury.

jury *n.* group of people sworn to give a verdict on a case in a court of law.

just *a.* giving proper consideration to the claims of all concerned; right in amount etc., deserved. —*adv.* exactly; by only a short amount etc.; only a moment ago; (*colloq.*) merely; really. **justly** *adv.*, **justness** *n.*

justice *n.* just treatment, fairness; legal proceedings; magistrate; judge. **Justice of the Peace,** citizen serving as a magistrate.

justiciary *n.* one who administers justice.

justifiable *a.* able to be justified. **justifiably** *adv.*

justify *v.t.* show to be right or just or reasonable; be sufficient reason for; adjust (a line of type) to fill a space neatly. **justification** *n.*

jut *v.i.* (p.t. *jutted*) project.

jute *n.* fibre from the bark of certain tropical plants.

juvenile *a.* youthful, childish; for young people. —*n.* young person. **juvenility** *n.*

juxtapose *v.t.* put (things) side by side. **juxtaposition** *n.*

K

Kaiser *n.* title of German and Austrian emperors until 1918.

kale *n.* cabbage with curly leaves.

kaleidoscope /-ˈlaɪ-/ *n.* toy tube containing mirrors and coloured fragments reflected to produce changing patterns. **kaleidoscopic** *a.*

kampong *n.* Malayan enclosure or village.

kangaroo *n.* Australian marsupial that jumps along on its strong hind legs. **~ court,** court formed illegally by a group to settle disputes among themselves.

kaolin *n.* fine white clay used in porcelain and medicine.

kapok *n.* fluffy fibre used for padding things.

karate /kəˈrɑtɪ/ *n.* Japanese system of unarmed combat using the hands and feet as weapons.

kauri /ˈkaʊrɪ/ *n.* coniferous New Zealand tree yielding **kauri-gum.**

kayak /ˈkaɪ-/ *n.* small covered canoe, esp. of Eskimos.

kc/s *abbr.* kilocycle(s) per second.

kebabs /kɪˈbæ-/ *n.pl.* small pieces of meat cooked on a skewer.

kedgeree *n.* cooked dish of rice and fish or eggs.

keel *n.* timber or steel structure along the base of a ship. —*v.t./i.* overturn; become tilted.

keen¹ *a.* (*-er*, *-est*) sharp; penetrating; piercingly cold; intense; very eager. **~ on,** (*colloq.*) liking greatly. **keenly** *adv.*, **keenness** *n.*

keen² *n.* Irish funeral song with wailing. —*v.i.* utter this; wail.

keep *v.t./i.* (p.t. *kept*) remain or cause to remain in a specified state or position; prevent, detain; put aside for a future time; pay due regard to; celebrate; protect; continue to have; provide with food and other necessities; own and look after (animals); manage (a shop etc.); have in stock or for sale; make regular entries in (a diary, accounts, etc.); continue doing something; remain in good condition. —*n.* person's food and other necessities; strongly fortified structure in a castle. **for keeps,** (*colloq.*) permanently. **~ house,** look after a house or household. **~ up,** progress at the same pace as others; continue; maintain.

keeper *n.* person who keeps or looks after something, custodian.

keeping *n.* custody, charge. **in ~ with,** suited to.

keepsake *n.* thing kept in memory of the giver.

keg *n.* small barrel. **~ beer,** beer from sealed metal kegs.

kelp *n.* large brown seaweed.

kelvin *n.* degree of the **Kelvin scale** of temperature which has zero at absolute zero ($-273.15\,°C$).

ken *n.* range of sight or knowledge. —*v.t.* (p.t. *kenned*) (*Sc.*) know.

kennel *n.* shelter for a dog; pack of dogs; (*pl.*) boarding place for dogs.

kept *see* **keep.**

kerb *n.* stone edging to a pavement.

kerchief *n.* square scarf worn on the head.

kerfuffle *n.* (*colloq.*) fuss, commotion.

kernel *n.* softer part inside the shell of a nut or stone of fruit; seed within a husk; central or important part.

kerosene *n.* paraffin oil.

kestrel *n.* a kind of small falcon.

ketch *n.* two-masted sailing-boat.

ketchup *n.* thick sauce made from tomatoes and vinegar.

kettle *n.* metal container with a spout and handle, for boiling water in.

kettledrum *n.* drum with parchment stretched over a large metal bowl.

key *n.* piece of metal shaped for moving the bolt of a lock, tightening a spring, etc.; thing giving access or control or insight; set of answers to problems; word or system for interpreting a code etc.; system of related notes in music; style; roughness of surface to help adhesion; lever for a finger to press on a piano, typewriter, etc. —*v.t.* link closely; roughen (a surface) to help adhesion. **~-ring** *n.* ring on which keys are threaded. **~ up,** stimulate, make nervously tense.

keyboard *n.* set of keys on a piano etc.

keyhole *n.* hole by which a key is put into a lock.

keynote *n.* note on which a key in music is based; prevailing tone.

keystone *n.* central stone of an arch, locking others into position.

keyword *n.* key to a cipher etc.

kg *abbr.* kilogram(s).

K.G.B. *abbr.* secret police of the U.S.S.R.

khaki *a. & n.* dull brownish-yellow, colour of military uniforms.

kHz *abbr.* kilohertz.

kibbutz /-ˈbʊts/ *n.* (pl. *-im*) communal settlement in Israel.

kick *v.t./i.* strike or propel with the foot; score (a goal) by kicking a ball; (of a gun) recoil when fired. —*n.* act of kicking; blow with the foot; (*colloq.*) thrill, interest. **~-off** *n.* start of a football game. **~-starter** *n.* lever pressed with the foot to start a motor-cycle. **~ up,** (*colloq.*) create (a fuss or noise).

kickback *n.* recoil.

kid *n.* young goat; leather made from its skin; (*sl.*) child. —*v.t./i.* (p.t. *kidded*) (*sl.*) hoax, tease.

kiddy *n.* (*sl.*) child.

kidnap *v.t.* (p.t. *kidnapped*) carry off (a person) illegally in order to obtain a ransom. **kidnapper** *n.*

kidney *n.* (pl. *-eys*) either of a pair of organs that remove waste products from the blood and secrete urine. **~ bean,** French bean; runner bean. **~ dish,** oval dish indented at one side.

kill *v.t.* cause the death of; put an end to; spend (time) unprofitably by waiting. —*n.* killing; animal(s) killed by a hunter. **killer** *n.*

killing *a.* (*colloq.*) very amusing.

killjoy *n.* person who spoils the enjoyment of others.

kiln *n.* oven for hardening or drying things (e.g. pottery, hops).

kilo /ˈkiːləʊ/ *n.* (pl. *-os*) kilogram.

kilo- *pref.* one thousand.

kilocycle *n.* 1000 cycles as a unit of wave frequency; kilohertz.

kilogram *n.* unit of weight or mass in the metric system (2·205 lb).

kilohertz *n.* unit of frequency of electromagnetic waves, = 1000 cycles per second.

kilometre /ˈkɪl- *or* -ˈlɒm-/ *n.* 1000 metres (0·62 mile).

kilovolt *n.* 1000 volts.

kilowatt *n.* 1000 watts.

kilt *n.* knee-length pleated skirt of tartan wool, esp. as part of Highland man's dress. **kilted** *a.*

kimono *n.* (pl. *-os*) loose Japanese robe worn with a sash; dressing-gown resembling this.

kin *n.* person's relatives.

kind[1] *n.* class of similar things. **a ~ of,** thing belonging approximately to (a class named). **in ~,** (of payment) in goods etc. not money. **of a ~,** similar.

kind[2] *a.* (*-er, -est*) gentle and considerate towards others. **~-hearted** *a.*, **kindness** *n.*

kindergarten *n.* school for very young children.

kindle[1] *v.t./i.* set on fire; arouse, stimulate; become kindled.

kindle[2] *v.i.* (of rabbits) produce offspring.

kindling *n.* small pieces of wood for lighting fires.

kindly *a.* (*-ier, -iest*) kind. —*adv.* in a kind way; please. **kindliness** *n.*

kindred *n.* kin. —*a.* related; of similar kind.

kinetic *a.* of movement.

king *n.* male ruler of a country by right of birth; man or thing regarded as supreme in some way; chess piece to be protected from checkmate; playing-card next above queen. **~-size,** **~-sized** *adjs.* extra large. **kingly** *a.*, **kingship** *n.*

kingcup *n.* marsh marigold.

kingdom *n.* country ruled by a king or queen; division of the natural world. **~-come** *n.* (*sl.*) next world.

kingfisher *n.* small blue bird that dives to catch fish.

kingpin *n.* indispensable person or thing.

kink *n.* short twist in thread or wire etc.; mental peculiarity. —*v.t./i.* form or cause to form kink(s). **kinky** *a.*

kinsfolk *n.pl.* kin. **kinsman** *n.*, **kinswoman** *n.fem.*

kiosk *n.* booth where newspapers or refreshments are sold, or containing a public telephone.

kip *n. & v.i.* (p.t. *kipped*) (*sl.*) sleep.

kipper *n.* smoked herring.

kirk *n.* (*Sc.*) church.

kirsch /kɪəʃ/ *n.* colourless liqueur made from wild cherries.

kismet *n.* destiny, fate.

kiss *n. & v.t./i.* touch or caress with the lips.

kit *n.* outfit of clothing, tools, etc.; set of parts to be assembled. —*v.t.* (p.t. *kitted*) equip with kit.

kitbag *n.* bag for holding kit.

kitchen *n.* room where meals are prepared. **~ garden,** vegetable garden.

kitchenette *n.* small kitchen.

kite *n.* large bird of the hawk family; light framework on a string, for flying in the wind as a toy.

kith *n.* **~ and kin,** relatives.

kitten *n.* young of cat, hare, rabbit, or ferret. **kittenish** *a.*

kitty *n.* communal fund.

kiwi *n.* (pl. *-is*) New Zealand bird that does not fly.

kleptomania *n.* tendency to steal things without desire to use or profit by them. **kleptomaniac** *n.*

km *abbr.* kilometre(s).

knack *n.* ability to do something skilfully.

knacker *n.* person who buys and slaughters useless horses.

knapsack *n.* bag worn strapped on the back.

knave *n.* (*old use*) rogue; jack in playing-cards. **knavish** *a.*

knead *v.t./i.* press and stretch (dough) with the hands; massage with similar movements.

knee *n.* joint between the thigh and the lower part of the leg; part of a garment covering this. —*v.t.* (p.t. *kneed*) touch or strike with the knee. **knees-up** *n.* (*colloq.*) lively party with dancing.

kneecap *n.* small bone over the front of the knee; covering for the knee.

kneel *v.i.* (p.t. *knelt*) lower one's body to rest on the knees with legs bent back, esp. in reverence.

knell *n.* sound of a bell tolled after a death or at a funeral.

knelt *see* **kneel.**

knew *see* **know.**

knickerbockers *n.pl.* loose breeches gathered in at the knee.

knickers *n.pl.* woman's or girl's undergarment for the lower part of the body.

knick-knack *n.* small ornament.

knife *n.* (pl. *knives*) cutting instrument with a sharp blade and a handle. —*v.t.* cut or stab with a knife.

knight *n.* man given a rank below baronet, with the title 'Sir'; chess piece usu. with the form of a horse's head. —*v.t.* confer a knighthood on.

knighthood *n.* rank of knight.

knit *v.t./i.* (p.t. *knitted* or *knit*) form (yarn) into fabric of interlocking loops; make in this way; grow together so as to unite. **~ one's brow,** frown. **knitter** *n.*

knitwear *n.* knitted garments.

knob *n.* rounded projecting part, esp. as a handle; small lump. **knobby** *a.*, **knobbly** *a.*

knock *v.t./i.* strike with an audible sharp blow; strike a door etc. to summon a person or gain admittance; drive or make by knocking; (of an engine) make an abnormal thumping or rattling noise; (*sl.*) criticize insultingly. —*n.*

act or sound of knocking; sharp blow. ∼ **about,** treat roughly; wander casually. ∼ **down,** dispose of (an article) at auction. ∼**-down** *a.* (of price) very low. ∼**-kneed** *a.* having an abnormal inward curvature of the legs at the knees. ∼ **off,** (*colloq.*) cease work; complete quickly; (*sl.*) steal. ∼ **out,** make unconscious by a blow on the head; eliminate; exhaust, disable. ∼**-out** *a.* & *n.* knocking a person etc. out; (*sl.*) outstanding or irresistible person or thing. ∼ **up,** rouse by knocking at a door; make or arrange hastily; score (runs) at cricket; make exhausted or ill. ∼**-up** *n.* practice or casual game at tennis etc.

knocker *n.* one who knocks; hinged flap for rapping on a door.

knoll /nəʊl/ *n.* hillock, mound.

knot *n.* intertwining of one or more pieces of thread or rope etc. as a fastening; tangle; hard mass esp. where a branch joins a tree-trunk; round spot in timber; cluster; unit of speed used by ships and aircraft, = one nautical mile per hour. —*v.t./i.* (p.t. *knotted*) tie or fasten with a knot; entangle.

knotty *a.* (-ier, -iest) full of knots; puzzling, difficult.

know *v.t./i.* (p.t. *knew*, p.p. *known*) have in one's mind or memory; feel certain; recognize, be familiar with; understand. **in the** ∼, (*colloq.*) having inside information. ∼**-all** *n.* person who behaves as if he knows everything. ∼**-how** *n.* practical knowledge or skill.

knowable *a.* able to be known.

knowledge *n.* knowing about things; all a person knows; all that is known, body of information.

knowledgeable *a.* well-informed.

knuckle *n.* finger-joint; animal's knee-joint or part joining the leg to the foot, esp. as meat. —*v.i.* ∼ **under,** yield, submit.

knuckleduster *n.* metal device worn over the knuckles in fighting, esp. to increase the injury done by a blow.

koala /kəʊˈɑ-/ *n.* ∼ **bear,** Australian tree-climbing animal with thick grey fur.

kohl /kəʊl/ *n.* powder used to darken the eye-lids.

kookaburra *n.* Australian giant kingfisher.

koppie *n.* (*S.Afr.*) small hill.

Koran /-rɑn/ *n.* sacred book of Muslims containing the revelations of Muhammad.

kosher /ˈkəʊ-/ *a.* conforming to Jewish dietary laws.

kowtow *v.i.* behave with exaggerated respect.

k.p.h. *abbr.* kilometres per hour.

kraal /krɑl/ *n.* (*S.Afr.*) fenced village of huts; enclosure.

Kremlin *n.* government of the U.S.S.R.

Krugerrand /ˈkruːɡərɑnt/ *n.* South African gold coin bearing a portrait of President Kruger.

kudos *n.* (*colloq.*) honour and glory.

kung fu Chinese form of unarmed combat similar to karate.

Kurd *n.* member of a pastoral people of south-west Asia. **Kurdish** *a.*

kV *abbr.* kilovolt(s).

kW *abbr.* kilowatt(s).

L

L *abbr.* learner.

l *abbr.* litre(s).

lab *n.* (*colloq.*) laboratory.

label *n.* note fixed on or beside an object to show its nature, destination, etc. —*v.t.* (p.t. *labelled*) fix a label to; describe as.

labial *a.* of the lips.

laboratory *n.* room or building equipped for scientific work.

laborious *a.* needing or showing much effort. **laboriously** *adv.*

labour *n.* work, exertion; contractions of the womb at childbirth; workers. —*v.t./i.* work hard; progress or operate with difficulty; emphasize lengthily.

Labour *a.* & *n.* (of) the U.K. political party representing the interests of workers. **Labour-ite** *n.*

laboured *a.* showing signs of great effort, not spontaneous.

labourer *n.* person employed to do unskilled work.

Labrador *n.* dog of the retriever breed with a black or golden coat.

laburnum *n.* tree with hanging clusters of yellow flowers.

labyrinth *n.* maze. **labyrinthine** *a.*

lace *n.* ornamental openwork fabric or trimming; cord etc. threaded through holes or hooks to pull opposite edges together. —*v.t.* fasten with lace(s); intertwine; add a dash of spirits to (drink).

lacerate *v.t.* injure (flesh) by tearing; wound (feelings). **laceration** *n.*

lachrymal *a.* of tears.

lachrymose *a.* tearful.

lack *n.* state or fact of not having something. —*v.t.* be without.

lackadaisical *a.* lacking vigour or determination, unenthusiastic.

lackey *n.* (pl. *-eys*) footman, servant; servile follower.

lacking *a.* undesirably absent.

laconic *a.* terse. **laconically** *adv.*

lacquer *n.* hard glossy varnish. —*v.t.* coat with lacquer.

lacrosse *n.* team game using a netted crook to carry a ball.

lacuna *n.* (pl. *-ae*) gap.

lacy *a.* of or like lace.

lad *n.* boy, young fellow.

ladder *n.* set of cross-bars between uprights,

used as a means of climbing; vertical ladder-like flaw where stitches become undone in a stocking etc. —*v.t./i.* cause or develop a ladder (in).

laden *a.* loaded.

lading *n.* cargo.

ladle *n.* deep long-handled spoon for transferring liquids. —*v.t.* transfer with a ladle.

lady *n.* woman, esp. of good social position; well-mannered woman; *L~*, title of wives, widows, or daughters of certain noblemen. **Lady chapel,** chapel (within a church) dedicated to the Virgin Mary. **~-in-waiting** *n.* lady attending a queen or princess. **ladylike** *a.*

ladybird *n.* small flying beetle, usu. red with black spots.

ladyship *n.* title used of or to a woman with rank of *Lady*.

lag[1] *v.i.* (p.t. *lagged*) go too slow, not keep up. —*n.* lagging, delay.

lag[2] *v.t.* (p.t. *lagged*) encase in material that prevents loss of heat.

lag[3] *n.* old *~*, (*sl.*) convict.

lager /ˈlɑː-/ *n.* light beer.

laggard *n.* person who lags behind.

lagoon *n.* salt-water lake beside a sea; fresh-water lake beside a river or larger lake.

laid see **lay**[3].

lain see **lie**[2].

lair *n.* sheltered place where a wild animal regularly sleeps or rests; person's hiding-place.

laird *n.* (*Sc.*) landowner.

laissez-faire /leɪseɪˈfeə(r)/ *n.* policy of non-interference.

laity /ˈleɪtɪ/ *n.* laymen.

lake *n.* large body of water surrounded by land.

lakh *n.* (in India) one hundred thousand.

lama *n.* Buddhist priest in Tibet and Mongolia.

lamasery /-ˈmɑː-/ *n.* monastery of lamas.

lamb *n.* young sheep; its flesh as food; gentle or endearing person. —*v.i.* give birth to a lamb.

lambaste /-ˈbeɪ-/ *v.t.* (*colloq.*) thrash; repri-mand severely.

lambswool *n.* soft fine wool.

lame *a.* (*-er, -est*) unable to walk normally; weak, unconvincing. —*v.t.* make lame. **lamely** *adv.*, **lameness** *n.*

lamé /ˈlɑːmeɪ/ *n.* fabric with gold or silver thread interwoven.

lament *n.* passionate expression of grief; song or poem expressing grief. —*v.t./i.* feel or express grief or regret. **lamentation** *n.*

lamentable /ˈlæ-/ *a.* regrettable, deplorable. **lamentably** *adv.*

lamented *a.* mourned for.

laminate /-ət/ *n.* laminated material.

laminated *a.* made of layers joined one upon another.

Lammas *n.* first day of August.

lamp *n.* device for giving light. **~-post** *n.* tall post of a street lamp.

lampoon *n.* piece of writing that attacks a person by ridiculing him. —*v.t.* ridicule in a lampoon.

lamprey *n.* (pl. *-eys*) small eel-like water animal.

lampshade *n.* shade placed over a lamp to screen its light.

lance *n.* long spear. —*v.t.* prick or cut open with a lancet. **~-corporal** *n.* N.C.O. ranking below corporal.

lancer *n.* soldier of a regiment formerly armed with lances.

lancet *n.* surgeon's pointed two-edged knife; tall narrow pointed arch or window.

land *n.* part of earth's surface not covered by water; expanse of this; ground, soil. —*v.t./i.* set or go ashore; come or bring (an aircraft) down to the surface of land or water; bring to or reach a place or situation; deal (a person) a blow; bring (a fish) to land; obtain (a prize, appointment, etc.). **~-locked** *a.* surrounded by land.

landed *a.* owning land; consisting of land.

landfall *n.* approach to land after a journey by sea or air.

landing *n.* coming or bringing ashore or to ground; place for this; level area at the top of one or more flights of stairs. **~-stage** *n.* plat-form for landing from a boat.

landlady *n.* woman who lets rooms to tenants or who keeps an inn or boarding-house.

landlord *n.* person who lets land or a house or room to a tenant; one who keeps an inn or boarding-house.

landlubber *n.* (*colloq.*) person not accustomed to the sea and seamanship.

landmark *n.* conspicuous feature of a land-scape; event marking a stage in a thing's history.

landrail *n.* corncrake.

landscape *n.* scenery of a land area; picture of this. —*v.t.* lay out (an area) attractively with natural-looking features.

landslide *n.* sliding down of a mass of land on a slope; overwhelming majority of votes.

landsman *n.* (pl. *-men*) person who is not a sailor.

landward *a. & adv.* towards the land. **landwards** *adv.*

lane *n.* narrow road, track, or passage; strip of road for a single line of traffic; track to which ships or aircraft etc. must keep.

language *n.* words and their use; system of this used by a nation or group.

languid *a.* lacking vigour or vitality. **languidly** *adv.*

languish *v.i.* lose or lack vitality; live under miserable conditions.

languishing *a.* putting on a languid look.

languor *n.* state of being languid. **languorous** *n.*

lank *a.* tall and lean; straight and limp.

lanky *a.* (*-ier, -iest*) ungracefully tall and lean. **lankiness** *n.*

lanolin *n.* fat extracted from sheep's wool, used in ointments.

lantern *n.* transparent case for holding and shielding a light outdoors. **~-jawed** *a.* having long thin jaws.

lanyard *n.* short rope for securing things on

a ship; cord for hanging a whistle etc. round the neck or shoulder.

lap[1] *n.* flat area over the thighs of a seated person; overlap; single circuit; section of a journey. —*v.t./i.* (p.t. *lapped*) wrap round; overlap; be lap(s) ahead of (a competitor in a race). **~-dog** *n.* small pampered dog.

lap[2] *v.t./i.* (p.t. *lapped*) take up (liquid) by movements of tongue; flow (against) with ripples.

lapel *n.* flap folded back at the front of a coat etc.

lapidary *a.* of stones.

lapis lazuli blue semi-precious stone.

Laplander *n.* native of Lapland.

Lapp *n.* Laplander; language of Lapland.

lapse *v.i.* fail to maintain one's position or standard; become void or no longer valid. —*n.* slight error; lapsing; passage of time.

lapwing *n.* peewit.

larceny *n.* theft of personal goods.

larch *n.* deciduous tree of the pine family.

lard *n.* white greasy substance prepared from pig-fat, used in cooking. —*v.t.* put strips of fat bacon in or on (meat etc.) before cooking; interlard. **lardy** *a.*

larder *n.* room or cupboard for storing food.

large *a.* (*-er, -est*) of great size or extent. —*adv.* in a large way. **at ~,** free to roam about; in general. **largeness** *n.*

largely *adv.* to a great extent.

largesse *n.* money or gifts generously given.

lariat *n.* lasso; rope for tethering a horse etc.

lark[1] *n.* small brown bird, skylark.

lark[2] *n.* lighthearted adventurous action; amusing incident. —*v.i.* play about light-heartedly.

larkspur *n.* plant with spur-shaped blue or pink flowers.

larrikin *n.* (*Austr.*) lout, hooligan.

larva *n.* (pl. *-vae*) insect in the first stage after coming out of the egg. **larval** *a.*

laryngitis *n.* inflammation of larynx.

larynx *n.* part of the throat containing the vocal cords.

lasagne /-ˈsænje/ *n.pl.* pasta in ribbon-like strips.

Lascar *n.* seaman from islands south-east of India.

lascivious /-ˈsɪv-/ *a.* lustful. **lasciviously** *adv.*, **lasciviousness** *n.*

laser /ˈleɪ-/ *n.* device emitting an intense narrow beam of light.

lash *v.t./i.* move in a whip-like movement; beat with a whip; strike violently; fasten with a cord etc. —*n.* flexible part of a whip; stroke with this; eyelash. **~ out,** attack with blows or words; spend lavishly.

lashings *n.pl.* (*sl.*) a lot.

lass, lassie *ns.* (*Sc. & N. Engl.*) girl, young woman.

lassitude *n.* tiredness, listlessness.

lasso *n.* (pl. *-oes*) rope with a noose for catching cattle. —*v.t.* (p.t. *lassoed*, pres.p. *lassoing*) catch with a lasso.

last[1] *n.* foot-shaped block used in making and repairing shoes.

last[2] *a. & adv.* coming after all others; most recent(ly). —*n.* last person or thing. **at ~,** **at long ~,** in the end, after much delay. **~ post,** military bugle-call sounded at sunset or military funerals. **~ straw,** slight addition to difficulties, making them unbearable. **Last Supper,** meal eaten by Christ and his disciples on the eve of his crucifixion. **~ trump,** trumpet to wake the dead on Judgement Day. **~ word,** final statement in a dispute; latest fashion. **on its ~ legs,** near the end of its usefulness.

last[3] *v.t./i.* continue, endure; suffice for a period of time.

lastly *adv.* finally.

latch *n.* bar lifted from its catch by a lever, used to fasten a gate etc.; spring-lock that catches when a door is closed. —*v.t./i.* fasten with a latch.

latchkey *n.* key of an outer door.

late *a. & adv.* (*-er, -est*) after the proper or usual time; far on in a day or night or period; recent; no longer living or holding a position. **of ~,** lately. **lateness** *n.*

lately *adv.* recently.

latent *a.* existing but not active or developed or visible.

lateral *a.* of, at, to, or from the side(s). **laterally** *adv.*

latex *n.* milky fluid from certain plants, esp. the rubber-tree; similar synthetic substance.

lath /læθ/ *n.* (pl. *laths*) narrow thin strip of wood, e.g. in trellis.

lathe /leɪð/ *n.* machine for holding and turning pieces of wood or metal etc. while they are worked on.

lather *n.* froth from soap and water; frothy sweat. —*v.t./i.* cover with or form lather.

Latin *n.* language of the ancient Romans. —*a.* of or in Latin; speaking a language based on Latin.

latitude *n.* distance of a place from the equator, measured in degrees; region; freedom from restrictions.

latrine *n.* lavatory in a camp or barracks.

latter *a.* mentioned after another; nearer to the end. **~-day** *a.* modern, recent.

latterly *adv.* recently; nowadays.

lattice *n.* framework of crossed strips. **~ window,** one with this.

laud *v.t. & n.* praise.

laudable *a.* praiseworthy. **laudably** *adv.*

laudanum /ˈlɒdnəm/ *n.* opium prepared for use as a sedative.

laudatory /ˈlɔ-/ *a.* praising.

laugh *v.t./i.* make sounds and movements of the face that express lively amusement or amused scorn; have these emotions; treat with a laugh. —*n.* act or manner of laughing; (*colloq.*) amusing incident. **laughing-stock** *n.* person or thing that is ridiculed.

laughable *a.* ridiculous.

laughter *n.* laughing.

launch[1] *v.t./i.* send forth; put or go into action;

cause (a ship) to slide into the water. —*n.* process of launching something. **~ out,** spend lavishly; start an ambitious enterprise.

launch² *n.* large motor boat.

launder *v.t.* wash and iron (clothes etc.).

launderette *n.* establishment fitted with washing-machines to be used for a fee.

laundress *n.* woman whose job is to launder clothes etc.

laundry *n.* place where clothes etc. are laundered; batch of clothes etc. sent to or from this.

Laureate /ˈlo-/ *a.* **Poet ~,** poet appointed to write poems for State occasions.

laurel /ˈlo-/ *n.* evergreen shrub with smooth glossy leaves; (*pl.*) victories or honours gained.

lav *n.* (*colloq.*) lavatory.

lava *n.* flowing or hardened molten rock from a volcano.

lavatory *n.* pan (usu. a fixture) into which urine and faeces are discharged for disposal; room etc. equipped with this.

lavender *n.* shrub with fragrant purple flowers; light purple. **~-water** *n.* delicate perfume made from lavender.

lavish *a.* giving or producing something in large quantities; plentiful. —*v.t.* bestow lavishly. **lavishly** *adv.*, **lavishness** *n.*

law *n.* rule(s) established by authority or custom; their influence or operation; statement of what always happens in certain circumstances. **~-abiding** *a.* obeying the law.

lawcourt *n.* room or building where legal cases are heard and judged.

lawful *a.* permitted or recognized by law. **lawfully** *adv.*

lawless *a.* disregarding the law, uncontrolled. **lawlessness** *n.*

lawn¹ *n.* fine woven cotton or synthetic fabric.

lawn² *n.* area of closely cut grass. **~-mower** *n.* machine for cutting the grass of lawns. **~ tennis** (see *tennis*).

lawsuit *n.* process of bringing a problem or claim etc. before a court of law for settlement.

lawyer *n.* person trained and qualified in legal matters.

lax *a.* slack, not strict or severe. **laxly** *adv.*, **laxity** *n.*

laxative *a.* & *n.* (medicine) stimulating the bowels to empty.

lay¹ *n.* (*old use*) poem meant to be sung, ballad.

lay² *a.* not ordained into the clergy; non-professional.

lay³ *v.t./i.* (p.t. **laid**) place; arrange ready for use; cause to be in a certain condition; cause to subside; present for consideration; stake; (of a hen) produce (an egg or eggs) from the body; (*incorrect use*) = lie². —*n.* way a thing lies. **~ about one,** hit out on all sides. **~ hold of,** grasp. **~ into,** (*sl.*) thrash; reprimand harshly. **~ off,** discharge (workmen) temporarily through lack of work; (*colloq.*) cease. **~-off** *n.* temporary discharge. **~ out,** arrange according to a plan; prepare (a body) for burial; spend (money) for a purpose; knock

unconscious. **~ up,** store; cause (a person) to be ill. **~ waste,** destroy the crops and buildings of (an area).

layabout *n.* loafer, one who lazily avoids working for a living.

lay-by *n.* extra strip of road beside a carriageway, where vehicles may stop without obstructing traffic.

layer *n.* one who lays something; one thickness of material laid over a surface. —*v.t.* arrange in layers; propagate (a plant) by fastening down an attached shoot to take root.

layette *n.* outfit for a new-born baby.

lay figure artist's jointed wooden model of the human body.

layman *n.* (pl. **-men**) non-professional person.

layout *n.* arrangement of parts etc. according to a plan.

laze *v.i.* spend time idly or in idle relaxation. —*n.* act or period of lazing.

lazy *a.* (**-ier, -iest**) unwilling to work, doing little work; showing lack of energy. **~-bones** *n.* lazy person. **~-tongs** *n.* zigzag levers for picking up distant objects. **lazily** *adv.*, **laziness** *n.*

lb *abbr.* pound(s) weight.

leach *v.t./i.* percolate (liquid) through soil or ore etc.; remove (soluble matter) or be removed in this way.

lead¹ /lid/ *v.t./i.* (p.t. **led**) guide; influence into an action, opinion, or state; be a route or means of access; pass (one's life); be in first place in, be ahead; make one's start; be the first player in card-game, play as one's first card. —*n.* guidance; clue; leading place, amount by which one competitor is in front; wire conveying electric current; strap or cord for leading an animal; act or right of playing the first card in card-game; this card; chief part in a play or other performance; its player. **~ up to,** serve as introduction to or preparation for; direct conversation towards. **leading article,** newspaper article giving the editor's opinions. **leading question,** one worded so that it prompts the desired answer.

lead² /led/ *n.* heavy grey metal; graphite as the writing-substance in a pencil; lump of lead used for sounding depths; (*pl.*) strips of lead. **swing the ~,** (*sl.*) pretend to be ill in order to avoid work.

leaden /ˈle-/ *a.* made of lead; heavy, slow as if weighted with lead; dark grey.

leader *n.* person or thing that leads; leading article. **leadership** *n.*

leaf *n.* flat (usu. green) organ growing from the stem, branch, or root of a plant; single thickness of paper as a page of a book; very thin sheet of metal; hinged flap or extra section of a table. —*v.i.* **~ through,** turn over the leaves of (a book). **~-mould** *n.* soil or compost consisting of decayed leaves.

leafless *a.* having no leaves.

leaflet *n.* small leaf of a plant; printed sheet of paper giving information.

leafy *a.* with many leaves.

league[1] *n.* (*old use*) measure of travelling-distance, about 3 miles.

league[2] *n.* union of people or countries; association of sports clubs which compete against each other for a championship; class of contestants. —*v.i.* form a league. **in ~ with,** allied or conspiring with.

leak *n.* hole through which liquid or gas makes its way wrongly; liquid etc. passing through this; process of leaking; similar escape of an electric charge; disclosure of secret information. —*v.t./i.* escape or let out from a container; disclose; become known. **leakage** *n.*, **leaky** *a.*

lean[1] *a.* (-er, -est) without much flesh; (of meat) with little or no fat; scanty. —*n.* lean part of meat. **leanness** *n.*

lean[2] *v.t./i.* (p.t. *leaned*, p.p. *leant*) put or be in a sloping position; rest against for support; depend on for help. **~ on,** (*colloq.*) seek to influence by intimidating. **~-to** *n.* shed etc. abutting against the side of a building.

leaning *n.* inclination, preference.

leap *v.t./i.* (p.t. *leaped*, p.p. *leapt*) jump vigorously. —*n.* vigorous jump. **~ year,** year with an extra day (29 Feb.).

leap-frog *n.* game in which each player in turn vaults over another who is bending down. —*v.t./i.* (p.t. *-frogged*) perform this vault (over); overtake alternately.

learn *v.t./i.* (p.t. *learned* or *learnt*) gain knowledge of or skill in; become aware of; (*joc.* or *incorrect*) teach. **learner** *n.*

learned /-nɪd/ *a.* having or showing great learning.

learning *n.* knowledge obtained by study.

lease *n.* contract allowing the use of land or a building for a specified time. —*v.t.* allow, obtain, or hold by lease. **leasehold** *n.*, **leaseholder** *n.*

leash *n.* dog's lead; thong for holding hounds under restraint. —*v.t.* hold on a leash.

least *a.* smallest in amount or degree; lowest in importance. —*n.* least amount etc. —*adv.* in the least degree.

leather *n.* material made from animal skins by tanning or a similar process; piece of soft leather for polishing with.

leathery *a.* tough as leather.

leave *v.t./i.* (p.t. *left*) go away (from); go away finally or permanently; let remain; deposit; entrust with; abandon. —*n.* permission; official permission to be absent from duty, period for which this lasts. **on ~,** absent in this way. **take one's ~,** say farewell and go away.

leaven /ˈle-/ *n.* substance (e.g. yeast) used to produce fermentation in dough; enlivening influence. —*v.t.* add leaven to; enliven.

leavings *n.pl.* what is left.

lecher *n.* lecherous man.

lechery *n.* unrestrained indulgence in sexual lust. **lecherous** *a.*

lectern *n.* stand with a sloping top to hold a Bible etc. to be read from.

lecture *n.* speech giving information about a subject; lengthy reproof or warning. —*v.t./i.* give lecture(s); give a lengthy reproof etc. to. **lecturer** *n.*, **lectureship** *n.*

led *see* **lead**[1].

ledge *n.* narrow horizontal projection; narrow shelf.

ledger *n.* book used as an account-book or to record trading transactions.

lee *n.* sheltered side, shelter in this.

leech *n.* small blood-sucking worm.

leek *n.* plant related to the onion, with a cylindrical white bulb.

leer *v.i.* look slyly or maliciously or lustfully. —*n.* leering look.

lees *n.pl.* sediment in wine.

leeward /ˈli-, *nautical pr.* ˈlu-/ *a. & n.* (on) the side away from the wind.

leeway *n.* ship's sideways drift from its course. **make up ~,** make up one's lost time or position.

left[1] *see* **leave**. **~-overs** *n.pl.* things remaining when the rest is finished.

left[2] *a. & adv.* of, on, or to the side or region opposite right. —*n.* left side or region; left hand or foot; people supporting a more extreme form of socialism than others in their group. **~-handed** *a.* using the left hand.

leftist *a. & n.* (member) of the left wing of a political party.

leg *n.* one of the limbs on which an animal stands or moves; part of a garment covering a person's leg; projecting support of piece of furniture; one section of a journey or contest; side of a cricket field opposite the off side and behind the batsman. —*v.t.* (p.t. *legged*) **~ it,** (*colloq.*) walk or run rapidly, go on foot. **~-pull** *n.* (*colloq.*) hoax.

legacy *n.* thing left to someone in a will, or handed down by a predecessor.

legal *a.* of or based on law; authorized or required by law. **legally** *adv.*, **legality** *n.*

legalize *v.t.* make legal.

legate /-ət/ *n.* envoy.

legatee *n.* recipient of a legacy.

legation *n.* diplomatic minister and his staff; their headquarters.

legend *n.* story handed down from the past; such stories collectively; inscription on a coin or medal.

legendary *a.* of or described in legend; (*colloq.*) famous.

leger /ˈledʒ-/ *a.* **~ line,** short line added to a musical staff for notes above or below it.

legerdemain /ledʒədəˈmeɪn/ *n.* sleight of hand.

leggings *n.pl.* protective coverings for the legs from knee to ankle.

legible *a.* clear enough to be deciphered, readable. **legibly** *adv.*, **legibility** *n.*

legion *n.* division of the ancient Roman army; organized group; multitude.

legislate *v.i.* make laws.

legislation *n.* legislating; law(s) made.

legislative *a.* making laws.

legislator *n.* member of a legislature.

legislature *n.* country's legislative assembly.

legitimate *a.* in accordance with a law or rule; justifiable; born of parents married to each other. **legitimately** *adv.*, **legitimacy** *n.*

legitimize *v.t.* make legitimate.

legless *a.* without legs.

legume /ˈleg-/ *n.* leguminous plant; pod of this.

leguminous *a.* of the family of plants bearing seeds in pods.

leisure *n.* time free from work, in which one can do what one chooses. **at one's ~,** when one has time.

leisured *a.* having plenty of leisure.

leisurely *a. & adv.* without hurry.

lemming *n.* mouse-like rodent of arctic regions (said to rush headlong into the sea in its migration, and drown).

lemon *n.* oval fruit with acid juice; tree bearing it; its pale yellow colour. **lemony** *a.*

lemonade *n.* lemon-flavoured soft drink.

lemur /ˈliːmə(r)/ *n.* monkey-like animal of Madagascar.

lend *v.t.* (p.t. *lent*) give or allow to use temporarily; provide (money) temporarily in return for payment of interest; contribute as a help or effect. **~ itself to,** be suitable for. **lender** *n.*

length *n.* measurement or extent from end to end; great extent; piece (of cloth etc.). **at ~,** after or taking a long time.

lengthen *v.t./i.* make or become longer.

lengthways *adv.* in the direction of thing's length. **lengthwise** *adv. & a.*

lengthy *a.* (-ier, -iest) very long; long and boring. **lengthily** *adv.*

lenient *a.* merciful, not punishing severely. **leniently** *adv.*, **lenience** *n.*

lens *n.* piece of glass or similar substance shaped for use in an optical instrument; transparent part of the eye, behind the pupil.

lent *see* **lend.**

Lent *n.* Christian period of fasting and repentance, the 40 weekdays before Easter. **Lenten** *a.*

lentil *n.* a kind of bean.

leonine *a.* of or like a lion.

leopard *n.* large flesh-eating animal of the cat family, with a dark-spotted yellowish or a black coat. **leopardess** *n.fem.*

leotard /ˈliːəʊ-/ *n.* close-fitting garment worn by acrobats etc.

leper *n.* person with leprosy.

leprechaun *n.* (in Irish folklore) elf resembling a little old man.

leprosy *n.* infectious disease affecting the skin and nerves and causing deformities. **leprous** *a.*

lesbian *n.* homosexual woman. —*a.* **lesbianism** *n.*

lesion *n.* harmful change in the tissue of an organ of the body.

less *a.* not so much of; smaller in amount or degree. —*adv.* to a smaller extent. —*n.* smaller amount. —*prep.* minus, deducting.

lessee *n.* person holding property by lease.

lessen *v.t./i.* make or become less.

lesser *a.* not so great as the other.

lesson *n.* thing to be learnt by a pupil; amount of teaching given at one time; experience by which one can learn; passage from the Bible read aloud in church.

lessor *n.* person who lets property on lease.

lest *conj.* (for fear) that.

let[1] *n.* stoppage.

let[2] *v.t./i.* (p.t. *let*, pres.p. *letting*) allow or cause to; allow or cause to come, go, or pass; allow the use of (rooms or land) in return for payment. —*v.aux.* (used in requests, commands, assumptions, or challenges). —*n.* letting of property etc. **~ alone,** refrain from interfering with or doing; not to mention. **~ down,** let out air from (a balloon, tyre, etc.); fail to support, disappoint. **~-down** *n.* disappointment. **~ in for,** involve in. **~ off,** fire (a gun); cause to explode; ignite (a firework); excuse from; give little or no punishment to. **~ on,** (*sl.*) reveal a secret. **~ up,** (*colloq.*) relax. **~-up** *n.*

lethal *a.* causing death.

lethargy *n.* extreme lack of energy or vitality. **lethargic** *a.*, **lethargically** *adv.*

letter *n.* symbol representing a speech-sound; written message, usu. sent by post; strict interpretation (of a law etc.). —*v.t./i.* inscribe letters (on). **~-box** *n.* slit in a door, with a movable flap, through which letters are delivered; post-box.

letterhead *n.* printed heading on stationery; stationery with this.

lettuce *n.* plant with broad crisp leaves used as salad.

leucocyte *n.* white blood-cell.

leukaemia *n.* disease in which white corpuscles multiply uncontrollably.

Levant /lɪˈvæ-/ *n.* countries and islands of the eastern Mediterranean. **Levantine** /ˈlevəntaɪn/ *a. & n.*

level *a.* horizontal; without projections or hollows; on a level with; steady, uniform. —*n.* horizontal line or plane; device for testing this; measured height or value etc.; relative position; level surface or area. —*v.t./i.* (p.t. *levelled*) make or become level; knock down (a building); aim (a gun, missile, or accusation etc.). **~ crossing,** place where a road and railway cross at the same level. **~-headed** *a.* mentally well-balanced, sensible. **leveller** *n.*

lever *n.* bar pivoted on a fixed point to lift something; pivoted handle used to operate machinery. —*v.t./i.* use a lever; lift by this.

leverage *n.* action or power of a lever; power, influence.

leveret /ˈlev-/ *n.* young hare.

leviathan /lɪˈvaɪ-/ *n.* thing of enormous size and power.

levitate *v.t./i.* rise or cause to rise and float in the air. **levitation** *n.*

levity *n.* humorous attitude.

levy *v.t.* impose (payment) or collect (an army etc.) by authority or force. —*n.* levying; payment levied.

lewd *a.* (-er, -est) indecent, treating sexual

matters vulgarly; lascivious. **lewdly** *adv.*, **lewdness** *n.*

lexicography *n.* process of compiling a dictionary. **lexicographer** *n.*

lexicon *n.* dictionary, esp. of Greek.

liability *n.* being liable; (*colloq.*) disadvantage; (*pl.*) debts, obligations.

liable *a.* held responsible by law, legally obliged to pay a tax or penalty etc.; likely to do or suffer something.

liaise *v.i.* (*colloq.*) act as liaison.

liaison *n.* communication and co-operation; person who acts as a link or go-between.

liar *n.* person who tells lies.

libel *n.* published false statement that damages a person's reputation; act of publishing it. —*v.t.* (p.t. *libelled*) publish a libel against. **libellous** *a.*

liberal *a.* generous; tolerant. **liberally** *adv.*, **liberality** *n.*

Liberal *a. & n.* (member) of the U.K. political party favouring moderate reforms. **Liberalism** *n.*

liberalize *v.t.* make less strict. **liberalization** *n.*

liberate *v.t.* set free, esp. from oppression. **liberation** *n.*, **liberator** *n.*

libertine /-tin/ *n.* man who lives an irresponsible immoral life.

liberty *n.* freedom. **take the ~,** venture. **take liberties,** behave with undue freedom or familiarity.

libido /-'bid-/ *n.* (pl. *-os*) emotional energy or urge, esp. of sexual desire.

librarian *n.* person in charge of or assisting in a library.

library *n.* collection of books for consulting or borrowing; room or building containing these; similar collection of records, films, etc.

libretto *n.* (pl. *-os*) words of opera or other long musical work.

lice *see* **louse**.

licence *n.* official permit to own or do something; permission; disregard of rules etc.

license *v.t.* grant a licence to or for.

licensee *n.* holder of a licence.

licentiate *n.* holder of a certificate of competence in a profession.

licentious /-'senʃəs/ *a.* sexually immoral. **licentiousness** *n.*

lichen /'laɪkən/ *n.* dry-looking plant that grows on rocks etc.

lich-gate *n.* roofed gateway to a churchyard.

lick *v.t./i.* pass the tongue over; (of waves or flame) touch lightly; (*sl.*) defeat. —*n.* act of licking; blow with a stick etc.; slight application (of paint etc.); (*sl.*) fast pace. **~ into shape,** make presentable or efficient.

lid *n.* hinged or removable cover for a box, pot, etc.; eyelid.

lido /'lid-/ *n.* (pl. *-os*) public open-air swimming-pool or beach.

lie[1] *n.* statement the speaker knows to be untrue. —*v.i.* (p.t. *lied*, pres.p. *lying*) tell lie(s). **give the ~ to,** show to be untrue.

lie[2] *v.t./i.* (p.t. *lay*, p.p. *lain*, pres.p. *lying*) have or put one's body in a flat or resting position

on a surface; be at rest on something; be in a specified state; be situated; exist; be admissible or able to be upheld as a lawsuit or appeal. —*n.* way a thing lies. **~ low,** conceal oneself or one's intentions.

liege *n.* (*old use*) vassal, subject; feudal lord.

lieu /lju/ *n.* **in ~,** instead.

lieutenant /lef'ten-/ *n.* army officer next below captain; naval officer next below lieutenant-commander; rank just below a specified officer; chief assistant.

life *n.* (pl. *lives*) being alive, animals' and plants' ability to function and grow; period of this; living things; liveliness; activities or manner of living; biography. **~ cycle,** series of forms into which a living thing changes. **~-guard** *n.* expert swimmer employed to rescue bathers who are in danger. **~-jacket** *n.* jacket of buoyant material to keep a person afloat. **~-preserver** *n.* short heavy stick as a defensive weapon; lifebelt, life-jacket. **~-size, ~-sized** *adjs.* of the same size etc. as a real person.

lifebelt *n.* belt of buoyant material to keep a person afloat.

lifeboat *n.* boat constructed for going to help people in danger on the sea near a coast; ship's boat for emergency use.

lifebuoy *n.* buoyant device to keep a person afloat.

lifeless *a.* without life; dead; unconscious; lacking liveliness.

lifelike *n.* exactly like a real person or thing.

lifeline *n.* rope etc. used in rescue; vital means of communication.

lifelong *a.* for all one's life.

lifetime *n.* duration of a person's life.

lift *v.t./i.* raise; take up; rise, (of fog etc.) disperse; remove (restrictions) (*colloq.*) steal. —*n.* lifting; apparatus for transporting people or goods from one level to another, esp. in a building; free ride in a motor vehicle; feeling of elation. **~-off** *n.* vertical take-off of a spacecraft etc.

ligament *n.* tough flexible tissue holding bones together.

ligature *n.* thing that ties something, esp. in surgical operations.

light[1] *n.* thing that stimulates sight, a kind of radiation; brightness, light part of a picture etc.; source of light, electric lamp; flame or spark; enlightenment; aspect, way a thing appears to the mind. —*a.* full of light, not in darkness; pale. —*v.t./i.* (p.t. *lit* or *lighted*) set burning, begin to burn; provide with light; brighten. **bring to ~,** reveal. **come to ~,** be revealed. **~ up,** put lights on at dusk; brighten; make or become animated; begin to smoke a pipe or cigar or cigarette. **~-year** *n.* distance light travels in one year, about 6 million million miles.

light[2] *a.* (*-er*, *-est*) having little weight; not heavy, easy to lift or carry or do; of less than average weight or force or intensity; cheerful; not profound or serious; (of food) easy to digest. —*adv.* lightly, with little load.

∼-fingered a. apt to steal. **∼-headed** a. feeling slightly faint; delirious. **∼-hearted** a. cheerful. **make ∼ of**, treat as unimportant. **lightly** adv., **lightness** n.

light³ v.i. (p.t. *lit.* or *lighted*) **∼ on**, find accidentally. **∼ out**, (sl.) depart.

lighten¹ v.t./i. shed light on; make or become brighter; flash with lightning.

lighten² v.t./i. make or become less heavy.

lighter¹ n. device for lighting cigarettes and cigars.

lighter² n. flat-bottomed boat for transporting goods between ship and wharf. **lighterman** n.

lighthouse n. tower with a beacon light to warn or guide ships.

lighting n. means of providing light; the light itself.

lightning n. flash of bright light produced from cloud by natural electricity. —a. very quick. **like ∼**, with very great speed.

lights n.pl. lungs of certain animals, used as animal food.

lightship n. moored or anchored ship with a beacon light, serving as a lighthouse.

lightweight a. not having great weight or influence. —n. lightweight person; boxing-weight (60 kg).

like¹ a. having the qualities or appearance of; characteristic of; in a suitable state or right mood for. —prep. in the manner of, to the same degree as. —conj. (colloq.) as; (U.S.) as if. —adv. (colloq.) likely. —n. person or thing like another. **∼-minded** a. having similar tastes or opinions.

like² v.t. find pleasant or satisfactory; wish for. **likes** n.pl. things one likes or prefers.

likeable a. pleasant, easy to like.

likelihood n. probability.

likely a. (-ier, -iest) such as may reasonably be expected to occur or be true; seeming to be suitable or have a chance of success. —adv. probably. **not ∼**, (colloq.) certainly not. **likeliness** n.

liken v.t. point out the likeness of (one thing to another).

likeness n. being like; copy, portrait.

likewise adv. also; in the same way.

liking n. what one likes; one's feeling that one likes a thing.

lilac n. shrub with fragrant purple or white flowers; pale purple. —a. pale purple.

lilliputian /-'pjuː-/ a. very small.

lilt n. light pleasant rhythm; song with this. **lilting** a.

lily n. plant growing from a bulb, with large white or reddish flowers.

limb n. projecting part of an animal body, used in movement or in grasping things; large branch of a tree; mischievous child. **out on a ∼**, isolated.

limber a. flexible, supple. —v.t./i. **∼ up**, exercise in preparation for athletic activity.

limbo¹ n. intermediate inactive or neglected state.

limbo² n. (pl. -os) West Indian dance in which the dancer bends back to pass below a bar.

lime¹ n. white substance used in making cement etc.

lime² n. round yellowish-green fruit like a lemon; its colour.

lime³ n. tree with heart-shaped leaves. **∼-tree** n.

limelight n. great publicity.

limerick n. a type of humorous poem with five lines.

limestone n. a kind of rock from which lime is obtained.

limit n. point beyond which something does not continue; greatest amount allowed. —v.t./i. set or serve as a limit, keep within limits. **limitation** n.

limousine n. luxurious car.

limp¹ v.i. walk or proceed lamely. —n. limping walk.

limp² a. (-er, -est) not stiff or firm; wilting. **limply** adv., **limpness** n.

limpet n. small shellfish that sticks tightly to rocks.

limpid a. (of liquids) clear.

linchpin n. pin passed through the end of an axle to secure a wheel; person or thing vital to something.

linctus n. soothing cough-medicine.

linden n. lime-tree.

line¹ n. long narrow mark; outline; boundary; one of a set of military fieldworks; row of people or things; row of words on a page or in a poem; brief letter; service of ships, buses, or aircraft; series, several generations of a family; direction, course; railway track; type of activity, business, or goods; piece of cord for a particular purpose; electrical or telephone cable, connection by this; *the L∼*, the equator. —v.t. mark with lines; arrange in line(s). **get a ∼ on**, (colloq.) discover information about. **in ∼ with**, in accordance with.

line² v.t. cover the inside surface of. **∼ one's pockets**, make money, esp. in underhand or dishonest ways.

lineage /'lɪnɪɪdʒ/ n. line of ancestors or descendants.

lineal a. of or in a line.

lineaments n.pl. features of the face.

linear a. of a line, of length; arranged in a line.

linen n. cloth made of flax; household articles (e.g. sheets, table-cloths) formerly made of this.

liner¹ n. ship or aircraft of a regular line.

liner² n. removable lining.

linesman n. (pl. -men) umpire's assistant at the boundary line; workman who tests railway lines or repairs electrical or telephone cables.

ling¹ n. a kind of heather.

ling² n. sea-fish of north Europe.

linger v.i. stay on as if reluctant to leave; dawdle.

lingerie /'læ̃ʒəri/ n. women's underwear.

lingo n. (pl. -oes) (joc. or derog.) language.

lingua franca language used between people of an area where several languages are spoken.

linguist n. person who knows foreign languages well.

linguistic *a.* of language.

linguistics *n.* study of languages and their structure.

liniment *n.* embrocation.

lining *n.* layer of material or substance covering an inner surface.

link *n.* one ring of a chain; person or thing connecting others. —*v.t.* connect; intertwine. **linkage** *n.*

links *n.* or *n.pl.* golf-course.

linnet *n.* a kind of finch.

lino *n.* linoleum.

linocut *n.* design cut in relief on a block of linoleum; print made from this.

linoleum *n.* a kind of smooth covering for floors.

linseed *n.* seed of flax.

lint *n.* soft fabric for dressing wounds; fluff.

lintel *n.* horizontal timber or stone over a doorway etc.

lion *n.* large flesh-eating animal of the cat family. **~'s share,** largest part. **lioness** *n.fem.*

lionize *v.t.* treat as a celebrity.

lip *n.* either of the fleshy edges of the mouth-opening; edge of a container or opening; slight projection shaped for pouring from. **~-read** *v.t./i.* understand (what is said) from movements of a speaker's lips. **pay ~-service,** state approval insincerely. **lipped** *a.*

lipsalve *n.* ointment for the lips.

lipstick *n.* cosmetic for colouring the lips; stick of this.

liquefy *v.t./i.* make or become liquid. **liquefaction** *n.*

liqueur /lɪˈkjʊə(r)/ *n.* strong alcoholic spirit with fragrant flavouring.

liquid *n.* flowing substance like water or oil. —*a.* in the form of liquid; (of sound) flowing pleasantly; (of assets) easy to convert into cash. **liquidity** *n.*

liquidate *v.t.* pay and settle (a debt); close down (a business) and divide its assets between creditors; get rid of, esp. by killing. **liquidation** *n.*, **liquidator** *n.*

liquidize *v.t.* reduce to a liquid state. **liquidizer** *n.*

liquor *n.* alcoholic drink; juice from cooked food.

liquorice *n.* black substance used in medicine and as a sweet; plant from whose root it is made.

lira *n.* (pl. *lire*, pr. ˈlɪəreɪ) unit of money in Italy and Turkey.

lisle *n.* fine smooth cotton thread used esp. for stockings.

lisp *n.* speech defect in which *s* and *z* are pronounced like *th.* —*v.t./i.* speak or utter with a lisp.

lissom *a.* lithe.

list¹ *n.* written or printed series of names, items, figures, etc. —*v.t.* make a list of; enter in a list. **enter the lists,** make or accept a challenge in a controversy etc.

list² *v.i.* (of a ship) lean over to one side. —*n.* listing position.

listen *v.i.* make an effort to hear something; pay attention; be persuaded by advice or a request. **~ in,** overhear a conversation; listen to a broadcast. **listener** *n.*

listless *a.* without energy or enthusiasm. **listlessly** *adv.*, **listlessness** *n.*

lit *see* **light**¹, **light**³.

litany *n.* a set form of prayer.

litchi /ˈliːtʃiː/ *n.* (pl. *-is*) fruit with sweet white pulp in a thin brown shell; tree bearing this.

literacy *n.* being literate.

literal *a.* taking the primary meaning of a word or words, not a metaphorical or exaggerated one. **literally** *adv.*, **literalness** *n.*

literary *a.* of literature.

literate *a.* able to read and write.

literature *n.* writings, esp. great novels, poetry, and plays.

lithe *a.* supple, agile.

lithograph /ˈlɪθə-/ *n.* picture printed by lithography.

lithography /-ˈθɒg-/ *n.* printing from a design on a smooth surface. **lithographic** *a.*

litigant *n.* person involved in or initiating a lawsuit.

litigation *n.* lawsuit(s).

litmus *n.* blue colouring-matter that is turned red by acids and restored to blue by alkalis. **~-paper** *n.* paper stained with this.

litre *n.* metric unit of capacity (about 1¾ pints) for measuring liquids.

litter *n.* rubbish left lying about; straw etc. put down as bedding for animals; young animals born at one birth. —*v.t.* scatter as litter; make untidy by litter; give birth to (a litter of young).

little *a.* small in size, amount, or intensity etc. —*n.* small amount, time, or distance. —*adv.* to a small extent; not at all.

liturgy *n.* set form of public worship used in churches. **liturgical** *a.*

live¹ /laɪv/ *a.* alive; burning; unexploded; charged with electricity; (of broadcasts) transmitted while actually happening, not recorded. **~ wire,** energetic forceful person.

live² /lɪv/ *v.t./i.* have life, remain alive; have one's dwelling-place; conduct (one's life) in a certain way. **~ down,** live until (scandal etc.) is forgotten. **~ it up,** live in a lively extravagant way. **~ on,** keep oneself alive by. **liveable** *a.*

livelihood *n.* means of earning or providing enough food etc. to sustain life.

livelong *a.* **the ~ day,** the whole day.

lively *a.* (*-ier*, *-iest*) full of energy or action. **liveliness** *n.*

liven *v.t./i.* make or become lively.

liver *n.* large organ in the abdomen, secreting bile; animal's liver as food; dark reddish brown.

liveried *a.* wearing livery.

livery *n.* distinctive uniform worn by male servants or by members of the London trade guilds.

livestock *n.* farm animals.

livid *a.* of the colour of lead, bluish-grey; (*colloq.*) furiously angry.

living *a.* having life, not dead; (of rock) not detached from the earth; (of likeness) exact. —*n.* being alive; manner of life; livelihood. **~-room** *n.* room for general daytime use.

lizard *n.* reptile with four legs and a long tail.

llama *n.* South American animal related to the camel but with no hump.

lo *int.* (*old use*) see.

loach *n.* small freshwater fish.

load *n.* thing or quantity carried; amount of electric current supplied by a generating station or carried by a circuit; burden of responsibility or worry; (*pl.*, *colloq.*) plenty. —*v.t./i.* put a load in or on; receive a load; fill heavily; weight; put ammunition into (a gun) or film into (a camera). **loader** *n.*

loaf¹ *n.* (pl. *loaves*) mass of bread shaped in one piece; (*sl.*) head.

loaf² *v.i.* spend time idly, stand or saunter about. **loafer** *n.*

loam *n.* rich soil. **loamy** *a.*

loan *n.* lending; thing lent, esp. money. —*v.t.* (*colloq.*) lend.

loath *a.* unwilling.

loathe *v.t.* feel hatred and disgust for. **loathing** *n.*, **loathsome** *a.*

lob *v.t.* (p.t. *lobbed*) send or strike (a ball) slowly in a high arc. —*n.* lobbed ball.

lobar /ˈləʊ-/ *a.* of a lobe, esp. of the lung.

lobby *n.* porch, entrance-hall, ante-room; body of people lobbying an M.P. or seeking to influence legislation. —*v.t.* seek to persuade (an M.P.) to support one's cause.

lobe *n.* rounded part or projection; lower soft part of the ear.

lobelia *n.* low-growing garden plant used esp. for edging.

lobster *n.* large shellfish that turns scarlet when boiled; its flesh as food. **~-pot** *n.*

local *a.* of or affecting a particular place or small area. —*n.* inhabitant of a particular district; (*colloq.*) public house of a neighbourhood. **~ colour**, details added to a story etc. to give a realistic background. **~ government**, administration of a district by elected representatives of people who live there. **locally** *adv.*

locale /-ˈkɑl/ *n.* scene of event.

locality *n.* thing's position; site, neighbourhood.

localized *a.* local not general, confined within an area.

locate *v.t.* discover the position of; situate in a particular location.

location *n.* locating; place where a thing is situated. **on ~**, (of filming) in a suitable environment, not in a film studio.

loch /lox/ *n.* (*Sc.*) lake, arm of the sea.

lock¹ *n.* portion of hair that hangs together; (*pl.*) hair.

lock² *n.* device (able to be opened by a key) for fastening a door or lid etc.; mechanism for exploding a charge in a gun; gated section of a canal where the water-level can be changed; secure hold; interlocking; turning of a vehicle's front wheels by use of the steering-wheel. —*v.t./i.* fasten with a lock; shut into a locked place; store inaccessibly; make or become rigidly fixed. **~ out,** shut out by locking a door. **~-out** *n.* employer's procedure of locking out employees during a dispute. **~-up** *n.* lockable premises; room or building where prisoners can be detained temporarily.

lockable *a.* able to be locked.

locker *n.* small cupboard or compartment where things can be stowed securely.

locket *n.* small ornamental case worn on a chain round the neck.

lockjaw *n.* form of tetanus in which the jaws become rigidly closed.

locksmith *n.* maker and mender of locks.

locomotion *n.* ability to move from place to place.

locomotive *n.* railway engine. —*a.* of locomotion.

locum *n.* doctor or clergyman deputizing for one who is absent.

locus *n.* (pl. *-ci*, pr. *-saɪ*) thing's exact place; line or curve etc. formed by certain points or by the movement of a point or line.

locust *n.* a kind of grasshopper that devours vegetation.

locution *n.* word or phrase.

lode *n.* vein of metal ore.

lodestar *n.* star (esp. the pole-star) used as a guide in navigation.

lodge *n.* small country house, esp. at the entrance to a park etc.; porter's room at the entrance to a building; members or meeting-place of a branch of certain societies; beaver's or otter's lair. —*v.t./i.* provide with sleeping-quarters or temporary accommodation; live as a lodger; deposit; be or become embedded.

lodger *n.* person paying for accommodation in another's house.

lodging *n.* place where one lodges; (*pl.*) room(s) rented for living in.

loft *n.* space under the roof of a house, stable, or barn; gallery in a church etc. —*v.t.* hit (a ball) in a high arc.

lofty *a.* (*-ier*, *-iest*) very tall; noble; haughty. **loftily** *adv.*

log¹ *n.* piece cut from a trunk or branch of a tree; device for gauging a ship's speed; log-book, entry in this. —*v.t.* (p.t. *logged*) enter (facts) in a log-book. **~-book** *n.* book in which details of a voyage or journey are recorded. **~-rolling** *n.* unprincipled assistance to each other's progress.

log² *n.* logarithm.

loganberry *n.* large dark-red fruit resembling a blackberry.

logarithm *n.* one of a series of numbers set out in tables, used to simplify calculations. **logarithmic** *a.*

loggerheads *n.pl.* **at ~**, disagreeing or quarrelling.

loggia /ˈlodʒjə/ *n.* open-sided gallery or arcade.

logging *n.* (*U.S.*) work of cutting down forest trees for timber.

logic *n.* science or method of reasoning; correct reasoning.

logical *a.* of or according to logic; reasonable; reasoning correctly. **logically** *adv.*, **logicality** *n.*

logistics /-ˈdʒɪ-/ *n.* organization of supplies and services.

logo /ˈləʊ-/ *n.* (pl. *-os*) printed design used as an emblem.

loin *n.* side and back of the body between ribs and hip-bone.

loiter *v.i.* linger, stand about idly. **loiterer** *n.*

loll *v.i.* stand, sit, or rest lazily; hang loosely.

lollipop *n.* large usu. flat boiled sweet on a small stick.

lollop *v.i.* (p.t. *lolloped*) (*colloq.*) flop; move in clumsy bounds.

lolly *n.* (*colloq.*) lollipop; (*Austral.*) sweet; (*sl.*) money.

Londoner *n.* native or inhabitant of London.

lone *a.* solitary.

lonely *a.* solitary; sad because lacking friends or companions; not much frequented. **loneliness** *n.*

loner *n.* person who prefers not to associate with others.

lonesome *a.* lonely.

long[1] *a.* (*-er*, *-est*) of great or specified length. *—adv.* for a long time; throughout a specified time. **as** *or* **so ~ as**, provided that. **~-distance** *a.* travelling or operated between distant places. **~ face**, dismal expression. **~ johns**, (*colloq.*) underpants or knickers with long legs. **~-lived** *a.* living or lasting for a long time. **~ odds**, very uneven odds. **~-playing record**, one playing for about 10 to 30 minutes on each side. **~-range** *a.* having a relatively long range; relating to a long period of future time. **~-shore** *a.* found or employed on the shore. **~ shot**, wild guess or venture. **~-sighted** *a.* able to see clearly only what is at a distance. **~-standing** *a.* having existed for a long time. **~-suffering** *a.* bearing provocation patiently. **~-term** *a.* of or for a long period. **~ ton** (see *ton*). **~ wave**, radio wave of more than 1000 metres wavelength. **~-winded** *a.* talking or writing at tedious length.

long[2] *v.i.* feel a longing.

longevity /-ˈdʒev-/ *n.* long life.

longhand *n.* ordinary writing, not shorthand or typing etc.

longhorn *n.* one of a breed of cattle with long horns.

longing *n.* intense persistent wish.

longitude /ˈlɒndʒ-/ *n.* distance east or west (measured in degrees on a map) from the Greenwich meridian.

longitudinal /lɒndʒɪ-/ *a.* of longitude; of length, lengthwise. **longitudinally** *adv.*

loo *n.* (*colloq.*) lavatory.

loofah *n.* dried pod of a gourd, used as a rough sponge.

look *v.t./i.* use or direct one's eyes in order to see, search, or examine; face; seem. *—n.* act of looking; inspection, search; appearance. **~ after,** take care of; attend to. **~ down on,** despise. **~ forward to,** await eagerly. **~ in,** make a short visit; (*colloq.*) watch television. **~-in** *n.* chance of participation. **~ into,** investigate. **~ on,** be a spectator. **~ out,** be vigilant; select by inspection. **~-out** *n.* watch; watcher; observation-post; prospect; person's own concern. **~ up,** search for information about; improve in prospects; go to visit. **~ up to,** admire and respect.

looker-on *n.* (pl. *lookers-on*) mere spectator.

looking-glass *n.* mirror.

loom[1] *n.* apparatus for weaving cloth.

loom[2] *v.i.* appear, esp. close at hand or with a threatening aspect.

loon *n.* a kind of diving-bird.

loony *n.* (*sl.*) lunatic. *—a.* (*sl.*) crazy. **~-bin** *n.* (*sl.*) mental institution.

loop *n.* curve that is U-shaped or crosses itself; thing shaped like this, esp. length of cord or wire etc. fastened at the crossing. *—v.t./i.* form into loop(s); fasten or join with loop(s); enclose in a loop. **~ the loop,** fly in a vertical circle, turning upside down between climb and dive.

loophole *n.* narrow opening in the wall of a fort etc.; means of evading a rule or contract.

loose *a.* (*-er*, *-est*) not tied or restrained; not rigidly fixed or held together; not held or packed or contained in something; slack; not closely packed; inexact, approximate; promiscuous. *—adv.* loosely. *—v.t.* release; untie, loosen. **at a ~ end,** without a definite occupation. **~ box,** stall in which a horse can move about. **~-leaf** *a.* with each page separate and removable. **loosely** *adv.*, **looseness** *n.*

loosen *v.t./i.* make or become loose or looser.

loot *n.* goods taken from an enemy or by theft. *—v.t./i.* take loot (from); take as loot. **looter** *n.*

lop *v.t.* (p.t. *lopped*) cut branches or twigs of; cut off.

lope *v.i.* run with a long bounding stride. *—n.* this stride.

lop-eared *a.* with drooping ears.

lopsided *a.* with one side lower, smaller, or heavier than the other.

loquacious *a.* talkative. **loquaciously** *adv.*, **loquacity** *n.*

lord *n.* master, ruler; nobleman; title of certain peers or high officials; *the Lord*, God; *Our Lord*, Christ. *—v.t.* domineer. **Lord's Supper,** Eucharist.

lordly *a.* suitable for a lord; haughty, imperious.

lordship *n.* title used of or to a man with the rank of *Lord*.

lore *n.* body of traditions and knowledge.

lorgnette /-ˈnjet/ *n.* eye-glasses or opera-glasses held to the eyes on a long handle.

lorry *n.* large strong motor vehicle for transporting heavy loads.

lose *v.t./i.* (p.t. *lost*) cease to have or maintain; become unable to find or follow; fail to obtain or catch; get rid of; be defeated in a contest etc.; suffer loss (of); cause loss of; (of a clock) become slow. **loser** *n.*

loss *n.* losing; person or thing or amount etc.

lost; disadvantage caused by losing something. **be at a** ~, be puzzled, not know what to do or say. ~**-leader** n. popular article sold at a loss to attract customers.

lost see lose. —a. strayed or separated from its owner.

lot[1] n. one of a set of objects used in making a selection by methods depending on chance; this method of selecting; choice resulting from it; person's share or destiny; piece of land; item being sold at auction.

lot[2] n. number of people or things of the same kind; (colloq.) large number or amount; much; the ~, the total quantity.

loth a. = loath.

lotion n. medicinal or cosmetic liquid applied to the skin.

lottery n. system of raising money by selling numbered tickets and giving prizes to holders of numbers drawn at random; thing where the outcome is governed by luck.

lotto n. game like bingo but with numbers drawn instead of called.

lotus n. (pl. -uses) tropical water-lily; mythical fruit.

loud a. (-er, -est) producing much noise, easily heard; gaudy. —adv. loudly. ~ **hailer,** electronically operated megaphone. **out** ~, aloud. **loudly** adv., **loudness** n.

loudspeaker n. apparatus (esp. part of a radio) that converts electrical impulses into audible sound.

lough /lox/ n. (Ir.) = loch.

lounge v.i. loll, sit or stand about idly. —n. sitting-room; waiting-room at an airport etc. ~ **suit,** man's ordinary suit for day wear. **lounger** n.

lour /lαʊə(r)/ v.i. scowl; (of the sky) look dark and threatening.

louse n. (pl. lice) small parasitic insect; (pl. louses) contemptible person.

lousy a. (-ier, -iest) infested with lice; (sl.) very bad.

lout n. clumsy ill-mannered young man. **loutish** a.

louvre /ˈluː-/ n. one of a set of overlapping slats arranged to admit air but exclude light or rain. **louvred** a.

lovable a. easy to love.

love n. warm liking or affection; loved person; (in games) no score, nil. —v.t. feel love for; like greatly. **in** ~, feeling (esp. sexual) love for another person. ~ **affair,** romantic or sexual relationship between people who are in love. ~**-bird** n. small parakeet that shows great affection for its mate. ~**-child** n. illegitimate child.

loveless a. without love.

lovelorn a. pining with love.

lovely a. (-ier, -iest) beautiful, attractive; (colloq.) delightful. **loveliness** n.

lover n. person (esp. man) in love with another or having an illicit love affair; one who likes or enjoys something.

lovesick a. languishing because of love.

loving a. feeling or showing love. **lovingly** adv.

low[1] n. deep sound made by cattle. —v.i. make this sound.

low[2] a. (-er, -est) not high, not extending or lying far up; ranking below others; ignoble, vulgar; less than normal in amount or intensity; with slow vibrations, not loud or shrill; lacking vigour, depressed. —n. low level; area of low pressure. —adv. in, at, or to a low level. **Low Church,** section of the Church of England giving a low place to ritual and the authority of priests. ~**class** a. of low quality or social class. ~**down** a. dishonourable; (n., sl.) true facts. ~**-key** a. restrained, not intense or emotional. ~ **season,** season that is least busy. **Low Sunday,** next Sunday after Easter.

lowbrow a. not intellectual or cultured. —n. lowbrow person.

lower[1] a. & adv. see low[2]. —v.t./i. let or haul down; make or become lower; direct (one's gaze) downwards. ~ **case,** letters (for printing or typing) that are not capitals. ~ **deck,** petty officers and lower ranks.

lower[2] v.i. = lour.

lowlands n.pl. low-lying land. **lowland** a., **lowlander** n.

lowly a. (-ier, -iest) of humble rank or condition. **lowliness** n.

loyal a. firm in one's allegiance. **loyally** adv., **loyalty** n.

loyalist n. person who is loyal, esp. while others revolt.

lozenge n. four-sided diamond-shaped figure; small tablet to be dissolved in the mouth.

Ltd. abbr. Limited.

lubricant n. lubricating substance.

lubricate v.t. oil or grease (machinery etc.). **lubrication** n.

lucerne n. clover-like plant.

lucid a. clearly expressed; sane. **lucidly** adv., **lucidity** n.

luck n. good or bad fortune; chance thought of as a force bringing this.

luckless a. unlucky.

lucky a. (-ier, -iest) having, bringing, or resulting from good luck. **luckily** adv.

lucrative a. producing much money.

lucre n. (derog.) money.

ludicrous a. ridiculous.

ludo n. simple game played with counters on a special board.

luff v.i. bring a ship's head towards the wind.

lug[1] v.t. (p.t. lugged) drag or carry with great effort.

lug[2] n. ear-like projection.

luggage n. suitcases and bags etc. holding a traveller's possessions.

lugubrious /-ˈɡuː-/ a. dismal, mournful. **lugubriously** adv.

lukewarm a. only slightly warm; not enthusiastic.

lull v.t./i. soothe or send to sleep; calm; become quiet. —n. period of quiet or inactivity.

lullaby n. soothing song sung to put a child to sleep.

lumbago *n.* rheumatic pain in muscles of the loins.

lumbar *a.* of or in the loins.

lumber *n.* useless or unwanted articles, esp. furniture; (*U.S.*) timber sawn into planks. —*v.t./i.* encumber; fill up (space) inconveniently; move heavily and clumsily.

lumberjack *n.* (*U.S.*) workman cutting or conveying lumber.

luminescent *a.* emitting light without heat. **luminescence** *n.*

luminous *a.* emitting light, glowing in the dark. **luminosity** *n.*

lump[1] *n.* hard or compact mass; swelling; heavy dull person; (*sl.*) great quantity. —*v.t.* put or consider together, treat as alike. **~ sum,** money paid as a single amount.

lump[2] *v.t.* **~ it,** (*colloq.*) put up with a thing one dislikes.

lumpy *a.* (-*ier*, -*iest*) full of lumps; covered in lumps. **lumpiness** *n.*

lunacy *n.* insanity; great folly.

lunar *a.* of the moon. **~ month,** period between new moons (29½ days), four weeks.

lunatic *n.* person who is insane or very foolish or reckless.

lunch *n.* midday meal; mid-morning snack. —*v.t./i.* eat lunch, entertain to lunch.

luncheon *n.* lunch. **~ meat,** tinned cured meat ready for serving.

lung *n.* either of the pair of breathing-organs in the chest of man and most vertebrates.

lunge /lʌndʒ/ *n.* sudden forward movement of the body; thrust. —*v.i.* make this movement.

lupin *n.* garden plant with tall spikes of flowers.

lurch[1] *n.* **leave in the ~,** leave (a person) in difficulties.

lurch[2] *v.i. & n.* (make) an unsteady swaying movement, stagger.

lurcher *n.* dog that is a cross between a collie and a greyhound.

lure /ljʊə(r)/ *v.t.* entice. —*n.* enticement; bait or decoy to attract wild animals.

lurid *a.* in glaring colours; vivid and sensational or shocking. **luridly** *adv.*, **luridness** *n.*

lurk *v.i.* wait furtively or keeping out of sight; be latent.

luscious *a.* delicious.

lush[1] *a.* (of grass etc.) growing thickly and strongly; luxurious. **lushly** *adv.*, **lushness** *n.*

lush[2] *v.t.* **~ up,** (*sl.*) ply with drink or good food etc. —*n.* (*U.S. sl.*) drunkard.

lust *n.* intense sexual desire; any intense desire. —*v.i.* feel lust. **lustful** *a.*, **lustfully** *adv.*

lustre *n.* soft brightness of a surface; glory; metallic glaze on pottery. **lustrous** *a.*

lusty *a.* (-*ier*, -*iest*) strong and vigorous. **lustily** *adv.*, **lustiness** *n.*

lute *n.* guitar-like instrument of the 14th–17th centuries.

Lutheran *a.* of the Protestant reformer Martin Luther or his teachings.

luxuriant *a.* growing profusely. **luxuriantly** *adv.*, **luxuriance** *n.*

luxuriate *v.i.* feel great enjoyment in something.

luxurious *a.* supplied with luxuries, very comfortable. **luxuriously** *adv.*, **luxuriousness** *n.*

luxury *n.* choice and costly surroundings, food, etc.; self-indulgence; thing that is enjoyable but not essential.

lych /lɪtʃ/ *n.* = lich.

lying *see* lie[1], lie[2].

lymph /lɪmf/ *n.* colourless fluid from body tissue or organs. **lymphatic** *a.*

lynch *v.t.* execute or punish violently by a mob, without trial.

lynx *n.* wild animal of the cat family with spotted fur and keen sight.

lyre *n.* ancient musical instrument with strings in a U-shaped frame. **~-bird** *n.* Australian bird with a lyre-shaped tail.

lyric *a.* of poetry that expresses the poet's thoughts and feelings. —*n.* lyric poem; words of a song.

lyrical *a.* resembling or using language suitable for lyric poetry; (*colloq.*) expressing oneself enthusiastically. **lyrically** *adv.*

M

m. *abbr.* metre(s); mile(s); million(s).

ma *n.* (*vulg.*) mother.

M.A. *abbr.* Master of Arts.

ma'am /mæm/ *n.* madam.

mac *n.* (*colloq.*) mackintosh.

macabre /-ˈkɑbr/ *a.* gruesome.

macadam *n.* layers of broken stone used in road-making.

macadamized *a.* made with macadam.

macaroni *n.* tube-shaped pasta.

macaroon *n.* biscuit or small cake made with ground almonds.

macaw *n.* American parrot.

mace[1] *n.* ceremonial staff carried or placed before an official.

mace[2] *n.* spice made from the dried outer covering of nutmeg.

Mach /mɑk/ *n.* **~ number,** ratio of the speed of a moving body to the speed of sound.

machiavellian /mæk-/ *a.* elaborately cunning or deceitful.

machinations /mæʃ-/ *n.pl.* clever scheming.

machine *n.* apparatus for applying mechanical power; thing (e.g. a bicycle, aircraft) operated by this; controlling system of an organization. —*v.t.* produce or work on with a machine. **~-gun** *n.* mounted mechanically-operated gun that can fire continuously; (*v.t.*) shoot at with this.

machinery *n.* machines; mechanism.

machinist *n.* person who makes or works machinery.

mackerel *n.* (pl. *mackerel*) edible sea-fish.

mackintosh *n.* cloth waterproofed with rubber; raincoat.

macrobiotic *a.* of or involving a diet intended to prolong life.

mad *a.* (*madder*, *maddest*) having a disordered mind, not sane; extremely foolish; wildly enthusiastic; frenzied; (*colloq.*) very annoyed. **like ~,** with great haste or energy or enthusiasm. **madly** *adv.*, **madness** *n.*

madam *n.* polite form of address to a woman.

madcap *a. & n.* wildly impulsive (person).

madden *v.t.* make mad or angry.

made *see* **make.**

madhouse *n.* (*colloq.*) mental institution; scene of confused uproar.

madman *n.* (pl. *-men*) man who is mad.

madonna *n.* picture or statue of the Virgin Mary.

madrigal *n.* part-song for voices.

madwoman *n.* (pl. *-women*) woman who is mad.

maelstrom /ˈmeɪl-/ *n.* great whirlpool.

maestro /ˈmaɪ-/ *n.* (pl. *-i*) great conductor or composer of music; master of any art.

magazine *n.* paper-covered illustrated periodical; store for ammunition, explosives, etc.; chamber holding cartridges in a gun, slides in a projector, etc.

magenta *a. & n.* purplish-red.

maggot *n.* larva, esp. of the bluebottle. **maggoty** *a.*

Magi /ˈmeɪdʒaɪ/ *n.pl.* the 'wise men' from the East who brought offerings to Christ at Bethlehem.

magic *n.* supposed art of controlling things by supernatural power. **magical** *a.*, **magically** *adv.*

magician *n.* person skilled in magic.

magisterial /-ˈtɪər-/ *a.* of a magistrate; imperious. **magisterially** *adv.*

magistrate *n.* official or citizen with authority to hold preliminary hearings and judge minor cases.

magnanimous /-ˈnæn-/ *a.* noble and generous in conduct, not petty. **magnanimously** *adv.*, **magnanimity** *n.*

magnate *n.* wealthy influential person, esp. in business.

magnesia /-ʃə/ *n.* compound of magnesium used in medicine.

magnesium *n.* white metal that burns with an intensely bright flame.

magnet *n.* piece of iron or steel that can attract iron and point north when suspended; thing exerting powerful attraction.

magnetic *a.* having the properties of a magnet; produced or acting by magnetism. **~ tape,** strip of plastic with magnetic particles, used in sound-recording, computers, etc. **magnetically** *adv.*

magnetism *n.* properties and effects of magnetic substances; great charm and attraction.

magnetize *v.t.* make magnetic; attract. **magnetization** *n.*

magneto /-ˈniː-/ *n.* (pl. *-os*) small electric generator using magnets.

magnification *n.* magnifying.

magnificent *a.* splendid in appearance etc.; excellent in quality. **magnificently** *adv.*, **magnificence** *n.*

magnify *v.t.* make (an object) appear larger by use of a lens; exaggerate. **magnifier** *n.*

magnitude *n.* largeness, size; importance.

magnolia *n.* tree with large wax-like white or pink flowers.

magnum *n.* bottle holding two quarts of wine or spirits.

magpie *n.* noisy bird with black-and-white plumage; person who collects objects at random.

Magyar *a. & n.* (member, language) of a people now predominant in Hungary.

maharajah *n.* former title of certain Indian princes.

maharishi /-ˈrɪʃɪ/ *n.* Hindu man of great wisdom.

mahatma *n.* (in India etc.) title of a man regarded with reverence.

mahogany *n.* very hard reddish-brown wood; its colour.

maid *n.* woman servant doing indoor work; (*old use*) maiden.

maiden *n.* (*old use*) girl, young unmarried woman, virgin; *—a.* unmarried; first. **~ name,** woman's family name before she married. **~ over,** over in cricket in which no runs are scored. **maidenly** *adj.*, **maidenhood** *n.*

maidenhair *n.* fern with very thin stalks and delicate foliage.

mail[1] *n.* = post[3]. *—v.t.* send by post. **~ order,** order for goods to be sent by post.

mail[2] *n.* body-armour made of metal rings or chains.

maim *v.t.* wound or injure so that a part of the body is useless.

main *a.* principal, most important, greatest in size or extent. *—n.* main pipe or channel in a public system for conveying water, gas, or (*pl.*) electricity. **in the ~,** for the most part. **mainly** *adv.*

mainland *n.* country or continent without its adjacent islands.

mainspring *n.* chief spring of a watch or clock; chief motivating force.

mainstay *n.* strong cable securing the principal mast; chief support.

mainstream *n.* dominant trend of opinion or style etc.

maintain *v.t.* cause to continue, keep in existence; keep in repair; bear the expenses of; assert as true.

maintenance *n.* process of maintaining something; provision of means to support life, allowance of money for this.

maisonette *n.* small house; part of a house (usu. not all on one floor) used as a separate dwelling.

maize *n.* tall cereal plant bearing grain on large cobs; its grain.

majestic *a.* stately and dignified, imposing. **majestically** *adv.*

majesty *n.* impressive stateliness; sovereign power; title of a king or queen.

major *a.* greater; very important; (of a musical scale) with a semitone above the third and seventh notes. —*n.* army officer next below lieutenant-colonel; officer in charge of a section of band instruments. —*v.i.* (*U.S.*) specialize (in a subject) at college. **~-domo** *n.* (pl. *-os*) head steward of a great household. **~-general** *n.* army officer next below lieutenant-general.

majority *n.* greatest part of a group or class; number by which votes for one party etc. exceed those for the next or for all combined; age when a person legally becomes adult.

make *v.t./i.* (p.t. *made*) form, prepare, produce; cause to exist or be or become; succeed in arriving at or achieving; gain, acquire; reckon to be; compel; perform (an action etc.); ensure the success of. —*n.* making, way a thing is made; manufacture, brand. **~ believe,** pretend. **~-believe** *a.* pretended; (*n.*) pretence. **~ do,** manage with something not fully satisfactory. **~ for,** proceed towards, try to reach; tend to bring about. **~ good,** become successful; fulfil; repair or pay compensation for. **~ love,** embrace in courtship; have sexual intercourse. **~ much of,** treat as important; give much flattering attention to. **~ off,** go away hastily. **~ off with,** carry away, steal. **~ out,** write out (a list etc.); manage to see or understand; assert to be. **~ over,** transfer the ownership of. **~ shift,** = make do. **~ up,** form, constitute; prepare; invent (a story etc.); compensate (for a loss etc.); become reconciled after (a quarrel); complete (an amount) to supply what is lacking; apply cosmetics to. **~-up** *n.* cosmetics applied to the skin esp. of the face; way a thing is made; person's character. **~ up one's mind,** decide. **~ up to,** curry favour with.

maker *n.* one who makes something. **makeshift** *a. & n.* (thing) used as a temporary or improvised substitute.

makeweight *n.* thing or amount added to make up for a deficiency.

making *n.* **be the ~ of,** be the main factor in the success of. **have the makings of,** have the qualities for becoming.

malachite /ˈmæləkaɪt/ *n.* green mineral.

maladjusted *a.* not happily adapted to one's circumstances. **maladjustment** *n.*

maladministration *n.* bad management of business or public affairs.

malady *n.* illness, disease.

malaise /-ˈleɪz/ *n.* feeling of illness or uneasiness.

malapropism /ˈmæl-/ *n.* comical confusion of words.

malaria *n.* disease causing a recurring fever. **malarial** *a.*

Malay *a. & n.* (member, language) of a people of Malaya and Indonesia.

malcontent /ˈmæ-/ *n.* discontented person.

male *a.* of the sex that can beget offspring by fertilizing egg-cells produced by a female; (of a plant) having flowers that contain pollen-bearing organs not seeds. —*n.* male person, animal, or plant.

malefactor /ˈmælɪ-/ *n.* wrongdoer.

malevolent /-ˈlev-/ *a.* wishing harm to others. **malevolently** *adv.*, **malevolence** *n.*

malformation *n.* faulty formation. **malformed** *a.*

malfunction *n.* faulty functioning. —*v.i.* function faultily.

malice *n.* desire to harm others or to tease.

malicious *a.* showing malice. **maliciously** *adv.*

malign /-ˈlaɪn/ *a.* harmful; showing malice. —*v.t.* say unpleasant and untrue things about. **malignity** /-ˈlɪg-/ *n.*

malignant *a.* showing great ill-will; (of a tumour) growing harmfully and uncontrollably. **malignantly** *adv.*, **malignancy** *n.*

malinger *v.i.* pretend illness in order to avoid work. **malingerer** *n.*

mallard *n.* wild duck, male of which has a glossy green head.

malleable *a.* able to be hammered or pressed into shape; easy to influence. **malleability** *n.*

mallet *n.* hammer, usu. of wood; similarly shaped instrument with a long handle for striking the ball in croquet or polo.

mallow *n.* wild plant with hairy stems and leaves.

malmsey /ˈmɑm-/ *n.* a kind of strong sweet wine.

malnutrition *n.* insufficient nutrition.

malodorous /-ˈloʊ-/ *a.* stinking.

malpractice *n.* wrongdoing.

malt *n.* barley or other grain prepared for brewing or distilling; (*colloq.*) beer or whisky made with this. **malted milk,** drink made from dried milk and malt.

maltreat *v.t.* ill-treat. **maltreatment** *n.*

mama /-ˈmɑ/ *n.* (*old use*) mother.

mamba *n.* poisonous South African tree-snake.

mamma /-ˈmɑ/ *n.* (*old use*) mother.

mammal *n.* member of the class of animals that suckle their young. **mammalian** /-ˈmeɪl-/ *a.*

mammary *a.* of the breasts.

Mammon *n.* wealth personified.

mammoth *n.* large extinct elephant with curved tusks. —*a.* huge.

mammy *n.* (*children's colloq.*) mother.

man *n.* (pl. *men*) human being, animal with the power of articulate speech and upright posture; mankind; adult male person; individual person; male servant or employee; ordinary soldier etc., not an officer; one of the small objects used in board-games. —*v.t.* (p.t. *manned*) supply with people to guard or operate something. **~-hour** *n.* one hour's work by one person. **~-hunt** *n.* organized search for a person, esp. a criminal. **~ in the street,** ordinary person, not an expert. **~ made** *a.* made by man not by nature, synthetic. **~ of the world,** man experienced in the ways of society. **~-of-war** *n.* warship. **~-sized** *a.* adequate for a man. **~ to man,** with frankness.

manacle *n.* & *v.t.* handcuff.

manage *v.t./i.* have control of; be manager of; operate (a tool etc.) effectively; contrive; deal with (a person) tactfully. **manageable** *a.*

management *n.* managing; people engaged in managing a business.

manager *n.* person in charge of a business etc. **manageress** *n.fem.*, **managerial** /-'dʒɪər-/ *a.*

mandarin *n.* senior influential official; a kind of small orange.

Mandarin *n.* standard spoken Chinese language.

mandate *n.* authority to perform certain tasks.

mandatory /'mæ-/ *a.* compulsory.

mandible *n.* jaw.

mandolin *n.* guitar-like musical instrument.

mandrake *n.* poisonous plant with a large yellow fruit.

mane *n.* long hair on a horse's or lion's neck.

manful *a.* brave, resolute. **manfully** *adv.*

manganese *n.* hard brittle grey metal or its black oxide.

mange *n.* skin-disease affecting hairy animals.

mangel-wurzel *n.* large beet used as cattle-food.

manger *n.* open trough in a stable etc. for horses or cattle to feed from.

mangle¹ *n.* wringer. —*v.t.* press (clothes etc.) in a mangle.

mangle² *v.t.* damage by cutting or crushing roughly, mutilate.

mango *n.* (pl. *-oes*) tropical fruit with juicy flesh; tree bearing it.

mangrove *n.* tropical tree or shrub growing in shore-mud and swamps.

mangy *a.* having mange; squalid.

manhandle *v.t.* move by human effort alone; treat roughly.

manhole *n.* opening through which a person can enter a drain etc. to inspect it.

manhood *n.* state of being a man; manly qualities; men of a country.

mania *n.* violent madness; extreme enthusiasm for something.

maniac *n.* person with a mania.

maniacal /mə'naɪ-/ *a.* of or like a mania or maniac.

manic /'mæ-/ *a.* of or affected by mania.

manicure *n.* cosmetic treatment of finger-nails. —*v.t.* apply such treatment to. **manicurist** *n.*

manifest *a.* clear and unmistakable. —*v.t.* show clearly, give signs of. —*n.* list of cargo or passengers carried by a ship or aircraft. **manifestation** *n.*

manifesto *n.* (pl. *-os*) public declaration of principles and policy.

manifold *a.* of many kinds. —*n.* (in a machine) pipe or chamber with several openings.

manikin *n.* little man, dwarf.

manilla *n.* brown paper used for wrapping and for envelopes.

manioc /'mæ-/ *n.* cassava; flour made from this.

manipulate *v.t.* handle or manage in a skilful or cunning way. **manipulation** *n.*, **manipulator** *n.*

mankind *n.* human beings in general.

manly *a.* brave, strong; considered suitable for a man. **manliness** *n.*

manna *n.* (in the Bible) substance miraculously supplied as food to the Israelites in the wilderness.

mannequin /-kɪn/ *n.* woman who models clothes.

manner *n.* way a thing is done or happens; person's way of behaving towards others; kind, sort; (*pl.*) polite social behaviour.

mannered *a.* having manners of a certain kind; full of mannerisms.

mannerism *n.* distinctive personal habit or way of doing something.

mannish *a.* having masculine characteristics.

manœuvre *n.* planned movement of a vehicle, body of troops, etc.; skilful or crafty proceeding. —*v.t./i.* perform manœuvre(s); move or guide skilfully or craftily.

manor *n.* large country house, usu. with landed estate.

manpower *n.* number of people available for work or service.

manse *n.* church minister's house, esp. in Scotland.

manservant *n.* (pl. *menservants*) male servant.

mansion *n.* large stately house.

manslaughter *n.* act of killing a person unlawfully but not intentionally, or by negligence.

mantelpiece *n.* shelf above a fire-place.

mantilla *n.* Spanish lace veil worn over a woman's hair and shoulders.

mantis *n.* grasshopper-like insect.

mantle *n.* loose cloak; covering.

manual *a.* of the hands; done or operated by the hand(s). —*n.* handbook; organ keyboard played with the hands. **manually** *adv.*

manufacture *v.t.* make or produce (goods) on a large scale by machinery; invent. —*n.* process of manufacturing. **manufacturer** *n.*

manure *n.* substance, esp. dung, used as a fertilizer. —*v.t.* apply manure to.

manuscript *n.* thing written by hand, not typed or printed.

Manx *a.* & *n.* (language) of the Isle of Man.

many *a.* numerous. —*n.* many people or things.

Maori /'maʊ-/ *n.* & *a.* (pl. *-is*) (member, language) of the brown aboriginal race in New Zealand.

map *n.* representation of earth's surface or a part of it, or of the heavens. —*v.t.* (p.t. *mapped*) make a map of. **~ out**, plan in detail.

maple *n.* a kind of tree with broad leaves.

mar *v.t.* (p.t. *marred*) damage, spoil.

maraschino /-'ski-/ *n.* liqueur made from cherries.

marathon *n.* long-distance foot-race; long test of endurance.

marauding *a.* & *n.* going about in search of plunder. **marauder** *n.*

marble *n.* a kind of limestone that can be polished; piece of sculpture in this; small ball of glass or clay used in children's games.

marcasite /'mɑːkəsaɪt/ *n.* crystals of a form of iron, used in jewellery.

March *n.* third month of the year.

march *v.t./i.* walk in a regular rhythm or an

organized column; walk purposefully; cause to march or walk; progress steadily. —*n.* act of marching; distance covered by marching; music suitable for marching to; progress. **marcher** *n.*

marches *n.pl.* boundary regions.

marchioness /-ʃən-/ *n.* wife or widow of a marquis; woman with the rank of marquis.

mare *n.* female of horse or related animal. ∼**'s nest,** discovery that turns out to be false or worthless.

margarine /-dʒə- *or* -gə-/ *n.* substance made from animal or vegetable fat and used like butter.

marge *n.* (*colloq.*) margarine.

margin *n.* edge or border of surface; blank space round printed or written matter on a page; amount over the essential minimum.

marginal *a.* of or in a margin; near a limit; only very slight. ∼ **constituency,** one where an M.P.'s majority is too small for the seat to be regarded as safe. **marginally** *adv.*

marguerite /-ˈriːt/ *n.* large daisy.

marigold *n.* garden plant with golden daisy-like flowers.

marijuana /-ˈhwɑnə/ *n.* dried hemp, smoked as a hallucinogenic drug.

marina /-ˈriː-/ *n.* harbour for yachts and pleasure-boats.

marinade /-ˈneɪd/ *n.* seasoned flavoured liquid in which meat or fish is steeped before being cooked. —*v.t.* steep in marinade.

marine *a.* of the sea; of shipping. —*n.* a country's shipping; member of a body of troops trained to serve on land or sea.

mariner /ˈmæ-/ *n.* sailor, seaman.

marionette *n.* puppet worked by strings.

marital /ˈmæ-/ *a.* of marriage, of husband and wife.

maritime *a.* living or found near the sea; of seafaring.

marjoram *n.* herb with fragrant leaves.

mark[1] *n.* unit of money in Germany.

mark[2] *n.* thing that visibly breaks the uniformity of a surface; distinguishing feature; thing indicating the presence of a quality or feeling etc.; symbol; unit awarded for merit of a performance or piece of work; target; line or object serving to indicate position. —*v.t./i.* make a mark on; characterize; assign marks of merit to; notice, watch carefully; keep close to and ready to hamper (an opponent in football etc.). ∼ **time,** move the feet as if marching but without advancing.

marked *a.* clearly noticeable. **markedly** /-kɪdlɪ/ *adv.*

marker *n.* person or object that marks something.

market *n.* gathering for the sale of provisions, livestock, etc.; place where this is held; demand (for a commodity etc.). —*v.t./i.* buy or sell in a market; offer for sale. ∼ **garden,** one in which vegetables are grown for market. **on the** ∼, offered for sale.

marking *n.* mark(s); colouring of an animal's skin, feathers, or fur.

marksman *n.* (pl. -*men*) person who is a skilled shot. **marksmanship** *n.*

marmalade *n.* a kind of jam made from citrus fruit, esp. oranges.

marmoset *n.* small bushy-tailed monkey of tropical America.

marmot *n.* small burrowing animal of the squirrel family.

maroon[1] *n.* brownish-red colour; explosive device used as a warning signal. —*a.* brownish-red.

maroon[2] *v.t.* put and leave (a person) ashore in a desolate place; leave stranded.

marquee /-ˈkiː/ *n.* large tent used for a party or exhibition etc.

marquetry /-kɪt-/ *n.* inlaid work.

marquis *n.* nobleman ranking between duke and earl or count.

marriage *n.* state in which a man and woman are formally united for the purpose of living together; act or ceremony of marrying.

marriageable *a.* suitable or old enough for marriage.

marrow *n.* soft fatty substance in the cavities of bones; a type of gourd used as a vegetable.

marry *v.t./i.* unite or give or take in marriage; put (things) together.

marsh *n.* low-lying watery ground. ∼ **marigold,** a kind of large buttercup. **marshy** *a.*

marshal *n.* officer of high or the highest rank; official arranging ceremonies, controlling procedure at races, etc. —*v.t.* (p.t. *marshalled*) arrange in proper order; assemble; usher.

marshmallow *n.* soft sweet made from sugar, egg-white, and gelatine.

marsupial *n.* animal that carries its young in a pouch.

mart *n.* market.

marten *n.* weasel-like animal with thick soft fur.

martial *a.* of war, warlike. ∼ **law,** military government suspending ordinary law.

Martian *a.* & *n.* (inhabitant) of the planet Mars.

martin *n.* bird of the swallow family.

martinet *n.* person who demands strict obedience.

martyr *n.* person who undergoes death or suffering for his beliefs. —*v.t.* kill or torment as a martyr. **be a** ∼ **to,** suffer constantly from (an ailment). **martyrdom** *n.*

marvel *n.* wonderful thing. —*v.i.* (p.t. *marvelled*) feel wonder.

marvellous *a.* wonderful.

Marxism *n.* theories of the German socialist writer Karl Marx, on which Communism is based. **Marxist** *a.* & *n.*

marzipan *n.* edible paste made from ground almonds.

mascara *n.* cosmetic for darkening the eyelashes.

mascot *n.* thing believed to bring good luck to its owner; figurine mounted on a car etc.

masculine *a.* of, like, or suitable for men; of the grammatical form suitable for the names of males. —*n.* masculine word. **masculinity** *n.*

mash *n.* soft mixture of grain or bran; (*colloq.*) mashed potatoes. —*v.t.* beat or crush into a soft mixture.

mask *n.* covering worn over the face as a disguise or protection; respirator worn over the face; replica of the face; face or head of a fox. —*v.t.* cover with a mask; disguise, screen, conceal.

masochism /ˈmæsək-/ *n.* pleasure in suffering physical or mental pain. **masochist** *n.*, **masochistic** *a.*

mason *n.* person who builds or works with stone.

Mason *n.* freemason. **Masonic** /-ˈson-/ *a.*, **Masonry** *n.*

masonry *n.* mason's work; stonework.

masquerade *n.* false show or pretence. —*v.i.* pretend to be what one is not.

mass¹ *n.* celebration (esp. in R.C. church) of the Eucharist; form of service used in this.

mass² *n.* coherent unit of matter; large quantity or heap or expanse; quantity of matter a body contains (called *weight* in non-technical usage); *the masses*, ordinary people. —*v.t./i.* gather or assemble into a mass. **~-produce** *v.t.* manufacture in large quantities by a standardized process. **~ production.**

massacre *n.* great slaughter. —*v.t.* slaughter in large numbers.

massage *n.* rubbing and kneading the body to reduce pain or stiffness. —*v.t.* treat in this way.

masseur /-ˈsɜ(r)/ *n.* man who practises massage professionally. **masseuse** /-ˈsɜz/ *n.fem.*

massif /ˈmæ-/ *n.* central mass of mountain heights.

massive *a.* large and heavy or solid; huge. **massiveness** *n.*

mast¹ *n.* tall pole, esp. supporting a ship's sails.

mast² *n.* fruit of beech, oak, chestnut, etc., used as food for pigs.

mastectomy *n.* surgical removal of a breast.

master *n.* man who has control of people or things; employer; male teacher; person with very great skill, great artist; captain of a merchant ship; thing from which a series of copies is made; *M~*, title of a boy not old enough to be called *Mr*. —*v.t.* bring under control; acquire knowledge or skill in. **~-key** *n.* key that opens a number of different locks. **~-mind** *n.* person with outstanding mental ability or directing an enterprise; (*v.t.*) plan and direct. **Master of Arts** etc., person with a high university degree. **~-stroke** *n.* very skilful act of policy.

masterful *a.* domineering. **masterfully** *adv.*

masterly *a.* very skilful.

masterpiece *n.* outstanding piece of work.

mastery *n.* complete control, supremacy; thorough knowledge or skill.

masticate *v.t.* chew. **mastication** *n.*

mastiff *n.* large strong dog.

mastoid *n.* part of a bone behind the ear.

masturbate *v.t./i.* stimulate the genitals (of) manually. **masturbation** *n.*

mat *n.* piece of material placed on a floor or

other surface as an ornament or to protect it from damage. —*v.t./i.* (p.t. *matted*) make or become tangled to form a thick mass.

matador *n.* bull-fighter.

match¹ *n.* short piece of wood or pasteboard tipped with material that catches fire when rubbed on a rough surface.

match² *n.* contest in a game or sport; person or thing exactly like or corresponding or equal to another; matrimonial alliance. —*v.t./i.* set against each other in a contest; equal in ability or achievement; be alike; find a thing similar or corresponding to.

matchbox *n.* box for holding matches.

matchless *a.* unequalled.

matchmaking *n.* scheming to arrange marriages. **matchmaker** *n.*

matchstick *n.* stick of match.

matchwood *n.* wood that splinters easily; wood broken into splinters.

mate¹ *n.* companion or fellow worker; male or female of mated animals; merchant ship's officer next below master. —*v.t./i.* put or come together as a pair or as corresponding; come or bring (animals) together to breed.

mate² *n.* situation in chess where capture of a king is inevitable.

material *n.* that from which something is or can be made; cloth, fabric. —*a.* of matter; of the physical (not spiritual) world; significant. **materially** *adv.*

materialism *n.* belief that only the material world exists; excessive concern with material possessions. **materialist** *n.*, **materialistic** *a.*

materialize *v.i.* appear, become visible; become a fact, happen. **materialization** *n.*

maternal *a.* of a mother; motherly; related through one's mother. **maternally** *adv.*

maternity *n.* motherhood; (*attrib.*) of or for women in pregnancy and childbirth.

matey *a.* (*colloq.*) friendly.

mathematician *n.* person skilled in mathematics.

mathematics *n.* & *n.pl.* science of numbers, quantities, and measurements. **mathematical** *a.*, **mathematically** *adv.*

maths *n.* & *n.pl.* (*colloq.*) mathematics.

matinée /-neɪ/ *n.* afternoon performance. **~ coat,** baby's jacket.

matins *n.* (in the Church of England) service of morning prayer.

matriarch /ˈmeɪ-/ *n.* female head of a family or tribe. **matriarchal** *a.*

matriarchy /ˈmeɪ-/ *n.* social organization in which the mother is head of the family.

matriculate *v.t./i.* admit or be admitted to a university. **matriculation** *n.*

matrimony *n.* marriage. **matrimonial** *a.*

matrix /ˈmeɪ-/ *n.* (pl. *matrices*, pr. -ɪsiz) mould in which a thing is cast or shaped.

matron *n.* married woman; woman in charge of domestic affairs or nursing in a school etc.; (*former use*) senior nursing officer in a hospital.

matronly *a.* like or suitable for a dignified married woman.

matt *a.* (of a surface) dull, not shiny.

matter *n.* that which occupies space in the visible world; specified substance, material, or things; business etc. being discussed; pus. —*v.i.* be of importance. **∼-of-fact** *a.* strictly factual, not imaginative or emotional. **no ∼,** it is of no importance. **what is the ∼?,** what is amiss?

matting *n.* mats, material for making these.

mattock *n.* agricultural tool with a blade at right angles to the handle.

mattress *n.* fabric case filled with padding or springy material, used on or as a bed.

maturation *n.* maturing.

mature *a.* fully grown or developed; (of a bill of exchange etc.) due for payment. —*v.t./i.* make or become mature. **maturity** *n.*

maudlin *a.* sentimental in a silly or tearful way.

maul *v.t.* treat roughly, injure by rough handling.

Maundy *n.* distribution of **Maundy money** (special silver coins) to the poor on **Maundy Thursday** (Thursday before Easter).

mausoleum *n.* magnificent tomb.

mauve /məʊv/ *a.* & *n.* pale purple.

maverick *n.* unorthodox or undisciplined person.

maw *n.* jaws, mouth, or stomach of a voracious animal.

mawkish *a.* sentimental in a sickly way.

maxim *n.* sentence giving a general truth or rule of conduct.

maximize *v.t.* increase to a maximum.

maximum *a.* & *n.* (pl. *-ima*) greatest (amount) possible.

may[1] *v.aux.* (p.t. *might*) used to express a wish, possibility, or permission.

may[2] *n.* hawthorn blossom.

May *n.* fifth month of the year. **∼ Day,** first day of May.

maybe *adv.* perhaps.

mayday *n.* international radio signal of distress.

mayfly *n.* insect with long hair-like tails, living in spring.

mayhem *n.* violent action.

mayonnaise /-ˈneɪz/ *n.* creamy sauce made with eggs and oil.

mayor *n.* head of the municipal corporation of a city or borough.

mayoress *n.* mayor's wife, or other lady with her ceremonial duties.

maypole *n.* tall pole for dancing round on May Day.

maze *n.* complex and baffling network of paths, lines, etc.

mazurka *n.* lively Polish dance.

me *pron.* objective case of *I.*

mead *n.* alcoholic drink made from fermented honey and water.

meadow *n.* field of grass.

meadowsweet *n.* meadow plant with fragrant creamy-white flowers.

meagre *a.* scant in amount.

meal[1] *n.* occasion when food is eaten; the food itself.

meal[2] *n.* coarsely ground grain.

mealy *a.* of or like meal. **∼-mouthed** *a.* trying excessively to avoid offending people.

mean[1] *a.* (*-er, -est*) poor in quality or appearance; low in rank; unkind; selfish; miserly. **meanly** *adv.,* **meanness** *n.*

mean[2] *a.* & *n.* (thing) midway between two extremes; average. **∼ time,** intervening time.

mean[3] *v.t.* (p.t. *meant*) intend; have as equivalent word(s) in the same or another language; entail, involve, be likely to result in.

meander *v.i.* follow a winding course; wander in a leisurely way. —*n.* winding course.

meaning *n.* what is meant. —*a.* full of a certain meaning, expressive. **meaningful** *a.,* **meaningless** *a.*

means *n.* that by which a result is brought about. —*n.pl.* resources. **by all ∼,** certainly. **by no ∼,** not nearly. **∼ test,** official inquiry to establish neediness before giving help from public funds.

meant *see* **mean**[3].

meantime *adv.* meanwhile.

meanwhile *adv.* in the intervening period; at the same time.

measles *n.* infectious disease producing small red spots on the body.

measly *a.* (*sl.*) meagre.

measurable *a.* able to be measured.

measure *n.* size or quantity found by measuring; extent; unit, standard, device, or system used in measuring; rhythm; suitable action taken for a purpose, (proposed) law. —*v.t./i.* find the size etc. of by comparison with a fixed unit or known standard; be of a certain size; mark or deal (a measured amount). **∼ one's length,** fall flat on the ground. **∼ up to,** reach the standard required by.

measured *a.* rhythmical; carefully considered.

measurement *n.* measuring; size etc. found by measuring.

meat *n.* animal flesh as food (usu. excluding fish and poultry).

meaty *a.* (*-ier, -iest*) like meat; full of meat; full of subject-matter.

mechanic *n.* skilled workman who uses or repairs machines or tools.

mechanical *a.* of or worked by machinery; done without conscious thought. **mechanically** *adv.*

mechanics *n.* study of motion and force; science of machinery. —*n.pl.* mechanism, way a thing functions.

mechanism *n.* way a machine works; its parts.

mechanize *v.t.* equip with machinery. **mechanized** *a.* (of troops) equipped with armoured vehicles. **mechanization** *n.*

medal *n.* coin-like piece of metal commemorating an event or awarded for an achievement.

medallion /-ˈdæ-/ *n.* large medal; circular ornamental design.

medallist *n.* winner of a medal.

meddle *v.i.* interfere in people's affairs; tinker. **meddler** *n.*

meddlesome *a.* often meddling.

media *see* **medium.** —*n.pl.* **the ∼,** newspapers

and broadcasting as conveying information to the public.

mediaeval *a.* = medieval.

medial *a.* situated in the middle.

median *a.* in or passing through the middle. —*n.* median point or line.

mediate *v.t./i.* act as peacemaker between disputants; bring about (a settlement) thus. **mediation** *n.*, **mediator** *n.*

medical *a.* of the science of medicine; involving doctors and their work. —*n.* (*colloq.*) medical examination. **medically** *adv.*

medicament /-ˈdɪk-/ *n.* any medicine, ointment, etc.

medicate *v.t.* treat with a medicinal substance. **medication** *n.*

medicinal *a.* having healing properties. **medicinally** *adv.*

medicine *n.* science of the prevention and cure of disease; substance used to treat disease. **∼-man** *n.* witch-doctor.

medieval *a.* of the Middle Ages.

mediocre /mi-/ *a.* of medium quality; second-rate. **mediocrity** *n.*

meditate *v.t.* think deeply and quietly; plan. **meditation** *n.*

meditative *a.* meditating, full of meditation. **meditatively** *adv.*

Mediterranean *a.* & *n.* (of) the sea between Europe and North Africa.

medium *n.* (pl. *media*) middle size, quality, etc.; substance or surroundings in which a thing exists or moves or is produced; agency, means; (pl. *mediums*) person who claims ability to communicate with the spirits of the dead.

medlar *n.* apple-like fruit eaten when decaying; tree bearing this.

medley *n.* (pl. *-eys*) assortment; excerpts of music from various sources.

meek *a.* (*-er*, *-est*) quiet and obedient, not protesting. **meekly** *adv.*, **meekness** n.

meerschaum /-ʃəm/ *n.* tobacco-pipe with a white clay bowl.

meet[1] *a.* (*old use*) suitable, proper.

meet[2] *v.t./i.* (p.t. *met*) come face to face or into contact (with); go to be present at the arrival of; make the acquaintance of; become perceptible to; experience; satisfy (needs etc.). —*n.* assembly for a hunt etc.

meeting *n.* coming together; an assembly for discussion or (of Quakers) worship. **∼-place** *n.*

mega- *pref.* large; one million (as in *megavolts*, *megawatts*).

megahertz *n.* one million cycles per second, as a unit of frequency of electromagnetic waves.

megalomania *n.* excessive self-esteem, esp. as a form of insanity.

megaphone *n.* funnel-shaped device for amplifying and directing a speaker's voice.

megaton *n.* unit of explosive power equal to one million tons of TNT.

melamine /-min/ *n.* resilient kind of plastic.

melancholia /-ˈkəʊ-/ *n.* mental depression. **melancholic** /-ˈkol-/ *a.*

melancholy *n.* mental depression, sadness; gloom. —*a.* sad, gloomy.

mêlée /ˈmeleɪ/ *n.* confused fight; muddle.

mellow *a.* (*-er*, *-est*) (of fruit) ripe and sweet; (of sound or colour) soft and rich; (of persons) having become kindly, e.g. with age. —*v.t./i.* make or become mellow. **mellowly** *adv.*, **mellowness** *n.*

melodic /-ˈlod-/ *a.* of melody.

melodious *a.* full of melody.

melodrama *n.* sensational or emotional drama. **melodramatic** *a.*, **melodramatically** *adv.*

melody *n.* sweet music; main part in a piece of harmonized music; song.

melon *n.* large sweet fruit of various gourds.

melt *v.t./i.* make into or become liquid, esp. by heat; soften through pity or love; fade away.

member *n.* person or thing belonging to a particular group or society. **Member of Parliament,** constituency's elected representative in the House of Commons. **membership** *n.*

membrane *n.* thin flexible skin-like tissue.

memento *n.* (pl. *-oes*) souvenir.

memo *n.* (pl. *-os*) (*colloq.*) memorandum.

memoir /-mwɑ(r)/ *n.* written account of events etc. that one remembers.

memorable *a.* worth remembering, easy to remember.

memorandum *n.* (pl. *-da*) note written for future use as a reminder; informal written message from one colleague to another.

memorial *n.* object or custom etc. established in memory of an event or person(s). —*a.* serving as a memorial.

memorize *v.t.* learn (a thing) so as to know it from memory.

memory *n.* ability to remember things; thing(s) remembered. **from ∼,** remembered without the aid of notes etc. **in ∼ of,** in honour of a person or thing remembered with respect.

men *see* **man.**

menace *n.* threat; annoying or troublesome person or thing. —*v.t.* threaten. **menacingly** *adv.*

ménage /meɪˈnɑʒ/ *n.* household.

menagerie *n.* collection of wild or strange animals for exhibition.

mend *v.t./i.* repair; stitch up (torn fabric); make or become better. —*n.* repaired place. **on the ∼,** becoming better after illness etc. **mender** *n.*

mendacious *a.* untruthful. **mendaciously** *adv.*, **mendacity** /-ˈdæ-/ *n.*

mendicant *a.* begging. —*n.* beggar.

menfolk *n.* men in general; men of one's family.

menhir /ˈmenhɪə(r)/ *n.* tall stone set up in prehistoric times.

menial /ˈmi-/ *a.* lowly, degrading. —*n.* (*derog.*) servant, person who does humble tasks.

meningitis /-ˈdʒaɪ-/ *n.* inflammation of the membranes covering the brain and spinal cord.

menopause /ˈmen-/ *n.* time of life when a woman finally ceases to menstruate. **menopausal** *a.*

menstrual *a.* of or in menstruation.

menstruate v.i. experience a monthly discharge of blood from the womb. **menstruation** n.

mental a. of, in, or performed by the mind; (colloq.) mad. ∼ **deficiency,** lack of normal intelligence through imperfect mental development. ∼ **home** or **hospital,** establishment for the care of patients suffering from mental illness. **mentally** adv.

mentality n. person's mental ability or characteristic attitude of mind.

menthol n. camphor-like substance.

mentholated a. impregnated with menthol.

mention v.t. speak or write about briefly; refer to by name. —n. act of mentioning, being mentioned.

mentor n. trusted adviser.

menu /ˈmen-/ n. (pl. -us) list of dishes to be served.

mercantile a. trading, of trade or merchants.

mercenary a. working merely for money or other reward; grasping; (of soldiers) hired to serve a foreign country. —n. professional soldier hired by a foreign country.

merchandise n. goods bought and sold or for sale. —v.t./i. trade; promote sales of (goods).

merchant n. wholesale trader; (U.S. & Sc.) retail trader; (sl.) person fond of a certain activity. ∼ **bank,** one dealing in commercial loans and the financing of businesses. ∼ **navy,** shipping employed in commerce. ∼ **ship,** ship carrying merchandise.

merciful a. showing mercy; giving relief from pain and suffering.

mercifully adv. in a merciful way; (colloq.) thank goodness.

merciless a. showing no mercy. **mercilessly** adv.

mercurial a. of or caused by mercury; lively in temperament; liable to sudden changes of mood.

mercury n. heavy silvery usu. liquid metal, used in thermometers and barometers etc. **mercuric** a.

mercy n. kindness shown to an offender or enemy etc. who is in one's power; merciful act.

mere[1] a. no more or no better than what is specified. **merest** a. very small or insignificant. **merely** adv.

mere[2] n. lake.

merge v.t./i. combine into a whole; blend gradually.

merger n. combining of commercial companies etc. into one.

meridian /-ˈrɪd-/ n. great semicircle on the globe, passing through the North and South Poles.

meringue /-ˈræŋ/ n. baked mixture of sugar and white of egg; small cake of this.

merino /-ˈriː-/ n. (pl. -os) a kind of sheep with fine soft wool; soft woollen fabric.

merit n. feature or quality that deserves praise; excellence, worthiness. —v.t. (p.t. **merited**) deserve.

meritorious a. deserving praise.

mermaid n., **merman** n. (pl. -men) imaginary half-human sea creature with a fish's tail instead of legs.

merry a. (-ier, -iest) cheerful and lively, joyous. **make** ∼, hold lively festivities. ∼**-go-round** n. revolving machine at a fun-fair, with models of horses or cars etc. to ride on. ∼**-making** n. lively festivities. **merrily** adv., **merriment** n.

mesh n. space between threads in net or a sieve or wire screen etc.; network fabric. —v.i. (of a toothed wheel) engage with another.

mesmerize v.t. hypnotize, dominate the attention or will of.

mess n. dirty or untidy condition; unpleasant or untidy thing(s); something spilt; difficult or confused situation, trouble; (in the armed forces) group who take meals together, their dining-room. —v.t./i. make untidy or dirty; muddle, bungle; potter; (in the armed forces) take meals with a group. **make a** ∼ **of,** bungle. ∼ **with,** tinker with.

message n. spoken or written communication; moral or social teaching.

messenger n. bearer of a message.

Messiah n. deliverer expected by Jews; Christ as this. **Messianic** /-sɪˈæn-/ a.

Messrs. see **Mr.**

messy a. (-ier, -iest) untidy or dirty, slovenly. **messily** adv., **messiness** n.

met see **meet**[2].

metabolism /-ˈtæ-/ n. process by which nutrition takes place.

metal n. any of a class of mineral substances such as gold, silver, iron, etc., or an alloy of these. —a. made of metal.

metalled a. made or mended with road-metal (see **road**).

metallic a. of or like metal.

metallurgy /-ˈtæl-/ n. science of extracting and working metals. **metallurgical** a., **metallurgist** n.

metamorphosis /-ˈmɔf-/ n. (pl. -phoses) change of form or character.

metaphor n. transferred use of a word or phrase, suggesting comparison with its basic meaning (e.g. the evening of one's life, food for thought). **metaphorical** a., **metaphorically** adv.

metaphysics n. branch of philosophy dealing with the nature of existence and of knowledge. **metaphysical** a.

mete v.t. ∼ **out,** deal out.

meteor n. small mass of matter from outer space.

meteoric a. of meteors; swift and brilliant.

meteorite n. meteor fallen to earth.

meteorology n. study of atmospheric conditions esp. in order to forecast weather. **meteorological** a., **meteorologist** n.

meter[1] n. device measuring and indicating the quantity supplied, distance travelled, time elapsed, etc. —v.t. measure by a meter.

meter[2] n. (U.S.) = metre.

methane /ˈmiːθeɪn/ n. colourless inflammable gas.

method n. procedure or way of doing something; orderliness.

methodical /-ˈθɒd-/ a. orderly, systematic. **methodically** adv.

Methodist n. member of a Protestant religious

denomination based on the teachings of John and Charles Wesley. **Methodism** *n*.

meths *n*. (*colloq*.) methylated spirit.

methylated *a*. ∼ **spirit,** form of alcohol used as a solvent and for heating.

meticulous *a*. very careful and exact. **meticulously** *adv*., **meticulousness** *n*.

metre *n*. metric unit of length (about 39.4 inches); rhythm in poetry.

metric *a*. of or using the metric system; of poetic metre. ∼ **system,** decimal system of weights and measures, using the metre, litre, and gram as units.

metrical *a*. of or composed in rhythmic metre, not prose.

metrication *n*. conversion to the metric system.

metronome *n*. device sounding a click at a regular interval, used to indicate tempo while practising music.

metropolis /-'trop-/ *n*. chief city of country or region.

metropolitan *a*. of a metropolis.

mettle *n*. courage, strength of character. **on one's** ∼, determined to show one's courage or ability.

mettlesome *a*. spirited, brave.

mew *n*. cat's characteristic cry. —*v.i.* make this sound.

mews *n*. set of former stables now converted into dwellings or garages etc.

mezzanine /'metsənin/ *n*. extra storey set between two others.

mezzo-soprano *n*. singer with a voice between soprano and contralto.

mezzotint *n*. a kind of engraving.

mg *abbr*. milligram(s).

MHz *abbr*. megahertz.

miaow *n*. & *v.i.* = mew.

miasma /mɪ'æz-/ *n*. unpleasant or unwholesome air.

mica /'maɪ-/ *n*. mineral substance used as an electrical insulator.

mice *see* **mouse.**

Michaelmas /'mɪkəl-/ *n*. feast of St. Michael (29 Sept.).

mickey *n*. **take the** ∼ **out of,** (*sl.*) tease, ridicule.

micro- *pref*. extremely small; one millionth part of (as in *microgram*).

microbe *n*. micro-organism.

microchip *n*. small piece of silicon holding a complex electronic circuit.

microcosm *n*. community or complex resembling something else but on a very small scale.

microfiche /-fiʃ/ *n*. (pl. -*fiche*) sheet of microfilm that can be filed like an index-card.

microfilm *n*. length of film bearing a photograph of written or printed matter in greatly reduced size. —*v.t.* photograph on this.

micro-organism *n*. organism invisible to the naked eye.

microphone *n*. instrument for picking up sound waves for recording, amplifying, or broadcasting.

microprocessor *n*. miniature computer (or a unit of this) consisting of one or more microchips.

microscope *n*. instrument with lenses that magnify very small things and make them visible.

microscopic *a*. of a microscope; extremely small; too small to be visible without using a microscope.

microwave *n*. electromagnetic wave of length between about 50 cm and 1 mm.

mid *a*. middle.

midday *n*. middle of the day; noon.

midden *n*. dung-heap, rubbish-heap.

middle *a*. occurring at an equal distance from extremes or outer limits. —*n*. middle point, position, area, etc. **in the** ∼ **of,** half-way through (an activity). ∼**-aged** *a*. between youth and old age. **Middle Ages,** about A.D. 1000–1400. ∼ **class,** class of society between upper and working classes. **Middle East,** area from Egypt to Iran inclusive.

middleman *n*. (pl. -*men*) trader handling a commodity between producer and consumer.

middleweight *n*. boxing-weight (75 kg).

middling *a*. moderately good.

midge *n*. small biting insect.

midget *n*. extremely small person or thing. —*a*. extremely small.

Midlands *n.pl*. inland counties of central England. **midland** *a*.

midnight *n*. 12 o'clock at night; time near this.

midriff *n*. front part of the body just above the waist.

midshipman *n*. (pl. -*men*) naval rank just below sub-lieutenant.

midst *n*. **in the** ∼ **of,** in the middle of; among, surrounded by.

midsummer *n*. middle of the summer, about 21 June.

midway *adv*. half-way.

midwife *n*. (pl. -*wives*) person trained to assist women in child-birth.

midwifery /-wɪfrɪ/ *n*. work of a midwife.

midwinter *n*. middle of the winter, about 22 Dec.

mien /min/ *n*. person's manner or bearing.

might[1] *n*. great strength or power. **with** ∼ **and main,** with all one's power and energy.

might[2] *see* **may**[1]. —*v.aux*. (used to request permission or (like *may*) to express possibility).

mighty *a*. (-*ier*, -*iest*) very strong or powerful; very great.

mignonette /mɪnjən-/ *n*. plant with fragrant grey-green leaves.

migraine /'miɡ-/ *n*. severe form of headache.

migrant /'maɪ-/ *a*. & *n*. migrating (person or animal).

migrate *v.i.* leave one place and settle in another; (of animals) go from one place to another at each season. **migration** *n*., **migratory** /'maɪ-/ *a*.

mike *n*. (*colloq*.) microphone.

milch *a*. ∼ **cow,** cow kept for its milk; person or organization as an easy source of money.

mild *a*. (-*er*, -*est*) moderate in intensity,

not harsh or drastic; gentle; not strongly flavoured. **mildly** *adv.*, **mildness** *n.*

mildew *n.* tiny fungus forming a white coating on things exposed to damp. **mildewed** *a.*

mile *n.* measure of length, 1760 yds (about 1.609 km); (*colloq.*) great distance. **nautical ~,** unit used in navigation, 2025 yds (1.852 km).

mileage *n.* distance in miles.

milestone *n.* stone beside a road, showing the distance in miles to a certain place; significant event or stage reached.

milieu /ˈmiljə/ *n.* (pl. *-eus*) environment, surroundings.

militant *a.* & *n.* (person) prepared to take aggressive action. **militancy** *n.*

military *a.* of soldiers or the army or all armed forces.

militate *v.i.* serve as a strong influence.

militia /-ʃə/ *n.* a military force, esp. of trained civilians available in an emergency.

milk *n.* white fluid secreted by female mammals as food for their young; cow's milk as food for human beings; milk-like liquid. —*v.t.* draw milk from; exploit. **~ shake,** frothy drink of flavoured milk. **~-teeth** *n.pl.* first (temporary) teeth in young mammals. **milker** *n.*

milkmaid *n.* (*old use*) woman who milks cows.

milkman *n.* (pl. *-men*) man who delivers milk to customers.

milksop *n.* weakling.

milky *a.* of or like milk; containing much milk. **Milky Way,** broad luminous band of stars.

mill *n.* machinery for grinding something or for processing specified material; building containing this. —*v.t./i.* grind or produce in a mill; produce grooves in (metal); move in a confused mass. **miller** *n.*

millennium *n.* (pl. *-ums*) period of 1000 years; future period of great happiness for everyone.

millepede *n.* small crawling creature with many legs.

millet *n.* tall cereal plant; its small seeds.

milli- *pref.* one thousandth part of (as in *milligram, millilitre, millimetre*).

milliner *n.* person who makes or sells women's hats. **millinery,** milliner's work or goods.

million *n.* one thousand thousand (1,000,000). **millionth** *a.* & *n.*

millionaire *n.* person who possesses a million pounds.

millstone *n.* heavy circular stone used in grinding corn; great burden that impedes progress.

milometer /-ˈlom-/ *n.* instrument measuring the distance in miles travelled by a vehicle.

milt *n.* sperm discharged by a male fish over eggs laid by the female.

mime *n.* acting with gestures without words. —*v.t./i.* act with mime.

mimic *v.t.* (p.t. *mimicked*) imitate, esp. playfully or for entertainment. —*n.* person who is clever at mimicking others. **mimicry** *n.*

mimosa *n.* tropical shrub with small ball-shaped flowers.

minaret *n.* tall slender tower on or beside a mosque.

mince *v.t./i.* cut into small pieces in a mincer; walk or speak with affected refinement. —*n.* mincemeat. **~ pie,** pie containing mincemeat. **not to ~ matters,** to speak bluntly.

mincemeat *n.* mixture of dried fruit, sugar, etc., used in pies. **make ~ of,** defeat utterly.

mincer *n.* machine with revolving blades for cutting food into very small pieces.

mind *n.* ability to be aware of things and to think and reason, originating in the brain; a person's attention, remembrance, intention, or opinion; sanity. —*v.t./i.* have charge of; object to; bear in mind, feel concern about; remember and be careful (about).

minded *a.* having inclinations or interests of a certain kind.

minder *n.* person whose job is to have charge of something.

mindful *a.* taking thought or care (of something).

mindless *a.* without a mind, without intelligence.

mine[1] *a.* & *poss.pron.* belonging to me.

mine[2] *n.* excavation for extracting metal or coal etc.; abundant source; receptacle filled with explosive material, laid in or on the ground or in water. —*v.t./i.* dig for minerals, extract in this way; lay explosive mines in.

minefield *n.* area where explosive mines have been laid.

miner *n.* person who works in a mine.

mineral *n.* inorganic natural substance; ore etc. obtained by mining; fizzy soft drink. —*a.* of or containing minerals. **~ water,** water naturally containing dissolved mineral salts or gases; fizzy soft drink.

mineralogy /-ˈræl-/ *n.* study of minerals. **mineralogist** *n.*

minestrone /mɪnɪˈstrəʊnɪ/ *n.* Italian soup containing chopped vegetables and pasta.

minesweeper *n.* ship for clearing away mines laid in the sea.

mineworker *n.* miner.

mingle *v.t./i.* mix, blend; go about among.

mingy *a.* (*colloq.*) mean, stingy.

mini- *pref.* miniature.

miniature *a.* very small, on a small scale. —*n.* small-scale portrait, copy, or model.

miniaturize *v.t.* make miniature, produce in a very small version. **miniaturization** *n.*

minibus *n.* small bus-like vehicle with seats for only a few people.

minim *n.* note in music, lasting half as long as a semibreve; one sixtieth of a fluid drachm.

minimal *a.* very small, least possible. **minimally** *adv.*

minimize *v.t.* reduce to a minimum; represent as small or unimportant.

minimum *a.* & *n.* (pl. *-ima*) smallest (amount) possible.

minion *n.* (*derog.*) subordinate assistant.

minister *n.* head of a government department; senior diplomatic representative; clergyman, esp. Presbyterian or Nonconformist. —*v.i.* **~ to,** attend to the needs of. **ministerial** /-ˈtɪər-/ *a.*

ministry *n.* government department headed by a minister; period of government under one premier; work of a clergyman.

mink *n.* small stoat-like animal; its valuable fur; coat made of this.

minnow *n.* small fish of the carp family.

Minoan /mɪn-/ *a. & n.* (person) of the Cretan Bronze-Age civilization.

minor *a.* lesser; not very important; (of a musical scale) with a semitone above the second note. —*n.* person not yet legally of adult age.

minority *n.* smallest part of a group or class; small group differing from others; age when a person is not yet legally adult.

Minster *n.* name given to certain large or important churches.

minstrel *n.* medieval singer and musician.

mint[1] *n.* place authorized to make a country's coins; vast amount (of money); —*v.t.* make (coins) by stamping metal. **in ~ condition,** new-looking.

mint[2] *n.* plant with fragrant leaves used for flavouring; peppermint, sweet flavoured with this.

minuet *n.* slow stately dance.

minus *prep.* reduced by subtraction of; below zero; (*colloq.*) without. —*a.* less than zero; less than the amount indicated.

minuscule /ˈmɪn-/ *a.* extremely small.

minute[1] /ˈmɪnɪt/ *n.* one sixtieth of an hour or degree; moment of time; (*pl.*) official summary of an assembly's proceedings. —*v.t.* record in the minutes of an assembly.

minute[2] /maɪˈnjuːt/ *a.* extremely small; very precise. **minutely** *adv.*

minutiae /mɪˈnjuːʃɪ/ *n.pl.* very small details.

minx *n.* cheeky or mischievous girl.

miracle *n.* event so remarkable that it is attributed to a supernatural agency; remarkable occurrence or specimen. **miraculous** /-ˈræ-/ *a.*, **miraculously** *adv.*

mirage /ˈmɪrɑːʒ/ *n.* optical illusion caused by atmospheric conditions.

mire *n.* swampy ground, bog; mud or sticky dirt.

mirror *n.* piece of glass coated on one side so that reflections can be seen in it. —*v.t.* reflect in or as if in a mirror.

mirth *n.* merriment, laughter. **mirthful** *a.*, **mirthless** *a.*

mis- *pref.* badly, wrongly.

misadventure *n.* piece of bad luck.

misanthrope /ˈmɪs-/ *n.* misanthropist.

misanthropy /-ˈsæn-/ *n.* dislike of people in general. **misanthropist** *n.*, **misanthropic** /-ˈθrɒp-/ *a.*

misapprehend *v.t.* misunderstand. **misapprehension** *n.*

misappropriate *v.t.* take dishonestly. **misappropriation** *n.*

misbehave *v.i.* behave badly. **misbehaviour** *n.*

miscalculate *v.t./i.* calculate incorrectly. **miscalculation** *n.*

miscarriage *n.* abortion occurring naturally; process of miscarrying.

miscarry *v.i.* have a miscarriage; go wrong or astray, be unsuccessful.

miscellaneous *a.* assorted.

miscellany /-ˈsel-/ *n.* collection of assorted items.

mischance *n.* misfortune.

mischief *n.* children's annoying but not malicious conduct; playful malice; harm, damage.

mischievous *a.* full of mischief. **mischievously** *adv.*, **mischievousness** *n.*

misconception *n.* wrong interpretation.

misconduct *n.* bad behaviour; mismanagement.

misconstrue /-ˈstruː/ *v.t.* misinterpret. **misconstruction** *n.*

miscreant /-krɪə-/ *n.* wrongdoer.

misdeed *n.* wrongful act.

misdemeanour *n.* misdeed.

miser *n.* person who hoards money and spends as little as possible. **miserly** *a.*, **miserliness** *n.*

miserable *a.* full of misery; wretchedly poor in quality or surroundings etc. **miserably** *adv.*

misericord /-ˈze-/ *n.* projection under a hinged seat in a choir stall.

misery *n.* great unhappiness or discomfort; (*colloq.*) discontented or disagreeable person.

misfire *v.i.* (of a gun or engine) fail to fire correctly; go wrong.

misfit *n.* thing that does not fit; person not well suited to his work or environment.

misfortune *n.* bad luck, unfortunate event.

misgiving *n.* feeling of doubt or slight fear or mistrust.

misguided *a.* mistaken in one's opinions or actions.

mishap *n.* unlucky accident.

misinterpret *v.t.* interpret incorrectly. **misinterpretation** *n.*

misjudge *v.t.* form a wrong opinion or estimate of. **misjudgement** *n.*

mislay *v.t.* (*p.t. mislaid*) lose temporarily.

mislead *v.t.* (*p.t. misled*) cause to form a wrong impression.

mismanage *v.t.* manage badly or wrongly. **mismanagement** *n.*

misnomer *n.* wrongly applied name or description.

misogynist /-ˈsɒdʒɪ-/ *n.* person who hates women.

misplace *v.t.* put in a wrong place; place (confidence etc.) unwisely.

misprint *n.* error in printing.

misquote *v.t.* quote incorrectly. **misquotation** *n.*

misrepresent *v.t.* represent in a false way. **misrepresentation** *n.*

misrule *n.* bad government.

miss *v.t./i.* fail to hit, catch, see, hear, understand, etc.; lack; notice or regret the absence or loss of; avoid; (of an engine) misfire. —*n.* failure to hit or attain what is aimed at.

Miss *n.* (*pl. Misses*) title of a girl or unmarried woman.

missal *n.* book containing prayers used in Mass in the R.C. Church.

misshapen *a.* badly shaped.

missile *n.* object or weapon suitable for projecting at a target.

missing *a.* not present; not in its place, lost.

mission *n.* task that a person or group is sent to perform; this group; missionaries' headquarters.

missionary *n.* person sent to spread Christian faith in a community.

missive *n.* written message sent to someone.

misspell *v.t.* (p.t. *misspelt*) spell incorrectly.

misspend *v.t.* (p.t. *misspent*) spend badly or unwisely.

mist *n.* water vapour near the ground or clouding a window etc.; thing resembling this. —*v.t./i.* cover or become covered with mist.

mistake *n.* incorrect idea or opinion; thing done incorrectly. —*v.t.* (p.t. *mistook*, p.p. *mistaken*) misunderstand; choose or identify wrongly. **mistaken** *a.* wrong in opinion; unwise. **mistakenly** *adv.*

mistime *v.t.* say or do (a thing) at a wrong time.

mistletoe *n.* plant with white berries, growing on trees.

mistress *n.* woman who has control of people or things; female teacher; man's illicit female lover.

mistrust *v.t.* feel no trust in. —*n.* lack of trust. **mistrustful** *a.*

misty *a.* (-ier, -iest) full of mist; indistinct. **mistily** *adv.*, **mistiness** *n.*

misunderstand *v.t.* (p.t. *-stood*) fail to understand correctly. **misunderstanding** *n.*

misuse[1] /-'juz/ *v.t.* use wrongly; treat badly.

misuse[2] /-'jus/ *n.* wrong use.

mite *n.* very small spider-like animal; small creature, esp. a child; small contribution.

mitigate *v.t.* make seem less serious or severe. **mitigation** *n.*

mitre /'maɪtə(r)/ *n.* pointed head-dress of bishops and abbots; join with tapered ends that form a right angle. —*v.t.* join in this way.

mitt *n.* mitten.

mitten *n.* glove with no partitions between the fingers, or leaving the finger-tips bare.

mix *v.t./i.* put (different things) together so that they are no longer distinct; prepare by doing this; combine, blend. —*n.* mixture. **~ up**, mix thoroughly; confuse. **mixer** *n.*

mixed *a.* composed of various elements, or of people from different races or social classes; of or for both sexes. **~-up** *a.* (*colloq.*) not well adjusted emotionally.

mixture *n.* thing made by mixing; process of mixing things.

ml *abbr.* millilitre(s).

mm *abbr.* millimetre(s).

mnemonic /nɪ'mon-/ *a.* & *n.* (verse etc.) aiding the memory.

moan *n.* low mournful sound; grumble. —*v.t./i.* make or utter with a moan. **moaner** *n.*

moat *n.* deep wide usu. water-filled ditch round a castle or house etc. **moated** *a.* surrounded by a moat.

mob *n.* large disorderly crowd; (*sl.*) gang. —*v.t.* (p.t. *mobbed*) crowd round in great numbers.

mobile *a.* able to move or be moved easily. —*n.* artistic structure for hanging so that its parts move in currents of air. **mobility** *n.*

mobilize *v.t./i.* assemble (troops etc.) for active service. **mobilization** *n.*

moccasin /'mok-/ *n.* soft leather shoe, stitched round the vamp.

mocha /'məʊkə/ *n.* a kind of coffee.

mock *v.t./i.* make fun of by imitating; jeer; defy contemptuously. —*a.* sham, imitation. **~-up** *n.* model for use in testing or study.

mockery *n.* mocking, ridicule; absurd or unsatisfactory imitation.

mode *n.* way a thing is done; current fashion.

model *n.* three-dimensional reproduction, usu. on a smaller scale; design, style; exemplary person or thing; person employed to pose for an artist or display clothes in a shop etc. by wearing them. —*a.* exemplary. —*v.t./i.* (p.t. *modelled*) make a model of; shape; design or plan in accordance with a model; work as artist's or fashion model, display (clothes) thus.

moderate[1] /-ət/ *a.* medium; not extreme or excessive. —*n.* holder of moderate views. **moderately** *adv.*

moderate[2] /-eɪt/ *v.t./i.* make or become moderate or less intense.

moderation *n.* moderating. **in ~,** in moderate amounts.

moderator *n.* Presbyterian minister presiding over a church assembly.

modern *a.* of present or recent times; in current style. **modernity** /-'dɜ-/ *n.*

modernize *v.t.* make modern, adapt to modern ways. **modernization** *n.*

modest *a.* not vain or boastful; moderate in size etc., not showy; showing regard for conventional decencies. **modestly** *adv.*, **modesty** *n.*

modicum *n.* small amount.

modify *v.t.* make less severe; make partial changes in; qualify by describing. **modification** *n.*

modish /'məʊ-/ *a.* fashionable.

modulate *v.t./i.* regulate, moderate; vary in tone or pitch. **modulation** *n.*

module *n.* standardized part or independent unit in furniture or a building or spacecraft etc.

mogul /'məʊ-/ *n.* (*colloq.*) important or influential person.

mohair *n.* fine silky hair of the angora goat; yarn or fabric made from this.

Mohammedan *a.* & *n.* Muslim.

moist *a.* (-er, -est) slightly wet. **moistness** *n.*

moisten *v.t./i.* make or become moist.

moisture *n.* water or other liquid diffused through a substance or as vapour or condensed on a surface.

moisturize *v.t.* make (skin) less dry. **moisturizer** *n.*

molar *n.* back tooth with a broad top, used in chewing.

molasses *n.* syrup from raw sugar; (*U.S.*) treacle.

mole[1] *n.* small dark spot on human skin.

mole[2] *n.* breakwater or causeway built out into the sea.

mole[3] *n.* small burrowing animal with dark fur.

molehill *n.* mound of earth thrown up by a mole.

molecule /ˈmolɪ-/ *n.* very small unit (usu. a group of atoms) of a substance. **molecular** /-ˈlek-/ *a.*

molest *v.t.* pester in a hostile way or so as to cause injury. **molestation** *n.*

mollify *v.t.* soothe the anger of. **mollification** *n.*

mollusc *n.* animal with a soft body and often a hard shell.

mollycoddle *v.t.* coddle excessively.

molten *a.* liquefied by heat.

moment *n.* point or brief portion of time; importance.

momentary /ˈməʊ-/ *a.* lasting only a moment. **momentarily** *adv.*

momentous /-ˈmen-/ *a.* of great importance.

momentum *n.* impetus gained by a moving body.

monarch *n.* ruler with the title of king, queen, emperor, or empress. **monarchic** /-ˈnɑk-/ *a.*, **monarchical** *a.*

monarchy *n.* form of government with a monarch as the supreme ruler.

monastery *n.* residence of a community of monks.

monastic /-ˈnæs-/ *a.* of monks or monasteries. **monasticism** *n.* monks' way of life.

Monday *n.* day after Sunday.

monetarist /ˈmʌnɪ-/ *n.* person who advocates control of the money supply in order to curb inflation.

monetary /ˈmʌnɪ-/ *a.* of money or currency.

money *n.* current coins; coins and banknotes; (pl. *-eys*) any form of currency; wealth. ~ **order,** printed order for payment of a specified sum, issued by the Post Office. ~**-spinner** *n.* profitable thing.

moneyed /ˈmʌnɪd/ *a.* wealthy.

Mongol *a.* & *n.* Mongolian.

mongol *n.* person suffering from mongolism.

mongolism *n.* abnormal congenital condition causing a broad face and mental deficiency.

mongoose *n.* (pl. *-gooses*) stoat-like tropical animal that can attack and kill snakes.

mongrel *n.* animal (esp. a dog) of mixed breed. —*a.* of mixed origin or character.

monitor *n.* pupil with special duties in a school; device used to observe or test the operation of something. —*v.t.* keep watch over, record and test or control.

monk *n.* member of a male community living apart from the world under the rules of a religious order.

monkey *n.* (pl. *-eys*) animal of a group closely related to man; mischievous person. —*v.i.* (p.t. *monkeyed*) tamper mischievously. ~**-nut** *n.* peanut. ~**-puzzle,** evergreen tree with narrow stiff leaves on interlaced branches. ~**-wrench** *n.* wrench with an adjustable jaw.

mono *a.* & *n.* (pl. *-os*) monophonic (sound or recording).

monochrome *a.* done in only one colour, black-and-white.

monocle *n.* eye-glass for one eye only.

monogamy *n.* system of being married to only one person at a time.

monogram *n.* two or more letters (esp. a person's initials) combined in one design. **monogrammed** *a.*

monograph *n.* scholarly treatise on a single subject.

monologue *n.* long speech.

monophonic /-ˈfon-/ *a.* using only one transmission channel for reproduction of sound.

monoplane *n.* aeroplane with only one set of wings.

monopolize *v.t.* have a monopoly of; not allow others to share in. **monopolization** *n.*

monopoly *n.* sole possession or control of something, esp. of trade in a commodity.

monorail *n.* railway in which the track is a single rail.

monosyllable *n.* word of one syllable. **monosyllabic** /-ˈlæ-/ *a.*

monotheism /ˈmonəθiːɪzm/ *n.* doctrine that there is only one God.

monotone *n.* level unchanging tone of voice.

monotonous *a.* lacking in variety or variation; dull because of this. **monotonously** *adv.*, **monotony** *n.*

Monsignor /-ˈsinjɔ(r)/ *n.* title of certain R.C. priests and officials.

monsoon *n.* seasonal wind in South Asia; rainy season accompanying the south-west monsoon.

monster *n.* thing that is huge or very abnormal in form; huge ugly or frightening creature; very cruel or wicked person.

monstrance *n.* framed holder used in the R.C. Church for exposing the Host for veneration.

monstrosity *n.* monstrous thing.

monstrous *a.* like a monster, huge; outrageous, absurd.

montage /ˈmontaʒ/ *n.* making of a composite picture from pieces of others; this picture; joining of disconnected shots in a cinema film.

montbretia /monˈbriːʃə/ *n.* plant of the iris family with small orange-coloured flowers.

month *n.* any of the twelve portions into which the year is divided; period of four weeks.

monthly *a.* & *adv.* (produced or occurring) once a month. —*n.* monthly periodical.

monument *n.* thing (esp. a structure) commemorating a person or event etc.; structure of historical importance.

monumental /-ˈmen-/ *a.* of or serving as a monument; massive; extremely great.

moo *n.* cow's low deep cry. —*v.i.* make this sound.

mooch *v.i.* (*sl.*) walk slowly and aimlessly.

mood *n.* temporary state of mind or spirits; fit of bad temper or depression; verb-form showing whether it is a statement, command, etc.

moody *a.* (*-ier, -iest*) gloomy, sullen; liable to become like this. **moodily** *adv.*, **moodiness** *n.*

moon *n.* earth's satellite, made visible by light it reflects from the sun; natural satellite of any planet. —*v.i.* behave dreamily.

moonbeam *n.* ray of moonlight.

moonlight *n.* light from the moon.

moonlighting n. (colloq.) having two paid jobs, one by day and the other in the evening.

moonlit a. lit by the moon.

moonstone n. pearly semi-precious stone.

moor¹ n. stretch of open uncultivated land with low shrubs.

moor² v.t. secure (a boat etc.) to a fixed object by means of cable(s).

Moor n. member of a Muslim people of north-west Africa. **Moorish** a.

moorhen n. small water-bird.

moorings n.pl. cables or place for mooring a boat.

moose n. (pl. moose) elk of North America.

moot a. debatable. —v.t. raise (a question) for discussion.

mop n. pad or bundle of yarn on a stick, used for cleaning things; thick mass of hair. —v.t. (p.t. mopped) clean with a mop; wipe away. ～ **up**, wipe up with a mop or cloth etc.; clear an area of the remnants of enemy troops, after victory.

mope v.i. be unhappy and listless.

moped /ˈməʊped/ n. motorized bicycle.

moquette /-ˈket/ n. upholstery fabric with loops or pile.

moraine n. mass of stones etc. carried and deposited by a glacier.

moral a. concerned with right and wrong conduct; virtuous. —n. moral lesson or principle; (pl.) person's moral habits, esp. sexual conduct. ～ **certainty**, virtual certainty. ～ **support**, encouragement. ～ **victory**, a triumph though without concrete gain. **morally** adv.

morale /-ˈrɑl/ n. state of a person's or group's spirits and confidence.

moralist n. person who expresses or teaches moral principles.

morality n. moral principles or rules; goodness or rightness.

moralize v.i. talk or write about the morality of something.

morass /-ˈræs/ n. marsh, bog; complex entanglement.

moratorium n. (pl. -ums) temporary agreed ban on an activity.

morbid a. preoccupied with gloomy or unpleasant things; unhealthy. **morbidly** adv., **morbidness** n., **morbidity** n.

mordant a. (of wit etc.) caustic.

more a. greater in quantity or intensity etc. —n. greater amount or number. —adv. to a greater extent; again. ～ **or less**, approximately.

moreover adv. besides.

morganatic /-ˈnæ-/ a. ～ **marriage**, one where a woman of low rank does not take her husband's high rank.

morgue /mɔg/ n. mortuary.

moribund /ˈmo-/ a. in a dying state.

Mormon n. member of a Christian sect founded in 1830 in the U.S.A.

morning n. part of the day from dawn to noon or the midday meal. ～ **star**, Venus or other bright star seen in the east before sunrise.

morocco n. goatskin leather of the kind originally made in Morocco; imitation of this.

moron n. adult with intelligence equal to that of a child of 8–12 years old; (colloq.) very stupid person.

morose /-ˈrəʊs/ a. gloomy and unsociable, sullen. **morosely** adv., **moroseness** n.

morphia n. morphine.

morphine /-fin/ n. drug made from opium, used to relieve pain.

morris a. ～ **dance**, English folk-dance by men in costume.

morrow n. (old use) next day.

Morse n. ～ **code**, code of signals using short and long sounds or flashes of light.

morsel n. small amount; small piece of food.

mortal a. subject to death; fatal; deadly. —n. person subject to death, human being. **mortally** adv.

mortality n. being mortal; loss of life on a large scale; death-rate.

mortar n. mixture of lime or cement with sand and water, used for joining bricks or stones; hard bowl in which substances are pounded with a pestle; short cannon. ～**board** n. stiff square cap worn as part of academic dress.

mortgage n. loan for purchase of property, in which the property itself is pledged as security; agreement effecting this. —v.t. pledge (property) as security thus.

mortify v.t./i. humiliate greatly; (of flesh) become gangrenous. **mortification** n.

mortise n. hole in one part of a framework shaped to receive the end of another part. ～ **lock**, lock set in (not on) a door.

mortuary n. place where dead bodies may be kept temporarily.

mosaic n. pattern or picture made with small pieces of glass or stone of different colours.

Moslem a. & n. = Muslim.

mosque n. Muslim place of worship.

mosquito n. (pl. -oes) a kind of gnat.

moss n. small flowerless plant forming a dense growth in moist places. **mossy** a.

most a. greatest in quantity or intensity etc. —n. greatest amount or number. —adv. to the greatest extent; very. **at ～**, not more than. **for the ～ part**, in most cases; in most of its extent. **make the ～ of**, use or represent to the best advantage.

mostly adv. for the most part.

motel n. roadside hotel providing accommodation for motorists and their vehicles.

moth n. insect like a butterfly but usu. flying at night; similar insect whose larvae feed on cloth or fur. ～**ball** n. small ball of pungent substance for keeping moths away from clothes. ～**eaten** a. damaged by the larvae of moths.

mother n. female parent; title of the female head of a religious community. —v.t. look after in a motherly way. ～**in-law** n. (pl. ～s-in-law) mother of one's wife or husband. ～**of-pearl** n. pearly substance lining shells of oysters and mussels etc. **Mother's Day**, Mothering Sunday. ～ **tongue**, one's native language. **Mothering Sunday,** fourth Sunday in Lent, with the custom of giving a gift to one's mother. **motherhood** n.

motherland n. one's native country.

motherless a. without a living mother.

motherly a. showing a mother's kindness. **motherliness** n.

motif /-'tif/ n. recurring design, feature, or melody; ornament sewn on a dress etc.

motion n. moving; movement; formal proposal put to a meeting for discussion; emptying of the bowels, faeces. —v.t./i. make a gesture directing (a person) to do something.

motionless a. not moving.

motivate v.t. supply a motive to; cause to feel active interest. **motivation** n.

motive n. that which induces a person to act in a certain way. —a. producing movement or action.

motley a. multi-coloured; assorted.

motor n. machine supplying motive power; motor car. —a. producing motion; driven by a motor. —v.t./i. go or convey in a motor car. ∼ **bike,** (colloq.) motor cycle. ∼ **car,** low short-bodied motor vehicle. ∼ **cycle,** motor-driven cycle that cannot be driven by pedals. ∼**cyclist** n. rider of a motor cycle. ∼ **vehicle,** vehicle with a motor engine, for use on ordinary roads.

motorcade n. (U.S.) procession or parade of motor vehicles.

motorist n. driver of a motor car.

motorize v.t. equip with motor(s) or motor vehicles.

motorway n. road constructed and controlled for fast motor traffic.

mottled a. patterned with irregular patches of colour.

motto n. (pl. -oes) short sentence or phrase expressing an ideal or rule of conduct; maxim, riddle, etc., inside a paper cracker.

mould[1] n. hollow container into which a liquid substance is poured to set or cool in a desired shape; pudding etc. made in this. —v.t. shape; guide or control the development of.

mould[2] n. furry growth of tiny fungi on a damp substance.

mould[3] n. soft fine earth rich in organic matter.

moulder[1] n. workman who makes moulds for casting metal.

moulder[2] v.i. decay and rot away.

moulding n. moulded thing, esp. an ornamental strip of plaster etc.

mouldy a. covered with mould; stale; (sl.) worthless.

moult /məu-/ v.i. shed feathers, hair, or skin before new growth. —n. process of moulting.

mound n. mass of piled-up earth or small stones; small hill.

mount[1] n. mountain, hill.

mount[2] v.t./i. go up; get or put on a horse etc. for riding; increase; fix on or in support(s) or setting; organize, arrange. —n. horse for riding; thing on which something is fixed for support etc.

mountain n. mass of land rising to a great height, esp. over 1000 ft.; large heap or pile. ∼ **ash,** rowan tree.

mountaineer n. climber of mountains. **mountaineering** n.

mountainous a. full of mountains; huge.

mountebank /'mauntɪ-/ n. charlatan.

Mountie n. member of the Royal Canadian Mounted Police.

mourn v.t./i. feel or express sorrow or regret about (a dead person or lost thing). **mourner** n.

mournful a. sorrowful. **mournfully** adv., **mournfulness** n.

mourning n. dark clothes worn as a conventional sign of bereavement.

mouse n. (pl. mice) small rodent with a long tail; quiet timid person.

mousetrap n. trap for mice.

moussaka /mʊˈsɑ-/ n. Greek dish of minced meat and aubergine.

mousse /mus/ n. soft creamy dish.

moustache /məˈstɑʃ/ n. hair allowed to grow on a man's upper lip.

mousy a. dull greyish-brown; quiet and timid.

mouth[1] /-θ/ n. opening in the face through which food is taken in and sounds uttered; opening of a bag, cave, cannon, etc.; place where a river enters the sea. ∼**-organ** n. small wind-instrument played by blowing and sucking.

mouth[2] /-ð/ v.t./i. form (words) soundlessly with the lips; declaim pompously or with exaggerated distinctness.

mouthful n. amount that fills the mouth.

mouthpiece n. part of an instrument placed between or near the lips; person speaking on behalf of others.

mouthwash n. liquid for cleansing the mouth.

movable a. able to be moved.

move v.t./i. change or cause to change in place or position or attitude; change one's residence; progress; provoke reaction or emotion in; take action; put to a meeting for discussion. —n. act of moving; moving of a piece in chess etc.; calculated action. **on the** ∼, moving. **mover** n.

movement n. moving; move; moving parts; group's organized actions to achieve a purpose, the group itself; section of a long piece of music.

movie n. (U.S.) cinema film.

moving a. arousing pity or sympathy.

mow v.t. (p.p. mown) cut down (grass or grain etc.); cut grass etc. from. ∼ **down,** kill or destroy by a moving force. **mower** n.

M.P. abbr. Member of Parliament.

m.p.h. abbr. miles per hour.

Mr. n. (pl. Messrs.) title prefixed to a man's name.

Mrs. n. (pl. Mrs.) title prefixed to a married woman's name.

Ms. /mɪz/ n. title prefixed to a woman's name without distinction of married or unmarried status.

Mt. abbr. Mount.

much *a. & n.* (existing in) great quantity. —*adv.* in a great degree; to a great extent.

muck *n.* farmyard manure; (*colloq.*) dirt, a mess. —*v.t.* make dirty; mess. ∼ **in,** (*sl.*) share tasks etc. equally. ∼ **out,** remove muck from. ∼**-raking** *n.* seeking and exposing scandal.

mucky *a.*

mucous *a.* like or covered with mucus.

mucus *n.* slimy substance coating the inner surface of hollow organs of the body.

mud *n.* wet soft earth. ∼**-slinging** *n.* (*sl.*) attacking a reputation.

muddle *v.t./i.* confuse, mix up; progress in a haphazard way. —*n.* muddled condition or things.

muddy *a.* (-*ier*, -*iest*) like mud, full of mud; not clear or pure.—*v.t.* make muddy. **muddiness** *n.*

mudguard *n.* curved cover above the wheel of cycle etc. to protect the rider from the mud it throws up.

mudlark *n.* child who plays in mud; person who scavenges articles from mud.

muesli /ˈmuzlɪ/ *n.* food of mixed crushed cereals, dried fruit, nuts, etc.

muezzin /muˈɛz-/ *n.* man who proclaims the hours of prayer for Muslims.

muff[1] *n.* tube-shaped usu. furry covering for the hands.

muff[2] *v.t.* (*colloq.*) bungle.

muffin *n.* light round cake eaten toasted and buttered.

muffle *v.t.* wrap for warmth or protection, or to deaden sound; make less loud or less distinct.

muffler *n.* scarf worn for warmth.

mufti *n.* plain clothes worn by one who has the right to wear uniform.

mug[1] *n.* large drinking-vessel with a handle, for use without a saucer; (*sl.*) face; (*sl.*) person who is easily deceived. —*v.t.* (p.t. *mugged*) rob (a person) with violence, esp. in a public place. **mugger** *n.*

mug[2] *v.t.* (p.t. *mugged*) ∼ **up,** (*sl.*) learn (a subject) by studying hard.

muggy *a.* (of weather) oppressively damp and warm.

mulatto *n.* (pl. -*os*) person with one white and one black parent.

mulberry *n.* purple or white fruit resembling a blackberry; tree bearing this; dull purplish-red.

mulch *n.* mixture of wet straw, leaves, etc., spread on ground to protect plants or retain moisture. —*v.t.* cover with mulch.

mulct *v.t.* take money from (a person) by a fine, taxation, etc.

mule[1] *n.* animal that is the offspring of a horse and a donkey, known for its stubbornness.

mule[2] *n.* backless slipper.

mulish *a.* stubborn. **mulishly** *adv.*, **mulishness** *n.*

mull[1] *v.t.* heat (wine etc.) with sugar and spices, as a drink.

mull[2] *v.t.* ∼ **over,** think over.

mull[3] *n.* (*Sc.*) promontory.

mullein /-lɪn/ *n.* herb with spikes of yellow flowers.

mullet *n.* small edible sea-fish.

mulligatawny *n.* curry-flavoured soup.

mullion *n.* upright usu. stone strip between the panes of a tall window.

multi- *pref.* many.

multifarious /-ˈfeər-/ *a.* very varied.

multimillionaire *n.* person with a fortune of several million pounds.

multinational *a. & n.* (business company) operating in several countries.

multiple *a.* having or affecting many parts. —*n.* quantity containing another a number of times without remainder.

multiplication *n.* multiplying.

multiplicity *n.* great variety.

multiply *v.t./i.* take a quantity a specified number of times and find the quantity produced; increase in number. **multiplier** *n.*

multitude *n.* great number of things or people.

multitudinous *a.* very numerous.

mum[1] *a.* (*colloq.*) silent.

mum[2] *n.* (*colloq.*) mother.

mumble *v.t./i.* speak or utter indistinctly. —*n.* indistinct speech.

mumbo-jumbo *n.* meaningless ritual; deliberately obscure language.

mummify *v.t.* preserve (a corpse) by embalming as in ancient Egypt.

mummy[1] *n.* corpse embalmed and wrapped for burial esp. in ancient Egypt.

mummy[2] *n.* (*colloq.*) mother.

mumps *n.* virus disease with painful swellings in the neck.

munch *v.t.* chew vigorously.

mundane *a.* dull, routine; worldly.

municipal *a.* of a town or city.

municipality /-ˈpæl-/ *n.* self-governing town or district.

munificent *a.* splendidly generous. **munificently** *adv.*, **munificence** *n.*

munitions *n.pl.* weapons, ammunition, etc., used in war.

mural *a.* of or on a wall. —*n.* a painting made on a wall.

murder *n.* intentional unlawful killing. —*v.t.* kill intentionally and unlawfully; (*colloq.*) ruin by bad performance. **murderer** *n.*, **murderess** *n.fem.*

murderous *a.* involving or capable of murder.

murky *a.* (-*ier*, -*iest*) dark, gloomy.

murmur *n.* low continuous sound; softly spoken words. —*v.t./i.* make a murmur; speak or utter softly.

muscatel *n.* a kind of raisin.

muscle *n.* strip of fibrous tissue able to contract and relax and so move a part of an animal body; muscular power; strength. —*v.i.* ∼ **in** (*U.S. sl.*) force one's way.

muscular *a.* of muscles; having well-developed muscles. **muscularity** *n.*

muse *v.i.* ponder.

Muse *n.* one of the nine sister goddesses in Greek and Roman mythology, presiding over branches of learning and the arts.

museum *n.* place where objects of historical interest are collected and displayed.

mush *n.* soft pulp.

mushroom n. edible fungus with a stem and a domed cap, noted for its rapid growth; fawn colour. —v.i. spring up in large numbers; rise and spread in a mushroom shape.

mushy a. as or like mush; feebly sentimental. **mushiness** n.

music n. pleasing arrangement of sounds of one or more voices or instruments; written form of this. **~-hall** n. variety entertainment.

musical a. of or involving music; fond of or skilled in music; sweet-sounding. —n. light play with songs and dancing. **musically** adv.

musician n. person skilled in music.

musk n. substance secreted by certain animals or produced synthetically, used in perfumes. **musky** a.

musket n. long-barrelled gun formerly used by infantry. **musketeer** n. soldier armed with this.

Muslim a. of the Islamic faith, based on Muhammad's teaching. —n. believer in this faith.

muslin n. a kind of thin cotton cloth.

musquash n. rat-like North American water animal; its fur.

mussel n. a kind of bivalve mollusc.

must[1] v.aux. (used to express necessity or obligation, certainty, or insistence). —n. (colloq.) thing that must be done or visited etc.

must[2] n. grape-juice etc. undergoing fermentation; new wine.

mustang n. wild horse of Mexico and California.

mustard n. plant with yellow flowers and sharp-tasting seeds; these seeds ground to paste as a condiment; dark yellow.

muster v.t./i. assemble, gather. —n. gathering of people or things. **pass ~**, be accepted as adequate.

musty a. (-ier, -iest) smelling mouldy, stale. **mustiness** n.

mutable a. liable to change, fickle. **mutability** n.

mutant a. & n. (living thing) differing from its parents as a result of genetic change.

mutation n. change in form; mutant.

mute a. silent; dumb. —n. dumb person; device deadening the sound of a musical instrument. —v.t. deaden or muffle the sound of. **mutely** adv.

mutilate v.t. injure or disfigure by cutting off a part. **mutilation** n.

mutineer n. person who mutinies.

mutinous a. rebellious, ready to mutiny. **mutinously** adv.

mutiny n. open rebellion against authority, esp. by members of the armed forces. —v.i. engage in mutiny.

mutt n. (sl.) stupid person.

mutter v.t./i. speak or utter in a low unclear tone; utter subdued grumbles. —n. muttering.

mutton n. flesh of sheep as food.

mutual a. felt or done by each to the other; (colloq.) common to two or more. **mutually** adv.

muzzle n. projecting nose and jaws of certain animals; open end of a firearm; strap etc. over an animal's head to prevent it from biting or feeding. —v.t. put a muzzle on; prevent from expressing opinions freely.

muzzy a. dazed, feeling stupefied. **muzziness** n.

my a. belonging to me.

myopic /-'op-/ a. short-sighted.

myriad /'mɪrɪ-/ n. vast number.

myrmidon /'mɜ-/ n. henchman.

myrrh[1] /mɜ(r)/ n. gum resin used in perfumes, medicines, and incense.

myrrh[2] /mɜr/ n. white-flowered herb.

myrtle n. evergreen shrub.

myself pron. emphatic and reflexive form of I and me.

mysterious a. full of mystery, puzzling. **mysteriously** adv.

mystery n. a matter that remains unexplained or secret; quality of being unexplained or obscure; story dealing with a puzzling crime.

mystic a. having a hidden or symbolic meaning, esp. in religion; inspiring a sense of mystery and awe. —n. person who seeks to obtain union with God by spiritual contemplation. **mystical** a., **mystically** adv., **mysticism** n.

mystify v.t. cause to feel puzzled. **mystification** n.

mystique /-'tik/ n. aura of mystery or mystical power.

myth n. traditional tale(s) containing beliefs about ancient times or natural events; imaginary person or thing. **mythical** a.

mythology n. myths; study of myths. **mythological** a.

myxomatosis /-'təʊ-/ n. fatal virus disease of rabbits.

N

N. abbr. north; northern.

nab v.t. (p.t. **nabbed**) (sl.) catch in wrongdoing, arrest; seize.

nadir /'neɪdɪə(r)/ n. lowest point.

nag[1] n. (colloq.) horse.

nag[2] v.t./i. (p.t. **nagged**) find fault or scold continually; (of pain etc.) be felt persistently.

naiad /'naɪæd/ n. water-nymph.

nail n. layer of horny substance over the outer tip of a finger or toe; claw; small metal spike. —v.t. fasten with nail(s); catch, arrest. **on the ~**, (esp. of payment) without delay.

naïve /naɪ'iv/ a. showing lack of experience or of informed judgement. **naïvely** adv., **naïvety**, **naïveté** /-vteɪ/ ns.

naked a. without clothes on; without coverings or ornamentation. **~ eye**, the eye unassisted

by a telescope or microscope etc. **nakedly**
adv., **nakedness** *n.*

namby-pamby *a.* & *n.* feeble or unmanly
(person).

name *n.* word(s) by which a person, place, or
thing is known or indicated; reputation. —*v.t.*
give as a name; nominate, specify.

nameless *a.* not named.

namely *adv.* that is to say, specifically.

namesake *n.* person or thing with the same
name as another.

nanny *n.* child's nurse. **∼-goat** *n.* female
goat.

nap[1] *n.* short sleep, esp. during the day. —*v.i.*
(p.t. *napped*) have a nap. **catch a person
napping**, catch him unawares.

nap[2] *n.* short raised fibres on the surface of
cloth or leather.

nap[3] *n.* a card-game; betting all one's money on
one chance, tipster's choice for this. **go ∼,**
stake everything.

napalm /ˈneɪpɑm/ *n.* jelly-like petrol substance
used in incendiary bombs.

nape *n.* back part of neck.

naphtha /ˈnæf-/ *n.* inflammable oil.

naphthalene /ˈnæf-/ *n.* pungent white substance
obtained from coal-tar.

napkin *n.* square piece of cloth or paper used to
protect clothes or for wiping one's lips at
meals; piece of cloth worn by a baby to
absorb or retain its excreta.

nappy *n.* baby's napkin.

narcissus *n.* (pl. *-cissi*) flower of the group
including the daffodil.

narcotic /-ˈkot-/ *a.* & *n.* (drug) causing sleep or
drowsiness.

narrate *v.t.* tell (a story), give an account of.
narration *n.*, **narrator** *n.*

narrative /ˈnæ-/ *n.* spoken or written account of
something. —*a.* in this form.

narrow *a.* (*-er*, *-est*) small across, not wide; with
little margin or scope or variety. —*v.t./i.*
make or become narrower. **∼-minded** *a.*
having intolerant views. **narrowly** *adv.*,
narrowness *n.*

narwhal /-wəl/ *n.* Arctic whale with a spirally
grooved tusk.

nasal *a.* of the nose; sounding as if breath came
out through the nose. **nasally** *adv.*

nasturtium *n.* trailing garden plant with
orange, red, or yellow flowers.

nasty *a.* (*-ier*, *-iest*) unpleasant; unkind;
difficult. **nastily** *adv.*, **nastiness** *n.*

natal /ˈneɪ-/ *a.* of or from one's birth.

nation *n.* people of mainly common descent
and history usu. inhabiting a particular
country under one government.

national *a.* of a nation; common to a whole
nation. —*n.* citizen or subject of a particular
country. **nationally** *adv.*

nationalism *n.* patriotic feeling; policy of
national independence. **nationalist** *n.*,
nationalistic *a.*

nationality *n.* condition of belonging to a
particular nation.

nationalize *v.t.* convert (industries etc.) from

private to government ownership. **nationali-
zation** *n.*

native *a.* natural; belonging to a place by birth
or to a person because of his birth-place,
grown or produced in a specified place; of
natives. —*n.* person born in a specified place;
local inhabitant.

nativity *n.* birth; *the N∼*, that of Christ.

natter *v.i.* & *n.* (*colloq.*) chat.

natty *a.* (*-ier*, *-iest*) neat and trim, dapper
nattily *adv.*

natural *a.* of or produced by nature; normal,
not seeming artificial or affected; (of a note in
music) neither sharp nor flat. —*n.* person or
thing that seems naturally suited for something; natural note in music, sign indicating
this; pale fawn colour. **∼ history,** study of
animal and plant life. **naturally** *adv.*, **natural-
ness** *n.*

naturalism *n.* realism in art and literature
naturalistic *a.*

naturalist *n.* expert in natural history.

naturalize *v.t.* admit (a person of foreign birth)
to full citizenship of a country; introduce and
acclimatize (an animal or plant) into a
country. **naturalization** *n.*

nature *n.* the world with all its features and
living things; physical power producing these
kind, sort; complex of innate characteristics
all that makes a thing what it is.

-natured *a.* having a nature of a certain kind

naturist *n.* nudist. **naturism** *n.*

naught *n.* (*old use*) nothing.

naughty *a.* (*-ier*, *-iest*) behaving badly, dis
obedient; slightly indecent. **naughtily** *adv.*
naughtiness *n.*

nausea *n.* feeling of sickness.

nauseate *v.t.* affect with nausea.

nauseous *a.* causing nausea.

nautical *a.* of sailors or seamanship. **naval** *a.* o
a navy.

nave *n.* body of a church apart from the
chancel, aisles, and transepts.

navel *n.* small hollow in the centre of the
abdomen.

navigable *a.* suitable for ships to sail in; able t
be steered and sailed.

navigate *v.t.* sail in or through (a sea or rive
etc.); direct the course of (a ship or vehicl
etc.). **navigation** *n.*, **navigator** *n.*

navvy *n.* labourer making roads etc. wher
digging is necessary.

navy *n.* a country's warships; officers and me
of these; navy blue. **∼ blue,** very dark blue.

nay *adv.* (*old use*) no.

Nazi *n.* (pl. *-is*) member of the Nationa
Socialist party in Germany, brought to powe
by Hitler. **Nazism** *n.*

N.B. *abbr.* (Latin *nota bene*) note well.

N.C.O. *abbr.* non-commissioned officer.

neap *n.* **∼ tide,** tide when there is least rise an
fall of water.

Neapolitan *a.* & *n.* (native or inhabitant) o
Naples. **∼ ice,** ice cream made in layers o
different colours and flavours.

near *adv.* at, to, or within a short distance o

interval; nearly. —*prep.* near to. —*a.* with only a short distance or interval between; closely related; with little margin; of the left side of a horse, vehicle, or road; stingy. —*v.t./i.* draw near. **∼by,** not far away. **Near East,** Middle East. **nearness** *n.*

nearby *a.* near in position.

nearly *adv.* closely; almost.

neat *a.* (*-er, -est*) clean and orderly in appearance or workmanship; undiluted. **neatly** *adv.*, **neatness** *n.*

neaten *v.t.* make neat.

nebula *n.* (pl. *-ae*) bright or dark patch in the sky caused by distant stars or a cloud of gas or dust.

nebulous *a.* indistinct.

necessarily /ˈnes-/ *adv.* as a necessary result, inevitably.

necessary *a.* essential in order to achieve something; happening or existing by necessity. **necessaries** *n.pl.* things without which life cannot be maintained or is harsh.

necessitate *v.t.* make necessary; involve as a condition or result.

necessitous *a.* needy.

necessity *n.* state or fact of being necessary; necessary thing; compelling power of circumstances; state of need or hardship.

neck *n.* narrow part connecting the head to the body; part of a garment round this; narrow part of a bottle, cavity, etc. **∼ and neck,** running level in a race.

necklace *n.* string of precious stones or beads etc. worn round the neck.

necklet *n.* necklace; fur worn round the neck.

neckline *n.* outline formed by the edge of a garment at the neck.

necktie *n.* man's tie.

necromancy /ˈnek-/ *n.* art of predicting things by communicating with the dead. **necromancer** *n.*

necropolis /-ˈkrop-/ *n.* ancient cemetery.

nectar *n.* sweet fluid from plants, collected by bees; any delicious drink.

nectarine /-rɪn/ *n.* a kind of peach with no down on the skin.

née /neɪ/ *a.* born (used in stating a married woman's maiden name).

need *n.* requirement; state of great difficulty or misfortune; poverty. —*v.t./i.* be in need of, require; be obliged.

needful *a.* necessary.

needle *n.* small thin pointed piece of steel used in sewing; thing shaped like this; pointer of a compass or gauge. —*v.t.* annoy, provoke.

needless *a.* unnecessary.

needlework *n.* sewing or embroidery.

needy *a.* (*-ier, -iest*) lacking the necessaries of life, very poor.

nefarious /nɪˈfeər-/ *a.* wicked.

negate /-ˈgeɪt/ *v.t.* nullify, disprove. **negation** *n.*

negative *a.* expressing or implying denial, refusal, or prohibition; not positive; (of a quantity) less than zero; (of a battery terminal) through which electric current leaves. —*n.* negative statement or word; negative quality or quantity; photograph with lights and shades or colours reversed, from which positive pictures can be obtained. —*v.t.* veto; contradict; neutralize (an effect). **negatively** *adv.*

neglect *v.t.* pay insufficient or no attention to; fail to take proper care of; omit (to do something). —*n.* neglecting, being neglected. **neglectful** *a.*

négligé /ˈneglɪʒeɪ/ *n.* woman's flimsy ornamental dressing-gown.

negligence *n.* lack of proper care or attention. **negligent** *a.*

negligible *a.* too small to be worth taking into account.

negotiable *a.* able to be negotiated.

negotiate *v.t./i.* hold a discussion so as to reach agreement; arrange by such discussion; exchange (a cheque or bonds etc.) for money; get past (an obstacle) successfully. **negotiation** *n.*, **negotiator** *n.*

Negro *n.* (pl. *-oes*) member of the black-skinned race that originated in Africa. **Negress** *n.fem.*

Negroid *a. & n.* (person) having the physical characteristics of Negroes.

neigh /neɪ/ *n.* horse's long high-pitched cry. —*v.i.* make this cry.

neighbour *n.* person or thing living or situated near or next to another.

neighbourhood *n.* district. **in the ∼ of,** near, approximately.

neighbouring *a.* living or situated near by.

neighbourly *a.* kind and friendly towards neighbours.

neither /ˈnaɪ- or ˈniː-/ *a. & pron.* not either. —*adv. & conj.* not either; also not.

nelson *n.* a kind of hold in wrestling.

nemesis /ˈnemɪ-/ *n.* inevitable retribution.

neolithic *a.* of the later part of the Stone Age.

neon *n.* a kind of gas much used in illuminated signs.

nephew *n.* one's brother's or sister's son.

nepotism /ˈnepə-/ *n.* favouritism shown to relatives in appointing them to jobs.

nerve *n.* fibre carrying impulses of sensation or movement between the brain or spinal cord and a part of the body; courage; (*colloq.*) impudent boldness; (*pl.*) nervousness, effect of mental stress. —*v.t.* give courage to.

nervous *a.* of the nerves; easily agitated or frightened; slightly afraid. **nervously** *adv.*, **nervousness** *n.*

nervy *a.* nervous.

nest *n.* structure or place in which a bird lays eggs and shelters its young; breeding-place, lair; snug place, shelter; set of articles (esp. tables) designed to fit inside each other. —*v.i.* make or have a nest. **∼-egg** *n.* sum of money saved for future use.

nestle *v.i.* press oneself comfortably into a soft place; lie sheltered.

nestling *n.* bird too young to leave the nest.

net[1] *n.* open-work material of thread, cord, or wire etc.; piece of this used for a particular purpose. —*v.t.* (p.t. *netted*) make by forming threads into a net; place nets in or on; catch in or as if in a net.

net[2] *a.* remaining after all deductions; (of weight) not including wrappings etc. —*v.t.* (p.t. *netted*) obtain or yield as net profit.

netball *n.* team game in which a ball has to be thrown into a high net.

nether /ˈneð-/ *a.* lower.

nethermost /ˈneð-/ *a.* lowest.

netting *n.* netted fabric.

nettle *n.* wild plant with leaves that sting and redden the skin when touched; similar non-stinging plant. —*v.t.* irritate, provoke. **∼-rash** *n.* eruption on skin like that caused by nettles.

network *n.* arrangement with intersecting lines; complex system.

neuralgia *n.* sharp pain along a nerve, esp. in the head or face. **neuralgic** *a.*

neurology *n.* study of nerve systems. **neurological** *a.*, **neurologist** *n.*

neurosis *n.* (pl. *-oses*) mental disorder sometimes with physical symptoms but with no evidence of disease.

neurotic *a.* of or caused by a neurosis; subject to abnormal anxieties or obsessive behaviour. —*n.* neurotic person. **neurotically** *adv.*

neuter *a.* (of words) neither masculine nor feminine; (of plants) without male or female parts; (of insects) sexually undeveloped, sterile. —*n.* neuter word, plant, or insect; castrated animal. —*v.t.* castrate.

neutral *a.* not supporting either side in a conflict; without distinctive or positive characteristics. —*n.* neutral person, country, or colour; neutral gear. **∼ gear,** position of gear mechanism in which the engine is disconnected from driven parts. **neutrally** *adv.*, **neutrality** *n.*

neutralize *v.t.* make ineffective. **neutralization** *n.*

neutron *n.* nuclear particle with no electric charge. **∼ bomb,** nuclear bomb that kills people by intense radiation but does little damage to buildings etc.

never *adv.* at no time, on no occasion; not; (*colloq.*) surely not. **∼ mind,** do not be troubled.

nevertheless *adv.* & *conj.* in spite of this.

new *a.* (*-er, -est*) not existing before, recently made or discovered or experienced etc.; unfamiliar, unaccustomed. —*adv.* newly, recently. **∼ moon,** moon seen as a crescent. **New Testament** (see *Testament*). **New World,** the Americas. **∼ year,** first days of January. **New Year's Day,** 1 Jan. **New Year's Eve,** 31 Dec.

newcomer *n.* one who has arrived recently.

newel *n.* top or bottom post of the handrail of a stair; central pillar of a winding stair.

newfangled *a.* objectionably new in method or style.

newly *adv.* recently, freshly. **∼-wed** *a.* & *n.* recently married (person).

news *n.* new or interesting information about recent events; broadcast report of this.

newsagent *n.* shopkeeper who sells newspapers.

newsletter *n.* informal printed report containing news of interest to members of a club etc.

newspaper *n.* printed usu. daily or weekly publication containing news reports; sheets of paper forming this.

newsprint *n.* type of paper on which newspapers are printed.

newsreel *n.* cinema film showing current items of news.

newt *n.* small lizard-like amphibious creature.

next *a.* nearest in position or time etc.; soonest come to. —*adv.* in the next place or degree; on the next occasion. —*n.* next person or thing. **∼ best,** second best. **∼ door,** in the next house or room. **∼ door to,** almost. **∼ of kin,** one's closest relative. **∼ world,** life after death.

nexus *n.* (pl. *-uses*) connected group or series.

nib *n.* metal point of a pen.

nibble *v.t./i.* take small quick or gentle bites (at). —*n.* small quick bite. **nibbler** *n.*

nice *a.* (*-er, -est*) pleasant, satisfactory; (*iron.*) difficult, bad; needing precision and care; fastidious. **nicely** *adv.*, **niceness** *n.*

nicety /ˈnaɪsɪtɪ/ *n.* precision; detail. **to a ∼,** exactly.

niche /nɪtʃ/ *n.* shallow recess esp. in a wall; suitable position in life or employment.

nick *n.* small cut or notch; (*sl.*) police station, prison. —*v.t.* make a nick in; (*sl.*) steal; (*sl.*) arrest. **in good ∼,** (*colloq.*) in good condition. **in the ∼ of time,** only just in time.

nickel *n.* hard silvery-white metal used in alloys; (*U.S.*) 5-cent piece.

nickname *n.* name given humorously to a person or thing. —*v.t.* give as a nickname.

nicotine /-tin/ *n.* poisonous substance found in tobacco.

niece *n.* one's brother's or sister's daughter.

niggardly *a.* stingy.

niggle *v.i.* fuss over details.

nigh /naɪ/ *adv.* & *prep.* near.

night *n.* dark hours between sunset and sunrise; nightfall; specified night or evening. **∼-club** *n.* club open at night, providing meals and entertainment. **∼-life** *n.* entertainments available in public places at night. **∼-light** *n.* faint light kept burning in a bedroom at night. **∼-school** *n.* instruction provided in the evening. **∼-watchman** *n.* man employed to keep watch at night in a building that is closed.

nightcap *n.* soft cap formerly worn in bed; drink taken just before going to bed.

nightdress *n.* woman's or child's loose garment for sleeping in.

nightfall *n.* onset of night.

nightgown *n.* nightdress.

nightingale *n.* small thrush, male of which sings melodiously.

nightjar *n.* night-flying bird with a harsh cry.

nightly *a.* & *adv.* (happening) at night or every night.

nightmare *n.* unpleasant dream or (*colloq.*) experience.

nightshade *n.* plant with poisonous berries.

nightshirt *n.* man's or boy's long shirt for sleeping in.

nil *n.* nothing.

nimble *a.* (*-er*, *-est*) able to move quickly. **nimbly** *adv.*

nincompoop *n.* foolish person.

nine *a.* & *n.* one more than eight (9, IX). **ninth** *a.* & *n.*

ninepins *n.* game of skittles played with nine objects.

nineteen *a.* & *n.* one more than eighteen (19, XIX). **nineteenth** *a.* & *n.*

ninety *a.* & *n.* nine times ten (90, XC). **ninetieth** *a.* & *n.*

nip¹ *v.t./i.* (p.t. *nipped*) pinch or squeeze sharply; bite quickly with the front teeth; pain or harm with biting cold; (*sl.*) go quickly. —*n.* sharp pinch, squeeze, or bite; biting coldness.

nip² *n.* small drink of spirits.

nipper *n.* (*sl.*) young boy or girl; claw of a lobster etc.; (*pl.*) pincers, forceps.

nipple *n.* small projection at the centre of a breast; similar protuberance; teat of a feeding-bottle.

nippy *a.* (*-ier*, *-iest*) (*colloq.*) nimble, quick; bitingly cold.

nirvana /nɜ'vɑː-/ *n.* (in Buddhism and Hinduism) state of perfect bliss achieved by the soul.

nisi /'naɪsaɪ/ *a.* **decree ～,** conditional order for divorce.

nit *n.* egg of a louse or similar parasite.

nitrate *n.* substance formed from nitric acid, esp. used as a fertilizer.

nitric /'naɪ-/ *a.* **～ acid,** corrosive acid containing nitrogen.

nitrogen *n.* gas forming about four-fifths of the atmosphere.

nitro-glycerine *n.* a kind of powerful explosive.

nitrous /'naɪ-/ *a.* **～ oxide,** gas used as an anaesthetic.

nitty-gritty *n.* (*sl.*) basic facts or realities of a matter.

nitwit *n.* (*colloq.*) stupid or foolish person.

no *a.* not any; not a. —*adv.* (used as a denial or refusal of something); not at all. —*n.* (pl. *noes*) negative reply, vote against a proposal. **～-ball** *n.* unlawfully delivered ball in cricket etc. **～ man's land,** area not firmly assigned to anyone, esp. between opposing armies. **～ one,** no person, nobody.

No. *or* **no.** *abbr.* number.

nob¹ *n.* (*sl.*) head.

nob² *n.* (*sl.*) person of high rank.

nobble *v.t.* (*sl.*) get hold of, tamper with or influence dishonestly.

nobility *n.* nobleness of mind or character, or of rank; titled people.

noble *a.* (*-er*, *-est*) aristocratic; possessing excellent qualities, esp. of character, not mean or petty; imposing. —*n.* member of the nobility. **nobly** *adv.*, **nobleness** *n.*

nobleman, noblewoman *ns.* (pl. *-men*, *-women*) member of the nobility.

nobody *pron.* no person. —*n.* person of no importance.

nocturnal *a.* of or happening in or active in the night.

nocturne *n.* dreamy piece of music.

nod *v.t./i.* (p.t. *nodded*) move the head down and up quickly, indicate (agreement or casual greeting) thus; let the head droop, be drowsy; bend and sway. —*n.* nodding movement esp. in agreement or greeting.

node *n.* knob-like swelling; point on a stem where a leaf or bud grows out.

nodule /'nɒd-/ *n.* small rounded lump, small node.

Noel /-'el/ *n.* (in carols) Christmas.

noggin *n.* measure of alcohol, usu. one quarter of a pint.

noise *n.* sound, esp. loud or harsh or undesired. —*v.t.* spread (a rumour etc.). **noiseless** *a.*

noisy *a.* (*-ier*, *-iest*) making much noise. **noisily** *adv.*

nomad *n.* member of a tribe that roams seeking pasture for its animals; wanderer. **nomadic** *a.*

nom de plume /nom də 'pluːm/ writer's pseudonym.

nomenclature /-'menklə-/ *n.* system of names, e.g. in a science.

nominal *a.* in name only; (of a fee) very small. **～ value,** face value of a coin etc. **nominally** *adv.*

nominate *v.t.* name as candidate for or future holder of an office; appoint as a place or date. **nomination** *n.*, **nominator** *n.*

nominative /'nom-/ *n.* form of a noun used when it is the subject of a verb.

nominee *n.* person nominated.

non- *pref.* not.

nonagenarian *n.* person in his or her nineties.

nonchalant /'nonʃ-/ *a.* calm and casual. **nonchalantly** *adv.*, **nonchalance** *n.*

non-commissioned *a.* not holding a commission.

non-committal *a.* not revealing one's opinion.

non compos mentis insane.

non-conformist *n.* person not conforming to established practices; *N～*, member of a Protestant sect not conforming to Anglican practices.

nondescript *a.* lacking distinctive characteristics and therefore not easy to classify.

none *pron.* not any; no person(s). —*adv.* not at all.

nonentity /-'nen-/ *n.* person of no importance.

non-event *n.* event that was expected to be important but proves disappointing.

nonplussed *a.* completely perplexed.

nonsense *n.* words put together in a way that does not make sense; foolish talk or behaviour. **nonsensical** /-'sen-/ *a.*

non sequitur /non 'sek-/ conclusion that does not follow from the evidence given.

non-starter *n.* horse entered for a race but not running in it; person or idea etc. not worth considering for a purpose.

non-stop *a.* & *adv.* not ceasing; (of a train etc.) not stopping at intermediate places.

noodles *n.pl.* pasta in narrow strips, used in soups etc.

nook *n.* secluded place or corner, recess.

noon *n.* twelve o'clock in the day, midday.

noose *n.* loop of rope etc. with a knot that tightens when pulled.

nor *conj.* & *adv.* and not.

Nordic *a.* of a tall blond blue-eyed racial type.

norm *n.* standard.

normal *a.* conforming to what is standard or usual; free from mental or emotional disorders. **normally** *adv.*, **normality** *n.*

Norman *a.* & *n.* (member) of a former people of Normandy.

Norse *a.* & *n.* (language) of ancient Norway or Scandinavia. **Norseman** *n.* (pl. -men).

north *n.* point or direction to the left of person facing east; northern part. —*a.* in the north; (of wind) from the north. —*adv.* towards the north. ∼-**east** *n.* point or direction midway between north and east. ∼-**easterly** *a.* & *n.*, ∼-**eastern** *a.* ∼-**west** *n.* point or direction midway between north and west. ∼-**westerly** *a.* & *n.*, ∼-**western** *a.*

northerly *a.* towards or blowing from the north.

northern *a.* of or in the north.

northerner *n.* native of the north.

northernmost *a.* furthest north.

northward *a.* towards the north. **northwards** *adv.*

Norwegian *a.* & *n.* (native, language) of Norway.

Nos. *or* **nos.** *abbr.* numbers.

nose *n.* organ at the front of the head, used in breathing and smelling; sense of smell; open end of a tube; front end or projecting part. —*v.t./i.* detect or search by use of the sense of smell; push one's nose against or into; push one's way cautiously ahead.

nosebag *n.* bag of fodder for hanging on a horse's head.

nosebleed *n.* bleeding from the nose.

nosedive *n.* steep downward plunge, esp. of an aeroplane. —*v.i.* make this plunge.

nosegay *n.* small bunch of flowers.

nosey *a.* (-ier, -iest) (*sl.*) inquisitive. **nosily** *adv.*, **nosiness** *n.*

nostalgia *n.* sentimental memory of or longing for things of the past. **nostalgic** *a.*, **nostalgically** *adv.*

nostril *n.* either of the two openings in the nose.

nostrum *n.* (pl. *-ums*) quack remedy.

not *adv.* expressing a negative or denial or refusal.

notability *n.* being notable; notable person.

notable *a.* worthy of notice, remarkable, eminent. —*n.* eminent person. **notably** *adv.*

notary *n.* ∼ **public**, person authorized to witness the signing of documents and perform other formal transactions.

notation *n.* system of signs or symbols representing numbers, quantities, musical notes, etc.

notch *n.* V-shaped cut or indentation. —*v.t.* make notch(es) in. ∼ **up**, score, achieve.

note *n.* brief record written down to aid memory; short or informal letter; memorandum; formal diplomatic communication; short written comment; written or printed promise to pay money; banknote; musical tone of definite pitch; symbol representing the pitch and duration of a musical sound; one of the keys on a piano etc.; significant sound, indication of feelings etc.; eminence; notice, attention. —*v.t.* notice, pay attention to; write down.

notebook *n.* book with blank pages on which to write memoranda.

noted *a.* famous, well-known.

notepaper *n.* paper for writing letters on.

noteworthy *a.* worthy of notice, remarkable.

nothing *n.* no thing, not anything; no amount, nought; non-existence; person or thing of no importance. —*adv.* not at all.

notice *n.* intimation, warning; formal announcement of the termination of an agreement or employment; written or printed information displayed; attention, observation; review in a newspaper. —*v.t.* perceive; take notice of; remark upon. ∼-**board** *n.* board on which notices may be displayed. **take** ∼, show interest. **take no** ∼ (**of**), pay no attention (to).

noticeable *a.* easily seen or noticed. **noticeably** *adv.*

notifiable *a.* that must be notified.

notify *v.t.* inform; report, make known. **notification** *n.*

notion *n.* concept; idea; understanding; intention.

notional *a.* hypothetical. **notionally** *adv.*

notorious *a.* well known, esp. unfavourably. **notoriously** *adv.*, **notoriety** /-ˈraɪətɪ/ *n.*

notwithstanding *prep.* in spite of. —*adv.* nevertheless.

nougat /ˈnuːgɑː/ *n.* chewy sweet.

nought *n.* the figure 0; nothing.

noun *n.* word used as the name of a person, place, or thing.

nourish *v.t.* keep alive and well by food; foster or cherish (a feeling).

nourishment *n.* nourishing; food.

nous /naʊs/ *n.* (*colloq.*) common sense.

nova /ˈnəʊ-/ *n.* (pl. *-as*) star that suddenly becomes much brighter for a short time.

novel *n.* book-length story. —*a.* of a new kind.

novelist *n.* writer of novels.

novelty *n.* novel thing or quality; small unusual object.

November *n.* eleventh month of the year.

novice *n.* inexperienced person; probationary member of a religious order. **noviciate** *n.*

now *adv.* at the time when or of which one is writing or speaking; immediately; (without temporal sense) I wonder or am telling you —*conj.* as a consequence of or simultaneously with the fact that. —*n.* the present time. ∼ **and again,** ∼ **and then,** occasionally.

nowadays *adv.* in present times.

nowhere *adv.* not anywhere.

noxious *a.* unpleasant and harmful.

nozzle *n.* vent or spout of a hosepipe etc.

nuance /ˈnjuːɑːns/ *n.* shade of meaning.

nub *n.* small lump; central point or core of a matter or problem.

nubile *a.* marriageable.

nuclear *a.* of a nucleus; of the nuclei of atoms; using energy released or absorbed during reactions in these.

nucleus *n.* (pl. *-lei*, pr. *-lıaı*) central part or thing round which others are collected; central positively charged portion of an atom.

nude *a.* not clothed, naked. —*n.* nude human figure in a picture etc. **nudity** *n.*

nudge *v.t.* poke (a person) gently with one's elbow to attract his attention quietly; push slightly or gradually. —*n.* this movement.

nudist *n.* person who believes that going un-clothed is good for the health. **nudism** *n.*

nugget *n.* rough lump of gold or platinum found in the earth.

nuisance *n.* annoying person or thing.

null *a.* having no legal force. **nullity** *n.*

nullify *v.t.* make null; neutralize the effect of. **nullification** *n.*

numb *a.* deprived of power to feel or move. —*v.t.* make numb. **numbly** *adv.*, **numbness** *n.*

number *n.* symbol or word indicating how many; numeral assigned to a person or thing; single issue of a magazine; item; total; category 'singular' or 'plural' in grammar. —*v.t.* count; amount to; mark or distinguish with a number. **~-plate** *n.* plate on a motor vehicle, bearing its registration number.

numeral *n.* written symbol of a number.

numerate *a.* having a good basic understanding of mathematics and science. **numeracy** *n.*

numeration *n.* numbering.

numerator *n.* number written above the line in a vulgar fraction.

numerical *a.* of number(s).

numerous *a.* great in number.

numismatics /-'mæ-/ *n.* study of coins. **numismatist** /-'mɪz-/ *n.*

nun *n.* member of a female community living apart from the world under the rules of a religious order.

nunnery *n.* residence of a community of nuns.

nuptial *a.* of marriage or a wedding. **nuptials** *n.pl.* wedding ceremony.

nurse *n.* person trained to look after sick or injured people; woman employed to take charge of young children. —*v.t./i.* work as a nurse, act as nurse (to); feed at the breast or udder; hold carefully; give special care to. **nursing home,** privately run hospital or home for invalids.

nursemaid *n.* young woman employed to take charge of young children.

nursery *n.* room(s) for young children; place where young plants are reared. **~ rhyme,** traditional verse for children. **~ school,** school for children below normal school age.

nurture *v.t.* nourish, rear; bring up. —*n.* nurturing.

nut *n.* fruit with a hard shell round an edible kernel; this kernel; small lump; small threaded metal ring for use with a bolt.

nutcrackers *n.pl.* pincers for cracking nuts.

nuthatch *n.* small climbing bird.

nutmeg *n.* hard fragrant tropical seed ground or grated as spice.

nutrient /'nju-/ *a. & n.* nourishing (substance).

nutriment *n.* nourishment.

nutrition *n.* nourishment. **nutritional** *a.*, **nutritionally** *adv.*

nutritious *a.* nourishing.

nutritive *a. & n.* nourishing (substance).

nutshell *n.* hard shell of nut. **in a ~,** expressed very briefly.

nutty *a.* full of nuts; tasting like nuts.

nuzzle *v.t.* press or rub gently with the nose.

nylon *n.* very light strong synthetic fibre; fabric made of this.

nymph *n.* mythological semi-divine maiden living in the sea or woods; young insect.

N.Z. *abbr.* New Zealand.

O

oaf *n.* (pl. *oafs*) awkward lout.

oak *n.* deciduous forest tree bearing acorns; its hard wood. **~-apple** *n.* = gall³. **oaken** *a.*

O.A.P. *abbr.* old-age pensioner.

oar *n.* pole with a flat blade used to propel a boat by its leverage against water; oarsman. **put one's ~ in,** interfere.

oarsman *n.* (pl. *-men*) rower.

oasis *n.* (pl. *oases*) fertile spot in a desert, with a spring or well of water.

oast *n.* kiln for drying hops. **~-house** *n.* building containing this.

oatcake *n.* thin cake made of oatmeal.

oath *n.* solemn promise, appealing to God or a revered object as witness; swear-word.

oatmeal *n.* ground oats; greyish-fawn colour.

oats *n.* hardy cereal plant; its grain.

obbligato /-'gɑ-/ *n.* (pl. *-os*) important accompanying part in music.

obdurate /'ob-/ *a.* stubborn. **obdurately** *adv.*, **obduracy** *n.*

obedient *a.* doing what one is told to do. **obediently** *adv.*, **obedience** *n.*

obeisance /-'beɪ-/ *n.* bow or curtsy.

obelisk /'ob-/ *n.* tall pillar set up as a monument.

obese /-'biːs/ *a.* very fat. **obesity** *n.*

obey *v.t./i.* do what is commanded (by).

obituary *n.* printed statement of person's death (esp. in a newspaper), often with a brief biography.

object¹ /'ob-/ *n.* something solid that can be seen or touched; person or thing to which an action or feeling is directed; purpose, intention; noun etc. acted upon by a transitive verb or preposition. **no ~,** not an important or limiting factor. **~ lesson,** practical illustration of a principle.

object[2] /-ˈdʒekt/ v.t. state that one is opposed to, protest. **objector** n.

objection n. disapproval, opposition; statement of this; reason for objecting.

objectionable a. causing objections; unpleasant. **objectionably** adv.

objective a. not influenced by personal feelings or opinions; of the form of a word used when it is the object of a verb or preposition. —n. thing one is trying to achieve, reach, or capture. **objectively** adv.

objet d'art /obʒeɪ ˈdɑ(r)/ (pl. objets d'art) small artistic object.

obligation n. being obliged to do something; what one must do to comply with an agreement or law etc. **under an ~,** owing gratitude.

obligatory /-ˈlɪg-/ a. compulsory.

oblige v.t. compel; help or gratify by a small service.

obliged a. indebted.

obliging a. polite and helpful.

oblique a. slanting; indirect. **obliquely** adv.

obliterate v.t. blot out, destroy. **obliteration** n.

oblivion n. state of being forgotten; state of being oblivious.

oblivious a. unaware.

oblong a. & n. (having) rectangular shape with length greater than breadth.

obnoxious a. very unpleasant.

oboe n. woodwind instrument of treble pitch. **oboist** n.

obscene a. indecent in a repulsive or offensive way. **obscenely** adv., **obscenity** /-ˈsen-/ n.

obscure a. dark, indistinct; remote from observation; not famous; not easily understood. —v.t. make obscure, conceal. **obscurely** adv., **obscurity** n.

obsequies /ˈobsɪkwɪz/ n.pl. funeral rites.

obsequious /-ˈsi-/ a. excessively respectful. **obsequiously** adv.

observance n. keeping of a law, custom, or festival.

observant a. quick at noticing.

observation n. observing; remark.

observatory n. building equipped for observation of stars or weather.

observe v.t. perceive, watch carefully; pay attention to; keep or celebrate (a festival); remark. **observer** n.

obsess v.t. occupy the thoughts of continually.

obsession n. state of being obsessed; persistent idea.

obsessive a. of, causing, or showing obsession. **obsessively** adv.

obsolescent a. becoming obsolete. **obsolescence** n.

obsolete a. no longer used.

obstacle n. thing that obstructs progress. **~ race,** race in which obstacles have to be passed.

obstetrics n. branch of medicine and surgery dealing with childbirth. **obstetric, obstetrical** adjs., **obstetrician** n.

obstinate a. not easily persuaded or influenced or overcome. **obstinately** adv., **obstinacy** n.

obstreperous a. noisy, unruly.

obstruct v.t. prevent or hinder the movement or progress of or along.

obstruction n. obstructing; thing that obstructs.

obstructive a. causing obstruction.

obtain v.t./i. get, come into possession of; be in use as a rule or custom.

obtainable a. able to be obtained.

obtrude v.t. force (one's ideas or oneself) upon others. **obtrusion** n.

obtrusive a. obtruding oneself, unpleasantly noticeable.

obtuse a. of blunt shape, (of an angle) more than 90° but less than 180°; slow at understanding. **obtusely** adv., **obtuseness** n.

obverse /ˈob-/ n. side of a coin bearing a head or the principal design.

obviate v.t. make unnecessary.

obvious a. easy to perceive or understand. **obviously** adv.

occasion n. time at which a particular event takes place; special event; opportunity; need or cause. —v.t. cause. **on ~,** occasionally.

occasional a. happening sometimes but not frequently; for a special occasion. **occasionally** adv.

Occident n. the West, the western world. **occidental** a.

occlude v.t. stop up, obstruct.

occlusion n. upward movement of a mass of warm air caused by a cold front overtaking it.

occult /-ˈkʌ-/ a. secret; supernatural.

occupant n. person occupying a place or dwelling. **occupancy** n.

occupation n. occupying; taking or holding possession by force; activity that keeps a person busy; employment.

occupational a. of or caused by one's employment. **~ therapy,** creative activities designed to assist recovery from certain illnesses.

occupy v.t. dwell in; take possession of (a country or site etc.), esp. by force; fill (a space or position); keep filled with activity. **occupier** n.

occur v.i. (p.t. occurred) come into being as an event or process; exist in a specified place or conditions. **~ to,** come into the mind of.

occurrence n. occurring; incident, event.

ocean n. sea surrounding the continents of the earth. **oceanic** a.

oceanography n. study of the ocean.

ocelot /ˈosɪ-/ n. leopard-like animal of Central and South America; its fur.

ochre n. type of clay used as pigment; pale brownish-yellow.

o'clock adv. by the clock.

octagon n. geometric figure with eight sides. **octagonal** /-ˈtæ-/ a.

octane n. hydrocarbon occurring in petrol.

octave n. note six whole tones above or below a given note; interval or series of notes between these.

octet n. group of eight voices or instruments; music for these.

October *n.* tenth month of the year.

octogenarian /-'neər-/ *n.* person in his or her eighties.

octopus *n.* (pl. *-puses*) sea animal with eight tentacles.

ocular *a.* of, for, or by the eyes.

oculist *n.* specialist in the treatment of eye disorders and defects.

odd *a.* (*-er*, *-est*) (of a number) not exactly divisible by 2; from a pair or set of which the other(s) are lacking; exceeding a round number or amount; not regular; unusual. **oddly** *adv.*, **oddness** *n.*

oddity *n.* strangeness; unusual person or thing.

oddment *n.* thing left over, isolated article.

odds *n.pl.* probability, esp. expressed as a ratio; ratio between amounts staked by parties to a bet. **at ~ with**, in conflict with. **no ~,** no difference. **~ and ends**, oddments.

ode *n.* type of poem addressed to a person or celebrating an event.

odious *a.* hateful. **odiously** *adv.*, **odiousness** *n.*

odium *n.* widespread hatred or disgust towards a person or actions.

odour *n.* smell. **odorous** *a.*

odourless *a.* without a smell.

odyssey *n.* (pl. *-eys*) long adventurous journey.

oedema /i'di:mə/ *n.* excess fluid in tissues, causing swelling.

oesophagus /i'sof-/ *n.* gullet.

of *prep.* belonging to; from; composed or made from; concerning; for, involving; so as to bring separation or relief from; (*colloq.*) during.

off *adv.* away; out of position, disconnected; not operating, cancelled; completely; situated as regards money or supplies; (of food) beginning to decay. *—prep.* away from; below the normal standard of. *—a.* of the right-hand side of a horse, vehicle, or road etc. **~-beat** *a.* unusual, unconventional. **~ chance,** remote possibility. **~ colour,** not in the best of health. **~-licence** *n.* licence to sell alcohol for consumption away from the premises; shop with this. **~-load** *v.t.* unload. **~-putting** *a.* (*colloq.*) repellent. **~-stage** *a.* & *adv.* beside a stage and not visible to the audience. **~-white** *a.* not quite pure white.

offal *n.* edible organs from an animal carcass.

offence *n.* illegal act; feeling of annoyance or resentment.

offend *v.t./i.* cause offence to; do wrong. **offender** *n.*

offensive *a.* causing offence, insulting; disgusting; used in attacking, aggressive. *—n.* aggressive action. **take the ~,** begin hostilities. **offensively** *adv.*, **offensiveness** *n.*

offer *v.t./i.* (p.t. *offered*) present for acceptance or refusal, or for consideration or use; state what one is willing to do or pay or give; show an intention. *—n.* expression of willingness to do, give, or pay something; amount offered.

offering *n.* gift, contribution.

offhand *a.* without previous thought or preparation; unceremonious, casual. *—adv.* in an offhand way. **offhanded** *a.*

office *n.* room or building used for clerical and similar work; position of authority or trust; service; (*pl.*) rooms equipped for household work or as bathrooms etc.

officer *n.* official; person holding authority on a ship or (esp. with a commission) in the armed services; policeman.

official *a.* of office or officials; authorized. *—n.* person holding office. **officially** *n.*

officiate *v.i.* act in an official capacity, be in charge.

officious *a.* asserting one's authority, bossy. **officiously** *adv.*

offing *n.* **in the ~**, not far off in distance or time.

offset *v.t.* (p.t. *-set*, pres.p. *-setting*) counterbalance, compensate for. *—n.* offshoot; method of printing by transferring ink to and from a rubber surface.

offshoot *n.* side shoot; subsidiary product.

offside *a.* & *adv.* in a position where one may not legally play the ball (in football etc.).

offspring *n.* (pl. *-spring*) person's child or children; animal's young.

often *adv.* many times, at short intervals; in many instances.

ogle *v.t.* eye flirtatiously.

ogre *n.* cruel or man-eating giant in fairy-tales etc.; terrifying person.

oh *int.* exclamation of delight or pain, or used for emphasis.

ohm /əʊm/ *n.* unit of electrical resistance.

oil *n.* thick slippery liquid that will not dissolve in water; petroleum, a form of this; oil-colour. *—v.t.* lubricate or treat with oil. **~-colour, ~-paint** *ns.* paint made by mixing pigment in oil. **~-painting** *n.* picture painted in this.

oilfield *n.* area where oil is found in the ground.

oilskin *n.* cloth waterproofed by treatment with oil etc.; (*pl.*) waterproof clothing made of this.

oily *a.* (*-ier*, *-iest*) of or like oil; covered in oil, full of oil; unpleasantly smooth and ingratiating in manner. **oiliness** *n.*

ointment *n.* paste for rubbing on skin to heal it.

O.K., okay *a.* & *adv.* (*colloq.*) all right.

okapi /-'ka:-/ *n.* (pl. *-is*) giraffe-like animal of Central Africa.

old *a.* (*-er*, *-est*) having lived or existed or been known etc. for a long time; of specified age; shabby from age or wear; former, not recent or modern; (*colloq.*) regarded with affection. **~ age**, later part of life. **~-fashioned** *a.* in or according to old fashions. **~ maid**, elderly spinster. **Old Testament** (see *testament*). **~-time** *a.* belonging to former times. **~ wives' tale**, traditional but foolish belief. **Old World**, Europe, Asia, and Africa. **oldness** *n.*

olden *a.* (*old use*) former, not recent.

oleander /əʊli'æ-/ *n.* flowering shrub of Mediterranean regions.

olfactory /-'fæ-/ *a.* concerned with smelling.

oligarchy *n.* form of government where power is in the hands of a small group.

olive *n.* small oval fruit from which an oil (*olive oil*) is obtained; tree bearing this; greenish colour. —*a.* of this colour; (of the complexion) yellowish-brown. **~-branch** *n.* thing done or offered to show one's desire to make peace.

Olympian *a.* of Olympus; majestic and imposing in manner.

Olympic *a.* of the **~ Games,** international sports competitions held every fourth year. **Olympics** *n.pl.* Olympic Games.

ombudsman *n.* (pl. *-men*) official appointed to investigate people's complaints about maladministration by public authorities.

omega *n.* last letter of the Greek alphabet, = o.

omelette *n.* dish of beaten eggs cooked in a frying-pan.

omen *n.* event regarded as a prophetic sign.

ominous /ˈom-/ *a.* seeming as if trouble is imminent.

omit *v.t.* (p.t. *omitted*) leave out, not include; leave not done, neglect (to do something). **omission** *n.*

omnibus *n.* bus; comprehensive publication containing several items.

omnipotent /omˈnɪp-/ *a.* having unlimited or very great power. **omnipotence** *n.*

omniscient /-ˈnɪʃənt/ *a.* knowing everything, having very extensive knowledge. **omniscience** *n.*

omnivorous /-ˈnɪv-/ *a.* feeding on all kinds of food.

on *prep.* supported by, attached to, covering; using as a basis or reason etc.; close to; towards; (of time) exactly at, during; in the state or process of; concerning; added to. —*adv.* so as to be on or covering something; further forward, towards something; with continued movement or action; operating, taking place. **be** *or* **keep ~ at,** (*colloq.*) nag. **~ and off,** from time to time.

once *adv., conj., & n.* on one occasion, one time or occurrence; at all, as soon as; formerly. **~-over** *n.* (*colloq.*) rapid inspection. **~ upon a time,** at some vague time in the past.

oncoming *a.* approaching.

one *a.* single, individual, forming a unity. —*n.* smallest whole number (1, I); single thing or person; (*colloq.*) blow. —*pron.* person; any person (esp. used by a speaker or writer of himself as representing people in general). **~ another,** each other. **~ day,** at some unspecified date. **~-sided** *a.* unfair, prejudiced. **~-upmanship** *n.* art of maintaining a psychological advantage over others. **~-way street,** street where traffic may move in one direction only.

onerous /ˈon-/ *a.* burdensome.

oneself *pron.* emphatic and reflexive form of *one*.

onion *n.* vegetable with a bulb that has a strong taste and smell.

onlooker *n.* spectator.

only *a.* being the one specimen or all the specimens of a class, sole. —*adv.* without anything or anyone else; and that is all; no longer ago than. —*conj.* but then. **~ too,** extremely.

onomatopoeia /-ˈpiə/ *n.* formation of words that imitate the sound of what they stand for.

onrush *n.* onward rush.

onset *n.* beginning; attack.

onslaught *n.* fierce attack.

onus /ˈəʊ-/ *n.* duty or responsibility of doing something.

onward *adv. & a.* with an advancing motion; further on. **onwards** *adv.*

onyx /ˈonɪks/ *n.* stone like marble with colours in layers.

ooh *int.* exclamation of surprise, pleasure, or pain.

ooze *v.t./i.* trickle or flow out slowly; exude. —*n.* wet mud.

opacity /-ˈpæ-/ *n.* being opaque.

opal *n.* iridescent quartz-like stone often used as a gem.

opalescent /-ˈles-/ *a.* iridescent like an opal. **opalescence** *n.*

opaque *a.* not clear, not transparent.

OPEC *abbr.* Organization of Petroleum Exporting Countries.

open *a.* able to be entered, not closed or sealed or locked; not covered or concealed or restricted; spread out, unfolded; frank; not yet decided; available; willing to receive; (of a cheque) not crossed. —*v.t./i.* make or become open or more open; begin, establish. **in the ~ air,** not in a house or building etc. **~-ended** *a.* with no fixed limit. **~-handed** *a.* giving generously. **~-heart** *a.* (of surgery) with the heart exposed and blood circulating through a bypass. **~ house,** hospitality to all comers. **~ letter,** one addressed to a person by name but printed in a newspaper. **~-plan** *a.* without partition walls or fences. **~ secret,** one known to so many people that it is no longer secret. **~ verdict,** one not specifying whether a crime is involved. **~-work** *n.* pattern with spaces between threads or strips. **openness** *n.*

opener *n.* device for opening tins or bottles etc.

opening *n.* gap, place where a thing opens; beginning; opportunity.

openly *adv.* publicly, frankly.

opera *see* **opus.** —*n.* play(s) in which words are sung to music. **~-glasses** *n.pl.* small binoculars.

operable *a.* able to be operated.

operate *v.t./i.* be in action; produce an effect; control the functioning of; perform an operation on.

operatic *a.* of or like opera.

operation *n.* operating; way a thing works; piece of work; military action; piece of surgery.

operational *a.* of or used in operations; able to function.

operative /ˈop-/ *a.* working, functioning; of surgical operations. —*n.* worker, esp. in a factory.

operator *n.* person who operates a machine or business; one who connects lines at a telephone exchange.

operetta *n.* short or light opera.

ophthalmic *a.* of or for the eyes.

ophthalmology *n.* study of the eye and its diseases. **ophthalmologist** *n.*

opiate /ˈəʊ-/ *n.* sedative containing opium; thing that soothes feelings.

opinion *n.* belief or judgement held without actual proof; what one thinks on a particular point.

opinionated *a.* holding strong opinions obstinately.

opium *n.* narcotic drug made from the juice of certain poppies.

opossum *n.* small furry marsupial.

opponent *n.* one who opposes another.

opportune *a.* (of time) favourable; well-timed. **opportunely** *adv.*

opportunist *n.* person who grasps opportunities. **opportunism** *n.*

opportunity *n.* circumstances suitable for a particular purpose.

oppose *v.t.* argue or fight against; place opposite; place or be in opposition to; contrast.

opposite *a.* facing, on the further side; of a contrary kind, as different as possible from. —*n.* opposite thing or person. —*adv. & prep.* in an opposite position or direction (to). **one's ~ number,** person holding a similar position to oneself in another group.

opposition *n.* antagonism, resistance; placing or being placed opposite; people opposing something; *the O~,* the chief parliamentary party opposed to that in office.

oppress *v.t.* govern harshly; treat with continual harshness; weigh down with cares or unhappiness. **oppression** *n.*, **oppressor** *n.*

oppressive *a.* oppressing; hard to endure; sultry and tiring. **oppressively** *adv.*, **oppressiveness** *n.*

opprobrious /-ˈprəʊ-/ *a.* abusive.

opprobrium /-ˈprəʊ-/ *n.* great disgrace from shameful conduct.

opt *v.i.* make a choice. **~ out,** choose not to participate.

optic *a.* of the eye or sight.

optical *a.* of or aiding sight; visual. **~ illusion,** mental misinterpretation caused by a thing's deceptive appearance. **optically** *adv.*

optician *n.* maker or seller of spectacles.

optics *n.* study of sight and of light as its medium.

optimal *a.* optimum.

optimism *n.* tendency to take a hopeful view of things. **optimist** *n.*, **optimistic** *a.*, **optimistically** *adv.*

optimum *a. & n.* best or most favourable (conditions, amount, etc.).

option *n.* freedom to choose; thing that is or may be chosen; right to buy or sell a thing within a limited time.

optional *a.* not compulsory. **optionally** *adv.*

opulent /ˈɒp-/ *a.* wealthy; abundant. **opulently** *adv.*, **opulence** *n.*

opus /ˈəʊ-/ *n.* (pl. *opera,* pr. ˈɒp-) numbered musical composition.

or *conj.* as an alternative; because if not; also known as.

oracle *n.* place where the ancient Greeks con-sulted a god; the reply received; person or thing giving wise guidance. **oracular** /-ˈræ-/ *a.*

oral *a.* spoken not written; of the mouth, taken by mouth. —*n.* (*colloq.*) spoken examination. **orally** *adv.*

orange *n.* round juicy citrus fruit with reddish-yellow peel; this colour. —*a.* reddish-yellow. **~-stick** *n.* small thin stick for manicuring the nails.

orangeade *n.* orange-flavoured soft drink.

orang-utan /-ˈut-/ *n.* large ape of Borneo and Sumatra.

oration *n.* long speech, esp. of a ceremonial kind.

orator *n.* person who makes public speeches, skilful speaker.

oratorio *n.* (pl. *-os*) musical composition for voices and orchestra, usu. with a biblical theme.

oratory[1] *n.* art of public speaking; eloquent speech. **oratorical** /-ˈto-/ *a.*

oratory[2] *n.* small chapel.

orb *n.* sphere, globe.

orbit *n.* curved path of a planet, satellite, or spacecraft round another; sphere of influence. —*v.t./i.* move in an orbit (round).

orchard *n.* piece of land planted with fruit-trees; these trees.

orchestra *n.* large body of people playing various musical instruments; part of a theatre (between stalls and stage) where these sit. **orchestral** *a.*

orchestrate *v.t.* compose or arrange (music) for an orchestra; coordinate deliberately. **orchestration** *n.*

orchid *n.* a kind of showy often irregularly shaped flower.

orchis *n.* orchid, esp. a wild one.

ordain *v.t.* appoint ceremonially to the Christian ministry; destine; decree authoritatively.

ordeal /-ˈdil/ *n.* difficult experience.

order *n.* way things are placed in relation to each other; proper or usual sequence; efficient state; law-abiding state; system of rules or procedure; command; request to supply goods etc., things supplied; written instruction or permission; rank; kind, quality; monastic organization; company to which distinguished people are admitted as an honour; its insignia; style of classical architecture; (*pl.*) holy orders. —*v.t.* arrange in order; command; give an order for (goods etc.). **holy orders,** status of an ordained clergyman. **in ~ to** *or* **that,** with the purpose of or intention that.

orderly *a.* in due order; not unruly; of or for military business. —*n.* soldier assisting an officer; hospital attendant. **orderliness** *n.*

ordinal *a.* **~ numbers,** those defining position in a series (*first, second,* etc.).

ordinance *n.* decree.

ordinary *a.* usual, not exceptional. **ordinarily** *adv.*

ordination *n.* ordaining.

ordnance *n.* military materials; department

dealing with these. **Ordnance Survey,** official survey of Great Britain, preparing maps.

ore *n.* solid rock or mineral from which metal is obtained.

organ *n.* musical instrument with pipes supplied with wind by bellows and sounded by keys; distinct part with a specific function in an animal or plant body; medium of communication, esp. a newspaper.

organdie *n.* fine translucent usu. stiff cotton fabric.

organic *a.* of bodily organ(s); of or formed from living things; organized as a system of related parts. **organically** *adv.*

organism *n.* a living being, individual animal or plant.

organist *n.* person who plays the organ.

organization *n.* organizing; organized system or body of people. **organizational** *a.*

organize *v.t.* arrange systematically; make arrangements for; form (people) into an association for a common purpose. **organizer** *n.*

organza *n.* thin stiff transparent dress-fabric.

orgasm *n.* climax of sexual excitement.

orgy *n.* wild revelry; unrestrained activity.

Orient *n.* the East, the eastern world.

oriental *a.* of the Orient.

Oriental *n.* native of the Orient.

orientate *v.t.* place or determine the position of (a thing) with regard to points of the compass. ∼ **oneself,** get one's bearings; become accustomed to a new situation. **orientation** *n.*

orienteering *n.* sport of finding one's way across country by map and compass.

orifice *n.* opening of a cavity etc.

origami /-ˈgɑ-/ *n.* Japanese art of folding paper into attractive shapes.

origin *n.* point, source, or cause from which a thing begins its existence; ancestry, parentage.

original *a.* existing from the first, earliest; being the first form of something; new in character or design; inventive, creative. —*n.* first form, thing from which another is copied. **originally** *adv.*, **originality** *n.*

originate *v.t./i.* bring or come into being. **origination** *n.*, **originator** *n.*

oriole /ˈɔr-/ *n.* bird with black and yellow plumage.

ormolu /ˈɔm-/ *n.* gilded bronze; gold-coloured alloy of copper; things made of this.

ornament *n.* decorative object or detail; decoration. —*v.t.* decorate with ornament(s). **ornamentation** *n.*

ornamental *a.* serving as an ornament. **ornamentally** *adv.*

ornate *a.* elaborately ornamented.

ornithology *n.* study of birds. **ornithological** *a.*, **ornithologist** *n.*

orphan *n.* child whose parents are dead. —*v.t.* make (a child) an orphan.

orphanage *n.* institution where orphans are housed and cared for.

orthodontics *n.* correction of irregularities in teeth. **orthodontic** *a.*, **orthodontist** *n.*

orthodox *a.* of or holding conventional or currently accepted beliefs, esp. in religion. **Orthodox Church,** Eastern or Greek Church.

orthopaedics /-ˈpi-/ *n.* surgical correction of deformities in bones or muscles. **orthopaedic** *a.*, **orthopaedist** *n.*

oscillate /ˈos-/ *v.t./i.* move to and fro; vary. **oscillation** *n.*

osier /ˈəʊz-/ *n.* willow with flexible twigs; twig of this.

osmosis /ozˈməʊ-/ *n.* diffusion of fluid through a porous partition into another fluid.

osprey *n.* (pl. *-eys*) large bird preying on fish in inland waters.

ossify *v.t./i.* turn into bone, harden; make or become rigid and unprogressive. **ossification** *n.*

ostensible *a.* pretended, used as a pretext. **ostensibly** *adv.*

ostentation *n.* showy display intended to impress people. **ostentatious** *a.*, **ostentatiously** *adv.*

osteopath *n.* practitioner who treats certain diseases and abnormalities by manipulating bones and muscles. **osteopathic** *a.*, **osteopathy** /-ˈop-/ *n.*

ostracize *v.t.* refuse to associate with. **ostracism** *n.*

ostrich *n.* large swift-running African bird, unable to fly.

other *a.* alternative, additional, being the remaining one of a set of two or more; not the same. —*n. & pron.* the other person or thing. —*adv.* otherwise. **the ∼ day** *or* **week,** a few days or weeks ago. **the ∼ world,** life after death.

otherwise *adv.* in a different way; in other respects; if circumstances are or were different.

otter *n.* fish-eating water animal with thick brown fur.

ottoman *n.* long cushioned backless seat; storage box with a padded top.

Ottoman *a.* of the former Turkish empire.

ouch *int.* exclamation of pain.

ought *v.aux.* expressing duty, rightness, advisability, or strong probability.

ounce *n.* unit of weight, one sixteenth of a pound (about 28 grams). **fluid ∼,** one twentieth (in U.S.A., one sixteenth) of a pint.

our *a.*, **ours** *poss.pron.* belonging to us.

ourselves *pron.* emphatic and reflexive form of *we* and *us.*

oust /aʊ-/ *v.t.* drive out, eject.

out *adv.* away from or not in a place; not at home; not in effective action, no longer in fashion or office; on strike; no longer burning; in error; no longer visible; not possible; unconscious; into the open, so as to be heard or seen; unfolded; completely; in finished form. —*prep.* out of. —*n.* way of escape. **be ∼ to,** be intending to. **∼-and-out** *a.* thorough, extreme. **∼ of,** from within or among; beyond the range of; without a supply of; (of an animal) having as its dam. **∼ of date,** no longer fashionable or current or valid. **∼ of**

doors, in the open air. ~ **of the way,** no longer an obstacle; remote; unusual. ~**-patient** *n.* person visiting a hospital for treatment but not remaining resident there. ~**-tray** *n.* tray for documents that are ready for dispatch.

out- *pref.* more than, so as to exceed.

outback *n.* (*Austral.*) remote inland districts.

outbid *v.t.* (p.t. *-bid*, pres.p. *-bidding*) bid higher than.

outboard *a.* (of a motor) attached to the outside of a boat.

outbreak *n.* breaking out of anger or war or disease etc.

outbuilding *n.* outhouse.

outburst *n.* explosion of feeling.

outcast *n.* person driven out of a group or by society.

outcome *n.* result of an event.

outcrop *n.* part of an underlying layer of rock that projects on the surface of the ground.

outcry *n.* loud cry; strong protest.

outdated *a.* out of date.

outdo *v.t.* (p.t. *-did*, p.p. *-done*) be or do better than.

outdoor *a.* of or for use in the open air. **outdoors** *adv.*

outer *a.* further from the centre or inside; exterior, external.

outermost *adv.* furthest outward.

outfit *n.* set of clothes or equipment.

outfitter *n.* supplier of equipment or men's clothing.

outflank *v.t.* get round the flank of (an enemy).

outflow *n.* outward flow.

outgoing *a.* going out; sociable.

outgoings *n.pl.* expenditure.

outgrow *v.t.* (p.t. *-grew*, p.p. *-grown*) grow faster than; grow too large for.

outgrowth *n.* thing growing out of another.

outhouse *n.* shed, barn, etc.

outing *n.* pleasure-trip.

outlandish *a.* looking or sounding strange or foreign.

outlast *v.t.* last longer than.

outlaw *n.* person punished (in the Middle Ages) by being placed outside the protection of the law. —*v.t.* make (a person) an outlaw; declare illegal.

outlay *n.* money etc. spent.

outlet *n.* way out; means for giving vent to energies or feelings; market for goods.

outline *n.* line(s) showing a shape or boundary; summary. —*v.t.* draw or describe in outline; mark the outline of.

outlive *v.t.* live longer than.

outlook *n.* view, prospect; mental attitude; future prospects.

outlying *a.* remote.

outmanœuvre *v.t.* outdo in manœuvring.

outmoded *a.* no longer fashionable.

outmost *a.* outermost; uttermost.

outnumber *v.t.* exceed in number.

outpost *n.* outlying settlement or detachment of troops.

output *n.* amount of electrical power etc. produced.

outrage *n.* act that shocks public opinion; violation of rights. —*v.t.* shock and anger greatly.

outrageous *a.* greatly exceeding what is moderate or reasonable, shocking. **outrageously** *adv.*

outrank *v.t.* be of higher rank than.

outrider *n.* mounted attendant or motor-cyclist riding as guard.

outrigger *n.* beam or spar projecting over a ship's side; stabilizing strip of wood fixed outside and parallel to a canoe; boat with either of these.

outright *adv.* completely, not gradually; frankly. —*a.* thorough, complete.

outset *n.* beginning.

outshine *v.t.* (p.t. *-shone*) surpass in splendour or excellence.

outside *n.* outer side, surface, or part. —*a.* of or from the outside; (of price) greatest possible. —*adv.* on, at, or to the outside. —*prep.* on, at, or to the outside of; other than.

outsider *n.* non-member of a group; horse etc. thought to have no chance in a contest.

outsize *a.* much larger than average.

outskirts *n.pl.* outer districts.

outspoken *a.* very frank.

outstanding *a.* conspicuous; exceptionally good; not yet paid or settled. **outstandingly** *adv.*

outstretched *a.* stretched out.

outstrip *v.t.* (p.t. *-stripped*) run faster or further than; surpass.

outvote *v.t.* defeat by a majority of votes.

outward *a.* on or to the outside. —*adv.* outwards. **outwardly** *adv.*, **outwards** *adv.*

outweigh *v.t.* be of greater weight or importance than.

outwit *v.t.* (p.t. *-witted*) defeat by one's craftiness.

outwork *n.* advanced or detached part of a fortification.

outworn *a.* worn out.

ouzel /ˈuːz-/ *n.* small bird of the thrush family; diving bird.

ova *see* **ovum.**

oval *n.* & *a.* (of) rounded symmetrical shape longer than it is broad.

ovary *n.* organ producing egg-cells; that part of a pistil from which fruit is formed. **ovarian** *a.*

ovation *n.* enthusiastic applause.

oven *n.* enclosed chamber in which things are cooked or heated.

over *prep.* in or to a position higher than; above and across; throughout, during; transmitted by; concerning; more than; in superiority to. —*adv.* outwards and downwards from the brink or an upright position etc.; from one side or end etc. to the other; across a space or distance; besides; with repetition; at an end. —*n.* series of 6 (or 8) balls bowled in cricket.

over- *pref.* above; excessively.

overall *n.* garment worn to protect other clothing, which it covers; (*pl.*) one-piece garment of this kind covering the body and legs. —*a.* total; taking all aspects into account. —*adv.* taken as a whole.

overarm *a. & adv.* with the arm brought forward and down from above shoulder level.

overawe *v.t.* overcome with awe.

overbalance *v.t./i.* lose balance and fall; cause to do this.

overbearing *a.* domineering.

overboard *adv.* from a ship into the water.

overbook *v.t.* book too many passengers or vehicles for.

overcast *a.* covered with cloud.

overcharge *v.t.* charge too much; fill too full.

overcoat *n.* warm outdoor coat.

overcome *v.t./i.* win a victory over; succeed in subduing or dealing with; be victorious; make helpless.

overdo *v.t.* (p.t. *-did*, p.p. *-done*) do too much; cook too long.

overdose *n.* too large a dose.

overdraft *n.* overdrawing of a bank account; amount of this.

overdraw *v.t.* (p.t. *-drew*, p.p. *-drawn*) draw more from (a bank account) than the amount credited.

overdrive *n.* mechanism providing an extra gear above top gear.

overdue *a.* not paid or arrived etc. by the due time.

overestimate *v.t.* form too high an estimate of.

overflow *v.t./i.* flow over the edge or limits (of). —*n.* what overflows; outlet for excess liquid.

overgrown *a.* grown too large; covered with weeds etc.

overhand *a. & adv.* overarm.

overhang *v.t./i.* (p.t. *-hung*) jut out over. —*n.* overhanging part.

overhaul *v.t.* examine and repair; overtake. —*n.* examination and repair.

overhead *a. & adv.* above the level of one's head; in the sky.

overheads *n.pl.* expenses involved in running a business etc.

overhear *v.t.* (p.t. *-heard*) hear accidentally or without the speaker's knowledge or intention.

overjoyed *a.* filled with great joy.

overkill *n.* surplus of capacity for destruction above what is needed to defeat or destroy an enemy.

overland *a. & adv.* (travelling) by land.

overlap *v.t./i.* (p.t. *-lapped*) extend beyond the edge of; coincide partially. —*n.* overlapping; part or amount that overlaps.

overleaf *adv.* on the other side of a leaf of a book etc.

overload *v.t.* put too great a load on or in. —*n.* load that is too great.

overlook *v.t.* have a view over; oversee; fail to observe or consider; ignore, not punish.

overlord *n.* supreme lord.

overman *v.t.* (p.t. *-manned*) provide with too many people as workmen or crew.

overnight *adv. & a.* during a night.

overpass *n.* road crossing another by means of a bridge.

overpay *v.t.* (p.t. *-paid*) pay too highly.

overpower *v.t.* overcome by greater strength or numbers.

overpowering *a.* (of heat or feelings) extremely intense.

overrate *v.t.* have too high an opinion of.

overreach *v.refl.* ∼ **oneself**, fail through being too ambitious.

override *v.t.* (p.t. *-rode*, p.p. *-ridden*) overrule; prevail over; intervene and cancel the operation of.

overrider *n.* vertical attachment on the bumper of a car.

overripe *a.* too ripe.

overrule *v.t.* set aside (a decision etc.) by using one's authority.

overrun *v.t.* (p.t. *-ran*, p.p. *-run*, pres.p. *-running*) spread over and occupy or injure; exceed (a limit).

overseas *a. & adv.* across or beyond the sea, abroad.

oversee *v.t.* (p.t. *-saw*, p.p. *-seen*) superintend. **overseer** *n.*

oversew *v.t.* (p.p. *-sewn*) sew (edges) together so that each stitch lies over the edges.

overshadow *v.t.* cast a shadow over; cause to seem unimportant in comparison.

overshoe *n.* shoe worn over another as a protection against wet etc.

overshoot *v.t.* (p.t. *-shot*) pass beyond (a target or limit etc.).

oversight *n.* supervision; unintentional omission or mistake.

oversized *a.* of more than the usual size.

oversleep *v.i.* (p.t. *-slept*) sleep longer than one intended.

overspill *n.* what spills over; district's surplus population seeking accommodation elsewhere.

overstay *v.t.* ∼ **one's welcome**, stay so long that one is no longer welcome.

oversteer *v.i.* (of a car) tend to turn more sharply than was intended. —*n.* this tendency.

overstep *v.t.* (p.t. *-stepped*) go beyond (a limit).

overt *a.* done or shown openly. **overtly** *adv.*

overtake *v.t.* (p.t. *-took*, p.p. *-taken*) come abreast or level with; pass (a moving person or thing).

overtax *v.t.* levy excessive taxes on; put too great a burden on.

overthrow *v.t.* (p.t. *-threw*, p.p. *-thrown*) cause the downfall of. —*n.* downfall, defeat.

overtime *adv.* in addition to regular working hours. —*n.* time worked thus; payment for this.

overtone *n.* additional quality or implication.

overture *n.* orchestral composition forming a prelude to an opera or ballet etc.; (*pl.*) friendly approach, formal proposal.

overturn *v.t./i.* turn over; fall down or over, cause to fall.

overweight *a.* weighing too much.

overwhelm *v.t.* bury beneath a huge mass; overcome completely; make helpless with emotion.

overwhelming *a.* irresistible through force of numbers or amount or influence.

overwork *v.t./i.* work too hard; make excessive use of. —*n.* excessive work causing exhaustion.

overwrought /-ˈrɔt/ *a.* in a state of nervous agitation through over-excitement.

ovoid /ˈəʊ-/ *a.* egg-shaped, oval.

ovulate /ˈɒv-/ *v.i.* produce or discharge an egg-cell from an ovary. **ovulation** *n.*

ovule /ˈəʊ-/ *n.* germ-cell of a plant.

ovum /ˈəʊ-/ *n.* (pl. *ova*) egg-cell.

owe *v.t.* be under an obligation to pay or repay or render; have (a thing) as the result of the action of another person or cause.

owing *a.* owed and not yet paid. ~ **to,** caused by; because of.

owl *n.* bird of prey with large eyes, usu. flying at night.

own[1] *a.* belonging to oneself or itself. **get one's ~ back,** (*colloq.*) have one's revenge. **hold one's ~,** maintain one's position, not lose strength. **of one's ~,** belonging to oneself. **on one's ~,** alone; independently.

own[2] *v.t.* have as one's property; acknowledge ownership of; confess. ~ **up,** (*colloq.*) confess.

owner *n.* one who owns something as his property. **ownership** *n.*

ox *n.* (pl. *oxen*) animal of or related to the kind kept as domestic cattle; fully grown bullock.

oxidation *n.* process of combining with oxygen.

oxide *n.* compound of oxygen and one other element.

oxidize *v.t./i.* combine with oxygen; coat with an oxide; make or become rusty. **oxidization** *n.*

oxtail *n.* tail of an ox, used to make soup or stew.

oxygen *n.* colourless gas existing in air.

oyster *n.* shellfish used as food.

ozone *n.* form of oxygen.

P

pace *n.* single step in walking or running; rate of progress. —*v.t./i.* walk steadily or to and fro; measure by pacing; set the pace for. ~-**maker** *n.* runner etc. who sets the pace for another; electrical device stimulating heart contractions.

pacific *a.* making or loving peace. **pacifically** *adv.*

Pacific *a. & n.* (of) the ~ **Ocean** (west of the American continent).

pacifist *n.* person totally opposed to war. **pacifism** *n.*

pacify *v.t.* calm and soothe; establish peace in. **pacification** *n.*

pack *n.* collection of things wrapped or tied for carrying or selling; set of playing-cards; group of hounds or wolves; set; large amount or collection. —*v.t./i.* put into or fill a container; press or crowd together, fill (a space) thus; cover or protect with something pressed tightly. ~ **off,** send away. **send packing,** dismiss abruptly. **packer** *n.*

package *n.* parcel; box etc. in which goods are packed; package deal. —*v.t.* put together in a package. ~ **deal,** set of proposals offered or accepted as a whole. ~ **holiday,** one with set arrangements at an inclusive price.

packet *n.* small package; (*colloq.*) large sum of money; mail-boat.

pact *n.* agreement, treaty.

pad[1] *n.* piece of padding; set of sheets of paper fastened together at one edge; soft fleshy part under an animal's paw; flat surface for use by helicopters or for launching rockets. —*v.t./i.* (p.t. *padded*) put padding on or into; fill out.

pad[2] *v.i.* (p.t. *padded*) walk softly or steadily.

padding *n.* soft material used to protect against jarring, add bulk, absorb fluid, etc.

paddle[1] *n.* short oar used without a rowlock; thing shaped like this; board of a paddle-wheel. —*v.t./i.* propel by use of paddle(s); row gently. ~-**steamer** *n.* one driven by paddle-wheel(s). ~-**wheel** *n.* wheel with boards round its rim that drive a boat by pressing against the water as the wheel revolves.

paddle[2] *v.t./i.* walk with bare feet in shallow water for pleasure; dabble (feet or hands) in water.

paddock *n.* small field where horses are kept; enclosure for horses or racing-cars at a race-course.

paddy[1] *n.* (*colloq.*) rage, temper.

paddy[2] *n.* rice-field; growing rice.

padlock *n.* detachable lock with a U-shaped bar secured through the object fastened. —*v.t.* fasten with a padlock.

paean /ˈpiən/ *n.* song of triumph.

paediatrics /pi-/ *n.* study of children's diseases. **paediatric** *a.,* **paediatrician** /-ˈtrɪʃən/ *n.*

pagan *a. & n.* heathen.

page[1] *n.* sheet of paper in a book or newspaper etc.; one side of this.

page[2] *n.* liveried boy or man employed as a door attendant or to go on errands etc.; boy attendant of a bride or person of rank.

pageant /ˈpædʒ-/ *n.* public show or procession, esp. with people in costume.

pagoda *n.* Hindu temple or Buddhist tower in India, China, etc.

paid *see* **pay.** —*a.* **put ~ to,** (*colloq.*) end (hopes or prospects etc.).

pail *n.* bucket.

pain *n.* unpleasant feeling caused by injury or disease of the body; mental suffering; (*pl.*) careful effort. —*v.t.* cause pain to.

painful *a.* causing or suffering pain; laborious. **painfully** *adv.,* **painfulness** *n.*

painless *a.* not causing pain. **painlessly** *adv.*

painstaking *a.* very careful.

paint *n.* colouring-matter for applying in liquid form to a surface; (*pl.*) tubes or cakes of paint. —*v.t.* coat with paint; portray by using paint(s) or in words; apply (liquid) to.

painter[1] *n.* person who paints as artist or decorator.

painter[2] *n.* rope attached to a boat's bow for tying it up.

painting *n.* painted picture.

pair *n.* set of two things or people, couple; article consisting of two joined corresponding parts; other member of a pair. —*v.t./i.* arrange or be arranged in pair(s); (of animals) mate.

pal *n.* (*colloq.*) friend. **pally** *a.*

palace *n.* official residence of a sovereign, archbishop, or bishop; splendid mansion.

palaeolithic /pælɪə-/ *a.* of the early part of the Stone Age.

palatable *a.* pleasant to the taste or mind.

palate *n.* roof of the mouth; sense of taste.

palatial /-'leɪʃ-/ *a.* of or like a palace.

palaver /-'lɑ-/ *n.* (*colloq.*) fuss.

pale[1] *a.* (-*er*, -*est*) (of face) having less colour than normal; (of colour or light) faint. —*v.t./i.* turn pale. **palely** *adv.*, **paleness** *n.*

pale[2] *n.* stake forming part of a fence; boundary. **beyond the ~,** outside the bounds of acceptable behaviour.

Palestinian *a.* & *n.* (native) of Palestine.

palette *n.* board on which an artist mixes colours. **~-knife,** blade with a handle, used for spreading paint or for smoothing soft substances in cookery.

paling *n.* railing(s).

palisade *n.* fence of pointed stakes.

pall /pol/ *n.* cloth spread over a coffin; heavy dark covering. —*v.i.* become uninteresting.

pallbearer *n.* one of the people helping to carry or walking beside the coffin at a funeral.

pallet[1] *n.* straw-stuffed mattress; hard narrow or makeshift bed.

pallet[2] *n.* tray or platform for goods being lifted or stored.

palliasse *n.* straw-stuffed mattress.

palliative /'pæ-/ *a.* & *n.* (thing) reducing bad effects.

pallid *a.* pale, esp. from illness. **pallidness** *n.*, **pallor** *n.*

palm *n.* inner surface of the hand; part of a glove covering this; tree of warm and tropical climates, with large leaves and no branches; symbol of victory. —*v.t.* conceal in one's hand; get (a thing) accepted by fraud. **Palm Sunday,** Sunday before Easter. **~-tree** *n.*

palmist *n.* person who tells people's fortunes or characters from lines in their palms. **palmistry** *n.*

palmy *a.* (-*ier*, -*iest*) flourishing.

palpable *a.* able to be touched or felt; obvious. **palpably** *adv.*, **palpability** *n.*

palpitate *v.i.* throb rapidly; quiver with fear or excitement. **palpitation** *n.*

palsy *n.* paralysis, esp. with involuntary tremors. **palsied** *a.*

paltry *a.* (-*ier*, -*iest*) worthless.

pampas *n.* vast grassy plains in South America; tall ornamental grass.

pamper *v.t.* treat very indulgently.

pamphlet *n.* leaflet or paper-covered booklet.

pan[1] *n.* metal or earthenware vessel with a flat base, used in cooking; similar vessel; bowl of a pair of scales; bowl of a water-closet. —*v.t.* (p.t. *panned*) wash (gravel) in a pan in searching for gold; (*colloq.*) criticize severely.

pan[2] *v.t./i.* (p.t. *panned*) turn horizontally in filming.

pan- *pref.* all-, whole.

panacea /-'sɪə/ *n.* remedy for all kinds of diseases or troubles.

panache /-'næʃ/ *n.* confident stylish manner.

panama *n.* hat of fine straw-like material; a kind of woven fabric.

panatella *n.* thin cigar.

pancake *n.* thin round cake of fried batter; thing shaped like this.

panchromatic *a.* sensitive to all colours of the visible spectrum.

pancreas *n.* gland near the stomach, discharging insulin into the blood.

panda *n.* large bear-like black-and-white animal of south-west China; racoon-like animal of India. **~ car,** police patrol car.

pandemonium *n.* uproar.

pander *v.i.* **~ to,** gratify by satisfying a weakness or vulgar taste.

pane *n.* sheet of glass in a window or door.

panegyric /-'dʒɪ-/ *n.* piece of written or spoken praise.

panel *n.* distinct usu. rectangular section; strip of board etc. forming this; group assembled to discuss or decide something; list of jurors, jury. —*v.t.* (p.t. *panelled*) cover or decorate with panels.

panelling *n.* series of wooden panels in a wall; wood used for making panels.

panellist *n.* member of a panel.

pang *n.* sudden sharp pain.

panic *n.* sudden strong fear. —*v.t./i.* (p.t. *panicked*) affect or be affected with panic. **~-stricken, ~-struck** *adjs.*

panicle *n.* loose branching cluster of flowers.

pannier *n.* large basket carried by a donkey etc.; bag fitted on a motor cycle.

panoply *n.* splendid array.

panorama *n.* view of a wide area or set of events. **panoramic** *a.*

pansy *n.* garden flower of violet family with broad petals.

pant *v.t./i.* breathe with short quick breaths; utter breathlessly; be extremely eager.

pantaloons *n.pl.* (*joc.* & *U.S.*) trousers.

pantechnicon /-'tek-/ *n.* large van for transporting furniture.

panther *n.* leopard.

panties *n.pl.* (*colloq.*) short knickers.

pantile *n.* curved roof-tile.

pantomime *n.* Christmas play based on a fairy-tale; mime. —*v.t./i.* mime.

pantry *n.* room for storing china, glass, etc.; larder.

pants *n.pl.* (*colloq.*) trousers, underpants, knickers.

pap *n.* soft food suitable for infants or invalids; pulp.

papa /-ˈpɑ/ *n.* (*old use*) father.

papacy *n.* position or authority of the pope.

papal *a.* of the pope or papacy.

papaw /-ˈpɔ/ *n.* edible fruit of a palm-like tropical tree; this tree.

paper *n.* substance manufactured in thin sheets from wood fibre, rags, etc., used for writing on, wrapping things, etc.; newspaper; set of examination questions; document; essay, dissertation. —*v.t.* cover (walls etc.) with wallpaper. **on ∼,** in writing; when judged from written or printed evidence.

paperback *a.* & *n.* (book) bound in flexible paper binding.

paperweight *n.* small heavy object to hold loose papers down.

papery *a.* like paper in texture.

papier mâché /ˈpæpjeɪ ˈmæʃeɪ/ moulded paper pulp used for making small objects.

papist *n.* (*derog.*) Roman Catholic.

paprika /ˈpæ-/ *n.* red pepper.

papyrus *n.* reed-like water-plan from which the ancient Egyptians made a kind of paper; this paper; (pl. *-ri*) manuscript written on this.

par *n.* average or normal amount or condition etc.; equal footing.

parable *n.* story told to illustrate a moral or spiritual truth.

parabola /-ˈræ-/ *n.* curve like the path of object thrown up and falling back to earth.

parachute *n.* umbrella-shaped device used to slow the descent of a person or object dropping from a great height. —*v.t./i.* descend or drop by parachute. **parachutist** *n.*

parade *n.* formal assembly of troops for inspection etc.; place for this; procession; ostentatious display; public square or promenade. —*v.t./i.* assemble for parade; march or walk with display; make a display of.

paradise *n.* heaven; Eden.

paradox *n.* statement that seems self-contradictory but contains a truth. **paradoxical** *a.*, **paradoxically** *adv.*

paraffin *n.* oil from petroleum or shale, used as fuel. **liquid ∼,** tasteless form of this used as a mild laxative. **∼ wax,** solid paraffin.

paragon *n.* apparently perfect person or thing.

paragraph *n.* one or more sentences on a single theme, beginning on a new (usu. indented) line. —*v.t.* arrange in paragraphs.

parakeet *n.* a kind of small parrot.

parallax *n.* apparent difference in an object's position when viewed from different points.

parallel *a.* (of lines or planes) going continuously at the same distance from each other; similar, corresponding. —*n.* parallel line or thing; line on a map or globe, drawn parallel to the equator; comparison, analogy. —*v.t./i.* (p.t. *paralleled*) be parallel to; compare. **parallelism** *n.*

parallelogram *n.* four-sided geometric figure with its opposite sides parallel to each other.

paralyse *v.t.* affect with paralysis; bring to a standstill.

paralysis *n.* loss of power of movement, inability to move normally. **paralytic** /-ˈlɪt-/ *a.* & *n.*

parameter /-ˈræ-/ *n.* variable quantity or quality that restricts what it characterizes.

paramilitary *a.* organized like a military force.

paramount *a.* chief in importance.

paranoia *n.* mental disorder in which a person has delusions; abnormal tendency to mistrust others. **paranoiac** *a.*

parapet *n.* low protective wall along the edge of a balcony or bridge.

paraphernalia /-ˈneɪ-/ *n.* numerous belongings or pieces of equipment.

paraphrase *v.t.* express in other words. —*n.* rewording in this way.

paraplegia /-ˈpli-/ *n.* paralysis of the legs and part or all of the trunk. **paraplegic** *a.* & *n.*

paraquat /ˈpæ-/ *n.* extremely poisonous weed-killer.

parasite *n.* animal or plant living on or in another; person living off another or others and giving no useful return. **parasitic** /-ˈsɪt-/ *a.*

parasol *n.* light umbrella used to give shade from the sun.

paratrooper *n.* member of paratroops.

paratroops *n.pl.* troops trained to descend by parachute.

paratyphoid *n.* fever like typhoid but milder.

parboil *v.t.* cook partially by boiling.

parcel *n.* thing(s) wrapped for carrying or post; piece of land. —*v.t.* (p.t. *parcelled*) wrap as a parcel; divide into portions.

parch *v.t.* make hot and dry; make thirsty.

parchment *n.* heavy paper-like material made from animal skins; paper resembling this.

pardon *n.* forgiveness. —*v.t.* (p.t. *pardoned*) forgive. **pardonable** *a.*, **pardonably** *adv.*

pare /peə(r)/ *v.t.* trim the edges of; peel; reduce little by little.

parent *n.* one who has produced offspring; ancestor; source from which other things are derived. **parental** /-ˈren-/ *a.*, **parenthood** *n.*

parentage *n.* descent from parents.

parenthesis /-ˈren-/ *n.* (pl. *-theses*) word, phrase, or sentence inserted into a passage that is grammatically complete without it; brackets (like these) placed round this. **parenthetic** /-ˈθet-/ *a.*, **parenthetical** *a.*, **parenthetically** *adv.*

pariah /pəˈraɪə or ˈpærɪə/ *n.* outcast.

parings /ˈpeər-/ *n.pl.* pieces pared off.

parish *n.* area (within a diocese) with its own church and clergyman; local-government area within a county.

parishioner *n.* inhabitant of a parish.

Parisian /-ˈrɪz-/ *a.* & *n.* (native) of Paris.

parity /ˈpæ-/ *n.* equality.

park *n.* public garden or recreation ground; enclosed land attached to a country house or mansion; parking area. —*v.t.* place and leave (a vehicle etc.) temporarily.

parka *n.* a type of thick jacket with a hood attached.

parkin *n.* gingerbread made with oatmeal and treacle.

parky *a.* (*sl.*, of weather) chilly.

parley *n.* (pl. *-eys*) discussion, esp. between enemies, to settle a dispute. —*v.i.* (p.t. *parleyed*) hold a parley.

parliament *n.* assembly that makes a country's laws. **parliamentary** *a.*

parlour *n.* sitting-room.

parlourmaid *n.* maid who waits on a household at meals.

parochial /-'rəʊk-/ *a.* of a church parish; interested in a limited area only.

parody *n.* comic or grotesque imitation. —*v.t.* make a parody of.

parole /-'rəʊl/ *n.* person's word of honour; release of a prisoner before the end of his sentence on condition of good behaviour. —*v.t.* release in this way.

paroxysm /'pæ-/ *n.* spasm; outburst of laughter, rage, etc.

parquet /-keɪ/ *n.* flooring of wooden blocks arranged in a pattern.

parrot *n.* tropical bird with a short hooked bill; unintelligent imitator.

parry *v.t.* ward off (a blow); evade (a question) skilfully. —*n.* parrying.

parse *v.t.* explain the grammatical form and function of.

parsec *n.* unit of distance used in astronomy, about 3½ light-years.

parsimonious /-'məʊ-/ *a.* stingy, very sparing. **parsimoniously** *adv.*, **parsimony** /'pɑ-/ *n.*

parsley *n.* herb with crinkled green leaves.

parsnip *n.* vegetable with a large yellowish tapering root.

parson *n.* (*colloq.*) clergyman.

parsonage *n.* rectory, vicarage.

part *n.* some but not all; distinct portion; component; portion allotted, share; character assigned to an actor in a play etc.; melody assigned to one voice or instrument in a group; region; side in an agreement or dispute. —*adv.* partly. —*v.t./i.* separate, divide. **in good ~,** without taking offence. **in ~,** partly. **~ of speech,** word's grammatical class (noun, verb, adjective, etc.). **~ with,** give up possession of, hand over.

partake *v.i.* (p.t. *-took*, p.p. *-taken*) participate; take a portion, esp. of food. **partaker** *n.*

Parthian *a.* **~ shot,** sharp remark made by a person as he departs.

partial *a.* in part but not complete or total. **be ~ to,** have a strong liking for. **partially** *adv.*

partiality /-ʃɪ'æl-/ *n.* bias, favouritism; strong liking.

participate *v.i.* have a share, take part in something. **participation** *n.*

participle *n.* word formed from a verb, as a **past ~** (e.g. *burnt*, *frightened*), **present ~** (e.g. *burning*, *frightening*). **participial** *a.*

particle *n.* very small portion of matter; minor part of speech.

particoloured *a.* coloured partly in one colour, partly in another.

particular *a.* relating to one person or thing and not others; special, exceptional; carefully insisting on certain standards. —*n.* detail; piece of information. **in ~,** particularly, especially; specifically. **particularly** *adv.*, **particularity** *n.*

particularize *v.t./i.* specify, name specially or one by one.

parting *n.* leave-taking; line from which hair is combed in different directions.

partisan /-'zæn or 'pɑ-/ *n.* strong supporter; guerrilla. **partisanship** *n.*

partition *n.* division into parts; part formed thus; structure dividing a room or space, thin wall. —*v.t.* divide into parts or by a partition.

partly *a.* partially.

partner *n.* person sharing with another or others in an activity; one of a pair, esp. in dancing or games. —*v.t.* be the partner of; put together as partners. **partnership** *n.*

partridge *n.* game-bird with brown feathers and a plump body.

parturition *n.* process of giving birth to young; childbirth.

party *n.* social gathering; group travelling or working as a unit; group united in support of a cause or policy, esp. in politics; person(s) forming one side in an agreement or dispute; one who shares in an action or plan etc.; (*joc.*) person. **~ line,** shared telephone line; set policy of a political party. **~ wall,** wall common to two buildings or rooms.

paschal /-sk-/ *a.* of the Passover; of Easter.

pass *v.t./i.* (p.t. *passed*) move onward or past; go or cause to go to another person or place; send (a ball) to another player in football etc.; discharge from the body as excreta; change from one state into another; happen; occupy (time); be accepted, be currently known; be allowed or tolerated; examine and declare satisfactory; achieve the required standard in a test; go beyond; utter; (in cards) refuse one's turn. —*n.* passing; movement made with the hands or thing held; permit to enter or leave; gap in mountains, allowing passage to the other side; critical state of affairs. **make a ~ at,** (*colloq.*) try to attract sexually. **~ away,** cease; die. **~ out,** (*colloq.*) become unconscious. **~ over,** disregard. **~ up,** (*colloq.*) refuse to accept (an opportunity etc.).

passable *a.* able to be traversed; just satisfactory. **passably** *adv.*

passage *n.* passing; right to pass or be a passenger; way through, esp. with a wall on each side; tube-like structure; section of a literary or musical work. **~ of arms,** fight, dispute. **passageway** *n.*

passbook *n.* book recording a customer's deposits and withdrawals from a bank etc.

passenger *n.* person (other than the driver, pilot, or crew) travelling in a vehicle, train, ship, or aircraft; ineffective member of a team.

passer-by *n.* (pl. *passers-by*) person who happens to be going past.

passion *n.* strong emotion; sexual love; great enthusiasm; *the P~,* sufferings of Christ on the Cross. **~-flower** *n.* climbing plant with a flower suggesting the instruments of the Passion. **~-fruit** *n.* edible fruit of some kinds of this.

passionate *a.* full of passion, intense. **passionately** *adv.*

passive *a.* acted upon and not active; inert; not resisting; lacking initiative or forceful qualities. **passively** *adv.*, **passiveness** *n.*, **passivity** /-ˈsɪv-/ *n.*

passkey *n.* key to a door or gate; master-key.

Passover *n.* Jewish festival commemorating the escape of Jews from slavery in Egypt; paschal lamb.

passport *n.* official document for use by a person travelling abroad.

password *n.* secret word(s), knowledge of which distinguishes friend from enemy.

past *a.* belonging to the time before the present, gone by. —*n.* past time or events; person's past life. —*prep. & adv.* beyond. **~ master,** thorough master, expert.

pasta *n.* dried paste made with flour, produced in various shapes; cooked dish made with this.

paste *n.* moist fairly stiff mixture; adhesive; edible doughy substance; hard glass-like substance used in imitation gems. —*v.t.* fasten or coat with paste; (*sl.*) thrash.

pasteboard *n.* cardboard.

pastel *n.* chalk-like crayon; drawing made with this; light delicate shade of colour.

pastern *n.* part of a horse's foot between fetlock and hoof.

pasteurize *v.t.* sterilize (milk) partially. **pasteurization** *n.*

pastiche /-ˈtiːʃ/ *n.* musical or other composition made up of selections from various sources.

pastille *n.* small flavoured sweet for sucking; lozenge.

pastime *n.* something done to pass time pleasantly.

pastor *n.* clergyman in charge of a church or congregation.

pastoral *a.* of country life; of a pastor, of spiritual guidance.

pastry *n.* dough made of flour, fat, and water, used for making pies etc.; article(s) made with this.

pasturage *n.* pasture-land.

pasture *n.* land covered with grass etc. suitable for grazing cattle; this grass. —*v.t.* graze, put (animals) to graze.

pasty[1] /ˈpæ-/ *n.* pastry with sweet or savoury filling, baked without a dish.

pasty[2] /ˈpeɪ-/ *a.* of or like paste; unhealthily pale.

pat *v.t.* (p.t. *patted*) tap gently with an open hand or something flat. —*n.* patting movement; sound of this; small mass of a soft substance. —*adv. & a.* known and ready. **stand ~,** stick firmly to one's decision.

patch *n.* piece put on, esp. in mending; distinct area or period; piece of ground. —*v.t.* put patch(es) on; piece (things) together. **not a ~ on,** (*colloq.*) not nearly as good as. **~ up,** repair; settle (a quarrel etc.).

patchwork *n.* needlework in which small pieces of cloth are joined decoratively; thing made of assorted pieces.

patchy *a.* existing in patches; uneven in quality. **patchily** *adv.*, **patchiness** *n.*

pate *n.* (*old use*) head.

pâté /ˈpæteɪ/ *n.* paste of meat etc.

patent[1] /ˈpeɪ-/ *a.* obvious; patented. —*v.t.* obtain or hold a patent for. **~ leather,** leather with glossy varnished surface. **patently** *adv.*

patent[2] /ˈpæ- or ˈpeɪ-/ *n.* official right to be the sole maker or user of an invention or process; invention etc. protected by this.

patentee /peɪ- or pæ-/ *n.* holder of a patent.

paternal *a.* of a father; fatherly; related through one's father. **paternally** *adv.*

paternalism *n.* policy of making kindly provision for people's needs but giving them no responsibility. **paternalistic** *a.*

paternity *n.* fatherhood.

path *n.* way by which people pass on foot; line along which a person or thing moves; course of action.

pathetic *a.* arousing pity or sadness; miserably inadequate. **pathetically** *adv.*

pathology *n.* study of disease. **pathological** *a.*, **pathologist** *n.*

pathos /ˈpeɪ-/ *n.* pathetic quality.

patience *n.* calm endurance of annoyance or delay etc.; perseverance; card-game for one player.

patient *a.* showing patience. —*n.* person treated by a doctor or dentist etc. **patiently** *adv.*

patina *n.* attractive green incrustation on old bronze or gloss on old woodwork.

patio *n.* (pl. *-os*) paved courtyard.

patois /ˈpætwɑː/ *n.* dialect.

patriarch /ˈpeɪ-/ *n.* male head of a family or tribe; bishop of high rank in certain Churches. **patriarchal** *a.*

patrician *n.* member of the aristocracy, esp. in ancient Rome. —*a.* aristocratic.

patrimony /ˈpæ-/ *n.* heritage.

patriot /ˈpæ- or ˈpeɪ-/ *n.* patriotic person.

patriotic /pæ- or peɪ-/ *a.* loyally supporting one's country. **patriotically** *adv.*, **patriotism** *n.*

patrol *v.t.* walk or travel regularly through (an area or building) to see that all is well. —*n.* patrolling; person(s) patrolling; unit in a Scout or Guide company.

patron /ˈpeɪ-/ *n.* person giving influential or financial support to a cause; regular customer. **~ saint,** saint regarded as a protector. **patroness** *n.fem.*

patronage /ˈpæ-/ *n.* patron's support; patronizing behaviour.

patronize /ˈpæ-/ *v.t.* act as patron to; treat in a condescending way.

patter[1] *v.i.* make a series of quick tapping sounds; run with short quick steps. —*n.* pattering sound.

patter[2] *n.* rapid glib speech.

pattern *n.* decorative design; model, design, or instructions showing how a thing is to be made; sample of cloth etc.; excellent example;

regular manner in which things occur. **patterned** *a.*

patty *n.* small pie or pasty.

paucity *n.* smallness of quantity.

paunch *n.* belly; protruding abdomen.

pauper *n.* very poor person.

pause *n.* temporary stop. —*v.i.* make a pause.

pave *v.t.* cover (a road or path etc.) with stones or concrete to make a hard surface. **∼ the way,** prepare the way for changes etc.

pavement *n.* paved surface; paved path at the side of a road.

pavilion *n.* building on a sports ground for use by players and spectators; ornamental building.

paw *n.* foot of an animal that has claws; (*colloq.*) hand. —*v.t.* strike with a paw; scrape (the ground) with a hoof; (*colloq.*) touch with the hands.

pawky *a.* (*-ier, -iest*) drily humorous. **pawkily** *adv.*, **pawkiness** *n.*

pawl *n.* lever with a catch that engages with the notches of a ratchet.

pawn[1] *n.* chess-man of the smallest size and value; person whose actions are controlled by others.

pawn[2] *v.t.* deposit with a pawnbroker as security for money borrowed. —*n.* thing deposited as a pledge. **∼-shop** *n.* pawnbroker's premises.

pawnbroker *n.* person licensed to lend money on the security of personal property deposited with him.

pay *v.t./i.* (p.t. *paid*) give (money) in return for goods or services; give what is owed; be profitable or worth while; bestow; suffer (a penalty); let out (a rope) by slackening it. —*n.* payment; wages. **in the ∼ of,** employed by. **∼-as-you-earn,** method of collecting income tax by deducting it at source from wages or interest etc. **∼ off,** pay in full and be free from (a debt) or discharge (an employee); yield good results. **∼-off** *n.* (*sl.*) payment; reward, retribution, climax. **∼ out,** punish, be revenged on. **∼ up,** pay in full; pay what is demanded. **payer** *n.*

payable *a.* which must or may be paid.

P.A.Y.E. *abbr.* pay-as-you-earn.

payee *n.* person to whom money is paid or is to be paid.

payload *n.* aircraft's or rocket's total load.

paymaster *n.* official who pays troops or workmen etc. **Paymaster General,** head of the Treasury department through which payments are made.

payment *n.* paying; money etc. paid.

payola *n.* bribe or bribery offered in return for dishonest use of influence to promote a commercial product.

payroll *n.* list of a firm's employees receiving regular pay.

pea *n.* plant bearing seeds in pods; its round seed used as a vegetable. **∼-green** *a.* & *n.* bright green.

peace *n.* state of freedom from war or disturbance; treaty ending a war.

peaceable *a.* fond of peace, not quarrelsome; peaceful. **peaceably** *adv.*

peaceful *a.* characterized by peace. **peacefully** *adv.*, **peacefulness** *n.*

peacemaker *n.* person who brings about peace.

peach *n.* round juicy fruit with a rough stone; tree bearing this; its yellowish-pink colour; (*sl.*) greatly admired person or thing.

peacock *n.* male bird with splendid plumage and a long fan-like tail. **peahen** *n.fem.*

peak *n.* pointed top, esp. of a mountain; projecting part of the edge of a cap; point of highest value or intensity etc. **peaked** *a.*

peaky *a.* looking drawn and sickly.

peal *n.* sound of ringing bell(s); set of bells with different notes; loud burst of thunder or laughter. —*v.t./i.* sound in a peal.

peanut *n.* plant bearing underground pods with two edible seeds; this seed; (*pl.*) very trivial sum of money.

pear *n.* rounded fruit tapering towards the stalk; tree bearing this.

pearl *n.* round usu. white gem formed inside the shell of certain oysters; thing resembling this in shape or value or colour. **∼ barley,** barley grains ground small. **pearly** *a.*

peasant *n.* person working on the land, esp. in the Middle Ages.

peat *n.* decomposed vegetable matter from bogs etc., used in horticulture or as fuel. **peaty** *a.*

pebble *n.* small smooth round stone; rock-crystal used for spectacle lenses. **pebbly** *a.*

peccadillo *n.* (pl. *-oes*) trivial offence.

peck[1] *n.* measure of capacity for dry goods (= 2 gallons); a lot.

peck[2] *v.t./i.* strike, nip, or pick up with the beak; kiss hastily. —*n.* pecking movement.

peckish *a.* (*colloq.*) hungry.

pectin *n.* gelatinous substance found in fruits etc., causing jam to set.

pectoral *a.* of, in, or on the chest or breast.

peculation /pek-/ *n.* embezzlement.

peculiar *a.* strange, eccentric; belonging exclusively to one person or place or thing; special. **peculiarly** *adv.*, **peculiarity** *n.*

pecuniary /-ˈkju-/ *a.* of or in money.

pedagogue /-gog/ *n.* (*derog.*) person who teaches pedantically.

pedal *n.* lever operated by the foot in a vehicle or machine, or in certain musical instruments. —*v.t./i.* (p.t. *pedalled*) work the pedal(s) of; operate by pedals.

pedant /ˈped-/ *n.* pedantic person. **pedantry** *n.*

pedantic /-ˈdæ-/ *a.* insisting on strict observance of rules and details in presenting knowledge; parading one's learning. **pedantically** *adv.*

peddle *v.t.* sell (goods) as a pedlar.

pedestal *n.* base supporting a column or statue etc.

pedestrian *n.* person walking, esp. in a street. —*a.* of or for pedestrians; unimaginative, dull.

pedicure /ˈped-/ *n.* care or treatment of the feet and toe-nails.

pedigree *n.* line or list of (esp. distinguished) ancestors. —*a.* (of an animal) of recorded and pure breeding.

pediment *n.* triangular part crowning the front of a building.

pedlar *n.* person who goes from house to house selling small articles.

peek *v.i. & n.* peep, glance.

peel *n.* skin of certain fruits and vegetables etc. —*v.t./i.* remove the peel of; strip off; come off in strips or layers, lose skin or bark etc. thus. ~ **off,** veer away from a formation. **peeler** *n.*, **peelings** *n.pl.*

peep¹ *v.i.* look through a narrow opening; look quickly or surreptitiously; show slightly. —*n.* brief or surreptitious look. **~-hole** *n.* small hole to peep through.

peep² *n. & v.t.* cheep.

peer¹ *v.i.* look searchingly or with difficulty or effort.

peer² *n.* duke, marquis, earl, viscount, or baron; one who is the equal of another in rank or merit etc. **peeress** *n.fem.*

peerage *n.* peers as a group; rank of peer or peeress.

peerless *a.* without equal, superb.

peeved *a.* (*sl.*) annoyed.

peevish *a.* irritable. **peevishly** *adv.*, **peevishness** *n.*

peewit *n.* a kind of plover.

peg *n.* wooden or metal pin or stake; clip for holding clothes on a washing-line; drink or measure of spirits. —*v.t.* (p.t. *pegged*) fix or mark by means of peg(s); keep (wages or prices) at a fixed level. **off the ~,** (of clothes) ready-made. **~ away,** work diligently. **~ out,** (*sl.*) die.

pejorative /-ˈdʒɒ-/ *a.* derogatory.

peke *n.* Pekingese dog.

Pekingese *n.* dog of a breed with short legs, flat face, and silky hair.

pelican *n.* water-bird with a pouch in its long bill for storing fish. **~ crossing,** pedestrian crossing with lights operated by pedestrians.

pellet *n.* small round mass of a substance; small shot. **pelleted** *a.*

pell-mell *a. & adv.* in a hurrying disorderly manner, headlong.

pellucid /-ˈljuː-/ *a.* very clear.

pelmet *n.* ornamental strip above a window etc.

pelt¹ *n.* an animal skin.

pelt² *v.t./i.* throw missiles at; (of rain etc.) come down fast; run fast. **at full ~,** as fast as possible.

pelvis *n.* framework of bones round the body below the waist.

pen¹ *n.* small fenced enclosure, esp. for animals. —*v.t.* (p.t. *penned*) shut in or as if in a pen.

pen² *n.* device with a metal point for writing with ink. —*v.t.* (p.t. *penned*) write (a letter etc.). **~-friend** *n.* friend with whom a person corresponds without meeting. **~-name** *n.* author's pseudonym.

penal *a.* of or involving punishment.

penalize *v.t.* inflict a penalty on; put at a disadvantage. **penalization** *n.*

penalty *n.* punishment for breaking a law or rule or contract; disadvantage resulting from an action or quality.

penance *n.* act performed as an expression of penitence.

pence *see* **penny.**

penchant /ˈpɑ̃ʃɑ̃/ *n.* liking.

pencil *n.* instrument containing graphite, used for drawing or writing. —*v.t.* (p.t. *pencilled*) write, draw, or mark with a pencil.

pendant *n.* ornament hung from a chain round the neck.

pendent *a.* hanging.

pending *a.* waiting to be decided or settled. —*prep.* during; until.

pendulous *a.* hanging loosely.

pendulum *n.* weight hung from a cord and swinging freely; rod with a weighted end that regulates a clock's movement.

penetrable *a.* able to be penetrated. **penetrability** *n.*

penetrate *v.t./i.* make a way into or through, pierce; see into or through. **penetration** *n.*

penetrating *a.* showing great insight; (of sound) piercing.

penguin *n.* flightless sea-bird of Antarctic regions, with flippers used for swimming.

penicillin /-ˈsɪl-/ *n.* antibiotic obtained from mould fungi.

peninsula *n.* piece of land almost surrounded by water. **peninsular** *a.*

penis /ˈpiː-/ *n.* organ by which a male animal copulates and urinates.

penitent *a.* feeling or showing regret that one has done wrong. —*n.* penitent person. **penitently** *adv.*, **penitence** *n.*

penitential /-ˈten-/ *a.* of penitence or penance.

penitentiary /-ˈtenʃ-/ *n.* (*U.S.*) federal prison or State prison.

pennant *n.* ship's long tapering flag.

penniless *a.* having no money, destitute.

pennon *n.* flag, esp. a long triangular or forked one; long streamer on a ship.

penny *n.* (pl. *pennies* for separate coins, *pence* for a sum of money) British bronze coin worth $\frac{1}{100}$ of £1; former coin worth $\frac{1}{12}$ of a shilling.

pension¹ *n.* income consisting of a periodic payment made in consideration of past service or on retirement or widowhood etc. —*v.t.* pay a pension to. **~ off,** dismiss with a pension.

pension² /ˈpɑ̃sɪɒ̃/ *n.* boarding-house on the Continent.

pensionable *a.* entitled or (of a job) entitling one to a pension.

pensioner *n.* person who receives a pension.

pensive *a.* deep in thought. **pensively** *adv.*, **pensiveness** *n.*

pent *a.* shut in a confined space. **~-up** *a.*

pentagon *n.* geometric figure with five sides. **pentagonal** /-ˈtæg-/ *a.*

pentameter /-ˈtæm-/ *n.* line of verse with five metrical feet.

Pentateuch /-tjuːk/ *n.* first five books of the Old Testament.

pentathlon *n.* athletic contest involving five events.

Pentecost *n.* Jewish harvest festival, 50 days after second day of Passover; Whit Sunday.

penthouse *n.* sloping roof supported against the wall of a building; dwelling (usu. with a terrace) on the roof of a tall building.

penultimate *a.* last but one.

penury /ˈpenjʊərɪ/ *n.* poverty.

peony *n.* garden plant with large round red, pink, or white flowers.

people *n.pl.* human beings; persons; subjects of a State; persons without special rank; parents or other relatives. —*n.* persons composing a race or nation or community. —*v.t.* fill with people, populate.

pep *n.* vigour. —*v.t.* (p.t. *pepped*) fill with vigour, enliven. ～ **talk,** talk urging great effort.

peplum *n.* short flounce from the waist of a garment.

pepper *n.* hot-tasting seasoning-powder made from the dried berries of certain plants; capsicum. —*v.t.* sprinkle with pepper; pelt; sprinkle. ～-**and-salt** *a.* of mingled dark and light.

peppercorn *n.* dried black berry from which pepper is made. ～ **rent,** very low rent.

peppermint *n.* a kind of mint with strong fragrant oil; this oil; sweet flavoured with this.

peppery *a.* like pepper; containing much pepper; hot-tempered.

peptic *a.* of digestion.

per *prep.* for each; in accordance with; by means of. ～ **annum,** for each year. ～ **cent,** in or for every hundred.

perambulate *v.t./i.* walk through or round (an area). **perambulation** *n.*

perambulator *n.* child's pram.

perceive *v.t.* become aware of, see or notice.

percentage *n.* rate or proportion per hundred; proportion, part.

perceptible *a.* able to be perceived. **perceptibly** *adv.*

perception *n.* perceiving, ability to perceive.

perceptive *a.* showing insight and understanding. **perceptively** *adv.*, **perceptiveness** *n.*, **perceptivity** *n.*

perch[1] *n.* bird's resting-place, rod etc. for this; high seat. —*v.t./i.* rest or place on or as if on a perch.

perch[2] *n.* (pl. *perch*) edible freshwater fish with spiny fins.

perchance *n.* (*old use*) perhaps.

percipient *a.* perceptive. **percipience** *n.*

percolate *v.t./i.* filter, esp. through small holes; prepare in a percolator. **percolation** *n.*

percolator *n.* coffee-pot in which boiling water is circulated repeatedly through ground coffee held in a perforated drum.

percussion *n.* striking of one object against another. ～ **instrument,** musical instrument (e.g. drum, cymbals) played by striking.

perdition *n.* eternal damnation.

peregrination *n.* travelling.

peregrine *n.* a kind of falcon.

peremptory /-ˈrem-/ *a.* imperious. **peremptorily** *adv.*

perennial *a.* lasting a long time or for ever; constantly recurring; (of plants) living for several years. —*n.* perennial plant. **perennially** *adv.*

perfect[1] /ˈpɜ-/ *a.* complete, entire; faultless, excellent; exact. **perfectly** *adv.*

perfect[2] /-ˈfekt/ *v.t.* make perfect.

perfection *n.* making or being perfect; person or thing considered perfect. **to** ～, perfectly.

perfectionist *n.* person who seeks perfection.

perfidious /-ˈfid-/ *a.* treacherous, disloyal. **perfidy** /ˈpɜ-/ *n.*

perforate *v.t.* make hole(s) through; penetrate. **perforation** *n.*

perforce *adv.* by force of circumstances, necessarily.

perform *v.t./i.* carry into effect; go through (a piece of music, ceremony, etc.); function; act in a play, sing or play an instrument or do tricks etc. before an audience. **performer** *n.*, **performance** *n.*

perfume *n.* sweet smell; fragrant liquid for applying to the body. —*v.t.* give a sweet smell to; apply perfume to.

perfumery /-ˈfju-/ *n.* perfumes.

perfunctory /-ˈfʌ-/ *a.* done or doing things without much care or interest. **perfunctorily** *adv.*

pergola /ˈpɜ-/ *n.* arch of trellis-work with climbing plants trained over it.

perhaps *adv.* it may be, possibly.

peril *n.* serious danger.

perilous *a.* full of risk, dangerous. **perilously** *adv.*

perimeter /-ˈrim-/ *n.* outer edge of an area; length of this.

period *n.* length or portion of time; occurrence of menstruation; sentence; full stop in punctuation. —*a.* (of dress or furniture) belonging to a past age.

periodic *a.* happening at intervals.

periodical *a.* periodic. —*n.* magazine etc. published at regular intervals. **periodically** *adv.*

peripatetic /-ˈtet-/ *a.* going from place to place.

peripheral /-ˈrif-/ *a.* of or on the periphery; of minor but not central importance to something.

periphery /-ˈrif-/ *n.* boundary, edge; fringes of a subject etc.

periphrasis /-ˈrif-/ *n.* (pl. *-ases*) circumlocution.

periscope *n.* tube with mirror(s) by which a person in a trench or submarine etc. can see things otherwise out of sight.

perish *v.t./i.* suffer destruction, die; rot; distress or wither by cold or exposure.

perishable *a.* liable to decay or go bad in a short time.

periwinkle[1] *n.* trailing plant with blue or white flowers.

periwinkle[2] *n.* winkle.

perjure *v.refl.* ～ **oneself,** make a perjured statement.

perjured *a.* involving perjury.

perjury *n.* deliberate giving of false evidence while under oath; this evidence.

perk[1] *v.t./i.* **~ up,** (*colloq.*) cheer or brighten or smarten up.

perk[2] *n.* (*colloq.*) perquisite.

perm[1] *n.* permanent artificial wave in the hair. —*v.t.* give a perm to.

perm[2] *n.* permutation. —*v.t.* make a permutation of.

permafrost *n.* permanently frozen subsoil in arctic regions.

permanent *a.* lasting indefinitely. **permanently** *adv.*, **permanence** *n.*, **permanency** *n.*

permeable *a.* able to be permeated by fluids etc. **permeability** *n.*

permeate *v.t.* pass or flow into every part of. **permeation** *n.*

permissible *a.* allowable.

permission *n.* consent or authorization to do something.

permissive *a.* giving permission; tolerant, esp. in social and sexual matters. **permissiveness** *n.*

permit[1] /-ˈmɪt/ *v.t.* (p.t. *permitted*) give permission to or for; make possible.

permit[2] /ˈpɜ-/ *n.* written permission, esp. for entry to a place.

permutation *n.* variation of the order of or choice from a set of things.

pernicious *a.* harmful.

peroration *n.* lengthy speech; last part of this.

peroxide *n.* compound of hydrogen used to bleach hair. —*v.t.* bleach with this.

perpendicular *a.* at an angle of 90° to a line or surface; upright, vertical. —*n.* perpendicular line or direction. **perpendicularly** *adv.*

perpetrate *v.t.* commit (a crime), be guilty of (a blunder). **perpetration** *n.*, **perpetrator** *n.*

perpetual *a.* lasting, not ceasing. **perpetually** *adv.*

perpetuate *v.t.* preserve from being forgotten or from going out of use. **perpetuation** *n.*

perpetuity /-ˈtju-/ *n.* **in ~,** for ever.

perplex *v.t.* bewilder, puzzle.

perplexity *n.* bewilderment.

perquisite *n.* profit or privilege given in addition to wages.

perry *n.* drink resembling cider, made from fermented pears.

persecute *v.t.* treat with hostility esp. because of religious beliefs; harass. **persecution** *n.*, **persecutor** *n.*

persevere *v.i.* continue steadfastly in spite of difficulties. **perseverance** *n.*

Persian *a.* & *n.* (native, language) of Persia.

persiflage /-flɑʒ/ *n.* banter.

persist *v.i.* continue firmly or obstinately; continue to exist. **persistent** *a.*, **persistently** *adv.*, **persistence** *n.*, **persistency** *n.*

person *n.* individual human or divine being; one's body; (in grammar) one of the three classes of personal pronouns and verb-forms, referring to the person(s) speaking, spoken to, or spoken of. **in ~,** physically present.

personable /ˈpɜ-/ *a.* good-looking.

personage *n.* person, esp. an important one.

persona grata /-sɔʊnə ˈgrɑ-/ (pl. *-nae -tae*, pr. *-ni -ti*) acceptable person. **persona non grata,** unacceptable person.

personal *a.* of one's own; of or involving a person's private life; referring to a person; done in person. **personally** *adv.*

personality *n.* person's distinctive character; person with distinctive qualities; celebrity; (*pl.*) personal remarks.

personify *v.t.* represent in human form or as having human characteristics; embody in one's behaviour. **personification** *n.*

personnel *n.* employees, staff.

perspective *n.* art of drawing so as to give an effect of solidity and relative position; apparent relationship between visible objects as to position, distance, etc. **in ~,** according to the rules of perspective; not distorting a thing's relative importance.

perspicacious *a.* showing great insight. **perspicaciously** *adv.*, **perspicacity** *n.*

perspicuous *a.* expressed or expressing things clearly. **perspicuity** *n.*

perspire *v.i.* sweat. **perspiration** *n.*

persuade *v.t.* cause (a person) to believe or do something by reasoning with him.

persuasion *n.* persuading; persuasiveness; belief.

persuasive *a.* able or trying to persuade people. **persuasively** *adv.*, **persuasiveness** *n.*

pert *a.* cheeky; (*U.S.*) lively. **pertly** *adv.*, **pertness** *n.*

pertain *v.i.* be relevant; belong as a part.

pertinacious *a.* persistent and determined. **pertinaciously** *adv.*, **pertinacity** *n.*

pertinent *a.* pertaining, relevant. **pertinently** *adv.*, **pertinence** *n.*

perturb *v.t.* disturb greatly, make uneasy. **perturbation** *n.*

peruse /-ˈruz/ *v.t.* read carefully. **perusal** *n.*

pervade *v.t.* spread throughout (a thing). **pervasive** *a.*

perverse *a.* obstinately doing something different from what is reasonable or required. **perversely** *adv.*, **perverseness** *n.*, **perversity** *n.*

pervert[1] /-ˈvɜt/ *v.t.* misapply, lead astray, corrupt. **perversion** *n.*

pervert[2] /ˈpɜ-/ *n.* perverted person.

peseta /-ˈseɪ-/ *n.* unit of money in Spain.

pessimism *n.* tendency to take a gloomy view of things. **pessimist** *n.*, **pessimistic** *a.*, **pessimistically** *adv.*

pest *n.* troublesome person or thing; insect or animal harmful to plants, stored food, etc.

pester *v.t.* annoy continually, esp. with requests or questions.

pesticide *n.* substance used to destroy harmful insects etc.

pestilence *n.* deadly epidemic disease.

pestle *n.* club-shaped instrument for pounding things to powder.

pet *n.* tame animal treated with affection; darling, favourite. —*a.* kept as a pet; favourite. —*v.t.* (p.t. *petted*) treat with affection; fondle. **~ name,** name used affectionately.

petal *n.* one of the bright or delicately coloured outer parts of a flower-head.

peter *v.i.* **~ out,** dwindle away.

petersham *n.* strong corded ribbon.

petite /pə'tiːt/ *a.* of small dainty build.

petition *n.* formal written request, esp. one signed by many people. —*v.t.* make a petition to. **petitioner** *n.*

petrel *n.* a kind of sea-bird.

petrify *v.t./i.* change into a stony mass; paralyse with astonishment or fear. **petrifaction** *n.*

petrochemical *n.* chemical substance obtained from petroleum or gas.

petrodollar *n.* dollar earned by a petroleum-exporting country.

petrol *n.* inflammable liquid made from petroleum for use as fuel in internal combustion engines.

petroleum *n.* mineral oil found underground, refined for use as fuel or in dry-cleaning etc. ~ **jelly,** greasy substance obtained from petroleum, used as a lubricant.

petticoat *n.* dress-length undergarment worn hanging from the shoulders or waist beneath a dress or skirt.

pettifogging *a.* trivial; quibbling about unimportant details.

petting *n.* affectionate treatment; fondling.

pettish *a.* peevish, irritable. **pettishly** *adv.*, **pettishness** *n.*

petty *a.* (*-ier, -iest*) unimportant; minor, on a small scale; small-minded. ~ **cash,** money kept by an office etc. for or from small payments. ~ **officer,** N.C.O. in the Navy.

petulant *a.* peevish. **petulantly** *adv.*, **petulance** *n.*

petunia *n.* garden plant with funnel-shaped flowers.

pew *n.* long bench-like seat in a church.

pewter *n.* grey alloy of tin with lead or other metal; articles made of this.

phaeton /'feɪt-/ *n.* old type of open horse-drawn carriage.

phalanx *n.* compact mass esp. of people.

phallic /'fæ-/ *a.* of the penis as symbolizing generative power.

phantasm *n.* phantom.

phantom *n.* ghost.

Pharaoh /'feərəʊ/ *n.* title of the king of ancient Egypt.

Pharisee *n.* member of an ancient Jewish sect; self-righteous person. **pharisaical** /-'seɪɪ-/ *a.*

pharmaceutical /-'sjuːt-/ *a.* of or engaged in pharmacy.

pharmacist *n.* person skilled in pharmacy.

pharmacy *n.* preparation and dispensing of medicinal drugs; pharmacist's shop, dispensary.

pharynx /'fæ-/ *n.* cavity at the back of the nose and throat.

phase *n.* stage of change or development. —*v.t.* carry out (a programme etc.) in stages. ~ **out,** take gradually out of use.

pheasant *n.* game-bird with bright feathers.

phenobarbitone *n.* sedative drug.

phenomenal *a.* extraordinary, remarkable. **phenomenally** *adv.*

phenomenon *n.* (pl. *-ena*) fact, occurrence, or change perceived by the senses or the mind; remarkable person or thing.

phial /'faɪəl/ *n.* small bottle.

philander *v.i.* (of a man) flirt. **philanderer** *n.*

philanthropy *n.* love of mankind, esp. shown in benevolent acts. **philanthropist** *n.*, **philanthropic** /-'θrɒp-/ *a.*, **philanthropically** *adv.*

philately /-'lætə-/ *n.* stamp-collecting. **philatelist** *n.*

philharmonic /-lɑm-/ *a.* (in names of orchestras etc.) devoted to music.

Philippine *a.* of the Philippine Islands.

philistine /-taɪn/ *a.* & *n.* uncultured (person).

philology *n.* study of languages. **philologist** *n.*, **philological** *a.*

philosopher *n.* person skilled in philosophy; philosophical person.

philosophical *a.* of philosophy; bearing misfortune calmly. **philosophically** *adv.*

philosophy *n.* system or study of the basic truths and principles of the universe, life, and morals, and of human understanding of these; person's principles.

philtre *n.* magic potion.

phlebitis /flɪ'baɪ-/ *n.* inflammation of the walls of a vein.

phlegm /flem/ *n.* thick mucus in the bronchial passages, ejected by coughing.

phlegmatic /fleg-/ *a.* not easily excited or agitated; sluggish, apathetic. **phlegmatically** *adv.*

phlox /flɒks/ *n.* plant bearing a cluster of red, purple, or white flowers.

phobia *n.* lasting abnormal fear or great dislike.

Phoenician /fɪ'nɪʃ-/ *a.* & *n.* (member, language) of an ancient Semitic people of the east Mediterranean.

phoenix /'fiːn-/ *n.* mythical Arabian bird said to burn itself and rise young again from its ashes.

phone *n.* & *v.t./i.* (*colloq.*) telephone.

phonetic *a.* of or representing speech-sounds; (of spelling) corresponding to pronunciation. **phonetically** *adv.*

phoney *a.* (*-ier, -iest*) (*sl.*) sham. —*n.* (*sl.*) phoney person or thing.

phosphate *n.* fertilizer containing phosphorus.

phosphorescent *a.* luminous. **phosphorescence** *n.*

phosphorus *n.* non-metallic chemical element; wax-like form of this appearing luminous in the dark.

photo *n.* (pl. *-os*) (*colloq.*) photograph.

photocopy *n.* photographed copy of a document. —*v.t.* make a photocopy of. **photocopier** *n.*

photoelectric *a.* ~ **cell,** electronic device emitting an electric current when light falls on it.

photogenic /-'dʒen-/ *a.* coming out attractively in photographs.

photograph *n.* picture formed by the chemical action of light or other radiation on sensitive material. —*v.t./i.* take a photograph of; come out (well or badly) when photographed. **photographer** *n.*, **photography** *n.*, **photographic** *a.*, **photographically** *adv.*

photosynthesis /-'sɪn-/ *n.* process by which green plants use sunlight to convert carbon dioxide and water into complex substances.

phrase *n.* group of words forming a unit, esp. within a sentence or clause; unit in a melody. —*v.t.* express in words; divide (music) into phrases. **phrasal** *a.*

phraseology *n.* the way something is worded. **phraseological** *a.*

phut *adv.* **go** ~, burst or explode with this sound; (*colloq.*) come to nothing.

physic *n.* (*old use*) medicine.

physical *a.* of the body; of matter or the laws of nature; of physics. ~ **chemistry,** use of physics to study substances and their reactions. ~ **geography,** study of earth's natural features. **physically** *adv.*

physician *n.* doctor, esp. one specializing in medicine as distinct from surgery.

physicist *n.* expert in physics.

physics *n.* study of the properties and interactions of matter and energy.

physiognomy /-¹on-/ *n.* features of a person's face.

physiology *n.* study of the bodily functions of living organisms. **physiological** *a.*, **physiologist** *n.*

physiotherapy *n.* treatment of an injury etc. by massage and exercises. **physiotherapist** *n.*

physique /-¹zik/ *n.* person's physical build and muscular development.

pi /paɪ/ *n.* Greek letter π used as a symbol for the ratio of a circle's circumference to its diameter (about 3·14).

pianist *n.* person who plays the piano.

piano *n.* (pl. *-os*) musical instrument with metal strings struck by hammers operated by pressing the keys of a keyboard.

pianoforte /-¹fɔtɪ/ *n.* piano.

piazza /pɪ¹ætsə/ *n.* public square in an Italian town.

pibroch /¹pibrok/ *n.* martial or funeral music for bagpipes.

piccalilli *n.* pickle of chopped vegetables and hot spices.

piccaninny *n.* Black child; Australian Aboriginal child.

piccolo *n.* (pl. *-os*) small flute.

pick¹ *n.* pickaxe; plectrum.

pick² *v.t./i.* use a pointed instrument or the fingers or beak etc. to make (a hole) in or remove bits from (a thing); detach (flower or fruit) from the plant bearing it; select. —*n.* picking; selection; best part. ~**-a-back** *adv.* carried on the shoulders or on top of a larger object. ~ **a lock,** open it with a tool other than a key. ~ **a pocket,** steal its contents. ~ **a quarrel,** provoke one deliberately. ~ **holes in,** find fault with. ~ **off,** pluck off; shoot or destroy one by one. ~ **out,** select as a target, esp. for harassment. ~ **up,** lift or take up; call for and take away; acquire or become acquainted with casually; succeed in seeing or hearing by use of apparatus; recover health, improve; recover (speed). ~**-up** *n.* acquaintance met casually; small open motor truck; stylus-holder in a record-player. **picker** *n.*

pickaxe *n.* heavy tool with a pointed iron bar mounted at right angles to its handle, used for breaking ground etc.

picket *n.* pointed stake set in the ground; party of sentries; person(s) stationed by trade unionists to dissuade others from entering a building etc. during a strike. —*v.t.* (p.t. *picketed*) secure or enclose with stake(s); station or act as a picket on (a building etc.).

pickings *n.pl.* scraps of good food etc. remaining; odd gains or perquisites.

pickle *n.* vegetables preserved in vinegar or brine; this liquid; (*colloq.*) plight, mess. —*v.t.* preserve in pickle.

pickpocket *n.* thief who picks people's pockets.

picnic *n.* informal outdoor meal. —*v.i.* (p.t. *picnicked*) take part in a picnic. **picnicker** *n.*

picot /¹pikəʊ/ *n.* small loop of twisted thread in an ornamental edging.

Pict *n.* member of an ancient people of north Britain. **Pictish** *a.*

pictorial *a.* of or in or like a picture or pictures; illustrated. —*n.* newspaper etc. with many pictures.

picture *n.* representation of person(s) or object(s) etc. made by painting, drawing, or photography etc.; thing that looks beautiful; scene; description; cinema film. —*v.t.* depict; imagine.

picturesque /-¹resk/ *a.* forming a pleasant scene; (of words or description) very expressive.

pidgin *a.* ~ **English,** simplified form of English with elements of a local language.

pie *n.* baked dish of meat, fish, or fruit covered with pastry or other crust.

piebald *a.* (of a horse) with irregular patches of white and dark colour.

piece *n.* part, portion; thing regarded as a unit; musical, literary, or artistic composition; coin; small object used in board-games; slice of bread; unit of work. —*v.t.* make by putting pieces together. **of a** ~, of the same kind; consistent. ~**-work** *n.* work paid according to the quantity done.

piecemeal *a. & adv.* done piece by piece, part at a time.

pied /paɪd/ *a.* particoloured.

pied-à-terre /pjeɪt-ɑ-¹teə(r)/ *n.* (pl. *pieds-à-terre*, pr. pjeɪt-) small place for use as temporary quarters when needed.

pier *n.* structure built out into the sea, esp. as a promenade; pillar or similar structure supporting an arch or bridge.

pierce *v.t.* go into or through like a sharp-pointed instrument; make (a hole) in; force one's way into or through.

piercing *a.* (of cold or wind) penetrating sharply; (of sound) shrilly audible.

piety *n.* piousness.

piffle *n.* (*sl.*) nonsense.

pig *n.* animal with short legs, cloven hooves, and blunt snout; (*colloq.*) greedy or unpleasant person; pig-iron. ~**-headed** *a.* obstinate, stubborn. ~**-iron** *n.* crude iron from a smelting-furnace.

pigeon *n.* bird of the dove family; (*colloq.*) person's business or responsibility.

pigeon-hole *n.* small compartment in a desk or cabinet. —*v.t.* put away for future consideration or indefinitely; classify.

piggery *n.* pig-breeding establishment; pigsty.

piggy *a.* like a pig. **~-back** *adv.* pick-a-back. **~ bank**, money-box shaped like a pig.

piglet *n.* young pig.

pigment *n.* colouring-matter. —*v.t.* colour (skin or tissue) with natural colouring-matter. **pigmentation** *n.*

pigskin *n.* leather made from the skin of pigs.

pigsty *n.* partly covered pen for pigs.

pigtail *n.* long hair worn in a plait at the back of the head.

pike *n.* long wooden shaft with a pointed metal head; peaked summit; (pl. *pike*) large voracious freshwater fish.

pikelet *n.* crumpet.

pikestaff *n.* **plain as a ~**, quite plain or obvious.

pilaster /-ˈlæ-/ *n.* rectangular usu. ornamental column.

pilchard *n.* small sea-fish related to the herring.

pile[1] *n.* a number of things lying one upon another; heap; pyre; (*colloq.*) large amount; lofty building. —*v.t./i.* heap, stack, load; crowd. **~ up**, accumulate; run aground; crash (vehicle). **~-up** *n.* collision of several vehicles.

pile[2] *n.* heavy beam driven vertically into ground as a support for a building or bridge.

pile[3] *n.* cut or uncut loops on the surface of fabric.

pile[4] *n.* haemorrhoid.

pilfer *v.t./i.* steal (small items or in small quantities). **pilferage** *n.*

pilgrim *n.* person who travels to a sacred place as an act of religious devotion. **pilgrimage** *n.*

pill *n.* small ball or piece of medicinal substance for swallowing whole.

pillage *n.* & *v.t.* plunder.

pillar *n.* vertical structure used as a support or ornament; thing resembling this. **~-box** *n.* hollow pillar about 5 ft. high into which letters may be posted.

pillbox *n.* small round box for pills; thing shaped like this.

pillion *n.* saddle for a passenger seated behind the driver of a motor cycle. **ride ~**, ride on this.

pillory *n.* wooden frame with holes for the head and hands, in which offenders were formerly placed for exposure to public ridicule. —*v.t.* expose to public ridicule or scorn.

pillow *n.* cushion used (esp. in bed) for supporting the head. —*v.t.* rest on or as if on a pillow.

pillowcase, pillowslip *ns.* cloth cover for a pillow.

pilot *n.* person who operates an aircraft's flying-controls; person qualified to steer ships into or out of a harbour; guide. —*v.t.* (p.t. *piloted*) act as pilot of; guide. **~-light** *n.* small burning jet of gas which lights a larger burner; electric indicator light.

pimp *n.* man who solicits clients for a prostitute or brothel.

pimpernel /ˈpɪm-/ *n.* wild plant with small red, blue, or white flowers.

pimple *n.* small inflamed spot on the skin. **pimply** *a.*

pin *n.* short pointed piece of metal usu. with a round broadened head, used for fastening things together; peg or stake of wood or metal. —*v.t.* (p.t. *pinned*) fasten with pin(s); transfix; hold down and make unable to move; attach, fix. **~ down**, establish clearly; bind by a promise. **~-point** *v.t.* locate precisely. **pins and needles**, tingling sensation. **~-stripe** *n.* very narrow stripe on cloth. **~-table** *n.* board for pinball. **~-up** *n.* (*colloq.*) picture of an attractive or famous person.

pinafore *n.* apron. **~ dress**, dress without collar or sleeves, worn over a blouse or jumper.

pinball *n.* game played with a ball on a sloping board set with pins or targets.

pince-nez /ˈpæs neɪ/ *n.* (pl. *pince-nez*) pair of glasses that clip on the nose.

pincers *n.* tool with pivoted jaws for gripping and pulling things; claw-like part of a lobster etc.

pinch *v.t./i.* squeeze between two surfaces, esp. between finger and thumb; stint; (*sl.*) steal; (*sl.*) arrest. —*n.* pinching; stress of circumstances; small amount. **at a ~**, in time of difficulty or necessity.

pincushion *n.* small pad for sticking pins in to keep them ready for use.

pine[1] *n.* evergreen tree with needle-shaped leaves; its wood.

pine[2] *v.i.* lose strength through grief or yearning; feel an intense longing.

pineapple *n.* large juicy tropical fruit; plant bearing this.

ping *n.* short sharp ringing sound. —*v.i.* make this sound. **pinger** *n.*

ping-pong *n.* table tennis.

pinion[1] *n.* bird's wing. —*v.t.* restrain by holding or binding the arms or legs.

pinion[2] *n.* small cog-wheel.

pink[1] *a.* pale red. —*n.* pink colour; garden plant with fragrant pink, white, or variegated flowers. **in the ~**, (*sl.*) in very good health. **pinkness** *n.*

pink[2] *v.t.* pierce slightly; cut a zigzag edge on (fabric).

pink[3] *v.i.* (of an engine) make slight explosive sounds when running imperfectly.

pinnacle *n.* pointed ornament on a roof; peak; highest point.

pinprick *n.* small annoyance.

pint *n.* measure for liquids, one eighth of a gallon.

pioneer *n.* person who is one of the first to explore a new region or subject. —*v.t./i.* be a pioneer (in).

pious *a.* devout in religion; ostentatiously virtuous. **piously** *adv.*, **piousness** *n.*

pip[1] *n.* small seed in fruit.

pip[2] *n.* spot on a domino, dice, or playing-card; star on an army officer's uniform.

pip[3] *v.t.* (p.t. *pipped*) (*colloq.*) hit with a shot; defeat.

pip[4] *n.* short high-pitched sound.

pipe *n.* tube through which something can flow;

tube by which sound is produced, (*pl.*) bag-pipes; narrow tube with a bowl at one end for smoking tobacco. —*v.t.* convey through pipe(s); transmit (music etc.) by wire or cable; play (music) on pipe(s); lead by sounding pipe(s); utter in a shrill voice; ornament with piping. ~-**dream** *n.* impractical hope or scheme.

pipeline *n.* long pipe for conveying petroleum etc. to a distance; channel of supply or information. **in the** ~, on the way, in preparation.

piper *n.* player of pipe(s).

pipette *n.* slender tube for transferring or measuring small amounts of liquid.

piping *n.* length of pipe; pipes; ornamental pipe-like fold or line. ~ **hot,** very hot.

pipit *n.* small bird resembling a lark.

pippin *n.* a kind of apple.

piquant /ˈpiːk-/ *a.* pleasantly sharp in taste or smell; mentally stimulating. **piquantly** *adv.*, **piquancy** *n.*

pique /piːk/ *v.t.* hurt the pride of; stimulate (curiosity etc.). —*n.* feeling of hurt pride.

piqué /ˈpiːkeɪ/ *n.* firm usu. cotton fabric with a corded effect.

piranha /pɪˈrɑːnjə/ *n.* fierce tropical American freshwater fish.

pirate *n.* person on a ship who robs another ship at sea or raids a coast; one who infringes copyright or business rights, or broadcasts without due authorization. **piratical** *a.*, **piracy** /ˈpaɪ-/ *n.*

pirouette /-rʊˈet/ *n.* & *v.i.* spin on the toe in dancing.

pistachio /-ˈtɑːʃ-/ *n.* (pl. *-os*) a kind of nut.

piste /piːst/ *n.* ski-track.

pistil *n.* seed-producing part of a flower.

pistol *n.* small gun.

piston *n.* sliding disc or cylinder inside a tube, esp. as part of an engine or pump.

pit *n.* hole in the ground; coal-mine; sunken area; seats on the ground floor of a theatre, behind the stalls; place where race-cars are refuelled etc. during a race. —*v.t.* (p.t. *pitted*) make pits or depressions in; match or set in competition.

pitch[1] *n.* dark tarry substance. ~-**black,** ~-**dark** *adjs.*

pitch[2] *v.t./i.* throw; erect (a tent or camp); set at a particular slope or level; fall heavily, strike the ground; (of a ship or vehicle) plunge forward and back alternately; (*sl.*) tell (a yarn or excuse). —*n.* process of pitching; steepness; intensity; degree of highness or lowness of a music-note or voice; place where a street trader or performer is stationed; playing-field. ~ **into,** (*colloq.*) attack or reprimand vigorously.

pitchblende *n.* mineral ore (uranium oxide) yielding radium.

pitched *a.* ~ **battle,** one fought from prepared positions.

pitcher[1] *n.* baseball player who delivers the ball to the batter.

pitcher[2] *n.* large usu. earthenware jug.

pitchfork *n.* long-handled fork for lifting and tossing hay. —*v.t.* thrust (a person) into a position or office etc.

piteous *a.* deserving or arousing pity. **piteously** *adv.*

pitfall *n.* unsuspected danger or difficulty.

pith *n.* spongy tissue in stems or fruits; essential part.

pithy *a.* (*-ier*, *-iest*) like pith, containing much pith; brief and full of meaning. **pithily** *adv.*

pitiable *a.* pitiful. **pitiably** *adv.*

pitiful *a.* deserving or arousing pity or contempt. **pitifully** *adv.*

pitiless *a.* showing no pity.

piton /ˈpiːton/ *n.* spike or peg used in rock-climbing.

pittance *n.* very small allowance of money.

pituitary /-ˈtjuː-/ *a.* ~ **gland,** gland at the base of the brain, with important influence on bodily growth and functions.

pity *n.* feeling of sorrow for another's suffering; cause for regret. —*v.t.* feel pity for. **take** ~ **on,** pity and try to help.

pivot *n.* central point or shaft on which a thing turns or swings. —*v.t./i.* (p.t. *pivoted*) turn or place to turn on a pivot. **pivotal** *a.*

pixie *n.* a kind of fairy. ~ **hood,** woman's or child's pointed hood.

pizza /ˈpiːtsə/ *n.* layer of dough baked with a savoury topping.

pizzicato /pɪtsɪˈkɑː-/ *adv.* by plucking the strings of a violin etc. instead of using the bow.

placard *n.* poster or similar notice. —*v.t.* put up placards on.

placate *v.t.* conciliate. **placatory** /-ˈkeɪt-/ *a.*

place *n.* particular part of space or of an area or book etc.; particular town, district, building, etc.; position; duty appropriate to one's rank; step in reasoning. —*v.t.* put into a place, find a place for; locate, identify; put or give (an order for goods etc.). **be placed,** (in a race) be among the first three.

placebo /-ˈsiː-/ *n.* (pl. *-os*) harmless substance given as medicine, esp. to humour a patient.

placement *n.* placing.

placenta /-ˈsen-/ *n.* (pl. *-as*) organ that develops in the womb during pregnancy and nourishes the foetus. **placental** *a.*

placid *a.* calm and peaceful, not easily upset. **placidly** *adv.*, **placidity** *n.*

placket *n.* opening in a skirt to make it easy to put on and take off.

plagiarize /ˈpleɪdʒ-/ *v.t.* take and use (another's writings etc.) as one's own. **plagiarism** *n.*

plague *n.* deadly contagious disease; infestation; (*colloq.*) nuisance. —*v.t.* annoy, pester.

plaice *n.* (pl. *plaice*) a kind of flat-fish used as food.

plaid /plæd, *Sc. pr.* pleɪd/ *n.* long piece of woollen cloth worn as part of Highland costume; tartan pattern.

plain *a.* (*-er*, *-est*) unmistakable, easy to see or hear or understand; not elaborate or luxurious; in exact terms, candid; ordinary, without affectation; not good-looking. —*adv.* plainly. —*n.* large area of level country;

ordinary stitch in knitting. ∼ **clothes,** civilian clothes, not a uniform. **plainly** *adv.*, **plainness** *n.*

plainsong *n.* medieval type of church music for voices, without regular rhythm.

plaintiff *n.* party that brings an action in a court of law.

plaintive *a.* sounding sad. **plaintively** *adv.*

plait /plæt/ *v.t.* weave (three or more strands) into one rope-like length. —*n.* something plaited.

plan *n.* diagram showing the relative position of parts of a building or town etc.; method thought out in advance. —*v.t./i.* (p.t. *planned*) make a plan (of). **planner** *n.*

plane[1] *n.* tall spreading tree with broad leaves.

plane[2] *n.* level surface; imaginary surface of this kind; level of thought or existence or development; aeroplane. —*a.* level.

plane[3] *n.* tool for smoothing wood or metal by paring shavings from it. —*v.t.* smooth or pare with this.

planet *n.* one of the heavenly bodies moving round the sun. **planetary** *a.*

plangent /'plændʒ-/ *a.* resonant, loud and mournful.

plank *n.* long flat piece of timber.

plankton *n.* minute forms of organic life floating in the sea or in rivers and lakes.

plant *n.* living organism with neither the power of movement nor special organs of digestion; small plant as distinct from a tree or shrub; factory; its machinery. —*v.t.* place in soil for growing; place in position. **planter** *n.*

plantation *n.* area planted with trees or cultivated plants; estate on which cotton, tobacco, or tea etc. is cultivated.

plaque /-k/ *n.* strip of metal or porcelain fixed on a wall as an ornament or memorial; film on teeth.

plasma *n.* colourless fluid part of blood; a kind of gas.

plaster *n.* soft mixture of lime, sand, and water etc. used for coating walls; plaster of Paris, cast made from this; sticking-plaster. —*v.t.* cover with plaster; coat, daub, make smooth with a fixative. ∼ **of Paris,** white paste made from gypsum. **plasterer** *n.*

plastic *a.* able to be moulded; giving form to clay or wax etc.; made of plastic. —*n.* synthetic substance moulded to a permanent shape. ∼ **surgery,** operation(s) to replace injured or defective external tissue. **plasticity** *n.*

Plasticine *n.* [P] plastic substance used for modelling.

plate *n.* almost flat usu. circular utensil for holding food; articles of gold, silver, or other metal; flat thin sheet of metal, glass, or other material; illustration on special paper in a book; that part of a denture which fits against the palate or gums; (*colloq.*) denture. —*v.t.* cover or coat with metal. **plateful** *n.* (pl. *-fuls*).

plateau *n.* (pl. *-eaux*, pr. *-əʊz*) area of level high ground; steady state following an increase.

platelayer *n.* person who fixes and repairs railway rails.

platen /'plæ-/ *n.* roller of a typewriter, against which the paper is held.

platform *n.* raised level surface or area, esp. from which a speaker addresses an audience.

platinum *n.* silver-white metal that does not tarnish. ∼ **blonde,** woman with very light blonde hair.

platitude *n.* commonplace remark.

platonic *a.* ∼ **love,** affection (not involving sexual love) between a man and a woman.

platoon *n.* subdivision of a military company.

platter *n.* large plate for food.

platypus *n.* (pl. *-puses*) Australian animal with a duck-like beak that lays eggs but suckles its young.

plaudits *n.pl.* applause, expression of approval.

plausible *a.* seeming probable but not proved; persuasive but deceptive. **plausibly** *adv.*, **plausibility** *n.*

play *v.t./i.* occupy oneself in (a game) or in other recreational activity; compete against in a game; move (a piece) or put (a card) or strike (a ball) in a game; act in a drama etc., act the part of; perform (music), perform on (a musical instrument); cause (a record-player or recording etc.) to produce sound; move lightly, allow (light or water) to fall on something; allow (a hooked fish) to struggle against the line. —*n.* playing; activity, operation; literary work for stage or broadcast performance; free movement. ∼ **at,** perform in a trivial or half-hearted way. ∼ **down,** minimize the importance of. ∼**-group** *n.* group of young children who play together under supervision. ∼ **off,** oppose (one person) against another to serve one's own interests. ∼ **on,** affect and make use of (a person's sympathy). ∼ **on words,** pun. ∼**-pen** *n.* portable enclosure for a young child to play in. ∼ **safe,** not take risks. ∼ **the game,** behave honourably. ∼ **up,** play vigorously; (*colloq.*) be unruly, annoy by doing this. ∼ **up to,** try to encourage or win the favour of by flattery. **player** *n.*

playboy *n.* pleasure-loving usu. rich man.

playfellow *n.* playmate.

playful *a.* full of fun; in a mood for play, not serious. **playfully** *adv.*, **playfulness** *n.*

playground *n.* piece of ground for children to play in.

playing-card *n.* one of a pack or set of (usu. 52) pieces of pasteboard used in card-games.

playing-field *n.* field used for outdoor games.

playmate *n.* child's companion in play.

plaything *n.* toy.

playwright *n.* writer of plays.

P.L.C. *abbr.* public limited company.

plea *n.* defendant's answer (esp. 'guilty' or 'not guilty') to a charge in a lawcourt; appeal, entreaty; excuse.

plead *v.t./i.* give as one's plea; put forward (a case) in a lawcourt; make an appeal or entreaty; put forward as an excuse.

pleasant *a.* pleasing; having an agreeable manner. **pleasantly** *adv.*, **pleasantness** *n.*

pleasantry *n.* humorous remark.

please *v.t./i.* give pleasure to; be so kind as to; think fit. —*adv.* polite word of request. ∼ **oneself,** do as one chooses.

pleased *a.* feeling or showing pleasure or satisfaction.

pleasurable *a.* causing pleasure. **pleasurably** *adv.*

pleasure *n.* feeling of satisfaction or joy; source of this; choice, desire.

pleat *n.* flat fold of cloth. —*v.t.* make a pleat or pleats in.

plebeian /-ˈbiən/ *a.* & *n.* (member) of the lower social classes.

plebiscite /ˈplebɪsɪt/ *n.* referendum.

plectrum *n.* small piece of metal, bone, or ivory for plucking the strings of a musical instrument.

pledge *n.* thing deposited as a guarantee (e.g. that a debt will be paid) and liable to be forfeited in case of failure; token of something; solemn promise. —*v.t.* deposit as a pledge; promise solemnly; drink a toast to.

plenary /ˈpli-/ *a.* entire; attended by all members.

plenipotentiary /-ˈten-/ *a.* & *n.* (envoy) with full powers to take action.

plentiful *a.* existing in large amounts. **plentifully** *adv.*

plenty *n.* enough and more. —*adv.* (*colloq.*) quite, fully.

pleonasm /ˈpliən-/ *n.* expression in which certain words are redundant, as in *a false untruth.*

plethora /ˈpleθ-/ *n.* over-abundance.

pleurisy *n.* inflammation of the membrane round the lungs.

pliable *a.* flexible. **pliability** *n.*, **pliancy** *n.*

pliers *n.pl.* pincers with flat surfaces for gripping things.

plight[1] *n.* predicament.

plight[2] *v.t.* (*old use*) pledge, promise.

plimsoll *n.* canvas sports shoe.

Plimsoll *n.* ∼ **line,** ∼ **mark,** mark on a ship's side showing the legal water-level when loaded.

plinth *n.* slab forming the base of a column or a support for a vase etc.

plod *v.i.* (p.t. *plodded*) walk doggedly, trudge; work slowly but steadily. **plodder** *n.*

plonk *n.* (*sl.*) cheap or inferior wine.

plop *n.* & *v.i.* (p.t. *plopped*) sound like something small dropping into water with no splash.

plot *n.* small piece of land; story in a play or novel or film; conspiracy, secret plan. —*v.t./i.* (p.t. *plotted*) make a map or chart of, mark on this; plan secretly. **plotter** *n.*

plough *n.* implement for cutting furrows in soil and turning it up. —*v.t./i.* cut or turn up (soil etc.) with a plough; make one's way laboriously. **ploughman** *n.*

ploughshare *n.* cutting-blade of a plough.

plover /ˈplʌv-/ *n.* a wading bird.

ploy *n.* (*colloq.*) occupation; cunning manœuvre.

pluck *v.t.* pull at or out or off; pick (a flower etc.); strip (a bird) of its feathers. —*n.* plucking movement; courage. ∼ **up courage,** summon up one's courage.

plucky *a.* (*-ier, -iest*) showing pluck, brave. **pluckily** *adv.*

plug *n.* thing fitting into and stopping or filling a hole or cavity; device of this kind (usu. with pins) for making an electrical connection. —*v.t./i.* (p.t. *plugged*) put a plug into; (*sl.*) shoot, strike; (*colloq.*) -work diligently; (*colloq.*) seek to popularize by constant commendation. ∼ **in,** connect electrically by putting a plug into a socket.

plum *n.* fruit with sweet pulp round a pointed stone; tree bearing this; reddish-purple; something desirable, the best. ∼ **cake,** ∼ **pudding,** one containing raisins.

plumage /ˈplu-/ *n.* bird's feathers.

plumb *n.* lead weight hung on a cord (*plumbline*), used for testing depths or verticality. —*adv.* exactly; (*U.S. colloq.*) completely. —*v.t.* measure or test with a plumb-line; reach (depths); get to the bottom of; work or fit (things) as a plumber.

plumber *n.* person whose job is to fit and repair plumbing.

plumbing *n.* system of water-pipes, cisterns, and drainage-pipes etc. in a building.

plume *n.* feather, esp. as an ornament; thing(s) resembling this. —*v.t./refl.* preen. **plumed** *a.*

plummet *n.* plumb, plumb-line. —*v.i.* (p.t. *plummeted*) fall steeply.

plummy *a.* (of the voice) sounding affectedly rich in tone.

plump *a.* (*-er, -est*) having a full rounded shape. —*v.t./i.* make or become plump; plunge abruptly. ∼ **for,** choose, decide on. **plumpness** *n.*

plunder *v.t.* rob. —*n.* plundering; goods etc. acquired by this.

plunge *v.t./i.* thrust or go forcefully into something; dive; go down suddenly; gamble heavily. —*n.* plunging, dive.

plunger *n.* thing that works with a plunging movement.

plural *n.* form of a noun or verb used in referring to more than one person or thing. —*a.* of this form; of more than one. **plurality** *n.*

plus *prep.* with the addition of; above zero; (*colloq.*) with. —*a.* more than zero; more than the amount indicated. —*n.* the sign +; advantage. ∼**-fours** *n.pl.* knickerbockers worn esp. by golfers.

plush *n.* cloth with a long soft nap. —*a.* made of plush; plushy.

plushy *a.* luxurious.

plutocrat *n.* person who is powerful because of his wealth. **plutocratic** *a.*

plutonium *n.* radioactive substance used in nuclear weapons and reactors.

ply[1] *n.* thickness or layer of wood or cloth etc.; plywood.

ply[2] *v.t./i.* use or wield (a tool etc.); work (at a trade); keep offering or supplying; go to and fro regularly or looking for custom.

plywood *n.* board made by gluing layers with the grain crosswise.

p.m. *abbr.* (Latin *post meridiem*) after noon.

P.M. *abbr.* Prime Minister.

pneumatic /nju-/ *a.* filled with or operated by compressed air. **pneumatically** *adv.*

pneumonia /nju-/ *n.* inflammation of one or both lungs.

P.O. *abbr.* postal order; Post Office.

poach *v.t./i.* cook (an egg without its shell) in or over boiling water; simmer in a small amount of liquid; take (game or fish) illegally; trespass, encroach. **poacher** *n.*

pocket *n.* small bag-like part in or on a garment; one's resources of money; pouch-like compartment; isolated group or area. —*a.* suitable for carrying in one's pocket. —*v.t.* put into one's pocket; appropriate. **in** *or* **out of** ~, having made a profit or loss. ~**-book** *n.* notebook; small book-like case for money or papers. ~**-money** *n.* money for small personal expenses; money allowed to children. **pocketful** *n.* (pl. *-fuls*).

pock-marked *a.* marked by scars or pits.

pod *n.* long narrow seed-case.

podgy *a.* (*-ier*, *-iest*) short and fat. **podginess** *n.*

poem *n.* literary composition in verse.

poet *n.* writer of poems. **poetess** *n.fem.*

poetic, poetical *adjs.* of or like poetry. **poetically** *adv.*

poetry *n.* poems; poet's work; quality that pleases the mind similarly.

pogrom /ˈpɒg-/ *n.* organized massacre.

poignant /ˈpɔɪn-/ *a.* arousing sympathy, moving; keenly felt. **poignantly** *adv.*, **poignancy** *n.*

point *n.* tapered or sharp end, tip; promontory; dot used as a punctuation mark; particular place, moment, or stage; unit of measurement or value or scoring; item, detail; characteristic; chief or important feature; effectiveness; electrical socket; movable rail for directing a train from one line to another. —*v.t./i.* aim, direct (a finger or weapon etc.); have a certain direction; indicate; sharpen; fill in (joints of brickwork) with mortar or cement. **on the** ~ **of,** on the verge of (an action). ~**-blank** *a.* aimed or fired at very close range; (of a remark) direct; (*adv.*) in a point-blank manner. ~**-duty** *n.* that of a policeman stationed to regulate traffic. ~ **of view,** way of looking at a matter. ~ **out,** draw attention to. ~**-to-point** *n.* horse-race over a course defined only by landmarks. ~ **up,** emphasize. **to the** ~, relevant(ly).

pointed *a.* tapering to a point; (of a remark or manner) emphasized, clearly aimed at a person or thing. **pointedly** *adv.*

pointer *n.* thing that points to something; dog that points towards game which it scents.

pointless *a.* having no purpose or meaning. **pointlessly** *adv.*

poise *v.t./i.* balance; hold suspended or supported. —*n.* balance; dignified self-assured manner. **poised** *a.*

poison *n.* substance that can destroy life or harm health. —*v.t.* give poison to, kill with poison; put poison on or in; corrupt, fill with prejudice. **poisoner** *n.*, **poisonous** *a.*

poke *v.t./i.* thrust with the end of a finger or stick etc.; thrust forward; search, pry. —*n.* poking movement. ~ **fun at,** ridicule.

poker[1] *n.* stiff metal rod for stirring up a fire.

poker[2] *n.* gambling card-game. ~**-face** *n.* one that does not reveal thoughts or feelings.

poky *a.* (*-ier*, *-iest*) small and cramped.

polar *a.* of or near the North or South Pole; of a pole of a magnet. ~ **bear,** white bear of Arctic regions.

polarize *v.t./i.* confine similar vibrations of (light-waves) to one direction or plane; give magnetic poles to; set at opposite extremes of opinion. **polarization** *n.*

pole[1] *n.* long rod or post. —*v.t.* push along by using a pole. ~**-axe** *n.* battleaxe; implement for slaughtering cattle; (*v.t.*) strike down with this.

pole[2] *n.* north (*North Pole*) or south (*South Pole*) end of earth's axis; point in the sky opposite either of these; one of the opposite ends of a magnet or terminals of an electric cell or battery. ~**-star** *n.* star near the North Pole in the sky.

Pole *n.* Polish person.

polecat *n.* small animal of the weasel family; (*U.S.*) skunk.

polemic /-ˈlem-/ *n.* verbal attack on a belief or opinion.

police *n.* civil force responsible for keeping public order. —*v.t.* keep order in by means of police. ~ **state,** country where political police supervise and control citizens' activities. **policeman** *n.* (pl. *-men*), **policewoman** *n.* (pl. *-women*).

policy[1] *n.* course or general plan of action.

policy[2] *n.* insurance contract.

polio /ˈpəʊ-/ *n.* (*colloq.*) poliomyelitis.

poliomyelitis /pəʊ-/ *n.* infectious disease causing temporary or permanent paralysis.

Polish *a.* & *n.* (native, language) of Poland.

polish *v.t./i.* make or become smooth and glossy by rubbing; make (work) better by adding improvements. —*n.* smoothness and glossiness; polishing, substance used for this; high degree of elegance. ~ **off,** finish off. **polisher** *n.*

polished *a.* (of manner or performance) elegant, perfected.

polite *a.* having good manners, socially correct; refined. **politely** *adv.*, **politeness** *n.*

politic *a.* prudent. **body** ~, the State.

political *a.* of or involving politics; of the way a country is governed. **politically** *adv.*

politician *n.* person engaged in politics, Member of Parliament.

politics *n.* science and art of government; political affairs or life. —*n.pl.* political principles.

polka *n.* lively dance for couples. ~ **dots,** round evenly spaced dots on fabric.

poll *n.* voting or votes at an election; place for this; estimate of public opinion made by questioning people. —*v.t./i.* cast one's vote; receive as votes; cut off the horns of (cattle) or the top of (a tree etc.).

pollack *n.* sea-fish related to cod.

pollard *v.t.* poll (a tree) to produce a close head of young branches. —*n.* pollarded tree; hornless animal.

pollen *n.* fertilizing powder from the anthers of flowers.

pollinate *v.t.* fertilize with pollen. **pollination** *n.*

pollute —*v.t.* make dirty or impure. **pollution** *n.*, **pollutant** *n.*

polo *n.* game like hockey played by teams on horseback. ⁓ **neck,** high round turned-over collar.

polony *n.* sausage made of partly cooked pork.

poltergeist /-ɡaɪst/ *n.* spirit that throws things about noisily.

polyanthus *n.* (pl. *-thuses* or *-thus*) a kind of cultivated primrose.

polychrome *a.* multicoloured.

polyester *n.* synthetic resin or fibre.

polygamy /-ˈlɪɡ-/ *n.* system of having more than one wife at a time. **polygamist** *n.*, **polygamous** *a.*

polyglot *a.* knowing or using several languages.

polygon *n.* geometric figure with many sides. **polygonal** *a.*

polymer *n.* compound whose molecule is formed from a large number of simple molecules.

polymerize *v.t./i.* combine into a polymer. **polymerization** *n.*

polyp *n.* simple organism with a tube-shaped body; abnormal growth projecting from mucous membrane.

polystyrene /-ˈstaɪ-/ *n.* a kind of plastic.

polytechnic *n.* institution giving education and training in many subjects at an advanced level.

polythene *n.* a kind of tough light plastic.

pomander /-ˈmæn-/ *n.* ball of mixed sweet-smelling substances.

pomegranate /ˈpɒmɪ-/ *n.* tropical fruit with many seeds; tree bearing this.

Pomeranian *n.* dog of a small silky-haired breed.

pommel /ˈpʌm-/ *n.* knob on the hilt of a sword; upward projection on a saddle.

pomp *n.* stately and splendid ceremonial.

pom-pom *n.* = pompon.

pompon *n.* decorative tuft or ball.

pompous *a.* full of ostentatious dignity and self-importance. **pompously** *adv.*, **pomposity** *n.*

poncho *n.* (pl. *-os*) type of cloak made like a blanket with a hole for the head.

pond *n.* small area of still water.

ponder *v.t./i.* be deep in thought; think over.

ponderous *a.* heavy, unwieldy; laborious. **ponderously** *adv.*

pong *n.* & *v.i.* (*sl.*) stink.

pontifical *a.* pompously dogmatic.

pontificate *v.i.* speak in a pontifical way.

pontoon¹ *n.* a kind of flat-bottomed boat. ⁓ **bridge,** temporary bridge supported on boats or hollow cylinders.

pontoon² *n.* a kind of card-game.

pony *n.* horse of any small breed. ⁓**tail** *n.* long hair drawn back and tied to hang down. ⁓**trekking** *n.* riding across country on ponies for pleasure.

poodle *n.* dog with thick curly hair.

pool¹ *n.* small area of still water; puddle; swimming-pool.

pool² *n.* common fund or supply of things for sharing; game resembling snooker; (*pl.*) football pools. —*v.t.* put into a common fund or supply, for sharing.

poop *n.* ship's stern; raised deck at the stern.

poor *a.* (*-er*, *-est*) having little money or means; not abundant; not very good; pitiable. **poorness** *n.*

poorly *adv.* in a poor way, badly. —*a.* unwell.

pop¹ *n.* small explosive sound; fizzy drink. —*v.t./i.* (p.t. popped) make or cause to make a pop; put or come or go quickly.

pop² *n.* (*colloq.*) father.

pop³ *a.* in a popular modern style. —*n.* pop record or music.

popcorn *n.* maize heated to burst and form puffy balls.

pope *n.* bishop of Rome, head of the R.C. Church.

popgun *n.* child's gun that shoots with a popping sound.

poplar *n.* tall slender tree.

poplin *n.* plain woven usu. cotton fabric.

poppet *n.* (*colloq.*) darling.

poppy *n.* plant with showy flowers and milky juice.

populace *n.* the general public.

popular *a.* liked or enjoyed or used etc. by many people; of or for the general public. **popularly** *adv.*, **popularity** *n.*

popularize *v.t.* make generally liked; present in a popular non-technical form. **popularization** *n.*

populate *v.t.* fill with a population.

population *n.* inhabitants of an area.

populous *a.* thickly populated.

porcelain *n.* fine china.

porch *n.* roofed shelter over the entrance of a building.

porcupine *n.* small animal covered with protective spines.

pore¹ *n.* tiny opening on skin or on a leaf, for emitting or taking in moisture.

pore² *v.i.* ⁓ **over,** study closely.

pork *n.* unsalted pig-meat.

pornography *n.* writings or pictures intended to stimulate erotic feelings by portraying sexual activity. **pornographic** *a.*

porous *a.* containing pores; permeable by fluid or air. **porosity** *n.*

porphyry /-fɪrɪ/ *n.* rock containing mineral crystals.

porpoise /-pəs/ *n.* small whale with a blunt rounded snout.

porridge *n.* food made by boiling oatmeal etc. to a thick paste.

port¹ *n.* harbour; town with this; place where

goods pass in and out of a country by ship or aircraft.

port² *n.* opening in a ship's side; porthole.

port³ *n.* left-hand side of a ship or aircraft. —*v.t.* turn this way.

port⁴ *n.* strong sweet usu. dark-red wine.

portable *a.* able to be carried.

portal *n.* door or entrance, esp. an imposing one.

portcullis *n.* vertical grating that slides down in grooves to block the gateway to a castle.

portend *v.t.* foreshadow.

portent /ˈpɔ-/ *n.* omen, significant sign. **portentous** /-ˈten-/ *a.*

porter¹ *n.* door-keeper of a large building.

porter² *n.* person employed to carry luggage or goods.

porterage *n.* services of a porter.

portfolio *n.* (pl. *-os*) case for loose sheets of paper; set of investments; position of a minister of State.

porthole *n.* window-like structure in the side of a ship or aircraft.

portico *n.* (pl. *-oes*) columns supporting a roof to form a porch or similar structure.

portion *n.* part, share; amount of food for one person; one's destiny. —*v.t.* divide into portions; distribute in portions.

portly *a.* (*-ier*, *-iest*) stout and dignified. **portliness** *n.*

portmanteau *n.* (pl. *-eaus*) a kind of trunk for clothes.

portrait *n.* picture of a person or animal; description.

portray *v.t.* make a picture of; describe; represent in a play etc. **portrayal** *n.*

Portuguese *a.* & *n.* (native, language) of Portugal.

pose *v.t./i.* put into or take a particular attitude; pretend to be; put forward, present (a problem etc.). —*n.* attitude in which someone is posed; pretence.

poser *n.* puzzling problem.

poseur /-ˈzɜ(r)/ *n.* person who poses or behaves affectedly.

posh *a.* (*sl.*) very smart, luxurious.

position *n.* place occupied by or intended for a person or thing; posture; situation; status; job. —*v.t.* place.

positive *a.* definite; explicit; constructive; (of a quantity) greater than zero; (of a battery terminal) through which electric current enters; (of a photograph) with lights, shades, or colours as in the subject, not reversed. —*n.* positive quality or quantity or photograph. **positively** *adv.*, **positiveness** *n.*

posse /ˈposɪ/ *n.* body of constables, strong force or company.

possess *v.t.* hold as belonging to oneself; dominate the mind of. **∼ oneself of,** take. **possessor** *n.*

possession *n.* possessing; thing possessed. **take ∼ of,** become the owner or possessor of.

possessive *a.* of or indicating possession; desiring to possess things. **possessively** *adv.*, **possessiveness** *n.*

possible *a.* capable of existing or happening or being done etc. **possibly** *adv.*, **possibility** *n.*

possum *n.* opossum.

post¹ *n.* piece of timber or metal set upright in the ground etc. to support something or mark a position. —*v.t.* display (a notice etc.), announce thus.

post² *n.* place of duty; outpost of soldiers; trading-station; job. —*v.t.* place, station. **last ∼,** (see *last²*).

post³ *n.* official conveyance of letters etc.; the letters etc. conveyed. —*v.t.* put into a post-box or post office for transmission; enter in an official ledger. **keep me posted,** keep me informed. **∼-box** *n.* box into which letters are inserted for transmission. **∼-code** *n.* group of letters and figures in a postal address to assist sorting. **∼-haste** *adv.* with great haste. **Post Office,** public department responsible for postal services. **∼ office,** building or room where postal business is carried on.

post- *pref.* after.

postage *n.* charge for sending something by post.

postal *a.* of the post; by post. **∼ order,** a kind of money order.

postcard *n.* card for sending messages by post without an envelope.

poster *n.* large sheet of paper announcing or advertising something, for display in a public place.

poste restante /pəʊst ˈrestãt/ post office department where letters are kept until called for.

posterior *a.* situated behind or at the back. —*n.* buttocks.

posterity *n.* future generations.

postern /ˈpos-/ *n.* small entrance at the back or side of a fortress etc.

posthumous /ˈpos-/ *a.* (of a child) born after its father's death; published or awarded after a person's death. **posthumously** *adv.*

postman *n.* (pl. *-men*) person who delivers or collects letters etc.

postmark *n.* official mark stamped on something sent by post, giving place and date of marking.

postmaster, postmistress *ns.* person in charge of a post office.

post-mortem *a.* & *n.* (examination) made after death.

postpone *v.t.* keep (an event etc.) from occurring until a later time. **postponement** *n.*

postscript *n.* additional paragraph at the end of a letter etc.

postulant *n.* candidate for admission to a religious order.

postulate¹ /-eɪt/ *v.t.* assume to be true, esp. as a basis for reasoning. **postulation** *n.*

postulate² /-ət/ *n.* thing postulated.

posture *n.* attitude of the body. —*v.i.* assume a posture, esp. for effect. **postural** *a.*

posy *n.* small bunch of flowers.

pot¹ *n.* vessel for holding liquids or solids, or for cooking in; (*sl.*) large amount. —*v.t.* (p.t. *potted*) put into a pot; send (a ball in billiards etc.) into a pocket; (*colloq.*) abridge; shoot, kill by a pot-shot. **go to ~,** (*sl.*) deteriorate, become ruined. **~-belly** *n.* protuberant belly. **~-boiler** *n.* literary or artistic work produced merely to make a living. **pot luck,** whatever is available for a meal. **~-shot** *n.* shot aimed casually.

pot[2] *n.* (*sl.*) marijuana.

potash *n.* potassium carbonate.

potassium *n.* soft silvery-white metallic element.

potato *n.* (pl. *-oes*) plant with starchy tubers that are used as food; one of these tubers.

potent /ˈpəʊ-/ *a.* having great natural power; having a strong effect. **potency** *n.*

potentate /ˈpəʊ-/ *n.* monarch, ruler.

potential *a.* & *n.* (ability etc.) capable of being developed or used. **potentially** *adv.*, **potentiality** *n.*

pot-hole *n.* hole formed underground by the action of water; hole in a road-surface.

pot-holing *n.* exploration of underground pot-holes. **pot-holer** *n.*

potion *n.* liquid for drinking as a medicine or drug.

pot-pourri *n.* scented mixture of dried petals and spices; medley.

potted *see* **pot**[1]. —*a.* preserved in a pot. **~ meat,** meat paste.

potter[1] *n.* maker of pottery.

potter[2] *v.i.* work on trivial tasks in a leisurely way.

pottery *n.* vessels and other objects made of baked clay; potter's work or workshop.

potty *a.* (*-ier, -iest*) (*sl.*) trivial; crazy.

pouch *n.* small bag or bag-like formation. —*v.t./i.* put into a pouch; overhang in a pouch-like shape.

pouffe /puf/ *n.* padded stool.

poulterer *n.* dealer in poultry.

poultice /ˈpəʊ-/ *n.* soft usu. hot dressing applied to a sore or inflamed part. —*v.t.* put a poultice on.

poultry /ˈpəʊ-/ *n.* domestic fowls.

pounce *v.i.* swoop down on and grasp or attack. —*n.* pouncing movement.

pound[1] *n.* measure of weight, 16 oz. avoirdupois (0.454 kg) or 12 oz. troy (0.373 kg); unit of money in Britain and certain other countries.

pound[2] *n.* enclosure where stray animals, or vehicles officially removed, are kept until claimed.

pound[3] *v.t./i.* beat or crush with heavy strokes; make one's way heavily; (of the heart) beat heavily.

poundage *n.* charge or commission per £ or per pound weight.

pour *v.t./i.* flow, cause to flow; rain heavily; send out freely.

pout[1] *v.t./i.* push out one's lips, (of lips) be pushed out, esp. in annoyance. —*n.* pouting expression.

pout[2] *n.* sea fish related to cod; eel-like freshwater fish.

poverty *n.* state of being poor; scarcity, lack; inferiority.

powder *n.* mass of fine dry particles; medicine or cosmetic in this form; gunpowder. —*v.t.* cover with powder. **powdery** *a.*

powdered *a.* made into powder.

power *n.* ability to do something; vigour, strength; control, influence, authority; influential person or country etc.; product of a number multiplied by itself a given number of times; mechanical or electrical energy; electricity supply. **~-station** *n.* building where electrical power is generated for distribution.

powered *a.* equipped with mechanical or electrical power.

powerful *a.* having great power or influence. **powerfully** *adv.*

powerless *a.* without power to take action, wholly unable.

powwow *n.* meeting for discussion.

practicable *a.* able to be done. **practicability** *n.*

practical *a.* involving activity as distinct from study or theory; suitable for use; clever at doing and making things; virtual. **~ joke,** humorous trick played on a person. **practicality** *n.*

practically *adv.* in a practical way; virtually, almost.

practice *n.* action as opposed to theory; habitual action, custom; repeated exercise to improve skill; professional work, doctor's or lawyer's business. **out of ~,** not lately practised in a skill.

practise *v.t./i.* do something repeatedly to become or remain skilful; carry out in action, do habitually; (of a doctor or lawyer) perform professional work.

practised *a.* experienced.

practitioner *n.* professional or practical worker, esp. in medicine.

pragmatic *a.* treating things from a practical point of view. **pragmatically** *adv.*, **pragmatism** *n.*

prairie *n.* large treeless tract of grassland, esp. in North America.

praise *v.t.* express approval or admiration of; honour (God) in words. —*n.* praising; approval expressed in words.

praiseworthy *a.* deserving praise.

praline /ˈprɑːlin/ *n.* sweet made by browning nuts in syrup.

pram *n.* four-wheeled carriage for a baby.

prance *v.i.* move springily.

prank *n.* piece of mischief.

prattle *v.i.* chatter in a childish way. —*n.* childish chatter.

prawn *n.* edible shellfish like a large shrimp.

pray *v.t./i.* say prayers; entreat.

prayer *n.* solemn request or thanksgiving to God; set form of words used in this; act of praying; entreaty. **~-book** *n.* book of set prayers.

pre- *pref.* before; beforehand.

preach *v.t./i.* deliver a sermon; expound (the Gospel etc.); speak in favour of, advocate. **preacher** *n.*

preamble /-ˈæm-/ *n.* preliminary statement, introductory section.

pre-arrange *v.t.* arrange beforehand. **pre-arrangement** *n.*

precarious /-ˈkeər-/ *a.* unsafe, not secure. **precariously** *adv.*

precaution *n.* something done in advance to avoid a risk. **precautionary** *a.*

precede *v.t.* come or go or place before in time or order etc.

precedence /ˈpres-/ *n.* priority.

precedent /ˈpres-/ *n.* previous case serving as an example to be followed.

precentor /-ˈsen-/ *n.* clergyman in charge of music at a cathedral.

precept /ˈpri-/ *n.* command, rule of conduct.

precinct *n.* enclosed area, esp. round a place of worship; district where traffic is prohibited in a town; (*pl.*) environs.

precious *a.* of great value; beloved; affectedly refined. —*adv.* (*colloq.*) very. ∼ **stone,** small valuable piece of mineral.

precipice *n.* very steep or vertical face of a cliff or rock.

precipitate[1] /-teɪt/ *v.t.* throw headlong; send rapidly into a certain state; cause to happen suddenly or soon; cause (a substance) to be deposited. **precipitation** *n.*

precipitate[2] /-tət/ *n.* substance deposited from a solution etc. —*a.* headlong, violently hurried; hasty, rash. **precipitately** *adv.*

precipitous /-ˈsɪp-/ *a.* very steep.

précis /ˈpreɪsiː/ *n.* (pl. *précis*, pr. -siz) summary. —*v.t.* make a précis of.

precise *a.* exact; correct and clearly stated. **precisely** *adv.*, **precision** *n.*

preclude *v.t.* exclude the possibility of, prevent.

precocious /-ˈkəʊʃ-/ *a.* having developed abilities earlier than is usual; developed thus. **precociously** *adv.*, **precocity** /-ˈkos-/ *n.*

preconceived *a.* (of an idea) formed beforehand. **preconception** *n.*

precursor *n.* forerunner.

predator /ˈpredə-/ *n.* predatory animal.

predatory /ˈpredə-/ *a.* preying upon others.

predecease *v.t.* die earlier than (another person).

predecessor *n.* former holder of an office or position; ancestor.

predestine *v.t.* destine beforehand, appoint as if by fate. **predestination** *n.*

predicament /-ˈdɪk-/ *n.* difficult situation.

predicate *n.* the part of a sentence that says something about the subject (e.g. 'is short' in *life is short*).

predicative /-ˈdɪk-/ *a.* forming the predicate or part of this. **predicatively** *adv.*

predict *v.t.* foretell. **prediction** *n.*, **predictor** *n.*

predilection *n.* special liking.

predispose *v.t.* influence in advance; render liable or inclined (e.g. to a disease). **predisposition** *n.*

predominate *v.i.* be greater than others in number or intensity etc.; exert control. **predominant** *a.*, **predominantly** *adv.*, **predominance** *n.*

pre-eminent *a.* excelling others, outstanding. **pre-eminently** *adv.*, **pre-eminence** *n.*

pre-empt *v.t.* take (a thing) before anyone else can do so. **pre-emption** *n.*, **pre-emptive** *a.*

preen *v.t.* smooth (feathers) with the beak. ∼ **oneself,** groom oneself; show self-satisfaction.

prefab *n.* (*colloq.*) prefabricated building.

prefabricated *a.* manufactured in sections for assembly on a site. **prefabrication** *n.*

preface *n.* introductory statement. —*v.t.* introduce with a preface; lead up to (an event).

prefect *n.* senior pupil authorized to maintain discipline in a school; administrative official in certain countries.

prefer *v.t.* (p.t. *preferred*) choose as more desirable, like better; put forward (an accusation); promote (a person).

preferable /ˈpref-/ *a.* more desirable. **preferably** *adv.*

preference /ˈpref-/ *n.* preferring; thing preferred; prior right; favouring.

preferential *a.* giving preference.

preferment *n.* promotion.

prefix *n.* (pl. -*ixes*) word or syllable placed in front of a word to add to or change its meaning. —*v.t.* add as a prefix or introduction.

pregnant *a.* having a child or young developing in the womb; full of meaning. **pregnancy** *n.*

prehensile /-ˈhensaɪl/ *a.* able to grasp things.

prehistoric *a.* of the ancient period before written records were made. **prehistory** *n.* prehistoric matters or times.

prejudge *v.t.* form a judgement on before knowing all the facts.

prejudice *n.* unreasoning opinion or dislike; harm to rights. —*v.t.* cause to have a prejudice; harm the rights of. **prejudiced** *a.*

prejudicial *a.* harmful to rights or interests.

prelate /ˈprel-/ *n.* clergyman of high rank.

preliminary *a.* & *n.* (action or event etc.) preceding and preparing for a main action or event.

prelude *n.* action or event preceding and leading up to another; introductory part or piece of music.

premature /ˈprem-/ *a.* coming or done before the usual or proper time. **prematurely** *adv.*

premeditated *a.* planned beforehand. **premeditation** *n.*

premier /ˈprem-/ *a.* first in importance or order or time. —*n.* Prime Minister. **premiership** *n.*

première /ˈpremjeə(r)/ *n.* first public performance.

premises *n.pl.* house or other building and its grounds.

premiss *n.* statement on which reasoning is based.

premium *n.* amount or instalment paid for an insurance policy; extra sum added to a wage or charge; fee for instruction. **at a** ∼, above the nominal or usual price; highly esteemed. **Premium Bond,** government security paying no interest but offering a periodical chance of a cash prize. **put a** ∼ **on,** provide an incentive to (an action etc.).

premonition /pri-/ *n.* presentiment.

preoccupation *n.* being preoccupied; thing that fills one's thoughts.

preoccupied *a.* mentally engrossed and inattentive to other things.

prep *n.* (see *preparation*). ~ **school,** preparatory school.

preparation *n.* preparing; thing done to make ready; substance prepared for use; (also *prep*) work set for a pupil to do outside lessons.

preparatory /-ˈpæ-/ *a.* preparing for something. —*adv.* in a preparatory way. ~ **school,** school where pupils are prepared for a higher school or (*U.S.*) for college.

prepare *v.t./i.* make or get ready. **prepared to,** ready and willing to.

prepay *v.t.* (p.t. *-paid*) pay beforehand. **prepayment** *n.*

preponderate *v.i.* be greater in number or intensity etc. **preponderant** *a.,* **preponderantly** *adv.,* **preponderance** *n.*

preposition *n.* word used with a noun or pronoun to show position, time, or means (e.g. *at* home, *by* train).

prepossessing *a.* attractive.

preposterous *a.* utterly absurd, outrageous.

prerequisite *a.* & *n.* (thing) required before something can happen.

prerogative *n.* right or privilege belonging to a person or group.

Presbyterian *a.* & *n.* (member) of a Church governed by elders all of equal rank, esp. the national Church of Scotland.

prescribe *v.t.* advise the use of (a medicine etc.); lay down as a course or rule to be followed.

prescript /ˈpri-/ *n.* rule, command.

prescription *n.* prescribing; doctor's written instructions for the preparation and use of a medicine.

presence *n.* being present; person's bearing; person or thing that is or seems present. ~ **of mind,** ability to act sensibly in a crisis.

present[1] /ˈprez-/ *a.* being in the place in question; existing or being dealt with now. —*n.* present time, time now passing. **at** ~, now. **for the** ~, for now, temporarily.

present[2] /ˈprez-/ *n.* gift.

present[3] /-ˈzent/ *v.t.* give as a gift or award; offer for acceptance; introduce; bring to the public; show, reveal; aim (a weapon). ~ **arms,** bring a rifle vertically in front of the body as a salute. **presenter** *n.*

presentable *a.* fit to be presented, of good appearance.

presentation *n.* presenting; thing presented.

presentiment /-ˈzent-/ *n.* feeling of something about to happen, foreboding.

presently *adv.* soon; (*Sc.* & *U.S.*) now.

preservation *n.* preserving.

preservative *a.* preserving. —*n.* substance that preserves perishable food.

preserve *v.t.* keep safe or unchanged or in existence; treat (food) to prevent decay. —*n.* area where game or fish are preserved for private use; interests etc. regarded as one person's domain; (also *pl.*) jam. **preserver** *n.*

preside *v.i.* be president or chairman; have the position of control.

president *n.* head of an institution or club

etc.; head of a republic. **presidency** *n.,* **presidential** *a.*

press *v.t./i.* apply weight or force against; squeeze; make by pressing; flatten, smooth; iron (clothes etc.); urge, force; throng closely. —*n.* process of pressing; throng; instrument for pressing something; printing-press, printing or publishing firm; newspapers and periodicals, people involved in writing or producing these. **be pressed for,** have barely enough of. ~ **conference,** interview before a number of reporters. ~ **cutting,** report etc. cut from a newspaper. ~**-stud** *n.* small fastener with two parts that engage when pressed together.

pressing *a.* urgent; urging something strongly. —*n.* thing made by pressing; gramophone record or series of these made at one time.

pressure *n.* exertion of force against a thing; this force, that of the atmosphere; compelling or oppressive influence. —*v.t.* pressurize (a person). ~**-cooker** *n.* pan for cooking things quickly by steam under high pressure. ~ **group,** organized group seeking to exert influence by intensive concerted action.

pressurize *v.t.* try to compel into an action; maintain a constant atmospheric pressure in (a compartment). **pressurization** *n.*

prestige /-ˈtiʒ/ *n.* respect resulting from good reputation or achievements.

prestigious /-ˈtɪdʒ-/ *a.* having or giving prestige.

presumably *adv.* it may be presumed.

presume *v.t./i.* suppose to be true; take the liberty (to do something); be presumptuous. ~ **on,** take liberties because of. **presumption** *n.*

presumptive *a.* giving grounds for presumption.

presumptuous *a.* behaving with impudent boldness; acting beyond one's authority. **presumptuously** *adv.,* **presumptuousness** *n.*

presuppose *v.t.* assume beforehand; involve the existence etc. of. **presupposition** *n.*

pretence *n.* pretending, make-believe; claim (e.g. to merit or knowledge).

pretend *v.t./i.* create a false impression of (in play or deception); claim falsely that one has or is something; lay claim. **pretender** *n.*

pretension *n.* asserting of a claim; pretentiousness.

pretentious *a.* claiming great merit or importance, showy. **pretentiously** *adv.,* **pretentiousness** *n.*

preternatural /pri-/ *a.* beyond what is natural. **preternaturally** *adv.*

pretext /ˈpri-/ *n.* reason put forward to conceal one's true reason.

pretty *a.* (*-ier, -iest*) attractive in a delicate way. —*adv.* fairly, moderately. **a** ~ **penny,** much money. **prettily** *adv.,* **prettiness** *n.*

pretzel *n.* salted biscuit.

prevail *v.i.* be victorious, gain the mastery; be the most usual. ~ **on,** persuade.

prevalent *a.* existing generally, widespread. **prevalence** *n.*

prevaricate *v.i.* speak evasively or misleadingly. **prevarication** *n.,* **prevaricator** *n.*

prevent *v.t.* keep from happening; keep from doing something. **prevention** *n.*, **preventable** *a.*

preventative *a.* & *n.* preventive.

preventive *a.* & *n.* (thing) preventing something.

preview *n.* advance view.

previous *a.* coming before in time or order; done or acting prematurely. **previously** *adv.*

prey *n.* animal hunted or killed by another for food; victim. —*v.i.* ~ **on,** seek or take as prey; cause worry to. **bird of** ~, one that kills and eats animals.

price *n.* amount of money for which a thing is bought or sold; what must be given or done etc. to achieve something. —*v.t.* fix, find, or estimate the price of.

priceless *a.* invaluable; (*sl.*) very amusing or absurd.

pricey *a.* (*colloq.*) expensive.

prick *v.t./i.* pierce slightly; feel a pricking sensation; erect (the ears). —*n.* act of pricking; sensation of being pricked. ~ **up one's ears,** listen alertly.

prickle *n.* small thorn; pointed spine on a hedgehog etc.; pricking sensation. —*v.t./i.* feel or cause a pricking sensation.

prickly *a.* having prickles; irritable, touchy. **prickliness** *n.*

pride *n.* feeling of pleasure or satisfaction about one's actions or qualities or possessions etc.; source of this; proper sense of one's dignity; group (of lions). —*v.refl.* ~ **oneself on,** be proud of. ~ **of place,** most prominent position.

priest *n.* clergyman; official of a non-Christian religion. **priestess** *n.fem.*, **priesthood** *n.*, **priestly** *a.*

prig *n.* self-righteous person. **priggish** *a.*, **priggishness** *n.*

prim *a.* (*primmer*, *primmest*) stiffly formal and precise; disliking what is rough or improper. **primly** *adv.*, **primness** *n.*

prima /ˈpriː-/ *a.* ~ **ballerina,** chief ballerina. ~ **donna,** chief female singer in opera.

prima facie /praɪmə ˈfeɪʃi/ at first sight; based on a first impression.

primal /ˈpraɪ-/ *a.* primitive, primeval; fundamental.

primary *a.* first in time, order, or importance. ~ **colours,** those from which others can be made by mixing. ~ **education,** ~ **school,** that in which the rudiments of knowledge are taught. **primarily** /ˈpraɪmə-/ *adv.*

primate /ˈpraɪ-/ *n.* archbishop; member of the highly developed order of animals that includes man, apes, and monkeys.

prime[1] *a.* chief; first-rate; fundamental. ~ **minister,** chief minister in a government. ~ **number,** number that can be divided exactly only by itself and unity.

prime[2] *v.t.* prepare for use or action; provide with information, or with food and drink, in preparation for something.

primer[1] *n.* substance used to prime a surface for painting.

primer[2] *n.* elementary textbook.

primeval /-ˈmiːv-/ *a.* of the earliest times of the world.

primitive *a.* of or at an early stage of civilization; simple, crude.

primogeniture /praɪməˈdʒen-/ *n.* system by which an eldest son inherits all his parents' property.

primordial /praɪ-/ *a.* primeval.

primrose *n.* pale yellow spring flower; its colour.

primula *n.* perennial plant of a kind that includes the primrose.

prince *n.* male member of a royal family, (in Britain) sovereign's son or grandson.

princely *a.* like a prince; splendid, generous.

princess *n.* female member of a royal family, (in Britain) sovereign's daughter or granddaughter; prince's wife.

principal *a.* first in rank or importance. —*n.* head of certain schools or colleges; person with highest authority or playing the leading part; capital sum as distinct from interest or income.

principality *n.* country ruled by a prince; *the P*~, Wales.

principally *adv.* mainly.

principle *n.* general truth or doctrine used as a basis of reasoning or a guide to action; general or scientific law shown or used in the working of a machine etc. **in** ~, as regards the main elements. **on** ~, because of one's principles of conduct.

print *v.t.* press (a mark) on a surface, impress (a surface etc.) in this way; produce by applying inked type to paper; write with unjoined letters; produce a positive picture from (a photographic negative etc.) by transmission of light. —*n.* mark left by pressing; printed lettering or words; printed design or picture or fabric. **in** ~, available from the publisher. **out of** ~, no longer in print. ~-**out** *n.* output in printed form from a computer. **printed circuit,** electric circuit with lines of conducting material printed on a flat sheet (instead of wires).

printer *n.* person who prints books or newspapers etc.

prior[1] *a.* coming before in time or order or importance. ~ **to,** before.

prior[2] *n.* monk who is head of a religious house or order, or (in an abbey) ranking next below an abbot. **prioress** *n.fem.*

priority *n.* being earlier or more important, right to be first; thing that should be treated as most important.

priory *n.* monastery or nunnery governed by a prior or prioress.

prise *v.t.* force out or open by leverage.

prism *n.* solid geometric shape with ends that are equal and parallel; transparent object of this shape with refracting surfaces.

prismatic *a.* of or like a prism; (of colours) rainbow-like.

prison *n.* building used to confine people convicted of crimes; place of custody or confinement; imprisonment.

prisoner *n.* person kept in prison; captive; person in confinement.

prissy *a.* prim.

pristine /-tin/ *a.* in its original and unspoilt condition.

privacy /ˈprɪv-/ *n.* being private.

private *a.* belonging to a person or group, not public; confidential; secluded; not part of a public service. —*n.* soldier of the lowest rank. **in ~,** privately. **privately** *adv.*

privation /praɪ-/ *n.* loss, lack; hardship.

privet *n.* bushy evergreen shrub much used for hedges.

privilege *n.* special right granted to a person or group. **privileged** *a.*

privy *a.* (*old use*) secret, private. —*n.* (*old use* & *U.S.*) lavatory. **be ~ to,** know about (secret plans etc.). **Privy Council,** sovereign's body of advisers. **~ purse,** allowance to the sovereign from public revenue.

prize[1] *n.* award for victory or superiority; thing that can be won. —*a.* winning a prize; excellent. —*v.t.* value highly. **~-fighter** *n.* professional boxer.

prize[2] *n.* ship or property captured at sea during a war.

prize[3] *v.t.* = prise.

pro *prep.* **~ and con,** for and against. —*n.* **pros and cons,** arguments for and against something.

pro- *pref.* in favour of.

probable *a.* likely to happen or be true. **probably** *adv.*, **probability** *n.*

probate /ˈprəʊ-/ *n.* official process of proving that a will is valid; certified copy of a will, handed to executors.

probation *n.* testing of behaviour or abilities; system whereby certain offenders are supervised by an official (**~ officer**) instead of being imprisoned. **probationary** *a.*

probationer *n.* person undergoing a probationary period, esp. in training to be a hospital nurse.

probe *n.* blunt surgical instrument for exploring a wound; device used similarly; unmanned exploratory spacecraft; investigation. —*v.t.* explore with a probe; investigate.

probity /ˈprəʊ-/ *n.* honesty.

problem *n.* something difficult to deal with or understand; thing to be solved or dealt with. **problematic, problematical** /-ˈmæ-/ *adjs.*

proboscis /-ˈbɒsɪs/ *n.* long flexible snout; insect's elongated mouthpart used for sucking things.

procedure *n.* series of actions done to accomplish something. **procedural** *a.*

proceed *v.i.* go forward or onward; continue; start a lawsuit; come forth, originate.

proceedings *n.pl.* what takes place, esp. at a formal meeting; published report of a conference; lawsuit.

proceeds /ˈprəʊ-/ *n.pl.* profit from a sale or performance etc.

process[1] /ˈprəʊ-/ *n.* series of operations used in making or manufacturing something; pro-

cedure; series of changes or events; lawsuit; natural projection. —*v.t.* subject to a process; deal with.

process[2] /-ˈses/ *v.i.* (*colloq.*) go in procession.

procession *n.* number of people or vehicles or boats etc. going along in an orderly line.

proclaim *v.t.* announce publicly; make known as being. **proclamation** *n.*

proclivity /-ˈklɪv-/ *n.* tendency.

procrastinate *v.i.* postpone action. **procrastination** *n.*

procreate *v.t.* beget or generate (offspring). **procreation** *n.*

proctor *n.* university official with disciplinary powers.

procurator /ˈprɒk-/ *n.* **~ fiscal,** (in Scotland) public prosecutor and coroner of a district.

procure *v.t.* obtain by care or effort, acquire. **procurement** *n.*

prod *v.t./i.* (p.t. *prodded*) poke; stimulate to action. —*n.* prodding action; stimulus; pointed instrument for prodding things.

prodigal *a.* wasteful, extravagant. **prodigally** *adv.*, **prodigality** *n.*

prodigious /-ˈdɪdʒ-/ *a.* amazing; enormous. **prodigiously** *adv.*

prodigy *n.* person with exceptional qualities or abilities; wonderful thing.

produce[1] /-ˈdjuːs/ *v.t.* bring forward for inspection; bring (a performance etc.) before the public; direct the acting of (a play); bring into existence, cause; manufacture; extend (a line). **producer** *n.*, **production** *n.*

produce[2] /ˈprɒd-/ *n.* amount or thing(s) produced.

product *n.* thing produced; result obtained by multiplying two quantities together.

productive *a.* producing things, esp. in large quantities.

productivity *n.* efficiency in industrial production.

profane *a.* secular, not sacred; irreverent, blasphemous. —*v.t.* treat irreverently. **profanely** *adv.*, **profanity** /-ˈfæ-/ *n.*

profess *v.t.* state that one has (a quality etc.), pretend; affirm one's faith in (a religion).

profession *n.* occupation, esp. one that requires advanced learning; people engaged in this; declaration.

professional *a.* of or belonging to a profession; showing the skill of a trained person; doing specified work etc. for payment, not as a pastime. —*n.* professional worker or player etc. **professionally** *adv.*

professor *n.* university teacher of the highest rank.

proffer *v.t.* & *n.* offer.

proficient *a.* competent, skilled. **proficiently** *adv.*, **proficiency** *n.*

profile *n.* side view, esp. of the face; short account of a person's character or career.

profit *n.* advantage, benefit; money gained. —*v.t./i.* (p.t. *profited*) obtain a profit; bring advantage to.

profitable *a.* bringing profit. **profitably** *adv.*, **profitability** *n.*

profiteer *n.* person who makes excessive profits. **profiteering** *n.*

profligate *a.* wasteful, extravagant; dissolute. —*n.* profligate person. **profligacy** *n.*

profound *a.* intense; showing or needing great insight. **profoundly** *adv.*, **profundity** *n.*

profuse *a.* lavish; plentiful. **profusely** *adv.*, **profuseness** *n.*

profusion *n.* abundance.

progenitor /-'dʒen-/ *n.* ancestor.

progeny /'prodʒ-/ *n.* offspring.

prognosis /-'gnəʊ-/ *n.* (pl. *-oses*) forecast, esp. of the course of a disease.

prognostication *n.* forecast.

program *n.* (*U.S.*) = programme; series of coded instructions for a computer. —*v.t.* (p.t. *programmed*) instruct (a computer) by means of this. **programmer** *n.*

programme *n.* plan of procedure; list of events or of items in an entertainment; these events etc.; broadcast performance.

progress¹ /'prəʊ-/ *n.* forward or onward movement; advance, development. **in ~,** taking place.

progress² /-'gres/ *v.i.* make progress; develop. **progression** *n.*

progressive *a.* making continuous progress; favouring progress or reform; (of a disease) gradually increasing in its effect. **progressively** *adv.*

prohibit *v.t.* forbid. **prohibition** *n.*

prohibitive *a.* prohibiting; intended to prevent the use or purchase of something.

project¹ /-'dʒe-/ *v.t./i.* extend outwards; cast, throw; imagine (oneself etc.) in another situation or time; plan.

project² /'prodʒ-/ *n.* plan, undertaking; task involving research.

projectile *n.* missile.

projection *n.* process of projecting something; thing projecting from a surface; representation on a plane surface of earth's surface; estimate of future situations based on a study of present ones.

projectionist *n.* person who operates a projector.

projector *n.* apparatus for projecting images on to a screen.

prolapse¹ /-'læ-/ *v.i.* slip forward and down out of place.

prolapse² /'prəʊ-/ *n.* prolapsing of an organ of the body.

proletariat /prəʊlɪ'teər-/ *n.* working-class people. **proletarian** *a.* & *n.*

proliferate *v.i.* produce new growth or offspring rapidly, multiply. **proliferation** *n.*

prolific *a.* producing things abundantly. **prolifically** *adv.*

prologue /-log/ *n.* introduction to a poem or play etc.

prolong *v.t.* lengthen in extent or duration. **prolongation** *n.*

prolonged *a.* continuing for a long time.

prom *n.* (*colloq.*) promenade along a sea front; promenade concert.

promenade /-'nɑd/ *n.* leisurely walk in a public place; paved public walk (esp. along a sea front). —*v.t./i.* go or take for a promenade. **~ concert,** one where part of the audience is not seated and can move about.

prominent *a.* projecting; conspicuous; important, well-known. **prominently** *adv.*, **prominence** *n.*

promiscuous *a.* indiscriminate; having sexual relations with many people. **promiscuously** *adv.*, **promiscuity** /-'kju-/ *n.*

promise *n.* declaration that one will give or do or not do a certain thing; indication of what will occur or of future good results. —*v.t./i.* make a promise (to); say that one will do or give (a thing); seem likely, produce expectation of. **~ well,** offer good prospects.

promising *a.* likely to turn out well or produce good results.

promissory /'prom-/ *a.* conveying a promise.

promontory *n.* high land jutting out into the sea or a lake.

promote *v.t.* raise to a higher rank or office; help the progress of; publicize in order to sell. **promotion** *n.*, **promoter** *n.*

prompt *a.* done or doing something without delay; punctual. —*adv.* punctually. —*v.t.* incite; assist (an actor or speaker) by supplying words. **promptly** *adv.*, **promptness** *n.*, **promptitude** *n.*

prompter *n.* person stationed off-stage to prompt actors.

promulgate /'prom-/ *v.t.* make known to the public. **promulgation** *n.*

prone *a.* lying face downwards; likely to do or suffer something.

prong *n.* one of the projecting pointed parts of a fork. **pronged** *a.*

pronoun *n.* word used as a substitute for a noun (e.g. *I, me, who, which*).

pronounce *v.t.* utter (a sound or word) distinctly or in a certain way; declare. **pronunciation** *n.*

pronounced *a.* noticeable.

pronouncement *n.* declaration.

proof *n.* evidence that something is true or valid or exists; standard of strength for distilled alcoholic liquors; trial impression of printed matter for correction. —*a.* able to resist penetration or damage. —*v.t.* make (fabric) proof against something (e.g. water).

prop¹ *n.* & *v.t.* (p.t. *propped*) support to prevent something from falling or sagging or failing.

prop² *n.* (*colloq.*) a stage property.

propaganda *n.* publicity intended to persuade or convince people.

propagate *v.t.* breed or reproduce from parent stock; spread (news etc.); transmit. **propagation** *n.*, **propagator** *n.*

propel *v.t.* (p.t. *propelled*) push forward, give onward movement to. **propellent** *a.*

propellant *n.* thing that propels something.

propeller *n.* revolving device with blades, for propelling a ship or aircraft.

propensity *n.* tendency; inclination.

proper *a.* suitable; correct; conforming to social conventions; (*colloq.*) thorough. **~ fraction,** fraction that is less than unity, with the numerator less than the denominator. ~ **name** *or* **noun,** name of an individual person or thing.

property *n.* thing(s) owned; real estate, land; movable object used on the stage in a play etc.; quality, characteristic.

prophecy *n.* power of prophesying; statement prophesying something.

prophesy *v.t./i.* foretell (what will happen).

prophet *n.* person who foretells the future; religious teacher inspired by God; *the P~,* Muhammad. **prophetess** *n.fem.*

prophetic, prophetical *adjs.* prophesying. **prophetically** *adv.*

propinquity *n.* nearness.

propitiate /-ˈprɪʃ-/ *v.t.* win the favour of. **propitiation** *n.,* **propitiatory** *a.*

propitious /-ˈprɪʃəs/ *a.* giving a good omen, favourable. **propitiously** *adv.,* **propitiousness** *n.*

proportion *n.* fraction or share of a whole; ratio; correct relation in size or amount or degree; (*pl.*) dimensions. **proportional** *a.,* **proportionally** *adv.*

proportionate *a.* in due proportion. **proportionately** *adv.*

proposal *n.* proposing of something; thing proposed; request to marry the person asking.

propose *v.t./i.* put forward for consideration; have and declare as one's plan; nominate as a candidate; make a proposal of marriage. **proposer** *n.*

proposition *n.* statement; proposal, scheme proposed; (*colloq.*) undertaking. *—v.t.* (*colloq.*) put a proposal to.

propound *v.t.* put forward for consideration.

proprietary *a.* made and sold by a particular firm, usu. under a patent; of an owner or ownership.

proprietor /-ˈpraɪə-/ *n.* owner of a business. **proprietress** *n.fem.,* **proprietorial** *a.*

propriety /-ˈpraɪə-/ *n.* being proper or suitable; correctness of behaviour.

propulsion *n.* process of propelling or being propelled.

pro rata /-ˈrɑ-/ proportional(ly).

prosaic *a.* plain and ordinary, unimaginative. **prosaically** *adv.*

proscribe *v.t.* forbid by law.

prose *n.* written or spoken language not in verse form.

prosecute *v.t.* take legal proceedings against (a person) for a crime; carry on, conduct. **prosecution** *n.,* **prosecutor** *n.*

proselyte /ˈprɒsəl-/ *n.* Gentile convert to the Jewish faith.

prosody /ˈprɒs-/ *n.* study of verse-forms and poetic metres.

prospect[1] /ˈprɒs-/ *n.* view; what one is to expect; chance of success or advancement.

prospect[2] /-ˈspekt/ *v.i.* explore in search of something. **prospector** *n.*

prospective *a.* expected to be or to occur; future, possible.

prospectus *n.* printed document advertising the chief features of a school, business enterprise, etc.

prosper *v.i.* be successful, thrive.

prosperous *a.* financially successful. **prosperity** *n.*

prostate *n.* ~ **gland,** gland round the neck of the bladder in males. **prostatic** *a.*

prosthesis /ˈprɒs-/ *n.* (pl. *-theses*) artificial limb or similar appliance. **prosthetic** /-ˈθet-/ *a.*

prostitute *n.* woman who engages in promiscuous sexual intercourse for payment. *—v.t.* make a prostitute of; put (talent etc.) to an unworthy use. **prostitution** *n.*

prostrate[1] /ˈprɒs-/ *a.* face downwards; lying horizontally; overcome, exhausted.

prostrate[2] /-ˈtreɪt/ *v.t.* cause to be prostrate. **prostration** *n.*

protagonist *n.* one of the chief contenders; (*incorrect use*) supporter.

protect *v.t.* keep from harm or injury. **protection** *n.,* **protector** *n.*

protective *a.* protecting, giving protection. **protectively** *adv.*

protectorate *n.* country that is under the official protection and partial control of a stronger one.

protégé /ˈproteʒeɪ/ *n.* (fem. *-ée*) person under the protection or patronage of another.

protein /-tin/ *n.* organic compound containing nitrogen, forming an essential part of animals' food.

protest[1] /ˈprəʊ-/ *n.* statement or action indicating disapproval.

protest[2] /-ˈtest/ *v.t./i.* express disapproval; declare firmly.

Protestant *n.* member of one of the western Churches that are separated from the Roman Catholic Church. **Protestantism** *n.*

protestation *n.* firm declaration.

protocol *n.* etiquette applying to rank or status; draft of a treaty.

proton *n.* particle of matter with a positive electric charge.

protoplasm *n.* colourless jelly-like substance, the main constituent of all organic cells and tissues.

prototype *n.* original example from which others are developed; trial model (e.g. of an aircraft).

protract *v.t.* prolong in duration. **protraction** *n.*

protractor *n.* instrument for measuring angles, usu. a semicircle marked off in degrees.

protrude *v.t./i.* project, stick out. **protrusion** *n.*

protuberance *n.* bulging part.

protuberant *a.* bulging outwards.

proud *a.* (*-er, -est*) full of pride. *—adv.* **do a person ~,** (*colloq.*) treat him lavishly. **proudly** *adv.*

provable *a.* able to be proved.

prove *v.t./i.* give or be proof of; be found to be; (of unbaked dough) rise. ~ **oneself,** show that one has the required abilities.

proven *a.* proved.

provenance *n.* place of origin.

provender *n.* fodder; (*joc.*) food.

proverb *n.* short well-known saying.

proverbial *a.* of or mentioned in a proverb; well-known. **proverbially** *adv.*

provide *v.t./i.* cause to have possession or use of; supply the necessities of life; make preparations. **provider** *n.*

provided *conj.* on condition (that).

providence *n.* being provident; God's or nature's care and protection; *P~*, God.

provident *a.* showing wise forethought for future needs, thrifty.

providential *a.* happening very luckily. **providentially** *adv.*

providing *conj.* = provided.

province *n.* administrative division of a country; district under an archbishop's charge; range of learning or responsibility; (*pl.*) all parts of a country outside its capital city.

provincial *a.* of a province or provinces; having limited interests and narrow-minded views. —*n.* inhabitant of province(s).

provision *n.* process of providing things, esp. for future needs; stipulation in a treaty or contract etc.; (*pl.*) supply of food and drink.

provisional *a.* arranged temporarily. **provisionally** *adv.*

proviso /-ˈvaɪ-/ *n.* (pl. *-os*) stipulation.

provoke *v.t.* make angry; rouse to action; produce as a reaction or effect. **provocation** *n.*, **provocative** /-ˈvok-/ *a.*, **provocatively** *adv.*

provoking *a.* annoying.

provost /ˈprov-/ *n.* head of certain colleges or cathedral chapters; head of a municipal corporation or burgh in Scotland.

prow /praʊ/ *n.* projecting front part of a ship or boat.

prowess /ˈpraʊ-/ *n.* great ability or daring.

prowl *v.t./i.* go about stealthily or restlessly. —*n.* act of prowling. **prowler** *n.*

proximate *a.* nearest.

proximity *n.* nearness.

proxy *n.* person authorized to represent or act for another; use of such a person.

prude *n.* person of exaggerated propriety, one who is easily shocked. **prudery** *n.*

prudent *a.* showing carefulness and foresight. **prudently** *adv.*, **prudence** *n.*

prudential *a.* prudent.

prudish *a.* showing prudery. **prudishly** *adv.*, **prudishness** *n.*

prune[1] *n.* dried plum.

prune[2] *v.t.* trim by cutting away dead or unwanted parts; reduce.

prurient *a.* having or arising from lewd thoughts. **prurience** *n.*

prussic *a.* ~ **acid,** highly poisonous acid.

pry[1] *v.i.* inquire or peer impertinently (often furtively).

pry[2] *v.t.* (*U.S.*) prise.

P.S. *abbr.* postscript.

psalm *n.* sacred song, esp. from the Book of Psalms in the Old Testament.

psalmist *n.* writer of psalms.

psalter *n.* copy of the Book of Psalms.

pseudo- /sjuː-/ *pref.* false.

pseudonym *n.* fictitious name, esp. used by an author.

psoriasis /səˈraɪ-/ *n.* skin disease causing scaly red patches.

psychedelic /-ˈdel-/ *a.* full of vivid or luminous colours.

psychiatry /sɪˈkaɪə-/ *n.* study and treatment of mental disease. **psychiatrist** *n.*, **psychiatric** /-kɪˈæ-/ *a.*

psychic *a.* psychical; able to exercise psychical powers.

psychical *a.* of the soul or mind; of phenomena that seem to be outside physical and natural laws. **psychically** *adv.*

psycho-analyse *v.t.* treat by psycho-analysis. **psycho-analyst** *n.*

psycho-analysis *n.* method of examining and treating mental conditions by investigating the interaction of conscious and unconscious elements.

psychology *n.* study of the mind and how it works; mental characteristics. **psychological** *a.*, **psychologically** *adv.*, **psychologist** *n.*

psychopath *n.* person suffering from a severe mental disorder. **psychopathic** *a.*

psychosis *n.* (pl. *-oses*) severe mental disorder involving a person's whole personality.

psychosomatic /-ˈmæt-/ *a.* (of illness) caused or aggravated by mental stress.

psychotherapy *n.* treatment of mental disorders by the use of psychological methods.

pt. *abbr.* pint.

ptarmigan /ˈtɑː-/ *n.* bird of the grouse family with plumage that turns white in winter.

pterodactyl /te-/ *n.* extinct reptile with wings.

pub *n.* (*colloq.*) public house.

puberty *n.* stage in life at which a person's reproductive organs become able to function.

pubic *a.* of the abdomen at the lower front part of the pelvis.

public *a.* of, for, or known to people in general. —*n.* members of a community in general. **in ~,** openly, not in private. ~ **house,** building (other than a hotel) licensed to sell alcoholic drinks (not only with meals). ~ **school,** secondary school for fee-paying pupils; (in Scotland, U.S.A., etc.) school managed by public authorities. **~-spirited** *a.* showing readiness to do things for the benefit of people in general. **publicly** *adv.*

publican *n.* keeper of a public house; (in the Bible) tax-collector.

publication *n.* publishing; published book or newspaper etc.

publicity *n.* public attention directed upon a person or thing; process of attracting this.

publicize *v.t.* bring to the attention of the public.

publish *v.t.* issue copies of (a book etc.) to the public; make generally known. **publisher** *n.*

puce *a.* & *n.* brownish purple.

puck *n.* hard rubber disc used in ice hockey.

pucker *v.t./i.* & *n.* wrinkle.

puckish *a.* impish.

pudding *n.* baked, boiled, or steamed dish containing or enclosed in a mixture of flour and other ingredients; sweet course of a meal; a kind of sausage.

puddle *n.* small pool of rainwater or of liquid on a surface.

pudgy *a.* (-ier, -iest) podgy.

puerile /ˈpjʊərail/ *a.* childish. **puerility** /-ˈril-/ *n.*

puff *n.* short light blowing of breath, wind, smoke, etc.; round soft mass; soft pad for applying powder to the skin; piece of advertising. —*v.t./i.* send (air etc.) or come out in puffs; breathe hard, pant; make or become inflated, swell. **∼ pastry,** very light flaky pastry.

puffin *n.* sea-bird with a short striped bill.

puffy *a.* puffed out, swollen. **puffiness** *n.*

pug *n.* dog of a dwarf breed resembling the bulldog. **∼-nosed** *a.* having a short fairly flat nose.

pugilist /ˈpjudʒ-/ *n.* professional boxer. **pugilism** *n.*

pugnacious *a.* eager to fight, aggressive. **pugnaciously** *adv.*, **pugnacity** *n.*

puissance /ˈpwis-/ *n.* test of a horse's ability to jump high obstacles.

pull *v.t./i.* exert force upon (a thing) so as to move it towards oneself or the source of the force; remove or damage or check by pulling; exert a pulling or driving force; attract. —*n.* act or force of pulling; means of exerting influence; deep drink; draw at a pipe etc. **∼ a person's leg,** tease him. **∼ down,** demolish; weaken the health of. **∼ in,** (of a vehicle etc.) move towards the side of the road or into a stopping-place. **∼-in** *n.* place for doing this. **∼ off,** succeed in doing or achieving. **∼ oneself together,** regain one's self-control. **∼ one's punches,** avoid using full force. **∼ one's weight,** do one's fair share of work. **∼ out,** withdraw; (of a vehicle etc.) move away from the side of a road or a stopping-place. **∼ through,** come or bring successfully through an illness or difficulty. **∼ up,** stop; reprimand.

pullet *n.* young hen.

pulley *n.* (pl. -eys) wheel over which a rope etc. passes, used in lifting things or to drive an endless belt.

pullover *n.* sweater (with or without sleeves) with no fastenings.

pulmonary /ˈpʌl-/ *a.* of the lungs.

pulp *n.* soft moist part (esp. of fruit) or substance. —*v.t./i.* reduce or become reduced to pulp. **pulpy** *a.*

pulpit *n.* raised enclosed platform in a church, for preaching from.

pulsate *v.i.* expand and contract rhythmically; vibrate. **pulsation** *n.*

pulse[1] *n.* rhythmical throbbing of arteries as blood is propelled along them, esp. as felt in the wrists or temples etc.; single beat or throb. —*v.i.* pulsate.

pulse[2] *n.* edible seed of beans, peas, lentils, etc.

pulverize *v.t./i.* crush into powder; become powder; defeat thoroughly. **pulverization** *n.*

puma *n.* large brown American animal of the cat family.

pumice /ˈpʌm-/ *n.* solidified lava used for rubbing stains from the skin or as powder for polishing things. **∼-stone** *n.* piece of this.

pummel *v.t.* (p.t. *pummelled*) strike repeatedly esp. with the fists.

pump[1] *n.* machine for raising water, or for moving liquid, gas, or air. —*v.t./i.* use a pump; move or inflate or empty by using a pump; move vigorously up and down; pour forth; question persistently to obtain information.

pump[2] *n.* light shoe; plimsoll.

pumpkin *n.* large round orange-coloured fruit of a vine.

pun *n.* humorous use of a word to suggest another that sounds the same. **punning** *a.* & *n.*

punch[1] *v.t./i.* strike with the fist; (sl.) vigour; device for perforate, cut (a hole etc.) with a device. —*n.* blow with the fist; (sl.) vigour; device for cutting holes or impressing a design in metal or leather etc. **∼-drunk** *a.* stupefied by being severely punched. **∼ line,** words giving the climax of a joke. **∼-up** *n.* fight with fists, brawl.

punch[2] *n.* drink made of wine or spirits mixed with fruit juices etc. **∼-bowl** *n.*

punctilious *a.* very careful about details; conscientious. **punctiliously** *adv.*, **punctiliousness** *n.*

punctual *a.* arriving or doing things at the appointed time. **punctually** *adv.*, **punctuality** *n.*

punctuate *v.t.* insert the appropriate marks in written material to separate sentences etc.; interrupt at intervals. **punctuation** *n.*

puncture *n.* small hole made by something sharp, esp. accidentally in a pneumatic tyre. —*v.t./i.* make a puncture in; suffer a puncture.

pundit *n.* learned expert.

pungent /ˈpʌndʒ-/ *a.* having a strong sharp taste or smell; (of remarks) biting. **pungently** *adv.*, **pungency** *n.*

punish *v.t.* cause (an offender) to suffer for his offence; inflict a penalty for; treat roughly. **punishment** *n.*

punishable *a.* liable to be punished.

punitive /ˈpju-/ *a.* inflicting or intended to inflict punishment.

punk *n.* (sl.) worthless stuff, a worthless person. —*a.* (sl.) worthless; of punk rock or its devotees. **∼ rock,** type of pop music involving outrage and shock effects.

punnet *n.* small chip (basket) or similar container for fruit etc.

punt[1] *n.* shallow flat-bottomed boat with broad square ends. —*v.t./i.* propel (a punt) by thrusting with a pole against the bottom of a river; carry or travel in a punt.

punt[2] *v.t.* kick (a dropped football) before it touches the ground. —*n.* this kick.

punt[3] *v.i.* lay a stake against the bank in certain card-games; bet on a horse etc. **punter** *n.*

puny *a.* (-ier, -iest) undersized; feeble.

pup *n.* young dog; young wolf, rat, or seal. —*v.i.* (p.t. *pupped*) give birth to pup(s).

pupa /ˈpju-/ *n.* (pl. -ae, pr. -i) chrysalis. **pupal** *a.*

pupil *n.* person who is taught by another; opening in the centre of the iris of the eye.

puppet *n.* a kind of doll made to move by various means as an entertainment; person whose actions are controlled by another.

puppy *n.* young dog.

purchase *v.t.* buy. —*n.* buying; thing bought; firm hold to pull or raise something, leverage. **purchaser** *n.*

purdah *n.* Muslim or Hindu system of secluding women.

pure *a.* (*-er, -est*) not mixed with any other substances; mere; free from evil or sin; chaste; (of mathematics or sciences) dealing with theory, not with practical applications. **pureness** *n.*

purée /-reɪ/ *n.* pulped fruit or vegetables etc. —*v.t.* make into purée.

purely *adv.* in a pure way; entirely; only.

purgative *n.* strong laxative.

purgatory *n.* place or condition of suffering, esp. (in R.C. belief) in which souls undergo purification.

purge *v.t.* clear the bowels of by a purgative; rid of people or things regarded as undesirable; atone for (an offence). —*n.* process of purging.

purify *v.t.* make pure, cleanse from impurities. **purification** *n.*, **purifier** *n.*

purist *n.* stickler for correctness.

Puritan *n.* member of those English Protestants (16th–17th centuries) who wanted simpler church ceremonies and gravity in behaviour. **puritan** *n.* person who is strict in morals and regards certain pleasures as sinful. **puritanical** *a.*

purity *n.* pureness.

purl *n.* a kind of knitting-stitch. —*v.t./i.* produce this stitch (in).

purler *n.* (*colloq.*) headlong fall.

purlieus /-ljuz/ *n.pl.* outskirts.

purloin *v.t.* steal.

purple *a.* & *n.* (of) a colour made by mixing red and blue.

purport[1] /ˈpɜ-/ *n.* meaning.

purport[2] /-ˈpɔt/ *v.t.* have as its purport; pretend, be intended to seem. **purportedly** *adv.*

purpose *n.* intended result of effort; intention to act, determination. —*v.t.* intend. **on ~,** by intention not by chance. **~-built** *a.* built for a particular purpose. **to no ~,** with no result.

purposeful *a.* having or showing a conscious purpose, with determination. **purposefully** *adv.*, **purposefulness** *n.*

purposely *adv.* on purpose.

purr *n.* low vibrant sound that a cat makes when pleased; similar sound. —*v.i.* make this sound.

purse *n.* small pouch for carrying money; (*U.S.*) handbag; money, funds. —*v.t.* pucker (one's lips).

purser *n.* ship's officer in charge of accounts.

pursuance *n.* performance (of duties etc.).

pursue *v.t.* chase in order to catch or kill; afflict continually; continue, proceed along; engage in. **pursuer** *n.*

pursuit *n.* pursuing; activity to which one gives time or effort.

purvey *v.t.* supply (articles of food) as a trader. **purveyor** *n.*

pus *n.* thick yellowish matter produced by infected tissue.

push *v.t./i.* move away by exerting force; thrust forward; make (one's way) forcibly; make a vigorous effort; make demands on the abilities or tolerance of; urge; sell (drugs) illegally. —*n.* act of pushing; force exerted by this; vigorous effort; self-assertion, determination to get on. **give** *or* **get the ~,** (*sl.*) dismiss or be dismissed. **~-chair** *n.* folding chair on wheels, in which a child can be pushed along. **~ off,** (*sl.*) go away.

pushful *a.* self-assertive, determined to get on. **pushfulness** *n.*

pushing *a.* pushful.

pusillanimous /-ˈlæn-/ *a.* timid, cowardly. **pusillanimity** /-ˈnɪm-/ *n.*

puss *n.* cat.

pussy *n.* (*children's use*) cat. **~ willow,** willow with furry catkins.

pussyfoot *v.i.* (*U.S.*) move stealthily; act cautiously.

pustule *n.* pimple, blister.

put *v.t./i.* (p.t. *put*, pres.p. *putting*) cause to occupy or be in a certain place, position, state, or relationship; estimate; express, phrase; impose (as a tax etc.); lay (blame) on; throw (the shot or weight) as an athletic exercise; (of ships) proceed. —*n.* throw of the shot or weight. **~ by,** save for future use. **~ down,** suppress by force or authority; snub; have (an animal) killed; record in writing; reckon, consider. **~ in,** make (an appearance); spend (time) working. **~ in for,** apply for. **~ off,** postpone; dissuade, repel. **~ out,** disconcert; inconvenience; extinguish; dislocate. **~ up,** construct, build; raise the price of; provide (money etc.); present as an idea or proposal; give or receive accommodation; attempt or offer (resistance etc.) **~-up job,** scheme concocted fraudulently. **~ up to,** instigate (a person) in. **~ up with,** endure, tolerate.

putative /ˈpjuː-/ *a.* reputed, supposed.

putrefy *v.i.* rot. **putrefaction** *n.*

putrid *a.* rotten; stinking.

putt /pʌt/ *v.t.* strike (a golf-ball) gently to make it roll along the ground. —*n.* this stroke. **putter** *n.* club used for this.

puttee *n.* strip of cloth wound spirally from ankle to knee for protection and support.

putty *n.* soft paste that sets hard, used for fixing glass in frames, filling up holes, etc.

puzzle *n.* question that is difficult to answer, problem; problem or toy designed to test knowledge or ingenuity. —*v.t./i.* cause to think hard; use hard thought, solve by this. **puzzlement** *n.*

pygmy *n.* person or thing of unusually small size; **P~,** member of a dwarf negroid African people. —*a.* very small.

pyjamas /-ˈdʒɑ-/ *n.pl.* loose jacket and trousers esp. for sleeping in.

pylon *n.* tall lattice-work structure used for carrying electricity cables or as a boundary.

pyramid *n.* structure with sloping sides that meet at the top, esp. built by ancient Egyptians as a tomb or by Aztecs and Mayas as a platform for a temple. **pyramidal** /-'ræm-/ *a.*

pyre *n.* pile of wood etc. for burning a dead body as part of a funeral rite.

Pyrenean /pɪrə'nɪən/ *a.* of the Pyrenees.

pyrethrum /paɪ'ri:-/ *n.* a kind of chrysanthemum; insecticide from its dried flowers.

pyromaniac /paɪrə'meɪ-/ *n.* person with an uncontrollable impulse to set things on fire.

pyrotechnics *n.pl.* firework display. **pyrotechnic** *a.*

Pyrrhic /'pɪrɪk/ *a.* ∼ **victory,** one gained at too great a cost.

python *n.* large snake that crushes its prey.

pyx *n.* vessel in which bread consecrated for the Eucharist is kept; box in which specimen coins are deposited at the Royal Mint.

Q

Q.C. *abbr.* Queen's Counsel.

qt. *abbr.* quart(s).

qua /kweɪ/ *conj.* in the capacity of.

quack[1] *n.* duck's harsh cry. —*v.i.* make this sound.

quack[2] *n.* person who falsely claims to have medical skill or remedies.

quad /kwod/ *n.* (*colloq.*) quadrangle; quadraphonic; quadruplet.

quadrangle /'kwod-/ *n.* four-sided court bordered by large buildings.

quadrant /'kwod-/ *n.* one quarter of a circle or of its circumference; graduated instrument for taking angular measurements.

quadraphonic /kwod-/ *a. & n.* (sound-reproduction) using four transmission channels.

quadratic /kwod-/ *a. & n.* (equation) involving the second and no higher power of an unknown quantity or variable.

quadrennial /kwod-/ *a.* happening every fourth year; lasting four years.

quadrilateral /kwod-/ *n.* geometric figure with four sides.

quadruped /'kwod-/ *n.* four-footed animal.

quadruple /'kwod-/ *a.* having four parts or members; four times as much as. —*v.t./i.* increase by four times its amount.

quadruplet /'kwod-/ *n.* one of four children born at one birth.

quaff /kwof/ *v.t.* drink in large draughts.

quagmire /'kwæ-/ *n.* bog, marsh.

quail[1] *n.* bird related to the partridge.

quail[2] *v.i.* flinch, show fear.

quaint *a.* (*-er, -est*) odd in a pleasing way. **quaintly** *adv.*, **quaintness** *n.*

quake *v.i.* shake or tremble, esp. with fear. —*n.* (*colloq.*) earthquake.

Quaker *n.* member of the Society of Friends (a Christian sect with no written creed or ordained ministers).

qualification *n.* qualifying; thing that qualifies a person to do something; thing that limits a meaning.

qualify *v.t./i.* make or become competent or eligible or legally entitled to do something; limit the meaning of; attribute a quality to. **qualifier** *n.*

qualitative /'kwol-/ *a.* of or concerned with quality.

quality *n.* degree or level of excellence; characteristic, something that is special in a person or thing.

qualm /kwɑm/ *n.* misgiving, pang of conscience.

quandary /'kwon-/ *n.* state of perplexity, difficult situation.

quango *n.* (pl. *-os*) administrative body (outside the Civil Service) with senior members appointed by the government.

quantify *v.t.* express as a quantity. **quantifiable** *a.*

quantitative /'kwon-/ *a.* of or concerned with quantity.

quantity *n.* amount or number of things; ability to be measured; (*pl.*) large amounts. **in ∼,** in large amounts. ∼ **surveyor,** person who measures and prices building-work.

quantum /'kwon-/ *n.* ∼ **theory,** theory of physics based on the assumption that energy exists in indivisible units.

quarantine /-tin/ *n.* isolation imposed on those who have been exposed to an infection which they could spread. —*v.t.* put into quarantine.

quarrel *n.* angry disagreement. —*v.i.* (p.t. *quarrelled*) engage in a quarrel.

quarrelsome *a.* liable to quarrel.

quarry[1] *n.* intended prey or victim; thing sought or pursued.

quarry[2] *n.* open excavation from which stone or slate etc. is obtained. —*v.t./i.* obtain from a quarry; search for information.

quart *n.* quarter of a gallon, two pints.

quarter *n.* one of four equal parts; this amount; (*U.S. & Canada*) quarter of a dollar, 25 cents; grain-measure of 8 bushels; fourth part of a year, for which payments are due on *quarter-day*; point of time 15 minutes before or after every hour; direction, district; mercy towards an enemy or opponent; (*pl.*) lodgings, accommodation. —*v.t.* divide into quarters; place (a symbol) in a coat of arms; put (soldiers etc.) into lodgings; (of a dog) search systematically. ∼**-final** *n.* contest preceding a semifinal. ∼**-light** *n.* small triangular window in a motor vehicle.

quarterdeck *n.* part of a ship's upper deck nearest the stern.

quarterly *a. & adv.* (produced or occurring) once in every quarter of a year. —*n.* quarterly periodical.

quartermaster *n.* regimental officer in charge of

stores etc.; naval petty officer in charge of steering and signals.

quartet *n.* group of four instruments or voices; music for these.

quarto *n.* a size of paper.

quartz *n.* a kind of hard mineral.

quasar /ˈkweɪ-/ *n.* star-like object that is the source of intense electromagnetic radiation.

quash *v.t.* annul; suppress.

quasi- /ˈkweɪzaɪ/ *pref.* seeming to be but not really so.

quatercentenary /kwætɜsenˈti-/ *n.* 400th anniversary.

quatrain /ˈkwot-/ *n.* stanza of four lines.

quaver *v.t./i.* tremble, vibrate; speak or utter in a trembling voice. —*n.* trembling sound; note in music, half a crotchet.

quay /ki/ *n.* landing-place built for ships to load or unload alongside. **quayside** *n.*

queasy *a.* feeling or liable to feel slightly sick; squeamish. **queasiness** *n.*

queen *n.* female ruler of a country by right of birth; king's wife; woman or thing regarded as supreme in some way; piece in chess; playing-card bearing a picture of a queen; fertile female of bee or ant etc. —*v.t./i.* convert (a pawn in chess) to a queen, be converted thus. **∼ it,** behave as if supreme. **∼ mother,** dowager queen who is the reigning sovereign's mother. **Queen's Counsel,** counsel to the Crown. **queenly** *a.*

queer *a.* (-*er*, -*est*) strange, odd, eccentric; slightly ill or faint; (*sl.*) homosexual. —*n.* (*sl.*) homosexual. —*v.t.* spoil. **∼ a person's pitch,** spoil his chances.

quell *v.t.* suppress.

quench *v.t.* extinguish (a fire or flame) satisfy (one's thirst) by drinking something; cool by water.

quern *n.* hand-mill for grinding corn or pepper.

querulous /ˈkwe-/ *a.* complaining peevishly. **querulously** *adv.*, **querulousness** *n.*

query *n.* question; question mark. —*v.t.* ask a question or express doubt about.

quest *n.* seeking, search.

question *n.* sentence requesting information or an answer; matter for discussion or solution; raising of doubt. —*v.t.* ask or raise question(s) about. **in ∼,** being referred to or discussed or disputed. **no ∼ of,** no possibility of. **out of the ∼,** completely impracticable. **∼ mark,** punctuation mark ? placed after a question.

questionable *a.* open to doubt.

questionnaire *n.* list of questions seeking information.

queue *n.* line or series of people waiting for something. —*v.i.* (pres.p. *queuing*) wait in a queue.

quibble *n.* petty objection. —*v.i.* make petty objections.

quiche /kiʃ/ *n.* open tart, usu. with a savoury filling.

quick *a.* (-*er*, -*est*) taking only a short time; able to notice or learn or think quickly; (of temper) easily roused; (*old use*) alive. —*n.*

sensitive flesh below the nails. **quickly** *adv.*, **quickness** *n.*

quicken *v.t./i.* make or become quicker or livelier; reach the stage of pregnancy (the *quickening*) when the foetus makes movements that can be felt by the mother.

quicklime *n.* = lime¹.

quicksand *n.* area of loose wet deep sand into which heavy objects will sink.

quicksilver *n.* mercury.

quid¹ *n.* (pl. *quid*) (*sl.*) £1.

quid² *n.* lump of tobacco for chewing.

quiescent /kwɪˈes- *or* kwaɪ-/ *a.* inactive, quiet. **quiescence** *n.*

quiet *a.* (-*er*, -*est*) with little or no sound; free from disturbance or vigorous activity; silent; subdued. —*n.* quietness. —*v.t./i.* quieten. **on the ∼,** unobtrusively, secretly. **quietly** *adv.*, **quietness** *n.*

quieten *v.t./i.* make or become quiet.

quietude /ˈkwaɪ-/ *n.* quietness.

quiff *n.* upright tuft of hair.

quill *n.* large wing- or tail-feather; thing (esp. old type of pen) made from this; one of a porcupine's spines.

quilt *n.* padded bed-cover. —*v.t.* line with padding and fix with cross-lines of stitching.

quin *n.* quintuplet.

quince *n.* hard yellowish fruit; tree bearing this.

quincentenary /-ˈti-/ *n.* 500th anniversary.

quinine /-ˈnin/ *n.* bitter-tasting medicine.

quinquennial *a.* happening every fifth year; lasting five years.

quinsy *n.* abscess on a tonsil.

quintessence *n.* essence; perfect example of a quality.

quintet *n.* group of five instruments or voices; music for these.

quintuplet /-ˈtju-/ *n.* one of five children born at one birth.

quip *n.* witty or sarcastic remark. —*v.t.* (p.t. *quipped*) utter as a quip.

quirk *n.* a peculiarity of behaviour; trick of fate.

quisling *n.* traitor who collaborates with an enemy occupying his country.

quit *v.t./i.* (p.t. *quitted*) go away from; leave; abandon; (*colloq.*) cease. —*a.* rid. **quitter** *n.*

quite *adv.* completely; somewhat; really, actually; (as an answer) I agree. **∼ a few,** a considerable number.

quits *a.* on even terms after retaliation or repayment.

quiver¹ *n.* case for holding arrows.

quiver² *v.i.* shake or vibrate with a slight rapid motion. —*n.* quivering movement or sound.

quixotic /-ˈsot-/ *a.* chivalrous and unselfish. **quixotically** *adv.*

quiz *n.* (pl. *quizzes*) series of questions testing knowledge, esp. as an entertainment. —*v.t.* (p.t. *quizzed*) interrogate; (*old use*) stare at.

quizzical *a.* done in a questioning way, esp. humorously. **quizzically** *adv.*

quod *n.* (*sl.*) prison.

quoit /kɔɪt/ *n.* ring of metal or rubber etc. thrown to encircle a peg in the game of *quoits*.

quorum *n.* minimum number of people that must be present to constitute a valid meeting.

quota *n.* fixed share; maximum number or amount that may be admitted, manufactured, etc.

quotation *n.* quoting; passage or price quoted.

~-marks *n.pl.* punctuation marks (' ' or " ") enclosing words quoted.

quote *v.t./i.* repeat words from a book or speech; mention in support of a statement; state the price of, estimate.

quoth /kwəʊθ/ (*old use*) said.

quotient /ˈkwəʊʃənt/ *n.* result of a division sum.

R

rabbi /-baɪ/ *n.* (pl. *-is*) religious leader of a Jewish congregation.

rabbinical /-ˈbɪn-/ *a.* of rabbis or Jewish doctrines or law.

rabbit *n.* burrowing animal with long ears and a short furry tail.

rabble *n.* disorderly crowd, mob.

rabid /ˈræ-/ *a.* furious, fanatical; affected with rabies. **rabidity** *n.*

rabies /ˈreɪbiz/ *n.* contagious fatal virus disease of dogs etc., that can be transmitted to man.

race[1] *n.* contest of speed; strong fast current of water; channel for balls in a ball-bearing; (*pl.*) series of races for horses or dogs. *—v.t./i.* compete in a race (with); engage in horse-racing; move or operate at full or excessive speed. **~-track** *n.* track for horse or car etc. races.

race[2] *n.* one of the great divisions of mankind with certain inherited physical characteristics in common; large group of people related by common descent; genus, species, breed, or variety of animals or plants.

racecourse *n.* ground where horse-races are run.

racehorse *n.* horse bred for racing.

racial *a.* of or based on race. **racially** *adv.*

racialism *n.* belief in the superiority of a particular race; antagonism between races. **racialist** *a.* & *n.*

racism *n.* racialism; theory that human abilities are determined by race. **racist** *a.* & *n.*

rack[1] *n.* framework, usu. with bars or pegs, for keeping or placing things on; bar or rail with teeth or cogs that engage with those of a wheel or gear etc.; instrument of torture on which people were tied and stretched. *—v.t.* inflict great torment on. **~ one's brains**, think hard about a problem.

rack[2] *n.* **~ and ruin**, destruction.

rack[3] *v.t.* draw (wine or beer) off the lees.

racket[1] *n.* stringed bat used in tennis and similar games; (*pl.*) ball-game played with rackets in a four-walled court.

racket[2] *n.* din, noisy fuss; fraudulent business or other activity; (*sl.*) line of business, dodge.

racketeer *n.* person who operates a fraudulent business etc.

raconteur /-ˈtɜ(r)/ *n.* person who is good at telling anecdotes.

racy *a.* (*-ier*, *-iest*) spirited and vigorous in style. **racily** *adv.*

radar *n.* system for detecting objects by means of radio waves.

radial *a.* of rays or radii; having spokes or lines etc. that radiate from a central point.

radiant *a.* emitting rays of light or heat; emitted in rays; looking very bright and happy. **radiantly** *adv.*, **radiance** *n.*

radiate *v.t./i.* spread outwards from a central point; send or be sent out in rays.

radiation *n.* process of radiating; sending out of rays and atomic particles characteristic of radioactive substances; these rays and particles.

radiator *n.* apparatus that radiates heat, esp. a metal case through which steam or hot water circulates; engine-cooling apparatus.

radical *a.* fundamental; drastic, thorough; holding extremist views. *—n.* person desiring radical reforms or holding radical views. **radically** *adv.*

radicle *n.* embryo root (e.g. of pea or bean).

radio *n.* (pl. *-os*) process of sending and receiving messages etc. by electromagnetic waves without a connecting wire; transmitter or receiver for this; sound-broadcasting, station for this. *—a.* of or involving radio. *—v.t.* send, signal, or communicate by radio.

radioactive *a.* sending out radiation that produces electrical and chemical effects. **radioactivity** *n.*

radio-carbon *n.* radioactive form of carbon used in dating ancient organic remains.

radiogram *n.* combined radio and record-player.

radiography /-ˈɒg-/ *n.* production of X-ray photographs. **radiographer** *n.*

radiology /-ˈɒl-/ *n.* study of X-rays and similar radiation. **radiologist** *n.*

radiotherapy *n.* treatment of disease by X-rays or similar radiation.

radish *n.* plant with a crisp hot-tasting root that is eaten raw.

radium *n.* radioactive metal obtained from pitchblende.

radius *n.* (pl. *-dii*, pr. *-dɪaɪ*) straight line from the centre to the circumference of a circle or sphere; its length; distance from a centre; bone in the forearm.

R.A.F. *abbr.* Royal Air Force.

raffia *n.* strips of fibre from the leaves of a kind of palm-tree.

raffish *a.* looking vulgarly flashy or rakish. **raffishness** *n.*

raffle *n.* lottery with an object as the prize. *—v.t.* offer as the prize in a raffle.

raft *n.* flat floating structure of timber etc., used as a boat.

rafter *n.* one of the sloping beams forming the framework of a roof.

rag¹ *n.* torn or worn piece of woven fabric; (*derog.*) newspaper; (*pl.*) old and torn clothes.

rag² *v.t.* (p.t. *ragged*) (*sl.*) tease. —*n.* (*sl.*) practical joke, piece of fun; students' carnival in aid of charity.

ragamuffin *n.* person in ragged dirty clothes.

rage *n.* violent anger; craze, fashion. —*v.i.* show violent anger; (of a storm or battle) continue furiously.

ragged /-gɪd/ *a.* torn, frayed; wearing torn clothes; jagged; faulty, lacking uniformity.

raglan *n.* type of sleeve joined to a garment by sloping seams.

ragout /ˈræguˈ/ *n.* stew of meat and vegetables.

ragtime *n.* a form of jazz music with much syncopation.

raid *n.* brief attack to destroy or seize or steal something; surprise visit by police etc. to arrest suspected people or seize illicit goods. —*v.t.* make a raid on. **raider** *n.*

rail¹ *n.* horizontal or sloping bar; one of the lines of metal bars on which trains or trams run; railway(s). —*v.t.* fit or protect with a rail.

rail² *n.* small wading bird.

rail³ *v.i.* utter angry reproaches.

railing *n.* fence of rails supported on upright metal bars.

raillery *n.* banter, joking.

railroad *n.* (*U.S.*) railway.—*v.t.* force into hasty action.

railway *n.* set of rails on which trains run; system of transport using these. **railwayman** *n.* (pl. *-men*).

raiment *n.* (*old use*) clothing.

rain *n.* atmospheric moisture falling as separate drops; a fall or spell of this; shower of things. —*v.t./i.* send down or fall as or like rain.

rainbow *n.* arch of colours formed in rain or spray by the sun's rays.

raincoat *n.* water-resistant coat.

raindrop *n.* single drop of rain.

rainfall *n.* total amount of rain falling in a given time.

rainwater *n.* water that has fallen as rain.

rainy *a.* (*-ier*, *-iest*) in or on which much rain falls.

raise *v.t.* bring to or towards a higher level or an upright position; cause, rouse; breed, grow; bring up (a child or family); collect, procure; end (a siege). —*n.* (*U.S.*) increase in salary etc. **raising agent,** substance that makes bread etc. swell in cooking.

raisin *n.* dried grape.

raison d'être /reɪzɔ̃ ˈdeɪtr/ reason for or purpose of a thing's existence.

rajah /ˈrɑdʒə/ *n.* Indian prince.

rake¹ *n.* tool with prongs for drawing together hay etc. or for smoothing loose soil; implement used similarly. —*v.t.* gather or smooth with a rake; search; direct (gunfire, a scrutiny, etc.) along. **~-off** *n.* (*colloq.*) commission, share of profits. **~ up,** revive the memory of (an unpleasant incident).

rake² *n.* backward slope of an object. —*v.t.* set at a sloping angle.

rake³ *n.* man who lives an irresponsible and immoral life.

rakish *a.* like a rake (= rake³); jaunty.

rally *v.t./i.* bring or come together for a united effort; reassemble for effort after defeat; rouse, revive; recover strength. —*n.* act of rallying, recovery; series of strokes in tennis etc.; mass meeting; driving competition over public roads.

ram *n.* uncastrated male sheep; striking or plunging device. —*v.t.* (p.t. *rammed*) strike or push heavily, crash against. **rammer** *n.*

Ramadan /-ˈdan/ *n.* ninth month of the Muslim year, when Muslims fast during daylight hours.

ramble *n.* walk taken for pleasure. —*v.i.* take a ramble; wander, straggle; talk or write disconnectedly. **rambler** *n.*

ramekin /ˈræmɪ-/ *n.* small mould for baking an individual portion of food.

ramification *n.* part of a complex structure or scheme etc.

ramp¹ *n.* slope joining two levels; movable set of stairs for entering or leaving an aircraft.

ramp² *n.* (*sl.*) swindle, racket.

rampage¹ /-ˈpeɪdʒ/ *v.i.* behave or race about violently.

rampage² /ˈræm-/ *n.* violent behaviour. **on the ~,** rampaging.

rampant *a.* flourishing excessively, unrestrained; (of a heraldic animal) standing on one hind leg with the opposite foreleg raised.

rampart *n.* broad-topped defensive wall or bank of earth.

ramrod *n.* like a ~, stiff and straight.

ramshackle *n.* tumbledown, rickety.

ran *see* **run**.

ranch *n.* cattle-breeding establishment in North America; farm where certain other animals are bred. —*v.i.* farm on a ranch. **rancher** *n.*

rancid *a.* smelling or tasting like stale fat. **rancidity** *n.*

rancour /-kə(r)/ *n.* bitter feeling or ill will. **rancorous** *a.*

rand *n.* unit of money in South African countries.

random *a.* done or made etc. at random.—*n.* **at ~,** without a particular aim or purpose. **randomness** *n.*

randy *a.* (*-ier*, *-iest*) lustful; (*Sc.*) boisterous. **randiness** *n.*

rang *see* **ring**².

range *n.* line or series of things; limits between which something operates or varies; distance a thing can travel or be effective; distance to an objective; large open area for grazing or hunting; place with targets for shooting-practice; fireplace with ovens etc. for cooking in. —*v.t./i.* arrange in row(s) etc.; extend, reach; vary between limits; wander, go about a place. **~-finder** *n.* device for calculating the distance to a target etc.

ranger n. keeper of a royal park or forest; *R~*, senior Guide.

rangy a. (-ier, -iest) tall and thin.

rank¹ n. line of people or things; place in a scale of quality or value etc.; high social position; (*pl.*) ordinary soldiers, not officers. —*v.t./i.* arrange in a rank; assign a rank to; have a certain rank. **the ~ and file,** the ordinary people of an organization.

rank² a. (-er, -est) growing too thickly and coarsely; full of weeds; foul-smelling; unmistakably bad, out-and-out. **rankness** n.

rankle v.i. cause lasting resentment.

ransack v.t. search thoroughly or roughly; rob or pillage (a place).

ransom n. price demanded or paid for the release of a captive. —*v.t.* demand or pay ransom for.

rant v.i. make a violent speech.

rap n. quick sharp blow; knocking sound; (*sl.*) blame, punishment. —*v.t./i.* (p.t. *rapped*) strike with a rap; make a knocking sound; (*sl.*) reprimand. **~ out,** say sharply.

rapacious a. grasping, plundering and robbing others. **rapacity** a.

rape¹ v.t. have sexual intercourse with (a woman) without her consent. —n. this act or crime.

rape² n. plant grown as food for sheep and for its seed from which oil is obtained.

rapid a. quick, swift. **rapidly** adv., **rapidity** n.

rapids n.pl. swift current where a river-bed slopes steeply.

rapier n. thin light double-edged sword, used for thrusting.

rapist n. person who commits rape.

rapport /-ˈpɔ(r)/ n. harmonious understanding relationship.

rapt a. very intent and absorbed, enraptured. **raptly** adv.

rapture n. intense delight. **rapturous** a., **rapturously** adv.

rare¹ a. (-er, -est) very uncommon; exceptionally good; of low density. **rarely** adv., **rareness** n.

rare² a. (-er, -est) (of meat) cooked lightly not thoroughly.

rarebit n. Welsh ~, melted or toasted cheese on toast.

rarefied /ˈreərɪfaɪd/ a. (of air etc.) of low density, thin.

raring a. (*colloq.*) eager (to go etc.).

rarity n. rareness; rare thing.

rascal n. dishonest or mischievous person. **rascally** adv.

raschel /rəˈʃel/ n. loosely knitted textile fabric.

rash¹ n. eruption of spots or patches on the skin.

rash² a. (-er, -est) acting or done without due consideration of the risks. **rashly** adv., **rashness** n.

rasher n. slice of bacon or ham.

rasp n. coarse file; rough grating sound. —*v.t./i.* scrape with a rasp; utter with or make a grating sound or effect.

raspberry n. edible red berry; plant bearing this; (*sl.*) vulgar sound of disapproval.

Rastafarian /-ˈfeər-/ n. member of a Jamaican sect.

rat n. rodent like a mouse but larger; scoundrel, treacherous deserter. —*v.i.* (p.t. *ratted*) ~ **on,** desert treacherously. ~ **race,** fiercely competitive struggle for success.

ratafia /-ˈfiə/ n. liqueur or biscuit flavoured with fruit kernels.

ratchet n. bar or wheel with notches in which a pawl engages to prevent backward movement.

rate n. standard of reckoning, ratio of one quantity or amount etc. to another; rapidity; local tax assessed on the value of land and buildings, (*pl.*) amount payable. —*v.t./i.* estimate the worth or value of; consider, regard as; (*U.S.*) deserve; levy rates on, value for this purpose. **at any ~,** no matter what happens; at least.

rateable a. liable to or assessed for rates (= local tax).

ratepayer n. person liable to pay rates (= local tax).

rather adv. slightly; more exactly; by preference; emphatically yes.

ratify v.t. confirm (an agreement etc.) formally. **ratification** n.

rating n. level at which a thing is rated; amount payable as local rates; non-commissioned sailor.

ratio /ˈreɪʃɪəʊ/ n. (pl. -os) relationship between two amounts, reckoned as the number of times one contains the other.

ration n. fixed allowance of food etc. —*v.t.* limit to a ration.

rational a. able to reason; sane; based on reasoning, not unreasonable. **rationally** adv., **rationality** n.

rationale /-ˈnɑl/ n. fundamental reason; logical basis.

rationalize v.t. make logical and consistent; invent a rational explanation for; make more efficient by reorganizing. **rationalization** n.

rattle v.t./i. make or cause to make a rapid series of short hard sounds; (*sl.*) make nervous. —n. rattling sound; device or toy for making this; noise. ~ **off,** utter rapidly.

rattlesnake n. poisonous American snake with a rattling tail.

rattling a. that rattles; vigorous, brisk. —adv. (*colloq.*) very.

ratty a. (-ier, -iest) (*sl.*) angry.

raucous a. loud and harsh. **raucously** adv., **raucousness** n.

raunchy a. (-ier, -iest) (*U.S.*) slovenly, disreputable; coarsely outspoken; boisterous. **raunchily** adv.

ravage v.t. do great damage to.

ravages n.pl. damage.

rave v.i. talk wildly or furiously; speak with rapturous enthusiasm.

ravel v.t./i. (p.t. *ravelled*) tangle.

raven n. large black bird with a hoarse cry. —a. (of hair) glossy black.

ravening /ˈræ-/ a. hungrily seeking prey.

ravenous a. very hungry. **ravenously** adv.

ravine /-'vin/ n. deep narrow gorge.

raving a. completely (mad); notable.

ravioli n. Italian dish of small pasta cases containing meat.

ravish v.t. rape; enrapture.

raw a. (-er, -est) not cooked; not yet processed or manufactured; (of alcohol) undiluted; crude, lacking finish; inexperienced, untrained; stripped of skin, sensitive because of this; (of an edge of cloth) with loose threads; (of weather) damp and chilly. —n. raw sensitive patch of skin. ∼-**boned** a. gaunt. ∼ **deal**, unfair treatment. **rawness** n.

rawhide n. untanned leather.

ray[1] n. single line or narrow beam of radiation; trace (of hope etc.); radiating line or part or thing.

ray[2] n. large sea-fish used as food; skate.

rayon n. synthetic fibre or fabric, made from cellulose.

raze v.t. tear down (a building).

razor n. sharp-edged instrument used esp. for shaving hair from the skin.

razzle n. **on the** ∼, (sl.) on the spree.

R.C. abbr. Roman Catholic.

re /ri/ prep. concerning.

re- pref. again; back again.

reach v.t./i. extend, be continuous; go as far as, arrive at; stretch out a hand in order to touch or take; establish communication with; achieve, attain. —n. distance over which a person or thing can reach; extent of abilities etc.; section of a river or canal. **reachable** a.

react v.i. cause or undergo a reaction.

reaction n. response to a stimulus or act or situation etc.; chemical change produced by substances acting upon each other; occurrence of one condition after a period of the opposite.

reactionary a. & n. (person) opposed to progress and reform.

reactor n. apparatus for the production of nuclear energy.

read /rid/ v.t./i. (p.t. read, pr. red) understand the meaning of (written or printed words or symbols); speak (such words etc.) aloud; study or discover by reading; interpret mentally; have as wording; (of an instrument) indicate as a measurement. —n. (colloq.) session of reading.

readable a. pleasant to read; legible.

readdress v.t. redirect by altering the address.

reader n. person who reads; senior lecturer at a university; book containing passages for reading as an exercise; device producing a readable image from a microfilm etc.

readily adv. willingly; easily.

readiness n. being ready.

readjust v.t./i. adjust again; adapt oneself again. **readjustment** n.

ready a. (-ier, -iest) fit or available for action or use; willing; about or inclined (to do something); quick. —adv. beforehand. **at the** ∼, ready for action. ∼-**made** a. (of clothes) made in standard sizes, not to individual orders. ∼

reckoner, collection of answers to calculations commonly needed in business etc.

reagent /rɪ'eɪ-/ n. substance used to produce a chemical reaction.

real a. existing as a thing or occurring as a fact; genuine, natural; (of property) immovable, as land or houses. —adv. (Sc. & U.S. colloq.) really, very.

realism n. representing or viewing things as they are in reality. **realist** n.

realistic a. showing realism; (of wages or prices) paying the worker or seller adequately. **realistically** adv.

reality n. quality of being real; thing or all that is real and not imagination or fantasy.

realize v.t. be or become aware of; accept as a fact; fulfil (a hope or plan); obtain money by selling (securities etc.); fetch as a price. **realization** n.

really adv. in fact; thoroughly; indeed, I assure you, I protest.

realm n. kingdom; field of activity or interest.

ream n. quantity of paper (usu. 500 sheets); (pl.) great quantity of written matter.

reap v.t. cut (grain etc.) as harvest; receive as the consequence of actions. **reaper** n.

reappear v.i. appear again.

reappraisal n. new appraisal.

rear[1] n. back part. —a. situated at the rear. **bring up the** ∼, be last in an advancing line. ∼-**admiral** n. naval officer next below viceadmiral. **rearmost** a.

rear[2] v.t./i. bring up (children); breed and look after (animals); cultivate (crops); set up; (of a horse etc.) raise itself on its hind legs; extend to a great height.

rearguard n. troops protecting an army's rear.

rearm v.t./i. arm again. **rearmament** n.

rearrange v.t. arrange in a different way. **rearrangement** n.

reason n. motive, cause, justification; ability to think and draw conclusions; sanity; good sense or judgement, what is right or practical or possible. —v.t./i. use one's ability to think and draw conclusions. ∼ **with,** try to persuade by argument.

reasonable a. ready to use or listen to reason; in accordance with reason, logical; moderate, not expensive. **reasonably** adv.

reassemble v.t./i. assemble again.

reassure v.t. restore confidence to, remove the fears or doubts of. **reassurance** n.

rebate /'ri-/ n. partial refund.

rebel[1] /'reb-/ n. person who rebels.

rebel[2] /-'bel/ v.i. (p.t. rebelled) fight against or refuse allegiance to one's established government; resist control, refuse to obey. **rebellion** n., **rebellious** a.

rebound[1] /-'baʊnd/ v.i. spring back after impact.

rebound[2] /'ri-/ n. act of rebounding. **on the** ∼, while rebounding; while still reacting to a disappointment etc.

rebuff v.t. & n. snub.

rebuild v.t. (p.t. rebuilt) build again after destruction.

rebuke *v.t.* reprove. —*n.* reproof.

rebut *v.t.* (p.t. *rebutted*) disprove. **rebuttal** *n.*

recalcitrant /-ˈkæl-/ *a.* obstinately disobedient. **recalcitrance** *n.*

recall *v.t.* summon to return; remember, cause oneself to remember. —*n.* recalling, being recalled.

recant *v.t./i.* withdraw and reject (one's former statement or belief). **recantation** *n.*

recap /ˈriː-/ *v.t.* (p.t. *recapped*) (*colloq.*) recapitulate. —*n.* (*colloq.*) recapitulation.

recapitulate *v.t./i.* state again the main points of (a statement or discussion). **recapitulation** *n.*

recapture *v.t.* capture again. —*n.* recapturing.

recce /ˈrekɪ/ *n.* (*colloq.*) reconnaissance.

recede *v.i.* go or shrink back; become more distant; slope backwards.

receipt /-ˈsiːt/ *n.* act of receiving; written acknowledgement that something has been received or money paid. —*v.t.* mark (a bill) as having been paid.

receive *v.t.* acquire, accept, or take in (a thing offered or sent or given); experience, be treated with; allow to enter; greet on arrival.

receiver *n.* person or thing that receives something; one who receives stolen goods; official who administers a bankrupt or insane person's property; apparatus that receives broadcast signals and converts them into sound or a picture; the part of a telephone that receives incoming sound.

recent *a.* happening or begun in a time shortly before the present. **recently** *adv.*

receptacle *n.* thing for holding what is put into it.

reception *n.* act or process or way of receiving; assembly held to receive guests; place where clients etc. are received on arrival.

receptionist *n.* person employed to receive and direct clients etc.

receptive *a.* quick to receive ideas. **receptiveness** *n.*, **receptivity** *n.*

recess /-ˈses/ *n.* part or space set back from the line of a wall or room etc.; temporary cessation from business. —*v.t.* make a recess in or of.

recession *n.* receding from a point or level; temporary decline in economic activity or prosperity.

recessive *a.* tending to recede.

recherché /rəˈʃeəʃeɪ/ *a.* devised or selected with care; far-fetched.

recidivist /-ˈsɪd-/ *n.* person who persistently relapses into crime.

recipe *n.* directions for preparing a dish etc. in cookery; way of achieving something.

recipient *n.* person who receives something.

reciprocal *a.* both given and received. —*n.* mathematical expression related to another as $\frac{2}{3}$ is related to $\frac{3}{2}$. **reciprocally** *adv.*, **reciprocity** *n.*

reciprocate *v.i.* give and receive; make a return for something; move backward and forward alternately. **reciprocation** *n.*

recital *n.* reciting; long account of events; musical entertainment.

recitation *n.* reciting; thing recited.

recitative /-ˈtiːv/ *n.* narrative or dialogue sung in a rhythm imitating that of ordinary speech.

recite *v.t.* repeat aloud from memory; state (facts) in order.

reckless *a.* wildly impulsive. **recklessly** *adv.*, **recklessness** *n.*

reckon *v.t./i.* count up; include in a total or class; have as one's opinion; rely. ∼ **with,** take into account.

reckoner *n.* aid to reckoning.

reclaim *v.t.* take action to recover possession of; make (flooded or waste land) usable. **reclamation** *n.*

recline *v.t./i.* lean (one's body), lie down.

recluse /-ˈkluːs/ *n.* person who avoids social life.

recognition *n.* recognizing.

recognizance /-ˈkɒg-/ *n.* pledge made to a lawcourt or magistrate; surety for this.

recognize *v.t.* know again from one's previous experience; realize, admit; acknowledge as genuine or valid or worthy. **recognizable** *a.*

recoil *v.i.* spring back; shrink in fear or disgust; have an adverse effect (on the originator). —*n.* act of recoiling.

recollect /rek-/ *v.t.* remember, call to mind. **recollection** *n.*

recommend *v.t.* advise; praise as worthy of employment or use etc.; (of qualities etc.) make acceptable or desirable. **recommendation** *n.*

recompense /ˈrek-/ *v.t.* make a repayment to, compensate. —*n.* repayment.

reconcile *v.t.* make friendly after an estrangement; induce to tolerate something unwelcome; make compatible. **reconciliation** *n.*

recondite /ˈrekəndaɪt/ *a.* obscure, dealing with an obscure subject.

recondition *v.t.* overhaul, repair.

reconnaissance /-ˈkɒnɪs-/ *n.* preliminary survey, esp. exploration of an area for military purposes.

reconnoitre *v.t./i.* (pres.p. *-tring*) make a reconnaissance (of).

reconsider *v.t./i.* consider again, esp. for a possible change of decision. **reconsideration** *n.*

reconstitute *v.t.* reconstruct; restore to its original form. **reconstitution** *n.*

reconstruct *v.t.* construct or build or enact again. **reconstruction** *n.*

record[1] /-ˈkɔːd/ *v.t.* set down in writing or other permanent form; preserve (sound) on a disc or magnetic tape for later reproduction; (of a measuring instrument) indicate, register.

record[2] /ˈrek-/ *n.* information set down in writing or other permanent form; document etc. bearing this; disc bearing recorded sound; facts known about a person's past; best performance or most remarkable event etc. of its kind. —*a.* best or most extreme hitherto recorded. **off the ∼,** unofficially or not for publication. **∼-player** *n.* apparatus for reproducing recorded sound from discs.

recorder *n.* person or thing that records something; judge in certain lawcourts; a kind of flute.

recordist /-ˈkɔ-/ n. person who records sounds.

recount v.t. narrate, tell in detail.

re-count v.t. count again. —n. second or subsequent counting.

recoup /-ˈkup/ v.t. reimburse or compensate (for).

recourse n. source of help. **have ∼ to,** turn to for help.

recover v.t./i. regain possession or use or control of; obtain as compensation; return to health or consciousness. **recovery** n.

recreation /rek-/ n. pastime; relaxation. **recreational** a.

recrimination n. angry accusation in retaliation. **recriminatory** a.

recrudesce /-ˈdes/ v.i. (of disease or discontent) break out again. **recrudescence** n.

recruit n. new member, esp. of the armed forces. —v.t. form (an army etc.) by enlisting recruits; enlist as a recruit; refresh (one's strength etc.). **recruitment** n.

rectal a. of the rectum.

rectangle n. geometric figure with four sides and four right angles, esp. with adjacent sides unequal in length. **rectangular** a.

rectify v.t. put right; purify, refine; convert to direct current. **rectification** n.

rectilinear a. bounded by straight lines.

rectitude n. correctness of behaviour or procedure.

rector n. clergyman in charge of a parish; head of certain schools, colleges, and universities.

rectory n. house of a rector.

rectum n. last section of the intestine, between colon and anus.

recumbent a. lying down, reclining.

recuperate v.t./i. recover (health, strength, or losses). **recuperation** n.

recuperative a. of recuperation.

recur v.i. (p.t. *recurred*) happen again or repeatedly.

recurrent /-ˈkʌ-/ a. recurring. **recurrence** n.

recurve v.t./i. bend backwards.

recycle v.t./i. convert (waste material) for re-use.

red a. (*redder, reddest*) of or like the colour of blood; (of hair) reddish-brown; Communist, favouring Communism. —n. red colour or thing; Communist. **in the ∼,** having a debit balance, in debt. **∼ carpet,** privileged treatment for an important visitor. **Red Cross,** international organization for the care of people wounded in war or afflicted by great natural disasters. **∼-handed** a. in the act of crime. **∼ herring,** misleading clue or diversion. **∼-hot** a. glowing red from heat; (of news) completely new. **Red Indian,** North American Indian, with reddish skin. **∼-letter day,** day of a very joyful occurrence. **∼ light,** signal to stop; danger-signal. **∼ tape,** excessive formalities in official transactions. **redly** adv., **redness** n.

redbreast n. robin.

redbrick a. (of universities) founded in the 19th century or later.

redden v.t./i. make or become red.

reddish a. rather red.

redeem v.t. buy back; convert (tokens etc.) into goods or cash; reclaim; save from the consequences of sin; make up for (faults). **redemption** n.

Redeemer n. Christ, who redeemed mankind.

redeploy v.t. send to a new place or task. **redeployment** n.

redhead n. person with red hair.

rediffusion n. relaying of broadcasts, from a central receiver.

redirect v.t. direct or send to another place. **redirection** n.

redolent a. smelling strongly; reminiscent, suggestive. **redolence** n.

redouble v.t. double again.

redoubt n. outwork without flanking defences.

redoubtable /-ˈdaʊt-/ a. formidable.

redound v.i. come back as an advantage or disadvantage, accrue.

redress v.i. set right. —n. reparation, amends.

redstart n. song-bird with a red tail.

reduce v.t./i. make or become less; make lower in rank; slim; subdue; bring into a specified state; convert into a simpler or more general form; restore (a fractured bone) to its proper position. **reduction** n., **reducible** a.

redundant a. superfluous; no longer needed. **redundancy** n.

reduplicate v.t. repeat (a letter or syllable). **reduplication** n.

redwood n. very tall evergreen Californian tree; its reddish wood.

re-echo v.t./i. echo; echo repeatedly; resound.

reed n. water or marsh plant with tall hollow stems; its stem; vibrating part producing sound in certain wind instruments.

reedy a. (of the voice) having a thin high tone. **reediness** n.

reef n. ridge of rock or sand etc. reaching to or near the surface of water; one of the strips at the top or bottom of a sail, that can be drawn in when there is a high wind. —v.t. shorten (a sail) by drawing in a reef. **∼-knot** n. symmetrical double knot.

reefer n. thick double-breasted jacket; (*sl.*) marijuana cigarette.

reek n. strong usu. unpleasant smell. —v.i. smell strongly.

reel n. cylinder or similar device on which something is wound; lively Scottish or folk dance. —v.t./i. wind on or off a reel; stagger. **∼ off,** rattle off without effort.

refectory /-ˈfek-/ n. dining-room of a monastery or college etc.

refer v.t./i. (p.t. *referred*) **∼ to,** mention; direct to an authority or specialist; turn to for information.

referee n. umpire, esp. in football and boxing; person to whom disputes are referred for decision; person willing to testify to the character or ability of one applying for a job. —v.t. (p.t. *refereed*) act as referee in (a match etc.).

reference n. act of referring; mention; relation, correspondence; direction to a source of information, this source; testimonial; person willing to testify to another's character, ability, etc. **in** *or* **with ～ to,** in connection with, about. **～ book,** book providing information for reference. **～ library,** one containing books that can be consulted but not taken away.

referendum *n.* (pl. *-ums*) referring of a question to the people for decision by a general vote.

referral /-'fɜ-/ *n.* referring.

refill[1] /-'fɪl/ *v.t./i.* fill again.

refill[2] /'ri-/ *n.* second or later filling; material used for this.

refine *v.t.* remove impurities or defects from; make elegant or cultured. **refined** *a.*

refinement *n.* refining; elegance of behaviour; improvement added to something; fine distinction.

refiner *n.* one who refines crude oil or metal or sugar etc.

refinery *n.* establishment where crude substances are refined.

refit[1] /-'fɪt/ *v.t.* (p.t. *refitted*) renew or repair the fittings of. **refitment** *n.*

refit[2] /'ri-/ *n.* refitment.

reflate *v.t.* restore (a financial system) after deflation. **reflation** *n.*, **reflationary** *a.*

reflect *v.t./i.* throw back (light, heat, or sound), be thrown back; show an image of; correspond to in appearance or effect; bring (credit or discredit); bring discredit; think deeply, remind oneself of past events.

reflective *a.* reflecting; thoughtful.

reflector *n.* thing that reflects light or heat.

reflex /'ri-/ *n.* reflex action; reflex camera. —*a.* bent backwards. **～ action,** involuntary or instinctive movement in response to a stimulus. **～ angle,** angle of more than 180°. **～ camera,** one in which the image given by the lens is reflected to the viewfinder.

reflexive *a.* & *n.* (word or form) showing that the action of the verb is performed on its subject (e.g. *he washed himself*).

reform *v.t./i.* improve by removing faults. —*n.* reforming. **reformer** *n.*

reformation *n.* reforming; *the R～,* 16th-century movement for reform of certain practices in the Church of Rome, resulting in the establishment of Reformed or Protestant Churches.

refract *v.t.* bend (a ray of light) where it enters water or glass etc. obliquely. **refraction** *n.*, **refractor** *n.*, **refractive** *a.*

refractory *a.* resisting control or discipline; resistant to treatment or heat.

refrain[1] *n.* recurring lines of a song; music for these.

refrain[2] *v.i.* keep oneself from doing something.

refresh *v.t.* restore the vigour of by food or drink or rest; stimulate (a person's memory) by reminding him.

refresher *n.* **～ course,** course of instruction to renew or increase a qualified person's knowledge.

refreshing *a.* restoring vigour, cooling; interesting because of its novelty.

refreshment *n.* process of refreshing; thing that refreshes, (usu. *pl.*) food and drink.

refrigerate *v.t.* make extremely cold, esp. in order to preserve and store (food). **refrigeration** *n.*

refrigerator *n.* cabinet or room in which food is stored at a very low temperature.

refuel *v.t.* (p.t. *refuelled*) replenish the fuel supply of.

refuge *n.* shelter from pursuit or danger or trouble.

refugee *n.* person who has left his home and seeks refuge (e.g. from war or persecution) elsewhere.

refund[1] /-'fʌnd/ *v.t.* pay back.

refund[2] /'ri-/ *n.* repayment, money refunded.

refurbish *v.t.* make clean or bright again, redecorate.

refuse[1] /-'fjuz/ *v.t./i.* say or show that one is unwilling to accept or give or do (what is asked or required). **refusal** *n.*

refuse[2] /'ref-/ *n.* waste material.

refute *v.t.* prove (a statement or person) to be wrong. **refutation** *n.*

regain *v.t.* obtain again after loss; reach again.

regal *a.* like or fit for a king. **regally** *adv.*, **regality** *n.*

regale *v.t.* feed or entertain well.

regalia /-'geɪ-/ *n.pl.* emblems of royalty or rank.

regard *v.t.* look steadily at; consider to be. —*n.* steady gaze; heed; respect; (*pl.*) kindly greetings conveyed in a message. **as regards,** regarding.

regarding *prep.* with reference to.

regardless *adv.* heedlessly.

regatta *n.* boat or yacht races organized as a sporting event.

regency *n.* rule by a regent; period of this; *the R～,* 1810–20 in England.

regenerate *v.t.* give new life or vigour to. **regeneration** *n.*

regent *n.* person appointed to rule while the monarch is a minor or ill or absent.

reggae /'regeɪ/ *n.* West Indian style of music.

regime /reɪ'ʒim/ *n.* method or system of government or adminstration.

regiment *n.* permanent unit of an army; operational unit of artillery, tanks, etc.; large array or number of things. —*v.t.* organize rigidly. **regimentation** *n.*

regimental *a.* of an army regiment.

regimentals *n.pl.* regimental uniform.

Regina /rɪ'dʒaɪ-/ *n.* reigning queen.

region *n.* continuous part of a surface or space or body; administrative division of a country. **in the ～ of,** approximately. **regional** *a.*

register *n.* official list; mechanical device indicating numbers or speed etc.; adjustable plate regulating the size of an opening; range of a voice or musical instrument. —*v.t./i.* enter in a register; record in writing, present for consideration; notice and remember; indicate, record; make an impression. **～ office,** place where records of births, marriages, and deaths are kept and marriages are performed by a registrar. **registration** *n.*

registrar *n.* official responsible for keeping written records; judicial and administrative officer of the High Court; hospital doctor ranking just below specialist.

registry *n.* registration; place where written records are kept. ~ **office,** register office.

regression *n.* relapse to an earlier or more primitive state. **regressive** *a.*

regret *n.* feeling of sorrow about a loss, or of annoyance or repentance. —*v.t.* (p.t. *regretted*) feel regret about. **regretful** *a.*, **regretfully** *adv.*

regrettable *a.* that is to be regretted. **regrettably** *adv.*

regular *a.* acting or occurring or done in a uniform manner or constantly at a fixed time or interval; conforming to a rule or habit; even, symmetrical; forming a country's permanent armed forces; (*colloq.*) thorough. —*n.* regular soldier etc.; (*colloq.*) regular customer or visitor etc. **regularly** *adv.*, **regularity** *n.*

regularize *v.t.* make regular; make lawful or correct. **regularization** *n.*

regulate *v.t.* control by rules; adjust to work correctly or according to one's requirements. **regulator** *n.*

regulation *n.* process of regulating; rule.

regurgitate *v.t.* bring (swallowed food) up again to the mouth; cast out again. **regurgitation** *n.*

rehabilitate *v.t.* restore to a normal life or good condition. **rehabilitation** *n.*

rehash[1] /-'hæʃ/ *v.t.* put (old material) into a new form with no great change or improvement.

rehash[2] /'ri-/ *n.* rehashing; thing made of rehashed material.

rehearse *v.t./i.* practise or train beforehand; enumerate. **rehearsal** *n.*

rehouse *v.t.* provide with new accommodation.

reign *n.* sovereignty, rule. —*v.i.* rule as king or queen; be supreme.

reimburse *v.t.* repay (a person), refund. **reimbursement** *n.*

rein *n.* (also *pl.*) long narrow strap fastened to the bit of a bridle, used to guide or check a horse; means of control. —*v.t.* check or control with reins.

reincarnation *n.* incarnation of the soul in another body after death of the first. **reincarnate** *a.* & *v.t.*

reindeer *n.* (pl. *reindeer*) deer of arctic regions, with large antlers.

reinforce *v.t.* strengthen with additional men or material or quantity. **reinforcement** *n.*

reinstate *v.t.* restore to a previous position. **reinstatement** *n.*

reiterate *v.t.* say or do again or repeatedly. **reiteration** *n.*

reject[1] /-'dʒekt/ *v.t.* refuse to accept; react against. **rejection** *n.*

reject[2] /'ri-/ *n.* person or thing rejected.

rejig *v.t.* (p.t. *rejigged*) re-equip for a new type of work.

rejoice *v.t./i.* feel or show great joy; gladden.

rejoin *v.t.* join again; say in answer, retort.

rejoinder *n.* answer, retort.

rejuvenate *v.t.* restore youthful appearance or vigour to. **rejuvenation** *n.*

relapse *v.i.* fall back into a previous state; become worse after improvement. —*n.* relapsing.

relate *v.t./i.* narrate; establish a relation between; have a connection with; establish a successful relationship.

related *a.* having a common descent or origin.

relation *n.* similarity connecting persons or things; relative; narrating; (*pl.*) dealings with others; (*pl.*) sexual intercourse. **relationship** *n.*

relative *a.* considered in relation to something else; having a connection; (in grammar) referring to an earlier noun or clause or sentence. —*n.* person related to another by descent or marriage; relative pronoun or adverb. **relatively** *adv.*

relativity *n.* being relative; Einstein's theory of the universe, showing that all motion is relative and treating time as a fourth dimension related to space.

relax *v.t./i.* make or become less tight or less tense or less strict; rest from work, indulge in recreation. **relaxation** *n.*

relay[1] /'ri-/ *n.* fresh set of people etc. to replace those who have completed a spell of work; fresh supply of material; relay race; relayed message or transmission; device relaying things. ~ **race,** race between teams in which each person in turn covers a part of the total distance.

relay[2] /-'leɪ/ *v.t.* (p.t. *relayed*) receive and pass on or re-transmit (a message, broadcast, etc.).

release *v.t.* set free; remove from a fixed position; issue (information etc.) to the public or (a film) for general exhibition. —*n.* releasing; handle or catch etc. that unfastens something; information or a film etc. released to the public.

relegate /'rel-/ *v.t.* consign to a less important place or state or group. **relegation** *n.*

relent *v.i.* become less severe or more lenient. **relentless** *a.*

relevant /'rel-/ *a.* related to the matter in hand. **relevance** *n.*

reliable *a.* able to be relied on; consistently good. **reliably** *adv.*, **reliability** *n.*

reliance *n.* relying; trust, confidence. **reliant** *a.*

relic *n.* thing that survives from earlier times; (*pl.*) remains.

relief *n.* ease given by reduction or removal of pain or anxiety etc.; thing that breaks up monotony; assistance to those in need; person replacing one who is on duty; bus etc. supplementing an ordinary service; raising of a siege; carving or moulding in which the design projects from a surface; similar effect given by colour or shading. ~ **road,** road by which traffic can avoid a congested area.

relieve *v.t.* give or bring relief to; release from a task or duty; raise the siege of. ~ **oneself,** urinate or defecate.

religion *n.* belief in the existence of a superhuman controlling power, usu. expressed in worship; influence compared to religious faith.

religious *a.* of religion; believing in a religion and carrying out its practices; of a monastic order; very conscientious. **religiously** *adv.*

relinquish *v.t.* give up, cease from. **relinquishment** *n.*

reliquary /'rel-/ *n.* receptacle for relic(s) of a holy person.

relish *n.* great enjoyment of something; appetizing flavour, thing giving this. — *v.t.* enjoy greatly.

relocate *v.t.* move to a different place. **relocation** *n.*

reluctant *a.* unwilling, grudging one's consent. **reluctantly** *adv.*, **reluctance** *n.*

rely *v.i.* ∼ **on,** trust confidently, depend on for help etc.

remain *v.i.* be in the same place or condition during further time; be there after other parts have been used or removed.

remainder *n.* remaining people or things or part; quantity left after subtraction or division. — *v.t.* dispose of unsold copies of (a book) at a reduced price.

remains *n.pl.* what remains, surviving parts; dead body.

remand /-'mɑ-/ *v.t.* send back (a prisoner) into custody while further evidence is sought. — *n.* remanding. **on ∼,** remanded.

remark *n.* spoken or written comment, thing said. — *v.t./i.* make a remark, say; notice.

remarkable *a.* worth noticing, unusual. **remarkably** *adv.*

remedy *n.* thing that cures or relieves a disease or puts right a matter. — *v.t.* be a remedy for, put right. **remedial** /-'mi-/ *a.*

remember *v.t.* keep in one's mind and recall at will; think of and make a present to; mention as sending greetings. ∼ **oneself,** remember one's intentions or behave suitably after a lapse. **remembrance** *n.*

remind *v.t.* cause to remember.

reminder *n.* thing that reminds someone, letter sent as this.

reminisce *v.i.* think or talk about past events.

reminiscence *n.* reminiscing; thing reminiscent of something else; (usu. *pl.*) account of what one remembers.

reminiscent *a.* inclined to reminisce; having characteristics that remind one (of something). **reminiscently** *adv.*

remiss /-'mɪs/ *a.* negligent.

remission *n.* remitting of a debt or penalty; reduction of force or intensity.

remit *v.t./i.* (p.t. *remitted*) cancel (a debt or punishment); make or become less intense; send (money etc.); refer (a matter for decision) to an authority; postpone.

remittance *n.* sending of money; money sent.

remnant *n.* small remaining quantity; surviving trace.

remonstrate /'rem-/ *v.i.* make a protest. **remonstrance** /-'mon-/ *n.*

remorse *n.* deep regret for one's wrongdoing.

remorseful *a.*, **remorsefully** *adv.*

remorseless *a.* relentless.

remote *a.* far away in place or time; not close; slight. **remotely** *adv.*, **remoteness** *n.*

removable *a.* able to be removed.

remove *v.t.* take off or away from its place; dismiss from office; get rid of. — *n.* degree of remoteness or difference; stage; form or division in certain schools. **remover** *n.*, **removal** *n.*

removed *a.* separated, distant. **once** *or* **twice** etc. **∼,** (of cousins) separated by one or by two etc. generations.

remunerate *v.t.* pay or reward for services. **remuneration** *n.*

remunerative /-'mju-/ *a.* giving good remuneration, profitable.

Renaissance /-'neɪsəns/ *n.* revival of art and learning in Europe in the 14th–16th centuries.

renal /'ri-/ *a.* of the kidneys.

rend *v.t./i.* (p.t. *rent*) tear.

render *v.t.* give, esp. in return; present or send in (a bill etc.); cause to become; give a performance of; translate; melt down (fat).

rendezvous /'rondeɪvu/ *n.* (pl. *-vous,* pr. *-vuz*) pre-arranged meeting or meeting-place. — *v.i.* meet at a rendezvous.

rendition *n.* way something is rendered or performed.

renegade /'reni-/ *n.* person who deserts from a group or cause etc.

renege /-'nig/ *v.i.* fail to keep a promise or agreement.

renew *v.t.* restore to its original state; replace with a fresh thing or supply; get or make or give again. **renewal** *n.*

renewable *a.* able to be renewed.

rennet *n.* substance used to curdle milk in making cheese or junket.

renounce *v.t.* give up formally; refuse to abide by. **renouncement** *n.*

renovate /'ren-/ *v.t.* repair, restore to good condition. **renovation** *n.*, **renovator** *n.*

renown /-'naʊn/ *n.* fame.

renowned /-'naʊnd/ *a.* famous.

rent[1] *see* **rend.** — *n.* torn place.

rent[2] *n.* periodical payment for use of land, rooms, machinery, etc. — *v.t.* pay or receive rent for.

rental *n.* rent; renting.

renunciation *n.* renouncing.

reorganize *v.t.* organize in a new way. **reorganization** *n.*

rep[1] *n.* upholstery fabric with a corded effect.

rep[2] *n.* (*colloq.*) business firm's travelling representative.

rep[3] *n.* (*colloq.*) repertory.

repair[1] *v.t.* put into good condition after damage or wear; make amends for. — *n.* process of repairing; repaired place; condition as regards being repaired. **repairer** *n.*

repair[2] *v.i.* go.

reparation *n.* making amends; (*pl.*) compensation for war damage.

repartee *n.* witty reply; ability to make witty replies.

repast /-'pɑ-/ *n.* (*formal*) a meal.

repatriate *v.t.* send or bring back (a person) to his own country. **repatriation** *n.*

repay *v.t.* (p.t. *repaid*) pay back. **repayment** *n.*, **repayable** *a.*

repeal *v.t.* withdraw (a law) officially. —*n.* repealing of a law.

repeat *v.t./i.* say or do or produce or occur again; tell (a thing told to oneself) to another person. —*n.* repeating; thing repeated. ∼ **itself**, recur. ∼ **oneself**, say or do the same thing again. **repeatable** *a.*

repeatedly *adv.* again and again.

repeater *n.* device that repeats a signal.

repel *v.t.* (p.t. *repelled*) drive away; be impossible for (a substance) to penetrate; be repulsive or distasteful to. **repellent** *a.* & *n.*

repent *v.t./i.* feel regret about (what one has done or failed to do). **repentance** *n.*, **repentant** *a.*

repercussion *n.* recoil; echo; indirect effect or reaction.

repertoire /-twɑ(r)/ *n.* stock of songs, plays, etc., that a person or company is prepared to perform.

repertory /ˈrep-/ *n.* repertoire; theatrical performances of various plays for short periods by one company (∼ *company*).

repetition *n.* repeating; instance of this.

repetitious *a.* repetitive.

repetitive *a.* characterized by repetition. **repetitively** *adv.*

replace *v.t.* put back in its place; take the place of; provide a substitute for. **replacement** *n.*, **replaceable** *a.*

replay[1] /-ˈpleɪ/ *v.t.* play again.

replay[2] /ˈri-/ *n.* replaying.

replenish *v.t.* refill; renew (a supply etc.). **replenishment** *n.*

replete *a.* well stocked; full, gorged. **repletion** *n.*

replica *n.* exact reproduction.

reply *v.t./i.* & *n.* answer.

report *v.t./i.* give an account of; tell as news; make a formal complaint about; present oneself as having arrived. —*n.* spoken or written account; written statement about a pupil's or employee's work etc.; rumour; explosive sound.

reportage /-tɑʒ/ *n.* reporting of news, style of this.

reportedly *adv.* according to reports.

reporter *n.* person employed to report news etc. for publication or broadcasting.

repose[1] *n.* rest, sleep; tranquillity. —*v.t./i.* rest, lie.

repose[2] *v.t.* place (trust etc.) in.

repository *n.* storage place.

repossess *v.t.* take back (goods) when hire-purchase payments have not been made. **repossession** *n.*

repp *n.* = rep[1].

reprehend /repri-/ *v.t.* rebuke.

reprehensible /repri-/ *a.* deserving rebuke. **reprehensibly** *adv.*

represent *v.t.* show in a picture or play etc.; describe or declare (to be); state (facts); symbolize; be an example or embodiment of;

act as deputy or agent or spokesman for. **representation** *n.*

representative *a.* typical of a group or class; based on or consisting of elected representatives. —*n.* sample, specimen; person's or firm's agent; person chosen to represent others.

repress *v.t.* suppress, keep (emotions) from finding an outlet. **repression** *n.*, **repressive** *a.*

reprieve *n.* postponement or cancellation of punishment (esp. death sentence); temporary relief from trouble. —*v.t.* give a reprieve to.

reprimand *v.t.* & *n.* rebuke.

reprint[1] /-ˈpri-/ *v.t.* print again.

reprint[2] /ˈri-/ *n.* reprinting; book reprinted.

reprisal *n.* act of retaliation.

reproach *v.t.* express disapproval to (a person) for a fault or offence. —*n.* act or instance of reproaching; thing that brings discredit. **reproachful** *a.*, **reproachfully** *adv.*

reprobate /ˈrep-/ *n.* immoral or unprincipled person.

reproduce *v.t./i.* produce again; produce a copy or representation of; produce further members of the same species. **reproduction** *n.*

reproductive *a.* of reproduction.

reproof *n.* expression of condemnation for a fault or offence.

reprove *v.t.* give a reproof to.

reptile *n.* member of the class of animals with a backbone and relatively short legs or no legs. **reptilian** /-ˈtɪl-/ *a.*

republic *n.* country in which the supreme power is held by the people or their representatives.

republican *a.* of or advocating a republic. —*n.* person advocating republican government; *R*∼, member of one of the two main political parties in the U.S.A.

repudiate *v.t.* reject or disown utterly, deny. **repudiation** *n.*

repugnant *a.* distasteful, objectionable. **repugnance** *n.*

repulse *v.t.* drive back (an attacking force); reject, rebuff. —*n.*

repulsion *n.* repelling; strong feeling of distaste, revulsion.

repulsive *a.* arousing disgust; able to repel.

reputable /ˈrep-/ *a.* having a good reputation, respected.

reputation *n.* what is generally believed about a person or thing; general recognition for one's abilities or achievements.

repute /-ˈpjut/ *n.* reputation.

reputed *a.* said or thought to be. **reputedly** *adv.* by repute.

request *n.* asking for something; thing asked for. —*v.t.* ask (for).

requiem /ˈrekwɪem/ *n.* special Mass for the repose of the soul(s) of the dead; music for this.

require *v.t.* need, depend on for success or fulfilment; order, oblige.

requirement *n.* need.

requisite /ˈrek-/ *a.* required, necessary. —*n.* thing needed.

requisition *n.* formal written demand, order

laying claim to use of property or materials. —*v.t.* demand or order by this.

reredos /'rɪədos/ *n.* ornamental screen covering the wall above the back of an altar.

resale *n.* sale to another person of something one has bought.

rescind /-'sɪnd/ *v.t.* repeal or cancel (a law or rule etc.). **rescission** *n.*

rescue *v.t.* save or bring away from danger or capture etc. —*n.* rescuing. **rescuer** *n.*

research /-'sɜːtʃ/ *n.* study and investigation, esp. to discover new facts. —*v.t./i.* perform research (into). **researcher** *n.*

resemble *v.t.* be like. **resemblance** *n.*

resent *v.t.* feel displeased and indignant about. **resentment** *n.*, **resentful** *a.*, **resentfully** *adv.*

reservation *n.* reserving; reserved seat or accommodation etc.; limitation on one's agreement; strip of land between carriageways of a road; (*U.S.*) area reserved for Indian occupation.

reserve *v.t.* put aside for future or special use; order or set aside for a particular person; retain; postpone. —*n.* thing reserved for future or special use, extra stock kept available; (also *pl.*) forces outside the regular armed services; extra player chosen in case a substitute is needed in a team; reservation between carriageways; limitation on one's agreement; reserve price; tendency to avoid showing feelings or cordiality. **in ~,** unused and available. **~ price,** lowest price acceptable for a thing to be sold at an auction etc.

reserved *a.* (of a person) showing reserve of manner.

reservist *n.* member of reserve forces.

reservoir /'rezəvwɑ(r)/ *n.* natural or artificial lake that is a source or store of water to a town etc.; container for a supply of fluid; store of information.

reside *v.i.* dwell; (of a quality or power) be present or vested (in a person).

residence *n.* residing; dwelling. **in ~,** living in a specified place to perform one's work.

resident *a.* residing, in residence. —*n.* permanent inhabitant; (at a hotel) person staying overnight.

residential *a.* containing dwellings; of or based on residence.

residual /-'zɪd-/ *a.* left over as a residue. **residually** *adv.*

residuary /-'zɪd-/ *a.* residual; of the residue of an estate.

residue /'rez-/ *n.* what is left over.

residuum /rɪ'zɪdjʊʌm/ *n.* (pl. *-dua*) residue.

resign *v.t./i.* give up (one's job or property or claim etc.). **~ oneself to,** be ready to accept and endure. **resignation** *n.*

resigned *a.* having resigned oneself. **resignedly** /-'zaɪnɪd-/ *adv.*

resilient /-'zɪl-/ *a.* springy; readily recovering from shock etc. **resiliently** *adv.*, **resilience** *n.*

resin *n.* sticky substance from plants and certain trees; similar substance made synthetically, used in plastics. **resinous** *a.*

resist *v.t./i.* oppose; use force to prevent something from happening or being successful; be undamaged or unaffected by; prevent from penetrating; refrain from accepting or yielding to. **resistance** *n.*, **resistant** *a.*

resistivity *n.* resistance to the passage of electric current.

resistor *n.* device having resistance to the passage of electric current.

resolute *a.* showing great determination. **resolutely** *adv.*, **resoluteness** *n.*

resolution *n.* resolving; great determination; formal statement of a committee's opinion.

resolve *v.t./i.* decide firmly; solve or settle (a problem or doubts); separate into constituent parts. —*n.* thing one has decided to do; great determination.

resonant /'rez-/ *a.* resounding, echoing. **resonance** *n.*

resort *v.i.* turn for help, adopt as an expedient; go customarily. —*n.* expedient, resorting to this; place resorted to; popular holiday place.

resound *v.i.* fill a place or be filled with sound; echo.

resounding *a.* (of an event) notable.

resource *n.* something to which one can turn for help; ingenuity; (*pl.*) available assets, source of wealth to a country.

resourceful *a.* clever at finding ways of doing things. **resourcefully** *adv.*, **resourcefulness** *n.*

respect *n.* admiration felt towards a person or thing that has good qualities or achievements; politeness arising from this; attention, consideration; relation, reference; particular detail or aspect; (*pl.*) polite greetings. —*v.t.* feel or show respect for. **respecter** *n.*

respectable *a.* of moderately good social standing; honest and decent; considerable. **respectably** *adv.*, **respectability** *n.*

respectful *a.* showing respect. **respectfully** *adv.*

respecting *prep.* concerning.

respective *a.* belonging to each as an individual.

respectively *adv.* for each separately; in the order mentioned.

respiration *n.* breathing.

respirator *n.* device worn over the nose and mouth to purify air before it is inhaled; device for giving artificial respiration.

respiratory /'res-/ *a.* of respiration.

respire *v.t./i.* breathe.

respite /'respaɪt/ *n.* interval of rest or relief; permitted delay.

resplendent *a.* brilliant with colour or decorations. **resplendently** *adv.*

respond *v.i.* make an answer. **~ to,** act or react in answer to or because of.

respondent *n.* defendant in a lawsuit, esp. in a divorce case.

response *n.* answer; act, feeling, or movement produced by a stimulus or another's action.

responsibility *n.* being responsible; thing for which one is responsible.

responsible *a.* obliged to take care of something or to carry out a duty, liable to be blamed for loss or failure etc.; having to account for one's actions; capable of rational conduct; trustworthy; involving important duties; being the cause of something. **responsibly** *adv.*

responsive *a.* responding well to an influence. **responsiveness** *n.*

rest[1] *v.t./i.* be still; cease from activity or working, esp. in order to regain vigour; cause or allow to do this; (of a matter) be left without further discussion; place or be placed for support; rely; (of a look) alight, be directed. —*n.* inactivity or sleep, esp. to regain vigour; prop or support for an object; interval of silence between notes in music, sign indicating this.

rest[2] *v.i.* be left in the hands or charge of; remain in a specified state. —*n.* **the ∼,** the remaining part; the others.

restaurant /'restərɑ̃/ *n.* place where meals can be bought and eaten.

restful *a.* giving rest or a feeling of rest. **restfully** *adv.*, **restfulness** *n.*

restitution *n.* restoring of a thing to its proper owner or original state; compensation.

restive *a.* restless; impatient because of delay or restraint. **restiveness** *n.*

restless *a.* unable to rest or be still. **restlessly** *adv.*, **restlessness** *n.*

restoration *n.* restoring; *the R∼,* reestablishment of the monarchy in Britain in 1660.

restorative /-'stɒ-/ *a.* restoring health or strength. —*n.* restorative food or medicine or treatment.

restore *v.t.* bring back to its original state (e.g. by repairing), or to good health or vigour; put back in a former position. **restorer** *n.*

restrain *v.t.* hold back from movement or action, keep under control. **restraint** *n.*

restrict *v.t.* put a limit on, subject to limitations. **restriction** *n.*

restrictive *a.* restricting. **∼ practices,** those preventing labour or materials from being used in the most efficient way.

result *n.* product of an activity or operation or calculation; score, marks, or name of the winner in a sports event or competition. —*v.i.* occur or have as a result.

resultant *a.* occurring as a result.

resume *v.t./i.* get or take again; begin again after stopping. **resumption** *n.*

résumé /'rezjumeɪ/ *n.* summary.

resurgence *n.* revival after destruction or disappearance.

resurrect *v.t.* bring back into use.

resurrection *n.* rising from the dead (*the R∼,* that of Christ); revival after disuse.

resuscitate /-'sʌsɪ-/ *v.t./i.* revive. **resuscitation** *n.*

retail *n.* selling of goods to the public (not for resale). —*a. & adv.* in the retail trade. —*v.t./i.* sell or be sold in the retail trade; relate details of. **retailer** *n.*

retain *v.t.* keep, esp. in one's possession or memory or in use; hold in place.

retainer *n.* fee paid to retain services; (*old use*) servant, attendant.

retaliate *v.i.* repay an injury or insult etc. by inflicting one in return. **retaliation** *n.*, **retaliatory** /-'tæljə-/ *a.*

retard *v.t.* cause delay to. **retardation** *n.*

retarded *a.* backward in mental or physical development.

retch /retʃ/ *v.i.* strain one's throat as if vomiting.

retention *n.* retaining.

retentive *a.* able to retain things.

rethink *v.t.* (p.t. *rethought*) reconsider; plan again and differently.

reticent /'retɪ-/ *a.* not revealing one's thoughts. **reticence** *n.*

retina /'retɪ-/ *n.* (pl. *-as*) membrane at the back of the eyeball, sensitive to light.

retinue *n.* attendants accompanying an important person.

retire *v.t./i.* give up one's regular work because of age; cause (an employee) to do this; withdraw, retreat; go to bed. **retirement** *n.*

retiring *a.* shy, avoiding society.

retort[1] *v.t./i.* make (as) a witty or angry reply. —*n.* retorting; reply of this kind.

retort[2] *n.* vessel (usu. glass) with a long downward-bent neck, used in distilling liquids; vessel used in making gas or steel.

retouch *v.t.* touch up (a picture or photograph).

retrace *v.t.* trace back to the source. **∼ one's steps,** go back the way one came.

retract *v.t./i.* withdraw. **retraction** *n.*, **retractor** *n.*, **retractable** *a.*

retreat *v.i.* withdraw, esp. after defeat or when faced with difficulty. —*n.* retreating, withdrawal; military signal for this; place of shelter or seclusion.

retrench *v.t./i.* reduce the amount of (expenditure or operations). **retrenchment** *n.*

retrial *n.* trial of a lawsuit again.

retribution /retrɪ-/ *n.* deserved punishment. **retributive** /-'trɪb-/ *a.*

retrieve *v.t.* regain possession of; find and extract or bring back; set right (an error etc.). —*n.* possibility of recovery. **retrieval** *n.*

retrievable *a.* able to be retrieved.

retriever *n.* dog of a breed used to retrieve game.

retroactive *a.* operating retrospectively.

retrograde *a.* going backwards; reverting to an inferior state.

retrogress *v.i.* move backwards, deteriorate. **retrogression** *n.*, **retrogressive** *a.*

retro-rocket *n.* auxiliary rocket used for slowing a spacecraft.

retrospect *n.* **in ∼,** when one looks back on a past event.

retrospective *a.* looking back on the past; (of a law etc.) made to apply to the past as well as the future. **retrospectively** *adv.*

retroussé /rə'truseɪ/ *a.* (of the nose) turned up at the tip.

retroverted *a.* turned backwards. **retroversion** *n.*

return *v.t./i.* come or go back; bring, give, put, or send back; say in reply; elect as an M.P. —*n.* returning; profit; return ticket; return match; formal report submitted by order. **∼ match,** second match between the same opponents. **∼ ticket,** ticket for a journey to a place and back again.

returnable *a.* that can or must be returned.

reunion *n.* social gathering of people who were formerly associated.

reusable *a.* able to be used again.

rev *n.* (*colloq.*) revolution of an engine. —*v.t./i.* (p.t. *revved*) (*colloq.*) cause (an engine) to run quickly; (of an engine) revolve.

Rev. *abbr.* Reverend.

revamp *v.t.* renovate, give a new appearance to.

Revd. *abbr.* Reverend.

reveal *v.t.* make visible by uncovering; make known.

reveille /rɪˈvælɪ/ *n.* military waking signal.

revel *v.i.* (p.t. *revelled*) take great delight; hold revels. **revels** *n.pl.* lively festivities, merry-making. **reveller** *n.*, **revelry** *n.*

revelation *n.* revealing; thing revealed, esp. something surprising.

revenge *n.* punishment, injury inflicted in return for what one has suffered; desire to inflict this; opportunity to defeat a victorious opponent. —*v.t.* avenge.

revengeful *a.* eager for revenge.

revenue *n.* country's income from taxes etc.

reverberate *v.t./i.* echo, resound. **reverberation** *n.*

revere /-ˈvɪə(r)/ *v.t.* feel deep respect or religious veneration for.

reverence *n.* feeling of awe and respect or veneration. —*v.t.* feel or show reverence for.

reverend *a.* deserving to be treated with respect; *R∼*, title of a clergyman or (*R∼ Mother*) of the head of a convent.

reverent *a.* feeling or showing reverence. **reverently** *adv.*

reverie /ˈrevərɪ/ *n.* daydream.

revers /rɪˈvɪə(r)/ *n.* (pl. *revers*, pr. -ˈvɪəz) turned-back front edge at the neck of a jacket or bodice.

reversal *n.* reversing.

reverse *a.* facing or moving in the opposite direction; opposite in character or order; upside down. —*v.t./i.* turn the other way round or up or inside out; convert to the opposite kind or effect; annul (a decree etc.); move in the opposite direction, travel backwards. —*n.* reverse side or effect; piece of misfortune. **reversely** *adv.*, **reversible** *a.*

revert *v.i.* return to a former condition or habit; return to a subject in talk etc.; (of property etc.) pass to another holder when its present holder relinquishes it. **reversion** *n.*, **reversionary** *a.*

revetment /-ˈvet-/ *n.* facing of masonry on a rampart etc.

review *n.* general survey of events or a subject; reconsideration; ceremonial inspection of troops etc.; report assessing the merits of a book or play etc. —*v.t.* make or write a review of. **reviewer** *n.*

revile *v.t.* criticize angrily in abusive language. **revilement** *n.*

revise *v.t.* re-examine and alter or correct; study again (work already learnt) in preparation for an examination. **revision** *n.*

revivalist *n.* person who seeks to promote religious fervour.

revive *v.t./i.* come or bring back to life or consciousness or vigour, or into use. **revival** *n.*

revoke *v.t./i.* withdraw (a decree or licence etc.); fail to follow suit in a card-game when able to do so.

revolt *v.t./i.* take part in a rebellion; be in a mood of protest or defiance; cause strong disgust in. —*n.* act or state of rebelling; sense of disgust.

revolting *a.* in revolt; causing disgust.

revolution *n.* revolving, single complete orbit or rotation; complete change of method or conditions; substitution of a new system of government, esp. by force.

revolutionary *a.* involving a great change; of political revolution. —*n.* person who begins or supports a political revolution.

revolutionize *v.t.* alter completely.

revolve *v.t./i.* turn round; move in an orbit; turn over (a problem etc.) in one's mind.

revolver *n.* a kind of pistol.

revue *n.* entertainment consisting of a series of items.

revulsion *n.* strong disgust; sudden violent change of feeling.

reward *n.* something given or received in return for a service or merit etc. —*v.t.* give a reward to.

rewrite *v.t.* (p.t. *rewrote*, p.p. *rewritten*) write again in a different form or style.

Rex *n.* reigning king.

rhapsodize *v.i.* talk or write about something ecstatically.

rhapsody *n.* ecstatic written or spoken statement; romantic musical composition. **rhapsodical** *a.*

rheostat /ˈrɪə-/ *n.* device for varying the resistance to electric current.

rhesus *n.* small Indian monkey used in biological experiments. **Rhesus factor,** substance usu. present in blood (*Rhesus-positive*, containing this; *Rhesus-negative*, not containing it).

rhetoric /ˈret-/ *n.* art of using words impressively, esp. in public speaking; impressive language.

rhetorical /rɪˈto-/ *a.* expressed so as to sound impressive. **∼ question,** one phrased as a question for dramatic effect, not seeking an answer. **rhetorically** *adv.*

rheumatic *a.* of or affected with rheumatism. **rheumaticky** *a.*

rheumatics *n.pl.* (*colloq.*) rheumatism.

rheumatism *n.* disease causing pain in the joints, muscles, or fibrous tissue.

rheumatoid *a.* having the character of rheumatism.

rhinestone *n.* imitation diamond.

rhino *n.* (pl. *rhino* or *-os*) (*sl.*) rhinoceros.

rhinoceros *n.* (pl. *-oses*) large thick-skinned animal with one horn or two horns on its nose.

rhizome /'raɪ-/ *n.* root-like stem producing roots and shoots.

rhododendron *n.* shrub with clusters of trumpet-shaped flowers.

rhomboid *a.* like a rhombus.

rhombus *n.* quadrilateral with opposite sides and angles equal (and not right angles).

rhubarb *n.* garden plant with red leaf-stalks that are used like fruit.

rhyme *n.* identity of sound between words or syllables; word providing a rhyme to another; poem with line-endings that rhyme. *v.t./i.* form a rhyme; have rhymes; treat as rhyming.

rhythm *n.* pattern produced by emphasis and duration of notes in music or of syllables in words, or by a regular succession of movements or events. **rhythmic** *a.*, **rhythmical** *a.*, **rhythmically** *adv.*

rib *n.* one of the curved bones round the chest; structural part resembling this; pattern of raised lines in knitting. —*v.t.* (p.t. *ribbed*) support with ribs; knit as rib; (*colloq.*) tease.

ribald /'rɪbəld/ *a.* humorous in a cheerful but vulgar or disrespectful way. **ribaldry** *n.*

riband /'rɪb-/ *n.* ribbon.

ribbed *a.* with raised ridges.

ribbon *n.* band of silky material used for decoration or tying things; strip resembling this.

rice *n.* cereal plant grown in marshes in hot countries, with seeds used as food; these seeds.

rich *a.* (-*er*, -*est*) having much wealth; made of costly materials; abundant; containing a large proportion of something (e.g. fat, fuel); (of soil) fertile; (of colour or sound or smell) pleasantly deep and strong; highly amusing. **riches** *n.pl.* much money or valuable possessions. **richness** *n.*

richly *adv.* in a rich way; fully, thoroughly.

rick[1] *n.* built stack of hay etc.

rick[2] *n.* slight sprain or strain. —*v.t.* sprain or strain slightly.

rickets *n.* children's disease causing softening and deformity of the bones.

rickety *a.* shaky, insecure.

rickrack *n.* zigzag braid used for trimming.

rickshaw *n.* two-wheeled hooded vehicle used in the Far East, drawn by one or more people.

ricochet /'rɪkəʃeɪ/ *n.* & *v.i.* (p.t. *ricocheted*, pr. -ʃeɪd) rebound from a surface after striking it with a glancing blow.

rid *v.t.* (p.t. *rid*, pres.p. *ridding*) free from something unpleasant or unwanted. **get ~ of**, cause to go away; free oneself of.

riddance *n.* ridding. **good ~,** welcome freedom from a person or thing one is rid of.

ridden *see* **ride.** —*a.* full of, dominated by.

riddle[1] *n.* question etc. designed to test ingenuity or give amusement in finding its answer or meaning; something puzzling or mysterious.

riddle[2] *n.* coarse sieve. —*v.t.* pass through a riddle; pierce with many holes; permeate thoroughly.

ride *v.t./i.* (p.t. *rode*, p.p. *ridden*) sit on and be carried by (a horse or bicycle etc.) or in a car etc.; be supported on, float; yield to (a blow) to reduce its impact. —*n.* spell of riding; journey in a vehicle; track for riding on; feel of a ride. **~ up,** (of a garment) work upwards when worn.

rider *n.* one who rides a horse etc.; additional statement.

ridge *n.* narrow raised strip; line where two upward slopes meet; elongated region of high barometric pressure. **ridged** *a.*

ridicule /'rɪd-/ *n.* making or being made to seem ridiculous. —*v.t.* subject to ridicule, make fun of.

ridiculous /-'dɪk-/ *a.* deserving to be laughed at, esp. in a malicious or scornful way; not worth serious consideration. **ridiculously** *adv.*

riding-light *n.* light shown by a ship riding at anchor.

rife *a.* occurring frequently, widespread. **~ with,** full of (rumours etc.).

riffle *v.t./i.* flex and release (pages etc.) in quick succession.

riff-raff *n.* rabble; disreputable people.

rifle *n.* a kind of gun with a long barrel. —*v.t.* search and rob; cut spiral grooves in (a gun-barrel).

rift *n.* cleft in earth or rock; crack, split; breach in friendly relations. **~-valley** *n.* steep-sided valley formed by subsidence.

rig[1] *v.t.* (p.t. *rigged*) provide with clothes or equipment; fit (a ship) with spars, sails, ropes, etc.; set up (a structure), esp. in a makeshift way. —*n.* way a ship's masts and sails etc. are arranged; equipment (e.g. for drilling an oil-well); (*colloq.*) outfit. **~-out** *n.* (*colloq.*) outfit.

rig[2] *v.t.* (p.t. *rigged*) manage or control fraudulently.

rigging *n.* ropes etc. used to support a ship's masts and sails.

right *a.* morally good; in accordance with justice; proper; correct, true; in a good or normal condition; of or on the side of the body which in most people has the more-used hand. —*n.* what is just; something one is entitled to; right hand or foot; people supporting more conservative or traditional policies than others in their group. —*v.t.* restore to a proper or correct or upright position; set right. —*adv.* on or towards the right-hand side; directly; (*colloq.*) immediately; completely; exactly; rightly; all right. **in the ~,** having truth or justice on one's side. **~ angle,** angle of 90°. **~ away,** immediately. **~-hand man,** indispensable or chief assistant. **~-handed** *a.* using the right hand. **~ of way,** right to pass over another's land; path subject to this; right to proceed while another vehicle must wait. **rightly** *adv.*, **rightness** *n.*

righteous *a.* doing what is morally right, making a show of this; morally justifiable. **righteously** *adv.*, **righteousness** *n.*

rightful *a.* just, proper, legal. **rightfully** *adv.*

rightist *a.* & *n.* (member) of the right wing of a political party.

rigid *a.* stiff, not bending or yielding; strict, inflexible. **rigidly** *adv.* **rigidity** *n.*

rigmarole /ˈrɪgmərəʊl/ *n.* long rambling statement; complicated formal procedure.

rigor /ˈraɪ-/ *n.* ~ **mortis,** stiffening of the body after death.

rigour /ˈrɪg-/ *n.* strictness, severity; harshness of weather or conditions. **rigorous** *a.,* **rigorously** *adv.*

rile *v.t.* (*colloq.*) annoy.

rill *n.* small stream.

rim *n.* edge or border of something more or less circular. **rimmed** *a.*

rime *n.* frost.

rimed /raɪmd/ *a.* coated with frost.

rimless *a.* (of spectacles) made without frames.

rind /raɪnd/ *n.* tough outer layer or skin on fruit, cheese, bacon, etc.

ring[1] *n.* outline of a circle; thing shaped like this; small circular metal band worn on a finger; enclosure for a circus or sports event or cattle-show etc.; combination of people acting together to control operations or policy; *the* ~, bookmakers. —*v.t.* put a ring on or round; surround.

ring[2] *v.t./i.* (p.t. *rang,* p.p. *rung*) give out a loud clear resonant sound; cause (a bell) to do this; signal by ringing; be filled with sound; telephone; (*colloq.*) alter and sell (a stolen vehicle). —*n.* act or sound of ringing; specified tone or feeling of a statement etc.; (*colloq.*) telephone call. ~ **off,** end a telephone call. ~ **the changes,** vary things. ~ **up,** make a telephone call.

ringer *n.* person who rings bells; (*U.S.*) racehorse etc. fraudulently substituted for another; person's double.

ringleader *n.* person who leads others in wrongdoing or riot etc.

ringlet *n.* long tubular curl.

ringside *n.* area beside a boxing ring. ~ **seat,** position from which one has a clear view of the scene of action.

ringworm *n.* skin disease producing round scaly patches on the skin.

rink *n.* skating-rink.

rinse *v.t.* wash lightly; wash out soap etc. from. —*n.* process of rinsing; solution washed through hair to tint or condition it.

riot *n.* wild disturbance by a crowd of people; profuse display; (*colloq.*) very amusing person or thing. —*v.i.* take part in a riot or disorderly revelry. **read the Riot Act,** insist that noise or disobedience must cease. **run** ~, behave in an unruly way; grow in an uncontrolled way.

riotous /ˈraɪ-/ *a.* disorderly, unruly; boisterous. **riotously** *adv.*

rip *v.t./i.* (p.t. *ripped*) tear apart; remove by pulling roughly; become torn; rush along. —*n.* act of ripping; torn place. **let** ~, refrain from checking the speed or progress of; speak violently. ~**cord** *n.* cord for pulling to release a parachute. ~ **off,** (*sl.*) defraud; steal. (~**off** *n.*) ~**roaring** *a.* wildly noisy. **ripper** *n.*

R.I.P. *abbr.* (Latin *requiescat* (or *requiescant*) *in pace*) rest in peace.

ripe *a.* (*-er, -est*) ready to be gathered and used; matured; (of age) advanced; ready. **ripeness** *n.*

ripen *v.t./i.* make or become ripe.

riposte /rɪˈpɒst/ *n.* quick counter-stroke or retort. —*v.i.* deliver a riposte.

ripple *n.* small wave(s); gentle sound that rises and falls. —*v.t./i.* form ripples (in).

rise *v.i.* (p.t. *rose,* p.p. *risen*) come or go or extend upwards; get up from lying or sitting or kneeling, get out of bed; cease to sit for business; become upright; come to life again after death; rebel; become higher; increase; have its origin or source. —*n.* act or amount of rising, increase; upward slope; increase in wages. **get** *or* **take a** ~ **out of,** draw into a display of annoyance. **give** ~ **to,** cause.

riser *n.* person or thing that rises; vertical piece between treads of a staircase.

rising *n.* revolt. —*a.* ~ **five** etc., nearing the age of five. ~ **generation,** young people, those who are growing up.

risk *n.* possibility of meeting danger or suffering harm; person or thing representing a source of risk. —*v.t.* expose to the chance of injury or loss; accept the risk of.

risky *a.* (*-ier, -iest*) full of risk. **riskily** *adv.,* **riskiness** *n.*

risotto *n.* (pl. *-os*) dish of rice containing chopped meat or fish etc.

risqué /ˈrɪskeɪ/ *a.* slightly indecent.

rissole *n.* fried cake of minced meat.

rite *n.* ritual.

ritual *n.* series of actions used in a religious or other ceremony. —*a.* of or done as a ritual. **ritually** *adv.*

rival *n.* person or thing competing with another or that can equal another. —*a.* being a rival or rivals. —*v.t.* (p.t. *rivalled*) be a rival of; seem as good as. **rivalry** *n.*

riven /ˈrɪv-/ *a.* split, torn violently.

river *n.* large natural stream of water; great flow.

rivet /ˈrɪv-/ *n.* nail or bolt for holding pieces of metal together, with its end pressed down to form a head when in place. —*v.t.* (p.t. *riveted*) fasten with or press down as a rivet; make immovable; attract and hold (the attention of). **riveter** *n.*

Riviera /rɪvɪˈeərə/ *n.* coastal region of southeast France, Monaco, and north-west Italy.

rivulet *n.* small stream.

roach *n.* (pl. *roach*) small freshwater fish of the carp family.

road *n.* way by which people or vehicles may pass between places, esp. one with a prepared surface; way of reaching something. **on the** ~, travelling. ~**hog** *n.* reckless or inconsiderate driver. ~**house** *n.* inn, club, or restaurant on a main road in the country. ~**metal** *n.* broken stone for making the foundation of a road or railway. ~**works** *n.pl.* construction or repair of roads.

roadside *n.* border of a road.

roadway *n.* road, esp. as distinct from a foot-path beside it.

roadworthy *a.* (of a vehicle) fit to be used on a road. **roadworthiness** *n.*

roam *v.t./i.* & *n.* wander.

roan *n.* horse with a dark coat sprinkled with white or grey hairs.

roar *n.* long deep sound like that made by a lion; loud laughter. —*v.t./i.* give a roar; express in this way. **roarer** *n.*

roaring *a.* noisy; briskly active.

roast *v.t./i.* cook (meat) in an oven or by exposure to heat; expose to great heat; undergo roasting. —*n.* roast meat; joint of meat for roasting.

rob *v.t.* (p.t. *robbed*) steal from; take unlawfully; deprive. **robber** *n.*, **robbery** *n.*

robe *n.* long loose esp. ceremonial garment. —*v.t.* dress in a robe.

robin *n.* brown red-breasted bird.

robot /ˈrəʊbɒt/ *n.* machine resembling and acting like a person; piece of apparatus operated by remote control.

robust /-ˈbʌst/ *a.* strong, vigorous. **robustly** *adv.*, **robustness** *n.*

rock[1] *n.* hard part of earth's crust, below the soil; mass of this, large stone or boulder; hard sugar sweet made in cylindrical sticks. **on the rocks**, (*colloq.*) short of money; (of a drink) served neat with ice cubes. **∼-bottom** *a.* (*colloq.*) very low. **∼-cake** *n.* small fruit cake with a rugged surface.

rock[2] *v.t./i.* move to and fro while supported; disturb greatly by shock. —*n.* rocking movement; a kind of modern music usu. with a strong beat. **∼ 'n roll**, form of rock music with elements of blues.

rocker *n.* thing that rocks; pivoting switch.

rockery *n.* collection of rough stones with soil between them on which small plants are grown.

rocket *n.* firework that shoots into the air when ignited and then explodes; structure that flies by expelling burning gases, propelling a bomb or spacecraft; (*sl.*) reprimand. —*v.i.* (p.t. *rocketed*) move rapidly upwards or away.

rocketry *n.* science or practice of rocket propulsion.

rocky *a.* (-*ier*, -*iest*) of or like rock; full of rock; unsteady.

rococo /rəˈkəʊ-/ *a.* & *n.* (of or in) an ornate style of decoration in Europe in the 18th century.

rod *n.* slender straight round stick or metal bar; fishing-rod.

rode *see* **ride.**

rodent *n.* animal with strong front teeth for gnawing things.

rodeo /-ˈdeɪəʊ/ *n.* (pl. -*os*) round-up of ranch cattle for branding etc.; exhibition of cowboys' skill in handling animals.

roe[1] *n.* mass of eggs in a female fish's ovary (*hard* ∼); male fish's milt (*soft* ∼).

roe[2] *n.* (pl. *roe* or *roes*) a kind of small deer. **roebuck** *n.* male roe.

rogations *n.pl.* litany for use on **Rogation Days,** the three days before Ascension Day. **Rogation Sunday,** Sunday before this.

roger *int.* (in signalling) message received and understood.

rogue *n.* dishonest or unprincipled or mischievous person; wild animal living apart from the herd. **roguery** *n.*

roguish *a.* mischievous; playful. **roguishly** *adv.*, **roguishness** *n.*

roistering *a.* & *n.* merrymaking noisily. **roisterer** *n.*

role *n.* actor's part; person's or thing's function.

roll *v.t./i.* move (on a surface) on wheels or by turning over and over; turn on an axis or over and over; form into a cylindrical or spherical shape; flatten with a roller; rock from side to side; undulate; move or pass steadily; make a long continuous vibrating sound; (*U.S. sl.*) attack and rob (a person). —*n.* cylinder formed by turning flexible material over and over upon itself; thing with this shape, undulation; small individual portion of bread baked in a rounded shape, this with filling; official list or register; rolling movement or sound. **be rolling (in money),** (*colloq.*) be wealthy. **∼-call** *n.* calling of a list of names to check that all are present. **rolled gold,** thin coating of gold on another metal. **rolling-pin** *n.* roller for flattening dough. **rolling-stock** *n.* railway engines and carriages, wagons, etc. **rolling stone,** person who does not settle in one place.

roller *n.* cylinder rolled over things to flatten or spread them, or on which something is wound; long swelling wave. **∼-coaster** *n.* switchback at a fair etc. **∼-skate** *n.* (see *skate*[2]). **∼-skating** *n.* skating on roller-skates. **∼ towel** *n.* towel with its ends joined to make it continuous, hung over a roller.

rollicking *a.* full of boisterous high spirits.

rollmop *n.* rolled pickled herring fillet.

roly-poly *n.* pudding of suet pastry spread with jam, rolled up, and boiled. —*a.* plump, podgy.

Roman *a.* & *n.* (native, inhabitant) of Rome or of the ancient Roman republic or empire; Roman Catholic. **∼ Catholic,** (member) of the Church that acknowledges the Pope as its head. **∼ Catholicism** faith of the Roman Catholic Church. **∼ numerals,** letters representing numbers (I = 1, V = 5, etc.).

roman *n.* plain upright type (not italic).

romance /-ˈmæns/ *n.* imaginative story or literature; romantic situation, event, or atmosphere; love story, love affair resembling this; picturesque exaggeration. —*v.i.* distort the truth or invent imaginatively. **Romance languages,** those descended from Latin.

Romanesque /-ˈnesk/ *a.* & *n.* (of or in) a style of art and architecture in Europe about 1050–1200.

romantic *a.* appealing to the emotions by its imaginative or heroic or picturesque quality;

involving a love affair; enjoying romantic situations etc. —*n.* romantic person. **romantically** *adv.*

Romany *a.* & *n.* gypsy; (of) the gypsy language.

romp *v.i.* play about in a lively way; (*colloq.*) go along easily. —*n.* spell of romping.

rompers *n.pl.* young child's one-piece garment.

rondo *n.* (pl. -*os*) piece of music with a recurring theme.

rood *n.* crucifix, esp. on a rood-screen; quarter of an acre. **Holy Rood,** (*old use*) Cross of Christ. **∼-screen** *n.* carved screen separating nave from chancel.

roof *n.* (pl. *roofs*) upper covering of a building, car, cavity, etc. —*v.t.* cover with a roof; be the roof of.

rook[1] *n.* a kind of crow.—*v.t.* swindle, charge an extortionate price.

rook[2] *n.* chess piece with a top shaped like battlements.

rookery *n.* colony of rooks; their nesting-place; colony or breeding-place of penguins or seals.

room *n.* space that is or could be occupied; enclosed part of a building; scope to allow something; (*pl.*) set of rooms as lodgings.

roomy *a.* able to contain much.

roost *n.* place where birds perch or rest. —*v.i.* perch, esp. for sleep.

rooster *n.* (*U.S.*) domestic cock.

root[1] *n.* part of a plant that attaches it to the earth and absorbs water and nourishment from the soil; embedded part of hair, tooth, etc.; source, basis; language-element from which words have been made; number in relation to another which it produces when multiplied by itself a specified number of times; (*pl.*) emotional attachment to a place. —*v.t./i.* take root, cause to do this; cause to stand fixed and unmoving. **∼ out** *or* **up,** drag or dig up by the roots; get rid of. **take ∼,** send down roots; become established.

root[2] *v.t./i.* (of an animal) turn up ground with the snout or beak in search of food; rummage, extract; (*U.S. sl.*) give support by applause.

rootless *a.* without roots.

rope *n.* strong thick cord; thing resembling this. —*v.t.* fasten or secure with rope; fence off with rope(s). **know** *or* **show the ropes,** know or show the procedure. **∼ in,** persuade to take part in an activity.

ropy *a.* (-*ier*, -*iest*) forming long sticky threads; (*colloq.*) poor in quality. **ropiness** *n.*

rorqual /-kəl/ *n.* whale with a dorsal fin.

rosary *n.* rose-garden; set series of prayers used in the R.C. Church; string of beads for keeping count in this.

rose[1] *n.* ornamental usu. fragrant flower; bush or shrub bearing this; deep pink; sprinkling-nozzle. **∼ window,** circular window with tracery.

rose[2] *see* **rise.**

rosé /ˈrəʊzeɪ/ *n.* light pink wine.

roseate /-zɪeɪt/ *a.* deep pink, rosy.

rosebud *n.* bud of a rose.

rosemary *n.* shrub with fragrant leaves used to flavour food.

rosette *n.* rose-shaped badge or ornament.

rosewood *n.* fragrant close-grained wood used for making furniture.

rosin /ˈrɒz-/ *n.* a kind of resin.

roster /ˈrɒs-/ *n.* list showing people's turns of duty etc.

rostrum /ˈrɒs-/ *n.* platform for one person.

rosy *a.* (-*ier*, -*iest*) deep pink; promising, hopeful. **rosily** *adv.*, **rosiness** *n.*

rot *v.t./i.* (p.t. *rotted*) lose its original form by chemical action caused by bacteria or fungi etc.; cause to do this; perish through lack of use. —*n.* rotting, rottenness; (*sl.*) nonsense; series of failures.

rota *n.* list of duties to be done or people to do them in rotation.

rotary *a.* acting by rotating.

rotate *v.t./i.* revolve; arrange or occur or deal with in a recurrent series. **rotation** *n.*, **rotatory** /ˈrəʊ-/ *a.*

rote *n.* **by ∼,** by memory without thought of the meaning; by a fixed procedure.

rotisserie /-ˈtɪs-/ *n.* cooking-device for roasting food on a revolving spit.

rotor *n.* rotating part.

rotten *a.* rotted, breaking easily from age or use; morally corrupt; (*colloq.*) worthless, unpleasant. **rottenness** *n.*

rotter *n.* (*sl.*) contemptible person.

rotund /-ˈtʌnd/ *a.* rounded, plump. **rotundity** *n.*

rotunda *n.* circular domed building or hall.

rouble /ˈruːbəl/ *n.* unit of money in Russia.

roué /ˈruːeɪ/ *n.* dissolute elderly man.

rouge /ruːʒ/ *n.* reddish cosmetic colouring for the cheeks; fine red powder for polishing metal. —*v.t.* colour with rouge.

rough *a.* (-*er*, -*est*) having an uneven or irregular surface; coarse in texture; not gentle or careful, violent, (of weather) stormy; not perfected or detailed; approximate. —*adv.* roughly; in rough conditions. —*n.* rough thing or state; rough ground; ruffian. —*v.t.* make rough. **∼-and-ready** *a.* full of rough vigour; rough but effective. **∼-and-tumble** *n.* haphazard struggle. **∼ diamond,** diamond not yet cut; person of good nature but lacking polished manners. **∼ it,** do without ordinary comforts. **∼ out,** plan or sketch roughly. **roughly** *adv.*, **roughness** *n.*

roughage *n.* indigestible material in food-plants that stimulates the action of the intestines.

roughcast *n.* plaster of lime and gravel used on buildings. —*v.t.* (p.t. *roughcast*) coat with this.

roughen *v.t./i.* make or become rough.

roughshod *a.* (of a horse) having shoes with the nail-heads left projecting. **ride ∼ over,** treat inconsiderately or arrogantly.

roulette /ruːˈlet/ *n.* gambling game played with a small ball on a revolving disc.

round *a.* (-*er*, -*est*) having a curved shape or outline; circular, spherical, or cylindrical; complete. —*n.* round object; slice of bread cut across a loaf; circular or recurring course or series; song for two or more voices that start at different times; shot(s) from one or more firearms, ammunition for this; one section of a competition or struggle or boxing-match. —*prep.* so as to circle or enclose; visiting in a series; to all points of interest in. —*adv.* in a circle or curve; by a circuitous route; so as to face in a different direction; round a place or group; to a person's house etc.; into consciousness after unconsciousness. —*v.t./i.* make or become round; make into a round figure or number; travel round. **in the ~,** with all sides visible. **~ about,** near by; approximately, **~ figure** *or* **number,** approximation without odd units. **~ on,** make an attack or retort in retaliation. **~ robin,** statement signed by a number of people. **~ the clock,** continuously through day and night. **~ up,** gather into one place **~-up** *n.*

roundabout *n.* merry-go-round; road junction with a circular island round which traffic has to pass in one direction. —*a.* indirect.

rounders *n.* team game played with bat and ball, in which players have to run round a circuit. **rounder** *n.* unit of scoring in this.

Roundhead *n.* supporter of the Parliamentary party in the English Civil War.

roundly *a.* thoroughly, severely; in a rounded shape.

roundsman *n.* (pl. *-men*) tradesman's employee delivering goods on a regular route.

roundworm *n.* worm with a rounded body.

rouse *v.t./i.* wake; cause to become active or excited.

rousing *a.* vigorous, stirring.

roustabout *n.* labourer on an oil rig.

rout[1] *n.* utter defeat; disorderly retreat. —*v.t.* defeat completely; put to flight.

rout[2] *v.t./i.* fetch (out); rummage.

route *n.* course or way from starting-point to finishing point. —*v.t.* (pres.p. *routeing*) send by a specified route. **~ march,** training-march for troops.

routine /ruˈtin/ *n.* standard procedure; set sequence of movements. —*a.* in accordance with routine. **routinely** *adv.*

roux /ru/ *n.* mixture of heated fat and flour as a basis for a sauce.

rove *v.t./i.* wander.

row[1] /rəʊ/ *n.* people or things in a line.

row[2] /rəʊ/ *v.t./i.* propel (a boat) by using oars; carry in a boat that one rows. —*n.* spell of rowing. **~-boat** *n.*, **rowing-boat** *n.*

row[3] /raʊ/ *n.* (*colloq.*) loud noise; quarrel, angry argument; scolding. —*v.t./i.* (*colloq.*) quarrel, argue angrily; scold.

rowan /ˈrəʊ-/ *n.* tree bearing hanging clusters of red berries.

rowdy /ˈraʊ-/ *a.* (*-ier, -iest*) noisy and disorderly. —*n.* rowdy person. **rowdily** *adv.*, **rowdiness** *n.*

rowlock /ˈrɒl-/ *n.* device on the side of a boat securing and forming a fulcrum for an oar.

royal *a.* of or suited to a king or queen; of the

family or in the service or under the patronage of royalty; splendid, of exceptional size. —*n.* (*colloq.*) member of a royal family. **~ blue,** bright blue. **royally** *adv.*

Royalist *n.* supporter of the monarchy in the English Civil War.

royalty *n.* being royal; royal person(s); payment by a mining or oil company to the landowner; payment to an author etc. for each copy or performance of his work, or to a patentee for use of his patent.

R.S.V.P. *abbr.* (French *répondez s'il vous plaît*) please reply.

Rt. Hon. *abbr.* Right Honourable.

Rt. Rev., Rt. Revd. *abbr.* Right Reverend.

rub *v.t./i.* (p.t. *rubbed*) press against a surface and slide to and fro; polish, clean, dry, or make sore etc. by rubbing. —*n.* act or process of rubbing; difficulty. **~ it in,** emphasize or remind a person constantly of an unpleasant fact. **~ out,** remove (marks etc.) by using a rubber.

rubber[1] *n.* tough elastic substance made from the juice of certain plants or synthetically; piece of this for rubbing out pencil or ink marks; device for rubbing things. **~-stamp** *v.t.* approve automatically without consideration.

rubber[2] *n.* match of three successive games at bridge or whist.

rubberize *v.t.* treat or coat with rubber.

rubbery *a.* like rubber.

rubbish *n.* waste or worthless material; nonsense. **rubbishy** *a.*

rubble *n.* waste or rough fragments of stone or brick etc.

rubicund /ˈruː-/ *a.* (of the complexion) red, ruddy.

rubric /ˈruː-/ *n.* words put as a heading or note of explanation.

ruby *n.* red gem; deep red colour. —*a.* deep red.

ruche /ruʃ/ *n.* fabric gathered as trimming. —*v.t.* gather thus.

ruck *v.t./i.* & *n.* crease, wrinkle.

rucksack *n.* capacious bag carried on the back in hiking etc.

ructions *n.pl.* (*colloq.*) protests and noisy arguments, a row.

rudder *n.* vertical piece of metal or wood hinged to the stern of a boat or aircraft, used for steering.

ruddy *a.* (*-ier, -iest*) reddish. **ruddily** *adv.*, **ruddiness** *n.*

rude *a.* (*-er, -est*) impolite, showing no respect; primitive, roughly made; hearty; startling. **rudely** *adv.*, **rudeness** *n.*

rudiment *n.* rudimentary part or organ; (*pl.*) basic or elementary principles.

rudimentary *a.* incompletely developed; basic, elementary.

rue[1] *n.* shrub with bitter leaves formerly used in medicine.

rue[2] *v.t.* repent, regret.

rueful *a.* showing or feeling good-humoured regret. **ruefully** *adv.*

ruff[1] *n.* pleated frill worn round the neck in

the 16th century; projecting or coloured ring of feathers or fur round a bird's or animal's neck; bird of the sandpiper family.

ruff² *v.t./i.* trump in a card-game. —*n.* trumping.

ruffian *n.* violent lawless person.

ruffle *v.t./i.* disturb the smoothness (of); upset the calmness or even temper of. —*n.* gathered frill.

rug *n.* thick floor-mat; piece of thick warm fabric used as a covering.

Rugby *n.* = ~ **football**, a kind of football played with an oval ball which may be kicked or carried.

rugged /-gɪd/ *a.* uneven, irregular, craggy; rough but kindly. **ruggedly** *adv.*, **ruggedness** *n.*

rugger *n.* (*sl.*) Rugby football.

ruin *n.* severe damage or destruction; complete loss of one's fortune or prospects; broken remains of something; cause of ruin. —*v.t.* cause ruin to; reduce to ruins.

ruinous *a.* bringing ruin; in ruins, ruined. **ruinously** *adv.*

rule *n.* statement of what can or should or must be done in certain circumstances or in a game; dominant custom; governing, control; ruler used by carpenters etc. —*v.t./i.* have authoritative control (over), govern; keep under control; give an authoritative decision; draw (a line) using a ruler or other straight edge, mark parallel lines on. **as a** ~, usually. ~ **of thumb**, rough practical method of procedure. ~ **out**, exclude as irrelevant or ineligible.

ruler *n.* person who rules; straight strip used in measuring or for drawing straight lines.

rum¹ *n.* alcoholic spirit distilled from sugar-cane or molasses.

rum² *a.* (*colloq.*) strange, odd.

rumba *n.* ballroom dance of Cuban origin.

rumble¹ *v.i.* make a deep heavy continuous sound; utter in a deep voice. —*n.* rumbling sound.

rumble² *v.t.* (*sl.*) detect the true character of; see through (a deception).

ruminant /ˈruː-/ *n.* animal that chews the cud. —*a.* ruminating.

ruminate /ˈruː-/ *v.i.* chew the cud; meditate, ponder. **rumination** *n.*, **ruminative** /ˈruː-/ *a.*

rummage *v.i.* & *n.* search by disarranging things. ~ **sale**, jumble sale.

rummy *n.* card-game in which players try to form sets or sequences of cards.

rumour *n.* information spread by talking but not certainly true. **be rumoured**, be spread as a rumour.

rump *n.* buttocks; corresponding part of a bird.

rumple *v.t./i.* make or become crumpled; make untidy.

rumpus *n.* (*colloq.*) uproar, angry dispute.

run *v.t./i.* (p.t. *ran*, p.p. *run*, pres.p. *running*) move with quick steps and with always at least one foot off the ground; go smoothly or swiftly; compete in a race or contest; spread; flow, exude liquid; function; travel or convey from one point to another; extend; be current

or valid; be in a specified condition; cause to run; manage, organize; own and use (a vehicle etc.); (of a newspaper) print as an item; sew loosely or quickly. —*n.* spell or course of running; point scored in cricket or baseball; ladder in fabric; continuous stretch or sequence; general demand for goods etc.; general type or class of things; enclosure where domestic animals can range; track (e.g. for skiing); permission to make unrestricted use of something. **in** *or* **out of the running**, with a good *or* with no chance of winning. **in the long** ~, in the end, over a long period. **on the** ~, fleeing. ~ **across**, happen to meet or find. ~ **a blockade**, pass through it. ~ **a risk**, take a risk. ~ **a temperature**, be feverish. ~ **away**, leave quickly or secretly. ~ **down**, stop because not rewound; reduce the numbers of; knock down with a moving vehicle or ship; discover after searching; speak of in a slighting way; *be* ~ *down*, be weak or exhausted. ~**-down** *n.* detailed analysis. ~ **into**, collide with; happen to meet. ~ **off**, produce (copies etc.) on a machine. ~**-of-the-mill** *a.* ordinary. ~ **on**, talk continually. ~ **out**, become used up. ~ **out of**, have used up (one's stock). ~ **over**, knock down or crush with a vehicle. ~ **up**, allow (a bill) to mount. ~**-up** *n.* period leading up to an event.

runaway *n.* person who has run away. —*a.* having run away or become out of control; (of victory) won easily.

rune *n.* any of the letters in an early Germanic alphabet. **runic** *a.*

rung¹ *n.* cross-piece of a ladder etc.

rung² *see* **ring**².

runner *n.* person or animal that runs; messenger; creeping stem that roots; groove, strip, or roller etc. for a thing to move on; long narrow strip of carpet or ornamental cloth. ~ **bean**, climbing bean. ~**-up** *n.* one who finishes second in a competition.

runny *a.* semi-liquid; tending to flow or exude fluid.

runt *n.* undersized person or animal.

runway *n.* prepared surface on which aircraft may take off and land.

rupee /ruːˈpiː/ *n.* unit of money in India, Pakistan, etc.

rupture *n.* breaking, breach; abdominal hernia. —*v.t./i.* burst, break; cause hernia in.

rural *a.* of or in or like the countryside. ~ **dean**, (see *dean*).

ruse /ruːz/ *n.* deception, trick.

rush¹ *n.* marsh plant with a slender pithy stem.

rush² *v.t./i.* go or come or convey with great speed; act hastily; force into hasty action; attack or capture with a sudden assault. —*n.* rushing, instance of this; period of great activity; (*colloq.*) first print of a cinema film before editing. ~**-hour** *n.* one of the times of day when traffic is busiest.

rusk *n.* a kind of biscuit.

russet *a.* soft reddish-brown. —*n.* russet colour; a kind of apple with a rough skin.

rust *n.* brownish corrosive coating formed on

iron exposed to moisture; reddish-brown; plant disease with rust-coloured spots. —*v.t./i.* make or become rusty. **∼-proof** *a.*, **rustless** *a.*

rustic *a.* of or like country life or people; made of rough timber or untrimmed branches.

rusticate *v.i.* settle in the country. **rustication** *n.*

rustle *v.t./i.* make a sound like paper being crumpled, cause to do this; (*U.S.*) steal (horses or cattle). —*n.* rustling sound. **∼ up**, (*colloq.*) prepare, produce. **rustler** *n.*

rusty *a.* (*-ier, -iest*) affected with rust; rust-coloured; having lost quality by lack of use. **rustiness** *n.*

rut[1] *n.* deep track made by wheels; habitual usu. dull course of life. **rutted** *a.*

rut[2] *n.* periodic sexual excitement of a male deer, goat, etc. —*v.i.* (p.t. *rutted*) be affected with this.

ruthless *a.* having no pity. **ruthlessly** *adv.*, **ruthlessness** *n.*

rye *n.* a kind of cereal; whisky made from rye.

S

S. *abbr.* south.

sabbath *n.* day of religious services and abstinence from work (Saturday for Jews, Sunday for Christians).

sabbatical /-'bæt-/ *a.* of or like the sabbath. **∼ leave,** leave granted at intervals to a university professor etc. for study and travel.

sabotage /-tɑʒ/ *n.* wilful damage to machinery or materials, or disruption of work. —*v.t.* commit sabotage on; make useless. **saboteur** /-'tɜ(r)/ *n.*

sabre /'seɪbə(r)/ *n.* curved sword.

sac *n.* bag-like part in an animal or plant.

saccharin /-rɪn/ *n.* very sweet substance used instead of sugar.

saccharine /-rɪn/ *a.* intensely and unpleasantly sweet.

sachet /'sæʃeɪ/ *n.* small bag with a flap; small sealed pack.

sack[1] *n.* large bag of strong coarse fabric; *the* **∼**, (*colloq.*) dismissal from one's employment. —*v.t.* put into a sack or sacks; (*colloq.*) dismiss. **sackful** *n.* (pl. *-fuls*).

sack[2] *v.t.* plunder (a captured town) violently. —*n.* this act or process.

sackcloth, sacking *ns.* coarse fabric for making sacks.

sacrament *n.* any of the symbolic Christian religious ceremonies; consecrated elements in the Eucharist. **sacramental** *a.*

sacred *a.* holy; dedicated (to a person or purpose); connected with religion; sacrosanct. **∼ cow,** idea etc. which its supporters will not allow to be criticized.

sacrifice *n.* slaughter of a victim or presenting of a gift to win a god's favour; this victim or gift; giving up of a valued thing for the sake of something else; thing given up, loss entailed. —*v.t.* offer or kill or give up as a sacrifice. **sacrificial** *a.*

sacrilege /-lɪdʒ/ *n.* disrespect to a sacred thing. **sacrilegious** *a.*

sacristan *n.* person in charge of the contents of a church.

sacristy *n.* place where sacred vessels are kept in a church.

sacrosanct *a.* reverenced or respected and not to be harmed.

sad *a.* (*sadder, saddest*) showing or causing sorrow; regrettable; (of cake etc.) dense from not having risen. **sadly** *adv.*, **sadness** *n.*

sadden *v.t./i.* make or become sad.

saddle *n.* seat for a rider; ridge of high land between two peaks; joint of meat consisting of the two loins. —*v.t.* put a saddle on (an animal); burden with a task. **in the ∼,** in a controlling position.

saddler *n.* person who makes or deals in saddles and harness.

saddlery *n.* saddler's trade or goods.

sadism /'seɪ-/ *n.* enjoyment of inflicting or watching cruelty. **sadist** *n.*, **sadistic** /sə'dɪs-/ *a.*, **sadistically** *adv.*

safari /sə'fɑrɪ/ *n.* expedition to hunt or observe wild animals. **∼ park,** park where exotic wild animals are kept in the open for visitors to see.

safe *a.* (*-er, -est*) free from risk or danger; providing security. —*adv.* safely. —*n.* strong locked cupboard for valuables; ventilated cabinet for storing food. **∼ deposit,** building containing safes and strong-rooms for hire.

safeguard *n.* means of protection. —*v.t.* protect.

safety *n.* being safe, freedom from risk or danger. **∼-pin** *n.* brooch-like pin with a guard protecting and securing the point. **∼-valve** *n.* valve that opens automatically to relieve excessive pressure in a steam boiler; harmless outlet for excitement etc.

saffron *n.* orange-coloured stigmas of a kind of crocus, used to colour and flavour food; colour of these.

sag *v.i.* (p.t. *sagged*) droop or curve down in the middle under weight or pressure. —*n.* sagging.

saga /'sɑ-/ *n.* long story.

sagacious /-'geɪ-/ *a.* showing wisdom. **sagaciously** *adv.*, **sagacity** /-'gæ-/ *n.*

sage[1] *n.* herb with fragrant grey-green leaves used to flavour food.

sage[2] *a.* wise, esp. from experience. —*n.* wise man. **sagely** *adv.*

sago /'seɪ-/ *n.* starchy food in hard white grains, used in puddings.

said *see* **say.**

sail *n.* piece of fabric spread to catch the wind

and drive a ship or boat along; journey by ship or boat; arm of a windmill. —*v.t./i.* travel on water by use of sails or engine-power; start on a voyage; control the sailing of; move smoothly. **sailing-ship** *n.*

sailcloth *n.* canvas for sails; strong canvas-like dress-material.

sailor *n.* member of a ship's crew; traveller considered as liable (*bad* ∼), or not liable (*good* ∼) to sea-sickness.

saint *n.* holy person, esp. one venerated by the R.C. or Orthodox Church; soul in paradise; member of the Christian Church; very good or patient or unselfish person. **sainthood** *n.*, **saintly** *a.* **saintliness** *n.*

sake *n.* **for the** ∼ **of,** in order to please or honour (a person) or to get or keep (a thing).

salaam /-'lɑm/ *n.* Oriental salutation, a low bow. —*v.t./i.* make a salaam to.

salacious /-'leɪ-/ *a.* lewd, erotic. **salaciously** *adv.*, **salaciousness** *n.*, **salacity** /-'læ-/ *n.*

salad *n.* cold dish of one or more chopped or sliced (usu. raw) vegetables.

salamander /'sæ-/ *n.* lizard-like animal.

salami /-'lɑ-/ *n.* strongly flavoured Italian sausage.

salaried /-rɪd/ *a.* receiving a salary.

salary *n.* fixed regular (usu. monthly or quar-terly) payment by employer to employee.

sale *n.* selling; event at which goods are sold; disposal of a shop's stock at reduced prices. **for** *or* **on** ∼**,** offered for purchase.

saleable /-ləb-/ *a.* fit to be sold, likely to find a purchaser.

saleroom *n.* room where auctions are held.

salesman, saleswoman, salesperson *ns.* (pl. -*men*, -*women*) one employed to sell goods.

salesmanship *n.* skill at selling.

salient /'seɪ-/ *a.* projecting, most noticeable. —*n.* projecting part.

saline /'seɪlaɪn/ *a.* salty, containing salt(s). **salinity** /sə'lɪn-/ *n.*

saliva /-'laɪ-/ *n.* colourless liquid that forms in the mouth.

salivary /-'laɪ-/ *a.* of or producing saliva.

salivate /'sælɪ-/ *v.i.* produce saliva. **salivation** *n.*

sallow[1] /-ləʊ/ *a.* (-*er*, -*est*) (of the complexion) yellowish. **sallowness** *n.*

sallow[2] /-ləʊ/ *n.* low-growing willow.

sally *n.* sudden rush in attack; excursion; lively or witty remark. —*v.i.* ∼ **forth** *or* **out,** make a sally (in attack) or excursion.

salmi *n.* ragout or casserole, esp. of game-birds.

salmon *n.* (pl. *salmon*) large fish with pinkish flesh; salmon-pink. ∼**-pink** *a.* & *n.* yellowish-pink. ∼ **trout,** trout resembling salmon.

salon /'sælɔ̃/ *n.* elegant room for receiving guests; room or establishment where a hair-dresser or couturier etc. receives clients.

saloon *n.* public room for a specified purpose, or on board ship; (*U.S.*) public bar; saloon car. ∼ **car,** car for a driver and passengers, with a closed body.

salsify /'sæl-/ *n.* plant with a long fleshy root used as a vegetable.

salt *n.* sodium chloride obtained from mines or by evaporation from sea-water, used to season and preserve food; chemical com-pound of a metal and an acid; salt-cellar; (*pl.*) substance resembling salt in form, esp. a laxative. —*a.* tasting of salt; impregnated with salt. —*v.t.* season with salt; preserve in salt; make (a mine) appear rich by fraudu-lently inserting precious metal before it is viewed. **old** ∼**,** experienced sailor. ∼ **away,** put aside for the future. ∼**-cellar** *n.* dish or perforated pot holding salt for use at meals.

salty *a.*, **saltiness** *n.*

saltire /'sæ-/ *n.* a cross (×) dividing a shield into four parts.

saltpetre *n.* salty white powder used in gun-powder, in medicine, and in preserving meat.

salubrious /-'lu-/ *a.* health-giving. **salubrity** *n.*

saluki /-'lu-/ *n.* (pl. -*is*) tall swift silky-coated dog.

salutary /'sæ-/ *a.* producing a beneficial or wholesome effect.

salutation *n.* word(s) or gesture of greeting; expression of respect.

salute *n.* gesture of respect or greeting. —*v.t.* make a salute to.

salvage *n.* rescue of a ship or its cargo from loss at sea, or of property from fire etc.; saving and use of waste material; items saved thus. —*v.t.* save from loss or for use as salvage.

salvation *n.* saving from disaster, esp. from sin and its spiritual consequences.

salve *n.* soothing ointment; thing that soothes. —*v.t.* soothe (conscience etc.).

salver *n.* a kind of small tray.

salvo *n.* (pl. -*oes*) firing of guns simultaneously; volley of applause.

sal volatile /və'lætɪlɪ/ flavoured solution of ammonium carbonate, drunk as a remedy for faintness.

same *a.* being of one kind, not changed or different; previously mentioned; *the* ∼**,** the same thing, in the same manner. **sameness** *n.*

samovar *n.* metal urn for making tea, used esp. in Russia.

sampan *n.* small boat used along coasts and rivers of China.

samphire *n.* plant with fragrant fleshy leaves, growing on cliffs.

sample *n.* small separated part showing the quality of the whole; specimen. —*v.t.* test by taking a sample or getting an experience of.

sampler *n.* thing that takes samples; piece of embroidery worked in various stitches to show one's skill.

sanatorium *n.* (pl. -*ums*) establishment for treating chronic diseases or convalescents; room or building for sick persons in a school etc.

sanctify *v.t.* make holy or sacred. **sanctification** *n.*

sanctimonious /-'məʊ-/ *a.* making a show of righteousness or piety. **sanctimoniously** *adv.*, **sanctimoniousness** *n.*

sanction *n.* permission, approval; penalty im-posed on a country or organization. —*v.t.* give sanction to, authorize.

sanctity *n.* sacredness, holiness.

sanctuary *n.* sacred place; part of a chancel containing the altar; place where birds or wild animals are protected; refuge.

sanctum *n.* holy place; person's private room.

sand *n.* very fine loose fragments of crushed rock; (*pl.*) expanse of sand, sandbank. —*v.t.* sprinkle or cover with sand; smooth with sand or sandpaper. **~-blast** *v.t.* treat with a jet of sand driven by compressed air or steam.

sandal *n.* light shoe with straps or thongs. **sandalled** *a.*

sandalwood *n.* a kind of scented wood.

sandbag *n.* bag filled with sand, used to protect a wall or building. —*v.t.* (p.t. -*bagged*) protect with sandbags.

sandbank *n.* underwater deposit of sand.

sandpaper *n.* paper with a coating of sand or other abrasive substance, used for smoothing surfaces. —*v.t.* smooth with this.

sandpiper *n.* bird inhabiting wet sandy places.

sandstone *n.* rock formed of compressed sand.

sandstorm *n.* desert storm of wind with blown sand.

sandwich *n.* two or more slices of bread with a layer of filling between; thing arranged like this. —*v.t.* put between two others.

sandy *a.* like sand; covered with sand; yellowish-red.

sane *a.* (-*er*, -*est*) having a sound mind, not mad; sensible and practical. **sanely** *adv.*

sang *see* **sing.**

sang-froid /sä'frwɑ/ *n.* calmness in danger or difficulty.

sanguinary /'sæŋgwɪn-/ *a.* full of bloodshed; bloodthirsty.

sanguine /-gwɪn/ *a.* optimistic.

sanitary *a.* of hygiene; hygienic; of sanitation.

sanitation *n.* arrangements to protect public health, esp. drainage and disposal of sewage.

sanity *n.* condition of being sane.

sank *see* **sink.**

Sanskrit *n.* ancient Indo-European language.

sap[1] *n.* vital liquid in plants; (*sl.*) foolish person. —*v.t.* (p.t. *sapped*) exhaust gradually.

sap[2] *n.* trench or tunnel dug to get closer to an enemy.

sapele /-'pilɪ/ *n.* mahogany-like wood; tree producing this.

sapling *n.* young tree.

sapphire *n.* transparent blue precious stone; its colour. —*a.* bright blue.

saprophyte /'sæ-/ *n.* fungus or related plant living on decayed matter. **saprophytic** /-'fɪt-/ *a.*

Saracen /'sæ-/ *n.* Arab or Muslim of the time of the Crusades.

sarcasm *n.* ironical remark; use of such remarks. **sarcastic** *a.*, **sarcastically** *adv.*

sarcophagus /-'kof-/ *n.* (pl. -*gi*, pr. -gɑɪ) stone coffin.

sardine *n.* young pilchard or similar small fish.

sardonic *a.* humorous in a grim or sarcastic way. **sardonically** *adv.*

sari *n.* (pl. -*is*) length of cloth draped round the body, worn as the main garment by Hindu women.

sarong *n.* strip of cloth worn round the body, esp. in Malaya and Java.

sarsen *n.* sandstone boulder.

sartorial *a.* of tailoring; of men's clothing.

sash[1] *n.* long strip of cloth worn round the body at the waist or over one shoulder.

sash[2] *n.* frame holding a glass pane of a window and sliding up and down in grooves. **~-cord** *n.* cord attaching a balancing-weight at each end of this. **~-window** *n.*

Sassenach /'sæsənæk/ *n.* (*Sc.* & *Irish*) Englishman.

sat *see* **sit.**

Satanic /-'tæn-/ *a.* of Satan.

satanic /-'tæn-/ *a.* devilish, hellish.

Satanism /'seɪ-/ *n.* worship of Satan.

satchel *n.* bag for carrying school books or other light articles, hung over the shoulder(s).

sate *v.t.* satiate.

sateen /-'tin/ *n.* closely woven cotton fabric resembling satin.

satellite *n.* heavenly or artificial body revolving round a planet; person's hanger-on; country that is subservient to another.

satiate /'seɪʃɪeɪt/ *v.t.* satisfy fully, glut. **satiation** *n.*

satiety /sə'taɪətɪ/ *n.* condition of being satiated.

satin *n.* silky material that is glossy on one side. —*a.* smooth as satin. **satiny** *a.*

satinette *n.* satin-like fabric.

satinwood *n.* smooth hard wood; tropical tree yielding this.

satire *n.* use of ridicule, irony, or sarcasm; novel or play etc. that ridicules something. **satirical** /-'tɪ-/ *a.*, **satirically** *adv.*

satirize *v.t.* attack with satire; describe satirically. **satirist** *n.*

satisfactory *a.* satisfying an expectation or need, adequate. **satisfactorily** *adv.*

satisfy *v.t.* give (a person) what he wants or needs; make pleased or contented; end (a demand etc.) by giving what is required; provide with sufficient proof, convince; pay (a creditor). **satisfaction** *n.*

satsuma /'sæ-/ *n.* a kind of mandarin orange.

saturate *v.t.* make thoroughly wet; cause to absorb or accept as much as possible. **saturation** *n.*

Saturday *n.* day after Friday.

saturnalia /-'neɪ-/ *n.* wild revelry.

saturnine /-naɪn/ *a.* having a gloomy or forbidding appearance.

satyr /-tə(r)/ *n.* woodland god in classical mythology, with a goat's ears, tail, and legs.

sauce *n.* liquid or semi-liquid preparation added to food to give flavour or richness; (*sl.*) impudence.

saucepan *n.* metal cooking-pot with a long handle, used for boiling things over heat.

saucer *n.* curved dish on which a cup stands; thing shaped like this.

saucy *a.* (-*ier*, -*iest*) impudent; jaunty. **saucily** *adv.*, **sauciness** *n.*

sauerkraut /ˈsaʊəkraʊt/ *n.* chopped pickled cabbage.

sauna /ˈsɔ-/ *n.* Finnish-style steam bath.

saunter *v.i. & n.* stroll.

saurian /ˈsɔ-/ *a.* of or like a lizard. —*n.* animal of the lizard family.

sausage *n.* minced seasoned meat in a tubular case of thin skin.

savage *a.* uncivilized; wild and fierce; cruel and hostile; (*colloq.*) very angry. —*n.* member of an uncivilized tribe. —*v.t.* maul savagely. **savagely** *adv.*, **savageness** *n.*, **savagery** *n.*

savannah /-ˈvænə/ *n.* grassy plain in hot regions.

save *v.t./i.* rescue, keep from danger or harm or capture; avoid wasting; keep for future use, put aside money thus; relieve (a person) from (trouble etc.); prevent the scoring of (a goal etc.). —*n.* act of saving in football etc. **saver** *n.*

saving *prep.* except.

savings *n.pl.* money put aside for future use.

saviour *n.* person who rescues people from harm or danger; *the* or *our S~*, Christ as saviour of mankind.

savory *n.* spicy herb.

savour *n.* flavour; smell. —*v.t./i.* have a certain savour; taste or smell with enjoyment.

savoury *a.* having an appetizing taste or smell; salty or piquant and not sweet in flavour. —*n.* savoury dish, esp. at the end of a meal.

savoy *n.* a kind of cabbage.

saw[1] *see* **see**[1].

saw[2] *n.* tool with a zigzag edge for cutting wood or metal. —*v.t./i.* (p.t. *sawed*, p.p. *sawn*) cut with a saw; make a to-and-fro movement.

sawdust *n.* powdery fragments of wood, made in sawing timber.

sawfish *n.* large sea-fish with a jagged blade-like snout.

sawmill *n.* mill where timber is cut into planks etc.

sawyer *n.* workman who saws timber.

sawn *see* **saw**[2].

sax *n.* (*colloq.*) saxophone.

saxe *n.* **~-blue**, greyish-blue.

saxifrage *n.* a kind of rock plant.

Saxon *n. & a.* (member, language) of a Germanic people who occupied parts of England in the 5th–6th centuries.

saxophone *n.* brass wind instrument with finger-operated keys.

say *v.t./i.* (p.t. *said*, pr. sed) utter, recite; express in words, state; give as an opinion or argument or excuse; suppose as a possibility etc. —*n.* power to decide. **I ~!**, expression of surprise or admiration, or used to call attention.

saying *n.* well-known phrase or proverb or other statement.

scab *n.* crust forming over a sore; skin-disease or plant-disease causing similar roughness; (*colloq., derog.*) blackleg. **scabby** *a.*

scabbard *n.* sheath of a sword etc.

scabies /ˈskeɪbiz/ *n.* contagious skin-disease causing itching.

scabious /ˈskeɪbɪəs/ *n.* herbaceous plant with clustered flowers.

scaffold *n.* wooden platform for the execution of criminals; scaffolding. —*v.t.* fit scaffolding to.

scaffolding *n.* poles and planks providing platforms for workmen building or repairing a house etc.

scalable *a.* able to be scaled.

scald *v.t.* injure or pain with hot liquid or steam; heat (milk) to near boiling-point; cleanse with boiling water. —*n.* injury to the skin by scalding.

scale[1] *n.* one of the overlapping plates of horny membrane protecting the skin of fishes and reptiles; thing resembling this; incrustation caused by hard water or forming on teeth. —*v.t./i.* remove scale(s) from; come off in scales. **scaly** *a.*

scale[2] *n.* pan of a balance; (*pl.*) instrument for weighing things.

scale[3] *n.* ordered series of units or qualities etc. for measuring or classifying things; fixed series of notes in a system of music; relative size or extent. —*v.t.* climb; represent in measurements or extent in proportion to the size of the original.

scallop /ˈskɒl-/ *n.* shellfish with hinged fan-shaped shells; one shell of this; (*pl.*) semi-circular curves as an ornamental edging. **scalloped** *a.*

scallywag *n.* (*sl.*) rascal.

scalp *n.* skin of the head excluding the face. —*v.t.* cut the scalp from.

scalpel /ˈskæ-/ *n.* surgeon's small straight knife.

scamp *n.* rascal. —*v.t.* do (work) hastily and inadequately.

scamper *v.i.* run hastily or in play. —*n.* scampering run.

scampi *n.pl.* large prawns.

scan *v.t./i.* (p.t. *scanned*) look at all parts of, esp. quickly; pass a radar or electronic beam over; analyse the rhythm of (verse); (of verse) have a regular rhythm. —*n.* scanning. **scanner** *n.*

scandal *n.* something disgraceful; gossip about wrong-doing. **scandalous** *a.*, **scandalously** *adv.*

scandalize *v.t.* shock by scandal.

scandalmonger *n.* person who invents or spreads scandal.

Scandinavian *a. & n.* (native) of Scandinavia.

scansion *n.* scanning of verse.

scant *a.* scanty, insufficient.

scanty *a.* (*-ier, -iest*) small in amount or extent; barely enough. **scantily** *adv.*, **scantiness** *n.*

scapegoat *n.* person made to bear blame that should fall on others.

scapula *n.* (pl. *-lae*) shoulder-blade.

scar *n.* mark left by damage, esp. where a wound or sore has healed. —*v.t./i.* (p.t. *scarred*) mark with a scar; form scar(s).

scarab /ˈskæ-/ *n.* carving of a beetle, used in ancient Egypt as a charm.

scarce *a.* (*-er, -est*) not enough to supply a demand, rare. **make oneself ~**, (*colloq.*) go away.

scarcely *adv.* only just, almost not; not, surely not.

scarcity *n.* being scarce, shortage.

scare *v.t./i.* frighten; become frightened. —*n.* fright, alarm.

scarecrow *n.* figure dressed in old clothes and set up to scare birds away from crops.

scaremonger *n.* alarmist.

scarf *n.* (pl. *scarves*) piece or strip of material worn round the neck or tied over a woman's head.

scarify /ˈskæ-/ *v.t.* make slight cuts in; criticize harshly.

scarlet *a. & n.* brilliant red. ~ **fever,** infectious fever producing a scarlet rash.

scarp *n.* steep slope on a hillside.

scarper *v.i.* (*sl.*) run away.

scary *a.* (-ier, -iest) frightening; easily frightened.

scathing /ˈskeɪð-/ *a.* (of criticism) very severe.

scatter *v.t./i.* throw or put here and there; cover thus; go or send in different directions. —*n.* small scattered amount. ~**-brain** *n.* person who is frivolous or careless and unsystematic. ~**-brained** *a.*

scatty *a.* (-ier, -iest) (*sl.*) crazy.

scaup /skɔp/ *n.* a kind of duck.

scavenge *v.t./i.* search for (usable objects) among rubbish etc.; (of animals) search for decaying flesh as food. **scavenger** *n.*

scenario /-ˈnɑr-/ *n.* (pl. *-os*) script or summary of a film or play; imagined sequence of events.

scene *n.* place of an event; piece of continuous action in a play or film; dramatic outburst of temper or emotion; stage scenery; landscape or view or incident as seen; (*sl.*) area of activity. **behind the scenes,** hidden from public view.

scenery *n.* general (esp. picturesque) appearance of a landscape; structures used on a theatre stage to represent the scene of action.

scenic /ˈsi-/ *a.* picturesque.

scent *n.* pleasant smell; liquid perfume; animal's trail perceptible to a hound's sense of smell; animal's sense of smell. —*v.t.* discover by smell; suspect the presence or existence of; apply scent to, make fragrant.

sceptic /ˈskep-/ *n.* sceptical person.

sceptical /ˈskep-/ *a.* unwilling to believe things. **sceptically** *adv.*, **scepticism** *n.*

sceptre *n.* ornamental rod carried as a symbol of sovereignty.

schedule /ˈʃedjul/ *n.* programme or timetable of events. —*v.t.* appoint in a schedule.

schematic /ski-/ *a.* in the form of a diagram. **schematically** *adv.*

scheme *n.* plan of work or action. —*v.t./i.* make plans, plot. **schemer** *n.*

scherzo /ˈskeərtsəʊ/ *n.* (pl. *-os*) lively musical composition or passage.

schism /ˈsɪzm/ *n.* division into opposing groups through difference in belief or opinion. **schismatic** /-ˈmæt-/ *a. & n.*

schizoid *a.* like or suffering from schizophrenia. —*n.* schizoid person.

schizophrenia /-ˈfri-/ *n.* mental disorder in which a person is unable to act or reason rationally. **schizophrenic** /-ˈfren-/ *a. & n.*

scholar *n.* person with great learning; academic person; holder of a scholarship. **scholarly** *a.*, **scholarliness** *n.*

scholarship *n.* grant of money towards education; great learning; scholars' methods and achievements.

scholastic /-ˈlæs-/ *a.* of schools or education; academic.

school[1] *n.* shoal of fish or whales.

school[2] *n.* institution for educating children or giving instruction; group of philosophers, artists, etc., following the same principles. —*v.t.* train, discipline. **schoolboy** *n.*, **schoolchild** *n.* (pl. *-children*), **schoolgirl** *n.*

schoolmaster, schoolmistress *ns.* male or female schoolteacher.

schoolteacher *n.* teacher in a school.

schooner /ˈsku-/ *n.* a kind of sailing-ship; measure for sherry etc.

sciatic /saɪˈæ-/ *a.* of the hip or the ~ **nerve** (nerve running from pelvis to thigh). **sciatica** *n.* pain in this nerve or region.

science *n.* branch of knowledge requiring systematic study and method, esp. dealing with substances, life, and natural laws. **scientific** *a.*, **scientifically** *adv.*

scientist *n.* expert in science(s).

scilla /ˈsɪlə/ *n.* plant with small blue hanging flowers.

scimitar /ˈsɪm-/ *n.* short curved Oriental sword.

scintillate *v.i.* sparkle, spark; be brilliant in wit etc. **scintillation** *n.*

scion /ˈsaɪən/ *n.* shoot, esp. cut for grafting; descendant.

scissors *n.pl.* cutting instrument with two pivoted blades.

sclerosis *n.* abnormal hardening of tissue.

scoff[1] *v.i.* speak contemptuously, jeer. **scoffer** *n.*

scoff[2] *v.t.* (*sl.*) eat quickly.

scold *v.t.* rebuke (esp. a child or servant). **scolding** *n.*

sconce *n.* ornamental bracket on a wall, holding a light.

scone /skon *or* skəʊn/ *n.* a kind of soft flat cake baked quickly and eaten buttered.

scoop *n.* deep shovel-like tool; a kind of ladle; scooping movement; piece of news published by one newspaper before its rivals. —*v.t.* lift or hollow with (or as if with) a scoop; forestall with a news scoop.

scoot *v.i.* run, dart.

scooter *n.* child's toy vehicle with a footboard and long steering-handle; a kind of lightweight motor cycle. **scooterist** *n.*

scope *n.* range of a subject etc.; opportunity, outlet.

scorch *v.t./i.* burn or become burnt on the surface; (*sl.*) travel very fast. **scorching** *a.* (*colloq.*) extremely hot.

score *n.* number of points gained in a game or competition; set of twenty; line or mark cut into something; written or printed music showing the notes on a series of staves.

—*v.t./i.* gain (points etc.) in a game or competition; keep a record of the score; achieve; cut a line or mark into; write or compose as a musical score. **on the ∼ of,** for the reason of. **∼ off,** humiliate by a clever remark. **∼ out,** cross out. **scorer** *n.*

scorn *n.* strong contempt. —*v.t.* feel or show scorn for; reject with scorn. **scornful** *a.*, **scornfully** *adv.*, **scornfulness** *n.*

scorpion *n.* small animal of the spider group with lobster-like claws and a sting in its long tail.

Scot *n.* native of Scotland.

Scotch *a.* Scottish. —*n.* Scottish dialect; Scotch whisky. **∼ cap,** man's wide beret.

scotch *v.t.* put an end to (a rumour).

scot-free *a.* unharmed, not punished; free of charge.

Scots *a.* Scottish. —*n.* Scottish dialect. **Scotsman** *n.*, **Scotswoman** *n.*

Scottish *a.* of Scotland or its people or their form of the English language.

scoundrel *n.* dishonest or unprincipled person.

scour[1] *v.t.* cleanse or brighten by rubbing; clear out (a channel etc.) by flowing water; purge drastically. —*n.* scouring; action of water on a channel etc. **scourer** *n.*

scour[2] *v.t.* search thoroughly.

scourge /skɜːdʒ/ *n.* whip; great affliction. —*v.t.* flog; afflict greatly.

Scouse *a. & n.* (native, dialect) of Liverpool.

scout[1] *n.* person sent to gather information, esp. about enemy movements etc. —*v.i.* act as scout, search.

scout[2] *v.t.* reject (an idea) scornfully.

Scout *n.* member of the Scout Association, an organization for boys.

scowl *n.* sullen or angry frown. —*v.i.* make a scowl.

scrabble *v.i.* scratch with the hands or feet; grope busily.

scrag *n.* bony part of an animal's carcass as food.

scraggy *a.* (*-ier, -iest*) lean and bony.

scram *v.imper.* (*sl.*) go away.

scramble *v.t./i.* clamber; move hastily or awkwardly; struggle to do or obtain something; mix indiscriminately; cook (eggs) by mixing the contents and heating the mixture; make (a telephone conversation etc.) unintelligible except by means of a special receiver, by altering its transmission frequency. —*n.* scrambling walk or movement; eager struggle; motor-cycle race over rough ground. **scrambler** *n.*

scrap[1] *n.* fragment, remnant; waste material; discarded metal suitable for being reprocessed. —*v.t.* (p.t. *scrapped*) discard as useless. **∼-book** *n.* book in which to mount newspaper cuttings or similar souvenirs.

scrap[2] *n. & v.i.* (*colloq.*) fight, quarrel.

scrape *v.t./i.* clean, smooth, or damage by passing a hard edge across a surface; pass (an edge) across in this way; dig by scraping; make the sound of scraping; get along or through etc. with difficulty, esp. while

(almost) touching; obtain or amass with difficulty; be very economical. —*n.* scraping movement or sound; scraped place; thinly applied layer of butter; awkward situation resulting from an escapade. **scraper** *n.*

scrapings *n.pl.* fragments produced by scraping.

scrappy *a.* (*-ier, -iest*) made up of scraps or disconnected elements.

scratch *v.t./i.* cut a shallow line or wound on (a surface) with something sharp; form by scratching; scrape with the fingernails; make a thin scraping sound; obtain with difficulty; withdraw from a race or competition. —*n.* mark, wound, or sound made by scratching; spell of scratching; line from which competitors start in a race when they receive no handicap. —*a.* collected from what is available; receiving no handicap. **start from ∼,** start at the very beginning or with no advantage or preparation. **up to ∼,** up to the required standard. **scratchy** *a.*

scrawl *n.* bad handwriting; something written in this. —*v.t./i.* write in a scrawl.

scrawny *a.* (*-ier, -iest*) scraggy.

scream *v.t./i.* make a long piercing cry or sound; utter in a screaming tone. —*n.* screaming cry or sound; (*sl.*) extremely amusing person or thing.

scree *n.* mass of loose stones on a mountain side.

screech *n.* harsh high-pitched scream or sound. —*v.t./i.* make or utter with a screech. **∼-owl** *n.* owl that makes a screeching cry.

screed *n.* tiresomely long list or letter etc.

screen *n.* upright structure used to conceal or protect or divide something; anything serving a similar purpose; windscreen; blank surface on which pictures or cinema films or television transmissions etc. are projected; large sieve. —*v.t.* shelter, conceal; protect from discovery or deserved blame; show (images etc.) on a screen; sieve; examine for the presence or absence of a disease or quality or potential loyalty etc.

screw *n.* metal pin with a spiral ridge round its length, fastened by turning; thing twisted to tighten or press something; propeller, esp. of a ship or motor boat; act of screwing; (*sl.*) wage, salary. —*v.t./i.* fasten or tighten with screw(s); turn (a screw); twist, become twisted; oppress, extort; (*sl.*) extort money from.

screwdriver *n.* tool for turning screws.

screwy *a.* (*-ier, -iest*) (*sl.*) crazy.

scribble *v.t./i.* write hurriedly or carelessly; make meaningless marks. —*n.* something scribbled.

scribe *n.* person who (before the invention of printing) made copies of writings; (in New Testament times) professional religious scholar.

scrimmage *n.* confused struggle.

scrimp *v.t./i.* skimp.

scrimshank *v.i.* shirk work, malinger.

scrip *n.* extra share(s) (in a business) issued instead of a dividend.

script *n.* handwriting; style of printed characters resembling this; text of a play or film or broadcast talk etc.

scripture *n.* any sacred writings; S~ or *the Scriptures*, those of the Christians (Old and New Testaments) or the Jews (Old Testament). **scriptural** *a.*

scroll *n.* roll of paper or parchment; ornamental design in this shape.

scrotum /ˈskrəʊ-/ *n.* (pl. -ta) pouch of skin enclosing the testicles.

scrounge *v.t./i.* cadge; collect by foraging. **scrounger** *n.*

scrub[1] *n.* vegetation consisting of stunted trees and shrubs; land covered with this.

scrub[2] *v.t./i.* (p.t. *scrubbed*) rub hard esp. with something coarse or bristly. —*n.* process of scrubbing.

scrubby *a.* (-ier, -iest) small and mean or shabby.

scruff *n.* back of the neck.

scruffy *a.* (-ier, -iest) shabby and untidy. **scruffily** *adv.*, **scruffiness** *n.*

scrum *n.* scrummage; confused struggle.

scrummage *n.* grouping of forwards in Rugby football to struggle for possession of the ball by pushing.

scrumping *n.* (*colloq.*) stealing apples from trees.

scrumptious *a.* (*colloq.*) delicious.

scrunch *v.t./i.* crunch.

scruple *n.* doubt about doing something, produced by one's conscience. —*v.t.* hesitate because of scruples.

scrupulous *a.* very conscientious or careful. **scrupulously** *adv.*, **scrupulousness** *n.*, **scrupulosity** *n.*

scrutinize *v.t.* make a scrutiny of.

scrutiny *n.* careful look or examination.

scuba /ˈskjuː-/ *n.* self-contained underwater breathing apparatus.

scud *v.i.* (p.t. *scudded*) move along fast and smoothly.

scuff *v.t./i.* scrape or drag (one's feet) in walking; mark or scrape by doing this.

scuffle *n.* confused struggle or fight. —*v.i.* take part in a scuffle.

scull *n.* one of a pair of small oars; oar that rests on a boat's stern, worked with a screw-like movement. —*v.t./i.* row with scull(s).

scullery *n.* room where dishes etc. are washed.

sculpt *v.t./i.* (*colloq.*) sculpture.

sculptor *n.* maker of sculptures.

sculpture *n.* art of carving or modelling in wood or stone etc.; work made thus. —*v.t./i.* represent in or decorate with sculpture; be a sculptor.

scum *n.* layer of impurities or froth etc. on the surface of a liquid; worthless person(s).

scupper *n.* opening in a ship's side to drain water from the deck. —*v.t.* (*sl.*) sink (a ship) deliberately, wreck.

scurf *n.* flakes of dry skin, esp. from the scalp; similar scaly matter.

scurrilous /ˈskʌ-/ *a.* abusive and insulting; coarsely humorous. **scurrilously** *adv.*, **scurrility** *n.*

scurry *v.i.* run hurriedly, scamper. —*n.* scurrying, rush.

scurvy *n.* disease caused by lack of vitamin C in the diet.

scut *n.* short tail of a rabbit, hare, or deer.

scutter *v.i. & n.* (*colloq.*) scurry.

scuttle[1] *n.* box or bucket for holding coal in a room; part of a car body between the windscreen and the bonnet.

scuttle[2] *n.* small opening with a lid, esp. in a ship's deck or side. —*v.t.* sink (a ship) by letting in water.

scuttle[3] *v.i. & n.* scurry.

scythe /saɪð/ *n.* implement with a curved blade on a long handle, for cutting long grass or grain.

sea *n.* expanse of salt water surrounding the continents; section of this; large inland lake; waves of the sea; vast expanse. **at ~**, in a ship on the sea; perplexed. **by ~**, carried by ship. **~-green** *a. & n.* bluish-green. **~-horse** *n.* small fish with a horse-like head. **~-level** *n.* level corresponding to the mean level of the sea's surface. **~-lion** *n.* a kind of large seal. **~-mew** *n.* gull. **~-urchin** *n.* sea animal with a round spiky shell.

seaboard *n.* coast.

seafarer *n.* seafaring person.

seafaring *a. & n.* working or travelling on the sea.

seafood *n.* fish or shellfish from the sea eaten as food.

seagoing *a.* for sea voyages; seafaring.

seagull *n.* gull.

seal[1] *n.* amphibious sea animal with thick fur or bristles.

seal[2] *n.* engraved piece of metal etc. used to stamp a design; its impression; action or event etc. serving to confirm or guarantee something; paper sticker resembling a postage stamp; thing used to close an opening very tightly. —*v.t./i.* affix a seal to; close or coat so as to prevent penetration; stick down; settle, decide (e.g. a bargain). **~ off**, prevent access to (an area).

sealant *n.* substance for coating a surface to make it watertight.

sealing-wax *n.* a kind of wax used for impressing with a design.

sealskin *n.* seal's skin or fur used as a clothing material.

seam *n.* line where two edges join; layer of coal etc. in the ground. —*v.t.* join by a seam.

seaman *n.* (pl. -men) sailor; person skilled in seafaring. **seamanship** *n.*

seamstress /ˈsem-/ *n.* woman whose job is sewing things.

seamy *a.* **~ side**, unattractive or disreputable side (of life).

seance /ˈseɪɑ̃s/ *n.* spiritualist meeting.

seaplane *n.* aeroplane designed to take off from and land on water.

seaport *n.* port on the coast.

sear *v.t.* scorch, burn.

search *v.t./i.* look or feel or go over (a person

or place etc.) in order to find something. —*n.* process of searching. **searcher** *n.*

searchlight *n.* outdoor lamp with a powerful beam; its beam.

seascape *n.* picture or view of the sea.

seasick *a.* made sick by the motion of a ship. **seasickness** *n.*

seaside *n.* sea-coast, esp. as a place for holidays.

season *n.* section of the year associated with a type of weather; time when something is common or plentiful, or when an activity takes place. —*v.t./i.* give extra flavour to (food); dry or treat until ready for use. ∼-**ticket** *n.* ticket valid for any number of journeys or performances etc. in a specified period.

seasonable *a.* suitable for the season; timely. **seasonably** *adv.*

seasonal *a.* of a season or seasons; varying with the seasons.

seasoned *a.* (of people) experienced.

seasoning *n.* substance used to season food.

seat *n.* thing made or used for sitting on; horizontal part of a chair etc. on which a sitter's body rests; place as member of a committee or parliament etc.; buttocks, part of a garment covering these; place where something is based; country mansion; manner of sitting on a horse etc. —*v.t.* cause to sit; have seats for; put (machinery etc.) on its support. ∼-**belt** *n.* strap securing a person to his seat in a vehicle or aircraft. **be seated,** sit down.

seaward *a. & adv.* towards the sea. **seawards** *adv.*

seaweed *n.* any plant that grows in the sea.

seaworthy *a.* (of ships) fit for a sea voyage.

sebaceous /-ˈbeɪʃəs/ *a.* secreting an oily or greasy substance.

secateurs /-ˈtɜz *or* ˈsek-/ *n.pl.* clippers for pruning plants.

secede /-ˈsid/ *v.i.* withdraw from membership. **secession** *n.*

seclude *v.t.* keep (a person) apart from others. **secluded** *a.* screened from view. **seclusion** *n.*

second[1] /ˈsek-/ *a.* next after the first; following the first; secondary; inferior. —*n.* second thing, class, etc.; attendant of a person taking part in a duel or boxing-match; sixtieth part of a minute of time or (in measuring angles) degree. —*v.t.* assist; state one's support of (a proposal) formally. ∼-**best** *a.* next to the best in quality; inferior. ∼-**class** *a. & adv.* next or inferior to first-class in quality etc. ∼ **cousin** (see *cousin*). **at** ∼ **hand,** indirectly, not from the original source. ∼-**hand** *a.* bought after use by a previous owner; dealing in used goods. ∼ **nature,** habit or characteristic that has become automatic. ∼-**rate** *a.* inferior in quality. ∼ **sight,** supposed power to foresee future events.

second[2] /-ˈkond/ *v.t.* transfer temporarily to another job or department. **secondment** *n.*

secondary *a.* coming after or derived from what is primary. ∼ **colours,** those obtained by mixing two primary colours. ∼ **education,**

∼**school,** that for children who have received primary education. **secondarily** *adv.*

secondly *adv.* second.

secret *a.* kept or intended to be kept from the knowledge or view of most people; operating secretly. —*n.* something secret; mystery; thing not widely understood. **in** ∼, secretly. ∼ **police,** police force operating secretly for political purposes. **Secret Service,** government department conducting espionage. **secretly** *adv.*, **secrecy** *n.*

secretaire /sekrɪˈteə(r)/ *n.* writing-desk with drawers.

secretariat /-ˈteər-/ *n.* administrative office or department.

secretary /ˈsekrətrɪ/ *n.* person employed to help deal with correspondence and routine office-work; official in charge of an organization's correspondence; ambassador's or government minister's chief assistant. **Secretary of State,** head of a major government department. **secretarial** *a.*

secrete /-ˈkrit/ *v.t.* put into a place of concealment; produce by secretion. **secretor** *n.*

secretion /-ˈkri-/ *n.* process of secreting; production of a substance within the body; this substance.

secretive /ˈsik-/ *a.* making a secret of things. **secretively** *adv.*, **secretiveness** *n.*

sect *n.* group with beliefs that differ from those generally accepted.

sectarian /-ˈteər-/ *a.* of a sect or sects; narrow-mindedly promoting the interests of one's sect.

section *n.* distinct part; cross-section; process of cutting something surgically. —*v.t.* divide into sections.

sectional *a.* of a section or sections; made in sections.

sector *n.* part of an area; branch of an activity; section of a circular area between two lines drawn from its centre to its circumference.

secular *a.* of worldly (not religious or spiritual) matters.

secure *a.* safe, esp. against attack; certain not to slip or fail. —*v.t.* make secure; fasten securely; obtain; guarantee by pledging something as security. **securely** *adv.*

security *n.* safety; safety of a country or organization against espionage or theft or other danger; thing serving as a pledge; certificate showing ownership of financial stocks etc.

sedan /-ˈdæn/ *n.* sedan-chair; (*U.S.*) saloon car. ∼-**chair** *n.* enclosed chair (17th–18th centuries) carried on two poles by bearers.

sedate[1] *a.* calm and dignified. **sedately** *adv.*, **sedateness** *n.*

sedate[2] *v.t.* treat with sedatives. **sedation** *n.*

sedative /ˈsed-/ *a.* having a calming effect. —*n.* sedative drug or influence.

sedentary /ˈsed-/ *a.* seated; (of work) done while sitting.

sedge *n.* grass-like plant(s) growing in marshes or by water.

sediment *n.* particles of solid matter in a liquid

or carried by water or wind. **sedimentary** /-'ment-/ a.

sedition /sɪ'dɪʃən/ n. words or actions inciting people to rebellion. **seditious** a., **seditiously** adv.

seduce v.t. persuade (esp. into wrongdoing) by offering temptations; tempt immorally into sexual intercourse. **seducer** n., **seduction** n., **seductive** a.

sedulous /'sed-/ diligent and persevering. **sedulously** adv.

see[1] v.t./i. (p.t. saw, p.p. seen) perceive with the eye(s) or mind; understand; consider; be a spectator of; look at for information; meet; discover; experience, undergo; grant or obtain an interview with; escort; make sure. ～ **through,** not be deceived by; not abandon before completion. ～ **to,** attend to. **seeing that,** in view of the fact that, because.

see[2] n. position or district of a bishop or archbishop.

seed n. (pl. seeds or seed) plant's fertilized ovule; semen, milt; (old use) descendants; something from which a tendency etc. can develop; (colloq.) seeded player. —v.t./i. produce seed; sprinkle with seeds; remove seeds from; name (a strong player) as not to be matched against others named thus until the later rounds of a tournament. **go** or **run to** ～, cease flowering as seed develops; become shabby or less efficient. ～**-cake** n. cake flavoured with caraway seeds. ～**-pearl** n. very small pearl.

seedless a. not containing seeds.

seedling n. very young plant growing from a seed.

seedy a. (-ier, -iest) full of seeds; looking shabby and disreputable; (colloq.) feeling slightly ill.

seek v.t. (p.t. sought) try to find or obtain; try (to do something). ～ **out,** seek specially. **seeker** n.

seem v.i. appear to be or exist or be true.

seemly a. in accordance with accepted standards of good taste.

seen see **see**[1].

seep v.i. ooze slowly out or through. **seepage** n.

seer n. prophet, person who sees visions.

seersucker n. fabric woven with a puckered surface.

see-saw n. children's amusement consisting of a long board balanced on a central support so that persons sitting on each end can make the ends go up and down alternately; constantly repeated up-and-down change. —v.i. make this movement or change.

seethe v.i. bubble or surge as in boiling; be very agitated or excited.

segment n. part cut off or marked off or separable from others; part of a circle or sphere cut off by a straight line or plane. **segmented** a.

segregate v.t. put apart from others. **segregation** n.

seine /seɪn/ n. a kind of fishing-net that hangs from floats.

seismic /'saɪz-/ a. of earthquake(s).

seismograph /'saɪz-/ n. instrument for recording earthquakes.

seize v.t./i. take hold of forcibly or suddenly or eagerly; take possession of by force or legal right; affect suddenly; seize up. ～ **on,** make use of eagerly. ～ **up,** become stuck because of friction or undue heat.

seizure n. seizing; sudden attack of apoplexy or epilepsy etc.

seldom adv. rarely, not often.

select v.t. pick out as best or most suitable. —a. chosen, esp. for excellence; exclusive. **selector** n.

selection n. selecting; people or things selected; collection of this from which to choose.

selective a. chosen or choosing carefully. **selectively** adv., **selectivity** n.

self n. (pl. selves) person as an individual; person's special nature; one's own advantage or interests; (joc. or in commerce) myself, herself, himself, etc. —a. of the same colour or material as that used for the whole.

self- pref. of or to or done by oneself or itself. ～**-assurance** n., ～**-assured** a. being self-confident. ～**-catering** a. catering for oneself. ～**-centred** a. thinking chiefly of oneself or one's own affairs. ～**-command** n. self-control. ～**-confidence** n., ～**-confident** a. being confident of one's own abilities. ～**-conscious** a., ～**-consciousness** n. being embarrassed or unnatural in manner from knowing that one is observed. ～**-contained** a. complete in itself, having all the necessary facilities; able to do without the company of others. ～**-control** n., ～**-controlled** a. being able to control one's behaviour and not act emotionally. ～**-denial** n. deliberately going without things one would like to have. ～**-evident** a. clear without proof or explanation. ～**-important** a. having a high opinion of one's own importance, pompous. ～**-indulgent** a. greatly indulging one's own desires for comfort and pleasure. ～**-interest** n. one's own advantage. ～**-made** a. having risen from poverty or obscurity to success by one's own efforts. ～**-portrait** n. artist's portrait of himself; writer's account of himself. ～**-possessed** a., ～**-possession** n. being calm and dignified. ～**-raising** a. (of flour) containing a raising agent. ～**-reliance** n., ～**-reliant** a. relying on one's own abilities and resources. ～**-respect** n. proper regard for oneself and one's own dignity and principles etc. ～**-righteous** a. smugly sure of one's own righteousness. ～**-sacrifice** n., ～**-sacrificing** a. sacrificing one's own interests so that others may benefit. ～**-satisfaction** n., ～**-satisfied** a. being pleased with oneself and one's achievements. ～**-seeking** a. & n. seeking to promote one's own interests rather than those of others. ～**-service** a. at which customers help themselves and pay a cashier for goods etc. taken. ～**-styled** a. using a name or description one has adopted without right. ～**-sufficient** a. able to provide what one needs without outside help. ～**-willed** a. obstinately doing what one wishes.

selfish *a.* acting or done according to one's own interests and needs without regard to those of others; keeping good things for oneself. **selfishly** *adv.*, **selfishness** *n.*

selfless *a.* unselfish.

selfsame *a.* the very same.

sell *v.t./i.* (p.t. *sold*) transfer the ownership of (goods etc.) in exchange for money; keep (goods) for sale; promote sales of; (of goods) find buyers; have a specified price; persuade into accepting (an idea etc.). —*n.* manner of selling; (*colloq.*) deception, disappointment. ∼ **off**, dispose of by selling, esp. at a reduced price. ∼ **out**, dispose of all one's stock etc. by selling; betray. ∼**-out** *n.* selling of all tickets for a show etc.; betrayal. ∼ **up**, sell one's house or business etc. **seller** *n.*

selvage *n.* edge of cloth woven so that it does not unravel.

selvedge *n.* = selvage.

semantic *a.* of meaning in language. **semantically** *adv.*

semantics *n.* study of meaning. —*n.pl.* meaning(s), connotation.

semaphore *n.* system of signalling by means of the arms; signalling device with mechanical arms. —*v.t./i.* signal by semaphore.

semblance *n.* outward appearance, show; resemblance.

semen /ˈsiː-/ *n.* sperm-bearing fluid produced by male animals.

semester /-ˈmes-/ *n.* half-year term in an American university.

semi- *pref.* half; partly.

semibreve *n.* note in music, equal to two minims.

semicircle *n.* half of a circle. **semicircular** *a.*

semicolon *n.* punctuation-mark ; .

semiconductor *n.* substance that conducts electricity in certain conditions.

semi-detached *a.* (of a house) joined to another on one side but not on the other.

semifinal *n.* match or round preceding the final.

semifinalist *n.* competitor in a semifinal.

seminal /ˈsem-/ *a.* of seed or semen; giving rise to new developments.

seminar /ˈsem-/ *n.* small class for advanced discussion and research.

seminary /ˈsem-/ *n.* training college for priests or rabbis.

semi-precious *a.* (of a gem-stone) less valuable than those called precious.

semiquaver *n.* note in music, equal to half a quaver.

Semite /ˈsiːmaɪt/ *n.* member of the group of races that includes Jews and Arabs. **Semitic** /-ˈmɪt-/ *a.*

semitone *n.* half a tone in music.

semolina /-ˈliː-/ *n.* hard particles left when wheat is ground and sifted, used to make puddings.

senate *n.* governing council in ancient Rome; upper house of certain parliaments (e.g. U.S.A., France); governing body of certain universities.

senator *n.* member of a senate.

send *v.t./i.* (p.t. *sent*) order or cause to go to a certain destination; send a message; cause to move or go or become. ∼ **for**, order to come or be brought. ∼**-off** *n.* friendly demonstration at a person's departure. ∼ **up**, (*colloq.*) make fun of by imitating. ∼**-up** *n.*

senile /ˈsiːnaɪl/ *a.* weak in body or mind because of old age; characteristic of old people. **senility** /sɪˈnɪl-/ *n.*

senior *a.* older; higher in rank or authority; for older children. —*n.* senior person; member of a senior school. ∼ **citizen,** elderly person. ∼ **service,** the Navy. **seniority** *n.*

senna *n.* dried pods or leaves of a tropical tree, used as a laxative.

sensation *n.* feeling produced by stimulation of a sense-organ or of the mind; great excitement or admiration aroused in a number of people, person or thing producing this.

sensational *a.* causing great excitement or admiration. **sensationally** *adv.*

sense *n.* any of the special powers (sight, hearing, smell, taste, touch) by which a living thing becomes aware of the external world; ability to perceive or be conscious of a thing; practical wisdom; meaning; (*pl.*) consciousness, sanity. —*v.t.* perceive by one of the senses or by a mental impression; (of a machine) detect. **make** ∼, have a meaning; be a sensible idea. **make** ∼ **of,** find a meaning in. ∼**-organ** *n.* any of the organs by which the body becomes aware of the external world.

senseless *a.* foolish; unconscious.

sensibility *n.* sensitiveness.

sensible *a.* having or showing good sense; aware. **sensibly** *adv.*

sensitive *a.* affected by something; receiving impressions or responding to stimuli easily; easily hurt or offended; requiring tact. **sensitively** *adv.*, **sensitivity** *n.*

sensitize *v.t.* make sensitive.

sensor *n.* device that responds to a certain stimulus.

sensory *a.* of the senses; receiving and transmitting sensations.

sensual *a.* gratifying to the body; indulging oneself with physical pleasures. **sensually** *adv.*, **sensuality** *n.*

sensuous *a.* affecting the senses pleasantly. **sensuously** *adv.*

sent *see* **send.**

sentence *n.* set of words making a single complete statement; punishment awarded by a lawcourt; declaration of this. —*v.t.* pass sentence on; declare condemned (to punishment).

sententious /-ˈtenʃəs/ *a.* putting on an air of wisdom; dull and moralizing. **sententiously** *adv.*, **sententiousness** *n.*

sentient /ˈsenʃənt/ *a.* capable of perceiving and feeling things. **sentiently** *adv.*, **sentience** *n.*

sentiment *n.* mental feeling; opinion; sentimentality.

sentimental *a.* full of romantic or nostalgic feeling. **sentimentally** *adv.*, **sentimentality** *n.*

sentinel *n.* sentry.

sentry n. soldier posted to keep watch and guard something.

sepal /'sep-/ n. one of the leaf-like parts forming a calyx.

separable a. able to be separated.

separate[1] /-ət/ a. not joined or united with others. **separates** n.pl. items of outer clothing for wearing in various combinations. **separately** adv.

separate[2] /-eɪt/ v.t./i. divide, keep apart; become separate; go different ways; cease to live together as a married couple. **separation** n., **separator** n.

separatist n. person who favours separation from a larger (esp. political) unit. **separatism** n.

sepia /'si:-/ n. brown colouring-matter; rich reddish-brown.

sepsis n. septic condition.

September n. ninth month of the year.

septet n. group of seven instruments or voices; music for these.

septic a. infected with harmful microorganisms. **~ tank,** tank in which sewage is liquefied by bacterial activity.

septicaemia /-'si:m-/ n. blood-poisoning.

septuagenarian /-'neər-/ n. person in his or her seventies.

Septuagint n. Greek version of the Old Testament.

septum n. (pl. -a) partition between two cavities (e.g. in the nose).

sepulchral /-'pʌl-/ a. of a tomb; dismal; (of a voice) sounding deep and hollow.

sepulchre /'sepʌlkə(r)/ n. tomb.

sequel n. what follows, esp. as a result; novel or film etc. continuing the story of an earlier one.

sequence n. following of one thing after another; series, set of things belonging next to each other in a particular order; section dealing with one topic in a cinema film.

sequential /-'kwenʃəl/ a. forming a sequence; occurring as a result. **sequentially** adv.

sequester /-'kwes-/ v.t. seclude; confiscate.

sequin n. circular spangle. **sequinned** a.

sequoia /-'kwɔɪə/ n. Californian tree growing to a great height.

seraglio /-'rɑːljəʊ/ n. (pl. -os) harem of a Muslim palace.

seraph n. (pl. -im) member of the highest order of angels in ancient Christian belief.

seraphic /-'ræf-/ a. like a seraph, angelic. **seraphically** adv.

serenade n. song or tune played by a lover to his lady, or suitable for this. —v.t. sing or play a serenade to.

serendipity /-'dɪp-/ n. making of pleasant discoveries by accident.

serene a. calm and cheerful. **Serene Highness,** title of members of certain royal families. **serenely** adv., **serenity** /-'ren-/ n.

serf n. medieval farm labourer forced to work for his landowner; oppressed labourer. **serfdom** n.

serge n. strong twilled fabric.

sergeant n. army N.C.O. ranking just above corporal; police officer ranking just below inspector. **~-major** n. warrant officer assisting an adjutant.

serial n. story presented in a series of instalments. —a. of or forming a series.

serialize v.t. produce as a serial.

seriatim /serɪ'eɪ-/ adv. point by point in sequence.

series n. (pl. series) number of things of the same kind, or related to each other, occurring or arranged or produced in order.

serio-comic a. partly serious and partly comic.

serious a. solemn; sincere; important; not slight. **seriously** adv., **seriousness** n.

serjeant-at-arms n. official of a court or city etc., with ceremonial duties.

sermon n. talk on a religious or moral subject, esp. during a religious service.

sermonize v.i. give a long moralizing talk.

serpent n. snake, esp. a large one.

serpentine a. twisting like a snake.

serrated /-'reɪtɪd/ a. having a series of small projections. **serration** n.

serried /'serɪd/ a. arranged in a close series.

serum n. (pl. sera or -ums) fluid that remains when blood has clotted; this used for inoculation; watery fluid from animal tissue.

servant n. person employed to do domestic work in a household or as an attendant; employee.

serve v.t./i. perform or provide services for; be employed (in the army etc.); be suitable (for); spend due time in, undergo; (of a male animal) copulate with; present (food etc.) for others to consume; attend to (customers); (of food) be enough for; set the ball in play at tennis etc., produce thus; deliver (a legal writ etc.) to (a person); treat in a certain way. —n. service in tennis etc. **server** n.

service n. act of serving; being a servant; working for an employer; department of people employed by the Crown or a public organization; (pl.) armed forces; system that performs work for customers or supplies public needs; assistance, beneficial act; meeting for worship of God, religious ceremony; set of dishes etc. for serving a meal; game in which one serves in tennis etc.; maintenance and repair of machinery. —v.t. maintain and repair (machinery); supply with service(s); pay the interest on (a loan). **~ area,** area beside a motorway where petrol and refreshment etc. are available. **~ flat,** flat where domestic service is provided by the management. **~ road,** road giving access to houses etc. but not for use by through traffic. **~ station,** place where petrol etc. is available, beside a road.

serviceable a. usable; hard-wearing.

serviceman, servicewoman ns. (pl. -men, -women) member of the armed services.

serviette n. table-napkin.

servile a. menial; excessively submissive. **servilely** adv., **servility** n.

servitude n. condition of being forced to work for others, with no freedom.

servo- *pref.* power-assisted.

sesame /ˈsesəmɪ/ *n.* tropical plant with seeds that yield oil or are used as food; its seeds.

session *n.* meeting(s) for discussing or deciding something; period spent in an activity; academic year in certain universities; governing body of a Presbyterian church.

set *v.t./i.* (p.t. *set*, pres.p. *setting*) put, place, fix in position or readiness; provide a tune for; make or become hard or firm or established; fix or appoint (a date etc.); arrange and protect (a broken bone) for healing; fix (hair) while it is damp; place (a jewel) in a framework; establish; assign as something to be done; put into a specified state; have a certain movement; be brought towards or below the horizon by earth's movement; (in dances) face another dancer and make certain steps. —*n.* people or things grouped as similar or forming a unit; games forming part of a match in tennis etc.; radio or television receiver; way a thing sets or is set; process of setting hair; scenery or stage for a play or film; (also *sett*) badger's burrow; (also *sett*) paving-block. **be ~ on**, be determined about. **~ about,** begin (a task); attack. **~ back,** halt or slow the progress of; (*sl.*) cost (a person) a specified amount. **~back** *n.* setting back of progress. **~ by the ears,** cause to argue or quarrel. **~ eyes on,** catch sight of. **~ fire to,** cause to burn. **~ forth,** set out. **~ in,** become established. **~ off,** begin a journey; cause to begin; ignite, cause to explode; improve the appearance of by contrast. **~ out,** declare, make known; begin a journey. **~ sail,** hoist sail(s); begin a voyage. **~ square,** right-angled triangular drawing-instrument. **~ theory,** study of sets of things in mathematics without regard to their individual constituents. **~ to,** begin doing something vigorously; begin fighting or arguing. **~to** *n.* fight; argument. **~-up** *n.* (*colloq.*) structure of an organization.

sett *n.* (see **set** *n.*)

settee *n.* long seat with a back and usu. arms, for two or more people.

setter *n.* person or thing that sets something; dog of a long-haired breed.

settle[1] *n.* wooden seat with a high back and arms.

settle[2] *v.t./i.* place so as to stay in position; establish, become established; make one's home; occupy (a previously unoccupied area); sink, come to rest; arrange as desired or conclusively, deal with; make or become calm or orderly; pay (a bill etc.); bestow legally. **~ up,** pay what is owing. **settler** *n.*

settlement *n.* settling; business or financial arrangement; amount or property settled legally on a person; place occupied by settlers.

seven *a. & n.* one more than six (7, VII).

seventh *a. & n.*

seventeen *a. & n.* one more than sixteen (17, XVII). **seventeenth** *a. & n.*

seventy *a. & n.* seven times ten (70, LXX). **seventieth** *a. & n.*

sever /ˈsev-/ *v.t./i.* cut or break off. **severance** *n.*

several *a.* a few, more than two but not many; separate, individual. —*pron.* several people or things.

severally *adv.* separately.

severe /-ˈvɪə(r)/ *a.* (*-er, -est*) strict; without sympathy; intense, forceful; (of style) plain, without decoration. **severely** *adv.*, **severity** *n.*

sew /səʊ/ *v.t./i.* (p.t. *sewed*, p.p. *sewn* or *sewed*) fasten by passing thread through material, using a threaded needle or an awl etc.; make or fasten (a thing) by sewing.

sewage /ˈsjuː-/ *n.* liquid waste drained from houses etc. for disposal. **~-farm** *n.* farm where sewage is treated and used as manure. **~-works** *n.* place where sewage is purified.

sewer[1] /ˈsəʊ-/ *n.* one who sews.

sewer[2] /ˈsjuː-/ *n.* drain for carrying sewage. —*v.t.* drain with sewers.

sewerage /ˈsjuː-/ *n.* system of sewers.

sewing-machine *n.* machine for sewing or stitching things.

sewn *see* **sew.**

sex *n.* either of the two main groups (*male* and *female*) into which living things are placed according to their reproductive functions; fact of belonging to one of these; sexual feelings or impulses or intercourse. —*v.t.* judge the sex of. **sexer** *n.*

sexagenarian /-ˈneər-/ *n.* person in his or her sixties.

sexist *a.* discriminating in favour of members of one sex; assuming a person's abilities and social functions are predetermined by his or her sex. —*n.* person who does this. **sexism** *n.*

sexless *a.* lacking sex, neuter; not involving sexual feelings.

sexology *n.* study of human sexual relationships. **sexological** *a.*, **sexologist** *n.*

sextant *n.* instrument for finding one's position by measuring the height of the sun etc.

sextet *n.* group of six instruments or voices; music for these.

sextile /-taɪl/ *a.* (of stars) in the position 60° distant from each other.

sexton *n.* official in charge of a church and churchyard.

sextuplet /-ˈtjuː-/ *n.* one of six children born at one birth.

sexual *a.* of sex or the sexes; (of reproduction) occurring by fusion of male and female cells. **~ intercourse,** copulation, insertion of the penis into the vagina. **sexually** *adv.*, **sexuality** *n.*

sexy *a.* (*-ier, -iest*) sexually attractive or stimulating.

sez = says. **~ you,** (*sl.*) that is your opinion but I disagree.

S.F. *abbr.* science fiction.

sh *int.* hush.

shabby *a.* (*-ier, -iest*) worn or used and not in good condition; poorly dressed; unfair, dishonourable. **shabbily** *adv.*, **shabbiness** *n.*

shack *n.* roughly-built hut or shed.

shackle *n.* one of a pair of iron rings joined by a chain, for fastening a prisoner's wrists or ankles. —*v.t.* put shackles on; impede, restrict.

shade *n.* comparative darkness; place sheltered from the sun; colour, degree or depth of this; differing variety; small amount; ghost; screen or cover used to block or moderate light; (*U.S.*) window-blind; (*pl.*) darkness of night or evening. —*v.t./i.* block the rays of; give shade to; darken (parts of a drawing etc.); pass gradually into another colour or variety.

shadow *n.* shade; patch of this where a body blocks light-rays; person's inseparable companion; slight trace; gloom. —*v.t.* cast shadow over; follow and watch secretly. **~boxing** *n.* boxing against an imaginary opponent as a form of training. **Shadow Cabinet**, members of the Opposition party acting as spokesmen on ministerial topics (so *S~ Chancellor* etc.). **shadower** *n.*, **shadowy** *a.*

shady *a.* (-ier, -iest) giving shade; situated in shade; disreputable, not completely honest.

shaft *n.* arrow, spear; long slender straight part of a thing; long bar; large axle; vertical or sloping passage or opening.

shag *n.* shaggy mass; strong coarse tobacco; cormorant.

shaggy *a.* (-ier, -iest) having long rough hair or fibre; (of hair etc.) rough and thick. **~dog story**, lengthy anecdote with a twist of humour at the end. **shagginess** *n.*

shah *n.* king of Iran.

shake *v.t./i.* (p.t. *shook*, p.p. *shaken*) move quickly up and down or to and fro; dislodge by doing this; shock; make less firm; (of the voice) become uneven; (*colloq.*) shake hands. —*n.* shaking, being shaken; shock; milk shake. **in a brace of shakes**, (*colloq.*) very quickly. **~ down**, become harmoniously adjusted; sleep in an improvised bed. **~ hands**, clasp right hands in greeting or parting or agreement. **shaker** *n.*

shakedown *n.* process of shaking down; improvised bed.

Shakespearian *a.* of Shakespeare.

shaky *a.* (-ier, -iest) shaking, unsteady; unreliable. **shakily** *adv.*, **shakiness** *n.*

shale *n.* slate-like stone.

shall *v.aux.* (*shalt* is used with *thou*), used with *I* and *we* to express future tense, and with other words in promises or statements of obligation.

shallot /-ˈlot/ *n.* onion-like plant.

shallow *a.* (-er, -est) of little depth; superficial. —*n.* shallow place. —*v.t./i.* make or become shallow. **shallowness** *n.*

shalt *see* shall.

sham *n.* pretence; thing that is not genuine. —*a.* pretended; not genuine. —*v.t./i.* (p.t. *shammed*) pretend; pretend to be.

shamble *v.i.* & *n.* walk or run in a shuffling or lazy way.

shambles *n.pl.* scene or condition of great bloodshed or disorder.

shame *n.* painful mental feeling aroused by having done something wrong or dishonourable or ridiculous; ability to feel this; person or thing causing shame; something regrettable. —*v.t.* bring shame on; make ashamed; compel by arousing shame. **shameful** *adv.*, **shamefully** *adv.*, **shameless** *a.*, **shamelessly** *adv.*

shamefaced *a.* looking ashamed.

shampoo *n.* liquid used to lather and wash hair; similar preparation for cleaning upholstery etc.; process of shampooing. —*v.t.* wash or clean with shampoo.

shamrock *n.* clover-like plant.

shandy *n.* mixed drink of beer and ginger-beer or lemonade.

shanghai /-ˈhaɪ/ *v.t.* (p.t. *shanghaied*, pres.p. *shanghaiing*) take (a person) by force or trickery and compel him to do something.

shank *n.* leg, esp. from knee to ankle; thing's shaft or stem.

shan't = shall not.

shantung *n.* soft Chinese silk.

shanty[1] *n.* shack. **~ town,** town consisting of shanties.

shanty[2] *n.* sailors' traditional song.

shape *n.* area or form with a definite outline; form, condition; orderly arrangement; jelly etc. shaped in a mould. —*v.t.* give shape to; develop into a certain condition. **shapeless** *a.*, **shapelessness** *n.*

shapely *a.* (-ier, -iest) having a pleasant shape. **shapeliness** *n.*

share *n.* part of an amount or task etc. that one is entitled to have or do; one of the equal parts forming a business company's capital and entitling the holder to a proportion of the profits; ploughshare. —*v.t./i.* give or have a share (of). **~out** *n.* division into shares. **shareholder** *n.*, **sharer** *n.*

shark *n.* large voracious sea-fish; person who ruthlessly extorts money, swindler.

sharp *a.* (-er, -est) having a fine edge or point capable of cutting; peaked, pointed; abrupt, not gradual; well-defined; intense, (of temper) irritable; (of tastes or smells) causing a smarting sensation; having an alert mind, intelligent; unscrupulous; vigorous, brisk; (in music) above the correct pitch, (of a note or key) a semitone above natural pitch. —*adv.* punctually, speedily; suddenly; at a sharp angle; above the correct pitch in music. —*n.* sharp note in music; symbol for this; (*colloq.*) swindler. **sharply** *adv.*, **sharpness** *n.*

sharpen *v.t./i.* make or become sharp or sharper. **sharpener** *n.*

sharper *n.* swindler, esp. at cards.

sharpshooter *n.* marksman.

shatter *v.t./i.* break violently into small pieces; destroy utterly; upset the calmness of.

shave *v.t./i.* scrape (growing hair) off the skin; clear (the chin etc.) of hair thus; cut thin slices from (wood etc.); graze gently in passing; reduce (costs etc.). —*n.* shaving of hair from the face. **shaver** *n.*

shaven *a.* shaved.

shaving *n.* thin strip of wood etc. shaved off.

shawl *n.* large piece of soft fabric worn round the shoulders or wrapped round a baby as a covering.

she *pron.* female (or thing personified as female) previously mentioned. —*n.* female animal.

sheaf *n.* (pl. *sheaves*) bundle of things laid lengthwise together; tied bundle of corn-stalks.

shear *v.t./i.* (p.p. *shorn* or *sheared*) cut or trim with shears or other sharp device; strip bare, deprive; break because of strain. **shearer** *n.*

shears *n.pl.* large cutting-instrument shaped like scissors.

shearwater *n.* sea-bird with long wings.

sheath *n.* close-fitting cover, esp. for a blade or tool. ∼-**knife** *n.* dagger-like knife carried in a sheath.

sheathe /ʃiδ/ *v.t.* put into a case; encase in a covering.

shed[1] *n.* building for storing or sheltering things, or for use as a workshop.

shed[2] *v.t.* (p.t. *shed*, pres.p. *shedding*) lose by a natural falling off; take off; allow to fall or flow.

sheen *n.* gloss, lustre.

sheep *n.* (pl. *sheep*) grass-eating animal with a thick fleecy coat. ∼ **dog** *n.* dog trained to guard and herd sheep.

sheepish *a.* bashful, embarrassed. **sheepishly** *adv.*, **sheepishness** *n.*

sheepshank *n.* knot used to shorten a rope without cutting it.

sheepskin *n.* sheep's skin with the fleece on; leather of sheep's skin.

sheer[1] *a.* pure, not mixed or qualified; very steep, with no slope; (of fabric) very thin, transparent. —*adv.* directly, straight up or down.

sheer[2] *v.i.* swerve from a course.

sheet *n.* rectangular piece of cotton or similar fabric used in pairs as inner bedclothes; large thin piece of glass, metal, etc.; piece of paper for writing or printing on; wide expanse of water, flame, etc.; rope or chain securing the lower corner of a sail. ∼-**anchor** *n.* thing on which one depends for security or stability.

sheikh /ʃeɪk/ *n.* leader of an Arab tribe or village. **sheikhdom** *n.* his territory.

shekel *n.* unit of money in Israel; (*pl.*, *colloq.*) money, riches.

sheldrake *n.* (pl. *shelduck*) wild duck living on coasts. **shelduck** *n.* female sheldrake.

shelf *n.* (pl. *shelves*) board or slab fastened horizontally for things to be placed on; thing resembling this, ledge. ∼-**mark** *n.* number marked on a book to show its place in a library.

shell *n.* hard outer covering of eggs, nut-kernels, and of animals such as snails and tortoises; firm frame-work or covering; light racing-boat; metal case filled with explosive, for firing from a large gun. —*v.t.* remove the shell(s) of; fire explosive shells at. ∼-**pink** *a.* & *n.* delicate pale pink. ∼-**shock** *n.* nervous breakdown from exposure to battle conditions.

shellac *n.* resinous substance used in varnish. —*v.t.* (p.t. *shellacked*) coat with this.

shellfish *n.* water animal that has a shell.

shelter *n.* structure that shields against danger, wind, rain, etc.; refuge, shielded condition. —*v.t.* provide with shelter; protect from blame, trouble, etc.; find or take shelter.

shelve *v.t./i.* arrange on a shelf; fit with shelves; put aside for later consideration or permanently; slope.

shemozzle *n.* (*sl.*) rumpus, brawl.

shenanigans *n.pl.* (*U.S. sl.*) high-spirited behaviour; trickery.

shepherd *n.* man who tends a flock of sheep. —*v.t.* guide (people). ∼'**s pie**, pie of minced meat topped with mashed potato. **shepherdess** *n.fem.*

sherbet *n.* weak sweet fruit-juice; fizzy sweet drink, powder from which this is made; flavoured water-ice.

sheriff *n.* Crown's chief executive officer in a county; chief judge of a district in Scotland; (*U.S.*) chief law-enforcing officer of a county.

Sherpa *n.* member of a Himalayan people of Nepal and Tibet.

sherry *n.* strong white wine orig. from southern Spain.

shibboleth *n.* old slogan or principle still considered essential by some member of a party.

shield *n.* piece of defensive armour carried on the arm to protect the body; trophy in the form of this; protective structure. —*v.t.* protect, screen; protect from discovery.

shift *v.t./i.* change or move from one position to another; change form or character; transfer (blame etc.); (*sl.*) move quickly; manage to do something. —*n.* change of place or form etc.; set of workers who start work when another set finishes; time for which they work; evasion; scheme; woman's straight-cut dress. **make** ∼, (see *make*).

shiftless *a.* lazy and inefficient.

shifty *a.* (-*ier*, -*iest*) evasive, not straight-forward; untrustworthy.

shilling *n.* former British coin (= 5p).

shilly-shally *v.i.* be unable to make up one's mind firmly.

shimmer *v.i.* & *n.* shine with a soft quivering light.

shin *n.* front of the leg below the knee; lower foreleg, esp. as a cut of beef. —*v.i.* (p.t. *shinned*) ∼ **up**, climb.

shindy *n.* (*colloq.*) din, brawl.

shine *v.t./i.* (p.t. *shone*) give out or reflect light, be bright; excel; cause to shine; (*colloq.*, p.t. *shined*) polish. —*n.* brightness; high polish.

shingle[1] *n.* wooden roof-tile. —*v.t.* roof with shingles; cut (a woman's hair) in a short tapered style.

shingle[2] *n.* small rounded pebbles; stretch of these, esp. on a shore.

shingles *n.* disease with a rash of small blisters.

shinty *n.* game resembling hockey.

shiny *a.* (-*ier*, -*iest*) shining, glossy.

ship *n.* large sea-going vessel. —*v.t.* (p.t. *shipped*) put or take on board a ship; transport. **shipper** *n.*

shipbuilding *n.* business of constructing ships. **shipbuilder** *n.*

shipmate *n.* person travelling or working on the same ship as another.

shipment *n.* shipping of goods; consignment shipped.

shipping *n.* ships collectively.

shipshape *adv.* & *a.* in good order, tidy.

shipwreck *n.* destruction of a ship by storm or striking rock etc. **shipwrecked** *a.*

shipyard *n.* shipbuilding establishment.

shire *n.* county; (*Austr.*) rural area with its own elected council. **~-horse** *n.* horse of a heavy powerful breed.

shirk *v.t./i.* avoid (duty or work etc.) selfishly. **shirker** *n.*

shirr *v.t.* gather (cloth) with parallel threads running through it.

shirt *n.* man's loose-fitting garment of cotton or silk etc. for the upper part of the body; woman's similar garment.

shirtwaister *n.* woman's dress with the bodice shaped like a shirt.

shirty *a.* (*sl.*) annoyed, angry.

shiver[1] *v.i.* tremble slightly esp. with cold or fear. —*n.* shivering movement.

shiver[2] *v.t./i.* shatter.

shoal[1] *n.* great number of fish swimming together. —*v.i.* form shoals.

shoal[2] *n.* shallow place; underwater sandbank; (*pl.*) hidden dangers. —*v.i.* become shallower.

shock[1] *n.* bushy mass of hair.

shock[2] *n.* effect of a violent impact or shake; sudden violent effect on the mind or emotions; acute weakness caused by injury, pain, or mental shock; effect of a sudden discharge of electricity through the body. —*v.t./i.* cause to suffer shock or a shock; horrify, disgust, seem scandalous to (a person).

shocker *n.* (*colloq.*) shocking person or thing.

shod *see* **shoe.**

shoddy *a.* fibre or cloth made from old shredded cloth. —*a.* (*-ier, -iest*) of poor quality. **shoddily** *adv.,* **shoddiness** *n.*

shoe *n.* outer covering for a person's foot, with a fairly stiff sole; thing like this in appearance or use; horseshoe; part of a brake that presses against a wheel or its drum. —*v.t.* (p.t. **shod,** pres.p. **shoeing**) fit with a shoe or shoes. **on a ~-string,** with only a small amount of capital. **~-tree** *n.* shaped block for keeping a shoe in shape.

shoehorn *n.* curved piece of stiff material for easing one's heel into the back of a shoe.

shoelace *n.* cord for fastening together the edges of a shoe's uppers.

shoemaker *n.* person whose trade is making or mending shoes.

shoeshine *n.* (*U.S.*) polishing of shoes.

shone *see* **shine.**

shoo *int.* sound uttered to frighten animals away. —*v.t.* drive away by this.

shook *see* **shake.**

shoot *v.t./i.* (p.t. **shot**) fire (a gun etc., or a missile); kill or wound with a missile from a gun etc.; hunt with a gun for sport; send out or move swiftly; (of a plant) put forth buds or shoots; slide (a bolt) into or out of its fastening; have one's boat move swiftly over or through; take a shot at goal; photograph, film. —*n.* young branch or new growth of a plant; expedition for hunting game, land where this is held. **~ up,** rise suddenly; grow rapidly. **shooting star,** small meteor seen to move quickly. **shooting-stick** *n.* walking-stick with a small folding seat in the handle.

shop *n.* building or room where goods or services are sold to the public; workshop; one's own work as a subject of conversation. —*v.t./i.* (p.t. **shopped**) go into a shop or shops to buy things; (*sl.*) inform against. **~ around,** look for the best bargain. **~-floor** *n.* workers as distinct from management or senior union officials. **~-soiled** *a.* soiled from being on display in a shop. **~-steward** *n.* trade union official elected by fellow workers as their spokesman. **~-worn** *a.* shop-soiled.

shopkeeper *n.* person who owns or manages a shop.

shoplifter *n.* person who steals goods that are displayed in a shop. **shoplifting** *n.*

shopper *n.* person who shops; bag for holding shopping.

shopping *n.* buying goods in shops; goods bought.

shore[1] *n.* land along the edge of a sea or lake.

shore[2] *v.t.* prop or support with a length of timber.

shorn *see* **shear.**

short *a.* (*-er, -est*) measuring little from end to end in space or time; not lasting; insufficient; having insufficient; concise, brief; curt; (of drink) small and concentrated, made with spirits; (of pastry) crisp and easily crumbled. —*adv.* abruptly. —*n.* (*colloq.*) short drink; short circuit; (*pl.*) trousers that do not reach the knee. —*v.t./i.* (*colloq.*) short-circuit. **for ~,** as an abbreviation. **in ~,** expressed briefly. **~-change** *v.t.* cheat, esp. by giving insufficient change. **~ circuit,** connection (usu. a fault) in an electrical circuit where current flows by a shorter route than the normal one. **~-circuit** *v.t.* cause a short circuit in; bypass. **~ cut,** route or method quicker than the normal one. **~-handed** *a.* having an insufficient number of workers. **~-list** *v.t.* put on a short list from which a final choice will be made. **~-lived** *a.* living or lasting for only a short time. **~ odds,** nearly even odds in betting. **~-sighted** *a.* able to see clearly only what is close; lacking foresight. **~ ton,** (see *ton*). **~ wave,** radio wave of about 10 to 100 metres wavelength.

shortage *n.* lack, insufficiency.

shortbread *n.* rich sweet biscuit.

shortcake *n.* shortbread.

shortcoming *n.* failure to reach a required standard; fault.

shorten *v.t./i.* make or become shorter.

shortfall *n.* deficit.

shorthand *n.* method of writing rapidly with quickly made symbols.

shortly *adv.* after a short time; in a few words; curtly.

shot *see* **shoot.** —*a.* (of fabric) made so that different colours show at different angles. —*n.* firing of a gun etc.; sound of this; person of specified skill in shooting; missile(s) for a cannon or gun etc.; heavy ball thrown as a sport; attempt to hit something or reach a target; launching of a spacecraft; stroke in tennis or cricket or billiards etc.; attempt; injection; photograph; (*colloq.*) dram of spirits. **like a ~,** without hesitation. **~-gun** *n.* gun for firing small shot at close range. **~-gun wedding,** one that is enforced, esp. because the bride is pregnant.

should *v.aux.* used to express duty or obligation, possible or expected future event, or (with *I* and *we*) a polite statement or a conditional or indefinite clause.

shoulder *n.* part of the body where the arm, foreleg, or wing is attached; part of the human body between this and the neck; animal's upper foreleg as a joint of meat; projection compared to the human shoulder. —*v.t./i.* push with one's shoulder; take (a burden) on one's shoulders; take (blame or responsibility) on oneself. **~ arms,** hold a rifle with the barrel against one's shoulder. **~-blade** *n.* large flat bone of the shoulder.

shout *n.* loud cry or utterance. —*v.t./i.* utter a shout; call loudly. **~ down,** silence by shouting.

shove *n.* rough push. —*v.t./i.* push roughly; (*colloq.*) put.

shovel *n.* spade-like tool for scooping earth etc.; mechanical scoop. —*v.t.* (p.t. *shovelled*) shift or clear with or as if with a shovel; scoop roughly.

shoveller *n.* duck with a broad shovel-like beak.

show *v.t./i.* (p.t. *showed*, p.p. *shown*) allow or cause to be seen, offer for inspection or viewing; demonstrate, point out, prove; cause to understand; conduct; present an image of; treat with (kindness, interest, etc.); be able to be seen. —*n.* process of showing; display, public exhibition or (*colloq.*) performance; outward appearance; (*sl.*) business, undertaking. **~-down** *n.* final test; disclosure of intentions or conditions etc. **~-jumping** *n.* competitive sport of riding horses to jump over obstacles. **~ off,** display well or proudly or ostentatiously; try to impress people. **~ of hands,** raising of hands in voting. **~-piece** *n.* excellent specimen used for exhibition. **~-room** *n.* room where goods are displayed for inspection. **~ up,** make or be clearly visible; reveal (a fault etc.); (*colloq.*) be present.

shower *n.* brief fall of rain or of snow, bullets, stones, etc.; sudden influx of letters or gifts etc.; device or cabinet in which water is sprayed on a person's body; wash in this; (*U.S.*) party for giving presents esp. to a bride-to-be. —*v.t./i.* pour down or send or come in a shower; wash oneself in sprayed water.

showerproof *a.* (of fabric) able to keep out slight rain. —*v.t.* make showerproof.

showery *a.* with showers of rain.

showman *n.* (pl. -*men*) organizer of circuses or similar entertainments.

showmanship *n.* skill in presenting entertainment or goods etc. well.

shown *see* **show.**

showy *a.* (-*ier*, -*iest*) making a good display; brilliant, gaudy. **showily** *adv.*

shrank *see* **shrink.**

shrapnel *n.* artillery shell containing bullets or pieces of metal which it scatters on exploding; these pieces.

shred *n.* small piece torn or cut from something; small amount. —*v.t.* (p.t. *shredded*) tear or cut into shreds. **shredder** *n.*

shrew *n.* small mouse-like animal; shrewish woman.

shrewd *a.* (-*er*, -*est*) showing sound judgement, clever. **shrewdly** *adv.*, **shrewdness** *n.*

shrewish *a.* sharp-tempered and scolding.

shriek *n.* shrill cry or scream. —*v.t./i.* utter (with) a shriek.

shrift *n.* **short ~,** curt treatment.

shrike *n.* bird with a strong hooked beak.

shrill *a.* (-*er*, -*est*) piercing and high-pitched in sound. **shrilly** *adv.*, **shrillness** *n.*

shrimp *n.* small edible shellfish, pink when boiled; (*colloq.*) very small person.

shrimping *n.* catching shrimps.

shrine *n.* sacred or revered place.

shrink *v.t./i.* (p.t. *shrank*, p.p. *shrunk*) make or become smaller; draw back to avoid something. **~ from,** be unwilling to.

shrinkage *n.* shrinking of textile fabric.

shrivel *v.t./i.* (p.t. *shrivelled*) shrink and wrinkle from great heat or cold or lack of moisture.

shroud *n.* cloth wrapping a dead body for burial; thing that conceals; one of the ropes supporting a ship's mast. —*v.t.* wrap in a shroud; protect or conceal in wrappings; conceal.

Shrove *n.* **~ Tuesday,** day before Ash Wednesday.

shrub *n.* woody plant smaller than a tree. **shrubby** *a.*

shrubbery *n.* area planted with shrubs.

shrug *v.t./i.* (p.t. *shrugged*) raise (one's shoulders) as a gesture of indifference or doubt or helplessness. —*n.* this movement.

shrunk *see* **shrink.**

shrunken *a.* having shrunk.

shudder *v.i.* shiver or shake violently. —*n.* this movement.

shuffle *v.t./i.* walk without lifting one's feet clear of the ground; rearrange, jumble; keep shifting one's position; get rid of (a burden etc.) shiftily. —*n.* shuffling movement or walk; rearrangement.

shuffleboard *n.* game in which discs are driven over a marked surface.

shun *v.t.* (p.t. *shunned*) avoid.

shunt *v.t./i.* move (a train) to a side track; divert. —*n.* act of shunting; (*sl.*) collision in which a vehicle knocks the back of the one in front of it.

shush *int.* & *v.t./i.* (*colloq.*) hush.

shut *v.t./i.* (p.t. *shut*, pres.p. *shutting*) move (a door or window etc.) into position to block an opening; be moved thus; prevent access to (a place); bring or fold parts of (a thing) together; trap or exclude by shutting something. —*a.* (*sl.*) rid. **∼ down**, cease working or business; cause to do this. **∼-down** *n.* this process. **∼ up**, shut securely; (*colloq.*) stop or cease talking or making a noise, silence.

shutter *n.* screen that can be closed over a window; device that opens and closes the aperture of a camera. **shuttered** *a.*

shuttle *n.* thread-holder, esp. one carrying the weft-thread in weaving; vehicle used in a shuttle service; shuttlecock. —*v.t./i.* move or travel or send to and fro. **∼ service,** transport service going to and fro.

shuttlecock *n.* small rounded object struck to and fro in badminton.

shy[1] *a.* (*-er*, *-est*) timid and lacking self-confidence. —*v.t.* jump or move suddenly in alarm. **shyly** *adv.*, **shyness** *n.*

shy[2] *v.t./n.* throw.

SI *abbr.* Système International (French, = International System of Units).

Siamese *a.* & *n.* (native, language) of Siam (= Thailand). **∼ cat,** cat with pale fur and darker face. **∼ twins,** twins whose bodies are joined at birth.

sibilant *a.* sounding like a hiss. —*n.* sibilant speech-sound (e.g. *s*, *sh*).

sibling *n.* brother or sister.

sic /sik/ *adv.* used or spelt in the way quoted.

Sicilian *a.* & *n.* (native) of Sicily.

sick *a.* unwell; vomiting; likely to vomit; distressed, disgusted; finding amusement in misfortune or morbid subjects. **∼ of,** bored with. **∼-room** *n.* room ready for or occupied by a sick person.

sicken *v.t./i.* become ill; make or become distressed or disgusted. **be sickening for,** be in the first stages of (a disease).

sickle *n.* curved blade used for cutting corn etc.; thing shaped like this.

sickly *a.* (*-ier*, *-iest*) unhealthy; causing sickness or distaste; weak.

sickness *n.* illness; vomiting.

side *n.* surface of an object, esp. one that is not the top, bottom, front, back, or end; bounding line of a plane figure; either of the two halves into which something is divided; part near an edge; slope of a hill or ridge; region next to a person or thing; aspect of a problem etc.; one of two opposing groups or teams etc.; (*sl.*) conceit. —*a.* at or on the side. —*v.i.* join forces (with a person) in a dispute. **on the ∼,** as a sideline; as a surreptitious activity. **∼ by side,** close together. **∼-drum** *n.* small double-headed drum. **∼-effect** *n.* secondary (usu. bad) effect. **∼-saddle** *n.* saddle on which a woman rider sits with both legs on the same side of the horse; (*adv.*) sitting thus. **∼-show** *n.* small show forming part of a large one.

∼-step *v.t.* avoid by stepping sideways; evade. **∼-stroke** *n.* stroke used in swimming on one's side. **∼-track** *v.t.* divert. **∼-whiskers** *n.pl.* whiskers on the cheek.

sideboard *n.* flat-topped piece of dining-room furniture with drawers and cupboards for china etc.; (*pl.*, *sl.*) side-whiskers.

sideburns *n.pl.* short side-whiskers.

sidecar *n.* small vehicle seating a passenger, attached to the side of a motor cycle.

sidelight *n.* light from or on one side; minor or casual light shed on a subject.

sideline *n.* thing done in addition to one's main activity; (*pl.*) lines bounding the sides of a football pitch etc., place for spectators.

sidelong *a.* & *adv.* sideways.

sidereal /saɪˈdɪər-/ *a.* of or measured by the stars.

sidesman *n.* (pl. *-men*) assistant churchwarden.

sidewalk *n.* (*U.S.*) pavement.

sideways *adv.* & *a.* to or from one side; with one side forward.

siding *n.* short track by the side of a railway, used in shunting.

sidle *v.i.* advance in a timid, furtive, or cringing way.

siege *n.* surrounding and blockading of a place by armed forces, in order to capture it.

sienna /sɪˈe-/ *n.* a kind of clay used as colouring-matter. **burnt ∼,** reddish-brown. **raw ∼,** brownish-yellow.

sierra /sɪˈe-/ *n.* chain of mountains with jagged peaks in Spain or Spanish America.

siesta /sɪˈe-/ *n.* afternoon nap or rest, esp. in hot countries.

sieve /sɪv/ *n.* utensil with a wire mesh or gauze through which liquids or fine particles can pass. —*v.t.* put through a sieve.

sift *v.t./i.* sieve; sprinkle lightly; examine carefully and select or analyse; fall as if from a sieve. **sifter** *n.*

sigh *n.* long deep breath given out audibly in sadness, tiredness, relief, etc. —*v.t./i.* give or express with a sigh; make a similar sound; yearn.

sight *n.* ability to see; seeing, being seen; thing seen or worth seeing; unsightly thing; (*colloq.*) great amount; device looked through to aim or observe with a gun or telescope etc.; precise aim with this. —*v.t.* get a sight of; aim or observe with a gun-sight etc. **at** *or* **on ∼,** as soon as seen. **∼-reading** *n.* playing or singing music without preliminary study of the score.

sightless *a.* blind.

sightseeing *n.* visiting places of interest. **sightseer** *n.*

sign *n.* something perceived that suggests the existence of a fact or quality or condition; symbol; sign-board; notice displayed; action or gesture conveying information or a command etc.; any of the twelve divisions of the zodiac. —*v.t./i.* make a sign; write (one's name) on a document, convey or engage or acknowledge by this.

signal *n.* sign or gesture giving information or a command; object placed to give notice or warning; sequence of electrical impulses or radio waves transmitted or received. —*v.t./i.* (p.t. *signalled*) make a signal or signals; communicate with or announce thus. —*a.* noteworthy. **~-box** *n.* small railway building with signalling apparatus. **signaller** *n.*, **signally** *adv.*

signalize *v.t.* make noteworthy.

signalman *n.* (pl. *-men*) person responsible for displaying naval signals or for operating railway signals.

signatory /ˈsɪg-/ *n.* one of the parties who sign an agreement.

signature *n.* person's name or initials written by himself in signing something; section of a book made from one sheet folded and cut; indication of key or tempo, following the clef in a musical score. **~ tune,** tune used to announce a particular performer or programme.

signboard *n.* board bearing the name or device of a shop etc.

signet *n.* person's seal used with or instead of a signature. **~-ring** *n.* finger-ring with an engraved design.

significance *n.* meaning; importance. **significant** *a.*, **significantly** *adv.*

signification *n.* meaning.

signify *v.t./i.* be a sign or symbol of; have as a meaning; make known; matter.

signpost *n.* post with arms showing the direction of certain places. —*v.t.* provide with signpost(s).

Sikh /sik/ *n.* member of a certain Indian religious sect.

silage /ˈsaɪ-/ *n.* green fodder stored and fermented in a silo.

silence *n.* absence of sound or of speaking. —*v.t.* make silent.

silencer *n.* device for reducing sound.

silent *a.* without sound; not speaking. **silently** *adv.*

silhouette /sɪluˈet/ *n.* dark shadow or outline seen against a light background. —*v.t.* show as a silhouette.

silica *n.* compound of silicon occurring as quartz and in sandstone etc.

silicate *n.* compound of silicon.

silicon /-kən/ *n.* chemical substance found in the earth's crust in its compound forms. **~ chip,** microchip.

silicone /-kəʊn/ *n.* organic compound of silicon, used in paint, varnish, and lubricants.

silicosis /-ˈkəʊ-/ *n.* lung disease caused by inhaling dust that contains silica.

silk *n.* fine strong soft fibre produced by silkworms; thread or cloth made from it or resembling this. **take ~,** become a Queen's Counsel, entitled to wear a silk gown. **silky** *a.*

silken *a.* like silk.

silkworm *n.* caterpillar which feeds on mulberry leaves and spins its cocoon of silk.

sill *n.* strip of stone, wood, or metal at the base of a door or window.

silly *a.* (*-ier, -iest*) lacking good sense, foolish, unwise; feeble-minded; (of a fieldsman's position in cricket) close to the batsman. —*n.* (*colloq.*) foolish person. **~-billy** *n.* (*colloq.*) foolish person. **silliness** *n.*

silo /ˈsaɪ-/ *n.* (pl. *-os*) pit or airtight structure for holding silage; pit or tower for storing grain or cement or radioactive waste; underground place where a missile is kept ready for firing.

silt *n.* sediment deposited by water in a channel or harbour etc. —*v.t./i.* block or become blocked with silt.

silver *n.* shiny white precious metal; coins or articles made of this; coins made of an alloy resembling it; household cutlery; colour of silver. —*a.* made of or coloured like silver. **~-fish** *n.* small insect with a fish-like body. **~ jubilee, ~ wedding,** 25th anniversary.

silverside *n.* joint of beef cut from the haunch, below topside.

silversmith *n.* person whose trade is making articles in silver.

silvery *a.* like silver; having a clear gentle ringing sound.

simian /ˈsɪm-/ *a.* monkey-like.

similar *a.* like, alike; resembling but not the same; of the same kind or amount. **similarly** *adv.*, **similarity** *n.*

simile /ˈsɪmɪlɪ/ *n.* figure of speech in which one thing is compared to another.

similitude /-ˈmɪl-/ *n.* similarity.

simmer *v.t./i.* boil very gently; be in a state of barely suppressed anger or excitement. **~ down,** become less excited.

simnel *n.* **~ cake,** rich cake covered with marzipan and decorated.

simper *v.i.* smile in an affected way. —*n.* affected smile.

simple *a.* (*-er, -est*) of one element or kind; not complicated or showy or luxurious; unsophisticated, without cunning; feeble-minded. **simply** *adv.*, **simplicity** *n.*

simpleton *n.* foolish or half-witted person.

simplify *v.t.* make simple; make easy to do or understand. **simplification** *n.*

simulate *v.t.* pretend; imitate the form or condition of. **simulation** *n.*, **simulator** *n.*

simultaneous *a.* occurring or operating at the same time. **simultaneously** *adv.*, **simultaneity** /-ˈnɪə-/ *n.*

sin *n.* breaking of a religious or moral law, act which does this; serious fault or offence. —*v.i.* (p.t. *sinned*) commit a sin.

since *prep.* after; from (a specified time) until now. —*conj.* from the time that; because. —*adv.* since that time.

sincere *a.* free from pretence or deceit. **sincerely** *adv.*, **sincerity** *n.*

sine /saɪn/ *n.* ratio of the length of one side of a right-angled triangle to the hypotenuse. .

sinecure /ˈsaɪ-/ *n.* position of profit or honour with no work attached.

sine die /saɪnɪ daɪɪ/ indefinitely, with no appointed date.

sinew *n.* tough fibrous tissue joining muscle to bone; tendon; (pl.) muscles, strength. **sinewy** *a.*

sinful *a.* full of sin, wicked. **sinfully** *adv.*, **sinfulness** *n.*

sing *v.t./i.* (p.t. *sang*, p.p. *sung*) make musical sounds with the voice; perform (a song); make a humming sound. **singer** *n.*

singe /-ndʒ/ *v.t./i.* (pres.p. *singeing*) burn slightly; burn the ends or edges of. —*n.* slight burn.

single *a.* one only, not double or multiple; designed for one person or thing; taken separately; unmarried; having only one circle of petals; (of a ticket) valid for an outward journey only. —*n.* one person or thing; room etc. for one person; single ticket; pop record with one piece of music on each side; (usu. *pl.*) game with one player on each side. —*v.t.* choose or distinguish from others. ∼ **combat,** duel. ∼ **cream,** thin cream. ∼ **figures,** numbers from 1 to 9. ∼**-handed** *a.* without help from others. ∼**-minded** *a.* with one's mind set on a single purpose. **singly** *adv.*

singlet *n.* vest; athlete's shirt resembling a vest.

singleton /-ŋgəl-/ *n.* thing that occurs singly.

singsong *a.* with a monotonous rise and fall of the voice. —*n.* singsong manner; informal singing by a group of people.

singular *n.* form of a noun or verb used in referring to one person or thing. —*a.* of this form; uncommon, extraordinary. **singularly** *adv.*, **singularity** *n.*

singularize *v.t.* make different from others.

sinister *a.* suggestive of evil; involving wickedness.

sink *v.t./i.* (p.t. *sank*, p.p. *sunk*) fall or come gradually downwards; fall below the surface of water or the sea etc.; pass into a less active condition; lose value or strength etc.; cause or allow to sink; dig (a well), bore (a shaft); engrave (a die); send (a ball) into a pocket or hole; invest (money). —*n.* fixed basin with a drainage pipe; cesspool. ∼ **in,** become understood.

sinker *n.* weight used to sink a fishing-line etc.

sinner *n.* person who sins.

sinuous *a.* curving undulating.

sinus /ˈsaɪ-/ *n.* (pl. *-uses*) cavity in bone or tissue, esp. that connecting with the nostrils.

sip *n.* & *v.t./i.* (p.t. *sipped*) drink in small mouthfuls.

siphon /ˈsaɪ-/ *n.* bent pipe or tube used for transferring liquid by utilizing atmospheric pressure; bottle from which soda water etc. is forced out by pressure of gas. —*v.t./i.* flow or draw out through a siphon; take from a source.

sir *n.* polite form of address to a man; *S*∼, title of a knight or baronet.

sire /saɪə(r)/ *n.* (*old use*) father, male ancestor; polite form of address to a king; animal's male parent. —*v.t.* beget.

siren *n.* device that makes a loud prolonged sound as a signal; dangerously fascinating woman.

sirloin *n.* upper (best) part of loin of beef.

sirocco *n.* (pl. *-os*) hot wind that reaches Italy from Africa.

sisal /ˈsaɪs-/ *n.* rope-fibre made from the leaves of a tropical plant; this plant.

siskin *n.* bird related to the goldfinch.

sissy *n.* effeminate or cowardly person.

sister *n.* daughter of the same parents as another person; woman who is a fellow member of a group or Church etc.; nun; female hospital nurse in authority over others. ∼**-in-law** *n.* (pl. ∼*s-in-law*) sister of one's husband or wife; wife of one's brother. **sisterly** *adj.*

sisterhood *n.* relationship of sisters; order of nuns; society of women doing religious or charitable work.

sit *v.t./i.* (p.t. *sat*, pres.p. *sitting*) take or be in a position with the body resting more or less upright on the buttocks; cause to sit; pose for a portrait; (of birds) perch, (of animals) rest with legs bent and body on the ground; (of birds) remain on the nest to hatch eggs; be situated, lie; be a candidate (for); occupy a seat as member of a committee etc.; (of a committee etc.) hold a session. ∼**-in** *n.* occupation of a building etc. as a form of protest.

sitar /ˈsɪtɑ(r)/ *n.* guitar-like Indian musical instrument.

site *n.* ground on which a building etc. stands or stood or is to stand, or where an event takes or took or is to take place. —*v.t.* locate, provide with a site.

sitter *n.* person sitting; sitting hen; baby-sitter; (*sl.*) easy catch or shot.

sitting *see* **sit.** —*n.* time during which a person or assembly etc. sits; clutch of eggs. ∼**-room** *n.* room used for sitting in, not a bedroom. ∼ **tenant,** one already in occupation of rented accommodation etc.

situate *v.t.* place or put in a certain position. **be situated,** be in a certain position.

situation *n.* place (with its surroundings) occupied by something; set of circumstances; position of employment.

six *a.* & *n.* one more than five (6, VI). **at sixes and sevens,** in disorder. **sixth** *a.* & *n.*

sixpence *n.* sum of 6 pence; (*old use*) coin worth this. **sixpenny** *a.*

sixteen *n.* one more than fifteen (16, XVI). **sixteenth** *a.* & *n.*

sixty *a.* & *n.* six times ten (60, LX). **sixtieth** *a.* & *n.*

size[1] *n.* relative bigness, extent; one of the series of standard measurements in which things are made and sold. —*v.t.* group according to size. ∼ **up,** estimate the size of; (*colloq.*) form a judgement of.

size[2] *n.* gluey solution used to glaze paper or stiffen textiles etc. —*v.t.* treat with size.

sizeable *a.* large; fairly large.

sizzle *v.i.* make a hissing sound like that of frying.

skate[1] *n.* (pl. *skate*) large flat-fish.

skate[2] *n.* one of a pair of blades or (*roller-*∼) sets of wheels attached to boots or shoes for gliding over ice or a hard surface. —*v.t./i.* move or perform on skates. ∼ **over,** make only a passing reference to. **skater** *n.*

skateboard *n.* small board with wheels like those of roller-skates, for riding on while standing.

skein /skeɪn/ *n.* loosely coiled bundle of yarn; flock of wild geese etc. in flight.

skeletal *a.* of or like a skeleton.

skeleton *n.* hard supporting structure of an animal body; any supporting structure; framework. **~ crew** *or* **staff,** one with staff reduced to a minimum. **~ key,** key made so as to fit many locks.

skep *n.* wooden or wicker basket; straw or wicker beehive.

sketch *n.* rough drawing or painting; brief account; short usu. comic play. —*v.t./i.* make a sketch or sketches (of). **~-map** *n.* roughly drawn map.

sketchy *a.* (*-ier, -iest*) rough and not detailed or substantial. **sketchily** *adv.,* **sketchiness** *n.*

skew *a.* slanting, askew. —*v.t./i.* make skew; turn or twist round. **on the ~,** askew.

skewbald *a.* (of an animal) with irregular patches of white and another colour.

skewer *n.* pin thrust through meat to hold it compactly in cooking. —*v.t.* pierce or hold in place thus.

ski /skiː/ *n.* (pl. *-is*) one of a pair of long narrow strips of wood etc. fixed under the feet for travelling over snow. —*v.i.* (p.t. *ski'd,* pres.p. *skiing*) travel on skis. **skier** *n.*

skid *v.i.* (p.t. *skidded*) (of a vehicle) slide uncontrollably. —*n.* skidding movement; plank etc. over which heavy objects may be dragged or rolled; helicopter's runner for use in landing; wedge acting as a brake on the wheel of a cart. **~-pan** *n.* surface used for practising control of skidding vehicles.

skiff *n.* small light row-boat.

skilful *a.* having or showing great skill. **skilfully** *adv.*

skill *n.* ability to do something well. **skilled** *a.*

skillet *n.* (*U.S.*) frying-pan; (*old use*) cooking-pot shaped like this.

skim *v.t./i.* (p.t. *skimmed*) take (matter) from the surface of (liquid); glide; read quickly.

skimp *v.t./i.* supply or use rather less than what is necessary.

skimpy *a.* (*-ier, -iest*) scanty. **skimpily** *adv.,* **skimpiness** *n.*

skin *n.* flexible continuous covering of the human or other animal body; material made from animal skin; complexion; outer layer; skin-like film on liquid. —*v.t./i.* (p.t. *skinned*) strip skin from; become covered with new skin. **~-diving** *n.* sport of swimming under water with flippers and breathing apparatus. **~-diver** *n.*

skinflint *n.* miserly person.

skinny *a.* (*-ier, -iest*) very thin; miserly.

skint *a.* (*sl.*) with no money left.

skip¹ *v.t./i.* (p.t. *skipped*) move lightly, esp. taking two steps with each foot in turn; jump with a skipping-rope; omit; (*sl.*) go away hastily or secretly. —*n.* skipping movement.

skip² *n.* cage or bucket for raising and lowering

things in a quarry etc.; large container for builders' rubbish etc.

skip³ *n.* skep.

skipper *n.* & *v.t.* captain.

skipping-rope *n.* rope turned over the head and under the feet while jumping in play or exercise.

skirl *n.* shrill sound characteristic of bagpipes. —*v.i.* make this sound.

skirmish *n.* minor fight or conflict. —*v.i.* take part in a skirmish.

skirt *n.* woman's garment hanging from the waist; this part of a garment; similar part; cut of beef from the lower flank. —*v.t.* go or be along the edge of.

skirting-board *n.* narrow board round the bottom of a room-wall.

skit *n.* short parody.

skittish *a.* frisky.

skittle *n.* one of the wooden pins set up to be bowled down with a ball or disc in the game of *skittles.* —*v.t.* **~ out,** get (batsmen) out rapidly.

skive *v.i.* (*sl.*) dodge a duty.

skivvy *n.* (*colloq.*) lowly female servant.

skua *n.* large seagull.

skulduggery *n.* (*colloq.*) trickery.

skulk *v.i.* loiter stealthily.

skull *n.* bony framework of the head; representation of this. **~-cap** *n.* small cap with no peak.

skunk *n.* black bushy-tailed American animal able to spray an evil-smelling liquid; (*sl.*) contemptible person.

sky *n.* region of the clouds or upper air; weather shown by this. —*v.t.* (p.t. *skied,* pres.p. *skying*) hit (a ball) high. **~-blue** *a.* & *n.* bright clear blue.

skylark *n.* lark that soars while singing. —*v.i.* play mischievously.

skylight *n.* window set in the line of a roof or ceiling.

skyscraper *n.* very tall building.

slab *n.* broad flat piece of something solid.

slack¹ *a.* (*-er, -est*) not tight or tense; slow, sluggish; negligent. —*n.* slack part of a rope etc. —*v.t./i.* slacken; be lazy about work. **slacker** *n.,* **slackly** *adv.,* **slackness** *n.*

slack² *n.* coal-dust or fragments left when coal is screened.

slacken *v.t./i.* make or become slack.

slacks *n.pl.* trousers for casual wear.

slag *n.* solid waste matter left when metal has been separated from ore by smelting. **~-heap** *n.* mound of waste matter.

slain *see* **slay.**

slake *v.t.* satisfy or make (thirst) less strong; combine (lime) with water.

slalom /ˈslɑː-/ *n.* ski-race down a zig-zag course; obstacle race in canoes.

slam *v.t./i.* (p.t. *slammed*) shut forcefully and noisily; put or hit forcefully; (*sl.*) criticize severely. —*n.* slamming noise; winning of 12 or 13 tricks in the game of bridge.

slander *n.* false statement uttered maliciously that damages a person's reputation; crime of uttering this. —*v.t.* utter a slander about. **slanderous** *a.*

slang *n.* words or phrases or particular meanings of these used very informally for vividness or novelty. —*v.t.* use abusive language to. **slangy** *a.*

slant *v.t./i.* slope; present (news etc.) from a particular point of view. —*n.* slope; way news etc. is slanted, bias. **slantwise** *adv.*

slap *v.t./i.* (p.t. *slapped*) strike with the open hand or with something flat; place forcefully or carelessly. —*n.* slapping blow. —*adv.* with a slap, directly. **∼-happy** *a.* (*colloq.*) cheerfully casual. **∼-up** *a.* (*sl.*) first-class.

slapdash *a.* hasty and careless.

slapstick *n.* comedy with boisterous activities.

slash *v.t./i.* make a sweeping stroke; strike thus; slit (a garment) ornamentally; reduce drastically; criticize vigorously. —*n.* slashing stroke; cut.

slat *n.* one of the thin narrow over-lapping strips arranged to form a screen.

slate *n.* rock that splits easily into smooth flat blue-grey plates; piece of this used as roofing-material or (formerly) for writing on. —*v.t.* cover with slates; (*colloq.*) criticize or rebuke severely.

slattern *n.* slovenly woman. **slatternly** *a.*

slaughter *v.t.* kill (animals) for food; kill ruthlessly or in great numbers. —*n.* this process.

slaughterhouse *n.* place where animals are killed for food.

Slav *a. & n.* (member) of any of the peoples of East and Central Europe who speak a Slavonic language.

slave *n.* person who is the property of another and is obliged to work for him; victim of or to a dominating influence; drudge. —*v.i.* work very hard. **∼-driver** *n.* person who makes others work very hard. **∼-driving** *n.*

slaver /ˈsleɪ-/ *v.i.* have saliva flowing from the mouth.

slavery *n.* existence or condition of slaves; very hard work.

slavish *a.* excessively submissive or imitative. **slavishly** *adv.*

Slavonic /-ˈvon-/ *a. & n.* (of) the group of languages including Russian and Polish.

slay *v.t.* (p.t. *slain*, p.p. *slew*) kill.

sleazy *a.* (-*ier*, -*iest*) (*colloq.*) dirty and slovenly.

sledge *n.* narrow cart with runners instead of wheels, used on snow or for sliding.

sledge-hammer *n.* large heavy hammer.

sleek *a.* (-*er*, -*est*) smooth and glossy; looking well-fed and thriving. —*v.t.* make sleek by smoothing. **sleekness** *n.*

sleep *n.* natural condition of rest with unconsciousness and relaxation of muscles; spell of this. —*v.t./i.* (p.t. *slept*) be or spend (time) in a state of sleep; provide with sleeping accommodation. **∼-walker** *n.*, **∼-walking** *n.* (person) walking about while asleep.

sleeper *n.* one who sleeps; one of the beams on which the rails of a railway etc. rest; railway coach fitted for sleeping in; berth in this.

sleeping-bag *n.* padded bag for sleeping in.

sleepless *a.* without sleep.

sleepy *a.* (-*ier*, -*iest*) feeling or showing a desire to sleep; without stir or bustle; (of fruit) tasteless from being over-ripe. **sleepily** *adv.*, **sleepiness** *n.*

sleet *n.* snow and rain falling simultaneously; hail or snow that melts while falling. —*v.i.* fall as sleet. **sleety** *a.*

sleeve *n.* part of a garment covering the arm or part of it; tube-like cover; cover for a record. **up one's ∼,** concealed but available. **sleeveless** *a.* without sleeves.

sleigh /sleɪ/ *n.* sledge, esp. as a passenger vehicle drawn by horses. **sleighing** *n.*

sleight /slaɪt/ *n.* **∼ of hand,** skill in using the hands to perform conjuring tricks etc.

slender *a.* slim and graceful; small in amount. **slenderness** *n.*

slept *see* **sleep.**

sleuth /sluːθ/ *n.* detective.

slew[1] *v.t./i.* turn or swing round.

slew[2] *see* **slay.**

slice *n.* thin broad piece (or a wedge) cut from something; portion; implement for lifting or serving fish etc.; slicing stroke. —*v.t./i.* cut, esp. into slices; strike (a ball in golf) badly so that it spins away from the direction intended. **slicer** *n.*

slick *a.* quick and cunning; smooth in manner; slippery. —*n.* slippery place; patch of oil on the sea. —*v.t.* make sleek.

slicker *n.* (*U.S. colloq.*) smooth stylish townsman.

slide *v.t./i.* (p.t. *slid*) move or cause to move along a smooth surface touching it always with the same part; move or pass smoothly. —*n.* act of sliding; smooth slope down which people or things can slide; sliding part; piece of glass for holding an object under a microscope; picture for showing on a screen by means of a projector; hinged clip for holding hair in place. **∼-rule** *n.* ruler used for making calculations, having a sliding central strip and marked with logarithmic scales. **sliding scale,** scale of fees or taxes etc. that varies according to the variation of some standard.

slight *a.* (-*er*, -*est*) not much or great or thorough; slender. —*v.t. & n.* insult by treating with lack of respect. **slightly** *adv.*, **slightness** *n.*

slim *a.* (*slimmer*, *slimmest*) of small girth or thickness; small, insufficient. —*v.t./i.* (p.t. *slimmed*) make (oneself) slimmer by dieting, exercise, etc. **slimmer** *n.*, **slimness** *n.*

slime *n.* unpleasant thick slippery liquid substance. **slimy** *a.*, **slimily** *adv.*, **sliminess** *n.*

sling *n.* belt or chain or bandage etc. looped round an object to support, or lift it; looped strap used to throw a stone etc. —*v.t.* (p.t. *slung*) suspend or lift or hurl with a sling; (*colloq.*) throw.

slink *v.i.* (p.t. *slunk*) move in a stealthy or shamefaced way.

slinky *a.* smooth and sinuous.

slip *v.t./i.* (p.t. *slipped*) slide accidentally; lose one's balance thus; go or put smoothly;

escape hold or capture; detach, release; become detached from. —*n.* act of slipping; accidental or casual mistake; loose covering; petticoat; slipway; strip of thin wood or paper; fielding position in cricket; liquid containing clay for coating pottery. **give a person the ~,** escape from or avoid him. **~-knot** *n.* one that slides easily or that can be undone by pulling. **~-road** *n.* road for entering or leaving a motorway or other main road. **~-stream** *n.* current of air driven backward as something is propelled forward. **~ up,** (*colloq.*) make an accidental or casual mistake. **~-up** *n.*

slipper *n.* light loose shoe for indoor wear.

slippery *n.* smooth or wet and difficult to hold or causing slipping; (of a person) not trustworthy.

slippy *a.* (*colloq.*) slippery. **look ~,** (*colloq.*) make haste.

slipshod *a.* done or doing things carelessly.

slipway *n.* sloping structure on which boats are landed or ships built or repaired.

slit *n.* narrow straight cut or opening. —*v.t.* (p.t. *slitted*) cut a slit in; cut into strips.

slither *v.i.* slide unsteadily.

sliver /ˈslɪv-/ *n.* small thin strip.

slobber *v.i.* slaver, dribble.

sloe *n.* blackthorn; its small dark plum-like fruit.

slog *v.t./i.* (p.t. *slogged*) hit hard; work or walk hard and steadily. —*n.* hard hit; spell of hard steady work or walking. **slogger** *n.*

slogan *n.* word or phrase adopted as a motto or in advertising.

sloop *n.* small ship with one mast.

slop *v.t./i.* (p.t. *slopped*) spill; splash liquid on; plod clumsily. —*n.* weak unappetizing liquid; slopped liquid; (*pl.*) liquid refuse. **~-basin** *n.* basin for receiving dregs from teacups at the table.

slope *v.t./i.* lie or lay or turn at an angle from the horizontal or vertical. —*n.* sloping surface or ground or direction; amount by which a thing slopes. **~ off,** (*sl.*) go away.

sloppy *a.* (-*ier*, -*iest*) liquid and splashing easily; slipshod; weakly sentimental. **sloppily** *adv.,* **sloppiness** *n.*

slosh *v.t./i.* (*colloq.*) splash, pour clumsily; (*sl.*) hit. —*n.* (*colloq.*) splashing sound; (*sl.*) blow.

slot *n.* narrow opening through which something is to be put; groove or slit in which something fits; position in a series or scheme. —*v.t./i.* (p.t. *slotted*) make slot(s) in; put or fit into a slot. **~-machine** *n.* machine operated by inserting a coin into a slot.

sloth /sləʊθ/ *n.* laziness; slow-moving animal of tropical America.

slothful *a.* lazy. **slothfully** *adv.*

slouch *v.i.* stand, sit, or move in a lazy awkward way. —*n.* slouching movement or posture.

slough[1] /slaʊ/ *n.* swamp, marsh.

slough[2] /slʌf/ *v.t./i.* shed (skin); be shed in this way.

slovenly /ˈslʌv-/ *a.* careless and untidy. **slovenliness** *n.*

slow *a.* (-*er*, -*est*) not quick or fast; showing an earlier time than the correct one; stupid. —*adv.* slowly. —*v.t./i.* reduce the speed (of). **slowly** *adv.,* **slowness** *n.*

slowcoach *n.* person who is slow in his actions or work.

slow-worm *n.* small legless lizard.

slub *n.* lump in yarn or thread.

sludge *n.* thick mud.

slug[1] *n.* small slimy animal like a snail without a shell; small lump of metal; bullet of irregular shape.

slug[2] *v.t.* (p.t. *slugged*) (*U.S.*) hit hard.

sluggard *n.* slow or lazy person.

sluggish *a.* slow-moving, not lively. **sluggishly** *adv.,* **sluggishness** *n.*

sluice /slus/ *n.* sliding gate controlling a flow of water; this water; channel carrying off water; place where objects are rinsed; act of sluicing. —*v.t./i.* flood, scour, or rinse with a flow of water; fit with sluices.

slum *n.* squalid district.

slumber *v.i. & n.* sleep. **slumberer** *n.*

slumming *n.* visiting a slum; living like inhabitants of slums.

slump *n.* sudden great fall in prices or demand. —*v.i.* undergo a slump; sit or flop down slackly.

slung *see* **sling.**

slunk *see* **slink.**

slur *v.t./i.* (p.t. *slurred*) write, pronounce, or sound with each letter or sound running into the next; pass lightly over (a fact); (*U.S.*) speak ill of. —*n.* slurred letter or sound; curved line marking notes to be slurred in music; discredit.

slurp *v.t./i. & n.* (*colloq.*) (make) a noisy sucking sound.

slurry /ˈslʌ-/ *n.* thin mud; thin liquid cement.

slush *n.* partly melted snow on the ground; silly sentimental talk or writing. **~ fund,** fund for an illegal purpose, e.g. bribery. **slushy** *a.*

slut *n.* slovenly woman. **sluttish** *a.*

sly *a.* (*slyer, slyest*) unpleasantly cunning and secret; mischievous and knowing. **on the ~,** secretly. **slyly** *adv.,* **slyness** *n.*

smack[1] *n.* slap; hard hit; loud kiss. —*v.t./i.* slap, hit hard; close and part (lips) noisily. —*adv.* (*colloq.*) slap.

smack[2] *n. & v.i.* (have) a slight flavour or trace.

smack[3] *n.* single-masted boat.

small *a.* (-*er*, -*est*) not large or great; doing things on a small scale; petty. —*n.* narrowest part (of the back); (*pl., colloq.*) small articles of laundry, esp. underwear. —*adv.* in a small way. **~-minded** *a.* narrow or selfish in outlook. **~ talk,** social conversation on unimportant subjects. **~-time** *a.* of an unimportant level. **smallness** *n.*

smallholding *n.* small piece of agricultural land. **smallholder** *n.*

smallpox *n.* disease with pustules that often leave bad scars.

smarmy *a.* (-*ier*, -*iest*) (*colloq.*) ingratiating, fulsome. **smarminess** *n.*

smart *a.* (-*er*, -*est*) neat and elegant; clever;

forceful, brisk. —v.i. & n. (feel) a stinging pain. **smartly** adv., **smartness** n.

smarten v.t./i. make or become smarter.

smash v.t./i. break noisily into pieces; strike forcefully; crash; overthrow; ruin, become ruined. —n. act or sound of smashing; collision; disaster; ruin.

smashing a. (colloq.) excellent.

smattering n. slight knowledge.

smear v.t./i. spread with a greasy or dirty substance; try to damage the reputation of. —n. thing smeared; mark made by this; attempt to damage a reputation.

smell n. ability to perceive things by their action on the sense-organs of the nose; quality perceived thus; unpleasant quality of this kind; act of smelling. —v.t./i. (p.t. smelt) perceive the smell of; detect or test thus; give off a smell. **smelly** a.

smelling-salts n.pl. solid preparation of ammonia to be sniffed as a remedy for faintness.

smelt[1] see smell.

smelt[2] v.t. heat and melt (ore) to extract metal; obtain (metal) thus.

smelt[3] n. small fish related to the salmon.

smile n. facial expression indicating pleasure or amusement, with lips stretched and their ends upturned. —v.t./i. give a smile; express by smiling; look favourable.

smirch v.t. & n. smear, soil; discredit.

smirk n. self-satisfied smile. —v.i. give a smirk.

smite v.t./i. (p.t. smote, p.p. smitten) hit hard; affect suddenly.

smith n. person who makes things in metal; blacksmith.

smithereens n.pl. small fragments.

smithy n. blacksmith; his workshop.

smitten see smite.

smock n. loose overall. —v.t. ornament with smocking.

smocking n. decoration of close gathers stitched ornamentally.

smoke n. visible vapour given off by a burning substance; spell of smoking tobacco; (sl.) cigarette, cigar. —v.t./i. give out smoke or steam; (of a chimney) send smoke into a room; darken or preserve with smoke; draw smoke from (a cigarette or cigar or pipe) into the mouth; do this as a habit. **~-screen** n. thing intended to disguise or conceal activities. **smoky** a.

smokeless a. with little or no smoke.

smoker n. person who smokes tobacco as a habit.

smooth a. (-er, -est) having an even surface with no projections; not harsh in sound or taste; moving evenly without bumping; pleasantly polite but perhaps insincere. —v.t./i. make or become smooth. **smoothly** adv., **smoothness** n.

smote see smite.

smother v.t./i. suffocate, stifle; cover thickly; suppress. —n. dense cloud of dust or smoke.

smoulder v.i. burn slowly with smoke but no flame; burn inwardly with concealed anger etc.

smudge n. dirty or blurred mark. —v.t./i. make a smudge on or with; become smudged; blur. **smudgy** a.

smug a. (smugger, smuggest) self-satisfied. **smugly** adv., **smugness** n.

smuggle v.t. convey secretly; bring (goods) illegally into or out of a country, esp. without paying customs duties. **smuggler** n.

smut n. small flake of soot; small black mark; indecent talk or pictures or stories. **smutty** a.

snack n. small or casual meal. **~-bar** n. place where snacks are sold.

snaffle n. horse's bit without a curb. —v.t. (sl.) take for oneself.

snag n. jagged projection; tear caused by this. —v.t./i. (p.t. snagged) catch or tear on a snag.

snail n. soft-bodied animal with a shell that can enclose its whole body. **~'s pace,** very slow pace.

snake n. reptile with a long narrow body and no legs. —v.i. move in a winding course. **snaky** a.

snakeskin n. leather made from snakes' skins.

snap v.t./i. (p.t. snapped) make or cause to make a sharp cracking sound; break suddenly; bite at with a snatching movement; speak with sudden irritation; move smartly; take a snapshot of. —n. act or sound of snapping; fastener that closes with a snap; small crisp biscuit; sudden brief spell of cold weather; snapshot; S~, card-game in which players call 'snap' when two similar cards are exposed. —adv. with a snapping sound. —a. sudden, done or arranged at short notice. **~ up,** take eagerly.

snapdragon n. garden plant with flowers that have a mouth-like opening.

snapper n. any of several sea-fish used as food.

snappy a. (-ier, -iest) (colloq.) irritable; brisk; neat and elegant. **snappily** adv., **snappiness** n.

snapshot n. photograph taken informally or casually.

snare n. trap, usu. with a noose; one of the strings stretched across a side-drum to produce a rattling effect. —v.t. trap in a snare.

snarl[1] v.t./i. growl angrily with teeth bared; speak or utter in a bad-tempered way. —n. act or sound of snarling.

snarl[2] v.t./i. & n. tangle.

snatch v.t./i. seize quickly or eagerly. —n. act of snatching; short or brief part.

snazzy a. (sl.) stylish.

sneak v.t./i. go or convey or (sl.) steal furtively; (school sl.) tell tales. —n. (school sl.) telltale.

sneakers n.pl. (U.S.) soft-soled shoes.

sneaking a. persistent but not openly acknowledged.

sneer n. scornful expression or remark. —v.i. show contempt by a sneer.

sneeze n. sudden audible involuntary expulsion of air through the nose. —v.i. give a sneeze.

snib n. fastening or catch of a window etc.

snick v.t. make a small cut in; hit (a ball) with a light glancing blow. —n. cut or blow of this kind.

snicker v.i. & n. snigger.

snide *a.* (*colloq.*) sneering slyly.

sniff *v.t./i.* draw air audibly through the nose; draw in as one breathes; try the smell of. —*n.* act or sound of sniffing. **sniffer** *n.*

sniffle *v.i.* sniff slightly or repeatedly. —*n.* this act or sound.

snigger *n.* & *v.i.* (give) a sly giggle.

snip *v.t./i.* (p.t. *snipped*) cut with scissors or shears in small quick strokes. —*n.* act or sound of snipping; piece snipped off; (*sl.*) bargain, certainty, easy task.

snipe *n.* (pl. *snipe*) wading-bird with a long straight bill. —*v.i.* fire shots from a hiding-place; make sly critical remarks. **sniper** *n.*

snippet *n.* small piece.

snitch *v.t.* (*sl.*) steal.

snivel *v.i.* (p.t. *snivelled*) cry in a miserable whining way.

snob *n.* person with an exaggerated respect for social position or wealth or certain tastes and who despises those he considers inferior. **snobbery** *n.*, **snobbish** *a.*

snood *n.* loose bag-like ornament in which a woman's hair is held at the back.

snook *n.* **cock a** ～, (*sl.*) make a contemptuous gesture.

snooker *n.* game played on a billiard-table with 15 red and 6 other coloured balls.

snoop *v.i.* (*colloq.*) pry. **snooper** *n.*

snooty *a.* (*colloq.*) haughty and contemptuous. **snootily** *adv.*

snooze *n.* & *v.i.* nap.

snore *n.* snorting or grunting sound made during sleep. —*v.i.* make such sounds. **snorer** *n.*

snorkel *n.* device by which an underwater swimmer or submarine can take in and expel air.

snorkelling *n.* swimming with a snorkel.

snort *n.* rough sound made by forcing breath through the nose, esp. in indignation. —*v.i.* make a snort.

snout *n.* animal's long projecting nose or nose and jaws; projecting front part.

snow *n.* frozen atmospheric vapour falling to earth in white flakes; fall or layer of snow. —*v.i.* fall as or like snow. ～**-plough** *n.* device for clearing roads etc. by pushing snow aside. **snowed under,** covered with snow; overwhelmed with a mass of letters etc. **snowstorm** *n.*, **snowy** *a.*

snowball *n.* snow pressed into a compact mass for throwing in play. —*v.t./i.* throw snowballs (at); increase in size or intensity.

snowdrop *n.* plant with small hanging white flowers blooming in spring.

snowflake *n.* flake of snow.

snowman *n.* (pl. *-men*) figure made of snow.

snub[1] *v.t.* (p.t. *snubbed*) reject (a person) unkindly or contemptuously. —*n.* treatment of this kind.

snub[2] *a.* (of the nose) short and stumpy. ～**-nosed** *a.*

snuff[1] *n.* powdered tobacco for sniffing up the nostrils.

snuff[2] *v.t.* put out (a candle) by covering or pinching the flame. ～ **it,** (*sl.*) die. **snuffer** *n.*

snuffle *v.i.* breathe with a noisy sniff. —*n.* snuffling sound.

snug *a.* (*snugger*, *snuggest*) cosy; close-fitting. **snugly** *a.*

snuggle *v.t./i.* nestle, cuddle.

so *adv.* & *conj.* to the extent or in the manner or with the result indicated; very; for that reason; also. —*pron.* that, the same thing. ～**and-so** *n.* person or thing that need not be named; (*colloq.*) disliked person. ～**-called** *a.* called (wrongly) by that name. ～ **long!**, (*colloq.*) goodbye. ～**-so** *a.* & *adv.* (*colloq.*) only moderately good or well. ～ **that,** in order that.

soak *v.t./i.* place or lie in liquid so as to become thoroughly wet; (of liquid) penetrate; absorb; (*sl.*) extort money from. —*n.* process of soaking; (*sl.*) heavy drinker.

soap *n.* substance used in washing and cleaning things, made of fat or oil and an alkali. —*v.t.* apply soap to. ～ **opera,** (*U.S. colloq.*) sentimental broadcast serial. **soapy** *a.*

soapstone *n.* steatite.

soapsuds *n.pl.* froth of soapy water.

soar *v.i.* rise high esp. in flight.

sob *n.* uneven drawing of breath when weeping or gasping. —*v.t./i.* (p.t. *sobbed*) weep or breathe or utter with sobs.

sober *a.* not intoxicated; serious, not frivolous; (of colour) not bright. —*v.t./i.* make or become sober. **soberly** *adv.*, **sobriety** /-ˈbraɪə-/ *n.*

sobriquet /ˈsəʊbrɪkeɪ/ *n.* nickname.

soccer *n.* (*colloq.*) Association football.

sociable *a.* fond of company; characterized by friendly companionship. **sociably** *adv.*, **sociability** *n.*

social *a.* living in an organized community; of society or its organization; sociable. —*n.* social gathering. ～ **science,** study of society and social relationships. ～ **security,** State assistance for those who lack economic security. ～ **services,** welfare services provided by the State. ～ **worker,** person trained to help people with social problems. **socially** *adv.*

socialism *n.* political and economic theory that resources, industries, and transport should be owned and managed by the State. **socialist** *n.*, **socialistic** *a.*

socialite *n.* person prominent in fashionable society.

socialize *v.t./i.* organize in a socialistic manner; behave sociably. **socialization** *n.*

society *n.* organized community; system of living in this; people of the higher social classes; mixing with other people; group organized for a common purpose. **Society of Friends,** Quakers. **Society of Jesus,** Jesuits.

sociology *n.* study of human society or of social problems. **sociological** *a.*, **sociologist** *n.*

sock[1] *n.* short stocking not reaching the knee; loose insole.

sock[2] *v.t.* (*sl.*) hit forcefully. —*n.* (*sl.*) forceful blow.

socket *n.* hollow into which something fits. **socketed** *a.*

sockeye *n.* a kind of salmon.

sod *n.* turf; a piece of this.

soda *n.* compound of sodium in common use, esp. sodium carbonate (*washing-~*), bicarbonate (*baking-~*) or hydroxide (*caustic ~*); soda-water. **~-water** *n.* water made fizzy by being charged with carbon dioxide under pressure.

sodden *a.* made very wet.

sodium *n.* soft silver-white metallic element. **~ lamp,** lamp giving a yellow light from an electrical discharge in sodium vapour.

sofa *n.* long upholstered seat with a back and raised ends.

soffit *n.* under-surface of a lintel or arch etc.

soft *a.* (*-er, -est*) not hard or firm or rough; not loud; gentle; flabby, feeble; easily influenced, tender-hearted; silly; not bright or dazzling; (*sl.*) easy; (of drinks) non-alcoholic; (of water) free from mineral salts that prevent soap from lathering; (of drugs) not likely to cause addiction; (of currency) likely to drop suddenly in value. **~ fruit,** small stoneless fruit (e.g. raspberry). **~ spot,** feeling of affection. **softly** *adv.,* **softness** *n.*

soften *v.t./i.* make or become soft or softer. **softener** *n.*

software *n.* computer programs or tapes containing these (as distinct from machinery or *hardware*).

soggy *a.* (*-ier, -iest*) sodden; moist and heavy. **sogginess** *n.*

soigné /ˈswɑnjeɪ/ *a.* (fem. *soignée*) well-groomed and sophisticated.

soil[1] *n.* loose earth; ground as territory.

soil[2] *v.t./i.* make or become dirty.

sojourn /ˈsɒdʒən/ *n.* temporary stay. —*v.i.* stay temporarily.

solace /ˈsɒl-/ *v.t. & n.* comfort in distress.

solar *a.* of or from the sun; reckoned by the sun. **~ plexus,** network of nerves at the pit of the stomach; this area. **~ system,** sun with the heavenly bodies that revolve round it.

solarium /-ˈleər-/ *n.* (pl. *-ia*) room or balcony where sunlight can be enjoyed for medical use or for pleasure.

sold *see* **sell.**

solder *n.* soft alloy used to cement metal parts together. —*v.t.* join with solder.

soldier *n.* member of an army. —*v.i.* serve as a soldier. **~ on,** (*colloq.*) persevere doggedly. **soldierly** *a.*

soldiery *n.* soldiers collectively.

sole[1] *n.* under-surface of a foot; part of a shoe or stocking etc. covering this. —*v.t.* put a sole on.

sole[2] *n.* flat-fish used as food.

sole[3] *a.* one and only; belonging exclusively to one person or group. **solely** *adv.*

solecism /ˈsɒlɪs-/ *n.* mistake in the use of language; social blunder.

solemn *a.* not smiling or cheerful; formal and dignified. **solemnly** *adv.,* **solemnity** *n.*

solemnize *v.t.* celebrate (a festival etc.); perform with formal rites. **solemnization** *n.*

solenoid /ˈsəʊ- *or* ˈsɒl-/ *n.* coil of wire magnetized by electric current.

sol-fa *n.* system of syllables (*doh, ray, me,* etc.) representing the notes of a musical scale.

solicit *v.t./i.* seek to obtain by asking (for). **solicitation** *n.*

solicitor *n.* lawyer who advises clients and instructs barristers.

solicitous /-ˈlɪs-/ *a.* anxious about a person's welfare or comfort. **solicitously** *adv.,* **solicitude** *n.*

solid *a.* keeping its shape, firm; not liquid or gas; not hollow; of the same substance throughout; continuous; of solids; with three dimensions; sound and reliable; unanimous. —*n.* solid substance or body or food. **~-state** *a.* using transistors (which use the electronic properties of solids). **solidly** *adv.,* **solidity** *n.*

solidarity *n.* unity resulting from common aims or interests etc.

solidify *v.t./i.* make or become solid.

soliloquize *v.i.* utter a soliloquy.

soliloquy /-ˈlɪləkwɪ/ *n.* speech made aloud to oneself.

solitaire *n.* gem set by itself; game played on a special board by one person who removes objects after jumping others over them; (*U.S.*) card-game of patience.

solitary *a.* alone; single; not frequented, lonely. —*n.* recluse.

solitude *n.* being solitary.

solo *n.* (pl. *-os*) music for a single voice or instrument; unaccompanied performance or flight etc. —*a.* alone.

soloist *n.* performer of a solo.

solstice *n.* either of the times (about 21 June and 22 Dec.) or points reached when the sun is furthest from the equator.

soluble *a.* able to be dissolved; able to be solved. **solubility** *n.*

solution *n.* liquid containing something dissolved; process of dissolving; process of solving a problem etc.; answer found.

solvable *a.* able to be solved.

solve *v.t.* find the answer to. **solver** *n.*

solvent *a.* having enough money to pay one's debts etc.; able to dissolve another substance. —*n.* liquid used for dissolving something. **solvency** *n.*

sombre *a.* dark, gloomy. **sombrely** *adv.*

sombrero /-ˈbreər-/ *n.* (pl. *-os*) man's hat with a very wide brim.

some *a.* unspecified quantity or number of; unknown, unnamed; considerable quantity; approximately; (*sl.*) remarkable. —*pron.* some persons or things.

somebody *n. & pron.* unspecified person; person of importance.

somehow *adv.* in an unspecified or unexplained manner; by one means or another.

someone *n. & pron.* somebody.

somersault /ˈsʌməsɔlt/ *n. & v.i.* leap or roll turning one's body upside down and over.

something *n. & pron.* unspecified thing or extent; important or praiseworthy thing. **~ like,** rather like; approximately.

sometime *a. & adv.* former(ly).

sometimes *adv.* at some times but not all the time.

somewhat *adv.* to some extent.

somewhere *adv.* at, in, or to an unspecified place.

somnambulist /-'næm-/ *n.* sleepwalker.

somnolent /'som-/ *a.* sleepy; asleep. **somnolence** *n.*

son *n.* male in relation to his parents. **~-in-law** *n.* (pl. *sons-in-law*) daughter's husband.

sonar /'səʊ-/ *n.* device for detecting objects under water by reflection of sound-waves.

sonata /-'nɑ-/ *n.* musical composition for one instrument or two, usu. in several movements.

sonatina /-'ti-/ *n.* simple or short sonata.

song *n.* singing; music for singing. **going for a ~**, being sold very cheaply. **~-bird** *n.* bird with a musical cry.

songster *n.* singer; song-bird.

sonic *a.* of sound-waves.

sonnet *n.* type of poem of 14 lines.

sonny *n.* (*colloq.*) form of address to a boy or young man.

sonorous /'son-/ *a.* resonant.

soon *adv.* (*-er*, *-est*) in a short time; early; readily. **sooner or later**, at some time, eventually.

soot *n.* black powdery substance in smoke. **sooty** *a.*

soothe /suð/ *v.t.* calm, ease (pain etc.). **soothing** *a.*, **soothingly** *adv.*

soothsayer /-θ-/ *n.* prophet.

sop *n.* piece of bread dipped in liquid before being eaten or cooked; concession to pacify a troublesome person. *—v.t.* (p.t. *sopped*) dip in liquid; soak up (liquid).

sophisticated *a.* characteristic of or experienced in fashionable life and its ways; complicated, elaborate. **sophistication** *n.*

sophistry *n.* clever and subtle but perhaps misleading reasoning.

soporific *a.* tending to cause sleep. *—n.* soporific drug etc.

sopping *a.* very wet, drenched.

soppy *a.* (*-ier*, *-iest*) very wet; (*colloq.*) sentimental in a sickly way.

soprano *n.* (pl. *-os*) highest female or boy's singing-voice; music for this.

sorbet *n.* flavoured water-ice.

sorcerer *n.* magician. **sorceress** *n.fem.*, **sorcery** *n.*

sordid *a.* dirty, squalid; (of motives etc.) not honourable, mercenary. **sordidly** *adv.*, **sordidness** *n.*

sore *a.* (*-er*, *-est*) causing or suffering pain from injury or disease; (*old use*) serious; distressed, vexed. *—n.* sore place; source of distress or annoyance. **sorely** *adv.*, **soreness** *n.*

sorrel[1] /'so-/ *n.* sharp-tasting herb.

sorrel[2] /'so-/ *a.* light reddish-brown.

sorrow *n.* mental suffering caused by loss or disappointment etc.; thing causing this. *—v.i.* feel sorrow, grieve. **sorrowful** *a.*, **sorrowfully** *adv.*

sorry *a.* (*-ier*, *-iest*) feeling pity or regret or sympathy; wretched.

sort *n.* particular kind or variety; (*colloq.*) person of a specified character. *—v.t.* arrange according to sort or size or destination etc. **out of sorts**, slightly unwell or depressed.

sortie *n.* sally by troops from a besieged place; flight of an aircraft on a military operation.

SOS international code-signal of distress. *—n.* urgent appeal for help.

sotto voce /sotəʊ 'vəʊtʃi/ in an undertone.

soufflé /'sufleɪ/ *n.* light dish made with beaten egg-white.

sought *see* **seek.**

soul *n.* person's spiritual or immortal element; mental, moral, or emotional nature; personification, pattern (of honesty etc.); person; American Black culture. **~ music**, emotional style of jazz-playing.

soulful *a.* showing deep feeling, emotional. **soulfully** *adv.*

soulless *a.* lacking sensitivity or noble qualities; dull.

sound[1] *n.* vibrations of air detectable (at certain frequencies) by the ear; sensation produced by these; what is or may be heard. *—v.t./i.* produce or cause to produce sound; utter, pronounce; seem when heard; test by noting the sound produced. **~ barrier**, high resistance of air to objects moving at speeds near that of sound. **sounding-board** *n.* board to reflect sound or increase resonance. **sounder** *n.*

sound[2] *a.* (*-er*, *-est*) healthy; not diseased or damaged; secure; correct, well-founded; thorough. *—adv.* soundly. **soundly** *adv.*, **soundness** *n.*

sound[3] *v.t.* test the depth or quality of the bottom of (a river or sea etc.), esp. by a weighted line; examine with a probe. **sounder** *n.*

sound[4] *n.* strait.

soup *n.* liquid food made from stewed meat or vegetables etc. *—v.t.* **~ up**, (*colloq.*) increase the power of (an engine etc.). **in the ~**, (*sl.*) in difficulties. **~-kitchen** *n.* place where soup etc. is supplied free to the needy.

soupçon /'supsɔ̃/ *n.* trace.

sour *a.* (*-er*, *-est*) tasting sharp like unripe fruit; not fresh, tasting or smelling stale; (of soil) excessively acid; bad-tempered. *—n.* acid drink. *—v.t./i.* make or become sour. **sourly** *adv.*, **sourness** *n.*

source *n.* place from which something comes or is obtained; river's starting-point; person or book etc. supplying information.

sourpuss *n.* (*sl.*) bad-tempered person.

souse *v.t.* steep in pickle; drench.

south *n.* point or direction to the right of a person facing east; southern part. *—a.* in the south; (of wind) from the south. *—adv.* towards the south. **~-east** *n.* point or direction midway between south and east. (**~-easterly** *a.* & *n.*, **~-eastern** *a.*) **~-west** *n.* point or direction midway between south and west. **~-westerly** *a.* & *n.*, **~-western** *a.*

southerly /'sʌ-/ *a.* towards or blowing from the south.

southern *a.* of or in the south.

southerner *n.* native of the south.

southernmost *a.* furthest south.

southpaw *n.* (*colloq.*) left-handed person.

southward *a.* towards the south. **southwards** *adv.*

souvenir /suvə'nɪə(r)/ *n.* thing serving as a reminder of an incident or place visited.

sou'wester *n.* waterproof usu. oil-skin hat with a broad flap at the back.

sovereign *n.* king or queen who is the supreme ruler of a country; British gold coin nominally worth £1. —*a.* supreme; (of a State) independent; very effective. **sovereignty** *n.*

soviet /'səʊv-/ *n.* elected council in the U.S.S.R. **Soviet** *a.* of the **Soviet Union** (= U.S.S.R.).

sow[1] /səʊ/ *v.t.* (p.t. *sowed*, p.p. *sowed* or *sown*) plant or scatter (seed) for growth; plant seed in; implant (ideas etc.). **sower** *n.*

sow[2] /saʊ/ *n.* adult female pig.

soy *n.* soya bean.

soya *n.* ~ **bean**, bean from which an edible oil and flour are obtained.

spa *n.* place with a curative mineral spring.

space *n.* boundless expanse in which all objects exist and move; portion of this; empty area or extent; universe beyond earth's atmosphere; interval. —*v.t.* arrange with spaces between.

spacecraft *n.* (pl. *-craft*) vehicle for travelling in outer space.

spacious *a.* providing much space, roomy. **spaciousness** *n.*

spade[1] *n.* tool for digging ground, with a broad metal blade on a handle; tool of similar shape for other purposes.

spade[2] *n.* playing-card of the suit marked with black figures shaped like an inverted heart with a small stem.

spadework *n.* hard preparatory work.

spaghetti *n.* pasta made in thin sticks.

span[1] *n.* extent from end to end; distance (about 9 inches or 23 cm) between the tips of the thumb and little finger when these are stretched apart; distance or part between the uprights of an arch or bridge. —*v.t.* (p.t. *spanned*) extend or reach across.

span[2] *see* **spick.**

spandrel *n.* area between the curves of adjoining arches.

spangle *n.* small piece of glittering material ornamenting a dress etc. —*v.t.* cover with spangles or sparkling objects.

Spaniard *n.* native of Spain.

spaniel *n.* a kind of dog with drooping ears and a silky coat.

Spanish *a.* & *n.* (language) of Spain.

spank *v.t.* slap on the buttocks.

spanking *a.* (*colloq.*) brisk.

spanner *n.* tool for gripping and turning the nut on a screw etc.

spar[1] *n.* strong pole used as a ship's mast or yard or boom.

spar[2] *n.* mineral that splits easily.

spar[3] *v.i.* (p.t. *sparred*) box, esp. for practice; quarrel, argue.

spare *v.t./i.* refrain from hurting or harming; use with restraint; be able to afford to give. —*a.* additional to what is usually needed or used, kept in reserve; thin, lean; small in quantity. —*n.* extra thing kept in reserve. **sparely** *adv.*, **spareness** *n.*

sparing /'speər-/ *a.* economical, not generous or wasteful.

spark *n.* fiery particle; flash of light produced by an electrical discharge; particle (of energy, genius, etc.). —*v.t./i.* give off spark(s). **~ off**, trigger off.

sparkle *v.i.* shine with flashes of light; show brilliant wit or liveliness. —*n.* sparkling light or brightness.

sparkler *n.* sparking firework.

sparkling *a.* (of wine) effervescent.

sparrow *n.* small brownish-grey bird.

sparse *a.* thinly scattered, not dense. **sparsely** *adv.*, **sparseness** *n.*, **sparsity** *n.*

spartan *a.* (of conditions) simple and sometimes harsh.

spasm *n.* strong involuntary contraction of a muscle; sudden brief spell of activity or emotion etc.

spasmodic *a.* of or occurring in spasms. **spasmodically** *adv.*

spastic *a.* physically disabled by cerebral palsy which causes jerky or involuntary movements. —*n.* person suffering from this condition. **spasticity** *n.*

spat[1] *see* **spit**[1].

spat[2] *n.* short gaiter.

spate *n.* sudden flood.

spathe /speɪð/ *n.* large petal-like part of a flower, surrounding a central spike.

spatial /'speɪʃəl/ *a.* of or existing in space. **spatially** *adv.*

spatter *v.t./i.* scatter or fall in small drops (on). —*n.* splash(es); sound of spattering.

spatula *n.* knife-like tool with a blunt blade; medical instrument for pressing down the tongue.

spatulate *a.* with a broad rounded end.

spawn *n.* eggs of fish or frogs or shellfish; (*derog.*) offspring; thread-like matter from which fungi grow. —*v.t./i.* deposit spawn; produce from spawn; generate.

spay *v.t.* sterilize (a female animal) by removing the ovaries.

speak *v.t.* (p.t. *spoke*, p.p. *spoken*) utter (words) in an ordinary voice; say something; converse; express by speaking; be evidence of something.

speaker *n.* person who speaks, one who makes a speech; loudspeaker; *S*~, person presiding over the House of Commons or a similar assembly.

spear *n.* weapon for hurling, with a long shaft and pointed tip; pointed stem. —*v.t.* pierce with or as if with a spear.

spearhead *n.* foremost part of an advancing force. —*v.t.* be the spearhead of.

spearmint *n.* a kind of mint.

spec *n.* **on ~**, (*colloq.*) as a speculation, without being certain.

special *a.* of a particular kind; for a particular purpose; exceptional. **specially** *adv.*

specialist *n.* expert in a particular branch of a subject, esp. of medicine.

speciality /-ˈæl-/ *n.* special quality or product or activity.

specialize *v.t./i.* be or become a specialist; adapt for a particular purpose. **specialization** *n.*

species /ˈspiːʃiz/ *n.* (pl. *species*) group of similar animals or plants within a genus; kind.

specific *a.* particular, clearly distinguished from others; exact, not vague. —*n.* specific aspect or influence; remedy for a specific disease etc. **~ gravity,** ratio between the weight of a substance and that of the same volume of water or air. **specifically** *adv.*

specification *n.* specifying; details describing a thing to be made or done.

specify *v.t.* mention definitely; include in specifications.

specimen *n.* part or individual taken as an example or for examination or testing.

specious /ˈspiː-/ *a.* seeming good or sound but lacking real merit. **speciously** *adv.*, **speciousness** *n.*

speck *n.* small spot or particle.

speckle *n.* small spot, esp. as a natural marking. **speckled** *a.*

specs *n.pl.* (*colloq.*) spectacles.

spectacle *n.* impressive sight; lavish public show; ridiculous sight; (*pl.*) pair of lenses set in a frame, worn to assist sight or protect the eyes.

spectacular *a.* impressive. —*n.* spectacular performance or production. **spectacularly** *adv.*

spectator *n.* person who watches a show or game or incident.

spectral *a.* of or like a spectre; of the spectrum.

spectre *n.* ghost; haunting fear.

spectrum *n.* (pl. *-tra*) bands of colour or sound forming a series according to their wavelengths; entire range of ideas etc.

speculate *v.i.* form opinions by guessing; buy in the hope of making a profit but with risk of loss. **speculation** *n.*, **speculator** *n.*, **speculative** *a.*

speculum *n.* medical instrument for looking into bodily cavities.

sped *see* **speed.**

speech *n.* act or power or manner of speaking; spoken communication, esp. to an audience; language, dialect.

speechless *a.* unable to speak because of great emotion.

speed *n.* rate of time at which something moves or operates; rapidity. —*v.t./i.* (p.t. *sped*) move, pass, or send quickly; (p.t. *speeded*) travel at an illegal or dangerous speed. **~ up,** move or operate at a greater speed. **~-up** *n.*

speedboat *n.* fast motor-boat.

speedometer /-ˈdom-/ *n.* device in a motor vehicle, showing its speed.

speedway *n.* arena for motor-cycle racing; (*U.S.*) fast motor-road.

speedwell *n.* wild plant with small blue flowers.

speedy *a.* (*-ier*, *-iest*) rapid. **speedily** *adv.*, **speediness** *n.*

speleology /spelɪ-/ *n.* exploration and study of caves. **speleological** *a.*, **speleologist** *n.*

spell¹ *n.* words supposed to have magic power; their influence; fascination, attraction.

spell² *v.t./i.* (p.t. *spelt*) give in their correct sequence the letters that form (a word); produce as a result. **~ out,** spell aloud; state explicitly. **speller** *n.*

spell³ *n.* period of time or weather or activity. —*v.t.* take turns with (a person) in work etc.

spellbound *a.* entranced.

spelt¹ *see* **spell**².

spelt² *n.* a kind of wheat.

spencer *n.* woman's undergarment like a thin jumper.

spend *v.t.* (p.t. *spent*) pay out (money) in buying something; use for a certain purpose; use up; pass (time etc.). **spender** *n.*

spendthrift *n.* wasteful spender.

spent *see* **spend.**

sperm *n.* (pl. *sperms* or *sperm*) male reproductive cell; semen. **~ whale,** a kind of large whale.

spermicidal *a.* killing sperm.

spew *v.t./i.* vomit; cast out in a stream.

sphagnum *n.* moss growing on bogs.

sphere *n.* perfectly round solid geometric figure or object; field of action or influence etc.

spherical *a.* shaped like a sphere.

sphincter *n.* ring of muscle controlling an opening in the body.

sphinx *n.* **the S~,** winged monster in Greek mythology; stone statue with a lion's body and human or ram's head, esp. in ancient Egypt; enigmatic person.

spice *n.* flavouring-substance(s) (obtained from plants) with a strong taste or smell; thing that adds zest. —*v.t.* flavour with spice. **spicy** *a.*

spick *a.* **~ and span,** neat and clean.

spider *n.* small animal (not an insect) with a segmented body and eight jointed legs, living on insects. **spidery** *a.*

spiel /spiːl/ *n.* (*U.S. sl.*) glib or lengthy speech.

spigot *n.* plug stopping the vent-hole of a cask or controlling the flow of a tap.

spike *n.* pointed thing; pointed piece of metal. —*v.t.* put spikes on; pierce or fasten with a spike; (*colloq.*) add alcohol to (drink). **~ a person's guns,** thwart him. **spiky** *a.*

spill¹ *n.* thin strip of wood or paper for transferring flame.

spill² *v.t./i.* (p.t. *spilt*) cause or allow to run over the edge of a container; become spilt. —*n.* fall. **~ the beans,** (*sl.*) reveal information indiscreetly. **spillage** *n.*

spin *v.t./i.* (p.t. *spun*, pres.p. *spinning*) turn rapidly on its axis; draw out and twist into threads; make (yarn etc.) thus. —*n.* spinning movement; short drive for pleasure. **~-drier** *n.* machine for drying washed articles by spinning them in a rotating drum. **~-off** *n.* incidental benefit. **~ out,** prolong. **spinner** *n.*

spina bifida /spaɪnə ˈbɪf-/ congenital defect of the spine, in which membranes protrude.

spinach *n.* vegetable with dark-green leaves.

spinal *a.* of the spine.

spindle *n.* rod on which thread is wound in spinning; revolving pin or axis; shrub or tree with pink or red berries.

spindly *a.* long or tall and thin.

spindrift *n.* sea-spray.

spine *n.* backbone; needle-like projection; part of a book where the pages are hinged.

spineless *a.* having no backbone; lacking determination.

spinet /-'net/ *n.* a kind of small harpsichord.

spinnaker /ˈspɪn-/ *n.* large extra sail on a racing-yacht.

spinney *n.* (pl. -eys) thicket.

spinning-wheel *n.* household device for spinning fibre into yarn.

spinster *n.* unmarried woman.

spiny *a.* full of spines, prickly.

spiral *a.* forming a continuous winding curve round a central point or axis. —*n.* spiral line or thing; continuous increase or decrease in two or more quantities alternately. —*v.i.* (p.t. *spiralled*) move in a spiral course. **spirally** *adv.*

spire *n.* tall pointed structure esp. on a church tower.

spirit *n.* mind or animating principle as distinct from body; soul; ghost; person's nature; characteristic quality; real meaning; liveliness, boldness; distilled extract; *the S~*, the Holy Spirit; (*pl.*) person's feeling of cheerfulness or depression; (*pl.*) strong distilled alcoholic drink. —*v.t.* carry off swiftly and mysteriously. **~-lamp** *n.* lamp that burns methylated spirit or similar fluid. **~-level** *n.* sealed glass tube containing an air-bubble in liquid, used to test levelness.

spirited *a.* lively, bold; having the mental spirit(s) specified. **spiritedly** *adv.*

spiritual *a.* of the human spirit or soul; of the Church or religion. —*n.* religious folk-song of American Blacks. **spiritually** *adv.*, **spirituality** *n.*

spiritualism *n.* attempted communication with spirits of the dead. **spiritualist** *n.*

spirituous *a.* strongly alcoholic.

spit[1] *v.t./i.* (p.t. *spat* or *spit*, pres.p. *spitting*) eject from the mouth; eject saliva; make a spitting sound in anger or hostility; (of rain) fall lightly. —*n.* spittle; act of spitting; (also *spitting image*) exact likeness.

spit[2] *n.* metal spike holding meat while it is roasted; narrow strip of land projecting into the sea. —*v.t.* (p.t. *spitted*) pierce with or as if with a spit.

spit[3] *n.* spade's depth of earth.

spite *n.* malicious desire to hurt or annoy someone. —*v.t.* hurt or annoy from spite. **in ~ of,** not being prevented by. **spiteful** *a.*, **spitefully** *adv.*, **spitefulness** *n.*

spittle *n.* saliva.

spittoon *n.* receptacle for spitting into.

spiv *n.* (*sl.*) smartly dressed person who makes money shadily.

splash *v.t./i.* cause (liquid) to fly about in drops; move or fall or wet with such drops; decorate with irregular patches of colour etc.; display in large print; spend (money) freely. —*n.* act or mark or sound of splashing; (*colloq.*) dash of soda-water etc.; patch of colour or light; striking display. **splashy** *a.*

splatter *v.t./i.* & *n.* splash, spatter.

splay *v.t./i.* spread apart; slant outwards or inwards. —*a.* splayed.

spleen *n.* abdominal organ of the body, involved in maintaining the proper condition of the blood.

splendid *a.* brilliant, very impressive; excellent. **splendidly** *adv.*

splendour *n.* splendid appearance.

splice *v.t.* join by interweaving or overlapping the ends.

splint *n.* rigid framework preventing a limb etc. from movement, e.g. while a broken bone heals. —*v.t.* secure with a splint.

splinter *n.* thin sharp piece of broken wood etc. —*v.t./i.* break into splinters. **~ group,** small group that has broken away from a larger one.

split *v.t./i.* (p.t. *split*, pres.p. *splitting*) break or come apart, esp. lengthwise; divide, share; (*sl.*) reveal a secret. —*n.* splitting; split thing or place; (*pl.*) acrobatic position with legs stretched fully apart along the floor. **~ one's sides,** laugh very heartily. **~ second,** very brief moment.

splotch *v.t.* & *n.* splash, blotch.

splurge *n.* ostentatious display, esp. of wealth. —*v.i.* make a splurge, spend money freely.

splutter *v.t./i.* make a rapid series of spitting sounds; speak or utter incoherently. —*n.* spluttering sound.

spoil *v.t./i.* (p.t. & p.p. *spoilt* or *spoiled*) damage, make useless or unsatisfactory; become unfit for use; harm the character of (a person) by being indulgent. —*n.* (also *pl.*) plunder; perquisites. **~-sport** *n.* person who spoils others' enjoyment. **be spoiling for,** (*colloq.*) desire (a fight etc.) eagerly.

spoke[1] *n.* one of the bars connecting the hub to the rim of a wheel.

spoke[2], **spoken** *see* speak.

spokesman *n.* (pl. -*men*) person who speaks on behalf of a group.

spoliation *n.* pillaging.

sponge *n.* water animal with a porous structure; its skeleton, or a similar substance, esp. used for washing or cleaning or padding; sponge-cake; wash with a sponge. —*v.t./i.* wipe or wash with a sponge; cadge, live off the generosity of others. **~-bag** *n.* waterproof bag for toilet articles. **~-cake** *n.*, **~ pudding** *n.*, one with a light open texture. **spongeable** *a.*, **spongy** *a.*

sponger *n.* person who sponges on others.

sponsor *n.* person who makes himself responsible for a trainee etc., introduces legislation, or contributes to charity in return for another's activity; godparent; one who provides funds for a broadcast, sporting event, etc. —*v.t.* act as sponsor for. **sponsorship** *n.*

spontaneous *a.* resulting from natural impulse;

not caused or suggested from outside. **spontaneously** *adv.*, **spontaneity** /-ˈnɪə-/ *n.*

spoof *n.* (*colloq.*) hoax, parody.

spook *n.* (*colloq.*) ghost. **spooky** *a.*

spool *n.* reel on which something is wound.

spoon *n.* utensil with a rounded bowl and a handle, used for conveying food to the mouth or for stirring things; amount it contains. —*v.t.* take or lift with a spoon; hit (a ball) feebly upwards. **~-feed** *v.t.* (p.t. *-fed*) feed from a spoon; give excessive help to. **spoonful** *n.* (pl. *-fuls*).

spoonbill *n.* wading bird with a broad flat tip to its bill.

spoonerism *n.* accidental interchange of the initial letters of two words.

spoor *n.* track or scent left by an animal.

sporadic *a.* occurring here and there, scattered. **sporadically** *adv.*

spore *n.* one of the tiny reproductive cells of fungi, ferns, etc.

sporran *n.* pouch worn hanging in front of a kilt.

sport *n.* athletic (esp. outdoor) activity; game(s), pastime(s); amusement, fun; (*sl.*) sportsmanlike person; animal or plant that differs strikingly from its parent(s). —*v.t./i.* play, amuse oneself; wear. **sports car,** open low-built fast car. **sports coat,** man's jacket for informal wear.

sporting *a.* of or interested in sport; like a sportsman. **~ chance,** reasonable chance of success.

sportive *a.* playful. **sportively** *adv.*

sportsman *n.* (pl. *-men*), **sportswoman** *n.fem.* (pl. *-women*) one who takes part in sports; one who plays fairly and generously. **sportsmanship** *n.*

sporty *a.* (*colloq.*) sporting; dashing.

spot *n.* round mark or stain; pimple; place; drop; (*colloq.*) small amount; spotlight. —*v.t./i.* (p.t. *spotted*) mark with a spot or spots; rain slightly; (*colloq.*) notice; watch for and take note of. **in a ~,** (*colloq.*) in difficulties. **on the ~,** without delay or change of place; alert; (*colloq.*) compelled to take action or justify oneself. **~ check,** random check. **spotter** *n.*

spotless *a.* free from stain or blemish. **spotlessly** *adv.*

spotlight *n.* lamp or its beam directed on a small area. —*v.t.* (p.t. *-lighted*) direct a spotlight on; draw attention to.

spotty *a.* marked with spots.

spouse *n.* person's husband or wife.

spout *n.* projecting tube through which liquid is poured or conveyed; jet of liquid. —*v.t./i.* come or send out forcefully as a jet of liquid; utter or speak lengthily. **up the ~,** (*sl.*) broken, ruined, in a hopeless condition.

sprain *v.t.* injure by wrenching violently. —*n.* this injury.

sprang see **spring**.

sprat *n.* small herring-like fish.

sprawl *v.t./i.* sit, lie, or fall with arms and legs spread loosely; spread out irregularly —*n.* sprawling attitude or arrangement.

spray[1] *n.* single shoot or branch with its leaves and flowers; decorative bunch of cut flowers; ornament in similar form.

spray[2] *n.* water or other liquid dispersed in very small drops; liquid for spraying; device for spraying liquid. —*v.t./i.* come or send out as spray; wet with liquid thus. **sprayer** *n.*

spread *v.t./i.* (p.t. *spread*) open out; become longer or wider; cover the surface of; apply as a layer; be able to be spread; make or become widely known or felt or suffered; distribute, become distributed. —*n.* spreading; extent, expanse; expansion; bedspread; (*colloq.*) lavish meal; thing's range; paste for spreading on bread. **~ eagle,** figure of an eagle with legs and wings spread, as an emblem. **~-eagle** *v.t.* spread out like this.

spree *n.* (*colloq.*) lively outing, piece of fun.

sprig[1] *n.* twig.

sprig[2] *n.* small headless tack.

sprightly *a.* (*-ier, -iest*) lively, full of energy. **sprightliness** *n.*

spring *v.t./i.* (p.t. *sprang*, p.p. *sprung*) jump; move rapidly; issue, arise; become warped or split; produce or cause to operate suddenly; contrive the escape of (a prisoner). —*n.* act of springing, jump; device that reverts to its original position after being compressed or tightened or stretched, used to drive clockwork or (in groups) make a seat etc. more comfortable; elasticity; place where water or oil flows naturally from the ground; season between winter and summer. **~-clean** *v.t./i.* clean (one's home etc.) thoroughly. **~ tide,** tide when there is the largest rise and fall of water.

springboard *n.* flexible board giving impetus to a gymnast or diver.

springbok *n.* South African gazelle.

springtime *n.* season of spring.

springy *a.* (*-ier, -iest*) able to spring back easily after being squeezed or stretched. **springiness** *n.*

sprinkle *v.t./i.* scatter or fall in drops or particles on (a surface). —*n.* light shower. **sprinkler** *n.*

sprinkling *n.* something sprinkled; a few here and there.

sprint *v.i.* & *n.* run or swim etc. at full speed. **sprinter** *n.*

sprit *n.* small diagonal spar.

sprite *n.* elf, fairy, or goblin.

sprocket *n.* projection engaging with links on a chain etc.

sprout *v.t./i.* begin to grow or appear; put forth. —*n.* plant's shoot.

spruce[1] *a.* neat, smart. —*v.t.* smarten. **sprucely** *adv.*, **spruceness** *n.*

spruce[2] *n.* a kind of fir.

sprung see **spring**. —*a.* fitted with springs.

spry *a.* (*spryer, spryest*) active, lively. **spryly** *adv.*, **spryness** *n.*

spud *n.* narrow spade; (*sl.*) potato.

spume *n.* froth.

spun see **spin**.

spunk *n.* (*sl.*) courage.

spur *n.* pricking-device worn on a horseman's heel; stimulus, incentive; projection; branch road or railway. —*v.t.* (p.t. *spurred*) urge on (a horse) by pricking it with one's spurs; urge on, incite; stimulate. **on the ~ of the moment,** on impulse. **win one's spurs,** prove one's ability.

spurge *n.* plant or bush with a bitter milky juice.

spurious *a.* not genuine or authentic. **spuriously** *adv.*, **spuriousness** *n.*

spurt *v.t./i.* gush; send out (liquid) suddenly; increase speed suddenly. —*n.* sudden gush; short burst of activity; sudden increase in speed.

sputter *v.i. & n.* splutter.

spy *n.* person who secretly watches or gathers information. —*v.t./i.* catch sight of; be a spy, watch secretly. ~ **out,** explore secretly.

sq. *abbr.* square.

squab /-ob/ *n.* young pigeon; a kind of firmly padded cushion or seatback.

squabble *v.i.* quarrel pettily or noisily. —*n.* quarrel of this kind.

squad *n.* small group working or being trained together.

squadron *n.* division (two troops) of a cavalry unit or armoured formation; detachment of warships; unit (10 to 18 aircraft) of the R.A.F.

squalid *a.* dirty and unpleasant; morally degrading. **squalidly** *adv.*, **squalor** *n.*

squall *n.* harsh cry or scream; sudden storm or wind. —*v.i.* utter a squall. **squally** *a.*

squander *v.i.* spend wastefully.

square *n.* geometric figure with four equal sides and four right angles; area or object shaped like this; L-shaped or T-shaped object for making or testing right angles; product obtained when a number is multiplied by itself; (in astrology) aspect of two planets 90° apart; (*sl.*) person considered old-fashioned or conventional. —*a.* of square shape; right-angled; of or using units expressing the measure of an area; properly arranged; equal, not owed or owing anything; straight-forward; honest; (of a meal) substantial; (*sl.*) old-fashioned, conventional. —*adv.* squarely, directly. —*v.t./i.* make right-angled; mark with squares; place evenly; multiply by itself; settle (an account etc.); make or be consistent; (*colloq.*) bribe. ~ **root,** number of which a given number is the square. ~ **up to,** face in a fighting attitude; face resolutely. **squarely** *adv.*, **squareness** *n.*

squash[1] *v.t./i.* crush, squeeze or become squeezed flat or into pulp; suppress; silence with a crushing reply. —*n.* crowd of people squashed together; fruit-flavoured soft drink; (also ~ *rackets*) game played with rackets and a small ball in a closed court. **squashy** *a.*

squash[2] *n.* a kind of gourd.

squat *v.t./i.* (p.t. *squatted*) sit on one's heels; crouch; (*colloq.*) sit; be a squatter (in). —*n.* squatting posture; being a squatter, place occupied thus. —*a.* dumpy.

squatter *n.* person who takes unauthorized

possession of unoccupied premises; (*Austr.*) sheep-farmer.

squaw *n.* North American Indian woman or wife.

squawk *n.* loud harsh cry. —*v.t./i.* make or utter with a squawk.

squeak *n.* short high-pitched cry or sound. —*v.t./i.* make or utter with a squeak. **narrow ~,** (*colloq.*) narrow escape. **squeaky** *a.*

squeal *n.* long shrill cry or sound. —*v.t./i.* make or utter with a squeal; (*sl.*) protest sharply; (*sl.*) become an informer.

squeamish *a.* easily disgusted; over-scrupulous. **squeamishness** *n.*

squeegee *n.* rubber tool for sweeping or squeezing away moisture. —*v.t.* treat with this.

squeeze *v.t./i.* exert pressure on; treat thus to extract moisture; force into or through, force one's way, crowd; produce by pressure or effort or compulsion; extort money etc. from. —*n.* squeezing; affectionate clasp or hug; drops produced by squeezing; crowd, crush, pressure of this; hardship or difficulty caused by shortage of money or time; restrictions on borrowing. **squeezer** *n.*

squelch *v.i. & n.* sound like someone treading in thick mud.

squib *n.* small exploding firework.

squid *n.* sea creature with ten arms round its mouth.

squiggle *n.* short curly line.

squint *v.i.* have one eye turned abnormally from the line of gaze of the other; look sideways or through a small opening. —*n.* squinting condition of an eye; sideways glance; (*colloq.*) look. —*a.* (*colloq.*) askew.

squire *n.* country gentleman, esp. landowner; (*colloq.*) sir.

squirm *v.i.* wriggle; feel embarrassment. —*n.* wriggle.

squirrel *n.* small tree-climbing animal with a bushy tail.

squirt *v.t./i.* send out (liquid) or be sent out in a jet; wet thus. —*n.* syringe; jet of liquid; (*colloq.*) small or unimportant self-assertive fellow.

St. *abbr.* Saint; Street.

stab *v.t.* (p.t. *stabbed*) pierce, wound or kill with something pointed; poke. —*n.* act of stabbing; wound made thus; sensation of being stabbed; (*colloq.*) attempt.

stabilize /ˈsteɪ-/ *v.t./i.* make or become stable. **stabilization** *n.*, **stabilizer** *n.*

stable[1] *a.* (-*er*, -*est*) firmly fixed or established, not easily shaken or decomposed or destroyed. **stably** *adv.*, **stability** *n.*

stable[2] *n.* building in which horses are kept; establishment for training racehorses; horses, people, or products etc. from the same establishment. —*v.t.* put or keep in a stable. ~ **boy,** ~**lad** *ns.* person who works in a stable.

staccato /-ˈkɑː-/ *a. & adv.* in a sharp disconnected manner.

stack *n.* orderly pile or heap or similar arrangement; (*colloq.*) large quantity; number of chimneys standing together; isolated chimney.

—*v.t.* arrange in a stack or stacks; arrange (cards) secretly for cheating.

stadium *n.* sports ground surrounded by tiers of seats for spectators.

staff *n.* stick or pole used as a weapon, support, measuring-rod, or symbol of authority; group of assistants responsible to a manager or superior officer; people in authority within an organization, or doing administrative work; (*pl. staves*) set of five horizontal lines on which music is written. —*v.t.* provide with a staff of people.

stag *n.* fully grown male deer. ∼-**beetle** *n.* beetle with branched projecting mouth-parts. ∼-**party** *n.* party of men only.

stage *n.* raised floor or platform; one on which plays etc. are performed; theatrical work or profession; division of or point reached in a process or journey etc.; separable section of a rocket. —*v.t.* present on the stage; arrange and carry out. **go on the** ∼, become an actor or actress. ∼-**coach** *n.* (*old use*) horse-drawn coach running regularly between two places. ∼ **fright,** nervousness on facing an audience. ∼ **whisper,** one meant to be overheard.

stager *n.* **old** ∼, experienced person.

stagger *v.t./i.* move or go unsteadily; shock deeply; place in an alternating arrangement; arrange so as not to coincide exactly. —*n.* staggering movement.

staggering *a.* astonishing.

staging *n.* scaffolding; platform. ∼ **post,** regular stopping-place on a long journey.

stagnant *a.* not flowing, still and stale; without activity.

stagnate *v.i.* be stagnant; become dull from inactivity. **stagnation** *n.*

staid *a.* steady and serious.

stain *v.t./i.* discolour, become discoloured; blemish; colour with a penetrating pigment. —*n.* mark caused by staining; blemish; liquid for staining things.

stainless *a.* free from stains. ∼ **steel,** steel containing chromium and not liable to rust or tarnish.

stair *n.* one of a flight of fixed indoor steps; (*pl.*) a flight of these.

staircase *n.* stairs and their supporting structure.

stairway *n.* staircase.

stake *n.* pointed stick or post for driving into the ground; post to which a person was tied for execution by being burnt alive; money etc. wagered; share or interest in an enterprise etc. —*v.t.* fasten or support or mark with a stake or stakes; wager; (*U.S. colloq.*) give financial or other support to. **at** ∼, being risked. ∼ **a claim,** claim a right to something.

stalactite *n.* deposit of calcium carbonate hanging like an icicle.

stalagmite *n.* deposit of calcium carbonate standing like a pillar.

stale *a.* (-*er*, -*est*) not fresh; unpleasant or uninteresting from lack of freshness; spoilt by too much practice. —*v.t./i.* make or become stale. **staleness** *n.*

stalemate *n.* drawn position in chess; drawn contest; deadlock.

stalk[1] *n.* stem or similar supporting part.

stalk[2] *v.t./i.* walk in a stately or imposing manner; track or pursue stealthily. **stalker** *n.*

stalking-horse *n.* person or thing used to conceal one's intentions.

stall *n.* stable, cow-house; compartment in this; compartment for one person; enclosed seat in a church etc.; one of the set of seats nearest the stage in a theatre; booth or stand where goods are displayed for sale; stalling of an aircraft. —*v.t./i.* place or keep in a stall; (of an engine) stop suddenly from an overload or from lack of fuel; (of an aircraft) begin to drop because the speed is too low; cause to stall; stave off (a person or request) in order to gain time.

stallion *n.* uncastrated male horse.

stalwart /ˈstɔl-/ *a.* sturdy; strong and faithful. —*n.* stalwart person.

stamen /ˈstei-/ *n.* pollen-bearing part of a flower.

stamina *n.* ability to withstand long physical or mental strain.

stammer *v.t./i.* speak with involuntary pauses or repetitions of a syllable. —*n.* this act or tendency.

stamp *v.t./i.* bring (one's foot) down heavily on the ground; press so as to cut or leave a mark or pattern, make (a mark etc.) thus; fix a postage or other stamp to; give a specified character to. —*n.* act or sound of stamping; instrument for stamping a mark etc., this mark; small adhesive label for affixing to an envelope or document to show the amount paid as postage or a fee etc.; similar decorative label; characteristic indication of quality. ∼ **out,** extinguish by stamping; suppress by force.

stampede *n.* sudden rush of animals or people. —*v.t./i.* take part in a stampede; cause to do this or to act hurriedly.

stance *n.* manner of standing.

stanch *v.t.* restrain the flow of (blood etc.) or from (a wound).

stanchion *n.* upright post or support.

stand *v.t./i.* (p.t. *stood*) have, take, or keep a stationary upright position; be situated; place, set upright; remain; stay firm or valid; offer oneself for election; undergo; steer a specified course in sailing; endure; provide at one's own expense. —*n.* stationary condition; position taken up; resistance to attack; halt to give a performance; rack, pedestal; raised structure with seats at a sports ground etc.; stall for goods; standing-place for vehicles; (*U.S.*) witness-box. ∼ **a chance,** have a chance of success. ∼ **by,** look on without interfering; stand ready for action; side with in a dispute; support in a difficulty; keep to (a promise etc.). ∼-**by** *a. & n.* (person or thing) available as a substitute. ∼ **down,** withdraw. ∼ **for,** represent; (*colloq.*) tolerate. ∼ **in,** deputize. ∼-**in** *n.* deputy, substitute. ∼-**offish** *a.* (*colloq.*) aloof. ∼ **on,** insist on formal observance of. ∼ **one's**

ground, not yield. ~ **to**, be ready for action. ~ **to reason**, be logical. ~ **up for**, speak in defence of. ~ **up to**, resist courageously; be strong enough to endure.

standard *n.* thing against which something may be compared for testing or measurement; average quality; required level of quality or proficiency; distinctive flag; upright support; shrub grafted on an upright stem. —*a.* serving as or conforming to a standard; of average or usual quality. ~ **lamp**, household lamp set on a tall pillar on a base.

standardize *v.t.* cause to conform to a standard. **standardization** *n.*

standing *n.* status; duration.

standpoint *n.* point of view.

standstill *n.* inability to proceed.

stank *see* **stink.**

stanza *n.* verse of poetry.

staple[1] *n.* U-shaped spike for holding something in place; bent piece of metal or wire driven into papers and clenched to fasten them. —*v.t.* secure with staple(s). **stapler** *n.*

staple[2] *a. & n.* principal or standard (food or product etc.).

star *n.* celestial body appearing as a point of light; this regarded as influencing human affairs; figure or object with rays; asterisk; star-shaped mark indicating a category of excellence; brilliant person, famous actor or performer etc. —*v.t./i.* (p.t. *starred*) put an asterisk beside (an item); present or perform as a star actor. ~**-gazing** *n.* (*joc.*) studying the stars.

starboard *n.* right-hand side of a ship or aircraft. —*v.t.* turn this way.

starch *n.* white carbohydrate; preparation of this or other substances for stiffening fabrics; stiffness of manner. —*v.t.* stiffen with starch. **starchy** *a.*

stardom *n.* being a star actor etc.

stare *v.t./i.* gaze fixedly esp. in astonishment. —*n.* staring gaze.

starfish *n.* star-shaped sea creature.

stark *a.* (-*er*, -*est*) desolate, bare; sharply evident; downright; naked; (*old use*) stiff. —*adv.* completely. **starkly** *adv.*, **starkness** *n.*

starlight *n.* light from the stars.

starling *n.* noisy bird with glossy black speckled feathers.

starlit *a.* lit by starlight.

starry *a.* set with stars; shining like stars. ~**eyed** *a.* romantically enthusiastic; eager but impractical.

start *v.t./i.* begin, cause to begin; begin operating; begin a journey; found; make a sudden movement, esp. from pain or surprise; spring suddenly; rouse (game etc.) from its covert. —*n.* beginning; place where a race etc. starts; advantage gained or allowed in starting; sudden movement of pain or surprise. **starter** *n.*

startle *v.t.* shock, surprise.

starve *v.t./i.* die or suffer acutely from lack of food; cause to do this; suffer or cause to suffer for lack (of something needed); force by

starvation; (*colloq.*) feel very hungry or cold. **starvation** *n.*

stash *v.t.* (*sl.*) stow.

state *n.* mode of being, with regard to characteristics or circumstances; excited or agitated condition of mind; grand imposing style; (often *S*~) political community under one government or forming part of a federation; civil government. —*a.* of or involving the State; involving ceremony, for ceremonial occasions. —*v.t.* express in words; specify.

stateless *a.* not a citizen or subject of any country.

stately *a.* (-*ier*, -*iest*) dignified, grand. **stateliness** *n.*

statement *n.* process of stating; thing stated; formal account of facts; written report of a financial account.

stateroom *n.* room used on ceremonial occasions; passenger's private compartment on a ship.

statesman *n.* (pl. -*men*) person who is skilled or prominent in managing State affairs. **stateswoman** *n.fem.*, **statesmanship** *n.*

static *a.* of force acting by weight without motion; stationary; not changing. —*n.* atmospherics; (also ~ **electricity**) electricity present in a body, not flowing as current.

statics *n.* branch of physics dealing with bodies at rest or forces in equilibrium.

station *n.* place where a person or thing stands or is stationed; place where a public service or specialized activity is based; broadcasting establishment with its own frequency; stopping-place on a railway with buildings for passengers or goods or both; status; (*Austr.*) large farming estate, sheep-run. —*v.t.* put at or in a certain place for a purpose.

stationary *a.* not moving; not movable.

stationer *n.* dealer in stationery.

stationery *n.* writing-paper, envelopes, labels, etc.

statistic *n.* item of information expressed in numbers. **statistics** *n.* science of collecting and interpreting information based on the numbers of things. **statistical** *a.*, **statistically** *adv.*

statistician *n.* expert in statistics.

statuary *n.* statues.

statue *n.* sculptured, cast, or moulded figure.

statuesque *a.* like a statue in size or dignity or stillness.

statuette *n.* small statue.

stature *n.* bodily height; greatness gained by ability or achievement.

status /ˈsteɪ-/ *n.* (pl. -*uses*) person's position or rank in relation to others; high rank or prestige. ~ **quo**, previous state of affairs.

statute *n.* law passed by Parliament or a similar body; one of the rules of an institution.

statutory /ˈstætʃ-/ *a.* fixed or done or required by statute.

staunch *a.* (-*er*, -*est*) firm in opinion or loyalty. **staunchly** *adv.*

stave *n.* one of the strips of wood forming the

side of a cask or tub; staff in music. —v.t. (p.t. & p.p. *stove* or *staved*) dent, break a hole in. ~ **off,** (p.t. *staved*) ward off.

stay[1] *n.* rope or wire holding a mast or spar etc.; any prop or support; (*pl., old use*) corset.

stay[2] *v.t./i.* continue in the same place or state; remain or dwell temporarily; satisfy temporarily; postpone; pause; show endurance. —*n.* period of temporary dwelling or visiting; postponement. ~ **away from,** not go to. ~ **the course,** be able to reach the end of it.

S.T.D. *abbr.* subscriber trunk dialling.

stead /sted/ *n.* **in a person's** *or* **thing's** ~, instead of him or it. **stand in good** ~, be of great service to.

steadfast *a.* firm and not changing or yielding. **steadfastly** *adv.*

steady *a.* (-*ier*, -*iest*) firmly supported or balanced, not shaking; regular, uniform; dependable, not excitable. —*n.* (*U.S. colloq.*) regular boy-friend or girl-friend. —*adv.* steadily. —*v.t./i.* make or become steady. **steadily** *adv.*, **steadiness** *n.*

steak *n.* slice of meat (esp. beef) or fish, usu. grilled or fried.

steal *v.t.* (p.t. *stole*, p.p. *stolen*) take (property) dishonestly; obtain by a trick or surreptitiously; move stealthily. ~ **a march on,** gain an advantage over (a person), esp. slyly. ~ **the show,** outshine other performers unexpectedly.

stealth *n.* stealthiness.

stealthy *a.* (-*ier*, -*iest*) quiet so as to avoid notice. **stealthily** *adv.*, **stealthiness** *n.*

steam *n.* gas into which water is changed by boiling; this as motive power; energy, power. —*v.t./i.* give out steam; cook or treat by steam; move by the power of steam; cover or become covered by steam. ~**-engine** *n.* engine or locomotive driven by steam. **steamy** *a.*

steamer *n.* steam-driven ship; container in which things are cooked or heated by steam.

steamroller *n.* heavy slow-moving engine with a large roller, used in road-making.

steamship *n.* steam-driven ship.

steatite /ˈstɪə-/ *n.* greyish talc that feels smooth and soapy.

steed *n.* (*poetical*) horse.

steel *n.* very strong alloy of iron and carbon; tapered steel rod for sharpening knives. —*v.t.* make resolute. ~ **wool,** mass of fine shavings of steel used as an abrasive. **steely** *a.*, **steeliness** *n.*

steep[1] *v.t./i.* soak in liquid; permeate thoroughly.

steep[2] *a.* (-*er*, -*est*) sloping sharply not gradually; (*colloq.*, of price) unreasonably high. **steeply** *adv.*, **steepness** *n.*

steepen *v.t./i.* make or become steeper.

steeple *n.* tall tower with a spire, rising above a church roof.

steeplechase *n.* horse-race across country or with fences to jump; cross-country race for runners. **steeplechaser** *n.*, **steeplechasing** *n.*

steeplejack *n.* person who climbs tall chimneys etc. to do repairs.

steer[1] *n.* young male ox, esp. bullock.

steer[2] *v.t./i.* direct the course of, guide by mechanism; be able to be steered. ~ **clear of,** avoid.

steerage *n.* steering.

steersman *n.* (pl. -*men*) person who steers a ship.

stellar *a.* of a star or stars.

stem[1] *n.* supporting usu. cylindrical part, esp. of a plant, flower, leaf, or fruit; main usu. unchanging part of a noun or verb; ship's bows. —*v.i.* (p.t. *stemmed*) ~ **from,** have as its source.

stem[2] *v.t./i.* (p.t. *stemmed*) restrain the flow or movement of; dam.

stench *n.* foul smell.

stencil *n.* sheet of metal or card etc. with a cut-out design, painted or inked over to reproduce this on the surface below; design reproduced thus. —*v.t.* (p.t. *stencilled*) produce or ornament by this.

stenographer *n.* shorthand-writer.

stenography *n.* shorthand.

stentorian /-ˈtɔr-/ *a.* (of a voice) extremely loud.

step *v.t./i.* (p.t. *stepped*) lift and set down a foot or alternate feet; move a short distance thus; progress. —*n.* complete movement of a foot and leg in stepping; distance covered thus; short distance; pattern of steps in dancing; sound of a step; one of a series of actions; level surface for placing the foot on in climbing; stage in a scale of promotion or precedence; (*pl.*) step-ladder. **in** ~, stepping in time with others; conforming. **out of** ~, not in step. ~ **in,** intervene, ~**-ladder** *n.* short ladder with a supporting framework. ~ **up,** increase.

step- *pref.* related by re-marriage of a parent, as **stepfather, stepmother, stepson,** etc. *ns.*

steppe *n.* grassy plain, esp. in south-east Europe and Siberia.

stepping-stone *n.* raised stone for stepping on in crossing a stream etc.; means of progress.

stereo /ˈste-/ *n.* (pl. -*os*) stereophonic sound or record-player etc.; stereoscopic effect.

stereophonic /sterɪəˈfon-/ *a.* using two transmission channels so as to give the effect of naturally distributed sound.

stereoscopic /ste-/ *a.* giving a three-dimensional effect.

stereotype /ˈste-/ *n.* printing-plate cast from a mould of type; standardized conventional idea or character etc. **stereotyped** *a.* standardized and hackneyed.

sterile /ˈste-/ *a.* barren; free from living microorganisms; unproductive. **sterility** *n.*

sterilize /ˈste-/ *v.t.* make sterile; make unable to produce offspring, esp. by removal or obstruction of reproductive organs. **sterilization** *n.*

sterling *n.* British money. —*a.* genuine, of standard purity; excellent, of solid worth.

stern[1] *a.* (-*er*, -*est*) strict and severe, not kindly or cheerful. **sternly** *adv.*, **sternness** *n.*

stern[2] *n.* rear of a boat or ship.

steroid /ˈstɪər-/ n. any of a group of organic compounds that includes certain hormones.

stertorous /ˈstɜ-/ a. making a snoring or rasping sound. **stertorously** adv.

stet v.imper. let it stand as written or printed.

stethoscope n. instrument for listening to sounds within the body, e.g. breathing and heart-beats.

stetson n. hat with a wide brim and high crown.

stevedore /-vd-/ n. man employed in loading and unloading ships.

stew v.t./i. cook by simmering in a closed vessel; (sl.) study hard. —n. dish (esp. of meat) made by stewing; (colloq.) state of great anxiety. **stewed** a. (of tea) strong and bitter from infusing too long.

steward n. person employed to manage an estate or great house etc.; passengers' attendant and waiter on a ship, aircraft, or train; official at a race-meeting or show etc. **stewardess** n. female steward on a ship etc.

stick[1] n. short relatively slender piece of wood; thing shaped like this; walking-stick; implement used to propel the ball in hockey, polo, etc.; punishment by caning or beating.

stick[2] v.t./i. (p.t. **stuck**) thrust (a thing) into something; stab; (colloq.) put; fix or be fixed by glue or suction etc.; jam; (colloq.) remain in a specified place, not progress; (sl.) endure. ~ **at it,** (colloq.) continue one's efforts. ~**-in-the-mud** n. person who will not adopt new ideas etc. ~ **out,** stand above the surrounding surface; be conspicuous; (colloq.) persist in one's demands. ~ **to,** remain faithful to; keep to (a subject or position etc.). ~ **to one's guns,** not yield. ~ **up for,** (colloq.) stand up for.

sticker n. adhesive label or sign.

sticking-plaster n. adhesive fabric for covering small cuts.

stickleback n. small fish with sharp spines on its back.

stickler n. ~ **for,** one who insists on.

sticky a. (-ier, -iest) sticking to what is touched; humid; (colloq.) making objections; (sl.) very unpleasant. **stickily** adv., **stickiness** n.

stiff a. (-er, -est) not bending or moving or flowing easily; difficult; formal in manner; (of wind) blowing briskly; (of a drink etc.) strong; (of a price or penalty) severe. ~**-necked** a. obstinate; haughty. **stiffly** adv., **stiffness** n.

stiffen v.t./i. make or become stiff. **stiffener** n.

stifle v.t./i. suffocate; feel or cause to feel unable to breathe; restrain, suppress.

stigma n. (pl. -as) mark of shame; part of a pistil; (pl. stigmata) mark corresponding to one of those left on Christ's crucified body.

stigmatize v.t. brand as something disgraceful.

stile n. steps or bars for people to climb over a fence.

stiletto n. (pl. -os) dagger with a narrow blade; pointed implement.

still[1] a. with little or no motion or sound; (of drinks) not fizzy. —n. silence and calm; photograph, esp. single one from a cinema film. —adv. without moving; then or now as before; nevertheless; in a greater amount or degree. ~ **birth,** birth in which the child is born dead. ~ **life,** painting of things such as cut flowers or fruit. **stillness** n.

still[2] n. distilling apparatus. ~**-room** n. housekeeper's store-room.

stillborn a. born dead.

stilted a. stiffly formal.

stilts n.pl. pair of poles with footrests, enabling the user to walk with feet at a distance above the ground; piles or posts on which a building stands.

stimulant a. stimulating. —n. stimulating drug or drink.

stimulate v.t. make more active; apply a stimulus to. **stimulation** n., **stimulator** n., **stimulative** a.

stimulus n. (pl. -li, pr. -laɪ) something that rouses a person or thing to activity or energy.

sting n. sharp wounding part or organ of an insect or plant etc.; wound made thus; its infliction; sharp bodily or mental pain, wounding effect. —v.t./i. (p.t. **stung**) wound or affect with a sting; feel or cause sharp pain; stimulate sharply; (sl.) overcharge, extort money from.

stingy /-dʒɪ/ a. (-ier, -iest) spending, giving, or given grudgingly or in small amounts. **stinginess** n.

stink n. offensive smell; (colloq.) offensive fuss. —v.t./i. (p.t. & p.p. **stank** or **stunk**) give off a stink; seem very unpleasant or dishonest. ~ **out,** fill with or drive out by an offensive smell.

stinker n. (sl.) something offensive or severe or difficult to do.

stint v.t. restrict to a small allowance. —n. limitation of supply or effort; allotted amount of work.

stipend /ˈstaɪ-/ n. salary.

stipendiary /stɪˈpen-/ a. receiving a stipend.

stipple v.t. paint, draw, or engrave in small dots.

stipulate v.t./i. demand or insist (on) as part of an agreement. **stipulation** n.

stir v.t./i. (p.t. **stirred**) move; mix (a substance) by moving a spoon etc. round in it; stimulate, excite. —n. act or process of stirring; commotion, excitement.

stirrup n. support for a rider's foot, hanging from the saddle. ~**-pump** n. small portable pump for extinguishing small fires.

stitch n. single movement of a thread in and out of fabric etc. in sewing, or of a needle or hook in knitting or crochet; loop made thus; method of making a stitch; least bit of clothing; sudden pain in muscles at the side of the body. —v.t./i. sew; join or close with stitches. **in stitches,** (colloq.) laughing uncontrollably.

stoat n. animal of the weasel family, with brown fur that turns white in winter.

stock n. amount of something available for use or selling; livestock; lineage; money lent to a government at fixed interest; business company's capital, portion of this held by an investor; person's standing in the opinion of others; liquid made by stewing bones, meat, fish, or vegetables; garden plant with fragrant flowers; growing plant into which a graft is inserted; base, holder, or handle of an implement or machine; cravat worn as part of riding-kit; piece of black or purple fabric worn hanging from a clerical collar; (*pl.*) framework on which a ship rests during construction; (*pl.*) wooden frame with holes for a seated person's legs, used like the pillory. —*a.* stocked and regularly available; commonly used. —*v.t.* keep in stock; provide with a supply. ~-**car** *n.* car used in racing where deliberate bumping is allowed. **Stock Exchange,** place where stocks and shares are publicly bought and sold; association of dealers conducting such business. ~-**in-trade** *n.* all the requisites for carrying on a trade or business. ~ **market,** Stock Exchange; transactions there. ~-**still** *a.* motionless. **take** ~, make an inventory (of stock or resources). ~-**taking** *n.*

stockade *n.* protective fence.

stockbreeder *n.* farmer who raises livestock. **stockbreeding** *n.*

stockbroker *n.* person who buys and sells stocks and shares (from stockjobbers) on behalf of customers.

stockinet *n.* fine machine-knitted fabric used for underwear etc.

stocking *n.* close-fitting covering for the foot and leg. ~-**stitch** *n.* alternate rows of plain and purl in knitting.

stockist *n.* firm that stocks certain goods.

stockjobber *n.* member of the Stock Exchange who buys and sells stocks and shares, dealing with stockbrokers (not with the public).

stockpile *n.* accumulated stock of goods etc. kept in reserve. —*v.t.* accumulate a stockpile of.

stocky *a.* (-*ier, -iest*) short and solidly built. **stockily** *adv.*, **stockiness** *n.*

stodge *n.* (*colloq.*) stodgy food.

stodgy *a.* (-*ier, -iest*) (of food) heavy and filling; dull.

stoep /stup/ *n.* (*S. Afr.*) veranda.

stoic /ˈstəʊɪk/ *n.* stoical person.

stoical /ˈstəʊ-/ *a.* calm and uncomplaining. **stoically** *adv.*, **stoicism** /-sɪzm/ *n.*

stoke *v.t.* tend and put fuel on (a fire etc.). **stoker** *n.*

stole[1] *n.* clergyman's vestment, a long strip of fabric hung round the neck; woman's wide scarf-like garment.

stole[2], **stolen** see **steal**.

stolid *a.* not excitable. **stolidly** *adv.*, **stolidity** *n.*

stomach *n.* internal organ in which the first part of digestion occurs; abdomen; appetite. —*v.t.* endure, tolerate. ~-**ache** *n.* pain in the belly or bowels.

stomp *v.i.* tread heavily.

stone *n.* piece of rock; this shaped or used for a purpose; stones or rock as a substance or material; precious stone; small piece of hard substance formed in the bladder or kidney etc.; hard case round the kernel of certain fruits; grape-seed; (pl. *stone*) unit of weight, 14 lb. —*a.* made of stone. —*v.t.* pelt with stones; remove stones from (fruit). **Stone Age,** prehistoric period when weapons and tools were made of stone.

stone- *pref.* completely (~-*cold*).

stonemason *n.* person who cuts and shapes stone or builds in stone.

stonewall *v.i.* bat in cricket without trying to score runs; give non-committal replies.

stonework *n.* stone construction.

stony *a.* (-*ier, -iest*) full of stones; hard, unfeeling; unresponsive. ~-**broke** *a.* (*sl.*) = broke. **stonily** *adv.*

stood see **stand.**

stooge *n.* comedian's assistant; subordinate who does routine work; person who is another's puppet. —*v.i.* (*sl.*) act as a stooge.

stool *n.* movable seat without arms or raised back; footstool; base of a plant, from which new stems etc. shoot; (*pl.*) faeces. ~-**pigeon** *n.* decoy, esp. to trap a criminal.

stoop *v.t./i.* bend forwards and down; condescend; lower oneself morally. —*n.* stooping posture.

stop *v.t./i.* (p.t. *stopped*) put an end to movement, progress, or operation (of); (*colloq.*) stay; keep back; refuse to give or allow; close by plugging or obstructing; fill a cavity in (a tooth); press a string or block a hole in a musical instrument in order to obtain the desired pitch. —*n.* stopping; place where a train or bus etc. stops regularly; punctuation-mark, full-stop; thing that stops or regulates motion; row of organ-pipes providing tones of one quality, knob etc. controlling these; key or lever regulating a wind-instrument's pitch; one of the standard sizes of aperture in an adjustable lens. ~ **down,** reduce the aperture of a lens. ~-**press** *n.* late news inserted in a newspaper after printing has begun. ~-**watch** *n.* watch with mechanism for starting and stopping at will.

stopcock *n.* valve regulating the flow in a pipe etc.; handle adjusting this.

stopgap *n.* temporary substitute.

stoppage *n.* stopping; obstruction.

stopper *n.* plug for closing a bottle etc. —*v.t.* close with a stopper.

storage *n.* storing. ~ **heater,** electric radiator accumulating heat in off-peak periods.

store *n.* supply of something available for use; large shop; store-house; device in a computer for storing retrievable information. —*v.t.* collect and keep for future use; stock with something useful; deposit in a warehouse. **in** ~, being stored; destined to happen, imminent. **set** ~ **by,** value greatly. ~-**room** *n.* room used for storing things.

storehouse *n.* place where things are stored.

storey *n.* (pl. -*eys*) one horizontal section of a building. **storeyed** *a.*

stork *n.* large wading-bird.

storm *n.* disturbance of the atmosphere with strong winds and usu. rain or snow; violent shower (of missiles etc.); great outbreak (of anger or abuse etc.); violent military attack. —*v.t./i.* rage, be violent; attack or capture by storm. **stormy** *a.*

story[1] *n.* account of an incident or series of incidents (true or invented); material for this; (*colloq.*) lie.

story[2] *n.* = storey.

stoup /stup/ *n.* stone basin for holy water.

stout *a.* (*-er, -est*) of considerable thickness or strength; fat; brave and resolute. —*n.* a kind of strong dark beer. **stoutly** *adv.*, **stoutness** *n.*

stove[1] *n.* apparatus containing one or more ovens; closed apparatus used for heating rooms etc. ∼**-enamel** *n.* heat-proof enamel.

stove[2] *see* **stave.**

stow *v.t.* place in a receptacle for storage. ∼ **away,** conceal oneself as a stowaway.

stowaway *n.* person who conceals himself on a ship etc. so as to travel without charge or unseen.

straddle *v.t./i.* sit or stand (across) with legs wide apart; stand or place (things) in a line across.

straggle *v.i.* grow or spread untidily; wander separately; lag behind others. **straggler** *n.*, **straggly** *a.*

straight *a.* (*-er, -est*) extending or moving in one direction, not curved or bent; correctly or tidily arranged; in unbroken succession; honest, frank; not modified or elaborate; without additions. —*adv.* in a straight line; direct; without delay; frankly. —*n.* straight part. **go** ∼, live honestly after being a criminal. ∼ **away,** without delay. ∼ **face,** not smiling. ∼ **fight,** contest between only two candidates. ∼ **off,** without hesitation. **straightness** *n.*

straighten *v.t./i.* make or become straight.

straightforward *a.* honest, frank; without complications. **straightforwardly** *adv.*

strain[1] *n.* lineage; variety or breed of animals etc.; slight or inherited tendency in a character.

strain[2] *v.t./i.* stretch tightly, make taut; injure by excessive stretching or over-exertion; hold in a tight embrace; make an intense effort (with); pass through a sieve or similar device to separate solids from the liquid containing them. —*n.* straining, force exerted thus; injury or exhaustion caused by straining; severe demand on strength or resources; passage from a tune; tone or style of something written or spoken. **strainer** *n.*

strained *a.* (of manner etc.) produced by effort not by genuine feeling. ∼ **relations,** unpleasant tension between people.

strait *a.* (*old use*) narrow, restricted. —*n.* (also *pl.*) narrow stretch of water connecting two seas; (*pl.*) difficult state of affairs. ∼**-jacket** *n.* strong jacket-like garment put round a violent person to restrain his arms; (*v.t.*) restrict severely. ∼**-laced** *a.* very prim and proper.

straitened *a.* (of conditions) poverty-stricken.

strake *n.* line of planking or metal plates from stem to stern of a boat.

strand[1] *n.* single thread; one of those twisted to form a cable or yarn etc.; lock of hair.

strand[2] *n.* shore. —*v.t./i.* run aground; leave in difficulties.

strange *a.* (*-er, -est*) not familiar, not well-known; alien; unusual, surprising; fresh, unaccustomed. **strangely** *adv.*, **strangeness** *n.*

stranger *n.* one who is strange to a place or company or experience.

strangle *v.t./i.* kill or be killed by squeezing the throat; restrict the proper growth or operation or utterance of. **strangler** *n.*

stranglehold *n.* strangling grip.

strangulate *v.t.* compress (a vein etc.) so that nothing can pass through.

strangulation *n.* strangling; strangulating.

strap *n.* strip of leather or other flexible material for holding things together or in place, or supporting something. —*v.t.* (p.t. *strapped*) secure with strap(s).

strapping *a.* tall and healthy-looking. —*n.* straps; sticking-plaster etc. used for binding injuries.

strata *see* **stratum.**

stratagem *n.* cunning method of achieving something; trick.

strategic *a.* of strategy; giving an advantage; (of weapons) very long-range. **strategical** *a.*, **strategically** *adv.*

strategist /ˈstræ-/*n.* expert in strategy.

strategy *n.* planning and directing of the whole operation of a campaign or war; plan, policy.

stratified *a.* arranged in strata. **stratification** *n.*

stratosphere /ˈstræ-/ *n.* layer of the atmosphere about 10–60 km above the earth's surface.

stratum /ˈstrɑ-/ *n.* (pl. *strata*) one of a series of layers or levels.

straw *n.* dry cut stalks of grain used as material for bedding, fodder, etc.; single piece of this; narrow straw-like tube for sucking up liquid in drinking. ∼ **poll,** (*U.S.*) unofficial poll as a test of general feeling.

strawberry *n.* soft juicy edible red fruit with yellow seeds on the surface. ∼ **mark,** red birthmark.

stray *v.i.* leave one's group or proper place aimlessly; wander; deviate from a direct course or subject. —*a.* having strayed; isolated. —*n.* stray person or thing or domestic animal.

streak *n.* thin line or band of a different colour or substance from its surroundings; element, trait; spell, series. —*v.t./i.* mark with streaks; move very rapidly. **streaky** *a.*

stream *n.* body of water flowing in its bed; flow of liquid or things or people; current or direction of this; (in certain schools) section into which children of the same level of ability are placed. —*v.t./i.* flow or move as a stream; emit a stream of, run with liquid; float or wave at full length; arrange (school-children) in streams. **on** ∼, in active operation or production.

streamer *n.* long narrow flag; strip of ribbon or paper etc. attached at one or both ends.

streamline *v.t.* give a smooth even shape that offers least resistance to movement through water or air; make more efficient by simplifying, removing superfluities, etc.

street *n.* public road in a town or village, with houses on one or both sides.

streetcar *n.* (*U.S.*) tram.

strength *n.* quality of being strong; its intensity; person's or thing's strong point; number of people present or available, full complement. **on the ~ of,** relying on as a basis or support.

strengthen *v.t./i.* make or become stronger.

strenuous *a.* making or requiring great effort. **strenuously** *adv.*, **strenuousness** *n.*

stress *n.* emphasis; extra force used on a sound in speech or music; pressure, tension, strain. —*v.t.* lay stress on.

stretch *v.t./i.* pull out tightly or into a greater extent; be able or tend to become stretched; be continuous; thrust out one's limbs and tighten the muscles; make demands on the abilities of; strain, exaggerate. —*n.* stretching; ability to be stretched; continuous expanse or period. —*a.* able to be stretched. **at a ~,** continuously. **~ a point,** agree to something not normally allowed.

stretcher *n.* framework for carrying a sick or injured person in a lying position; device for stretching or bracing things.

strew *v.t.* (p.t. *strewed*, p.p. *strewn* or *strewed*) scatter over a surface; cover with scattered things.

striation /straɪˈeɪʃən/ *n.* one of a series of ridges or furrows or linear marks. **striated** *a.*

stricken *a.* affected with or overcome by an illness, shock, or grief.

strict *a.* (-*er*, -*est*) precisely limited or defined; without exception or deviation; requiring or giving complete obedience or exactitude. **strictly** *adv.*, **strictness** *n.*

stricture *n.* severe criticism; abnormal constriction.

stride *v.t./i.* (p.t. *strode*, p.p. *stridden*) walk with long steps; stand astride. —*n.* single long step; manner of striding; progress.

strident /ˈstraɪ-/ *a.* loud and harsh. **stridently** *adv.*, **stridency** *n.*

strife *n.* quarrelling, conflict.

strike *v.t./i.* (p.t. *struck*) bring or come into sudden hard contact with; inflict (a blow), knock; attack suddenly; afflict; produce by striking or pressing something; ignite (a match) by friction; agree on (a bargain); indicate (the hour) or be indicated by a sound; reach (gold or mineral oil etc.) by digging or drilling; occur to the mind of, produce a mental impression on; lower or take down (a flag or tent etc.); stop work in protest; proceed in a certain direction; arrive at (an average or balance); assume (an attitude) dramatically. —*n.* act or instance of striking; attack; workers' refusal to work as a protest. **on ~,** (of workers) striking. **~ off** *or* **out,** cross out. **~ up,** begin playing or singing; start (a friendship etc.) casually.

strikebound *a.* immobilized by a workers' strike.

striker *n.* person or thing that strikes; worker

who is on strike; football player whose main function is to try to score goals.

striking *a.* sure to be noticed, attractive and impressive. **strikingly** *adv.*

string *n.* narrow cord; piece of this or similar material used to fasten or pull something; stretched piece of catgut or wire etc. in a musical instrument, vibrated to produce tones; set of objects strung together; series; (*pl.*) conditions insisted upon; (*pl.*) stringed instruments, (*sing. attrib.*) of or for these. —*v.t./i.* (p.t. *strung*) fit or fasten with string(s); thread on a string; trim tough fibre from (beans). **pull strings,** use one's influence. **~ along,** (*colloq.*) deceive; go along (with). **~-course** *n.* projecting line of bricks etc. round a building. **~ out,** spread out in a line.

stringed *a.* (of musical instruments) having strings that are played by touch or with a bow or plectrum.

stringent /-ndʒ-/ *a.* strict, with firm restrictions. **stringently** *adv.*, **stringency** *n.*

stringy *a.* like string; fibrous.

strip¹ *v.t./i.* (p.t. *stripped*) remove (clothes or coverings or parts etc.); pull or tear away (from); undress; deprive, e.g. of property or titles. **~ club,** club where strip-tease performances are given. **~-tease** *n.* entertainment in which a performer gradually undresses. **stripper** *n.*

strip² *n.* long narrow piece or area. **comic ~** *or* **~ cartoon,** sequence of cartoons. **~ lighting,** lighting by long tubular fluorescent lamps.

stripe *n.* long narrow band on a surface, differing in colour or texture from its surroundings; chevron on a sleeve, indicating rank. **striped** *a.*, **stripy** *a.*

stripling *n.* a youth.

strive *v.i.* (p.t. *strove*, p.p. *striven*) make great efforts; carry on a conflict.

strobe *n.* (*colloq.*) stroboscope.

stroboscope *n.* apparatus for producing a rapidly flashing bright light.

strode *see* **stride.**

stroke¹ *n.* act of striking something; single movement or action or effort; particular sequence of movements (e.g. in swimming); oarsman nearest the stern of a racing-boat; mark made by a movement of a pen or paint-brush etc.; sound made by a clock striking; attack of apoplexy or paralysis. —*v.t.* act as stroke to (a boat or crew).

stroke² *v.t.* pass the hand gently along the surface of. —*n.* act of stroking.

stroll *v.i. & n.* walk in a leisurely way. **stroller** *n.*

strong *a.* (-*er*, -*est*) capable of exerting or resisting great power; powerful through numbers or resources or quality; concentrated; containing much alcohol; having a considerable effect; having a specified number of members; (of verbs) changing the vowel in the past tense (e.g. *strike/struck*). —*adv.* strongly. **~-box** *n.* strongly made box for storing valuables. **~ language,** forcible language, oaths or swearing. **~-minded** *a.*

determined. **∼-point** *n.* specially fortified position. **∼-room** *n.* room designed for storage and protection of valuables. **strongly** *adv.*

stronghold *n.* fortified place; centre of support for a cause.

strontium *n.* silver-white metallic element.

strop *n.* device (esp. a strip of leather) for sharpening razors. —*v.t.* (p.t. *stropped*) sharpen on or with a strop.

stroppy *a.* (*sl.*) bad-tempered, awkward to deal with.

strove *see* **strive.**

struck *see* **strike.** —*a.* **∼ on,** (*sl.*) impressed with, liking.

structure *n.* way a thing is constructed or organized; thing's supporting framework or essential parts; constructed thing, complex whole. **structural** *a.*, **structurally** *adv.*

struggle *v.i.* move in a vigorous effort to get free; make one's way or a living etc. with difficulty; make a vigorous effort. —*n.* spell of struggling; vigorous effort; hard contest.

strum *v.t./i.* (p.t. *strummed*) play unskilfully or monotonously on (a musical instrument). —*n.* sound made by strumming.

strung *see* **string.** —*a.* **∼ up,** mentally tense or excited.

strut *n.* bar of wood or metal supporting something; strutting walk. —*v.i.* (p.t. *strutted*) walk in a pompous self-satisfied way.

strychnine /ˈstrɪknin/ *n.* bitter highly poisonous substance.

stub *n.* short stump; counterfoil of a cheque or receipt etc. —*v.t.* (p.t. *stubbed*) strike (one's toe) against a hard object; extinguish (a cigarette) by pressure. **stubby** *a.*

stubble *n.* lower ends of corn-stalks left in the ground after harvest; short stiff growth of hair or beard, esp. growing after shaving.

stubborn *a.* obstinate; not easy to deal with. **stubbornly** *adv.*, **stubbornness** *n.*

stucco *n.* plaster or cement used for coating walls or moulding into decorations. **stuccoed** *a.*

stuck *see* **stick²**. —*a.* unable to move; (of an animal) that has been stabbed or had its throat cut. **∼-up** *a.* (*sl.*) conceited; snobbish.

stud¹ *n.* projecting nail-head or similar knob on a surface; device like a button on a shank used e.g. to fasten a detachable shirt-collar. —*v.t.* (p.t. *studded*) decorate with studs or precious stones; strengthen with studs.

stud² *n.* horses kept for breeding; establishment keeping these.

student *n.* person engaged in studying something, esp. at a college or university.

studied *a.* deliberate and artificial.

studio *n.* (pl. *-os*) work-room of a painter, photographer, etc.; room or premises where cinema films are made; room from which broadcasts are transmitted or where recordings are made. **∼ couch,** divan-like couch convertible into a bed. **∼ flat,** one-room flat with a kitchen and bathroom.

studious *a.* involving study; spending much time in study; deliberate and careful. **studiously** *adv.*, **studiousness** *n.*

study *n.* process of studying; its subject; work presenting the results of studying a subject; musical composition designed to develop a player's skill; preliminary drawing; room used for work that involves studying. —*v.t./i.* give one's attention to acquiring knowledge of (a subject); examine attentively; give care and consideration to.

stuff *n.* material; (*sl.*) unnamed things, belongings, subjects, etc.; (*sl.*) trash. —*v.t./i.* fill or pack tightly; fill with padding or stuffing; eat greedily.

stuffing *n.* padding used to fill something; savoury mixture put inside poultry, rolled meat, etc., before cooking.

stuffy *a.* (-ier, -iest) lacking fresh air or ventilation; dull; (*colloq.*) old-fashioned and narrow-minded; (*colloq.*) showing annoyance. **stuffily** *adv.*, **stuffiness** *n.*

stultify *v.t.* impair, make ineffective. **stultification** *n.*

stumble *v.i.* strike one's foot on something and lose one's balance; walk with frequent stumbles; make mistakes in speaking or playing music etc. —*n.* act of stumbling. **∼ across** *or* **on,** discover accidentally. **stumbling-block** *n.* obstacle, thing causing difficulty.

stump *n.* base of a tree left in the ground when the rest has gone; similar remnant of a something cut or broken or worn down; one of the three uprights of a wicket in cricket. —*v.t./i.* walk stiffly or noisily; put out (a batsman) by dislodging the bails; (*colloq.*) baffle. **∼ up,** (*sl.*) produce or pay over (money required).

stumpy *a.* (-ier, -iest) short and thick. **stumpiness** *n.*

stun *v.t.* (p.t. *stunned*) knock senseless; daze by the impact of emotion.

stung *see* **sting.**

stunk *see* **stink.**

stunning *a.* (*colloq.*) very attractive.

stunt¹ *v.t.* hinder the growth or development of.

stunt² *n.* (*colloq.*) something unusual or difficult done as a performance or to attract attention. **∼ flying,** aerobatics.

stupefy *v.t.* dull the wits or senses of; stun with astonishment. **stupefaction** *n.*

stupendous *a.* amazing; exceedingly great. **stupendously** *adv.*

stupid *a.* not clever; slow at learning or understanding; in a state of stupor. **stupidly** *adv.*, **stupidity** *n.*

stupor *n.* dazed almost unconscious condition.

sturdy *a.* (-ier, -iest) strongly built, hardy, vigorous. **sturdily** *adv.*, **sturdiness** *n.*

sturgeon *n.* (pl. *sturgeon*) large shark-like fish.

stutter *v.t./i.* & *n.* stammer, esp. repeating consonants.

sty *n.* pigsty.

stye *n.* inflamed swelling on the edge of the eyelid.

style *n.* manner of writing or speaking or doing

something; shape, design; elegance; narrow extension of a plant's ovary. —*v.t.* design, shape, or arrange, esp. fashionably. **in ~**, elegantly, luxuriously.

stylish *a.* fashionable, elegant. **stylishly** *adv.*, **stylishness** *n.*

stylist *n.* person who has or aims at a good style; person who styles things.

stylistic *a.* of literary or artistic style. **stylistically** *adv.*

stylized *a.* made to conform to a conventional style.

stylus *n.* (pl. *-uses*) needle-like device for cutting or following a groove in a record.

stymie /ˈstaɪmɪ/ *v.t.* (pres.p. *stymieing*) thwart.

styptic *a.* checking bleeding by causing blood-vessels to contract.

suasion *n.* persuasion.

suave /swɑv/ *a.* smooth-mannered. **suavely** *adv.*, **suavity** *n.*

sub *n.* (*colloq.*) submarine; subscription; substitute.

sub- *pref.* under; subordinate.

subaltern /ˈsʌb-/ *n.* army officer below the rank of captain.

subaqua *a.* (of sport etc.) taking place under water.

subcommittee *n.* committee formed for a special purpose from some members of a main committee.

subconscious *a. & n.* (of) our own mental activities of which we are not aware. **subconsciously** *adv.*

subcontinent *n.* large land-mass forming part of a continent.

subcontract *v.t./i.* give or accept a contract to carry out all or part of another contract. **subcontractor** *n.*

subdivide *v.t.* divide into smaller parts after a first division. **subdivision** *n.*

subdue *v.t.* overcome, bring under control; make quieter or less intense.

subhuman *a.* less than human; not fully human.

subject[1] /ˈsʌb-/ *a.* not politically independent. —*n.* person subject to a particular political rule or ruler; person or thing being discussed, represented, or studied; word(s) in a sentence that name who or what does the action or undergoes what is stated by the verb; theme or chief phrase in a sonata etc. **~-matter** *n.* matter treated in a book or speech etc. **~ to**, owing obedience to; liable to; depending upon as a condition.

subject[2] /-ˈdʒekt/ *v.t.* bring (a country) under one's control; cause to undergo. **subjection** *n.*

subjective *a.* existing in a person's mind and not produced by things outside it; dependent on personal taste or views etc. **subjectively** *adv.*

subjoin *v.t.* add at the end.

subjugate *v.t.* bring (a country) into subjection. **subjugation** *n.*

subjunctive *a. & n.* (of) the form of a verb used in expressing what is imagined, wished, or possible.

sublet *v.t.* (p.t. *sublet*, pres.p. *subletting*) let (rooms etc. that one holds by lease) to a tenant.

sublimate /ˈsʌb-/ *v.t.* divert the energy of (an emotion or impulse) into a culturally higher activity. **sublimation** *n.*

sublime *a.* most exalted; most extreme or impressive. **sublimely** *adv.*, **sublimity** *n.*

subliminal *a.* below the level of conscious awareness.

submarine *a.* under the surface of the sea. —*n.* vessel that can operate under water.

submerge *v.t./i.* put or go below the surface of water or other liquid; flood. **submergence** *n.*, **submersion** *n.*

submicroscopic *a.* too small to be seen by an ordinary microscope.

submission *n.* submitting; theory or statement etc. submitted; being submissive, obedience.

submissive *a.* submitting to authority. **submissively** *adv.*, **submissiveness** *n.*

submit *v.t./i.* (p.t. *submitted*) yield to another's authority or control, surrender; subject to a process; present for consideration or decision.

subnormal *a.* below normal level.

subordinate[1] /-nət/ *a.* of lesser importance or rank; working under another's control or authority. —*n.* subordinate person.

subordinate[2] /-neɪt/ *v.t.* make subordinate; treat as of lesser importance. **subordination** *n.*

suborn *v.t.* induce by bribery to commit perjury or other unlawful act. **subornation** *n.*

subpoena /sʌbˈpiːnə/ *n.* writ commanding a person to appear in a lawcourt. —*v.t.* (p.t. *subpoenaed*) summon with a subpoena.

subscribe *v.t./i.* pay (a subscription); sign. **~ to** a theory etc., express agreement. **subscriber** *n.*

subscription *n.* sum of money contributed; fee for membership etc.; process of subscribing.

subsection *n.* division of a section.

subsequent *a.* coming after in time or order. **subsequently** *adv.*

subservient *a.* subordinate; servile. **subserviently** *adv.*, **subservience** *n.*

subside *v.i.* sink, esp. to a lower or normal level; become less intense. **subsidence** /ˈsʌbsɪ-/ *n.*

subsidiary *a.* of secondary importance; (of a business company) controlled by another. —*n.* subsidiary thing.

subsidize *v.t.* pay a subsidy to or for.

subsidy *n.* money contributed to an industry or other cause needing help, or to keep prices at a desired level.

subsist *v.i.* exist; continue to exist; keep oneself alive. **subsistence** *n.*

subsoil *n.* soil lying immediately below the surface layer.

subsonic *a.* of or flying at speeds less than that of sound.

substance *n.* matter with more or less uniform properties; particular kind of this; essence of something spoken or written; reality, solidity.

substantial *a.* of solid material or structure; of considerable amount or intensity or validity; possessing much property or wealth; in essentials. **substantially** *adv.*

substantiate v.t. support with evidence, prove. **substantiation** n.

substantive[1] /-'stæn-/ a. (of military rank) permanent.

substantive[2] /'sʌb-/ n. noun.

substitute n. person or thing that acts or serves in place of another. —v.t./i. put or use or (colloq.) serve as a substitute. **substitution** n.

subsume v.t. bring or include under a particular classification.

subtenant n. person to whom a room etc. is sublet. **subtenancy** n.

subterfuge n. trick used to avoid blame or defeat etc.

subterranean a. underground.

subtitle n. subordinate title; caption on a cinema film.

subtle /'sʌtl/ a. (-er, -est) slight and difficult to detect or identify; making fine distinctions; ingenious. **subtly** adv., **subtlety** /'sʌtltɪ/ n.

subtopia /-'təʊ-/ n. unsightly suburbs.

subtotal n. total of part of a group of figures.

subtract v.t. remove (a part or quantity or number) from a greater one. **subtraction** n.

subtropical a. of regions bordering on the tropics.

suburb n. residential district lying outside the central part of a town. **suburban** a.

suburbia n. suburbs and their inhabitants.

subvention n. subsidy.

subvert v.t. overthrow the authority of, esp. by weakening people's trust. **subversion** n., **subversive** a.

subway n. underground passage; (U.S.) underground railway.

succeed v.t./i. be successful; come next to; take the place previously filled by, come by inheritance or in due order.

success n. favourable outcome; attainment of what was desired or attempted, or of wealth, fame, or position; successful person or thing. **successful** a. having success. **successfully** adv.

succession n. following in order; series of people or things following each other; succeeding to a throne or other position. **in** ∼, one after another.

successive a. following in succession. **successively** adv.

successor n. person who succeeds another.

succinct /sək'sɪŋkt/ a. concise and clear. **succinctly** adv.

succour /'sʌk-/ v.t. & n. help.

succulent a. juicy; (of plants) having thick fleshy leaves or stems. —n. succulent plant.

succumb v.i. give way to something overpowering.

such a. of the same or that kind or degree; so great or intense. —pron. that. ∼**-and-such** a. particular but not now specified.

suchlike a. (colloq.) of the same kind.

suck v.t. draw (liquid or air etc.) into the mouth; draw liquid from; squeeze in the mouth by using the tongue; draw in. —n. act or process of sucking. ∼ **up to**, (sl.) toady to.

sucker n. organ or device that can adhere to a surface by suction; shoot coming up from

a tree's or shrub's root or underground stem; (sl.) person who is easily deceived.

suckle v.t./i. feed at the breast.

suction n. sucking; production of a partial vacuum so that external atmospheric pressure forces fluid etc. into the vacant space or causes adhesion.

sudden a. happening or done quickly or without warning. **all of a** ∼, suddenly. **suddenly** adv., **suddenness** n.

suds n.pl. soapsuds.

sue v.t./i. (pres.p. suing) take legal proceedings against; make an application.

suede /sweɪd/ n. leather with the flesh side rubbed into a velvety nap.

suet n. hard white fat from round an animal's kidneys, used in cooking. **suety** a.

suffer v.t./i. feel or undergo or be subjected to (pain, loss, damage, etc.); permit; tolerate. **suffering** n.

sufferance n. **on** ∼, tolerated but only grudgingly.

suffice /-'faɪs/ v.t. be enough (for).

sufficient a. enough. **sufficiently** adv., **sufficiency** n.

suffix n. (pl. -ixes) letter(s) added at the end of a word to make another word.

suffocate v.t./i. kill by stopping the breathing; cause discomfort to by making breathing difficult; be suffocated. **suffocation** n.

suffragan /-gən/ n. ∼ **bishop**, bishop consecrated to help another with administration; bishop in relation to an archbishop.

suffrage n. right to vote in political elections.

suffragette n. woman who (in the early 20th century) agitated for women's suffrage.

suffuse v.t. spread throughout or over. **suffusion** n.

sugar n. sweet crystalline substance obtained from the juices of various plants. ∼ **soap**, abrasive compound for cleaning paint. **sugary** a.

suggest v.t. cause (an idea etc.) to be present in the mind; propose for acceptance or rejection.

suggestible a. easily influenced by people's suggestions. **suggestibility** n.

suggestion n. suggesting; thing suggested; slight trace.

suggestive a. conveying a suggestion; suggesting something indecent. **suggestively** adv.

suicidal /-'saɪ-/ a. of or involving suicide; liable to commit suicide.

suicide n. intentional killing of oneself; person who commits suicide; act destructive to one's own interests. **commit** ∼, kill oneself intentionally.

suit n. set of clothing, esp. jacket and trousers or skirt; any of the four sets (spades, hearts, diamonds, clubs) into which a pack of cards is divided; lawsuit. —v.t. meet the demands or needs of; make or be suitable or convenient for; give a pleasing appearance upon.

suitable a. right for the purpose or occasion. **suitably** adv., **suitability** n.

suitcase n. rectangular case for carrying clothes.

suite *n.* set of rooms or furniture; retinue; set of musical pieces.

suitor *n.* man who is courting a woman.

sulk *v.i.* be sullen because of resentment or bad temper. **sulks** *n.pl.* fit of sulking. **sulky** *a.*, **sulkily** *adv.*, **sulkiness** *n.*

sullen *a.* gloomy and unresponsive because of resentment or bad temper; dark and dismal. **sullenly** *adv.*, **sullenness** *n.*

sully *v.t.* stain, blemish.

sulphate *n.* salt of sulphuric acid.

sulphonamide /-'fon-/ *n.* a kind of antibiotic drug.

sulphur *n.* pale yellow non-metallic element. **sulphurous** /'sʌlfʊər-/ *a.*

sulphuric /-'fjʊər-/ *a.* **~ acid,** strong corrosive acid.

sultan *n.* ruler of certain Muslim countries.

sultana *n.* seedless raisin.

sultanate /'sʌl-/ *n.* sultan's territory.

sultry *a.* (*-ier*, *-iest*) hot and humid; (of a woman) of dark mysterious beauty. **sultriness** *n.*

sum *n.* total; amount of money; problem in arithmetic. —*v.t.* (p.t. *summed*) find the sum of. **~ up,** give the total of; summarize; form an opinion of.

summarize *v.t.* make or be a summary of.

summary *n.* statement giving the main points of something. —*a.* brief, giving the main points only; without delay; without attention to details or formalities. **summarily** *adv.*

summer *n.* warmest season of the year. **~house** *n.* light building in a garden or park, providing shade in summer. **~-time** *n.* summer. **~ time,** time shown by clocks put forward in summer to give long light evenings. **summery** *a.*

summit *n.* highest point; top of a mountain; (also **~ conference** etc.) conference between heads of States. **summitry** *n.*

summon *v.t.* send for (a person); order to appear in a lawcourt; gather together (one's courage etc.); call upon to do something.

summons *n.* command summoning a person; written order to appear in a lawcourt. —*v.t.* serve with a summons.

sump *n.* reservoir of oil in a petrol engine; hole or low area into which liquid drains.

sumptuous *a.* splendid and costly-looking. **sumptuously** *adv.*

sun *n.* heavenly body round which the earth travels; light or warmth from this; any fixed star. —*v.t.* (p.t. *sunned*) expose to the sun.

sunbathe *v.i.* expose one's body to the sun.

sunbeam *n.* ray of sun.

sunburn *n.* tanning or inflammation caused by exposure to sun. **sunburnt** *a.*

sundae /-deɪ/ *n.* dish of ice cream and crushed fruit, nuts, syrup, etc.

Sunday *n.* first day of the week. **~ school,** school for religious instruction of children, held on Sundays.

sunder *v.t.* break or tear apart.

sundew *n.* bog-plant with hairs secreting moisture that traps insects.

sundial *n.* device that shows the time by means of a shadow on a scaled dial.

sundown *n.* sunset.

sundry /-drɪ/ *a.* various. **all and ~,** everyone. **sundries** *n.pl.* various small items.

sunflower *n.* tall garden plant bearing large yellow flowers.

sung *see* **sing.**

sunk, sunken *see* **sink.** —*adjs.* below the level of the surrounding surface. **~ fence,** ditch strengthened by a wall, forming a boundary.

sunlight *n.* light from the sun.

sunny *a.* (*-ier*, *-iest*) full of sunshine; cheerful. **sunnily** *adv.*

sunrise *n.* rising of the sun.

sunset *n.* setting of the sun; sky full of colour at sunset.

sunshade *n.* parasol; awning.

sunshine *n.* direct sunlight.

sunspot *n.* dark patch observed on the sun's surface; (*colloq.*) place with a sunny climate.

sunstroke *n.* illness caused by too much exposure to sun.

sup *v.t./i.* (p.t. *supped*) take (liquid) by sips or spoonfuls; eat supper. —*n.* mouthful of liquid.

super *a.* (*sl.*) excellent, superb.

superannuate *v.t.* discharge into retirement with a pension. **superannuation** *n.*

superb *a.* of the most impressive or splendid kind. **superbly** *adv.*

supercharge *v.t.* increase the power of (an engine) by a device that forces extra air or fuel into it. **supercharger** *n.*

supercilious /-'sɪl-/ *a.* haughty and superior. **superciliously** *adv.*

supererogation *n.* doing of more than is required by duty.

superficial *a.* of or on the surface, not deep or penetrating. **superficially** *adv.*, **superficiality** *n.*

superfluous *a.* more than is required. **superfluously** *adv.*, **superfluity** /-'flu-/ *n.*

superhuman *a.* beyond ordinary human capacity or power; higher than humanity, divine.

superimpose *v.t.* place on top of something else. **superimposition** *n.*

superintend *v.t.* supervise. **superintendence** *n.*

superintendent *n.* supervisor; police officer next above inspector.

superior *a.* higher in position or rank; better, greater; showing that one feels wiser or better etc. than others. —*n.* person or thing of higher rank or ability or quality; head of a monastery etc. **superiority** *n.*

superlative *a.* of the highest degree or quality; of the grammatical form expressing 'most'. —*n.* superlative form. **superlatively** *adv.*

superman *n.* (pl. *-men*) man of superhuman powers.

supermarket *n.* very large self-service shop.

supernatural *a.* of or involving a power above the forces of nature. **supernaturally** *adv.*

supernumerary *a.* & *n.* extra.

superphosphate *n.* fertilizer containing phosphates.

superpower *n.* extremely powerful nation.

superscript *a.* written just above and to the right of a word or figure or symbol.

superscription *n.* word(s) written at the top or on the outside.

supersede *v.t.* take the place of; put or use in place of.

supersonic *a.* of or flying at speeds greater than that of sound.

superstition *n.* belief in magical and similar influences; idea or practice based on this; widely held but wrong idea. **superstitious** *a.*, **superstitiously** *adv.*

superstore *n.* large supermarket.

superstructure *n.* structure that rests on something else.

supertanker *n.* very large tanker.

supervene *v.i.* occur as an interruption or a change. **supervention** *n.*

supervise *v.t.* direct and inspect. **supervision** *n.*, **supervisor** *n.*, **supervisory** /ˈsuː-/ *a.*

supine /ˈsuːpaɪn/ *a.* lying face upwards; indolent. **supinely** *adv.*

supper *n.* evening meal, last meal of the day.

supplant *v.t.* oust and take the place of.

supple *a.* bending easily. **supplely** *adv.*, **suppleness** *n.*

supplement *n.* thing added as an extra part or to make up for a deficiency. —*v.t.* provide or be a supplement to.

supplementary *a.* serving as a supplement.

suppliant /ˈsʌplɪ-/ *n.* & *a.* (person) asking humbly for something.

supplicate *v.t.* ask humbly for; beseech. **supplication** *n.*

supply *v.t.* give or provide with, make available; satisfy (a need). —*n.* supplying; stock, amount provided or available.

support *v.t.* keep from falling or sinking or failing; bear the weight of; strengthen; supply with necessaries; help, encourage; endure, tolerate. —*n.* act of supporting; person or thing that supports. **supporter** *n.*

suppose *v.t.* be inclined to think; assume or accept to be true; consider as a proposal; presuppose. **be supposed to,** be expected to; have as a duty.

supposedly /-zɪd-/ *adv.* according to supposition.

supposition *n.* process of supposing; what is supposed.

suppositious /-ˈzɪʃəs/ *a.* hypothetical.

supposititious *a.* substituted for the real thing, spurious.

suppository /-ˈpɒz-/ *n.* solid piece of medicinal substance placed in the rectum, vagina, or urethra and left to melt.

suppress *v.t.* put an end to the activity or existence of; keep from being known. **suppression** *n.* **suppressor** *n.*

suppurate /-pjʊər-/ *v.i.* form pus, fester. **suppuration** *n.*

supra- *pref.* above, over.

supreme *a.* highest in authority, rank, importance, or quality. **supremely** *adv.*, **supremacy** /-ˈprem-/ *n.*

surcharge *n.* additional charge; extra or excessive load. —*v.t.* make a surcharge on or to; overload.

surd *n.* mathematical quantity (esp. a root) that cannot be expressed in finite terms of whole numbers or quantities.

sure *a.* (*-er*, *-est*) having firm reasons for belief, convinced; reliable, unfailing. —*adv.* (*U.S. colloq.*) certainly. **~-footed** *a.* never slipping or stumbling. **make ~,** act so as to be certain; feel confident (perhaps mistakenly). **sureness** *n.*

surely *adv.* in a sure manner; (used for emphasis) that must be right; (as an answer) certainly.

surety /ˈʃʊətɪ/ *n.* guarantee; guarantor of a person's promise.

surf *n.* white foam of waves. **~-board** *n.* narrow board for riding over surf. **~-riding** *or* **surfing** *ns.* this sport.

surface *n.* outside or outward appearance of something; any side of an object; uppermost area, top. —*a.* of or on the surface. —*v.t./i.* put a specified surface on; come or bring to the surface; (*colloq.*) wake. **~ mail,** mail carried by sea not by air.

surfeit /ˈsɜːfɪt/ *n.* too much, esp. of food or drink. —*v.t.* cause to take too much of something; satiate, cloy.

surge *v.i.* move forward in or like waves; increase in volume or intensity. —*n.* wave(s); surging movement or increase.

surgeon *n.* doctor (esp. a specialist) who performs surgical operations.

surgery *n.* treatment by cutting or manipulation of affected parts of the body; place where or times when a doctor or dentist or an M.P. etc. is available for consultation. **surgical** *a.*, **surgically** *adv.*

surly *a.* (*-ier*, *-iest*) bad-tempered and unfriendly. **surliness** *n.*

surmise /-ˈmaɪz/ *v.t./i.* & *n.* conjecture.

surmount *v.t.* overcome (a difficulty); get over (an obstacle); be on the top of.

surname *n.* name held by all members of a family. —*v.t.* give as a surname.

surpass *v.t.* outdo; excel.

surplice *n.* loose white vestment worn over a cassock.

surplus *n.* amount left over after what is needed has been used; excess of revenue over expenditure.

surprise *n.* emotion aroused by something sudden or unexpected; thing causing this; process of catching a person etc. unprepared. —*v.t.* cause to feel surprise; come upon or attack unexpectedly; startle thus.

surrealism *n.* style of art and literature seeking to express what is in the subconscious mind. **surrealist** *n.*, **surrealistic** *a.*

surrender *v.t./i.* hand over, give into another's power or control, esp. under compulsion; give (oneself) up. —*n.* surrendering.

surreptitious *a.* acting or done stealthily. **surreptitiously** *adv.*

surrogate /ˈsʌrəgeɪt/ *n.* deputy.

surround *v.t.* come, lie, or be all round;

place all round, encircle. —*n.* border, edging.

surroundings *n.pl.* things or conditions around a person or place.

surveillance /-'veɪl-/ *n.* supervision; close watch.

survey[1] /-'veɪ/ *v.t.* look at and take a general view of; make or present a general examination of (a subject); examine the condition of (a building); measure and map out.

survey[2] /'sɜ-/ *n.* general look at or examination of something; report or map produced by surveying.

surveyor *n.* person whose job is to survey land or buildings.

survival *n.* surviving; thing that has survived from an earlier time.

survive *v.t./i.* continue to live or exist; remain alive or in existence after. **survivor** *n.*

susceptible /-'sep-/ *a.* easily affected; falling in love easily. **~ of,** able to undergo (proof etc.). **~ to,** liable to be affected by. **susceptibility** *n.*

susceptive /-'sep-/ *a.* susceptible.

suspect[1] /-'spekt/ *v.t.* have an impression of the existence or presence of; mistrust; feel to be guilty but have little or no proof.

suspect[2] /'sʌs-/ *n.* person suspected of a crime etc. —*a.* suspected, open to suspicion.

suspend *v.t.* hang up; keep from falling or sinking in air or liquid; postpone; stop temporarily; deprive temporarily of a position or right.

suspender *n.* attachment to hold up a sock or stocking by its top.

suspense *n.* anxious uncertainty while awaiting an event etc.

suspension *n.* suspending; means by which a vehicle is supported on its axles. **~ bridge,** bridge suspended from cables that pass over supports at each end.

suspicion *n.* suspecting; partial or unconfirmed belief; slight trace.

suspicious *a.* feeling or causing suspicion. **suspiciously** *adv.*

sustain *v.t.* support; keep alive; keep (a sound or effort) going continuously; undergo; endure without giving way; uphold the validity of.

sustenance *n.* process of sustaining life by food; food, nourishment.

suture /'su-/ *n.* surgical stitching of a wound; stitch or thread used in this. —*v.t.* stitch (a wound).

suzerain /'suːzəreɪn/ *n.* country or ruler with some authority over a self-governing country; overlord. **suzerainty** *n.*

svelte *a.* slender and graceful.

swab /-ob/ *n.* mop or pad for cleansing, drying, or absorbing things; specimen of a secretion taken with this. —*v.t.* (p.t. *swabbed*) cleanse or wipe with a swab.

swaddle /'swo-/ *v.t.* swathe in wraps or warm garments.

swag *n.* loot; carved festoon; (*Austr.*) bundle of belongings carried by a tramp etc. **swagman** *n.*

swagger *v.i.* walk or behave with aggressive

pride. —*n.* this gait or manner. —*a.* (*colloq.*) smart, fashionable.

Swahili /-'hiːlɪ/ *n.* Bantu language widely used in East Africa.

swallow[1] *v.t./i.* cause or allow to go down one's throat; work throat-muscles in doing this; take in and engulf or absorb; accept. —*n.* act of swallowing; amount swallowed.

swallow[2] *n.* small migratory bird with a forked tail. **~-dive** *n.* dive with arms outspread at the start.

swam *see* **swim.**

swamp *n.* marsh. —*v.t.* flood, drench or submerge in water; overwhelm with a mass or number of things. **swampy** *a.*

swan *n.* large usu. white water-bird with a long slender neck. **~-song** *n.* person's last performance or achievement etc.

swank *n.* (*colloq.*) boastful person or behaviour; ostentation. —*v.i.* (*colloq.*) behave with swank.

swansdown *n.* swan's fine soft down, used for trimmings.

swap *v.t./i.* (p.t. *swapped*) & *n.* (*colloq.*) exchange.

swarm[1] *n.* large cluster of people, insects (esp. bees), etc. —*v.i.* cluster, move in a swarm; be crowded or overrun.

swarm[2] *v.i.* **~ up,** climb by gripping with arms and legs.

swarthy /'swɔːðɪ/ *a.* (-ier, -iest) having a dark complexion.

swashbuckling *a.* & *n.* swaggering boldly.

swastika /'swɒs-/ *n.* symbol formed by a cross with ends bent at right angles.

swat *v.t.* (p.t. *swatted*) hit hard with something flat. **swatter** *n.*

swath /-əθ/ *n.* (pl. *swaths*, pr. -əðz) strip cut in one sweep or passage by a scythe or mowing-machine; line of wheat etc. cut thus.

swathe /-eɪð/ *v.t.* wrap with layers of coverings.

sway *v.t./i.* swing gently, lean to and fro; influence the opinions of; waver in one's opinion. —*n.* swaying movement; influence.

swear *v.t./i.* (p.t. *swore*, p.p. *sworn*) state or promise on oath; state emphatically; cause to take an oath; use curses or profane language. **~ by,** (*colloq.*) have great confidence in. **~-word** *n.* profane or indecent word used in anger etc.

sweat *n.* moisture given off by the body through the pores; state of sweating, or (*colloq.*) of great anxiety; (*colloq.*) laborious task; moisture forming in drops on a surface. —*v.t./i.* exude sweat or as sweat; be in a state of great anxiety; work long and hard. **sweated labour,** labour of workers with poor pay and conditions. **sweaty** *a.*

sweater *n.* jumper, pullover.

swede *n.* large yellow variety of turnip.

Swede *n.* native of Sweden.

Swedish *a.* & *n.* (language) of Sweden.

sweep *v.t./i.* (p.t. *swept*) clear away with or as if with a broom or brush; clean or clear (a surface) thus; move or remove by pushing; go smoothly and swiftly or majestically;

extend in a continuous line or slope; pass lightly or quickly over or along etc.; make (a bow or curtsy) smoothly. —*n.* sweeping movement or line or slope; act of sweeping; chimney-sweep; sweepstake. ~ **the board,** win all the prizes. **sweeper** *n.*

sweeping *a.* of great scope, comprehensive; making no exceptions.

sweepstake *n.* form of gambling in which the money staked is divided among those who have drawn numbered tickets for the winners; race etc. with such betting.

sweet *a.* (*-er, -est*) tasting as if containing sugar, not bitter or savoury; fragrant; melodious; fresh, not stale; pleasant; beloved; (*colloq.*) charming. —*n.* small shaped piece of sweet substance; sweet dish forming one course of a meal; beloved person. ~ **pea,** climbing plant with fragrant flowers. ~ **tooth,** liking for sweet things. **sweetly** *adv.*, **sweetness** *n.*

sweetbread *n.* animal's thymus gland or pancreas used as food.

sweeten *v.t./i.* make or become sweet or sweeter. **sweetener** *n.*

sweetheart *n.* either of a pair of people in love with each other.

sweetmeal *a.* of sweetened wholemeal.

sweetmeat *n.* sweet; very small fancy cake.

swell *v.t./i.* (p.t. *swelled*, p.p. *swollen* or *swelled*) make or become larger from pressure within; curve outwards; make or become greater in amount or intensity. —*n.* act or state of swelling; heaving of the sea; gradual increase in loudness; (*colloq.*) person of high social position. —*a.* (*colloq.*) smart, excellent. **swelled head,** (*sl.*) conceit.

swelling *n.* swollen place on the body.

swelter *v.i.* be uncomfortably hot.

swept *see* **sweep.**

swerve *v.t./i.* turn aside from a straight course. —*n.* swerving movement or direction.

swift *a.* (*-er, -est*) quick, rapid. —*n.* swiftly flying bird with narrow wings. **swiftly** *adv.*, **swiftness** *n.*

swig *v.t./i.* (p.t. *swigged*) & *n.* (*colloq.*) drink, swallow.

swill *v.t./i.* pour water over or through; wash, rinse; (of water) pour; drink greedily. —*n.* rinse; sloppy food fed to pigs.

swim *v.t./i.* (p.t. *swam*, p.p. *swum*) travel through water by movements of the body; cross by swimming; float; be covered with liquid; seem to be whirling or waving; be dizzy. —*n.* act or period of swimming. **in the ~,** active in or knowing what is going on. **~-suit** *n.* garment worn for swimming. **swimming-bath, swimming-pool** *ns.* artificial pool for swimming in. **swimmer** *n.*

swimmingly *adv.* with easy unobstructed progress.

swindle *v.t.* cheat in a business transaction; obtain by fraud. —*n.* piece of swindling; fraudulent person or thing. **swindler** *n.*

swine *n.pl.* pigs. —*n.* (pl. *swine*) (*colloq.*) hated person or thing.

swineherd *n.* (*old use*) person taking care of a number of pigs.

swing *v.t./i.* (p.t. *swung*) move to and fro while hanging or supported; hang by its end(s); turn in a curve; walk or run or lift etc. with an easy rhythmical movement; change from one mood or opinion to another; influence decisively; (*sl.*) be executed by hanging; play (music) with a swing rhythm. —*n.* act, movement, or extent of swinging; seat slung by ropes or chains for swinging in; jazz with the time of the melody varied. **in full ~,** with activity at its greatest. ~ **bridge,** bridge that can be swung aside for ships to pass. ~ **the lead,** (see *lead*²). **~-wing** *n.* aircraft wing that can be moved to slant backwards. **swinger** *n.*

swingeing /-ndʒɪŋ/ *a.* forcible; huge in amount or scope.

swipe *v.t./i.* (*colloq.*) hit with a swinging blow; snatch, steal. —*n.* (*colloq.*) swinging blow.

swirl *v.t./i.* & *n.* whirl, flow with a whirling movement.

swish *v.t./i.* move or strike with a hissing sound. —*n.* swishing sound. —*a.* (*colloq.*) smart, fashionable.

Swiss *a.* & *n.* (native) of Switzerland; ~ **roll,** thin flat sponge-cake spread with jam etc. and rolled up.

switch *n.* device operated to turn electric current on or off; (*pl.*) railway points; flexible stick or rod, whip; tress of hair tied at one end; shift in opinion or method etc. —*v.t./i.* turn (on or off) by means of a switch; transfer, divert; change; whip with a switch; swing round quickly; snatch suddenly.

switchback *n.* railway used for amusement at a fun-fair, with alternate steep ascents and descents; road with similar slopes.

switchboard *n.* panel of switches for making telephone connections or operating electric circuits.

swivel *n.* link or pivot enabling one part to revolve without turning another. —*v.t./i.* (p.t. *swivelled*) turn on or as if on a swivel.

swizzle *n.* (*colloq.*) frothy mixed alcoholic drink; (*sl.*) swindle, disappointment. **~-stick** *n.* stick for stirring a drink.

swollen *see* **swell.**

swoon *v.i.* & *n.* faint.

swoop *v.i.* make a sudden downward rush, attack suddenly. —*n.* swooping movement or attack.

swop *v.t./i.* (p.t. *swopped*) & *n.* = swap.

sword *n.* weapon with a long blade and a hilt.

swordfish *n.* sea-fish with a long sword-like upper jaw.

swore *see* **swear.**

sworn *see* **swear.** —*a.* open and determined in devotion or enmity.

swot *v.t./i.* (p.t. *swotted*) (*school sl.*) study hard. —*n.* (*school sl.*) hard study; person who studies hard.

swum *see* **swim.**

swung *see* **swing.**

sybarite /ˈsɪbəraɪt/ *n.* person who is excessively fond of comfort and luxury. **sybaritic** /-ˈrɪt-/ *a.*

sycamore *n.* large tree of the maple family.

sycophant /'sɪk-/ *n.* person who tries to win favour by flattery. **sycophantic** *a.*, **sycophantically** *adv.*

syllable *n.* unit of sound in a word. **syllabic** *a.*, **syllabically** *adv.*

syllabub *n.* dish of whipped cream flavoured with wine.

syllabus *n.* (pl. *-buses*) statement of the subjects to be covered by a course of study.

syllogism *n.* form of reasoning in which a conclusion is reached from two statements.

sylph *n.* slender girl or woman.

symbiosis *n.* (pl. *-oses*) relationship of different organisms living in close association. **symbiotic** *a.*

symbol *n.* thing regarded as suggesting something; mark or sign with a special meaning.

symbolic, symbolical *adjs.* of, using, or used as a symbol. **symbolically** *adv.*

symbolism *n.* use of symbols to express things.

symbolize *v.t./i.* be a symbol of; represent by means of a symbol.

symmetry *n.* state of having parts that correspond in size, shape, and position on either side of a dividing line or round a centre. **symmetrical** *a.*, **symmetrically** *adv.*

sympathetic *a.* feeling or showing or resulting from sympathy; likeable. **sympathetically** *adv.*

sympathize *v.i.* feel or express sympathy. **sympathizer** *n.*

sympathy *n.* sharing or ability to share another's emotions or sensations; pity or tenderness towards a sufferer; liking for each other. **be in ~ with,** feel approval of (an opinion or desire).

symphony *n.* long elaborate musical composition for a full orchestra. **symphonic** *a.*

symposium *n.* (pl. *-ia*) meeting for discussing a particular subject.

symptom *n.* sign of the existence of a condition.

symptomatic *a.* serving as a symptom.

synagogue /'sɪnəgog/ *n.* building for public Jewish worship.

synchromesh *n.* device that makes parts of a gear revolve at the same speed while becoming engaged.

synchronize *v.t./i.* occur or exist or operate at the same time; cause to do this; cause (clocks etc.) to show the same time. **synchronization** *n.*

syncopate *v.t.* change the beats or accents in (music). **syncopation** *n.*

syncope /'sɪŋkəpɪ/ *n.* faint, fainting.

syndicate[1] /-kət/ *n.* association of people or firms to carry out a business undertaking.

syndicate[2] /-keɪt/ *v.t./i.* combine into a syndicate; publish through an agency that supplies material to many newspapers etc. simultaneously. **syndication** *n.*

syndrome *n.* combination of signs, symptoms, behaviour, etc. characteristic of a specified condition.

synod /'sɪn-/ *n.* council of senior clergy or church officials.

synonym *n.* word or phrase meaning the same as another in the same language.

synonymous /-'non-/ *a.* equivalent in meaning.

synopsis *n.* (pl. *-opses*) summary, brief general survey.

syntax *n.* way words are arranged to form phrases and sentences. **syntactic** *a.*, **syntactically** *adv.*

synthesis *n.* (pl. *-theses*) combining; artificial production of a substance that occurs naturally.

synthesize *v.t.* make by synthesis.

synthetic *a.* made by synthesis, manufactured; artificial. —*n.* synthetic substance or fabric. **synthetically** *n.*

syphilis *n.* a venereal disease.

syringa *n.* shrub with scented flowers.

syringe /sɪ'rɪndʒ/ *n.* device for drawing in liquid and forcing it out in a fine stream. —*v.t.* wash out or spray with a syringe.

syrup *n.* thick sweet liquid; water sweetened with sugar. **syrupy** *n.*

system *n.* set of connected things that form a whole or work together; animal body as a whole; set of rules or practices used together; method of classification or notation or measurement; orderliness. **systems analysis,** analysis of an operation in order to decide how a computer may perform it. **systems analyst,** expert in this.

systematic *a.* methodical; according to a plan, not casually or at random. **systematically** *adv.*

systematize *v.t.* arrange according to a system. **systematization** *n.*

systemic /-'tem-/ *a.* of the body as a whole; (of a fungicide etc.) entering a plant's tissues.

T

tab *n.* small projecting flap or strip. **keep a ~ or tabs on,** (*colloq.*) keep under observation. **pick up the ~,** (*U.S. colloq.*) be the one who pays the bill.

tabard /'tæ-/ *n.* short sleeveless tunic-like garment.

tabby *n.* cat with grey or brown fur and dark stripes.

tabernacle *n.* (in the Bible) portable shrine used by the Jews in the wilderness; (R.C. Church) receptacle for the Eucharist; Non-conformist or Mormon meeting-place for worship.

table *n.* piece of furniture with a flat top supported on one or more legs; food provided at table; list of facts or figures arranged systematically, esp. in columns, (*pl.*) those showing the products of numbers taken in pairs. —*v.t.* submit (a motion or report) for discussion. **at ~,** while taking a meal at the table. **~-cloth** *n.* cloth for covering a table

tableau 532 **talisman**

esp. at meals. ~ **tennis,** game like lawn tennis played on a table.

tableau /ˈtæbləʊ/ n. (pl. -eaux pr. -əʊz) silent motionless group arranged to represent a scene; dramatic or picturesque scene.

table d'hôte /tɑbl ˈdəʊt/ (of a meal) served at a fixed inclusive price.

tableland n. plateau of land.

tablespoon n. large spoon for serving food; amount held by this. **tablespoonful** n. (pl. -fuls).

tablet n. slab bearing an inscription etc.; small flat piece of a solid substance; measured amount of a drug compressed into a solid form.

tabloid n. newspaper with pages half the size of larger ones.

taboo n. ban or prohibition made by religion or social custom. —a. prohibited by a taboo.

tabular a. arranged in a table or list.

tabulate v.t. arrange in tabular form. **tabulation** n.

tabulator n. device on a typewriter for advancing to a series of set positions in tabular work.

tachograph /ˈtæk-/ n. device in a motor vehicle to record speed and travel-time.

tacit /ˈtæs-/ a. implied or understood without being put into words. **tacitly** a.

taciturn /ˈtæs-/ a. saying very little. **taciturnity** n.

tack¹ n. small broad-headed nail; long temporary stitch; sailing ship's oblique course; course of action or policy. —v.t./i. nail with tack(s); stitch with tacks; add as an extra thing; sail a zigzag course.

tack² n. harness, saddles, etc.

tackle n. set of ropes and pulleys for lifting weights or working sails; equipment for a task or sport; act of tackling in football etc. —v.t. try to deal with or overcome (an opponent or problem etc.); intercept (an opponent who has the ball in football etc.). **tackler** n.

tacky a. (of paint etc.) sticky, not quite dry. **tackiness** n.

tact n. skill in avoiding offence or in winning goodwill. **tactful** a., **tactfully** adv.

tactic n. piece of tactics.

tactical a. of tactics; planning or planned skilfully; (of weapons) for use in a battle or at close quarters. **tactically** adv.

tactician n. expert in tactics.

tactics n. art of placing or manœuvring forces skilfully in a battle. —n.pl. manœuvring; procedure adopted to achieve something.

tactile a. of or using the sense of touch.

tactless a. lacking in tact. **tactlessly** adv., **tactlessness** n.

tadpole n. larva of a frog or toad etc. at the stage when it has gills and a tail.

taffeta n. shiny silk-like fabric.

taffrail n. rail round a vessel's stern.

tag¹ n. metal or plastic point on a shoelace etc.; label; ragged end or projection; much-used phrase or quotation. —v.t./i. (p.t. tagged) label; attach, add.

tag² n. children's chasing-game.

tail n. animal's hindmost part, esp. when extending beyond its body; rear or hanging or inferior part; (sl.) person tailing another; (pl.) tailcoat; tails, reverse of a coin, turned upwards after being tossed. —v.t./i. remove the stalks of; (sl.) follow closely, shadow. ~ **away,** = tail off. **~-end** n. hindmost or very last part. **~-gate** n. rear door in a motor vehicle. ~ **off,** become fewer or smaller or slighter; end inconclusively.

tailcoat n. man's coat with the skirt tapering and divided at the back.

tailless a. having no tail.

tailor n. maker of men's clothes, esp. to order. —v.t. make (clothes) as a tailor; make in a simple well-fitted design; make or adapt for a special purpose. **~-made** a., **tailoress** n.fem.

tailplane n. horizontal part of an aeroplane's tail.

taint n. trace of decay or infection or other bad quality. —v.t. affect with a taint.

take v.t./i. (p.t. took, p.p. taken) lay hold of; get possession of, capture; be successful or effective; make use of; indulge in; occupy (a position), esp. as one's right; obtain; buy regularly; require; cause to come or go with one; carry, remove; be affected by, catch (fire); experience or exert (a feeling or effort); find out and record; accept, endure; perform, deal with; study or teach (a subject); make a photograph (of). —n. amount taken or caught; instance of photographing a scene for a cinema film. **be taken by** or **with,** find attractive. **be taken ill,** become ill. ~ **after,** resemble (a parent etc.). ~ **back,** withdraw (a statement). ~ **in,** include; make (a garment etc.) smaller; understand; deceive, cheat. ~ **life,** kill. ~ **off,** take (clothing etc.) from the body; mimic humorously; leave the ground and become airborne. ~ **oneself off,** depart. **~-off** n. humorous mimicry; process of becoming airborne. ~ **on,** acquire; undertake; engage (an employee); accept as an opponent; (colloq.) show great emotion. ~ **one's time,** not hurry. ~ **over,** take control of. **(~over** n.). ~ **part,** share in an activity. ~ **sides,** support one side or another. ~ **to,** adopt as a habit or custom; go to as a refuge; develop a liking or ability for. ~ **up,** take as a hobby or business or protégé; occupy (time or space); begin (residence etc.); resume; interrupt or question (a speaker); accept (an offer). ~ **up with,** begin to associate with. **taker** n.

taking a. attractive, captivating.

takings n.pl. money taken in business.

talc n. a kind of smooth mineral; talcum powder.

talcum n. talc. ~ **powder,** talc powdered and usu. perfumed for use on the skin.

tale n. narrative, story; report spread by gossip.

talent n. special or very great ability; ancient unit of money.

talented a. having talent.

talisman n. (pl. -mans) object supposed to bring good luck.

talk *v.t./i.* convey or exchange ideas by spoken words; express in words; use (a specified language) in talking; affect or influence by talking. —*n.* talking; style of speech; informal lecture; rumour. ~ **over,** discuss. **talking-to** *n.* reproof. **talker** *n.*

talkative *a.* talking very much.

tall *a.* (-*er*, -*est*) of great or specified height; ~ **order,** (*colloq.*) difficult task. ~ **story,** (*colloq.*) one that is hard to believe. **tallness** *n.*

tallboy *n.* tall chest of drawers.

tallow *n.* animal fat used to make candles, lubricants, etc.

tally *n.* total of a debt or score. —*v.i.* correspond.

tally-ho *int.* huntsman's cry on sighting the fox.

Talmud *n.* body of Jewish law and tradition. **Talmudic** *a.*

talon *n.* bird's large claw.

tamarind *n.* tropical tree; its acid fruit.

tamarisk *n.* evergreen shrub with feathery branches.

tambourine *n.* percussion instrument with jingling metal discs.

tame *a.* (-*er*, -*est*) (of animals) gentle and not afraid of human beings; docile; not exciting. —*v.t.* make tame or manageable. **tamely** *adv.*, **tameness** *n.*

tamer *n.* person who tames and trains wild animals.

Tamil *n.* member or language of a people of south India and Sri Lanka.

tam-o'-shanter *n.* beret with a soft full top.

tamp *v.t.* pack down tightly.

tamper *v.i.* ~ **with,** meddle or interfere with.

tampon *n.* plug of absorbent material inserted into the body.

tan *v.t./i.* (p.t. *tanned*) convert (hide) into leather by treating it with tannin or mineral salts; make or become brown by exposure to sun; (*sl.*) thrash. —*n.* yellowish-brown; brown colour in sun-tanned skin; tree-bark used in tanning hides. —*a.* yellowish-brown.

tandem *n.* bicycle with seats and pedals for two or more people one behind another. —*adv.* one behind another. **in** ~, arranged thus.

tang *n.* strong taste or flavour or smell; projection by which a knife-blade etc. is held in its handle. **tangy** *a.*

tangent *n.* straight line that touches the outside of a curve without intersecting it. **go off at a** ~, diverge suddenly from a line of thought etc. **tangential** *a.*

tangerine /-'rin/ *n.* a kind of small orange; its colour.

tangible *a.* able to be perceived by touch; clear and definite, real. **tangibly** *adv.*, **tangibility** *n.*

tangle *v.t./i.* twist into a confused mass; entangle; become involved in conflict with. —*n.* tangled mass or condition.

tango *n.* (pl. -*os*) ballroom dance with gliding steps.

tank *n.* large container for liquid or gas; armoured fighting vehicle moving on caterpillar tracks.

tankard *n.* large one-handled usu. metal drinking-vessel.

tanker *n.* ship or aircraft or vehicle for carrying liquid in bulk.

tanner *n.* person who tans hides into leather.

tannery *n.* place where hides are tanned into leather.

tannic *a.* ~ **acid,** tannin.

tannin *n.* substance obtained from tree-barks etc. (also found in tea), used in tanning and dyeing.

tansy *n.* plant with yellow flowers.

tantalize *v.t.* torment by the sight of something desired but kept out of reach or withheld.

tantamount *a.* equivalent.

tantrum *n.* outburst of bad temper.

tap[1] *n.* tubular plug with a device for allowing liquid to flow through; connection for tapping a telephone. —*v.t.* (p.t. *tapped*) fit a tap into; draw off through a tap or incision; obtain supplies etc. or information from; cut a screw-thread in (a cavity); fit a listening device in (a telephone circuit). **on** ~, available for use. ~**-root** *n.* plant's chief root.

tap[2] *v.t./i.* (p.t. *tapped*) knock gently. —*n.* light blow; sound of this. ~**-dance** *n.* dance in which the feet tap an elaborate rhythm.

tape *n.* narrow strip of woven cotton etc. for tying or fastening or labelling things; pieces of this stretched across a race-track at the finishing-line; narrow continuous strip of paper etc.; magnetic tape; tape-measure; tape-recording. —*v.t.* tie or fasten with tape; record on magnetic tape. **have a thing taped,** (*sl.*) understand it fully, have an organized method of dealing with it. ~**-measure** *n.* strip of tape or flexible metal etc. marked for measuring length. ~**-recorder** *n.* apparatus for recording and playing back sounds on magnetic tape. ~**-recording** *n.*

taper *n.* thin candle; wax-coated wick for conveying flame. —*v.t./i.* make or become gradually narrower. ~ **off,** diminish.

tapestry *n.* textile fabric woven or embroidered ornamentally.

tapeworm *n.* tape-like worm living as a parasite in intestines.

tapioca *n.* starchy grains obtained from cassava, used in making puddings.

tapir /'teɪpə(r)/ *n.* small pig-like animal with a long snout.

tappet *n.* projection used in machinery to tap against something.

tar *n.* thick dark inflammable liquid distilled from wood or coal etc.; similar substance formed by burning tobacco. —*v.t.* (p.t. *tarred*) coat with tar.

tarantula /-'ræn-/ *n.* large black south European spider; large hairy tropical spider.

tardy *a.* (-*ier*, -*iest*) slow to act or move or happen; behind time. **tardily** *adv.*, **tardiness** *n.*

tare[1] /teə(r)/ *n.* a kind of vetch.

tare[2] /teə(r)/ *n.* allowance for the weight of the container or vehicle weighed with the goods it holds.

target *n.* object or mark to be hit in shooting etc.; person or thing against which criticism is directed; objective, minimum result desired.

tariff *n.* list of fixed charges; duty to be paid.

Tarmac *n.* [P.] broken stone or slag mixed with tar. **tarmac** *n.* area surfaced with this. **tarmacked** *a.*

tarn *n.* small mountain lake.

tarnish *v.t./i.* lose or cause (metal) to lose lustre; blemish (a reputation). —*n.* loss of lustre; blemish.

tarot /ˈtærəʊ/ *n.* game played with a pack of 78 cards which are also used for fortune-telling.

tarpaulin *n.* waterproof canvas.

tarragon *n.* aromatic herb.

tarry[1] /ˈtɑr-/ *a.* of or like tar.

tarry[2] /ˈtæ-/ *v.i.* (*old use*) delay.

tarsier *n.* small monkey-like animal of the East Indies.

tart[1] *a.* (-*er*, -*est*) acid in taste or manner. **tartly** *adv.*, **tartness** *n.*

tart[2] *n.* pie with fruit or sweet filling; piece of pastry with jam etc. on top; (*sl.*) prostitute. —*v.t.* ~ **up**, (*colloq.*) dress gaudily, smarten up.

tartan *n.* pattern (orig. of a Scottish clan) with coloured stripes crossing at right angles; cloth with this.

tartar *n.* hard deposit forming on teeth; deposit formed by fermentation in a wine-cask.

Tartar *n.* member of a group of Central Asian peoples; bad-tempered or difficult person.

tartare *a.* ~ **sauce**, sauce of mayonnaise, chopped gherkins, etc.

task *n.* piece of work to be done. —*v.t.* make great demands upon (a person's powers). **take to** ~, rebuke. ~ **force**, group specially organized for a special task.

taskmaster *n.* person considered with regard to the way he imposes tasks.

tassel *n.* ornamental bunch of hanging threads; tassel-like head of maize etc. **tasselled** *a.*

taste *n.* sensation caused in the tongue by things placed upon it; ability to perceive this; small quantity (of food or drink); slight experience; liking; ability to perceive and enjoy what is beautiful or to know what is fitting. —*v.t./i.* discover or test the flavour of in one's mouth; have a certain flavour; experience. **taster** *n.*

tasteful *a.* showing good taste. **tastefully** *adv.*, **tastefulness** *n.*

tasteless *a.* having no flavour; showing poor taste. **tastelessly** *adv.*, **tastelessness** *n.*

tasty *a.* (-*ier*, -*iest*) having a strong flavour, appetizing.

tat[1] *v.t./i.* (p.t. *tatted*) do or make by tatting.

tat[2] *see* **tit**[2].

tattered *a.* ragged.

tatters *n.pl.* torn pieces.

tatting *n.* a kind of lace made by hand with a small shuttle; process of making this.

tattle *v.i.* chatter idly, reveal information thus. —*n.* idle chatter.

tattoo[1] *n.* drum or bugle signal recalling soldiers to quarters in the evening; elabora-tion of this with music and marching, as an entertainment; tapping sound.

tattoo[2] *v.t.* mark (skin) by puncturing it and inserting pigments; make (a pattern) thus. —*n.* tattooed pattern.

tatty *a.* (-*ier*, -*iest*) ragged, shabby and untidy; tawdry. **tattily** *adv.*, **tattiness** *n.*

taught *see* **teach.**

taunt *v.t.* jeer at provocatively. —*n.* taunting remark.

taut *a.* stretched firmly, not slack.

tauten *v.t./i.* make or become taut.

tautology *n.* pleonasm, esp. using a word or phrase of the same grammatical function (e.g. *free, gratis, and for nothing*). **tautological** *a.*, **tautologous** *a.*

tavern *n.* (*old use*) inn, public house.

tawdry *a.* (-*ier*, -*iest*) showy but without real value. **tawdrily** *adv.*, **tawdriness** *n.*

tawny *a.* orange-brown.

tax *n.* money to be paid by people or firms to a government; thing that makes a heavy demand. —*v.t.* impose a tax on; require to pay tax; make heavy demands on; pay tax on. ~ **with**, accuse of. **taxation** *n.*, **taxable** *a.*

taxi *n.* (pl. -*is*) car that plies for hire. —*v.i.* (p.t. *taxied*, pres.p. *taxiing*) (of an aircraft) move along ground or water under its own power. ~-**cab** *n.* taxi.

taxidermy /ˈtæks-/ *n.* process of preparing, stuffing, and mounting the skins of animals in lifelike form. **taxidermist** *n.*

taxonomy *n.* scientific classification of organisms. **taxonomist** *n.*

taxpayer *n.* person who pays tax (esp. income tax).

T.B. *abbr.* (*colloq.*) tuberculosis.

tea *n.* dried leaves of a tropical evergreen shrub; hot drink made by infusing these (or other substances) in boiling water; afternoon or early evening meal at which tea is drunk. ~-**bag** *n.* small porous bag holding a portion of tea for infusion. ~-**break** *n.* interruption of work allowed for drinking tea. ~-**chest** *n.* wooden box in which tea is exported. ~-**leaf** *n.* leaf of tea, esp. after infusion. ~-**rose** *n.* rose with scent like tea. ~-**set** *n.* set of cups and plates etc. for serving tea. ~-**shop** *n.* shop where·tea is served to the public. ~-**towel** *n.* towel for drying washed crockery etc.

teacake *n.* bun for serving toasted and buttered.

teach *v.t./i.* (p.t. *taught*) impart information or skill to (a person) or about (a subject); put forward as a fact or principle; (*colloq.*) deter by punishment. **teachable** *a.*, **teacher** *n.*

teacup *n.* cup from which tea is drunk.

teak *n.* strong heavy wood of an Asian evergreen tree; this tree.

teal *n.* (pl. *teal*) a kind of duck.

team *n.* set of players; set of people working together; animals harnessed to draw a vehicle etc. —*v.t./i.* combine into a team or set. ~-**work** *n.* organized co-operation.

teapot *n.* vessel with a spout, in which tea is made.

tear[1] /teə(r)/ *v.t./i.* (p.t. *tore*, p.p. *torn*) pull forcibly apart or away or to pieces; make (a hole etc.) thus; become torn; run, walk, or travel hurriedly. —*n.* hole etc. torn.

tear[2] /tɪə(r)/ *n.* drop of liquid forming in the eye from grief or other emotion or irritation by fumes etc. **in tears,** with tears flowing. **~-gas** *n.* gas causing severe irritation of the eyes.

tearaway *n.* impetuous hooligan.

tearful *a.* shedding or ready to shed tears. **tearfully** *adv.*

tearing *a.* violent, overwhelming.

tease *v.t.* try to provoke in a playful or unkind way; pick into separate strands; brush up nap on (cloth). —*n.* person fond of teasing others.

teasel *n.* plant with bristly heads; device for brushing nap.

teaser *n.* (*colloq.*) difficult problem.

teaspoon *n.* small spoon for stirring tea etc.; amount held by this. **teaspoonful** *n.* (pl. *-fuls*).

teat *n.* nipple on a milk-secreting organ; device of rubber etc. on a feeding-bottle, through which the contents are sucked.

technical *a.* of the mechanical arts and applied sciences; of a particular subject or craft etc.; using technical terms; in a strict legal sense. **technically** *adv.*, **technicality** *n.*

technician *n.* expert in the techniques of a subject or craft; skilled mechanic.

technique /-'niːk/ *n.* method of doing or performing something.

technology *n.* study of mechanical arts and applied sciences; these subjects; their application in industry etc. **technological** *a.*, **technologically** *adv.*, **technologist** *n.*

teddy-bear *n.* toy bear.

tedious /'tiː-/ *a.* tiresome because of length, slowness, or dullness. **tediously** *adv.*, **tediousness** *n.*, **tedium** *n.*

tee *n.* cleared space from which a golf-ball is driven at the start of play; small heap of sand or piece of wood for supporting this ball; mark aimed at in quoits, bowls, and curling. —*v.t.* (p.t. *teed*) place (a ball) on a tee.

teem[1] *v.i.* be full of; be present in large numbers.

teem[2] *v.i.* (of water or rain) pour.

teenager *n.* person in his or her teens.

teens *n.pl.* years of age from 13 to 19. **teen-age** *a.*, **teen-aged** *a.*

teeny *a.* (*-ier, -iest*) (*colloq.*) tiny.

tee-shirt *n.* = T-shirt.

teeter *v.i.* stand or move unsteadily.

teeth *see* **tooth.**

teethe *v.i.* (of a baby) have its first teeth appear through the gums. **teething troubles,** problems in the early stages of an enterprise.

teetotal *a.* abstaining completely from alcohol. **teetotaller** *n.*

telecommunications *n.pl.* means of communication over long distances, by telephone, radio, etc.

telegram *n.* message sent by telegraph.

telegraph *n.* system or apparatus for sending written messages, esp. by electrical impulses along wires. —*v.t.* send (a message) or communicate with (a person) thus.

telegraphist /-'leg-/ *n.* person employed in telegraphy.

telegraphy /-'leg-/ *n.* communication by telegraph. **telegraphic** *a.*

telepathy /-'lep-/ *n.* communication between minds other than by the known senses. **telepathic** *a.*, **telepath** /'tel-/, **telepathist** /-'lep-/ *ns.*

telephone *n.* system of transmitting speech etc. by wire or radio; instrument used in this. —*v.t.* send (a message) or speak to (a person) by telephone. **telephonic** /-'fon-/ *a.*, **telephony** /-'lef-/ *n.*

telephonist /-'lef-/ *n.* operator at a telephone exchange or switchboard.

telephoto *a.* **~ lens,** lens producing a large image of a distant object for photography.

teleprinter *n.* telegraph instrument for sending and receiving typewritten messages.

telescope *n.* optical instrument for making distant objects appear larger. —*v.t./i.* make or become shorter by sliding each adjacent section inside the next; compress or become compressed forcibly. **telescopic** *a.*, **telescopically** *adv.*

televise *v.t.* transmit by television.

television *n.* system for reproducing on a screen a view of scenes etc. by radio transmission; televised programmes; (also **~ set**) apparatus with a screen for receiving these.

telex *n.* system of telegraphy using teleprinters and public transmission lines. —*v.t.* send (a message) or communicate with (a person) by telex.

tell *v.t./i.* (p.t. *told*) make known, esp. in written or spoken words; give information to; utter; reveal a secret; decide; distinguish; produce an effect; count; direct, order. **~ off,** (*colloq.*) reprimand; count off or detach for duty. **~-tale** *n.* person who tells tales; mechanical indicator. **~ tales,** reveal secrets.

teller *n.* person giving an account of something; person appointed to count votes; bank cashier.

telling *a.* having a noticeable effect.

telly *n.* (*colloq.*) television.

temerity /-'me-/ *n.* audacity.

temp *n.* (*colloq.*) temporary employee.

temper *n.* state of mind as regards calmness or anger; fit of anger; calmness under provocation; condition of tempered metal. —*v.t.* bring (metal or clay) to the required hardness or consistency; moderate the effects of.

temperament *n.* person's nature as it controls his behaviour.

temperamental *a.* of or in temperament; having fits of excitable or moody behaviour. **temperamentally** *adv.*

temperance *n.* self-restraint; total abstinence from alcohol.

temperate *a.* self-restrained, moderate; (of climate) without extremes of heat and cold. **temperately** *adv.*

temperature *n.* intensity of heat or cold, esp. as

shown by a thermometer; body temperature above normal.

tempest *n.* violent storm.

tempestuous *a.* stormy.

template *n.* pattern or gauge for cutting metal, stone, etc.

temple[1] *n.* building dedicated to the presence or service of god(s). **Inner Temple, Middle Temple**, two Inns of Court in London.

temple[2] *n.* flat part between forehead and ear.

tempo *n.* (pl. *-os* or *-i*) time, speed, or rhythm of a piece of music; rate of motion or activity.

temporal *a.* secular; of or denoting time; of the temple(s) of the head.

temporary *a.* lasting for a limited time, not permanent. **temporarily** *adv.*

temporize *v.i.* avoid committing oneself in order to gain time. **temporization** *n.*

tempt *v.t.* persuade or try to persuade by the prospect of pleasure or advantage; arouse a desire in; risk provoking (fate) by rashness. **temptation** *n.*, **tempter** *n.*, **temptress** *n.fem.*

ten *a.* & *n.* one more than nine (10, X).

tenable /ˈten-/ *a.* able to be defended; (of an office) able to be held. **tenability** *n.*

tenacious *a.* holding or clinging or sticking firmly. **tenaciously** *adv.*, **tenacity** *n.*

tenancy /ˈten-/ *n.* use of land or a building etc. as a tenant.

tenant *n.* person who rents land or a building etc. from a landlord; (in law) occupant, owner.

tenantry /ˈten-/ *n.* tenants.

tench *n.* (pl. *tench*) fish of the carp family.

tend[1] *v.t.* take care of.

tend[2] *v.i.* have a specified tendency.

tendency *n.* way a person or thing is likely to be or behave or become; thing's direction.

tendentious *a.* aimed at helping a cause, not impartial.

tender[1] *a.* not tough or hard; easily damaged, delicate; painful when touched; easily moved to pity or sympathy; loving, gentle. **tenderly** *adv.*, **tenderness** *n.*

tender[2] *v.t./i.* offer formally; make a tender for. —*n.* formal offer to supply goods or carry out work at a stated price. **legal ∼**, currency that must, by law, be accepted in payment.

tender[3] *n.* vessel or vehicle conveying goods or passengers to and from a larger one; truck attached to a steam locomotive, carrying fuel and water etc.

tenderfoot *n.* inexperienced person.

tenderize *v.t.* make more tender.

tenderloin *n.* middle part of pork loin.

tendon *n.* strip of strong tissue connecting a muscle to a bone etc.

tendril *n.* thread-like part by which a climbing plant clings; slender curl of hair etc.

tenement *n.* dwelling-house; large house let in portions to tenants; rented flat or room.

tenet /ˈten-/ *n.* firm belief or principle.

tenfold *a.* & *adv.* ten times as much or as many.

tenner *n.* (*colloq.*) £10.

tennis *n.* ball-game played with rackets over a net, with a soft ball on an open court (*lawn*

tennis) or with a hard ball in a walled court (*real tennis*).

tenon *n.* projection shaped to fit into a mortise.

tenor *n.* general course or meaning; highest ordinary adult male singing-voice; music for this. —*a.* of tenor pitch.

tenpin *a.* ∼ **bowling**, game similar to ninepins.

tense[1] *n.* any of the forms of a verb that indicate the time of the action.

tense[2] *a.* (*-er*, *-est*) stretched tightly; with muscles tight in anticipation. —*v.t./i.* make or become tense. **tensely** *adv.*, **tenseness** *n.*

tensile /-saɪl/ *a.* of tension; capable of being stretched.

tension *n.* stretching; tenseness, esp. of feelings; effect produced by forces pulling against each other; electromotive force; unit of measurement in knitting.

tent *n.* portable shelter or dwelling made of canvas etc.

tentacle *n.* slender flexible part of certain animals, used for feeling or grasping things.

tentative /ˈten-/ *a.* hesitant, not definite; done as a trial. **tentatively** *adv.*

tenterhooks *n.pl.* **on ∼**, in suspense because of uncertainty.

tenth *a.* & *n.* next after ninth. **tenthly** *adv.*

tenuous *a.* very thin; very slight. **tenuousness** *n.*, **tenuity** /-ˈnju-/ *n.*

tenure /ˈten-/ *n.* holding of office or of land or accommodation etc.

tepid *a.* slightly warm, lukewarm. **tepidity** *n.*

tercentenary /-ˈtin-/ *n.* 300th anniversary.

term *n.* time for which something lasts, fixed or limited period; period of weeks during which instruction is given in a school etc. or in which a lawcourt holds sessions; each quantity or expression in a mathematical series or ratio etc.; word or phrase; (*pl.*) stipulations, conditions offered or accepted; (*pl.*) relation between people.

termagant *n.* bullying woman.

terminable *a.* able to be terminated.

terminal *a.* of or forming an end; of or in the last stage of a fatal disease; of or done each term. —*n.* terminating point or part; terminus; building where air passengers arrive and depart; point of connection in an electric circuit or device, or of input or output to a computer etc. **terminally** *adv.*

terminate *v.t./i.* end. **termination** *n.*

terminology *n.* technical terms of a subject. **terminological** *a.*

terminus *n.* (pl. *-i*) end; last stopping-place.

termite *n.* small insect that is very destructive to timber.

tern *n.* sea-bird with long wings.

terrace *n.* raised level place, esp. one of a series; paved area beside a house; row of houses joined by party walls.

terracotta *n.* brownish-red unglazed pottery; its colour.

terra firma dry land, the ground.

terrain /-ˈreɪn/ *n.* land with regard to its natural features.

terrapin *n.* edible freshwater tortoise.

terrestrial /-'res-/ *a.* of the earth; of or living on land.

terrible *a.* appalling, distressing; (*colloq.*) very bad. **terribly** *adv.*

terrier *n.* small active dog.

terrific *a.* (*colloq.*) of great size; excellent. **terrifically** *adv.*

terrify *v.t.* fill with terror.

terrine /-'rin/ *n.* pâté or similar food; earthenware dish for this.

territorial *a.* of territory.

Territorial *n.* member of the ∼ **Army, a** volunteer reserve force.

territory *n.* land under the control of a person or State or city etc.; sphere of action or thought; *T*∼, area forming part of the U.S.A., Australia, or Canada, but not ranking as a State or province.

terror *n.* extreme fear; terrifying person or thing; (*colloq.*) troublesome person or thing.

terrorism *n.* use of violence and intimidation. **terrorist** *n.*

terrorize *v.t.* fill with terror; coerce by terrorism. **terrorization** *n.*

terry *a.* looped cotton fabric used for towels etc.

terse *a.* concise, curt. **tersely** *adv.*, **terseness** *n.*

tertiary /'tɜ:ʃəri/ *a.* next after secondary.

tessellated *a.* resembling mosaic.

test *n.* something done to discover a person's or thing's qualities or abilities etc.; examination (esp. in a school) on a limited subject; (*colloq.*) test match. —*v.t.* subject to a test. ∼ **match,** one of a series of cricket or Rugby football matches between teams of certain countries. ∼**tube** *n.* tube of thin glass with one end closed, used in laboratories. **tester** *n.*

testament *n.* a will; written statement of beliefs. **Old Testament,** books of the Bible telling the history and beliefs of the Jews. **New Testament,** those telling the life and teachings of Christ.

testamentary /-'men-/ *a.* of or given in a person's will.

testate *a.* having left a valid will at death.

testator /-'teɪ-/ *n.* person who has made a will. **testatrix** *n.fem.*

testes *see* **testis.**

testicle *n.* male organ that secretes spermbearing fluid (in man, each of the two enclosed in the scrotum, behind the penis).

testify *v.t./i.* bear witness to; give evidence; be evidence of.

testimonial *n.* formal statement testifying to character, abilities, etc.; gift showing appreciation.

testimony *n.* declaration (esp. under oath); supporting evidence.

testis *n.* (pl. *testes*) testicle.

testy *a.* irritable. **testily** *adv.*

tetanus /'tet-/ *n.* disease in which muscles contract and stiffen, caused by bacteria.

tetchy *a.* peevish, irritable.

tête-à-tête /teɪtɑ'teɪt/ *n.* private conversation, esp. between two people. —*a. & adv.* together in private.

tether *n.* rope etc. fastening an animal so that it can graze. —*v.t.* fasten with a tether. **at the end of one's** ∼, having reached the limit of one's endurance.

tetrahedron /-'hi-/ *n.* solid with four sides, pyramid with a triangular base.

Teutonic /tju'ton-/ *a.* of Germanic peoples or their languages.

text *n.* wording; main body of a book as distinct from illustrations or notes etc.; sentence from Scripture used as the subject of a sermon; book prescribed for study. **textual** *a.*

textbook *n.* book of information for use in studying a subject.

textile *n.* woven or machine-knitted fabric. —*a.* of textiles.

texture *n.* way a fabric etc. feels to the touch.

thalidomide /-'lɪd-/ *n.* sedative drug found to have caused malformation of babies' limbs.

than *conj.* used to introduce the second element in a comparison.

thank *v.t.* express gratitude to. ∼**offering** *n.* offering made as an act of thanks. ∼ **you,** polite expression of thanks. **thanks** *n.pl.* expressions of gratitude (*colloq.*) thank you. **thanks to,** on account of, because of.

thankful *a.* feeling or expressing gratitude. **thankfully** *adv.*

thankless *a.* not likely to win thanks.

thanksgiving *n.* expression of gratitude, esp. to God.

that *a. & pron.* (pl. *those*) the (person or thing) referred to; further or less obvious (one) of two. —*adv.* to such an extent. —*rel.pron.* used to introduce a defining clause. —*conj.* introducing a dependent clause.

thatch *n.* roof made of straw or reeds etc. —*v.t.* roof with thatch. **thatcher** *n.*

thaw *v.t./i.* pass into an unfrozen state; become less cool or less formal in manner; cause to thaw. —*n.* thawing, weather that thaws ice etc.

the *a.* applied to a noun standing for a specific person or thing, or one or all of a kind, or (pr. ðɪ) used to emphasize excellence or importance; (of prices) per. —*adv.* in that degree, by that amount.

theatre *n.* building or outdoor structure for the performance of plays etc.; room or hall for lectures etc. with seats in tiers; room where surgical operations are performed; plays and acting; (of weapons) intermediate between tactical and strategic.

theatrical *a.* of or for the theatre; exaggerated for effect. **theatricals** *n.pl.* theatrical (esp. amateur) performances. **theatrically** *adv.*

thee *pron.* objective case of *thou.*

theft *n.* stealing.

their *a.,* **theirs** *poss. pron.* belonging to them.

them *pron.* objective case of *they.*

theme *n.* subject being discussed; melody which is repeated. **thematic** /-'mæt-/ *a.*

themselves *pron.* emphatic and reflexive form of *they* and *them.*

then *adv.* at that time; next, and also; in that case. —*a. & n.* (of) that time.

thence *adv*. from that place or source.

thenceforth *adv*. from then on.

theodolite /θɪ'ɒd-/ *n*. surveying instrument for measuring angles.

theology *n*. study or system of religion. **theological** *a*., **theologian** /-'ləʊ-/ *n*.

theorem *n*. mathematical statement to be proved by reasoning.

theoretical *a*. based on theory only. **theoretically** *adv*.

theorist *n*. person who theorizes.

theorize *v.i*. form theories.

theory *n*. set of ideas formulated to explain something; opinion, supposition; statement of the principles of a subject.

theosophy /-'ɒs-/ *n*. system of philosophy that aims at direct knowledge of God by spiritual ecstasy and contemplation. **theosophical** *a*.

therapeutic /θerə'pju-/ *a*. curative. **therapeutically** *adv*.

therapist *n*. specialist in therapy.

therapy *n*. curative treatment; physiotherapy; psychotherapy.

there *adv*. in, at, or to that place; at that point; in that matter; introducing a sentence where the verb comes before its subject. —*n*. that place. —*int*. exclamation of satisfaction or dismay or consolation.

thereabouts *adv*. near there.

thereafter *adv*. after that.

thereby *adv*. by that means.

therefore *adv*. for that reason.

thereof *adv*. of that.

thereto *adv*. to that.

thereupon *adv*. in consequence of that, because of that.

therm *n*. unit of heat esp. in a gas supply (= 100,000 thermal units).

thermal *a*. of or using heat; warm, hot. —*n*. rising current of hot air.

thermionic *a*. ∼ **valve**, vacuum tube in which heated electrodes emit a flow of electrons.

thermodynamics *n*. science of the relationship between heat and other forms of energy.

thermometer *n*. instrument (esp. a graduated glass tube) for measuring heat.

thermonuclear *a*. of or using nuclear reactions that occur only at very high temperatures.

thermoplastic *a*. & *n*. (substance) becoming soft when heated and hardening when cooled.

Thermos *n*. [P.] vacuum flask.

thermostat *n*. device that regulates temperature automatically. **thermostatic** *a*., **thermostatically** *adv*.

thesaurus /θɪ'sɔrəs/ *n*. (pl. -ri, pr. rɑɪ) comprehensive referencebook; dictionary of synonyms.

these *see* **this**.

thesis *n*. (pl. **theses**, pr. 'θisiz) theory put forward and supported by reasoning; lengthy written essay submitted for a university degree.

thews *n.pl*. muscular strength.

they *pron*. people or things mentioned or unspecified.

thick *a*. (-er, -est) of great or specified distance between opposite surfaces; broad; having units that are numerous or crowded, dense; fairly stiff in consistency; stupid; hoarse; (*colloq*.) on terms of close association. —*adv*. thickly. —*n*. busiest part. ∼**-skinned** *a*. not sensitive to criticism or snubs. **thickly** *adv*., **thickness** *n*.

thicken *v.t./i*. make or become thicker.

thicket *n*. close group of shrubs and small trees etc.

thickset *a*. set or growing close together; stocky, burly.

thief *n*. (pl. **thieves**) one who steals. **thievish** *a*., **thievery** *n*.

thieve *v.t./i*. be a thief; steal.

thigh *n*. upper part of the leg, between hip and knee.

thimble *n*. cap of metal etc. worn on the end of the finger to protect it in sewing.

thin *a*. (*thinner, thinnest*) of small thickness; not thick; lean, not plump; lacking substance, weak. —*adv*. thinly. —*v.t*. (p.t. *thinned*) make or become thinner. ∼ **out**, make or become fewer or less crowded. ∼**-skinned** *a*. over-sensitive to criticism or snubs. **thinly** *adv*., **thinness** *n*., **thinner** *n*.

thine *a*. & *poss.pron*. (*old use*) belonging to thee.

thing *n*. whatever is or may be perceived, known, or thought about; act, fact, idea, task, etc.; item; inanimate object; creature; (*pl*.) belongings, utensils, circumstances; *the* ∼, what is proper or fashionable.

think *v.t./i*. (p.t. **thought**) exercise the mind, form connected ideas; form or have as an idea or opinion or plan. —*n*. (*colloq*.) act of thinking. ∼ **better of it**, change one's mind after thought. ∼ **nothing of**, consider unremarkable. ∼ **over**, reach a decision by thinking. ∼**-tank** *n*. group providing ideas and advice on national or commercial problems. **thinker** *n*.

third *a*. next after second. —*n*. third thing, class, etc.; one of three equal parts. ∼ **degree**, (*U.S.*) long severe questioning by police. ∼ **rate** *a*. very inferior in quality. **Third World**, countries of Asia, Africa, and Latin America not politically aligned with Communist or Western nations. **thirdly** *adv*.

thirst *n*. feeling caused by a desire to drink; strong desire. —*v.i*. feel a thirst. **thirsty** *a*., **thirstily** *adv*.

thirteen *a*. & *n*. one more than twelve (13, XIII). **thirteenth** *a*. & *n*.

thirty *a*. three times ten (30, XXX). **thirtieth** *a*. & *n*.

this *a*. & *pron*. (pl. **these**) the (person or thing) near or present or mentioned; present day or time.

thistle *n*. prickly plant.

thistledown *n*. very light fluff on thistle seeds.

thither *adv*. (*old use*) to or towards that place.

thole *n*. peg set in a boat's gunwale to serve as a rowlock.

thong *n*. strip of leather used as a fastening or lash etc.

thorax *n*. part of the body between head or neck and abdomen. **thoracic** *a*.

thorn *n*. small sharp pointed projection on a plant; thorn-bearing tree or shrub. **thorny** *a*.

thorough *a*. complete in every way; detailed, not superficial. **thoroughly** *adv.*, **thoroughness** *n*.

thoroughbred *a*. & *n*. (horse etc.) bred of pure or pedigree stock.

thoroughfare *n*. public way open at both ends.

thoroughgoing *a*. thorough.

those *see* **that**.

thou *pron*. (*old use*) you.

though *conj*. in spite of the fact that, even supposing. —*adv.* (*colloq.*) however.

thought *see* **think**. —*n*. process or power or way of thinking; idea etc. produced by thinking; intention; consideration.

thoughtful *a*. thinking deeply; thought out carefully; considerate. **thoughtfully** *adv.*, **thoughtfulness** *n*.

thoughtless *a*. not alert to possible consequences; inconsiderate. **thoughtlessly** *adv.*, **thoughtlessness** *n*.

thousand *a*. & *n*. ten hundred (1000, M). **thousandth** *a*. & *n*.

thrall *n*. bondage. **thraldom** *n*.

thrash *v.t.* beat, esp. with a stick or whip; defeat thoroughly; thresh; make flailing movements. **~ out,** discuss thoroughly.

thread *n*. thin length of any substance; spun cotton or wool etc. used in sewing, knitting, or making cloth; thing compared to this; spiral ridge of a screw. —*v.t.* pass a thread through; pass (a strip) through or round something; make (one's way) through a crowd or streets etc. **threader** *n*.

threadbare *a*. with nap worn and threads visible; shabbily dressed.

threadworm *n*. small thread-like worm, esp. found in the rectum of children.

threat *n*. expression of intention to punish, hurt, or harm; person or thing thought likely to bring harm or danger.

threaten *v.t.* make or be a threat (to).

three *a*. & *n*. one more than two (3, III). **~quarter** *n*. player with a position just behind the half-backs in Rugby football.

threefold *a*. & *adv.* three times as much or as many.

threepence /θrep-/ *n*. sum of three pence. **threepenny** *a*.

threescore *n*. (*old use*) sixty.

threesome *n*. three together, trio.

thresh *v.t./i.* beat out (grain) from husks of corn; make flailing movements.

threshold *n*. piece of wood or stone forming the bottom of a doorway; point of entry; lowest limit at which a stimulus is perceptible; highest limit at which pain is bearable.

threw *see* **throw**.

thrice *adv*. (*old use*) three times.

thrift *n*. economical management of resources; plant with pink flowers. **thrifty** *a.*, **thriftily** *adv*.

thrill *n*. nervous tremor caused by emotion or sensation; wave of feeling or excitement. —*v.t./i.* feel or cause to feel a thrill.

thriller *n*. exciting story or play etc., esp. involving crime.

thrips *n*. (pl. *thrips*) insect harmful to plants.

thrive *v.i.* (p.t. *throve* or *thrived*, p.p. *thrived* or *thriven*) grow or develop well and vigorously; prosper.

throat *n*. front of the neck; passage from mouth to oesophagus or lungs; narrow passage.

throaty *a*. uttered deep in the throat; hoarse. **throatily** *adv*.

throb *v.i.* (p.t. *throbbed*) (of the heart or pulse) beat with more than usual force; vibrate or sound with a persistent rhythm. —*n*. throbbing beat or sound.

throes *n.pl.* severe pangs of pain. **in the ~ of,** struggling with the task of.

thrombosis *n*. formation of a clot of blood in a blood-vessel or organ of the body.

throne *n*. seat for a king, queen, or bishop etc. on ceremonial occasions; sovereign power.

throng *n*. crowded mass of people. —*v.t./i.* come or go or press in a throng; fill with a throng.

throstle *n*. a thrush.

throttle *n*. valve controlling the flow of fuel or steam etc. to an engine; lever controlling this. —*v.t.* strangle.

through *prep*. & *adv*. from end to end or side to side (of), entering at one point and coming out at another; among; from beginning to end (of); so as to have finished, so as to have passed (an examination); so as to be connected by telephone (to); by the agency, means, or fault of; (*U.S.*) up to and including. —*a*. going through; passing without stopping.

throughout *prep*. & *adv*. right through, from beginning to end (of).

throve *see* **thrive**.

throw *v.t.* (p.t. *threw*, p.p. *thrown*) send with some force through the air or in a certain direction; hurl to the ground; cause to fall; put (clothes etc.) on or off hastily; shape (pottery) on a wheel; cause to be in a certain state; (*colloq.*) disconcert; cause to extend; operate (a switch or lever); have (a fit or tantrum); (*colloq.*) give (a party). —*n*. act of throwing; distance something is thrown. **~ away,** part with as useless or unwanted; fail to make use of. **~-away** *a*. to be thrown away after use. **~-back** *n*. animal etc. showing characteristics of an ancestor that is earlier than its parents. **~ in the towel,** = throw up the sponge. **~ out,** discard; reject. **~ over,** desert, abandon. **~ up,** raise, erect; bring to notice; resign from; vomit. **~ up the sponge,** admit defeat or failure. **thrower** *n*.

thrum *v.t./i.* (p.t. *thrummed*) strum, sound monotonously. —*n*. thrumming sound.

thrush[1] *n*. song-bird, esp. one with a speckled breast.

thrush[2] *n*. fungoid infection of the throat (esp. in children); similar infection of the vagina.

thrust *v.t./i.* (p.t. *thrust*) push forcibly; make

a forward stroke with a sword etc. —*n.* thrusting movement or force; hostile remark aimed at a person etc.

thud *n.* dull low sound like that of a blow. —*v.i.* (p.t. *thudded*) make or fall with a thud.

thug *n.* vicious ruffian.

thumb *n.* short thick finger set apart from the other four. —*v.t.* wear or soil or turn (pages etc.) with the thumbs; request (a lift) by signalling with one's thumb. **~-index** *n.* set of marked notches showing where to open a book to find a particular section. **under the ~ of,** completely under the influence of.

thumbscrew *n.* former instrument of torture for squeezing the thumb; screw turned by the thumb.

thump *v.t./i.* strike or knock heavily (esp. with the fist), thud. —*n.* heavy blow; sound of thumping.

thumping *a.* (*colloq.*) large.

thunder *n.* loud noise that accompanies lightning; similar sound. —*v.t./i.* sound with or like thunder; utter loudly; make a forceful attack in words. **steal a person's ~,** forestall him. **thundery** *a.*

thunderbolt *n.* imaginary missile thought of as sent to earth with a lightning-flash; startling formidable event or statement.

thunderclap *n.* clap of thunder.

thunderous *a.* like thunder.

thunderstorm *n.* storm accompanied by thunder.

thunderstruck *a.* amazed.

Thursday *n.* day after Wednesday.

thus *adv.* in this way; as a result of this; to this extent.

thwack *v.t./i.* strike with a heavy blow. —*n.* this blow or sound.

thwart *v.t.* prevent from doing what is intended or from being accomplished. —*n.* oarsman's bench across a boat.

thy *a.* (*old use*) belonging to thee.

thyme /taɪm/ *n.* herb with fragrant leaves.

thymus *n.* ductless gland near the base of the neck.

thyroid *a. & n.* **~ gland,** large ductless gland in the neck.

thyself *pron.* emphatic and reflexive form of *thou* and *thee.*

tiara /tɪˈɑː-/ *n.* woman's jewelled crescent-shaped head-dress.

tic *n.* involuntary muscular twitch.

tick[1] *n.* regular clicking sound, esp. made by a clock or watch; (*colloq.*) moment; small mark placed against an item in a list etc., esp. to show that it is correct. —*v.t./i.* (of a clock etc.) make a series of ticks; mark with a tick. **~ off,** (*sl.*) reprimand. **~ over,** (of an engine) idle. **~-tack** *n.* semaphore signalling by racecourse bookmakers. **~-tock** *n.* ticking of a large clock.

tick[2] *n.* blood-sucking mite or parasitic insect.

tick[3] *n.* case of a mattress or pillow etc., holding the filling.

tick[4] *n.* (*colloq.*) financial credit.

ticker *n.* (*colloq.*) watch; teleprinter; (*joc.*) heart. **~-tape** *n.* (*U.S.*) paper tape from a teleprinter etc.

ticket *n.* marked piece of card or paper entitling the holder to a certain right (e.g. to travel by train etc.); certificate of qualification as a ship's master or pilot etc.; label; notification of a traffic offence; *the ~,* (*sl.*) the correct or desirable thing. —*v.t.* (p.t. *ticketed*) put a ticket on.

ticking *n.* strong fabric for making ticks for mattresses, pillows, etc.

tickle *v.t./i.* touch or stroke lightly so as to cause a slight tingling sensation; feel this sensation; amuse, please. —*n.* act or sensation of tickling.

ticklish *a.* sensitive to tickling; (of a problem) requiring careful handling.

tidal *a.* of or affected by tides.

tidbit *n.* (*U.S.*) titbit.

tiddler *n.* (*colloq.*) small fish, esp. stickleback or minnow; unusually small thing.

tiddly-winks *n.pl.* game of flicking small counters into a receptacle.

tide *n.* sea's regular rise and fall; trend of feeling or events etc.; (*old use*) season. —*v.t./i.* float with the tide. **~ over,** help temporarily.

tidings *n.pl.* news.

tidy *a.* (-*ier*, -*iest*) neat and orderly; (*colloq.*) considerable. —*v.t.* make tidy. **tidily** *adv.*, **tidiness** *n.*

tie *v.t./i.* (pres.p. *tying*) attach or fasten with cord etc.; form into a knot or bow; unite; make the same score as another competitor; restrict, limit. —*n.* cord etc. used for tying something; strip of material worn below the collar and knotted at the front of the neck; thing that unites or restricts; equality of score between competitors; sports match between two of a set of teams or players. **~-clip** *n.,* **~-pin** *n.* ornamental clip or pin for holding a necktie in place. **~ in,** link or (of information etc.) agree or be connected with something else. **~ up,** fasten with cord etc.; make (money etc.) not readily available for use; occupy fully. **~-up** *n.* connection, link.

tied *a.* (of a public house) bound to supply only one brewer's beer; (of a house) for occupation only by a person working for its owner.

tier *n.* any of a series of rows or ranks or units of a structure placed one above the other.

tiff *n.* petty quarrel.

tiffin *n.* midday meal in India etc.

tiger *n.* large striped animal of the cat family. **~-cat** *n.* animal resembling this; large Australian marsupial cat. **~-lily** *n.* orange lily with dark spots.

tight *a.* (-*er*, -*est*) held or fastened firmly, fitting closely, hard to move or undo; with things or people arranged closely together; tense, strict, with nothing slack or spare; (of money etc.) severely restricted; stingy; (*colloq.*) drunk. —*adv.* tightly. **~ corner,** difficult situation. **~-fisted** *a.* stingy. **tightly** *adv.,* **tightness** *n.*

tighten *v.t./i.* make or become tighter.

tightrope *n.* tightly stretched rope on which acrobats perform.

tights *n.pl.* garment (esp. worn in place of stockings) covering the legs and lower part of the body.

tigress *n.* female tiger.

tile *n.* thin slab of baked clay etc. used in rows for covering roofs, walls, or floors. —*v.t.* cover with tiles.

till[1] *v.t.* prepare and use (land) for growing crops.

till[2] *prep. & conj.* up to (a specified time).

till[3] *n.* receptacle for money behind the counter in a shop or bank etc.

tiller *n.* bar by which a rudder is turned.

tilt *v.t./i.* move into a sloping position; run or thrust with a lance in jousting. —*n.* process of tilting; sloping position. **at full ~,** at full speed or force.

timber *n.* wood prepared for use in building or carpentry; trees suitable for this; piece of wood or wooden beam used in constructing a house or ship.

timbered *a.* constructed of timber or with a timber framework; (of land) wooded.

timbre /ˈtæbr/ *n.* characteristic quality of the sound of a voice or instrument.

time *n.* all the years of the past, present, and future; point or portion of this; occasion, instance; allotted or available or measured time; rhythm in music; (*pl.*) contemporary circumstances; (*pl.*, in multiplication or comparison) taken a number of times. —*v.t.* choose the time for; measure the time taken by. **behind the times,** out of date. **for the ~ being,** until another arrangement is made. **from ~ to ~,** at intervals. **in no ~,** very rapidly. **in ~,** not late; eventually. **on ~,** punctually. **~ bomb,** bomb that can be set to explode after an interval. **~ exposure,** long photographic exposure. **~-honoured** *a.* respected because of antiquity, traditional. **~ lag** *n.* interval between two connected events. **~ zone,** region (between parallels of longitude) where a common standard time is used.

timekeeper *n.* person who times something or records workmen's hours of work; person in respect of punctuality; clock or watch in respect of accuracy.

timeless *a.* not affected by the passage of time. **timelessness** *n.*

timely *a.* occurring at just the right time. **timeliness** *n.*

timepiece *n.* clock or watch.

timer *n.* person or device that measures the time taken.

timetable *n.* list showing the times at which certain events take place.

timid *a.* easily alarmed, not bold, shy. **timidly** *adv.,* **timidity** *n.*

timing *n.* way something is timed.

timorous *a.* timid. **timorously** *adv.,* **timorousness** *n.*

timpani /ˈtɪmpəni/ *n.pl.* kettledrums. **timpanist** *n.*

tin *n.* silvery-white metal; (also **~ plate**) iron or steel sheets coated with tin; box or other container made of this, one in which food is sealed for preservation. —*v.t.* (p.t. *tinned*) coat with tin; seal (food) into a tin. **~-pan alley,** world of the composers and publishers etc. of popular music. **tinny** *a.*

tincture *n.* solution of a medicinal substance in alcohol; slight tinge. —*v.t.* tinge.

tinder *n.* any dry substance that catches fire easily

tine /taɪn/ *n.* prong or point of a fork, harrow, or antler.

tinge *v.t.* (pres.p. *tingeing*) colour slightly; give a slight trace of an element or quality to. —*n.* slight colouring or trace.

tingle *v.i.* have a slight pricking or stinging sensation. —*n.* this sensation.

tinker *n.* travelling mender of pots and pans; mischievous person or animal. —*v.i.* work at something casually trying to repair or improve it.

tinkle *n.* series of short light ringing sounds. —*v.t./i.* make or cause to make a tinkle.

tinpot *a.* (*derog.*) cheap, inferior.

tinsel *n.* glittering decorative metallic strips or threads.

tint *n.* variety or slight trace of a colour. —*v.t.* colour slightly.

tiny *a.* (*-ier, -iest*) very small.

tip[1] *n.* end, esp. of something small or tapering. —*v.t.* (p.t. *tipped*) provide with a tip.

tip[2] *v.t./i.* (p.t. *tipped*) tilt, topple; discharge (a thing's contents) by tilting; strike lightly; name as a likely winner; make a small present of money to, esp. in acknowledgement of services. —*n.* small money present; private or special and useful information or advice; slight tilt or push; place where rubbish etc. is tipped. **~ off,** give a warning or hint or inside information to. **~-off** *n.* such a warning etc. **~ the wink,** give a private signal or information to (a person). **tipper** *n.*

tippet *n.* small cape or collar of fur etc.

tipple *v.t./i.* drink (wine or spirits etc.) repeatedly. —*n.* (*colloq.*) alcoholic or other drink.

tipster *n.* person who gives tips about racehorses etc.

tiptoe *v.i.* (p.t. *tiptoeing*) walk very quietly or carefully.

tiptop *a.* (*colloq.*) first-rate.

tipsy *a.* slightly drunk.

tirade *n.* long angry piece of criticism or denunciation.

tire[1] *v.t./i.* make or become tired.

tire[2] *n.* (*U.S.*) tyre.

tired *a.* feeling a desire to sleep or rest. **~ of,** having had enough of and feeling impatient or bored.

tireless *a.* not tiring easily. **tirelessly** *adv.*

tiresome *a.* annoying.

tiro /ˈtaɪr-/ *n.* (pl. *-os*) beginner.

tissue /ˈtɪʃu/ *n.* substance forming an animal or plant body; tissue-paper; disposable piece of soft absorbent paper used as a handkerchief etc.; fine gauzy fabric; interwoven series (of lies etc.). **~-paper** *n.* very thin soft paper used for packing things.

tit[1] *n.* any of several small birds.

tit[2] *n.* ~ **for tat,** equivalent given in retaliation.

tit[3] *n.* (*vulg.*) breast, nipple.

titanic /taɪˈtæn-/ *a.* gigantic.

titbit *n.* choice bit of food or item of information.

tithe *n.* one tenth of the annual produce of agriculture etc., formerly paid to the Church.

Titian /ˈtɪʃən/ *a.* (of hair) auburn.

titillate *v.t.* excite or stimulate pleasantly. **titillation** *n.*

titivate *v.t./i.* (*colloq.*) smarten up, put finishing touches to. **titivation** *n.*

title *n.* name of a book, poem, or picture etc.; word denoting rank or office, or used in speaking of or to the holder; legal right to ownership of property; championship in sport; ~**-deed** *n.* legal document proving a person's title to a property. ~**-page** *n.* page at the beginning of a book giving the title, author's name, etc. ~**-role** *n.* part in a play etc. from which the title is taken.

titled *a.* having a title of nobility.

titter *n.* high-pitched giggle. —*v.i.* give a titter.

tittle-tattle *v.i.* & *n.* tattle.

titular *a.* of or belonging to a title; having the title of ruler etc. but without real authority.

tizzy *n.* (*sl.*) state of nervous agitation or confusion.

T.N.T. *abbr.* trinitrotoluene, a powerful explosive.

to *prep.* towards, so as to approach or reach or be in (a position or state etc.); as far as; as compared with, in respect of; for (a person or thing) to hold or possess or be affected by. —(with a verb) forming an infinitive, or expressing purpose or consequence etc.; used alone when the infinitive is understood. —*adv.* to a closed or almost closed position or a standstill; into a state of consciousness or activity. ~ **and fro,** backwards and forwards. ~**-be** soon to become. ~**-do** *n.* fuss.

toad *n.* frog-like animal living chiefly on land. ~ **in the hole,** sausages baked in batter.

toadflax *n.* wild plant with yellow or purple flowers.

toadstool *n.* fungus (usu. poisonous) with a round top on a stalk.

toady *n.* sycophant. —*v.i.* behave sycophantically.

toast *n.* toasted bread; person or thing in whose honour a company is requested to drink; this request or instance of drinking. —*v.t./i.* brown or warm by placing before a fire etc.; honour or pledge good wishes to by drinking.

toaster *n.* electrical device for toasting bread.

tobacco *n.* plant with leaves that are used for smoking or snuff; its prepared leaves.

tobacconist *n.* shopkeeper who sells cigarettes etc.

toboggan *n.* small sledge used for sliding downhill. **tobogganing** *n.*

toby jug mug or jug in the form of an old man with a three-cornered hat.

toccata /-ˈkɑ-/ *n.* showy composition for a piano or organ etc.

tocsin *n.* bell rung as an alarmsignal; signal of disaster.

today *n.* & *adv.* (on) this present day; (at) the present time.

toddle *v.i.* (of a young child) walk with short unsteady steps.

toddler *n.* child who has only recently learnt to walk.

toddy *n.* sweetened drink of spirits and hot water.

toe *n.* any of the divisions (five in man) of the front part of the foot; part of a shoe or stocking covering the toes; lower end or tip of a tool etc.—*v.t.* touch with the toe(s); make or repair the toe(s) of. **be on one's toes,** be alert or eager. ~**-cap** *n.* outer covering of the toe of a boot or shoe. ~**-hold** *n.* slight foothold. ~ **the line,** conform to the requirements of one's party.

toff *n.* (*sl.*) distinguished or well-dressed person.

toffee *n.* sweet made with heated butter and sugar. ~**-apple** *n.* toffee-coated apple on a stick.

tog *v.t.* (p.t. *togged*) (*sl.*) ~ **out** or **up,** dress. **togs** *n.pl.* (*sl.*) clothes.

toga *n.* loose outer garment worn by men in ancient Rome.

together *adv.* in or into company or conjunction, towards each other; one with another; simultaneously; in unbroken succession.

toggle *n.* short piece of wood or metal etc. passed through a loop as a fastening device. ~**-switch** *n.* switch operated by a projecting lever.

toil *v.i.* work or move laboriously. —*n.* laborious work.

toilet *n.* process of dressing and grooming oneself; lavatory. ~ **water,** scented lotion for the skin.

toiletries *n.pl.* articles used in washing and grooming oneself.

token *n.* sign, symbol, evidence; keepsake; voucher that can be exchanged for goods; coin-like device for operating a machine or making certain payments. —*a.* serving as a token or pledge but often on a small scale.

told *see* **tell.** —*a.* **all** ~, counting everything or everyone.

tolerable *a.* endurable; passable. **tolerably** *adv.*

tolerance *n.* willingness to tolerate a person or thing; permitted variation. **tolerant** *a.*, **tolerantly** *adv.*

tolerate *v.t.* permit without protest or interference; bear (pain etc.), not be harmed by. **toleration** *n.*

toll[1] /təʊl/ *n.* tax paid for the use of a public road or harbour etc.; loss or damage caused by a disaster etc.

toll[2] /təʊl/ *v.t./i.* ring with slow strokes, esp. for a death or funeral. —*n.* stroke of a tolling bell.

tom *n.* tom-cat. ~**-cat** *n.* male cat.

tomahawk *n.* light axe used by North American Indians; (*Austr.*) hatchet.

tomato *n.* (pl. *-oes*) plant bearing glossy red

or yellow fruit used as a vegetable; this fruit.

tomb /tuːm/ *n.* grave or other place of burial.

tombola /-ˈbəʊ-/ *n.* lottery resembling bingo.

tomboy *n.* girl who enjoys rough noisy recreations.

tombstone *n.* memorial stone set up over a grave.

tome /təʊm/ *n.* large book.

tomfool *a.* & *n.* extremely foolish (person). **tomfoolery** *n.*

tommy-gun *n.* portable machine-gun.

tommy-rot *n.* (*sl.*) nonsense.

tomorrow *n.* & *adv.* (on) the day after today; (in) the near future.

tom-tom *n.* drum beaten with the hands; tall drum used in jazz bands.

ton *n.* measure of weight, either 2240 lb (*long* ~) or 2000 lb (*short* ~); unit of volume in shipping; (*colloq.*) large amount; (*sl.*) speed of 100 m.p.h. **metric** ~, tonne.

tone *n.* musical or vocal sound, esp. with reference to its pitch and quality and strength; manner of expression in speaking or writing; full interval between one note and the next in an octave; proper firmness of bodily organs and tissues; tint, shade of colour; general spirit or character. —*v.t./i.* give a tone of sound or colour to; harmonize in colour; give proper firmness to (muscles or skin etc.). ~-**deaf** *a.* unable to perceive differences of musical pitch. ~ **down**, make less strong or less harsh. **tonal** *a.*, **tonally** *adv.*, **tonality** *n.*

toneless *a.* without positive tone, not expressive. **tonelessly** *adv.*

tongs *n.pl.* instrument with two arms used for grasping things.

tongue *n.* muscular organ in the mouth, used in tasting and swallowing and (in man) speaking; tongue of an ox etc. as food; ability to speak, manner of speaking; language; projecting strip; tapering jet of flame. —*v.i.* produce a staccato or other effect in a wind instrument by using the tongue. ~-**tied** *a.* silent from shyness etc. ~-**twister** *n.* sequence of words difficult to pronounce quickly and correctly. **with one's** ~ **in one's cheek,** speaking with sly sarcasm.

tonic *n.* medicine etc. with an invigorating effect; keynote in music; tonic water. —*a.* toning muscles etc., invigorating. ~ **water,** mineral water, esp. flavoured with quinine.

tonight *n.* & *adv.* (on) the present evening or night, or that of today.

tonnage *n.* ship's carrying-capacity expressed in tons; charge per ton for carrying cargo.

tonne /tʌn *or* ˈtʌnɪ/ *n.* metric ton, 1000 kg.

tonsil *n.* either of two small organs near the root of the tongue.

tonsillitis *n.* inflammation of the tonsils.

tonsure /ˈtonʃə(r)/ *n.* shaving the top or all of the head as a clerical or monastic symbol; this shaven area. **tonsured** *a.*

too *adv.* to a greater extent than is desirable; (*colloq.*) very; also.

took *see* **take.**

tool *n.* thing used for working on something; person used by another for his own purposes. —*v.t./i.* shape or ornament with a tool; equip with tools; (*sl.*) drive or ride in a leisurely way.

toot *n.* short sound produced by a horn or whistle etc. —*v.t./i.* make or cause to make a toot.

tooth *n.* (pl. *teeth*) each of the hard white bony structures in the jaws, used in biting and chewing things; tooth-like part or projection; liking for a particular food. **in the teeth of,** in spite of; in opposition to. ~-**comb** *n.* comb with fine close-set teeth. **toothed** *a.*

toothache *n.* ache in a tooth.

toothbrush *n.* brush for cleaning the teeth.

toothless *a.* having no teeth.

toothpaste *n.* paste for cleaning the teeth.

toothpick *n.* small pointed instrument for removing bits of food from between the teeth.

toothy *a.* having many or large teeth.

tootle *v.t./i.* toot gently.

top[1] *n.* highest point or part or position; upper surface; utmost degree or intensity; thing forming the upper part or covering; garment for the upper part of the body. —*a.* highest in position or rank etc. —*v.t.* (p.t. *topped*) provide or be a top for; reach the top of; be higher than; add as a final thing; remove the top of; strike (a golfball) above its centre. **on** ~ **of,** in addition to. ~ **coat,** overcoat. ~ **dog,** (*sl.*) master, victor. ~-**dressing** *n.* application of fertilizer on the top of soil. ~ **hat,** man's stiff black or grey hat worn with formal dress. ~-**heavy** *a.* over-weighted at the top and liable to fall over. ~-**notch** *a.* (*colloq.*) first-rate. ~ **secret,** of the highest category of secrecy. ~ **up,** fill up (something half empty).

top[2] *n.* toy that spins on its point when set in motion.

topaz *n.* semi-precious stone of various colours, esp. yellow.

topi /ˈtəʊpɪ/ *n.* light pith sun-helmet.

topiary /ˈtəʊ-/ *a.* & *n.* (of) the art of clipping shrubs etc. into ornamental shapes.

topic *a.* subject of a discussion or written work.

topical *a.* having reference to current events. **topically** *adv.*, **topicality** *n.*

topknot *n.* tuft, crest, or bow etc. on top of the head.

topless *a.* leaving or having the breasts bare.

topmost *a.* highest.

topography /-ˈpog-/ *n.* local geography, position of the rivers, roads, buildings, etc., of a place or district. **topographical** *a.*

topper *n.* (*colloq.*) top hat.

topple *v.t./i.* be unsteady and fall; cause to do this.

topside *n.* beef from the upper part of the haunch.

topsoil *n.* top layer of the soil.

topsy-turvy *adv.* & *a.* upside down; in or into great disorder.

toque /təʊk/ *n.* woman's brimless hat with a high crown.

tor *n.* hill or rocky peak.

torch *n.* small hand-held electric lamp; burning

piece of wood etc. carried as a light. **torch-light** *n.*

tore *see* **tear**[1].

toreador /ˈtɒ-/ *n.* fighter (esp. on horseback) in a bullfight.

torment[1] /ˈtɔ-/ *n.* severe suffering; cause of this.

torment[2] /-ˈment/ *v.t.* subject to torment or annoyances. **tormentor** *n.*

torn *see* **tear**[1].

tornado /-ˈneɪ-/ *n.* (pl. *-oes*) violent destructive whirlwind.

torpedo *n.* (pl. *-oes*) explosive underwater missile. —*v.t.* attack or destroy with a torpedo; wreck (a plan etc.) suddenly.

torpid *a.* sluggish and inactive. **torpidly** *adv.*, **torpidity** *n.*

torpor *n.* sluggish condition.

torque /tɔk/ *n.* force causing rotation in mechanism; ancient twisted metal necklace.

torrent *n.* rushing stream or flow; downpour. **torrential** /-ˈrenʃəl/ *a.*

torrid /ˈtɒ-/ *a.* intensely hot.

torsion *n.* twisting, spiral twist.

torso *n.* (pl. *-os*) trunk of the human body.

tort *n.* any private or civil wrong (other than breach of contract) for which damages may be claimed.

tortoise /-təs/ *n.* slow-moving land or fresh-water reptile with its body enclosed in a hard shell.

tortoiseshell /ˈtɔːtəʃel/ *n.* mottled yellowish-brown shell of certain turtles, used for making combs etc. ~ **cat** etc., one with mottled colouring.

tortuous *a.* full of twists and turns. **tortuously** *adv.*, **tortuosity** *n.*

torture *n.* severe pain; infliction of this as a punishment or means of coercion. —*v.t.* inflict torture upon; force out of its natural shape etc. **torturer** *n.*

Tory *n. & a.* (*colloq.*) Conservative.

toss *v.t./i.* throw lightly; send (a coin) spinning in the air to settle a question by the way it falls; throw or roll about from side to side; coat (food) by gently shaking it in dressing etc. —*n.* tossing action or movement or process. ~ **off,** drink rapidly; finish or compose rapidly. ~**-up** *n.* tossing of a coin; even chance.

tot[1] *n.* small child; (*colloq.*) small quantity of spirits.

tot[2] *v.t./i.* (p.t. *totted*) ~ **up,** (*colloq.*) add up.

total *a.* including everything or everyone; complete. —*n.* total amount.—*v.t./i.* (p.t. *totalled*) reckon the total of; amount to. **totally** *adv.*, **totality** *n.*

totalitarian /-ˈteər-/ *a.* of a regime in which no rival parties or loyalties are permitted.

totalizator *n.* device that automatically registers bets staked, with a view to dividing the total amount among those betting on the winner.

totalize *v.t.* find the total of.

tote[1] *n.* (*sl.*) totalizator.

tote[2] *v.t.* (*U.S.*) carry.

totem *n.* animal etc. adopted by North American Indians as the emblem of a clan or family; image of this. ~**-pole** *n.* pole carved or painted with totems.

totter *v.i.* walk or rock unsteadily. —*n.* tottering walk or movement. **tottery** *a.*

toucan /ˈtuː-/ *n.* tropical American bird with an immense beak.

touch *v.t./i.* be or come or bring together so that there is no space between; put one's hand etc. on (a thing) lightly; press or strike lightly; reach; equal in excellence; meddle with; involve oneself in; affect slightly; rouse sympathy in; (*sl.*) persuade to give money as a loan or gift. —*n.* act or fact or manner of touching; ability to perceive things through touching them; small thing done in producing a piece of work; style of workmanship; relationship of communication or knowledge; slight trace; part of a football field outside the touch-lines; (*sl.*) act of obtaining money from a person. ~**-and-go** *a.* uncertain as regards result. ~ **down,** touch the ball on the ground behind the goal-line in Rugby football; (of an aircraft) land. (**touchdown** *n.*). ~**-line** *n.* side limit of a football field. ~ **off,** cause to explode; start (a process). ~ **on,** mention briefly. ~**-typing** *n.* typewriting without looking at the keys. ~ **up,** improve by making small additions.

touché /ˈtuːʃeɪ/ *int.* acknowledgement of a hit in fencing, or of a valid criticism.

touching *a.* rousing kindly feelings or pity. —*prep.* concerning.

touchstone *n.* standard or criterion by which something is judged.

touchy *a.* easily offended.

tough *a.* (*-er, -est*) hard to break or cut or chew; hardy; unyielding, resolute; difficult; (*colloq.*, of luck) hard. —*n.* rough violent person. **toughness** *n.*

toughen *v.t./i.* make or become tough or tougher.

toupee /ˈtuːpeɪ/ *n.* wig, artificial patch of hair.

tour *n.* journey through a place, visiting things of interest or giving performances. —*v.t./i.* make a tour (of). **on** ~, touring.

tourism *n.* organized touring or other services for tourists.

tourist *n.* person travelling or visiting a place for recreation.

tourmaline /ˈtʊəməlin/ *n.* mineral possessing unusual electric properties and used as a gem.

tournament *n.* contest of skill involving a series of matches.

tournedos /ˈtʊənədəʊ/ *n.* (pl. *-os*) small piece of fillet of beef.

tousle /ˈtaʊ-/ *v.t.* make (hair etc.) untidy by ruffling.

tout /taʊt/ *v.t./i.* try to obtain orders (for goods or services); pester people to buy. —*n.* person who touts, tipster touting information.

tow[1] /təʊ/ *n.* coarse fibres of flax or hemp.

tow[2] /təʊ/ *v.t.* pull along behind one. —*n.* act of towing. ~**-path** *n.*, **towing-path** *n.* path beside a canal or river, orig. for use when a horse tows a barge etc.

toward *prep.* towards.

towards *prep.* in the direction of; in relation to; as a contribution to; near, approaching.

towel *n.* piece of absorbent material for drying oneself or wiping things dry. —*v.t.* (p.t. *towelled*) rub with a towel.

towelling *n.* fabric for towels.

tower *n.* tall usu. square or circular structure, esp. as part of a church or castle etc. —*v.i.* be of great height. ~ **of strength,** source of strong reliable support.

towering *a.* (of rage) intense.

town *n.* collection of dwellings and other buildings (larger than a village); its inhabitants; central business and shopping area; London. **go to** ~, (*colloq.*) do something lavishly or with enthusiasm. ~ **hall,** building containing local government offices etc. **townsman** *n.*, **townswoman** *n.fem.*

townee *n.* (*derog.*) inhabitant of a town.

township *n.* (esp. *Austr.* & *N.Z.*) small town; (*U.S.* & *Canada*) division of a county, district six miles square.

toxic *a.* of or caused by poison; poisonous. **toxicity** /-ˈɪsɪ-/ *n.*

toxin *n.* poisonous substance, esp. formed in the body.

toy *n.* thing to play with; (*attrib.*, of a dog) of a diminutive variety. —*v.i.* ~ **with,** handle idly; deal with (a thing) without seriousness.

toyshop *n.* shop that sells toys.

trace¹ *n.* track or mark left behind; sign of what has existed or occurred; very small quantity. —*v.t.* follow or discover by observing marks or other evidence; mark out; copy by using tracing-paper or carbon paper. **tracer** *n.*

trace² *n.* each of the two side-straps or ropes etc. by which a horse draws a vehicle. **kick over the traces,** become insubordinate or reckless.

traceable *a.* able to be traced.

tracery *n.* open-work pattern in stone; similar decorative pattern of lines.

trachea /trəˈkiə/ *n.* windpipe.

tracheotomy /treɪkɪˈɒt-/ *n.* opening made surgically into the trachea from the surface of the neck.

tracing *n.* copy of a map or drawing etc. made by tracing it. ~-**paper** *n.* transparent paper used in this.

track *n.* mark(s) left by a moving person or thing; course; path, rough road; particular section on a record or recording-tape; continuous line of railway; continuous band round the wheels of a tank or tractor etc. —*v.t.* follow the track of, find or observe thus. **keep** *or* **lose** ~ **of,** keep or fail to keep oneself informed about. **make tracks,** (*sl.*) go away. ~ **suit,** loose warm suit worn by an athlete etc. during practice. **tracker** *n.*

tract¹ *n.* stretch of land; system of connected parts of the body, along which something passes.

tract² *n.* pamphlet with a short essay, esp. on a religious subject.

tractable *a.* easy to deal with or control, docile. **tractability** *n.*

traction *n.* pulling. ~-**engine** *n.* engine for pulling a heavy load along a road etc.

tractor *n.* powerful motor vehicle for pulling heavy equipment.

trade *n.* exchange of goods for money or other goods; business of a particular kind, people engaged in this; trading. —*v.t./i.* engage in trade, buy and sell; exchange (goods) in trading. ~ **in,** give (a used article) as partial payment for another article. (~-**in** *n.*). ~ **mark,** manufacturer's or trader's registered emblem or name etc. used to identify his goods. ~ **on,** use (esp. unscrupulously) for one's own advantage. **Trades Union Congress,** association of representatives of British trade unions. ~ **union,** (pl. ~ *unions*) organized association of employees formed to protect and promote their common interests. ~-**unionist** *n.* member of a trade union. ~ **wind,** constant wind blowing towards the equator from the north-east or south-east. **trader** *n.*

tradesman *n.* (pl. *-men*) person engaged in trade; shopkeeper; roundsman.

trading *n.* buying and selling. ~ **estate,** area designed to be occupied by a group of industrial and commercial firms.

tradition *n.* belief or custom handed down from one generation to another; long-established procedure; handing down of beliefs etc. **traditional** *a.*, **traditionally** *adv.*

traditionalist *n.* person who upholds traditional beliefs etc.

traffic *n.* vehicles, ships, or aircraft moving along a route; trading. —*v.t./i.* (p.t. *trafficked*) trade. ~-**lights** *n.pl.* automatic signal controlling traffic at a junction etc. by means of coloured lights. ~ **warden,** official who assists police in controlling the movement and parking of road vehicles. **trafficker** *n.*

tragedian /-ˈdʒi-/ *n.* writer of or actor in tragedies.

tragedy *n.* serious drama with unhappy events or a sad ending; event causing great sadness.

tragic *a.* of or in tragedy; sorrowful; causing great sadness. **tragical** *a.*, **tragically** *adv.*

trail *v.t./i.* drag behind, esp. on the ground; hang loosely; (of a plant) grow lengthily downwards or along the ground; move wearily; lag, straggle; diminish, become fainter; track. —*n.* thing that trails; line of people or things following something; mark left, track, trace; beaten path.

trailer *n.* truck etc. designed to be hauled by a vehicle; short extract from a film etc., shown in advance to advertise it.

train *n.* railway engine with linked carriages or trucks; people or animals moving in a line; retinue; sequence of things; part of a long robe that trails behind the wearer; line of combustible material placed to lead fire to an explosive. —*v.t./i.* bring or come to a desired standard of efficiency or condition or behaviour etc. by instruction and practice;

teach to do something; aim (a gun etc.); cause (a plant) to grow in the required direction. **in ~**, in preparation. **trainer** n.

trainable a. able to be trained.

trainee n. person being trained.

traipse v.i. (colloq.) trudge.

trait /treɪ/ n. characteristic.

traitor n. person who behaves disloyally, esp. to his country. **traitorous** a.

trajectory /ˈtræ-/ n. path of a bullet or rocket or other body moving under certain forces.

tram n. public passenger vehicle running on rails laid in the road.

tramcar n. tram.

tramlines n.pl. rails on which a tram runs; (colloq.) pair of parallel side-lines in tennis etc.

trammel n. a kind of fishing-net; (pl.) hampering influence. —v.t. (p.t. trammelled) hamper.

tramp v.t./i. walk with heavy footsteps; go on foot across (an area); trample. —n. sound of heavy footsteps; long walk; vagrant; cargo boat that does not travel a regular route.

trample v.t./i. tread repeatedly, crush or harm by treading.

trampoline /-lin/ n. canvas sheet attached by springs to a frame, used for jumping on in acrobatic leaps.

trance n. sleep-like or dreamy state.

tranquil a. calm and undisturbed. **tranquilly** adv., **tranquillity** n.

tranquillize v.t. calm.

tranquillizer n. drug used to relieve anxiety and induce calmness.

transact v.t. perform or carry out (business etc.). **transaction** n.

transatlantic a. on or from the other side of the Atlantic; crossing the Atlantic.

transcend /-ˈsend/ v.t. go beyond the range of (experience, belief, etc.); surpass. **transcendent** a.

transcendental a. transcendent; abstract, obscure, visionary.

transcribe v.t. copy in writing; record (sound) for reproduction; arrange (music) for a different instrument etc. **transcription** n.

transcript n. written or recorded copy.

transducer n. device that receives waves or other variations from one system and conveys related ones to another.

transept n. part lying at right angles to the nave in a church.

transfer[1] /-ˈfɜ(r)/ v.t./i. (p.t. transferred) convey or move or hand over from one place or person or application etc. to another. **transference** /ˈtræ-/ n., **transferable** a.

transfer[2] /ˈtræ-/ n. process of transferring; document transferring property or a right; design for transferring from one surface to another; paper bearing this.

transfigure v.t. change in appearance to something nobler or more beautiful. **transfiguration** n.

transfix v.t. pierce through, impale; make motionless with fear or astonishment.

transform v.t./i. change greatly in appearance

or character; change the voltage of (electric current). **transformation** n., **transformer** n.

transfuse v.t. give a transfusion of or to.

transfusion n. injection of blood or other fluid into a blood-vessel.

transgress v.t./i. break (a rule or law); go beyond (a limitation); (old use) sin. **transgression** n., **transgressor** n.

transient /-zɪənt/ a. passing away quickly, not lasting. **transience** n.

transistor n. very small semi-conductor device performing the same functions as a thermionic valve; portable radio set using transistors. **transistorized** a.

transit n. process of going or conveying across, over, or through. —v.t. (p.t. transited) make a transit across.

transition n. process of changing from one state or style etc. to another. **transitional** a.

transitory a. lasting only briefly.

translate v.t./i. express in another language or other words; be able to be translated; transfer. **translation** n., **translator** n., **translatable** a.

transliterate v.t. convert to the letters of another alphabet. **transliteration** n.

translucent a. allowing light to pass through but not transparent. **translucence** n.

transmigration n. migration; passing of the soul into another body after a person's death.

transmission n. transmitting; broadcast; gear transmitting power from engine to axle.

transmit v.t. (p.t. transmitted) send or pass on from one person, place, or thing to another; send out (a signal or programme etc.) by telegraph wire or radio waves. **transmitter** n.

transmogrify v.t. (joc.) transform. **transmogrification** n.

transmute v.t. change in form or substance. **transmutation** n.

transom n. horizontal bar across the top of a door or window; small window above a door or another window.

transparency /-ˈpæ-/ n. being transparent; photographic slide, esp. on film not glass.

transparent /-ˈpæ- or -ˈpeər-/ a. able to be seen through; easily understood, obvious. **transparently** adv.

transpire v.i. become known; (colloq.) happen; (of plants) give off watery vapour from leaves etc. **transpiration** n.

transplant[1] /-ˈplɑ-/ v.t./i. remove and re-plant or establish elsewhere; transfer (living tissue). **transplantation** n.

transplant[2] /ˈtræ-/ n. transplanting of tissue; thing transplanted.

transport[1] /-ˈpɔt/ v.t. convey from one place to another. **transportation** n., **transporter** n.

transport[2] /ˈtræ-/ n. process of transporting; means of conveyance; ship or aircraft for carrying troops or supplies; (pl.) condition of strong emotion.

transported a. carried away by strong emotion.

transpose v.t. cause (two or more things) to change places; change the position of; put (music) into a different key. **transposition** n.

transubstantiation *n.* conversion of the elements in the Eucharist to the body and blood of Christ.

transuranic /-'ræn-/ *a.* belonging to a group of radioactive elements whose atoms are heavier than those of uranium.

transverse *a.* crosswise.

transvestism *n.* dressing in clothing of the opposite sex. **transvestite** *n.*

trap *n.* device for catching and holding an animal; anything by which an unsuspecting person is captured or outwitted; trapdoor; compartment with a hinged flap from which a dog is released in racing; curved section of a pipe holding liquid to prevent foul gases from coming upwards; two-wheeled horse-drawn carriage. —*v.t.* (p.t. *trapped*) catch or hold in a trap.

trapdoor *n.* door in a floor, ceiling, or roof.

trapeze *n.* a kind of swing on which acrobatics are performed.

trapezium /-'piz-/ *n.* quadrilateral with two opposite sides parallel.

trapezoid /'træp-/ *n.* quadrilateral with no sides parallel; (*U.S.*) trapezium.

trapper *n.* person who traps animals, esp. for furs.

trappings *n.pl.* accessories; adjuncts.

Trappist *n.* member of a monastic order noted for silence.

traps *n.pl.* percussion instruments in a jazz band.

trash *n.* worthless stuff. **trashy** *a.*

trauma /'trɔ-/ *n.* wound, injury; emotional shock producing a lasting effect. **traumatic** *a.*

travel *v.t./i.* (p.t. *travelled*) go from one place to another; journey along or through; go from place to place as a salesman. —*n.* travelling, esp. abroad. **traveller** *n.*

traverse[1] /-'vɜs/ *v.t.* travel or lie or extend across.

traverse[2] /'træv-/ *n.* thing that lies across another; zigzag course, each leg of this; lateral movement; steep slope that has to be crossed from side to side.

travesty /'træv-/ *n.* absurd or inferior imitation. —*v.t.* make or be a travesty of.

trawl *n.* large wide-mouthed fishing-net. —*v.t./i.* fish or catch with a trawl.

trawler *n.* boat used in trawling.

tray *n.* flat utensil on which small articles are placed for display or carrying; open receptacle for holding correspondence in an office; tray-like compartment.

treacherous *a.* showing treachery; not to be relied on, deceptive. **treacherously** *adv.*

treachery *n.* betrayal of a person or cause; act of disloyalty.

treacle *n.* thick sticky liquid produced when sugar is refined. **treacly** *a.*

tread *v.t./i.* (p.t. *trod*, p.p. *trodden*) set one's foot down; walk, step; walk on, press or crush with the feet. —*n.* manner or sound of walking; horizontal surface of a stair; part of a wheel or tyre etc. that touches the ground.

~ **water,** keep upright in water by making treading movements.

treadle *n.* lever worked by the foot to drive a wheel. —*v.i.* work a treadle.

treadmill *n.* wide mill-wheel formerly turned by people treading on steps fixed round its edge; tiring monotonous routine work.

treason *n.* treachery towards one's country or its ruler.

treasonable *a.* involving treason.

treasure *n.* collection of precious metals or gems; highly valued object or person. —*v.t.* value highly; store as precious. ~ **trove,** treasure of unknown ownership, found hidden; something very desirable that a person finds.

treasurer *n.* person in charge of the funds of an institution.

treasury *n.* place where treasure is kept; *the T*~, department managing a country's revenue.

treat *v.t./i.* act or behave towards or deal with in a certain way; give medical treatment to; subject to a chemical or other process; buy a meal etc. for (a person) in order to give pleasure; negotiate terms. —*n.* something special that gives pleasure; treating of others to food etc.

treatise *n.* written work dealing with one subject.

treatment *n.* manner of dealing with a person or thing; something done to relieve illness etc.

treaty *n.* formal agreement made, esp. between countries.

treble *a.* three times as much or as many; (of a voice) high-pitched, soprano. —*n.* treble quantity or thing; treble voice, person with this. **trebly** *adv.*

tree *n.* perennial plant with a single thick stem; framework of wood for various purposes. —*v.t.* force to take refuge up a tree. **treeless** *a.*

trefoil /'tref-/ *n.* plant with three leaflets (e.g. clover); thing shaped like this.

trek *n.* long arduous journey. —*v.i.* (p.t. *trekked*) make a trek.

trellis *n.* light framework of crossing strips of wood etc. used to support climbing plants.

tremble *v.i.* shake involuntarily, esp. from fear or cold etc.; quiver; feel very anxious. —*n.* trembling movement.

tremendous *a.* immense; (*colloq.*) excellent. **tremendously** *adv.*

tremolo *n.* (pl. *-os*) trembling effect in music or singing.

tremor *n.* slight trembling movement; thrill of fear etc.

tremulous *a.* trembling, quivering.

trench *n.* deep ditch. ~ **coat,** belted coat or raincoat resembling military uniform.

trenchant *a.* (of comments, policies, etc.) strong and effective.

trend *n.* thing's continuing tendency. ~**-setter** *n.* person who leads the way in fashion etc.

trendy *a.* (*-ier*, *-iest*) (*colloq.*) following the latest trends of fashion. **trendily** *adv.*, **trendiness** *n.*

trepidation *n.* nervousness.

trespass *v.i.* enter land or property unlawfully; intrude; (*old use*) sin. —*n.* act of trespassing; (*old use*) sin. **trespasser** *n.*

tress *n.* lock of hair.

trestle *n.* one of a set of supports on which a board is rested to form a table; braced framework supporting a bridge. **∼-table** *n.*

trews *n.pl.* close-fitting usu. tartan trousers.

tri- *pref.* three times, triple.

trial *n.* examination in a lawcourt by a judge to decide an issue, esp. the guilt or innocence of an accused person; process of testing qualities or performance; person or thing that tries one's patience, hardship. **on ∼,** undergoing a trial.

triangle *n.* geometric figure with three sides and three angles; thing shaped like this; triangular steel rod struck with another rod as a percussion instrument.

triangular *a.* shaped like a triangle; involving three people.

triangulation *n.* measurement or mapping of an area by means of a network of triangles.

tribe *n.* racial group (esp. in a primitive culture) living as a community under one or more chiefs; set or class of people. **tribal** *a.*, **tribesman** *n.*

tribulation *n.* great affliction.

tribunal /traɪ-/ *n.* board of officials appointed to adjudicate on a particular problem.

tributary *a.* & *n.* (stream) flowing into a larger stream or a lake.

tribute *n.* something said or done as a mark of respect; payment that one country or ruler was formerly obliged to pay to another.

trice *n.* **in a ∼,** in an instant.

trichology /trɪk-/ *n.* study of hair and its diseases. **trichologist** *n.*

trick *n.* something done to deceive or outwit someone; deception, illusion; technique, best way of doing something; feat of skill; mannerism; mischievous or discreditable act; cards played in one round of a card-game; this round, a point gained from it; person's turn of duty (usu. for two hours) at a ship's helm. —*v.t.* deceive or persuade by a trick; deck, decorate. **do the ∼,** (*colloq.*) achieve what is required.

trickery *n.* use of tricks, deception.

trickle *v.t./i.* flow or cause to flow in a thin stream; come or go slowly or gradually. —*n.* trickling flow.

trickster *n.* person who tricks people.

tricky *a.* crafty, deceitful; requiring careful handling. **trickiness** *n.*

tricolour /ˈtrɪk-/ *n.* flag with three colours in stripes.

tricot /ˈtriːkəʊ/ *n.* fine jersey fabric.

tricycle *n.* three-wheeled pedal-driven vehicle.

trident /ˈtraɪ-/ *n.* three-pronged fish-spear carried as a symbol of power over the sea.

Tridentine /trɪˈdentaɪn/ *a.* of traditional Roman Catholic orthodoxy.

triennial /traɪˈen-/ *a.* happening every third year; lasting three years.

trier *n.* person who tries hard.

trifle *n.* thing of only slight value or importance; very small amount, esp. of money; sweet dish of sponge-cake soaked in wine or jelly etc. and topped with custard and cream. —*v.t.* behave or talk frivolously. **∼ with,** toy with. **trifler** *n.*

trifling *a.* trivial.

trigger *n.* small lever for releasing a spring, esp. to fire a gun. —*v.t.* (also **∼ off**) set in action, cause.

trigonometry /-ˈnom-/ *n.* branch of mathematics dealing with the relationship of sides and angles of triangles etc.

trilateral /traɪ-/ *a.* having three sides or three participants.

trilby *n.* man's soft felt hat.

trilingual /-gwəl/ *a.* speaking or using three languages.

trill *n.* vibrating sound, esp. in music or singing. —*v.t./i.* sound or sing with a trill.

trilogy /ˈtrɪl-/ *n.* group of three related literary or operatic works.

trim *a.* (**trimmer, trimmest**) neat and orderly. —*v.t.* (p.t. **trimmed**) remove irregular parts; reduce or neaten by cutting; ornament; make (a boat or aircraft) evenly balanced by distributing its load; arrange (sails) to suit the wind. —*n.* condition as regards readiness or fitness; ornamentation; colour or type of upholstery etc. in a car; trimming of hair etc. **trimly** *adv.*, **trimness** *n.*

trimaran /ˈtraɪ-/ *n.* vessel like a catamaran, with three hulls.

trimming *n.* thing added as a decoration; (*pl.*) pieces cut off when something is trimmed.

trine *n.* & *a.* (astrological aspect) of two planets one-third of the zodiac (= 120°) apart.

trinity *n.* group of three; **the T∼,** the three persons of the Godhead (Father, Son, Holy Spirit) as constituting one God.

trinket *n.* small fancy article or piece of jewellery.

trio *n.* (pl. *-os*) group or set of three; music for three instruments or voices.

trip *v.t./i.* (p.t. **tripped**) go lightly and quickly; stumble, cause to do this; make or cause to make a blunder; release (a switch etc.) so as to operate a mechanism. —*n.* journey or excursion, esp. for pleasure; (*colloq.*) visionary experience caused by a drug; stumble; device for tripping a mechanism. **∼-wire** *n.* wire stretched along the ground, operating a warning device or a mine etc. if disturbed.

tripartite /-ˈtraɪ-/ *a.* consisting of three parts.

tripe *n.* stomach of an ox etc. as food; (*sl.*) worthless thing, nonsense.

triple *a.* having three parts or members; three times as much as. —*v.t./i.* increase by three times its amount. **∼ time,** rhythm of music with three beats to the bar.

triplet *n.* one of three children born at one birth; set of three.

triplicate *a.* & *n.* existing in three examples. **in ∼,** as three identical copies.

tripod /ˈtraɪ-/ *n.* three-legged stand.

tripos /ˈtraɪpɒs/ *n.* final examination for the B.A. degree at Cambridge University.

tripper *n.* person who goes on a pleasure trip. **trippery** *a.*

triptych /ˈtrɪptɪk/ *n.* picture or carving with three panels fixed or hinged side by side.

trisect *v.t.* divide into three equal parts. **trisection** *n.*

trite *a.* hackneyed.

triumph *n.* fact of being successful or victorious; joy at this; great success. —*v.i.* be successful or victorious, rejoice at this. **triumphant** *a.*, **triumphantly** *adv.*

triumphal *a.* celebrating or commemorating a triumph.

trivet /ˈtrɪv-/ *n.* iron usu. three-legged stand for a kettle or pot etc. placed over a fire.

trivial *a.* of only small value or importance. **trivially** *adv.*, **triviality** *n.*

trod, trodden *see* **tread.**

troglodyte /ˈtrɒg-/ *n.* cave-dweller.

troll[1] /trəʊl/ *v.t./i.* sing in a carefree way; fish by drawing bait along.

troll[2] /trəʊl/ *n.* giant or dwarf in Scandinavian mythology.

trolley *n.* (pl. *-eys*) platform on wheels for transporting goods; small cart; small table on wheels for transporting food or articles. **~-bus** *n.* bus powered by electricity from an overhead wire.

trollop *n.* slatternly woman.

trombone *n.* large brass wind instrument with a sliding tube.

troop *n.* company of people or animals; cavalry or artillery unit; Scout company. —*v.t./i.* assemble or go as a troop or in great numbers. **trooping the colour,** ceremony of carrying the regimental flag along ranks of soldiers.

trooper *n.* soldier in a cavalry or armoured unit; (*U.S.*) member of a State police force.

trophy *n.* thing taken in war or hunting etc. as a souvenir of success; object awarded as a prize.

tropic *n.* line of latitude 23° 27′ north or south of the equator; (*pl.*) region between these, with a hot climate. **tropical** *a.*

troposphere /ˈtrɒp-/ *n.* layer of the atmosphere extending from earth's surface to the stratosphere.

trot *n.* running action of a horse etc.; moderate running-pace. —*v.t./i.* (p.t. *trotted*) go or cause to go at a trot. **~ out,** (*colloq.*) produce.

Trotskyism *n.* principles of the Russian revolutionary leader Leon Trotsky. **Trotskyist** *n.*

trotter *n.* animal's foot as food.

trouble *n.* difficulty, distress, misfortune; cause of this; conflict; inconvenience, exertion; unpleasantness involving punishment or rebuke; faulty functioning. —*v.t./i.* cause trouble to; make or be disturbed or worried; use much care and effort.

troublesome *a.* causing trouble.

trough /trɒf/ *n.* long narrow open receptacle, esp. for holding water or food for animals; depression between two waves or ridges; elongated region of low atmospheric pressure.

trounce *v.t.* thrash; defeat heavily.

troupe /truːp/ *n.* company of actors or other performers.

trouper /ˈtruː-/ *n.* member of a troupe; staunch colleague.

trousers *n.pl.* two-legged outer garment reaching from the waist usu. to the ankles.

trousseau /ˈtruːsəʊ/ *n.* (pl. *-eaux,* pr. *-əʊz*) bride's collection of clothing etc. to begin married life.

trout *n.* (pl. *trout*) freshwater fish valued as food and game.

trowel *n.* small spade-like tool with a curved blade; similar tool with a flat blade for spreading mortar etc.

truant *n.* person who absents himself from school or work etc. without leave. **play ~,** stay away as a truant. **truancy** *n.*

truce *n.* agreement to cease hostilities temporarily.

truck[1] *n.* open container on wheels for transporting loads; open railway wagon; lorry.

truck[2] *n.* dealings.

truckle *v.i.* submit obsequiously. **~-bed** *n.* low bed on wheels, kept under another.

truculent /ˈtrʌkjʊ-/ *a.* defiant and aggressive. **truculently** *adv.*, **truculence** *n.*

trudge *v.i.* walk laboriously. —*n.* laborious walk.

true *a.* (*-er, -est*) in accordance with fact or correct principles or an accepted standard; genuine; exact, accurate; loyal, faithful. —*adv.* truly, accurately. **trueness** *n.*

truffle *n.* rich-flavoured underground fungus valued as a delicacy; soft chocolate sweet.

trug *n.* gardener's shallow basket.

truism *n.* statement that is obviously true, esp. a hackneyed one.

truly *adv.* truthfully; genuinely; faithfully.

trump[1] *n.* (*old use*) sound of a trumpet.

trump[2] *n.* playing-card of a suit temporarily ranking above others; (*colloq.*) person who behaves in a helpful or useful way. —*v.t.* **~ up,** invent fraudulently.

trumpery *a.* showy but worthless.

trumpet *n.* metal wind instrument with a flared tube; thing shaped like this. —*v.t./i.* (p.t. *trumpeted*) blow or proclaim by a trumpet; (of an elephant) make a loud sound with its trunk. **trumpeter** *n.*

truncate *v.t.* shorten by cutting off the end. **truncation** *n.*

truncheon *n.* short thick stick carried as a weapon.

trundle *v.t./i.* roll along, move along heavily on wheels.

trunk *n.* tree's main stem; body apart from head and limbs; large box with a hinged lid, for transporting or storing clothes etc.; elephant's long flexible nose; (*U.S.*) boot of a car (*pl.*) shorts for swimming etc.. **~-call** *n.* long-distance inland telephone call. **~-road** *n.* important main road.

truss *n.* bundle of hay or straw; cluster of flowers or fruit; framework of beams or bars supporting a roof etc.; padded belt or other device worn to support a hernia. —*v.t.* tie securely; support with trusses.

trust *n.* firm belief in the reliability or truth or strength etc. of a person or thing; confident expectation; responsibility arising from being entrusted with something; property legally entrusted to someone with instructions for its use; association of business firms, formed to reduce or defeat competition. —*v.t./i.* have or place trust in; entrust; hope earnestly. **in ~, on ~,** held as a trust. **on ~,** accepted without investigation. **~ to,** rely on. **trustful** *a.*, **trust-fully** *adv.*, **trustfulness** *n.*

trustee *n.* person who administers property held as a trust; one of a group managing the business affairs of an institution.

trustworthy *a.* worthy of trust.

trusty *a.* trustworthy.

truth *n.* quality of being true; something that is true.

truthful *a.* habitually telling the truth; true. **truthfully** *adv.*, **truthfulness** *n.*

try *v.t./i.* attempt; test, esp. by use; attempt to open (a door etc.); be a strain on; hold a trial of. —*n.* attempt; touchdown in Rugby football, entitling the player's side to a kick at goal. **~ on,** put (a garment) on to see if it fits. **~ out,** test by use. **~-out** *n.*

trying *a.* annoying.

tryst /trɪst/ *n.* (*old use*) appointed meeting, esp. of sweethearts.

tsar /zɑ(r)/ *n.* title of the former emperor of Russia.

tsetse /ˈtsetsɪ/ *n.* African fly that transmits disease by its bite.

T-shirt *n.* simple shirt usu. of knitted cotton.

T-square *n.* T-shaped instrument for measuring or obtaining right angles.

tub *n.* open usu. round container.

tuba /ˈtjuː-/ *n.* large low-pitched brass wind instrument.

tubby *a.* (-*ier*, -*iest*) short and fat. **tubbiness** *n.*

tube *n.* long hollow cylinder; thing shaped like this; (*colloq.*) underground railway system in London.

tuber *n.* short thick rounded root or underground stem from which shoots will grow.

tubercular /-ˈbɜː-/ *a.* of or affected with tuberculosis.

tuberculosis *n.* infectious wasting disease, esp. affecting lungs.

tuberose *n.* tropical plant with fragrant white flowers.

tuberous *a.* of or like a tuber; bearing tubers.

tubing *n.* tubes; a length of tube.

tubular /ˈtjuː-/ *a.* tube-shaped.

T.U.C. *abbr.* Trades Union Congress.

tuck *n.* flat fold stitched in a garment etc. —*v.t./i.* put a tuck or tucks in; turn into or under something so as to be concealed or held in place; cover or put away compactly. **~ in** *or* **into,** (*sl.*) eat heartily. **~-shop** *n.* shop selling sweets and cake etc. to schoolchildren.

tucker *n.* (*Austr. colloq.*) food.

Tuesday *n.* day after Monday.

tufa /ˈtjuː-/ *n.* a kind of coarse rock.

tuft *n.* bunch of threads or grass or hair etc. held or growing together at the base. **tufted** *a.*

tug *v.t./i.* (p.t. **tugged**) pull vigorously; tow. —*n.* vigorous pull; small powerful boat for towing others. **~ of war,** contest of strength in which two teams pull opposite ways on a rope.

tuition *n.* process of teaching; instruction.

tulip *n.* garden plant with a cup-shaped flower. **~-tree** *n.* tree with tulip-like flowers.

tulle /tjuːl/ *n.* fine silky net fabric used for veils and dresses.

tumble *v.t./i.* fall; cause to fall; roll or push or move in a disorderly way; rumple. —*n.* fall; untidy state. **~-drier** *n.* machine for drying washing in a heated rotating drum. **~ to,** (*colloq.*) realize, grasp the meaning of.

tumbledown *a.* dilapidated.

tumbler *n.* pigeon that throws itself over backwards in flight; drinking-glass with no handle or foot; pivoted piece in a lock etc. **~-drier** *n.* tumble-drier.

tumbrel *n.* open cart used for carrying condemned persons to the guillotine during the French Revolution.

tummy *n.* (*colloq.*) stomach.

tumour *n.* abnormal mass of new tissue growing in or on the body.

tumult *n.* uproar; conflict of emotions.

tumultuous /-ˈmʌl-/ *a.* making an uproar.

tun *n.* large cask.

tuna /ˈtjuː-/ *n.* (pl. *tuna*) tunny; its flesh as food.

tundra *n.* vast level Arctic regions where the subsoil is frozen.

tune *n.* melody. —*v.t.* put (a musical instrument) in tune; set (a radio) to the desired wavelength; adjust (an engine) to run smoothly. **in ~,** playing or singing at the correct musical pitch; harmonious. **out of ~,** not in tune. **~ up,** bring musical instruments to the correct or uniform pitch. **tuner** *n.*

tuneful *a.* melodious.

tuneless *a.* without a tune.

tungsten *n.* heavy grey metallic element.

tunic *n.* close-fitting jacket worn as part of a uniform; loose garment reaching to the hips or knees.

tuning-fork *n.* two-pronged steel device giving a particular note (usu. middle C) when struck.

tunnel *n.* underground passage. —*v.t./i.* (p.t. **tunnelled**) make a tunnel (through), make (one's way) thus.

tunny *n.* large edible sea-fish.

turban *n.* Muslim or Sikh man's head-dress of a scarf wound round a cap; woman's hat resembling this.

turbid *a.* (of liquids) muddy, not clear; disordered. **turbidity** *n.*

turbine /-baɪn/ *n.* machine or motor driven by a wheel that is turned by a flow of water or gas.

turbo- *pref.* using a turbine; driven by such engines.

turbot *n.* large flat sea-fish valued as food.

turbulent *a.* in a state of commotion or unrest;

moving unevenly. **turbulently** *adv.*, **turbulence** *n.*

tureen /tjʊ'rin/ *n.* deep covered dish from which soup is served.

turf *n.* (pl. *turfs* or *turves*) short grass and the soil just below it; piece of this; slab of peat for fuel; *the* ∼, racecourse, horse-racing. —*v.t.* lay (ground) with turf. ∼ **accountant,** bookmaker. ∼ **out,** (*sl.*) throw out.

turgid *a.* swollen and not flexible; (of language) pompous, not flowing easily. **turgidly** *adv.*, **turgidity** *n.*

Turk *n.* native of Turkey.

turkey *n.* (pl. *-eys*) large bird reared for its flesh.

Turkish *a.* & *n.* (language) of Turkey. ∼ **bath,** exposure of the body to hot air or steam. ∼ **delight,** sweet consisting of flavoured gelatine coated in powdered sugar. ∼ **towel,** towel made in terry towelling.

turmeric /'tɜ-/ *n.* plant of the ginger family; its powdered root.

turmoil *n.* state of great disturbance or confusion.

turn *v.t./i.* move round a point or axis, or so that a different side is presented; take or give a new direction (to); aim; pass round (a point); pass (a certain hour or age); send, put; change in form or appearance etc.; make or become sour or nauseated; shape in a lathe; give an elegant form to. —*n.* process of turning; change of direction or condition etc.; angle, bend or corner in a road; character, tendency; service of a specified kind; opportunity or obligation coming in succession; short performance in an entertainment; (*colloq.*) attack of illness, momentary nervous shock. **in** ∼, in succession. **out of** ∼, before or after one's proper turn; indiscreetly, presumptuously. **to a** ∼, so as to be cooked perfectly. ∼ **against,** make or become hostile to. ∼ **down,** fold down; turn a knob or tap to reduce the volume or flow of; reject. ∼ **in,** hand in; (*colloq.*) go to bed; (*colloq.*) abandon (work etc.). ∼ **off,** (*or on*), turn a tap or switch to stop (*or* start) the flow or operation of; (*colloq.*) cause to lose (*or to* feel) interest. ∼ **out,** expel; turn off (a light etc.); equip, dress; produce by work; empty and search or clean; (*colloq.*) come out; summon (a military guard) for duty; prove to be the case eventually. ∼-**out** *n.* process of turning out a room etc.; number of people attending a public or social function; thing arrayed, outfit. ∼ **the tables,** reverse a situation and put oneself in a superior position. ∼ **up,** discover; be found; make one's appearance; happen; turn a knob or tap to increase the volume or flow of; (*colloq.*) sicken. ∼-**up** *n.* turned-up part, esp. at the lower end of a trouser-leg; (*colloq.*) unexpected event.

turncoat *n.* person who changes his principles.

turner *n.* person who works with a lathe. **turnery** *n.* his work or products.

turning *n.* place where one road meets another, forming a corner. ∼-**point** *n.* point at which a decisive change takes place.

turnip *n.* plant with a round white root used as a vegetable or as fodder; its root.

turnover *n.* pasty with pastry folded to enclose filling; amount of money taken in a business; rate of replacement.

turnpike *n.* (*old use* & *U.S.*) road on which toll is collected at gates.

turnstile *n.* revolving barrier for admitting people to a building etc. one at a time.

turntable *n.* circular revolving platform.

turpentine *n.* oil used for thinning paint and as a solvent.

turpitude *n.* wickedness.

turps *n.* (*colloq.*) turpentine.

turquoise /-kwɔɪz/ *n.* blue-green precious stone; its colour.

turret *n.* small tower-like structure. **turreted** *a.*

turtle *n.* sea-creature like a tortoise. **turn** ∼, capsize. ∼-**dove** *n.* wild dove noted for its soft cooing. ∼-**neck** *n.* high round close-fitting neckline.

tusk *n.* one of the pair of long pointed teeth projecting outside the mouth in certain animals.

tussle *v.i.* & *n.* struggle, conflict.

tussock *n.* tuft or clump of grass.

tussore /'tʌs-/ *n.* strong but coarse silk.

tutelage /'tjutɪ-/ *n.* guardianship; tuition.

tutor *n.* private or university teacher. —*v.t./i.* act as tutor (to), teach.

tutorial /-'tɔ-/ *a.* of a tutor. —*n.* student's session with a tutor.

tutu /'tutu/ *n.* dancer's short skirt made of layers of frills.

tuxedo /tʌk'si-/ *n.* (pl. *-os*) (*U.S.*) dinner-jacket.

T.V. *abbr.* television.

twaddle *n.* nonsense.

twain *a.* & *n.* (*old use*) two.

twang *n.* sharp ringing sound like that made by a tense wire when plucked; nasal intonation. —*v.t./i.* make or cause to make a twang.

tweak *v.t.* & *n.* pinch, twist, or pull with a sharp jerk.

twee *a.* affectedly dainty or quaint.

tweed *n.* twilled usu. woollen fabric; (*pl.*) clothes made of tweed.

tweet *n.* & *v.i.* chirp.

tweeter *n.* loudspeaker for reproducing high-frequency signals.

tweezers *n.pl.* small pincers for picking up or pulling very small things.

twelve *a.* & *n.* one more than eleven (12, XII). **twelfth** *a.* & *n.*

twenty *a.* & *n.* twice ten. ∼-**five** *n.* line or area twenty-five yards from a goal-line. **twentieth** *a.* & *n.*

twerp *n.* (*sl.*) stupid or insignificant person.

twice *adv.* two times; in double amount or degree.

twiddle *v.t.* twist idly about. —*n.* act of twiddling. ∼ **one's thumbs,** twist them idly, have nothing to do. **twiddly** *a.*

twig¹ *n.* small shoot issuing from a branch or stem.

twig² *v.t./i.* (p.t. *twigged*) (*colloq.*) realize, grasp the meaning of.

twilight *n.* light from the sky when the sun is below the horizon (esp. after sunset); period of this.

twill *n.* fabric woven so that parallel diagonal lines are produced. **twilled** *a.*

twin *n.* one of two children or animals born at one birth; one of a pair that are exactly alike. —*a.* being a twin or twins. —*v.t./i.* (p.t. *twinned*) combine as a pair.

twine *n.* strong thread or string. —*v.t./i.* twist; wind or coil.

twinge *n.* slight or brief pang.

twinkle *v.i.* shine with a light that flickers rapidly; move with short rapid movements. —*n.* twinkling light or look or movement.

twirl *v.t./i.* twist lightly or rapidly. —*n.* twirling movement; twirled mark. **twirly** *a.*

twist *v.t./i.* wind (strands etc.) round each other, esp. to form a single cord; make by doing this; give a spiral form to; take a spiral course, bend round; rotate; wrench out of its normal shape; distort; (*sl.*) swindle. —*n.* process of twisting; thing formed by twisting; peculiar tendency of mind or character; (*sl.*) swindle. **twister** *n.*

twit[1] *v.t.* (p.t. *twitted*) taunt.

twit[2] *n.* (*sl.*) foolish or insignificant person.

twitch *v.t./i.* pull with a light jerk; quiver or contract spasmodically. —*n.* twitching movement.

twitter *v.i.* make light chirping sounds; talk rapidly in an anxious or nervous way. —*n.* twittering.

two *a. & n.* one more than one (2, II). **be in ～ minds**, be undecided. **～faced** *a.* insincere, deceitful. **～piece** *n.* suit of clothes or a woman's swim-suit consisting of two separate parts.

twofold *a. & adv.* twice as much or as many.

twopence /ˈtʌp-/ *n.* sum of two pence. **twopenny** *a.*

twosome *n.* two together, pair.

tycoon *n.* magnate.

tying *see* **tie.**

tyke *n.* objectionable fellow.

Tynwald /ˈtɪnwold/ *n.* governing assembly of the Isle of Man.

type *n.* kind, class; typical example or instance; (*colloq.*) person of specified character; small block with a raised letter etc. used in printing; set or kind of these. —*v.t./i.* classify according to type; write with a typewriter. **～cast** *v.t.* cast (an actor) in a role appropriate to his nature or previous successful roles.

typescript *n.* typewritten document.

typewriter *n.* machine for producing print-like characters on paper, by pressing keys. **typewritten** *a.*

typhoid *n.* **～ fever,** serious infectious feverish disease.

typhoon *n.* violent hurricane.

typhus *n.* infectious feverish disease transmitted by parasites.

typical *a.* having the distinctive qualities of a particular type of person or thing. **typically** *adv.*

typify *v.t.* be a representative specimen of.

typist *n.* person who types.

typography *n.* art, practice, or style of printing. **typographical** *a.*

tyrannize /ˈtɪ-/ *v.i.* rule as or like a tyrant.

tyranny /ˈtɪ-/ *n.* government by a tyrant; tyrannical use of power.

tyrant /ˈtaɪ-/ *n.* ruler or other person who uses his power in a harsh, demanding, or oppressive way. **tyrannical** /tɪˈræn-/ *a.*, **tyrannically** *adv.*, **tyrannous** /ˈtɪ-/ *a.*

tyre *n.* covering round the rim of a wheel to absorb shocks.

tyro *n.* (pl. *-os*) = tiro.

U

ubiquitous /juˈbɪk-/ *a.* found everywhere. **ubiquity** *n.*

udder *n.* bag-like milk-secreting organ of a cow, goat, etc.

UFO *abbr.* unidentified flying object.

ugly *a.* (*-ier*, *-iest*) unpleasant to look at or hear; threatening, hostile. **ugliness** *n.*

U.H.F. *abbr.* ultra-high frequency.

U.K. *abbr.* United Kingdom.

ukulele /jukəˈleɪlɪ/ *n.* small four-stringed guitar.

ulcer *n.* open sore. **ulcerous** *a.*

ulcerated *a.* affected with ulcer(s). **ulceration** *n.*

ulterior *a.* beyond what is obvious or admitted.

ultimate *a.* last, final; fundamental. **ultimately** *adv.*

ultimatum *n.* (pl. *-ums*) final demand, with a threat of hostile action if this is rejected.

ultra- *pref.* beyond; extremely.

ultramarine *a. & n.* deep bright blue.

ultrasonic *a.* above the range of normal human hearing.

ultraviolet *a.* of or using radiation with a wavelength shorter than that of visible light-rays.

umbel *n.* flower-cluster with stalks of nearly equal length.

umber *n.* natural brownish colouring-matter. **burnt ～,** reddish brown.

umbilical /-ˈbɪl-/ *a.* of the navel. **～ cord,** flexible tube connecting the placenta to the navel of a foetus.

umbrage *n.* feeling of being offended. **take ～,** take offence.

umbrella *n.* portable protection against rain, circle of fabric on a folding framework of spokes attached to a central stick.

umpire *n.* person appointed to supervise a game or contest etc. and see that rules are observed. —*v.t.* act as umpire in.

umpteen *a.* (*sl.*) very many. **umpteenth** *a.*

U.N. *abbr.* United Nations.

'un *pron.* (*colloq.*) one.

un- *pref.* not; reversing the action indicated by a verb, e.g. *unlock*.

The number of words with this prefix is almost unlimited and many of those whose meaning is obvious are not listed below.

unable *a.* not able.

unaccountable *a.* unable to be accounted for; not having to account for one's actions etc. **unaccountably** *adv.*

unadopted *a.* (of a road) not maintained by a local authority.

unadulterated *a.* pure, complete.

unalloyed /-ˈlɔɪd/ *a.* pure.

unanimous *a.* all agreeing; agreed by all. **unanimously** *adv.*, **unanimity** /-ˈnɪm-/ *a.*

unarmed *a.* without weapons.

unasked *a.* without being requested.

unassuming *a.* not arrogant, unpretentious.

unavoidable *a.* unable to be avoided. **unavoidably** *adv.*

unaware *a.* not aware.

unawares *adv.* unexpectedly; without noticing.

unbalanced *a.* not balanced; mentally unsound.

unbearable *a.* not bearable, unable to be endured.

unbeatable *a.* impossible to defeat or surpass.

unbeaten *a.* not defeated, not surpassed.

unbeknown *a.* (*colloq.*) unknown.

unbend *v.t./i.* (p.t. *unbent*) change from a bent position; become relaxed or affable.

unbending *a.* inflexible, refusing to alter one's demands.

unbiased *a.* not biased.

unbidden *a.* not commanded or invited.

unblock *v.t.* remove an obstruction from.

unbolt *v.t.* release (a door) by drawing back the bolt(s).

unborn *a.* not yet born.

unbounded *a.* without limits.

unbridled *a.* unrestrained.

unburden *v.refl.* **~ oneself**, reveal one's thoughts and feelings.

uncalled-for *a.* given or done impertinently or unjustifiably.

uncanny *a.* (-*ier*, -*iest*) strange and rather frightening; extraordinary. **uncannily** *adv.*

unceasing *a.* not ceasing.

unceremonious *a.* without proper formality or dignity.

uncertain *a.* not known or not knowing certainly; not to be depended on; changeable. **uncertainly** *adv.*, **uncertainty** *n.*

unchristian *a.* contrary to Christian principles, uncharitable.

uncial /ˈʌnsɪəl/ *a.* of or using written capital letters as found in 4th–8th century manuscripts. —*n.* uncial letter.

uncle *n.* brother or brother-in-law of one's father or mother.

uncoil *v.t./i.* unwind.

uncommon *a.* not common, unusual.

uncompromising /-ˈkɒmprəmaɪz-/ *a.* not allowing or not seeking compromise, inflexible.

unconditional *a.* not subject to conditions. **unconditionally** *adv.*

unconscionable /-ʃən-/ *a.* unscrupulous; contrary to what one's conscience feels is right.

unconscious *a.* not conscious; not aware; done without conscious intention. **unconsciously** *adv.*, **unconsciousness** *n.*

uncooperative *a.* not co-operative.

uncork *v.t.* pull the cork from.

uncouple *v.t.* disconnect (things joined by a coupling).

uncouth /-ˈkuθ/ *a.* awkward in manner, boorish.

uncover *v.t.* remove a covering from; reveal, expose.

unction *n.* anointing with oil, esp. as a religious rite; pretended earnestness, excessive politeness.

unctuous *a.* having an oily manner; smugly virtuous. **unctuously** *adv.*

undecided *a.* not yet certain; not yet having made up one's mind.

undeniable *a.* impossible to deny, undoubtedly true. **undeniably** *adv.*

under *prep.* in or to a position or rank etc. lower than; less than; governed or controlled by; subjected to; in accordance with; designated by. —*adv.* in or to a lower position or subordinate condition; in or into a state of unconsciousness; below a certain quantity, rank, or age etc. **~ age**, not old enough, esp. for some legal right; not yet of adult status. **~ way**, making progress.

under- *pref.* below; lower, subordinate; insufficiently.

underarm *a. & adv.* in the armpit; with the hand brought forwards and upwards.

undercarriage *n.* aircraft's landing-wheels and their supports.

underclothes *n.pl.* underwear.

undercoat *n.* layer of paint used under a finishing coat.

undercover *a.* done or doing things secretly.

undercurrent *n.* current flowing below a surface; underlying feeling or influence or trend.

undercut *v.t.* (p.t. *undercut*) cut away the part below; sell or work for a lower price than.

underdog *n.* person etc. in an inferior or subordinate position.

underdone *a.* not thoroughly cooked.

underestimate *v.t.* make too low an estimate of. **underestimation** *n.*

underfoot *adv.* on the ground; under one's feet.

undergarment *n.* piece of underwear.

undergo *v.t.* (p.t. -*went*, p.p. -*gone*) experience; be subjected to.

undergraduate *n.* university student who has not yet taken a degree.

underground[1] /-ˈgraʊ-/ *adv.* under the surface of the ground; in secret, into secrecy or hiding.

underground[2] /ˈʌn-/ *a.* under the surface of the ground; secret. —*n.* underground railway.

undergrowth *n.* shrubs and bushes growing closely, esp. under trees.

underhand[1] /ˈʌn-/ a. done or doing things slyly or secretly; underarm.

underhand[2] /-ˈhæ-/ adv. in an underhand way. **underhandedly** adv.

underlay n. layer of material laid under another as a support.

underlie v.t. (p.t. -lay, p.p. -lain, pres.p. -lying) lie or exist beneath; be the basis of. **underlying** a.

underline v.t. draw a line under; emphasize.

underling n. subordinate.

undermine v.t. make a hollow or tunnel beneath; weaken gradually.

underneath prep. & adv. below or on the inside of (a thing).

underpaid a. paid too little.

underpants n.pl. man's under-garment covering the lower part of the body and part of the legs.

underpass n. road passing under another.

underprivileged a. not having the normal standard of living or rights in a community.

underrate v.t. underestimate.

underripe a. not fully ripe.

underseal v.t. coat the lower surface of (a vehicle) with a protective layer.

undersell v.t. (p.t. -sold) sell at a lower price than.

undersigned a. who has or have signed this document.

undersized a. of less than the usual size.

underskirt n. skirt for wearing beneath another; petticoat.

underslung a. supported from above.

understand v.t./i. (p.t. -stood) see the meaning or importance of; know the ways or workings of; know the explanation; infer; take for granted. **understandable** a.

understanding a. showing insight or sympathy. —n. ability to understand; intelligence; sympathetic insight; agreement, harmony of feeling; thing agreed.

understatement n. statement representing a thing as less than it really is.

understeer v.i. (of a car) tend to turn less sharply than was intended. —n. this tendency.

understudy n. actor who studies another's part in order to be able to take his place if necessary. —v.t. study in this way.

undertake v.t. (p.t. -took, p.p. -taken) agree or promise (to do something); make oneself responsible for.

undertaker n. one whose business is to organize funerals.

undertaking n. work etc. undertaken; promise, guarantee; undertaker's work.

undertone n. low or subdued tone; underlying quality or feeling.

undertow /-təʊ/ n. current below the sea's surface, moving in the opposite direction to the surface current.

undervalue v.t. put too low a value on.

underwater a. & adv. (situated, used, or done) beneath the surface of water.

underwear n. garments worn under indoor clothing.

underweight a. weighing too little.

underwent see undergo.

underworld n. (in mythology) abode of spirits of the dead, under the earth; part of society habitually involved in crime.

underwrite v.t. (p.t. -wrote, p.p. -written) accept liability under (an insurance policy); undertake to finance. **underwriter** n.

undeserved a. not deserved. **undeservedly** /-vɪdlɪ/ adv.

undesirable a. not desirable, objectionable. **undesirably** adv.

undeveloped a. not developed.

undies n.pl. (colloq.) women's underwear.

undo v.t. (p.t. -did, p.p. -done) unfasten, unwrap; cancel the effect of, ruin.

undone a. unfastened; not done; (old use) brought to ruin.

undoubted a. not disputed. **undoubtedly** adv.

undress v.t./i. take clothes off.

undue a. excessive.

undulate v.t./i. have or cause to have a wavy movement or appearance. **undulation** n.

unduly adv. excessively.

undying a. everlasting.

unearth v.t. uncover or bring out from the ground; find by searching.

unearthly a. not of this earth; mysterious and frightening; (colloq.) absurdly early or inconvenient.

uneasy a. not comfortable; not confident; worrying. **uneasily** adv., **uneasiness** n.

uneconomic a. not profitable.

unemployed a. having no employment; without a paid job; not in use. **unemployment** n.

unending a. endless.

unequal a. not equal. **unequally** adv.

unequivocal a. clear and not ambiguous. **unequivocally** adv.

unerring /-ˈɜr-/ a. making no mistake.

uneven a. not level, not smooth; not uniform. **unevenly** adv., **unevenness** n.

unexampled a. without precedent.

unexceptionable a. with which no fault can be found.

unexceptional a. not exceptional.

unexpected a. not expected. **unexpectedly** adv.

unfailing a. constant, reliable.

unfair a. not impartial, not in accordance with justice. **unfairly** adv., **unfairness** n.

unfaithful a. not loyal; having committed adultery. **unfaithfully** adv., **unfaithfulness** n.

unfasten v.t. open the fastening(s) of.

unfeeling a. lacking sensitivity; not sympathetic. **unfeelingly** adv.

unfit a. unsuitable; not in perfect health or physical condition. —v.t. (p.t. unfitted) make unsuitable.

unfold v.t./i. open, spread out; become known.

unforgettable a. impossible to forget.

unfortunate a. having bad luck; regrettable. **unfortunately** adv.

unfounded a. with no basis.

unfrock v.t. deprive (a priest) of his priesthood.

unfurl v.t./i. unroll; spread out.

ungainly *adv.* awkward-looking, not graceful. **ungainliness** *n.*

ungodly *a.* not reverencing God; wicked; (*colloq.*) outrageous.

ungrateful *a.* not grateful.

unguarded *a.* not guarded; incautious.

unguent /ˈʌŋgwənt/ *n.* ointment, lubricant.

unhappy *a.* (*-ier, -iest*) not happy, sad; unfortunate; unsuitable. **unhappily** *adv.*, **unhappiness** *n.*

unhealthy *a.* (*-ier, -iest*) not healthy; harmful to health. **unhealthily** *adv.*

unhinge *v.t.* cause to become mentally unbalanced.

unholy *a.* (*-ier, -iest*) wicked, irreverent; (*colloq.*) very great.

unhook *v.t.* detach from hook(s); unfasten by releasing hook(s).

unhorse *v.t.* throw or drag (a rider) from a horse.

unicorn *n.* mythical horse-like animal with one straight horn on its forehead.

uniform *n.* distinctive clothing identifying the wearer as a member of an organization or group. —*a.* always the same. **uniformly** *adv.*, **uniformity** *n.*

unify *v.t.* unite. **unification** *n.*

unilateral *a.* done by or affecting one person or group etc. and not another. **unilaterally** *adv.*

unimpeachable *a.* completely trustworthy.

union *n.* uniting, being united; a whole formed by uniting parts; association; trade union (see *trade*). **Union Jack,** national flag of the U.K.

unionist *n.* member of a trade union; supporter of trade unions; one who favours union.

unique *a.* being the only one of its kind; unequalled. **uniquely** *adv.*

unisex *a.* designed in a style suitable for people of either sex.

unison *n.* in **∼,** all together; sounding or singing together.

unit *n.* individual thing, person, or group, esp. as part of a complex whole; fixed quantity used as a standard in terms of which other quantities are expressed or for which a stated charge is made. **∼ trust,** investment company paying dividends calculated on the average return from the various securities which they hold.

Unitarian /-ˈteər-/ *n.* member of a Christian sect maintaining that God is one person not a Trinity.

unitary *a.* of a unit or units.

unite *v.t./i.* join together, make or become one; act together, cooperate.

unity *n.* state of being one or a unit; complex whole; number one in mathematics; agreement.

universal *a.* of or for or done by all. **universally** *adv.*

universe *n.* all existing things, including the earth and its creatures and all the heavenly bodies.

university *n.* educational institution providing facilities for advanced learning.

unjust *a.* not just or fair. **unjustly** *adv.*

unkempt *a.* looking untidy or neglected.

unkind *a.* not kind, harsh. **unkindly** *adv.*, **unkindness** *n.*

unknown *a.* not known.

unleash *v.t.* release, let loose.

unless *conj.* if . . . not, except when.

unlike *a.* not like. —*prep.* differently from.

unlikely *a.* not likely to happen or be true or be successful.

unlimited *a.* not limited, very great in number or quantity.

unload *v.t./i.* remove a load or cargo (from); get rid of; remove the charge from (a gun).

unlock *v.t.* release the lock of (a door etc.); release by unlocking.

unlucky *a.* (*-ier, -iest*) not lucky. **unluckily** *adv.*

unman *v.t.* (p.t. *unmanned*) weaken the self-control or courage of (a man).

unmanned *a.* operated without a crew.

unmarried *a.* not married.

unmask *v.t./i.* remove a mask (from); expose the true character of.

unmentionable *a.* not fit to be spoken of.

unmistakable *a.* clear, not able to be doubted or mistaken for another. **unmistakably** *adv.*

unmitigated *a.* not modified, absolute.

unmoved *a.* not moved, not persuaded, not affected by emotion.

unnatural *a.* not natural; not normal. **unnaturally** *adv.*

unnecessary *a.* not necessary; more than is necessary. **unnecessarily** *adv.*

unnerve *v.t.* cause to lose courage or determination.

unnumbered *a.* not marked with a number; countless.

unobtrusive *a.* not making oneself or itself noticed.

unofficial *a.* not official. **unofficially** *adv.*

unpack *v.t./i.* open and remove the contents of (a suitcase etc.); take out from its packaging.

unparalleled *a.* never yet equalled.

unpick *v.t.* undo the stitching of.

unpleasant *a.* not pleasant. **unpleasantly** *adv.*, **unpleasantness** *n.*

unpopular *a.* not liked by most people. **unpopularity** *n.*

unprecedented /-ˈpres-/ *a.* for which there is no precedent; unparalleled.

unpremeditated *a.* not planned beforehand.

unprepared *a.* not prepared beforehand; not ready or not equipped to do something.

unprepossessing *a.* unattractive.

unpretentious *a.* not pretentious, not showy or pompous.

unprincipled *a.* without good moral principles, unscrupulous.

unprofessional *a.* not professional; contrary to the standards of behaviour for members of a profession. **unprofessionally** *adv.*

unqualified *a.* not qualified; not restricted or modified.

unquestionable *a.* too clear to be doubted. **unquestionably** *adv.*

unquote (direction in dictation etc.) mark the end of the quotation.

unravel *v.t./i.* (p.t. *unravelled*) disentangle; undo (knitted fabric); become unravelled.

unreel *v.t./i.* unwind from a reel.

unrelieved *a.* not relieved; without anything to give variation.

unremitting *a.* not ceasing.

unrequited /-ˈkwaɪ-/ *a.* (of love) not returned or rewarded.

unreservedly /-vɪdlɪ/ *adv.* without reservation, completely.

unrest *n.* restlessness, agitation.

unrivalled *a.* having no equal, incomparable.

unroll *v.t./i.* open after being rolled.

unruly *a.* not easy to control, disorderly. **unruliness** *n.*

unsaddle *v.t.* remove the saddle from.

unsaid *a.* not spoken or expressed.

unsavoury *a.* disagreeable to the taste or smell; morally disgusting.

unscathed /-ˈskeɪðd/ *a.* without suffering any injury.

unscramble *v.t.* sort out; make (a scrambled transmission) intelligible.

unscrew *v.t.* loosen (a screw etc.); unfasten by removing screw(s).

unscripted *a.* without a prepared script.

unscrupulous *a.* not prevented by scruples of conscience.

unseat *v.t.* dislodge (a rider); remove from a parliamentary seat.

unseemly *a.* not seemly, improper.

unseen *a.* not seen. —*n.* passage for unprepared translation from a foreign language.

unselfish *a.* not selfish; considering others' needs before one's own.

unsettle *v.t.* make uneasy, disturb.

unsettled *a.* (of weather) changeable.

unshakeable *a.* firm.

unsightly *a.* not pleasant to look at, ugly. **unsightliness** *n.*

unsigned *a.* not signed.

unskilled *a.* not having or needing skill or special training.

unsociable *a.* not sociable.

unsocial *a.* not sociable; not conforming to normal social practices.

unsolicited *a.* not requested.

unsophisticated *a.* simple and natural or naïve.

unsound *a.* not sound or strong, not free from defects. **of ∼ mind,** insane.

unsparing *a.* giving lavishly.

unspeakable *a.* too bad to be described in words.

unstable *a.* not stable; mentally or emotionally unbalanced.

unsteady *a.* not steady. **unsteadily** *adv.*, **unsteadiness** *n.*

unstinted *a.* given lavishly.

unstuck *a.* detached after being stuck on or together. **come ∼,** (*colloq.*) suffer disaster, fail.

unstudied *a.* natural in manner.

unsuccessful *a.* not successful. **unsuccessfully** *adv.*

unsuitable *a.* not suitable. **unsuitably** *adv.*

unsullied *a.* not sullied, pure.

unsuspecting *a.* feeling no suspicion.

unthinkable *a.* too bad or too unlikely to be thought about.

unthinking *a.* thoughtless.

untidy *a.* (*-ier, -iest*) not tidy. **untidily** *adv.*, **untidiness** *n.*

untie *v.t.* unfasten; release from being tied up.

until *prep. & conj.* = till².

untimely *a.* inopportune; premature.

untiring *a.* not becoming tired.

unto *prep.* (*old use*) to.

untold *a.* not told; too much or too many to be counted.

untouchable *a.* not able or not allowed to be touched. —*n.* member of the lowest Hindu caste in India.

untoward /-ˈwɒd/ *a.* inconvenient.

untraceable *a.* unable to be traced.

untried *a.* not yet tried or tested.

untrue *a.* not true, contrary to facts; not loyal. **untruly** *adv.*

untruth *n.* untrue statement, lie; lack of truth. **untruthful** *a.*, **untruthfully** *adv.*

unused *a.* not yet used.

unusual *a.* not usual; remarkable, rare. **unusually** *adv.*

unutterable *a.* too great to be expressed in words. **unutterably** *adv.*

unvarnished *a.* not varnished; plain and straightforward.

unveil *v.t./i.* remove a veil (from); remove concealing drapery from; disclose, make publicly known.

unversed *a.* ∼ **in,** not experienced in.

unwanted *a.* not wanted.

unwarrantable *a.* unjustifiable.

unwarranted *a.* unjustified, unauthorized.

unwary *a.* not cautious.

unwell *a.* not in good health.

unwieldy *a.* awkward to move or control because of its size, shape, or weight.

unwilling *a.* not willing.

unwind *v.t./i.* (p.t. *unwound*) draw out or become drawn out from being wound; (*colloq.*) relax from work or tension.

unwise *a.* not wise, foolish. **unwisely** *adv.*

unwitting *a.* unaware; unintentional. **unwittingly** *adv.*

unwonted /-ˈwəʊ-/ *a.* not customary, not usual. **unwontedly** *adv.*

unworldly *a.* not worldly, spiritually-minded. **unworldliness** *n.*

unworn *a.* not yet worn.

unworthy *a.* worthless; not deserving; unsuitable to the character (of a person or thing).

unwrap *v.t./i.* (p.t. *unwrapped*) open from being wrapped.

unwritten *a.* not written down; based on custom not statute.

up *adv.* to a vertical position; to, in, or at a higher place or state etc.; to a larger size; as far as a stated place, time, or amount; out of bed; into activity or efficiency; into pieces, apart; compactly; (*colloq.*) amiss, happening.

—*prep.* up-wards along or through or into; at a higher part of. —*a.* directed upwards; travelling towards a central place. —*v.t./i.* (p.t. *upped*) raise; pick up; get up (and do something). **time is ~,** is finished. **~-end** *v.t./i.* set or rise up on end. **~ in,** (*colloq.*) knowledgeable about. **ups and downs,** alternate good and bad fortune. **~ to,** occupied with, doing; required as a duty or obligation from; capable of. **~ to date,** in accordance with current fashion or information. **~-to-date** *a.*

upbraid *v.t.* reproach.

upbringing *n.* training and education during childhood.

update *v.t.* bring up to date.

upgrade *v.t.* raise to higher grade.

upheaval *n.* sudden heaving upwards; violent disturbance.

uphill *a. & adv.* going or sloping upwards.

uphold *v.t.* (p.t. *upheld*) support.

upholster *v.t.* put fabric covering, padding, etc., on (furniture).

upholstery *n.* work of upholstering furniture, material used in this.

upkeep *n.* keeping (a thing) in good condition and repair; cost of this.

upland *n. & a.* (of) higher or inland parts of a country.

uplift[1] /-'lɪ-/ *v.t.* raise.

uplift[2] /'ʌp-/ *n.* being raised; mentally elevating influence.

upon *prep.* on.

upper *a.* higher in place or position or rank. —*n.* part of a boot or shoe above the sole. **~ case,** capital letters in printing or typing. **~ hand,** mastery, dominance.

uppermost *a. & adv.* in, on, or to the top or most prominent position.

upright *a.* in a vertical position; (of a piano) with vertical strings; strictly honest or honourable. —*n.* post or rod etc. placed upright, esp. as a support.

uprising *n.* rebellion.

uproar *n.* outburst of noise and excitement or anger.

uproarious *a.* very noisy, with loud laughter. **uproariously** *adv.*

uproot *v.t.* pull out of the ground together with its roots; force to leave an established place.

upset[1] /-'set/ *v.t./i.* (p.t. *upset*, pres.p. *upsetting*) overturn; disrupt; distress; disturb the temper or digestion of.

upset[2] /'ʌp-/ *n.* upsetting.

upshot *n.* outcome.

upside down with the upper part underneath; in great disorder.

upstage *adv. & a.* nearer the back of a theatre stage. —*v.t.* divert attention from, outshine.

upstairs *adv. & a.* to or on a higher floor.

upstanding *a.* strong and healthy, well set up.

upstart *n.* person newly risen to a high position, esp. one who behaves arrogantly.

upstream *a. & adv.* in the direction from which a stream flows.

upsurge *n.* upward surge, rise.

uptake *n.* **quick in the ~,** quick to understand what is meant.

uptight *a.* (*colloq.*) nervously tense; annoyed.

upturn[1] /-'tɜn/ *v.t.* turn up or upwards or upside down.

upturn[2] /'ʌp-/ *n.* upheaval; upward trend.

upward *a.* moving or leading up.

upwards *adv.* towards a higher place etc.

uranium *n.* heavy grey metal used as a source of nuclear energy.

urban *a.* of a city or town.

urbane *a.* having smooth manners. **urbanely** *adv.*, **urbanity** *n.*

urbanize *v.t.* change (a place) into a town-like area. **urbanization** *n.*

urchin *n.* mischievous or raggedly dressed boy; sea-urchin.

Urdu /'ʊədu/ *n.* language related to Hindi, used in Pakistan.

ureter /jʊə'ri-/ *n.* duct from the kidney to the bladder.

urethra /jʊə'ri-/ *n.* duct by which urine is discharged from the body.

urge *v.t.* drive onward, encourage to proceed; recommend strongly or earnestly. —*n.* feeling or desire urging a person to do something.

urgent *a.* needing or calling for immediate attention or action. **urgently** *adv.*, **urgency** *n.*

urinal /'jʊərɪ-/ *n.* receptacle or structure for receiving urine.

urinate /'jʊər-/ *v.i.* discharge urine from the body.

urine /'jʊərɪn/ *n.* waste liquid which collects in the bladder and is discharged from the body. **urinary** *a.*

urn *n.* a kind of vase, esp. for holding a cremated person's ashes; large metal container with a tap, for keeping water etc. hot.

us *pron.* objective case of *we.*

U.S., U.S.A. *abbr.* United States of America.

usable *a.* able or fit to be used.

usage *n.* manner of using or treating something; customary practice.

use[1] /-z/ *v.t.* cause to act or to serve for a purpose or as an instrument or material; treat; exploit selfishly. **~ up,** use the whole or the remainder of; tire out. **user** *n.*

use[2] /-s/ *n.* using, being used; power of using; purpose for which a thing is used. **make ~ of,** use, exploit.

used[1] /-zd/ *a.* second-hand.

used[2] /-st/ *p.t.* was or were accustomed. —*a.* **~ to,** familiar with by practice or habit.

useful *a.* usable for a practical purpose; able to produce good results. **usefully** *adv.*, **usefulness** *n.*

useless *a.* not usable, not useful. **uselessly** *adv.*, **uselessness** *n.*

usher *n.* person who shows people to their seats in a public hall etc. or into someone's presence; official acting as doorkeeper in a lawcourt. —*v.t.* lead, escort.

usherette *n.* woman who ushers people to seats in a cinema etc.

U.S.S.R. *abbr.* Union of Soviet Socialist Republics.

usual *a.* such as happens or is done or used etc. in many or most instances. **usually** *adv.*

usurer /'juʒ-/ *n.* person who lends money at excessively high rates.

usurp *v.t.* take (power, position, or right) wrongfully or by force. **usurpation** *n.*, **usurper** *n.*

usury /'juʒ-/ *n.* lending of money at excessively high rates of interest.

utensil *n.* instrument or container, esp. for domestic use.

uterus *n.* womb. **uterine** /-aɪn/ *a.*

utilitarian *a.* designed to be useful rather than decorative or luxurious, severely practical.

utility *n.* usefulness; useful thing. —*a.* severely practical.

utilize *v.t.* use, find a use for. **utilization** *n.*

utmost *a. & n.* furthest, greatest, or extreme (point or degree etc.).

Utopia *n.* imaginary place or state where all is perfect. **Utopian** *a.*

utter[1] *a.* complete, absolute. **utterly** *adv.*

utter[2] *v.t.* make (a sound or words) with the mouth or voice; speak; put (a forged banknote or coin etc.) into circulation. **utterance** *n.*

uttermost *a. & n.* = utmost.

uvula /'juːvjʊ-/ *n.* small fleshy projection hanging at the back of the throat.

uxorious *a.* excessively fond of one's wife.

V

V *abbr.* volt(s).

vac *n.* (*colloq.*) vacation; vacuum cleaner.

vacancy *n.* state of being vacant; vacant place or position etc.

vacant *a.* empty, not filled or occupied; showing no intelligence or interest. **vacantly** *adv.*

vacate *v.t.* cease to occupy.

vacation *n.* interval between terms in universities and lawcourts; (*U.S.*) holiday; vacating of a place etc. —*v.i.* (*U.S.*) spend a holiday.

vaccinate *n.* inoculate with a vaccine. **vaccination** *n.*

vaccine /'væksɪn/ *n.* preparation that gives immunity from an infection when introduced into the bloodstream. **vaccination** *n.*

vacillate /'væs-/ *v.i.* keep changing one's mind, waver. **vacillation** *n.*

vacuous *a.* inane; expressionless. **vacuously** *adv.*, **vacuousness** *n.*, **vacuity** /-'kju-/ *n.*

vacuum *n.* (pl. *-cua* or *-cuums*) space from which air has been removed; absence of normal contents. —*v.t./i.* (*colloq.*) clean with a vacuum cleaner. ∼ **cleaner,** electrical apparatus that takes up dust etc. by suction. ∼ **flask,** container for keeping liquids hot or cold.

vade-mecum /vɑːdɪ'meɪ-/ *n.* handbook.

vagabond *n.* wanderer; vagrant, esp. an idle or dishonest one.

vagary /'veɪg-/ *n.* capricious act or idea or fluctuation.

vagina /-'dʒaɪnə/ *n.* passage leading from the vulva to the womb in females. **vaginal** *a.*

vagrant /'veɪg-/ *n.* person without a settled home or regular work. **vagrancy** *n.*

vague *a.* (-*er*, -*est*) not clearly expressed or perceived or identified; not expressing oneself clearly. **vaguely** *adv.*, **vagueness** *n.*

vain *a.* (-*er*, -*est*) conceited; having no value or significance; useless, futile. **in** ∼, uselessly. **vainly** *adv.*

valance /'væl-/ *n.* short curtain or hanging frill.

vale *n.* valley.

valediction /vælɪ-/ *n.* farewell. **valedictory** *a.*

valence /'veɪ-/ *n.* combining-power of an atom as compared with that of the hydrogen atom.

valency /'veɪ-/ *n.* unit of the combining-power of atoms.

valentine *n.* sweetheart chosen on St. Valentine's Day (14 Feb.); greetings-card sent to one's valentine.

valerian /-'lɪər-/ *n.* strong-smelling herb with pink or white flowers.

valet /'vælɪt *or* -leɪ/ *n.* man's personal attendant who takes care of clothes etc. —*v.t.* (p.t. *valeted*) act as valet to.

valetudinarian /-'neər-/ *n.* person who pays excessive attention to preserving his health.

valiant *a.* brave. **valiantly** *adv.*

valid *a.* having legal force, legally usable; (of reasoning) sound, logical. **validity** *n.*

validate *v.t.* make valid, confirm. **validation** *n.*

valley *n.* (pl. *-eys*) low area between hills; region drained by a river.

valour *n.* bravery, esp. in fighting.

valse *n.* = waltz.

valuable *a.* of great value or worth.

valuables *n.pl.* valuable things.

valuation *n.* estimation or estimate of a thing's worth.

value *n.* amount of money or other commodity etc. considered equivalent to something else; usefulness, importance; thing's ability to serve a purpose or cause an effect; amount etc. denoted by a symbol; (*pl.*) principles considered important. —*v.t.* estimate the value of; consider to be of great worth. ∼ **added tax,** tax on the amount by which a thing's value has been increased at each stage of its production.

valueless *a.* having no value.

valuer *n.* person who estimates values professionally.

valve *n.* device controlling flow through a pipe; structure allowing blood to flow in one direction only; device to vary the length of the tube in a trumpet etc.; each half of the hinged shell of an oyster etc.; thermionic valve.

valvular *a.* of the valves of the heart or blood-vessels.

vamp[1] *n.* upper front part of a boot or shoe. —*v.t./i.* improvise (esp. a musical accompaniment).

vamp[2] *n.* woman who is an unscrupulous flirt. —*v.t./i.* behave as a vamp (to).

vampire *n.* ghost or reanimated body supposed to suck blood.

van[1] *n.* covered vehicle for transporting goods etc.; railway carriage for luggage or goods.

van[2] *n.* vanguard, forefront.

vandal *n.* person who damages things wilfully. **vandalism** *n.*

vandalize *v.t.* damage wilfully.

vane *n.* weather-vane; blade of a propeller etc.

vanguard *n.* foremost part of an advancing army etc.

vanilla *n.* a kind of flavouring, esp. obtained from the pods of a tropical orchid.

vanish *v.i.* disappear completely.

vanity *n.* conceit; worthlessness, worthless thing. ∼ **bag** or **case,** woman's small bag or case for carrying cosmetics etc.

vanquish *v.i.* conquer.

vantage *n.* advantage (esp. as a score in tennis). ∼**-point** *n.* position giving a good view.

vapid *a.* insipid, uninteresting.

vaporize *v.t./i.* convert or be converted into vapour. **vaporization** *n.*

vapour *n.* moisture or other substance suspended in air; air-like substance into which certain liquids or solids are converted by heating.

variable *a.* varying. —*n.* thing that varies. **variability** *n.*

variance *n.* **at** ∼, disagreeing.

variant *a.* differing. —*n.* variant form or spelling etc.

variation *n.* varying, extent of this; variant; repetition of a melody in a different form.

varicoloured /ˈveər-/ *a.* variegated; of various colours.

varicose /ˈvæ-/ *a.* (of veins) permanently swollen. **varicosity** *n.*

varied *a.* of different sorts.

variegated /ˈveərɪg-/ *a.* having irregular patches of colours.

variety *n.* quality of not being the same; quantity of different things; class of things differing from others in their general group; member of such a class; entertainment with a series of short performances.

various *a.* of several kinds; several. **variously** *adv.*

varnish *n.* liquid that dries to form a shiny transparent coating on wood etc.; paint used on the nails. —*v.t.* coat with varnish.

vary *v.t./i.* make or be or become different.

vascular *a.* of vessels or ducts for conveying blood or sap.

vase /vɑz/ *n.* open vessel used for holding cut flowers or as an ornament.

vasectomy *n.* surgical removal of part of the ducts that carry semen from the testicles, esp. as a method of birth control.

vassal *n.* humble servant or subordinate.

vast *a.* very great in area or size. **vastly** *adv.*, **vastness** *n.*

vat *n.* large tank for liquids.

V.A.T. *abbr.* value added tax.

vaudeville /ˈvɔdə-/ *n.* variety entertainment.

vault[1] *n.* arched roof; cellar used as a storage-place; burial chamber. **vaulted** *a.*

vault[2] *v.t./i. & n.* jump, esp. while resting on the hand(s) or with the help of a pole. **vaulting-horse** *n.* padded structure for vaulting over.

vaunt *v.t./i. & n.* boast.

veal *n.* calf's flesh as food.

vector *n.* thing (e.g. velocity) that has both magnitude and direction; carrier of an infection.

veer *v.i.* change direction.

vegan /ˈviː-/ *n.* person who eats no meat or animal products.

vegetable *n.* plant grown for food. —*a.* of or from plants.

vegetarian *n.* person who eats no meat.

vegetate *v.i.* live an uneventful life.

vegetation *n.* plants collectively.

vehement /ˈviːm-/ *a.* showing strong feeling. **vehemently** *adv.*, **vehemence** *n.*

vehicle /ˈviːɪk-/ *n.* conveyance for transporting passengers or goods on land or in space; means by which something is expressed or displayed. **vehicular** /-ˈhɪk-/ *a.*

veil *n.* piece of fine net or other fabric worn as part of a head-dress or to protect or conceal the face. —*v.t.* cover with or as if with a veil. **take the** ∼, become a nun.

vein *n.* any of the blood-vessels conveying blood towards the heart; thread-like structure; narrow streak in marble or layer in rock etc.; mood, manner. **veined** *a.*

veld /velt/ *n.* open grassland in South Africa.

vellum *n.* fine parchment; smooth writing-paper.

velocity *n.* speed.

velour /-ˈlʊə(r)/ *n.* plush-like fabric.

velvet *n.* woven fabric with thick short pile on one side. **on** ∼, in an advantageous or prosperous position. **velvety** *a.*

velveteen *n.* cotton velvet.

venal /ˈviː-/ *a.* able to be bribed; influenced by bribery. **venality** *n.*

vend *v.t.* sell, offer for sale. **vendor** *n.*

vendetta *n.* feud.

vending-machine *n.* slot-machine where small articles are obtained.

veneer *n.* thin covering layer of fine wood; superficial show of a quality. —*v.t.* cover with a veneer.

venerate *v.t.* respect deeply; honour as hallowed or sacred. **veneration** *n.*, **venerable** *a.*

venereal /-ˈnɪər-/ *a.* (of infections) contracted by sexual intercourse with an infected person.

Venetian *a. & n.* (native) of Venice. ∼ **blind,** window blind of adjustable horizontal slats.

vengeance *n.* retaliation. **with a** ∼, in an extreme degree.

vengeful *a.* seeking vengeance.

venial /ˈviː-/ *a.* (of a sin) pardonable, not serious. **veniality** *n.*

venison *n.* deer's flesh as food.

venom *n.* poisonous fluid secreted by certain snakes etc.; bitter feeling or language, hatred. **venomous** *a.*

vent[1] *n.* slit at the lower edge of the back or side of a coat.

vent[2] *n.* opening allowing air or liquid etc. to pass through. —*v.t.* make a vent in; give vent to. **give ∼ to,** give an outlet to (feelings etc.), express freely.

ventilate *v.t.* cause air to enter or circulate freely in; express publicly. **ventilation** *n.*

ventilator *n.* device for ventilating a room etc.

ventral *a.* of or on the abdomen.

ventricle *n.* cavity, esp. in the heart or brain.

ventriloquist /-ˈtrɪl-/ *n.* entertainer who can produce voice-sounds so that they seem to come from a puppet etc. **ventriloquism** *n.*

venture *n.* undertaking that involves risk. —*v.t./i.* dare; dare to go or utter. **at a ∼,** at random.

venturesome *a.* daring.

venue /ˈven-/ *n.* appointed place for a meeting etc.

veracious /-ˈreɪ-/ *a.* truthful; true. **veraciously** *adv.,* **veracity** /-ˈræ-/ *n.*

veranda *n.* roofed terrace.

verb *n.* word indicating action or occurrence or being.

verbal *a.* of or in words; spoken; of a verb. **verbally** *adv.*

verbatim /-ˈbeɪ-/ *adv.* & *a.* in exactly the same words.

verbena /-ˈbiː-/ *n.* vervain; cultivated variety of this.

verbiage /ˈvɜː-/ *n.* excessive number of words.

verbose /-ˈbəʊs/ *a.* using more words than are needed. **verbosely** *adv.,* **verbosity** /-ˈbɒs-/ *n.*

verdant *a.* (of grass etc.) green.

verdict *n.* decision reached by a jury; decision or opinion reached after testing something.

verdigris /-grɪs/ *n.* green deposit forming on copper or brass.

verge *n.* extreme edge, brink; grass edging of a road etc. —*v.i.* **∼ on,** border on.

verger *n.* person who is caretaker and attendant in a church.

verify *v.t.* check the truth or correctness of. **verification** *n.*

verily *adv.* (*old use*) in truth.

verisimilitude /-ˈmɪl-/ *n.* appearance of being true.

veritable *a.* real, rightly named.

verity *n.* (*old use*) truth.

vermicelli /-ˈsel-/ *n.* pasta made in slender threads.

vermiform *a.* worm-like in shape.

vermilion *a.* & *n.* bright red.

vermin *n.* common animal or insect regarded as a pest.

verminous *a.* infested with vermin.

vermouth /-məθ/ *n.* white wine flavoured with herbs.

vernacular *n.* ordinary language of a country or district.

vernal *a.* of or occurring in spring.

verruca /-ˈruː-/ *n.* wart or wart-like swelling, esp. on the foot.

versatile *a.* able to do or be used for many different things. **versatility** *n.*

verse *n.* metrical (not prose) composition; group of lines forming a unit in a poem or hymn; numbered division of a Bible chapter.

versed *a.* **∼ in,** experienced in.

versicle *n.* each of the short sentences said or sung by the clergyman in the liturgy.

version *n.* particular account of a matter; translation; special or variant form.

versus *prep.* against.

vertebra *n.* (pl. *-brae,* pr. -bri) each segment of the backbone. **vertebral** *a.*

vertebrate /-ˈbrət/ *n.* animal that has a backbone.

vertex *n.* (pl. *vertices*) highest point of a hill etc.; apex.

vertical *a.* perpendicular to the horizontal, upright. —*n.* vertical line or position. **vertically** *adv.,* **verticality** *n.*

vertigo *n.* dizziness.

vervain *n.* tall wild plant with hairy leaves and small flowers.

verve *n.* enthusiasm, vigour.

very *adv.* in a high degree, extremely; exactly. —*a.* actual, truly such; extreme. **∼ well,** expression of consent.

vesicle /ˈves-/ *n.* small hollow structure in a plant or animal body; blister.

vespers *n.pl.* R.C. Church service held in the evening.

vessel *n.* structure designed to travel on water and carry people or goods; hollow receptacle esp. for liquid; tube-like structure conveying blood or other fluid in the body of an animal or plant.

vest *n.* undergarment covering the trunk of the body; (*U.S.* & *shop use*) waistcoat. —*v.t.* confer or furnish with (power) as a firm or legal right. **vested interest,** advantageous right securely held by a person or group.

vestibule *n.* entrance hall; porch.

vestige *n.* trace, small remaining bit; very small amount.

vestigial /-ˈtɪdʒ-/ *a.* remaining as a vestige.

vestment *n.* ceremonial robe, esp. of clergy or a church choir.

vestry *n.* room attached to a church, where vestments are kept and clergy etc. robe themselves.

vet *n.* veterinary surgeon. —*v.t.* (p.t. *vetted*) examine critically for faults or errors etc.

vetch *n.* plant of the pea family used as fodder for cattle.

veteran *n.* person with long experience, esp. in the armed forces. **∼ car,** car made before 1916 or before 1905.

veterinary /ˈvet-/ *a.* of or for the treatment of diseases and disorders of animals. **∼ surgeon,** person skilled in such treatment.

veto /ˈviːtəʊ/ *n.* (pl. *-oes*) authoritative rejection of something proposed; right to make this. —*v.t.* reject by a veto.

vex *v.t.* annoy. **vexed question,** problem that is much discussed. **vexation** *n.*, **vexatious** *a.*

V.H.F. *abbr.* very high frequency.

via *prep.* by way of, through.

viable *a.* capable of living or surviving; practicable. **viability** *n.*

viaduct *n.* long bridge-like structure carrying a road or railway over a valley etc.

vial *n.* small bottle.

viands /ˈvaɪ-/ *n.pl.* articles of food.

vibrant *a.* vibrating, resonant, thrilling with energy.

vibraphone /ˈvaɪ-/ *n.* percussion instrument like a xylophone but with a vibrating effect.

vibrate *v.t./i.* move rapidly and continuously to and fro; resound, sound with rapid slight variation of pitch. **vibration** *n.*, **vibrator** *n.*, **vibratory** /ˈvaɪ-/ *a.*

vicar *n.* clergyman in charge of a parish.

vicarage *n.* house of a vicar.

vicarious /-ˈkeər-/ *a.* felt through sharing imaginatively in the feelings or activities etc. of another person. **vicariously** *adv.*

vice[1] *n.* great wickedness; a form of this; criminal and immoral practices.

vice[2] *n.* instrument with two jaws for holding things firmly.

vice[3] /ˈvaɪsɪ/ *prep.* in place of.

vice- *pref.* substitute or deputy for; next in rank to.

viceroy *n.* person governing a colony etc. as the sovereign's representative.

vice versa /vaɪsɪ ˈvɜ-/ with terms the other way round.

vicinity /-ˈsɪn-/ *n.* surrounding district. **in the ∼ (of),** near.

vicious /ˈvɪʃəs/ *a.* brutal, strongly spiteful; savage and dangerous. **∼ circle,** bad situation producing effects that produce or intensify its original cause. **viciously** *adv.*

vicissitude /-ˈsɪs-/ *n.* change of circumstances or luck.

victim *n.* person injured or killed or made to suffer; living creature killed as a religious sacrifice.

victimize *v.t.* single out to suffer ill treatment. **victimization** *n.*

victor *n.* winner.

Victorian *a.* & *n.* (person) of the reign of Queen Victoria (1837–1901).

victorious *a.* having gained victory.

victory *n.* success achieved by gaining mastery over opponent(s) or having the highest score.

victualler /ˈvɪtlə(r)/ *n.* person who supplies victuals. **licensed ∼,** licensee of a public house.

victuals /ˈvɪtlz/ *n.pl.* foods.

vicuña /-ˈkunjə/ *n.* South American animal related to the llama; soft cloth made from its wool, imitation of this.

video /ˈvɪdɪəʊ/ *n.* recording or broadcasting of pictures.

videotape *n.* magnetic tape suitable for recording television pictures and sound.

vie *v.i.* (pres.p. *vying*) carry on a rivalry, compete.

view *n.* range of vision; things within this; fine scenery; visual or mental survey; mental attitude, opinion. —*v.t./i.* survey with the eyes or mind; watch television; regard, consider. **in ∼ of,** having regard to, considering. **on ∼,** displayed for inspection. **with a ∼ to,** with the hope or intention of. **viewer** *n.*

viewfinder *n.* device on a camera showing the extent of the area being photographed.

viewpoint *n.* point of view.

vigil /ˈvɪdʒ-/ *n.* staying awake to keep watch or pray; period of this; eve of a religious festival.

vigilant *a.* watchful. **vigilantly** *adv.*, **vigilance** *n.*

vigilante /-ˈlæntɪ/ *n.* member of a self-appointed group trying to prevent crime etc. in a disorderly community.

vignette /viˈnjet/ *n.* portrait with the background gradually shaded off; short description.

vigour *n.* active physical or mental strength; forcefulness. **vigorous** *a.*, **vigorously** *adv.*, **vigorousness** *n.*

Viking /ˈvaɪ-/ *n.* ancient Scandinavian trader and pirate.

vile *a.* extremely disgusting or despicable. **vilely** *adv.*, **vileness** *n.*

vilify /ˈvɪl-/ *v.t.* say evil things about. **vilification** *n.*

villa *n.* house in a suburban or residential district; country house in Italy or France; seaside house used for holidays.

village *n.* collection of houses etc. in a country district.

villager *n.* inhabitant of a village.

villain *n.* wicked person. **villainous** *a.*, **villainy** *n.*

villein /-lɪn/ *n.* medieval serf.

vim *n.* (*colloq.*) vigour.

vinaigrette /vɪnɪˈgret/ *n.* small bottle for smelling-salts. **∼ sauce,** salad dressing of oil and vinegar.

vindicate *v.t.* clear of blame; justify. **vindication** *n.*

vindictive *a.* showing a desire for vengeance. **vindictively** *adv.*, **vindictiveness** *n.*

vine *n.* climbing or trailing woody-stemmed plant whose fruit is the grape.

vinegar *n.* sour liquid made from wine, malt, etc., by fermentation. **vinegary** *a.*

vineyard /ˈvɪn-/ *n.* plantation of vines for wine-making.

vintage *n.* gathering of grapes for wine-making; season of this; wine from a season's grapes, esp. when of high quality; date when something was produced or existed. —*a.* of high quality, esp. from a past period. **∼ car,** car made between 1917 and 1930.

vintner *n.* wine-merchant.

vinyl /ˈvaɪnɪl/ *n.* a kind of plastic.

viol /ˈvaɪəl/ *n.* medieval musical instrument resembling a violin.

viola[1] /vɪˈəʊlə/ *n.* musical instrument resembling a violin but of lower pitch.

viola[2] /ˈvaɪələ/ *n.* plant of the genus to which violets belong.

violate v.t. break (an oath or treaty etc.); treat (a sacred place) irreverently; disturb; rape. **violation** n., **violator** n.

violent a. involving great force or strength or intensity; (of death) caused by external force, not natural. **violently** adv., **violence** n.

violet n. small wild or garden plant, often with purple flowers; bluish-purple colour. —a. bluish-purple.

violin n. musical instrument with four strings of treble pitch, played with a bow. **violinist** n.

violoncello /-ˈtʃel-/ n. (pl. -os) cello.

V.I.P. abbr. very important person.

viper n. small poisonous snake.

virago /-ˈrɑː-/ n. (pl. -os) shrewish bullying woman.

viral /ˈvaɪ-/ a. of a virus.

virgin n. person (esp. a woman) who has never had sexual intercourse; the V~, the Virgin Mary, mother of Christ. —a. virginal; spotless, undefiled; untouched, not yet used. **virginal** a., **virginity** n.

virginals n.pl. earliest form of harpsichord.

virile /ˈvɪraɪl/ a. having masculine strength or procreative power. **virility** n.

virology /vaɪˈrɒl-/ n. study of viruses. **virologist** n.

virtual a. being so in effect though not in name. **virtually** adv.

virtue n. moral excellence, goodness; chastity; good characteristic. **by** or **in ~ of**, because of.

virtuoso n. (pl. -si) expert performer. **virtuosity** /-ˈɒs-/ n.

virtuous a. showing moral virtue, chaste. **virtuously** adv., **virtuousness** n.

virulent /ˈvɪrʊ-/ a. (of poison or disease) extremely strong or violent; bitterly hostile. **virulently** adv., **virulence** n.

virus n. (pl. -uses) organism (smaller than a bacterium) capable of causing disease.

visa /ˈviːzə/ n. official mark on a passport, permitting the holder to enter a specified country. **visaed** a.

visage /ˈvɪz-/ n. person's face.

vis-à-vis /viːz-ɑː-ˈviː/ adv. & prep. facing one another; as compared with.

viscera /ˈvɪsərə/ n.pl. internal organs of the body.

viscid /ˈvɪsɪd/ a. thick and gluey. **viscidity** n.

viscose n. viscous cellulose; fabric made from this.

viscount /ˈvaɪk-/ n. nobleman ranking between earl and baron; courtesy title of earl's eldest son. **viscountess** n.fem.

viscous a. thick and gluey. **viscosity** n.

visibility n. state of being visible; range of vision as determined by conditions of light etc.

visible a. able to be seen or noticed. **visibly** adv.

vision n. ability to see, sight; thing seen in the imagination or a dream etc.; imaginative insight; foresight; person or sight of unusual beauty.

visionary a. fanciful; not practical. —n. person with visionary ideas.

visit v.t./i. go or come to see (a person or place)

socially or as a sightseer or on business etc.; stay temporarily with or at; (in the Bible) inflict punishment for. —n. act of visiting. **visitor** n.

visitant n. visitor, esp. a supernatural one.

visitation n. official visit; trouble looked upon as punishment from God.

visor /ˈvaɪz-/ n. movable front part of a helmet, covering the face; shading device at the top of a vehicle's windscreen.

vista n. extensive view, esp. seen through a long opening.

visual a. of or from or used in seeing. **visually** adv.

visualize v.t. form a mental picture of. **visualization** n.

vital a. connected with or essential to life; essential to a thing's existence or success; full of vitality. **~ statistics**, those relating to population figures or births and deaths; (colloq.) measurements of a woman's bust, waist, and hips. **vitals** n.pl. vital parts of the body (e.g. heart, lungs). **vitally** adv.

vitality n. liveliness, persistent energy.

vitalize v.t. put life or vitality into.

vitamin /ˈvɪt-/ n. any of the organic substances present in food and essential to nutrition.

vitaminize v.t. add vitamins to.

vitiate /ˈvɪʃɪ-/ v.t. make imperfect or ineffective. **vitiation** n.

vitreous a. having a glass-like texture or finish.

vitrify v.t./i. change into a glassy substance, esp. by heat. **vitrifaction** n.

vitriol n. sulphuric acid or one of its salts; savagely hostile remarks. **vitriolic** a.

vituperate /vɪˈtjuː-/ v.i. use abusive language. **vituperation** n., **vituperative** a.

vivacious /-ˈveɪ-/ a. lively, high-spirited. **vivaciously** adv., **vivacity** n.

viva voce /vaɪvə ˈvəʊtʃɪ/ spoken examination.

vivid a. bright and strong; clear; (of imagination) lively. **vividly** adv., **vividness** n.

vivisection n. performance of surgical experiments on living animals.

vixen n. female fox.

viz. adv. namely.

vizier /-ˈzɪə(r)/ n. official of high rank in certain Muslim countries.

vocabulary n. list of words with their meanings; words known or used by a person or group.

vocal a. of or for or uttered by the voice. —n. piece of sung music. **vocally** adv.

vocalist n. singer.

vocalize v.t. utter.

vocation n. feeling of being called by God to a certain career; natural liking for a certain type of work; trade, profession. **vocational** a.

vociferate v.t./i. say loudly, shout. **vociferation** n.

vociferous a. making a great outcry. **vociferously** adv.

vodka n. alcoholic spirit distilled chiefly from rye.

vogue /vəʊg/ n. current fashion; popularity. **in ~**, in fashion.

voice n. sounds formed in the larynx and

uttered by the mouth; ability to produce these; expressed opinion, right to express an opinion; set of verbal forms that show the relation of the subject to the action. —*v.t.* put into words, express; utter.

void *a.* empty; not valid. —*n.* empty space, emptiness. —*v.t.* make void; excrete.

voile *n.* very thin dress-fabric.

volatile /ˈvol-/ *a.* evaporating rapidly; lively, changing quickly in mood. **volatility** *n.*

vol-au-vent /vol-əʊ-ˈvã/ *n.* puff pastry case filled with a savoury mixture.

volcano *n.* (pl. *-oes*) mountain or hill with openings through which lava, gases, etc., are or have been expelled. **volcanic** *a.*

vole *n.* small rat-like animal.

volition /-ˈlɪʃ-/ *n.* use of one's own will in making a decision etc.

volley *n.* (pl. *-eys*) simultaneous discharge of missiles etc.; outburst of questions or other words; return of the ball in tennis etc. before it touches the ground. —*v.t.* send in a volley.

volt /vəʊlt/ *n.* unit of electromotive force.

voltage *n.* electromotive force expressed in volts.

volte-face /volt-ˈfɑs/ *n.* complete change of attitude to something.

voluble *a.* speaking or spoken with a great flow of words. **volubly** *adv.*, **volubility** *n.*

volume *n.* book; amount of space occupied or contained by a three-dimensional object; size, amount; strength of sound.

voluminous /-ˈlju-/ *a.* having great volume, bulky; copious.

voluntary *a.* done, given, or acting of one's own free will; working or done without payment; maintained by voluntary work or contributions. —*n.* organ solo at a church service. **voluntarily** *n.*

volunteer *n.* person who offers to do something; one who enrols voluntarily for military service. —*v.t./i.* undertake or offer voluntarily; be a volunteer.

voluptuous *a.* full of or fond of luxury and the pleasures of life; having a full attractive figure. **voluptuously** *adv.*, **voluptuousness** *n.*

vomit *v.t./i.* (p.t. *vomited*) eject (matter) from the stomach through the mouth. —*n.* vomited matter.

voodoo *n.* form of religion based on witchcraft, esp. in the West Indies. **voodooism** *n.*

voracious *a.* greedy in eating, ravenous; desiring much. **voraciously** *adv.*, **voracity** *n.*

vortex *n.* (pl. *-ices* or *-exes*) whirlpool; whirlwind.

vote *n.* formal expression of one's opinion or choice on a matter under discussion; choice etc. expressed thus; right to vote. —*v.t./i.* express or decide or support etc. by a vote. **voter** *n.*

votive *a.* given in fulfilment of a vow.

vouch *v.i.* ~ **for**, guarantee the accuracy or reliability etc. of.

voucher *n.* a kind of receipt; document issued for payment and exchangeable for certain goods or services.

vouchsafe *v.t.* give or grant in a gracious or condescending way.

vow *n.* solemn promise, esp. in the form of an oath to a deity or saint. —*v.t.* promise solemnly.

vowel *n.* speech-sound made without audible stopping of the breath; letter(s) representing this.

voyage *n.* journey made by water or in space. —*v.i.* make a voyage. **voyager** *n.*

voyeur /vwɑˈjɜ/ *n.* person who obtains sexual gratification by looking at the sexual acts or organs of others.

vulcanize *v.t.* strengthen (rubber etc.) by treating with sulphur. **vulcanization** *n.*

vulgar *a.* lacking refinement or good taste; commonly used but incorrect. ~ **fraction,** one represented by numbers above and below a line. **vulgarly** *adv.*, **vulgarity** *n.*

vulgarism *n.* vulgar word(s) etc.

vulgarize *v.t.* make vulgar; spoil by making ordinary or too well known. **vulgarization** *n.*

Vulgate *n.* 4th-century Latin version of the Bible.

vulnerable *a.* able to be hurt or injured; exposed to danger or criticism. **vulnerability** *n.*

vulture *n.* large bird of prey that lives on the flesh of dead animals.

vulva *n.* external parts of the female genital organs.

vying *see* **vie.**

W

W. *abbr.* watt(s); west.

wad *n.* pad of soft material; bunch of papers or banknotes. —*v.t.* (p.t. *wadded*) pad.

wadding *n.* padding.

waddle *v.i.* & *n.* walk with short steps and a swaying movement.

wade *v.t./i.* walk through water or mud etc., walk across (a stream); make one's way slowly and laboriously (through work etc.). **wader** *n.*

waders *n.pl.* high waterproof boots worn in fishing etc.

wafer *n.* thin light biscuit; small thin slice.

waffle[1] *n.* (*colloq.*) vague wordy talk or writing. —*v.i.* (*colloq.*) talk or write waffle.

waffle[2] *n.* small cake of batter eaten hot, cooked in a **waffle-iron.**

waft *v.t./i.* carry or travel lightly through air or over water. —*n.* wafted odour.

wag *v.t./i.* (p.t. *wagged*) shake briskly to and fro. —*n.* wagging movement; waggish person.

wage[1] *v.t.* engage in (war).

wage[2] *n.*, **wages** *n.pl.* regular payment to an employee for his work.

wager *n. & v.t./i.* bet.

waggish *a.* joking.

waggle *v.t./i. & n.* wag.

waggon *n.* = wagon.

wagon *n.* four-wheeled goods-vehicle pulled by horses or oxen; open railway-truck; trolley for carrying food etc.

wagoner *n.* driver of a wagon.

wagtail *n.* small bird with a long tail that wags up and down.

waif *n.* homeless helpless person, esp. an abandoned child.

wail *v.t./i. & n.* (utter) a long sad cry; lament.

wain *n.* (*old use*) farm wagon.

wainscot *n.* wooden panelling in a room. **wainscoting** *n.*

waist *n.* part of the human body between ribs and hips; part of a garment covering this; narrow middle part.

waistcoat *n.* close-fitting waist-length sleeveless jacket.

waistline *n.* outline or size of the waist.

wait *v.t./i.* postpone an action until a specified time or event occurs; be postponed; wait on people at a meal; pause. —*n.* act or period of waiting; (*pl.*, *old use*) carol-singers. **~ on,** hand food and drink to (persons) at a meal; fetch and carry things for; pay a respectful visit to. **waiting-list** *n.* list of people waiting for something. **waiting-room** *n.* room provided for people waiting.

waiter *n.* man employed to serve food and drink to customers at tables in a restaurant etc. **waitress** *n.fem.*

waive *v.t.* refrain from using (a right etc.), dispense with.

wake[1] *v.t./i.* (p.t. *woke*, p.p. *woken*) cease to sleep; cause to cease sleeping; evoke. —*n.* (*Irish*) watch by a corpse before burial; attendant lamentations and merrymaking; (*pl.*) annual holiday in industrial northern England. **~ up,** wake; make or become alert.

wake[2] *n.* track left on water's surface by a ship etc.; air-currents left behind a moving aircraft etc. **in the ~ of,** behind; following.

wakeful *a.* unable to sleep; sleepless.

waken *v.t./i.* wake.

walk *v.t./i.* progress by setting down one foot and then lifting the other(s) in turn; travel over in this way; cause to walk, accompany in walking; (of a ghost) appear. —*n.* journey on foot; manner or style of walking; place or route for walking. **~ of life,** social rank; occupation. **~ out,** depart suddenly and angrily; go on strike suddenly. (**~-out** *n.*). **~ out on,** desert. **~-over** *n.* easy victory or achievement.

walkabout *n.* informal stroll among a crowd by a royal person etc.; (*Austr.*) Aboriginal's period of wandering in the bush.

walker *n.* person who walks; framework to assist walking.

walkie-talkie *n.* small portable radio transmitter and receiver.

walking-stick *n.* stick carried or used as a support when walking.

walkway *n.* passage, wide path.

wall *n.* continuous upright structure forming one side of a building or room or area; thing like this in form or function. —*v.t.* surround or enclose with a wall. **go to the ~,** suffer defeat or failure or ruin.

wallaby *n.* small species of kangaroo.

wallet *n.* small flat folding case for banknotes or small documents.

wall-eyed *a.* with eyes showing white abnormally, as in a squint.

wallflower *n.* garden plant with fragrant flowers.

wallop *v.t.* (p.t. *walloped*) (*sl.*) thrash, hit hard. —*n.* (*sl.*) heavy blow; beer or other drink.

wallow *v.i.* roll in mud or water etc. —*n.* act of wallowing. **~ in,** take unrestrained pleasure in.

wallpaper *n.* paper for covering the interior walls of rooms.

walnut *n.* nut containing a wrinkled edible kernel; tree bearing this; its wood.

walrus *n.* large seal-like arctic animal with long tusks.

waltz *n.* ballroom dance in triple time; music for this. —*v.i.* dance a waltz; (*colloq.*) move gaily or casually.

wan /won/ *a.* pallid. **wanly** *adv.*, **wanness** *n.*

wand *n.* slender rod, esp. associated with the working of magic.

wander *v.i.* go from place to place with no settled route or purpose; (of a road or river) wind; stray; digress. —*n.* act of wandering. **wanderer** *n.*

wanderlust *n.* strong desire to travel.

wane *v.i.* decrease in vigour or importance; (of the moon) show a decreasing bright area after being full. **on the ~,** waning.

wangle *v.t.* (*sl.*) obtain or arrange by using trickery or scheming. —*n.* (*sl.*) act of wangling.

want *v.t./i.* desire; need; lack; be without the necessaries of life; fall short of. —*n.* desire; need; lack.

wanted *a.* (of a suspected criminal) sought by the police.

wanting *a.* lacking, deficient.

wanton /'won-/ *a.* irresponsible, lacking proper restraint.

war *n.* strife (esp. between countries) involving military, naval, or air attacks; open hostility; strong effort to combat crime, disease, or poverty etc. **at ~,** engaged in a war. **on the ~-path,** seeking hostile confrontation or revenge.

warble *v.t./i.* sing, esp. with a gentle trilling note as certain birds do. —*n.* warbling sound. **warbler** *n.*

ward *n.* room with beds for a group of patients in a hospital; division of a city or town, electing a councillor to represent it; person (esp. a child) under the care of a guardian or lawcourt; one of the notches or projections in a lock or its key. —v.t. ～ off, keep (a danger etc.) at a distance.

warden n. official with supervisory duties; churchwarden.

warder n. prison officer.

wardrobe n. large cupboard for storing hanging clothes; stock of clothes or costumes.

wardroom n. officers' room in a warship.

ware n. manufactured goods (esp. pottery) of the kind specified; (pl.) articles offered for sale.

warehouse n. building for storing goods or furniture.

warfare n. making war, fighting.

warhead n. explosive head of a missile etc.

warlike a. fond of making war, aggressive; of or for war.

warm a. (-er, -est) moderately hot; providing warmth; enthusiastic, hearty; kindly and affectionate. —v.t./i. make or become warm. ～-blooded a. having blood that remains warm permanently. ～-hearted a. having a kindly and affectionate disposition. ～ to, become cordial towards (a person) or more animated about (a task). ～ up, warm; reheat; prepare for exercise etc. by practice beforehand; make or become more lively. **warmly** adv., **warmness** n.

warming-pan n. covered metal pan formerly filled with hot coals and used to warm beds.

warmonger n. person who seeks to bring about war.

warmth n. warmness.

warn v.t. inform about a present or future danger or difficulty etc., advise about action in this. ～ off, tell (a person) to keep away or to avoid (a thing).

warning n. thing that serves to warn a person.

warp /wɔp/ v.t./i. make or become bent by uneven shrinkage or expansion; distort, pervert. —n. warped condition; lengthwise threads in a loom.

warrant /ˈwo-/ n. written authorization; voucher; justification for an action etc.; proof, guarantee. —v.t. serve as a warrant for, justify; prove, guarantee. ～-officer n. member of the armed services ranking between commissioned officers and N.C.O.s.

warranty n. guarantee; authority or justification for an action etc.

warren n. piece of ground with many burrows where rabbits live and breed; building or district with many winding passages.

warring a. engaged in a war.

warrior n. person who fights in a battle.

warship n. ship for use in war.

wart n. small hard abnormal growth. ～-hog n. African pig with wart-like growths on its face.

wartime n. period when a war is being waged.

wary /ˈweərɪ/ a. (-ier, -iest) cautious, looking out for possible danger or difficulty. **warily** adv., **wariness** n.

was see **be**.

wash v.t./i. cleanse with water or other liquid; wash oneself or clothes etc.; be washable; flow past or against or over; carry by flowing;

coat thinly with paint; (colloq., of reasoning) be valid. —n. process of washing or being washed; clothes etc. to be washed; disturbed water or air behind a moving ship or aircraft etc.; liquid food for pigs; thin coating of paint. ～-basin n. bowl (usu. fixed to a wall) for washing one's hands and face. ～ one's hands of, refuse to take responsibility for. ～ out, wash (clothes etc.); make (a sport) impossible by heavy rainfall; (colloq.) cancel. ～-out n. (sl.) complete failure. ～-room n. (U.S.) lavatory. ～-stand n. piece of furniture to hold a basin and jug of water for washing. ～-tub n. tub for washing clothes. ～ up, wash (dishes etc.) after use; cast up on the shore; (U.S.) wash oneself.

washable a. able to be washed without suffering damage.

washer n. ring of rubber or metal etc. placed between two surfaces to give tightness.

washed-out a. faded by washing; faded-looking; pallid.

washerwoman n. (pl. -women) woman whose occupation is washing clothes etc.

washing n. clothes etc. to be washed. ～-machine n. machine for washing these. ～-up n. dishes etc. for washing after use; process of washing these.

wasp n. stinging insect with a black-and-yellow striped body.

waspish a. making sharp or irritable comments. **waspishly** adv.

wassailing /ˈwosəl-/ n. (old use) making merry (esp. at Christmas) with drinking of spiced ale etc.

wast (old use with thou) = was.

wastage n. loss or diminution by waste; loss of employees by retirement or resignation.

waste v.t./i. use or be used extravagantly or without adequate result; fail to use; make or become gradually weaker. —a. left or thrown away because not wanted; (of land) unfit for use. —n. process of wasting; waste material or food etc.; waste land.

wasteful a. wasting things. **wastefully** adv., **wastefulness** n.

waster /ˈweɪ-/ n. wasteful person; (sl.) wastrel.

wastrel /ˈweɪ-/ n. good-for-nothing person.

watch v.t./i. look at, keep under observation; wait alertly, take heed; exercise protective care. —n. act of watching, constant observation or attention; sailor's period (usu. four hours) of duty, persons on duty in this; small portable device indicating the time. **on the ～,** waiting alertly. ～-dog n. dog kept to guard property; guardian of people's rights etc. ～-night service, religious service on the last day of the year. ～ out, be on one's guard. ～-tower n. tower from which observation can be kept. **watching-brief** n. brief of a barrister who is present during a lawsuit to advise a client not directly concerned in it. **watcher** n.

watchful a. watching closely. **watchfully** adv., **watchfulness** n.

watchmaker n. person who makes or repairs watches.

watchman *n.* (pl. *-men*) man employed to look after an empty building etc.

watchword *n.* word or phrase expressing a group's principles.

water *n.* colourless, odourless, tasteless liquid that is a compound of hydrogen and oxygen; this as supplied for domestic use; lake, sea; watery secretion, urine; watery preparation; level of the tide; transparency and lustre of a gem. —*v.t.* sprinkle, supply, or dilute with water; secrete tears or saliva. **by** ～**,** (of travel) in a boat etc. **in low** ～**,** short of money. ～**-biscuit** *n.* thin unsweetened biscuit. ～**butt** *n.* barrel used to catch rainwater. ～**closet** *n.* lavatory flushed by water. ～**-colour** *n.* artists' paint mixed with water (not oil); painting done with this. ～ **down,** dilute; make less forceful. ～**-glass** *n.* thick liquid used for coating eggs to preserve them. ～**ice** *n.* edible concoction of frozen flavoured water. ～**-lily** *n.* plant with broad floating leaves and large flowers that grows in water. ～**-line** *n.* line along which the surface of water touches a ship's side. ～**-main** *n.* main pipe in a water-supply system. ～**-meadow** *n.* meadow that is flooded periodically by a stream. ～**-melon** *n.* melon with red pulp and watery juice. ～**-mill** *n.* mill worked by a water-wheel. ～**-pistol** *n.* toy pistol that shoots a jet of water. ～ **polo,** game played by teams of swimmers with a ball like a football. ～**power** *n.* power obtained from flowing or falling water, used to drive machinery or generate electricity. ～**-rat** *n.* rat-like animal living beside a lake or stream. ～**-skiing** *n.* sport of skimming over water on flat boards while towed by a motor boat. ～**-splash** *n.* section of a road where vehicles must travel through a shallow stream or pool. ～**-table** *n.* level below which the ground is saturated with water. ～**-way** *n.* navigable channel. ～**-weed** *n.* weed growing in water. ～**-wheel** *n.* wheel turned by a flow of water to work machinery. ～**-wings** *n.pl.* floats worn on the shoulders by a person learning to swim.

waterbrash *n.* watery fluid brought up from the stomach.

watercourse *n.* stream, brook, or artificial waterway; its channel.

watercress *n.* a kind of cress that grows in streams and ponds.

watered *a.* (of silk) having an irregular wavy marking.

waterfall *n.* stream that falls from a height.

waterfront *n.* part of a town that borders on a river, lake, or sea.

watering-can *n.* container with a tubular spout, holding water for watering plants.

watering-place *n.* pool where animals drink; spa, seaside resort.

waterless *a.* without water.

waterlogged *a.* saturated with water.

watermark *n.* manufacturer's design in paper, visible when the paper is held against light.

waterproof *a.* unable to be penetrated by water.

—*n.* waterproof coat or cape. —*v.t.* make waterproof.

watershed *n.* line of high land separating two river-systems; turning-point in the course of events.

waterspout *n.* column of water between sea and cloud, formed by a whirlwind.

watertight *a.* made or fastened so that water cannot get in or out; impossible to set aside or disprove.

waterworks *n.* establishment with machinery etc. for supplying water to a district.

watery *a.* of or like water; containing too much water; (of colour) pale.

watt /wot/ *n.* unit of electric power.

wattage /ˈwot-/ *n.* amount of electric power, expressed in watts.

wattle[1] /ˈwo-/ *n.* interwoven sticks used as material for fences, walls, etc.; Australian acacia with golden flowers.

wattle[2] /ˈwo-/ *n.* fold of skin hanging from the neck of a turkey etc.

wave *n.* moving ridge of water; wave-like curve(s), e.g. in hair; advancing group; temporary increase of an influence or condition; act of waving; wave-like motion by which heat, light, sound, or electricity etc. is spread; single curve in this. —*v.t./i.* move loosely to and fro or up and down; move (one's arm etc.) thus as a signal; signal or express thus; give or have a wavy course or appearance.

waveband *n.* range of wavelengths.

wavelength *n.* distance between corresponding points in a sound wave or electromagnetic wave.

waver *v.i.* be or become unsteady; begin to give way; show hesitation or uncertainty. **waverer** *n.*

wavy *a.* (*-ier*, *-iest*) full of waves or wave-like curves.

wax[1] *n.* beeswax; any of various similar soft substances; polish containing this; (*colloq.*) gramophone record. —*v.t.* coat, polish, or treat with wax. **waxy** *a.*

wax[2] *v.i.* increase in vigour or importance; (of the moon) show an increasing bright area until becoming full.

waxen *a.* made of wax; like wax in paleness or smoothness.

waxwing *n.* small bird with red tips on some of its wing-feathers.

waxwork *n.* object modelled in wax, esp. life-like model of a person.

way *n.* line of communication between two places; route; travelling-distance; space free of obstacles so that people etc. can pass; progress; specified direction or aspect; method, style, manner; chosen or desired course of action; difference from a specified state or condition; (*pl.*) habits. —*adv.* (*colloq.*) far. **by the** ～**,** incidentally, as an irrelevant comment. **by** ～ **of,** as a substitute for or a form of. **in a** ～**,** to a limited extent; in some respects. **in the** ～**,** forming an obstacle or hindrance. **on one's** ～**,** in the process of travelling or approaching. **on the** ～**,** on one's way; (of a baby) conceived but not yet born. **under** ∿, (see *under*). ∿**-bill** *n.* list of the passengers or goods being carried by a vehicle. ∿**-out** *a.* (*colloq.*) exaggeratedly unusual.

wayfarer *n.* traveller, esp. on foot.

waylay *v.t.* (p.t. *-laid*) lie in wait for.

wayside *n.* side of a road or path.

wayward *a.* childishly self-willed, hard to control. **waywardness** *n.*

W.C. *abbr.* water-closet.

we *pron.* used by a person referring to himself and another or others; used instead of 'I' by a royal person in formal proclamations, and by the writer of an editorial article in a newspaper.

weak *a.* (*-er, -est*) lacking strength or power or number, easily broken or bent or defeated; not convincing; much diluted; (of verbs) forming the past tense by adding a suffix (e.g. *walk/walked*). ∿**-kneed** *a.,* ∿**-minded** *a.* lacking determination.

weaken *v.t./i.* make or become weaker.

weakling *n.* feeble person or animal.

weakly *adv.* in a weak manner. —*a.* sickly, not robust.

weakness *n.* state of being weak; weak point, fault; self-indulgent liking.

weal *n.* ridge raised on flesh esp. by the stroke of a rod or whip.

wealth *n.* riches; possession of these; great quantity.

wealthy *a.* (*-ier, -iest*) having wealth, rich.

wean *v.t.* accustom (a baby) to take food other than milk; cause to give up something gradually.

weapon *n.* thing designed or used for inflicting harm or damage; means of coercing someone.

wear[1] *v.t./i.* (p.t. *wore*, p.p. *worn*) have on the body, e.g. as clothing or ornament; damage gradually or become damaged on the surface by rubbing, make (a hole etc.) thus; endure continued use. —*n.* wearing, being worn; clothing; capacity to endure being used. ∿ **down,** exhaust or overcome (opposition etc.) by persistence. ∿ **off,** pass off gradually. ∿ **on,** (of time) pass gradually. ∿ **out,** use or be used until no longer usable. **wearer** *n.,* **wearable** *a.*

wear[2] *v.t./i.* (p.t. & p.p. *wore*) come or bring (a ship) about by turning its head away from the wind.

wearisome *a.* causing weariness.

weary *a.* (*-ier, -iest*) very tired; tiring, tedious. —*v.t./i.* make or become weary. **wearily** *adv.,* **weariness** *n.*

weasel *n.* small wild animal with a slender body and reddish-brown fur.

weather *n.* state of the atmosphere with reference to sunshine, rain, wind, etc. —*a.* windward. —*v.t./i.* dry or season by exposure to the action of the weather; become dried or worn etc. thus; sail to windward of; come safely through (a storm). **under the** ∿, feeling unwell or depressed. ∿**-beaten** *a.* bronzed

or worn by exposure to weather. ∿**-vane** *n.* weathercock.

weatherboard *n.* sloping board for keeping out rain.

weathercock *n.* revolving pointer (often in the form of a cockerel) mounted in a high place, turning easily to show the direction of the wind.

weave *v.t./i.* (p.t. *wove*, p.p. *woven*) make (fabric etc.) by passing crosswise threads or strips under and over lengthwise ones; form (thread etc.) into fabric thus; compose (a story etc.); move in an intricate course. —*n.* style or pattern of weaving. **weaver** *n.*

web *n.* network of fine strands made by a spider etc.; skin filling the spaces between the toes of ducks, frogs, etc. ∿**-footed** *a.* having toes joined by web. **webbed** *a.*

webbing *n.* strong band(s) of woven fabric used in upholstery etc.

wed *v.t./i.* (p.t. *wedded*) marry; unite. **wedded to,** devotedly attached to (an occupation, opinion, etc.).

wedding *n.* marriage ceremony and festivities. ∿**-cake** *n.,* ∿**-ring** *n.*

wedge *n.* piece of solid substance thick at one end and tapering to a thin edge at the other, thrust between things to force them apart or prevent free movement; thing shaped like this. —*v.t./i.* force apart or fix firmly with a wedge; crowd tightly; be immovable.

wedlock *n.* married state.

Wednesday *n.* day after Tuesday.

wee *a.* (*Sc.*) little; (*colloq.*) tiny.

weed *n.* wild plant growing where it is not wanted; thin weak-looking person. —*v.t./i.* uproot and remove weeds (from). ∿**-killer** *n.* substance used to destroy weeds. ∿ **out,** remove as inferior or undesirable. **weedy** *a.*

weeds *n.pl.* deep mourning formerly worn by widows.

week *n.* period of seven successive days, esp. from Sunday to Saturday; the six days between Sundays; the five days other than Saturday and Sunday; working-period during a week. ∿**-end** *n.* Saturday and Sunday.

weekday *n.* day other than Sunday.

weekly *a.* & *adv.* (produced or occurring) once a week. —*n.* weekly periodical.

weep *v.t./i.* (p.t. *wept*) shed (tears); shed or ooze (moisture) in drops. —*n.* spell of weeping.

weeping *a.* (of a tree) having drooping branches.

weevil *n.* small beetle that feeds on grain, nuts, tree-bark, etc.

weft *n.* crosswise threads in weaving.

weigh *v.t.* measure the weight of; have a specified weight; consider the relative importance of; have importance or influence; be burdensome. ∿ **anchor,** raise the anchor and start a voyage. ∿ **down,** bring or keep down by its weight; depress, oppress.

weighbridge *n.* weighing-machine with a plate set in a road etc. for weighing vehicles.

weight *n.* object's mass numerically expressed using a recognized scale of units; unit or system of units used thus; piece of metal of known weight used in weighing; heavy object; heaviness; load, burden; influence, convincing effect. —*v.t.* attach a weight to; hold down with a weight; burden; bias. **~-lifting** *n.* sport of lifting heavy weights. **weightless** *a.*, **weightlessness** *n.*

weighting *n.* extra pay given in special cases.

weighty *a.* (-ier, -iest) heavy; showing or deserving earnest thought; influential.

weir *n.* small dam built so that some of a stream's water flows over it; waterfall formed thus.

weird *a.* (-er, -est) uncanny, bizarre. **weirdly** *adv.*, **weirdness** *n.*

welcome *a.* received with pleasure; ungrudgingly permitted or given a right to. —*int.* greeting expressing pleasure at a person's coming. —*n.* greeting or reception, esp. a glad and kindly one. —*v.t.* give a welcome to; receive gladly.

weld *v.t./i.* unite or fuse (pieces of usu. heated metal) by hammering or pressure; make by welding; unite into a whole. —*n.* welded joint. **welder** *n.*

welfare *n.* well-being; organized efforts to ensure people's well-being. **Welfare State**, country with highly developed social services.

welkin *n.* (*poet.*) sky.

well[1] *n.* shaft dug or drilled to obtain water or oil etc.; enclosed shaft-like space. —*v.i.* rise or spring.

well[2] *adv.* (*better*, *best*) in a good manner or style, rightly; thoroughly; by a considerable margin; favourably, kindly; with good reason; easily; probably. —*a.* in good health; in a satisfactory state or position. —*int.* expressing surprise or relief or resignation etc., or said when one is hesitating. **as ~,** in addition; desirable; desirably. **as ~ as,** in addition to. **~-being** *n.* good health, happiness, and prosperity. **~-born** *a.* born of good family. **~-bred** *a.* showing good breeding; well-mannered. **~-disposed** *a.* having kindly or favourable feelings. **~-heeled** *a.* (*colloq.*) wealthy. **~-knit** *a.* having a compact body. **~-meaning** *a.*, **~-meant** *a.* acting or done with good intentions. **~ off,** in a satisfactory or good situation; fairly rich. **~-read** *a.* having read much literature. **~-spoken** *a.* speaking in a polite and correct way. **~-to-do** *a.* fairly rich. **~-wisher** *n.* person who wishes well to another.

wellington *n.* boot of rubber or other waterproof material.

wellnigh *adv.* almost.

Welsh *a.* & *n.* (language) of Wales. **~ rabbit** *or* **rarebit,** (see *rarebit*). **Welshman** *n.*, **Welshwoman** *n.*

welsh *v.i.* avoid paying one's debts; break an agreement. **welsher** *n.*

welt *n.* leather rim attaching the top of a boot or shoe to the sole; ribbed or strengthened border of a knitted garment; weal.

welter *v.i.* (of a ship etc.) be tossed to and fro on waves. —*n.* turmoil; disorderly mixture.

welterweight *n.* boxing-weight (67 kg).

wen *n.* benign tumour on the skin.

wench *n.* (*old use*) girl, young woman.

wend *v.t.* **~ one's way,** go.

went *see* **go.**

wept *see* **weep.**

were *see* **be.**

werewolf /ˈwɪə-/ *n.* (pl. -*wolves*) (in myths) person who at times turns into a wolf.

west *n.* point on the horizon where the sun sets; direction in which this lies; western part. —*a.* in the west; (of wind) from the west. —*adv.* towards the west. **go ~,** (*sl.*) be destroyed or lost or killed.

westerly *a.* towards or blowing from the west.

western *a.* of or in the west. —*n.* film or novel about cowboys in western North America.

westerner *n.* native or inhabitant of the west.

westernize *v.t.* make (an Oriental country etc.) more like a western one in ideas and institutions. **westernization** *n.*

westernmost *a.* furthest west.

westward *a.* towards the west. **westwards** *adv.*

wet *a.* (*wetter*, *wettest*) soaked or covered with water or other liquid; rainy; not dry; allowing the sale of alcohol; (*sl.*) lacking vitality. —*v.t.* (p.t. *wetted*) make wet. —*n.* moisture, water; wet weather. **~ blanket,** gloomy person. **~-nurse** *n.* woman employed to suckle another's child; (*v.t.*) act as wet-nurse to, coddle as if helpless. **~ suit,** porous garment worn by a skin-diver etc. **wetly** *adv.*, **wetness** *n.*

wether *n.* castrated ram.

whack *v.t.* & *n.* (*colloq.*) hit. **do one's ~,** (*sl.*) do one's share.

whacked *a.* (*colloq.*) tired out.

whacking *a.* & *adv.* very (large).

whale *n.* very large sea animal. **a ~ of a,** (*colloq.*) an exceedingly great or good (thing).

whalebone *n.* horny substance from the upper jaw of whales, formerly used as stiffening.

whaling *n.* hunting whales.

wham *int.* & *n.* sound of a forcible impact.

whang *v.t./i.* strike heavily and loudly. —*n.* whanging sound or blow.

wharf *n.* (pl. *wharfs*) landing-stage where ships load and unload.

wharfinger /-fɪndʒ-/ *n.* owner or manager of a wharf.

what *a.* asking for a statement of amount or number or kind; how great or remarkable; the or any that. —*pron.* what thing(s); what did you say? —*adv.* to what extent or degree. —*int.* exclamation of surprise. **~ about,** what is the news or your opinion about (a subject). **~'s what,** what things are useful or important etc. **what with,** on account of (various causes).

whatever *a.* of any kind or number. —*pron.* anything or everything; no matter what.

whatnot *n.* something trivial or indefinite; stand with shelves for small objects.

whatsoever *a.* & *pron.* whatever.

wheat *n.* grain from which flour is made; plant producing this.

wheatear *n.* a kind of small bird.

wheaten *a.* made from wheat-flour.

wheatmeal *n.* wholemeal.

wheedle *v.t.* coax.

wheel *n.* disc or circular frame that revolves on a shaft passing through its centre; thing resembling this; machine etc. using a wheel; wheel-like motion. —*v.t./i.* push or pull (a cart or bicycle etc.) along; turn; move in circles or curves. **at the ~,** driving a vehicle, directing a ship; in control of affairs. **~ and deal,** (*U.S.*) engage in scheming to exert influence.

wheelbarrow *n.* open container for moving small loads, with a wheel at one end.

wheelbase *n.* distance between a vehicle's front and rear axles.

wheelchair *n.* invalid's chair on wheels.

wheeze *v.i.* breathe with a hoarse whistling sound. —*n.* this sound.

whelk *n.* shellfish with a spiral shell.

whelp *n.* young dog, pup. —*v.t./i.* give birth to (a whelp or whelps).

when *adv.* at what time, on what occasion; at which time. —*conj.* at the time that; whenever; as soon as; although. —*pron.* what or which time.

whence *adv. & conj.* from where; from which.

whenever *conj. & adv.* at whatever time; every time that.

where *adv. & conj.* at or in which place or circumstances; in what respect; from what place or source; to what place. —*pron.* what place.

whereabouts *adv.* in or near what place. —*n.* a person's or thing's approximate location.

whereas *adv.* since it is the fact that; but in contrast.

whereby *adv.* by which.

wherefore *adv.* (*old use*) for what reason, for this reason.

wherein *adv.* in what, in which.

whereupon *adv.* after which, and then.

wherever *adv.* at or to whatever place.

wherewithal *n.* (*colloq.*) things (esp. money) needed for a purpose.

whet *v.t.* (p.t. *whetted*) sharpen by rubbing against a stone etc.; stimulate (appetite or interest).

whether *conj.* introducing an alternative possibility.

whetstone *n.* shaped stone used for sharpening tools.

whey *n.* watery liquid left when milk forms curds.

which *a. & pron.* what particular one(s) of a set; and that. —*relative pron.* thing or animal referred to.

whichever *a. & pron.* any which, that or those which.

whiff *n.* puff of air or odour etc.

Whig *n.* member of a former political party (succeeded by the Liberal Party).

while *n.* period of time; time spent in doing something. —*conj.* during the time that, as long as; although; on the other hand. —*v.t.* **~ away,** pass (time) in a leisurely or interesting way.

whilst *conj.* while.

whim *n.* sudden fancy.

whimper *v.i.* make feeble crying sounds. —*n.* whimpering sound.

whimsical *a.* impulsive and playful; fanciful, quaint. **whimsically** *adv.,* **whimsicality** *n.*

whinchat *n.* small brown bird.

whine *v.t./i.* make a long high complaining cry or a similar shrill sound; complain or utter with a whine. —*n.* whining sound or complaint. **whiner** *n.*

whinny *n.* gentle or joyful neigh. —*v.i.* utter a whinny.

whip *n.* cord or strip of leather on a handle, used for striking a person or animal; official appointed to maintain discipline of his party in Parliament, party discipline and instructions given by such officials; food made with whipped cream etc. —*v.t.* (p.t. *whipped*) strike or urge on with a whip; beat into a froth; move or take suddenly; oversew. **have the ~ hand,** have control. **~-round** *n.* appeal for contributions from a group. **~ up,** incite.

whipcord *n.* cord of tightly twisted strands; twilled fabric with prominent ridges.

whiplash *n.* lash of a whip; jerk.

whipper-snapper *n.* young insignificant presumptuous person.

whippet *n.* small dog resembling a greyhound, used for racing.

whipping-boy *n.* scapegoat.

whippy *a.* flexible, springy.

whirl *v.t./i.* swing or spin round and round; travel swiftly in a curved course; convey or go rapidly in a vehicle. —*n.* whirling movement; confused state; bustling activity.

whirligig *n.* whirling toy; merry-go-round.

whirlpool *n.* current of water whirling in a circle.

whirlwind *n.* mass of air whirling rapidly about a central point.

whirr *n.* continuous buzzing or vibrating sound. —*v.i.* make this sound.

whisk *v.t./i.* move with a quick light sweeping movement; convey or go rapidly; brush away lightly; beat into a froth. —*n.* whisking movement; instrument for beating eggs etc.; bunch of bristles etc. for brushing or flicking things.

whisker *n.* long hair-like bristle near the mouth of a cat etc.; (*pl.*) hair growing on a man's cheek. **whiskered** *a.,* **whiskery** *a.*

whiskey *n.* Irish whisky.

whisky *n.* spirit distilled from malted grain (esp. barley).

whisper *v.t./i.* speak or utter softly, not using the vocal cords; converse privately or secretly; rustle. —*n.* whispering sound or speech or remark; rumour.

whist *n.* card-game usu. for two pairs of players. **~ drive,** series of games of whist for a number of players.

whistle *n.* shrill sound made by blowing through a narrow opening between the lips; similar sound; instrument for producing this. —*v.t./i.* make this sound; signal or produce (a tune) in this way. **~-stop** *n.* (*U.S.*) brief stop (during a tour made by a politician etc.) e.g. for electioneering. **whistler** *n.*

whit *n.* least possible amount.

Whit *a.* of or close to ∼ **Sunday,** seventh Sunday after Easter, commemorating the descent of the Holy Spirit upon the Apostles.

white *a.* (-*er*, -*est*) of the very lightest colour, like snow or common salt; having a pale skin; pale from illness or fear etc. —*n.* white colour or thing; white person; transparent substance (white when cooked) round egg-yolk. ∼ **ant,** termite. ∼. **Christmas,** one with snow. ∼ **coffee,** coffee with milk or cream. ∼**-collar worker,** one not engaged in manual labour. ∼ **elephant,** useless possession. ∼ **horses,** white-crested waves on sea. ∼**-hot** *a.* (of metal) glowing white after heating. ∼ **lie,** harmless lie. **White Paper,** government report giving information on a subject. ∼ **sale,** sale of household linen. ∼ **slave,** woman tricked (and usu. sent abroad) into prostitution. ∼ **slavery,** this practice or state. ∼ **wine,** wine of yellow colour. **whitely** *adv.,* **whiteness** *n.*

whitebait *n.* (pl. *whitebait*) small silvery-white fish.

Whitehall *n.* British Government or the Civil Service.

whiten *v.t./i.* make or become white or whiter.

whitewash *n.* liquid containing quicklime or powdered chalk, used for painting walls or ceilings etc.; means of glossing over mistakes. —*v.t.* paint with whitewash; gloss over mistakes in.

whither *adv.* (*old use*) to what place.

whiting *n.* (pl. *whiting*) small sea-fish used as food.

whitlow *n.* small abscess under or affecting a nail.

Whitsun *n.* Whit Sunday and the days close to it.

Whitsunday *n.* (*Sc.*) a quarter-day, 15 May.

whittle *v.t.* trim (wood) by cutting thin slices from the surface; reduce by removing various amounts.

whiz *v.t./i.* (p.t. *whizzed*) make a sound like something moving at great speed through air; move very quickly. —*n.* whizzing sound. ∼**-kid** *n.* (*colloq.*) brilliant or successful young person.

who *pron.* what or which person(s)?; the particular person(s).

whoa *int.* command to a horse etc. to stop or stand still.

whodunit *n.* (*colloq.*) detective or mystery story or play etc.

whoever *pron.* any or every person who, no matter who.

whole *a.* with no part removed or left out; not injured or broken. —*n.* full amount, all parts or members; complete system made up of parts. **on the** ∼, considering everything; in respect of the whole though some details form exceptions. ∼**-hearted** *a.* without doubts or reservations. ∼ **number,** number consisting of one or more units with no fractions.

wholemeal *a.* made from the whole grain of wheat etc.

wholesale *n.* selling of goods in large quantities to be retailed by others. —*a.* & *adv.* in the wholesale trade; on a large scale. **wholesaler** *n.*

wholesome *a.* good for physical or mental health or well-being; healthy. **wholesomeness** *n.*

wholly *adv.* entirely.

whom *pron.* objective case of *who.*

whoop *v.i.* utter a loud cry of excitement. —*n.* this cry.

whoopee *int.* cry of exuberant joy.

whooping-cough *n.* infectious disease esp. of children, with a violent convulsive cough.

whoops *int.* (*colloq.*) exclamation of surprise or apology.

whopper *n.* (*sl.*) something very large.

whopping *a.* (*sl.*) very large.

whore /hɔ(r)/ *n.* prostitute; sexually immoral woman.

whorl *n.* coiled form, one turn of a spiral; circle of ridges in a fingerprint; ring of leaves or petals.

whose *pron.* of whom; of which.

why *adv.* for what reason or purpose?; on account of which. —*int.* exclamation of surprised discovery or recognition.

wick *n.* length of thread in a candle or lamp etc., by which the flame is kept supplied with melted grease or fuel.

wicked *a.* morally bad, offending against what is right; formidable, severe; mischievous. **wickedly** *adv.,* **wickedness** *n.*

wicker *n.* osiers or thin canes interwoven to make furniture or baskets etc. **wickerwork** *n.*

wicket *n.* set of three stumps and two bails used in cricket; part of a cricket ground between or near the two wickets; wicket-door, wicket-gate. ∼**-door** *n.,* ∼**-gate** *n.* small door or gate for use when a larger one is closed. ∼**-keeper** *n.* cricket fieldsman stationed just behind the batsman's wicket.

wide *a.* (-*er*, -*est*) measuring much from side to side; having a specified width; extending far; fully opened; far from the target. —*adv.* widely; far from the target. —*n.* bowled ball that passes beyond the batsman's reach in cricket. **to the** ∼, completely. ∼ **awake,** fully awake or (*colloq.*) alert. **widely** *adv.,* **wideness** *n.*

widen *v.t./i.* make or become wider.

widespread *a.* found or distributed over a wide area.

widgeon /ˈwɪdʒən/ *n.* wild duck.

widow *n.* woman whose husband has died and who has not remarried.

widowed *a.* made a widow or widower.

widower *n.* man whose wife has died and who has not remarried.

width *n.* wideness; distance from side to side; piece of material of full width as woven.

wield *v.t.* hold and use (a tool etc.); have and use (power).

wife *n.* (pl. *wives*) married woman in relation to her husband. **wifely** *a.*

wig *n.* covering of hair worn on the head.

wigging *n.* scolding.

wiggle *v.t./i. & n.* move repeatedly from side to side, wriggle.

wigwam *n.* conical tent as formerly used by North American Indians.

wild *a.* (*-er, -est*) living or growing in its original or natural state, not domesticated or tame or cultivated; not civilized; disorderly; stormy; full of strong unrestrained feeling; extremely foolish; random. —*adv.* in a wild manner. —*n.* (usu. *pl.*) waste place; districts far from civilization. **run ~,** grow or live without being controlled. **~-goose chase,** useless quest. **wildly** *adv.*, **wildness** *n.*

wildcat *a.* reckless; (of strikes) unofficial and irresponsible.

wildebeest /ˈwɪldɪbɪst/ *n.* gnu.

wilderness *n.* wild uncultivated area.

wildfire *n.* **spread like ~,** spread very fast.

wildfowl *n.* birds hunted as game.

wildlife *n.* wild animals.

wile *n.* piece of trickery. —*v.t.* **~ away,** = while away.

wilful *a.* intentional, not accidental; self-willed. **wilfully** *adv.*, **wilfulness** *n.*

will[1] *v.aux.* (*wilt* is used with *thou*) used with *I* and *we* to express promises or obligations, and with other words to express a future tense.

will[2] *n.* mental faculty by which a person decides upon and controls his own or others' actions; determination; that which is desired; person's attitude in wishing good or bad to others; written directions made by a person for disposal of his property after his death. —*v.t.* exercise one's willpower, influence by doing this; bequeath by a will. **at ~,** whenever one pleases. **have one's ~,** get what one desires. **with a ~,** vigorously. **~-power** *n.* control exercised by one's will.

willies *n.pl.* (*sl.*) nervous discomfort.

willing *a.* desiring to do what is required, not objecting; given or done readily. —*n.* willingness. **willingly** *adv.*, **willingness** *n.*

will-o'-the-wisp *n.* hope or aim that lures a person on but can never be fulfilled.

willow *n.* tree or shrub with flexible branches; its wood.

willowy *a.* full of willows; slender and supple.

willy-nilly *adv.* whether one desires it or not.

wilt[1] *see* **will**[1].

wilt[2] *v.t./i.* lose or cause to lose freshness and droop; become limp from exhaustion. —*n.* plant-disease that causes wilting.

wily /ˈwaɪlɪ/ *a.* (*-ier, -iest*) full of wiles, cunning. **wiliness** *n.*

wimple *n.* medieval head-dress covering all but the face.

win *v.t./i.* (p.t. *won*, pres.p. *winning*) be victorious (in); obtain as the result of a contest or bet etc., or by effort; gain the favour or support of. —*n.* victory esp. in a game.

wince *v.i.* make a slight movement from pain or embarrassment etc. —*n.* this movement.

winceyette *n.* cotton fabric with a soft downy surface.

winch *n.* machine for hoisting or pulling things by a cable that winds round a revolving drum. —*v.t.* hoist or pull with a winch.

wind[1] /wɪnd/ *n.* current of air; smell carried by this; gas in the stomach or intestines; breath as needed in exertion or speech etc.; orchestra's wind instruments; useless or boastful talk. —*v.t./i.* detect by the presence of a smell; cause to be out of breath. **get** *or* **have the ~ up,** (*sl.*) feel frightened. **get ~ of,** hear a hint or rumour of. **in the ~,** happening or about to happen. **like the ~,** very swiftly. **put the ~ up,** (*sl.*) frighten. **take the ~ out of a person's sails,** take away his advantage, frustrate him. **~-break** *n.* protective screen shielding something from the wind. **~-cheater** *n.* thin but wind-proof jacket. **~ instrument,** musical instrument sounded by a current of air, esp. by the player's breath. **~-jammer** *n.* merchant sailing-ship. **~-sock** *n.* canvas cylinder flown at an airfield to show the direction of the wind. **~-swept** *a.* exposed to strong winds.

wind[2] /waɪnd/ *v.t./i.* (p.t. *wound*, pr. waʊnd) move or go in a curving or spiral course; wrap closely around something or round upon itself; hoist or move by turning a windlass or handle etc.; wind up (a clock etc.). **~ up,** set or keep (a clock etc.) going by tightening its spring or adjusting its weights; bring or come to an end; settle the affairs of and close (a business company). **winding-sheet** *n.* sheet in which a corpse is wrapped for burial. **winder** *n.*

windbag *n.* (*colloq.*) person who talks lengthily.

windfall *n.* fruit blown off a tree by the wind; unexpected gain, esp. a sum of money.

windlass *n.* winch-like device using a rope or chain that winds round a horizontal roller.

windless *a.* without wind.

windmill *n.* mill worked by the action of wind on projecting parts that radiate from a shaft.

window *n.* opening in a wall etc. to admit light and often air, usu. filled with glass; this glass; space for display of goods behind the window of a shop; opening resembling a window. **~-box** *n.* trough fixed outside a window, for growing flowers etc. **~-dressing** *n.* arranging a display of goods in a shop-window; presentation of facts so as to give a favourable impression. **~-shopping** *n.* looking at displayed goods without buying.

windpipe *n.* air-passage from the throat to the bronchial tubes.

windscreen *n.* glass in the window at the front of a vehicle.

windshield *n.* (*U.S.*) windscreen.

windsurfing *n.* sport of surfing on a board to which a sail is fixed.

windward *a.* situated in the direction from which the wind blows. —*n.* this side or region.

windy *a.* (*-ier, -iest*) with much wind; exposed to winds; wordy; (*sl.*) frightened. **windiness** *n.*

wine *n.* fermented grape-juice as an alcoholic drink; fermented drink made from other fruits or plants; dark red. —*v.t./i.* drink wine; entertain with wine. **winy** *a.*

wineglass *n*. glass for drinking wine from.

wing *n*. one of a pair of projecting parts by which a bird or insect etc. is able to fly; one of the parts projecting widely from the sides of an aircraft; projecting part; body-work just above the wheel of a car; either end of a battle array; player at either end of the forward line in football or hockey etc., side part of playing-area in these games; extreme section of a political party; air-force unit of several squadrons; (*pl.*) sides of a theatre stage. —*v.t./i.* fly, travel by wings; wound slightly in the wing or arm. **on the** ∼, flying. **take** ∼, fly away. **under one's** ∼, under one's protection.

winged *a*. having wings.

wingless *a*. without wings.

wink *v.i.* blink one eye as a signal; shine with a light that flashes on and off or twinkles. —*n*. act of winking. **not a** ∼, no sleep at all. ∼ **at**, pretend not to notice (an illicit act etc.).

winker *n*. flashing indicator.

winkle *n*. edible sea-snail. —*v.t.* ∼ **out**, extract, prise out.

winner *n*. person or thing that wins; something successful.

winning *see* **win**. —*a*. charming, persuasive. ∼ **post** *n*. post marking the end of a race. **winnings** *n.pl.* money won in betting etc.

winnow *v.t.* fan or toss (grain) to free it of chaff; separate (chaff) thus; separate from inferior elements.

winsome *a*. charming.

winter *n*. coldest season of the year. —*v.i.* spend the winter. **wintry** *a*.

wipe *v.t.* clean or dry or remove by rubbing; spread thinly on a surface. —*n*. act of wiping. ∼ **out**, cancel; destroy completely.

wiper *n*. device that automatically wipes rain etc. from a windscreen.

wire *n*. strand of metal; length of this used for fencing, conducting electric current, etc. —*v.t.* provide or fasten or strengthen with wire(s). ∼**-haired** *a*. having stiff wiry hair.

wireless *n*. radio.

wiring *n*. system of wires for conducting electricity in a building.

wiry *a*. (-*ier*, -*iest*) like wire; lean but strong. **wiriness** *n*.

wisdom *n*. being wise, soundness of judgement; wise sayings. ∼ **tooth**, third and hindmost molar tooth, cut (if at all) after the age of 20.

wise[1] *a*. (-*er*, -*est*) showing soundness of judgement; having knowledge; (*sl.*) aware, informed. —*v.t.* (*sl.*) inform. **wisely** *adv*.

wise[2] *n*. (*old use*) way, manner.

wiseacre *n*. person who pretends to have great wisdom.

wisecrack *n*. (*colloq.*) witty remark. —*v.i.* (*colloq.*) make a wisecrack.

wish *n*. desire, mental aim; expression of desire. —*v.t./i.* have or express as a wish; hope or express hope about another person's welfare; (*colloq.*) foist.

wishbone *n*. forked bone between a bird's neck and breast.

wishful *a*. desiring. ∼ **thinking**, belief founded on wishes not facts.

wishy-washy *a*. weak in colour, character, etc.

wisp *n*. small separate bunch; small streak of smoke etc.; small thin person.

wistaria /-'teər-/ *n*. climbing shrub with hanging clusters of flowers.

wistful *a*. full of sad or vague longing. **wistfully** *adv*., **wistfulness** *n*.

wit[1] *n*. amusing ingenuity in expressing words or ideas; person who has this; intelligence. **at one's wits' end**, worried and not knowing what to do.

wit[2] *v.t./i.* (*old use*) **to** ∼, that is to say, namely.

witch *n*. person (esp. a woman) who practises witchcraft; bewitching woman. ∼**-doctor** *n*. tribal magician of a primitive people. ∼**-hazel** *n*. North American shrub with yellow flowers; astringent lotion made from its leaves and bark. ∼**-hunt** *n*. search to find and destroy or persecute persons thought to be witches or holders of unpopular views. **witchery** *n*.

witchcraft *n*. practice of magic.

with *prep*. in the company of, among; having, characterized by; using as an instrument or means; on the side of, of the same opinion as; in the charge of; at the same time as; in the same way or direction as; because of; under the conditions of; by addition or possession of; in regard to, towards. **be** ∼ **child**, (*old use*) be pregnant. ∼ **it**, (*colloq.*) up to date, appreciating current fashions etc.

withdraw *v.t./i.* (p.t. *withdrew*, p.p. *withdrawn*) take back or away; remove (deposited money) from a bank etc.; cancel (a statement); go away from a place or from company etc. **withdrawal** *n*.

withdrawn *a*. (of a person) unsociable.

wither *v.t./i.* shrivel, lose freshness or vitality; subdue by scorn.

withers *n.pl.* ridge between a horse's shoulder-blades.

withhold *v.t.* (p.t. *withheld*) refuse to give; restrain.

within *prep*. inside; not beyond the limit or scope of; in a time no longer than. —*adv*. inside.

without *prep*. not having; in the absence of; with no action of; (*old use*) outside. —*adv*. outside.

withstand *v.t.* (p.t. *withstood*) endure successfully.

withy /'wɪðɪ/ *n*. tough flexible willow branch or osier etc., used for tying things.

witness *n*. person who sees or hears something; one who gives evidence in a lawcourt; one who confirms another's signature; thing that serves as evidence. —*v.t.* be a witness of. ∼ **box** *n*. enclosure from which witnesses give evidence in a lawcourt.

witticism *n*. witty remark.

wittingly *adv*. intentionally.

witty *a*. (-*ier*, -*iest*) full of wit. **wittily** *adv*., **wittiness** *n*.

wives *see* **wife**.

wizard *n.* male witch, magician; person with amazing abilities. **wizardry** *n.*

wizened /ˈwɪzənd/ *a.* full of wrinkles, shrivelled with age.

woad *n.* blue dye formerly obtained from a plant; this plant.

wobble *v.i.* stand or move unsteadily; quiver. —*n.* wobbling movement; quiver. **wobbly** *a.*

wodge *n.* (*colloq.*) chunk, wedge.

woe *n.* sorrow, distress; trouble causing this, misfortune. **woeful** *a.*, **woefully** *adv.*, **woefulness** *n.*

woebegone *a.* looking unhappy.

woke, woken *see* **wake**¹.

wold *n.* (esp. in *pl.*) area of open upland country.

wolf *n.* (pl. *wolves*) fierce wild animal of the dog family; (*sl.*) man who aggressively seeks to attract women. —*v.t.* eat quickly and greedily. **cry** ~, raise false alarms. **keep the** ~ **from the door,** ward off hunger or starvation. ~**-whistle** *n.* man's admiring whistle at an attractive woman. **wolfish** *a.*

wolfhound *n.* large dog of a kind orig. used for hunting wolves.

wolverine /-riːn/ *n.* North American animal of the weasel family.

woman *n.* (pl. *women*) adult female person; women in general; (*colloq.*) charwoman. ~ **of the world,** woman experienced in the ways of society.

womanhood *n.* state of being a woman.

womanize *v.i.* (of a man) seek women's company for sexual purposes. **womanizer** *n.*

womanly *a.* having qualities considered characteristic of a woman. **womanliness** *n.*

womb /wuːm/ *n.* hollow organ in female mammals in which the young develop before birth.

wombat *n.* small bear-like Australian animal.

women *see* **woman.**

womenfolk *n.* women in general; women of one's family.

won *see* **win.**

wonder *n.* feeling of surprise and admiration or curiosity or bewilderment; remarkable thing. —*v.t./i.* feel wonder or surprise; desire to know; try to decide.

wonderful *a.* arousing admiration. **wonderfully** *adv.*

wonderland *n.* place full of wonderful things.

wonderment *n.* feeling of wonder.

wondrous *a.* (*old use*) wonderful.

wont /wəʊnt/ *a.* (*old use*) accustomed. —*n.* habitual custom.

won't = will not.

wonted /ˈwəʊntɪd/ *a.* customary.

woo *v.t.* (*old use*) court; try to achieve or obtain or coax.

wood *n.* tough fibrous substance of a tree; this cut for use; (also *pl.*) trees growing fairly densely over an area of ground; ball used in bowls; golf-club with a wooden head. **out of the** ~, clear of danger or difficulty. ~**-pigeon** *n.* a kind of large pigeon.

woodbine *n.* wild honeysuckle.

woodcock *n.* a kind of game-bird.

woodcut *n.* engraving made on wood; picture made from this.

wooded *a.* covered with trees.

wooden *a.* made of wood; showing no expression. **woodenly** *adv.*

woodland *n.* wooded country.

woodlouse *n.* (pl. *-lice*) small wingless creature with seven pairs of legs, living in decaying wood etc.

woodpecker *n.* bird that taps treetrunks with its beak to discover insects.

woodwind *n.* wind instruments made (or formerly made) of wood.

woodwork *n.* art or practice of making things from wood; wooden things or fittings.

woodworm *n.* larva of a kind of beetle that bores in wood.

woody *a.* like or consisting of wood; full of woods.

woof *n.* dog's gruff bark.

woofer *n.* loudspeaker for reproducing low-frequency signals.

wool *n.* fine soft hair from sheep or goats etc.; yarn or fabric made from this; thing resembling sheep's wool. **pull the** ~ **over someone's eyes,** deceive him. ~**-gathering** *n.* daydreaming.

woollen *a.* made of wool. **woollens** *n.pl.* woollen cloth or clothing.

woolly *a.* (*-ier, -iest*) covered with wool; like wool, woollen; vague. —*n.* (*colloq.*) woollen garment. **woolliness** *n.*

Woolsack *n.* large stuffed cushion on which the Lord Chancellor sits in the House of Lords.

word *n.* sound(s) expressing a meaning independently and forming a basic element of speech; this represented by letters or symbols; thing said; message, news; promise; command. —*v.t.* express in words. ~ **of honour,** promise made upon one's honour. ~ **of mouth,** spoken (not written) words. ~**-perfect** *a.* having memorized every word perfectly.

wording *n.* way a thing is worded.

wordy *a.* using too many words.

wore *see* **wear**¹, ².

work *n.* use of bodily or mental power in order to do or make something, esp. contrasted with play or recreation; thing to be undertaken; materials for use in a task; thing done or produced by work, result of action; employment; ornamentation of a certain kind, articles with this; things made of certain materials or with certain tools; (*pl.*) operations of building etc., operative parts of a machine, factory. —*v.t./i.* perform work; make efforts; be employed; operate, do this effectively; purchase (one's passage etc.) with one's labour; cause to work or function; bring about, accomplish; shape or knead or hammer etc. into a desired form or consistency; do or make by needlework, fretwork, etc.; excite progressively; make (a way) or pass or cause to pass gradually by effort; become (loose etc.) through repeated stress or pressure; be in motion; ferment. ~ **in,** find a place for, insert. **∼-in** *n.* take-over by workers of a factory etc. threatened with closure. **∼ off,** get rid of by activity. **∼ out,** find or solve by calculation; plan the details of; have a specified result. **∼-out** *n.* practice or test, esp. in boxing. **∼ to rule,** cause delay by over-strict observance of rules, as a form of protest. **∼ up,** bring gradually to a more developed state; excite progressively; advance (to a climax).

workable *a.* able to be done or used successfully.

worker *n.* person who works; member of the working class; neuter bee or ant etc. that does the work of the hive or colony.

workhouse *n.* former public institution where people unable to support themselves were housed.

working *a.* engaged in work, esp. manual labour, working-class. —*n.* excavation(s) made in mining, tunnelling, etc. **∼ class,** class of people who are employed for wages, esp. in manual or industrial work. **∼-class** *a.*

workman *n.* (pl. -*men*) man employed to do manual labour; person who works in a specified way.

workmanlike *a.* characteristic of a good workman, practical.

workmanship *n.* skill in working or in a thing produced.

workshop *n.* room or building in which manual work or manufacture etc. is carried on.

world *n.* universe, all that exists; earth, heavenly body like it; section of the earth; time or state or scene of human existence; people or things belonging to a certain class or sphere of activity; everything, all people; material things and occupations; very great amount. **∼-wide** *a.* extending through the whole world.

worldly *a.* of or concerned with earthly life or material gains, not spiritual. **∼-wise** *a.* shrewd in worldly affairs. **worldliness** *n.*

worm *n.* animal with a soft rounded or flattened body and no backbone or limbs; insignificant or contemptible person; spiral part of a screw. —*v.t./i.* move with a twisting movement like a worm; make (one's way) thus or insidiously; obtain by crafty persistence; rid of parasitic worms. **∼-cast** *n.* tubular pile of earth cast up by an earthworm to the surface of the ground. **∼-eaten** *a.* full of holes made by insect larvae. **wormy** *a.*

wormwood *n.* woody plant with a bitter flavour; bitter mortification.

worn *see* **wear**[1]. —*a.* damaged or altered by use or wear; looking exhausted. **∼-out** *a.*

worried *a.* feeling or showing worry.

worry *v.t./i.* be troublesome to; give way to anxiety; seize with the teeth and shake or pull about. —*n.* worried state, mental uneasiness; thing causing this. **worrier** *n.*

worse *a. & adv.* more bad, more badly, more evil or ill; less good, in or into less good health or condition or circumstances. —*n.* something worse.

worsen *v.t./i.* make or become worse.

worship *n.* reverence and respect paid to God or a god; adoration of or devotion to a person or thing; title of respect used of or to a mayor or certain magistrates. —*v.t./i.* (p.t. *worshipped*) honour as a deity, pay worship to; take part in an act of worship; idolize, treat with adoration. **worshipper** *n.*

worshipful *a.* (in titles) honourable.

worst *a. & adv.* most bad, most badly, least good. —*n.* worst part or feature or event etc. —*v.t.* defeat, outdo. **get the ∼ of,** be defeated in.

worsted /ˈwʊstɪd/ *n.* a kind of smooth woollen yarn or fabric.

worth *a.* having a specified value; giving a good return for, deserving; possessing as wealth. —*n.* value, merit, usefulness; amount that a specified sum will buy. **for all one is ∼,** (*colloq.*) with all one's energy. **∼ while** *or* **∼ one's while,** worth the time or effort needed.

worthless *a.* having no value or usefulness. **worthlessness** *n.*

worthwhile *a.* worth while.

worthy *a.* (-*ier*, -*iest*) having great merit; deserving. —*n.* worthy person. **worthily** *adv.,* **worthiness** *n.*

would *v.aux.* used in senses corresponding to *will*[1] in the past tense, conditional statements, questions, polite requests and statements, and to express probability or something that happens from time to time. **∼-be** *a.* desiring or pretending to be.

wound[1] /wuːnd/ *n.* injury done to tissue by a cut or blow; injury to feelings or reputation. —*v.t.* inflict a wound upon.

wound[2] /waʊnd/ *see* **wind**[2].

wove, woven *see* **weave**.

wow *int.* exclamation of astonishment. —*n.* (*sl.*) sensational success.

wrack *n.* seaweed cast up on the shore or growing there.

wraith *n.* ghost, spectral apparition of a living person.

wrangle *v.i.* argue or quarrel noisily. —*n.* noisy argument or quarrel.

wrap *v.t./i.* (p.t. *wrapped*) enclose in a soft or flexible covering; arrange (this covering) round (a person or thing). —*n.* shawl or cloak etc. worn for warmth. **be wrapped up in,** have one's attention deeply occupied by.

wrapper *n.* cover of paper etc. wrapped round something; loose dressing-gown.

wrapping *n.* material for wrapping things.

wrasse /ræs/ *n.* brightly coloured sea-fish.

wrath /rɒθ/ *n.* anger, indignation. **wrathful** *a.,* **wrathfully** *adv.*

wreak /riːk/ *v.t.* inflict (vengeance etc.).

wreath /riːθ/ *n.* (pl. -*ths*, pr. -ðz) flowers or leaves etc. fastened into a ring, used as a decoration or placed on a grave etc.; curving line of mist or smoke.

wreathe /riːð/ *v.t./i.* encircle; twist into a wreath; wind, curve.

wreck *n.* disabling or destruction, esp. of a ship by storms or accidental damage; ship that has suffered this; remains of a greatly damaged building or vehicle etc.; person whose health has been damaged or destroyed. —*v.t.* cause the wreck of; involve in shipwreck.

wreckage *n.* remains of something wrecked; process of wrecking.

wrecker *n.* person who wrecks something; one employed in demolition work.

wren *n.* very small bird.

Wren *n.* member of the W.R.N.S. (Women's Royal Naval Service).

wrench *v.t.* twist or pull violently round; damage or pull by twisting. —*n.* violent twisting pull; pain caused by parting; adjustable spanner-like tool.

wrest *v.t.* wrench away; obtain by effort or with difficulty; twist, distort.

wrestle *v.t./i.* fight (esp. as a sport) by grappling with and trying to throw an opponent to the ground; struggle to deal with. —*n.* wrestling-match; hard struggle.

wretch *n.* wretched or despicable person; rascal.

wretched /-ɪd/ *a.* miserable, unhappy; of poor quality; contemptible, displeasing. **wretchedly** *adv.*, **wretchedness** *n.*

wriggle *v.t./i.* move with short twisting movements; escape (out of a difficulty etc.) cunningly. —*n.* wriggling movement.

wring *v.t.* (p.t. *wrung*) twist and squeeze, esp. to remove liquid; remove (liquid) thus; squeeze firmly or forcibly; obtain with effort or difficulty. —*n.* wringing movement, squeeze, twist. **wringing wet,** so wet that moisture can be wrung from it.

wringer *n.* device with rollers between which washed clothes are passed to squeeze out water.

wrinkle *n.* small crease; small ridge or furrow in skin; (*colloq.*) useful hint. —*v.t./i.* form wrinkles (in).

wrist *n.* joint connecting hand and forearm; part of a garment covering this. **∼-watch** *n.* watch worn on a strap etc. round the wrist.

wristlet *n.* band or bracelet etc. worn round the wrist.

writ *n.* formal written authoritative command. **Holy Writ,** the Bible.

write *v.t./i.* (p.t. *wrote*, p.p. *written*, pres.p. *writing*) make letters or other symbols on a surface, esp. with a pen or pencil; form (letters etc.) thus; compose in written form, esp. for publication; be an author; write and send a letter. **∼ off,** cancel, recognize as lost. **∼-off** *n.* something written off as lost, vehicle too damaged to be worth repairing. **∼ up,** write an account of; write entries in. **∼-up** *n.* published account of something, review.

writer *n.* person who writes; author. **∼'s cramp,** cramp in the muscles of the hand.

writhe /raɪð/ *v.i.* twist one's body about, as in pain; wriggle; suffer because of shame or embarrassment.

writing *n.* handwriting; literary work. **in ∼,** in written form. **the ∼ on the wall,** an event signifying that something is doomed. **∼-paper** *n.* paper for writing (esp. letters) on.

written *see* **write.**

wrong *a.* morally bad; contrary to justice; incorrect, not true; not what is required or desirable; not in a good or normal condition. —*adv.* in a wrong manner or direction, mistakenly. —*n.* what is wrong, wrong action etc.; injustice. —*v.t.* do a wrong to, treat unjustly. **in the ∼,** not having truth or justice on one's side. **wrongly** *adv.*, **wrongness** *n.*

wrongdoer *n.* person who acts contrary to law or moral standards. **wrongdoing** *n.*

wrongful *a.* contrary to what is right or legal. **wrongfully** *adv.*

wrote *see* **write.**

wrought /rɔt/ (*old use*) = worked. —*a.* (of metals) shaped by hammering. **∼ iron,** iron made by forging or rolling, not cast.

wrung *see* **wring.**

wry *a.* (*wryer, wryest*) twisted or bent out of shape; contorted in disgust or disappointment; (of humour) dry and mocking. **wryly** *adv.*, **wryness** *n.*

wryneck *n.* small bird related to the woodpecker.

wych-elm *n.* elm with broad leaves and spreading branches.

X

xenophobia /zen-/ *n.* strong dislike or distrust of foreigners.

Xerox /ˈzɪər-/ *n.* [P.] a kind of photocopying process; copy produced by this. **xerox** *v.t.* copy in this way.

Xmas *n.* Christmas.

X-ray *n.* photograph or examination made by a kind of electromagnetic radiation (*X-rays*) that can penetrate solids. —*v.t.* photograph, examine, or treat by X-rays.

xylophone /ˈzaɪ-/ *n.* musical instrument with flat wooden bars struck with small hammers.

Y

yacht /yot/ *n.* light sailing-vessel for racing; vessel used for private pleasure excursions. **yachting** *n.*, **yachtsman** *n.* (pl. *-men*).

yak *n.* long-haired Asian ox.

yam *n.* tropical climbing plant; its edible starchy tuber; sweet potato.

yank *v.t.* (*colloq.*) pull sharply. —*n.* (*colloq.*) sharp pull.

Yank *n.* (*colloq.*) Yankee.

Yankee *n.* (*colloq.*) American; (*U.S.*) inhabitant of the northern States of the U.S.A.

yap *n.* shrill bark. —*v.i.* (p.t. *yapped*) bark shrilly.

yard[1] *n.* measure of length, = 3 feet (0.9144 metre); pole slung from a mast to support a sail. **~-arm** *n.* either end of a yard supporting a sail.

yard[2] *n.* piece of enclosed ground, esp. attached to a building; *the Y~*, (*colloq.*) Scotland Yard.

yardage *n.* length measured in yards.

yardstick *n.* standard of comparison.

yarn *n.* any spun thread; (*colloq.*) tale. —*v.i.* tell yarns.

yarrow *n.* plant with feathery leaves and strong-smelling flowers.

yashmak *n.* veil worn by Muslim women in certain countries.

yaw *v.i.* (of a ship or aircraft) fail to hold a straight course. —*n.* yawing.

yawl *n.* a kind of fishing-boat or sailing-boat.

yawn *v.i.* open the mouth wide and draw in breath, as when sleepy or bored; have a wide opening. —*n.* act of yawning.

yaws *n.* tropical skin-disease.

yd. *abbr.* yard. **yds.** *abbr.* yards.

ye *pron.* (*old use*) you.

yea /jeɪ/ *adv.* & *n.* (*old use*) yes.

year *n.* time taken by the earth to orbit the sun (about 365¼ days); period from 1 Jan. to 31 Dec. inclusive; consecutive period of twelve months; (*pl.*) age. **~-book** *n.* annual publication with current information about a subject.

yearling *n.* animal between 1 and 2 years old.

yearly *a.* happening, published, or payable once a year. —*adv.* annually.

yearn *v.i.* feel great longing.

yeast *n.* fungus used to cause fermentation in making beer and wine and as a raising agent.

yeasty *a.* frothy like yeast when it is developing.

yell *v.t./i.* & *n.* shout.

yellow *a.* of the colour of buttercups and ripe lemons; (*colloq.*) cowardly. —*n.* yellow colour or thing.

yellowhammer *n.* bird of the finch family with a yellow head, neck, and breast.

yellowish *a.* rather yellow.

yelp *n.* shrill yell or bark. —*v.i.* utter a yelp.

yen[1] *n.* (pl. *yen*) unit of money in Japan.

yen[2] *n.* longing, yearning.

yeoman /ˈjəʊ-/ *n.* (pl. *-men*) man who owns and farms a small estate. **Yeoman of the Guard**, member of the British sovereign's bodyguard, wearing Tudor dress as uniform. **~ service**, long useful service.

yes *adv.* & *n.* expression of agreement or consent, or of reply to a summons etc. **~-man** *n.* person who is always ready to agree with his superiors.

yesterday *n.* & *adv.* (on) the day before today; (in) the recent past.

yet *adv.* up to this or that time, still; besides; eventually; even; nevertheless. —*conj.* nevertheless, in spite of that.

yeti /ˈjetɪ/ *n.* (pl. *-is*) large man-like or bear-like animal said to exist in the Himalayas.

yew *n.* evergreen tree with dark needle-like leaves; its wood.

Yiddish *n.* language (based on a German dialect) used by Jews of central and eastern Europe.

yield *v.t./i.* give as fruit or gain or result; surrender, do what is asked or ordered; allow (victory, right of way, etc.) to another; be able to be forced out of the natural shape. —*n.* amount yielded or produced.

yodel *v.t./i.* (p.t. *yodelled*) sing, or utter a musical call, with a quickly alternating change of pitch. —*n.* yodelling cry. **yodeller** *n.*

yoga /ˈjəʊ-/ *n.* Hindu system of meditation and self-control.

yoghurt /ˈjɒg-/ *n.* food made of milk that has been thickened by the action of certain bacteria.

yoke *n.* wooden cross-piece fastened over the necks of two oxen pulling a cart or plough etc.; piece of wood shaped to fit a person's shoulders and hold a pail or other load slung from each end; top part of a garment; oppression, burdensome restraint. —*v.t.* harness with a yoke; unite.

yokel *n.* country fellow; bumpkin.

yolk /jəʊk/ *n.* round yellow internal part of an egg.

yon *a.* & *adv.* (*dialect*) yonder.

yonder *adv.* over there. —*a.* situated or able to be seen over there.

yore *n.* **of ~**, long ago.

yorker *n.* ball bowled to pitch just in front of the batsman.

Yorkshire *n.* **~ pudding**, baked batter pudding eaten with meat. **~ terrier**, terrier of a long-haired toy breed.

you *pron.* person(s) addressed; one, anyone, everyone. **you're**, you are.

young *a.* (*-er*, *-est*) having lived or existed for only a short time; youthful; having little experience. —*n.* offspring (before or soon after birth) of animals.

youngster *n.* young person, child.

your *a.*, **yours** *poss.pron.* belonging to you.

yourself *pron.* (pl. *yourselves*) emphatic and reflexive form of *you*.

youth *n.* (pl. *youths*, pr. juðz) state or period of being young; young man; young people. ~ **club,** club where leisure activities are provided for young people. ~ **hostel,** hostel providing cheap accommodation for young travellers.

youthful *a.* young; characteristic of young people. **youthfulness** *n.*

yowl *v.t./i.* & *n.* howl.

yo-yo *n.* (pl. *-os*) round toy that can be made to rise and fall on a string that winds round it.

yucca *n.* tall plant with white bell-like flowers and spiky leaves.

yule, yule-tide *ns.* (*old use*) Christmas festival.

Z

zany /ˈzeɪ-/ *a.* (*-ier, -iest*) crazily funny.

zeal *n.* enthusiasm, hearty and persistent effort.

zealous /ˈzel-/ *a.* full of zeal. **zealously** *adv.*

zealot /ˈzel-/ *n.* zealous person, fanatic.

zebra /ˈzi- or ˈzeb-/ *n.* African horse-like animal with black and white stripes. ~ **crossing** /ˈzeb-/, pedestrian crossing where the road is marked with broad white stripes.

zebu /ˈzibju/ *n.* humped ox.

zenith *n.* the part of the sky that is directly overhead; highest point.

zephyr /ˈzefə(r)/ *n.* soft gentle wind.

zero *n.* (pl. *-os*) nought, the figure 0; nil; point marked 0 on a graduated scale, temperature corresponding to this. ~ **hour,** hour at which something is timed to begin.

zest *n.* keen enjoyment or interest; orange or lemon peel as flavouring. **zestful** *a.*, **zestfully** *adv.*

zigzag *n.* line or course turning right and left alternately at sharp angles. —*a.* & *adv.* as or in a zigzag. —*v.i.* (p.t. *zigzagged*) move in a zigzag.

zinc *n.* bluish-white metal.

zinnia *n.* daisy-like garden plant with bright flowers.

Zionism *n.* movement that sought and achieved the founding of a Jewish homeland in Palestine. **Zionist** *n.*

zip *n.* short sharp sound; vigour, liveliness; zip-

fastener. —*v.t./i.* (p.t. *zipped*) open or close with a zip-fastener; move with the sound of 'zip' or at high speed. **Zip code,** (*U.S.*) postal code. ~**fastener** *n.* fastening device with projections that interlock when brought together by a sliding tab.

zipper *n.* zip-fastener.

zircon *n.* bluish-white gem cut from a translucent mineral.

zither *n.* shallow box-like stringed instrument played with the fingers.

zodiac *n.* (in astrology) band of the sky divided into twelve equal parts (*signs of the* ~) each named from a constellation formerly situated in it. **zodiacal** /-ˈdaɪ-/ *a.*

zombie *n.* (in voodoo) corpse said to have been revived by witchcraft; (*colloq.*) person who seems to have no mind or will.

zone *n.* area with particular characteristics, purpose, or use. —*v.t.* divide into zones; assign to a zone or zones. **zonal** *a.*

zoo *n.* place where wild animals are kept for exhibition and study.

zoology /zəʊˈol- or zʊˈol-/ *n.* study of animals. **zoological** *a.*, **zoologist** *n.*

zoom *v.i.* move quickly, esp. with a buzzing sound; rise quickly; (in photography) make a distant object appear gradually closer by means of a **zoom lens.**

Zulu *n.* (pl. *-us*) member or language of a Bantu people of South Africa.